P9-CBL-681

DISCARDED

POEMS ON AFFAIRS OF STATE

AUGUSTAN SATIRICAL VERSE, 1660–1714

Volume 6: 1697–1704

The Royal Family. Mezzotint engraving by Bernard Lens

Poems on Affairs of State

AUGUSTAN SATIRICAL VERSE, 1660–1714

VOLUME 6: 1697–1704

edited by

FRANK H. ELLIS

New Haven and London

YALE UNIVERSITY PRESS

1970

Library of Congress catalog card number: 63-7938
Standard book number: 300-01194-6
Designed by John O. C. McCrillis,
set in Baskerville type,
and printed in the United States of America by
Vail-Ballou Press, Binghamton, N.Y.

Distributed in Great Britain, Europe, and Africa by Yale University Press, Ltd., London; in Canada by McGill-Queen's University Press, Montreal; in Mexico by Centro Interamericano de Libros Academicos, Mexico City; in Australasia by Australia and New Zealand Book Co., Pty., Ltd., Artarmon, New South Wales; in India by UBS Publishers' Distributors Pvt., Ltd., Delhi; in Japan by John Weatherhill, Inc., Tokyo.

PREFACE

"The common aim of Prefaces" seems not to have changed since 1697 when the first preface to *Poems on Affairs of State* was written. It is still, as the editor said then, "to prepossess the Reader in favour of the Book."

"What is now publish'd," therefore, "is none of the trifling Performances of the Age," but a variorum edition of *The Dispensary,* a minor classic in the mock-epic mode, and eleven verse satires by Daniel Defoe, including two proposed additions to the canon, and the first edition of any kind of two poems by William Walsh, the friend of Dryden and young Alexander Pope, and a new poem by Joseph Addison, and five satires "never before printed." I am not as certain as the original editor that reading these works will "remove those pernicious Principles which lead us directly to Slavery [and will] promote a Publick and Generous Spirit," but there can be no doubt that they constitute "a just and secret History" of the years from 1697 to 1704.

The material for this volume could not have been assembled without the manuscript resources of the library of James M. Osborn or without the help of Margaret Crum, Department of Western MSS., Bodleian Library, David F. Foxon, late of the British Museum and now Reader in Textual Criticism, Oxford University, and Mary P. Pollard, Keeper of Rare Books, Trinity College, Dublin. It is a pleasure at last to be able to thank them publicly. Nor could the volume have been completed without the facilities of special collections on both sides of the Atlantic which David M. Lloyd, Ronald Hall, W. J. Smith, E. H. Sergeant, Dr. W. O. Hassall, John Alden, Carolyn E. Jakeman, Marjorie G. Wynne, Harriet C. Jameson, David A. Randall, Robert Rosenthal, James M. Wells, Edna C. Davis, Carey S. Bliss, and a dozen more librarians and county archivists made available to me.

The Portland MSS. in custody of the University of Nottingham Library are quoted with permission of His Grace the Duke of Portland and the Keeper of Manuscripts. Quotations from the Holkham

MSS. are made with the kind permission of the Earl of Leicester. Lord Downshire has given his consent for extracts to be made from the Trumbull MSS. in the Berkshire Record Office. The kindness of Sir Berwick Lechmere, Bart., has made it possible to quote from the Lechmere MSS. in the Worcestershire Record Office. The Cowper MSS. which were formerly at Panshanger are quoted by permission of the Hon. Lady Salmond and the Hertfordshire County Record Office. Manuscript material in the Royal College of Physicians of London was most generously made available by the Registrar and by the Harveian Librarian, L. M. Payne.

For exemplary research assistance by Carola Bradford Lea this acknowledgment is but a faint shadow of my gratitude. And Mrs. Carl A. Lohmann, by her continuing hospitality, has given new meaning to the phrase, "summer friend."

Professor J. H. Plumb, Christ's College, Cambridge, read the first half of this volume in typescript and provided invaluable intelligence concerning tactics to be pursued as well as booby-traps to be avoided. John Robert Moore, the distinguished Defoe scholar, and Basil Duke Henning, editor of *The House of Commons 1660–1690* for The History of Parliament Trust, were unfailingly responsive to cries for help. Many of the problems relating to the text of the poems were worked out in conversation with William J. Cameron, during the pleasant year which both of us enjoyed in New Haven. But most of all I am indebted to George deF. Lord, General Editor of the series, who has read and criticized the whole work. What I hope has emerged is something that he might like.

CONTENTS

Preface vii

List of Illustrations xiii

Works Frequently Cited xv

Introduction xxvii

1697

Thomas Brown, *A Satyr upon the French King* (28 October 1697) 3

Advice to a Painter (11–26 December 1697) 12

1698–1699

Joseph Addison, *The Play-House* (December 1698–April 1699) 29

1699

Arthur Mainwaring[?], *The Brawny Bishop's Complaint* (January–February 1699) 37

Daniel Defoe, *An Encomium upon a Parliament* (May[?] 1699) 43

Samuel Garth, *The Dispensary* (6–8 May 1699) 58

Sir Richard Blackmore, *A Satyr against Wit* (23 November 1699) 129

1700

Daniel Defoe, *The Pacificator* (15 February 1700) 157

Sir Charles Sedley, *Upon the Author of the Satyr against Wit* (27 February 1700) 181

Thomas Brown, *A Lent-Entertainment* (1700–02) 189

On My Lord Somers (April 1700) 195

John Dryden, *Prologue to "The Pilgrim"* (April 1700) 199

Edward Baynard[?], *Epitaph upon Mr. John Dryden* (11 June 1700) 206

A Conference between King William and the Earl of Sunderland (June 1700) 210

John Tutchin, *The Foreigners* (6 August 1700) 224

John Dennis[?], *The Reverse* (24 August 1700) 227

The Court (November 1700–March 1701) 248

1701

Daniel Defoe, *The True-Born Englishman* (December 1700–January 1701) 259
William Walsh[?], *The Worcester Cabal* (January 1701) 310
Daniel Defoe, *A New Satyr on the Parliament* (June[?] 1701) 318
Advice to a Painter. 1701 (July[?] 1701) 334
A Paradox in Praise of War (Before October 1701) 339
Daniel Defoe[?], *England's Late Jury* (November 1701) 343

1702

Bevil Higgons[?], *The Mourners* (March[?] 1702) 361
Thomas Smith[?], *Upon Sorrel* (March[?] 1702) 364
A Dialogue between the Illustrious Ladies, the Countesses of Albemarle and Orkney, Soon after the King's Death (March[?] 1702) 367
Daniel Defoe, *The Mock Mourners* (12 May 1702) 372
Daniel Defoe, *Reformation of Manners* (August[?] 1702) 398
John Dryden, *The Fourth Pastoral of Virgil, Englished by Mr. Dryden* (1697) 449
The Golden Age (November[?] 1702) 449
Daniel Defoe, *The Spanish Descent* (December[?] 1702) 467

1703

William Walsh, *The Golden Age Restor'd* (January 1703) 487
Henry Hall[?], *The Mitred Club* (January[?] 1703) 506
The Golden Age Revers'd (February 1703) 517
A Prophecy (June[?] 1703) 530
On Dr. Birch (June 1703[?]) 540
Daniel Defoe, *More Reformation. A Satyr upon Himself* (16 July 1703) 547
Daniel Defoe, *A Hymn to the Pillory* (29 July 1703) 585

1704

On the King of Spain's Voyage to Portugall (January[?] 1704) 609
On the 8th of March 1703/4 (March 1704) 613
Arthur Mainwaring[?], *An Address to Our Sovereign Lady* (5 April 1704) 615
The Seven Wise Men (January–March[?] 1704) 622
Daniel Defoe, *The Address* (April[?] 1704) 631

William Shippen, *Faction Display'd* (April[?] 1704) 648
Thomas Brown, *Upon the Anonymous Author of, Legion's Humble Address to the Lords* (May[?] 1704) 674
Thomas Brown, *To that Most Senseless Scondrel, the Author of Legion's Humble Address to the Lords* (May[?] 1704) 674
The Tryal of Skill: or, A New Session of the Poets (8 August 1704) 679

Textual Notes 713

Index of First Lines 801

General Index 802

LIST OF ILLUSTRATIONS

The Royal Family. A mezzotint engraving by Bernard Lens, printed by Edward Cooper. Courtesy of the Trustees of the British Museum. Frontispiece

Facing page

Peace Restored in Europe by King William III. Engraving by Paulus van Somer. Printroom Rijksmuseum, Amsterdam (F.M. 2980). 12

The Royal College of Physicians, Warwick Lane, London. Engraving by James S. Storer after a drawing by C. J. M. Whichelo. Courtesy of the New York Academy of Medicine Library. 63

Letter from Samuel Garth to Arthur Charlett, Master of University College, Oxford, postmarked April 20 [1700?], preserved in Bodl. MS Ballard XXIV, f. 68. 75

From *A Large and Accurate Map of the City of London . . . Actually Surveyed and Delineated by John Ogilby, Esq; His Majesties Cosmographer,* 1677. The College of Physicians, on Warwick Lane, is designated B37 and Apothecaries Hall, on Black Friars Lane, is at C1. Courtesy of the Trustees of the British Museum. 86

John Somers, baron Somers of Evesham. A mezzotint by John Smith after a portrait by Jonathan Richardson. 195

The Five Kentish Petitioners. Engraved by Robert White after drawings by Robert White. Courtesy of the Trustees of the British Museum. 336

The Death of William III. Anonymous engraving. Printroom Rijksmuseum, Amsterdam (F.M. 3022-A). 355

Brittania's Tears, a folio half-sheet, 1702. Courtesy of the Harvard College Library. 357

The Fall of William III. Engraved by Reinier Vinkeles after a drawing by Jacobus Buys. Printroom Rijksmuseum, Amsterdam (F.M. 3021-a). 364

The Bay of Cadiz. *Vues des Villes, Edifices & autres Choses remarqu-*

ables de l'Espagne & du Portugal, Leiden, Pierre Van Der Aa, n.d. Plate 88. Reproduced from a copy in the Yale University Library. 469

William and Mary. Medal by George Bower. Courtesy of the Trustees of the British Museum. 513

Benjamin Hoadly. A folio half-sheet, reprinting lines 145–48, 155–61, 9–18 of *Faction Display'd.* Courtesy of the Trustees of the British Museum. 651

Charing Cross and Northumberland House, a drawing by Antonio Canale (Canaletto) in The Minneapolis Institute of Arts. 653

John Toland(?) presenting the Act of Settlement to the Dowager Electress Sophia of Hanover, an anonymous engraving in the Sutherland Collection (B II 594). Courtesy of the Ashmolean Museum, Oxford. 659

WORKS FREQUENTLY CITED

In bibliographical references the place of publication is London unless otherwise stated. Classical references are to the Loeb Classical Library, William Heineman Ltd. and Harvard University Press.

Account of the Conduct: An Account of the Conduct of the Dowager Duchess of Marlborough, from Her First Coming to Court, to the Year 1710. In a Letter from Herself to My Lord———, 1742.

Ailesbury: *Memoirs of Thomas, Earl of Ailesbury Written by Himself,* 2 vols., 1890.

Alumni Oxonienses: Joseph Foster, *Alumni Oxonienses. The Members of the University of Oxford, 1500–1714,* 4 vols., Oxford, 1891–92.

Annals: Liber Annalium Collegii Medicorum Lond., vols. 1–7 (1518–1710).

Arber: Edward Arber, *The Term Catalogues 1668–1709,* 3 vols., Edward Arber, 1903–06.

Atterbury, *Works: The Miscellaneous Works of Bishop Atterbury with Historical Notes by J. Nichols,* 5 vols., 1789–98.

Aubrey: John Aubrey, *Brief Lives,* ed. Andrew Clark, 2 vols., Oxford, 1898.

Baker: David E. Baker, *Biographia Dramatica,* 3 vols. in 4, 1812.

Barrett: Charles R. B. Barrett, *The History of the Society of Apothecaries of London,* Elliot Stock, 1905.

Beatson: Robert Beatson, *A Political Index to the Histories of Great Britain and Ireland,* 3rd ed., 3 vols., 1806.

Beaven: Alfred B. Beaven, *The Aldermen of the City of London,* 2 vols., Eden Fisher & Co., 1908–13.

BIHR: Bulletin of the Institute of Historical Research, 42 vols., University of London, 1923– .

Biographia Britannica: Biographia Britannica: Or, The Lives of the Most Eminent Persons, 6 vols. in 7, 1747–66; 2nd ed., ed. Andrew Kippis, and others, 5 vols., 1778–93.

Blancard: Stephen Blancard [Blankaart], *A Physical Dictionary,* 3rd ed., 1697.

Bloom and James: J. H. Bloom and R. R. James, *Medical Practitioners in the Diocese of London . . . An Annotated List 1529–1725,* Cambridge, Cambridge University Press, 1935.

BM: British Museum, London.

Bodl.: Bodleian Library, Oxford University.

Boyer, *Annals:* Abel Boyer, *The History of the Reign of Queen Anne, Digested into Annals,* 11 vols., 1703–13.

Boyer, *History:* Abel Boyer, *The History of the Life and Reign of Queen Anne,* 1722.

British Diplomatic Representatives: David B. Horn, British Diplomatic *Representatives, 1689–1789,* Camden Society, 1932.

Browning: Andrew Browning, *Thomas Osborne, Earl of Danby and Duke of Leeds,* 3 vols., Glasgow, Jackson, Son & Co., 1944–51.

Burnet: Gilbert Burnet, *History of His Own Time,* 2 vols., 1724–34.

Burnet, 1823: *Bishop Burnet's History of His Own Time: With the Suppressed Passages of the First Volume, and Notes by the Earls of Dartmouth and Hardwicke, and Speaker Onslow,* 6 vols., Oxford, 1823.

Calamy, *Abridgement:* Edmund Calamy, *An Abridgement of Mr. Baxter's History of His Life and Times, With an Account of the Ministers who were Ejected after the Restauration of King Charles II,* 2nd ed., 2 vols., 1713.

Case: *A Bibliography of English Poetical Miscellanies 1521–1750,* ed. Arthur E. Case, Oxford, Bibliographical Society, 1935.

CBEL: The Cambridge Bibliography of English Literature, ed. Frederick W. Bateson, 5 vols., Cambridge, Cambridge University Press, 1940–57.

Chamberlayne: Edward Chamberlayne, *Angliae Notitia: Or, The Present State of England,* 19 vols., 1669–1704.

Chappell: William Chappell, *Popular Music of the Olden Time,* 2 vols., [1855–59].

Cibber, *Lives:* Theophilus Cibber [and Robert Shiels], *The Lives of the Poets,* 5 vols., 1753.

CJ: The Journals of the House of Commons.

Collins, 1741: Arthur Collins, *The Peerage of England,* 2nd ed., 4 vols., 1741.

Collins, 1812: *Collins's Peerage of England,* ed. Sir Egerton Brydges, 9 vols., 1812.

Cowper MSS.: Manuscripts formerly at Panshanger, Hertfordshire, now deposited in the Hertfordshire County Record Office, Hertford.

Coxe: *Private and Original Correspondence of Charles Talbot, Duke of Shrewsbury,* ed. William Coxe, 1821.

CSPD: Calendar of State Papers, Domestic Series, 1660–1702, ed. Mary Anne E. Greene, and others, 38 vols., H. M. Stationery Office, 1860–1964.

CTB: Calendar of Treasury Books, 1660–1704, ed. William A. Shaw, 19 vols. in 35, H. M. Stationery Office, 1904–38.

CTP: Calendar of Treasury Papers, 1557–1728, ed. Joseph Redington, 6 vols., 1868–89.

Culpeper: Nicholas Culpeper, *Pharmacopoeia Londinensis; or, The London Dispensatory,* 1695.

Dalrymple: Sir John Dalrymple, Baronet, *Memoirs of Great Britain and Ireland,* 3rd ed., 3 vols., 1790.

Dalton: *English Army Lists and Commission Registers, 1661–1714,* ed. Charles Dalton, 4 vols. in 2, Francis Edwards Ltd., 1960.

D'Auvergne, 1692: [Edward D'Auvergne], *A Relation of the Most Remarkable Transactions of the Last Campaigne . . . in the Spanish Netherlands, Anno Dom. 1692,* 1693.

D'Auvergne, 1693: Edward D'Auvergne, *The History of the Last Campagne in the Spanish Netherlands, Anno Dom. 1693,* 1693.

D'Auvergne, 1694: Edward D'Auvergne, *The History of the Campagne in the Spanish Netherlands, Anno Dom. 1694,* 1694.

D'Auvergne, 1695: Edward D'Auvergne, *The History of the Campagne in Flanders for the Year 1695,* 1696.

D'Auvergne, 1696: *The History of the Campagne in Flanders for the Year 1696,* 1696.

D'Auvergne, 1697: Edward D'Auvergne, *The History of the Campagne in Flanders, for the Year 1697,* 1698.

Defoe, *A Second Volume of the Writings: A Second Volume of the Writings of the Author of The True-Born Englishman,* 1705.

Defoe, *A True Collection: A True Collection of the Writings of the Author of The True Born English-man,* 1703.

Dennis, *Critical Works: The Critical Works of John Dennis,* ed. Edward N. Hooker, 2 vols., Baltimore, The Johns Hopkins Press, 1939–43.

DNB: The Dictionary of National Biography, ed. Sir Leslie Stephen and Sir Sidney Lee, 22 vols., Oxford University Press, 1949–50.

Downshire MSS.: Manuscripts of the Marquis of Downshire on deposit in the Berkshire Record Office, Reading.

Dryden, *Poems: The Poems of John Dryden,* ed. James Kinsley, 4 vols., Oxford, Clarendon Press, 1958.

Dryden, *Prose: The Critical and Miscellaneous Prose Works of John Dryden,* ed. Edmond Malone, 3 vols. in 4, 1800.

Dryden, *Works: The Works of John Dryden,* ed. Sir Walter Scott and George Saintsbury, 18 vols., Edinburgh, 1882–93.

Dryden, *Works* (California): *The Works of John Dryden,* ed. Edward N. Hooker, H. T. Swedenberg, Jr., Vinton A. Nearing, and others, Berkeley and Los Angeles, University of California Press, 1956– [in progress].

Echard: Laurence Echard, *The History of England from the Restoration of King Charles the Second to the Conclusion of the Reign of King James the Second,* 3 vols., 1707–18.

EHD: English Historical Documents 1660–1714, ed. Andrew Browning, Eyre & Spottiswoode, 1953.

Evelyn: *The Diary of John Evelyn,* ed. Esmond S. deBeer, 6 vols., Oxford, Clarendon Press, 1955.

Feiling: Keith Feiling, *A History of the Tory Party 1640–1714,* 2nd ed., Oxford, Clarendon Press, 1950.

Foss: Edward Foss, *The Judges of England,* 9 vols., 1848–64.

Foxcroft: *A Supplement to Burnet's History of My Own Time,* ed. Helen C. Foxcroft, Oxford, Clarendon Press, 1902.

Foxon: David F. Foxon, "Defoe: a specimen of a catalogue of verse 1701–1750," *The Library,* 20 (December 1965), 277–97.

GEC: George E. Cokayne, *The Complete Peerage,* ed. Vicary Gibbs, 13 vols. in 14, St. Catherine Press Ltd., 1910–59.

GEC, *Baronetage: Complete Baronetage,* ed. George E. Cokayne, 5 vols., Exeter, William Pollard & Co., 1900–06.

Genest: John Genest, *Some Account of the English Stage, from the Restoration in 1660–1830,* 10 vols., Bath, 1832.

Granger: James Granger, *A Biographical History of England,* 4 vols., 1769.

Grimblot: *Letters of William III and Louis XIV . . . 1697–1700,* ed. Paul Grimblot, 2 vols., 1848.

Hardwicke: *Miscellaneous State Papers from 1501 to 1726,* ed. Philip Yorke, 2nd earl of Hardwicke, 2 vols., 1778.

Harris: Brice Harris, *Charles Sackville, Sixth Earl of Dorset,* Urbana, University of Illinois Press, 1940.

Hearne: *Remarks and Collections of Thomas Hearne,* ed. C. E. Doble, and others, 11 vols., Oxford, Clarendon Press, 1884–1918.

HMC *Bagot MSS:* Historical Manuscripts Commission, *10th Report, Appendix, Part IV, The Manuscripts of Captain Josceline F. Bagot,* H. M. Stationery Office, 1885.

HMC *Bath MSS.:* Historical Manuscripts Commission, *Calendar of the Manuscripts of the Marquis of Bath Preserved at Longleat, Wiltshire,* 3 vols., H. M. Stationery Office, 1904–08.

HMC *Beaufort MSS.:* Historical Manuscripts Commission, *12th Report, Appendix, Part IX, The Manuscripts of the Duke of Beaufort,* H. M. Stationery Office, 1891.

HMC *Buccleuch & Queensberry MSS.:* Historical Manuscripts Commission, *The Manuscripts of the Duke of Buccleuch & Queensberry,* 2 vols. in 3, H. M. Stationery Office, 1897–1903.

HMC *Cowper MSS.:* Historical Manuscripts Commission, *The Manuscripts of the Earl Cowper, K.G., Preserved at Melbourne Hall, Derbyshire,* 3 vols., H. M. Stationery Office, 1888–89.

HMC *Downshire MSS.:* Historical Manuscripts Commission, *The Manuscripts of the Marquess of Downshire. Papers of Sir William Trumbull,* 1 vol. in 2, H. M. Stationery Office, 1924.

HMC *Finch MSS.:* Historical Manuscripts Commission, *Report on the Manuscripts of Allan George Finch,* 5 vols., H. M. Stationery Office, 1913– [in progress].

HMC *Hope Johnstone MSS.:* Historical Manuscripts Commission, *The Manuscripts of J. J. Hope Johnstone, Esq., of Annandale,* H. M. Stationery Office, 1897.

HMC *Kenyon MSS.:* Historical Manuscripts Commission, *The Manuscripts of Lord Kenyon,* H. M. Stationery Office, 1894.

HMC *Le Fleming MSS.:* Historical Manuscripts Commission, *The Manuscripts of S. H. Le Fleming, Esq., of Rydal Hall,* H. M. Stationery Office, 1890.

HMC *Lonsdale MSS.:* Historical Manuscripts Commission, *The Manuscripts of the Earl of Lonsdale,* H. M. Stationery Office, 1893.

HMC *Lords MSS.:* Historical Manuscripts Commission, *The Manuscripts of the House of Lords, 1678–1714,* 4 vols., 1887–94, New Series 10 vols., H. M. Stationery Office, 1900–53.

HMC *Ormonde MSS.:* Historical Manuscripts Commission, *The Manuscripts of the Marquis of Ormonde,* 2 vols., 1895–99, New Series 8 vols., H. M. Stationery Office, 1902–20.

HMC *Portland MSS.:* Historical Manuscripts Commission, *The Manuscripts of His Grace the Duke of Portland,* 10 vols., H. M. Stationery Office, 1891–1931.

HMC *Seventh Report: Seventh Report of the Royal Commission on Historical Manuscripts,* H. M. Stationery Office, 1879.

HMC *Townshend MSS.:* Historical Manuscripts Commission, *The Manuscripts of the Marquess Townshend,* H. M. Stationery Office, 1887.

Holkham MSS.: Manuscripts of the earl of Leicester at Holkham Hall, Wells, Norfolk.

Howell: *A Complete Collection of State Trials,* ed. Thomas B. Howell, 33 vols., 1816–26.

Jacob, *Historical Account:* [Giles Jacob], *An Historical Account of the Lives and Writings of our Most Considerable English Poets,* 1720.

Jacob, *Poetical Register:* [Giles Jacob], *The Poetical Register: Or, The Lives and Characters of the English Dramatic Poets,* 1719.

Japikse: *Correspondentie van Willem III en van Hans Willem Bentinck, Eersten Graaf van Portland,* ed. Nicolaas Japikse, 4 vols., 'S Gravenhage, M. Nijhoff, 1927–37.

JHM: Journal of the History of Medicine.

Johnson, *Lives:* Samuel Johnson, *The Lives of the English Poets,* ed. George Birkbeck Hill, 3 vols., Oxford, Clarendon Press, 1905.

Journey to London: [William King], *A Journey to London, In the Year, 1698 . . . Written Originally in French, by Monsieur Sorbiere,* 2nd ed., 1699.

Kennett: [White Kennett], *A Complete History of England,* 3 vols., 1706–19.

Kenyon: John P. Kenyon, *Robert Spencer, Earl of Sunderland, 1641–1702,* Longmans, Green, 1958.

Key: [1st t.p.] *The Genuine Works of Mr. Daniel D'Foe, Author of The True-born English-man, A Satyr . . . To which is added A Complete Key to the Whole, Never before Printed. Vol. I* [2nd t.p.] *A True Collection of the Writings of the Author of the True-born English-Man . . . Vol. I. The Third Edition,* [1710?], sig. *1–4 (Yale copy: Ik.D362.C703c).

Klopp: Onno Klopp, *Der Fall des Hauses Stuart,* 14 vols., Wien, 1875–88.

Lamberty: Guillaume de Lamberty, *Memoires pour servir à l'Histoire du XVIII Siècle,* 2nd ed., 14 vols., Amsterdam, 1734–40.

Lechmere MSS.: Manuscripts of Sir Ronald Lechmere, Baronet, on deposit in the Worcestershire Record Office, Worcester.

Lee: William Lee, *Daniel Defoe: His Life, and Recently Discovered Writings,* 3 vols., 1869.

Leicht: Wilhelm Josef Leicht, *Garth's Dispensary, Kritische Ausgabe,* Heidelberg, Carl Winter, 1905.

Le Neve: *Le Neve's Pedigrees of the Knights,* ed. George W. Marshall, Harleian Society, 1873.

Lilly MSS.: Manuscripts of the Lilly Library, Indiana University, Bloomington, Indiana.

Lillywhite: Bryant Lillywhite, *London Coffee Houses. A Reference Book,* G. Allen and Unwin, 1963.

LJ: The Journals of the House of Lords.

London Stage: The London Stage 1600–1800, ed. William Van Lennep, and others, 8 vols., Carbondale, Southern Illinois University Press, 1960– [in progress].

Lowndes: William T. Lowndes, *The Bibliographer's Manual,* ed. Henry G. Bohn, 6 vols., 1864.

Lucas: Theophilus Lucas, *Memoirs of the Lives, Intrigues, and Comical Adventures of the Most Famous Gamesters and Celebrated Sharpers in the Reigns of Charles II. James II. William III. and Queen Anne* (1714), ed. Cyril H. Hartmann, George Routledge & Sons, 1930.

Luttrell: Narcissus Luttrell, *A Brief Historical Relation of State Affairs from September 1678 to April 1714,* 6 vols., Oxford, 1857.

Macaulay: Thomas Babington Macaulay, *The History of England from the Accession of James II,* ed. Charles H. Firth, 6 vols., Macmillan & Co., 1913–15.

Macdonald: Hugh Macdonald, *John Dryden. A Bibliography of Early Editions and of Drydeniana,* Oxford, Clarendon Press, 1939.

Macky: *Memoirs of the Secret Services of John Macky,* ed. Spring Macky, 2nd ed., 1733.

Manley: [Delariviere Manley], *Secret Memoirs and Manners of Several Persons of Quality of Both Sexes. From the New Atalantis, An Island in the Mediteranean. Written Originally in Italian,* 2 vols., 1709.

Moore: John R. Moore, *A Checklist of the Writings of Daniel Defoe,* Bloomington, Indiana University Press, 1960.

Moore, *Daniel Defoe:* John R. Moore, *Daniel Defoe Citizen of the Modern World,* Chicago, University of Chicago Press, 1958.

Morden: [Robert Morden], *The New Description and State of England,* 1701.

Mottley: *Scanderbeg: Or, Love and Liberty. A Tragedy. Written by the late Thomas Whincop, Esq. To which are added A List of all the Dramatic Authors, with some Account of their Lives; and of all the Dramatic Pieces ever published in the English Language* [by John Mottley], 1747.

MS. Key: A manuscript key to Samuel Garth, *The Dispensary* (1699), preserved in the Historical Library, Yale University Medical Library.

Munk: William Munk, *The Roll of the Royal College of Physicians,* 2nd ed., 3 vols., 1878.

N&Q: Notes and Queries, ed. W. J. Thoms, and others, 214 vols., George Bell, 1849– .

Nash: Treadway R. Nash, *Collections for the History of Worcestershire,* 2 vols., 1781–82.

New Dictionary: B. E., *A New Dictionary of the Terms Ancient and Modern of the Canting Crew,* [1699].

Nichols, *Anecdotes:* John Nichols, *Literary Anecdotes of the Eighteenth Century,* 9 vols., 1812–15.

Nichols, *Illustrations:* John Nichols, *Illustrations of the Literary History of the Eighteenth Century,* 8 vols., 1817–58.

NLS: National Library of Scotland, Edinburgh.

Noble: Mark Noble, *A Biographical History of England, from the Revolution to the End of George I's Reign,* 3 vols., 1806.

Numerical Calculation: A Numerical Calculation of the Honourable Mem—rs As were Elected for the Ensuing Parl—nt, 1705 [folio half-sheet].

OED: The Oxford English Dictionary, ed. James A. H. Murray, and others, 13 vols., Oxford, Clarendon Press, 1933.

Ogg, *1–2:* David Ogg, *England in the Reign of Charles II,* 2nd ed., 2 vols., Oxford, Clarendon Press, 1956.

Ogg, *3:* David Ogg, *England in the Reign of James II and William III,* 2nd ed., Oxford, Clarendon Press, 1957.

Oldmixon: John Oldmixon, *The History of England during the Reigns of King William and Queen Mary, Queen Anne, King George I,* 1735.

Original Letters: Original Letters of Locke, Algernon Sidney, and Anthony Lord Shaftesbury, ed. T. Forster, 1830.

Osborn MSS.: Manuscripts of James M. Osborn, deposited in the Yale University Library.

Parl. Hist.: Cobbett's Parliamentary History of England, 36 vols., 1806–20.

Partridge: Eric Partridge, *A Dictionary of Slang and Unconventional English,* 4th ed., New York, Macmillan, 1951.

Pepys, *Corr.: Private Correspondence and Miscellaneous Papers of Samuel Pepys,* ed. J. R. Tanner, 2 vols., G. Bell, 1926.

Pepys, *Diary: The Diary of Samuel Pepys,* ed. Henry B. Wheatley, 8 vols. in 3, G. Bell & Sons, 1952.

Plomer: Henry R. Plomer, *A Dictionary of Printers and Booksellers . . . 1668–1725,* Oxford, Bibliographical Society, 1922.

POAS: Poems on Affairs of State, 1697–1716 (Case 211).

POAS, Yale: *Poems on Affairs of State,* ed. George deF. Lord, and others, 7 vols., New Haven, Yale University Press, 1963– [in progress].

Pope, *Corr.: The Correspondence of Alexander Pope,* ed. George Sherburn, 5 vols., Oxford, Clarendon Press, 1956.

Portland MSS.: Manuscripts of the Duke of Portland on deposit in the Department of Manuscripts, Nottingham University Library.

Prior, *Works: The Literary Works of Matthew Prior,* ed. H. Bunker Wright and Monroe K. Spears, 2 vols., Oxford, Clarendon Press, 1959.

PRO: Public Record Office, London.

PRSA: A New Collection of Poems Relating to State Affairs, from Oliver Cromwell to this Present Time: By the Greatest Wits of the Age, 1705.

Ralph: [James Ralph], *The History of England during the Reigns of King William, Queen Anne, and King George the First,* 2 vols., 1744–46.

RCP: Royal College of Physicians of London.

Rosenberg: Albert Rosenberg, *Sir Richard Blackmore, A Poet and Physician of the Augustan Age,* Lincoln, University of Nebraska Press, 1953.

Roxburghe Ballads: The Roxburghe Ballads, 9 vols. in 10, vols. 1–3 ed. William Chappell, vols. 4–9 ed. J. W. Ebsworth, Hertford (Ballad Society), 1871–99.

1718 Key: *A Compleat Key to the Eighth Edition of The Dispensary* (J. Roberts), 1718.

1709 Key: *A Compleat Key to The Dispensary* (H. Hills), 1709 (see p. 726, below).

Shaw: William A. Shaw, *The Knights of England,* 2 vols., Sherratt and Hughes, 1906.

Spence: Joseph Spence, *Observations, Anecdotes, and Characters of Books and Men Collected from Conversation,* ed. James M. Osborn, 2 vols., Oxford, Clarendon Press, 1966.

Spingarn: *Critical Essays of the Seventeenth Century,* ed. Joel E. Spingarn, 3 vols., Oxford, Clarendon Press, 1908.

Steele: *A Bibliography of Royal Proclamations of the Tudor and Stuart Sovereigns,* ed. Robert Steele, 2 vols., Oxford, Clarendon Press, 1910.

Strype: John Stowe, *A Survey of the Cities of London and Westminster,* ed. John Strype, 2 vols., 1720.

Survey of London: Charles R. Ashbee, and others, *The Survey of London,* 32 vols., London County Council, 1900– [in progress].

Swift, *Corr.: The Correspondence of Jonathan Swift,* ed. Sir Harold Williams, 5 vols., Oxford, Clarendon Press, 1963–65.

Swift, *Discourse:* Jonathan Swift, *A Discourse of the Contests and Dissentions between the Nobles and the Commons in Athens and Rome,* ed. Frank H. Ellis, Oxford, Clarendon Press, 1967.

Swift, *Journal:* Jonathan Swift, *Journal to Stella,* ed. Harold Williams, 2 vols., Oxford, Clarendon Press, 1948.

Swift, *Poems: The Poems of Jonathan Swift,* ed. Harold Williams, 3 vols., Oxford, Clarendon Press, 1937.

Swift, *Prose: The Prose Writings of Jonathan Swift,* ed. Herbert Davis, 13 vols., Oxford, Basil Blackwell, 1939–62.

TCD: Trinity College, Dublin.

Tilley: *A Dictionary of the Proverbs in England in the Sixteenth and Seventeenth Centuries,* ed. Morris P. Tilley, Ann Arbor, University of Michigan Press, 1950.

Tindal: Nicholas Tindal, *The History of England by Mr. Rapin de Thoyras. Continued from the Revolution to the Accession of King George II,* 3rd ed., 4 vols. in 5, 1743–47.

Trevelyan: George Macaulay Trevelyan, *England under Queen Anne,* 3 vols., Longmans, Green, 1930.

VCH, *Wiltshire:* The Victoria History of the Counties of England, *A History of Wiltshire,* ed. R. B. Pugh and Elizabeth Crittal, 8 vols., Institute of Historical Research, 1953–65.

Venn: *Alumni Cantabrigienses, Part I, From the Earliest Times to 1751,* ed. John Venn and J. A. Venn, 4 vols., Cambridge, Cambridge University Press, 1922–27.

Vernon: *Letters Illustrative of the Reign of William III from 1696 to 1708 Addressed to the Duke of Shrewsbury by James Vernon,* ed. G. P. R. James, 3 vols., 1841.

Walcott: Robert Walcott, *English Politics in the Early 18th Century,* Cambridge, Harvard University Press, 1956.

Wing: *Short-Title Catalogue . . . 1641–1700,* ed. Donald Wing, New York, Index Society, 1945–51.

Wood: Anthony à Wood, *Athenae Oxonienses. An Exact History of All the Writers and Bishops who have had their Education in the University of Oxford. To which are added The Fasti, or Annals of the said University,* ed. Philip Bliss, 4 vols., 1813–20.

Wood, *Life and Times: The Life and Times of Anthony Wood,* ed. Andrew Clark, 5 vols., Oxford, 1891–1900.

INTRODUCTION

I. 1697–1704

"If I was to name a time when the arts and polite literature were at their height in this nation," said Joseph Warton in 1756, "I should mention the latter end of King William, and the reign of Queen Anne." [1] This was also the opinion of Oliver Goldsmith, and Samuel Johnson boasted that through these reigns "no prosperous event passed undignified by poetry." [2] And—Johnson might have added—no misfeasance went unstigmatized by satire. The widening focus of satire, noticed in the Introduction to the third volume of this series (1682–85), had by this time been extended to take in almost everything, with some of the distortion inevitable in the wide-angle lens.

From 1660 to 1695 the volume of verse satire ebbed and flowed as censorship was tightened (May 1662, October 1679, February 1685) or relaxed (May 1679, March 1681), but from April 1695 (when the Licensing Act was allowed to expire) until August 1712 (when the newspaper tax was imposed), it just flowed. The days when Stephen College could be hanged, drawn, and quartered for publishing libelous verses (August 1681) and Algernon Sidney beheaded for mere possession of treasonable verse in manuscript (November 1683) were almost over. It was 1719 when John Matthews, the last English martyr to a free press, was hanged for printing *Vox Populi, Vox Dei*.[3] James II had believed that "command of the press [was] a prerogative inseparable from the sovereignity of his imperial crown",[4] but whatever he believed, William III did not even try to "command" the press. Instead he learned to use it (or to allow it to be used for him) to create and change public opinion, "not being able," as he explained to Antonie Heinsius, "to play any other game with these people than to engage them imperceptibily." [5]

1 *An Essay on the Writings and Genius of Pope,* 2 vols., 1756–82, *1,* 160–61.

2 *Collected Works of Oliver Goldsmith,* ed. Arthur Friedman, 5 vols., Oxford, Clarendon Press, 1966, *1,* 498; Johnson, *Lives, 2,* 186.

3 Laurence Hanson, *The Government and the Press, 1695–1753,* 1936, pp. 57–58.

4 *CSPD 1685,* p. 159, quoted in *POAS,* Yale, *4,* xxxvi.

5 Grimblot, *2,* 479.

The treaty that brought peace to England in September 1697 after nine years of war with France gave an enormous impetus to all the arts, including those of propaganda. Thomas Brown correctly predicted that "when Money *circulated* merrily, and Claret is to be had at the old Price, a new *Spirit* will appear abroad, Wit and Mirth will shake off their Fetters, and Parnassus, that has made such *heavy* returns of late Years, will trade considerably."[6] The exuberant "new *Spirit*," "tossing and sporting with the *Commonwealth*",[7] is reflected in the first poems of the present volume (which prints the poems in chronological order).

The brief period covered by this volume might best be represented as a system of major and minor watersheds: the treaty of Ryswick in September 1697, the opening of the first free out-patient clinic in London in April 1698, the shift from a Whig to a Tory ministry in 1699–1700, the death of Dryden on 1 May 1700, the death of William III and the accession of Queen Anne in March 1702, the declaration of war against France in May 1702. Most of the 47 poems in the volume cluster themselves about one or the other of these watersheds, some of which, evidently, are quite unrelated. But it is their number as well as their unrelatedness that provides the unusual variety in the poems they precipitated.

Cutting through all of these isolated barriers is one constant and growing current. This is a major shift in sensibility, which was institutionalized in the societies for the reformation of manners, reflected in the growth of sentimental comedy, and perfected in the manners and morals of Victorian England. It began at court in 1685, became a major interest of Queen Mary, was taken up by William upon the conclusion of hostilities in 1697 and by Queen Anne in 1702. It emerges in the present volume in Blackmore's *Satyr against Wit* (1699), in the anonymous *Tryal of Skill* (1704), and in half a dozen poems in between. It supplies in addition the theme for two of Defoe's major satires, *Reformation of Manners* (1702) and *More Reformation* (1703).

The careless obscenity so characteristic of the earlier volumes in

6 *Familiar Letters: Written by the Right Honourable John late Earl of Rochester, and Several Other Persons*, 1697, p. 226.

7 Swift, *Prose, 1*, 25. It was to prevent Leviathan wits like Thomas Brown and William Shippen "from tossing and sporting with the *Commonwealth*" that Swift undertook to provide them with *A Tale of a Tub*.

this series is heard less frequently in this one, most remarkably perhaps in the squib *Upon the Author of the Satyr against Wit* by Sir Charles Sedley, who was himself a not unreformed relic of the earlier generation.

II. The genre

In the two volumes of his anthology, *Political Ballads of the 17th and 18th Centuries,* published in 1860, W. Walker Wilkins found nothing worth reprinting between 1696 and 1707, which includes the period covered by the present volume. The reasons for this omission, however, are instructive. Wilkins was collecting folklore, mainly in the form of broadside ballads, of which there are no examples in the present volume. There are, however, four poems in this volume written in a modified ballad stanza. All of these are attributed to Defoe and one, *A New Satyr on the Parliament* (June [?] 1701) was called *The Ballad* in an early reprinting. But none of these poems qualify as "exponents of the *popular mind,*" in Wilkins' phrase.[8] On the contrary, they represent the highly self-conscious, informed responses of one sophisticated mind to four sessions of parliament, cast into ballad form to achieve certain artistic and propagandistic effects.

This in turn may remind us that satire is the cuckoo bird of the literary genres: it lays its eggs in the nests of other birds. Thus the poems in the present volume assume many of the forms made familiar in the previous volumes: the epistle, the mock-panegyric, the mock-epic, the paradox, the mock-pastoral, the vision, the prophecy, the hymn, the session of the poets, and at least one new one: the mock address to the throne (p. 615 below). Corresponding to this dazzling array of subgenres is an equally broad band of assumed occasional voices, or tones.

One of these is the high-moralistic, Old-Testament-prophetic, infallible-oracular tone which Defoe sometimes assumes and which so infuriated Swift: "so grave, sententious, dogmatical a Rogue, that there is no enduring him." [9] That this was only a pose assumed for purposes of satire seems to be confirmed by Defoe's acknowledgment that he was in fact "a plain and unpolish'd man." [10] At the

8 *Political Ballads of the 17th and 18th Centuries,* 2 vols., 1860, *1,* vi.

9 Swift, *Prose, 2,* 113; *3,* 13–14; cf. *Daniel the Prophet No Conjurer,* 1705, p. 3.

10 *Original Letters of Eminent Literary Men,* ed. Sir Henry Ellis, Camden Society, 1843, p. 323.

opposite end of the scale may be heard the plain, dry, matter-of-fact voice of the historian who condescends to stoop to the level of the keyhole to report to the reader the "Truth and Nakedness" behind the closed doors. This is the voice, for example, of William Shippen in *Faction Display'd* (April[?] 1704) and with all their differences of political bias and satiric technique, it is interesting to note that both Shippen and Defoe agree that satire must be true. " 'Tis the Criticks Objection to *Lucan,* that his Poem [*an Lucanus sit poeta*] is too Historical, but it must be said in his Defence," Shippen insisted, "that tho' for that Reason he may perhaps delight less; yet he certainly Instructs more, which is the better End of Poetry." [11] Defoe is more succinct: "the Satyr lies in the Truth, not in the ill Language," [12] he said, and here of course he had behind him the growing weight of the reformation of manners.

On the other hand, satire cannot tolerate too much high-mindedness. Crudity and deformity remain as essential to the genre in 1697–1704 as they did during the Restoration.[13] It seems eminently appropriate that Sir Richard Blackmore should be smacked in the face with a foul-smelling laurel wreath (p. 194 below). Perhaps the art of the satirist lies partly—in Sir Richard's own words—in knowing "Where . . . the Legislator ends, [and] the Comick Genius begins." [14]

Verse satire is a mixed art that derives from the prose pamphlet at one extreme and approaches imaginative literature at the other. Alexander Pope expressed it more wittily: "We find by Experience," he said, "that the same Humours which vent themselves in Summer in *Ballads* and *Sonnets,* are condens'd by the Winter's Cold into *Pamphlets* and *Speeches* for and against the *Ministry.*" [15]

That it cannot have mattered much to Defoe whether he cast a given work in verse or prose is indicated by *The Address* (April [?] 1704), which repeats in a version of the Cherrie-an-the-Slae stanza many of the arguments of a prose pamphlet, *Legion's Humble Address to the Lords,* probably published in the same month. Lines

11 *Faction Display'd, A Poem,* 1705, sig. A2v.

12 *The Dissenters Answer to the High-Church Challenge,* 1704, sig. A2r.

13 *POAS,* Yale, *1,* xliii.

14 Blackmore, *Essays upon Several Subjects,* 1716, p. 198.

15 *Peri Bathous, Or The Art of Sinking in Poetry* (1727), ed. Edna L. Steeves, New York, Columbia University Press, 1952, p. 14.

771–843 of *The True-Born Englishman* (January 1701) versify whole paragraphs of Locke's *Two Treatises of Government* (1690). And when it is recalled that 80,000 copies of one edition of *The True-Born Englishman* were sold at a penny and that there were as many as 50 editions in the first half of the century, some idea may be gained of the propaganda power of Defoe's verse, for none of Locke's prose pamphlets sold at this rate.

On the other hand, the fact that Defoe's satire versifies Locke's prose does not imply that Defoe's verse is inferior as verse. Coleridge has taught us to scorn "those who, reading but little poetry, are most stimulated with that species of it, which seems most distant from prose." [16] Verse satire is that species which lies nearest prose. It was observed sarcastically in 1683 that "'Tis a fine Age, when Mercinary Poets shall become Politicians, and their Plays business of State," [17] but this is literally what happened, and it would be silly to argue today that their poems and plays would have been better if the poets had stayed out of politics.

Nor does it seem fair to make autonomy the criterion of excellence for verse satire.[18] *Absalom and Achitophel* is not a better poem than *Faction Display'd* because it is less dependent upon its historical background. Neither poem in fact is even intelligible without some knowledge of its background. It is not the poems that have deteriorated with the passing of years, it is our knowledge of the background that has deteriorated. The editor of a series similar to *Poems on Affairs of State* in 1713 anticipated the present situation exactly. In offering his poems to the reader he hoped that "none will be thought wholly unworthy of being preserv'd. They are now in their Prime," he said, "when every person may understand what is allegorical; and, perhaps, in Time to come, may merit a Key, for Prosperity to judge of the Humour of this Age." [19]

III. The Poets

Daniel Defoe dominates the present volume much in the way that Andrew Marvell dominates the first volume in this series. Of the 47

[16] Cf. p. 261, below; S. T. Coleridge, *Biographia Literaria*, ed. J. Shawcross, 2 vols., Oxford, Clarendon Press, 1907, *1*, 51.

[17] *Some Reflections upon the Pretended Parallel in the Play called The Duke of Guise*, 1683, p 25.

[18] *POAS*, Yale, *1*, li–lii.

[19] *Tory Pills to Purge Whig Melancholy*, 2nd ed., 1715, sig. A2v.

poems here reprinted, 11 of them are by Defoe. Half of the total number of lines of verse in the volume are his. But even this proportion does not misrepresent Defoe's importance in the period. From 1697 to 1700 he was a volunteer propagandist for the Whig junto and from early 1701 until the death of William III in March 1702 he apparently enjoyed some kind of semi-official status as court poet. In the next reign, however, "an Exasperated Government," as he said himself, committed him to Newgate, from which he was ransomed and put back to work by Robert Harley, who needed Defoe's propaganda powers to put together a coalition of moderate Whigs and moderate Tories.

Quantity in itself, of course, will not determine whether Defoe is a considerable poet. This will have to wait the assessment of critics, but in the meantime it might be helpful to point out some pitfalls to be avoided.

There is no longer any necessity for dismissing Defoe as a venal hack. It was a good joke in *The Dunciad,* but Arthur L. Windsor pointed out more than a hundred years ago that it was Defoe's honesty, not his venality, that set him "un-abashed" in the pillory and in Newgate (twice).[20] The very inconsistencies of Defoe's political career have the shape of honesty. Though a passionate Williamite, he deplored the cruel treatment and insults that James II received at St. Germains. Though a Whig, he accepted the necessity for a standing army. Though a dissenter, he supported the bill to prevent occasional conformity—and then changed his mind and opposed it. Though a Protestant, he opposed the bill for preventing the growth of popery in Ireland. Though a loyal friend of Harley, he bitterly opposed Harley's terms for the treaty of Utrecht.[21] Probably the single most important clue to an understanding of Defoe's tangled career is the fact that he never could accept the necessity or even the usefulness of parties.[22]

Once the image of the shameless hack has been discarded, it should be possible to set out Defoe's satiric purposes in their true light. The present volume affords overwhelming evidence of the

20 Windsor, *Ethica: or, Characteristics of Men, Manners, and Books,* 1855, pp. 197–98.

21 [Defoe], *A Serious Inquiry into this Grand Question,* 1704, p. 23.

22 *Review,* [9] (9 September 1712), 23.

truth of what Defoe wrote in 1705 in the preface to the first collected volume of the *Review:*

> my firm Resolution in all I write to exalt Vertue, expose Vice, promote Truth, and help Men to serious Reflection, is my first moving Cause, and last directed End.[23]

A second important clue to an understanding of Defoe as a satirist is that he never could accept art as an end in itself, but only as a means to an end. And "The End of Satyr," he insisted, "is Reformation."[24]

The strangeness that the reader may feel when he first encounters Defoe's verse is partly the result of Defoe's rejection of conventional poetic diction. There is in Defoe almost none of the language that claims to be "poetical for no better reason, than that it would be intolerable in conversation or in prose."[25] And except for the four in modified ballad form, none of Defoe's satires adopt any of the subgenres mentioned above. It was James Joyce who pointed out that Defoe was the first English writer "to write without imitating or adapting foreign words, to create without literary models and . . . to devise for himself an artistic form which is perhaps without precedent."[26]

The second most important figure in the present volume is probably William Shippen, the "downright" Jacobite and member of parliament, who has long been known to be the author of *Faction Display'd* (1704) and *Moderation Display'd* (1705). Even the most casual reading of the scandals exposed in *Faction Display'd* will reveal the inappropriateness of the epithet "dreary," which is applied to it in *The Dictionary of National Biography,* and if the four earlier poems tentatively attributed to him (p. 13 below) turn out actually

23 *A Review of the Affairs of France,* 1705, sig. A3v; cf. "I . . . have often sacrific'd the Poet to the Reasoning Stile," *Jure Divino. A Satyr,* 1706, p. xxvi; "I could give you Similies, and Allegories . . . But I have chose a down-right Plainness," *Review,* 7 (24 June 1710), 149.

24 *The True-Born Englishman. A Satyr,* 1700, sig. A2r.

25 Coleridge, *Biographia Literaria,* ed. Shawcross, 2, 21.

26 "Daniel Defoe," trans. and ed. Joseph Prescott, Buffalo State University of New York, 1964, p. 27.

to be his, Shippen may well come to be recognized as a successor to Dryden, corresponding to Defoe as successor to Marvell.

But neither Defoe nor Shippen were awarded the laurel in the session of the poets which concludes the present volume. This honor went to Samuel Garth, M.D. In *The Dispensary* Garth had learned to play new tunes on the old closed couplet. One of his favorites was a pompous three-stress line, productive of mock-heroic effects:

> Unbounded in Exorbitance of Ill (textual note, 2, 48).
>
> A barren Superfluity of Words (2, 84).

And once at least he almost succeeded in shrinking the five stresses down to two:

> And Violence advances Charity (textual note, *1*, 132).

Garth also loved "romantic" words like "tender Pinion," and "sullen," and "Lustre." He taught a whole generation of poets, from Lady Mary Chudleigh [27] to Alexander Pope, to play these tunes and his popularity almost overcame the malice of party. Garth was a member of the Kit-Cat Club and a favorite of the Whig junto, but Pope dedicated to him his second pastoral; young Henry St. John admired his "Wit" and "living Verse," [28] and Edward Ward, a third Tory, summed it up in a couplet of his own:

> Dryden *and* Shadwell *held the Bays for Years,*
> *But both resign the Crown when* Garth *appears.*[29]

It was fairly well agreed that Garth was not only "one of the best Poets," [30] but also "one of the best-natured men of the age," [31] as Pope put it. Even after he had been created Lord Bolingbroke, St. John could recall that Garth was "the best natured ingenious wild man I ever knew." [32] And Henry Killigrew, Jr., another Tory, recalled after Garth's death that "no unhappy Person ever apply'd to him, but that he made use of the utmost of his Interest to ease their Pain and Anxiety." [33]

27 Lady Mary Chudleigh, *Poems on Several Occasions,* 1703, p. 63.
28 *A New Collection of Poems,* 1701, p. 103.
29 Ward, *The Secret History of Clubs,* 1709, p. 15.
30 Jacob, *Historical Account,* p. 58.
31 Spence, *1,* 44.
32 Bolingbroke, *Works,* 8 vols., 1809, *4,* 90.
33 Thomas Killigrew, *Miscellanea Aurea,* 1720, p. 2.

IV. This Volume

In the first volume of this series, the copy text for 43 of the 54 poems is in manuscript, and to avoid producing some kind of typographical pastiche, it was decided to modernize the text. In the present volume, however, the situation is exactly reversed: for 41 of the 47 poems the copy text is in print. Thus it was decided to retain the accidentals of the copy text.

All available witnesses to the text of each poem have been collated and the substantive variants recorded in the apparatus. Obvious errors, however, have not been recorded. Thus in *The Play-House* it is not recorded that line 58 in the copy text and a collateral manuscript read "our Eyes" and "their Eyes," respectively, for the context clearly requires a singular pronoun.

The 47 poems in the present volume were chosen, from about 500 possibilities, on the same principles as those stated in the Introduction to Volume IV.[34] In annotating these poems no attempt was made to be objective. The aim instead was to provide Tory commentary for a Tory poem and Whig commentary for a Whig poem. This may lead to contradiction, but more importantly it should enable the reader "to dwell rather upon Excellencies than Imperfections," as Addison recommended.[35]

34 *POAS*, Yale, *4*, xli.

35 *The Spectator*, No. 291, 2 February 1712.

The Politicians of *Parnassus* prate,
And Poets canvass the Affairs of State.

The Dispensary, 4, 21–22

1697

Thomas Brown

A Satyr upon the French King
(*28 October 1697*)

The night of 14 September 1697, when Matthew Prior brought to London the news of the signing of the Treaty of Ryswick, the guns at the Tower were discharged, the flag displayed, bells rung, and bonfires lit. But joy in London was by no means unconfined. Neither this poem nor the next one are celebratory; both in fact are almost desperate.

The present poem is a soliloquy. It begins in incredulity and ends in an obscene curse. The imagined speaker is a nonjuring Anglican parson, one of an estimated 400 who lost their livings in 1689 when they refused to take the oaths of allegiance to William and Mary. Thus the speaker is also a man of principle, albeit a quixotic principle: he refused "to admit that an absurd doctrine had been discredited by events" (Ogg, *3*, 234). The absurd doctrine was the Anglican doctrine of nonresistance, the belief that the authority of a *jure divino* king could not be resisted under any circumstances. What this principle had cost the speaker is set forth in lines 34–40, which constitute the emotional center of the poem: two rural benefices worth £160 a year, yielding a fat sufficiency for the parson, his wife, and daughter. In his impassioned recollection of this life, the tithe eggs were not collected; they flew in of their own accord.

Since 1689 the speaker has lived in London on pawn tickets, credit, and the hope of a second Stuart restoration. One of the favorite toasts at Sam's coffeehouse, which the speaker frequents, was "To the king's fast friend," meaning Louis XIV. For after James II had fled Ireland in 1690, it was obvious that he could not be restored without Louis and it was widely believed that Louis had engaged his *parole d'honneur* as a king not to make peace with the confederates until he had restored James to the throne of England (Tindal, *3*, 78). And it cannot be denied that Louis tried. But Louis' interests were never so simple, nor so single-minded, as James' and when the two came into conflict, James', of course, had to be sacrificed.

This occurred in December 1696 and became public knowledge in February 1697 when Louis ordered his plenipotentiaries to proceed to Ryswick to negotiate a treaty of peace with the confederates. The speaker of the present poem was not alone in being incredulous that Louis should seek a peace while four French armies remained undefeated in the field and Jean Bart's privateers operated freely out of Dunkirk to destroy confederate shipping. All of Europe was astonished at the concessions that Louis was willing to make at the conference table that summer. Now Louis pledged his *parole d'honneur*, *not* "pour le restablissement du Roy legitime en Angleterre," but "not to assist directly or indirectly any of the enemies" of William III. Yet even while the French plenipotentiaries at Ryswick were demanding the highest price for Louis' abandonment of James, "the Court of *France* did, to the last minute, assure King *James*, that they would never abandon his Interests." When Louis finally told Mary of Modena that he had signed the treaty, she was emboldened to reply that "She wished it might be such, as should raise his Glory, as much as it might settle his Repose" (Burnet, *2*, 203). It is amid the ruin of all his hopes, therefore, that the speaker in the present poem utters his diabolical curse of Louis: he condemns Louis to suffer the fate that he fears will be his own—teaching school or keeping a shop.

Thomas Brown must have begun to write this poem very soon after the news of the peace reached London. It was published in a folio half-sheet on 28 October 1697 (Luttrell copy, in the Newberry Library). Two days later Brown was arrested, along with Abel Roper, the publisher, for having violated "the new-made Treaty, between the two Crowns of *England* and *France*" (Oldmixon, p. 167). Brown and Roper were released on bail, and six months later, after serving a short sentence in Newgate, Brown was finally discharged. In the meantime, the poem had generated a Jacobite reply, in verse, by a "Mr. Stacy." This was *An Answer to the Satyr upon the French King*, another broadside, published on 13 November 1697 (Luttrell copy, in the Newberry Library). Brown's counterreply, in prose, *Mr.* Brown*'s Character of the Jacobite Clergy, found among his private Papers, and suppos'd to be writ upon the Occasion of Mr.* Stacy*'s Answer to the* Satyr *against the* French *King* (Brown, *Works*, 1711, *4*, 262–71), he wisely withheld from publication during his lifetime.

Next there appeared in *The Flying Post* for 23–25 November 1697 a *Petition of Tom Brown, who was taken up on account of the Satyr upon the French King* (Brown, *Works,* 1707, *1,* 94–95). This humorous defense of Brown was said by John Oldmixon to have been written by Charles Sackville, sixth earl of Dorset. "And by his Lordship's Intercession," Oldmixon goes on to say, "the whipping part [of Brown's sentence] was dispens'd with, and he was, after a short Confinement, set at liberty" (Oldmixon, p. 167). While he was still in Newgate, Brown added another work to the canon of prison literature. This was *Tho. Brown's Recantation of his Satyr on the French King* ("And has this Bitch, my Muse, trapan'd me?"), which was published immediately in a folio half-sheet dated 1697 (Wing B5074) and eventually found its way into Brown's *Works* (1720 [2nd t.p. dated 1719], *4,* 321–25). In this poem, Brown's imagination presents him with a too-vivid anticipation of a public whipping:

> I'm just as if at Cart's-Arse ty'd,
> With Hangman grinning by my Side,
> And Mob of all Sorts crowding round me,
> Advising Ketch to swinge me soundly.

During Brown's lifetime all sorts crowded round him to hear his conversation. His writing also is best when it most closely approximates the vocabulary and rhythms of the literary Alsatia in which he lived. He was, we are told by James Drake (Brown, *Works,* 1707, *1,* sig. A7v), "unambitious of a Reputation" as a poet, but his best poetry is like brilliant conversation, alternately witty, learned, obscene, inconsecutive, larded with Latin tags, underworld slang, and even, as in the present poem, the refrain of a current popular song.

A Satyr upon the French King

Written by a Non-Swearing Parson, and drop'd out of his Pocket at Samm's Coffee-House

Facit indignatio Versum.

And hast thou left Old *Jemmy* in the Lurch?
A plague confound the Doctors of thy Church!
Then to abandon poor *Italian Molly*—
Would I'd the firking of thy Bumm with Holly!
Next to discard the Virtuous Prince of *Wales,*
How suits this with the Honour of *Versailes?*
Fourthly, and Lastly, to renounce the *Turks,*
Why, this is the Devil, the Devil, and all his Works!
Were I thy Confessor, who am thy Martyr,
Dost think that I'de allow thee any Quarter?
No—thou shou'dst find what 'tis to be a Starter.
Lord! with what monstrous Lies, and senseless Shamms,
Have we been cullied all a-long at *Samms.*
Who cou'd have e're believ'd, unless in Spite,
Lewis le Grand wou'd turn rank *Williamite?*

3. *Italian Molly:* Maria d'Este (1658–1718), called Mary of Modena in England. When she became James's second wife in 1673, Louis XIV underwrote her dowry of 300,000 crowns.

4. *firking:* whipping.

5. *Prince of Wales:* James Francis Edward (1688–1766), the only son of James II.

7. *renounce the Turks:* His Most Christian Majesty's subvention of the infidel was frequently noticed in England (Luttrell, *3*, 44, 387–88, 433, 450). In 1697, however, while peace negotiations were under way at Ryswick, Louis' failure to create a diversion on the Rhine exposed the Turks to two crushing defeats—one at Azov in the Crimea and another at Zenta in Hungary—which afforded them "but too much reason to repent, when they [saw] themselves left in the Lurch" (D'Auvergne, 1697, p. 159).

8. *the Devil, the Devil, and all his Works:* the last line of a catch by Henry Purcell, "Let's live good honest lives," of which the music is recorded in *The Catch Club or Merry Companions* [1720?], Part II, p. 44.

11. *Starter:* a deserter from a principle or cause. *OED* cites this line.

13. *Samms:* Sam's coffeehouse in Ludgate Street near St. Paul's was known to be a center for the dissemination of Jacobite literature (HMC *Finch MSS.*, *3*, 365).

Thou, that hast Look'd so fierce, and Talk'd so bigg,
In thy Old Age to dwindle to a *Whigg!*
By Heaven, I see thou'rt in thy heart a Prigg.
I'de not be for a Million in thy Jerkin,
'Fore *George* thy Soul's no bigger than a Gerkin.
Hast thou for this spent so much *Ready Rhino?*
Now, what the Plague will become of *Jure Divino?*
A Change so monstrous I cou'd ne're have thought,
Though *Partridge* all his Stars to vouch it, brought.
S'life, I'le not take thy Honour for a Groat,
Ev'n Oaths, with thee, are only things of Course.
Thou, 'Zoons, thou art a Monarch for a Horse.
Of Kings distress'd thou art a fine Securer;
Thou make'st me Swear, that am a known *Non-Juror.*
But tho' I swear thus, as I said before,
Know, King, I'le place it all upon thy Score.
  Were *Job* alive, and banter'd by such Shufflers,
He'd out-rail *Oats,* and Curse both thee and *Boufflers.*

18. *Prigg:* a puritanical person; a precisian in religion, especially a nonconformist minister. *OED* cites this line.

20. *Gerkin:* a small cucumber used for pickling.

22. *Jure Divino:* the doctrine that kings derive their power from God alone, unlimited by any rights on the part of their subjects. *Jure* is monosyllabic.

24. *Partridge:* John Partridge (1644–1715), the *famigeratissimus* Whig astrologer and almanac-maker.

25–26. *Honour . . . Oaths:* Louis' *parole d'honneur* was a very flexible and useful diplomatic instrument: "After *Lewis* XIV. had been so stout as to declare, *He wou'd never sheath his Sword till he had plac'd King* James *upon the Throne again*" (Oldmixon, p. 55), he signed the treaty of Ryswick, the fourth article of which required him to give "his royal word not to assist directly or indirectly any of the enemies" of William III (HMC *Lords MSS., 4,* 234).

29. *Non-Juror:* Eight bishops and about 400 Anglican clergymen were deprived of their livings in 1689 when they refused to take the oaths of allegiance to William and Mary.

33. *Oats:* The railings of Titus Oates (1649–1705) in 1697 were indeed epical. He complained to the king that "he had run into debt £1600 . . . [that] he had afterwards incurred further debt, for which he was arrested, and must inevitably perish . . . [and that] He had a poor aged mother, to maintain, and his wife and family likely to be turned out of doors" (*CTP 1697–1701/2,* p. 116).

Boufflers: Louis François, duc de Boufflers (1644–1711), a marshal of France in command of one of Louis' armies in Flanders, played an important part in the peace negotiations in July 1697. In five conversations with the earl of Portland, the crucial phrase by which Louis agreed to recognize William as king of England was worked out. In London, however, it was believed that Louis had agreed to send James away to live in Rome (Luttrell, *4,* 253–54, 258–59).

For thee I've lost, if I can rightly scann 'em,
Two Livings worth full Eightscore Pounds *per Annum,*
Bonae & legalis Angliae Monetae;
But now I'm clearly routed by the Treaty.
Then Geese and Pigs my Table ne're did fail,
And Tyth-Eggs merrily flew in like hail;
My Barns with Corn, my Cellars cramm'd with Ale.
The Dice are chang'd, for now, as I'm a sinner,
The Devil, for me, knows where to buy a Dinner.
I might as soon, tho' I were ne're so willing,
Raise a whole Troop of Horse, as one poor Shilling.
My *Spouse,* Alas, must flaunt in Silks no more,
Pray Heaven, for Sustenance, she turn not Whore;
And Daughter *Peggy* too, in time, I fear,
Will learn to take a Stone up in her Ear.
My friends have basely left me with my place,
What's worse, my very Pimples bilk my face.
And frankly my Condition to disclose,
I most resent th'ungratitude of my Nose,
On which tho' I have spent of Wine such store,
It now looks paler than my Tavern score.
My double Chin's dismantled, and my Coat is
Past its best days, *in Verbo Sacerdotis.*
My Breeches too this morning, to my wonder,
I found grown Schismatics, and fallen assunder.
When first I came to Town with Houshold-Clogg,
Rings, Watch, and so forth, fairly went for Progg.
The Ancient *Fathers* next, in whom I boasted,
Were soon exchang'd for primitive Boil'd and Roasted.
Since 'tis no Sin of Books to be a Glutton,
I truck'd *St. Austin* for a Leg of Mutton.
Old *Jerom*'s Volumes next I made a Rape on,
And melted down that Father for a Capon.
When these were gone, my Bowels not to balk,

37. *Treaty:* The treaty of Ryswick was signed on 10 September 1697.
48. *take a Stone up in her Ear:* play the whore (Partridge, p. 834).
58. *Schismatics:* accented on the first syllable. *OED* cites this line.
60. *Progg:* food. *OED* cites this line.
64. *truck'd:* exchanged.

I trespass'd most *enormously* in Chalk.
But long I had not Quarter'd upon Tick,
E're Christian Faith, I found, grew monstrous sick:
And now, Alas! when my starv'd Entrails croke,
At *Partner How*'s I Dine and Sup on Smoke.
In fine, the Government may do its Will,
But I'm afraid my Guts will *Grumble* still.
  Dennis of Sicily, as Books relate, Sir,
When he was tumbled from the Regal State, Sir,
(Which, by the by, I hope will be your Fate, Sir,)
And his good Subjects left him in the lurch,
Turn'd Pedagogue, and *Tyranniz'd* in Birch:
Tho' thus the *Spark* was taken a pegg lower,
Some feeble signs of his old State he bore,
And Reign'd o're Boys, that Govern'd Men before.
For thee I wish some Punishment that worse is;
Since thou hast spoil'd my Prayers, now hear my Curses.
May thy Affairs (for so I wish by Heavens)
All the World o're, at Sixes ly and Sevens.
May *Conti* be impos'd on by the *Primate,*

68. *Chalk:* credit; referring to the custom in alehouses and inns of "ticking" or writing up with chalk a "score" or account of credit given. *OED* cites this line.

72. *Partner How's:* presumably a coffeehouse. Brown himself is consigned to "Dine on Smoak at *How*'s again" in *To the Quibling, Drib'ling, Scribling Poetaster, who has let himself out for Scandal to the Wits at Will's Coffee-House* ("Be not puff'd up with Punning, Friend of mine"), *Discommendatory Verses,* 1700, p. 13.

75–82. *Dennis of Sicily:* Dionysius II (?395–after 343 B.C.), the pupil of Plato and tyrant of Syracuse. There is a tradition that after his second deposition, in 343 B.C., he was allowed to retire to Corinth. "Here looking upon the humblest Station to be safest, he stooped to the meanest Things imaginable. . . . At last he turn'd a Pedagogue in his own Defence, and taught Children in the Highway, that he might either be seen in publick by those that fear'd him, or be more cheaply despis'd by those that fear'd him not" (*Justin's History of the World . . . Made English by Mr. T. Brown. The Second Edition,* 1713, p. 226).

80. *Spark:* an easily-angered bully; cf. "hot headed Sparks," Brown, *Works,* 1711, *4,* 263.

87–90. *Conti:* François-Louis de Bourbon, prince de Conti (1664–1709), was the candidate of Louis XIV for the throne of Poland left vacant by the death of Jan Sobieski in June 1696. Large bribes, administered by Louis' ambassador to Poland, Abbé Melchior de Polignac, secured Conti's election by the Polish diet in June 1697. He was duly proclaimed king of Poland by Cardinal Michal Radziejowski (1645–1705), archbishop of Gniezno and primate of Poland. Conti, however, was "passionnément amoureux" of one of Louis' natural daughters, the young wife of Louis III, duc de Bourbon-Condé, so he was in no hurry to leave Paris (Louis de Rouvroy, duc de

And forc'd, in haste, to leave the Northern Climate:
May he rely upon their Faith, and try it,
And have his Bellyfull of the *Polish Dyet.*
May *Maintenon,* tho' thou so long hast kept her,
With Brand-Venereal singe thy Royal Scepter.
May all the Poets, that thy Fame have scatter'd,
Un-god thee now, and Damn what once they flatter'd.
The Pope, and Thou, be never Cater Cousins,
And *Fistula's* thy Arse-hole seize by Dozens.
Thus far in Jest; but now, to pin the basket,
Mayst thou to *England* come, of *Jove* I ask it,
Thy wretched Fortune, *Lewis,* there to prop,
I hope thou'lt in the *Fryars* take a shop.
Turn Puny-Barber there, bleed lousy Carmen,
Cut Corns for Chimney-Sweepers, and such Vermin,

Saint-Simon, *Mémoires,* ed. Gonzague Truc, *1,* 395–96). When he had not left by mid-August, it was reported that the cardinal primate had already despaired of Conti's success and was preparing to go into retirement at Rome (Luttrell, *4,* 266). Conti's delay provided Frederick Augustus, elector of Saxony, with an opportunity he had been seeking since May 1697 when he publicly abjured Protestantism. By means of larger bribes and the presence of 8000 German troops drawn up on the Polish border, Frederick Augustus, "der Starke," as he was called, succeeded in getting himself crowned king of Poland at Cracow on 15 September 1697 by a bishop who had no power to do so. Ten days later Conti finally reached Danzig. But even after he had been able to bring into play another 5,000,000 *livres,* the Polish diet declared that they would "stand by and assist the king [Augustus II] to the utmost of their power" and Louis was reported to be "mightily exasperated" (Luttrell, *4,* 293, 287).

91. *Maintenon:* Françoise d'Aubigné, marquise de Maintenon (1635–1719) began her long career at the French court in 1669 as governess to Louis' bastards and ended it as governess to Louis himself. Since her marriage to Louis in January 1684 had been kept secret, she was commonly supposed to be his mistress (Luttrell, *2,* 523).

93. *Poets:* "The *French* King had taken *Namur* in the Campaign of 92, in Sight of the Army of the Allies, who were unable to raise the Siege. This was extolled by the Flatterers of that Prince, as a most inimitable Action; and the celebrated *Boileau* . . . composed an Ode on this Occasion in Imitation of *Pindar*" (Matthew Prior, *Miscellaneous Works,* ed. John Banks, 2 vols., 1740, *1,* 17). In 1695 Boileau's ode was reprinted with Prior's parody of it on facing pages.

95. *Pope:* After having broken diplomatic relations with the Vatican in 1688, and imprisoning the papal nuncio, Louis effected a reconciliation with Innocent XII (1615–1700) in November 1693 (Luttrell, *3,* 219).

97. *to pin the basket:* to settle the matter. *OED,* s.v. Basket, cites this line.

100. *Fryars:* Blackfriars, a precinct in the ward of Farringdon Within, between St. Paul's and Fleet Ditch, "well inhabited by Tradesmen" (Strype, *1,* [3]193).

101. *Carmen:* carters, carriers, traditionally "rude, exacting and quarrelsome" (Chamberlayne, 1700, p. 428).

Be forc'd to Trimm (for such I'me sure thy Fate is,)
Thy own *Hugonots,* and us *Non-Jurors,* gratis.
May *Savoy* likewise with thee hither pack,
And carry a Raree-Show upon his back.
May all this happen, as I've put my Pen to't,
And may all *Christian* People say *Amen* to't.

104. *Hugonots:* pronounced *à la française,* disyllabically, with accent on second syllable [yg-no′] (Edmund Huguet, *Dictionnaire de la langue française du sixième siècle,* 7 vols., Paris, 1925–1966, *4,* 515–16). Cf. textual notes, where the addition of "poor" represents an attempt to retain an iambic meter while pronouncing the word *à l'anglaise.*

105. *Savoy:* Víctor Amadeo II, duke of Savoy (1666–1732), whose wife was a granddaughter of Charles I, as well as a niece of Louis XIV, had been a hero in England when he recognized William as king. He joined the League of Augsburg and fought five campaigns against the French. In 1696, however, he capitulated to French pressure, accepted bribes to make a separate peace, and married his daughter to Louis' eldest grandson, Louis, duc de Bourgogne. His "Foul Play with the Allies and . . . Secret Correspondence with the *French* King" is related in *Memoires of the Transactions in Savoy during this War* (1697) (Wing M1673).

106. *Raree-Show:* a peep show carried about in a box; the early exhibitors of peep shows seem to have been Savoyards. *OED* cites this line.

Advice to a Painter
(*11–26 December 1697*)

Among the "other demonstrations of joy" that succeeded upon the signing of the treaty of Ryswick in September 1697 were "the Columns, the triumphal Archs, [and] the Obelises" that were ordered be made ready to welcome the king back to London. Samuel Garth imagined William's entrance in the style of a Roman emperor: "sitting in your Coach of State, adorned with Spoiles, your Coat embroidered with Palms, clad with Purple, crowned with laurel, a company of Captives comeing behind." Prints of William in Roman body armor and a full-bottomed wig were hawked about the streets (see illustration, p. 12), but the triumphal arches and "Obelises" were never to be completed. When William returned to England in November "he put a stop to it; He seemed," as Burnet goes on to say, "to have contracted an antipathy to all vain shows" (Burnet, 2, 205).

These maimed rites reflect perfectly the Tory patriot's feeling that there was really very little to celebrate in the fall of 1697. "Disgrac'd and discontent," his mood, as reflected in this anonymous *Advice to a Painter,* was that of an almost existentialist despair. This poem is no mere bill of complaints, or list of grievances to be patched up or put right. It implies an intrinsic rottenness that is essential to the human condition. The end of the poem does not envisage a reform; it imagines "Knaves in Embrio, and Rogues to come," who will "sell their Country in a closer way." The methods of corruption and betrayal will be refined and made safer, not eliminated.

Within the convention of the advice-to-a-painter genre, the poem commands a series of tableaux. This series begins at the top, with the king on the throne, flanked by the two main supports of the crown, the church and the law, the archbishop of Canterbury and the lord chancellor of England. Then it works its way through the king's favorites, the king's ministers, who were still legally *partes regis*

Peace Restored in Europe by King William III. Engraving by Paulus van Somer

corporis, and the king's loyal House of Commons. The series ends, at the bottom, in a subhuman swarm of "nameless Somethings,"

> Of yelping Yeas and No's, who poll by rote,
> And multiply the Unites of a Vote.
> (lines 135–36)

More particularly, the poem attacks placemen, the holders of lucrative offices in the gift of the crown. These ranged from sinecures like secretary to the lord chief justice in eyre of all his majesty's forests on the south side of the Trent (who was James Sloan [line 108]), to the chief executive officers of the state, like the chancellor of the exchequer, Charles Montagu (line 81). Since 1692 the Commons had failed three times to pass a bill to exclude placemen from sitting in the House. On the second occasion, in fact, the bill passed both houses of parliament and was vetoed by William in January 1694 in what Macaulay called "one of the most dangerous contests in which [William] ever engaged with his Parliament." It is Macaulay again who explained "That the patronage of the Crown was employed on an extensive scale for the purpose of influencing votes" (Macaulay, *5,* 2424, 2291).

The date of composition of the poem can be established within a few weeks. Lines 62–67 assume that Sunderland is still in office and therefore must have been written *before* 26 December 1697, when he resigned. Line 121 requires that Sunderland's son, Lord Spencer, have voted "for Armies" and must have been written *after* 11 December 1697, when, in the first vote taken on the bill for disbanding the army, a Whig motion to recommit was defeated (*CJ, 12,* 5).

The numerous references to this poem in *Faction Display'd* (pp. 660–63, below) suggest that it may have been written by William Shippen. The political orientation and certain stylistic preferences, in any case, are identical with *Faction Display'd,* and the possibility that *Advice to a Painter* (December 1697), *A Conference* (June 1700), *The Golden Age Revers'd* (February 1703), and *The Seven Wise Men* (January–March[?] 1704) are all the work of William Shippen is presently being studied.

In default of corroborating evidence, however, the author of *Advice to a Painter* remains anonymous. But the attribution to Swift (*DNB, 5,* 369) must have been made inadvertently, for there is no evidence that Swift wrote it. The poem elicited a spirited reply by Isaac Watts, *To David Polhill, Esq.* ("And must the Hero, that redeem'd our Land"), which was published first in *POAS,* 1703, 2, 469 and then in Watts, *Horae Lyricae,* 1706, pp. 182–88.

Advice to a Painter

What Hand, what Skill can form the Artful Piece,
To paint our Ruins in a proper Dress?
Inspire us, *Denham*'s Genius, while w'indite,
Urg'd by true Zeal to do our Country right;
As when the daring Artist, taught by you,
With Master-Strokes the first bold Landskip drew.
Here, Painter, here employ thy utmost Skill;
With War and Slav'ry the vast Canvas fill:
And that the Lines be easier understood,
Paint not with fading Colours, but with Blood;
Blood of our bravest Youth in Battel slain,
At *Steenkirk* and at *Landen*'s fatal Plain;
Or that which flow'd, and does just Heaven invoke,
When *Fenwick* yielded to the cruel Stroke.

3. *Denham:* Sir John Denham (1615–69) is invoked as the supposed author of *The Second Advice to a Painter,* of April 1666 (*POAS,* Yale, *1,* 34–53), the first satirical use of the advice-to-a-painter genre.

6. *the first bold Landskip:* the scene depicted in *The Second Advice to a Painter.* The wording may reflect the opening lines of that poem: "Nay, Painter, if thou dar'st design that fight/Which Waller only courage had to write."

12. *Steenkirk:* Steenkerke, a village on the Senne, 20 miles southwest of Brussels, was the scene of one of the confederates' worst defeats in the war of 1689–97. William ordered an attack on the French for 24 July 1692, but the failure of Count Solms to bring up reserves to support the initial successes turned the attack into a desperate retreat, during which Corporal Trim was "run over by a dragoon." The next morning the streets of Brussels were filled with the wounded for whom no room could be found in hospitals (D'Auvergne, 1692, pp. 36–49).

Landen: Landen and Neerwinden are two villages in the province of Liége between which William's army was deployed on 19 July 1693 when it sustained a massive onslaught by the French. The third cavalry charge broke the confederate line, and 5000 or 6000 men, including Count Solms, were killed in the subsequent rout (D'Auvergne, 1693, pp. 58–81). "Thus the *French* triumphed every where" (Burnet, *2,* 113).

14. *Fenwick:* Sir John Fenwick (1645?–97), the Jacobite conspirator, was beheaded on Tower Hill on 28 January 1697 for complicity in a plot to assassinate William III. In an attempt to secure his pardon, he had produced deeply compromising evidence against several Whig leaders and even those who had no doubt about his guilt deplored the summary manner in which justice was executed by an act of attainder passed by the Whig majority in both houses of parliament. This enabled the Tories

First draw the Hero seated on the Throne,
Spite of all Laws, himself observing none;
Let *English* Rights all gasping round him lie,
And native Freedom thrown neglected by:
On either Hand the Priest and Lawyer set,
Two fit Supporters of the Monarch's Seat.
There in a greazy Rotchet cloth'd, describe
The bulky Oracle of the Preaching Tribe;
That solid necessary Tool of State,
Profoundly Dull, Divinely Obstinate.
Here in polluted Robes just reeking, draw
Th'Adulterous Moderator of the Law;
Whose wrinkled Cheeks and sallow Looks proclaim,
The ill Effects of his distemper'd Flame.
If more you'd know, consult his friend *Tom Hobbs*
Who vamps him up with his Mercuriall Jobs.
Next cringing *Benting* place, whose Earth-born Race

---

to proclaim Fenwick as a martyr to Whig vindictiveness (cf. *On Sir John Fenwick* ["Here lie the Relicks of a martyr'd Knight,"] *POAS,* 1703, 2, 321). Harley violently opposed the attainder (Oldmixon, pp. 156–57).

15. *the Hero:* William III (1650–1702).

22. *The bulky Oracle:* Thomas Tenison (1636–1715), archbishop of Canterbury. His "moderation with dissenters" made him particularly unpopular with Tories. He voted for the attainder of Fenwick.

24. *Dull:* "James II spoke of [Tenison] as 'that dull man,' and the epithet stuck" (*DNB, 19,* 540).

26. *Th'Adulterous Moderator:* John Somers (1651–1716), created Baron Somers of Evesham in 1697, was lord chancellor of England. He was unmarried but the name of his mistress was said, in a folio half-sheet of 1694 entitled *Fathers nown Child* ("If you'll lend your Attention, I'll sing you a Song"), to be "Madam *Blount.*" *A Letter from the Grecian Coffee-house, In Answer to the Taunton-Dean Letter,* 1701, p. 7, mentions "his L———p's . . . keeping *Bl——t* in Jayle, while he lay with his Wife."

29. *Tom Hobbs:* Thomas Hobbes (d. 1698), the famous London surgeon, figures in *The Dispensary* (*6,* 163) as Guaiacum, a favorite specific for the French pox (Culpeper, p. 16).

31. *Benting:* Hans Willem Bentinck (1649–1709) was the younger son of a petty Dutch nobleman whose service to William of Orange began in childhood when he was appointed a page of honor at the court of the stadholder. It has been conjectured that "His personal beauty . . . not improbably was the cause of his early favour with the King, whose appreciation of its existence in the male sex resembled that of his ancestor James I" (GEC, *10,* 591). In 1677 he served as William's envoy to England to arrange the marriage with Princess Mary of York. At the Revolution he marched with William from Tor Bay to London at the head of his regiment of horse guards in the Dutch army. In April 1689 he was raised to the peerage as earl of Portland and in-

The Coronet and Garter does disgrace;
Of undescended Parentage, made great
By Chance, his Vertues not discover'd yet.
Patron o'th'Noblest Order, O be just
To thy Heroick Founder's injur'd Dust!
From his ignoble Neck thy Collar tear,
Let not his Breast thy Rays of Honour wear;
To black Designs and Lust let him remain
A servile Favorite, and Grants obtain:
While antient Honours sacred to the Crown
Are lavish'd to support the Minion.
Pale Envy rages in his canker'd Breast,
And to the *British* Name a Foe profest.
  Artist retire, 'twere Insolence too great

---

stalled knight of the garter in March 1697. "He could never bring himself to be acceptable to the *English* Nation" (Burnet, *2*, 5), and by 1697 he had already been displaced by Arnold Joost van Keppel, earl of Albemarle, as William's personal favorite.

35. *Patron o'th'Noblest Order:* The patron of the Order of the Garter is St. George, "and none of those Fabulous St. *Georges* as some have vainly fancied; but that famous Saint and Soldier of Christ, St. *George* of *Cappadocia*" (Chamberlayne, 1692, p. 1253).

36. *Founder:* The Order of the Garter was founded by Edward III in 1350.

37–38. *Collar . . . Rays:* "at high Feasts [members of the Order of the Garter] are to wear . . . a *Collar* of *pure Gold,* composed of Roses enamelled Red, within a Garter enamelled Blew, with the usual Motto ['Honi soit qui mal y pense'] in Letters of Gold . . . . Upon the left Shoulder . . . in all places of Assembly . . . they are to wear an Escutcheon of the Arms of St. *George,* that is, a *Cross with a Garter,* and this by an Order made, *April* 1626. That Ornament . . . about the said Escutcheon now worn, and called *The Star,* or rather, *The Sun in its Glory,* was at the same time enjoyned" (Chamberlayne, 1692, p. 1254).

40. *Grants:* Since 1689 the Tories in the House of Commons had been trying to divert the income from the forfeited estates of English and Irish Jacobites from the privy purse of the king into the public revenue to help defray the costs of the war. After the second such failure, in December 1690, William had promised to make no grants of the forfeited lands "till there be another Opportunity of settling that matter in Parliament" (*CJ, 10,* 536). Although there were six such opportunities in the next seven years, the matter was never settled. So William went ahead and made such lavish grants that some of them, as Bishop Burnet complained, "could hardly be excused, much less justified" (Burnet, *2,* 240). Portland received no less than 135,820 acres in Ireland, plus the manors of Denbigh, Bromfield, and Yale, traditionally reserved for the Prince of Wales (HMC *Lords MSS.,* New Series, *4,* 46). When the Commons forced him to revoke the latter grant, William gave Portland instead the forfeited Irish estates of Donogh Maccarthy, earl of Clancarty, who had followed James II into exile (*CJ, 11,* 390–91, 395, 409; Luttrell, *4,* 215). Earlier he had given him the manor of Swaden, worth £2000 a year (Luttrell, *3,* 472). As a result of William's benefactions, Portland was "supposed to be the richest Subject in *Europe*" (Macky, p. 62).

T'expose the Secrets of the Cabinet;
Or tell how they their looser Moments spend;
That Hellish Scene would all chast Ears offend.
For should you pry into the close Alcove,
And draw the Exercise of Royal Love,
Keppell and He are *Ganymede* and *Jove*.
Avert the Omen, Heaven! O may I ne'er
Purchase a Title at a Rate so dear:
In some mean Cottage let me die unknown,
Rather than thus be Darling of a Throne.
  Now Painter, even Art is at a stand,
For who can draw the *Proteus Sunderland?*
The deep Reserves of whose Apostate Mind,
No Skill can reach, no Principles can bind;
Whose working Brain does more Disguises bear
Than ever yet in Vision did appear.
A supple whispring Minister, ne'er just,
Trusted, yet always forfeiting his Trust,
And only constant to unnat'ral Lust.
For prostituted Faith alone made great,
And this is he who must support the Weight,
And prop the Ruins of a sinking State.
  Artist proceed, next the brib'd Senate draw,
That Arbitrary Body above Law;
Place Noise and Faction and Disorder there,

51. *Keppell:* Arnold Joost van Keppel (1670–1718), the eldest son of Oswald, heer van Keppel in Guelderland, attended William to England in 1688 as a page of honor and served successively as groom of the bedchamber and master of the robes. William made him grants of forfeited estates in Ireland which amounted to 108,634 acres, although he was then but a handsome young man "who had rendered no service whatever to his adopted country" (GEC, *1*, 92). Macky mentions that he was "King *William*'s constant Companion in all his Diversions and Pleasures"—"very infamous Pleasures," Swift added (Swift, *Prose, 5*, 259). On 10 February 1697 he had been created earl of Albemarle and in March 1698 Tallard reported to Louis XIV that he was rising in favor every day (Grimblot, *1*, 323).

57. *Sunderland:* Robert Spencer (1640–1702), second earl of Sunderland. Princess Anne told her sister in March 1688 that "Everybody knows how often this man turned backwards and forwards" (*DNB, 18*, 781). He twice served Charles II as secretary of state, but voted for the first exclusion bill. He was lord president of the council and secretary of state for James II, but betrayed his master's secrets to William of Orange. In April 1697 he had returned to public office as lord chamberlain and was appointed one of the lords justices of the realm who governed England in William's absence that summer.

And formal *Paul* set mumping in the Chair;
Once the chief Bulwark of the Church and State,
Their Darling once, but now their Fear and Hate:
So a rich Cordial, when its Virtue's spent,
Contributes to the Death it should prevent;
Of publick Treasure lavishly profuse,
Large Sums diverted to their private use;
By Places and by Bounty largely paid,
For Rights given up, and Liberty betray'd.
  Expose the Mercenary Herd to view,
And in the Front Imperious *Montague:*
With venal Wit, and prostituted Sense,
With matchless Pride and monstrous Impudence;
To whose successful Villanies we owe
All his own Ills, and all that others do.
Slavish Excises are his darling Sin,

71. *Paul:* Paul Foley (1645?–99) was a younger son of Thomas Foley, the ironmaster of Stourbridge. He represented Hereford city in the House of Commons (1689–99), was elected speaker in March 1695 and unanimously re-elected in November 1695. Like Robert Harley, he was nominally a Whig, but a Whig "mécontent" who made common cause with the Tories and opposed the attainder of Fenwick. Burnet called him "a man of vertue, and good principles, but morose and wilful" (Burnet, *2,* 109).

78. *Bounty:* a gift bestowed by the sovereign. The earliest citation in *OED* is dated 1708.

81. *Montague:* Charles Montagu (1661–1715) attracted the patronage of Charles Sackville, sixth earl of Dorset, almost immediately upon his graduation from Trinity College, Cambridge. He was appointed lord of the treasury in March 1692 and "came to have great notions, with relation to all the concerns of the Treasury, and of the Publick Funds" (Burnet, *2,* 108). In April 1694 he was made chancellor of the exchequer. In the House of Commons, where he sat for the borough of Maldon, Essex (1689–95) and Westminster (1695–1700), he "gained such a visible ascendant over all, that were zealous for the King's Service, that he gave the Law to the rest, which he always did with great spirit, but sometimes with too assuming an air" (Burnet, *2,* 218). Consequently, when the Tories learned that a Mr. Railton, to whom a grant had been passed of some £10,000 in recognizances forfeited in Ireland, was really a nominee of Montagu, they leaped to the attack, Montagu "being the person they have the greatest mind to lower, as one that stands in their way" (*CJ, 12,* 116; Vernon, *1,* 461). Seeing which way the wind was blowing, Montagu installed his brother in the profitable post of auditor of the exchequer when it fell vacant in September 1698 (Vernon, *2,* 165–67) and subsequently retired to it himself in November 1699.

86. *Excises:* The mounting costs of the war with France had required substantial increases in excise taxes. An Act for doubling the Duty of Excise upon Beer, Ale, and other Liquors received the royal assent in January 1691 (*CJ, 10,* 536), and under Montagu new taxes were imposed on salt (1694), sea-coal, glass, and tobacco pipes (1695), malt and leather (1697).

And 'Chequer-Bills the Product of his Brain;
No publick Profit but conduces most
To raise his Fortune at the publick Cost.
Orders and Precedents are Things of Course,
Too weak to interrupt his rapid Force;
Till Wiser Commons shall in time to come
Their Antient English *Principles resume,*
And give their base Corrupter his just Doom.
Thus have I seen a Whelp of Lion's Brood
Couch, fawn and lick his Keeper's Hand for Food,
Till in some lucky Hour the generous Beast,
By an insulting Lash, or some gross Fraud opprest,
His just Resentment terribly declares,
Disdains the Marks of Slavery he wears,
And his weak Feeder into pieces tears.
  Let *Gaffney*'s noble Hangman next advance,
And tell his Fears of Popery and *France;*
And for the blust'ring Pedant leave a space,

87. *'Chequer-Bills:* In April 1696 Montagu tacked to Harley's land bank bill clauses empowering the treasury to issue negotiable paper payable to bearer (7 & 8 William III c. 31). These were the first exchequer bills. Upon issue, they yielded no interest, but after they had been tendered in payment of any tax obligation and reissued by the Exchequer, they bore interest at 3*d.* per cent per day. Consequently a number of customs, excise, and treasury officials maintained a dangerous trade in forging endorsements.

94. *give . . . his just Doom:* i.e. impeach Montagu for procuring grants to himself of forfeited Irish estates (81 *n.*); cf. [Charles Davenant], *A Discourse upon Grants and Resumptions,* 1700, p. 357: *"when the People of* England *desire an Act of Resumption, the Work must begin with Impeaching Corrupt Ministers."*

95–101. *Whelp . . . Keeper:* In the somewhat strained terms of this metaphor, the "Whelp of Lion's Brood" is the House of Commons and its "Keeper" is Montagu.

102. *Gaffney's noble Hangman:* Thomas Coningsby (1656?–1729) was successively paymaster-general of William's forces in Ireland, one of the lords justices, and vice-treasurer of Ireland. He was created baron Coningsby of Clanbrassil in the Irish peerage in April 1692 and a year later was sworn as privy councillor. In December 1693 Richard Coote, earl of Bellamont, moved his impeachment in the House of Commons for crimes committed during his term of office as lord justice, 1690–92. The fourth article claimed that he ordered one Gaffney, a witness in a pending murder case, to be hanged without trial and without even a written order for his execution (*CJ, 11,* 33). Coningsby was saved from replying to the articles by a pardon under the king's hand (Luttrell, *3,* 310). In Parliament he represented Leominster, Herefordshire (1695–1717), but even among Whigs it was "not very well liked that my Lord Coningsby should be so insatiable as to have some new grant every session" (Vernon, *2,* 143–44).

104. *Pedant:* Marginalia in *ACKOP* identify the Pedant as Norris, presumably William Norris (1657–1702), of Speke, in Lancashire. He succeeded his elder brother

Who wears *Corinthian* Metal in his Face:
See where the florid warlike *Cutts* appears,
As brave and senseless as the Sword he wears.
Here *Sloan* baits *Seymour, Littleton, Jack How,*

Thomas as a Whig member for Liverpool (1695–1700). He signed the Association for defending the king in 1696, was active in the prosecution of Fenwick (*Norris Papers,* ed. Thomas Heywood, Manchester, 1846, pp. xii–xiii, where he is confused with his brother Thomas), and in April 1697 was mentioned for a post in the admiralty (Luttrell, *4,* 213). He was said to be "a violent man, but speaks well" (HMC *Kenyon MSS.,* p. 400).

105. *wears Corinthian Metal in his Face:* i.e. looks like a shameless debauchee.

106. *Cutts: John Cutts* (1661–1707), created baron Cutts of Gowran in the Irish peerage (December 1690), was one of England's authentic military heroes in the period between the crossing of the Boyne in July 1690 and Blenheim in August 1704. He earned his sobriquet, the Salamander, while leading 3000 fusiliers in the final assault on Namur in August 1695. He was also a poet and patron of literature to whom Richard Steele dedicated *The Christian Hero* (1701). But even his admirers found him "too much seized with vanity and self-conceit" (*DNB, 5,* 368) and his weakness was said to be "son attachement . . . à la personne du Roy Guillaume" (PRO 31/3 190, f. 35v). He secured election to parliament by 13 votes in a disputed election for Cambridgeshire which was almost overturned in the House (*CJ, 11,* 91–93). Thereafter he sat for Cambridgeshire until July 1702 and for Newport, Isle of Wight, until his death.

108. *Sloan:* James Sloan (d. 1704), "blustr'ing Sloan," as he is called in *A Description of the Chancellor of Ireland* ("With Negro Phyz and Impudence repleat") (Folger MS. M.b.12, f. 223), represented the rotten borough of Thetford, Norfolk (1696–1700), where the 32 burgesses demanded "fifty guineas for a vote" (Walcott, p. 16), in January 1696. He so distinguished himself in his first session that he "had like to have been call'd to the barr" for defending the king's veto of the members property qualification bill (Luttrell, *4,* 42–43). In February 1697 he was elected one of the commissioners of the public accounts in the room of Lord William Paulet (125 *n.*) (*CJ, 11,* 703–05) and in the following April he was made secretary to Thomas, Lord Wharton, chief justice in eyre south of Trent and one of the leading Whig magnates (Luttrell, *4,* 215). He voted for the attainder of Fenwick and against disbanding the army in January 1699 (Browning, *3,* 217).

Seymour: Sir Edward Seymour (1633–1708) of Berry Pomeroy, Devonshire, fourth baronet, explained to the prince of Orange in November 1688 that "the proud Duke" of Somerset represented a younger branch of *his* family. He was speaker of the House of Commons in the second parliament of Charles II and survived to sit in the third parliament of Queen Anne. He represented, alternately, the Devonshire boroughs of Totness (1661–81, 1685–87, 1695–98) and Exeter (1689–95, 1698–1708), but Czar "Seymskeyes Western Empire" as Defoe called it (HMC *Portland MSS., 4,* 222), controlled the election to several more seats in the House of Commons. Seymour refused to join the Association in 1696 and spoke in defense of Sir John Fenwick (Oldmixon, pp. 153, 158). Burnet called him "The ablest man of his party" (Burnet, *1,* 382).

Littleton: Sir Thomas Littleton (1647?–1710) of Stoke St. Milborough, Shropshire, third baronet, was the Whig member for New Woodstock, Oxfordshire (1689–1702) and a close associate of Montagu. He was appointed a lord of the treasury in May 1696,

And all the while old *Bowman* cries Bow Wow.
To *Palms* and *Strickland,* and the *Yorkshire* Crew
By *Smith* directed, the next Station's due.

---

and supported the attainder of Fenwick. In the next parliament (December 1698) he was elected speaker. Burnet called him "the vehementest arguer of them all" (Burnet, *1,* 389).

Jack How: John Grubham Howe (1657–1722), a younger brother of Sir Scrope Howe of Nottinghamshire, was from 1689 to 1698 a member for Cirencester, Gloucestershire, and subsequently served for county Gloucestershire (1698–1705). He began his career as a staunch Whig, like his brother, but soon became a violent Tory and partisan of Sir Edward Seymour. He refused to sign the Association in 1696 (Browning, *3,* 201), opposed the attainder of Fenwick, and with "a boldness of speech, which, till *then,* had never been heard in parliament . . . contributed more than any other man in the kingdom to embarrass the measures of the government" (*Gentleman's Magazine, 19* [August 1749], 364–65). One occasion on which "Littleton [baits] Jack How" is recorded in *The Gentleman's Magazine* (ibid.). He was "a tall, thin, pale-faced Man, with a very wild Look; brave in his Person, bold in expressing himself, a violent Enemy, a sure Friend, and seems always to be in a Hurry" (Macky, p. 118).

109. *old Bowman:* identified by one reader as "Boscowen" (BM MS. Sloane 3516, f. 160), presumably Hugh Boscawen (1625–1701), the Whig member for Cornwall (1660, 1668–1701) and Tregoney, Cornwall (1661–81), who distinguished himself by his opposition to James II. But the phrase also recalls Sir Roger L'Estrange (1616–1704), James II's licenser of the press: *"old Bowman Roger, with his little pack of inferiour Crape-gown-Men yelping after him" (Some Reflections upon the Pretended Parallel in the Play called The Duke of Guise,* 1683, p. 8). The joke may also depend upon the fact that one *"Bowman* . . . kept the *Dog-Tavern* in *Drury-Lane,"* which was a Jacobite center (Thomas Brown, *A Continuation or Second Part of the Letters from the Dead to the Living,* 2nd ed., 1707, p. 73; Luttrell, *3,* 484).

110. *Palms:* William Palmes, the member for Malton, Yorkshire (1668–1713), was a friend and partisan of the Whig magnate, Thomas, Lord Wharton. He controlled the borough of Malton and secured the second seat for his son-in-law, Sir William Strickland (Walcott, p. 202). In 1694 he had been mentioned for a commissionership of the treasury (Luttrell, *3,* 273), but the post went instead to John Smith (111 *n.*). He voted for the recoinage and for the attainder of Fenwick, both in 1696, and against disbanding the army in 1699.

Strickland: Sir William Strickland (1665–1724) of Boynton, Yorkshire, third baronet, was a Whig member for Malton, Yorkshire (1689–98, January 1701–08, 1722–24), the pocket borough of his father-in-law, William Palmes (110 *n.*), Yorkshire (1708–10), and Old Sarum, Wiltshire (1716–22); see *The Golden Age Revers'd,* 86 *n.,* below.

111. *Smith:* John Smith (1655–1723) had been a staunch Whig since 1678 when he was first elected for Ludgershall, in Wiltshire. Subsequently he represented Beeralston, Devonshire, and Andover, Hampshire (1695–1713). In 1694 he was appointed lord of the treasury and sworn of the privy council in May 1695. Later he served twice as chancellor of the exchequer and once as speaker of the House of Commons. James Vernon, who refers to him as "a leading man" in February 1698, also provides an example of his "inveterate Rancour." He was unalterably opposed to restoring Sunderland to the ministry after his resignation in December 1697 and told Montagu that "others might be as good-natured as they please, and forget all that was passed; but

Smith while he seems good-natur'd, frank and kind,
Betrays th'inveterate Rancour of his Mind.
To the Chit *Spencer,* Painter next be just,
That roiling wither'd Offspring of Forc'd Lust,
Which his unnatural Father grudg'd to spare
From his *Italian* Joys, and spoil'd his Heir;
From hence the aukward Politician came,
To Commonwealths, which he admires, a Shame,
And Slave to Kings, tho he abhors the Name.
He votes for Armies, talks for Liberty,
In th' House for Millions, out for Property:
Thus Father-like, with Flattery betrays
The Government which he pretends to raise.
Near him Lord *William* draw, whose well-stock'd Brain

---

for his part, he would never trust those who were capable of such practices, and he must leave those who would enter into such engagements" (Vernon, *1,* 484).

114. *Chit:* the young of a wild animal; a sprout, scion.

Spencer: Charles Spencer (1674–1722), second son of Robert Spencer, second earl of Sunderland, became Lord Spencer in 1688 upon the death of his older brother. He was a Whig member for Tiverton, Devonshire (1695–1702), a small borough in which his father "had a great deal of influence" (Walcott, p. 20). He was an enthusiastic partisan of Montagu and during the debate on Fenwick boldly proposed that bishops be excluded from voting (Vernon, *1,* 69).

117. *Italian Joys:* buggery; Thomas Brown called it "Cathedral Exercise, or Bestial backslidings" (*A Continuation or Second Part of the Letters from the Dead to the Living,* p. 180). Torcy reported to Louis XIV in 1687 that Sunderland "hait les femmes" (PRO Trans. 31/3 174, f. 134).

119. *Commonwealths . . . admires:* In 1712 Jonathan Swift found that Spencer "hath much fallen from the Height of those Republican Principles with which he began: For, in his Father's lifetime, while he was a Member of the House of Commons, he would often among his familiar Friends refuse the Title of Lord; (as he hath done to myself) swear that he would never be called otherwise than *Charles Spencer;* and hoped to see the Day, when there should not be a Peer in *England*" (Swift, *Prose, 7,* 9).

121. *votes for Armies:* On considering the king's speech at the opening of the first session of parliament after "the happy Conclusion" of the war, the first resolution, proposed by Robert Harley, was to disband all land forces raised since 1680 (*Parl. Hist., 5,* 1167–1169). Lord Spencer must have opposed this measure in a division of 11 December 1697 (*CJ, 12,* 5). His name also appears in a list of court Whigs who "voted for the army" (Browning, *3,* 217) in a division of January 1699.

125. *Lord William:* identified by marginal notes in *ALM* as William Paulet, second son of Charles Paulet, first duke of Bolton, who was one of the prime movers of the Revolution. Lord William, as he was styled by his courtesy title, became a personal friend of the junto lords and one of their leading henchmen in the House of Commons, where he sat for Hampshire (1689–90), Winchester (1690–1710, 1715–30) and

Outweighs his Index-Learning half a Grain.
  Next Painter draw our Politician *Boyle,*
That fawning Arse-worm with his cringing Smile;
Relations, Country, Court do all despise him,
He's grown so low ev'n Buggery can't raise him.
  With these as fellow Empricks in design,
Let *Wharton, Rich, Young, Clark,* and *Hobart* join;

New Lymington, Hampshire (1710–15). He was another one of the King's Friends who "voted for the army" in 1699. He frequently resorted to duels for the settlement of political differences (Luttrell, *2,* 599; *3,* 252; *4,* 337, 370; *5,* 623).

126. *his:* Lord Spencer's. Evelyn had remarked in 1688 that he was "a Youth of extraordinary hopes, very learned for his age & ingenious" (Evelyn, *4,* 595).

127. *Boyle:* Henry Boyle (d. 1725), third son of Charles Boyle, baron Clifford of Lanesborough, and the grandson of William Seymour, second duke of Somerset, and of Richard Boyle, second earl of Cork and first earl of Burlington, made "a considerable Figure in the *House* of *Commons*" where he sat for Tamworth, Staffordshire (1689–90), Cambridge University (1692–1705), and Westminster (1705–10). Although nominally a Tory—he voted against the recoinage bill and against the attainder of Fenwick—he subscribed to the Association to defend William III, voted against disbanding the army, and became in the next reign totally Whiggish. He was appointed lord of the treasury (1699–1701), privy councillor, and chancellor of the exchequer (1701–08). Macky's prediction that he "obliges every Body in the *Exchequer;* and in Time may prove a Great Man," was subsequently fulfilled when Boyle was appointed lord treasurer of Ireland (1704–10), lord lieutenant of the West Riding of Yorkshire (1704–15), secretary of state (1708–10), and raised to the peerage as baron Carleton of Carleton. Although said to be "agreeable amongst the Ladies," he died unmarried (Macky, p. 126).

128. *Arse-worm:* "a little diminutive Fellow" (*A New Dictionary* [1699], sig. B3r).

132. *Wharton:* Goodwin Wharton (1653–1704) was the second son of Philip, fourth baron Wharton, of Wharton in Westmorland, and the brother of "Honest Tom Wharton," the Whig magnate who became the first marquis. He was a wayward genius whose eccentricities included spiritualism, underwater salvage, and a two-volume autobiography preserved in BM Add. MSS. 20006 and 20007 (Bryan Dale, *The Good Lord Wharton,* 1901, pp. 21, 23). He began his parliamentary career in 1697 as an exclusionist member for East Grinstead, Sussex (1679–81), and subsequently represented Westmorland (1689–90), Malmesbury, Wiltshire (1690–95), Cockermouth, Cumberland (1695–98), and Buckinghamshire (1698–1704), all in the Whig interest. In 1696 he signed the Association twice, for Cockermouth and Malmesbury, both of which had returned him (Browning, *3,* 198, 211).

Rich: presumably Sir Robert Rich (1648–99), of Roos Hall, in Beccles, Suffolk, second baronet, and Whig member of parliament for the neighboring borough of Dunwich (1689–99). He was a member of the puritan family headed by the earls of Warwick and also a grandson of John Hampden. He served as a lord of the admiralty (1691–99), voted for the recoinage and against disbanding the army.

Young: Sir Walter Yonge (1653–1731), of Colyton, Devonshire, third baronet, represented the neighboring boroughs of Honiton (1679–81, 1690–1710) and Ashburton (1689–90) in parliament and long served as a commissioner of customs (1694–1701, 1714–31). He began his career as one of Shaftesbury's lieutenants, signed the Association in

And let not *Hawles* pass unregarded by.
'Twere endless to recount the meaner Fry
Of yelping Yeas and No's, who poll by rote,
And multiply the Unites of a Vote;
Opprest with Clamour, Truth and Justice flies,
And thus pursu'd, down-hunted Reason lies.
  Some few untainted Patriots still remain,
Who native Zeal and Probity retain;
These sullen draw, disgrac'd and discontent,
Mourning the Ruin which they can't prevent.
  But Painter hold—Reserve the vacant Room
For Knaves in Embrio, and Rogues to come;
Who undiscover'd, yet will us betray,
And sell their Country in a closer way.

1696, and on 18 January 1699 upon the third reading of Harley's bill for disbanding the army, he was a teller for the noes, along with Lord William Paulet (125 *n.*) (Browning, *3*, 199, 217; *CJ*, *12*, 440).

Clark: Edward Clarke (1649?–1710) of Chipley, the lifelong friend of John Locke, represented Taunton, Somerset (1690–1710), as a nominee and partisan of Somers (26 *n.*) (Walcott, p. 202). He was chosen one of the 24 original directors of the Bank of England in July 1694, but "desired to be excused" (Luttrell, *3*, 342, 351). He was auditor of the queen's household and from 1695 to 1700 served as a commissioner of the excise. He voted for the recoinage, for the attainder of Fenwick, and against disbanding the army in 1699.

Hobart: Sir Henry Hobart (1658?–98) of Blickling, Norfolk, fourth baronet, began his parliamentary career in 1681 as a Whig member for King's Lynn, Norfolk. Subsequently he sat for Norfolk (1689–90, 1695–98) and Beeralston, Devonshire (1694–95). He was prominent in the opposition to James II, served as gentleman of the horse to William at the Boyne (Collins, 1741, *4*, 399), and voted for the recoinage and the attainder of Fenwick in 1696. In April 1697 it was rumored that he was to join Sir Robert Rich (132 *n.*) on the admiralty board (Luttrell, *4*, 213), but Goodwin Wharton (132 *n.*) was appointed instead. In June of the same year he joined Sir Walter Yonge (132 *n.*) in the commission of the customs (Beatson, *2*, 356). In August 1698 he was killed in a duel with Oliver Le Neve (Vernon, *2*, 158).

133. *Hawles:* Sir John Hawles (1645–1716), of Salisbury and Lincoln's Inn, began his parliamentary career in the convention parliament as a member for Old Sarum, Wiltshire. Subsequently he was elected for Wilton, Wiltshire (1695–98), three Cornish boroughs: Michael (1698–1700), Truro (1701), St. Ives (1701–02), and Stockbridge, Hampshire (1705–10). Anthony à Wood called him "a great Williamite . . . but ill-natured, turbulent and inclining to a republic" (Wood, *4*, 1527 *n.*). Knighted in November 1695, he served as solicitor-general (1695–1702), signed the Association in 1696, and invariably voted Whig.

135. *poll by rote:* vote at the poll as they have been instructed or bribed.

136. *multiply:* Multiple voting was a frequent cause of disputed parliamentary elections; cf. *CJ*, *13*, 329.

1698

Joseph Addison

The Play-House
(December 1698–April 1699)

Although it is called *The Play-House. A Satyr* in most copies, Addison's poem is a satire in which a fascination for the stage in "all its Pomp and Pageantry" is revealed in every paragraph. Written only a year after Jeremy Collier had published *A Short View of the Immorality, and Profaneness of the English Stage, The Play-House* attacks neither the immorality nor the profaneness of the stage. It takes it for granted that when an actress plays a whore she is not playing a part and that when an actor works for "thrifty Rich" he may literally "stink" in his own clothes. Nowhere is it suggested that these conditions should be changed.

Addison's poem makes a sharp contrast with Robert Gould's satire, also called *The Play-House,* which was published in 1689 and reprinted with additions in 1709. Gould's poem is straightforward diatribe by an outsider:

> The *Play-house* is the Scandal of the *State;*
>
> the Stage . . .
> Is but a *Hot-Bed* rais'd to force up Whores:
> (*Works,* 2 vols., 1709, 2, 249, 252)

Addison's poem, on the other hand, is a satire on the stage from the inside: "But enter in, my Muse, the Stage survey."

After not having left Magdalen College, where he was a fellow, for more than two years, Addison visited London twice in 1698: 7 March–27 April and October–27 November (Peter Smithers, *The Life of Joseph Addison,* Oxford, Clarendon Press, 1954, pp. 41, 42). The visit that provided the occasion for the present poem is more likely to have been the second one, for then Addison could have seen Peter Motteux's opera, *The Island Princess,* at the Theatre Royal (*London Stage, 1,* 505). This play, based on John Fletcher's tragicomedy, meets all the requirements of *The Play-House:* it has two kings, each attended "with a numerous Train" (Stage Direction, II, iii), a "Stern exasperated Tyrant," a princess in constant jeopardy, clowns, "Dull Cits," and even an allusion to Amphion (*The Island Princess: Or, The Generous Portugueze: Made into an Opera,* 1736, p. 64).

Another performance which *The Play-House* suggests that Addison attended was that of the first play by a 21-year-old Anglo-Irishman recently arrived in London. The playwright was George Farquhar and the play was *Love and a Bottle,* a kind of parody of the genre in which Farquhar was later to excel. This was not a popular play (*London Stage, 1,* 507) and Addison's praise (line 38) may have been Farquhar's first favorable notice. Conversely, the tone of Addison's poem may owe something to Farquhar's scorn of Jeremy Collier's attitudinizing. In the epilogue to his play Farquhar insists that Collier's total effect has been to frighten one poor actress out of London:

> Yet for all this, we still are at a loss.
> O Collier! Collier! thou'st frighted away Miss *C*[*ros*]*s*.

Since Addison left Oxford for the last time in April 1699, it is probably safe to assume that *The Play-House* was written between November 1698, when *Love and a Bottle* succeeded *The Island Princess* at the Theatre Royal, and April 1699.

The Play-House

Near to the *Rose* where Punks in numbers flock
To pick up Cullies, to increase their Stock;
A Lofty Fabrick does the Sight Invade,
And stretches round the Place a pompous Shade;
Where sudden Shouts the Neighbourhood surprise,
And Thund'ring Claps, and dreadful Hissings rise.
Here Thrifty *Rich* hires Heroes by the Day,
And keeps his Mercenary Kings in Pay;
With deep-Mouth'd Actors fills the Vacant Scenes,
And draines the Town for Goddesses and Queens:
Here the Lewd Punk, with Crowns and Scepters Grac'd,
Teaches her Eyes a more Majestick Cast;
And Hungry Monarchs with a numerous Train
Of Suppliant Slaves, like *Sancho* Starve and Reign.
But enter in, my Muse, the Stage survey,
And all its Pomp and Pageantry display;
Trap-Doors and Pit-falls, from th'unfaithful Ground,
And Magic Walls, encompass it around:
On either side maim'd Temples fill our Eyes,
And Intermixt with Brothell-Houses rise;
Disjointed Palaces in order stand,

1. *the Rose:* The Rose Tavern, on the corner of Bridges and Russell streets, adjacent to the Theatre Royal, was a great resort for loose women and minor poets (*Letters from the Living to the Living,* 1703, p. 22).

Punks: "about the Third Act," Edward Ward relates, "the Mask'd Ladies . . . bolted from their Stews . . . sneak into the Pit and Eighteen-penny Gallery, without Tickets, at the Curtesie of the Door-Keepers" (*The Secret History of Clubs,* 1709, p. 144). The intrigues agreed upon in the theatre were frequently played out at the Rose, the best room of which is depicted in the third stage of *The Rake's Progress* (Robert Gould, *Works,* 1709, *2,* 229); cf. *The Dispensary, 4,* 2 *n.,* below.

3. *A Lofty Fabrick:* the Theatre Royal; cf. *The Dispensary, 4,* 1 *n.,* below.

4. *pompous Shade:* The phrase recurs in Pope, *An Essay on Man* (1733–34), IV, 304.

7. *Thrifty Rich:* Christopher Rich (d. 1714) was co-patentee of the Theatre Royal for more than 20 years (March 1688–November 1709). According to Colley Cibber, who was a member of his company, he was "a close subtle Man" who "gave the Actors more Liberty, and fewer Days Pay, than any of his Predecessors" (*An Apology for the Life,* ed. Robert W. Lowe, 2 vols., 1889, *1,* 252–53).

And Groves Obedient to the movers Hand,
O'er-shade the Stage, and flourish at Command.
A Stamp makes broken Towns and Trees entire:
So when *Amphion* struck the Vocal Lyre,
He saw the Spacious Circuit all around,
With crowding Woods, and rising Cities Crown'd.
  But next survey the Tyring-Room and see
False Titles, and promiscuous Quality
Confus'dly swarm, from Heroes and from Queens
To those that Swing in Clouds and fill Machines;
Their various Characters, they chuse with Art,
The Frowning Bully fits the Tyrants part:
Swoln Cheeks and Swagging Belly makes a Host;
Pale meager Looks, and hollow Voice, a Ghost;
From careful Brows, and heavy down-cast Eyes,
Dull Cits, and thick-scull'd Aldermen arise:
The Comick Tone, inspir'd by *Farquhar,* draws
At every Word, loud Laughter and Applause:
The Mincing Dame continues as before,
Her Character unchang'd, and Acts a Whore.
  Above the rest, the Prince with haughty stalks,
Magnificent in Purple Buskins walks:
The Royal Robes his awful Shoulders grace,
Profuse of Spangles and of Copper-Lace:
Officious Vassals, to his mighty Thigh,
Guiltless of Blood, th'unpointed Weapon tye:
Then the Gay Glittering Diadem put on,
Pondrous with Brass, and Starr'd with Bristoll stone.
His Royal Consort next consults her Glass
And out of twenty Boxes culls a Face;
The Whit'ning first her Sallow Looks besmears,

24. *A Stamp makes . . . entire:* On cue—a stamp of the foot(?)—the scenes are changed.

25. *Amphion:* a son of Zeus and Antiope who learned to play the lyre so well that stones and trees moved of their own accord to provide a walled setting for Thebes; cf. Marvell, *The First Anniversary of the Government under O.C.* (1655), 49.

34. *Swagging:* swaying heavily to and fro *(OED).*

42. *with haughty stalks:* Cf. Addison, *An Account of the Greatest English Poets, Works,* 2nd ed., 4 vols., 1730, *1,* 36: "But *Milton* next, with high and haughty stalks,/ Unfetter'd in majestick numbers walks."

49. *Bristoll stone:* rock crystals cut to imitate diamonds.

All Pale and Wan th'unfinish'd Form appears;
'Till on her Cheeks the Blushing Purple Glows,
And a false Virgin Modesty bestows.
Her ruddy Lips the Deep Vermillion dyes;
Length to her Brows the Pencils touch supplies,
And with black bending Arches Shades her Eyes.
Well pleas'd at last the Picture she beholds,
And Spots it o'er with Artificial Moles;
Her Countenance compleat, the Beaux she warms
With looks not hers, and spight of Nature, Charms.
   Thus Artfully their Persons they disguise,
'Till the last flourish bids the Curtain rise.
The Prince then enters on the Stage in State;
Behind, a Guard of Candle-Snuffers wait:
There, swoln with Empire, Terrible and fierce,
He shakes the Dome, and tears his Lungs with Verse:
His Subjects Tremble, the Submissive Pit,
Wrapt up in Silence and Attention, sit;
Till freed at length, he lays aside the weight
Of Publick Business, and Affairs of State:
Forgets his Pomp, Dead to Ambitious Fires,
And to some peaceful Brandy-Shop retires;
Where in full Gills his Anxious thoughts he drowns,
And quaffs away the cares that wait on Crowns.
   The Princess next her painted Charms displays,
Where every look the Pencils Art betrays.
The Callow 'Squire at distance Feeds his Eyes,
And silently for Paint and Patches Dies:
But if the Youth behind the Scenes Retreat,
He sees the blended Colours melt with heat,
And all the trickling Beauties run in Sweat.
The borrow'd Visage he admires no more,
And Nauseates every Charm he lov'd before:
So the same Spear, for double force Renown'd,
Apply'd the Remedy, that gave the Wound.

86–87. *Spear . . . Wound:* The spear was Achilles' and the victim was Telephos. The Delphic oracle, "He that wounded shall also heal," was correctly interpreted by Odysseus to mean the spear itself which had given the wound. When scrapings from the spear were applied, therefore, the wound healed (H. J. Rose, *A Handbook of Greek Mythology,* New York, E. P. Dutton, 1959, p. 233).

In tedious Lists 'twere endless to Engage,
And draw at length the Rabble of the Stage,
Where one for twenty Years, has giv'n Allarms,
And call'd Contending Monarchs to their Arms;
Another fills a more Important Post,
And rises every other night a Ghost.
Thro' the cleft Stage, his mealy Face he rears,
Then Stalks along, Groans thrice, and Disappears;
Others with Swords and Shields, the Soldiers Pride,
More than a thousand times have chang'd their Side,
And in a thousand fatal Battles Dy'd.
Thus several Persons, several Parts perform;
Pale Lovers whine, and Blustring Heroes Storm.
The Stern exasperated Tyrants rage,
Till the kind Bowl of Poyson clears the Stage.
Then Honours vanish, and Distinctions cease;
Then with Reluctance, haughty Queens undress.
Heroes no more their fading Lawrells boast,
And mighty Kings, in private Men are lost.
He, whom such Titles swell'd, such Power made proud,
To whom whole Realms, and Vanquish'd Nations bow'd,
Throws off the Gaudy Plume, the purple Train,
And in his own vile Tatters stinks again.

1699

Arthur Mainwaring[?]

The Brawny Bishop's Complaint (*January–February 1699*)

Gilbert Burnet (1643–1715), cashiered chaplain of Charles II, *eminence grise* of the Revolution, and William's latitudinarian bishop of Salisbury, was a frequent target for Tory satirists in four reigns. *The Brawny Bishop's Complaint* simply takes up and expands an insinuation in Dryden's characterization of Burnet as the noble Buzzard in the Fable of the Swallows from *The Hind and the Panther* (1687), *3*, 1145–46:

> Broad-back'd and Brawny, built for Loves delight,
> A Prophet form'd, to make a female Proselyte.

In 1698 Burnet had been much in the news. In June his second wife had died, leaving him with five children under the age of 10 years. Burnet commented on this event with typical bluntness: "At that time I saw it was convenient for me to marry again" (Foxcroft, p. 508). In the same month the king had appointed him preceptor to Prince William, duke of Gloucester, the nine-year-old heir apparent to the Princess Anne, and on 30 January 1699 Burnet had preached an eloquent sermon before the House of Lords in the Abbey church.

At this period of his life Burnet lived in a rented house in Windsor, which was within his diocese, but during sessions of parliament, when he stayed in town, "he failed not of preaching every *Sunday* Morning, in some Church or other in *London*" (Burnet, *2*, 721). Presumably, as the poem implies, he was also in the habit of preaching before the fashionable and influential congregation of St. James, Piccadilly. The unusual orientation of this church was well known:

> Accounts by visitors to St. James's during the eighteenth century stress the fashionable element in the congregation. John Evelyn remarked that a sermon which he had heard elsewhere on the subject of costly apparel would have been more appropriately

> delivered at 'St. James's or some other of the Theatrical Churches in Lond, where the Ladys and Women were so richly and wantonly dressed and full of Jewells.' James Macky complained that a stranger had to pay for a convenient seat so that 'it costs one almost as dear to see a Play,' but he still thought the church worth a visit 'on a Holiday or Sunday, when the fine Assembly of Beauties and Quality come there.'
>
> (*Survey of London, 29,* 36)

The church itself, which Sir Christopher Wren called "the most capacious" of those he had designed, had been consecrated only in 1684. Built to accommodate the court *faubourg* that was growing up around St. James's Square, it was richly furnished, with an excellent organ donated by Queen Mary, "a curious Font, and the Galleries well set off with Tapestries and *Persian* Carpets" (Strype, 2, ^{3}81). The same wealthy parishioners who provided this luxury, "also altered the pews to suit their convenience and sent carpenters to put up benches, and rails on the seats" (*Survey of London, 29,* 36), and this fact must have provided the occasion for the present poem.

Dryden enclosed a copy of the poem in a letter of 23 February [1699] to Elizabeth Steward, his literary cousin in the country:

> Though I have not leisure to thank you for the last trouble I gave you, yet haveing by me two lampoons lately made, I know not but they may be worth your reading; and therefore have presum'd to send them. I know not the authours; but the Town will be ghessing. The Ballad of The Pews, which are lately rais'd higher at St. James's church, is by some sayd to be Mr. Manwairing, or my Lord Peterborough: the Poem of The Confederates ["Ye vile traducers of the female kind"] some think to be Mr. Walsh: the copies are both lik'd.
>
> (Dryden, *Prose, 1,* ii, ^{1}109)

This letter has been repeatedly dated 1699/1700, but six of the surviving manuscripts of *The Brawny Bishop's Complaint* date the poem 1698/1699 and *The Confederates; or the first Happy Day of the Island Princess* (*POAS*, 1703, *2,* 248–50) celebrates the opening of Peter Motteux's adaptation of John Fletcher, *The Island Princess,* at Drury Lane late in 1698 (*London Stage, 1,* 505). Since Dryden describes the two lampoons as "lately written," he must be writing on 23 February 1699. As far as authorship is concerned, however, no evidence beyond Dryden's statement has yet been uncovered.

"Packington's Pound" is an old dance tune, the music of which is printed in Thomas D'Urfey, *Wit and Mirth: Or Pills to Purge Melancholy,* 1719, *4,* 20. Nightingale, the ballad man in Ben Jonson, *Bartholomew Fair,* claimed it was "spicke and span new" when he sang it in October 1614 at the Bankside (C. H. Herford, P. and E. Simpson, *Ben Jonson,* 11 vols., Oxford, 1925–1952, *10,* 199). The tune was very popular in the seventeenth century, "many ballads, both on political subjects and subjects of gallantry, having been adapted to it," as Edmund Malone has said (Dryden, *Prose, 1,* ii, [1]110, *n.* 9). *The Worcester Cabal* (p. 313, below) was written to the same tune and another song to the same tune in *POAS,* 1704, *3,* 272, is simply entitled *Packington's Pound* ("When the Joy of all Hearts, and Desire of all Eyes"). In 1728 John Gay appropriated the tune for an aria in *The Beggar's Opera* ("Thus Gamesters united in Friendship are found").

An Excellent New Ballad,

call'd,
The Brawny Bishop's Complaint.
To the Tune of Packington's Pound.

1.

When *Burnet* perceiv'd that the beautiful Dames,
Who flock to the Chappel of holy St. *James,*
On their Lovers above their kind Looks did bestow,
And smil'd not at him when he bellow'd below,
To the Princess he went
With a pious intent,
This dangerous Ill in the Church to prevent:
O Madam! said he, our Religion's quite lost,
If the Ladies thus ogle the Knights of the Toast.

2.

Your Highness observes how I labour and sweat,
Their Affections to raise, and new Flames to beget;
And sure when I preach, all the World will agree,
That their Ears and their Eyes should be pointed at me:

2. *the Chappel of holy St. James:* correctly identified in Dryden's letter of 23 February 1699 as "St. James's church" and not the chapel royal in the palace of St. James, as Edmund Malone supposed (Dryden, *Prose, 1,* ii, 1109).

4. *bellow'd:* Malone cites William Shippen, *Faction Display'd,* line 98, where Burnet boasts of his "thund'ring Voice" (ibid., 1111, *n.* 1).

5. Burnet's favor with Anne, princess of Denmark, began with his appointment in June 1698 as preceptor to William, duke of Gloucester (1689–1700), Anne's sole surviving child and heir apparent to the throne of England. Burnet filled this post so capably that "the Princess of *Denmark* ever after retained a peculiar Regard for him" (Burnet, *2,* 718).

9. *Knights of the Toast:* a festive society, whose ritual included drinking toasts in succession to the reigning beauties (W. J. Cameron, "John Dryden and Henry Heveningham," *N&Q, 202* [May 1957], 199–203).

12. *preach:* John Evelyn heard Burnet preach on 15 November 1674 "with such a floud of Eloquence, & fullnesse of matter as shew'd him to be a person of extraordinary parts" (Evelyn, *4,* 47–48).

But now I can find
No Beauty so kind,
My Parts to regard, or my Person to mind:
Nay, I scarce have a sight of one feminine Face,
But those of old *Oxford,* and ugly *Arglass.*

3.

These sorrowful Matrons with Hearts full of Truth,
Repent for the manifold Sins of their Youth:
The rest with their Tattle my Harmony spoil;
And *Burlington, Anglesey, Kingston* and *Boyle*
Their Minds entertain
With thoughts so profane,
'Tis a Mercy to find that at Church they contain;
Ev'n *Heveningham*'s Shape their weak Fancies intice,

18. *old Oxford:* Diana Kirke (d. 1719), of whom H. B. Wheatley claimed that "nothing more need be said than that she bore an inappropriate Christian name" (Pepys, *2,* 224 *n.*), became the second wife of Aubrey de Vere, twentieth earl of Oxford, shortly before 12 April 1673 (GEC, *10,* 260–61).

ugly Arglass: Honora Boyle (d. 1710), daughter of Michael Boyle, archbishop of Armagh and chancellor of Ireland, married first Thomas Cromwell, earl of Ardglass in Ireland and baron Cromwell in England (1653–82), then Francis Cuffe (1656–94), and finally Thomas Burdett (d. 1727) (GEC, *1,* 193).

22. *Burlington:* Juliana (1672–1750), daughter of Henry Noel and wife of Charles Boyle, second earl of Burlington and Cork (Dryden, *Prose, 1,* ii, 1116, *n.* 6).

Anglesey: Malone identifies her as Lady Catherine Darnley (1683–1743), natural daughter of James II by Catherine Sedley. Since she married James Annesley, fifth earl of Anglesey, on 28 October 1699 (Collins, 1741, *2,* 344), the attribution is probably correct (Dryden, *Prose, 1,* ii, 1116, *n.* 7).

Kingston: Malone (ibid., *n.* 8) identifies her as Mary, daughter of William Feilding, third earl of Denbigh, and first wife of Evelyn Pierrepoint, fifth earl of Kingston, but since she died in 1697 (GEC, *7,* 307), the reference must be to Anne, the dowager countess of Kingston (d. 1702), whose amorous inclinations are recorded in Holkham MS. 686, p. 266.

Boyle: Perhaps Arethusa, daughter of Charles Boyle, baron Clifford of Lanesborough, by his second wife, and half-sister to Charles Boyle, second earl of Burlington and Cork, and therefore, as Malone suggests, "likely to have been grouped with his lady" (Dryden, *Prose, 1,* ii, 1116, *n.* 9).

25. *contain:* refrain from expressing or yielding to passion; "But if they cannot contain, let them marry" (1 *Corinthians* 7:9).

26. Henry Heveningham (c. 1651–1700), was member of parliament for Dunwich, Suffolk, and held a minor post at court, where he was lieutenant of the band of gentlemen pensioners, the king's house guards. He was also, apparently, an occasional, or renegade, Knight of the Toast, for he is charged with profaning its mysteries and exposing its president "in rude Rhime." These rhymes were *An Epistle from Henry Heveningham to the Duke of Somerset at Newmarket* ("Since Manwaring and learned

And rather than me they will ogle the *Vice*.

4.

These Practices, Madam, my Preaching disgrace;
Shall Laymen enjoy the just Rights of my Place?
Then all may lament my Condition so hard,
Who thresh in the Pulpit without a Reward.
Therefore pray condescend
Such Disorders to end,
And from the ripe Vineyard those Labourers send;
Or build up the Seats that the Beauties may see
The Face of no brawny Pretender but me.

5.

The Princess by rude Importunity press'd,
Tho she laugh'd at his Reasons, allow'd his Request:
And now *Britain*'s Nymphs in this Protestant Reign
Are lock'd up at Pray'rs like the Virgins in *Spain;*
So they all are undone,
For as sure as a Gun,
Whenever a Woman is kept like a Nun,
If any kind Man from her Bondage will save her,
The Lady in Gratitude grants him the Favour.

Perry"), which have never been published, although the reply to them, *A Letter from J. P. to Colonel H. occasion'd by the Colonel's two late Letters* ("O *Harry,* canst thou find no Subject fit"), is printed in *POAS,* 1703, 2, 255. In those lines Heveningham is represented as an aging and impotent roué.

Shape: The best manuscripts read "Shape," but the grammar requires "Shapes" and *OED* cites *A New Dictionary,* sig. liv, "*Shapes,* said (often) to an ill-made Man," and T. Dyche and W. Pardon, *A New General English Dictionary,* 1735, "*Shapes,* a Cant Name for . . . an ill-made, irregular Lump of Flesh, &c." Heveningham was "a tall thin-gutted Mortal" (Thomas Brown, *Works,* 1707, 2, 10–11).

27. *the Vice:* Peregrine Bertie, second son of Robert Bertie, third earl of Lindsey, was vice-chamberlain of the royal household, a privy councillor, and Knight of the Toast. His feat of running the mall in St. James's Park eleven times in less than an hour to win a wager is recorded in Luttrell, 2, 98.

34. *the ripe Vineyard:* apparently an allusion to the parable of the wicked husbandmen (Mark 12:1–12), with the Knights of the Toast cast in the role of the usurping husbandmen and Burnet in the role of the excluded heir.

40. *Virgins in Spain:* Sympathy for the Spanish was widespread. It was explained to Joseph Spence that "Spanish ladies are of a constitution particularly apt to take fire. As they are more confined, they are fuller of passion than other women are" (Spence, 2, 536).

Daniel Defoe

An Encomium upon a Parliament (*May*[?] *1699*)

The parliament in the title is the fourth of William III, which a recent historian has called "a parliament more xenophobic and obstructive, more essentially 'country,' than any since the Revolution" (Kenyon, p. 307). More exactly, it is the first session of this parliament, which sat from 6 December 1698 to 4 May 1699, that is "encomionized" in the poem.

"Country," of course, means anti-court, and the intensity of hatred generated during this session would be difficult to exaggerate. William came to believe that he himself was the target, but it is more likely that power, rather than principle or personality, was the matter at issue (Coxe, p. 582; Vernon, 2, 245). John Toland was probably right when he concluded that "this party-business is . . . but a mere blind, for matters go on just as they did; where one left off, the other begins: in Tory out Whig, in Whig out Tory" (*The Art of Governing by Partys,* 1701, p. 99). In the winter of 1698–99, it was "in Tory out Whig."

The composition of William's fourth parliament had been determined in the general election of July–August 1698. "The New Country-Party," as the Whigs called it, campaigned everywhere against such perennially reliable bogeys as standing armies, corruption, and high taxes. One of their most successful election pamphlets, by "Mr. *Harley*'s Creature," John Toland, was entitled *The Danger of Mercenary Parliaments.* The New Country-Party was at first only a shaky coalition of "Old" Whigs (as they still preferred to be called), like the Harleys and the Foleys and their followers, and Tory high churchmen like Sir Edward Seymour and Sir Christopher Musgrave. What success they met with in the election was not immediately known. James Vernon, secretary of state, thought that the Whigs might retain "a considerable majority" (Vernon, 2, 149), but Somers, the lord chancellor, feared that the new parliament would be "somewhat difficult to be dealt with" (Coxe, p. 554).

There was even a rumor that Paul Foley would "mend his manners" and be put up again as speaker by the court Whigs. The opposition, on the other hand, was split among three candidates (*Song* ["A Courtier and a Taylor"], Folger MS. M.b.12, f. 203), so a Whig, Sir Thomas Littleton, was elected speaker by a large majority, 242–135. On 9 December 1698 the king, in his customary address from the throne, pointed out to the parliament that "two Things seem principally to require your Attention": the size of the military establishment and "further Progress toward discharging the Debts, which the Nation has contracted by reason of the long and expensive War." He also urged legislation on three matters of secondary importance: employing the poor, restoring trade, and discouraging vice and profaneness. After hearing an unusually large number of petitions about disputed elections, the House of Commons settled down to draft its reply to the king's address.

On the surface, therefore, the fourth parliament did not appear to be very different from the third, about which William had said:

> I cannot take Leave of so good a Parliament without publicly acknowledging the sense I have of the great Things you have done for My Safety and Honour, and for the Support and Welfare of My People.
>
> (*LJ, 16,* 344)

Beneath the surface, however, the situation was very different. The Whig junto was in the process of dissolution. On 8 September 1697, even before the treaty of Ryswick had been signed, Charles Talbot, twelfth earl of Shrewsbury, to whom the other members of the junto habitually deferred, resigned as secretary of state. William refused to accept the resignation, but in November Shrewsbury simply retired to the country. Sunderland predicted that "nothing but disorder, confusion, and groundless fears, and jealousies" would succeed upon Shrewsbury's retirement (Coxe, p. 535). This became apparent as soon as parliament convened, when the Whigs were unable to defeat the first resolution of the session, introduced by Robert Harley on 11 December 1697, to cut back the land forces to the level of 1680. In the same month Sunderland himself was forced to resign as lord chamberlain and that post too was left vacant. This time it was Robert Harley who observed that Sunderland's resignation would leave the Whig managers "very naked" (HMC *Portland MSS., 3,*

594). Since Sunderland was one of the few Englishmen whom he felt he could be free with, the king was displeased and embarrassed when the junto refused to take Sunderland back into the government (Grimblot, *1*, 213; *2*, 80; Vernon, *1*, 450, 471). The junto, on the other hand, were demanding a place for Thomas Wharton, Lord Wharton, who was anathema to the king. Finally, in September 1698, Charles Montagu, without even consulting the king or the other members of the junto, made evident his intention to resign his posts of chancellor of the exchequer and first lord of the treasury (cf. *Advice to a Painter,* 81 *n.,* above).

"Like the whole summer," as Evelyn observed, it was "a very darke, rainy gloomy Autumn" (Evelyn, *5*, 301). Somers wrote to Shrewsbury in October to say that

> There is not, at present, a face of government; and every body seeing the little credit those have with the king who are in employments, are naturally invited to endeavour to ruin or expose them.
>
> (Coxe, p. 560)

Toward this end Harley had ordered two more pamphlets against a standing army, "tim'd to appear," Defoe said, "just at the opening of the Parliament, and so industriously handed about, that they have been seen in the remotest Countries of *England* before they were published in *London*" (*A Brief Reply to the History of Standing Armies in England,* 1698, p. 25; cf. Vernon, *2*, 216).

The precise moment when the New Country-Party seized the initiative in the House of Commons can be stated with certainty. It occurred on 14 December 1698 when "they stopped the motion for a supply, till they had been in a committee to consider of the army both in England and Ireland" (Vernon, *2*, 235). "The business of the standing Army," as Toland observed, "finish'd all" (*A Collection of Several Pieces,* 1726, *2*, 341). On 16 December the earl of Ranelagh laid before the House estimates that showed that even after the cut-back to the level of 1680, 14,834 troops remained on the English establishment. The next day the House "acted as in a fury" (Grimblot, *2*, 216); without even a division they cut that figure in halves and Robert Harley, who had made the motion, was instructed to bring in a bill to disband all forces exceeding 7000 officers and men. John Grubham Howe's amendment that none but "natural-born Subjects of *England*" be included was also accepted without a division. This meant dismissal of the Dutch guards, which included the famous Blue Guards regiment, Portland's regiment of horse guards, and a troop of life guards, some 2500 men.

William thought this was not only "ruinous" in face of the "cauchemar perpetuel" of the Spanish succession and a claimant to the English throne at the French court, but also a personal affront to him. On 29 December 1698 Somers reported to Shrewsbury the shocking news that William was planning to give up the throne. He had in fact retired to Windsor to write his speech of abdication. Then he planned to convene the two houses of parliament on 4 January and make the following address:

> I came into this kingdom, at the desire of the nation, to save it from ruin, and to preserve your religion, your laws, and liberties. And, for that end, I have been obliged to maintain a long and burthensome war, for this kingdom, which, by the grace of God, and the bravery of this nation, is at present ended in a good peace, under which you may live happily and in quiet, provided you will contribute towards your own security, in the manner I had recommended to you, at the opening of the sessions. But seeing to the contrary, that you have so little regard to my advice, that you take no manner of care of your own security, and that you expose yourselves to evident ruin, by divesting yourselves of the only means for your defence, it would not be just or reasonable, that I should be witness of your ruin, not being able to do anything of myself to prevent it, it not being in my power to defend and protect you, which was the only view I had in coming to this country.
>
> (Coxe, pp. 574–75)

These words were to have been followed by the king's announcement of his "withdrawal" from the country. "It was one of Somers' most notable achievements," according to David Ogg, "that he induced the king to give up his intention of returning to Holland" (Ogg, *3*, 450).

Further evidence of the king's state of mind may be gained from his letter of 6 January 1699 to Antonie Heinsius, the grand pensionary of the Netherlands. "Matters in Parliament here," he said, "are taking a turn which drives me mad" (Grimblot, *2,* 233). A few days later Vernon noticed that the king was "not very right in his health. He neither eats nor sleeps so well as he used to" (Vernon, *2,* 250). Abandoned by "the gentlemen best affected to his . . . service" and even by his ministers (*CSPD 1698,* p. 428; Grimblot, *2,* 224), the king turned away from domestic concerns to foreign affairs, which were still his exclusive prerogative.

Meanwhile, the triumph of the New Country-Party was complete. The disbanding bill passed by a large majority, 221–154, and by February 1699 Vernon had to confess that "We are a dispersed routed party, [and] our opposers bear hard upon us" (Vernon, *2,* 262). Vernon also acknowledged that what was happening was a naked struggle for power, unencumbered by ideology. "The public has no place in our thoughts," he said, "but we are pushing at each other as fast as we can" (Vernon, *2,* 245, 265–66). This explains why the present poem is neither Whig nor Tory, or, more exactly, why it is anti-Whig and anti-Tory. It adopts a position very similar to that of the king's abdication speech, a position above party, which conforms very well to that "air of being a disinterested spectator who is moved to certain conclusions by the pure logic of circumstances," which James Sutherland described as Defoe's characteristic tone (*Defoe,* New York and Philadelphia, J. B. Lippincott, 1938, p. 62).

"This miserable session of Parliament," as the king called it, finally drew to an end on 4 May 1699 and William could look forward to a summer in Holland; "God knows how I long for that moment," he added (Grimblot, *2,* 324, 328).

Six manuscripts of the present poem, *ACDEHO,* date the poem 1699. Two more, *FG,* narrow it down to 1699/8, presumably meaning 1 January–24 March 1699. But a date before 25 March is impossible since the poem mentions events happening in April (lines 30 *n.,* 56–57 *n.*). Since "Petitions [still] lie . . . on the Table" (line 97), parliament is presumably still in session. But this seems to be contradicted by the fact that the poem taunts the parliament with begining good legislation but not finishing it (line 4). A date of composition for the poem very close to 4 May 1699, therefore, seems most likely. Edward Ward, *An Answer to An Encomium on a Parliament* ("Be silent, ye *Apollo*'s Brood") was published in *The Weekly*

Comedy for 10–17 May 1699 (and reprinted in *The Second Volume of the Writings of the Author of the London-Spy,* [October] 1703, p. 253).

The poem described as "*The Patriots—a Poem* (1702, folio)" in a list of works attributed to Defoe given to W. P. Trent by Thomas J. Wise or H. S. Foxwell (*New York Evening Post,* 21 September 1907) is probably [William Pittis], *The Patriots. A Poem, in Vindication of Several Worthy Members of the Late Parliament* ("Once more, my Muse, a generous Offring make"), a folio published in 1702 for R. Basset. *An Encomium upon a Parliament* was not called *The Patriots* until it was reprinted in *POAS,* 1703, 2. The evidence for Defoe's authorship, therefore, lies mainly in his quotation of the poem in later works (see lines 23–25 *n.* and 98–100 *n.,* below). While this kind of circumstantial evidence can never produce absolute certainty, it is, in the present case, convincing nonetheless. In fact, the existence of *An Encomium upon a Parliament,* dealing with the first session of the fourth parliament of William III, and of Defoe's *New Satyr on the Parliament* (p. 318, below), dealing with the fifth parliament in 1701, raises the question whether Defoe did not also write a similar attack on the second session of the fourth parliament, in 1700, which was even more damaging to his hero, the king.

An Encomium upon a Parliament

Ye worthy Patriots go on
    To heal the Nation's Sores,
Find all Mens Faults out but your own,
Begin good Laws, but finish none,
    And then shut up your Doors.

Fail not our Freedom to secure,
    And all our Friends disband,
And send those Fools to t'other Shore

1. *Patriot:* used "ironically for a factious disturber of the government" (*OED*). A "patriot" becomes a "statesman" as soon as he gets a "place" (42–43 *n.*, below).

4. Among half a dozen "reform" bills dropped during the session was one that may have particularly interested Defoe. It was a bill for suppressing the ill practices of pawnbrokers, ordered to be brought in on 2 March 1699 but never mentioned again. Another was a bill ordered to be brought in on 4 May, the day parliament was prorogued, by a committee appointed to inquire into the ill practices and abuses of the prisons of the king's bench and the Fleet (*CJ, 12,* 687), of which Defoe said later, "I had the Honour to be one of the first Complainers, and . . . to have had some Hand in the Dissolution of their monstrous Privileges" (*Review, 4* [8 April 1707], 100). White Kennett mentions another bill that was "unhappily dropt" (Kennett, *3,* 766). This was a bill for the conveying of lands, tenements, rents, tithes, and hereditaments to any college or school for the education of poor scholars or the advancement of learning. Oldmixon implies that Oxford University elected Sir Christopher Musgrave specifically to secure passage of this bill, which was ordered to be read a second time on 7 January, but then was heard of no more (Oldmixon, p. 193; *CJ, 12,* 368, 389). Cf. 72 *n.*, and 76 *n.*, below.

6. *Freedom to secure:* A French intelligence report of December 1698 explained that "the hope of the restoration of King James being entirely lost," the Tories "may speak and act more boldly for liberty" (Grimblot, *2,* 193). Accordingly, in the next month, Robert Harley maintained that the only alternative to disbanding the army was "keeping it up, shutting up the Exchequer, governing by sword and edicts" (HMC *Portland MSS., 3,* 601).

7. *Friends disband:* By the terms of John Grubham Howe's amendment to the disbanding bill, excluding all but "natural-born Subjects of *England*" from the armed forces, William had to order the famous Dutch guards regiments to return to Holland. Defoe may have witnessed their departure in March 1699: "it was a moving Sight to behold them marching from *St. James*'s Park, thro' *London* Streets, taking a long farewel of the Friends they left in *England* with Kisses and Tears in their Eyes; many of them having *English* Wives and Children, following them into a Land strange to them, after their Husbands and Fathers had spent so many Years in the Service of that Country, out of which they were now driven. Whoever had seen this as I did, must be shock'd, to hear it said, that the driving them away thus, gave great Satisfaction to the People" (Oldmixon, p. 186).

Who knew no better than to come o'er
   To help this grateful Land.

And may the next that hear us pray,
   And in Distress relieve us,
Go home like those without their Pay,
And with Contempt be sent away
   For having once believ'd us.

And if the *French* should e'er attempt
   This Nation to invade,
May they be damn'd that list again,
But lead your fam'd Militia on,
   To be like us betray'd.

As for the Crown you have bestow'd
   With all its Limitations,

10. *this grateful Land:* The five so-called "French" regiments, made up entirely of Huguenot refugees and now stationed in Ireland, also had to be disbanded. In June 1699 the king wrote to Henri de Massue de Ruvigny, earl of Galway and one of the lords justices of Ireland, who was himself a Huguenot exile: "It is not possible to be more sensibly touched than I am, at my not being able to do more for the poor refugee officers, who have served me with so much zeal and fidelity. I am afraid the good God will punish the ingratitude of this nation" (Grimblot, *2*, 333–34).

13. *without their Pay:* The situation of the foreign mercenary in the army on 25 March 1699, the day set by parliament for the disbanding, may be judged by the petition of three troopers in the earl of Macclesfield's regiment, two German and one Scottish, who claimed that they were "now disbanded, and barbarously used by their Officers, having their Horses and Accoutrements taken from them, which was given them by the King, and themselves stripped from the Waist upwards: That, being Aliens, and forced to leave this Kingdom; and having not One Peny to buy them Bread withal," they prayed some relief might be afforded them (*CJ, 12,* 650).

16–17. *French . . . invade:* Less than a year after the signing of the treaty of Ryswick, John Ellis, one of the undersecretaries of state, was already considering the possibility of another war with France (*CSPD 1698,* p. 387). In April 1699 reports of some "secret design" on the French coast (Luttrell, *4,* 503, 506, 508–09) became so insistent that the matter was debated in the House of Lords (*LJ, 16,* 448).

19. *fam'd Militia:* The legendary ineffectiveness of the militia was a constant source of amusement and the importance assigned to it as a consequence of disbanding the army had already been noticed in verse: "Then will our Prince, like *Mars* in warlike Guise,/Encamp at *Hounslow,* to shoot Butterflies" (*Aesop in Select Fables,* 1698, sig. E1r). On 1 February 1699 when the king gave his assent to the disbanding bill, he felt compelled to tell the parliament "plainly" that the nation was left "too much exposed" (*CJ, 12,* 468). To forestall any anxiety on the part of the Country members, Harley "was pretty quick in proposing, that for a further security of the nation, a bill should be brought in for better regulating the militia" (Vernon, *2,* 263).

22. *Limitations:* William of Orange was offered "the Crown and Royal Dignity of the Kingdoms of *England, France,* and *Ireland,*" not unconditionally, but "according

The meanest Prince in *Christendom*
Would never stir a Mile from home
To govern three such Nations.

The King himself, whom ye have call'd
Your Saviour in Distress,
You have his first Request deny'd,
And then his Royal Patience try'd
With a canting sham Address.

---

to the Resolution and Desire of the . . . Lords and Commons" contained in the Bill of Rights (1 William & Mary, sess. 2, c. 2). The main limitation was the abrogation of the dispensing power, the power claimed by James II of suspending the execution of the laws by regal authority.

23–25. These lines are quoted, with slight variants, as if from memory, in *Review*, *4* (3 February 1708), 610. Four years later in a *Review* devoted to the Hanoverian succession, Defoe adopted the same three lines as an epigraph to his essay, attributing them, again with characteristic inaccuracy, to "*Hymn to Parl.* 1698" (*Review*, [*9*] [14 October 1712], 43).

26–27. *call'd Your Saviour:* In the Bill of Rights (February 1689) William is called "the Prince of *Orange* (whom it hath pleased Almighty God to make the Glorious Instrument of delivering this Kingdom from Popery and arbitrary Power)." Exactly ten years later, the fourth parliament addressed the king in similar terms, referring to "the Labours you have sustained, and the Hazards you have run, in rescuing us from Popery and arbitrary Power, restoring our Liberties, and giving Peace and Quiet to all *Christendom*" (*CJ*, *12*, 481).

28. *first Request:* Even after the date for their departure had been set, William made a final attempt to keep the Dutch guards in England. On Saturday 18 March he sent Richard Jones, earl of Ranelagh, to the House of Commons with a message in his own handwriting, stating his intention "to send them away immediately, unless, out of Consideration to him, the House be disposed to find a Way for continuing them longer in his Service; which his Majesty would take very kindly" (*CJ*, *12*, 601–02). The House was not so disposed, however. Harley professed to be puzzled by the request and added sarcastically, "that he acquitted the ministers from having any hand in it" (Vernon, *2*, 269). John Grubham Howe insisted that the request was a reflection on his majesty's natural-born subjects. So a committee was appointed to draw up an address presenting the reasons why the House could not comply with the king's request.

29. *Patience try'd:* "on all sides," the king wrote to Heinsius in May 1699, "my patience is put to the trial" (Grimblot, *2*, 334). His resentment was public knowledge. Richard Lucas, the blind rector of St. Stephens', in Coleman Street, said in a sermon preached on 5 April 1699 that the king "was born to have his person exposed to his enemies abroad, and his patience tryed by his subjects at home" (Luttrell, *4*, 502).

30. *Address:* William told Heinsius that his attempt to keep the Dutch guards had produced only "a very impertinent address on the subject" (Grimblot, *2*, 310). The address is heavy with sarcasm:

> Most Gracious Sovereign, We, Your Majesty's most dutiful and loyal Subjects, the Commons in this present Parliament assembled, do, with unfeigned Zeal to Your Majesty's Person and Government (which God long preserve!), most humbly represent to Your Majesty; That the Passing the late Act for disbanding the Army

Ye are the Men that to be chose
  Would be at no Expences,
Who love no Friends, nor fear no Foes,
And have ways and means that no Man knows
  To mortify our Senses.

Ye are the Men that can condemn
  By Laws made *ex post facto,*
Who can make Knaves of honest Men,
And married Women turn again
  To be *Virgo et intacta.*

Go on to purify the Court,
  And damn the Men of Places,
Till decently you send them home,

---

gave great Satisfaction to Your Subjects; and the Readiness Your Majesty has expressed by your Message, to comply with the punctual Execution thereof, will prevent all Occasion of Distrust or Jealousy between Your Majesty and Your People. It is, Sir, to Your loyal Commons an unspeakable Grief, that Your Majesty should be advised to propose any thing in Your Message, to which they cannot consent, with due Regard to that Constitution Your Majesty came over to restore, and have so often exposed Your Royal Person to preserve; and did, in Your gracious Declaration, promise, that all those foreign Forces which came over with You should be sent back.

(*CJ, 12,* 604)

This last "offensive allusion," as Sir Keith Feiling has said, "was in effect a reproach, that he had violated his original Declaration of 1688" (Feiling, p. 331). A motion to leave it out lost by only six votes, 157–163, and a motion to recommit the entire address was lost, 156–175, so at length, on 24 April, it was presented to the king at Kensington.

36–37. *condemn . . . ex post facto:* The "honest Men" who were condemned ex post facto may be Defoe's friend Dalby Thomas and the projector, Thomas Neale, both of whom were accused in 1698(?) of embezzlement arising out of their management of a state lottery which had raised £1,000,000 for the government (*The Second Drawing of the Blank Tickets of the Million Adventure,* 1695 [Wing N351]; *A Further Account of the Proposals Made by Thomas Neale and Dalby Thomas, Esquires, for Exchanging the Blank Tickets in the Million Adventure,* 1695 [Wing N340]). Neale seems to have died in 1699, but Thomas was exonerated and knighted in 1703 (*DNB, 14,* 148; Luttrell, *4,* 543; *CTB 1700–1701,* p. 267; Le Neve, p. 483).

39–40. *married Women . . . intacta:* This may be a reference to the divorce case of Charles Gerard, second earl of Macclesfield, against his wife, Anne, the alleged mother of Richard Savage. It caused considerable stir in the last session of the third parliament because it was the first divorce bill to pass without a prior decree from an ecclesiastical court (*LJ, 16,* 224). The bill, while it could not restore the countess's virginity, did restore her fortune (*Parl. Hist., 5,* 1175).

42–43. *Men of Places:* It was evident early in the session that "Those . . . who are

And get your selves put in their room,
And then you'l change your Faces.

Go on to reestablish Trade,
And mend our Navigation,
Let *India India* invade,

---

in the possession of offices are to be tossed up and down" (Vernon, *2,* 241). In January when the Commons began to examine the state of the navy, it was again observed that "men in employments here stand slipperily" (*CSPD 1699–1700,* p. 37). Finally on 10 February, the storm broke. "The Commons . . . are in a rage," Tallard reported. "Instead of proceeding with the affair of the fleet, they attacked, by virtue of an Act of Parliament, which, to this hour, had never been [enforced], all those who were receivers of the king's money, saying that they cannot be chosen members of Parliament" (Grimblot, *2,* 277). Within the next 10 days, five members were expelled and new elections ordered. The reason for this, as Tallard explained, was simply "to diminish the Court party" (Grimblot, *2,* 289).

46. *reestablish Trade:* In his address at the opening of the session William had urged the parliament to employ its thoughts "about some good Bills for the Advancement of Trade." The commissioners of trade presented an elaborate report on the state of trade since 1670 with "Remedies" whereby the balance could be made more favorable to England (*CJ, 12,* 432–35). But almost the only practical result was a bill to prevent the export of wool from Ireland (10 & 11 William III c. 10). In his speech at the closing of the session, therefore, William allowed that "If any Thing shall be found wanting . . . towards the advancing of Trade . . . I cannot doubt but effectual Care will be taken of [it] next Winter" (*LJ, 16,* 466).

48. *India India invade:* In 1698 the East India Company offered the government a loan of £700,000 at 4 per cent to maintain the trading monopoly which it had enjoyed for 40 years. It was outbid, however, by a syndicate of bankers and merchants headed by Samuel Shepherd, who offered a loan of £2,000,000 at 8 per cent. In May 1698 Charles Montagu, chancellor of the exchequer, introduced a bill creating a new East India Company and allowing the old one three years to wind up its affairs. When this bill, tacked to a money bill, reached the House of Lords it was debated with such acrimony that Montagu himself regretted that he had proposed it. "Lord Godolphin said, aloud, that he would not give his vote for the new Company if they would give him the two millions which they promised to advance. Lord Rochester spoke of those who are at the head of it, as rogues and men who deserved to be hanged. But the Court party . . . prevailed by its numbers" (Grimblot, *2,* 61). The majority, however, was only 17 votes. In July 1698, to nearly everyone's amazement, the entire £2,000,000 was subscribed in three days and a new East India Company came into existence. It was freely predicted that "two East-India Company's in England could no more subsist, without destroying one the other, than two Kings, at the same time regnant in the same kingdom—that now a civil battle was to be fought, between the Old and the New Company" (John Bruce, *Annals of the Honorable East-India Company,* 3 vols., 1810, *3,* 256–57; cf. Grimblot, *2,* 62). Accordingly, on 27 February 1699, when the Whigs failed, 148–175, to defeat a Tory motion to bring in a bill for the relief of the old company, the stock of the new fell £2. When the same bill was finally thrown out upon another division, 149–139, the stock of the new company rose £6 (*CJ, 12,* 531, 557; Luttrell, *4,* 487, 492).

And borrow on Funds that will ne'er be paid,
And bankrupt all the Nation.

'Tis you that calculate our Gold,
And with a senseless Tone
Vote what you never understood,
That we might take them if we wou'd,
Or let them all alone.

Your Missives you send round about
With Mr. *Speaker*'s Letter,
To fetch Folks in, and find Folks out,

49. *Funds that will ne'er be paid:* As David Ogg explains, "what we now call the national debt was then thought of, not as an aggregate, but as a series of deficiencies, of greatly varying amounts, in the funds—deficiencies which, it was thought, could eventually be made good by taxation" (Ogg, *3*, 413). These deficiencies came into existence whenever the treasury overestimated the yield on new sources of revenue, such as a duty imposed on malt and related products in 1697 that was estimated to produce £800,000 a year. On this fund the public lent £1,400,000, but in its first year the levy yielded only £344,000, for a deficiency of £456,000. The anxious creditors, therefore, petitioned the House of Commons in March 1699 that "the Deficiency should be made good, and supplied, out of the First Aids to be granted in Parliament" (*CJ, 12*, 557). Defoe is expressing his doubt that these deficiencies, which Montagu estimated to amount to more than £10,000,000, would ever be made good.

51. *calculate our Gold:* On 14 February 1699 Commons read a report from the Commission of Trade, of which John Locke was a member, which pointed out that "over-valuing [gold] in the Currency of Guineas at 22*s.* is a Prejudice to this Kingdom in our Trade" and recommended a devaluation to 21*s.* 6*d.* (*CJ, 12*, 511). Two days later the House resolved that 7 & 8 William III c. 19 did not require anyone to take guineas at 22*s.* and the treasury ordered its revenue collectors to pay no more than 21*s.* 6*d.* (*CJ, 12*, 514; Luttrell, *4*, 484).

54. *them:* gold guineas.

56–57. *Missives . . . Letter:* On 6 April 1699 complaint was made on the floor of the House of Commons "of several Letters, sent into the Country, by *Henry Chivers*," the Tory member for Calne, Wiltshire, "wherein several of the Members of this House are not only reflected on, but misrepresented as to their Votes in this House" (*CJ, 12*, 632). Besides the letters, which are printed in the *Journal,* Chivers had sent into the country a handwritten list of the Whigs who had voted against the disbanding bill, like the one preserved in BM MS. Add. 28091 (Browning, *3*, 213). Chivers, who was absent, was ordered to attend the House on 14 April. When he failed to appear on that date, he was ordered to attend the next day. When he again failed to appear, a Whig motion to send for him in custody of the sergeant at arms was defeated 99–134. Chivers was next ordered to appear on 22 April. On this date the speaker read another letter from him stating that he was still indisposed, whereupon the House resolved that publishing the names of the members and reflecting upon them was a breach of privilege and ordered Chivers to attend on 27 April (*CJ, 12*, 643, 645, 661). No further action resulted.

Which Fools believe without dispute,
Because they know no better.

You borrow'd Ships and hir'd Men
The *Irish* to reduce,
Who will be paid the Lord knows when;
'Tis hop'd when e'er you want again,
You'l think of that Abuse.

Ye laid sham Taxes on our Malt,
On Salt, and Glass, and Leather,
To wheedle Coxcombs in to lend;
Then like true Cheats you drop the Fund,
And sink them all together.

And now y'are piously enclin'd
The Needy to employ;

61. *Ships:* Owners of ships chartered for transport during the Irish campaigns of 1689–91 were issued debentures (certificates of indebtedness) in 1695 which were still unpaid in July 1703 (*A Hymn to the Pillory,* 185, below).

66. *Malt:* The tax on malt was imposed in 1697 (8 & 9 William III c. 22).

67. *Salt:* The tax on salt, both domestic and imported, was tripled by a clause in Montagu's bill of May 1698 establishing the new East India Company (9 & 10 William III c. 44).

Glass: The tax on glass, both domestic and imported, was originally imposed in 1695 (6 & 7 William III c. 18). In 1698 it was cut in halves, but the demands of the local glassmakers remained so insistent and the costs of collection remained so high that on 1 April 1699 the Commons ordered a bill to be brought in taking off the remaining tax. As soon as this became known, the creditors of this fund petitioned the House either to retain the tax or to grant them "some other fund to pay the money they have lent thereon" (Luttrell, *4,* 505). At the same time the House ordered a report to be made on how much revenue the tax produced. The report, signed by "Daniel de Foe, Accomptant," showed that it cost £767 to collect £5124 in taxes (*CJ, 12,* 647). The House lost no time in ordering a bill to be engrossed which took off all taxes and duties on glass to be effective 1 August 1699. On this same date, of course, Defoe found himself without a job.

Leather: A tax on leather was first imposed in 1697 (8 & 9 William III c. 21). During the session of 1698–99 36 petitions were received from tanners, shoemakers, saddlers, glovers, cordwainers, tawers, girdlers, fellmongers, curriers, skinners, and collar makers, all claiming to have been ruined by the tax and praying relief in the premises. Instead, the Commons added a clause to a supply bill to provide "for the more easy raising the Duties upon Leather" (10 & 11 William III c. 21).

69. *drop the Fund:* While no funds had actually defaulted, on 4 March 1699 there was a deficit of £2,759,854 "for which no Provision [for refunding] is made" (*CJ, 12,* 548–49). Consequently, there must have been many anxious creditors in the City.

72. In his address at the opening of the session, the king urged that "some effectual expedient . . . be found for employing the Poor," but a bill for the better

You'd better much your time bestow
To pay the neglected Debts you owe,
  Which make them multiply.

Against Profaneness you declar'd,
  And then the Bill rejected;
And when your Arguments appear'd,
They were the worst that e'er were heard,
  And the best that we expected.

'Twas voted once, that for the Sin
  Of Whoring Men should die all;
But then 'twas wisely thought again,
The House would quickly grow so thin,
  They durst not stand the Tryal.

---

providing for the poor and setting them on work was allowed to die in committee after a second reading. In his address at the end of the session, therefore, William observed that "If any Thing shall be found wanting, for . . . the employing of the Poor . . . I cannot doubt but effectual Care will be taken of them next Winter" (*LJ, 16,* 466).

74. *neglected Debts:* The arrears due the army and navy were estimated to be nearly £3,000,000 (Luttrell, *4,* 469, 471, 502).

75. *them:* "The Needy." As in line 54 the syntax is telegraphic, but it is "the neglected Debts" that make "The Needy" multiply.

76. *Against Profaneness:* In his address at the opening of the session, the king hoped that the parliament would employ its "Thoughts about some good Bills for . . . the further discouraging of Vice and Profaneness" (*LJ, 16,* 352). Accordingly, on 2 January 1699, Sir John Philipps brought in a bill for the more effectual discouraging and suppressing of profaneness and all manner of vice and immorality. The bill narrowly survived its second reading, 134–124, and then was allowed to die quietly in committee (*CJ, 12,* 368, 387, 401–02). Robert Harley's brother Edward was scandalized by "Such an open appearing for vice" (HMC *Portland MSS.,* 3, 602). The king, therefore, was again required to say, in his speech proroguing the parliament, "If any Thing shall be found wanting, for . . . the suppressing of Vice . . . I cannot doubt but effectual Care will be taken of [it] next Winter" (*LJ, 16,* 466).

78. *Arguments:* The only argument against the bill was said to be the fact that it would profit the Whig justices of the peace "Who live by their Commission" (Edward Ward, *The Second Volume of the Writings,* 4th ed., 1709, p. 285).

81–82. *for . . . Whoring Men should die:* In the last session of the third parliament Sir John Philipps and Edward Harley had been ordered to bring in "a Bill for suppressing all sorts of *Debauchery;* but the Bill was clogg'd by a Clause of one of these two Members, which made not only Houses of ill Fame, but even Hackney-Coaches, where Suspicion might be had of unlawful Commerce between Men and Women, liable to the Law; Adultery was propos'd to be punished with Death" (Oldmixon, p. 175; *CJ, 12,* 132, 147, 155, 160).

King *Charles* the Second knew your aim,
And Places gave and Pensions;
And had King *William*'s Money flown,
His Majesty would soon have known
Your Consciences Dimensions.

But he has wisely given you up
To work your own Desires,
And, laying Arguments aside
As things that have in vain been try'd,
To Fasting, Calls, and Prayers.

Chorus.
Your Hours are choicely employ'd,
Your Petitions lie all on the Table,
With Funds Insufficient,
And Taxes Deficient,
And Debts which are innumerable.

For shame leave this wicked Employment,
Reform both your Manners and Lives;
You were never sent out
To make such a Rout,
Go home and look after your Wives.

97. All the petitions of the unemployed leather workers mentioned in 67 *n.* were, in the parliamentary formula, ordered to "lie upon the Table, to be perused by the Members of the House." Instead of providing some "Relief in the Premises," the Commons simply made it easier for the excise men to collect the tax.

98–100. Defoe quotes these lines in *Review, 8* (24 May 1712), 734.

98. *Funds Insufficient:* See 49 *n.* and 69 *n.*, above.

99. *Taxes Deficient:* The king wrote to Heinsius on 28 April 1699: "they have not even voted the wherewithal to supply the taxes that were granted, nor a single farthing to discharge any kind of debt; so that credit is gone" (Grimblot, 2, 324).

102. *Reform:* "It would be better, indeed, that parliament reformed themselves, and save that trouble to others; but corruption and partialities have taken fast hold of us" (Vernon, 2, 264).

105. The lines in the ballad that follow this one may be relevant as well:

> Gae hame and lie with yer wife
> And I wish that the first news I may hear,
> That she has taen your life.

(MacEdward Leach, *The Ballad Book,* New York & London, A. S. Barnes & Co., Yoseloff Ltd., 1955, p. 18).

Samuel Garth

The Dispensary (*6–8 May 1699*)

Mock-epic requires an occasion—some petty incident like the theft of a bucket or a lock of hair—that can be recounted in high heroic style to achieve the elevation necessary for descents into bathos. Such an occasion was vouchsafed to Samuel Garth, M.D., fellow of the Royal College of Physicians of London, in 1698, when a disaffected member of the College involved himself in a discreditable fracas with the personnel of the free out-patient clinic in the College. "The Description of the Battel," as Garth recalled in the preface to *The Dispensary,* "is grounded upon a Feud that hapned in the *Dispensary,* betwixt a Member of the College with his Retinue, and some of the Servants that attended there, to dispence the Medicines; and is so far real: tho' the Poetical Relation be fictitious."

The disaffected member must have been one of those "Apothecaries Physicians" who had joined forces with the Company of Apothecaries in its long battle to prevent the dispensary from opening. The dispensary itself, which finally did open in April 1698, was simply two rooms in the new College buildings on Warwick Lane, where charity patients were examined and medicines dispensed "at their intrinsick value." Nothing more is known of this obscure scuffle between the renegade physician in his velvet jacket and the laboratory assistants in their blue aprons, but without doubt it provided the occasion for "this small Performance," as Garth called it, which supplies such an important link between *Mac Flecknoe* and *The Dunciad.*

"The Original of this Difference," Garth went on to say, had "been of some standing, tho' it did not break out to Fury and Excess till the time of erecting the *Dispensary.*" It was, in fact, a difference of some thirty years' standing ("The background of the London dispensary," *JHM, 20* [July 1965], 197–212). Garth did not invent the battle imagery that dominates his poem; it was already current in 1670 when Christopher Merrett, the librarian of the College, complained that "the *Apothecaries* . . . have been constant underminers and enemies to our Profession and Corporation" (*A Short Reply to the Postscript, &c. of H.S.*, 1670, p. 5). The main reason for this hostility was that the relationship between the two professions was undergoing a drastic revision.

Collusion between physician and apothecary is a condition of life celebrated in the prologue to *The Canterbury Tales.* In fact, the normal relationship between physician and apothecary was both hierarchical and collusive. It was hierarchical because the physician was the master and the apothecary the servant, and collusive "For ech of hem made oother for to wynne." Toward the end of the seventeenth century, however, the London apothecaries appeared intent to upset this ancient subordination. By 1705 they finally won the right to practice medicine legally. The physicians, meanwhile, were on the defensive and insisted that the apothecaries aimed to reverse the traditional roles and make themselves "absolute Masters in *Physick,* and *Physicians* their Servants" (Christopher Merrett, *A Short View of the Frauds, and Abuses committed by Apothecaries,* 1669, p. 19). The apothecaries were correspondingly aggressive. They left their shops and began to visit "patients" at home, boasting that they could bring in or turn out whatever physician they pleased. It was widely recognized that "to get Business is a valuable part of Physick." So despite a statute of the College of Physicians that read, "He that bargains with Apothecaries . . . shall be fined forty Shillings," many physicians were found "to have so little honour, as to vye with one another for the Apothecaries favour" (*A Short Answer to a Late Book, Entituled, Tentamen Medicinale,* 1705, p. 32). These were the "Apothecaries Physicians," and they opposed the dispensary because the Company of Apothecaries wanted it to be opposed. Collusion, in short, was reinstated in some cases with the apothecary as master. This is reflected in contemporary descriptions of the new relationship: *"Apothecary, Physician* and *Patient,* appear like *Sharper, Sweetner and Cully"* (ibid.); the physician is "the *Apothecary*'s Under-Pick-Pocket" (*Observations upon the Case of William Rose,* 1704, p. 114).

The important point is that *The Dispensary* celebrates, not a battle between two bodies "Corporate and Politic" in the City of London—the College of Physicians and the Society of the Art and Mystery of Apothecaries—but a civil war between two factions within the College itself, the "Society-Physicians," as those loyal to the College were called, and the renegade "Apothecaries Physicians." Of the dozen or so enemies of the College that figure in *The Dispensary,* all but three are members of the College. This point is made perfectly clear in a pamphlet of 1701 that points out that

> Any *Citizen* who will give himself the *trouble* of *thinking,* will easily hence *discern* the reason of the *perpetual Dissensions* of the *College.* When one party would raise up its *reputation* by serving the *Publick* faithfully, the other strenuously oppose all *Projects* of that kind, to merit the favour of the *Apothecaries.*
> (*The Present State of Physick & Surgery in London,* 1701, p. 9)

From the day he was admitted to the College, Dr. Samuel Garth, of Peterhouse, Cambridge, was a loyal "Society-Physician." On 18 March 1692, "haveing spent some years in forreign campaignes & Hospitalls," he was examined in pathology by the president and censors of the College and "acquitted himself very well." Two months later he was examined in therapeutics and was "very well approved of." Comments like these, which are most infrequent in the *Annals* of the College, indicate that Garth's career was a success from the beginning.

Only three months after he was admitted a fellow, Garth was elected a delegate, or member of a kind of executive committee to "treate of all matters that belong to the honor or advantage of the Colledge" (*Annals,* 7, 60). The next year, 1694, he was appointed to read the Gulstonian lectures. In January 1695 he and Dr. John Bateman ("Celsus") were empowered "to act in everything, as they should think convenient" to prevent the College from sustaining any injury by the apothecaries bill, which was then pending in parliament (see below, Canto 2, 160 *n.*). Garth, therefore, may have been sitting in the gallery of the House of Lords when Sir William Williams ("Vagellius"), the attorney for the Company of Apothecaries, attacked the motives and impugned the honor of the College: "The Doctors," he said, "would not come to the poor without Fees, nor to the Rich, if at Dinner or in Bed, whilst [the apothecaries] came at all times, and gave their advice and physick to the poor for Nothing" (*Annals, 6,* 194). This is almost certainly the occasion that determined the College to promote and encourage an order of eight years' standing that "all Members thereof . . . shall give their advice *gratis* to all their sick neighboring Poor, when desired, within the City of *London*." For it was only when the dispensary had been finally established that the "Society-Physicians" could claim that they had "wiped off the Scandal they lay so long unjustly under" (*The Necessity and Usefulness of the Dispensaries* [1702], reprinted in *A Short Answer to a Late Book, Entituled, Tentamen Medicinale,* 1705, p. 77).

In April 1696 Garth was a member of a committee that presented William III with an address on the occasion of the assassination plot. In the following year he was appointed to deliver the Harveian oration, in which he made a bold appeal to the "Apothecaries Physicians" "to return again to unitie and concord; so all differences amongst us being buried, we may joyntly seek the advantage of our Societie" (*JHM, 18* [1963], 19). When oratory failed, Garth turned to ridicule and set about writing *The Dispensary.* "Nor had I ever attempted any thing in this kind," he said, "till finding the Animosities amongst the Members of the *College of Physicians* encreasing daily (notwithstanding the frequent Exhortations of our worthy President to the contrary) I was persuaded to attempt something of this nature, and to endeavour to Rally some of our disaffected Members into a sense of their Duty" (*1699*^{2}, sig. A1v).

Publication of *The Dispensary* was advertised in *The Post Boy* for 6–8 May 1699 and immediately enjoyed exceptional popular success; three editions were called for within five weeks. The work was almost equally a critical success. Abel Boyer, who had the advantage of being bilingual, declared that it "equall'd, if not exceeded the *Lutrin*," and this was also the opinion of Voltaire. Boyer even judged that "this little Piece is worth an Epick Poem" (Boyer, *Letters of Wit, Politicks, and Morality,* 1701, pp. 217–18; *Oeuvres Completes de Voltaire,* 70 vols., Kehl, 1784–89, *38,* 340). Best of all, it shut up the scoffers who had claimed that the subscribers to the dispensary were not as eminent as the "Apothecaries Physicians" who opposed it. There had, in fact, been some truth to this claim, for Dr. Edward Tyson, Fellow of the Royal Society and a distinguished anatomist, Dr. John Radcliffe, the most eminent physician of his age, Dr. Hugh Chamberlen, the fashionable "Man Midwife," and Sir Richard Blackmore, physician-in-ordinary to King William III and author of *Prince Arthur. An Heroick Poem. In Ten Books* (1695) and *King Arthur. An Heroick Poem. In Twelve Books* (1697), all had refused to subscribe to the dispensary. But after publication of *The Dispensary,* another critic could claim that there is not *"any part of* Physick, *even Poetry, which* [the "Society-Physicians"] *cannot pretend to, as well as the* other" (*The Present State of Physick,* 1701, sig. A2r). A third critic, however, while acknowledging that *The Dispensary* had "given the Day to the Collegiate Mortars," was still willing to lay two to one that "the Society in *Black-Fryars* will fling a Bomb out of theirs, as far as those in *Warwick-Lane,* since they are so well provided with Ammunition and Artillery" (*Letters from the Living to the Living,* 1703, p. [2]15). This was the first distant rumbling of Blackmore's *Satyr against Wit.*

Three of the many surviving "keys" to *The Dispensary* are cited in the notes that follow. These are a manuscript preserved in the Historical Library, Yale Medical Library (MS. Key); a printed version, *A Compleat Key to the Eighth Edition of The Dispensary* (*1718* Key), which was the last edition published during Garth's lifetime; and another printed version (*1709* Key), which is probably a plagiary of the *1718* Key with additions (see p. 726 below).

The Royal College of Physicians, Warwick Lane. Engraving by James S. Storer

The Dispensary

Canto 1

Speak, Goddess! since 'tis Thou that best canst tell,
How ancient Leagues to modern Discord fell;
Whence 'twas, Physicians were so frugal grown
Of others Lives, and lavish of their own;
How by a Journey to th'*Elysian* Plain
Peace triumph'd, and old Time return'd again.
Not far from that most celebrated Place,
Where angry Justice shews her awful Face;
Where little Villains must submit to Fate,
That great Ones may enjoy the World in state;
There stands a Dome, Majestick to the Sight,
And sumptuous Arches bear its oval Height;
A golden Globe plac'd high with artful Skill,
Seems, to the distant Sight, a gilded Pill:
This Pile was, by the pious Patron's Aim,
Rais'd for a Use as Noble as its Frame;
Nor did the learn'd Society decline
The Propagation of that great Design;

7. *that most celebrated Place:* "heinous Malefactors, as *Traitors, Murderers, Felons,* and the like . . . are tried in the Sessions-house in the *Old-Baily*" (Chamberlayne, 1700, pp. 409–10). The College of Physicians was separated from the Sessions House Yard only by London Wall (see illustration, p. 86).

11. *a Dome:* The part of the College facing Warwick Lane was the Cutlerian Theatre (see illustration, p. 63), the gift of Sir John Cutler. Although his statue in stone on the inside facade of the building bore the inscription, "Omnis CUTLERI cedat Labor Amphitheatro," this wealthy and provident merchant entered the entire amount of his £7000 benefaction to the College on his account books as a loan. Accordingly, in October 1695 his heirs were able to secure a writ of error ordering the College to repay the entire amount (RCP MS. 274, 18 October 1695).

15. *the pious Patron:* The letters patent creating the College of Physicians in 1518 were initiated by Thomas Linacre (1460?–1524), five other physicians, and Thomas Cardinal Wolsey. Linacre remained president of the College until his death and its meetings were held at his house in Knightrider Street. His monument in St. Paul's Cathedral states that "In hac urbe *Collegium Medicorum* fieri sua industria curavit" (*Biographia Britannica, 5,* 2972–73). Alexander Pope, however, thought that "the pious Patron" was Sir John Cutler (*1706* Huntington Library copy, p. 2), but the irony of this attribution is apparent from the preceding footnote.

In all her Mazes, Nature's Face they view'd,
And as she disappear'd, they still pursu'd.
They find her dubious now, and then as plain;
Here, she's too sparing; there, profusely vain.
Now she unfolds the faint, and dawning Strife
Of infant Atoms kindling into Life:
How ductile Matter new Meanders takes,
And slender Trains of twisting Fibres makes.
And how the Viscous seeks a closer Tone,
By just degrees to harden into Bone;
While the more Loose flow from the vital Urn,
And in full Tides of Purple Streams return;
How, from each Sluice, a briny Torrent pours,
T'extinguish feav'rish Heats with ambient Show'rs;
Whence their Mechanick Pow'rs the Spirits claim,
How great their Force, how delicate their Frame:
How the same Nerves are fashion'd to sustain
The greatest Pleasure, and the greatest Pain.
Why bileous Juice a golden Light puts on,
And Floods of Chyle in Silver Currents run.
How the dim Speck of Entity began
T'extend its recent Form, and stretch to Man.
To how minute an Origin we owe
Young *Ammon, Caesar,* and the Great *Nassau.*
Why paler Looks impetuous Rage proclaim,
And why chill Virgins redden into Flame.
Why Envy oft transforms with wan Disguise,
And why gay Mirth sits smiling in the Eyes.
All Ice why *Lucrece,* or *Sempronia,* fire,
Why *Scarsdale* rages to survive Desire.

19. *Mazes:* In his Harveian oration of 16 September 1697, Garth had said that "Physick . . . pursues nature through a thousand Windings and Maeanders" (*JHM, 18* [1963], 13).

26–28. *Fibres . . . Bone:* Connective tissue can become either fibrous to form tendons or mineralized to form hard, concentric circles of bone.

29. *the vital Urn:* the heart.

37. *bileous Juice:* Bile was one of the "four humours" of early physiology and was, until the eighteenth century, commonly called choler. "*Bilis* . . . is naturally Yellow" (Blancard, p. 27).

38. *Chyle:* "*Chylus* . . . a white Juice in the . . . *Intestines*" (Blancard, p. 44).

48. *Scarsdale:* Since the meaning of this line is not absolutely clear, even contemporary readers made wildly varying guesses at the identity of *S*———, ranging from

Whence *Milo*'s Vigour at th'*Olympick*'s shown,
Whence Tropes to *Finch,* or Impudence to *Sloan,*
Why *Atticus* polite, *Brutus* severe,

John Sheffield, marquess of Normanby (*1699*^{2} Chicago University copy) to "Southcott A Baud in So-ho" (*1699*^{3} RCP copy). Sir Charles Sedley (1639–1701), "one of the most licentious men of his age" (GEC, *Baronetage, 1,* 74 note b) and Henry Sidney, earl of Romney (1641–1704), "an old vitious illiterate Rake" (Swift, *Prose, 5,* 195), were also mentioned, but the best candidate is Robert Leke, third earl of Scarsdale (1654–1707). "He was always a Man of Pleasure more than Business, no Man loves the Company of Ladies more than he, or says less when he is in it, yet is successful in his Intrigues" (Macky, p. 81). He bequeathed £1000 to Anne Bracegirdle, the actress (GEC, *11,* 519 note b).

49. *Milo:* Milo of Croton (sixth century B.C.), the six-time winner of Olympic wrestling, was unopposed in his seventh appearance (Pausanias, *6,* 14).

50. *Finch:* Heneage Finch (1647?–1719) is Polytropos in *An Essay upon Satire (*1679) (*POAS,* Yale, *1,* 408). He was appointed solicitor-general in 1679 and elected to parliament as a Tory member for Oxford University (1678, 1689–98, 1701–03) and Guildford, Surrey (1685–87). Known as "silvertongued Finch," (GEC, *1,* 364), he was said to be "one of the greatest Orators in *England"* (Macky, p. 90), but Burnet thought that in summing up the crown's case against Lord Russell in 1683 he "shewed more of a vicious eloquence, in turning matters with some subtlety against the prisoners, than of solid or sincere reasoning" (Burnet, *1,* 555). Deprived of the solicitor-generalship by James II, Finch served as chief counsel for the seven bishops in June 1688. He held no office under William III and refused to subscribe to the Association for the defense of the king in 1696. In 1703 he was raised to the peerage as Lord Guernsey and sworn of the privy council.

Sloan: James Sloan; see above, *Advice to a Painter,* 108 *n.*

51. *Atticus:* Lord Somers. John Somers began his public career as a junior counsel for the defense of the seven bishops in June 1688. Just eight months later, as a member of the Convention Parliament for Worcester, he was made manager of the committee that drafted the Declaration of Rights. He was lord chancellor of England (1697–1700), president of the Royal Society (1699–1704), and "the general patron of the *literati"* (John Boyle, fifth earl of Orrery, *Remarks on the Life and Writings of Dr. Jonathan Swift,* 1752, pp. 92–93). John Locke and Isaac Newton were his friends and he corresponded with Jean LeClerc and Pierre Bayle. He was also, as Sunderland assured the king, "the life, the soul, and the spirit" of the Whig party (Hardwicke, *2,* 446). Hence it is strange that Garth should identify him with T. Pomponius Atticus (109–32 B.C.), who avoided politics but patronized the arts and cultivated the friendship of distinguished men: Cicero and Cornelius Nepos, Brutus and Mark Antony.

Brutus: Sir John Holt (1642–1710), one of the counsels assigned to defend Thomas Osborne, earl of Danby, at his impeachment trial in 1679. He was knighted in February 1686, served as a member for Beeralston, Devonshire, in the Convention Parliament, and in April 1689 was appointed lord chief justice of the king's bench. His Brutus-like "severity" is illustrated by the Knollys case, when, summoned before the House of Lords in February 1698, he refused on three different occasions to give reasons for his judgment, because, as he said, "I have ever given my opinion upon the greatest consideration and upon my conscience. I humbly beg pardon if I say I ought not by the law to be called to account for the reasons of my opinion. If we err, the judgment may be rectified by writ of error, but the law acquits us" (Howell, *12,* 1179–83).

Why *Methuen* muddy, *Montague* why clear.
  Hence 'tis we wait the wondrous Cause to find,
How Body acts upon impassive Mind.
How Fumes of Wine the thinking part can fire,
Past Hopes revive, and present Joys inspire:
Why our Complexions oft our Soul declare,
And how the Passions in the Features are.
How Touch and Harmony arise between
Corporeal Substances, and Things unseen.
With mighty Truths, mysterious to descry,
Which in the Womb of distant Causes lie.
  But now those great Enquiries are no more,
And Faction skulks, where Learning shone before:
The drooping Sciences neglected pine,
And *Paean*'s Beams with fading Lustre shine.
No Readers here with Hectick looks are found,
Or Eyes in Rheum, thro' midnight-watching drown'd:
The lonely Edifice in Sweats complains,
That nothing there but empty Silence reigns.
  This Place so fit for undisturb'd Repose,
The God of Sloth for his *Asylum* chose.

52. *Methuen:* John Methuen (1650?–1706), Whig member of parliament for Devizes, Wiltshire (1690–1706), envoy extraordinary to Portugal (1691–97), and lord chancellor of Ireland (1697–1703), was "a Man of Intrigue, but very muddy in his Conceptions, and not quickly understood in any Thing. In his Complexion and Manners, much of a *Spaniard;* a tall, Black Man" (Macky, p. 143). He is the subject of a particularly lilting song *To the Tune of Lilly Bolero* ("Two Opposite Parties do govern the House") (BM MS. Lansdowne 852, f. 96v).

Montague: Charles Montagu; see above, *Advice to a Painter,* 81 *n.*

54. *How Body acts upon . . . Mind:* The College of Physicians had been attacked for refusing to admit the solution to this problem proposed by "our Famous Countryman Sir *Kenelm Digby,* who in his Discourse at *Montpelier* [Wing D1435] hath sufficiently set forth the Doctrine of Operations at a distance, which who-ever denyes, must first deny his own Senses; and they are performed, he saith, by those small Bodies called *Atoms*" (Marchamont Nedham, *Medela Medicinae,* 1665, pp. 117–18).

64. *Faction:* The membership of the College was split almost exactly in halves by the dispensary quarrel; 53 members, of a total of 104, finally signed the agreement creating the dispensary.

65. *Sciences neglected:* Both parties to the dispensary controversy agreed that its effects had been deleterious. In his Harveian oration Garth had observed that "Physick it self is grown sick" (*JHM, 18* [1963], 13) and "the Malecontents" similarly complained of "the low and languishing State to which the College is at present reduc'd" (Bodl. MS. Rawl. D.391, f. 34).

66. *Paean:* physician to the Olympian gods, later identified with Apollo.

Upon a Couch of Down in these Abodes
The careless Deity supinely nods.
His leaden Limbs at gentle ease are laid,
With *Poppies* and dull *Nightshade* o'er him spread;
No Passions interrupt his easie Reign,
No Problems puzzle his lethargick Brain.
But dull Oblivion guards his peaceful Bed,
And lazy Fogs bedew his thoughtless Head.
  As at full length the pamper'd Monarch lay,
Batt'ning in Ease, and slumb'ring Life away:
A spightful Noise his downy Chains unties,
Hastes forward, and encreases as it flies.
  First, some to cleave the stubborn Flint engage,
Till urg'd by Blows, it sparkles into Rage.
Some temper Lute, some spacious Vessels move;
These Furnaces erect, and Those approve.
Here Phyals in nice Discipline are set,
There Gally-pots are rang'd in Alphabet.
In this place, Magazines of Pills you spy;
In that, like Forrage, Herbs in Bundles lye.
While lifted Pestles, brandish'd in the Air,
Descend in Peals, and Civil Wars declare.
Loud Stroaks, with pounding Spice, the Fabrick rend,
And Aromatick Clouds in Spires ascend.
  So when the *Cyclops*, o'er their Anvils sweat,
And their swol'n Sinews ecchoing Blows repeat;
From the *Vulcano*'s gross Eruptions rise,
And curling Sheets of Smoke obscure the Skies.
  The slumb'ring God amaz'd at this new Din,
Thrice strove to rise, and thrice sunk down agen.

85–96. The building of the dispensary is described in terms reminiscent of the raising of Pandemonium (*Paradise Lost, 1,* 670–730).

87. *temper Lute:* Lute is a clay "whereby Vessels for Distillation are cemented" (Blancard, p. 130). To "temper" lute is to bring it to a proper consistency by mixing with water and stirring.

101–04. Leicht (p. 140) cites Boileau, *Le Lutrin,* 2, 117–20:

> A ce triste discours, qu'un long soûpire acheve,
> La Mollesse en pleurant sur un bras se releve,
> Ouvre un oeil languissant, & d'une faible voix,
> Laisse tomber ces mots, qu'elle interrompt vingt fois.

Then, half erect, he rubb'd his op'ning Eyes,
And faulter'd thus betwixt half Words and Sighs:
  How impotent a Deity am I!
With Godhead born, but curs'd, that cannot die!
Thro' my Indulgence, Mortals hourly share
A grateful Negligence, and Ease from Care.
Lull'd in my Arms, how long have I with-held
The *Northern* Monarchs from the dusty Field.
How have I kept the *British* Fleet at ease,
From tempting the rough Dangers of the Seas.
Hibernia owns the mildness of my Reign,
And my Divinity's ador'd in *Spain.*
I Swains to *Sylvan* Solitudes convey,
Where stretch'd on Mossy Beds, they waste away,
In gentle inactivity, the day.
What marks of wondrous Clemency I've shown,
Some Rev'rend Worthies of the Gown can own.
Triumphant Plenty, with a chearful Grace,
Basks in their Eyes, and sparkles in their Face.
How sleek their Looks, how goodly is their Mien,
When big they strut behind a double Chin.
Each Faculty in Blandishments they lull,
Aspiring to be venerably dull.
No learn'd Debates molest their downy Trance,
Or discompose their pompous Ignorance:
But undisturb'd, they loiter Life away,
So wither, Green, and blossom in Decay.
Deep sunk in Down, they, by my gentle Care,
Avoid th'Inclemencies of Morning Air,
And leave to tatter'd Crape the Drudgery of Pray'r.
  Mankind my fond propitious Pow'r has try'd,
Too oft to own, too much to be deni'd.

107–17. Leicht (p. 141) cites *Le Lutrin, 2,* 123–28.
119–23. Leicht (p. 142) cites *Le Lutrin, 1,* 17–20.
130–32. Leicht (p. 142) cites *Le Lutrin, 1,* 21–24:

Sans sortir de leurs licts plus doux que leurs hermines,
Ces pieux Faineans faisoient chanter Matines,
Veilloient à bien disner, & laissoient, en leur lieu,
A des Chantres gagés le soin de loüer Dieu.

Textual note *1,* 132. *Urim:* Francis Atterbury (1662–1732).

And in return, I ask but some Recess,
T'enjoy th'entrancing Extasies of Peace.
But that, the Great *Nassau*'s Heroick Arms
Has long prevented with his loud Alarms.
Still my Indulgence with contempt he flies,
His Couch a Trench, his Canopy the Skies.
Nor Skies nor Seasons his Resolves controul,
Th'*Æquator* has no Heat, no Ice the *Pole*.
From Clime to Clime his wondrous Triumphs move,
And *Jove* grows jealous of his Realms above.
  But as the slothful God to yawn begun,
He shook off the dull Mist, and thus went on:
  Sometimes among the *Caspian* Cliffs I creep,
Where solitary Bats, and Swallows sleep.
Or if some Cloyster's Refuge I implore,
Where holy Drones o'er dying Tapers snore;
Still *Nassau*'s Arms a soft Repose deny,
Keep me awake, and follow where I fly.
  Since he has bless'd the weary World with Peace,
And with a Nod has bid *Bellona* cease:
I sought the Covert of some peaceful Cell,
Where silent Shades in harmless Raptures dwell;
That Rest might past Tranquility restore,
And Mortal never interrupt me more.
  'Twas here, alas! I thought I might Repose,
These Walls were that *Asylum* I had chose.
Nought underneath this Roof, but Damps are found,
Nought heard, but drowzy Beetles buzzing round.
Spread Cobwebs hide the Walls, and Dust the Floors,
And midnight Silence guards the noiseless Doors.
But now I find some enterprizing Brain,

137–44. *Nassau:* In a remarkable example of literary economy Garth praises William III in terms derived from Boileau's panegyric of Louis XIV, the hereditary enemy of the house of Orange-Nassau. Leicht (p. 143) cites *Le Lutrin, 2,* 133–44.

141–42. Cf. *Le Lutrin, 2,* 137–38:

> Rien ne peut arrester sa vigilante audace.
> L'Esté n'a point de feux, l'Hyver n'a point de glace.

153. *Peace:* News of the signing of the treaty of Ryswick reached London on 14 September 1697.

159–60. Leicht (p. 143) cites *Le Lutrin, 2,* 145–46.

Invents new Fancies to renew my Pain,
And labours to dissolve my easie Reign.
 With that, the God his darling *Phantom* calls,
And from his fault'ring Lips this Message falls:
 Since Mortals will dispute my Pow'r, I'll try
Who has the greatest Empire, they or I.
Find Envy out, some Prince's Court attend,
Most likely there you'l meet the famish'd Fiend.
Or in Cabals, or Camps, or at the Bar,
Or where ill Poets Pennyless confer,
Or in the Senate-house at *Westminster*.
Tell the bleak Fury what new Projects reign,
Among the Homicides of *Warwick-Lane*.
And what th'Event, unless her Care enclines
To blast their Hopes, and baffle their Designs.
 More he had spoke, but sudden Vapours rise,
And with their silken Cords tie down his Eyes.

Canto 2

 Soon as with gentle Sighs the ev'ning Breeze
Begun to whisper thro' the murm'ring Trees;
And Night to wrap in Shades the Mountains Heads,
While Winds lay hush'd in Subterranean Beds;
Officious *Phantom* did with speed prepare
To slide on tender Pinions through the Air.
He often sought the Summit of a Rock,
And oft the Hollow of some blasted Oak;

166. *new Fancies:* The opening of the dispensary was advertised in *The Post Boy* for 14–16 April 1698.

172. *Find Envy:* In a passage from Ariosto, *Orlando Furioso* (*14*, 75ff.), which Dryden had mentioned in 1693 (*Prose, 3*, 101), St. Michael finds Discord in a convent of friars.

181–82. La Mollesse, the prototype of Sloth, also falls to sleep at the conclusion of his speech. Leicht (p. 143) cites *Le Lutrin, 2*, 163–64.

1. Pope observed that "Lin. 1st . . . seems contradictory to lin. 4" (*1703* Victoria & Albert Museum copy).

1–2. *Breeze . . . Trees:* "Where-e'er you find *the cooling Western Breeze*,/In the next Line, it *whispers thro' the Trees*" (Pope, *An Essay on Criticism*, 350–51).

At length approaching where bleak Envy lay,
The hissing of her Snakes proclaim'd the way.
  Beneath the gloomy Covert of an Yew,
That taints the Grass with sickly Sweats of Dew;
No verdant Beauty entertains the Sight,
But baneful Hemlock, and cold Aconite;
There crawl'd the meagre Monster on the Ground,
And breath'd a livid Pestilence around:
A bald and bloted Toad-stool rais'd her Head;
The Plumes of boding Ravens were her Bed.
Down her wan Cheeks sulphureous Torrents flow,
And her red haggard Eyes with Fury glow.
Like *Ætna* with Metallick Steams oppress'd,
She breaths a blue Eruption from her Breast:
Then rends with canker'd Teeth the pregnant Scrolls,
Where Fame the Acts of Demi-Gods enrolls.
And as the rent Records in pieces fell,
Each Scrap did some immortal Action tell.
This show'd, how fix'd as Fate *Torquatus* stood,
That, the fam'd Passage of the *Granick* Flood.
The *Julian* Eagles here, their Wings display;
And there, all pale, th'expiring *Decii* lay.

9–10. Leicht (p. 144) cites *Le Lutrin, 1,* 41–42:

> La Discorde, à l'aspect d'un calme qui l'offence,
> Fait sifler ses serpens, s'excite à la vengeance.

17. *Toad-stool:* Cf. "Bald Toadstools," Blackmore, *King Arthur. An Heroick Poem* (1697), *6,* 451, p. 165; *12,* 77, p. 317.

27. *Torquatus:* T. Manlius Imperiosus Torquatus (fourth century B.C.), twice dictator and thrice consul of Rome. As a young military tribune he defeated in single combat a gigantic Gaul who had terrorized the Roman army (Livy, *6,* 42; *7,* 10).

28. *Granick Flood:* Alexander the Great's defeat of the armies of Darius on the Granicus River in northwest Turkey (334 B.C.) left all of Asia Minor open to invasion.

30. *Decii:* two generations of a plebeian family of the Decian gens, named Publius Decius Mus, who sacrificed their lives to save the Roman army in 340 and 295 B.C. (Livy, *8,* 9; *10,* 28). With lines 27, 29-31, cf. Dryden's translation of the *Aeneid, 6,* 824–25 (July 1697):

> Behold *Torquatus* the same track pursue;
> And next, the two devoted *Decii* view—
> The *Drusian* line, *Camillus* loaded home
> With Standards well redeem'd, and foreign Foes o'recome.
> (*6,* 1130–33)

This does *Camillus* as a God extol,
That points at *Manlius* in the Capitol.
How *Cochles* did the *Tyber*'s Surges brave,
How *Curtius* plung'd into the gaping Grave.
Great *Cyrus* here, the *Medes* and *Persians* join,
And there, the Glorious Battel of the *Boyn.*
  As th'airy Messenger the Fury spy'd,
A while his curdling Blood forgot to glide.
Confusion on his fainting Vitals hung,
And fault'ring Accents flutter'd on his Tongue.
At length, assuming Courage, he essay'd
T'inform the Fiend, then shrunk into a Shade.
  The Hag lay long revolving what might be
The blest Event of such an Embassy.
She blazons in dread Smiles her hideous Form,
So Light'ning gilds the unrelenting Storm.
Then she: Alas! how long in vain have I
Aim'd at those noble Ills the Fates deny:
Within this Isle for ever must I find
Disasters to distract my restless Mind?

31. *Camillus:* M. Furius Camillus (fourth century B.C.), five times dictator of Rome, was virtually deified as a second Romulus for defeating the Gauls and rebuilding the city.

32. *Manlius:* The story of M. Manlius Capitolinus being awakened by the sacred geese and rushing to the Capitol in time to stave off a surprise attack by the Gauls in 387 B.C., is recounted in Plutarch, *Camillus,* 27, and Livy, *5,* 47. With lines 32–33, cf. Garth's Harveian oration, in praise of William III: "You swim with Cocles, you delay with Fabius, and with Manlius your self alone withstands a Troop" (*JHM, 18* [1963], 17).

33. *Cochles:* P. Horatius Cocles held off the entire army of Porsenna the Etruscan until the wooden bridge across the Tiber could be destroyed. He then swam back to the Roman shore, even remembering to rescue his arms (Livy, *2,* 10).

34. *Curtius:* Marcus Curtius, the legendary hero, rode fully armed into a gulf which appeared in the Roman forum and which the oracle promised would not close until Rome's most valuable possession had been thrown into it. The gulf closed instantly (Livy, *1,* 6).

35. *Cyrus:* an Achaemenid sheikh who revolted successfully against his Median overlord, Astyages, in 550 B.C. and went on to conquer the entire Middle East.

36. *Boyn:* The decisive battle between the Dutch and English forces of William of Orange and the French and Irish troops of James II took place across the shallow river Boyne, about 25 miles northwest of Dublin, on 1 July 1690.

37. Pope observed that line 37 contradicts lines 38–39 (*1703* Victoria & Albert Museum copy).

Good *Tenison*'s Celestial Piety
At last has rais'd him to the Sacred See.
Somers does sick'ning Equity restore,
And helpless Orphans are oppress'd no more.
Pembroke to *Britain* endless Blessings brings;
He spoke; and Peace clap'd her Triumphant wings:
Great *Ormond* shines illustriously bright
With Blazes of Hereditary Light.
The noble Ardour of a Loyal Fire,
Inspires the generous Breast of *Devonshire*.
And *Macclesfield* is active to defend

51–69. Blackmore complains that *The Dispensary* has "little in't but Praise" (*A Satyr against Wit,* 181, below).

51. *Tenison:* Thomas Tenison (1636–1715) was consecrated archbishop of Canterbury on 16 May 1695.

53. *Somers:* See above, *1,* 51 *n.*

55. *Pembroke:* Thomas Herbert, eighth earl of Pembroke (1656?–1733), was much admired, both for his simple, unostentatious way of life, and for his virtuoso learning. "Without being of a Party," he was "yet esteemed by all Parties" (Macky, p. 22). Sunderland remarked that Pembroke was "as good a block of wood as a King can be cut out of" (Dalrymple, *3,* 2182). He was appointed to the privy council in October 1689, served as lord privy seal (1692–99), plenipotentiary to the Congress of Ryswick in 1697, and lord president of the council (May 1699–January 1702).

56. *clap'd her . . . wings:* Edward Ward borrows, or parodies, this phrase in *A Journey to Hell,* 2nd ed., 1700, p. 13: "envious Spirits . . . clap'd their pointed Wings, and with a Yell,/Gave 'em a dreadful Welcome into Hell."

57. *Ormond:* James Butler, second duke of Ormonde (1665–1745), grandson of the great duke of Ormonde who commanded Charles I's troops in Ireland and negotiated the restoration of Charles II, was one of the most popular men in England. He had fought at the king's side in all the major engagements of the war, as captain of the horse guards and lieutenant-general of the army. He was said to be "one of the most generous, princely, brave Men that ever was" (Macky, p. 10).

60. *Devonshire:* William Cavendish, fourth earl and first duke of Devonshire (1641–1707), was "the finest and handsomest Gentleman of his Time" (Macky, p. 18). One of the seven signers of the invitation to the prince of Orange in June 1688, he served as lord steward of the household throughout the reign. Like Archbishop Tenison (line 51) and the earl of Pembroke (line 55), he was one of the lords justices whom William appointed every year to govern England during his absence on the continent. His well-known generosity did not, apparently, extend to tradesmen; he was said to be "Of nice Honour in every Thing, but the paying his Tradesmen" (ibid.).

61. *Macclesfield:* Charles Gerard, second earl of Macclesfield (1659?–1701), after having been convicted of treason for complicity in the Rye House plot and pardoned by James II, served William III as colonel of a regiment of horse (1694–97) and of "Carabiniers" in the disastrous operation against Brest (June 1694). His "Friend" was the notorious Charles Mohun, baron Mohun of Okehampton, of whom it has been surmised that "few persons have been oftener tried for the crime of murder" (GEC, *9,* 28). To Mohun, Macclesfield left all his estates and made him his executor, "not

His Country, with the Zeal he loves his Friend.
Like *Leda*'s radiant Sons, divinely clear,
Portland and *Jersey* deck'd in Rays appear
To Guild, by turns, the Gallick Hemisphear.
Worth in Distress is rais'd by *Montague*,
Augustus listens if *Maecenas* sue.
And *Vernon*'s Vigilance no slumber takes,

---

doubting," as he said, "but that he is a man of that honour and so true an Englishman as always to have a regard for the true lovers of their country" (GEC, *8*, 331).

63. *Sons:* Castor and Pollux.

64. *Portland:* William appointed Portland as his first ambassador to France in October 1697. The preparations for his departure were extraordinarily lavish. The jewel office turned out two services of plate for his table and a coach of state was ordered to be made in Paris at a cost of £6000. Even his secretary, Matthew Prior, was allowed £300 for personal furnishings. The effects were equally gratifying. It was reported in February 1698 that "no ambassador before ever received so much civility from the French court" (Luttrell, *4*, 289, 326, 321, 344–45). Even the cynical St. Simon was impressed: "Les mêmes raisons qui avaient fait choisir Portland . . . le firent préferer à tout autre pour cette ambassade. On n'en pouvait nommer un plus distingué. Sa suite fut nombreuse et superbe, et sa dépense extrêmement magnifique en table, en chevaux, en livrées, en équipages, en meubles, en habits, en vaisselle, et en tout, et avec une recherche et une délicatesse exquise" (*Mémoires*, ed. Gonzague Truc, 7 vols., 1947, *1*, 473). A panegyric *To the Earl of Portland on his Embassy to France* ("What! Shall each Patron's rip'ning Smile infuse") is included in *POAS*, 1704, *3*, 375.

Jersey: Edward Villiers, earl of Jersey (1656–1711), a figure of great elegance and fashion, was the elder brother of Elizabeth Villiers, who had been William's mistress. He had recently been raised to the peerage (October 1697) and sworn to the privy council (November 1697). On 22 April 1698 William appointed him to succeed Portland, but with the rank of ambassador only, and he was already "making preparations so as to be able to leave" (Grimblot, *1*, 436). Although Jersey's preparations must have been considerably less elaborate than Portland's—he was given an advance of only £1300 (*CTB 1698–1699*, p. 313)—he did not reach Paris until August 1698 (Luttrell, *4*, 415).

66. *Montague:* See above, *Advice to a Painter*, 81 *n.*

67. *Augustus:* William III.

Maecenas: Charles Sackville, sixth earl of Dorset (1635–1706), was "the finest gentleman in the voluptuous court of Charles the Second, and in the gloomy one of King William" (Horace Walpole, *Catalogue of the Royal and Noble Authors*, 2nd ed., 2 vols., 1759, *2*, 96). He retired from political life in April 1697, but continued to afford patronage to Dryden, Wycherley, and Prior, as well as to the dunces, Thomas Shadwell, John Dennis, and Susanna Centlivre (Harris, pp. 173–94). G. Cilnius Maecenas (70?–8 B.C.), the patron of Virgil, Horace, and Propertius, was somewhat more discriminating, but no less dissolute (Seneca, *Ep.* 19, 114).

68. *Vernon:* James Vernon (1646–1727) was educated at Christ Church, Oxford, but entered parliament as a member for Cambridge University (1678–1679). Subsequently he became private secretary to the duke of Shrewsbury and was again elected to parliament (Penryn, Cornwall, 1695–98; Westminster, 1698–1702), where he became a staunch Whig. In December 1697 he succeeded Sir William Trumbull as secretary of

Sr

112

Duke street [?]
4 [illegible]

Sr Ed: Walrop, to whom I have many obligations, has added to them by giving mee this opportunity of assuring you of my humble service. I am ashamed that any thing besides ye sence of my own duty shoud remind mee of acquitting my self to you as I ought. You must give mee leave to remember yr ~~[illegible]~~ former civilitys to mee, since t'is naturall to you to forgett them. I have sub=scribed ye interpretation ye Town putts upon some names and abreviations in a late Poem you have been pleased to reade, and must take leave to tell you, that since by your approbation ~~[illegible]~~ of it you have made mee proud, you ought to send me somthing done by yr self to make mee humble. Tho I have made some Persons very angry with mee yet if I have any ways contributed to yr diversion, ye attempt I engaged in will ~~[illegible]~~ be repented of by

Sr

yr obliged Servant

S Garth

Colon — Birch
Horoscope — Haughton
Diasenna — Gillstorp ~~[illegible]~~
Colocynthis — Garner
2 Ascarides. Pierse and Arott [?]

} Apothecarys

Mirmillo — Gibbons
Querpo — Howe
City Bard — Sr R. Blackmore
Carus — Tyson
Umbra — Gold
Machaon — Sr Tho Millington

Physitians
Stentor — Goodall
Celsus — Bateman
Chiron — Gill
Psylas [?] — Chamberlen

} Vagellius — Sr Wi: Williams
C—t — Colt
R— — Roe
C—h — Colbatch
W—ly — Westly

Letter from Samuel Garth to Arthur Charlett, Master of University College, Oxford

Whilst Faction peeps abroad, and Anarchy awakes.
  Since by no Arts I therefore can defeat
The happy Enterprizes of the Great,
I'll calmly stoop to more inferiour things;
And try if my lov'd Snakes have Teeth or Stings.
  She said; and straight shrill *Colon*'s Person took,
In Morals loose, but most precise in Look.
Black-Fryar's Annals lately pleas'd to call
Him Warden of *Apothecaries-Hall.*
And, when so dignifi'd, he'd not forbear
That Operation which the Learn'd declare
Gives Cholicks ease, and makes the Ladies fair.
In starch'd Urbanity his Talent lies,
And Form the want of Intellects supplies.
Hourly his Learn'd Impertinence affords
A barren Superfluity of Words.
In haste he strides along to recompence
The want of Bus'ness with its vain Pretence.
The Fury thus assuming *Colon*'s Grace,
So slung her Arms, so shuffl'd in her Pace.
Onward she hastens to the fam'd Abodes,
Where *Horoscope* invokes th'infernal Gods;

---

state and was sworn of the privy council. As secretary of state he had custody of the signet, without which, for example, no payment could be made from the treasury, and also of the secret service funds, by which all intelligence operations were financed.

74. *Colon's Person took:* This condescension, whereby gods appear to mortals only in human form, is an epic convention (*Iliad, 2,* 16–22) which is also observed in *Le Lutrin.* Leicht (p. 147) cites *Le Lutrin, 1,* 54, where La Discorde "prend d'un vieux Chantre & la taille & la forme." The identity of Colon remains uncertain. In his letter to Charlett (see illustration, p. 75), Garth identified him as "Birch," and several readers made the same identification (*1699*[3] Yale copy [correcting an earlier annotation of "Leigh an Apoth"], *1703* Victoria & Albert Museum copy, *1706* Yale Medical Library copy 2). But Samuel Birch had not been "lately . . . Warden of *Apothecaries-Hall*" (2, 76–77, below). Among those who had, contemporary readers singled out two: Thomas Gardiner (*1699*[2] Chicago University copy, MS. Key), who had been renter warden in 1694–95, and Peter Gelsthorp (*1699*[3] Northwestern University copy and RCP copy), who had been renter warden in 1693–94 and upper warden in 1699–1700. But since Gelsthorp is Diasenna (*3,* 124 *n.*) and Gardiner probably is Colocynthis (*3,* 158 *n.*), Samuel Birch remains the most likely candidate

79. *That Operation:* glossed "Glister" (clyster) in *1699*[3] Victoria & Albert Museum copy.

90. *Horoscope:* Although in his letter to Charlett (see illustration, p. 75), Garth designated James Haughton as Horoscope, there is no doubt that Francis Bernard

And reach'd the Mansion where the Vulgar run
T'increase their Ills, and throng to be undone.
  This *Wight* all Mercenary Projects tries,
And knows, that to be Rich is to be Wise.
By useful Observations he can tell
The Sacred Charms, that in true Sterling dwell;

(1627–98) was the villain he had in mind when he wrote the poem. This has surprised some readers, like William Osler, who knew that Bernard was a distinguished practitioner, scholar, bibliophile, and physician to St. Bartholomew's Hospital. But Alexander Pope's annotation of this line provides the necessary clue; it reads: "Dr. Bernard formerly an Apothecary" (*1706* Huntington Library copy). Bernard's machinations on behalf of the Company of Apothecaries began early. Christopher Merrett was informed in 1670 "that *F*[rancis] *B*[ernard] an Apothecary, and active against the *R*[oyal] *S*[ociety] . . . shewed [the Company of Apothecaries] *H*[enry] *S*[tubbes'] Manuscripts against the *R*[oyal] *S*[ociety]" (*A Short Reply to the Postscript, &c. of H. S.*, 1670, p. 8). He was created M.D. by the archbishop of Canterbury in February 1678 and the degree was incorporated at Cambridge a few months later. In September 1680 he was elected an honorary member of the College of Physicians. Four years later he was elected renter warden of the Company of Apothecaries but paid a fine not to serve (Barrett, p. 106). In April 1687 he was admitted to the College of Physicians by the new charter of James II, whom he served as physician-in-ordinary. His career of disaffection to the College began almost immediately. In December of the same year he was fined 10*s.* for refusing to observe the Signetur statute (see below, *5*, 224 *n.*). In 1693 he complained about his place in a published list of members of the College. In December 1695 he refused to sign a £50 bond "to stand by the officers of the College" and observe its statutes (*Annals, 5,* 71; *6,* 59; *7,* 13). On this occasion he also "Transcribed with his own Hand from the College-Book, and delivered to [John Badger] for the Use and Service of the Company of Apothecaries" the list of those who did sign, as well as the list of subscribers to the dispensary (*A Short Answer to a Late Book, Entituled, Tentamen Medicinale,* 1705, p. 22). A year later he walked out of an extraordinary meeting of the College convened to promulgate the statutes of 1687 and when summoned to account for his "indecent and rude Carriage," declined to appear because the beadle had failed to sign the summons. In January 1697, along with William Gibbons (Mirmillo), George Howe, (Querpo), and Sir Richard Blackmore (a Bard) who called him "great *Bernardo* of Immortal Fame/For his Chirurgic Skill" (*King Arthur* [1697], *11,* 713–14, p. 312), he signed a petition to the visitors of the College, claiming that the new statutes had been enacted by "A prevailing Party" in the College "in a fraudulent and surreptitious Manner" (*Annals, 7,* 89, 95). On four different occasions he refused to subscribe £10 for the dispensary. It it not difficult to imagine why Garth misled Charlett concerning the identity of Horoscope. Bernard died on 9 February 1698 and on the principle of *nihil nisi bonum,* Garth may not have wished to attack a dead man. More importantly, on account of his politics, Bernard was popular at Oxford, and Garth may not have wished to offend his admirers. This seems to be confirmed by one of Thomas Tanner's correspondents who observed: "I'm sorry Dr. Bernard couldn't be spared. But I think Horoscope and Mirmillo touch not much Dr. Bernard and Gibbons, because very little particular" (Bodl. MS., Tanner 21, f. 90). Horoscopes cast by Bernard are preserved in BM MS. Sloane 1683.

91. *the Mansion:* Francis Bernard's shop was in Little Britain.

How Gold makes a *Patrician* of a Slave,
A Dwarf an *Atlas,* a *Thersites* brave.
It cancels all Defects, and in their Place
Finds Sense in *Brownlow,* Charms in Lady *Grace.*
It guides the Fancy, and directs the Mind;
No Bankrupt ever found a Fair One kind.
  So truly *Horoscope* its Virtue knows,
To this bright Idol 'tis, alone, he bows;
And fancies, that a Thousand Pound supplies
The want of Twenty thousand Qualities.
  Long has he been of that amphibious Fry,
Bold to Prescribe, and busie to Apply.
His Shop the gazing Vulgar's Eyes employs
With foreign Trinkets, and domestick Toys.
  Here, *Mummies* lay most reverendly stale,
And there, the *Tortois* hung her Coat o' Mail;
Not far from some huge *Shark*'s devouring Head,
The flying Fish their finny Pinions spread.
Aloft in Rows large Poppy Heads were strung,
And near, a scaly Alligator hung.
In this place, Drugs in musty Heaps decay'd,
In that, dri'd Bladders, and drawn Teeth were laid.
  An inner Room receives the numerous Shoals
Of such as Pay to be reputed Fools.
Globes stand by Globes, Volumns on Volumns lie,

98. *Thersites:* Deformed and cynical, Thersites provides anti-epic relief in the *Iliad,* 2, 212.

100. *Brownlow:* Sir William Brownlow, of Belton, Lincolnshire (1665–1701), fourth baronet, was a Whig member of parliament for Peterborough, Northamptonshire (1689–98) and Bishops Castle, Shropshire (1699–February 1700), and "an ordinary Councellor" (MS. Key).

Lady Grace: Lady Grace Pierrepoint (1635?–1703), hailed in Garth's Harveian oration as "a most noble heiresse of a noble paternal dowry" (*JHM, 18* [1963], 15), was the younger but only surviving daughter of Henry, first marquis of Dorchester and second earl of Kingston. In 1688 she gave the College of Physicians books worth £4000 from her father's library. She was said to be "not one of the handsomest Ladies in Town" (MS. Key).

111–18. Some details of Bernard's shop are borrowed from the "needy shop" of Romeo's apothecary (*Romeo and Juliet,* V.1.42–46).

121. *Volumns on Volumns:* Bernard was said to have assembled the largest collection of medical books in England (*A Catalogue of the Library of the late learned Dr. Francis Bernard,* 1698, sig. a2r).

And Planetary Schemes amuse the Eye.
The Sage, in Velvet Chair, here lolls at Ease,
To promise future Health for present Fees.
Then, as from *Tripod,* solemn Shams reveals,
And what the Stars know nothing of, foretels.
  One asks, how soon *Panthea* may be won,
And longs to feel the Marriage Fetters on.
Others, convinc'd by melancholy Proof,
Enquire when courteous Fates will strike 'em off.
  Some, by what means they may redress the Wrong,
When Fathers the Possession keep too long.
And some wou'd know the Issue of their Cause,
And whether Gold can sodder up its Flaws.
Poor pregnant *Laïs* his Advice would have,
To lose by Art what fruitful Nature gave:
And *Portia* old in Expectation grown,
Laments her barren Curse, and begs a Son.
Whilst *Iris,* his cosmetick *Wash,* must try,
To make her Bloom revive, and Lovers dye.
Some ask for Charms, and others Philtres choose,
To gain *Corinna,* and their Quartans lose.
Young *Hylas,* botch'd with Stains too foul to name,
In Cradle here renews his Youthful Frame:
Cloy'd with Desire, and surfeited with Charms,
A Hot-house he prefers to *Julia*'s Arms.
And old *Lucullus* wou'd th'*Arcanum* prove,
Of kindling in cold Veins the Sparks of Love.
  Bleak Envy these dull Frauds with Pleasure sees,
And wonders at the senseless Mysteries.
In *Colon*'s Voice she thus calls out aloud
On *Horoscope* environ'd by the Crowd:
  Forbear, forbear, thy vain Amusements cease;

137. *Portia:* To several readers, Portia suggested the childless Lady Anne, wife of Sir John Holt, lord chief justice of the king's bench (*1703* Yale Medical Library copy 1; *1706* Yale Medical Library copy 2 and Victoria & Albert Museum copy). But as Pope suggested in the case of Panthea (2, 127), these portraits are typical rather than particular (*1706* Huntington Library copy).

147. *Lucullus:* "Dr. King" (MS. Key) is Sir Edmund King, M.D. (1629–1709), who attended Charles II in his last illness, published a paper on the reproductive organs of men and rats (*Philosophical Transactions, 4* [17 October 1669], 1403), and served as physician to Sir Charles Sedley (BM MS. Sloane 4078, f. 215).

Thy *Wood-Cocks* from their *Gins* a while release;
And to that dire Misfortune listen well,
Which thou shou'dst fear to know, or I to tell.
'Tis true, Thou ever wast esteem'd by me
The Great *Alcides* of our Company.
When we with Noble Scorn resolv'd to ease
Our selves of all Parochial Offices;
And to our Wealthier Patients left the Care,
And draggl'd Dignity of Scavenger:
Such Zeal in that Affair thou didst express,
Nought cou'd be equal, but the great Success.
Now call to mind thy Gen'rous Prowess past,
Be what thou shou'dst, by thinking what thou wast.
The Faculty of *Warwick-Lane* Design,
If not to Storm, at least to Undermine:
Their Gates each day Ten thousand Night-caps crowd,
And Mortars utter their Attempts aloud.
If they shou'd once unmask our Mystery,
Each Nurse, e're long, wou'd be as Learn'd as We;
Our Art expos'd to ev'ry Vulgar Eye,

154. *Wood-Cocks:* Professional gamblers "make it their sole practise and employment to noose unwary woodcocks, and deprive them of their plumes" (Lucas, p. 200).

160. *Parochial Offices:* On 13 December 1694 the Company of Apothecaries petitioned the House of Commons to be relieved, as members of the College of Physicians already were, from the performance of all parish duties. A bill for exempting apothecaries from serving the offices of constable, scavenger, and other parish and ward offices, and from serving on juries, was subsequently introduced and received the royal assent on 11 February 1695 (*CJ, 11,* 186, 228), despite a petition from the lord mayor and common council of the city of London protesting that the bill was "very prejudicial" to the city. In their replication before the House of Commons, the apothecaries, including, it would seem, Dr. Francis Bernard, argued (1) that "their great Charity . . . to the Meaner Sort of People . . . [and] their *diligent Attendance* upon *Sick Persons* of all sorts, *Day and Night*" made it impossible for them to undertake additional responsibilities, (2) that "133,000 *Families* receive advantage by their *undisturb'd Attendance,*" and (3) that "they must needs have *as great Skill* as any *Physician;* for the *Physician* has only his *own Prescriptions,* whereas they see *those* of most of the best and learnedest *Physicians*" (*A Vindication of the Colledge of Physicians* [1695]). The College opposed this bill not only because it reflected upon their charity but also because it seemed to sanction the apothecaries' illegal practice of medicine.

169. *Ten thousand Night-caps:* During the first three years of its operation, the dispensary made up, at cost, 13,192 prescriptions; during the period February 1701–December 1704, this figure increased to 71,999 (*A Short Answer to a Late Book, Entituled, Tentamen Medicinale,* pp. 33–34).

And none, in Complaisance to us, would dye.
What if We claim their Right t'Assassinate,
Must they needs turn *Apothecaries* straight?
Prevent it, Gods! all Stratagems we try,
To crowd with new Inhabitants your Sky.
'Tis we who wait the Destinies Command,
To purge the troubl'd Air, and weed the Land.
And dare the *College* of *Physicians* aim
To equal our Fraternity in Fame?
Crabs Eyes as well with *Pearl* for Use may try,
Or *Highgate-Hill* with lofty *Pindus* vie:
So *Glow-worms* may compare with *Titan*'s Beams,
Or *Hare-Court* Pump with *Aganippe*'s Streams.
  Our Manufacture now they meanly sell,
And spightfully th'intrinsick Value tell:
Nay more, (but Heav'ns prevent) they'l force us soon,
To act with Conscience, and to be Undone.
  At this, fam'd *Horoscope* turn'd pale, and straight
In Silence tumbl'd from his Chair of State.
The Crowd in great Confusion sought the Door,
And left the *Magus* fainting on the Floor.
Whilst in his Breast the Fury breath'd a Storm,

176. *turn Apothecaries:* William Salmon claimed that "all their whole Design is, only to ruine the *Apothecaries* Trade, and get it into their own hands, and so (under the Umbrage of their *pretended Charity*) to make their own Fortunes by it . . ." (*A Rebuke to the Authors of a Blew-Book,* 1698, p. 30).

183. *Crabs Eyes . . . Pearl:* "Pearls are a wonderful strengthener to the heart, increase milk in Nurses, and amend it being naught; they restore such as are in Consumptions . . . preserve the body in health, and resist Fevers" (Culpeper, p. 51). Crabs' eyes, concretions found in the stomachs of crustaceans, were frequently substituted for pearls in prescriptions ([Edward Ward], *A Journey to H—,* Part II, 2nd ed., 1700, Canto *5,* 141, p. [10, misnumbered] 6).

184. *Highgate-Hill:* The elevation of Highgate Hill, in Hampstead, is 426 feet.

Pindus: "a mountain of Thessaly sacred to Apollo, and the Muses" (*1706* Yale Medical Library copy 2).

186. *Hare-Court: "Hare-Court,* has excellent Water; some people use *New River,* others *Thames Water" (Journey to London,* sig. D2r).

Aganippe: "A River sacred to the Muses" (*1706* Yale Medical Library copy 2).

188. *intrinsick Value:* The £530 contributed by the subscribers to the dispensary was to be "expended for preparing for and delivering Medicines to the said poor at their intrinsick values" (*Annals,* 7, 92).

195. Leicht (p. 150) cites *Le Lutrin, 1,* 81–82:

> Elle dit: & du vent de sa bouche profane,
> Lui soufle avec ces mots l'ardeur de la chicane.

Then sought her Cell, and reassum'd her Form.
Thus from the Sore altho' the Insect flies,
It leaves a Brood of Maggots in Disguise.
 Officious *Squirt* in haste forsook the Shop,
To succour the expiring *Horoscope.*
Oft he essay'd the *Magus* to restore,
By Salt of *Succinum's* prevailing Pow'r;
But still supine the solid Lumber lay,
An Image of scarce animated Clay;
Till Fates, indulgent when Disasters call,
Bethought th'Assistant of a Urinal;
Whose Steam the Wight no sooner did receive,
But rous'd, and bless'd the Stale Restorative.
The Springs of Life their former Vigour feel,
Such Zeal he had for that vile Utensil.
 So when the Great *Pelides, Thetis* found,
He knew the Fishy Smell, and th'Azure Goddess own'd.

Canto 3

 All Night the Sage in Pensive Tumults lay,
Complaining of the slow approach of Day;
Oft turn'd him round, and strove to think no more,
Of what shrill *Colon* spoke the Day before.
Cowslips and *Poppies* o'er his Eyes he spread,
And *Salmon's* Works he laid beneath his Head.

199. *Squirt:* Several readers identified Squirt as Perrott, an apothecary (*1699*[3] Royal College of Physicians copy), but most readers were satisfied with "Dr. Barnard's man" (*1700* Yale Medical Library copy; *1709* Key).

202. *Salt of Succinum:* amber salts. Amber "prevails against most diseases of the head" (Culpeper, p. 51).

211. *Pelides, Thetis found:* Aeneas recognized his mother, Venus, by her birds, *geminae columbae* (*Aeneid, 6,* 190–93).

5. *Cowslips and Poppies:* "The water of Cowslip-flowers . . . takes away pains in the head, the Vertigo and Megrim." "Syrups of Poppies provoke sleep" (Culpeper, pp. 88, 135).

6. *Salmon's Works:* William Salmon (1644–1713) was a "Quack Doctor, and indefatigable Scribbler" (*1709* Key) whom the College prosecuted more or less continuously for malpractice. Twenty of his works, plus 11 editions of *Salmon's Almanack,* are listed in Wing (S420–S457, A2314–A2324). When Thomas Gill and Richard Morton, the fellows of the College of Physicians who had been appointed the first "Curators" of

But all those Opiats still in vain he tries,
Sleep's gentle Image his Embraces flies.
Tumultuous Cares lay rouling in his Breast,
And thus his anxious Thoughts the Sage express'd:
  Oft has this Planet roul'd around the Sun,
Since to consult the Skies, I first begun:
Such my Applause, so mighty my Success,
I once thought my Predictions more than Guess.
But, doubtful as I am, I'll entertain
This Faith: there can be no Mistake in Gain.
For the dull World most Honour pay to those
Who on their Understanding most impose.
First Man creates, and then he fears the Elf,
Thus others cheat him not, but he himself:
He loaths the Substance, and he loves the Show,
'Tis hard e're to convince a Fool, He's so:
He hates Realities, and hugs the Cheat,
And still the Pleasure lies in the Deceit.
So Meteors flatter with a dazling Dye
Which no Existence has, but in the Eye.
At distance Prospects please us, but when near,
We find but desart Rocks and fleeting Air.
From Stratagem, to Stratagem we run,
And he knows most, who latest is undone.
  Mankind one day serene and free appear;
The next, they're cloudy, sullen, and severe:

---

the dispensary, published *The State of Physick in London* in April 1698, explaining the operation of the free out-patient clinic that had opened two months before, Salmon reacted with a violent *Rebuke to the Authors of A Blew-Book; call'd The State of Physick in London . . . Written in Behalf of the Apothecaries and Chirurgions of the City of London.* See above, 2, 176.

24. *the Pleasure lies in the Deceit:* "As in cheating there is a *Bonum utile,* so in being cheated there is a *Bonum jucundum,* the Impostor usually impressing an expectation on his Patients fancy, which doth not a little tickle his dull spleen" (*The Accomplisht Physician,* 1670, p. 2).

27. *At distance Prospects please us:* "Tis distance lends enchantment to the view. Campbell, Vide Pleasures of Hope [1799]" (*1706* Yale Medical Library copy 2, in a different hand from other annotation).

29. *From Stratagem, to Stratagem:* Nine stratagems for multiplying apothecaries' bills, including "creating diseases in easie mens Phansies, and so decoying them into courses of *Physick,*" are listed in Christopher Merrett, *A Short View of the Frauds, and Abuses Committed by Apothecaries,* 1669, pp. 13–14.

New Passions, new Opinions still excite,
And what they like at Noon, despise at Night:
They gain with Labour, what they quit with Ease,
And Health, for want to Change, grows a Disease.
Religion's bright Authority they dare,
And yet are Slaves to Superstitious Fear.
They Councel others, but themselves deceive,
And tho' they're Cozen'd still, they still believe.
  Shall I then, who with penetrating Sight
Inspect the Springs that guide each Appetite:
Who with unfathom'd Searches hourly pierce
The dark Recesses of the Universe,
Be Passive, whilst the Faculty pretend
Our Charter with unhallow'd Hands to rend?
If all the Fiends that in low Darkness reign,
Be not the Fictions of a sickly Brain,
That Project, the *Dispensary* they call,
Before the Moon can blunt her Horns, shall fall.
  With that, a Glance from mild *Aurora*'s Eyes,
Shoots thro' the Crystal Kingdoms of the Skies;
The Savage Kind in Forests cease to roam,
And Sots o'ercharg'd with nauseous Loads reel home.
Light's chearful Smiles o'er th'Azure Waste are spread,
And Miss from Inns o' Court bolts out unpaid.
The Sage transported at th'approaching Hour,
Imperiously thrice thunder'd on the Floor;
Officious *Squirt* that moment had access,
His Trust was great, his Vigilance no less.
To him thus *Horoscope:*
  My kind Companion in this dire Affair,
Which is more Light, since you assume a Share;

45. *Faculty:* The legal title of the College was "the President and College or Commonalty of the Faculty of Physick London." In one of his trials for malpractice, William Salmon's demurrer that the College had not been declared by its right name was allowed by the court (*Annals, 6,* 171–72).

46. *Charter:* The Master, Warden, and Society of the Art and Mystery of Apothecaries of the City of London was separated from the Grocers Company and incorporated by a charter of James I on 6 December 1617.

49–50. Leicht (p. 151) cites *Le Lutrin, 4,* 85: "Non, s'il n'est abattu, je ne sçaurois plus vivre."

57–60. Leicht (p. 151) cites *Le Lutrin, 4,* 5–8.

Fly with what haste you us'd to do of old,
When *Clyster* was in danger to be cold:
With Expedition on the Beadle call,
To summon all the Company to th'Hall.
  Away the trusty Coadjutor hies,
Swift as from Phyal Steam of *Harts-horn* flies.
The *Magus* in the int'rim mumbles o'er
Vile Terms of Art to some Infernal Pow'r,
And draws Mysterious Circles on the Floor.
But from the gloomy Vault no glaring Spright,
Ascends to blast the tender Bloom of Light.
No mystick Sounds from *Hell's* detested Womb,
In dusky Exhalations upwards come.
And now to raise an Altar He decrees,
To that devouring Harpy call'd *Disease;*
Then Flow'rs in Canisters he hastes to bring,
The wither'd Product of a blighted Spring,
With cold *Solanum* from the *Pontick* Shore,
The Roots of *Mandrake* and Black *Ellebore.*
And on the Structure next he heaps a Load
Of *Sassafras* in Chips, and *Mastick* Wood.

66. *the Beadle:* The Company of Apothecaries had elected a new beadle, John Brewster (d. 1708), in 1697, and appropriated £4 to buy him a new suit of clothes "against Lord Mayors Day."

67. Leicht (p. 152) cites *Le Lutrin, 4,* 103–04.

69. *Harts-horn:* Hartshorn, formerly an important source of ammonia, "resists Poyson and the Pestilence, provokes Urine, restores lost strength, brings forth both Birth and After-birth" (Culpeper, p. 49).

72. *And draws . . . Circles:* cf. "And drew dire Circles with her Magic Wand," Blackmore, *King Arthur* (1697), *12,* 85, p. 318.

81. *Solanum: "Solanum.* Nightshade, very cold and dry" (Culpeper, p. 38).

82. *Mandrake: "Mandragorae* . . . , a Root dangerous for its coldness, being cold in the fourth degree; the root is scarce, and dangerous for the vulgar to use; therefore I leave it to those that have skill" (Culpeper, p. 8).

Black Ellebore: "Black Hellebore, Bears-foot, or Christmas flowers: both this and the former [white hellebore] are hot and dry in the third degree . . . , purgeth Melancholy, resisteth Madness" (Culpeper, p. 6).

84. *Sassafras:* "Sassafras . . . is hot and dry in the second degree; it opens obstructions . . . breaks the stone, stays vomiting, provokes Urine, and is very profitable in the French Pox" (Culpeper, p. 16).

Mastick: a gum or resin exuded from the bark of *Pistacia lentiscus* and some other trees; "Mastick stays fluxes, being taken inwardly any way. Three or four small grains of Mastick, swallowed down whole at night going to bed, is an excellent remedy for

Then from the Compter he takes down the File,
And with Prescriptions lights the solemn Pile.
  Feebly the Flames on clumsie Wings aspire,
And smoth'ring Fogs of Smoke benight the Fire.
With Sorrow he beheld the sad Portent,
Then to the Hag these *Orizons* he sent:
  Disease! thou ever most propitious Pow'r,
Whose soft Indulgence we perceive each Hour;
Thou that wou'dst lay whole *States* and *Regions* waste,
Sooner than we thy *Cormorants* shou'd fast;
If, in return, all Diligence we pay
T'extend your Empire, and confirm your Sway,
Far as the weekly Bills can reach around,
From *Kent-street* end to fam'd St. *Giles's Pound;*
Behold this poor Libation with a Smile,
And let auspicious Light break through the Pile.
  He spoke; and on the Pyramid he laid
Bay-Leaves and Viper's Hearts, and thus he said:
  As These consume in this mysterious Fire,
So let the curs'd *Dispensary* expire;
And as Those crackle in the Flames, and die,
So let its Vessels burst, and Glasses fly.
  But a sinister Cricket straight was heard,
The Altar fell, the Off'ring disappear'd.

---

pains in the stomach . . . : being mixed with white Wine and the mouth washed with it, it cleanseth the Gums of corruption, and fastneth loose Teeth" (Culpeper, p. 77).

97. *Bills:* The bills of mortality, or official returns of deaths, began to be published weekly by the Company of Parish Clerks in 1592 for 109 parishes in and around London.

98. *Kent-street end:* Kent Street was the main thoroughfare leading southeast from London Bridge. It "ended" when it became the Dover road, in the vicinity of Lock Bridge, outside Southwark.

St. Giles's Pound: St. Giles Pound, located in what is now St. Giles Circus, marked the beginning of the Oxford road, the main route northwest.

102. *Bay-Leaves: "Laurus.* Bay-tree. The Leaves are hot and dry, resist drunkenness, they gently bind and help Diseases in the bladder, help the stinging of Bees and Wasps, mitigate the pain of the stomach, dry and heal, open obstructions of the Liver and Spleen, resist the Pestilence" (Culpeper, p. 30).

Viper's Hearts: Viper's flesh was thought to be a powerful antidote to poison and was also indicated for "vices of the Nerves" (Culpeper, p. 47), but viper's hearts do not appear in the pharmacopoeia. Perhaps they only characterize nonsubscribers to the dispensary.

104. Leicht (p. 153) cites Theocritus, II, 23–26.

As the fam'd Wight the Omen did regret,
Squirt brought the News the Company was met.
Nigh where *Fleet-Ditch* descends in sable Streams,
To wash his sooty *Naiads* in the *Thames;*
There stands a Structure on a rising Hill,
Where *Tyro's* take their Freedom out to kill.
Some Pictures in these dreadful Shambles tell,
How, by the *Delian* God, the *Pithon* fell;
And how *Medea* did the *Philter* brew,
That cou'd in *Æson's* Veins young force renew;
How sanguine Swains their Amorous Hours repent,
When Pleasure's past, and Pains are permanent;
And how frail Nymphs, oft by Abortion, aim
To lose a Substance, to preserve a Name.
Soon as each Member in his Rank was plac'd,
Th' Assembly *Diasenna* thus address'd:
My kind Confed'rates if my poor Intent,

111–13. *Fleet-Ditch . . . Hill:* Apothecaries Hall was, and is, located halfway up Ludgate Hill, off Water Lane (now called Blackfriars Lane), east of the mouth of Fleet Ditch (see illustration, p. 86).

114. *Tyro's:* "Apprentices" (*1706* Huntington Library copy).

115. *Pictures:* "Apothecaries hall . . . is a beautiful edifice . . . . The ceiling of the court-room and of the hall are ornamented with fretwork; the wall is wainscotted 14 feet high, and adorned with the bust of Dr. Gideon Delaun, apothecary to king James I. and with several pieces of good painting" (John Noorthouck, *A New History of London,* 1773, p. 621).

116. *the Delian God:* Apollo attacked and killed the monster, Python, as soon as he was born (Ovid, *Metamorphoses, 1,* 438–44).

117. *Medea:* By drawing out his blood and replacing it with a sort of witches' brew, Medea was able to restore Aeson to youthful virility (*ibid., 7,* 251–93).

124. *Diasenna: Garth* (see illustration, p. 75) identified Diasenna as Peter Gelsthorp (c. 1661–1719), a London apothecary who received an M.D. degree from Utrecht in 1687. He was admitted candidate of the College of Physicians in 1688 and elected a fellow in April 1691. Two years later he served as renter warden of the Company of Apothecaries. In December 1695 he refused to sign a £50 bond "to stand by the officers of the College" and at two meetings of the College in 1697 he "positively refused to subscribe" to the dispensary (*Annals, 7,* 13, 94, 117). In 1699 he was elected upper warden of the Company of Apothecaries and Master in 1701. Diasenna is a powerful cathartic. Nicholas Culpeper, who gives the prescription, also observes that "Out of question some body had formerly cursed the College for calling so violent a purge as this, HOLY POWDER; and therefore now they changed the name" (Culpeper, p. 154).

125–238. "Th' Assembly" in Apothecaries Hall parodies "the great consult" in Hell (*Paradise Lost, 2,* 50–298), with Diasenna, Colocynthis, and the elder Askaris, respec-

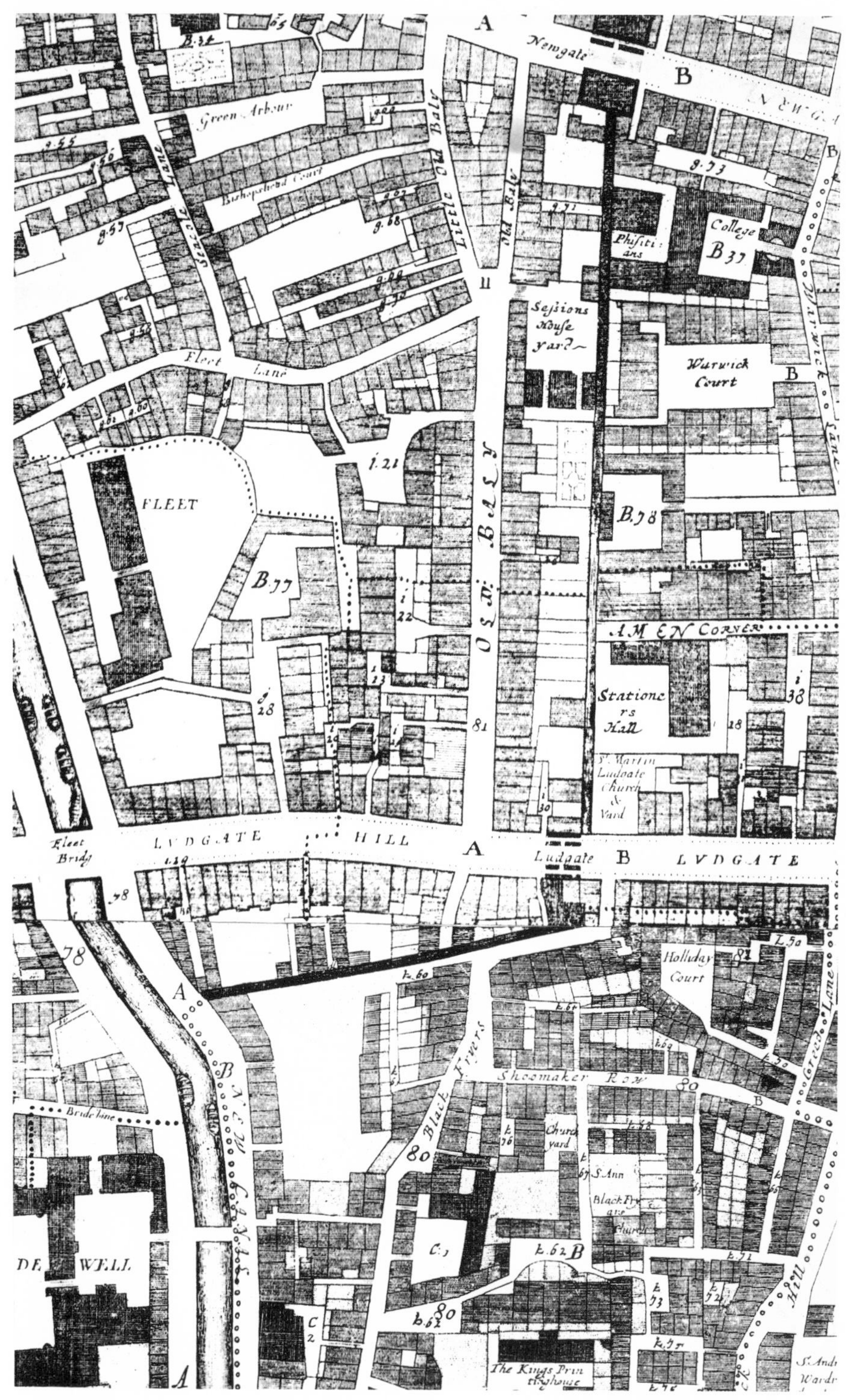

From *A Large and Accurate Map of the City of London . . . by John Ogilby, Esq.*
The College of Physicians is designated B37 and Apothecaries Hall is at C1

As 'tis sincere, had been but prevalent,
We here had met on some serene Design,
And on no other Bus'ness but to Dine;
The Faculty had still maintain'd their Sway,
And Interest had taught us to obey;
Then we'd this only Emulation known,
Who best cou'd fill his Purse, and thin the Town.
But now from gath'ring Clouds Destruction pours,
Which threatens with mad rage our *Halcyon* hours:
Mists from black Jealousies the Tempest form,
Whilst late Divisions reinforce the Storm.
Know, when these Feuds, like those at Law, are past,
The Winners will be Losers at the last.
Like Heroes in Sea-Fights we seek Renown,
To Fire some hostile Ship, we burn our own.
That Jugler which another's Slight will show,
But teaches how the World his own may know.
Thrice happy were those golden Days of old,
When dear as *Burgundy, Ptisans* were sold;
When Patients chose to die with better will,
Than live to pay th'*Apothecary*'s Bill.
And cheaper than for our Assistance call,
Might go to *Aix* or *Bourbon* Spring and Fall.
But now late Jars our Practices detect,
For Mines, when once discover'd, lose th'Effect.
Dissentions, like small Streams, are first begun,
Scarce seen they rise, but gather as they run:
So Lines that from their Parallel decline,
More they advance, the more they still dis-join.
'Tis therefore my Advice, in haste we send,
And beg the Faculty to be our Friend.
   As he revolving stood to speak the rest,
Rough *Colocynthis* thus his Rage exprest:

---

tively, in the roles of Belial, Moloch, and Mammon. Both meetings conclude in a hollow roar, appropriately described in epic simile.

144. *Ptisans:* French, *tisane;* a palatable decoction of nourishing and negligibly medicinal quality; originally, barley water.

158. *Colocynthis:* Garth identified Colocynthis as "Garner" (see illustration, p. 75), presumably Thomas Gardiner, who, as renter warden of the Company of Apothecaries in 1694–95, paid John Groenevelt £15 "to oppose the College" and support the

Thou Scandal of the mighty *Paean*'s Art,
At thy approach, the Springs of Nature start,
The Nerves unbrace: Nay, at the sight of thee,
A Scratch turns Cancer, th'Itch a Leprosie.
Cou'dst thou propose that we, the *Friends* o' Fates,
Who fill *Church-yards,* and who unpeople States,
Who baffle Nature, and dispose of Lives,
Whilst *Russel,* as we please, or starves, or thrives,
Shou'd e'er submit to their imperious Will,
Who out o' Consultation scarce can kill?
The tow'ring *Alps* shall sooner sink to Vales,
And *Leaches,* in our Glasses, swell to *Whales;*
Or *Norwich* trade in Implements of Steel,
And *Bromingham* in Stuffs and Druggets deal:
The Sick to th'Hundreds sooner shall repair,
And change the *Gravel-Pits* for *Essex* Air.
No, no, the Faculty shall soon confess
Our Force encreases, as our Funds grow less;
And what requir'd such Industry to raise,
We'll scatter into nothing as we please.
Thus they'll acknowledge, to Annihilate
Shews as immense a Pow'r as to Create.

Apothecaries' bill then pending in parliament. It was Gardiner as well who "wrote something in Answer" to *The State of Physick in London: With an Account of the Charitable Regulation made lately at the College,* 1698 (*A Short Answer to a Late Book, Entituled, Tentamen Medicinale,* pp. 27–29). Colocynthis, or coloquintida, is also a well-known cathartic.

166. *Russel:* William Russell (b. 1644?) was the famous undertaker in Cheapside who embalmed Dryden (*1706* Yale Medical Library copy 2); cf. *Epitaph upon Mr. John Dryden,* headnote, pp. 206–07, below.

171–72. *Norwich . . . Bromingham:* Norwich was "Famous for Druggets" and Birmingham "Noted for Steel-Ware made there" (*1706* Yale Medical Library copy 2).

173. *Hundreds:* A hundred is a subdivision of a county or shire having its own court; the hundreds of Kent and Essex were foggy, marshy places that were thought to be very unhealthful, "for here Strangers get a *Kentish* Ague that seldom forsakes them till it has laid them in their Graves" (Morden, p. 77).

174. *the Gravel-Pits:* Alexander Pope located these gravel pits in Kensington (*1706* Huntington Library copy), but there were others in Soho. The sick were lowered into them for therapeutic purposes. Cf. *Prologue by Sir John Falstaff* ("See Brittains, see, one half before your Eyes"): "worn out with acting Beaus and Wits,/You're all sent crawling to the Gravel pits,/Pretending Claps, there Languishing you lye" (Folger MS. M.b.12, f. 233).

Essex: See below, *4,* 198.

We'll raise our num'rous Cohorts, and oppose
The feeble Forces of our Pigmy Foes;
Whole Troops of Quacks shall join us on the Place,
From Great *Kirleus* down to *Doctor Case.*
Tho' such vile Rubbish sink, yet we shall rise;
Directors still secure the greatest Prize.
Such poor Supports serve only like a Stay;
The Tree once fix'd, its Rest is torn away.
  So Patriots in the times of Peace and Ease,
Forget the Fury of the late Disease:
Imaginary Dangers they create,
And loath th'*Elixir* which preserv'd the State.
  Arm therefore, gallant Friends, 'tis Honour's Call,
Or let us boldly Fight, or bravely Fall.
  To this the *Session* seem'd to give consent,
Much lik'd the War, but dreaded much th'Event.
At length, the growing Diff'rence to compose,
Two Brothers, nam'd *Ascarides,* arose.
Both had the Volubility of Tongue,
In Meaning faint, but in Opinion strong.
To speak they both assum'd a like Pretence,
But th'Elder gain'd his just Preeminence.
  Then he: 'Tis true, when Privilege and Right
Are once invaded, Honour bids us Fight.
But let us, to the Field before we move,
Know, if the Gods our Enterprize approve.
Suppose th'unthinking Faculty unvail,
What we, thro' wiser Conduct, wou'd conceal;
Is't Reason we shou'd quarrel with the Glass

184. *Kirleus:* Thomas Kirleus (d. 1696?) was a famous quack and physician-in-ordinary to Charles II.

Case: John Case was a quack pox doctor who lived "At the Golden Ball, and Lillies-Head," near Ludgate (*Journey to London,* p. 25). In 1693 he applied to the College to be licensed to practice medicine, "but was found so ignorant, that he understood not the Questions which were askt him in Latin . . . [and] nothing at all of Physick" (*Annals, 6,* 74).

198. *Ascarides:* Garth identified the Ascarides as "Pierce and Brother" (see illustration, p. 75), apothecaries in Covent Garden. Michael Pierce, the elder brother, who was apothecary to Princess Anne, qualified for inclusion in *The Dispensary* by encouraging Dr. John Badger in his attacks on the College of Physicians (*A Short Answer to a Late Book, Entituled, Tentamen Medicinale,* p. 28).

That shews the monstrous Features of our Face?
Or grant some grave Pretenders have of late
Thought fit an Innovation to create;
Soon they'll repent, what rashly they begun;
Tho' Projects please, Projectors are undone.
All Novelties must this Success expect,
When good, our Envy; and when bad, Neglect:
If things of Use were valu'd, there had been
Some Work-house where the *Monument* is seen.
Or if the Voice of Reason cou'd be heard,
E're this, Triumphal Arches had appear'd.
Then since no Veneration is allow'd,
Or to the real, or th'appearing Good;
The Project that we vainly apprehend,
Must, as it blindly rose, as vilely end.
Some Members of the Faculty there are,
Who Int'rest prudently to Oaths prefer.
Our Friendship with a servile Air they court,
And their Clandestine Arts are our Support.
Them we'll consult about this Enterprise,
And boldly Execute what they Advise.
  But from below (while such Resolves they took)

218. *the Monument:* "Not far from the Bridge, is the fatal Place where the dreadful Fire . . . first began; near which, is now erected (as was ordered by an Act of Parliament, immediately after the Fire) a Pillar in perpetual Memory thereof; It is of the *Dorick* Order, 202 Foot high . . . the Front whereof is curiously adorned with ingenious Emblems in *Basso Relievo,* the Work of that admirable Sculptor and Carver in Stone, Mr. *Gabriel Cibber,* another *Praxiteles*" (Chamberlayne, 1700, p. 414).

220. *Triumphal Arches:* See *Advice to a Painter,* headnote, p. 12 above.

225–26. *Oaths:* By the oath to which every candidate subscribed, members of the College of Physicians were enjoined not to "entertain familiarity with any one who studies in word or deed to subvert the State of the Colledge" (*The Statutes of the Colledge of Physicians London,* 1693, p. 80). More specifically the members were enjoined not to bargain with apothecaries for a share in the profit of medicines prescribed, nor to employ apothecaries who themselves practiced medicine (ibid., p. 160). By the new statutes enacted in September 1687, the members were further enjoined not to consult with an apothecary (see below, *5,* 108) and not to include directions in the prescriptions which they sent to apothecaries to be made up—this was the controversial "*Signetur*-Statute" (see below, *5,* 224). These laws must define the actual practices of the "Apothecaries Physicians" who opposed the opening of the dispensary.

231. *from below:* When Apothecaries Hall was rebuilt after the Great Fire of 1666, the old kitchen under the Great Hall was converted into "a *grand Laboratory*" where the new chemical medicines could be manufactured for the wholesale trade (Adrian

Some *Aurum Fulminans* the Fabrick shook.
The Champions, daunted at the Crack, retreat,
Regard their Safety, and their Rage forget.
So when at *Bathos* all the *Gyants* strove
T'invade the Skies, and wage a War with *Jove;*
Soon as the *Ass* of old *Silenus* bray'd,
The trembling Rebels in confusion fled.

Canto 4

Not far from that most famous Theater,
Where wandring Punks each Night at five repair;
Where Purple Emperors in Buskins tread,
And Rule imaginary Worlds for Bread;
Where *Bently,* by Old Writers, wealthy grew,
And *Briscoe* lately was undone by New:

Huyberts, *A Corner-Stone Laid towards the Building of a New Colledge,* 1675, p. 20; Barrett, p. 86).

232. *Aurum Fulminans:* Fulminate of gold is an explosive made by adding ammonia to a solution of auric chloride (BM MS. Sloane 179A, f. 76v). It was thought at the time to be "perhaps the most active Body in Nature" (*Bellum Medicinale,* 1701, p. 43).

235. *Bathos:* A deep valley in Arcadia, one alleged site of the war between the giants and the Greek gods (Pausanias, *8,* 29).

237. *the Ass of old Silenus:* The story probably derives from Paul Scarron, *Typhon ou La Gigantomachie. Poëme burlesque* (1664), a secondary source of *The Dispensary.* In the English translation by John Phillips, the lines read: "The silly Ass began to bray,/And Gyants fairly ran away" (*Typhon: Or, The Gyants Wars with the Gods. A Mock-Poem,* 1665, p. 86).

1. *Theater:* The King's Playhouse, or Theatre Royal, also called the Drury Lane Theatre, was actually situated between Drury Lane and Bridges Street, near Russell Street.

2. *wandring Punks:* "several *Courts* . . . give Passage into *Drury Lane* . . . all small, with narrow Passages, and not over well Inhabited; except some of them noted for the Reception of the kinder Sort of Females" (Strype, 2, 175).

5. *Bently:* Richard Bentley, the bookseller, occupied the Post House in Russell Street, near Covent Garden, from 1675 to 1697. In 1692 he reissued some 50 novels of the preceding 15 years (Plomer, pp. 31–32).

6. *Briscoe:* Samuel Briscoe began life as an apprentice to Richard Bentley and then set up his own shop in Russell Street at the corner of Charles Street opposite Will's coffee-house. He published Dryden, Wycherley, and Congreve. John Dunton mentions his "misfortunes" (MS. Key; Plomer, p. 50).

There triumphs a *Physician* of Renown,
To scarce a Mortal, but himself, unknown.
None e'er was plac'd more luckily than He,
For th'Exercise of such a Mystery.
When *Burgess* deafens all the list'ning press
With Peals of most Seraphick Emptiness;
Or when Mysterious *Freeman* mounts on high
To preach his Parish to a Lethargy:
This *Æsculapius* waits hard by, to ease
The *Martyrs* of such Christian Cruelties.
  Long has this happy Quarter of the Town,
For Lewdness, Wit, and Gallantry been known.
All Sorts meet here, of whatsoe'er Degree,
To blend and justle into Harmony.
The Politicians of *Parnassus* prate,
And Poets canvass the Affairs of State;
The Cits ne'er talk of Trade and Stock, but tell

7. *Physician:* William Gibbons (1649–1728), proceeded M.D. from St. John's College, Oxford, in 1683. The present text (*4*, 52–59) implies that he practiced medicine in Oxford for some years before going to London. He was elected a fellow of the College of Physicians in 1692 and almost immediately identified himself with the "Apothecaries Physicians." Thomas Brown said he "got all his Practice by taking Dr. *Lower's* House" in King Street, Covent Garden (*The Second Volume of Miscellaneous Works, Written by George, Late Duke of Buckingham,* 1705, p. 2123). In January 1695 he did "freely acknowledge that he had, and did promote the Apothecaries Bill" (see above, *2*, 160 *n.*), which was then under consideration in parliament (*Annals, 6,* 186). In December of the same year he refused to sign a £50 bond "to stand by the officers of the College." He walked out of the *comitia extraordinaria* convened in November 1696 to promulgate the new statutes and in January 1697 he joined Francis Bernard, George Howe, and Sir Richard Blackmore, who called him "one with *Aesculapian* Skill inspir'd" (*King Arthur* [1697], *4*, 490, p. 112), in signing a petition to the visitors of the College (see above, *2*, 90 *n.*). He did not, of course, subscribe to the dispensary. Despite all this, he was still, in March 1697, accused of malpractice by an apothecary (*Annals, 7,* 97). In 1727 he was described as "pretty old Dr. Gibbons (78), who did not receive fees with grief, but alacrity" (Nichols, *Illustrations, 2,* 801).

11. *Burgess:* Daniel Burgess (1645–1713), the "non Con. Parson" (MS. Key), attended Westminster School under Richard Busby, but left Magdalen Hall, Oxford, without taking a degree. He was ordained by the Dublin presbytery and in 1685 came to London, where he ministered to a large congregation at a hired meeting place in Bridges Street, Covent Garden. In 1695 the congregation moved to a meeting house in Russell Court, Drury Lane.

13. *Freeman:* Samuel Freeman (1644–1707) had been rector of St. Paul's, Covent Garden, since December 1689 (MS. Key). "He was a man of great pleasantry in conversation; but his performances in the pulpit were not equally admired" (Thomas Birch, *The Life of the Most Reverend Dr. John Tillotson,* 2nd ed., 1753, p. 212).

How *Virgil* writ, how bravely *Turnus* fell.
The Country Dames drive to *Hippolito*'s,
First find a Spark, and after lose a Nose.
The Lawyer for Lac'd Coat the Robe does quit,
He grows a Mad-man, and then turns a Wit.
And in the Cloister pensive *Strephon* waits,
Till *Chloe*'s Hackney comes, and then retreats;
And if th'ungenerous Nymph a Shaft lets fly
More fatally than from a sparkling Eye,
Mirmillo, that fam'd *Opifer,* is nigh.
Th'*Apothecaries* thither throng to Dine,
And want of Elbow-room's supply'd in Wine.
Cloy'd with Variety, they surfeit there,
Whilst the wan Patients on thin Gruel fare.
'Twas here the Champions of the Party met,
Of their Heroick Enterprize to treat.
Each Hero a tremendous Air put on,
And stern *Mirmillo* in these Words begun:
'Tis with concern, my Friends, I meet you here;
No Grievance you can know, but I must share.
'Tis plain, my Int'rest you've advanc'd so long,
Each Fee, tho' I was mute, wou'd find a Tongue.
And in return, tho' I have strove to rend
Those Statutes, which on Oath I should defend;
Yet that's a Trifle to a generous Mind,
Great Services, as great Returns should find.
And you'll perceive, this Hand, when Glory calls,
Can brandish Arms as well as Urinals.

25. *Hippolito's:* a chocolate house in Covent Garden (MS. Key).

33. *Mirmillo:* Garth identified Mirmillo as "Gibbons" (see illustration, p. 75); see above, *4, 7 n.*

Opifer: The motto of the Company of Apothecaries, *Opiferque Per Orbem Dicor* ("I am called an assistant throughout the world"), was ironically translated by the apothecaries as "the Doctor can do nothing without us" (Everard Maynwaring, *Praxis Medicorum Antiqua & Nova,* 1671, p. 67), and by the physicians as "sent forward and backward to *fetch and carry* the *Boles* and *Glasses*" *(The Present State of Physick and Surgery in London,* 1701, p. 8).

47. *Oath:* See above, *3,* 225–26 *n.* In his Harveian oration Garth had reminded his auditors that even "If Statutes, if Solemn Oaths are vain names," yet it is still to the self-interest of every member "to return again to unitie and concord" (*JHM, 18* [1963], 19).

Oxford and all her passing Bells can tell,
By this Right Arm, what mighty Numbers fell.
Whilst others meanly ask'd whole Months to slay,
I oft dispatch'd the Patient in a Day:
With Pen in hand I push'd to that degree,
I scarce had left a Wretch to give a Fee.
Some fell by *Laudanum,* and some by *Steel,*
And Death in ambush lay in ev'ry Pill.
For save or slay, this Privilege we claim,
Tho' Credit suffers, the Reward's the same.
What tho' the Art of Healing we pretend,
He that designs it least, is most a Friend.
Into the Right we err, and must confess,
To Oversights we often owe Success.
Thus *Bessus* got the Battel in the *Play,*
His glorious Cowardise restor'd the Day.
So the fam'd *Grecian* Piece ow'd its desert
To Chance, and not the labour'd Stroaks of Art.
Physicians, if they're wise, shou'd never think
Of any other Arms than Pen and Ink:
But th'Enemy, at their expence, shall find,
When Honour calls, I'll scorn to stay behind.
He said; and seal'd th'Engagement with a Kiss,
Which was return'd by Younger *Askaris;*

52. *passing Bells:* The most famous passing bell is that which tolls in John Donne, *Devotions upon Emergent Occasions,* 1624, No. 18, pp. 436–69.

58. *Laudanum . . . Steel:* "*Steel* [iron or steel filings administered internally], the *Jesuits Powder* [quinine], and *Laudanum* [opium], are become the three *Quack-Medicines* of this Age" (Gideon Harvey, *The Second Part of The Conclave of Physicians,* 1685, p. 42). Blackmore prescribed "spa-water and . . . tincture of steel daily" for the Rev. John Shower (Rosenberg, p. 31).

66. *Bessus:* Bessus is a *miles gloriosus* in Beaumont and Fletcher's *A King and No King* (1611). In the first scene he is told: "thou mean'st to flie, and thy fear making thee mistake, thou ran'st upon the enemy . . . thou art furious in running away, and I think, we owe thy fear for our victory" (*A King, and No King. As it is now Acted at the Theatre-Royal,* 1693, p. 2).

68. *the fam'd Grecian Piece:* The "Piece" is Protogenes' painting of Ialysos, a hero of Rhodes. Infuriated at his inability to depict hunting dogs foaming at the mouth, Protogenes threw his sponge at the work and "chance produced the effect of nature" (Pliny, *Natural History, 35,* 101–04). Garth could have read of this episode in Dryden, "A Parallel of Poetry and Painting," prefixed to C. A. Du Fresnoy, *De Arte Graphica* (1695) (Dryden, *Prose, 3,* 349).

75. *Younger Askaris:* See above, *3,* 198 *n.*

Who thus advanc'd: Each Word, Sir, you impart,
Has something killing in it, like your Art.
How much we to your boundless Friendship owe,
Our Files can speak, and your Prescriptions show.
Your Ink descends in such excessive Show'rs,
'Tis plain, you can regard no Health but ours.
Whilst poor Pretenders trifle o'er a Case,
You but appear, and give the *Coup de Grace.*
O that near *Xanthus* Banks you had but dwelt,
When *Ilium* first *Achaian* Fury felt,
The Flood had curs'd young *Peleus's* Arm in vain,
For troubling his choak'd Streams with heaps of slain.
No Trophies you had left for *Greeks* to raise,
Their ten Years Toil, you'd finish'd in ten Days.
Fate smiles on your Attempts, and when you list,
In vain the Cowards fly, or Brave resist.
Then let us Arm, we need not fear Success,
No Labours are too hard for *Hercules.*
Our military Ensigns we'll display;
Conquest pursues, where Courage leads the way.
To this Design sly *Querpo* did agree,

78. The apothecaries' "principal Art of all is, to cry up, and bring into *Patients* such unworthy *Physicians,* who through Covetousness do . . . comply with the *Apothecaries* Interest . . . which some of them call more expressly good *Apothecaries Physicians* . . . . Now this good *Apothecaries Physician,* they describe by his frequent though needless visits, but especially [by] the multitude of his Bills [prescriptions] . . . making an *Apothecaries* Shop in the *Patients* House, planting the Cupboards and Windows with Glasses and Galley-Pots" (Christopher Merrett, *A Short View of the Frauds, and Abuses Committed by Apothecaries,* 1670, pp. 14–15).

83. *Coup de Grace:* Alexander Pope explained this phrase as follows: "The Blow of Grace giv'n on the Stomach when Criminals are broken on the Wheel" (*1706* Huntington Library copy).

86. *curs'd:* The river Xanthus curses Achilles, the son of Peleus, in the *Iliad, 21,* 211–21.

96. *Querpo:* Garth designated Querpo as "How" (see illustration, p. 75) and Pope further identified him as "Dr. How Son of a Non Con Preacher" (*1706* Huntington Library copy). George Howe (c. 1655–1710) was the son of John Howe, the ejected divine who was defended in one controversy by Andrew Marvell and attacked by Daniel Defoe in another. George Howe studied medicine at Utrecht and was licensed by the College of Physicians in 1679. Then, like Francis Bernard, he was admitted a fellow of the College by the order of James II in 1687. He was frequently at odds with the College. On one occasion, when he was fined 2*s.* "for laughing at the president in the publick college, and being reproved, [he] answered slightingly, why may I not laugh" (*Annals, 6,* 51). He refused to sign the bond "to stand by the

A worthless Member of the Faculty;
Drain'd from an *Elder*'s Loins with awkard gust,
In Lees of Stale Hypocrisie and Lust.
His Sire's pretended pious Steps he treads,
And where the Doctor fails, the Saint succeeds.
A Conventicle flesh'd his greener Years,
And his full Age th'envenom'd Rancour shares.
Thus Boys hatch Game-Eggs under Birds o' prey,
To make the Fowl more furious for the Fray.
  Dull *Carus* next discover'd his intent,
With much ado explaining what he meant.
His Spirits stagnate like *Cocitus*'s Flood,
And nought but Calentures can warm his Blood.
In his chill Veins the sluggish Puddle flows,
And loads with lazy Fogs his sable Brows.
The brainless Wretch claims a Preeminence
In settling Lunaticks, and helping Sense.

---

officers of the College," walked out of the *comitia extraordinaria* called to promulgate the new statutes in November 1696, signed the petition of the malcontents to the visitors of the College in January 1697 (*Annals, 7*, 13, 86, 96), and twice refused to subscribe to the dispensary. Howe was the subject of another attack in 1699, in *The Second Tunbridge Lampoon* ("Not many miles from Tunbridge Town"), where he is represented as "formall worthless Querpo . . . Extorting fees for wrong advice" (BM MS. Sloane 1731A, f. 113). The phrase "in cuerpo" means, variously, without the outside garment so as to show the shape of the body, in undress, or naked.

106. *Carus:* Edward Tyson (1650–1708) (see illustration, p. 75) graduated M.D. from Corpus Christi College, Cambridge, in 1680. Three years later he was elected a fellow of the College of Physicians and appointed physician to Bridewell prison and Bethlehem Hospital for the insane. He was found guilty of contempt on one occasion for calling another member of the College a quack. On another occasion, when he was accused of writing his prescriptions in Latin in violation of one of the new statutes of 1687, "minding to be troublesome he answer'd they must prove he writ such bills, that he was not to accuse himself, neither could they bring him by all their discourse either to deny or to confess it" (*Annals, 5*, 93v–94). When it was discovered, during the crisis over the Apothecaries' bill in January 1695, that someone in the College was revealing to the apothecaries everything that was "discoursed and transacted" in the College, Tyson "absolutely refused" to enter into an obligation to maintain secrecy. Later that same year, when the College censors found William Wragg, an apothecary, guilty of malpractice, Tyson, who was one of the censors, refused to sign the complaint (*Annals, 6*, 186, 212). He refused to sign the £50 bond "to stand by the officers of the College," walked out of the *comitia extraordinaria* convened to promulgate the new statutes, and refused on four occasions to subscribe to the dispensary.

108. *Cocitus:* Only in Dante, *Inferno, 31*, 123, is the Cocytus sluggish and *cold*.

109. *Calentures:* Sp. *calentura*, fever, sunstroke.

So when Perfumes their fragrant Scent give o're,
Nought can their Odour, like a Jakes, restore.
When for Advice the Vulgar throng, he's found
With lumber of vile Books besieg'd around.
The gazing Fry acknowledge their Surprize,
Consulting less their Reason than their Eyes.
And He perceives it stands in greater stead,
To furnish well his Classes, than his Head.
Thus a weak State, by wise Distrust, enclines
To num'rous Stores, and Strength in Magazines.
So Fools are always most profuse of Words,
And Cowards never fail of longest Swords.
Abandon'd Authors here a Refuge meet,
And from the World, to Dust and Worms retreat.
Here Dregs and Sediment of Auctions reign,
Refuse of Fairs, and Gleanings of *Duck-lane;*
And up these shelves, much *Gothick* Lumber climbs,
With *Swiss* Philosophy, and *Danish* Rhimes.
And hither, rescu'd from the *Grocers,* come
More's Works entire, and endless Rheams of *Bloom.*
Where wou'd the long neglected *Collins* fly,
If bounteous *Carus* should refuse to buy?
But each vile Scribler's happy on this score,
He'll find some *Carus* still to read him o're.

121. *Classes* (sing. classis): stalls or carrels in a library; bookshelves on either side of and at right angles to a window.

129. *Duck-lane:* a street running southwest out of Smithfield; "taken up by Booksellers for old Books" (Strype, *1,* ³122).

133. *More:* Henry More (1614–87), the Cambridge mystic (*1699*³ Yale copy; MS. Key), published his collected works in 1679, *Henrici Mori Cantabrigiensis opera omnia* (Wing M2633).

Bloom: Richard Blome (c. 1621–1705), a "very foolish" author (MS. Key) and "Editor of Books by Subscription" (*1709* Key). Wing lists thirteen of these (B3205–3219), including a new and highly inaccurate edition of Guillim, *Display of Heraldry* (1660), *A Geographical Description of the Four Parts of the World* (1670), and *An Entire Body of Philosophy, according to the Principles of Renatus des Cartes* (1694).

134. *Collins:* Garth did not identify "*C——s,*" but nearly every contemporary reader filled in the blank as "Collins." (MS. Key, however, has "Ctesias"). Since Samuel Collins (1618–1710) was a distinguished anatomist, president of the College of Physicians in 1695, a Signetur-man (see below, *5,* 224 *n.*), and a subscriber to the dispensary, the joke must be limited to the fate of his two folio volumes published in 1685 as *A Systeme of Anatomy, treating of the Body of Man, Beasts, Birds, Fish, Insects, and Plants* (Wing C5387).

Nor must we the obsequious *Umbra* spare,
Who, soft by Nature, yet declar'd for War.
But when some Rival Pow'r invades a Right,
Flies set on Flies, and Turtles Turtles fight.
Else courteous *Umbra* to the last had been
Demurely meek, insipidly serene.
With Him, the present still some Virtues have,
The Vain are sprightly, and the Stupid, grave;
The Slothful, negligent; the Foppish, neat;
The Lewd are airy; and the Sly, discreet.
A Wren's an Eagle, a Baboon a Beau;
Colt a *Lycurgus,* and a *Phocion, Rowe.*

138. *Umbra:* Garth identified Umbra as "Gold" (see illustration, p. 75), presumably William Gold, or Gould (c. 1652–1714), who graduated M.D. from Wadham College, Oxford, and was elected a fellow of the College of Physicians in 1692. His medical specialty may be inferred from the fact that he is the subject of a satire entitled *On Don Quicksilver* ("A Certain Don, whom *Sol* and *Lune*") by Thomas Guidot in 1694 (Bodl. MS. Wood 429 [53]). A good "Apothecaries Physician," he refused to sign the £50 bond "to stand by the officers of the College," walked out of the *comitia extra-ordinaria* convened to promulgate the new statutes, and twice refused to subscribe to the dispensary (*Annals,* 7, 13, 86, 91, 94).

149. *Colt:* Henry Dutton Colt, of St. James, Westminster (c. 1646–1731), first baronet, was a Whig M.P. for Newport (1695–98), but switched to the New Country-Party and stood for Westminster against Charles Montagu and James Vernon in the election of July 1698. "He rails at courtiers," Vernon said, "and sets up for a national interest till he makes it a jest." But Colt built up a following among "the very scum of the town" which worried the secretary of state. Even Patch, the duke of Shrewsbury's footman, called himself a gentleman and voted for Colt. When Colt was defeated he immediately announced that he would enter a protest (Vernon, 2, 126, 137, 140). In the House of Commons, his petition was "heard, and laughed at, and voted false, vexatious and frivolous." It was observed that "no man a great while has more effectually exposed himself for want of common civility and common sense" (*CSPD 1698,* p. 430). As a result, the king ordered him to be put out of the commission of the peace for Westminster in December 1698 (Luttrell, *4,* 465). Colt finally secured election in Westminster (1701–02, 1705–08) and was reconciled to the Whigs. Long a favorite butt of the satirists, he figured in the *Tunbridge Lampoon* ("Our Ladies, fond of Love's soft Joyes") of 1690 (Osborn MS. Chest II, No. 1 [Phillipps 8301]) and twenty years later in *A Dialogue between Captain Tom and Sir H——y D——n C——t* ("Come, Fair Muse, of *Grub-street*"), a folio half-sheet that achieved two editions in 1710.

Lycurgus: the legendary lawgiver of Sparta (9th c. B.C.) whose life was written by Plutarch.

Phocion: an Athenian statesman and general (4th c. B.C.) whose life was written by Plutarch.

Rowe: Anthony Rowe (d. 1704) began his career by organizing a syndicate to lend Charles II £150,000 down and £162,000 a year for the privilege of farming the hearth money (*CTB 1698–1699,* p. 53). He subsequently raised a regiment of dragoons

Heroick Ardour now th'Assembly warms,
Each Combatant breaths nothing but Alarms.
For future Glory, while the Scheme is laid,
Fam'd *Horoscope* thus offers to disswade:
Since of each Enterprise th' Event's unknown,
We'll quit the Sword, and hearken to the Gown.
Nigh lives *Vagellius,* one reputed long,
For Strength of Lungs, and Pliancy of Tongue.
Which way He pleases, he can mould a Cause,
The Worst has Merits, and the Best has Flaws.
Five Guinea's make a Criminal to Day,
And ten to Morrow wipe the Stain away.
What ever he affirms is undeny'd,
Milo's the Lecher, *Clodius* th'Homicide.

---

in Essex for the service of the prince of Orange and was rewarded with a succession of sinecures at court, including clerk of the board of greencloth (1694–1704), worth £1000 a year. His parliamentary career is described in *A Prophecy,* 63 *n.,* below. He was also a racing enthusiast and invented two kinds of "calashes with carriages" (*CSPD 1693,* p. 192).

153. *Horoscope:* See above, *2,* 90 *n.*

154–56, 166–67. Leicht (p. 162) cites *Le Lutrin, 5,* 25–28:

> Mais le Vieillard condamne un projet inutile.
> Nos destins sont, dit-il, écrits chez la Sybile.
> Son antre n'est pas loin. Allons la consulter,
> Et subissons la loi qu'elle nous va dicter.

156. *Vagellius:* Contemporary readers were undecided: "Sr. Bartho. Sho[w]re, some say Sr. Tho. Powis" (MS. Key), and Pope added "Sergeant Darnell" (*1706* Huntington Library copy), but Garth identified Vagellius as Sir William Williams (1634–1700), whose "Pliancy" is demonstrated by his own comment on his own career: "We have all done amiss, and must wink at one another" (*Modern Reports or Select Cases Adjudged in the Courts of Kings Bench,* 12 vols., 1793–96, *5,* 463). As speaker of the House of Commons in 1680–81, he violently opposed Charles II. But as solicitor-general in the next reign, he prosecuted the seven bishops for James II, by whom he was knighted. In December 1688, however, he offered his services to the prince of Orange and found himself appointed to the committee that drafted the bill of rights. (William, however, found it necessary to remove him as solicitor-general). He was not returned to the fourth parliament of William III in 1698, but continued his practice at the bar until his death. He is the subject of a lampoon, *On Sir William Williams Sollicitor Generall* ("Williams thy Tame Submission suits thee more"), which is preserved in Portland MS. Pw V 52, pp. 369–70).

163. *Milo: T. Annius Milo Papianus* (d. 48 B.C.) murdered P. Clodius Pulcher in 52 B.C. Although defended by Cicero, he was convicted and exiled to Marseilles (Dio Cassius, *40,* 54).

Clodius: P. Clodius Pulcher (c. 93–52 B.C.) was publicly accused of incest with one sister and generally believed to have committed incest with two others, one of whom

Cato pernicious, *Cataline* a Saint,
Orford suspected, *Duncombe* innocent.
Let's then to Law, for 'tis by Fate decreed,
Vagellius, and our Mony, shall succeed.
Know, when I first invok'd *Disease* by Charms
T'assist, and be propitious to our Arms;
Ill Omens did the Sacrifice attend,
Nor wou'd the *Sybil* from her *Grott* ascend.
As *Horoscope* urg'd farther to be heard,
He thus was interrupted by a *Bard:*

---

was the notorious Clodia, Catullus's Lesbia (Plutarch, *Cicero,* 29). During an intrigue with the wife of Julius Caesar, he gained admission to Caesar's house disguised as a female lute player while Pompeia was celebrating the mysteries of the Bona Dea which no man was permitted to witness (Plutarch, *Caesar,* 9–10).

164. *Cato:* M. Porcius Cato Uticensis (95–46 B.C.), the outspoken and incorruptible Stoic "Saint" and patriot, supported Cicero in the Catiline conspiracy and was chiefly responsible for bringing the conspirators to trial and execution (Plutarch, *Cato the Younger,* 22–23).

Cataline: L. Sergius Catilina (c. 108–62 B.C.), famous for his sadistic debaucheries, violated the vestal, Fabia, murdered his stepson (Sallust, *Bellum Catilinae,* xiv–xv), and finally was killed leading revolted legions in an unsuccessful coup d'état.

165. *Orford:* Edward Russell, first earl of Orford (1653–1727), was commander-in-chief of the fleet and first lord of the admiralty during most of the war of 1689–97 and a member of the ruling Whig junto until his resignation in May 1699. He was the hero of the naval battle off La Hougue, Normandy, in May 1692, one of England's few successes of the war. When Louis XIV offered him £20,000 not to fight, but to maneuver, he reported the offer to the king. William told him to "Take the money, and beat them" (Noble, *1,* 189–90).

Duncombe: Charles Duncombe (c. 1648–1711) was a goldsmith, receiver-general of the excise, and member of parliament (*The True-Born Englishman,* 1046 *n.,* below). His "innocence" of a charge of forging endorsements to exchequer bills was established by one vote in the House of Lords and by a mistake in the information in the court of king's bench (Luttrell, *4,* 355, 480).

173. *a Bard:* Sir Richard Blackmore (1654–1729), "England's Arch-Poet," passed 13 years at St. Edmund Hall, Oxford, the last five of them as a tutor. He graduated M.D. from the University of Padua in 1684 (Rosenberg, p. 14), and like Francis Bernard (see above, *2,* 90) and George Howe (see above, *4,* 96), was admitted to the College of Physicians in April 1687 when the new charter of James II required that the number of fellows be increased from 40 to 80. Three months later, when the dispensary was first proposed, Blackmore aligned himself with those "Apothecaries Physicians" within the College who, for ten years, prevented it from opening. Blackmore, in fact, is the only one of the "Apothecaries Physicians" who has a perfect record of obstruction. He refused to sign the £50 bond "to stand by the Officers of the College," walked out on the *comitia extraordinaria* of 21 November 1696, signed the petition to the visitors of the College, and refused on four occasions to subscribe to the dispensary. He must, therefore, be considered the leader of the malcontents. This is confirmed by the fact that he was the first of the dissidents to be summoned before the president, Sir Thomas Millington, and the censors, for his "indecent and rude carriage" in refusing

In vain your Magick Mysteries you use,
Such sounds the *Sybil*'s Sacred Ears abuse.
These Lines the pale Divinity shall raise,
Such is the Pow'r of Sound, and Force of Lays:
Arms meet with Arms, Fauchions with Fauchions clash,
And sparks of Fire struck out from Armour flash.
Thick Clouds of Dust contending Warriours raise,
And hideous War o're all the Region brays.
Some raging ran with huge Herculean *Clubs,*
Some massy Balls of Brass, some mighty Tubs
Of Cynders bore.—
Naked and half burnt Hulls, with hideous wreck,
Affright the Skies, and fry the Ocean's back.
High Rocks of Snow, and sailing Hills of Ice,
Against each other with a mighty crash,
Driven by the Winds, in rude rencounter dash.
Blood, Brains, and Limbs the highest Walls distain,
And all around lay squallid Heaps of Slain.
As he went rumbling on, the *Fury* straight

to stay to hear the statutes read on 21 November 1696. On this occasion Blackmore defended himself by a remarkable evasion: the "Statutes were not then promulged, therefore he did not think them obligatory" (*Annals,* 7, 89). Blackmore published his first epic, *Prince Arthur. An Heroick Poem. In Ten Books,* in March 1695, adumbrating the exploits of prince William of Orange. Although Blackmore later complained that "the Muses . . . Had of the Royal Favour little Share" in William's reign (*The Kit-Cats, A Poem,* 1708, p. 4), William responded magnanimously by appointing Blackmore his physician-in-ordinary, a place worth £2000 a year, and conferring upon him the honor of knighthood on 18 March 1697. Only a few days later out came *King Arthur. An Heroick Poem. In Twelve Books,* two more than before, its title page advertising both of Blackmore's new honors. But there were to be no more honors from William, for someone convinced him that in *King Arthur,* "instead of . . . panegyricks of his person, [there] are plain, and bitter Satyrs on his Character" (New York Public Library MS. Hardwicke 33, p. 67).

178–92. "Verses of Sir Richard Blackmore . . . which our Poet here most wittily ridicules" (*1706* Yale Medical Library copy 2).

178–81. *King Arthur* (1697), *11,* 573–76, p. 307.

182–84. *King Arthur* (1697), *12,* 362–64, pp. 327–28. Line 364 actually reads "Of Cynders, some great Pots of Sulphur bore."

185–86. *Prince Arthur* (1695), *5,* 364–65, p. 138.

187–89. *Prince Arthur* (1695), *5,* 300–02, p. 136.

190–91. *King Arthur* (1697), *7,* 342–43, p. 189. Line 342 reads "Blood, Brains, and Limbs did the high Lines distain."

192. *rumbling:* Blackmore acknowledged that *"for the greatest part," Prince Arthur "was written in* Coffee-houses, *and in passing up and down the Streets"* in his carriage (*King Arthur* [1697], "The Preface," p. v); see below, Dryden, *Prologue to The Pilgrim,* 42.

Crawl'd in, her Limbs cou'd scarce support her Weight.
A noysom Rag her pensive Temples bound,
And faintly her parch'd Lips these Accents sound:
Mortal, how dar'st thou with such Lines address
My awful Seat, and trouble my Recess?
In *Essex* Marshy Hundreds is a Cell,
Where lazy Fogs, and drisling Vapours dwell:
Thither raw Damps on drooping Wings repair,
And shiv'ring Quartans shake the sickly Air.
There, when fatigu'd, some silent Hours I pass,
And substitute Physicians in my place.
Then dare not, for the future, once rehearse
Th'offensive Discord of such hideous Verse.
But in your Lines let Energy be found,
And learn to rise in Sense, and sink in Sound.
Harsh words, tho' pertinent, uncouth appear,
None please the Fancy, who offend the Ear.
In Sense and Numbers if you wou'd excel,
Read *Wycherley,* consider *Dryden* well.
In one, what vigorous Turns of Fancy shine,
In th'other, *Syrens* warble in each Line.
If *Dorset*'s sprightly Muse but touch the Lyre,
The *Smiles* and *Graces* melt in soft desire,
And little *Loves* confess their amorous Fire.
The *Tyber* now no gentle *Gallus* sees,
But smiling *Thames* enjoys his *Normanbys.*
And gentle *Isis* claims the Ivy Crown,

198. *Hundreds:* "The Air [of Essex] is healthful up in the Land, but in the Hundreds near the Sea, 'tis much inclinable to Agues" (Morden, p. 49).

201. *Quartans:* of a fever or ague: characterized by the recurrence of a paroxysm every fourth (in modern reckoning, every third) day.

211. *Wycherley:* "Mr. Wycherly, a Poet famous for solid Wit and Sense" (*1709* Key).

Dryden: "Mr. Dryden . . . who will ever be famous for good Versification" (*1709* Key).

214. *Dorset:* See above, 2, 67 *n.*

217. *Gallus:* C. Cornelius Gallus (c. 70–26 B.C.) wrote elegies to Lycoris, an actress, who deserted him for Mark Antony and provided Virgil with the occasion for his tenth eclogue: "neget quis carmina Gallo?" Ovid called him the best of the elegiac poets (*Tristia,* 5, 1), but only a few dubious fragments of his work have survived.

218. *Normanby:* John Sheffield (1648–1721), third earl of Mulgrave, marquis of Normanby, and, in Queen Anne's reign, duke of Buckingham, whose "sentiments with

To bind th'immortal Brows of *Addison.*
As tuneful *Congreve* trys his rural Strains,
Pan quits the Woods, the list'ning Fawns the Plains;
And *Philomel,* in Notes like his, complains.
And *Britain,* since *Pausanias* was writ,
Knows *Spartan* Virtue, and *Athenian* Wit.
When *Stepny* paints the Godlike Acts of Kings,
Or, what *Apollo* dictates, *Prior* sings:
The Banks of *Rhine* a pleas'd Attention show,
And Silver *Sequana* forgets to flow.

---

respect to women he picked up in the court of Charles," wrote elegies to a succession of Astraeas, Celias, and Silvias. Samuel Wesley called him the *"Perfection"* of English verse *(An Epistle to a Friend Concerning Poetry,* 1700, p. 6). A pirated edition of his works was published by Edmund Curll in 1721 and an authorized edition in two volumes folio, "overlooked" and corrected for the press by Alexander Pope, appeared in 1723.

220. *Addison:* By 1699 Joseph Addison (1672–1719) had published only half a dozen poems in English. One reader thought he was still a student at Magdalen College, Oxford (*1699*[3] College of Physicians copy). Actually he was a fellow of the college, having graduated M.A. in 1693. But he had been admitted to Dryden's circle and Dryden had paid him a handsome compliment in his "Postscript to the Reader" in *The Works of Virgil . . . Translated* (1697).

221. *Congreve:* By 1699 William Congreve (1670–1729) had written all his great plays except *The Way of the World* and had been acknowledged by Dryden as his successor (*To my Dear Friend Mr. Congreve* [1694], *Poems, 2,* 852). As Garth's lines imply, however, Congreve was prized mainly for his verse, *The Mourning Muse of Alexis. A Pastoral* (1695) and *The Birth of the Muse. A Poem* (1698). The *1709* Key describes him as "a Poet principally famous for his *Pastorals* and Dramatic *Writings."*

224. *Pausanias: Pausanias the Betrayer of His Country* is a tragedy by Richard Norton, published in May 1696 (Wing N1327). One reader called it "feeble" and attributed it to "Anth. Henly and Norton" *(1699*[3] College of Physicians copy).

226. *Stepny:* George Stepney (1663–1707) acquired repute as a poet while still an undergraduate at Trinity College, Cambridge, and was elected a fellow in 1687. He celebrated the marriage of Princess Anne to Prince George of Denmark in a Latin ode published in *Hymenaeus Cantabrigiensis* (1683), and then, in English, William's victories in Ireland *(An Epistle to Charles Montagu, Esq; on his Majesty's Voyage to Holland* [1691]), and the death of the queen (*A Poem Dedicated to the Blessed Memory of her late Gracious Majesty Queen Mary* [1695]). He was a career diplomat, serving mainly in Germany.

227. *Prior:* Matthew Prior (1664–1721) was a contemporary of Garth and Stepney at Cambridge. He graduated B.A. from St. John's College in 1686 and almost immediately achieved literary fame with *The Hind and the Panther transvers'd to the Story of the Country-Mouse and the City-Mouse* (1687), which he wrote in collaboration with Charles Montagu. The MS. Key calls him "a good Poet." Like Stepney, he was also a career diplomat, serving at The Hague (1693–97), at the congress of Ryswick (1697), and in Paris (1697–99).

229. *Sequana:* Seine.

Such just Examples carefully read o're,
Slide without falling, without straining soar.
Oft tho' your Stroaks surprize, you shou'd not choose,
A Theme so mighty for a Virgin Muse.
Long did *Apelles* his Fam'd Piece decline,
His *Alexander* was his last Design.
'Tis *Montague*'s rich Vein alone must prove,
None but a *Phidias* shou'd attempt a *Jove*.
The Fury said; and vanishing from Sight,
Cry'd out, To Arms; so left the Realms of Light.
The Combatants to th'Enterprize consent,
And the next day smil'd on the great Event.

Canto 5

When the still Night, with peaceful Poppies crown'd,
Had spread her shady Pinions o're the Ground;
And slumbring Chiefs of painted Triumphs dream,
While Groves and Streams are the soft Virgin's Theme.
The Surges gently dash against the Shoar,
Flocks quit the Plains, and Gally-Slaves the Oar.
Sleep shakes its downy Wing o're mortal Eyes,
Mirmillo is the only Wretch it Flies.
He finds no respite from his anxious Grief,
Then seeks, from this Soliloquy, relief:
Long have I reign'd unrival'd in the Town,

236. *Montague:* The literary career of Charles Montagu began, like Stepney's, when he was still an undergraduate in Trinity College, Cambridge, and contributed an ode on the marriage of Princess Anne to *Hymenaeus Cantabrigiensis* (1683). In 1685, by which time he had graduated M.A. and been elected a fellow of Trinity College, he published an elegy on the death of Charles II in *Moestissimae ac Laetissimae Academiae Cantabrigiensis affectus.* Then, in 1687, he collaborated with Matthew Prior in *The Hind and the Panther transvers'd* and in 1690 wrote *An Epistle to the Right Honourable Charles Earl of Dorset and Middlesex, Occasion'd by His Majesty's Victory in Ireland,* but thereafter his preoccupation was with politics; see above, *Advice to a Painter,* 81 *n.*

237. *Phidias:* Phidias (c. 500–432 B.C.) executed the colossal statue in ivory and gold of Zeus at Olympia, which was regarded as one of the wonders of ancient civilization (Strabo, *8,* 3, 30).

8. *Mirmillo:* See above, *4,* 33 *n.*

Glutted with Fees, and mighty in Renown.
There's none can dye with due Solemnity,
Unless his Pass-port first be sign'd by Me.
My arbitrary Bounty's undeny'd,
I give Reversions, and for Heirs provide.
None cou'd the tedious Nuptial State support,
But I, to make it easie, make it short.
I set the discontented Matrons free,
And Ransom Husbands from Captivity.
Then shall so useful a *Machin* as I
Engage in civil Broyls, I know not why?
No, I'll endeavour straight a Peace, and so
Preserve my Honour, and my Person too.
  But *Discord,* that still haunts with hideous Mien
Those dire Abodes where *Hymen* once has been,
O're-heard *Mirmillo* reas'ning in his Bed;
Then raging inwardly the Fury said:
  Have I so often banisht lazy Peace
From her dark Solitude, and lov'd Recess?
Have I made *South* and *Sherlock* disagree,
And puzzle Truth with learn'd Obscurity?
And does my faithful *Ferguson* profess
His Ardour still for Animosities?
Have I, *Britannia*'s Safety to insure,

25–27. Leicht (p. 165) cites *Le Lutrin, 1,* 25–28.

31. *South and Sherlock:* "Dr. *South,* Prebendary of *Westminster,* and Dr. *Sherlock* . . . Dean of St. *Paul*'s, and Master of the *Temple,* who wrote against one another about the *TRINITY;* and so managed the Controversy, that the Public were of Opinion, That the first proved there is but One *God;* and the other, That there are Three. The Dispute was ridiculed in a Ballad, to the Tune of *A Soldier and a Sailor, &c.*" (*1709* Key), which is included in *POAS,* Yale, *5*.

33. *Ferguson:* Robert Ferguson (c. 1638–1714), an ejected Anglican divine, was the "famous Plot-monger" (*1700* Yale Medical Library copy), "A non-Con. Parson who came over with the King, but suppos'd to be a Jesuit, who has writ severall seditious Libells against the Government, and thought to be among the Conspirators in the late Assassination Plot against his Majestie King William" (MS. Key). Previously, he had been involved in the Black Box controversy, the Rye House plot, Monmouth's rebellion, the Montgomery plot, and Fuller's plot.

35–36. *Britannia . . . Expos'd . . . to be more secure:* Defoe had developed the same paradox in *An Encomium upon a Parliament,* 6–7.

35–44. Leicht (p. 165) cites *Le Lutrin, 1,* 45–52:

> Quoi? dit-elle, d'un ton qui fit trembler les vitres,
> J'aurai pû jusqu'ici broüiller tous les Chapitres,

Expos'd her naked, to be more secure?
Have I made Parties opposite, unite,
In monstrous Leagues of amicable Spight
T'embroyl their Country, whilst the common Cry,
Is *Freedom*, but their Aim, the *Ministry*?
And shall a Dastard's Cowardise prevent
The War so long, I've labour'd to foment?
No, 'tis resolv'd, he either shall comply,
Or I'll renounce my wan Divinity.
  With that, the *Hag* approach'd *Mirmillo*'s Bed,
And taking *Querpo*'s meager Shape, She said:
  I come, altho' at Midnight, to dispel,
Those Tumults in your pensive Bosom dwell.
I dream't, but now, my Friend, that you were by;
Methought I saw your Tears, and heard you sigh.
O that 'twere but a Dream! But sure I find
Grief in your Looks, and Tempests in your Mind.
Speak, whence it is this late disorder flows,
That shakes your Soul, and troubles your Repose.
Erroneous Practice scarce cou'd give you pain,
Too well you know the Dead will ne're complain.
  What Looks discover, said the Homicide,
Wou'd be but too impertinent to hide.
My Stars direct me to decline the Fight;
The way to serve our Party, is to write.

Diviser Cordeliers, Carmes & Celestins?
J'aurai fait soûtenir un siege aux Augustins?
Et cette Eglise seule à mes ordres rebelle
Nourira dans son sein une paix éternelle?
Suis-je donc la Discorde & parmi les Mortels,
Qui voudra desormais encenser mes autels?

37. *Parties opposite, unite:* See above, *An Encomium upon a Parliament,* headnote, p. 43 above; cf. *Aesop in Select Fables,* 1698, sig. D5r: "*If there be no* Mysteries in Christianity, *it seems there are some in* Policy; *when* Jacobites *and* Commonwealths men, *who have mutually branded one another with the harshest Names that Malice and Rancour could invent, should now unite in a Design against the present Government, as a common Center.*"

45–46. Leicht (p. 166) cites *Le Lutrin, 1,* 53–54.

46. *Querpo:* See above, *4,* 96 *n.*

60. *write:* There may be a pun here on "write" meaning "to write pamphlets against the dispensary" and "write" meaning "to write frequent and expensive prescriptions,"

How many, said the Fury, had not split
On Shelves so fatal, if they ne're had writ!
Had *Colbatch* printed nothing of his own,
He had not been the *Saffold* o' the Town.
Asses and Owls, unseen, themselves betray,
If These attempt to Hoot, or Those to Bray.
Had *Wesley* never aim'd in Verse to please,
We had not rank'd him with our *Ogilbys*.

---

for *"Writing well,"* in apothecaries' language, meant "writing a very *long Prescription*" (*The Present State of Physick,* 1701, p. 4).

63. *Colbatch:* Sir John Colbatch (d. 1729) (see illustration, p. 75) "was first an Apothecary, now a foolish member of the Colledge, who has writ severall ~~indifferent~~ ridiculous Treatises in Physick & Chirurgery" (MS. Key). A member of the Company of Apothecaries and Mercers of Worcester, he moved to London in 1696 and was licensed to practice medicine by the College of Physicians in December of that year. In the same month he subscribed £10 to the dispensary, but in 1699 he became involved in a tedious controversy about *"Acids, Alkalies* and Hell knows what" ([Edward Ward], *A Journey to Hell,* 2nd ed., 1700, p. 29). Twenty-five editions of 11 different works of Colbatch are listed in Wing (C4991–C5015).

64. *Saffold:* Thomas Saffold (d. 1691), "at the Black-Ball and Lilly's Head . . . over against Ludgate-Church," was "a celebrated Empiric, whose Bills were formerly set up in all publick Diuretic Places in *London* and *Westminster,* to the great Comfort and Entertainment of idle Country Folks" (*1709* Key). He wrote his "Bills," or advertisements, "in senceless Rhime" (MS. Key).

67. *Wesley:* Samuel Wesley (1662–1735) was a fellow student of Daniel Defoe in Charles Morton's academy at Newington Green, a graduate of Exeter College, Oxford, rector of Epsworth, Lincolnshire, and father of John Wesley. He was said to be "very ingenious at oratory but like Cicero himself not skilfull in Poetry" (MS. Key). A less sympathetic source called him "a Divine who has wrote much Holy-Doggrel" (*1700* Yale Medical Library copy). This included *Maggots: Or Poems on Several Subjects never before Handled* (1685) and *The Life of Our Blessed Lord. An Heroic Poem* (1693).

68. *Ogilby:* John Ogilby (1600–76) was "one who translated Virgill very indifferently, so put, *per metonymiam sive synechdochen generis* for any ignorant Poet" (MS. Key). It is one of the anomalies of English literary history that Ogilby, "one of the prodigies" of one age (Edward Phillips, *Theatrum Poetarum,* 1675, p. 2114), should have become a generic term for bad poetry in the next. An autodidact with "an amazing proficiency in learning" (*Biographia Britannica, 5,* 3262), Ogilby was a successful and sometimes brilliant dancing master, theatrical producer, translator, publisher, book designer, and cartographer. In his lifetime "He never failed in what he undertook, but by his great industry and prudence went through it with profit and honour to himself" (Wood, *3,* 740–44, 996), but when he died, perhaps in the very month of his death, he was transformed into a commodity: "Much Heywood, Shirley, Ogleby there lay,/But loads of Sh——— almost chok'd the way" (*POAS,* Yale, *1,* 382). And it is only by metonymy that his name has survived. "Mr. *Ogilby* would have perhaps got some Reputation, if he had aspired no higher than *Reynard the Fox;* But having ventur'd to translate in Verse the sublimest *Latin* Poets, his Name will, as long as the *English* Tongue lives, signify a *Poetaster*" (*1709* Key).

Still Censures will on dull Pretenders fall,
A *Codrus* shou'd expect a *Juvenal.*
Ill Lines, but like ill Paintings, are allow'd,
To set off, and to recommend the good.
So *Diamonds* take a Lustre from their Foyle;
And to a *Bentley* 'tis, we owe a *Boyle.*
  Consider well the Talent you possess,
To strive to make it more wou'd make it less;
And recollect what Gratitude is due,
To those whose Party you abandon now.
To Them you owe your odd Magnificence,
But to your Stars your Penury of Sense.
Haspt in a Tombril, awkardly you've shin'd
With one fat Slave before, and none behind.
But soon, what They've exalted They'l discard,
And set up *Carus,* or the City *Bard.*
  Alarm'd at this, the *Heroe* Courage took,
And Storms of Terrour threaten'd in his Look.

70. *Codrus:* Virgil's rival poet; see *Eclogues, 5,* 11; *7,* 25–28.

74. *Bentley:* Richard Bentley (1662–1742), the classics scholar, was keeper of the library in St. James's Palace. His alleged discourtesy to Charles Boyle was known even in Europe (*Journey to London,* p. 23).

Boyle: Charles Boyle (1676–1731), eldest son of the third earl of Orrery, while still an undergraduate at Christ Church, Oxford, had been assigned to edit the epistles of Phalaris, which had been so admired by Sir William Temple in his *Essay on Ancient and Modern Learning* (1692). It was in the preface to this edition, published in December 1694, that Boyle claimed that Bentley, "pro singulari sua humanitate," had denied him access to an important manuscript in the library at St. James. In an appendix to the second edition of William Wotton's *Reflections upon Ancient and Modern Learning* (June 1697), Bentley demonstrated not only that Boyle's edition was amateurish and inadequate but that the epistles themselves were clumsy forgeries. "The Wits of *Christ-Church,*" George Smalridge, Francis Atterbury, and several undergraduates, concocted a reply to Bentley, entitled *Dr. Bentley's Dissertations . . . Examin'd,* and published it in March 1698, under the name of Charles Boyle, who by this time had left Oxford. "Boyle against Bentley," as it was called, was almost unanimously agreed to represent a triumph of *"Urbanity* and *good Manners"* over *"Sufficiency* and *Pedantry"* (*1709* Key). "Never," said Thomas Brown, had "Wit and Learning" triumphed "so gloriously over Dullness and Pedantry, as in that noble Book" (*Familiar and Courtly Letters, Written by Monsieur Voiture,* 1700, pp. 218–19). This was also the opinion of Jonathan Swift (*Prose, 1,* 164–65), but in fact, as R. C. Jebb has pointed out, "Garth has pilloried himself for ever by the couplet in which he celebrated Boyle's supposed triumph" (*DNB, 2,* 310).

84. *Carus:* See above, *4,* 106.

City Bard: See above, *4,* 173; Sir Richard Blackmore lived in Sadler's Hall, Cheapside (Rosenberg, p. 18).

My dread Resolves, he cry'd, I'll straight pursue;
The *Fury* satisfy'd, in Smiles withdrew.
In boding Dreams *Mirmillo* spent the Night,
And frightful Phantoms danc'd before his Sight.
At length gay Morn smiles in the Eastern Sky,
From rifling silent Graves the *Sextons* fly.
The rising Mists skud o'er the dewy Lawns,
The *Chaunter* at his early Matins yawns.
The *Vi'lets* ope their Buds, *Cowslips* their Bells,
And *Progne* her Complaint of *Tereus* tells.
As bold *Mirmillo* the gray Dawn descries,
Arm'd *Cap-a-pe,* where Honour calls, he flies,
And finds the Legions planted at their Post;
Where *Querpo* in his Armour shone the most.
His Shield was wrought, if we may credit Fame,
By *Mulciber,* the Mayor of *Bromigham.*
A Foliage of dissembl'd *Senna* Leaves,
Grav'd round its Brim, the wond'ring sight deceives.
Embost upon its Field, a Battle stood
Of *Leeches* spouting *Hemorrhoidal* Blood.
The Artist too exprest the solemn state
Of grave *Physicians* at a Consult met;

96. *Progne:* Progne's "Complaint" was that her husband, Tereus, had so rudely forced her sister, Philomela. She was changed into a swallow (Ovid, *Metamorphoses, 6,* 412–674).

101–12. *Shield:* Cf. *Iliad, 18,* 478–607; *Aeneid, 8,* 626–728.

102. *Mulciber:* "Every one knows that *Mulciber* was one of the Heathen Gods, otherwise called *Vulcan;* but 'tis the Opinion of many, that our Poet means here Mr. Tho[mas] Foley, a Lawyer of notable Parts" (*1709* Key). This Thomas Foley (1673–1733), was the grandson of Thomas Foley, the ironmaster of Stourbridge, a nephew of Paul Foley (*Advice to a Painter,* 71 *n.,* above), and brother-in-law of Robert Harley. A Tory member of parliament for Stafford (1694–1711), he was elevated to the peerage on 1 January 1712, as baron Foley of Kidderminster.

103. *dissembl'd Senna:* Myrtle leaves were commonly substituted in prescriptions requiring senna, a shrub of the genus *Cassia,* native in tropical regions (Christopher Merrett, *A Short View of the Frauds, and Abuses Committed by Apothecaries,* p. 8).

108. *a Consult:* Unscrupulous practice in consultation is described in Everard Maynwaring, *Praxis Medicorum Antiqua & Nova,* 1671, pp. 63–71. The new statutes of the College of Physicians, enacted in September 1687, tried to regulate this practice. One statute required that "If to visit the same sick person, two or more Phisicians shall meet together, let none prescribe any thing, nay let him not so much as hint what is to be done, in presence of the sick or by-standers, before with joynt counsel in private, it shall be concluded betwixt them; lest he seem too ambitiously to forestall Practice, and snatch the free opportunity of prescribing from all the rest" (*The Statutes of the Colledge of Physicians London,* 1693, p. 180).

About each Symptom how they Disagree,
But how unanimous in case of Fee.
And whilst one *Assassin* another plys
With starch'd Civilities, the Patient dyes.
  Beneath this Blazing Orb bright *Querpo* shone,
Himself an *Atlas*, and his Shield a Moon.
A Pestle for his Truncheon led the Van,
And his high Helmet was a Close-stool pan.
His Crest an *Ibis*, brandishing her Beak,
And winding in loose Folds her spiral Neck.
This, when the Young *Querpoïdes* beheld,
His Face in Nurse's Breast the Boy conceal'd,
Then peep't, and with th'effulgent Helm wou'd play,
But as the Monster gap'd he'd shrink away:
Thus sometimes Joy prevail'd, and sometimes Fear;
And Tears and Smiles alternate Passions were.
  But *Fame* that whispers each profound Design,
And tells the Consultations at the *Vine;*
And how at Church and Bar all gape and stretch,
If *Winnington* but plead, or *Onely* preach;

113–14. Querpo suggests Satan in *Paradise Lost, 1,* 283–87 and *4,* 987.

117. *Ibis:* "the original and necessity of [apothecaries'] employ was derived from the *Aegyptian* Bird *Ibis,* spouting Sea-water into its Breech for a Glyster" (*The Accomplisht Physician,* 1670, p. 53).

119–24. Cf. *Iliad, 6,* 466–70.

119. *Querpoïdes:* George Howe actually had two sons, John and Philip.

125. *Fame:* Leicht (p. 168) cites Ovid, *Metamorphoses, 9,* 136–40 and *Le Lutrin, 2,* 1–6 and *5,* 98–109.

126. *the Vine:* "By these Lines he ridicules Dr: Radcliffe who frequents the Vine Tavern" (MS. Key) in Longacre (see *The Golden Age Restor'd,* 77 *n.,* below). In later life Radcliffe preferred the Mitre (William Wadd, *Mems. Maxims, and Memoirs,* 1827, p. 226). If it is true that these lines ridicule Radcliffe, Garth would have had sufficient reason to do so. In December 1689 Radcliffe was expelled for "absenting himselfe from the College above twenty six tymes after [being] legally summoned and for his contemptuous slight of the College Comitia," but upon offering some "frivolous excuses" and paying a £10 fine, he was readmitted (*Annals, 5,* 108). He subsequently refused either to sign the £50 bond "to stand by the Officers of the College" or to subscribe to the dispensary (*Annals, 7,* 172).

128. *Winnington:* Sir Francis Winnington (1634–1700), "a Counsellor who stretches his argument to the full length in Pleading" (MS. Key), was a highly successful lawyer who served as solicitor-general (1674–79) and Tory member of parliament for New Windsor, Berkshire (1677–79), Worcester City (1679–81), and Tewkesbury, Gloucestershire (1692–98).

Onely: Nicholas Onely (c. 1640–1724), the son of a tavern porter in the Strand, was adopted by a gentleman of the same name and sent to Westminster School and Christ

On nimble Wings to *Warwick-Lane* repairs,
And what the Enemy intends, declares.
Disorder'd Murmurs thro' the College pass,
And pale Confusion glares in ev'ry Face.
In haste a Council's call'd, th'Occasion's great,
And quick as Thought, the summon'd Members meet,
Loud *Stentor* to th'Assembly had Access,
None aim'd at more, and none succeeded less.
True to Extreams, yet to dull Forms a Slave,
He's always dully gay, or vainly grave.
With Indignation, and a daring Air,
He paus'd a while, and thus address'd the Chair:
Machaon, whose Experience we adore,

Church, Oxford, whence he proceeded M.A. in 1664. He was made a prebendary of Westminster in 1672, master of the Savoy, and the minister of St. Margaret's, Westminster (1683) (G. F. Russell Barker and Alan H. Stenning, *The Record of Old Westminsters,* 2 vols., 1928, *2,* 702, 1105, Supplement p. 108). "Very tedious," is the comment of the MS. Key.

129. *Warwick-Lane:* See above, *1,* 11 *n.*

130. *the Enemy:* "The greatest enemies . . . Physicians have at present, are the Apothecaries." "If the Case be stated rightly, it will appear most evident, that we [physicians] are on the Defensive part, They the Aggressors" ([Daniel Coxe], *A Discourse Wherein the Interest of the Patient in Reference to Physick and Physicians is soberly debated,* 1669, pp. 5, A6v).

135. *Stentor:* the loudest of the Greeks at Troy (*Iliad, 5,* 785–86). Garth identifies him with Charles Goodall (1642–1712), who graduated M.D. at Cambridge in 1670 and was admitted a candidate of the College of Physicians in 1676. He promptly became an active defender and historian of the College, publishing *The Colledge of Physicians Vindicated* (1676) and *The Royal College of Physicians Founded and Established by Law* (1684). He was the Harveian orator in 1694 and censor in 1697 (Munk, *1,* 402).

141. *Machaon:* Machaon, the son of Aesculapius, was surgeon-general of the Greek forces at Troy (*Iliad, 2,* 732). Garth makes him the hero of *The Dispensary,* Sir Thomas Millington (1628–1704) (see illustration, p. 75). Millington was a king's scholar at Westminster and graduated A.B. from Trinity College, Cambridge, in 1649. Then he removed to Oxford where he became a student of Thomas Willis and participated in the meetings with Robert Boyle, John Wallis, and others, which led to the foundation of the Royal Society. He proceeded M.D. in 1659 and in the same year was elected a fellow of All Souls' College and a candidate of the College of Physicians. Admitted a fellow of the College of Physicians in 1672, "he soon became the delight of it; affable in his conversation, firm in his friendships, diligent and happy in his practice, candid and open in Consultations [see above, *5,* 108 *n.*], eloquent to an extraordinary degree in his publick Speeches" (*Annals, 7,* 211). He succeeded Willis as Sedleian professor of natural history in 1675 and was knighted in 1680. He succeeded Samuel Collins as president of the College of Physicians during the crisis over promulgation of the statutes. His first speech as president, although it was so "elegant and seasonable . . . and withall so acceptable to the College" that it was moved to enter it in the *Annals,*

Great as your matchless Merits, is your Pow'r.
At your approach, the baffl'd Tyrant *Death,*
Breaks his keen Shafts, and grinds his clashing Teeth;
To you we leave the Conduct of the Day,
What you command, your Vassals must obey.
If this dread Enterprize you wou'd decline,
We'll send to Treat, and stifle the Design.
But if my Arguments had force, we'd try
To scatter our audacious Foes, or die.
What *Stentor* offer'd was by most approv'd;
But sev'ral Voices sev'ral Methods mov'd.
At length th'adventrous *Heroes* all agree
T'expect the Foe, and act defensively.
Into the Shop their bold *Battalions* move,
And what their Chief commands the rest approve.
Down from the *Walls* they tear the *Shelves* in haste,
Which, on their Flank, for Pallisades are plac'd.
And then, behind the Compter rang'd, they stand,
Their Front so well secur'd t'obey Command.
And now the Scouts the adverse Host descry,
Blue Aprons in the Air for Colours fly:
With unresisted Force they urge their Way,

---

failed nonetheless to prevent 26 "Apothecaries Physicians," led by Sir Richard Blackmore and Francis Bernard, from walking out of the *comitia extraordinaria* of 21 November 1696, "though the President commanded them to stay to heare the Statutes read" (*Annals, 7,* 84, 86). Millington calmly proceeded with the promulgation of the statutes and at the next *comitia,* on 22 December 1696, led the College back to the long-postponed "Charitable Design" of the dispensary, and finally brought about its realization. He remained president of the College until his death and it was he who negotiated a settlement out of court of the claims of the heirs of Sir John Cutler against the College, for £2000 (see above, *1,* 11 *n.*) which "he himself, without the knowledge of the College, generously laid down" (*Annals, 7,* 182).

146. Cf. "when the President commanded me [to deliver the Harveian oration in 1697, Garth said], I esteemed it a Crime to oppose him, and therefore determined rather to hazard my Reputation, than neglect my duty; least I should seem to contemn his Authority, whose sole exhortation is to be complyed with" (*JHM, 18* [1963], 12).

155. *the Shop:* The battle takes place in the dispensary, which was simply two rooms in the College, one fitted out as a laboratory and the other furnished to receive patients and dispense medicines.

162. *Blue Aprons:* Blue aprons make appropriate battle flags for the apothecaries since they were the usual garb of apothecaries' apprentices. There was a further association of blue aprons with nonconformity (Oldmixon, p. 192), of which Garth may have been aware.

And find the Foe embattel'd in Array.
Then from their levell'd Syringes they pour
The liquid Volley of a missive Show'r.
Not Storms of Sleet, which o're the Baltick drive,
Push't on by *Northern* Gusts, such Horrour give.
Like Spouts in *Southern* Seas the Deluge broke,
And Numbers sunk beneath th'impetuous Stroak.
So when *Leviathans* Dispute the Reign,
And uncontrol'd Dominion of the Main;
From the rent Rocks whole *Coral* Groves are torn,
And Isles of *Sea-weed* on the Waves are born.
Such watry Stores from their spread Nostrils fly,
'Tis doubtful which is Sea, and which is Sky.
  And now the stagg'ring *Braves,* led by Despair,
Advance, and to return the Charge, prepare.
Each seizes for his Shield an ample *Scale,*
And the *Brass Weights* fly thick as showrs of Hail.
Whole heaps of Warriours welter on the Ground,
With Gally-Pots, and broken Phials crown'd;
And th'empty Vessels the Defeat resound.
Thus when some Storm its Chrystal Quarry rends,
And *Jove* in rattling Showrs of *Ice* descends;
Mount *Athos* shakes the Forests on his Brow,
Whilst down his wounded Sides fresh Torrents flow,
And Leaves and Limbs of Trees o'er-spread the Vale below.
  But now, all Order lost, promiscuous Blows
Confus'dly fall; perplex'd the Battel grows.
From *Stentor*'s sinewy Arm an Opiate flys,
And straight a deadly Sleep clos'd *Carus'* Eyes.
Chiron hit *Siphilus* with *Calomel,*

172. As Pope observes, this line "is taken intirely from Blackmore's *Pr*[*ince*] *Ar*[*thur,* *5,* 107] p. 130" (*1703* Victoria & Albert copy).

193. *Chiron:* A centaur distinguished for his knowledge of botany, medicine, and divination, Chiron was the tutor of Aesculapius (Ovid, *Metamorphoses, 2,* 630). Garth (see illustration, p. 75) identifies him as Thomas Gill, a subscriber to the dispensary who wrote *The State of Physick in London: With an Account of the Charitable Regulation made lately at the College of Physicians* (1698) and "cured Dr. [Ridley?] of the Clap" (MS. Key).

Siphilus: "Any Apothecary" (*1699*[3] College of Physicians copy), but *1703* Victoria & Albert Museum copy identifies him as "Ridly," presumably Humphrey Ridley (c. 1653–1708), who graduated M.D. from Leyden in 1679 and was admitted to the College

And scaly Crusts from his maim'd Fore-head fell.
At *Colon* great *Japix Rhubarb* flung,
Who with fierce Gripes, like those of Death, was stung;
And with a dauntless and disdainfull Mien
Hurl'd back Steel Pills, and hit Him on the Spleen.
Scribonius a vast *Eagle-stone* let fly
At *Psylas,* but *Lucina* put it by.
And *Querpo,* warm'd with more than mortal Rage,
Sprung thro' the Battel, *Stentor* to engage.

---

of Physicians in September 1692. In the same year he was appointed to deliver the Gulstonian lecture but failed to do so until summoned by the president. He also failed to subscribe to the dispensary (Munk, *1,* 490; *Annals, 6,* 97).

Calomel: mercurous chloride, or "protochloride" of mercury, used to cure syphilis.

194. *scaly Crusts:* syphilis "daubs [the] eye-brows . . . with crusty Scabs" (Gideon Harvey, *The Conclave of Physicians,* 2nd ed., 1686, p. 71).

195: *Colon:* See above, *2,* 74 *n.*

Japix: Iapis is the physician of Aeneas (*Aeneid, 12,* 391). Several readers identified him with Samuel Collins (MS. Key); see above, *4,* 134 *n.*

196. *fierce Gripes:* "Rhapontick, or Rhubarb of Pontus . . . will purge a little, but bind much" (Culpeper, p. 11).

199. *Scribonius:* Scribonius Largus Designatianus was a Roman physician (first century A.D.), who wrote *De compositione medicamentorum.* Most readers identified him as Martin Lister (c. 1638–1712), fellow of the Royal Society (1671), M.D. Oxford (1684), fellow of the College of Physicians (1687), and a subscriber to the dispensary, who wrote *De fontibus medicatis Angliae* (1682) (Wing L2518).

Eagle-stone: "Aetites, Or the stone with Child, because being hollow in the middle it contains another little stone within it, is found in an Eagles nest, and in many other places. This stone being bound to the left Arm of a woman with Child, stays their miscarriage or abortion: but when the time of their labour comes . . . bind it to the inside of their Thigh, and it brings forth the Child, and that (almost) without any pain at all" (Culpeper, p. 53).

200. *Psylas:* Garth apparently made up the name, perhaps suggested by the Psylli, a Libyan tribe skilled in the cure of snake-bite (Pausanias, *9,* 28; Pliny, *Hist. nat., 7,* 13–14). His readers had no difficulty in identifying Psylas as Hugh Chamberlen (1664–1728), "the famous man-mid-wife" (MS. Key). Upon his first examination for admission to the College of Physicians he was advised "to apply himselfe harder" to his studies at Trinity College, Cambridge. He was then created M.D. in October 1689 and admitted to the College but with the admonition that he "should more diligently apply himselfe to the Therapeutick part of Physick" (*Annals, 5,* 81v; *6,* 54). He immediately identified himself with the "Apothecaries Physicians," refusing to sign the bond "to stand by the Officers of the College," walking out of the *comitia extraordinaria* of 21 November 1696, and refusing on three occasions to subscribe to the dispensary, despite the assurance of his long and elegant epitaph in Westminster Abbey by Bishop Atterbury that he was "indole . . . propensâ ad munificentiam" (Munk, *1,* 506).

Lucina: "the Goddess of births" (MS. Key).

Fierce was the Onset, the Dispute was great,
Both cou'd not vanquish, Neither wou'd retreat.
Each Combatant his Adversary mauls
With batter'd *Bed-pans,* and stav'd *Urinals.*
But as bold *Stentor,* eager of Renown,
Design'd a fatal Stroak, he tumbl'd down;
And whilst the Victor hov'ring o'er him stood,
With Arms extended, thus the *Suppliant* su'd:
When Honour's lost, 'tis a Relief to die,
Death's but a sure Retreat from Infamy.
But to the lost, if Pity might be shown,
Reflect on young *Querpoïdes* thy Son;
Then pity mine; for such an Infant Grace,
Sports in his Eyes, and flatters in his Face.
If he was by, Compassion he'd create,
Or else lament his wretched Parent's Fate.
Thine is the Glory, and the Field is thine;
To Thee the lov'd *Dispens'ry* I resign.
The Chief at this the deadly Stroak declin'd,
And found Compassion pleading in his Mind.
But whilst He view'd with pity the Distress'd,
He spy'd *Signetur* writ upon his Breast.
Then tow'rds the Skies He toss'd his threat'ning Head,
And fir'd with mortal Indignation, said:

215. *pity mine:* Charles Goodall's son was Charles Goodall (1671–89), "a most ingenious young man of his age" (Wood, *4,* 256), whose *Poems and Translations written upon several Occasions and to several Persons by a late scholar of Eaton* (Wing G1092) was published in the year of his death.

220. Cf. *Aeneid, 12,* 937: "tua est Lavinia coniunx."

224. *Signetur:* One of the statutes adopted by the College of Physicians in September 1687 required that the directions for taking medicines prescribed by the member physicians should be left with the patient and *not* sent to the apothecary with the prescription itself, which was to be "only signed with some agreeable [appropriate] titles or apt notes for their distinction [by the patient]"—*solummodo ut titulis quibusdam congruentibus, aut notis ad eorum distinctionem apto signentur.* This was called "the *Signetur*-Statute" (*A Short Answer to a Late Book, Entituled, Tentamen Medicinale,* p. 23) and members of the College who observed it were "call'd by the Apothecaries Signetur-Men" (MS. Key). The purpose of this was to prevent the apothecaries from learning "with what design, intention, or for what uses the Remedies are prescribed" (*The Statutes of the Colledge of Physicians London,* 1693, pp. 187–89). The classical allusion is *Aeneid, 12,* 940–44.

Sooner than I'll from vow'd Revenge desist,
His *Holiness* shall turn a *Quietist.*
La Chase shall with the *Jansenists* agree,
The Inquisition wink at Heresy,
Faith stand unmov'd thro' *Stillingfleet*'s Defence
And *Lock* for Mystery abandon Sense.
With that, unsheathing an Incision Knife,
He offer'd at the prostrate *Stentor*'s Life.
But while his Thoughts that fatal Act decree,
Apollo interpos'd in form of Fee.
The Chief great *Paean*'s golden Tresses knew,
He own'd the God, and his rais'd Arm withdrew.
Thus often at the Temple-Stairs I've seen
Two Tritons of a rough Athletick Mien,
Sowrly dispute some quarrel of the Flood,
With Knuckles bruis'd, and Face besmear'd in Blood.
But at the first appearance of a Fare

228. *His Holiness:* Innocent XII (1691–1700).

Quietist: Quietism was a protestant and mystical movement within the Roman Catholic church in the seventeenth century. Its chief proponents were Miguel de Molinos, a Spanish priest resident in Rome, who wrote *Guida spirituale, che disinvolge l'anima e la conduce per l'interior camino all' acquisito della perfetta contemplazione e del ricco tesoro della pace interiore* (1675), and François de Salignac de la Mothe Fénelon, archbishop of Cambrai, who wrote an *Explication des Maximes des saintes sur la vie interieure* (1697).

229. *La Chase:* François de la Chaise (1624–1709), a Jesuit priest, was made confessor of Louis XIV in 1674. He was largely responsible for the revocation of the Edict of Nantes in 1685 and managed the controversy with the Jansenists. *Father La Chaise's Project for the Extirpation of Hereticks* (Wing L127) was published in 1688.

Jansenists: Jansenism was an evangelical reform movement within the Roman Catholic church, based on the *Augustinus* (1640) of Cornelius Jansen, bishop of Ypres. It was declared heretical in 1653.

231. *Stillingfleet:* Edward Stillingfleet (1635–99), "the Right Reverend and learned Divine . . . Bishop of Worcester and Pillar of the Protestant Religion" (MS. Key), defended the faith against what he believed to be the materialism of Locke. In a series of three pamphlets published in 1697–98 (Wing S5585, S5557, S5558), Stillingfleet argued that Locke's concept of "substance" in *An Essay concerning Humane Understanding* jeopardized the "Mystery" of the Trinity. Since Stillingfleet died on 27 March 1699, Garth presumably wrote these lines before that date.

232. *Lock:* John Locke (1632–1704), without abandoning "Sense," wrote a reply to each of Stillingfleet's pamphlets (Wing L2748A, L2749, L2753, L2754). The annotator who wrote "Lock, one who has writ so mysteriously that he has lost himself in the Clouds" (MS. Key) has exactly reversed the meaning of the line; cf. Hearne, *II*, 395: "it hath been allowed by all, that Locke had by much the advantage of the Bishop."

Both quit the Fray, and to their Oars repair.
The Heroe so his Enterprise recalls,
His Fist unclinches, and the Weapon falls.

Canto 6

While the shrill clangour of the Battel rings;
Auspicious *Health* appear'd on *Zephir*'s Wings;
She seem'd a Cherub most divinely bright,
More soft than Air, more gay than morning Light.
A Charm she takes from each excelling Fair,
And borrows *Cecil*'s Shape, and *Grafton*'s Air.
Her Eyes like *Ranelagh*'s their Beams dispence,
With *Churchill*'s Bloom, and *Berkley*'s Innocence.

1–2. Leicht (p. 171) cites *Le Lutrin, 6,* 1–5.

6. *Cecil: Frances Bennet* (1670–1713), youngest daughter of Simon Bennet of Beechampton, Buckinghamshire, was "about 13 years old" when she married James Cecil, fourth earl of Salisbury (Luttrell, *1,* 269). Widowed in October 1694, she became a celebrated toast and had her portrait painted by Godfrey Kneller. The dissolute Thomas Neale, when "dangerously ill" in August 1699, desired "in case of death" that "the countess of Salisbury's picture . . . be put into the coffin with him" (Luttrell, *4,* 543).

Grafton: Isabella Bennet (1667–1723), only child of Henry Bennet, first earl of Arlington, was married when she was only five years old to Henry Fitzroy, second son of Charles II by Barbara Villiers. She was widowed in October 1690 when Fitzroy, who had been created duke of Grafton, was mortally wounded during the seige of Cork. In October 1698 she married Sir Thomas Hanmer. Her picture is among the "Beauties" at Hampton Court. In the *Progress of Beauty* ("The God of Day descending from above"), *POAS,* 1698, *3,* 258, "*Grafton* leads the Stars."

7. *Ranelagh:* Margaret Cecil (1672–1728), fourth daughter of James Cecil, third earl of Salisbury. In 1691 she married John, Lord Stawell, who died in November 1692. She is "Beauteous *Stawel*" in *Progress of Beauty* (*POAS,* 1698, *3,* 259). In January 1696 she married Richard Jones, first earl of Ranelagh.

8. *Churchill:* Anne Churchill (1683–1716), second daughter of John, earl of Marlborough. "The Kit Cat and the Toasters,/Did never Care a Figg,/For any other Beauty, /Besides the little Whigg" (*Wit and Mirth: or Pills to Purge Melancholy,* 5 vols., 1699–1714, *5,* 277). She brought Charles, Lord Spencer, £20,000 when she married him in June 1700. Even Isaac Watts took time from writing hymns to celebrate her beauty in some broadside *Stanzas to My Lady Sunderland at Tunbridge-Wells* ("Fair Nymph, ascend to Beauty's Throne") in 1712.

Berkley: Jane Martha Temple (1672–1751), daughter of Sir John Temple of East Sheen, Surrey, was a maid of honor to Queen Mary. She married John Berkeley, third

From her bright Lips a vocal Musick falls,
As to *Machaon* thus the Goddess calls:
Enough th'atchievement of your Arms you've shown,
You seek a Triumph you shou'd blush to own.
Haste to th'*Elysian* Fields, those bless'd abodes,
Where *Harvy* sits among the Demi-Gods.
Consult that sacred Sage, He'll soon disclose
The method that must terminate these woes.
Let *Celsus* for that Enterprize prepare,
His conduct to the Shades shall be my care.
Aghast the Heroes stood dissolv'd in fear,
A Form so Heav'nly bright They cou'd not bear,
Celsus alone unmov'd, the Sight beheld,
The rest in pale confusion left the Field.

---

baron Berkeley of Stratton, in 1692, was widowed five years later, and in May 1700 became the second wife of the earl of Portland. "*B——y's . . .* Goodness . . . [which] cannot be but by her self exprest" is celebrated in *The Court at Kensington* (1700) ("Give me a Genius fill'd with soft Delight").

10. *Machaon:* See above, *5,* 141 *n.*

14. *Harvy:* William Harvey (1578–1657), *medicorum omnium apud Anglos princeps,* among his other benefactions to the College of Physicians endowed the Harveian oration. Delivering that oration in 1697, Garth said of its founder, "The Memory of that blessed Old man dayly revives, than whom no Age ever saw, nor perhaps ever will see one more learned. . . . Like to the Heavenly Inhabitants, [he] stood need to few, but was beneficial to very many, even to posterity, not only by teaching them divine Truths, but by makeing us all Heires of what he Left" (*JHM, 18* [1963], 14).

17. *Celsus:* One Celsus was a friend of Ovid (*Ex Ponto, 1,* 9) and this may have influenced Garth's choice of the name. But a more important one was A. Cornelius Celsus (first century A.D.), who wrote an encyclopedia of which five books of argiculture and eight books of medicine have survived. Several readers identified Celsus as Garth himself (*1699*[2] Newberry Library copy; MS. Key; *1706* Yale Medical Library copy 2). Garth, however (see illustration, p. 75), identified him as his friend John Bateman (d. 1728) and there seems to be no reason to doubt the ascription. "Bateman was first an apprentice to a draper (quaere): afterwards, when he came to the University, was servitor to Mr. [Francis] Johnson the master [of Univ. Coll.] and used to carry his wive's book under his armes after her to church" (Bodl. MS. Ballard 46, f. 166, quoted in Wood, *Life and Times, 2,* 145 *n.* 2). Bateman became a fellow of Merton College, Oxford, in 1663. There he became one of Anthony à Wood's drinking companions, delivered "a very eloquent oration" to "the prince of Aurange" in December 1670 when William received an honorary degree at Oxford, and finally graduated M.D. in 1682. He was elected a fellow of the College of Physicians in 1685, served as censor in 1687, 1690, and 1691, and was one of the original contributors to the dispensary. Thomas Hearne recalled that he "was always reckon'd an Excellent Scholar, & well vers'd in Physick . . . [and] an Honest Church of England Man . . . [who] translated one of Plutarch's Lives & may perhaps have done some other Things" (*1,* 230–31).

So when the Pigmies, marshal'd on the Plains,
Wage puny War against th'invading Cranes;
The Poppets to their bodkin Spears repair,
And scatter'd Feathers flutter in the Air.
But soon as e'er th'imperial Bird of Jove
Stoops on his sounding Pinions from above,
Among the Brakes, the Fairy Nation crowds,
And the *Strimonian* Squadron seeks the Clouds.
And now the Delegate prepares to go
And view the Wonders of the Realms below;
Then takes *Amomum* for the Golden Bough.
Thrice did the Goddess with her Sacred Wand
The Pavement strike; and straight at her Command
Th'obedient Surface opens, and descries
A deep Descent that leads to nether Skies.
Higeia to the silent Region tends;
And with his Heav'nly Guide the *Charge* descends.
Within the Chambers of the Globe they spy
The Beds where sleeping Vegetables lie,
Till the glad Summons of a Genial Ray
Unbinds the Glebe, and calls them out to Day.
Hence *Pancies* trick themselves in various Hew,

23–24. *Pigmies . . . Cranes:* Leicht (pp. 171–72) cites the *Iliad, 3,* 1–6, and *Le Lutrin, 1,* 113–16.

30. *Strimonian Squadron:* flights of cranes (*Aeneid, 10,* 265). The river Strymon, which divides Thrace and Macedonia, is a resort of cranes.

31. *Delegate:* The delegates are elected officers of the College of Physicians who, together with the president and vice-president constitute a kind of executive committee to "treate of all matters that belong to the honor or advantage of the Colledge" (*Annals, 7,* 60), which is exactly Celsus' mission in the poem. Bateman and Garth served as delegates during the years 1693–98.

33. *Amomum:* This mock-epic equivalent of moly (*Aeneid, 6,* 204–11) is as mysterious as its classical counterpart. "What the *Amomum* of the Ancients was, is uncertain; some will have it to be the Rose of *Jericho*. The Shops shew Two sorts of Seeds under the Name of *Amomum,* the first of which is black and round like *Pepper* or *Cubebs,* but has no sharp Taste. The other is a small and pale Seed; either of them is seldom used. Instead of the *Amomum* of the Ancients, they use Sweet-Cane" (Blancard, p. 9).

38. *Higeia: "the* Goddess *Health" (1718* Key).

44–47. Pope observed that these lines "are hinted from Blackmore," *Prince Arthur* (1695), *4,* 133–38, p. 97 (*1703* Victoria & Albert copy), but the similarity is not striking:

Hence grows the *Cedar,* hence the swelling *Vine*
Does round the *Elm* its purple Clusters twine.
Hence painted *Flowers* the smiling Gardens bless,

And hence *Junquils* derive their fragrant Dew.
Hence the *Carnation,* and the bashful *Rose*
Their Virgin Blushes to the Morn disclose.
Hence Arbours are with twining Greens aray'd,
T'oblige complaining Lovers with their Shade.
And hence on *Daphne*'s verdant Temples grow
Immortal Wreaths, for *Phoebus* and *Nassau.*
The Insects here their lingring Trance survive:
Benumn'd they seem, and doubtful if alive.
From Winter's fury hither they repair,
And stay for milder Skies and softer Air.
Down to these Cells obscener Reptils creep,
Where hateful *Nutes* and painted *Lizzards* sleep.
Where shiv'ring *Snakes* the Summer Solstice wait;
Unfurl their painted Folds, and slide in State.
Now, those profounder Regions they explore,
Where Metals ripen in vast Cakes of Oar.
Here, sullen to the Sight, at large is spread
The dull unwieldy Mass of lumpish Lead.
There, glimm'ring in their dawning Beds, are seen
The more aspiring Seeds of Sprightly Tin.
The Copper sparkles next in ruddy Streaks;
And in the Gloom betrays its glowing Cheeks.
The Silver then, with bright and burnish'd Grace,
Youth and a blooming Lustre in its Face,
To th'Arms of those more yeilding Metals flyes,
And in the Folds of their Embraces lyes.
So close they cling, so stubbornly retire;
Their Love's more violent than the Chymist's Fire.

Both with their fragrant Scent and gawdy Dress.
Hence the white *Lilly* in full Beauty grows,
Hence the blue *Violet,* and blushing *Rose.*

61. *Metals ripen:* The accepted scientific metaphor was that all metals represented different stages of unripened gold; cf. Dryden, *Annus Mirabilis,* 553–56:

As those who unripe veins in Mines explore,
On the rich bed again the warm turf lay,
Till time digests the yet imperfect Ore,
And know it will be Gold another day:

and the scientific references cited in Dryden, *Works* (California), *1,* 296.

Near These the Delegate with Wonder spies
Where living Floods of Merc'ry serpentize:
Where richest Metals their bright Beams put on,
While Silver Streams thro' Golden Channels run.
Here he observes the subterranean Cells,
Where wanton Nature sports in idle Shells.
Some *Helicoeids,* some *Conical* appear,
These, Miters emulate; Those, Turbans are:
Here Marcasites in various Figure wait,
To ripen to a true Metallick State:
Till Drops that from impending Rocks descend,
Their Substance petrifie, and Progress end.
Nigh, livid Seas of kindl'd Sulphur flow;
And, whilst enrag'd, their Fiery Surges glow:
Convulsions in the lab'ring Mountains rise,
Which hurl their melted Vitals to the Skies.
He views with Horror next the noisy Cave;
Where with hoarse dinn imprison'd Tempests rave:
Where Clam'rous Hurricanes attempt their Flight,
Or, whirling in tumultuous Eddies, fight.
And now the Goddess with her Charge descends,
Where scarce one cheerful Glimpse their Steps befriends.
Here his forsaken Seat old *Chaos* keeps;
And undisturb'd by Form, in Silence sleeps.
A grisly Wight, and hideous to the Eye;
An awkard Lump of shapeless Anarchy.
With sordid Age his Features are defac'd;
His Lands unpeopl'd, and his Countries waste.
Here Lumber, undeserving Light, is kept,
And *Philipps'* Bill to this dark Region's swept:

80. *Helicoeids:* things of a helicoid or spiral form. *OED* cites this line.

82. *Marcasites:* pyrites; supposed to be "the Seed or first Matter of Metals" (Ephraim Chambers, *Cyclopaedia,* 1728, *2,* 499).

96. *old Chaos:* Garth develops the comic potentialities of Milton's Chaos, "The other Shape . . . that shape had none," who "by decision more embroils the fray" (*Paradise Lost, 2,* 666–67, 908). Thus Pope's observation that the line "contradicts it self" (*1703* Victoria & Albert copy) is beside the point.

97. Cf. Cowley, *Davideis* (1656), 1, 80: "And undisturb'd by Moons in silence sleep": Dryden, *Mac Flecknoe* (1682), 72: "And undisturb'd by Watch, in silence sleep."

103. *Philipps' Bill:* In January 1699 Sir John Philipps of Picton Castle (c. 1660–1737), fourth baronet, the Tory member for Pembrokeshire, Wales (1695–December

Where Mushroom Libels silently retire;
And, soon as born, with Decency expire.
Upon a Couch of *Jett* in these Abodes,
Dull *Night,* his melancholy Consort, nods.
No Ways and Means their Cabinet employ;
But their dark Hours they waste in barren Joy.
  Nigh this Recess, with Terror they survey,
Where *Death* maintains his dread tyrannick Sway:
In the close Covert of a Cypress Grove,
Where *Goblins* frisk, and airy Spectres rove,
Yawns a dark Cave, most formidably wide;
And there the *Monarch*'s Triumphs are descry'd.
Within its dreadful Jaws those Furies wait,
Which execute the harsh Decrees of Fate.
  Febris is first: The *Hagg* relentless hears
The Virgin's Sighs; and sees the Infant's Tears.
In her parch'd Eye-balls fiery *Meteors* reign;
And restless Ferments revel in each Vein.
  Then *Hydrops* next appears amongst the *Throng;*
Bloated, and big, she slowly sails along.
But, like a Miser, in Excess she's poor;
And pines for Thirst amidst her wat'ry Store.
  Now loathsom *Lepra,* that offensive Spright,
With foul Eruptions stain'd, offends the Sight.
She's deaf to Beauty's soft-persuading Pow'r:
Nor can bright *Hebe*'s Charms her Bloom secure.
  Whilst meagre *Phthisis* gives a silent Blow;
Her Stroaks are sure; but her Advances slow.
No loud Alarms, nor fierce Assaults are shown:
She starves the *Fortress* first; then takes the *Town.*
  Behind stood Crouds of much inferiour Name,
Too num'rous to repeat, too foul to name;
The Vassals of their Monarch's Tyranny:
Who, at his Nod, on fatal Errands fly.
  Now *Celsus,* with his glorious Guide, invades

1701), introduced "a ridiculous senceless Bill" for suppressing vice and immorality (MS. Key), which was allowed to die in committee; see above, *An Encomium upon a Parliament,* 76 *n.*

107. *Night, his melancholy Consort:* Cf. *Paradise Lost,* 2, 960–63.

The silent Region of the fleeting shades,
Where Rocks and ruful Desarts are descry'd;
And sullen *Styx* rouls down his lazy Tide.
Then shews the Ferry-man the Plant he bore,
And claims his Passage to the further Shore.
To whom the *Stygian Pilot* smiling, said,
You need no Pass-port to demand our Aid.
Physicians never linger on this Strand:
Old *Charon* ne'er refuses their Command.
Our awful Monarch and his Consort owe
To them the Peopl'ing of their Realms below.
Then in his swarthy Hand he grasp'd his Oar,
Receiv'd his Guests aboard, and shov'd from Shoar.
  Now, as the Goddess and her Charge prepare
To breathe the Sweets of soft *Elysian* Air;
Upon the left they spy a pensive Shade,
Who on his bended Arm had rais'd his Head:
Pale Grief sate heavy on his careful Look:
To whom, not unconcern'd, thus *Celsus* spoke:
  Tell me, Thou much afflicted Shade, why Sighs
Burst from your Breast, and Torrents from your Eyes:
And who those mangl'd *Manes* are, which show
A sullen Satisfaction at your Woe?
  Since, said the Ghost, with Pity you'll attend,
Know, I'm *Guiacum,* once your valu'd Friend.
And on this barren Beach in Discontent,
Am doom'd to stay till th'angry Pow'rs relent.
Those *Spectres* seam'd with Scars that threaten there,
The Victims of my late ill Conduct are.
They vex with endless Clamours my Repose:
This wants his Palate; That demands his Nose:
And here they execute stern *Pluto*'s Will,
To ply me ev'ry moment with a Pill.

142. *the Plant:* amomum; see above, *6,* 33 *n.;* cf. *Aeneid, 6,* 406.

154. *a pensive Shade:* Thomas Hobbes, "the famous surgeon" who died in July 1698 (Luttrell, *4,* 401). The classical allusion is *Aeneid, 6,* 695.

163. *Guiacum:* "a Tree good against the French Pox" (*1703* Yale Medical Library copy 1). "*Guajacum Lignum vitae,* Dries, attenuates, causeth sweat, resisteth putrifaction, is admirable good for the French Pox" (Culpeper, p. 16). Garth's readers had no difficulty in recognizing Guiacum as "The late Mr. Hobbs" (MS. Key).

Then *Celsus* thus: O much lamented State!
How rigid is the Sentence you relate!
Methinks I recollect your former Air,
But ah, how much you're changed from what you were!
If Mortals e'er the *Stygian* Pow'rs cou'd bend,
Entreaties to their awful Seats I'd send.
But since no human Arts the Fates dissuade,
Direct me how to find bless'd *Harvy*'s Shade.
In vain th'unhappy Ghost still urg'd His stay;
Then rising from the Ground, he shew'd the way.
Nigh the dull Shoar a shapeless Mountain stood,
That with a dreadful Frown survey'd the Flood.
Its fearful Brow no lively Greens puts on,
No frisking Goats bound o'er the ridgy Stone.
To gain the Summit the bright Goddess try'd,
And *Celsus* follow'd, by degrees, his Guide.
Th'Ascent thus conquer'd, now They tow'r on high,
And taste th'Indulgence of a milder Sky.
Loose *Breezes* on their airy Pinions play,
And with refreshing Sweets perfume the way.
Cold Streams thro' flow'ry Meadows gently glide;
And as They pass, their painted Banks they chide.
These blissful Plains no Blights, nor Mildews fear,
The Flow'rs ne'er fade, and Shrubs are Myrtles there.
The *Delegate* observes, with wondring Eyes,
Ambrosial Dews descend, and Incense rise.
Then hastens onward to the pensive Grove,
The silent Mansion of disastrous Love.
No Winds but Sighs are there, no Floods but Tears,
Each conscious Tree a Tragick Signal bears.
Their wounded Bark records some broken Vow.
And Willough Garlands hang on ev'ry Bough.
His Mistress here in solitude he found,

204. *His Mistress:* Generalized to "Olivia" in later editions (*1703A–1718*), but identified by several readers as "Mrs. Tempest, his Quondam Mistress" (*1706* Yale Medical Library copy 2; *1706* Victoria & Albert Museum copy). Mrs. Tempest was "particularly admired" by William Walsh, who wrote an elegy upon her death in November 1703 and urged Pope to dedicate to her his Fourth Pastoral (Pope, *Poems, 1,* 88). Since Bateman's "Quondam Mistress" must have been dead in 1698–99 when Garth wrote these lines, she cannot have been Mrs. Tempest. The printed key settles the matter

Her down-cast Eyes fix'd on the silent Ground:
Her Dress neglected, and unbound her Hair,
She seem'd the mournful image of Despair.
How lately did this celebrated *Thing*
Blaze in the Box, and sparkle in the Ring,
Till the Greensickness and Love's force betray'd
To Death's remorsless arms th'unhappy Maid.
  Cold and confus'd the guilty Lover stood,
The Light forsook his Eyes, his Cheeks the Blood;
An icy horrour shiver'd in his Look,
Then softly in these gentle words, He spoke:
  Tell me, dear Shade, from whence such anxious care,
Your Looks disorder'd and your Bosom bare?
Why thus you languish like a drooping Flow'r,
Crush'd by the weight of some unfriendly shower.
Your pale Complexion your late Conduct tell,
O that instead of Trash you'd taken Steel!
  Then as he strove to clasp the fleeting *Fair*,
His empty Arms confess'd th'impassive Air.
From his Embrace th'unbody'd Spectre flies,
And as she mov'd, she chid him with her Eyes.
  They hasten now to that delightful Plain.
Where the glad *Manes* of the Bless'd remain:
Where *Harvy* gathers Simples to bestow
Immortal Youth on Heroes Shades below.
Soon as the bright *Higeia* was in view,
The Venerable Sage her Presence knew.

---

very nicely: "Whoever has the least Knowledge of the Town, and *Beau Monde*, will easily know where to fix" this fictitious name (*1718* Key). The classical allusion is *Aeneid, 6,* 450–55.

209. Leicht (p. 174) cites Dorset, *On the Countess of Dorchester* (1680) ("Tell me, Dorinda, why so gay"): "Wilt thou still sparkle in the Box,/Still ogle in the Ring?" (*POAS*, 1703, *2*, 480). The Ring was a circular track in Hyde Park for fashionable riding and driving.

221. *Trash:* adulterated drugs; cf. "Having occasion once to buy a great number of *Limons*, I enquired of the Merchant how he disposed of those that were rotten, and unsound; who Answered me, that nothing was lost, the Chymists and Apothecaries buying all that refuse Trash which he could not otherwayes vend, to make Oyls and Syrups" ([Daniel Coxe], *A Discourse wherein the Interest of the Patient in Reference to Physick and Physicians is Soberly Debated*, 1669, p. 59).

Steel: See above, *4, 58 n.*

228. *Simples:* medicinal herbs.

Thus He:
    Hail, blooming Goddess! Thou propitious Pow'r,
Whose Blessings Mortals next to Life implore.
Such Graces in your heav'nly Eyes appear,
That Cottages are Courts when you are there.
Mankind, as you vouchsafe to smile or frown,
Finds ease in Chains, or anguish in a Crown.
With just Resentments and Contempt you see
The mean Dissentions of the Faculty;
How sick'ning Physick hangs her pensive Head.
And what was once a Science, now's a Trade.
Her Son's ne'er rifle her Mysterious Store,
But study Nature less, and Lucre more.
    I show'd of old, how vital Currents glide,
And the *Meanders* of their refluent Tide.
Then, *Willis,* why spontaneous Actions here,
And whence involuntary Motions there:
And how the Spirits by mechanick Laws,
In wild Careers, tumultuous Riots cause.
Nor wou'd our *Wharton, Ent,* and *Glisson* lie

241. *sick'ning Physick:* Garth is attributing to the ghost of Harvey words which he himself spoke in his Harveian oration: "But we are faln into those times and places in which Physick it self is grown sick" (*JHM, 18* [1963], 13).

247. *Willis:* Thomas Willis (1621–75) was a farmer's son who graduated B.A. (1639) and M.B. (1646) from Christ Church, Oxford. About 1649 he joined the group at Oxford which became the Royal Society. In 1664 he was elected an honorary fellow of the College of Physicians. Although highly successful—Anthony à Wood said that no one had ever "got more money yearly than he" *(Athenae Oxonienses, 3,* 1051)—Willis was bitterly attacked. But a whole generation of anti-Galenical physicians called themselves Willisians. He was among the first to develop the implications of Harvey's discoveries and in the second of the two works to which Garth refers in the text, *Pathologiae cerebri et nervosi generis specimen* (1667) and *Affectionum quae dicuntur hystericae et hypochondriacae pathologia spasmodica* (1670), he elaborated the (correct) theory that epilepsy is caused by an "explosion" in the brain (Sir Charles Symonds, "Thomas Willis, F.R.S.," *The Royal Society,* ed. Sir Harold Hartley, 1960, p. 95).

251. *Wharton, Ent, and Glisson:* What Thomas Wharton (1614–73), Sir George Ent (1604–89), and Francis Glisson (1597–1677) have in common is that they were not only successful and even fashionable London physicians (and members of the College of Physicians), but also serious practitioners of what John Wallis called "the *New Philosophy*" and followed the lead of Harvey in basing their medical practice upon laboratory research. Wharton and Glisson made permanent contributions to the science of physiology, while Glisson and Ent were founding members of the Royal Society, which was dedicated to experimental science (Douglas McKie, "The origins and foundations of the Royal Society of London," *The Royal Society,* ed. Sir Harold

In the Abyss of blind Obscurity.
But now such wondrous Searches are forborn,
And *Paean*'s Art is by Divisions torn.
Then let your *Charge* attend, and I'll explain
How Physick her lost Lustre may regain.
  Haste, and the matchless *Atticus* Address;
From Heav'n, and great *Nassau* he has the Mace.
Th'oppress'd to his *Asylum* still repair;
Arts He supports, and Learning is his care.
He softens the harsh rigour of the Laws,
Blunts their keen Edge, and cuts their Harpy Claws;
And graciously he casts a pitying Eye
On the sad state of vertuous Poverty.
When e'er he speaks, Heav'ns! how the list'ning Throng
Dwells on the melting musick of his Tongue.
His Arguments are th'Emblems of his Mien,
Mild, but not faint, and forcing, tho' serene;
And when the power of Eloquence He'd try,
Here, Lightning strikes you; there, soft Breezes sigh.
  To him you must your sickly state refer,
Your Charter claims Him as your Visiter.

Hartley, 1960, p. 34). The ghost of Harvey now complains that their example is being ignored.

254. *Paean:* See above, *1,* 66 *n.*

257. *Atticus:* See above, *1,* 51 *n.*

259. *his Asylum:* Somers, who was unmarried, lived in the parish of St. Giles in the Fields, in Powis House, off Great Queen Street (Strype, 2, 175).

272. *Charter:* In March 1663 Charles II granted the College of Physicians a new charter "with confirmation of former privileges, and some additions" (*CSPD 1663–1664,* p. 95). It constituted the three top law officers of England, the lord high chancellor, and the chief justices of the court of king's bench and the court of common pleas as visitors to the College with the power "to receive, entertaine, heare, examine, adjudge and determine, alter, mitigate, reverse, or confirme all and every such Matter, Cause, Complaynt, Judgment, Decree or Sentence whatsoever which att any time hereafter shall come or bee brought before them" (Charles Goodall, *The Royal College of Physicians of London,* 1684, p. 102). Garth is telling his colleagues, in effect, to stop bickering over the dispensary and get back to work on medical research along the lines laid down by Harvey. His proposal of a visitation is both practical and ironical: practical because Somers, as a distinguished member of the Royal Society—he was elected its president in November 1699—could be expected to support exactly the solution Garth was proposing; and ironical because seven of the "Apothecaries Physicians," including Francis Bernard, George Howe, Sir Richard Blackmore, and William Gibbons, had already sought a visitation, unsuccessfully. They petitioned the

Your Wounds he'll close, and sov'reignly restore
Your Science to the height it had before.
  Then *Nassau*'s Health shall be your glorious Aim,
He shou'd be as Immortal as his Name.
Some Princes Claims from Devastations spring:
He condescends in pity to be King:
And when, amidst his *Olives* plac'd, He stands,
And governs more by Candour than Commands:
Ev'n then not less a Heroe he appears,
Than when his *Laurel* Diadem he wears.
  Wou'd but *Apollo* some great Bard inspire
With sacred veh'mence of Poetick Fire;
To celebrate in Song that God-like Power,
Which did the labouring Universe restore;
Fair *Albion*'s Cliffs wou'd Eccho to the Strain,
And praise the Arm that Conquer'd to regain
The Earth's repose, and Empire o'er the Main.
  Still may th'immortal Man his Cares repeat,
To make his Blessings endless as they're great:
Whilst *Malice* and *Ingratitude* confess
They've strove for Ruin long without success.
  Had some fam'd Hero of the *Latin* Blood,
Like *Julius* Great, and like *Octavius* Good,
But thus preserv'd the *Latian* Liberties,
Aspiring Columns soon had reach'd the Skies:
And whilst the Capitol with *Io*'s shook,
The Statues of the Guardian Gods had spoke.
  No more the Sage his Raptures cou'd pursue,
He paus'd; and *Celsus* with his Guide withdrew.

---

visitors in January 1697, seeking relief from "A prevailing Party" in the College, which had passed "severall grevious impracticable and illegall Statutes" (*Annals, 7,* 95). Receipt of the petition was acknowledged, but the petition was apparently ignored. Garth, therefore, is simply taking up the challenge of the "Apothecaries Physicians."

SIR RICHARD BLACKMORE

A Satyr against Wit
(23 November 1699)

By an instructive coincidence Blackmore's *Satyr against Wit* was published in the same month as Peter Motteux's translation of *The History of the Renown'd Don Quixote.* Before Blackmore began to practice medicine, in the 1680s, he had sought advice from Thomas Sydenham, who was then the most successful practitioner in London. Sydenham advised him to read Cervantes and it is not difficult to imagine Sir Richard Blackmore of Cheapside as the Don Quixote de la Mancha of English literature. Even by his admirers, he was "look'd upon as a sort of Mad man" (Hearne, *8,* 101).

No less than four windmills are tilted at in *A Satyr against Wit:* wit, of course, and obscenity, "science," and *The Dispensary.* It was the last of these which actually precipitated *A Satyr against Wit,* accurately described on the title page of a pirated Dublin edition as *"Design'd an Answer to a Poem Stil'd the Dispensary."* Blackmore had been leader of the "Apothecaries Physicians" in the College of Physicians who for 10 years had prevented the opening of a free out-patient clinic in the College. In *The Dispensary,* however, it is not Blackmore's obstructionist tactics, but his verses that Garth "most wittily ridicules" (see above, *The Dispensary, 4,* 173–237). As a consequence, Blackmore saw no need to defend his medical politics, although the last dozen lines of *A Satyr against Wit* refer unmistakably to the dispensary. What he did find it necessary to defend was his literary practice. And here he decided, quite rightly, that the best defense is a good offense. So he runs down *The Dispensary* as a satire "with little in't but Praise" (line 181), and as contraband goods stolen in France and illegally vended in England. And he rejects Dryden, whose "vigorous Turns" Garth had urged Blackmore to "consider" as a model, on account of the "leud Allay" (line 208) in his verses.

The year before *A Satyr against Wit* appeared, Jeremy Collier, a nonjuring clergyman under a sentence of outlawry, published *A*

Short View of the Immorality, and Profaneness of the English Stage, and then, as the story is commonly told, "The Pulpit [got] the better of the Stage." But as J. E. Spingarn has pointed out, "the victory had been achieved before Collier wrote; and in the year before the Revolution Sedley compared the change of public taste to the sudden whims of the English weather" (Spingarn, *1,* lxxxv). Sedley was "very unhappy, that the Ice that has borne so many Coaches and Carts, shou'd break with my Wheel barrow," but there was no doubt in his mind that the ice was breaking. "This suddain change," as he called it, was nothing less than a major shift in the sensibility of the English people, and Blackmore was one of the first to register and define it. In 1695, in his preface to *Prince Arthur. An Heroick Poem,* he discovered that wit is *"either* immodest *or* irreligious," and in the same year Colley Cibber tacked a sentimental ending onto his first play, *Love's Last Shift; or, The Fool in Fashion.* In *A Satyr against Wit* we are witnesses, delighted or horrified, according to our predilection, to the emergence of bourgeois morality:

> Therefore some just and wholesome Laws ordain,
> That may this wild Licentiousness restrain.
> (289–290)

These words, with their inevitable corollary, "Therefore let Satyr-Writers be supprest," (352) are merely a restatement of current government policy. In December 1698, in his speech at the opening of his fourth parliament, William had urged that "you will employ your Thoughts about some good Bills . . . for the further Discouraging of Vice and Profaneness."

As William's words imply, morality had been an affair of state for some time. John Evelyn, in fact, had noticed a change in the moral climate as soon as Charles II was buried, and James II "spoke openly against leudness, and expressed a detestation of drunkenness" (Burnet, *1,* 624). The Society for the Reformation of Manners was founded in 1690 and its informers began operations against "loose Persons" soon after (Strype, *2,* ²30).

William III turned to public morality as soon as he had brought the war to a conclusion. "I esteem it one of the greatest Advantages of the Peace," he said in December 1697, "that I shall now have Leisure . . . effectually to discourage Profaneness and Immorality" (*CJ, 12,* 1). Parliament responded with an Act for the more effectual suppressing of Blasphemy and Profaneness (9 & 10 William III c. 32), which was disappointing to the king because it simply established penalties for those who denied the doctrine of the Trinity. On his own side, the king kept up a steady barrage of proclamations and orders, "to prevent the Prophaneness and Immorality of the Stage," "not to act anything contrary to Religion and good Manners," and the like.

With all this encouragement, whole "Troops of *Informers*" sprang up to "serve God for *Gain*" and "pick *harmless words* out of Plays to indite the Players and squeez[e] Twenty Pound a Week out of them." Sir Harry Ashurst's coachman was fined for swearing at the chocolate house door and "a few poor Whores" were forced to shift their quarters. Otherwise, it was the theatre that was hardest hit. Both playhouses were presented as public nuisances by the grand jury of Middlesex county; actors were fined £10 for using indecent language on the stage, and Vanbrugh's new comedy, *The Provok'd Wife,* which had opened without incident in 1697, was presented as obscene only two years later. Vanbrugh was forced into the duller but safer work of adapting Beaumont and Fletcher and eventually into the peaceful province of architecture (Thomas Brown, *Letters from the Dead to the Living,* 2nd. ed., 1702, pp. 71, 73; *The Second Volume of Miscellaneous Works, Written by George, Late Duke of Buckingham,* 1705, p. 135; HMC *Cowper MSS.,* *2,* 434; Luttrell, *4,* 571, 712, 720).

In a poem entitled *A Satyr against Wit,* it is obviously relevant to determine what the poet meant by "Wit." During most of the poem the term is synonymous with obscenity and blasphemy. There are some contexts, however, where this equation does not hold (e.g. lines 97, 225, 315–16). Considering it simply as a literary commodity, Blackmore thinks of "Wit" as "intellectual Enameling," as he described it in his *Essay upon Wit* in 1716, or "a rich Embroidery of Flowers and Figures," something delightful but useless and unnecessary. Blackmore's stated literary ideals are by no means despicable. There is no reason why comedy, as Blackmore demanded, could not at the same time be "delightful, and promote Prudence and Sobriety of Manners" (*Essays upon Several Subjects,* 1716, pp. 192, 219), but the truth seems to be that Blackmore himself remained inaccessible to "delight" and responded only to didacticism. His values are not literary or aesthetic at all, but utilitarian: "the Labours of the meanest Persons," he said in this same *Essay upon Wit,* "are more valuable, because more useful, than . . . those, who apply themselves only, or principally, to divert and entertain the Fancy." Blackmore was aware that "Wit" is not *merely* "intellectual Enameling; besides this," he said, "it animates and warms a cold Sentiment, and makes it glow with Life and Vigor." Blackmore simply preferred "cold Sentiment" (ibid., pp. 214, 192–93).

Just beneath the surface of the dispensary quarrel there may lurk a more important difference of opinion between Garth and Blackmore on the subject of medical education and practice. Blackmore observed that logic and metaphysics had become *"the subject of much Raillery, and the great Abomination of the* Wits." For himself, on the contrary, he found that *"Logic and Metaphysicks, wherein I was carefully instructed in the University . . . fit a Man for any kind of Business or Profession, [better] than . . . all the Searches which I have made after the Reasons and Causes of* Natural Phaenomena" (*King Arthur* [1697], pp. x–xi). This depreciation of basic research contrasts sharply with the opinions of at least two of the dispensary physicians whom Blackmore opposed. Garth insisted that the study of medicine be based on "wondrous Searches" into the "wondrous Cause" of physiological phenomena (*The Dispensary, 1,* 53; *6,* 253) just as Daniel Coxe demanded "a Mass of Experiments" to establish the "unquestionable verities" (*A Discourse, Wherein the Interest of the Patient in Reference to Physick and Physicians is Soberly Debated,* 1669, pp. 199–200). Whereas Blackmore demanded that medical practice should be totally empirical, undertaken without preconceptions or hypotheses, Garth insisted that it should be accompanied by the constant testing of hypotheses in laboratory research. "Hypothesis" in science takes the place of "Wit" in literature as Blackmore's antithesis to "Sense" or common sense.

Ever since Sydenham advised Blackmore to read *Don Quixote,* there has been speculation as to what he meant. Samuel Johnson, who deplored "this foolish apophthegm," supposed that Sydenham meant that whether Blackmore read "Cervantes or Hippocrates he would be equally unqualified for practice" (*Lives, 2,* 236 *n.*). A better guess, however, is that Sydenham was warning Blackmore against what John Locke called "the romance way of physic." What Sydenham hated most in the practice of medicine was the intrusion of theories. "Beware of your imagination, he want[ed] to say; get rid of your fancies; let facts be facts; do not view nature in the light of your preconceived ideas" (Ludwig Edelstein, "Sydenham and Cervantes," *Essays in the History of Medicine presented to Professor Arturo Castiglioni,* Baltimore, 1944, p. 61). This is a lesson, from whatever source, that Blackmore learned very well. A dozen years later, in the preface to *King Arthur* (1697), he wrote:

> *I am so far faln out with all Hypotheses in* Philosophy, *and all Doctrines of Physic which are built upon them, that in such matters I am almost reduc'd to a* Sceptical Despair. . . . I am now inclin'd to think that 'tis an Injury to a Man of good Sense . . . to be hamper'd with any Hypothesis before he comes to the Practise of Physic.

John Locke was delighted with all this (*Works,* 10 vols., 1812, *9,* 426), but it seems obvious that without hypotheses, and without imagination and "fancies," medicine as a science would have been stillborn.

A Satyr against Wit, as Samuel Johnson has said, was "a proclamation of defiance," and it builds up in the last lines to an impressive climax of scorn for the witless subscribers to the dispensary: "Let 'em pound Drugs; they have no Brains to beat." And since it *was* "a proclamation of defiance," there can be no doubt that the poem "made a great noise" when it was published on 23 November 1699 (Jacob, *Historical Account,* p. 10; Dryden, *Works, 1,* 352; *The Post Man,* No. 680, 21–23 November 1699). Abel Boyer remembered very well "What Tumults, what Storms" it did raise (*Letters of Wit, Politicks, and Morality,* 1701, p. 250). More copies were needed even before the type for the first edition could be distributed, and a so-called third edition was advertised in *The Post Man,* No. 740, 18–20 April 1700.

At the same time the replies began to appear. A feeble and anonymous *Satyr upon a Late Pamphlet, Entituled, A Satyr against Wit* ("Who can unmov'd in stupid silence sit") was advertised in *The Post Boy* for 16–19 December 1699. *Extempore verses on the Author of the Satyr against Wit* ("This senceless Dunce great pains and labour took"), which circulated only in manuscript (BM MS. Sloane 1731A, f. 111), is equally anonymous and almost equally feeble. But these were only diversionary efforts. The first hint of the main counterattack occurs in Thomas Brown's letter "To Sir W. S———" dated 8 January [1700]:

> They talk of *Squibbing* him [Blackmore] with *Epigrams;* for my part, I think 'tis doing him too much *Honour,* and making him more considerable than he deserves; however, if they go on with it, I shall be not wanting to contribute my *Quota* to so Pious a Design.

"They" were the Honorable Charles Boyle and Sir Christopher Codrington, both of whom had reason to think themselves injured in the premises (lines 96–101, 248–51), and the pious design that they brought to perfection began to be advertised in *The Flying Post* for 24–27 February ([Thomas Brown], *Familiar and Courtly Letters,* 1700, pp. 219–220; Rosenberg, p. 49). To this work, which was entitled *Commendatory Verses, on the Author of the Two Arthurs and the Satyr against Wit; By Some of His Particular Friends,* Thomas Brown was induced to be the heaviest contributor, supplying eight or nine of a total of forty squibs.

A Satyr against Wit

Who can forbear, and tamely silent sit,
And see his Native Land undone by Wit?
Boast not, *Britannia,* of thy happy Peace,
What if Campaigns and Sea-Engagements cease?
Wit, a worse Plague, does mightily encrease.
Some monstrous Crimes to Ages past unknown,
Have surely pull'd this heavy Judgment down.
Fierce Insect-Wits draw out their noisy Swarms,
And threaten Ruin more than Foreign Arms.
O'er all the Land the hungry Locusts spread,
Gnaw every Plant, taint every flowry Bed,
And crop each budding Virtue's tender Head.
  How happy were the old unpolished Times,
As free from Wit as other modern Crimes?
As our Forefathers Vig'rous were and Brave;
So they were Virtuous, Wise, Discreet and Grave,
Detesting both alike the Wit and Knave.
They justly Wits and Fools believ'd the same,
And Jester was for both the common Name.
Their Minds for Empire form'd would never quit
Their noble Roughness, and dissolve in Wit.
For Business born and bred to Martial Toil,
They rais'd the Glory of *Britannia*'s Isle.
Then she her dreadful Ensigns did advance,
To curb *Iberia,* and to conquer *France.*
But this degenerate, loose and foolish Race
Are all turn'd Wits, and their great Stock debase.
Our Learning daily sinks, and Wit is grown
The senseless Conversation of the Town.
Enervated with this our Youth have lost

8–9. Cf. Swift, *Prose, 1,* 24: "The Wits of the present Age being so very numerous and penetrating, it seems, the Grandees of *Church* and *State* begin to fall under horrible Apprehensions, lest these Gentlemen, during the intervals of a long Peace, should find leisure to pick Holes in the weak sides of Religion and Government."

That stubborn Virtue, which we once could boast.
The Plague of Wit prevails; I fear 'tis vain
Now to attempt its Fury to restrain.
It takes Men in the Head, and in the Fit
They lose their Senses, and are gone in Wit.
By various ways their Frenzy they express,
Some with loose Lines run haring to the Press,
In Lewdness some are Wits, some only Wits in Dress.
Some seiz'd like *Gravar* with Convulsions, strain
Always to say fine Things, but strive in vain,
Urg'd with a dry *Tenesmus* of the Brain.
  Had but the People scar'd with Danger run
To shut up *Wills,* where first this Plague begun:
Had they the first infected Men convey'd
Strait to *Moorfields,* the Pest-house for the Head;
The wild Contagion might have been supprest,
Some few had fal'n but we had sav'd the rest.
An Act like this had been a good Defence
Against our great Mortality of Sense.
But now th'Infection spreads, the Bills run high,
At the last Gasp of Sense ten thousand ly.
We meet fine Youth in every House and Street,
With all the deadly Tokens out, of Wit.
  Vannine that look'd on all the Danger past,

37. *haring:* very fast (*OED*).

39. *Gravar:* unidentified.

41. *Tenesmus:* a continual inclination to void the contents of the bowels or bladder, accompanied by straining, but with little or no discharge.

43. *Wills:* Abel Boyer explains that since the English had no academies, the "*Beaux-Esprits*" had to meet "in Places of promiscuous Company, as *Coffee-houses*" and that among coffeehouses "*Will's* Coffee-house in *Covent-Garden,* holds the first Rank, as being consecrated to the Honour of *Apollo,* by the first-rate Wits that flourish'd in King *Charles* II's Reign." It was here, at the northwest corner of Russell and Bow streets, that Alexander Pope thrust himself in to see "the most celebrated wits of that time" presided over by "Mr. Dryden" (Spence, *1,* 29, 274). These included "Mr. *Wicherley,* Dr. *Garth,* Mr. *Congreve,* the Honorable Mr. *Boyle,* Colonel *Stanhope,* Mr. *Vanbruk,* Mr. *Cheek,* Mr. *Walsh,* Mr. *Burnaby,* Mr. *Rowe,* and some few others" (*Letters of Wit, Politicks, and Morality,* p. 216).

45. *Moorfields:* the site of Bethlehem Hospital for the insane, "vulgarly called *Bedlam*" (Strype, *1,* 2107).

50. *Bills:* See above, *The Dispensary, 3,* 97 *n.*

54. *Vannine:* identified by one reader (BM copy of *A* "The Second Edition") as Charles Gildon (see below, *The Pacificator,* 272 *n.*) and by another as Samuel Garth (University of Illinois copy of *A*).

Because he scap'd so long, is seiz'd at last.
By Pox and Hunger and by *Dryden* bit
He grins and snarles, and in his dogged Fit
Froths at the Mouth, a certain Sign of Wit.
Craper runs madly midst the sickest Crowd,
And fain would be infected, if he cou'd.
Under the Means he lies, frequents the Stage,
Is very leud, and does at Learning rage.
Pity that so much Labour should be lost
By such a healthful Constitution crost.
Against th'Assaults of Wit his Make is proof,
Still his strong Nature works the Poison off.
He still escapes, but yet is wondrous pleas'd,
Wit to recite, and to be thought Diseas'd.
So Hypocrites in Vice in this vile Town
To Wickedness pretend, that's not their own.
A Bantring Spirit has our Men possest,
And Wisdom is become a standing Jest.
Wit does of Virtue sure Destruction make;
Who can produce a Wit and not a Rake?
Wise Magistrates leud Wit do therefore hate,
The Bane of Virtue's Treason to the State.
While Honour fails and Honesty decays,
In vain we beat our Heads for Means and Ways.

59. *Craper:* One reader (BM copy of *A* "The Second Edition") identified Craper as Thomas Cheek (d. 1713?), "a Gentleman of above £2000 *per Annum,*" who enjoyed drinking with the Covent Garden wits and writing songs and prologues for his friends' works, including *The Dispensary* (*The Post Boy,* No. 746, 18–20 January 1700; *Discommendatory Verses* [1700], p. 16; *London Stage, 1,* 403, 454, 519; *The Select Works of Mr. John Dennis,* 1718, *2,* 330; *To My Friend, Dr. G—th, the Author of the Dispensary* ["To Praise your Healing Art would be in vain"]). This identification cannot be certain, however, for another reader (University of Illinois copy of *A*) identified Craper as "Drake." Besides being a distinguished candidate of the College of Physicians and subscriber to the dispensary, James Drake (1667–1707) was also an enthusiastic *littérateur.* He adapted for the stage two plays of John Fletcher as *The Sham Lawyer, or The Lucky Extravagant* (1697), which was "damnably acted at Drury Lane," and in 1699 he published a remarkable 367-page attack on Jeremy Collier entitled *The Antient and Modern Stage Survey'd,* which may be the subject of the reference in line 62.

61. *Under the Means:* a theological phrase applied here to a medical metaphor. "To live under the means of grace" is to live in such a manner that divine grace is imparted to the soul (*OED,* s.v. Mean, sb.2, 10e). Craper lives in a manner to invite the disease of wit.

65. *Make:* kind, sort, species.

What well-form'd Government or State can last,
When Wit has laid the Peoples Virtue wast?
The *Mob* of Wits is up to storm the Town,
To pull all Virtue and right Reason down.
Quite to subvert Religion's sacred Fence,
To set up Wit, and pull down common Sense.
Our Libraries they gut, and shouting bear
The Spoils of ruin'd Churches in the Air.
Their Captain *Tom* does at their Head appear,
And *Smalwood* in his Gown brings up the Rear.
Aloud the Church and Clergy they condemn,
Curse all their Order, and their God blaspheme.
Against all Springs of Learning they declare,
Against Religion's Nurseries, and swear
They will no *Alldridge, Mill,* or *Charlett* spare:

80. *wast:* On the variant, wast/waste, see Eric J. Dobson, *English Pronunciation 1500–1700,* 2 vols., Oxford, Clarendon Press, 1957, *2,* 465–69, 527 *n.* 1.

87. *Captain Tom:* Despite the fact that more than one reader (Huntington copy of *A* "The Second Edition") has identified Captain Tom as Thomas Brown and despite the fact that the preface to *Discommendatory Verses* claims that *"the Confederates at* Will's *Coffee-house* . . . have chosen *T— B——* for their Leader," Captain Tom is probably Charles Boyle or Sir Christopher Codrington. "Captain Tom" is a generic term for leader of a mob and Brown was by no means leader of the Covent Garden wits. Nor was he in the vanguard of the attack on Bentley (line 95), although he did join the wits as an irregular, sniping at Bentley in *The Life of Erasmus* which he contributed to a new issue of Sir Roger L'Estrange, *Twenty Select Colloquies out of Erasmus* [April] 1699, (sigs. b8r–c4v). It was Boyle and Codrington, however, who "set him at Work" and *A Short and True History of a Certain Captain-General* ("By Nature Small, and of a Dwarfish Breed") is about Codrington *(Discommendatory Verses,* sig. A2r, p. 1).

88. *Smalwood:* James Smalwood (d. 1719), the "Epigrammatic Parson," was graduated from Westminster School and Trinity College, Cambridge (Venn, *4,* 92). His reputation as wit was established early; *Mr. Smalwoods Verses to the Ladies When he was Praevaricator* ("After that Sort of Academick Wit"), dated 1681, is preserved in Folger MS. M.b.12, f. 73. He became chaplain to Henry Sidney, earl of Romney, "an old vitious illiterate Rake," and to the 1st Foot Guards. Among his published sermons is one (Wing S4007) preached in the field in June 1694. Smalwood responded to the attack here and in line 160 below with *To Sir R—— Bl——— upon his Unhappy Talent at Praising and Railing* ("Thine is the only Muse in *British* Ground") (*Commendatory Verses* [1700], p. 19).

93. *Alldridge:* Henry Aldrich (1647–1710) was dean of Christ Church, Oxford. Blackmore may not have known of his inadvertent part in precipitating the attack on Bentley. It was Aldrich's practice each year to assign one of his students to edit a classical text, a copy of which was then presented to every member of the college on New Year's day. In 1693 he assigned Charles Boyle, the eldest son of the third earl of Orrery, to edit the epistles of Phalaris (see above, *The Dispensary,* 5, 74 *n.*).

But the leud Crew affirm by all that's good
They'll ne'er disperse unless they've *Bently*'s Blood.
For that ill-natur'd Critic has undone
The rarest Piece of Wit that e'er was shown.
Till his rude Stroaks had thresh'd the empty Sheaf,
We thought there had been something else than Chaff.
Crown'd with Applause this Master Critic sits,
And round him ly the Spoils of ruin'd Wits.
How great a Man! What Rev'rence were his due,
Could he suppress the Critic's *Fastus* too?
As certain Words will Lunaticks enrage,
Who just before appear'd sedate and sage.
So do but *Lock* or *Books* or *Bentley* name,
The Wit's in clammy Sweats, or in a Flame.
  Horror and Shame! What would the Madmen have?
They dig up learned *Bernard*'s peaceful Grave.

Mill: John Mill (1645–1707) was a biblical scholar and principal of St. Edmund Hall, Oxford, where Blackmore passed 13 years as student and tutor. Bentley's first publication, which established his reputation, was a letter to John Mill, published as an appendix to Mill's edition of the *Chronicle of Malelas* (June 1691).

Charlett: Arthur Charlett (1655–1722) was a classics scholar and master of University College, Oxford.

95. *Bently:* Richard Bentley (1662–1742), the great classics scholar and butt of the Tory satirists, was the protégé of one Whig bishop and had been appointed keeper of the library in St. James's Palace in December 1693 by another

96–97. *undone/The rarest Piece of Wit: Dr. Bentley's Dissertations . . . Examin'd* was published in March 1698 under the name of Charles Boyle (see above, *The Dispensary, 5, 74 n.).* It was celebrated as a "very ingenious and learned book, penned in an elegant clean style" (Hearne, *II,* 364). But Bentley's reply, *A Dissertation upon the Epistles of Phalaris: with an Answer to the Objections of the Hon. Charles Boyle,* published in March 1699, effected "the most crushing blow that was ever dealt to insolent and aggressive sciolism" *(DNB, 2,* 310).

103. *Fastus:* pride, arrogance.

104. *certain Words:* Cf. "These two Words ["Presbytery" and "Commonwealth"], as if they carried some potent Charm, like some Notes of Musick, that strangely affect particular Persons, and as certain Accents vehemently disturb and enrage Lunaticks, had an unaccountable Influence upon many, who scar'd themselves with imaginary and phantastick Terrors" (Blackmore, *A True and Impartial History of the Conspiracy against the Person and Government of King William III,* 1723, p. 18).

106. *Lock:* John Locke "used to complement Blackmore highly for his skill in poetry" (Hearne, *II,* 395).

109. *Bernard:* Francis Bernard, physician to St. Bartholomew's Hospital, spoke five languages and owned the largest medical library ever collected in England (Wing B1992). He died in February 1698, 15 months before Garth published *The Dispensary,* in which he figures as Horoscope.

The Sacred-Urn of famous *Stillingfleet,*
We see prophan'd by the leud Sons of Wit.
The skilful *Tyson*'s Name they dare invade,
And yet they are undone without his Aid.
Tyson with base Reproaches they pursue,
Just as his *Moorfields* Patients use to do.
For next to Virtue, Learning they abhor,
Laugh at Discretion, but at Business more.
A Wit's an idle, wretched Fool of Parts,
That hates all Liberal and Mechanick Arts.
  Wit does enfeeble and debauch the Mind,
Before to Business or to Arts inclin'd.
How useless is a sauntring empty Wit,
Only to please with Jests at Dinner fit?
What hopeful Youths for Bar and Bench design'd,
Seduc'd by Wit have learned *Coke* declin'd?
For what has wit to do with Sense or Law?
Can that in Titles find or mend a Flaw?
Can Wit supply great *Treby*'s nervous Sense?
Or *Somers*' more than *Roman* Eloquence?
Which way has *Holt* gain'd Universal Fame?
What makes the World thy Praises, *Finch,* proclaim?

110. *Stillingfleet:* Edward Stillingfleet, the learned bishop of Worcester, who had been the patron of Richard Bentley, died in March 1699. He is mentioned (favorably) in *The Dispensary, 5,* 231.

112. *Tyson:* Edward Tyson, M.D. (1650–1708), fellow of the College of Physicians and master of the Bethlehem Hospital for the insane, was a distinguished anatomist and antiquarian. He figures prominently in *The Dispensary* (*4,* 106) as "Dull *Carus.*"

120–21. Cf. "Wits . . . *very rarely become eminently useful in any sort of Profession; for the most part they continue Triflers all their Days. . . . 'Tis remarkable that those Idle, and almost illiterate Young Men, that are call'd* Wits *in our Universities, are very inconsiderable Things elsewhere*" (Blackmore, *King Arthur. An Heroick Poem,* 1697, p. xi).

125. *Coke:* Sir Edward Coke (1552–1634), whose *Reports* and *Institutes* supplied the basis for seventeenth-century education in the law.

128. *Treby:* Sir George Treby (1644?–1700), one of the few learned men in the legal profession of the seventeenth-century (Evelyn, *5,* 438), served successively as solicitor-general, attorney-general, and chief justice of the court of common pleas. He is the subject of a panegyric in *POAS,* 1707, *4,* 365 ("As Indians, when a valu'd Hero dies").

129. *Somers:* See above, *The Dispensary, 1,* 51 *n.*

130. *Holt:* See above, *The Dispensary, 1,* 52 *n.*

131. *Finch:* See above, *The Dispensary, 1,* 50 *n.*

And charming *Powys,* what advanc'd thy Name?
'Twas Application, Knowledge of the Laws,
And your vast Fund of Sense, gain'd you Applause.
The Law will ne'er support the bant'ring Breed,
A *Sloan* may sometimes there, but Wits can ne'er succeed.
Radcliffe has Wit, and lavishes away
More in his Conversation every Day,
Than would supply a modern Writer's Play.
But 'tis not that, but the great Master's Skill,
Who with more Ease can cure, than *Colbatch* kill,
That does the grateful Realm with his Applauses fill.
Thy Learning *Gibbons,* and thy Judgment *How,*
Make you in envy'd Reputation grow.
This drew Invectives on you, all agree,
From the lean Small-craft of your Faculty.
Had you been Wits you had been both secure
From Business, and for Satyr too obscure,
Ill-natur'd, Arrogant, and very Poor.
But let Invectives still your Names assail,
Your Business is to Cure, and theirs to Rail.
Let 'em proceed and make your Names a Sport
In leud Lampoons, they've Time and Leisure for't.
Despise their Spite; the Thousands whom you raise

132. *Powys:* Sir Littleton Powys (1648?–1732) was another eloquent judge. Appointed to the Chester circuit in 1689, he was knighted in 1692 and raised to the court of exchequer in 1695. His "way of Speech" was said to outvy the Muses, "And ev'ry Period falling from his Tongue,/Reveals a Knowledge like his Reasons strong" ([William Pittis], *The Patriots* ["Once more, my Muse, a generous Offring make"] [1702], p. 11).

136. *Sloan:* See above, *Advice to a Painter,* 108 *n.*

137. *Radcliffe:* John Radcliffe (1650–1714) graduated B.A. from University College, Oxford, in 1669. He was then elected a fellow of Lincoln College and proceeded M.D. in 1682. Two years later he settled in Bow Street, Covent Garden, and soon became the most eminent general practitioner in London. "His conversation at this time was held in as much repute as his advice; and what with his pleasantry of discourse, and readiness of wit in making replies to any sort of questions, he was a diverting companion to the last degree. Insomuch that he was very often sent for, and presented with fees for pretended ailments, only for the gratification to hear him talk" (*Biographia Britannica,* 5, 3453).

141. *Colbatch:* See above, *The Dispensary,* 5, 63 *n.*

143. *Gibbons:* See above, *The Dispensary,* 4, 7 *n.*

How: See above, *The Dispensary,* 4, 96.

From threaten'd Death will bless you all their Days,
And spend the Breath you sav'd, in just and lasting Praise.
But Wit as now 'tis manag'd would undo
The Skill and Virtues we admire in you.
In *Garth* the Wit the Doctor has undone,
In *Smalwood* the Divine; Heav'ns guard poor *Addison.*
An able Senator is lost in *Moyle,*
And a fine Scholar sunk by Wit in *Boyle.*
After his foolish Rhimes both Friends and Foes
Conclude they know who did not write his Prose.
  Wit does our Schools and Colleges invade,
And has of Letters vast Destruction made.
Has laid the Muses choicest Gardens wast,
Broke their Inclosures and their Groves defac't.
We strive in Jests each other to exceed,
And shall e'er long forget to Write or Read.
Unless a Fund were settled once that cou'd
Make our deficient Sense and Learning good,
Nothing can be expected, for the Debt
By this loose Age contracted, is so great,
To set the Muses mortgag'd Acres free,
Our Bankrupt Sons must sell out-right the Fee.
The present Age has all their Treasure spent,
They can't the Int'rest pay at Five *per Cent.*
What to discharge it can we hope to raise

159. *Garth:* The success of *The Dispensary* encouraged detractors to belittle Garth's medical skill: "tho Poetry is a very pretty accomplishment, yet a Poet and a Physician are vastly different" (*Bellum Medicinale, or The Present State of Doctors and Apothecaries in London,* 1701, p. 9).

160. *Addison:* See above, *The Dispensary, 4,* 220 *n.*

161. *Moyle:* Walter Moyle (1672–1721) left Exeter College, Oxford, without taking a degree. He took up residence in the Middle Temple to read law, but soon moved to Covent Garden, loitered at Wills, and was praised by Dryden. "He quickly became acquainted with Mr. Congreve, Wycherley, and others . . . and among these was particularly distinguished by the vivacity of his wit" (*Biographia Britannica, 5,* 3192). He was elected a member of parliament for Saltash, Cornwall, in 1695, wrote against the standing army in 1697, but "avoided a second election" in order to devote himself to antiquarian pursuits.

162. *Boyle:* See 96–97 *n.,* above. Boyle's "Rhimes" were the admittedly "feeble" verses *To Dr. Garth, upon the Dispensary* ("Oh that some Genius, whose Poetick Vein"), the first of four commendatory poems that were published in all editions of *The Dispensary* after the first.

From *Durfey*'s, or from Poet *Dennis*'s Plays,
Or *Garth*'s Lampoon with little in't but Praise?
O *Somers, Talbot, Dorset, Montague,*
Grey, Sheffield, Cavendish, Pembroke, Vernon, you

180. *Durfey:* Thomas D'Urfey (1653–1723) was called "Sing-Song Durfey," but he stuttered—although he could speak plain "when he Swears 'G— Dam Me' "—and he made up for his diminutive size by an enormous output of verse: "Some 7953 Songs, 2250 Ballads, and 1956 Catches, besides Madrigals, Odes, and other Lyrick Copies of Verses"—not to mention 25 comedies that he wrote or adapted for the London stage (Thomas Brown, *Amusements Serious and Comical,* 1700, p. 51; George Fidge, *Wit for Money,* 1691, p. 20). Edward Ward claimed that D'Urfey "got some Reputation by turning of *Old Ditties* into *New Songs;* but lost it all by turning a *Spanish Romance* into an *English Stage-Play" (The London Spy,* No. 10, August 1699). The play was *The Comical History of Don Quixote,* which was cited both by the justices of the peace of Middlesex and by Jeremy Collier (Luttrell, *4,* 379; *A Short View of the Immorality, and Profaneness of the English Stage,* 1698, pp. 196–208). Swift set him down as "a Poet of vast Comprehension, an universal Genius, and most profound Learning" (*Prose, 1,* 22), but what posterity remembers is Addison's delightful recollection of Charles II leaning on D'Urfey's shoulder and "humming over a Song with him" (*The Guardian,* No. 67, 28 May 1713).

180. *Dennis:* See below, *The Pacificator,* 155 *n.* By 1699 John Dennis (1657–1734) had written only three plays, but the prologue to the first one, *A Plot, and No Plot, A Comedy* (1697), claimed that it had been written *"in some Coffee-house in* Exchange-alley," in ridicule of Blackmore's claim that *"the greatest part"* of *Prince Arthur* had been *"written in* Coffee-houses, *and in passing up and down the Streets" (King Arthur* [1697], p. v). In June 1696 Dennis published his *Remarks on a Book Entituled, Prince Arthur, an Heroick Poem* in which he complained that "the Action is nothing but an empty Fiction, of no manner of concern to us, without any kind of Instruction, and without any reasonable Meaning" (*Critical Works, 1,* 61). Blackmore acknowledged that there were *"considerable Defects"* in the poem, but insisted that its critics *"pretend to be displeas'd with* Prince Arthur, *because they have discover'd so many Faults in it: But there is good reason to believe they would have been more displeas'd, if they had discover'd fewer" (King Arthur* [1697], p. iii).

182. *Somers:* See above, *The Dispensary, 1,* 51 *n.*

Talbot: Charles Talbot, twelfth earl and first duke of Shrewsbury (1660–1718), was the namesake and godson of Charles II but deserted James II, mortgaged his estates for £40,000, and joined William of Orange in The Hague, landing with him at Torbay in November 1688. William, who called him "the *King of Hearts,"* made him his secretary of state (1689–90, 1694–December 1698), privy councillor, and lord chamberlain (October 1699–June 1700). *"Whigs* and *Tories* both spoke well" of him, but in William's reign he assumed leadership of the Whig junto. His effectiveness was severely limited, however, by real or feigned ill health and (unproved) accusations of treasonable correspondence with James II. He was "A Great Man," but with "Nothing of the Stiffness of a Statesman," and "generally beloved by the Ladies" (Macky, pp. 13, 15).

Dorset: See above, *The Dispensary, 2,* 67 *n.*

Montague: See above, *The Dispensary, 4,* 236 *n.*

183. *Grey:* presumably Thomas Grey, second earl of Stamford (1654–1720), "a very honest Man himself" (Macky, p. 72), whose only claim to dominion on Parnassus is that he was once the patron of Thomas Rymer (Curt A. Zimansky, *The Critical Works*

Who in *Parnassus* have Imperial Sway,
Whom all the Muses Subjects here obey,
Are in your Service and receive your Pay;
Exert your Soveraign Power, in Judgment sit
To regulate the Nation's Grievance, Wit.
Pity the cheated Folks that every Day
For Copper Wit good Sterling Silver pay.
If once the Muses Chequer would deny
To take false Wit, 'twould lose its currency.
Not a base Piece would pass, that pass'd before
Just wash'd with Sense, or thinly plated o'er.
  Set forth your Edict, let it be enjoyn'd
That all defective Species be recoyn'd.
St. Evremont and *Rymer* both are fit

---

of Thomas Rymer, New Haven, Yale University Press, 1956, p. xvi). A violent Whig who raised 400 horse and joined William of Orange in December 1688, he was rewarded by being appointed privy councillor (1694), one of the commissioners of trade and plantations (1695), and chancellor of the duchy of Lancaster (1697). In 1708 he was elected a fellow of the Royal Society.

Sheffield: See above, *The Dispensary, 4,* 218 *n.*

Cavendish: See above, *The Dispensary, 2,* 60 *n.*

Pembroke: See above, *The Dispensary, 2,* 55 *n.*

Vernon: See above, *The Dispensary, 2,* 68 *n.*

196. *Species be recoyn'd:* Cf. "After the Debates on this Subject, the House came to a Resolution, to recoin the Mony according to the Old Standard, both as to Weight and Fineness" ([Blackmore], *A Short History of the Last Parliament,* 1699, p. 30).

197. *St. Evremont:* Charles Marguetel de St. Denis de St. Évremond (1613?–1703), after a brilliant career as soldier, diplomat, and *littérateur,* fell into disfavor at court and fled France in 1661. In England he was welcomed by Charles II, who granted him a pension of £300 a year. He became the friend, not only of the rakes and royal mistresses, but of the poets Cowley and Waller, and of the philosophers Hobbes and—during visits to Holland—Spinoza. With his "satirical" smile and leather skullcap, he survived into the reign of William III—who remembered him only as "a major-general in the French service"—as an *arbiter elegantiarum* and memento of a more brilliant epoch.

Rymer: Thomas Rymer (1643?–1713), the dramatic critic and antiquarian, left Sidney Sussex College, Cambridge, without taking a degree and then read law at Gray's Inn. He published a translation of René Rapin's *Reflections sur la poëtique* in 1674 and his first critical work, *The Tragedies of the Last Age,* in 1677. In the latter year he also published *Edgar, or the English Monarch,* an unacted tragedy, in illustration of the "Aristotelian" rules and unities. Four years later during the Exclusion crisis, one of the Whig leaders encouraged him to compile *A General Draught and Prospect of Government in Europe* tracing the encroachment of parliaments upon the royal prerogative. Rymer's most important critical work, *A Short View of Tragedy,* appeared

To oversee the Coining of our Wit.
Let these be made the Masters of Essay,
They'll every Piece of Metal touch and weigh,
And tell which is too light, which has too much Allay.
'Tis true, that when the course and worthless Dross
Is purg'd away, there will be mighty Loss.
Ev'n *Congreve, Southern,* Manly *Wycherly,*
When thus refin'd will grievous Suff'rers be.
Into the melting Pot when *Dryden* comes,
What horrid Stench will rise, what noisome Fumes?
How will he shrink, when all his leud Allay,
And wicked Mixture shall be purg'd away?

---

in 1692, the same year in which he was appointed historiographer royal and began to compile the collection of treaties which became the *Foedera*. Blackmore, who also admired rules and unities, praised *"our own* excellent . . . *Mr.* Rymer" for having *"seen farther into them, than any of the* English Nation" (*Prince Arthur* [1695], sig. c1r).

203. *mighty Loss:* Cf. "the Farmer and Common Tradesman . . . abounded with Guineas which they receiv'd at Thirty Shillings. . . . [But] whatever Losses and Inconveniencys the People might suffer by the reducing of Guineas, yet the Mischiefs that arose . . . from not doing it, did infinitely over-balance those on the other side. Upon this the House resolv'd to lower the Price of Guineas . . . [to] Twenty two shillings" ([Blackmore], *A Short History of the Last Parliament,* 1699, pp. 33–34).

204. *Congreve:* See above, *The Dispensary, 4,* 221 *n.;* Congreve was an habitual offender in this respect. Alexander Pope, for example, told Spence that he "never knew anybody that had so much wit as Congreve" (Spence, *1,* 304).

Southern: Thomas Southerne (1659–1746) graduated from Trinity College, Dublin, in 1680 and had written seven plays by 1699, of which the most successful was *Oroonoko* (1696). His wit is attested by Dryden: "Yet those who blame thy Tale, commend thy wit;/So *Terence* Plotted; but so *Terence* Writ" *(Poems, 2,* 581).

Wycherly: See above, *The Dispensary, 4,* 211 *n.* As George Granville said, "He is not only the greatest *Wit,"* but "by the unanimous Assent of the World, is call'd, The *Manly Wycherley" (Letters of Wit, Politicks, and Morality,* pp. 254–56). *Manly* is the misanthropic hero in *The Plain Dealer* (1677)

206. *Dryden:* Cf. Henry Hall, *To Mr. Charles Hopkins upon my Lending Him Mr. Wallers Poems* (Leeds University MS. Brotherton Collection Lt.q.5, p. 51): "He [Dryden] first our native Language did refine,/Rugged & Rough, like mettle in the Mine,/He purg'd the Dross & Stampt it into Coin."

207. *noisome Fumes:* Cf. Dryden, *To the Pious Memory of the Accomplisht Young Lady Mrs. Anne Killigrew:*

> . . . why were we hurry'd down
> This lubrique and adult'rate age, . . .
> T'increase the steaming Ordures of the Stage?
> (*Poems, 1,* 461)

When once his boasted Heaps are melted down,
A Chest-full scarce will yield one Sterling Crown.
Those who will *Dennis* melt and think to find
A goodly Mass of Bullion left behind,
Do, as th'*Hibernian* Wit, who as 'tis told,
Burnt his gilt Leather to collect the Gold.
But what remains will be so pure, 'twill bear
Th'Examination of the most severe.
'Twill *Somers'* Scales and *Talbot*'s Test abide,
And with their Mark please all the World beside.
But when our Wit's call'd in, what will remain
The Muses learned Commerce to maintain?
How pensive will our Beaus and Ladies sit?
They'll mutiny for want of ready Wit.
That such a failure no Man may incense,
Let us erect a Bank for Wit and Sense.
A Bank whose current Bills may Payment make,
Till new Mill'd Wit shall from the *Mint* come back.
Let *Somers, Dorset, Sheffield, Montague,*
Lend but their Names, the Project then will do.
The Bank is fixt if these will under-write;
They pay the vastest Sums of Wit at sight.
These are good Men, in whom we all agree,
Their Notes for Wit are good Security.
Duncombs and *Claytons* in *Parnassus* all,

210–11. Cf. Dryden, Preface to *Troilus and Cressida* (1679): "if [Shakespeare's] embroideries were burnt down, there would still be silver at the bottom of the melting-pot" (*Prose, 1,* ii, 295).

213. *Bullion:* Cf. Wentworth Dillon, earl of Roscommon, *An Essay on Translated Verse* (1684), 53: "The weighty *Bullion* of *One Sterling Line*."

216–19. When he revised the poem in 1718 Blackmore deleted these lines, which Samuel Johnson called "an Abatement of the Censure" of Dryden and Dennis.

221. *Commerce to maintain:* Cf. " 'Twas plain, *England* could not subsist unless some Expedient was found out to support its Trade, till the New Mony return'd from the Mint" ([Blackmore], *A Short History of the Last Parliament,* p. 31).

226. *current Bills may Payment make:* Cf. "Parliament agreed, to augment and enlarge the Common Capital Stock of the Bank of *England* by admitting new Subscriptions . . . in Tallys and Bank Notes. . . . [Whereupon] the Credit of the Bank began to recover apace, till in a short time their Notes were all equal with, and their Bills that bore Interest, better than Mony" (ibid., pp. 50–51).

234. *Duncomb:* After serving as an apprentice to Edward Backwell, the leading goldsmith in London, Charles Duncombe set up in business for himself about 1675

Who cannot sink unless the Hill should fall.
Their Bills, tho' ne'er supported by Trustees,
Will through *Parnassus* circulate with ease.
If these come in, the Bank will quickly fill,
All will be scrambling up *Parnassus* Hill.
They'll crowd the Muses Hall and throng to write
Great sums of Wit, and will be Gainers by't.
Vanbrugh and *Congreve* both are Wealthy, they
Have Funds of Standard-Sense, need no Allay,
And yet mix'd Metal oft they pass away.
The Bank may safely their Subscriptions take,
But let 'em for their Reputation's sake,
Take care their Payments they in Sterling make.
Codron will under-write his *Indian* Wit,

"at the Grasshopper in Lombard Street." He soon became "immensely rich," a fact which was advertised in 1696 when, during the recoinage which made it difficult for most people to find "current money to carry on . . . the smalest concernes" (Evelyn, *5*, 245), Duncombe bought Helmsley Castle, the estate of the late duke of Buckingham, for £95,000 cash (Ralph, *2*, 778). He was knighted in October 1699 (Le Neve, p. 468).

Clayton: Sir Robert Clayton (1629–1707), another "poor boy," was apprenticed to his uncle, Robert Abbot, a London scrivener, and came to be "vastly rich" (Le Neve, p. 270), a director of the Bank of England, lord mayor (1679–80), and Whig member of parliament for London, or for the rotten borough of Bletchingley, in Surrey, which he owned.

236. *supported by Trustees: Cf.* "[Parliament] created Mony . . . by authorising the Lords of his Majesty's Treasury to issue out Bills from the Exchequer . . . to supply the place of our Silver Coin, which was call'd in to be new made. . . . By this means the Credit of the aforesaid Notes . . . dayly arose nearer to *Par* . . . and whereas the Trustees contracted with to exchange them for Mony, were before as a Premium allow'd Ten *per Cent.*, they have been since contented to do it for Four" ([Blackmore], *A Short History of the Last Parliament,* pp. 53–54). As Samuel Johnson observed, Blackmore "had lived in the City till he had learned its note" (*Lives, 2,* 328).

242. *Vanbrugh:* In 1699 Captain John Vanbrugh (1664–1726), as he was then known, was enjoying the success of his first plays, *The Relapse: or Virtue in Danger* (1696) and *The Provok'd Wife* (1697), and of his witty rejoinder to Collier's *Short View of the Immorality, and Profaneness of the English Stage,* which had attacked them both.

248. *Codron:* Christopher Codrington (1668–1710) was born in Barbados, educated at Christ Church, Oxford, "made all the campagnes during the war" as a captain in his majesty's foot guards (Luttrell, *4*, 430), and succeeded his father in May 1699 as governor general of the Leeward Islands. Before leaving to assume this post in August 1700, Codrington enjoyed a brief career in London as poet and wit, and even fought a duel about the etymology of a Greek word (*The Post Boy,* No. 840, 24–27 August 1700; BM MS. Add. 4245, f. 74). He contributed a set of commendatory verses to *The Dispensary* ("Ask me not, Friend, what I Approve or Blame"), which ridiculed Blackmore as "the City-Bard," and mobilized the Covent Garden wits to an effort of mock-commendation of *A Satyr against Wit.* In this work, *Commendatory Verses*

Far-fetch'd indeed, so 'twill the Ladies fit.
By Hearsay he's a Scholar, and they say
The Man's a sort of Wit too in his way.
Let 'em receive whatever *Prior* brings,
In nobler Strains no happy Genius sings.
'Tis Complaisance when to divert his Friends,
He to *facetious Fancies* condescends.
Tate will subscribe, but set no Payment-Day,
For his slow Muse you must with Patience stay,
He's honest, and as Wit comes in, will pay.
But how would all this new Contrivance Prize,
How high in value would their Actions rise?
Would *Freek* engraft his solid, manly Sense,
His Learning *Lock, Fleetwood* his Eloquence.

---

on the Author of the Two Arthurs and the Satyr against Wit (28 February 1700), Codrington's contribution appears first, in the place of honor. It is entitled *A Short and True History of the Author of the Satyr against Wit* ("By Nature meant, by Want a Pedant made").

255. *facetious Fancies:* The phrase is quoted from the first edition of *The Dispensary;* see *The Dispensary,* textual note *4,* 227.

256. *Tate:* Nahum Tate (1652–1715) graduated B.A. from Trinity College, Dublin, in 1672 and published his first volume of poems in London five years later. His version of Shakespeare's *King Lear,* with its happy ending, was first acted in 1681 and the next year he collaborated with Dryden to produce *The Second Part of Absalom and Achitophel (POAS,* Yale, *3,* 278). He succeeded Thomas Shadwell as poet laureate in November 1692 and his latest work, published only a few weeks before *A Satyr against Wit,* was "a curious ode" celebrating William's forty-ninth birthday (Luttrell, *4,* 579).

260. *Actions:* shares in the Bank for Wit and Sense, imagined to be a joint stock company.

261. *Freek:* John Freke left Oxford without taking a degree, studied law at the Middle Temple, and was one of the first supporters of Shaftesbury. In May 1676 he was committed to the Tower on charges of high treason for having written *The History of Insipids* ("Chaste, pious, prudent Charles the Second") *(POAS,* Yale, *1,* 243). He became a close friend and collaborator of John Locke in the 1690s and remained active in Whig propaganda at least until 1704 (*Philological Quarterly, 44* [October 1965], 472–83; *The Taunton-Dean Letter, from E*[*dward*] *C*[*larke*] *to J*[*ohn*] *F*[*reke*] *at the Grecian Coffee-House,* 1701; *A Poem on the Safe Arrival of the Spanish Monarch Charles III. to the British Shoar . . . Written by Mr. John Freke* ["Arise, Behold the Royal Fleet, whose Name"], 1704).

262. *Fleetwood:* William Fleetwood (1657?–1723) first achieved fame as a preacher by a sermon delivered in the chapel of King's College, Cambridge, whence he had graduated B.A. in 1679 and M.A. 1689 (Wing F1251). He was a staunch Whig, one of the king's chaplains-in-ordinary, rector of St. Augustine's in Watling Street, and a lecturer at St. Dunstan's in the West. Evelyn heard him preach at the latter church and pronounced it "a most excellent discourse" (Evelyn, *5,* 222).

The Bank when thus establish'd will supply
Small Places, for the little, loitt'ring Fry
That follow *Garth,* or at *Will Urwin*'s ply.
Their Station will be low, but ne'ertheless
For this Provision they should Thanks express:
'Tis sad to be a Wit and Dinnerless.
Tonson the great Wit-Jobber of the Age,
And all the Muses Broakers will engage
Their several Friends to cry the Actions up,
And all the railing Mouths of Envy stop.
Ye Lords who o'er the Muses Realm preside,
Their Int'rests manage and their Empire guide;
Regard your Care, regard the sacred State,
Laid by Invaders wast and desolate.
Tartars and *Scythians* have in barb'rous Bands
Riffled the Muses and o'er-run their Lands.
The Native Subjects, who in Peace enjoy'd
The happy Seat, are by the Sword destroy'd.
Gardens and Groves *Parnassus* did adorn,
Condemn'd to Thistles now, and curst with Thorn.
Instead of Flowers and Herbs of wholsom use,
It does rank Weeds and pois'nous Plants produce,
Fitter to be for *Witches* a Retreat,
Owls, Satyrs, Monkies, than the Muses Seat.
Ev'n these debauch'd by *Dryden* and his Crew,
Turn Bawds to Vice and wicked Aims pursue.
Therefore some just and wholesome Laws ordain,
That may this wild Licentiousness restrain.
To Virtue and to Merit have regard,
To punish learn, you know how to reward.

264. *the little, loitt'ring Fry:* Cf. *The Dunciad* (1742), *4,* 337–39: "a lazy lolling sort . . . Of ever-listless Loit'rers."

265. *Will Urwin:* proprietor of Will's coffeehouse, Bow Street (Lillywhite, pp. 655–59).

269. *Tonson:* By engaging Dryden to translate Virgil, the bookseller Jacob Tonson (1656?–1736) became in effect the first modern publisher. In May 1698 he was presented for printing two obscene plays, Congreve's *The Double Dealer,* and D'Urfey's *The Comical History of Don Quixote* (Luttrell, *4,* 379). For Blackmore he published *King Arthur* (1697) with A. & J. Churchill, and *A Short History of the Last Parliament* (1699), but not *Prince Arthur* (1695) or *A Satyr against Wit.*

287. *these:* the Muses.

Let those Corrections have, and not Applause,
That Heav'n affront and ridicule its Laws.
No sober Judge will Atheism e'er permit
To pass for Sense, or Blasphemy for Wit.
Declare that what's Obscene shall give Offence,
Let want of Decency be want of Sense.
Send out your Guards to scow'r the Ways and seize
The Footpads, Outlaws, Rogues and Rapparees,
That in the Muses Country rob and kill,
And make *Parnassus* worse than *Shooter*'s Hill.
Poetic Justice should on these be shown,
Or soon the Muses State must be undone.
For now an honest Man can't peep abroad,
And all chast Muses dread the dangerous Road.
If in *Parnassus* any *needy Wit*
Should filch and Petty Larceny commit,
If he should riffle Books, and Pilferer turn,
An Inch beside the Nose the *Felon* burn.
Let him distinguish'd by this Mark appear,
And in his Cheek a plain *Signetur* wear.
Chastise the Poets who our Laws invade,
And hold with *France* for Wit an Owling Trade.
Felonious *Garth* pursuing this Design,
Smuggles French Wit, as others Silks and Wine.

298. *Sense: "Immodest words* admit of no defence,/ For want of *Decency* is Want of *Sense*" (Roscommon, *An Essay on Translated Verse* [1684], 113–14).

302. *Shooter's Hill:* in Blackheath, a place of notorious danger to travelers on the Dover road. The bodies of executed criminals were left hanging there, which Pepys found "a filthy sight" (*Diary, 2,* 9).

303. *Poetic Justice:* J. E. Spingarn said that Jeremy Collier, *A Short View of the Profaneness, and Immorality of the English Stage* (1698), "follows the arguments of Blackmore pretty closely" and that "'Poetical justice' is the basis of his [Collier's] theory" (Spingarn, *1,* lxxxvi; *3,* 335).

310. *burn:* In the quarter-sessions at Old Bailey in the month before *A Satyr against Wit* was published, "six were burnt in the left cheek" (Luttrell, *4,* 572).

312. *Signetur:* See above, *The Dispensary, 5,* 224 *n.*

314. *Owling:* smuggling; cf. "many ill Men continued to export English Wool . . . to foreign Parts, to the unspeakable detriment of the Nation, notwithstanding the severe Laws that were in Force against such offenders" ([Blackmore], *A Short History of the Last Parliament,* p. 61).

316. *Silks:* Cf. "The Parliament likewise this Session [the third session of the third parliament of William III, 1697–98], apply'd themselves with great Diligence to discover such Offenders, who by fraudulent and surreptitious Ways had carry'd on a

But let his Suff'rings doubly be severe,
For he both steals it there, and runs it here.
Condemn all those who 'gainst the Muses Laws
Sollicit Votes, and canvas for Applause.
When *Torman* writes he rattles up and down,
And makes what Friends he can, to make the Town.
By Noise and Violence they force a Name,
For this leud Town has Setters too for Fame:
It is not Merit now that recommends,
But he's allow'd most Sense, that makes most Friends.
In Panegyrick let it be a Rule,
That for his Sense none praise a Wealthy Fool.
Dryden condemn, who taught Men how to make
Of Dunces Wits, an Angel of a Rake.
By Treats and Gifts our Youth may now commence
Wits without Brains, and Scholars without Sense.
They cry up *Darfel* for a Wit; to treat
Let him forbear, and they their Words will eat.
Great *Atticus* himself these men would curse,
Should *Atticus* appear without his Purse.
Of any Price you may bespeak a Name,
For Characters they cut, and retail Fame.
Bounty's the Measure of a Patron's Mind,
For they have still most Sense, that prove most kind.
Fame on Great Men's a Charge that still goes on,
For Wits, like Scriv'ners, take for *Pro* and *Con*.
Without his Gold what generous *Oran* writ,

secret Commerce with *France;* and to the great Damage of this Kingdom, had brought in for divers Years past, great quantitys of Alamodes and Lutestrings [kinds of silk]" ([Blackmore], *A Short History of the Last Parliament,* p. 61).

318. *runs:* imports illegally, smuggles. Earliest use cited by *OED,* s.v. *run,* 45c, is 1706.

321. *Torman:* To one reader (University of Illinois copy of *A*), Torman suggested Dr. Edward Baynard, but see below, 384 *n*.

333. *Darfel:* unidentified.

335. *Atticus:* John Somers; see above, *The Dispensary, 1,* 51 *n*.

338. *cut:* a pun on "cut" meaning "slandered, injured by gossip" (cf. "character assassins") and "cut" meaning "divided into small quantities and sold at higher unit price" (cf. French *tailler*).

343. *Oran:* Richard Norton, "a Person of Quality" and author of *Pausanias, The Betrayer of His Country* (1696), was recommended to Blackmore as a model of "*Athenian* Wit" in *The Dispensary, 4,* 224–25. Blackmore's emendation of this line

Had ne'er been Standard, sheer *Athenian* Wit.
Those who by Satyr would reform the Town,
Should have some little Merit of their own,
And not be Rakes themselves below Lampoon.
For all their Libels Panegyricks are,
They're still read backward like a Witch's Pray'r.
Elliot's Reproofs who does not make his Sport?
Who'll e'er repent that *Smalwood* does exhort?
Therefore let Satyr-Writers be supprest,
Or be reform'd by cautious *Dorset*'s Test.
'Tis only *Dorset*'s Judgment can command
Wit, the worst Weapon in a Madman's Hand.
The Biting Things by that great Master said,
Flow from rich Sense, but theirs from want of Bread.
Whatever is by them in Satyr writ

---

in *C* makes it possible to reconstruct the heavily cropped annotation in the University of Illinois copy of *A:* "[Norton] and [Hen]ly's Pausanias." Anthony Henley may have been added because he wrote the two songs in *Pausanias* which were set to music by Henry Purcell (*London Stage, 1,* 418, 461). Norton, who was the Whig member for Hampshire (1695–98, 1702–05), contributed *A Merry Ballad on the City Bard* ("In *London* City near *Cheapside*") to *Commendatory Verses* and was identified as "the Ballad-making Senator" in the reply (*Discommendatory Verses,* p. 25).

345. *reform the Town:* In the preface to the second edition, Garth recounted that he had undertaken *The Dispensary* in an "endeavour to Rally some of our disaffected Members [like Blackmore] into a Sense of their Duty."

348. *all their Libels Panegyricks are:* Cf. "The Slanders therefore and Invectives of these Men who heartily wish'd the Ruin of our Establishment, is an honourable and lasting Encomium on the Proceedings of this Assembly [the third parliament of William III]" ([Blackmore], *A Short History of the Last Parliament,* p. 64).

349. *read backward like a Witch's Pray'r:* Cf. Charles Sackville, earl of Dorset, *On Mr. Edward Howard Upon his British Princes,* 2–3: ". . . read it backward like a witch's prayer,/'Twill do as well" (*POAS,* Yale, *1,* 338).

350. *Elliot:* Presumably the "John Elliot of New Coll. LL.D" (Wood, *4,* 2279) whose sermon, *The Grace of God Asserted,* was published in 1695 (Wing E548a). Another possibility, however, is the infamous Robert Elliot, who graduated M.A. from the University of Edinburgh in 1668. This Elliot was deposed as minister of Lessuden, or St. Boswell's in Roxburghshire, in 1690, for refusing to take the oaths to William and Mary. When hired by Lord William Paulet to transcribe Burnet's *History of His Own Time,* he illicitly made extracts available to the nonjuror Charles Leslie (Hew Scott, *Fasti Ecclesiae Scoticanae,* 3 vols. in 6, Edinburgh and London, 1866–71, I, ii, 552; John Cockburn, *A Specimen of Some Free and Impartial Remarks on Publick Affairs and Particular Persons,* 1724, Preface, pp. 64–65).

353. *Dorset's Test:* "Those dang'rous weapons [pen and ink] should be kept from fools" (Charles Sackville, earl of Dorset, *On the Same Author upon his New Utopia,* 29; *POAS, Yale, 1,* 341).

Is Malice all, but his, excess of Wit.
To lash our Faults and Follies is his Aim;
Theirs is good Sense and Merit to defame.
In *Dorset* Wit (and therefore still 'twill please)
Is Constitution, but in them Disease.
  Care should be taken of the Impotent,
That in your Service have their Vigor spent.
They should have Pensions from the Muses State,
Too Old to Write, too Feeble to Translate.
But let the lusty Beggar-Wits that lurk
About the Hill, be seiz'd and set to Work.
Besides, some Youths Debauches will commit,
And surfeit by their undigested Wit.
Th'intoxicating Draught they cannot bear,
It takes their Heads before they are aware.
Weak Brothers by Excesses it appears
Have oft been laid up Months, and some whole Years.
By one Debauch a tender Wit was try'd,
And he 'tis known was likely to have dy'd.
That neither Sick nor Poor you may neglect,
For all the Muses *Invalids,* erect
An Hospital upon *Parnassus* Hill,
And settle Doctors there of Worth and Skill.
This Town can numbers for your Service spare,
That live obscure and of Success despair.
Fracar has many sour Invectives said,
And Jests upon his own Profession spred,
And with good Reason, 'twill not find him Bread.
And some such Doctors, sure you may persuade

384. *Fracar:* One reader (Huntington copy of *A* "The Second Edition") identified Fracar as "Baynard," presumably Dr. Edward Baynard (b. 1641?) and lines 385–86 seem to be reflected in Baynard's contribution to *Commendatory Verses,* entitled *Melancholy Reflections on the Deficiency of Useful Learning* ("Short are our Powers, tho' infinite our Will"). Blackmore's quarrel with Baynard must have been based on personal grounds, for professionally the two were equally intransigent. Baynard called one president of the College of Physicians "the son of A Whore" and refused to extend his support to another. He walked out of the meeting convened to promulgate the new statutes and repeatedly refused to subscribe to the dispensary (*Annals, 6,* 62; *7,* 86, 91; [John Badger], *A Catalogue of the Fellows and Other Members of the Royal College of Physicians,* 1695 [BM 777.l.2 [8]).

387. *some such Doctors:* Blackmore alludes to what the subscribers called "the Vilest

To labour at th'Apothecary's Trade.
They'll Med'cines make, and at the Mortar sweat,
Let 'em pound Drugs, they have no Brains to beat.

Objection" to the dispensary, namely, that with the exception of the president, Sir Thomas Millington, the members of the College of Physicians who subscribed to the dispensary were neither so distinguished nor so successful as some of those who refused to subscribe, namely, Dr. Edward Tyson, Fellow of the Royal Society and a distinguished anatomist, Dr. John Radcliffe, the most successful practitioner of the age, Dr. Hugh Chamberlen, the fashionable "Man Midwife," and Sir Richard Blackmore himself, physician-in-ordinary to William III.

1700

Daniel Defoe

The Pacificator
(15 February 1700)

September 1697 to May 1702, a brief interval of peace between two foreign wars, left the field open for intensified domestic strife in England. "The Age of the *Gracchi*," as Swift called it, was, like its classical counterpart, an age of factions: Jacobites *vs.* Williamites, the New Country-Party *vs.* the Whig junto, Church *vs.* stage, "Apothecaries Physicians" *vs.* "Society-Physicians," friends of Derby ale *vs.* enemies of Derby ale, Galenists *vs.* spagyrists, Cheapside *vs.* Covent Garden. It was even, as a Marxist critic has pointed out, an incident in the class struggle: bourgeois *vs.* aristocrat (Robert M. Krapp, *Science & Society, 10* [1946], 80–92). It remained for Defoe, in the present poem, to provide the right terms for the literary dimension of this conflict: "The Men of Sense against the Men of Wit" (line 59).

The poem opens with a fine, mock-heroic flourish: Englishmen are so contentious and quarrelsome that for lack of a better enemy they will fight each other. Civil war must again be close at hand, for the war of words has already begun between the Men of Sense and the Men of Wit (lines 1–60).

The body of the poem, lines 61–307, describes this war of words. The Men of Sense began the war (Blackmore, *Prince Arthur. An Heroick Poem,* 1695), but were beaten back by a massive counter-attack (Dennis, *Remarks on a Book Entituled, Prince Arthur, an Heroick Poem,* 1696). The Men of Sense rallied, however (Blackmore, *King Arthur. An Heroick Poem,* 1697; Collier, *A Short View of the Immorality, and Profaneness of the English Stage,* 1698), but Collier was overpowered and slain and the Men of Sense were again forced to retreat. The image of Collier lying in state, in *"Honours Truckle-bed"* (line 111), until the *parousia* of Sense, is one of the most delightful details in the poem.

The Men of Sense rallied again, however (Blackmore, *A Satyr against Wit,* 1699), and this time the Wits were "Disperc'd, Disgrac'd, and Overthrown" (line 305). Now, however, the speaker has learned that the Wits are preparing to mount another offensive (*Commendatory Verses, on the Author of the Two Arthurs and the Satyr against Wit*) and he intervenes, in the coda (lines 308–458), to demand that the destruction be stopped and the antagonists reconciled, for

> *United: Wit* and *Sense,* makes Science thrive,
> *Divided:* neither *Wit* nor *Sense* can live.
> (393–94)

He seeks some second Christ of Sense who will establish a commonwealth of wit on earth, who will show each poet "his proper Talent," and impose penalties for noncompliance, for bawdry, and for blasphemy. Although there is no evidence that it did so, it is not difficult to imagine Pope's mind working over this material and conceiving *The Dunciad.*

Although Defoe glances at political issues, such as the bitter struggle over the standing army (lines 33–36), the subject of the poem is literature and the tone remains light and fanciful—and witty. William Lee, in 1869, thought it was "one of Defoe's best productions in verse" and admired the "antithetic force and point" of lines 355–72 which define "wit" and "sense." Defoe's conception of wit as the spontaneous, subconscious element in creativeness, is much closer to Dryden's "school-distinction" of "Wit writing" than it is to Blackmore's concept of wit as "Enameling." Defoe clearly sympathizes with Blackmore's attack on blasphemy and profaneness—it was, after all, the policy of a government of which Defoe was the main propagandist—but he does not belittle wit itself. Nor does he belittle delight as an effect of literature. He knows that *"Sense-abstracted* has no Power to please" (line 362). He also knows that what he admires in poetry is exactly what Dryden admired in poetry, "turns . . . and lively images" (*Modern Language Notes, 44* [June 1929], 377–78). And although it is not without *longueurs, The Pacificator* frequently achieves both. It represents a remarkable advance over *An Encomium upon a Parliament* (1699) in the development of Defoe's poetic technique.

Defoe's opinion of the poem may be guessed from the fact that he did not include it, along with *The True-Born Englishman,* in *The Genuine Works* of 1703, but he did include it in *A Second Volume of the Writings of the Author of the True-Born Englishman* in 1705. *The Pacificator* is dated 15 February 1700 by the Luttrell copy in the Clark Library, Los Angeles; Luttrell added one of his infrequent comments, which sums up the poem very nicely: "Sharp upon the Several Poets."

The Pacificator

What *English* Man, without Concern, can see
The Approach of Bleeding *Britain*'s Destiny?
That Glorious Land which Justly did Preside,
For Wit and Wealth, o'r all the World beside?
In vain Victorious *NASSAU* did Advance
His Conquering Arms against the Power of *France,*
Since from those Conquests he is hardly come,
But here's a Civil War broke out at Home:
Britannia's Warlike Sons disturb the Isle,
Delighting one another to Dispoil,
Enur'd to Discord, Envy, and Debate,
Hereditary Frenzies of the State.
The Fruits of Ten Years War they now prevent,
By Civil Feuds, and Private Discontent.
The Peace We Gain'd! Does it so Cheap appear,
To Prize so Low, what We have bought so Dear?
The Blood, the Treasure, which has been Destroy'd!
Methinks We shou'd with War and Wounds be Cloy'd,
But 'twill not be, We cannot hope to find
That in the Birth which is not in the Kind:
For *Pride,* and *Strife,* are Natives of our Soil,
Freeholders born, and have Possess'd the Isle
Long before *Julius Caesar* Landed here,
Or *Picts,* or *Painted Brittons* did appear,

13. *Ten Years War:* It was actually a nine years' war. William of Orange published a declaration of reasons for his invasion of England in September 1688. Louis XIV responded in November by declaring war on the United Provinces and the war was concluded by the treaty of Ryswick, signed in September 1697.

17. *The Blood, the Treasure:* John Trenchard estimated the cost of the war to be "forty Millions of Money, and the Blood of three hundred thousand Men" (*An Argument, Shewing, That a Standing Army is Inconsistent with a Free Government,* 1697, p. 30), but modern estimates put the loss of life at 200,000 (*Cambridge Historical Journal, 11* [1954], 179). Charles Davenant's two estimates of the monetary cost, 60 millions and 41 millions, were subject to much ridicule, for "A mistake of 19 Millions is no small one" (*Some Remarks on the Bill for Taking, Examining and Stating the Publick Accounts,* 1702, p. 12).

A stubborn People, Barbarous and Rude;
Who, like the *Kentish Men,* were ne'r Subdu'd.
  Fierce *English Men,* in Blood and Wounds delight,
For want of Wars, with one another fight:
Nothing's so dangerous to them as Peace,
To feed the Flame, and nourish the Disease;
No Laws can this Contentious humour Curb,
Their Charter's such, they will themselves Disturb.
O *Julian, Julian,* who begun the Cry
Against our Safety, for our Liberty,
Who wou'd no Mercenary Troops allow,
Wou'd you Disband our Standing Army now?
Behold a Civil War is just at hand,
I'th' very bowels of your Native Land:
The strong Contention's grown to such a hight,
The Pen's already drawn, and has begun the fight.
The Pen's the certain Herald of a War,
And Points it out like any Blazing Star:

26. *the Kentish Men, were ne'r Subdu'd:* This seems to have been a commonplace; cf. [Thomas Baker], *Tunbridge-Walks; Or, The Yeoman of Kent,* 1736, p. 34. "Men born east of the river Medway . . . are said to have met [William] the Conqueror in a body, each carrying a green bough in his hand, the whole appearing like a moving wood; and thereby obtaining a confirmation of their ancient privileges" ([Francis Grose], *A Classical Dictionary of the Vulgar Tongue,* 2nd ed., 1788, sig. T2v).

33. *Julian:* Samuel Johnson (1649–1703), the "Arch Whig," was domestic chaplain to Lord William Russell in 1682 when he earned a place in *The Second Part of Absalom and Achitophel* by publishing *Julian the Apostate,* which demonstrated, in the words of the poem, "That Saints own no Allegiance to their Prince" (*POAS,* Yale, *3,* 300). In the next reign he was imprisoned, whipped, and degraded from the clergy for his republican writings. Even though he was said "to have done more towards paving the way for King William's Revolution, than any man in England besides" (Edmund Calamy, *An Historical Account of My Own Life,* ed. John T. Rutt, 2nd ed., 2 vols., 1830, *1,* 94), Johnson adhered firmly to "his darling doctrine of the power of the people over kings" and did not trust even William with the means of tyranny (*Hatton Correspondence,* ed. Edward M. Thompson, 2 vols., 1878, *2,* 213). Defoe seems to have attributed to Johnson three pamphlets against standing armies that he did not write: *An Argument Shewing that a Standing Army is Inconsistent with a Free Government* (1697), *A Second Part of the Argument Shewing that a Standing Army is Inconsistent with a Free Government* (1697), by John Trenchard and Walter Moyle, and *A Discourse concerning Militia's* (1697) , by Andrew Fletcher (*Some Reflections on a Pamphlet Lately Publish'd, Entituled, An Argument Shewing that a Standing Army is Inconsistent with a Free Government,* 1697, p. 17; *An Argument Shewing that a Standing Army, with Consent of Parliament, is not Inconsistent with a Free Government,* 1698, pp. 1–2). Defoe's emendation of this line in 1705 identifies the leaders in the Commons of the attack on the standing army.

Men Quarrel first, and Skirmish with ill Words,
And when they're heated then they draw their Swords;
As little Bawling Curs begin to Bark,
And bring the Mastive on you in the Dark.
We had some Jealousies of this last Year,
Both sides rais'd Forces, both in Arms appear;
But some Sage Doctors did them both Advise,
To make it up without Hostilities:
But the deep Quarrell's now of such a Nature,
As *Magna Charta* fights with *Alma Mater;*
The *Doctors fight,* and who shall heal the Matter?
The Dreadful Armies are Drawn out to fight,
Encamp'd at large in one anothers sight;
Their Standards are the *Red Rose* and the *White.*
Nothing but dire Destruction does Impend,
And who knows where the fatal Strife will end?
The Men of Sense against the Men of Wit,
Eternal fighting must determine it.
Great *Nokor* does the Men of Sense Command,
Prince *Arthur* Trailes a Pike at his Right Hand;
Heroic *Nokor* made the first Attack,
And threw *Drammatick Wit* upon its Back;
Sixteen Battalions of *Old Brittons* stand,
Enrich'd with Conquest from the *Neustrian Strand,*
Ready to Charge when he the Signal makes;
And thus the Bloody Combat undertakes.
His Sence was good, but see what Fate Decrees!
His hasty Talent threw him on his Knees,

61. *Nokor: B* adds a marginal note: "*Blackmore.*"

63. *the first Attack:* "Our Poets seem engag'd in a general *Confederacy* to ruin the End of their own Art, to expose *Religion* and *Virtue,* and bring *Vice* and *Corruption of Manners* into Esteem and Reputation. The Poets that write for the Stage (at least a great part of 'em) seem deeply concern'd in this Conspiracy. These are the *Champions* that charge *Religion* with such desperate Resolution, and have given it so many deep and ghastly Wounds. The Stage was an Outwork or Fort rais'd for the Protection and Security of the Temple, but the Poets that kept it, have revolted, and basely betray'd it, and what is worse, have turn'd all their *Force* and discharg'd all their *Artillery* against the Place their Duty was to defend" (Richard Blackmore, *Prince Arthur. An Heroick Poem,* 1695, sig. A1v).

66. *Neustria:* The Merovingian kingdom of Neustria included northwestern France and Burgundy.

A Storm of Words the Hero overtook,
Disorder'd all his Lines, and all his Squadrons broke,
The adverse Troops pour'd in their *Light Dragoons,*
Charg'd him with *Forty thousand Arm'd Lampoons;*
The Shock surpriz'd him into a Retreat,
And *Wits Gazette* Proclaim'd a huge Defeat;
Printed a List of Wounded and of Slain,
And bragg'd he ne'r cou'd Rally up again.
  But *Nokor,* like a Prudent General,
Resum'd new Courage from a seeming Foil,
The same Campagne again in Arms appear'd,
And what the *Prince* had lost, the *King* repair'd;
Apollo Knighted him upon the spot,
With other Royal Bounties I've forgot.
The Wits Commanders tho' they did retreat,
Will not allow it to be a Defeat;
Their Troops, they say, soon made a stand again,
Besides they lost but Thirteen thousand Men.
  Collier came next in order to the Charge,
His Squadrons thin, altho' his Front was large,
A modest Soldier, resolute and stout,
Arm'd with a Coat of Sense from head to foot;
No more than need, for he was hard put to't.

71. *Storm of Words:* The torrent stemmed mainly from John Dennis, *Remarks on a Book Entituled, Prince Arthur, An Heroick Poem* (1696), a work of 228 pages.

74. *Lampoons:* Three of these are included in [John Oldmixon], *Poems on Several Occasions,* 1696, pp. 61, 72–73, 103–04 (Rosenberg, pp. 27–28).

82. *the King: King Arthur. An Heroick Poem* was advertised in the *London Gazette,* No. 3272, 18–22 March 1697.

83. *Knighted:* William knighted Blackmore "in the bedchamber" on 18 March 1696/7 (William A. Shaw, *The Knights of England,* 2 vols., 1906, 2, 270). Blackmore's presentation of a copy of *Prince Arthur. An Heroick Poem* to the king (Rosenberg, p. 35), may be reflected by the official entry in the herald's office: "LOND. Richard Blackmore doctor of Phisick auctor of prince arthur Kted at Kensington 18 Mar. 1696–7 sworn Phisitian in Ordinary to his Majtie" (Le Neve, p. 458).

84. *other Royal Bounties:* Under a royal warrant dated 30 April 1697 Blackmore was granted an annual pension of £2000. The month before, he had been given "A chain and Medall of Gold of the Value of £150 . . . as a marke of his Majts. Grace and Favour for presenting his Maty. with his Bookes of Prince Arthur" (Rosenberg, pp. 34–35).

89. *Collier* (*Key*): Jeremy Collier, *A Short View of the Immorality, and Profaneness of the English Stage,* was published in 1698. The preface is dated 5 March 1698.

90. *large:* Despite its title, *A Short View* was a work of 288 pages.

He Charg'd the strongest Troops of all the Foes,
And gave them several signal Overthrows,
But over-power'd by multitudes of Wits,
By Number, not by Force oppress'd, retreats;
So Sense, to Noise and Nonsence, oft submits.
Collier's a calm and steady Combatant,
And push'd the forward Troops with brave Intent,
Modest, a Fault not known among his Tribe,
And honest too, too honest for a Bribe:
The Wits wou'd fain ha' bought his fury off,
And proffer'd him *Applause,* and Gold enough,
But 'twou'd not do, he boldly Charg'd again,
And by Ten thousand Wounds at last was slain.
Some say he was by his own Men betray'd,
And basely left alive among the Dead,
But I cannot understand how that can be,
For how can Treachery and Sense agree?
In *Honours Truckle-Bed* the Hero lies,
Till Sense again, *the Lord knows when,* shall rise.
Milburn, a Renegade from Wit, came on
And made a false Attack, and next to none;
The Hypocrite, in Sense, could not conceal
What Pride, and want of Brains, oblig'd him to reveal.
In him the Critick's ruin'd by the Poet,

94. *Charg'd the strongest Troops:* Although he snipes at minor figures like Otway and D'Urfey, Collier reserves his major attack for the major dramatists: Dryden, Congreve, and Vanbrugh.

96. *over-power'd by multitudes:* Fourteen replies to *A Short View* published in 1698 and three more in 1699 are listed in *CBEL, 2,* 400–01.

105. *boldly Charg'd again:* Collier published *A Defence of the Short View of the Profaneness and Immorality of the English Stage* in 1699. His *Second Defence of the Short View* did not appear until 10 February 1700, too late to be noticed in the present poem, which was published five days later.

113. *Milburn* (*Key*): Luke Milbourne (1649–1720) graduated B.A. from Pembroke College, Cambridge, in 1670. He was rector of Osmandiston, Norfolk (1677–1702) but lived in London, where he was a lecturer at St. Leonard's, Shoreditch. His "false Attack" on Dryden was entitled *Notes on Dryden's Virgil. In a Letter to a Friend. With an Essay on the Same Poet* (1698). "With an assurance which induced Pope to call him the fairest of critics, not content with criticising the production of Dryden, Milbourne," as Sir Walter Scott relates, "was so ill advised as to produce, and place in opposition to it, a rickety translation of his own" (Dryden, *Works, 1,* 333).

And *Virgil* gives his Testimony to it;
The Troops of Wit were so enrag'd to see,
This Priest Invade his own Fraternity,
They sent a Party out, by Silence led,
And without Answer shot the *Turn-Coat* Dead.
The Priest, the Rake, the Wit, strove all in vain,
For there, alas, he lies among the slain,
Memento Mori; see the Consequence,
When Rakes and Wits set up for Men of Sense.
But Sense still suffer'd, and the shock was rude,
For what can Valour do to Multitude?
The General sent for help both far and near,
To *Cowley, Milton, Ratcliff, Rochester,*

122. *shot the Turn-Coat Dead:* Dryden disposed of Milbourne in his preface to *Fables Ancient and Modern:* "His own translations of Virgil have answered his criticisms on mine. If (as they say, he has declared in print,) he prefers the version of Ogilby to mine, the world has made him the same compliment; for it is agreed on all hands, that he writes even below Ogilby. That, you will say, is not easily to be done; but what cannot Milbourne bring about? I am satisfied, however, that, while he and I live together, I shall not be thought the worst poet of the age" (*Prose, 3,* 645). These words, however, may have been published too late for Defoe to see them; Malone believed that *Fables Ancient and Modern* appeared "early in *February* 1699–1700," but it was not advertised until 5–7 March (*Prose, 3,* 647 *n.;* Macdonald, p. 62). In this case, Defoe may be referring to an earlier, anonymous attack on Milbourne, *A Vindication of the Memory, of the Late Excellent and Charitable Mr. Thomas Firmin, from the Injurious Reflections of Mr. Luke Milbourn, in his Sermon before the Court of Aldermen at St. Paul's Church, Aug. 28., 1698* (1699) (Wing V519).

130. *Ratcliff:* Alexander Radcliffe (d. 1697?) was born in Hampstead, Middlesex. He was admitted to Gray's Inn in November 1669, but in March 1672 abandoned the law for a captaincy in Colonel John Fitzgerald's regiment of foot (Dalton, *1,* 119). In the next year he published *Ovidius Exulans, or, Ovid Travestie,* the first of the verses that justify his inclusion here among the dead "*Giants* . . . of Wit and Sense." Two of the best of these (unprintable) remain in manuscript: *A Satyre upon Love and Women* ("Thou silly Fond besotted amorous Fool") (Rylands MS. Eng. 521, p. 20) and *Captaine Ratcliffs Debauch* ("When duns were Knocking at my door") (Edinburgh University MS. Dc.1.3, p. 8). He was an associate of Rochester and later "sharpers about town," including Thomas Brown. Within the fiction of Defoe's poem it is extremely unlikely that Blackmore would have sought Radcliffe's assistance. Not only was Radcliffe a Tory (Luttrell, *1,* 99), but Blackmore himself records the resistance of "all the Whimsical,/Half-craz'd, half-witted" fops and pedants "of the *R—t—ff* kind" to the growing influence of the Kit-Cat Club at the end of the century (*The Kit-Cats, A Poem* ["I Sing the Assembly's Rise, Encrease and Fame"], 1708, p. 7). Radcliffe died sometime before November 1697 (Arber, *3,* 40).

Rochester: John Wilmot, earl of Rochester (1648–80). This celebrated libertine and John Bunyan, the fanatic preacher, were among Defoe's literary models.

Waller, Roscommon, Howard, and to *Bhen,*
The Doubtful Fight the better to maintain;
Giants these were of Wit and Sense together,
But they were dead and gone *the Lord knows whether.*
The swift Express he then Commands to fly,
To *Dorset, Montague,* and *Normanby,*
To send their Aid, and save him from Defeat,
But their United Council was Retreat,
Reserve your Fortunes for a better Day;
So Sailors, when the Ship's a sinking, Pray.
These are the Sages who Preside o'r Sense,
And Laws to all the Common-wealth Dispence,
But Wealth and Ease anticipates our fate,
And makes our Heroes all degenerate;

131. *Roscommon:* Wentworth Dillon, fourth earl of Roscommon (1637–85), was numbered by Samuel Johnson "among the benefactors to English literature," but not apparently for his most famous work, *An Essay on Translated Verse* (1684), about which Johnson observed that "when the sum of Lord Roscommon's precepts is collected it will not be easy to discover how they can qualify their reader for a better performance of translation than might have been attained by his own reflections." The second edition of this work, in 1685, includes the first appreciation of *Paradise Lost* by one of "the sons/Of Belial."

Howard: Robert Howard (1626–98) was the sixth son of Thomas Howard, first earl of Berkshire, and Dryden's brother-in-law and collaborator. He was knighted for his bravery in action at Cropredy Bridge during the Civil Wars (Shaw, *2,* 218). At the restoration he was elected a member of parliament and appointed to the important post of auditor of the exchequer. At the revolution he was admitted to the privy council. His *Five New Plays,* of which *The Committee* (1662) had been the most successful, were published in 1692. He is the "inerrable" noble Sir Positive of *The Club-men of the House of Commons* ("Let Noble Sir Positive lead the Van") (*POAS,* Yale, *5*).

Bhen: Aphra Behn (1640–89), whom Edmund Gosse called the George Sand of the Restoration, was christened Ayfara Johnson. Her comedies were "very coarse" and very popular and she was equally successful as an intelligence agent and novelist. Some of the facts and fictions of her remarkable career are sorted out in W. J. Cameron, *New Light on Aphra Behn,* Auckland, 1961.

136. *Dorset: Key* reads *"Dryden, Montague, Normanby,"* but this is almost certainly a mistake. It is *"Dorset, Sheffield* [Normanby], *Montague"* who are to underwrite the Bank for Wit and Sense in *A Satyr against Wit* (228) and it is to *"Dorset*'s Judgment" alone that wit can be entrusted (354). Dryden, on the other hand, is reduced to "noisome Fumes" (207).

143–44. *Wealth and Ease . . . makes our Heroes all degenerate:* In April 1697 Dorset sold his office of lord chamberlain of his majesty's household to the earl of Sunderland for a figure variously estimated at £8000 to £12,500 and retired to cultivate his ease at Copt Hall and Knole (Harris, p. 132). Charles Montagu's reputation as a wit had been established while he was still an undergraduate at Trinity College, Cambridge, and was confirmed in 1687 when he collaborated with Matthew Prior to produce *The*

The Muses high Preferments they possess,
And now their Pay's so great their Pains decrease;
So *Russel* fought, so *Herbert* too fell on,
Till Lords of *Orford* made and *Torrington.*
  And now the Wits their Victory Proclaim,
Loaden with Spoils of Sense, and swell'd with Fame;
Their Plunder first they carefully bestow,
And then to spread their Conquest farther, go,
Their Troops divide, their Terror to extend,
And God knows where their Ravages will end.
Dennis Commanded the Forlorn of Wit,

Hind and the Panther Transvers'd to the Story of the Country Mouse and the City Mouse. Nothing that he wrote after November 1699 when he retired as first lord of the treasury to the post of auditor of the exchequer, worth £4000 a year, and was raised to the peerage as baron Halifax of Halifax, added anything to this reputation. Sheffield had established himself as a wit with *An Essay upon Satire* (1679), which he wrote in collaboration with Dryden, *The Character of a Tory, in Answer to that of a Trimmer* (1681), and *An Essay upon Poetry* (1682). Nothing that he wrote after May 1694, when he was made a privy councillor with a pension of £3000 and created marquess of Normanby, added anything to this reputation.

147. *Russel* (*Key*): Edward Russell (1653–1727), an admiral since May 1689 and hero of the victory off La Hougue in May 1692, saw no further sea duty after he was raised to the peerage as earl of Orford in May 1697.

Herbert (*Key*): Arthur Herbert (1647–1716) was commissioned as admiral in July 1680 and raised to the peerage as earl of Torrington in June 1689. He commanded the fleet that was defeated in July 1690 off Beachy Head. In December 1690 he was removed from his command and court-martialed on the grounds of refusing to engage the enemy. He was acquitted but never entrusted with another command.

155. *Dennis* (*Key*): John Dennis (1657–1734) was born in London, where his father was a successful saddler. He attended Harrow and graduated B.A. in 1679 from Caius College, Cambridge, whence he proceeded to Trinity Hall, Cambridge, and graduated M.A. four years later. After the Grand Tour, he returned to London to make his way as poet and critic. He was taken up by Normanby and Montagu, befriended by Congreve, Wycherley, and Walter Moyle, and admitted into Dryden's circle at Will's. He found out the errors of *Prince Arthur. An Heroick Poem* in *Remarks on a Book Entituled, Prince Arthur, an Heroick Poem* (1696) and those of *A Short View* in *The Usefulness of the Stage, to the Happiness of Mankind, to Government, and to Religion, Occasioned by a Late Book, Written by Jeremy Collier, M.A.* (1698). The latter work was presented by the grand jury of Middlesex as "a libell against the government, for asserting that the people of England are the most prone to rebellion of any in the world, and alwaies quarrelling among themselves, if not diverted by playes; upon which the court ordered an indictment against him, and the attorney generall to prosecute him" (Luttrell, *4*, 456). Already, it seems, Dennis was impoverished, for a week later, on 5 December 1698, Dr. William Aglionby told his friend Matthew Prior that he was going to give "three shillings to a poor poet. . . . The Grand Jury presented him some days ago, and 'tis fit we should do so too to enable him to answer them" (HMC *Bath MSS.*, *3*, 302). But this proved to be unnecessary, for the lord

A stiff Politish Critick, very fit
The open Country to over-run,
And find out all Mens Errors but his own;
His *Stony-Stratford Mistress* read his Fate,
A Slovens Fancy, and an Empty Pate.
But now Commission'd by the Jingling Train,
He has his Thousands, and Ten Thousands slain:
He, like the *Tartars,* who fore-run the *Turks,*
Easie to be distinguish'd by his Works,
With equal Havock, and destructive Hate,
Leaves all the Land he treads on Desolate;
He roots up Sense, and sows the Weeds of Wit,
And *Fops* and *Rakes,* ten thousand strong, submit.
Congreve and *Dryden, Hopkins* and *Motteaux,*
Durfey, and everlasting Fops, and Beaus,
Led up the Battel Fifty thousand strong,
Arm'd with *Burlesque, Bombast,* and *Bawdy-Song;*
Flesh'd with Great *Collier*'s Slaughter they led on,
Shouting *Victoria,* the Day's their own.

---

chancellor, Somers himself, "acquainted the king with the business" and the proceedings were stopped (BM Add. MS. 7121, f. 21, quoted in Hermann Lenz, *John Dennis sein Leben und seine Werke,* Halle, 1913, p. 31, *n.* 2).

159. *Stony-Stratford:* a village in Buckinghamshire, 65 miles northwest of London. The lady remains unidentified.

169. *Hopkins* (*Key*): Charles Hopkins (1664?–1700?), the son of a bishop of Londonderry, was educated at Trinity College, Dublin, and at Queens College, Cambridge, whence he graduated B.A. in 1688. He returned to Ireland to join the forces of the prince of Orange and was commissioned lieutenant in a regiment of foot in July 1694 (Dalton, *3,* 379). Four of his plays were produced and at least four volumes of his verse were published before he died at 36 as the result of "hard Drinking, and a too Passionate fondness for the fair Sex" (Jacob, *Historical Account,* p. 75). Dryden said that he wrote "naturally well, without art, or learning, or good sence" (*Works, 18,* 162).

Motteaux (*Key*): Peter Anthony Motteux (1663–1718), whose name Dennis rhymed with "Pothooks," was the translator of Rabelais and Cervantes and undertaker of the first literary miscellany in England, *The Gentleman's Journal* (January 1692–November 1694). Born in Rouen and christened Pierre Antoine le Motteux, he was a Huguenot who emigrated to England in 1685 when Louis revoked the edict of Nantes. Although literature was only an avocation—he was first a clerk-translator in the post office and later a merchant dealing in East Indian goods—the list of his published works, including 18 plays, occupies 18 pages in Robert N. Cunningham, "A bibliography of the writings of Peter Anthony Motteux," *Oxford Bibliographical Society Proceedings and Papers, 3* (1933), 317–36. In *The Town Display'd* (1701) ("My Dear *Amintor,* on a Summer's Day") he is condemned, along with Taverner and Pix, to be "Forgotten now, and in Futurity."

No Bounds to their Licentious Arms they know,
But Plunder all the Country as they go,
Kill, Ravish, Burn, Destroy, do what they please!
The *French* at *Swamerdam* were Fools to these.
The Cruelties they Exercis'd were such,
Amboyna's nothing, they've out-done the *Dutch;*
Never such Devastation sure was known,
A Man of Sense cou'd not be seen in Town.
Tonson, even Hackney *Tonson,* wou'd not Print,
A Book without Wits *Imprimatur* in't;
And as in Revolutions of the State,
Men strive the present things to imitate,
So when Wits, and Fops, had got the best,
Men Acquiesc'd, and took the Oaths and Test:
Few wou'd be Martyrs for their Understanding,
But all went over at the Prince's Landing;
So Story tells, in *Crook-back'd Richard*'s Time,
Folks wore false Humps to make them look like him.
  News, hasty News, the Post is just come in,
Nokor has Rally'd all his Troops again;
In a Pitch'd Field he met the haughty Foe,
And gave them there a total Overthrow,
The Slaughter's great, the Soldiers still pursue,
For they give Quarter but to very few;
Wits Routed, all the Beaus are quite undone,
Their General's slain, their Army's fled and gone.
See the uncertain fate of humane Things!
Change lays its fickle hands on States and Kings;
This bloody Battel has undone us all,

178. *Swamerdam:* "The *French* committed unheard of Barbarities at *Swammerdam* [1672]" ([Abel Boyer], *The History of King William the Third,* 1702, p. 30).

180. *Amboyna:* Amboina (now Ambon) was one of the Spice Islands (Moluccas) in modern Indonesia. In 1623 a number of English interlopers were tortured and put to death there by Dutch settlers and the memory of this massacre was kept alive as a patriotic slogan during the three Dutch wars (1652–74).

191. *Story:* Steele tells the same story in *The Spectator,* No. 32, 6 April 1711: "*Richard* the Third set up half the Backs of the Nation; and high Shoulders, as well as high Noses, were the Top of the Fashion."

194. *Rally'd . . . again:* Blackmore's *Satyr against Wit* appeared on 23 November 1699.

200. *General:* Cf. *A Satyr against Wit,* 87 *n.,* above.

Wit from its Glorious blazing Throne will fall,
For all the Flower of Gallantry, and Wit,
Was listed here, and overthrown in it.
The Florid *Garth* was General of Horse,
And lost his Life and Fame too, which was worse;
The Credit of this new Commander brought,
With hopes of Plunder, many a Coward out,
Who hitherto had very wisely chose,
The Name of Wits, but had declin'd the blows.
'Twas dismal to behold the Field of War,
What Desolation Wit has suffer'd there,
Whole Squadrons of Epick Horse appears,
Trod down by his Heroic Curassiers,
Garth lost his Darling Satyrick Dragoons,
And two Brigades of Light Horse, call'd *Lampoons,*
Old Soldiers all, well beaten to the Wars,
Known by their *Roughness, Ugliness,* and *Scars;*
Fellows, the like were never heard nor read of
"Wou'd bite sometimes, enough to bite one's Head off,
Nor cou'd their swiftness their Escape procure,
For *Nokor*'s Fury nothing cou'd endure:
Enrag'd with former Losses he fell on,
Resolv'd to Conquer, or be quite undone;
Whole Wings of Foreign Troops he overthrew,
Whom *Garth* from *France* to Wits assistance drew,
Something the Matter was those Troops betraid 'em;
He ill Procur'd them, or he had not Paid 'em;
'Twas a dull fancy in him to think fit,
To polish English Sense with Foreign Wit.
Among the Foot the Battel was severe,
For Wits best Troops were wisely planted there,
Led up by old Experienc'd Commanders,
As *Dryden, Congreve, Addison* and *Sanders.*

222. *bite one's Head off:* Defoe may be paraphrasing a line in Edmund Ashton, *On the Same Author* [Edward Howard] *upon His British Princes:*

Fellows that ne'er were heard or read of
(If thou writ'st on) will write thy head off.
(*POAS,* Yale, *I,* 340)

235. *Sanders* (*Key*): Charles Saunders, while still a schoolboy at Westminster, wrote "an indifferent T[ragedy]" called *Tamerlane the Great,* for which he "took the design

The Granadiers were known by their Blue Bonnets,
For they had been in *Scotland* making Sonnets:
Pun-Master-General *Durfey* led them on,
And with his Chattering Tunes the fight began.
His Orders were to Charge, and then retire,
And give the Body liberty to fire;
Ten Regiments of Plays stood on the Right,
Led on by General *Dryden* to the Fight;
The Tragedies had made some small pretence
To Mutiny, and so Revolt to Sense.
For *Dryden* had some Sense, till he thought fit
To Dote, and lately *Deviate into Wit;*
The Reason's plain, and he has found it true,
He *follow'd Wit which did too fast pursue.*
  The Left was form'd of seven large Brigades,
Of *Farces, Opera's,* and *Masquerades,*
With several little Bands of *Dogrel* Wit,
To Scowre the Ways, and Line the Hedges fit.
  Between these mighty Wings was rang'd in sight,
A solid Phalanx of Compounded Wit:
Ten thousand *Lyrick Foot,* all Gallant Beaus,
Arm'd with *soft Sighs,* with *Songs,* and *Billet-Doux.*
There was Eight thousand *Elegiack* Foot,
By *Briny Tears* and *Sullen Grief* made stout;
Five Pastoral Bands, lately bred up in Arms,
By Chanting *Gloriana*'s Mighty Charms,
And Thund'ring out King *WILLIAM*'s loud Alarms.
Pindarick Legions, seven I think appear'd
Like *Brandenburghers,* with Enchanted Beard,
For Lions Skins, and Whisker's late so fear'd.

. . . from a novel called Tamerlane and Asteria" (Genest, *1,* 291–92). Although Dryden, in an epilogue to the play, which was produced and published in 1681, called him "the first boy-poet of our age," Saunders appears to have published nothing more.

248. *Deviate into Wit:* Cf. "Sh—— never deviates into sense" (Dryden, *Mac Flecknoe,* 20).

250. *follow'd:* In a paragraph which he added to the preface in the second edition of *Tyrannick Love* (1672), Dryden observed that "Some foole . . . had charg'd me in *The Indian Emperour* with nonsense in these words: 'And follow fate which does too fast pursue.'" Dryden's explanation that he was alluding to *Aeneid,* XI, 695, "eludit gyro interior sequiturque sequentem," did not wholly stifle the merriment.

These were led up by able old Commanders,
As *Congreve, Hughs,* Soldiers Bred in *Flanders,*
With *Dennis, Durfey, Tuchin,* Dull *Motteaux,*
Brewer, Wessly, Pettys, Fops and *Beaus,*
Dull *Tate,* and Pious *Brady,* old *Traherne,*

268. *Hughs* (*Key*): John Hughes (1677–1720) was educated at a dissenting academy in London. At nineteen, as Samuel Johnson has said, "he drew the plan of a tragedy," *Amalsont, Queen of the Goths,* which was never acted. The genius of "This amiable man, and elegant author," seemed to his admirers "equally inclined to . . . music, poetry, and design" (Baker, *1*, i, 378), but Swift ranked him "among the *mediocribus* in prose as well as verse" (*Corr., 5,* 227).

269. *Tuchin* (*Key*): John Tutchin (1661?–1707) was educated at a dissenting academy at Stepney and published his first volume, *Poems on Several Occasions,* in 1685. In the same summer he joined in Monmouth's Rebellion but, less fortunate than Defoe, he was captured, tried before Jeffreys and sentenced to be whipped through every market town in Dorset. Jeffreys, however, was bribed to recommend a pardon and four years later Tutchin visited him during his last days in the Tower and wrote *A New Martyrology: or, The Bloody Assizes. . . . The Life and Death of George Lord Geffreys* (1689). In the same year he published *An Heroick Poem upon the Late Expedition of His Majesty to Rescue England from Popery, Tyranny, and Arbitrary Government.* During the next decade he published a series of pindaric odes on patriotic and didactic themes and was rewarded with a clerkship in the navy victualling office.

270. *Brewer* (*Key*): possibly Tom B——r, who published *Miscellany Poems on Several Subjects* (1702) and to whom a reference may be concealed in *The Examination, Tryal, and Condemnation of Rebellion Ob*[*servato*]*r,* 1703, p. 17: "[Tutchin] and one Mr. *B——r,* Deceas'd, joyn'd Heads together to write the Hymns for the *Calves-Head-Feasts.*"

Wessly (*Key*): Samuel Wesley; see *The Dispensary, 5,* 67 *n.,* above.

Pettys (*Key*): William Pittis (1674–1724) was the son of Thomas Pittis, D.D., the rector of St. Botolph's Bishopsgate. While still an undergraduate in New College, Oxford, he began to contribute verse to *The Gentleman's Journal* (July 1692). His prefatory poem to Motteux's edition of Rabelais, dated October 1693, indicates that by this time he was a fellow of New College. In 1695, however, he sold his fellowship (Oldmixon, p. 510) and moved into the Inner Temple, ostensibly to study medicine under Tyson, as he mentions at the end of *An Epistolary Poem to N. Tate, Esquire* (1696) ("Since evr'y Pen and evr'y Tongue employ"). In March 1697, along with four or five other "Drunken Fellows" who frequented the Rose Tavern, he undertook to edit *Miscellanies over Claret,* a literary miscellany modeled on *The Gentleman's Journal.* In May 1699 Pittis was "scandalized" in *An Elegy on the Death of the Author of the Characters &c. Of the Ladies Invention, who dyed on the 13th of this instant May at the Rose Spunging-house in Woodstreet* ("He's Dead! Lament ye *Mercuries* and *Hawkers*"). The next month, however, in his preface to *An Epistolary Poem to John Dryden, Esq.,* dated 13 June 1699, Pittis was able to boast that Dryden had looked over his poem before publication and sent him "obliging compliments" (Dryden, *Works, 18,* 229).

271. *Brady* (*Key*): Nicholas Brady (1659–1726), was born in Bandon, county Cork, but educated at Westminster School and Christ Church, Oxford, whence he graduated

Gildon, Tom Brown, and many a Subaltern;
Some Flying Troops were plac'd in Ambuscade,
Mock-Wits, Beau-Wits, and Wits in Masquerade;
Some *Amazonian* Troops of Female Wit,
For Ostentation, not for Combat fit;
The Witty *Davenant* appear'd there too,

B.A. in 1682. He was minister of St. Katherine Creechurch, in Aldgate (1691–96), and then vicar of Richmond, in Surrey, until his death. He was also one of William's chaplains-in-ordinary and collaborated with the poet laureate, Nahum Tate, to produce *A New Version of the Psalms of David* (Wing B2598) in 1696. This work, which was intended to supplant "that obsolete and ridiculous Version" made by Thomas Sternhold and John Hopkins in the reign of Edward VI (Cibber, *Lives, 4,* 63), became a partisan issue in December 1696 when William ordered it to be adopted "in all Churches . . . as shall think fit to receive the same" (*A Brief and Full Account of Mr. Tate's and Mr. Brady's New Version of the Psalms,* 1698, p. 7). Swift, for example, scorned to adopt "what Brady cribs/From Hopkins." Brady contributed an *Epigram, Occasion'd by the Passage in the Satyr against Wit, that Reflects upon Mr. Tate* ("Rail on, discourteous Knight. If modest *Tate*") to *Commendatory Verses* (1700).

Traherne (*Key*): Thomas Traherne (1637?–74), the "Son of a Shoe-maker in *Hereford,*" suffered from hallucinatory visions (John Aubrey, *Miscellanies,* 1696, p. 77). Although he published no poetry during his lifetime and not all of his poetry has yet been published (*Times Literary Supplement, 63* [8 October 1964], 928), he was also the last important metaphysical poet. He graduated B.A. from Brasenose College, Oxford, in 1656 and was appointed rector of Credenhill, near Hereford, the following year. In 1669 he became domestic chaplain to Sir Orlando Bridgeman, of Teddington, Middlesex, and spent the remaining years of his life in London and Teddington. All three of his works published before 1700 were anonymous, although *A Serious and Pathetical Contemplation of the Mercies of God* (1699) was announced in the preface to have been written by the chaplain to "the late Lord Keeper *Bridgman.*" But since neither Aubrey nor Anthony à Wood were aware that Traherne had written anything, it is remarkable that even his name should have been known to Defoe. His appearance here, among the "Pindarick Legions" of Will's coffeehouse and the Rose Tavern, may indicate that Defoe knew nothing more than his name.

272. *Gildon* (*Key*): Charles Gildon (1664–1724) was born in Gillingham, Dorsetshire, and educated for the Roman Catholic priesthood at Douai. But he abandoned divinity in 1684 and came up to London to establish himself as a scholar, wit, and critic. He joined the Rose Tavern circle of Brown and D'Urfey, became a deist (but was converted again, in 1697, to Anglican orthodoxy), and published a remarkably varied series of literary works. These included *The History of the Athenian Society* [n.d.], *Miscellaneous Letters and Essays on Several Subjects, Philosophical, Moral, Historical, Critical, Amorous, &c. in Prose and Verse* (1694), an edition of *The Miscellaneous Works of Charles Blount, Esq.* (1695) with a preface defending suicide, and *The Roman Brides Revenge. A Tragedy* (1697).

277. *Davenant* (*Key*): Charles Davenant (1656?–1714), the eldest son of Sir William D'Avenant, left Balliol College, Oxford, without taking a degree but was admitted to plead in doctors commons between 1674 and 1676 (Chamberlayne, 1674, pp. 2268–69;

Whose Wit's in Prose, but all *Incognito.*
There was one *Caledonian* Voluntier,
With some *Hibernian* Wits brought up the Rear;
The whole, as by the Musters may be seen,
Was Ninety seven thousand Fighting Men.
All these drawn up, and ready to Engage,
Old General *Dryden,* with a Pious Rage,
That the Great Work might with success go on,
First Sacrific'd to the *Emperor o' th' Moon;*
The Poet and the Priest alike in Fame,
"For Priests of all Religions are the same.
When *Nokor*'s Conquering Troops began t' appear,
They found a very warm Reception here,
He had Invok'd the *Gods of Wit* before,
And vow'd to make their Altars smoke once more,
With *Bloody Hecatombs* of Witty Gore.
Swifter than Lightning at their Host he flew,

1676, pp. 2239–40), a fact which makes his accepted birthdate seem impossibly late. How he acquired the necessary D.C.L. degree is also a mystery. Wood says he obtained it "by favour and money" from Cambridge or Dublin (Wood, *4,* 476), but "E" learned "From private information" that it was Cambridge (*Biographia Britannica, 3,* 1611). The records of neither university, however, mention Davenant's name. In 1675 he wrote *Circe. A Tragedy,* which was produced at the Duke of York's theatre and published two years later with a prologue by Dryden and an epilogue by Rochester. From 1678 to 1689 he enjoyed a place in the commission of the excise which paid £1000 a year. He was a Tory member for St. Ives, Cornwall (1685–87) and subsequently sat for Great Bedwin, Wiltshire (1698–1701). In 1694 he was appointed surveyor-general of the salt tax. Davenant's major interest, in fact, was public finance. Between 1695 and 1699 he published four important works in this field (Wing D311, D307, D306, D309) and four similar works which remained unpublished are preserved in BM MS. Harleian 1223. These works attracted the attention of Robert Harley and under Harley's patronage Davenant became the leading Tory propagandist at the end of the century, publishing *A Discourse upon Grants and Resumptions* (dated 1700 but published in November 1699) and *Essays* in March 1701. As such, of course, he became Defoe's chief antagonist.

278. *Incognito:* All of Davenant's works were published anonymously, but in most of them he is identified as "the Author of the Essay on Ways and Means."

279. *Caledonian Voluntier:* This is almost certainly Archibald Pitcairne (1652–1713), one of the most celebrated physicians in Europe and the greatest wit in Edinburgh, whom Defoe could have met during his tour of 1697. A Jacobite and atheist, he was regarded by the ignorant as an object of superstitious fear, "proud, Imperious and conceitie," but his "mirry knacks and wanton Stories" were repeated throughout the city (*The Life and death of Mirry Archie P: late Mountebanck of Edinburgh* ["The good Toun now may say alas"], Edinburgh University MS. La. II. 358).

288. Dryden, *Absalom and Achitophel* (1681), 99.

His Word was *Dorset, Dorset, Mountague,*
His Squadrons in Poetick Terror shone,
And whisper'd Death to Wit as they came on:
The strong Brigades of his Heroic Horse,
Dreadful for Sense, for Pointed Satyr worse,
Wing'd with Revenge, in fiery Raptures flew,
And dipt in Poison'd Gall the Darts they threw;
Nothing cou'd *Nokor*'s furious Troops withstand,
Nor cou'd he check them with his own Command.
The Troops of Wit, Disorder'd, and O'r-run,
Are Slain, Disperc'd, Disgrac'd, and Overthrown;
The Shouts of Triumph reach the distant Sky,
And *Nokor* lies Encamp'd in the Field of *Victory.*
  These are the doubtful dark Events of War,
But who *Britannia*'s Losses shall Repair?
For as when States in Civil Wars Engage,
Their Private Feuds and Passions to asswage,
The Publick suffers, harmless Subjects bear
The Plagues, and Famines, which attend the War.
So if we this Destructive War permit,
Britain will find the Consequence of it,
A Dearth of Sense, or else a Plague of Wit;
For Wit, by these Misfortunes desperate,
Begins to arm at an unusual rate,
Levies new Forces, gives Commissions out,
For several Regiments of Horse and Foot,
Recruits from every side come in amain,
From *Oxford, Cambridge, Will*'s, and *Warwick-lane,*

295. *Dorset, Dorset, Mountague* (*Key*): Defoe alludes to Blackmore's repeated invocation of these two important patrons in *A Satyr against Wit,* 182, 228, 352–55, 362–63.

307. *Victory:* Defoe represents *A Satyr against Wit* as a complete victory for Blackmore.

319. *Levies new Forces:* Defoe evidently was aware of the wits' design of "Squibbing" Blackmore "with Epigrams" in *Commendatory Verses,* published about 10 days after *The Pacificator.*

322. *Warwick-lane:* the site of the College of Physicians, from which several contributors to *Commendatory Verses* were recruited. Brown's friend, Dr. Edward Baynard, contributed *Melancholy Reflections on the Deficiency of Useful Learning* ("Short are our Powers, tho' infinite our Will"), and Dr. James Drake contributed *To Dr. Garth, on the Fourth Edition of His Incomparable Poem, The Dispensary* ("Bold thy Attempt, in these hard Times to raise"). A third squib, *To the Merry Poetaster at*

The scatter'd Troops too, from the last Defeat,
Begin to Halt, and check their swift Retreat:
In numerous Parties Wit appears again,
Talks of another Battel this *Campagne,*
Their strong Detachments o'r *Parnassus* range,
And meditate on nothing but Revenge.
  To whom shall we Apply, what Powers Invoke,
To deprecate the near impending stroke?
Ye Gods of Wit and Arts, their Minds inspire
With Thoughts of Peace, from your Pacifick Fire;
Engage some Neighbouring Powers to undertake
To Mediate Peace, for *Dear Britannia*'s sake;
Pity the Mother rifl'd of her Charms,
And make her Sons lay down Intestine Arms.
Preliminary Treaties first begin,
And may short Truce a lasting Peace let in,
Limits to Wits Unbounded Ocean place,
To which it may, and may no farther pass;
Fathom the unknown Depths of sullen Sense,
And Purge it from its Pride, and Insolence;
Your secret Influences interpose,
And make them all dispatch their *Plenipo's;*
Appoint *Parnassus* for a Place to meet,
Where all the Potentates of Wit may Treat,
Around the Hill let Troops of Muses stand,
To keep the Peace, and Guard the Sacred Land:
There let the high Pretensions be discuss'd,
And Heaven the fatal Differences adjust.
  Let either side abate of their Demands,
And both submit to Reason's high Commands,
For which way ere the Conquest shall encline,
The loss *Britannia* will at last be thine.
  Wit, like a hasty Flood, may over-run us,
And too much *Sense* has oftentimes undone us:
Wit is a Flux, a Looseness of the Brain,
And *Sense-abstract* has too much Pride to Reign:

Sadlers-hall, in Cheapside ("Unweildy Pedant, let thy awkward Muse"), which has since been attributed to Garth (*The Poetical Works,* 1773, p. 134), was thought at the time to be the work of Dr. Christopher Love Morley.

Wit-unconcoct is the Extreme of Sloth,
And too much *Sense* is the Extreme of both.
Abstracted-wit 'tis own'd is a Disease,
But *Sense-abstracted* has no Power to please:
For Sense like Water is but Wit condense,
And Wit like Air is rarify'd from Sense:
Meer Sense is sullen, stiff, and unpolite,
Meer Wit is apoplectick, thin, and light:
Wit is a King without a Parliament,
And *Sense* a Democratick Government:
Wit, like the *French,* where e'r it reigns Destroys,
And *Sense advanc'd* is apt to Tyrannize:
Wit without Sense is like the *Laughing-Evil,*
And *Sense* unmix'd with *Fancy* is the *Devil.*
Wit is a Standing Army Government,
And *Sense* a sullen stubborn *Parliament:*
Wit by its haste anticipates its Fate,
And so does *Sense* by being obstinate:
Wit without Sense in Verse is all but *Farce,*
Sense without Wit in Verse is all *mine Arse.*
Wit, like the *French,* Performs before it Thinks,
And Thoughtful *Sense* without Performance sinks:
Sense without *Wit* is flegmatick and pale,
And is all Head, forsooth, without a Tail:
Wit without *Sense* is cholerick and red,
Has Tail enough indeed, but has no Head.
Wit, like the Jangling Chimes, Rings all in One,
Till *Sense,* the Artist, sets them into Tune:
Wit, like the Belly, if it be not Fed,
Will starve the Members, and distract the Head.
Wit is the *Fruitful Womb* where Thoughts Conceive,
Sense is the *Vital Heat* which Life and Form must give:
Wit is the *Teeming Mother* brings them forth,
Sense is the *Active Father* gives them worth.
United: Wit and *Sense,* makes Science thrive,
Divided: neither *Wit* nor *Sense* can live;

377–78. "While the theologian usually speaks, as it were, in the indicative; the secular essayist . . . may favour what might be called a subjunctive mode of thought" (Ogg. *3,* 519).

For while the Parties eagerly contend,
The Mortal Strife must in their Mutual Ruin end.
  Listen, ye Powers, to *Lost Britannia*'s Prayer,
And either side to yielding Terms Prepare;
And if their Cases long Debates admit,
As how much Condescention shall be fit,
How far *Wits* Jurisdiction shall extend,
And where the stated Bounds of *Sense* shall end,
Let them to some known Head that strife submit,
Some Judge Infallible, some *Pope in Wit,*
His Triple Seat place on *Parnassus* Hill,
And from his Sentence suffer no Appeal:
Let the Great Balance in his Censure be,
And of the Treaty make him *Guarantee,*
Let him be the Director of the State,
And what he says, let both sides take for Fate:
Apollo's *Pastoral Charge* to him commit,
And make him *Grand Inquisitor* of Wit,
Let him to each his proper Talent show,
And tell them what they can, or cannot do,
That each may chuse the Part he can do well,
And let the Strife be only to Excel:
To their own Province let him all confine,
Doctors to Heal, to Preaching the Divine;
Dryden to Tragedy, let *Creech* Translate,

403. *to some known Head that strife submit:* Both *The Dispensary* (*6,* 257–74) and *A Satyr against Wit* (273 ff.) conclude in an appeal to the authority of the great magnates.

404. *Pope:* It has been observed that "a pope of wit is a remarkable appendage of a commonwealth" (Robert M. Krapp, *Science and Society, 10* [1946], 88).

419. *Creech* (*Key*): Thomas Creech (1659–1700) graduated B.A. from Wadham College, Oxford, in 1680. His speech, as Collector, "gain'd him great Reputation: which was shortly after highly rais'd by his incomparable translation into English Verse of *Lucretius*" (Hearne, *1,* 305). *T. Lucretius Carus the Epicurean Philosopher, His Six Books De natura rerum* was published at Oxford in 1682 and "commended to the world . . . by a copy of good English verses made by Tho. Browne the poet of Ch[rist] Ch[urch]" (Wood, *4,* 739). The second edition, in 1683, "was usher'd into the world by the recommendatory poems of John Dryden poet laureat, Tho. Flatman, N. Tate sometime of the univ. of Dublin, Aphora Bhen, Tho. Otway, John Evelin sen., Edm. Waller of Beconsfield, and two copies from Cambridge, one made by T. Adams fellow of King's college, and the other by Rich. Duke fellow of Trin." (Wood, *4,* 739). Thereafter, Creech published translations of Horace (1684), Theocritus (1684), and Manilius (1697). In 1683, "for his merits," he was elected a fellow of All Souls College.

Durfey make Ballads, Psalms and Hymns for *Tate:*
Let *Prior* Flatter Kings in Panegyrick,
Ratcliff Burlesque, and *Wicherly* be Lyrick:
Let *Congreve* write the Comick, *Foe* Lampoon,
Wessly the Banter, *Milburn* the Buffoon,
And the Transgressing Muse receive the Fate
Of Contumacy, Excommunicate.
Such as with Railing Spirits are possess'd,
The Muses Frenzy, let them be suppress'd,
Allow no Satyrs which receive their Date
From *Juno*'s Academy, *Billinsgate;*
No Banters, no Invective lines admit,
Where want of Manners, makes up want of Wit.
Such as are hardned in Poetick Crimes,
Let him give up to their own foolish Rhimes;
Let those Eternal Poets be Condemn'd,
To be Eternal Poets to the end:
Let *Dennis* still continue unpolite,
And no Man read what *Dull Motteux* shall write,
Reduce him to his Letter-Case and Whore,

He published in 1695 an edition of Lucretius "with very good Notes," which he dedicated to his friend Christopher Codrington, also a fellow of All Souls. "For all these his Deserts," Hearne continues, "he was not regarded by the Publick, and those who have the Disposal of Preferment: which wrought very much upon his Natural melancholly, and . . . heighten'd it to that degree, as to make him put an End to his own Life" (Hearne, *1*, 305). Creech made his will on 18 January 1699 and hanged himself in the garret of his lodgings five months later. Hearne's account neglects to mention what must have been at least a contributory cause of Creech's suicide and soon became the subject of a sensational pamphlet, *A Step to Oxford: Or, a Mad Essay on the Reverend Mr. Tho. Creech's Hanging Himself, (as 'tis said) for Love. With the Character of his Mistress* (1700). This work juxtaposes an uninformed account of Creech's death with ironical quotations from his own translations and from a conventional pastoral elegy, *Daphnis: Or, A Pastoral Elegy upon the Unfortunate Death of Mr. Thomas Creech* ("The Rosie Morning with prevailing Light"), which appeared in July 1700.

422. *Ratcliff (Key):* See line 130, above.

423. *Foe (Key):* "it is not certain whether he ever decided definitely whether his name was D. Foe or D. De Foe. In a legal document near the end of his life he signed himself Daniel Foe, Gentleman." The first public use of the prefix "De" is said to occur in October 1695 in an announcement in *The Post Boy* (Moore, *Daniel Defoe,* pp. 7–8, 347).

439. *Whore:* Motteux's death in a "Bawdy-house in Star-Court" became the subject of much speculation and a prolonged legal process in 1718 (Robert N. Cunningham, *Peter Anthony Motteux 1663–1718,* Oxford, 1933, pp. 190–93).

Let all Men shun him as they did before.
Let *Milburn* talk for what he can't Defend,
And Banter *Virgil* which he ne'r cou'd Mend;
Let all the little Fry of *Wit-Profaners*
Rest as they are, with neither Sense, nor Manners,
Forsaken of *Apollo*'s Influence,
With want of *Language,* and with want of *Pence:*
What Fools Indite, let none but Blockheads Read,
And may they write in vain, who write for Bread:
No Banters on the Sacred Text admit,
Nor *Bawdy Lines,* that *Blasphemy of Wit:*
To Standard Rules of Government Confine,
The Rate of every Bard, and Worth of every Line,
And let the Rays of their Ambition burn,
Those *Phaeton-Wits* who this Subjection scorn:
If they aspire to Invade the Government,
Bring them before the *Muses Parliament,*
No Universal Monarchy admit,
A *Common-wealth*'s the Government for Wit.

FINIS

Sir Charles Sedley

Upon the Author of the Satyr against Wit *(27 February 1700)*

Since Blackmore had scattered his shot so widely in *A Satyr against Wit,* it is appropriate that the wits should reply individually and collectively in *Commendatory Verses, on the Author of the Two Arthurs and the Satyr against Wit; By Some of His Particular Friends.* The pity is that so little wit could be mustered in defense of wit. Nor was the idea of an anthology of mock-panegyrics original with the "*Covent-Garden* Wits"; it repeats an earlier joke on Sir William Davenant entitled *Certain Verses Written by Several of the Authors Friends; to be Re-printed with the Second Edition of Gondibert* (1653). The title of *Commendatory Verses,* however, is both original and witty, but it requires a little explanation.

Blackmore had published *Prince Arthur. An Heroick Poem* in 1695 and *King Arthur. An Heroick Poem* in March 1697, but Henry and John Arthur were heroes of quite a different breed. They robbed the western mail in September 1698 and their subsequent fate was eagerly followed in the news sheets:

> *1 December 1698.* The two Arthurs, who robbed the mailes, are broke out of Newgate. . . .
> *13 December 1698.* . . . the two Arthurs are taken and committed to Salisbury goal [this was a false report].
> *31 December 1698.* The two Arthurs . . . were on Thursday night taken at a tavern by Doctors Commons, being discovered by one Bellenger, a companion of theirs.
>
> (Luttrell, *4,* 457, 461, 466)

Ichabod Dawks' account, in the best journalistic tradition, is rich in circumstantial detail:

> The two Arthurs . . . during the time of their Escape out of Newgate, Lodg'd in Black-friars, and went frequently about the Town in Grecians Habit . . . particularly the Day before they

were Taken they went through Newgate in a Coach, with the Glasses down; they have discovered the Person who helpt them to the Springs of Watches notched, fasten'd to a Bow, to file off the Iron Barrs, to facilitate their Escape, he being one Mr. *E*[*llis*], a Tobacconist, who is since taken and Committed to Newgate, where he is double Fetter'd.
(*Dawks News-Letter,* No. 398, p. 3, January 1699, quoted in Rosenberg, p. 50)

Public interest in the two Arthurs, which had subsided in March 1699 when John was found guilty and hanged but Henry acquitted, flared up again most conveniently just two weeks before publication of *A Satyr against Wit:*

14 November 1699. Saturday night last one Henry Arthur a noted highway man . . . quarelling with one Parry about paying the reckoning in a tavern, fought in Covent Garden, and was killed.

(Luttrell, *4,* 582)

The preface to *Commendatory Verses* is written in the person of Owen Swan, whom Thomas Brown called "the most sincere and honest Man/That e'er drew Wine in *Quart* or *Can.*" Swan was the proprietor of the Black Swan tavern, in Bartholomew Lane, near the Royal Exchange and the Bank of England, in the heart of the City. This fact made it possible to add a topographic dimension to the battle of "The Men of Sense against the Men of Wit," for Blackmore had localized the wits at Will's coffeehouse, well outside Temple Bar.

Swan first directs the attention of "all . . . Honourable CITIZENS"—and the word "citizen" itself was a term of opprobrium in 1700—to the existence of *"a certain Author"* who *"has writ twenty thousand Verses and upwards without one Grain of Wit in them; nay, he has declar'd open War against it."* Then he goes on to draw invidious comparisons between *"Those flashy Fellows, your* Covent-garden *Poets,"* who *"write for Fame and Immortality,"* and Blackmore, who *"writes for the Good of Trade. . . . His main design in writing the two* Arthurs, *whatever he pretended in his Preface, was only to help the poor Trunk-makers at a Pinch, when* Quarles *and* Ogilby *were all spent."* Swan, in effect, recommends Blackmore to succeed Elkanah Settle as the City Poet of London and to write a *"Panegyric upon Custard."*

Not all the authors of the 40 *Commendatory Verses* have been finally identified, but there is enough evidence to say that they include few figures of any literary importance: Richard Steele, certainly, and possibly John Dennis and William Walsh. It has been suggested that part of the strategy was to recruit authors who had been praised in *A Satyr against Wit.* While it is true that there is a squib by John Sheffield, earl of Mulgrave and marquis of Normanby, and possibly another by Vanbrugh (who is praised with reservations), in general such figures are more conspicuous by their absence: they include Charles Sackville, earl of Dorset, William Congreve, Matthew Prior, Willam Wycherley, and Thomas Southerne.

It has also been suggested that Sir Charles Sedley "may have been stirred to action because he was ignored in the *Satyr against Wit*" (Richard C. Boys, *Sir Richard Blackmore and the Wits,* University of Michigan Contributions in Modern Philology No. 13, Ann Arbor, 1949, pp. 51, 142). But there is no evidence for this surmise and it seems unlikely that Sir Charles Sedley of Southfleet, the fifth baronet, "whom Nature had furnished for the conversation of Princes," could be offended by the City Bard. He was, as he told his friend Dorset, "neither ambitious nor covetous" (Vivian de Sola Pinto, *Sir Charles Sedley,* London, Constable, 1927, p. 207).

If an alternate speculation may be entertained, Sir Charles Sedley might be imagined at this time as *The Maim'd Debauchee,* his skull fractured and his "Famous" pox now hopefully only a taunt, but still content to say, "Past Joys have more than paid what I endure," and

Thus Statesman-like I'le saucily impose,
 And, safe from Danger, valiantly advise;
Shelter'd in impotence, urge you to blows,
 And, being good for nothing else, be wise.

For the truth of the matter is that after Charles' death Sedley "seem'd to dislike the Town" and settled down to a useful career in the House of Commons as a member for New Romney, Kent, one of the Cinque Ports. Sedley had been one of Shaftesbury's "worthy" supporters in the first Whig parliament, but was absent on 21 May 1679 when the exclusion bill was defeated (J. R. Jones, "Shaftesbury's 'worthy men': a Whig view of the parliament of 1679," *Bulle-*

tin of the Institute of Historical Research, 30 [1957], 241; Andrew Browning and Doreen J. Milne, "An Exclusion bill division list," *Bulletin of the Institute of Historical Research, 23* [1950], 224). He was an early supporter of William of Orange, and lent him £4600 before parliament was convened to vote a supply (Pinto, *Sir Charles Sedley,* p. 203). But he almost invariably opposed the court during William's reign. He once complained that William kept "out of the reach of all whose places doe not afford them Six horses to follow him with" (ibid., p. 230).

His most famous speech, which was printed as a broadside and widely distributed, was made, in March 1690, against place men in the House of Commons, an issue to which the Tories frequently reverted in the reign of William III. His speech in January 1699 in support of Harley's bill cutting back the army to 7000 men must have been very influential because Sedley himself had supported a standing army in December 1693, "but that was War, and this is Peace," as he explained in his preamble (*Parl. Hist., 5,* 562–63, 795; *The Miscellaneous Works of the Honourable Sir Charles Sedley, Bart.,* 1702, p. 24). But it is chiefly as *The Maim'd Debauchee* that Sedley is seen in the last years of the reign, serving as chairman of one committee to bring in a bill to prevent the corrupt mixing and sophisticating of wine, and member of another to draft a bill for the more effectual suppressing of vice and immorality, two fields in which he could claim special competence (*CJ, 12,* 651, 401–02; Pinto, *Sir Charles Sedley,* p. 223); cf. *An Encomium upon a Parliament,* 76 *n.,* above).

In June 1691 Sedley's house in Bloomsbury Square had been searched "upon an information that the bishop of Ely was harboured there" (Luttrell, *2,* 158). Francis Turner, who had been deprived as bishop of Ely because he refused to take the oaths of allegiance to William and Mary, was then being sought for complicity in a plot to restore James II.

In 1695 Blackmore was employed by the Whig junto to write a history of another Jacobite plot to assassinate the king. Not only was he furnished with the raw material for the pamphlet, but the finished product was "perused and amended" by Somers, *chef de propagande* for the junto, and by Shrewsbury, the secretary of state who controlled all secret intelligence. The work was even subjected to "a second Correction" by Shrewsbury (Blackmore, *A True and Impar-*

tial History of the Conspiracy against the Person and Government of King William III, 1723, sig. A2v). On the other side, the name of "Sir Charles Sidley" appears in Shrewsbury's notes of "examinations, depositions, or informations" of Jacobites involved in the assassination plot (HMC *Buccleuch and Queensberry MSS., 2,* 319–20). In December 1698, therefore, while Sedley was supporting Harley and the New Country-Party in the House of Commons, Jacob Tonson was publishing Blackmore's *A Short History of the Last Parliament,* a propaganda piece for the Whig junto, which the New Country-Party was about to displace in power. These political differences, together with the natural antipathy of *The Maim'd Debauchee* for "some cold-complexion'd Sot . . . With his dull Morals," may explain how Sedley could be induced to lampoon Sir Richard Blackmore in the present poem.

Sedley, as Edmund Malone discovered long ago, is Lisideius in Dryden's *Essay of Dramatic Poesy* (Dryden, *Prose, 1,* i, 63–67), and Dryden's assessment of his friend's poetry is, for once, not outrageously extravagant. He called him "a more elegant Tibullus" (ibid., *1,* ii, 373), which is an interesting parallel since Tibullus was called the most correct of the Roman poets and no less a critic than Charles II predicted that "*Sedley*'s Stile, either in Writing, or Discourse, would be the Standard of the *English* Tongue" (*The Works of the Honourable Sir Charles Sedley, Bart.,* 2 vols., 1722, *1,* [1]5). It is also interesting that Daniel Defoe, who wrote "Some Account of the Life of Sir Charles Sedley" appended to Samuel Briscoe's edition of Sedley's works in 1722, found "nothing indecent or obscene" in all that Sedley wrote (ibid., pp. [1]8–9; Pinto, *Sir Charles Sedley,* p. 5). A recent writer on *Commendatory Verses* concludes that "Sedley's lines are perhaps the best" in that volume, and from this opinion it would be impossible to dissent (Richard C. Boys, *Sir Richard Blackmore and the Wits,* p. 55).

In *Commendatory Verses,* of which the Luttrell copy in the Clark Library is dated 28 February [1700], *Upon the Author of the Satyr against Wit* was put second, immediately following the contribution of the wits' "Captain Tom," Christopher Codrington (see *A Satyr against Wit,* 87 *n.,* above). It was answered in *Discommendatory Verses, on those which are truly Commendatory, on the Author of the Two Arthur's, and the Satyr against Wit,* the counterblast to *Commendatory Verses* published on 6 April 1700. There are 52 epigrams in *Discommendatory Verses,* at least one replying to each of the 40 in *Commendatory Verses.* The second piece in this volume, *To the Poetical Knight, who would have no Body spoil Paper but Himself* ("A Pox on Rhimes and Physick, *S*[*ed*]*l*[*e*]*y* cry'd"), besides mistakenly assuming that Sedley was a knight, loses its point in incoherence.

Upon the Author of the Satyr against Wit

A Grave Physician, us'd to write for Fees,
And spoil no Paper, but with *Recipe's,*
Is now turn'd Poet, rails against all Wit,
Except that Little found among the Great;
As if he thought true Wit and Sence were ty'd
To Men in Place, like Avarice, or Pride.
But in their Praise, so like a Quack he talks,
You'd swear he wanted for his *Christmas*-box.
With mangled Names old Stories he pollutes,
And to the present Time past Actions suits;
Amaz'd we find, in ev'ry Page he writes,
Members of Parliament with *Arthur*'s Knights.

2. *Recipe's:* L. *recipe,* take; used by physicians to sign prescriptions (abbreviated Rx). Cf. "This *new mode* of Practice is, to draw and frame medicines upon a *piece* of *Paper;* modelling them into *several* forms, and contriving them for *several* purposes; varying *pro re nata,* for every temperament and case, by *subtracting* and *adding* this and that variously, as the Prescriber *fansies*" (Everard Maynwaring, *Praxis Medicorum Antiqua & Nova,* 1671, p. 91).

4. *the Great:* Samuel Johnson similarly complained that Blackmore had "degraded himself by conferring that authority over the national taste, which he takes from the poets, upon men of high rank and wide influence, but of less wit and not greater virtue" (*Lives,* 2, 241).

8. *Christmas-box:* a box, usually of earthenware, in which contributions of money were solicited at Christmas by apprentices, carriers, watchmen, scavengers, and the like, the box being broken when full and the contents shared. Sedley's shaft is double-edged, however, for it also cuts Blackmore down to the level of a common apothecary. These tradesmen customarily presented their bills at Christmastime and this "mean and vile custom of going upon *Tick* 'till Christmas" was much complained of (*The Present State of Physick & Surgery in London,* 1701, p. 10; *Bellum Medicinale, Or The Present State of Doctors and Apothecaries in London,* 1701, p. 31).

12. Arthur's bold knights, in Blackmore's first two epics, bear such half-familiar names as *Cutar,* Major General John Cutts, baron Cutts of Gowran (I.), member for Cambridgeshire (1693–1702) and Newport, Isle of Wight (1702–07); *Erla,* Major General Thomas Erle, member for Wareham, Dorset, (1679–98, 1701–18) and Portsmouth, Hampshire (1698–1701); *Stannel,* Colonel James Stanley, member for Clitheroe, Lancashire (1685–87), Preston, Lancashire (1689–90), and Lancashire (1690–1703); *Trelon,* Major General Charles Trelawny, member for East Looe, Cornwall (1685–98) and Plymouth, Devonshire (1698–1713); and *Vebba,* Colonel John Webb, member for Ludgershall, Wiltshire (1695–1713, 1715–24) and Newport, Isle of Wight (1713–15). The first three of these remained solid Whigs, but Trelawny voted to impeach the

It is a common Pastime to Write Ill;
And Doctor, with the rest, e'en take thy fill;
Thy Satyr's harmless: 'Tis thy Prose that kills,
When thou Prescrib'st thy Potions and thy Pills.
Go on brave Doctor, a third Volume write,
And find us Paper while you make us Sh——.

---

junto lords and was blacklisted as a Poussineer in 1701, while Webb joined the Tories in the next reign.

17. *a third Volume:* Blackmore's next work was known to be in the press when the "*Covent-Garden* Wits" were composing their *Commendatory Verses* in December 1699–January 1700 ([Thomas Brown], *Occasion'd by the News that Sir R—— Bl——'s Paraphrase upon Job was in the Press* ["When *Job,* contending with the Devil, I saw"], *Commendatory Verses,* 1700, p. 8). It was advertised in *The London Gazette,* No. 3580, 29 February–4 March 1700, and a mock-advertisement was obligingly appended to *Commendatory Verses:* "Upon the Publishing of *Job* and *Habakkuk,* an Heroic Poem daily expected, but deferr'd upon Political Reasons, new Subscriptions will be open'd at *Will*'s Coffee-house in *Covent-garden,* and all Gentlemen, that are willing to Subscribe, are desired to send in their *Quota*'s."

18. *Sh——:* This line recalls "that notorious business in the balcony" at Oxford Kate's, in Bow Street, in 1663, when Sedley and his fellow debauchees "excrementized in the street." When fined £500 for this escapade in the court of common pleas, Sedley "made answer," to the lord chief justice "that he thought he was the first man that paid for shiting" (Wood, *Life and Times, 1,* 476–77).

Thomas Brown

A Lent-Entertainment: Or, A Merry Interview by Moon-light, betwixt a Ghost and the City-Bard (*1700–02*)

A Lent-Entertainment—Easter fell on 31 March in 1700—provides an example of the "vision" subgenre of which *The Mitred Club* in the present volume is another. In *A Lent-Entertainment* it is the ghost of Maevius that rises out of Hell to haunt Sir Richard Blackmore. Maevius and his congener Bavius "pessimi fuerunt poetae, inimici tam Horatio quam Virgilio." Virgil disposed of them in a single hexameter (*Eclogues* III, 90): "qui Bavium non odit amet tua carmina, Maevi". (If you haven't learned to despise Kerouac, you are ready for Ferlinghetti). Horace, however, devoted all of an *Epode* to cursing Maevius.

The situation in the present poem recalls the first book of *The Dunciad:* late at night, unable to write, Blackmore seeks inspiration from his own earlier work, when he is confronted by a visionary figure "of huge Size"—recalling the goddess Dulness' "ample Presence," which fills up the room. When he receives Maevius' sulphurous wreath—thrown full in his face—he is consecrated laureate of Hell. This crude variant of Flecknoe's consecration of Shadwell is evidently one more step toward the consecration of Lewis Theobald/Colley Cibber as the anti-Christ of wit.

If the 30-page issue of *Commendatory Verses* (1700) exists (see p. 755, below), then it may be supposed that *A Lent-Entertainment* (which occupies pp. 29–30 of the 1702 issue) was published in 1700, too late to be answered in *Discommendatory Verses,* of which the Luttrell copy is dated 6 April 1700. If the 30-page issue of *Commendatory Verses* (1700) is a ghost, then *A Lent-Entertainment* may have been written as late as 1702, when the second issue of *Commendatory Verses* was published.

A Lent-Entertainment:

Or, A Merry Interview by Moon-light, betwixt a Ghost and the City-Bard

Phoebus the witty, gay and bright,
Was sunk beneath his tedious Light,
And *Nature* had her Curtains drawn
O're half the World of Sable-lawn;
The *Fairies* in the gloomy Shade
Danc'd Minuets, while *Hobgoblins* play'd;
The weary *Clown* with Toil opprest
Renews his Strength by grateful Rest;
Not so the Bosoms of the *Great,*
Whom Guilt and Cares corrode and eat:
This swets beneath *Ambition*'s Itch,
And that by *Frauds* and *Rapines* rich;
T'other profusely wastes his Time,
Nay *cracks* his Brains to get a *Rhime;*
While *various* Mortals thus contrive
By Blood and Factions how to thrive;
No smaller Pangs our *Doctor* seiz'd
How to scan Verse, than cure Diseas'd;
He long implor'd *Apollo*'s Aid,
To save the *Sick,* and sing the *Dead;*
(To him both Attributes are due
Of *Poet,* and *Physician* too.)
The angry *God* his Incense spurn'd,
And in a Fury from him turn'd.
While the neglected *Altars* smoakt,
The *Priest* himself was almost choakt:
The *Bard,* sunk down with his Despair,
Blasphem'd all Wit, and tore his Hair;
But yet his Folly to evince,

2. *tedious: OED* quotes Samuel Johnson: "Wearisome by continuance."

He with *King Arthur* backt his *Prince,*
And humbly begging both their Aids,
He thus addrest the Royal Shades:
  Ye mighty *Heroes* of your Times,
Who cannot *Dye* but by my *Rhimes;*
'Tis too too much that you shou'd *frown,*
Since every Poet *knocks* me down;
Goodness waits always on the *Brave;*
Sure there's no Malice in the Grave:
Where have I done your Honours Wrong,
Either in Record, or in Song?
Alas, 'twas never in my *Will,*
And 'tis no Crime to have no *Skill.*
  As he proceded to rehearse
The *Hardships* put upon his Verse,
And humbly crav'd both *Arthurs* Leaves
To pin his Fame upon their Sleeves;
Lo! and 'twas *wondrous* to behold
(And can't be without *Terror* told)
Of huge Size, a *Laureat* Wight
Came prancing in from *Stygian*-night:
The wooden *Machine* at the Door
Neigh'd thrice, in Homage to his Power:
His ghastly Brows with *Bays* were bound,
The Product of *sulphureous* Ground;
His Eye-balls glow'd like red-hot *Bricks,*
And in his Hand a Quart of *Styx;*
Such *liquid* Flames, such *solid* Fire,
Many wou'd *fear,* but all admire.
The Bars, and Bolts, and Locks: Oh Wonder!
All of *themselves* burst quite asunder.
When he was to the Bed-side come,

30. *backt his Prince:* followed up *Prince Arthur. An Heroick Poem. In Ten Books,* [March] 1695, by publishing *King Arthur. An Heroick Poem. In Twelve Books,* in March 1697.

36. *every Poet knocks:* Cf. "The real Witts refus'd to take notice of Prince *Arthur* and King *Arthur*" ("Mr. *Dryden* to the Lord *D———,*" *Letters from the Dead to the Living,* 2nd ed., 1702, p. 44).

51–52. *Machine at the Door Neigh'd:* perhaps a door knocker in the form of a horse's head.

The *Bard* was struck with *Horror* dumb;
The *gentle* Ghost advanc'd his Arm,
And told him, *Brother,* there's no harm;
Come, thy *dejected* Spirits chear,
Who sings of *Heroes* shou'd not *fear.*
He wipt his Face, and trembling said:
  I was *surpris'd,* but not *afraid;*
Those verdant *Bays* that crown your Brows,
Your *Candour,* and your *Goodness* shows:
Poets are harmless, gay, and kind,
And shou'd be to each other blind;
Since you are then a *Son* of *Fame,*
Forgive my *Freedom*—What's your Name?
Tho' *scoundrel* Poets here harass us,
You look like *Praetor* of *Parnassus;*
And since a Bard of *t'other* World,
More *Goodness* has you hither hurld,
And you to my *Assistance* come,
To supersede my *rigid* Doom.
You know, wise Sir—Yes, very well,
Quoth *Spright,* that you're the *News* of Hell,
The *Scandal* of the *rhiming* Crew,
I *blush* to have been *rankt* with you;
My *Rhimes* with *me* were long since rotten,
And, but for *Arthurs,* quite forgotten;
In your *curs'd* Poems I *revive,*
And now again in *Scandal* live:
Pray what has poor *Habakkuk* done,
Thus to be *lasht* in your Lampoon?
His Character you shou'd have *spar'd,*
He was a *Prophet,* not a *Bard.*
Job too does in your Poems *languish*
And suffer almost *hellish* Anguish.

85. *rotten:* Horace called him "smelly Maevius" (*Epode X,* 2).

89. *Habakkuk:* Blackmore, *A Paraphrase on the Book of Job: As Likewise on the Songs of Moses, Deborah, David: On Four Select Psalms: Some Chapters of Isaiah, and the Third Chapter of Habakkuk,* was advertised in *The London Gazette,* No. 3580, 29 February–4 March 1700.

94. *hellish Anguish:* "Job complains more of his *ill* Usage from the *City Bard,* than all his other Afflictions, which the *Devil,* in Conjunction with his *Wife,* contriv'd to

Were he now *living,* and thy *Theme,*
He cou'd not help, but must *blaspheme.*
Sir, by your Favour, quoth the *Bard,*
Your *Censures* are unjust and hard;
I've done them *Honour,* as I think,
Or let my *Name* for ever stink.
Why that's most *certain,* quoth the Spright,
And thou'rt a *Coxcomb* by this Light,
So empty, sensless, and so dull,
Thou'rt every School-boy's Ridicule.
A damn'd *Reproach* to *Verse* and Prose,
As well as the *Gallenic* Dose.
What! saith the *Doctor,* in a Fury,
I no *Physician!*—I assure you
Diseases run from me affrighted;
My Skill's so great, that I am *Knighted;*
Such vast Discoveries I have made
Throughout the *Esculapean* Trade,
The *Cits* applaud, their *Wives* adore,
My numerous *Verse* and Medic Power.
Come, thou'rt a *Scoundrel,* quoth the Ghost;
Of *Wit* and *Cures* alike you boast;
Know, I am *Maevius,* that of old,
In *Thoughts* sublime, and *Matter* bold,
Did every *versifying* Ass,
By a Bar's length at least, *surpass;*
And only am *out-done* by you
In lofty *Noise* and *Nonsence* too.

---

lay upon him; and *Habakkuk* bewails the ignoble Captivity he lies under, with a *deeper* Resentment than that of his Country-men in *Chaldea*" (Brown, "To Madam *** upon sending her Sir Richard Blackmore's Job and Habakkuk," *Works,* 2nd ed., 1708 *1,* 1265–66).

102. *Coxcomb:* In his *Remarks on a Book Entituled Prince Arthur* (1695), Dennis had called Bavius and Maevius "Coxcombs in more than ordinary credit" (*Critical Works, 1,* 70).

114. Cf. "The Cheapside Hero . . . *Rhimes* as well as Prescribes" (Brown, "To a Physician in the Country; giving a true state of the Poetical War between *Cheap-side* and *Covent-Garden,*" *Works,* 2nd ed., 1708, *1,* 1261).

119–20. *every versifying Ass . . . surpass:* Dennis supposed that "a formidable Party in ancient *Rome* . . . thought [Bavius and Maevius] superiour both to *Horace* and *Virgil*" (*Critical Works, 1,* 70).

Then *Maevius* tore his wither'd Bays,
And threw 'em in the *Doctor*'s Face;
Who, being *scar'd* at such a Scene,
Has promis'd ne're to *Write* agen.

The Rt. Honble. John Lord Sommers.
J. Richardson pinx. 1713.
I. Smith fec.
Sold by J. Smith at the Lyon & Crown in Russell Street Covent Garden

John, Lord Somers. Mezzotint engraving by John Smith

On My Lord Somers
(April 1700)

Burnet called Somers "the Head of the Whigs" in 1700 and added that "the chief strength of the Party lay in his credit with the King" (*2*, 241). Somers had served William as his first solicitor-general in 1689, attorney-general in 1692, lord keeper of the great seal in 1693, and finally, in 1697, as lord high chancellor of England. In February 1698, in fact, William had complained to Portland that Somers was "le s[e]ul Ministre qui me reste présentement" (Japikse, *1*, 236). It was Somers to whom William wrote in August 1698 about the secret treaty with France and the Netherlands to partition the empire of Spain. And it was Somers, in January 1699, who dissuaded the king from abdicating in the crisis over the standing army. But as one leader after another of the Whig junto resigned from office in 1698–99, Somers was more and more exposed to attack.

The attack was particularly bitter because the Tories blamed Somers for having removed the justices of the peace who refused to sign the Association of 1696 and for having replaced them with "Upstarts" who wielded their influence in elections to secure majorities for the court Whigs. So when a New Country-Party of Tories and "old" Whigs achieved a solid majority in the session of December 1698–May 1699, Somers' resignation was demanded. But since William refused "to declare for one party more than for another," he could not be prevailed upon to part with his lord chancellor.

The crisis came in the second session of the fourth parliament. On 2 April 1700 a rampant Tory majority in the Commons sent up to the House of Lords a money bill to which was tacked a clause revoking the king's grants of forfeited estates in Ireland and ordering the rent from these estates diverted into the public treasury. These grants, which William had made very lavishly during the past 10 years, mainly to his favorite generals, who were foreigners, were highly unpopular. Ordering them to be resumed and tacking the resumption to a bill which, as James Vernon said, "carries with it the whole supply for the next year," precipitated the most serious constitutional and financial crisis of the reign (Vernon, *3*, 3).

Everyone recognized that the attack was directed against Somers, through whose office all the king's grants had been passed. There were even rumors that the Tories had agreed to throw out the resumption bill "upon condition that the Whigs [i.e. Somers] be discarded" (Vernon, *3*, 3, 8). For a time the king "seemed resolved to venture on all the ill consequences, that might follow the losing this Bill; tho' those," as Burnet knew, "would probably have been fatal" (*2*, 239). In the House of Lords, the bill "produc'd a long, perplex'd, and passionate Debate" (Ralph, *2*, 851). Since Somers had a bad cold—"And the worst construction possible was put on that"—his place on the woolsack was taken by Forde Grey, earl of Tankerville. The duke of Devonshire declared, prophetically, "et même avec serment," that the House of Commons with its money bills would be able to buy all the prerogatives of the lords and those of the king as well (Burnet, *2*, 239; BM MS. Add. 30000D, f. 123v.). But when the king withdrew his opposition on 10 April 1700, the lords voted 39–34 to accept the bill.

When this good news reached the Commons, the lobby was cleared of strangers, the doors locked, and the list of William's privy councillors laid before the house. The third name on the list was that of John, Lord Somers.

> At my Lord Chancellor's name a long debate arose, and all the great men on that [Tory] side spoke with a warmth against him; that his grant was exorbitant, that his ministry was partial and oppressive; that the ill answers they had received from the throne proceeded from his advice, and that it was not to be doubted but that he was the promoter of the opposition the Lords had given the bill.
>
> (Vernon, *3*, 21–22)

It is to the last point—Somers' Milonian attempt to divide the houses—that the present poem addresses itself. And whether or not it is true that Somers tried to effect a breach between the two houses, there can be no doubt that he was caught when the opposed houses fell back into agreement. On 27 April 1700 "the earl of Jersey, by order from his majestie, demanded of the lord chancellor the great seal, which his lordship delivered" (Luttrell, *4*, 639).

Since the epigram seems to require that Somers still be in office, it must have been written between 10 and 27 April 1700. There is no indication of its author. The same events are the subject of another epigram, *On Some Votes against the Lord S.* ("When Envy does at *Athens* rise"), which was published in *POAS*, 1703, *2*, 247, and attributed, in Bodl. MS. Add. B.105, f. 27, but nowhere else, to Matthew Prior.

On My Lord Somers

Blown up by Faction, and by Guilt Spurr'd on,
We read thy Fate O *Somers,* Thou'rt undone.
All thy Attempts against that Pow'r are vain,
By which some Kings have fallen, others Reign.
Vain thy Efforts the Houses to divide,
They'll close again and crush thy daring Pride.
Audacious Upstart! think on *Milo*'s End,
Wedg'd in that Timber which He strove to Rend.

3. *that Pow'r:* Nemesis, "the goddess of retribution, who brings down all immoderate good fortune, checks the presumption that attends it . . . , and is the punisher of extraordinary crimes" *(OED)*.

4. *some Kings:* e.g. *James II.*

others: e.g. William III.

5. *the Houses:* e.g. the House of Stuart and the House of Orange, or the House of Commons and the House of Lords.

7. *Upstart:* Belief in Somers' humble, or even doubtful, origins was widespread. His father was, in fact, a country gentleman living on his estate, Clifton, near Severn Stoke, Worcestershire. The father was also an attorney but apparently did not, as earlier biographers have said, manage the estates of Charles Talbot, earl (later duke) of Shrewsbury (Dorothy H. Somerville, *The King of Hearts,* London, Allen and Unwin, 1962, p. 19 *n.*).

Milo: the famous strong man of antiquity whose hands and feet were caught in a log that he was trying to split; "and caught in such a trap as that, he became food for wild beasts" (Strabo, *6,* i, 12).

7–8. *think . . . Rend:* Cf. Roscommon, *An Essay on Translated Verse* (1684), 87–88:

> 'Tis I that call, remember *Milo's End,*
> Wedg'd in that Timber which he strove to Rend.

John Dryden

Prologue to "The Pilgrim"
(April 1700)

The Dryden-Blackmore feud began in March 1695 with Blackmore's unprovoked sally in *Prince Arthur. An Heroick Poem.* Here the discharged laureate is introduced amid a crowd of patronage seekers at the gate of the lord chamberlain:

> *Laurus* amidst the meagre Crowd appear'd,
> An old, revolted, unbelieving Bard,
> Who throng'd, and shov'd, and prest, and would be heard.
> Distinguish'd by his louder craving Tone,
> So well to all the Muses Patrons known,
> He did the Voice of Modest Poets drown.
>
> (p. 167)

When Dryden failed to reply and even recanted some of his earlier work:

> What I have loosly, or profanely writ,
> Let them to Fires (their due desert) commit.
>
> (*Poems, 3,* 1435)

he inadvertently supplied Blackmore with the opportunity for a major attack. In *A Satyr against Wit* (November 1699) the entire corpus of Dryden's work is committed to the flames, purged of blasphemy and obscenity, and found to yield only a single silver crown (206–11).

Exactly five years after the first attack, Dryden, in the preface to *Fables Ancient and Modern* (February 1700), finally acknowledged the existence of "one B." who had written scurrilously against him. "As for the City Bard, or Knight Physician," Dryden went on to say, "I will deal the more civilly with his two Poems, because nothing ill is to be spoken of the Dead." And in *To My Honour'd Kinsman, John Driden, of Chesterton,* in the same volume, he reflected further on Blackmore's uncreating skills. Dryden's preoccupation with death was not accidental; he was, as he said, "an old decrepid Man," under the care of two villains of *The Dispensary: Guiacum* (Thomas Hobbes, Master of the Surgeons Company and a famous clap doctor) and *Mirmillo* (William Gibbons, "the Homicide"):

> *Guibbons* but guesses, nor is sure to save:
> But *Maurus* sweeps whole Parishes, and Peoples ev'ry Grave.
> And no more Mercy to Mankind will use,
> Than when he robb'd and murder'd *Maro*'s Muse.
> Wou'dst thou be soon dispatch'd, and perish whole?
> Trust *Maurus* with thy Life, and *M—lb—rn* with thy Soul.
>
> (82–87)

As Kinsley explains, " '*Maro*'s Muse' is the muse of epic poetry, outraged [i.e. fatally assaulted] by Blackmore's experiments in heroic Verse" (*Poems, 4,* 2070). "It was not for this noble Knight," Dryden asserted, "that I drew the Plan of an Epick Poem on King *Arthur* in my Preface to the Translation of *Juvenal*" from which Blackmore "plainly took his Hint" and then traduced his benefactor "in a Libel" (*Prose, 3,* 647).

In the last two weeks of March 1700 Blackmore struck back. Again turning Dryden's words against him, he reported that *"One of the most* Famous Poets *of the Stage has at last expresly own'd, that the* Charge *brought against him is* too just. *He has done it in* two Lines; *the* two best *he ever writ* . . . :

> What I have loosely, or prophanely writ,
> Let them to Fires, (their due Desert) commit."
>
> (*A Paraphrase on the Book of Job,* 1700, sig. a1r)

A few days later, on 11 April 1700, Dryden wrote to his literary cousin, Elizabeth Steward:

> Within this moneth, there will be playd for my profit, an old play of Fletchers, calld the Pilgrim, corrected by my good friend Mr. Vanbrook; to which I have added A New Masque, & am to write a New Prologue & Epilogue.
>
> (*Works, 18,* 179)

The prologue that Dryden wrote and Colley Cibber spoke on opening night at the Drury Lane theatre, probably on 29 April 1700, has very little to do with the play. What it does tell the audience is *not* to expect to find Sir Richard Blackmore presented in the play. All noted fools, the argument runs, expect to find themselves presented in a play, and Blackmore, because he played the fool and wrote three books, surely expects to be "shown." But it would be impossible to "characterize" him, "For no one Category can contain him." The latest of his roles, the argument concludes, is writer, and here Dryden joins himself to James II and William III as victims of the ingratitude of Sir Richard Blackmore, who

> Traduc'd Two Kings, their kindness to requite;
> One made the Doctor, and one dubb'd the Knight.

Thereafter, Dryden made sure that he had had the last word by dying on 1 May 1700, the night of the third performance, the traditional "third night," which had been reserved for his benefit (Macdonald, p. 135 *n.*).

PROLOGUE TO *"The Pilgrim"*

How wretched is the Fate of those who write!
Brought muzled to the Stage, for fear they bite.
Where, like *Tom Dove,* they stand the Common Foe;
Lugg'd by the *Critique,* Baited by the *Beau.*
Yet worse, their Brother *Poets* Damn the Play,
And Roar the loudest, tho' they never Pay.
The Fops are proud of Scandal, for they cry,
At every lewd, low Character,—That's I.
He who writes Letters to himself, wou'd Swear
The World forgot him, if he was not there.
What shou'd a Poet do? 'Tis hard for One
To pleasure all the Fools that wou'd be shown:
And yet not Two in Ten will pass the Town.
Most Coxcombs are not of the Laughing kind;
More goes to make a Fop, than Fops can find.
   Quack *Maurus,* tho' he never took Degrees

1. Cf. "How Bless'd is He, who leads a Country Life," the first line of *To My Honour'd Kinsman, John Driden, of Chesterton.* The juxtaposition of these two lines, among the last that he wrote, tells something about Dryden more important than most of the details that have been published about his life: the genius that compelled him to write and the fate that required him to earn a living combined to keep Dryden in London, but it is clear that like any good Augustan what he wanted was "a Country Life."

3. *Tom Dove:* the celebrated bear who performed at the stake in the Bear Garden. Other literary allusions to him, ranging from 1677 to 1696, are collected in *The Prologues and Epilogues of John Dryden,* ed. William B. Gardner, New York, Columbia University Press, 1951, p. 337.

9. *He who writes Letters to himself:* This may be a reference to Petulant in Congreve's *The Way of the World, a Comedy* (1700), concerning whom Witwoud says, "he [Petulant] would leave a Chocolate House and shortly return; thereupon he would send in for himself, that I mean, call for himself, wait for himself, nay and what's more, not finding himself, sometimes leave a Letter for himself" (ibid., pp. 337–38).

10. *there:* in the imagined play.

12. *shown:* represented in a play.

16. *Maurus: L.* Moor, Moorish; Negro. This is Dryden's pseudonym for Blackmore, which he first used in *To My Honour'd Kinsman* (line 83), as a retort to Blackmore's coinage of Laurus for Dryden in *Prince Arthur. An Heroick Poem* (1695) (p. 167). Dryden may or may not have known that Blackmore graduated B.A. from St. Edmund

In either of our Universities;
Yet to be shown by some kind Wit he looks,
Because he plaid the fool and writ Three Books.
But if he wou'd be worth a Poet's Pen,
He must be more a Fool, and write again:
For all the former Fustian stuff he wrote,
Was Dead-born Doggrel, or is quite forgot;
His Man of *Uz,* stript of his *Hebrew* Robe,
Is just the Proverb, and *As poor as* Job.
One wou'd have thought he cou'd no lower Jog;
But *Arthur* was a Level, *Job*'s a Bog.
There, tho' he crept, yet still he kept in sight;
But here, he flounders in, and sinks down right.
Had he prepar'd us, and been dull by Rule,
Tobit had first been turn'd to Ridicule:
But our bold *Britton,* without Fear or Awe,
O're-leaps at once, the whole *Apocrypha;*
Invades the *Psalms* with Rhymes, and leaves no room
For any Vandal *Hopkins* yet to come.
But what if, after all, this Godly Geer,
Is not so Senceless as it wou'd appear?
Our Mountebank has laid a deeper Train,

Hall, Oxford, in 1674, and M.A. two years later, but received his M.D. at Padua in 1684 (Rosenberg, pp. 7, 14). What he did know was that since Blackmore had no medical degree from Oxford or Cambridge, he could not have become a member of the College of Physicians if he had not been admitted under a new charter granted by James II in March 1687 extending membership to 40 physicians with degrees from foreign universities (HMC *House of Lords MSS., 2,* 121–27).

18. *to be shown . . . he looks:* He expects to be represented in a play, to be dramatized.

19. *Three Books: Prince Arthur. An Heroick Poem* (1695), *King Arthur. An Heroick Poem* (1697), and, to give its full title, *A Paraphrase on the Book of Job: As Likewise on the Songs of Moses, Deborah, David: on Four Select Psalms: Some Chapters of Isaiah, and the Third Chapter of Habakkuk* (1700), nearly everything, as Dryden saw, but *Bel and the Dragon* (cf. line 33, below).

35. *Hopkins:* John Hopkins (d. 1570), rector of Great Wallingfield, Suffolk, and a collaborator of Thomas Sternhold in *The Whole Booke of Psalmes Collected into Englysh* (1562) (STC 2430). Kinsley cites *The Second Part of Absalom and Achitophel* (1682), lines 402–03, where "dull and adlepated" Shadwell and Settle "Rhime below ev'n *David*'s Psalms translated" *(Poems, 1,* 282).

36. *Godly Geer:* pious cant, sanctimonious "stuff"; *OED,* s.v. Gear, sb. 11a, cites Dryden, *The Wife of Bath Her Tale,* 24–25, "For Priests with Pray'rs, and other godly Geer,/Have made the merry Goblins disappear."

His Cant, like *Merry Andrew*'s Noble Vein,
Cat-Call's the Sects, to draw 'em in for gain.
At leisure Hours, in Epique Song he deals,
Writes to the rumbling of his Coaches Wheels,
Prescribes in hast, and seldom kills by Rule,
But rides Triumphant between Stool and Stool.
Well, let him go; 'tis yet too early day,
To get himself a Place in Farce or Play.
We know not by what Name we should Arraign him,
For no one Category can contain him;
A Pedant, Canting Preacher, and a Quack,

39. *Merry Andrew:* a clown performing as a mountebank's assistant. Garth describes one in his Harveian oration of 1697: "A third [mountebank] haveing gathered a company together by the help of a Rope dancer, strutts and looks great, when happily down falls Tom Tumbler upon the gazeing croud and harms more than ever his Master cured" (*JHM, 18* [January 1963], 13).

41. *leisure Hours:* Dryden is paraphrasing the preface to *King Arthur* in which Blackmore explained that *Prince Arthur* had been "Begun, Carry'd on and Completed . . . in less than two years time, and by such catches and starts, and in such occasional, uncertain hours, as the Business of my Profession would afford me" (p. v). Upon which Dryden observed that "They who think too well of their own Performances, are apt to boast in their Prefaces how little Time their Works have cost them; and what other Business of more importance interfer'd: But the Reader will be as apt to ask the Question, Why they allow'd not a longer Time to make their Works more perfect?" (*Prose, 3,* 595).

42. *Writes to the rumbling:* Cf. *The Dispensary, 4,* 192 *n.,* above. Christopher Codrington had picked up the joke in *A Short and True History of the Author of the Satyr against Wit* ("By Nature meant, by Want a Pedant made"), the first poem in *Commendatory Verses:*

Next he turn'd Bard, and mounted on a Cart,
Whose hideous Rumbling made *Apollo* start.

49. *Pedant:* After taking his M.A. degree in June 1676, Blackmore remained at St. Edmund Hall, Oxford, as a tutor (Rosenberg, pp. 7–11). His detractors also accused him of having been for a time "a Country School-Master," "the only reproach," as Samuel Johnson has said, "which all the perspicacity of malice, animated by wit, has ever fixed upon his private life" (*Lives, 2,* 236).

Canting Preacher: "A Man had need have a great deal of time upon his hands," as John Dennis remarked, "to Examine a Poet's Politicks, or a Physician's Religion" (*Works, 1,* 52), but there is no evidence that Blackmore was anything but an orthodox member of the Church of England. Even his attendance at church, however, afforded matter for satire; a notice in *The Infallible Astrologer,* No. 4, for 13–20 November 1700, observed that on Sunday 17 November "Not one Physician [was] at Church, except the City-Bard, within the Bills of Mortality." Dryden may have heard the story that Blackmore had "married a rich Conventicler and by that means got a mighty Interest among the Whigs, and was knighted by King William, who always lov'd to conferr his Marks of Honour upon Persons disaffected to the Church of England"

Are Load enough to break one Asses Back:
At last, grown wanton, he presum'd to write,
Traduc'd Two Kings, their kindness to requite;
One made the Doctor, and one dubb'd the Knight.

(Hearne, *1,* 231–32). It has been observed that Blackmore is "the only poet, who ever suffered for having too much religion and morality" (Cibber, *Lives, 5,* 184).

53. *made the Doctor:* See 16 *n.,* above.

dubb'd the Knight: Samuel Johnson supposed that Blackmore had been knighted for political rather than for medical or poetical services: "The malignity of the wits attributed his knighthood to his new poem; but king William was not very studious of poetry, and Blackmore perhaps had other merit" (*Lives, 2,* 239–40). The entry in the herald's office, however, mentions only the "new poem": "LOND. RICHARD BLACKMORE doctor of Phisick auctor of prince arthur Kted at Kensington 18 Mar. 1696/7 sworn Phisitian in Ordinary to his Majtie" (Le Neve, p. 458; Luttrell, *4,* 199).

EDWARD BAYNARD[?]

Epitaph upon Mr. John Dryden (*11 June 1700*)

It has long been supposed that there are two, contradictory accounts of Dryden's funeral: Elizabeth Thomas' account and the true account. Elizabeth Thomas had forced herself upon Dryden's attention in 1699 by sending him copies of her verses. Her account of his funeral imagines a "velvet Hearse" and 18 mourning coaches lined up in Gerrard Street on Saturday, 4 May 1700 to accompany the mortal remains of John Dryden around the corner to St. Anne's Church:

> When just before they began to move, Lord *Jefferies,* with some of his rakish Companions, coming by, in Wine, ask'd whose Funeral? And being told; *What,* cries he! *shall* Dryden, *the greatest Honour and Ornament of the Nation, be buried after this private Manner? No, Gentlemen! let all that lov'd Mr.* Dryden, *and honour his Memory, alight and join with me in gaining my Lady's Consent, to let me have the Honour of his Interment, which shall be after another manner than this, and I will bestow £1000 on a Monument in the Abbey for him.*
> ([Elizabeth Thomas,] *Memoirs of the Life, Writings, and Amours of William Congreve,* 1730, p. ²4)

Whether or not the facts are true, this evocation of a great master written 30 years after his death by an abandoned poetaster in Fleet prison cannot fail to be affecting.

Elizabeth Thomas goes on to recount how the drunken Lord Jeffreys "order'd the Hearseman to carry the Corps to *Russell*'s an Undertaker in *Cheapside,*" how, the next morning, Lord Jeffreys had no recollection at all of this *boutade* and refused to pay for anything, how Russell then "threatened to bring home the Corps, and set it before [the] Door," and how the family was finally saved by the intervention of Samuel Garth, "a Man who entirely loved Mr. Dryden."

Harrowing as it is, Elizabeth Thomas' account is simply an imaginative expansion of the facts revealed by contemporary sources:

> [Monday 6 May 1700] Mr. Montague had given orders to bury him; some Lords thinking it would not be splendid enough, ordered him to be carried to Russel's. There he was embalmed and now lies in state at the Physicians College, and is to be buried with Chaucer, Cowley, &c. at Westminster Abbey on Monday next.
>
> (Bodl. MS. Ballard 4, f. 54)

> [Tuesday 14 May 1700] He says that Dryden was buried by the Bishop of Rochester at the Abbey on Monday; that the Kit Cat Club were at the charge of his funeral, which was not great [Russell's bill for the entire funeral, including "Covering the hearse with velvet," as Elizabeth Thomas remembered, amounted to £45 17s.], and that Mr. Montague had engaged to build him a fine monument. Dr. Garth made a Latin speech, and threw away some words and a great deal of false Latin in praise of the poet.
>
> (HMC *Fifth Report,* 1876, pp. 359–60)

The truth of the matter seems to be that Dryden was buried, "as his Virgil was printed, by subscription" (Pepys, *Corr., 1,* 344). He was buried at St. Anne's, Soho, on 2 May 1700 (*Athenaeum,* 77 [30 July and 27 August 1904], 145–46, 271), disinterred and embalmed by William Russell before 6 May. His body lay in state in the Cutlerian Theatre of the Royal College of Physicians until 13 May, when Samuel Garth pronounced a Latin oration, and Horace's thirtieth ode of the third book, "Exegi monumentum aere perennius," was sung to the accompaniment of a slow dirge. A funeral procession of more than 100 coaches, with countless mourners on horseback and afoot, then wound its way along Fleet Street and the Strand to Westminster Abbey.

To this procession there were two witnesses who recorded what they saw, one sympathetic and one hostile. The former was Edward Ward, who watched the procession from the foot of Chancery Lane and concluded that "No Ambassador from the greatest Emperour in the Universe, sent over with the most Welcome Embassy to the Throne of *England,* ever made his publick Entry to the Court, with half that Honour as the Corps of the Great *Dryden* did in its last *Exit* to the Grave" (*The London Spy,* 2 [April 1700], 5–8).

The hostile witness recorded his impressions in *A Description of Mr. Dryden's Funeral. A Poem* ("Of Kings Renown'd and Mighty Bards I write"), of which three folio editions were published in 1700 (Wing B5056–5058). With 31 lines added, the poem was included in *POAS,* 1703, *2,* 229–35. It has been attributed to Thomas Brown, but was written by John Tutchin. It was advertised in *The Foreigners* (1700), for publishing which Tutchin was arrested, and was included in a list of Tutchin's works published by M. Fabian in *The Apostates* ("Art thou, dear Israel! still the Butt of Fate?") (1701). But even this hostile, ill-natured account cannot conceal Tutchin's belief that, compared to "Poet *Squab,*" "All other Poets are not worth a Louse."

A month later, on 11 June 1700, the following mock-epitaph was found fixed on Dryden's tomb in the Abbey. It is attributed to Dr. Edward Baynard (*A Satyr against Wit,* 384*n.*, above) in BM MS. Add. 29921, f. 135. A less likely possibility is that it is the poem "On the Death of Mr. Dryden 1700," which is attributed to William Pittis in Bodl. MS. Rawl. J.4°.1, f. 249.

EPITAPH UPON MR. JOHN DRYDEN

John Dryden had Enemies three,
Old *Nick,* Sir *Dick,* and *Jeremy.*
The fustian knight was forc'd to yield,
The other two maintain'd the Field:
But had the Poet's Life been holier,
He 'ad beat the Devil and the Collier.

2. *Sir Dick:* "Sir Richard Blackmore" (*AG*).
Jeremy: "Mr. Ieremy Collier" (*G*).
6. *the Devil and the Collier: The Devil and the Collier* ("The Devil he was so Weather-beat") was a popular song; words and music are printed in *Wit and Mirth: Or, Pills to Purge Melancholy,* 1700, pp. 203–05.

A Conference
Between King William and the Earl of Sunderland.
In a Letter to a Friend.
June 1700.

This poem, with its fine scorn of party politics, can only be understood against the background of a major shift of power in the party politics of the reign of William III. "In such mysterious transactions" as these, as William Coxe observed, "we cannot expect to trace the real motives and real views of parties" (Coxe, p. 623). The French ambassador at the time was even less hopeful:

> Oserais-je vous dire, Sire [he asked, in cipher], qu'il n'y a rien de si difficile, que de suivre les affaires qu'on a en ce pays icy, ou l'on ny a ny règle ny ordre, ny rien de tout ce qui peut donner lieu de prendre des mesures.
>
> (PRO 31/3 185, f. 105)

But some details of these transactions have come to the surface.

What William wanted more than anything else at the beginning of 1700 was to avoid another disastrous session of parliament like that of December 1698–May 1699 described in Defoe's *An Encomium upon a Parliament*. So in January 1700 he asked Sunderland to invite Robert Harley, the leader of the New Country-Party in the House of Commons, to form a coalition ministry with Somers, now unquestionably the leader of the Whig junto, and Marlborough and Godolphin, both Tories (John P. Kenyon, *Robert Spencer, Earl of Sunderland, 1641–1702,* London and New York, Longmans, Green, 1958, p. 314). Harley apparently balked at forming a coalition government and insisted upon naming his own candidates for the important offices of the crown. At any rate, it soon became apparent that Somers had become the main target of the Tory attack in the House of Commons.

Still there was great surprise, on 27 April 1700, when Somers was suddenly dismissed from the highest office in England only 16 days after a motion in the House of Commons to address the king to remove Somers from his presence and councils forever had been defeated by the large margin of 61 votes. Nearly everyone, including Somers, believed that Sunderland had advised the king to dismiss the lord chancellor. A For Rent sign tacked up on the door of the lord chancellor's empty office bore the legend, "For particulars, apply to the earl of Sunderland" (BM MS. Add. 30000D, f. 164v).

It appears, however, that Sunderland could claim quite honestly that he had not advised the king to dismiss Somers. What he had advised the king to do was to make Somers resign. This is apparent from a letter of Charles Paulet, second duke of Bolton, to Somers, in September 1700:

> It looks as if Lord Sunderland [he said] was not so much dissatisfied with your being displaced, as he represented himself in the conversation with the Duke of Shrewsbury. . . . His complaint was, I find, that the method of doing it was not his; and that he thought it strange (as all the world did) to displace you, and not have somebody ready to put in; and was in hopes of finding a way to make your Lordship resign; which, he is in the right, must have been better for the King's affairs, as they designed it, but infinitely to your prejudice.
>
> (Hardwicke, 2, 439)

Burnet has recorded the king actually repeating Sunderland's words to Somers: "The first time that the Lord *Somers* had recovered so much health, as to come to Court, the King told him, it seemed necessary for his service, that he should part with the Seals, and he wished, that he would make the delivering them up his own Act" (Burnet 2, 242). Somers, however, refused to fall into the trap. His resignation would have been interpreted as an admission either of guilt or of weakness. So he told the king that with his majesty's permission he would keep the great seal in defiance of his enemies. But the king only shook his head a little and said, *"It must be so"* (Oldmixon, p. 208). Accordingly, on 26 April, the dull-witted earl of Jersey appeared in Somers' office and demanded the seals. Somers pointed out that he had forgotten to bring a warrant under the sign manual, so it was actually on the next day that Somers finally surrendered the seals of his office. Four days later, the first step toward the formation of a new Tory ministry was taken when Laurence

Hyde, earl of Rochester, wrote Harley asking to be allowed to wait on him in London (HMC *Portland MSS., 3,* 618–19).

William's action in dismissing Somers had been taken so precipitantly that he had in fact neglected to secure anyone to replace him. Robert Harley's original candidate for lord chancellor had apparently been John Methuen, the lord chancellor of Ireland and "Once very near being So in *England*" (Macky, p. 143; cf. BM MS. Add. 30000D, f. 167v). William, however, offered the great seal to one after another of the three ranking judges in England and was astounded to be refused in each case. By this time Sunderland "thought the King's affairs in so great a disorder" that he decided to retire to Althorp (Vernon, *3,* 44).

About the same time Harley switched his support to Sir Thomas Trevor, the king's attorney-general: "This has been a week of great fatigue," he wrote to his father on 11 May, "I have every day been with the Attorney General twice. At last he will not take it, which is a great disappointment" (HMC *Portland MSS., 3,* 619). On 14 May William granted Sunderland an audience to discuss the problem of Somers' successor. It is this meeting that provides the occasion for the present poem.

Three days later Shrewsbury returned to the attack on Sir Thomas Trevor, even threatening to have him removed from the attorney-generalship if he continued to refuse, but it was not until 21 May that Lord Rochester secured the agreement of Sir Nathan Wright, a little-known serjeant at law with "a fat broad Face, much marked with the Small-pox" (Macky, p. 41), to accept the post (BM MS. Add. 30000D, f. 176; Coxe, p. 621). On 23 June Rochester and Godolphin had an audience with the king at Hampton Court. William offered Rochester the lord lieutenancy of Ireland, but Rochester was holding out for lord high treasurer, an office that had been executed by commission since Rochester himself had been dismissed from it in January 1687. In September 1700 Henry Guy reported to Harley that Rochester and Godolphin had entirely made up their differences, and two months later a new Tory ministry was formed with Godolphin as first lord of the treasury and Rochester as lord lieutenant of Ireland. Finally, on 9 December 1700, Godolphin and Rochester took their seats in the privy council in the room of Montagu and Somers (BM MS. Add. 30000D, f. 212v; PRO 31/3 186, f. 40; HMC *Portland MSS., 3,* 626).

It is the contention of the present poem that the political merry-go-round is kept going only for the benefit of the riders. Sunderland argues that this

> . . . Changeing of Parties is still necessary
> According as Times and Conjunctures vary.
> (91–92)

But the king replies that

> There's no man among you, what ere he pretends,
> But laughs at the Publick and acts for Self Ends.
> (153–54)

Perhaps the poem comes closer than the fragmentary historical evidence to revealing "the real motives and real views of parties." On the other side, a very slight revision will show how close the poem is to the mocking tone and lilt of Gilbert and Sullivan:

> A Statesman's Conscience ought to be free
> And of what Religion he pleases to be, pleases to be,
> And of what Religion he pleases to be.

Three manuscripts of the poem preserve a postscript of varying length. Although it appears to be a later addition, it has been included in the textual apparatus, its lines numbered consecutively with the poem itself. The postscript repeats, rather than adds to, the poem in most details (cf. lines 10 and 169, 90 and 184). It seems to assume both a later date and a completely different stance than the original poem. The anonymous author of the poem is hostile to both parties, but the writer of the postscript damns the New Country-Party to a "Pox or a Rope." The writer of the poem calls Somers the best lord chancellor but he does not ignore his "Pentions and Bribes." The possibility that he is William Shippen, suggested by the references to *A Conference* in *Faction Display'd* (pp. 655, 666 below) and by the similarity of political orientation and stylistic preferences, is presently under investigation.

There is no reason to doubt that the poem was written in June 1700, the date that appears on five of the existing manuscripts.

A Conference
Between King William and the Earl of Sunderland.
in a Letter to a Friend.
June 1700.

Haveing thankt me so much for the Newes in my last,
This serves to acquaint you with what has since past.
The Count who lives in but not on the Square
Was Summon'd last week to the Court to repair,
Where he found the sad King to his Closet retreated,
Not more in the Dumps when at Landen defeated.
   Great Sir, said the Count, what is your Command?
Your Affaires I perceive are all at a Stand.
   Sacrament, swore the Monarch, thou hast me undone
And hast been a Traytor to Father and Son.
Just cause have I now the Proverb to quote,
Save a theif from the Gallows and he'l Cut your throat.
   Dread Sir, said the Count, tho the Proverb be true,

3. *the Square:* Sunderland occupied No. 31, in the southeast corner of St. James's Square (BM MS. Lansdowne 852, f. 41; *Survey of London, 29,* 187–89). "To live upon the square" is proverbial. George Stepney complained to Matthew Prior that "there is nothing but roguery and double dealing in this world and to live upon the square is the certain way of being cheated" (Charles K. Eves, *Matthew Prior,* New York, Columbia University Press, 1939, p. 61).

4. *last week:* The audience described in the poem was granted on Tuesday 14 May 1700. Vernon reported that Sunderland "is gone this day to Hampton Court, expecting that the King will make him put off his journey into the country, and that he will talk to him about the disposal of the seals" (Vernon, *3,* 48).

6. *Landen:* See *Advice to a Painter,* 12 *n.,* above.

8. *at a Stand:* Burnet recalled that "there was no direction at all" (*2,* 242–43) at this time and Harley not only complained that "we had no ministry, no right management of public affairs," but hinted darkly that "if the King did not mind it, a reformation would be wrought in a more disagreeable manner" (Vernon, *3,* 90–91).

10. *Traytor to Father:* Belief in Sunderland's betrayal of James II, long a fundamental article in the Jacobite creed, is "dismissed as patently silly" in J. P. Kenyon, "The earl of Sunderland and the Revolution of 1688," *Cambridge Historical Journal,* 11 (1955), 277.

11. *the Proverb: "Save a Thief from the Gallows and he will cut your Throat,* is a Proverb of our own Growth" (Thomas Brown, *The Second Volume of The Works,* 1707, p. 2223).

Yet tis very hard to be quoted by you.
Betraying your Father my Conscience does Sting,
But you by that Treason were made Brittains King.
  The Monarch surprizd with such a sharp touch
And Sensible of so Just a reproach,
Said, Fear not, my Lord, I'le no Secrets reveal,
Let me know how you like my dispose of the Seal.
  Not at all, said the Count, it is given to those
Who to absolute Monarchs are three sworn foes,
Men Learn'd in the Law but honest and brave,
Who the Guiltless won't hang nor the Guilty will Save
And such as will never the People Enslave;
That work's to be done by Methwyn my Knave.
  The Seal, said the King, is to Judges Committed
Till I with a Man for my turn can be fitted.
I have Pleas'd a few Lawyers but the rest of the Nation
I hear do talk high of a new Abdication.
Turning out my Lord Chancellor I confesse I repent

20. *dispose of the Seal:* Since it was term time, the office of lord chancellor could not long be left unfilled. After a week when no one could be found to succeed Somers, custody of the great seal was committed to Sir John Holt, lord chief justice of the court of king's bench, Sir George Treby, lord chief justice of the court of common pleas, and Sir Edward Ward, lord chief baron of the court of exchequer, "and they to seal all letters patents, commissions, grants, exemplifications, injunctions, writs, &c." (Luttrell, *4*, 641).

26. *Methwyn my Knave:* John Methuen owed to Sunderland both his own appointment as lord chancellor of Ireland and his son's appointment as resident in Lisbon. Not unexpectedly, therefore, he had joined Sunderland's other "Knaves" in attacking Montagu in the Commons in January 1698 (Kenyon, pp. 287, 303). He was nominally a Whig but in fact an opportunist who, as Somers said, was "equally the aversion of the whigs and tories" (Coxe, p. 558). He was also a protégé of Robert Harley and presumably Harley's candidate to succeed Somers (HMC *Portland MSS., 3*, 576–77, 641). As early as 30 April, in fact, it was rumored that he would be appointed to the chancellorship. Bonet believed that despite his inadequacy he would have secured the appointment a week later if the duke of Leeds had not come out of retirement to demonstrate to the king "l'insuffisance de cet homme" (BM MS. Add. 30000D, ff. 161v, 167v).

29. *Pleas'd a few Lawyers:* At the same time that he placed the great seal in the custody of Sir John Holt, the king issued another commission to Sir John Trevor, Master of the Rolls, and "the 9 other judges and masters in chancery, whereof 3 to be a quorum . . . and they to hear all causes, &c. in chancery; and so to continue till a lord chancellor or keeper be declared" (Luttrell, *4*, 641).

31. *repent:* Bonet reported on 7 May that "Sa Majesté est veritablement fachée d'avoir à present deposé un si habile et si fidelle Ministre" (BM MS. Add. 30000D, f. 168).

But since it is done, be what will the Event.
I never will doe like poor hen-hearted James,
Run away but first throw my great Seal in the Thames.
I designed to have given it to the man you were for,
Your Lillyburlero Irish Chancellor.
But he haveing bred up his Son at St. Omers,
Twere monstrous for him to succeed my Lord Sommers.
  The Count lookeing pale, cry'd, Then I must scower,
The Mobb have no mercy on those in their power.
I have sent my Son Spencer to tell all the Town
The remove of the Seal I lament and disown;
Twas not from my Lord taken, himself laid it down;
A better Lord Chancellor never was known.
But all the Town Swears my Son's a Court Spy
And therefore lay wagers what he sayes is a lye.
The removeing the Seal I advis'd and design'd;
Yet since you know it was your own mind,
To deny twas my Councell, pray Sir, be so kind.

36–37. Methuen's dependence upon Sunderland and his education of his son, Paul, at the English Jesuit college at St. Omers, are both mentioned in a particularly lilting song *To the Tune of Lilly Bolero* ("Two Opposite Parties do govern the House") preserved in BM MS. Lansdowne 852, f. 96v and in Trumbull MS. Add. 17. The following lines from two stanzas are relevant here:

He comitted his Sons to the Jesuits Care . . .
Methuen, Methuen, St. Omers Methuen.

And to shew You this was not done in a Heat . . .
He sent him to Rome to make him compleat.

Vernon, too, observed that there were "other considerations" that made it difficult for the king to "gratify" Methuen (Vernon, *3*, 64).

42. *lament and disown:* On 11 May Sunderland had found it "necessary to be understood, that it was always his notion that the King's business never could be so well carried on as by my Lord Chancellor, and his friends, and accordingly was always against my Lord's going out" (Vernon, *3*, 43).

43. *himself laid it down:* Although it flatly contradicted his claim that he opposed the dismissal of Somers, Sunderland may also have been responsible for the persistent (but totally false) rumor that Somers had resigned of his own free will. Tallard, for example, reported to Louis XIV on 26 April that "le Chancelier veut quitter, et que c'est le Roy son maistre seul qui l'a retenu jusqu'a cette heure" (PRO 31/3 185, f. 94).

44. *A better Lord Chancellor never:* Burnet similarly acknowledged that Somers was "in all respects the greatest Man I had ever known in that Post" (Burnet, *2*, 242).

47. *removeing the Seal I advis'd:* There seems to be no doubt that this is true; see headnote. Sunderland's only real complaint was "that the method of doing it was not his" (Hardwicke, *2*, 439).

To lye for your Service you'l me ready find.
You have been, said the King, to your Ministryes glory,
A Papist, A Protestant, A Whigg and A Tory,
And, my Lord, whoever his Religion forsakes,
Of Lying and Perjury no Scruple makes.
To Serve me I will not your Lordship should Lye;
To Serve you your Councell I cannot deny.
By displacing a Lord Chancellor so much Esteem'd,
More Credit I've lost than can ere be redeem'd.
With Shame and dishonor sure never before
Went the Great Seal a begging from door unto door.
Of the Seal till now it never was said
To take it when offer'd wise men were afraid.
My Lord, I must tell you I plainly have found
By taking your Councell I dayly lost ground
In the Peoples Affections; their murmurs require
That you and your Son from the Court should retire.
Leave the Court, said the Count, that is very hard
And for all my Service no grateful reward.
If he that serves God must obey the King,
It is to doe both an Impossible thing.
And of this Impossibility, the Cause
Is because King's Commands contradict Gods Laws.

52. *Papist:* "The Earl of Sunderland's famous conversion," as Edward Harley called it (HMC *Portland MSS.*, *3*, 414), occurred sometime before December 1687 and was made public in June 1688. His equally famous reconversion to Protestantism occurred in December 1688 (Kenyon, pp. 137–38, 168, 198, 228–29).

56. *your Councell I cannot deny:* referring back to line 49.

58. *Credit I've lost:* Tallard similarly reported on 8 May that William himself had derived no benefit from Somers' dismissal but had acted only to placate "le party anglican" in the House of Commons; "voila le conseil de M. de Sunderland entierement suivy," he observed (PRO 31/3 185, f. 102v).

60. *the Great Seal a begging:* The office of lord chancellor is known to have been refused by Sir John Holt and Sir George Treby, the two lord chief justices, and by Sir Thomas Trevor, the attorney-general. It was also reported to have been refused by the earl of Nottingham, by Sir John Powell, one of the justices of the court of common pleas, by "Mr. [Thomas] *Vernon,* the great Chancery Lawyer, [and] others of less fame" (Oldmixon, *4*, 210; BM MS. Add. 30000D, ff. 161, 165).

66. *from the Court should retire:* On 14 May, the day of Sunderland's audience with the king, Bonet reported (erroneously) that "Le Comte de Sunderland se retire à la Campagne." Bonet went on to explain that "On étudie ses demarches, parce qu'on le regarde comme un homme dangereux, et qu'on est bien aise de le voir loin de la cour" (BM MS. Add. 30000D, f. 173v).

When a Sovereign Princes Commands are evil,
He that obeys 'em must goe to the Devil.
My Changeing Religion you ought not to blame,
When Kings to Change theires do think it no Shame:
Your Father now liveing and Uncle now dead
Abjur'd the Religion in which they were bred.
If it be for the Peace and weal of a State
All Sorts of Religion to tollerate,
A publick Minister should have his mind
To no particular Religion Confin'd.
A Statesman's Conscience ought to be free
And of what Religion he pleases to be.
Instead of Plaindealing, he is prudently double,
And with matters of faith doth his Conscience nere trouble;
In all that he doth, pretends publick good,
But his private advantage is still understood.
He gets places for Knaves, but alwayes takes care
By private agreement the Profit to share.
His Changeing of Parties is still necessary
According as Times and Conjunctures vary;
Change of Winds and Stormes the Best Pilots force
Sometimes to Shift Sayles and alter their Course.
Sir, you have Chang'd mindes and ministers too
And the Torys Prefer'd when the Whiggs would not doe,
But finding the Torys still King James's freinds,
Took the Whiggs in again, to serve your own ends.
But ministers should not be valued the less,

77. *Father . . . Uncle:* James II, William's father-in-law, publicly abjured Protestantism in 1673; William's uncle, Charles II, privately acknowledged himself a Roman Catholic on his deathbed in 1685.

88. *private advantage:* On 21 May James Vernon commented on the "contest for places" as follows: "we see nothing aimed at but putting one another down only to rise upon their ruins, and the public is a sacrifice to self-interest" (Vernon, *3*, 56); cf. lines 153–54 below.

95. *Chang'd mindes and ministers:* William had made Danby his first minister in 1689, dismissed him in 1695 in favor of the Whig junto of Somers, Montagu, and Russell, and now was in the process of forming a new Tory ministry around Harley, Rochester, and Godolphin.

97. *Torys still King James's freinds:* This recalls Arthur Onslow's recollection that Sunderland had to explain to William "that it was very true, that the tories were better friends to monarchy than the whigs were, but then his majesty was to consider that he was not their monarch" (Burnet, 1823, *4*, 5 *n*).

If their Councells receiv'd Should not meet with Success.
An Honest Lord Chancellor may without doubt
For reasons of State sometimes be turn'd out.
When Princes would absolute be on the Throne,
They must trust their Conscience with those that have none,
And, when their Subjects deserve to be Slaves,
Turn out honest Ministers and prefer Knaves.
  My Lord, said the King, if these maxims be true,
The Seal should be given to none but to you.
But still all these Measures are false and unsafe,
And Montague's offers are greater by Half.
That Mushroom projector has far outdone you
And did undertake things you never durst doe.
Would I govern by force, hee'd an Army provide
That I might the three Kingdoms like Packhorses ride.
He, heading his Tools like some Turkish Bashaw,
The Old Company broke against Justice and law,
And, that he might ne're prove more faithfull then you,
He basely betray'd his dear friends of the New.

104. *Conscience:* "The *Chancellor* is said to be Keeper of the *King*'s *Conscience,* to Judge *secundum aequum & bonum,* according *to* Equity and Conscience" (Thomas Delaune, *The Present State of London,* 1681, p. 129).

110. *Montague's offers:* "I hear Mr. Montague has been lately with the King, and that they talked of affairs pretty freely. The King . . . [said that] those who shewed any zeal for his service might be assured of his favour, and as Mr. Montague had done him very acceptable services, and was still capable of doing more, he should have every reason to take it amiss if he found him cold and slack in it. Mr. Montague gave the king assurances of his readiness to serve him . . . [in any way] consistent with his friendship and obligations to my Lord Somers" (Vernon, *3,* 53).

113. *an Army provide:* Montagu stubbornly resisted disbanding the army in 1697–98, but seems to have opposed the bill "but faintly" in 1698–99 (Vernon, *1,* 465; *2,* 230, 236).

116. *The Old Company broke:* See *An Encomium upon a Parliament,* 48 *n.,* above.

118. *betray'd his dear friends of the New:* How Montagu betrayed the New East India Company is not clear. His bill creating the New Company allowed the Old East India Company to continue trading only until September 1701. On 8 March 1700, however, the king recommended to the governor and directors of the Old Company that a merger with the New Company "would be most for the interest of the India trade." He followed this up by giving his assent, on 11 April, to an act extending the corporate life of the Old Company, which discontented "the interested Whigs, both in the City and in the House" (Vernon, *3,* 25). As a result of all this, stock in the Old Company rose to a high of £144 a share (John Bruce, *Annals of the Honorable East-India Company,* 3 vols., 1810, *3,* 293–94). In the same session, however, further duties were laid upon silks and other commodities of the East Indies, which was obviously to the disadvantage of both Companies.

By Factions and Clubbs hee'd our ferments abate,
And pay the National Debts with Duncombs Estate.
In short there's no fence he would not break thorow,
Putts me on one thing to day, on another to morrow,
Till the Insolent, vain and Impolitick Elfe
Would make me as abject and mean as himself.
But, my Lord, that for once my whole mind you may know,
Pray mark well the truth I'me now goeing to shew.
Pembroke and Lounsdale, Godolphin and Lory,
Shrewsbury, Rumney, and Leeds, Whigg and Tory,

120. *Duncombs Estate:* In January–February 1698 Duncombe was expelled from the House of Commons and imprisoned in the Tower on charges of forging endorsements to exchequer bills. A bill was introduced to confiscate two-thirds of his estate, said to be worth £300,000, "for the use of the publick." The bill, in which Montagu was "hotly engaged," passed the lower house by 36 votes, but was defeated by one vote in the House of Lords (Luttrell, *4,* 346, 355; Vernon, *1,* 477; *CJ, 12,* 132–33).

123. *Elfe:* Montagu was short; cf. "Mr. Davenant, in his Resumption of Grants [Wing D304], sets that little elf in the truest light" (HMC *Cowper MSS.,* 2, 419).

127. *Lounsdale:* Sir John Lowther, first viscount Lonsdale (1655–1700), was a Whig courtier and placeman whom William appointed lord privy seal in March 1699.

Godolphin: Sidney Godolphin, baron (later earl) Godolphin (1645–1712), was invaluable as much for his colorlessness and inaccessibility as for his financial genius. He served as a lord of the treasury under both Charles II (1679–85) and James II (1687–88), remained first lord of the treasury under William III until 1696, and in December 1700 was reappointed to the treasury and made first minister of a new Tory administration (BM MS. Add. 17677UU, f. 364).

Lory: Laurence Hyde, first earl of Rochester (1641–1711) , was the second son of the first earl of Clarendon. He served Charles II as first lord of the treasury (1679–84) and his brother-in-law, James II, as lord high treasurer until January 1687 when he was dismissed for refusing to abjure Protestantism. The nominal leader of the Tory party during the next reign, he was restored to the privy council by William in March 1692, but held no public office until December 1700 when he was appointed lord lieutenant of Ireland. He had been closely associated with Sunderland and Godolphin since 1679 when the three of them formed the ministry of the "Chits." Burnet called him "the smoothest man in the Court," but violent and vain (GEC, *11,* 49–50; Burnet, *1,* 258).

128. *Rumney:* Henry Sidney, earl of Romney (1641–1704), served Charles II as envoy to the Hague (1679–81). In 1688 he signed and conveyed to William of Orange the secret invitation to invade England and thus became "the great *Wheel* on which the *Revolution* turned," as Burnet said. ("He had not a wheel to turn a mouse," Swift retorted, and Burnet ruefully acknowledged that for many years Sidney had been "drunk once a Day"). Subsequently he served as secretary of state (1690–92), lord lieutenant of Ireland (1692–95), master-general of the ordnance (1693–1702), and a lord justice during William's absences in 1697 and 1698. He was Sunderland's uncle, lifelong friend, and neighbor on St. James's Square (GEC, *11,* 83–84).

Leeds: Sir Thomas Osborne, first earl of Danby, marquis of Carmarthen, and duke of Leeds (1631–1712), served Charles II as lord high treasurer from 1673 until he was impeached for high treason in 1679. He signed the invitation to William of

My Keppell and Portland, with such forreign Slaves,
Are unthinking Proud fools or poor tricking Knaves.
Ranalagh, Blathwaite and Boyle I'le Skip ore
Least they smuggle the little that's yet left in Store,
Or like my Lord Orford make up their Accounts,
Though his Cowardly baseness their Cheating Surmounts.
Grim Coningsby should be Secure from all Pasquil,
Since none can express half the Crimes of a Rascal
Who by Murder makes Gaffny in Annals take place,
An Act well becoming his poisonous Race.
All my Train is reproach't with Jests and tart Gibes.

Orange in 1688 and served as lord president of the council from 1689 until he was again impeached, for accepting a bribe from the East India Company, in 1695. He was said to be "as cunning and unscrupulous in his decay as he was in the perfect vigour of his middle age" (GEC, *7*, 507–10).

129. *Keppell:* See *Advice to a Painter,* 51 *n.,* above.

Portland: See *Advice to a Painter,* 31 *n.,* above.

131. *Ranalagh:* Richard Jones, earl of Ranelagh in the Irish peerage (1641–1712), was "a young man of great parts, and as great vices" (Burnet, *1*, 266) who had made himself indispensable to Charles II. James II appointed him paymaster-general of the army, a post in which he was retained by William III and which enabled him at last to have "spent more Money, built more fine Houses, and laid out more on Houshold-Furniture and Gardening, than any other Nobleman in England" (Macky, p. 82).

Blathwaite: William Blathwayt (1649?–1717) occupied a less lucrative post than Ranelagh's, but he held it longer. He was secretary-at-war in four reigns (1683–1704).

Boyle: See *Advice to a Painter,* 127 *n.,* above.

133. *Lord Orford:* Edward Russell, earl of Orford (1653–1727), was a cousin of Lord William Russell, the Whig martyr, and one of the seven signers of the letter of invitation to William of Orange. He was the hero of a naval engagement off La Hougue, Normandy, in May 1692, which was one of the few victories in William's war. He is alleged to have made his fortune two years later by victualing the Mediterranean fleet of which he was in command (GEC, *10*, 77–81). His accounts were submitted to himself as treasurer of the navy (April 1689–November 1699) for approval by himself as first lord of the admiralty (May 1694–May 1699). Consequently, when he was impeached by the House of Commons in 1701, the articles claimed that "the said earl did receive great sums of the public money, issued out to him for the service of the Navy, which he hath converted to his own private use, and unlawfully and unjustly procured a privy seal or privy seals to discharge him from accompting to the public for the same . . . and that, for the advancing his own private interest, and securing himself from rendering any Accompt to the public, he the said Earl, during the said War, procured, enjoyed, and possessed, divers great offices, which were inconsistent, and in their nature improper to be executed by one and the same person" (*Parl. Hist.*, *5*, 1258–59).

135. *Coningsby:* See *Advice to a Painter,* 102 *n.,* above.

137. *Gaffny in Annals:* See *Advice to a Painter,* 102 *n.,* above.

Even Somers is branded with Pentions and Bribes,
But cheifly for keeping of other Mens Wives
And favouring Persons of dissolute Lives.
Vernon's by all Men beleived a meer Tool,
And Jersey's acknowledged to have ne're been at School.
In so wofull a Case there's no help in the Church,
That Jilt, ever leaving Us Kings in the lurch.
The Oxcheek of Lambeth with his deputy Blackcoats
(Like Prentices arm'd with Squibs, Crackers and Rockets)
Are all useless Blockheads and vain Empty fellows,
Fools enough to believe those fine tales which they tell us.
But herein with my Courtiers they are all of a Peice,
The one are not Swans if the other be Geese.
There's no man among you, what ere he pretends,
But laughs at the Publick and acts for Self Ends.
Wherefore henceforth you shall ne're be believ'd,
Nor Country nor Court by your Arts be deceiv'd.
I'le trust to my People, still constant and true,
While neither abus'd by such wretches as you.
And after my death they sha'nt split on like Shelves,
For I'le leave 'em of Age, fitt to govern themselves.
But of most Kings I find destruction the fate
Who made such as you their Ministers of State.

140. According to some of the rumors that were circulating, Somers had (1) embezzled £400 that had been appropriated for repairs to Windsor Castle, (2) shared in the profits from Captain Kidd's piracies, (3) procured grants of crown lands for himself under false names (BM Add. MS. 30000D, f. 159; [Charles Davenant], *The Old and Modern Whig Truly Represented,* 2nd ed., 1702, p. 21). Upon surrendering the great seal, Somers had been granted an annual pension of £4000 (BM MS. Add. 30000D, f. 161v).

141. *keeping of other Mens Wives:* See *Advice to a Painter,* 26 *n.,* above.

144. *Jersey:* Edward Villiers, first earl of Jersey (1656–1711), matriculated at St. John's College, Cambridge, on 17 March 1671, but left without taking a degree. His lack of intellect, however, was more than compensated by the fact that his sister, Elizabeth Villiers, was, until 1695, the mistress of William III. He was alleged to be "the Handle by which the great Turn" from the Whig junto to the Tory ministry of Godolphin and Rochester was accomplished in 1700 (Macky, p. 28).

147. *Oxcheek of Lambeth:* Thomas Tenison, archbishop of Canterbury, although a tall, "heavy Man" (Macky, p. 136), was no help at all when princes wished to be absolute. Swift, in fact, called him "The most good for Nothing Prelate I ever saw." His "moderation towards dissenters" put him "in the front of the battel all King *James*'s reign" (Burnet, *1,* 190).

Your Statesman and you were twins of one mother,
So perfectly well you resemble each other.
Which Sharp reply so confounded my Lord
He left his Majesty without speaking a word.

John Tutchin

The Foreigners
(6 August 1700)

The normal human hatred of foreigners was greatly aggravated in England, during the reign of a foreigner, by deliberate exploitation of xenophobia for political purposes. In 1693, for example, a Whig bill to naturalize foreign Protestants was defeated in the Commons simply by pointing out that it might open the gates to a flood of Dutch immigrants. Sir John Knight, the member for Bristol, who led the attack on the bill, shared the belief of Lemuel Gulliver that the Dutch were willing for monetary gain to forsake any principle "and on occasion *Christianity* too, as at *Japan.*" Like John Tutchin, Knight was also offended by the sound of foreign accents in the palaces of the kings of England; "there is no entering the courts of St. *James's* and *Whitehall,*" he said, "for the great Noise and Croaking of the *Frog-landers.*" So he concluded his speech "with this motion, that the *Serjeant* be commanded to open the Doors, and let us first Kick the Bill out of the HOUSE, and then Foreigners out of the KINGDOM" (*A Speech in the House of Commons, against the Naturalizing of Foreigners,* n.d., pp. 11, 16–17, 19).

As recently as April 1700 Tories in the House of Commons were clamoring to remove foreigners from all military commands and Sir Edward Seymour even proposed that they be excluded from the House of Lords as well (PRO 31/3 185, f. 81). It is doubtful that any less powerful emotion than xenophobia could have induced John Tutchin, a self-styled Whig martyr, to make common cause with an exploded pensionary of Charles II's like Sir Edward Seymour. John Dennis believed that the king himself was the object of Tutchin's attack (*The Reverse,* 155), and the republican tendency of *The Foreigners* is undeniable:

> If Kings are made the People to enthral,
> We had much better have no King at all.
> (176–77)

It is true that in *The Mouse Grown a Rat: or The Story of the City and Country Mouse, Newly Transposed, In a Discourse betwixt Bays, Johnson, and Smith* (1702), Tutchin speaks very bitterly of the "brave Heads [that] were lop't, to make a Bridg for K. *William* to come to the Imperial Crowns of these Kingdoms" (p. 26). But in *The Foreigners* he explicitly defends the king and even rewrites history to represent him as wildly acclaimed upon his landing at Tor Bay in 1688. He attributes all of England's troubles to "crafty Knaves at home," i.e. the Whig junto, and to "upstart Foreigners," particularly Hans Willem Bentinck van Diepenheim en Schoonheten, first earl of Portland, whom he designates "Bentir." The question whether any "Honours" are due a king is in the poem answered in the affirmative, at Portland's expense:

> Support your Rightful Monarch and his Crown,
> But pull this proud, this croaking Mortal down.
> (189–90)

Jacobites may have read these lines in quite a different sense, but it is doubtful that this was Tutchin's intention.

"Honours," however, is the operative word of the poem, which devolves upon an exhortation to the English nobility to resume their ancient honors and strip the foreign interlopers of the trappings—and the spoils—that accompany English titles.

The Mouse Grown a Rat reveals that Tutchin believed himself to be one of "the Chief Patriots and Sufferers" of the Revolution. He claimed to have "suffered Imprisonments, pecuniary Fines, and other Punishments, for asserting the Liberties of *England*" and to have "spent 13 or 14 years in a fruitless Attendance upon an ungrateful Court" (pp. 11, 13). In 1695 he was deprived of a minor post in the navy victualing office for bringing charges against the commissioners which he was unable to substantiate, and subsequently he was refused a place in the customs office (*The True-Born Englishman*, 641 *n.*, below; *The Mouse Grown a Rat*, 1702, p. 12).

Early in 1702, therefore, he was able to summarize his career as follows: ruined for his country in James' reign, starved for his country in William's reign, and liable to be hanged for his country in the next reign. While it would be fallacious to attribute the xenophobia of *The Foreigners* simply to Tutchin's failures, there can be no doubt that his conviction that he had been "basely and ungratefully dealt with" provides the poem with a powerful emotional undercurrent. Tutchin himself was aware that his obsessive concern for "the distressed Condition of [his] Dear and Native Land" would seem close to madness (*The Mouse Grown a Rat,* pp. 26–27).

The Foreigners, A Poem. Part I was advertised in *The Flying Post* for 31 July–1 August 1700 and published, according to the Luttrell copy preserved in the Brotherton Collection, University of Leeds, on 6 August 1700. Four days later, "Mr. Tutchin, author of a poem called The Foreigners, in which are reflections upon several great men, [was] taken into custody of a messenger" (Luttrell, *4,* 676), thus giving the lie to Abel Boyer, who proclaimed that "when as dull a Poet" as Tutchin "writes a low, pitiful Satyr, call'd the *Foreigners,* and levels his malicious Bolts at the two Favourite Lords, he is unregarded, and has nothing to fear but Contempt and Oblivion, the easie Punishment of *Scandal* without *Wit*" (*Letters of Wit, Politicks and Morality,* 1701, p. 251). Tutchin must have thought he had something more to fear than "Contempt and Oblivion," for, according to William Fuller, he escaped from the king's messenger and sought refuge in "a blind Ale-house, at the Windmill, by Mr. Bowyers, at Camberwel" (*Mr. William Fuller's Letter to Mr. John Tutchin,* 1703, p. 7).

Even though his poem was presented as a libel by a grand jury in the city of London on 28 August (Luttrell, *4,* 683), Tutchin need not have feared prosecution, for the attorney-general, Sir Thomas Trevor, advised the lords justices that since Tutchin had used "covert names" (Bentir and Keppech), no action against him could be sustained in the courts (BM MS. Add. 30000D, f. 253v). Defoe and Swift, of course, were using exactly the same technique, and Tutchin complained bitterly that they could publish the Legion *Memorial* and *A Discourse of the Contests and Dissensions* "without any Secretary of State's Warrant against either Authors or Publishers," whereas "if a Body happen to make a Ballad reflecting upon a Foreigner, that has run away with more than all the Honest Men in *England* have got since the Revolution, the Author is brought into jeopardy by Warrants and Presentments" (*The Mouse Grown a Rat,* p. 32).

What Tutchin could not escape was indictment by "The common

Beadle," satire. On 24 August 1700 appeared *The Reverse: Or, The Tables Turn'd. A Poem Written in Answer, Paragraph by Paragraph, to a Late Scurrilous and Malicious Medly of Rhimes Called the Foreigners.* This was presumably the work of John Dennis and is here printed on facing pages to *The Foreigners.*

While Dennis was content to answer *The Foreigners* "Paragraph by Paragraph," the anonymous author of *The Natives: An Answer to The Foreigners* ("No wonder Isra'l is depriv'd of Rest"), which was advertised in *The Post Boy* for 10–12 September 1700, went at it line by line. "Every line of this Poem," the title page boasts, *"is clos'd with the very same Word the* Foreigner *has made use of."* The result, "horrid dull stuff," as Lord Lexinton's correspondent called it, is admitted to lack the *"Coherence that otherwise it might have had"* (*CSPD 1700–1702,* pp. 118–19). The ultimate answer to *The Foreigners* had to wait until January 1701 when Defoe published *The True-Born Englishman,* the most popular poem of the reign.

Part II of *The Foreigners,* although not so designated on the title page, is *The Apostates: Or The Revolters. A Poem against Foreigners* ("Art thou, dear Israel! still the Butt of Fate"), which Tutchin published in August 1701.

John Dennis[?]

The Reverse
(24 August 1700)

A single phrase—celebrating the execution of Charles I on 30 January 1649 as "This Glorious Feat"—both betrays the republican tendency of *The Foreigners* and supplies the detail that John Dennis seized upon to polarize *The Reverse: Or, The Tables Turn'd. A Poem.* The ills that Tutchin had ascribed to "upstart Foreigners" Dennis attributes to an antecedent cause, the republicanism epitomized in the Calves' Head Club.

"This Calfs-head Club," according to a newsletter received by William Johnstone, earl of Annandale, in January 1700, "is some noblemen and gentlemen who meet at a tavern the 30th of January and instead of fasting have a great feast and among other things, as a symboll of the day, have a Calfs head served up in a dish like St. John Baptists head in a charger" (HMC *Hope Johnstone MSS.*, p. 116). Other sources fill in the details:

> an *Ax* hung up in the Clubb-Room [is] reverenced, as a Principal Symbol in this *Diabolical Sacrament.* Their Bill of Fare, was a large Dish of *Calves-Heads* dressed several ways; a large *Pike* with a small one in his Mouth, as an Emblem of Tyranny; a large *Cods-head,* by which they pretended to represent the Person of the *King* singly, as by the Calves-head before, they had done him, together with all them that had suffer'd in his Cause; a *Boars-head* with an *Apple* in its Mouth, to represent the King by this as *Bestial,* as by the others they had done, *Foolish* and *Tyrannical.* After the Repast was over, one of their Elders presented an *Eikon Basilike,* which was with great solemnity Burn'd upon the Table, whilst the *Anthems* were Singing. After this, another produc'd *Milton's Defensio Populi Anglicani,* upon which all lay'd their Hands, and made a Protestation in form of an Oath, for ever to stand by, and maintain; the Company wholly consisted of *Independants* and *Anabaptists.* (Edward Ward, *The Secret History of the Calves-Head Club,* 1703, p. 18)

Even the historian of the club found it difficult to believe in the reality of this republican black mass; "I was of Opinion at First," he said, "That the Story was purely contriv'd on purpose to render the *Republicans* more Odious," but the testimony of two witnesses convinced him that the account was true. John Milton was alleged to have been one of the founders of the club (but this is not confirmed by David Masson) and in 1703 the members were said to include J[ohn] T[utchin?], S. B., and J. S. (*A Continuation or Second Part of the Letters from the Dead to the Living,* 2nd ed., 1707, p. 120).

The strategy of Dennis' reply is to represent *The Foreigners* to be as much a product of the republican *"Faction"* as the barbarities of the calves' head feasts.

The Reverse was said to be published "This Day" in *The Post*

Boy, No. 839, 22–24 August 1700. It was first attributed to Dennis in *A Catalogue of the Library of the Late John Henry Wrenn,* ed. Harold B. Wrenn and Thomas J. Wise, 5 vols., Austin, Texas, 1920, 2, 53.

The Foreigners

Long time had *Israel* been disus'd from Rest,
Long had they been by Tyrants sore opprest;
Kings of all sorts they ignorantly crav'd,
And grew more stupid as they were enslav'd;
Yet want of Grace they impiously disown'd,
And still like Slaves beneath the Burden groan'd:
With languid Eyes their Race of Kings they view,
The Bad too many, and the Good too few;
Some rob'd their Houses, and destroy'd their Lives,
Ravish'd their Daughters, and debauch'd their Wives;
Prophan'd the Altars with polluted Loves,
And worship'd Idols in the Woods and Groves.
To Foreign Nations next they have recourse;
Striving to mend, they made their State much worse.
They first from *Hebron* all their Plagues did bring,
Cramm'd in the Single Person of a King;
From whose base Loins ten thousand Evils flow,
Which by Succession they must undergo.
Yet sense of Native Freedom still remains,
They fret and grumble underneath their Chains;
Incens'd enrag'd, their Passion do's arise,
Till at his Palace-Gate their Monarch dies.
This Glorious Feat was by the Fathers done,
Whose Children next depos'd his Tyrant Son,
Made him, like *Cain,* a murd'rous Wanderer,
Both of his Crimes, and of his Fortunes share.
But still resolv'd to split on Foreign Shelves,
Rather than venture once to trust Themselves,

1. *Israel:* England *(Absalom and Achitophel,* 7).

15. *Hebron:* Scotland *(Absalom and Achitophel,* 59).

16. *King:* James VI of Scotland was proclaimed James I, king of England, Scotland, and Ireland, on 24 March 1603.

17. *Evils flow:* James I was the father of Charles I, the grandfather of Charles II and James II, and great-grandfather of William III.

22. *Monarch dies:* Charles I was beheaded on a scaffold erected in front of his palace at Whitehall on 30 January 1649.

24. *Tyrant Son:* James II left London for the last time on 18 December 1688.

The Reverse

Israel had still, if *Israel* had been true,
Enjoy'd sweet Rest, and kept soft Peace in view;
Her Kings made awful, and their Subjects fear'd,
And *These* slept safe, while *Those* had wak'd and steer'd.
But Fears, Distrusts and Jealousies arose,
And Impious *Israelites* were *Israel*'s Foes;
As *Faction* at her Monarchs hiss'd aloud,
Shaking her *Snaky* Locks amidst the Croud.
Thence grew a Scene of undistinguish'd Crimes,
And nothing look'd like *Guilt* in *guilty* Times,
Whilst Murm'ring Fiends on *Tyrants* laid their ills,
And in their stead *obey'd* their *Tyrant* Wills.
  Her Queen deceas'd, and Virgin Sov'reign Dead,
Without the Pledges of the Nuptial Bed,
A Neighb'ring Land the Vacant Throne supply'd,
And lent with Tears, what she'd have kept with Pride,
Bless'd *Israel* with a Monarch Wise and Good,
Made her's, by *Choice,* by *Providence,* and *Blood.*
But Wealth nor Peace could Consecrate his Reign,
Her Childrens *Blessing* was her Childrens *Pain;*
Who in requital to the Race H'had run,
Return'd his *Goodness* with a *Martyr'd* Son.
Curs'd be the *Pen* that *dares* such Worth *defame,*
And give that *Murd'rous* Fact a *Glorious* Name,
Which Deaf to Pity scatters its Applause,
On what must *Damn* the *Praiser* with the *Cause.*
  The Father *Martyr'd,* and the Son *Misled*
By Counsels of a Land to which he fled,

13. *Queen:* Elizabeth I.
17. *Monarch:* James I.
22. *Martyr'd Son:* Charles I.
27. *Son:* James II.
28. *Land:* France.

To Foreign Courts and Councils do resort,
To find a King their Freedoms to support:
Of one for mighty Actions fam'd they're told,
Profoundly wise, and desperately bold,
Skilful in War, Successful still in Fight,
Had vanquish'd Hosts, and Armies put to flight;
And when the Storms of War and Battels cease,
Knew well to steer the Ship of State in Peace.
Him they approve, approaching to their sight,
Lov'd by the Gods, of Mankind the Delight.
The numerous Tribes resort to see him land,
Cover the Beach, and blacken all the Strand;
With loud Huzza's they welcome him on shore,
And for their Blessing do the Gods implore.
The *Sanhedrim* conven'd, at length debate
The sad Condition of their drooping State
And Sinking Church, just ready now to drown;
And with one Shout they do the Hero crown.
Ah Happy *Israel!* had there never come
Into his Councils crafty Knaves at home,
In combination with a Foreign Brood,
Sworn Foes to *Israel*'s Rights and *Israel*'s Good;
Who impiously foment Intestine Jars,
Exhaust our Treasure, and prolong our Wars;
Make *Israel*'s People to themselves a prey,

29–30. Of the eight great-grandparents of William of Orange, three were German, two were French, and one each was Scottish, Danish, and Italian (Florentine).

31. *one for mighty Actions fam'd:* See *The Mock Mourners,* 308 *n.,* below.

39. *see him land:* These lines may be ironical. William's landing near the village of Brixham, in Tor Bay, on 5 November 1688, could have been witnessed only by a few fisherman. An eyewitness described the occasion as follows: "There are sundry little Houses which belong unto Fisher-men, between the two Hills, at *Tor-Bay,* where we landed: The People of these Houses came running out at their Doors to see this happy Sight" (*An Exact Diary of the Late Expedition of His Illustrious Highness the Prince of Orange,* 1689, p. 37). Lines 39–40 actually describe Charles II's landing at Dover on 25 May 1660: "but the shore was so full of people to expect [his] coming, as that it was as black (which otherwise is white sand)" (Pepys, *Diary, 1,* 142); "The Joyfull People throng'd to see him Land,/Cov'ring the Beach, and blackning all the *Strand" (Absalom and Achitophel,* 271–72).

43. *Sanhedrim:* Parliament (*Absalom and Achitophel,* 390).

46. *Hero crown:* William III was crowned 11 April 1689.

48. *crafty Knaves:* the Whig junto, whom Tutchin calls "bold Invaders" in *The Mouse Grown a Rat* (1702), p. 26.

As taught to *Govern,* he forgot to Rule,
And held the Reins not *Temperate* or *Cool.*
What Method should misguided *Israel* chuse?
To trust *Herself* was ev'n *Herself* to *lose:*
Slow to correct, though eager to complain,
She could not regulate a faulty Reign.
When on Her injur'd side a Hero stood,
Foreign in *Birth,* but *Native* in his *Blood;*
And dar'd the Dangers of the Winds and Seas,
Vent'ring his Own to purchase *Israel*'s Ease.
  And just was *Israel*'s Joy to see him Land,
And view Deliv'rance *dawning* from his Hand,
Just was the Gift she gave him in return
For Death *despis'd,* and Hardships *nobly* Born,
For Wealth *deserted,* and for *Succours* brought,
Swift as *Our* Hopes, and daring as *His* Thought,
While the good Prince with Pious Sorrow griev'd,
And mourn'd *His* Fate, whose *Kingdoms* He reliev'd.
  Yet there were some who *shar'd* the Warriour's Aid,
That *murmur'd* at the *Gift* themselves had made,
That high in Trusts and Pensions from the State
Thought *their* Reward too *small,* and *His* too *great;*
As *Israel*'s Sov'reign *warm'd* 'em in his Breast,
And nurs'd the *Vip'rous* Tyrants of his Rest.
Amongst the Chief was *Seymour*'s haughty Mind,

32. *lose:* "For whosoever will save his life, shall lose it" (Matthew 16:25).

35. *Hero:* William of Orange.

41. *Gift:* the crown of England, Scotland, and Ireland.

46. *His:* James II's.

53. *haughty:* Sir Edward Seymour has been called "the most arrogant man that ever presided over . . . the House of Commons" (James A. Manning, *The Lives of the Speakers,* 1850, p. 362).

Mislead their King, and steal his Heart away:
United Intrests thus they do divide,
The State declines by Avarice and Pride;
Like Beasts of Prey they ravage all the Land,
Acquire Preferments, and usurp Command:
The Foreign Inmates the Housekeepers spoil,
And drain the Moisture of our fruitful Soil.
If to our Monarch there are Honours due,
Yet what with *Gibeonites* have we to do?
When Foreign States employ 'em for their Food,
To draw their Water, and to hew their Wood.
What Mushroom Honours do's our Soil afford!
One day a Begger, and the next a Lord.
What dastard Souls do *Jewish* Nobles wear!
The Commons such Affronts would never bear.
Let no Historian the sad Stories tell
Of thy base Sons, Oh servile *Israel!*
But thou, my Muse, more generous and brave,
Shalt their black Crimes from dark oblivion save;
To future Ages shalt their Sins disclose,
And brand with Infamy thy Nation's Foes.
  A Country lies, due East from *Judah*'s Shoar,
Where stormy Winds and noisy Billows roar;
A Land much differing from all other Soils,
Forc'd from the Sea, and buttress'd up with Piles.
No marble Quarrys bind the spungy Ground,
But Loads of Sand and Cockle-shells are found:

62. *Gibeonites:* the Dutch; cf. *The Second Part of Absalom and Achitophel,* 327: "What have the Men of *Hebron* here to doe?"

63–64. To avoid conquest, the Gibeonites tricked Joshua into a peace treaty. When the trick was discovered, Joshua spared the Gibeonites, but condemned them to be "hewers of wood, and drawers of water for the congregation" (Joshua 9:27).

66. *Lord:* Among the foreigners whom William raised to the English peerage were Friedrich Herman von Schönberg, Henri de Massue, marquis de Ruvigny, Godard van Reede de Ginkel, and Willem Hendrik van Nassau van Zuylesteyn.

75. *A Country:* the Netherlands.

77. *A Land much differing:* "They are a general *Sea Land,* the Great Bog of *Europe*" ([Edward Ward], *A Trip to Holland,* 1699, p. 3).

78. *Piles:* "the Foundation of all its building, is laid upon huge Piles" (ibid., p. 11).

79. *No marble Quarrys:* "Gold is a great deal more plentiful than Stones" (ibid., p. 3).

A *Sloven* of *Inhospitable* kind,
Prefer'd by Kings, yet ne'er to Monarch true,
A murm'ring, cunning, miserable *Jew,*
Who in return to Royal Bounty, sheds
His venom'd Insolence on Royal Heads,
Opposing Courts, that he by *Courts* may *rise,*
As he puts on the Patriot in Disguise.
If *Judah*'s Sons are false, and *Gibeon*'s just,
Gibeon has right to *share* in *Judah*'s *Trust;*
And serve abroad whom she at home rever'd,
By Gods approv'd of, and to Men endear'd.
Monarchs are *Fountains* whence all Honours flow,
(And Fountains where they please their Streams bestow)
And if all Titles issue from the Throne,
Sure they may *give,* since what they *give's* their *Own.*
But Malice other kinds of Doctrine spreads,
And makes the Crown *precarious* on their Heads.
Forbid it Heaven such Notions have a place
Amidst the Registers of *Jewish* Race,
Whose Pillory'd Printer blackens the designs,
And whose whip'd Author stains the very Lines.
A Sect of People seemingly precise,
Nor East, nor West, nor South, distinctly lies,
All Points of Wind the Murm'ring Sinners share,
And Whine, and Rail, and Plot in ev'ry Air.
No *God* they'd suffer, and no *King* obey.
But would the *People* by the *People* sway;

59. *by Courts may rise:* In 1698 Seymour's parliamentary career was summarized as follows: "some old Prostitute of the exploded Pension'd Parliament in *Charles* the Second's reign, who has from that time been tricking in the House in so shameful a manner, that the several Periods of his Life may be mark'd out by the Bargains he has made there, when the Court has come up to his price" (*A Collection of State Tracts,* 3 vols., 1705–07, 2, 653).

61. *Gibeon:* the Netherlands.

73. *Printer:* Ann Baldwin, publisher of *The Foreigners,* was the widow of Richard Baldwin, the Whig publisher, whom Thomas Brown called "the True, Primitive, Busie, Pragmatical, Prating, muttering *Dick Baldwin,*" the friend of "*Sam. Johnson* [and] Mr. *Touchin*" (*Letters from the Dead to the Living,* 2nd ed., 1702, pp. 17–18).

74. *Author:* Samuel Johnson; see *The Pacificator,* 33 *n.*

75. *Sect:* republicans.

Its Natives void of Honesty and Grace,
A Boorish, rude, and an inhumane Race;
From Nature's Excrement their Life is drawn,
Are born in Bogs, and nourish'd up from Spawn.
Their hard-smoak'd Beef is their continual Meat,
Which they with Rusk, their luscious Manna, eat;
Such Food with their chill stomachs best agrees,
They sing *Hosannah* to a Mare's-milk Cheese.
To supplicate no God, their Lips will move,
Who speaks in Thunder like Almighty *Jove,*
But watry Deities they do invoke,
Who from the Marshes most Divinely croak.
Their Land, as if asham'd their Crimes to see,
Dives down beneath the surface of the Sea.
Neptune, the God who do's the Seas command,
Ne'er stands on Tip-toe to descry their Land;
But seated on a Billow of the Sea,
With Ease their humble Marshes do's survey.
These are the Vermin do our State molest;
Eclipse our Glory, and disturb our Rest.
Bentir in the Inglorious Roll the first,
Bentir to this and future Ages curst,
Of mean Descent, yet insolently proud,
Shun'd by the Great, and hated by the Crowd;
Who neither Blood nor Parentage can boast,
And what he got the *Jewish* Nation lost:

82. *Boorish:* "The People are generally Boorish" (ibid., p. 6).

inhumane: "they are wholly the reverse of Humanity, as they are the backside of the whole World" (ibid., p. 10).

86. *Rusk:* slices of bread that have been browned and sometimes sweetened; formerly much used aboard ships.

101. *Bentir:* Hans Willem Bentinck, first earl of Portland; see *Advice to a Painter,* 31 *n.,* above.

Cursing their Kings, as if by Kings undone,
Yet wishing for *Five hundred* 'stead of *One.*
With these a Senseless, starving Scribler join'd,
Poor in his Purse, and restless in his Mind;
Yet proud of Parts he knew not how to show,
Turn'd out of Place, and despicably Low,
Whilst He to others Places laying Claim,
Lost what He had of Salary, and of Shame.
Stephens caress'd him, and Plain-dealing *Oates*
Fed him to Write his Anabaptist Notes.
A kind Assistance in a Lucky Time,
Which made *him* Preach as well as *he* could Rhime:
Such *Tutchin* was, an Evidential Scribe,
Fit for the Toil of one of *Oates* his Tribe,
Who Lash'd like *him,* like *him* could Snarl and Rail,
And shew his *Malice,* 'cause he shew'd his Tail.
Oh may the Calves-head Rioters, our Foes,
Still use *his* Rhimes, *his* lamentable Prose,
That Faction may be quieted and ceas'd,
Prais'd by so curs'd a *Poet,* and a *Priest.*
But, how can Factious Tempers be subdu'd,
When *Israel*'s Rabbis think such Tempers good?
When her High-Priests sit insolent in State,
And grumble at the Pow'rs that made 'em great,
Though from *Agrippa*'s Bounty they are rais'd,
To wear that *Vest* which they before disprais'd;

82. *wishing for Five hundred:* wishing to be ruled by the 513 members of the House of Commons rather than by one king.

83. *Scribler:* John Tutchin.

86. *Turn'd out:* See *The True-Born Englishman,* 641 *n.,* below.

89. *Stephens:* Edward Stephens (d. 1706) was a nonpracticing lawyer and unbeneficed clergyman who was known as "chaplain to the Calfs-head Club" (HMC *Hope Johnstone MSS.,* p. 116). He was an indefatigable controversialist (Wing S5414–5445). Defoe deals with his last *"to him unhappy, Libel* upon the Government, entitled, *A Letter to the Author of the Memorial of the Church of* England" in the preface to *Jure Divino. A Satyr* (1706).

90. *Write:* The allusion is presumably to a very amusing mock-sermon on the text, "Faith is the evidence of things not seen," by the most famous "Evidence" in English history, *A Sermon Preached in an Anabaptist Meeting in Wapping, on Sunday the 19th of February, by the Reverend T*[*itus*] *O*[*ates*] *D.D.,* 1699 (Wing O55).

95. Cf. *A Hymn to the Pillory,* 46 *n.,* below.

97. *Calves-head Rioters:* See headnote.

105. *Agrippa:* William III.

By lavish Grants whole Provinces he gains,
Made forfeit by the *Jewish* Peoples Pains;
Till angry *Sanhedrims* such Grants resume,
And from the Peacock take each borrow'd Plume.
Why should the *Gibeonites* our Land engross,
And aggrandize their Fortunes with our loss?
Let them in foreign States proudly command,
They have no Portion in the Promis'd Land,
Which immemorially has been decreed
To be the Birth-right of the *Jewish* Seed.
How ill do's *Bentir* in the Head appear
Of Warriours, who do *Jewish* Ensigns bear?
By such we're grown e'en Scandalous in War.
Our Fathers Trophies wore, and oft could tell
How by their Swords the mighty Thousands fell;
What mighty Deeds our Grandfathers had done,
What Battels fought, what Wreaths of Honour won:
Thro the extended Orb they purchas'd Fame,
The Nations trembling at their Awful Name:
Such wondrous Heroes our Fore-fathers were,
When we, base Souls! but Pigmies are in War:
By Foreign Chieftains we improve in Skill;

107. *lavish Grants:* See *Advice to a Painter,* 40 *n.,* above.

109. *Grants resume:* Parliament revoked all of William's grants of forfeited Irish estates on 11 April 1700 (see *On My Lord Somers,* headnote, pp. 195–96, above).

117. *Head:* Portland, who had been colonel of a Dutch regiment of horse guards, was commissioned lieutenant-general of the forces, both horse and foot, in the English army on 12 September 1690. He fought at the Boyne and through all the campaigns in Flanders and was promoted to general of the horse in June 1697 (Dalton, *3,* 164).

119. *Scandalous in War:* The duke of Schomberg observed to King William in 1690 that "La Nation Angloise est si delicatement élevée que d'abord qu'ils sont hors de leur pays, ils dépérissent partout où je les ay vu servir dans les pays étrangers les premières campagnes" (*CSPD 1689–1690,* p. 401; cited in Dalton, *3,* xi).

128. *Foreign Chieftains:* three of these were (1) Friedrich Herman von Schönberg, a German baron and marshal of France, whom William created duke of Schomberg in the English peerage; he was commander-in-chief of all William's forces in Ireland and was killed leading his troops across the Boyne on 1 July 1690; (2) a Dutchman, Hendrik van Nassau, count of Overkerke, whose father was an illegitimate son of Maurice, prince of Orange, William's great-uncle; he accompanied William to England in command of a Dutch guards regiment, was appointed William's master of the horse, fought at the Boyne, and seized Dublin for the king; in the following September he was commissioned lieutenant-general in the English army; (3) a French Huguenot, Henri de Massue, marquis de Ruvigny, who had been an aide-de-camp to Marshal Turenne; when his brother was killed at the Boyne, he joined the English army as a major-general of horse and became one of the heroes of the Irish war; William raised him to the peerage as viscount Galway in November 1692.

When ev'n *Hallastir*'s Gratitude is shown,
In wishing for the Fall of *Israel*'s Throne.
A Man well Skill'd in *Moses* Sacred Laws,
And too much learn'd for such senseless Cause,
Deserving *Love* for what he *truly knows,*
And *Hate* for the *Example* which he shows,
As His *Heart* laughs at what his *Hands* have took,
And loaths the *Shepherd* though he grasps the *Crook.*
Next *Levi*'s Son, a *Napthalite* appears,
Of *goodly Words,* but groundless in his Fears,
Still dreading the Excess of Regal Pow'r,
False, Discontented, Arrogant, and Sowr.
A Courtier once, for *Israel*'s Service fit,
Till *Grants refus'd* envenom'd all his *Wit,*
Made him oppose the finding *Means and Ways,*
And turn'd the Stream of Flatt'ry to Dispraise,
As he would have the Subjects Wrongs redress'd,
And lost the *Golden Key* which *Lock'd* his Breast.
  Distrusts like theirs our fretful Fathers seiz'd,
And urg'd a Rebel War to make 'em eas'd.
But Faith repos'd in Him our Wishes chose
Made us subdue another sort of Foes;

107. *Hallastir:* Gilbert Burnet, bishop of Salisbury, who is referred to below (209) as *"Hebron's* [Scotland's] *Priest"* because he was born in Edinburgh and educated at the University of Aberdeen. Burnet had long been identified with the "senseless Cause" (110) of republicanism: he performed the last offices for Lord Russell on the scaffold in 1683 and numbered among his other friends Algernon Sidney and Andrew Fletcher of Saltoun.

109. *Skill'd in Moses Sacred Laws:* In *The Usefulness of the Stage* (1698) Dennis mentions that Burnet's *History of the Reformation* is "deservedly celebrated by the learned World, where-ever *English* or *French* is known" (*Critical Works, 1,* 161).

115. *Levi's Son:* Sir Jonathan Trelawny, of Trelawne, Cornwall, third baronet (1650–1721), rector of St. Ives and vicar of Southill, is stigmatized in *The Tribe of Levi* ("Since Plagues were order'd for a Scourge to Men") (*POAS,* 1703, *2,* 177) as "a Spiritual Dragoon" for his aggressive action against Monmouth in 1685. He was consecrated bishop of Bristol the same year and was one of the seven bishops whom James II ordered to the Tower in 1688. Of these seven, only Trelawny and William Lloyd took the oaths of allegiance to William and Mary. Trelawny's translation to Exeter, which James had refused him, followed immediately. He sided with Princess Anne and the Churchills, however, in their quarrel with William in 1691–92 "and for the next ten years he held aloof from court" (*DNB, 19,* 1108). Korah, the son of Izhar, the son of Kohath, the son of Levi, is a rebel against Moses in Numbers 16:1.

127. *Him:* William of Orange.

We learn how to intrench, not how to kill:
For all our Charge are good Proficients made
In using both the Pickax and the Spade.
But in what Field have we a Conquest wrought?
In Ten Years War what Battel have we fought?
  If we a Foreign Slave may use in War,
Yet why in Council should that Slave appear?
If we with *Jewish* Treasure make him great,
Must it be done to undermine the State?
Where are the Antient Sages of Renown?
No *Magi* left, fit to advise the Crown?
Must we by Foreign Councils be undone?
Unhappy *Israel,* who such Measures takes,
And seeks for Statesmen in the Bogs and Lakes;
Who speak the Language of most abject Slaves,
Under the Conduct of our *Jewish* Knaves.
Our *Hebrew*'s murder'd in their hoarser Throats;
How ill their Tongues agree with *Jewish* Notes!
Their untun'd Prattle do's our Sense confound,
Which in our Princely Palaces do's sound;
The self-same Language the old Serpent spoke,
When misbelieving *Eve* the Apple took:
Of our first Mother why are we asham'd,
When by the self-same Rhetorick we are damn'd?
  But *Bentir,* not content with such Command,
To canton out the *Jewish* Nation's Land;
He do's extend to other Coasts his Pride,

133. *Ten Years War:* See *The Pacificator,* 13 *n.,* above.

135. *Council:* In 1700 two naturalized foreigners were members of the privy council: Portland, who had been appointed in February 1689, and Meinhardt, third duke of Schomberg, who had been appointed in May 1695. In addition, Henri de Massue, whom William had advanced from viscount to earl of Galway in 1697, had been a member of the Irish privy council since March 1692.

140. *Foreign Councils:* As Louis XIV instructed his ambassador in March 1698, "Those who have the greatest share in the confidence of that prince are foreigners, and consequently exposed to the hatred of the English" (Grimblot, *1,* 276).

149. *Language the old Serpent spoke:* the Serpent speaks Dutch in Joost van den Vondel, *Lucifer* (1654).

Instead of Natives, *Philistines* we slew,
And made the *Jebusite* adore the *Jew,*
When *Boyn* with Purple Torrents swell'd its Flood,
And *Ahgrim* swam, like *Golgotha,* in Blood.
  Yet those who Sav'd and Counsel'd us in War,
Must not in Peace at Council Board appear,
But in return for Conquest take Disgrace,
And Naturaliz'd, not have a Natives Place.
Oh! *Israel,* let it not in *Gath* be known,
Nor let thy *Gratitude* reach *Askalon,*
Publish it not, least Heathens know thy shame,
And *Philistins* deride thy Sacred Name!
Bentir has for thy Rights and Honours stood,
And made an *Israelite,* sought *Israel*'s good,
Dispell'd the Tempests gathering from a far,
And next *Agrippa* hush'd the Din of War.
Yet for the Language is the Man dispis'd,
Whilst he that has *no Thoughts* is ador'd and priz'd.
Beast, as thou art, impertinent in wrong,
Thou need'st no *Eve* to Damn *Thee* but thy Tongue;
Thy canker'd Malice, and thy fester'd Thoughts
Can turn the purest Vertues into Faults,
Whose rising Honours, and whose towring Fame,
Soar *high* in Merit, as thou *sink'st* in Shame.
  But Envy's not contented to Prophane
Agrippa's Friend, but dares his Master's Reign;
Under the Subject, it reviles the Prince,

129. *Philistines:* the Irish.

130. *Jebusite:* Roman Catholics; see *Absalom and Achitophel,* 86.

131. *Boyn:* William's passage of the Boyne on 1 July 1690 was his first victory over the French and Irish troops under the command of James II.

132. *Ahgrim:* The decisive battle of the war in Ireland was fought at Aughrim, county Galway, on 12 July 1691. The Dutchman, Godard van Reede de Ginkel, whom William had left in command of the English forces, succeeded in surrounding the Irish infantry, of whom 7000 are said to have been killed or wounded, against 4000 casualties on the other side (Ogg, *3,* 257–58).

137. *let it not:* "Tell it not in Gath, publish it not in the streets of Askelon; lest the daughters of the Philistines rejoice, lest the daughters of the uncircumcised triumph" (2 Samuel 1:20).

144. *hush'd the Din:* see *A Satyr upon the French King,* 33 *n.,* above.

146. *he that has no Thoughts:* Sir Edward Seymour [?].

147. *Beast:* John Tutchin.

154. *Agrippa's Friend:* Hans Willem Bentinck, first earl of Portland.

And other Kingdoms into Parts divide:
Unhappy *Hiram!* dismal is thy Song;
Tho born to Empire, thou art ever young!
Ever in Nonage, canst no Right transfer:
But who made *Bentir* thy Executor?
What mighty Power do's *Israel*'s Land afford?
What Power has made the famous *Bentir* Lord?
The Peoples Voice, and *Sanhedrim*'s Accord?
Are not the Rights of People still the same?
Did they e'er differ in or Place or Name?
Have not Mankind on equal Terms still stood,
Without Distinction, since the mighty Flood?
And have not *Hiram*'s Subjects a free Choice
To chuse a King by their united Voice?
If *Israel*'s People cou'd a Monarch chuse,
A living King at the same time refuse;
That *Hiram*'s People, shall it e'er be said,
Have not the Right of Choice when he is dead?
When no Successor to the Crown's in sight,
The Crown is certainly the Peoples Right.
If Kings are made the People to enthral,
We had much better have no King at all:
But Kings, appointed for the Common Good,
Always as Guardians to their People stood.
And Heaven allows the People sure a Power

156. *Kingdoms into Parts divide:* The second partition treaty among France, England, the Netherlands, and the Empire was signed for England by Portland (and Edward Villiers, earl of Jersey) on 21 February 1700. It was, as Andrew Fletcher said, "like an Alarum-Bell rung over all Europe" (*A Speech upon the State of the Nation, in April 1701,* n.d., p. 10). According to its terms, Archduke Charles, second son of Emperor Leopold I, was named heir to the throne of Spain. France was to get the Spanish possessions in Italy, of which the duchy of Milan was to be exchanged for the long-sought duchy of Lorraine. Holland was to get the barrier fortresses in the Spanish Netherlands as protection against the power of France. In September 1699 the Spanish ambassador to England protested so violently against "these operations and proceedings . . . contrary to the law of nature," as he claimed, that he was declared *persona non grata* and ordered to depart the country (Grimblot, 2, 355–56).

157. *Unhappy Hiram:* The problem of who was to succeed the childless Carlos II (1661–1700) on the throne of Spain was the "cauchemar perpetuel" which had already overlain the peace of Europe for 10 years.

And calls the truest Service an Offence.
Would Heav'n that *Hiram*'s Sickness would abate,
And he himself leave Heirs to *Sidon*'s State;
That Peace restor'd might have no other Face,
And War be known no more to Mortal Race.
But since our hopes are in appearance lost,
And Fate has *Israel*'s Vows and *Sidon*'s crost;
Since the good Prince nor Herbs nor Art can save,
And he must Childless yield to Nature's Grave,
What nobler Act could humane Mind perform,
Than to prevent and still the growing Storm,
Which from two fierce Pretenders else would rise
With Arms in hand disputing for the Prize;
As each had equal share in *Sidon*'s Reign
And each had *Sidon*'s Blood in ev'ry Vein.
What has *He* got, or what his Wisdom wrought,
But only Peace, and Peace was all he sought.
Egypt and *Syria* both as Brethren share,
Could *Syria* think her Lot divided fair,
And since they'r both Successors to the Throne,
Give *Egypt* what's *Her* Part, and like *Her own*.
  If King's are made the Product of our Choice,
And owe their Grandeur to the Peoples Voice,
Whence is their *Right Divine,* and whence is giv'n
A *Sacred* Pow'r, unless their *Voice* is *Heav'n*.

156. *the truest Service:* William's undertaking of the partition treaties. On 1 May 1699 he told Portland that "the welfare and the repose of all Europe may depend upon the negotiation which you have in hand with count Tallard" (Grimblot, *2*, 326). Portland, of course, acted only on the king's orders.

157. *Hiram's Sickness:* Carlos II was described as "that crazy King [of Spain], infirm alike in his Head and his Health" (Oldmixon, p. 214).

158. *Sidon:* Spain.

167. *Pretenders:* The leading claimants to the throne of Spain were the Habsburg Emperor Leopold I, Carlos' first cousin and brother-in-law, and the Bourbon Louis le Dauphin, Carlos' first cousin once removed.

171. *He:* William III, who told Defoe that "it was Essential to the Safety and Peace of *Europe,* that the Kingdom of *Spain* should never Devolve on one Hand to any Prince that was Emperor of *Germany,* or on the other Hand, to any Prince that was King of *France*" (*Review, 8* [28 April 1711], 59).

173. *Egypt and Syria:* France and the Empire. Leopold I refused to sign the second partition treaty and in August 1700 claimed the whole Spanish inheritance for himself (Luttrell, *4*, 680; Vernon, *3*, 131). Lines 174–76 urge him both to be content with the share of Spanish empire assigned to him in the partition treaty and to be willing to concede to France the equal share assigned to her.

To chuse such Kings as shall not them devour:
They know full well what best will serve themselves,
How to avoid the dang'rous Rocks and Shelves.
Unthinking *Israel!* Ah henceforth beware
How you entrust this faithless Wanderer!
He who another Kingdom can divide,
May set your Constitution soon aside,
And o'er your Liberties in Triumph ride.
Support your Rightful Monarch and his Crown,
But pull this proud, this croaking Mortal down.
Proceed, my Muse; the Story next relate
Of *Keppech* the Imperious Chit of State,
Mounted to Grandeur by the usual Course
Of Whoring, Pimping, or a Crime that's worse;
Of Foreign Birth, and undescended too,
Yet he, like *Bentir,* mighty Feats can do.
He robs our Treasure, to augment his State,
And *Jewish* Nobles on his Fortunes wait:
Our ravish'd Honours on his Shoulder wears,
And titles from our Antient Rolls he tears.

184–90. Quoted in *The Examination, Tryal, and Condemnation of Rebellion Ob[servato]r,* 1703, p. 21.

192. *Keppech:* Arnold Joost van Keppel, earl of Albemarle; see *Advice to a Painter,* 51 *n.,* above.

194. *Crime:* See *Advice to a Painter,* 117 *n.,* above.

198. *Jewish Nobles on his Fortunes wait:* John Granville, earl of Bath, devoted seven years to proving his claim to the estates and titles of George Monck, whom Charles II had created duke of Albemarle in 1660, and even "entered a caveat at the Great Seal against any grant of the title of Albemarle, upon pretence of its being promised to him by King Charles." Only a month later William chose to ignore this and created Keppel earl of Albemarle (Vernon, *1,* 192). Keppel's appointment as captain of the guard frustrated the ambition of the duke of Ormond, and even more recently his installation as knight of the garter had provided another occasion for the kind of "discours que la jalousie qu'on a ici contre les Etrangers inspire," for, as Bonet explained, the duke of Bolton, among others, "se flattoit d'obtenir cet honneur" (BM MS. Add. 30000D, ff. 174, 176; Grimblot, 2, 315).

199. *on his Shoulder:* Knights of the Bath wear "Upon the left Shoulder . . . an Escutcheon of the Arms of St. *George,* that is, a *Cross with a Garter*" (Chamberlayne, 1692, p. 1254).

200. *Antient Rolls:* in the charter and parliamentary rolls of the twelfth to fourteenth centuries the Albemarle title (Shakespeare's Aumerle), which derives from the town of Aumale in Normandy, is variously spelled Albemarle or Aumarle (GEC, *1,* 350–58).

God first appointed Kings, and God ordain'd
That should be fix'd which He alone sustain'd,
Well knowing from his Providential Mind,
That *Israel* could not *chuse,* since she was *Blind.*
Let her indeed *beware,* and truly dread
The Mischiefs which are falling on her Head,
Whilst she permits Audacious Slaves, to dare
That Providence, that made Her Kings its Care;
And lets a Servile Wretch for Servile Ends
Traduce Her Monarch, and Defame his Friends.
Amongst 'em shines a Youth of goodly Port,
Keppech the glorious Pride of *Israel's* Court,
By Nature form'd for Grandeur, and design'd
For Honours, the Rewards of such a Mind.
Noble his Birth, though Foreign is his Blood,
(For other Lands can shew a Noble Flood)
His Temper Courteous, though his Station Great,
As ev'ry Word flows affable and sweet,
And since *Agrippa's* plac'd him near his Heart,
It needs must be th' effect of *true* Desert.

184. *Israel . . . Blind:* Cf. Genesis 48:8–19.
189. *a Servile Wretch:* John Tutchin.

Was e'er a prudent People thus befool'd,
By upstart Foreigners thus basely gull'd?
Ye *Jewish* Nobles, boast no more your Race,
Or sacred Bays that did your Fathers grace!
In vain is Blood, or Parentages, when
Ribbons and Garters can ennoble Men.
To Chivalry you need have no recourse,
The gawdy Trappings make the Ass a Horse.
No more, no more your Antient Honours own,
By slavish *Gibeonites* you are outdone:
Or else your Antient Courage reassume,
And to assert your Honours once presume;
From off their Heads your ravish'd Lawrels tear,
And let them know what *Jewish* Nobles are.

206. *Ribbons and Garters:* Knights of the Bath "wear a Scarlet Ribbon Belt-wise" and knights of the garter wear "a *Blew Garter* deckt with *Gold, Pearl,* and *precious Stones* . . . daily on the left Leg" (Chamberlayne, 1692, pp. 1254, 1256).

213. *tear:* Cf. *Advice to a Painter,* 37, above.

And Thou Great Prince, from whose Auspicious Reign
We Triumph o'er the Land, and Rule the Main;
From whose Example we should Discords cease,
And learn to live in what Thou gav'st us, Peace.
Instead of these, whom *Common-wealth* Debates
Would render Enemies to *Israel*'s States,
Part with thy treach'rous *Jockey* from Thy side,
Nor let Thy Bounty more support his Pride;
Let *Hebron's Priest* from thy Embraces torn,
Preach *Anarchy* where *Anarchy* was born,
Whilst from Thy Righteous Throne we take our Laws,
And fear the Sovereign as we love the Cause;
As we the Blessings of thy Scepter share,
And truly know what *Jewish Monarchs* are.

205. *these:* foreigners.

207. *Jockey:* a crafty or fraudulent bargainer; a cheat who secures unfair advantage by adroit management; here Sir Edward Seymour; see lines 55–60 above.

209. *Hebron's Priest:* Gilbert Burnet; see lines 107–14.

The Court
(November 1700–March 1701)

Amid the rank proliferation of satire generated by the heat of parties and fertilized by the death of the Licensing Act in 1695, it was almost inevitable that there should appear *A Satyr against Satyrs* (1700) ("When Glittering Stars around bedeck the Sphere"). But here the the complaint, probably by Edward Ward, seems superficial and self-pitying:

> All Satyr's Vain, and 'tis the Poet's Curse,
> To be Despis'd, and have an Empty Purse.

In *The Court,* however, the complaint is more general:

> Cou'd ev'ry Man, my *Damon,* be so wise
> Only to Medle where his Talent lyes,
> Some wou'd not Wryte at all, and many less.
> (15–17)

This is one of the passages, moreover, that seem to reply to *The Pacificator.* In the first 18 lines of the poem, the author has been so successful in creating the illusion that something has gone before, that it is almost impossible to believe that *The Court* is not a reply to some other poem. This other poem, however, has not finally been identified. It can hardly be doubted, however, that the body of the poem, lines 19–62, is an expanded variation of lines 413–21 of *The Pacificator.* The differences between the two passages are instructive. Defoe is simply assigning poets to their "proper Talent," "*Dryden* to Tragedy," and so on. The author of *The Court* does the same thing, "To *Congreve* lofty Verse, to *Durfy* Song," but he also interprets "proper Talent" in another sense:

> Let *Ranelagh* with paint renew her Charms,
> And *Jeffry's* wanton it in *Windsor*'s Arms.
> (49–50)

But it is not as an early exemplar of a genre still important but no longer versified—the gossip column—that *The Court* is mainly interesting. The corrupt social and literary world implied by lines 19–62 is only one term of a contrast. In the concluding lines of the poem we are vouchsafed a rare glimpse into another world, the green world which is the repository of all the positive values of Augustan satire. It is these values, moreover, that not only characterize Augustan satire, but distinguish it, for example, from the satire of Donne or Byron. In this ideal world, "Swains . . . are Friends" and maidens are "yielding." In the real world, to point the contrast, "*Warwick* stab[s] his Friend" and "Nymphs" are "Virtuous out of Spight." The values of the green world are the stoic values of Virgil's second Georgic, Horace's second epode, and Martial's epigram, "De rusticatione" (2, 90). In *The Court* they are summarized in a couplet:

Many by Avarice, Pride or Lust are hurld,
But who Commands himself, Commands the World.
(61–62)

The goddess of satire is Honesty, and the Augustan satirist found her not in the city or at the universities, on the battlefield or in the inns of court, but in a little village "Contiguous to a Small, but Lofty Wood";

Beneath the Shadow of whose Spreading Trees,
Guarded by *Cottagers,* his *Goddess* Sees.
(John Tutchin, *A Search after Honesty,*
1697, p. 15)

The date of *The Court* can only be approximated. Line 42 refers to Box *vs.* Wells, which was tried at the king's bench on 16 November 1700. In two of the manuscripts the poem is dated "1700." It must have been written, therefore, between 16 November 1700 and 25 March 1701.

Concerning the author there is no evidence at all. What appears to be an attribution of the poem to John Tutchin in a paraphrase of *The Court* preserved in Bodl. MS. Rawl. poet. D.361 turns out to be something else. The lines are these:

Could every Man ahlas! be but soe wise,
Only to meddle where his tallent lyes; . . .

Collier would not turn Cato of his Age, . . .
Nor sawcy Tutchin dawbe, nor drawe the Court.

The last line is more likely to be a reference to Tutchin's arrest for reflecting upon "several great men" in *The Foreigners* (Luttrell, *4*, 676) than an attribution to him of *The Court*.

The Court

Damon forbear, and don't disturb your Muse,
You can't Correct the Coxcombs you accuse,
Some partial Judges of their harmless Rage
Out of Bravado rashly do ingage,
But many Pens, like *Wortley Montague*
Take an Affront, And yet beg pardon too.
Others I know, who in their Amorous fit,
Blaspheme Parnassus in their Bawdy Wit.
This Aims at Satyr, and in horrid Rhymes
Himself exposes, not the vicious times:
He shews his Mallice, but he cannot bite;
Others strain hard for ev'ry Line they write,
And after all the Throws they've had, 't'as been
Like a *Dutch womans* birth, a Souterkin.
Cou'd ev'ry Man, my *Damon,* be so wise
Only to Medle where his Talent lyes,
Some wou'd not Wryte at all, and many less,
Then We might bear the groaning of the Press.
  To diffrent Muses, diffrent Theams belong:
To *Congreve* lofty Verse, to *Durfy* Song.

3. *Rage:* Cf. *The Pacificator,* 8–9: "here's a Civil War broke out at Home:/*Britannia's* Warlike Sons disturb the Isle."

5. *Wortley Montague:* Although the exact allusion is lost, the reference is probably to Edward Wortley Montagu (1678–1761). A grandson of Edward, first earl of Sandwich, he left Trinity College, Cambridge, in the late 1690s, to indulge his literary tastes in London. In 1700 he undertook a grand tour of the continent, traveling part of the way, from Paris into Italy, with Joseph Addison. And although he long served as a Whig member of parliament for Huntingdon, Huntingdonshire (1705–13, 1722–34), Westminster (1715–22), and Peterborough, Northamptonshire (1734–61), a lord commissioner of the treasury, and an ambassador to the Ottoman Porte, he "never took any conspicuous part in politics" and is remembered chiefly as the husband of Pope's friend, Lady Mary Pierrepont, whom he married privately in 1712 (*DNB, 13,* 707).

13. *Throws:* an earlier form of "throes" (*OED* s.v. throe sb.).

14. *Souterkin: OED* cites John Cleveland, *A Character of a Diurnall-Maker* (1654): "There goes a Report of the Holland Women, that . . . they are delivered of a Sooterkin, not unlike to a Rat, which some imagine to be the Off-spring of the Stove."

16. *where his Talent lyes:* Cf. *The Pacificator,* 412–13: "Let him [*Grand Inquisitor* of Wit] to each his proper Talent show."

Lett Sharp *Architectus* Lampoon the Punk,
The Bawd, the Quidler, Buggerer, and the Drunk.
Let *Gallus* and *Catullus* Court the Fair
But *Caesar*'s Actions, must be *Pindar*'s Care.
Grave *Nestor* must support the tottring State,
And in the Councel cautiously debate.
Let *Lucan* soar beyond the Common reach,
Let florid *Cicero* preach, and *Zeno* teach.
In the black Croud of the litigious Hall
Let *Holt* decide, let *Sloan* and others bawl.
Let *Critic Dennis* from the Frenchman steal,
Let Fools be Beaus, whilst Wisemen are Genteel.
Let *Ratcliffe* Cure the feaver, *Wall* the Pox,
Germain and *Boucher* manage the false Box,

21. *Architectus: ABCD* identify him as "[Christopher] Codrington." "Architectus" may be the word over the etymology of which Codrington once fought a duel (BM MS. Add. 4245, f. 74). The "Lampoon" has not been identified.

22. *Quidler:* a palm-paddler (*Othello,* II.i.259); *OED* cites Richard Brome, *The City Wit (1653): "Cras.* How does she feel your hand? *Lin.* O, she does so quiddle it, shake it, and gripe it!"

23. *Gallus and Catullus: ABC* identify Gallus as "Hopkins." *AD* also identify Catullus as "Hopkins." Charles Hopkins' amatory verse includes *The History of Love: a Poem* (1695) and *The Art of Love* (1700). Cf. *The Pacificator,* 169 *n.,* above.

24. *Caesar:* William III.

Pindar: "[Sir Richard] Blackmore" (*ABCD*).

25. *Nestor:* "[Thomas Herbert, eighth earl of] Pembroke" (*ABCD*). A member of the privy council since October 1689, Pembroke was appointed lord president in May 1699.

27. *Lucan:* "[Samuel] Garth" (*ABCD*).

28. *Cicero:* "[Gilbert] Burnet" (*ABCD*).

Zeno: "[Richard] Bentley" (*ABCD*).

30. *Holt:* See *The Dispensary, 1,* 52 *n.,* above.

Sloan: See *Advice to a Painter,* 108 *n.,* above.

31. *Critic Dennis:* Cf. *The Pacificator,* 155–56 and n., above.

33. *Ratcliffe:* Dr. John Radcliffe; see *A Satyr against Wit,* 137 *n.,* above.

Wall: James Wall, a barber-surgeon (Bloom and James, pp. 41, 71, 72).

34. *Germain:* Sir John Germain (1650?–1718), baronet, was, according to one story, "the son of a private soldier in the life guards of William II, prince of Orange." According to another, "his parents kept an ordinary at Delft." In any case, when he came to England "at the time of the happy Revolution in 1688, he quickly advanced his fortune by being a great gamester." He was "very expert at L'Ombre, the manner of which game is . . . incomparably describ'd by Mr. Pope in his Hero-comical Poem, intitul'd *The Rape of the Lock*" (Lucas, p. 212). In 1690 he was charged with *"crim. con."* with Lady Mary Mordaunt, daughter and heiress of Henry Mordaunt, second earl of Peterborough, and wife of Thomas Howard, duke of Norfolk. Even though two witnesses deposed that they found Germain "between a pair of sheets with the dutchesse" (Luttrell, 2, 344), the House of Lords twice refused to grant the duke a

Let this one turn a Jilt, and that a Whore,
And *Duncomb* lavish his ill gotten Store.
Let *Cutts* be proud of seaven and twenty Scars,
All got alas! in the Low Country Wars,
Let empty *Settle* not to the Bays pretend,

---

divorce. Norfolk, therefore, brought suit against Germain for enticement and claimed £50,000 damages. The jury agreed that Germain was guilty, but found that the duke's loss in the duchess was only 100 marks (Luttrell, *2*, 623–24). Germain was knighted and made a baronet in 1698. In October 1706 he married, as his second wife, Elizabeth, the second daughter of Charles Berkeley, second earl of Berkeley, and Swift's friend, who survived into the next age to become the admirer of another adventurer, John Wilkes.

Boucher: Richard Bourchier, "a plaisterer's son, born [c. 1657] in Hartshorn-lane, near Charing Cross; but being not above 16 years old when his parents died . . . he was forced to shift for himself" (Lucas, p. 195). He shifted so well that he once won £500 on a single throw of the dice from John Sheffield, earl of Mulgrave, whose livery he had won as a footman. On other occasions he won £2500 from King William, 15,000 pistoles from Louis XIV, and £30,000 from Maximilian Emmanuel II, elector of Bavaria. With these winnings he purchased "a very pretty estate near Pershore in Worcestershire," where he was "decently interr'd" in 1702 (Lucas, pp. 197, 198, 202–03, 206–07).

the false Box: an "artificial," i.e. rigged, dice box is described in Lucas, p. 227.

36. *Duncomb:* See *A Satyr against Wit,* 234 *n.,* above; *The True-Born Englishman,* 1101 *n.,* below.

37–38. The implication of these lines is made explicit by the paraphrase in Rawl. poet. D.361, f. 203: "Let Cutts be proud of 27 Scarrs,/Some gott in Mars, but Most in Venus Warrs."

39. *Settle:* Elkanah Settle (1648–1724). His first play, *Cambyses King of Persia: A Tragedy,* was produced at Lincoln's Inn Fields about 1667, while he was still an undergraduate at Trinity College, Oxford. He proceeded to London without taking a degree and for a time "Spurr'd boldly on" as Dryden's "rival poet" and laureate of the Whig party, a phase of his career which was climaxed by his appointment as "organizer-in-chief of the pope burning procession on Queen Elizabeth's birthday (17 November 1680)" (*DNB*). He remained "empty" despite numerous apostasies: in 1681 he published *The Character of a Popish Successour, and what England may expect of such a one,* urging James' exclusion from the throne, and four years later he wrote *An Heroick Poem on the Coronation of the High and Mighty Monarch, James II. King of England, &c.* complaining that " 'twas *Exclusion* HELL's Foundation laid." After James' flight, he resumed his Whiggism and secured appointment as city poet of London in 1691. His pageants for lord mayor's day in 1692–95 and 1699–1701 are entitled *The Triumphs of London* (Wing S2721-2726). The last stage of his career is chronicled in *The Grove: or, the Rival Muses* ("Divine Thalia! Charmer of my Breast"):

> Unhappy Poet to have liv'd so long!
> A Play-wright once; for Profit and for Praise
> He drudg'd: But vanish'd are those golden Days.
> Expell'd the Stage, he met unhappy Times;
> And now for Bread composes Bellman's Rhymes.
> (*POAS,* 1707, *4,* 361)

Let *Morton* Rake, and *Warwick* Stab his Friend.
Whilst Worthless Dutchmen get all England's Riches
Let *Boxe*'s Wife, and hundred's more turn Bitches.
There be Grandees, whom 'tis not fit to Name
That make it Glory to Record their Shame.
Others transported with the Scandal grow,
And Wed those Whores that were prov'd so.
Portmore and *Orkney* Cupids Fort invade,

Settle's pretensions to the poet-laureateship must have been urged upon the unexpected death of Thomas Shadwell in November 1692. The pun is made possible by the fact that a settle is a long wooden bench, with arms and a high back, and a locker under the seat.

40. *Morton:* James Douglas, eleventh earl of Morton (c. 1652–1715), was an impoverished member of the Aberdour, Liddesdale, and Dalkeith branch of the Douglas family. He was both a supporter and pensioner of William of Orange. In June 1704 he was "tryed at the Old Baily for a rape; several of the Scotch nobility appeared in his behalf; and, the prosecution being look't upon as malitious, was acquitted" (Luttrell, *5*, 431).

Warwick: Edward Rich, earl of Warwick and Holland (1673–1701), was fleshed with hackney coachmen (Luttrell, *3*, 297) and killed his friend Richard Coote in Leicester Fields, following a drunken brawl at Locket's. He was tried in the House of Lords in March 1699 and found guilty of manslaughter, but "acquitted, the statute excusing a peer from being burnt in the hand" (Howell, *13*, 939–1032; Luttrell, *4*, 500).

41. *Dutchmen get:* See *Advice to a Painter,* 40 *n.,* above.

42. *Boxe's Wife:* "On Saturday [16 November 1700] was a tryal at the kings bench at nisi prius, upon an action brought by Mr. Box (druggist in Cheapside) against Mr. Wells of Hampshire, for lyeing with the formers wife, and a verdict was given for the plaintiff, and £100 damages; upon which the lord cheif justice Holt sent them out again, and then they brought in £60, which his lordship said was too much, considering she was first elop'd from her husband" (Luttrell, *4*, 709).

43. *Grandees:* "D. Norfolk, E: Macclesfield" (*C*).

46. *Wed those Whores:* Sir John Germain married the duchess of Norfolk in September 1701 after the House of Lords had finally granted the duke a divorce the year before. But Anne, countess of Macclesfield, could have had no expectation of marrying Richard Savage, fourth Earl Rivers, the father of her two illegitimate children, after the House of Lords had granted the earl of Macclesfield a divorce in March 1698. In 1700, however, she married Henry Brett, a friend of Colley Cibber and member of the circle at Will's coffeehouse.

47. *Portmore:* In August 1696 Sir David Colyear (c. 1656–1730), second baronet, married Catherine Sedley, the only child of Sir Charles Sedley and long the mistress of James II, whom James had created countess of Dorchester in January 1686. In June 1699 Colyear himself was created Lord Portmore and Blackness in the Scottish peerage.

Orkney: In November 1695 George Hamilton (1666–1737), fifth son of William Douglas, duke of Hamilton, and "much distinguished . . . as a Souldier" (Swift, *Prose, 5*, 261), married Elizabeth Villiers, daughter of Sir Edward Villiers, first cousin of Barbara Villiers, and *maîtresse en titre* to William III from the late 1670s to the death of Queen Mary in December 1694. On 3 January 1696 Hamilton was created earl of Orkney in the Scottish peerage.

And Marry what their Soveraign Princes made.
Let *Ranelagh* with paint renew her Charms,
And *Jeffry's* wanton it in *Windsor*'s Arms.
May *Williams* in the Horse dung find perfumes,
And hug her Coachman in her velvet Rooms.
Let some fair Nymph be Virtuous out of Spight,
Let *Thraso* brag, but let *Achilles* Fight.
Let *Garrat* at a Bottle spend the day,
Let *Swan* pun on, and Sir *George Humble* pay.

49. *Ranelagh:* On 11 January 1696 Richard Jones, earl of Ranelagh, married as his second wife Margaret Cecil (1672–1728), the dowager baroness Stawell; he was about 60 and she 24. She is alleged to have cuckolded the earl in "Swan passage . . . near Bloomsbury Square" (*A New Ballad,* BM MS. Add. 21094, f. 167).

50. *Jeffry's . . . Windsor's:* Lady Charlotte Herbert (1676?–1733), daughter of Philip Herbert, seventh earl of Pembroke, married John Jeffreys, second baron Jeffreys of Wem, in July 1688, at which time she was "a papist . . . said to be worth £70,000" (Luttrell, *1,* 451). Upon the death of her husband, she married Thomas Windsor, first viscount Windsor of Blackcastle in August 1703 (Luttrell, *5,* 293, 333).

51. *Williams:* There is no evidence to identify this Laurentian lady. One candidate, however, is Lady Ellen Williams, daughter of Robert Bulkeley, second viscount Bulkeley of Cashel, and widow of Sir William Williams, of Vaynol, Carnarvonshire, sixth and last baronet. When Sir William died without issue in January 1697 it was discovered that he had left his entire estate to the sons of his deceased friend, Sir Bourchier Wray. In "a great tryal at the exchequer" in June 1699, the heirs-at-law tried unsuccessfully to contest the will (GEC, *Baronetage, 1,* 198; *DNB, 21,* 462; Luttrell, *4,* 163, 531). "The Cabinet, Escritoire, and Dressing-table, in the Lady *Williams'* Chamber" happen to be mentioned in an earlier petition to the House of Commons (*CJ,* 12, 141).

54. *Thraso:* "[Arnold Joost van Keppel, first earl of] Albemarle" (*ABCD*); see *Advice to a Painter,* 51 *n.,* above.

Achilles: "[James Butler, second duke of] Ormond" (*BCD*).

55. *Garrat:* probably Sir Samuel Garrard (c. 1651–1725), of Lamer, Hertfordshire, fourth baronet, who succeeded to the baronetcy in January 1701 and became a prominent Tory politician: member of parliament for Agmondesham, Buckinghamshire (1701, 1702–10), alderman of Aldersgate ward (1702–22), sheriff (1702–03) and lord mayor (1709–10) of London, and president of Bridewell and Bethlehem Hospital (1721–25). By his second wife he had 12 children, of whom three survived him. He is "the *Drunken* Father" in Defoe, *An Elegy on the Author of The True-Born-English-Man* (August 1704), 326–38 *POAS,* Yale, *7.*

56. *Swan:* R. Swan, an habitué of Will's coffeehouse, was an Irishman with a taste for his native whisky. He was also, like Jonathan Swift, a collector and panegyrist of puns (Thomas Brown, *Familiar and Courtly Letters,* 1700, p. 257; Edward Ward, *The Secret History of Clubs,* 1709, p. 239). John Dennis agreed that "for the Management of Quibbles and Dice, there is no Man alive comes near him," but he was also "credibly inform'd that *Will. Urwin* has refus'd to take *Cunnudrums* of *S*—— for *Usquebaugh* any longer" (*A Pacquet from Wills,* 1701, p. 52; reprinted in *The Select Works of Mr. John Dennis,* 2 vols., 1718, *2,* 529).

Humble: Sir George Humble (c. 1670–1703), of London, third baronet, avoided

Let *Knipe* flog Boys, and let *Tom Browne* translate,
And each be easy in his various Fate.
Thô Men of Merrit may at theirs Repine,
They won't Act basely for an *Indian Mine*.
Many by Avarice, Pride or Lust are hurld,
But who Commands himself, Commands the World.
Lastly My Muse, this is not Our concern,
For whilst you others teach, your Self shou'd learn.
Damon and I alternative will prove
That Friendship by the Noblest Paths does move,
We Swains alone are Friends, We only love.
By purleing Rivers, or some grateful Shade
We Sing the Charming and the yielding Maid.
Ingenious Pens immortalize the Brave,
Yet rural Muses too their Beauties have.
For *Virgils Tytirus* has as many Charms
As when he rais'd his voyce to sing of Arms.
But my own Censures do my self Condemn,
In makeing others Characters, My Theme.
Then that my Crime I may no more pursue,
May you see *Cloris* smile, and so Adieu.
Let Our Augustus Rule the World in peace,
And may his Glory with his Hours increase.

---

one duel "about gaming" in August 1699 by begging his assailant's pardon, but was killed in another quarrel "at play" in March 1703 at the Blue Posts (Luttrell, *4*, 546; *5*, 278).

57. *Knipe:* Thomas Knipe (1638–1711) was educated at Westminster School and Christ Church, Oxford, whence he graduated B.A. in 1660 and M.A. 1663. In the interval between his degrees he began as an usher at his old school and eventually succeeded the legendary Richard Busby as headmaster in April 1695. He was a "strict disciplinarian" (*DNB, 11*, 272).

62. *Commands himself:* Cf. Horace, *Satires,* II, vii, 83: "Quisnam igitur liber? sapiens, sibi qui imperiosus."

72. *Tytirus:* "Dryden" (*ABCD*). Tityrus is Virgil's pastoral guise (Eclogues, I, 6–10). Lines 72–73 seem to mean that Dryden is just as effective in his translations of Virgil's pastorals as he was in "the long resounding Line" of the *Aeneid.*

78. *Augustus:* William III.

1701

Daniel Defoe

The True-Born Englishman
(December 1700–January 1701)

The etiology of *The True-Born Englishman* is best described by Defoe himself. In August 1700, he recalled, "there came out a vile abhor'd Pamphlet, in very ill Verse, written by one Mr. *Tutchin*, and call'd THE FOREIGNERS: In which the Author, *who he was I then knew not*, fell personally upon the King himself, and then upon the *Dutch* Nation; and after having reproach'd his Majesty with Crimes, that his worst Enemy could not think of without Horror, he sums up all in the odious Name of FOREIGNER. This fill'd me with a kind of Rage against the Book, and gave birth to a Trifle which I never could hope should have met with so general an Acceptation as it did, I mean, *The True-Born-Englishman*" (*An Appeal to Honour and Justice*, 1715, p. 6).

Defoe was proud of the unprecedented sale of his "Trifle" (see textual notes, pp. 762–63) but doubtful of its literary merit; it was, he said, "far from the best Satyre that was ever wrote." John Dunton, on the other hand, found it "the finest Piece of Wit that this Age has produc'd (except the Poem call'd *The Dispensary*") (*The Post Angel*, *1* [April 1701], 312) and this must have been the opinion of thousands of readers who bought the copies that poured from the press. It is dangerous to dissent from the *consensus gentium* in any case and the two most considerable poems in the present volume are undoubtedly *The Dispensary* and *The True-Born Englishman*. Yet it is not difficult to point out certain qualities of the latter which are essential to its success as propaganda but contribute nothing to its success as art.

The flaws of *The True-Born Englishman* were, in fact, made public almost immediately. William Pittis, who published *The True-Born Englishman: A Satyr, Answer'd* on 1 February 1701 (*The Post Boy*, No. 908, 30 January–1 February 1701), pointed out that the poem is flat and unmusical. "The Devil-a-bit of any Eccho comes from it," he complained. "The Beauty of Music," he went on to say, is indeed rarely heard in *The True-Born Englishman.* At its best it achieves the tones and rhythm of a quiet conversation:

> 'Tis worth observing, that we ne're complain'd
> Of Foreigners, nor of the Wealth they gain'd,
> Till all their Services were at an end.
>
> (973–75)

But there are vast reaches where Defoe simply "chops logick in heroic verse," as Dr. Johnson said of *Annus Mirabilis* (*Lives, 1,* 352). Defoe may have learned from Dryden how to reason in rhyme, but he is rarely so successful as Dryden in joining this to poetry (ibid., 469). Pittis calls him indifferently "our Poetical Man of Prose, or . . . our Prosaical Man of Poetry."

Measured by Defoe's intentions, however, Pittis' criticism is wholly beside the point. "All along," Defoe insisted in "A Explanatory Preface," "I have . . . strove rather to make the Thoughts Explicite, than the Poem correct." And in the body of the poem itself, he boasts that he had projected his "Thoughts" directly, not darkly involved in Old Testament allegory like Dryden:

> *No Parallel from* Hebrew *Stories take,*
> *Of God-like Kings my Similies to make:*
> *No borrow'd Names conceal my living Theam;*
> *But Names and Things directly I proclaim.*
>
> (921–24)

But this was a mistake; for whatever it may be in propaganda, "directness" is not a virtue in art. Critics from Aristotle to Sean O'Faolain have agreed that poets should tell their story in the most indirect way possible: "You have to make the point clear without stating it" (*Poetics,* 1456b).

Defoe was well acquainted with the "indirect" metaphysical style of the age immediately preceding his. He quotes Cowley in the Preface to *The True-Born Englishman* and alludes on several occasions in the body of the poem to John Cleveland, who had domesticated the metaphysical style to the purposes of political controversy. Pittis, however, insists that Defoe was ill-advised to invite comparison with Cleveland since he had not been "gifted with *Cleaveland's Wit*" (p. 31). Defoe experimented with metaphysical conceits in *The Pacificator,* as in the extended *definitio* of wit and sense (lines 355–

96). And occasionally he undertakes something like metaphysical wit in *The True-Born Englishman,*

> Some think of *England* 'twas our Saviour meant,
> The Gospel should to all the World be sent:
> Since when the blessed Sound did hither reach,
> They to all Nations might be said to Preach.
>
> (382–85)

But the effort seems more strained than illuminating, and Pittis found it downright "Presumptuous."

Perhaps it was Defoe's recognition of his own limitations that led him to seek another style for political controversy in verse, a style closer to prose than Cleveland's. "Closer to prose," of course, were the words that Horace used to describe his own style in satire and that Dryden expanded into a couplet in *Religio Laici:*

> And this unpolish'd, rugged verse, I chose,
> As fittest for discourse, and nearest prose.

But Defoe's style obviously does not derive from Horace; it is totally innocent of *os magna sonaturum.* It sticks as closely as possible to the style of political controversy in prose. By deliberately limiting himself to "pointed Truth . . . And down-right English," Defoe evolved a kind of stripped-down poetry of statement that is heard again in Cowper, for example. But by doing so, he cut himself off from the critics of his own age. To gain their approval he would have had to study to "make [his] Poem correct," as William Walsh was soon to advise the young Alexander Pope. But this, as noted before, he refused to do. As a result, Lord Halifax had to explain to the duchess of Marlborough that Defoe "has a great deal of Wit, [and] would write very well if his necessity's did not make him in too much haste to correct" (Blenheim MS. E36, cited by Henry L. Snyder, *Huntington Library Quarterly, 29* [November 1965], 57).

Pittis' final objection to *The True-Born Englishman* is interesting because it exposes the rhetorical design of the poem. Pittis complains that the conclusion "bears very little proportion to the Premises, for the Close of the Poem is fill'd with a Libel against Sir *Charles Duncomb* only." "What Plea has the Author to Justifie himself with," Pittis asks, "for Taxing above two Millions of People with a Folly which he only charg'd one in particular with?" (p. 87). This question, however, is easy to answer: Defoe has the best plea in the world, the plea of necessity. Duncombe's "Folly" is ingratitude; Duncombe provides an example of ingratitude that is indispensable to Defoe's strategy.

The True-Born Englishman begins with a list of the conventional vices attributed to national characters: "Rage rules the *Portuguese,* and Fraud the *Scotch*" (line 143), and so on. To these national stereotypes, of course, every English reader could be assumed to assent automatically. One by one, however, these vices are imputed to Englishmen (see line 368 *n.*); xenophobia is turned in upon itself. From the list of national vices, one is conspicuously lacking:

> *Satyr* be kind, and draw a silent Veil,
> Thy *Native England*'s Vices to conceal.
>
> (145–46)

But this is only a temporary, or rhetorical, "kindness," for the vice missing from the list, of course, turns out to be England's national vice, ingratitude, "the worst of Human Guilt,/The basest Action Mankind can commit" (lines 1108–09). Duncombe exemplifies ingratitude, and far from bearing "very little proportion to the Premises," he is anticipated in the opening lines of the poem.

Since the satirical portrait of Duncombe circulated in manuscript in 1699, there can be little doubt that Defoe built *The True-Born Englishman* around it, in much the same fashion that Pope built *An Epistle . . . to Dr. Arbuthnot* around the previously existing portraits of Atticus, Bufo, and Sporus. The pattern for this kind of poem, of which *Absalom and Achitophel* is the masterpiece, is at least as old as the anonymous satire *On the Prorogation* of 1671 with its satirical portrait of George Villiers, duke of Buckingham (*POAS,* Yale, *1*, 179).

Defoe was a propagandist, impatient of merely literary effects and insistent that "The End of Satyr is Reformation." Dryden, of course, had said the same thing: *"The true end of* Satyre, *is the amendment of Vices by correction"* (*Prose, 2,* 298). But it would be difficult to demonstrate that *Mac Flecknoe* was intended to "correct" Shadwell. Defoe, however, took his slogan seriously. His purposes in *The True-Born Englishman* were extraliterary. What he wanted to accomplish was nothing less than a reformation of the English character, the cultivation of a new way of feeling and behaving. He hoped his countrymen would "grow better-Natur'd from [his] ill-Natur'd Poem."

Defoe was appalled at "the vicious Tide" of xenophobia in England. *The Foreigners,* as he said, filled him with rage. As a propagandist he must have understood that nothing could resist this kind of force but another emotion equally powerful. The satirical portrait of Duncombe provides exactly this kind of antidote: "Search, *Satyr,* search, a deep Incision make;/The Poyson's strong" (lines 37–38). Hatred of foreigners is finally displaced by hatred of Duncombe's ingratitude, the sin against humanity. Righteous indignation turns out to be the only effective antidote against the poison of racism.

It is strange that the date of publication of *The True-Born Englishman* cannot be determined exactly. According to William Lee (p. xxviii), it was January 1701, but there is nothing to prove that the poem was not published in 1700, as the early editions are dated. The Yale copy of the second edition (*F*) is dated 23 January, so this represents a *terminus ad quem.* The first reference to the poem seems to be that in *The Post Angel* for January 1701, which was published on 1 February (see lines 806–07 *n.*). On the day before, there had appeared *An Answer to a Late Abusive Pamphlet, Intituled, The True-Born Englishman &c. Together with the True Character of a True Englishman* ("A Certain *Barber,* fraught with much Ill Nature"), a folio half-sheet dated 1700, but published, according to the Luttrell copy at Harvard, on 31 January 1701. On the verso is reprinted *A Character of Old England, in Allusion to a Piece of Tacitus de Vita Agricolae* ("The Free-born *English,* generous and wise"), which was first published in April 1681 and then reprinted in *POAS,* 1697, p. [1]131. One couplet in the original poem:

> Those guardian Laws with force to undermine,
> Can never be a prudent Kings design,

is clumsily altered to allude to events in 1701:

> To force that Guard with its worse *Foe* to joyn,
> Can never be a Prudent King's Design.

The king, however, had quite different designs for Defoe.

Thereafter, the angry replies reached a flood stage. All that can be done here is to list them:

2. [William Pittis] *The True-Born Englishman: A Satyr, Answer'd* [1 February] 1701.
3. *A Satyr, On a True Born Dutch-Skipper* ("Begot on Board some Fly-boat, Ship or Hoy") [February] 1701.
4. *The English Gentleman Justified* ("To search for Times in dark Oblivion Cast") [February] 1701.
5. *The True-born Welshman* ("Cot-splut-hur Nails! Shall hur sit dumb and mute") [1 March] 1701.
6. *The Female Critick: Or Letters in Drollery from Ladies to their Humble Servants. With a Letter to the Author of a Satyr call'd The True-born English-man* [March] 1701.
7. *English Men no Bastards: Or, A Satyr against the Author of The True-Born English-man* ("What makes an English Sat'rist loosely write") [17 May] 1701.
8. [John Tutchin] *The Apostates: Or, The Revolters* ("Art thou, dear Israel! still the Butt of Fate?") [November?] 1701.
9. "The True-Born Englishman" ("A Dispute once arose 'twixt an Ass and a Mule"), *Chaucer's Whims,* 1701.
10. *The Fable of the Cuckoo* ("A Princely Eagle that had long been Crown'd") [published early 1702 but dated] 1701.
11. [William Pittis?] *The True Born Hugonot: Or, Daniel de Foe. A Satyr* ("Are we then lost to Sense as well as Shame") [August] 1703.

There was one response to his poem, however, that must have been totally unexpected by Defoe. Fifteen years later he could still recall "How this Poem was the Occasion of my being known to his *Majesty;* how I was afterwards receiv'd by him; how Employ'd; and how, above my Capacity of deserving, Rewarded" (*An Appeal to Honour and Justice,* 1715, p. 6).

The True-Born Englishman

The Introduction.

Speak, *Satyr;* for there's none can tell like thee,
Whether 'tis Folly, Pride, or Knavery,
That makes this discontented Land appear
Less happy now in Times of Peace, than War:
Why Civil Feuds disturb the Nation more
Than all our Bloody Wars have done before.
  Fools out of Favour grudge at Knaves in Place,
And men are always honest in Disgrace:
The Court-Preferments make men Knaves in course:
But they which wou'd be in them wou'd be worse.
'Tis not at Foreigners that we repine,
Wou'd Foreigners their Perquisites resign:
The Grand Contention's plainly to be seen,
To get some men put out, and some put in.
For this our Senators make long Harangues,
And florid Members whet their polish'd Tongues.
Statesmen are always sick of one Disease;
And a good Pension gives them present Ease.
That's the Specifick makes them all content
With any King, and any Government.
Good Patriots at Court-Abuses rail,
And all the Nation's Grievances bewail:
But when the *Sov'reign Balsam*'s once appli'd,
The Zealot never fails to change his Side.
And when he must the *Golden Key* resign,

Title: The phrase is Shakespeare's (*Richard* II, I.iii.309).

5. *Civil Feuds:* See *The Pacificator,* headnote and lines 13–14, above.

13–14. Quoted in [Defoe], *A Serious Inquiry into This Grand Question,* 1704, p. 9, and *Review, 4* (20 March 1707), 65.

14. *To get . . . put in:* "The Parliament, in general, is much oblig'd to him for some Expressions in this Paragraph, and Mr. *H*[*arley*] in particular" (*The True-Born Englishman: A Satyr, Answer'd,* 1701, p. 5). It was during the second session of his fourth parliament (November 1699–April 1700) that William decided to dismiss Somers and form a new ministry around Harley, Rochester, and Godolphin.

25. *Golden Key:* The lord chamberlain of the king's household wears a gold key as

The *Railing Spirit* comes about again.
Who shall this Bubbl'd Nation disabuse,
While they their own Felicities refuse?
Who at the Wars have made such mighty Pother,
And now are falling out with one another;
With needless Fears the Jealous Nation fill,
And always have been sav'd against their Will:
Who Fifty Millions *Sterling* have disburs'd,
To be with Peace and too much Plenty curs'd.
Who their Old Monarch eagerly undo,
And yet uneasily obey the New.
Search, *Satyr,* search, a deep Incision make;
The Poyson's strong, the Antidote's too weak.
'Tis pointed Truth must manage this Dispute,
And down-right English *Englishmen* confute.
Whet thy just Anger at the Nation's Pride;
And with keen Phrase repel the Vicious Tide.
To *Englishmen* their own beginnings show,
And ask them why they slight their Neighbours so.
Go back to Elder Times, and Ages past,
And Nations into long Oblivion cast;
To Old *Britannia*'s Youthful Days retire,
And there for *True-Born Englishmen* enquire.
Britannia freely will disown the Name,
And hardly knows her self from whence they came:
Wonders that They of all men shou'd pretend
To *Birth* and *Blood,* and for a Name contend.
Go back to Causes where our Follies dwell,
And fetch the dark Original from Hell:
Speak, *Satyr,* for there's none like thee can tell.

---

the emblem of his office. The junto Whig, Shrewsbury, resigned from this office on 23 June 1700 and was replaced the next day by a Tory, Edward Villiers, earl of Jersey.

33. *Fifty Millions Sterling:* See *The Pacificator,* 17 *n.,* above.

35. *Old Monarch:* James II.

37. Cf. Charles Davenant, *Essays Upon I. The Ballance of Power,* [March] 1701, pp. 33–34: "our Distempers at Home must be first Cur'd: But in order to do this, the Sore must be Lanch'd, Prob'd, Search'd, and laid open."

Part I

Whereever God erects a House of Prayer,
The Devil always builds a Chappel there:
And 'twill be found upon Examination,
The latter has the largest Congregation:
For ever since he first debauch'd the Mind,
He made a perfect Conquest of Mankind.
With Uniformity of Service, he
Reigns with a general Aristocracy.
No Nonconforming Sects disturb his Reign,
For of his Yoak there's very few complain.
He knows the Genius and the Inclination,
And matches proper Sins for ev'ry Nation.
He needs no Standing-Army Government;
He always rules us by our own Consent:
His Laws are easy, and his gentle Sway
Makes it exceeding pleasant to obey.
The List of his Vicegerents and Commanders,
Outdoes your *Caesars,* or your *Alexanders.*
They never fail of his Infernal Aid,
And he's as certain ne're to be betray'd.
Through all the World they spread his vast Command,
And death's Eternal Empire's maintain'd.
They rule so politickly and so well,
As if they were Lords Justices of Hell,
Duly divided to debauch Mankind,
And plant Infernal Dictates in his Mind.

56–57. "An *English* Proverb" (*E*); Tilley G259. *The Female Critick,* 1701, p. 117, ridicules Defoe's "stately beginning with an old Saw."

68. *Standing-Army:* "The business of the standing Army," Toland said, did "quite ruin the credit of the Whig-Ministry" in 1698–99 (*A Collection of Several Pieces of Mr. John Toland,* 2 vols., 1726, 2, 341).

79. *Lords Justices:* Lords justices were appointed each year to rule England during William's visits to the Netherlands. In July 1700 two junto Whigs, Somers and Montagu, were replaced by Sir Nathan Wright, the new lord keeper of the great seal, and Forde Grey, earl of Tankerville, the new first lord of the treasury.

Pride, the First Peer, and President of Hell,
To his share *Spain,* the largest Province, fell.
The subtile Prince thought fittest to bestow
On these the Golden Mines of *Mexico;*
With all the Silver Mountains of *Peru;*
Wealth which would in wise hands the World undo:
Because he knew their Genius was such;
Too Lazy and too Haughty to be Rich.
So proud a People, so above their Fate,
That if reduc'd to beg, they'll beg in State.
Lavish of Money, to be counted Brave,
And Proudly starve, because they scorn to save.
Never was Nation in the World before,
So very Rich, and yet so very Poor.
Lust chose the Torrid Zone of *Italy,*
Where Blood ferments in Rapes and Sodomy:
Where swelling Veins o'reflow with livid Streams,
With Heat impregnate from *Vesuvian* Flames:
Whose flowing Sulphur forms Infernal Lakes,
And human Body of the Soil partakes.
There Nature ever burns with hot Desires.
Fann'd with Luxuriant Air from Subterranean Fires:
Here undisturb'd in Floods of scalding Lust,
Th'Infernal King reigns with Infernal Gust.
Drunk'ness, the Darling Favourite of Hell,
Chose *Germany* to rule; and rules so well,
No Subjects more obsequiously obey,
None please so well, or are so pleas'd as they.
The cunning Artist manages so well,
He lets them Bow to Heav'n, and Drink to Hell.
If but to Wine and him they Homage pay,
He cares not to what Deity they Pray,
What God they worship most, or in what way.
Whether by *Luther, Calvin,* or by *Rome,*
They sail for Heav'n, by Wine he steers them home.
Ungovern'd Passion settled first in *France,*

87. "how 'tis a *Wise* thing to *undo the World,* I can't imagine" (*The True-Born Englishman: A Satyr, Answer'd,* p. 10).

106. *Drunk'ness:* "the Spark has read *Heylin's Cosmography,* and taken the Character of Germany on trust from him" (ibid., p. 11). Cf. Peter Heylyn, *Cosmography in Four Books,* 1677, p. 339.

Where Mankind lives in haste, and thrives by Chance.
A *Dancing Nation,* Fickle and Untrue:
Have oft undone themselves, and others too:
Prompt the Infernal Dictates to obey,
And in Hell's Favour none more great than they.
  The *Pagan* World he blindly leads away,
And Personally rules with Arbitrary Sway:
The Mask thrown off, *Plain Devil* his Title stands;
And what elsewhere he Tempts, he there Commands.
There with full Gust th'Ambition of his Mind
Governs, as he of old in Heav'n design'd.
Worshipp'd as God, his *Painim Altars* smoke,
Embru'd with Blood of those that him Invoke.
  The rest by Deputies he rules as well,
And plants the distant Colonies of Hell.
By them his secret Power he maintains,
And binds the World in his Infernal Chains.
  By Zeal the *Irish;* and the *Rush* by Folly:
Fury the *Dane:* The *Swede* by Melancholly:
By stupid Ignorance, the *Muscovite:*
The *Chinese* by a *Child of Hell,* call'd Wit:
Wealth makes the *Persian* too Effeminate:
And Poverty the *Tartars* Desperate:
The *Turks* and *Moors* by *Mah'met* he subdues:
And God has giv'n him leave to rule the Jews:
Rage rules the *Portuguese;* and Fraud the *Scotch:*
Revenge the *Pole;* and Avarice the *Dutch.*
  Satyr be kind, and draw a silent Veil,
Thy *Native England*'s Vices to conceal:
Or if that Task's impossible to do,
At least be just, and show her Virtues too;
Too Great the first, Alas! the last too Few.
  England unknown as yet, unpeopled lay;
Happy, had she remain'd so to this day,
And not to ev'ry Nation been a Prey.
Her Open Harbours, and her Fertile Plains,
The Merchants Glory these, and those the Swains,
To ev'ry Barbarous Nation have betray'd her,
Who conquer her as oft as they Invade her.
So *Beauty guarded but by Innocence,*

That ruins her which should be her Defence.
  Ingratitude, a Devil of *Black Renown,*
Possess'd her very early for his own.
An Ugly, Surly, Sullen, Selfish Spirit,
Who Satan's worst Perfections does inherit:
Second to him in Malice and in Force,
All *Devil without,* and all within him *Worse.*
  He made her First-born Race to be so rude,
And suffer'd her to be so oft subdu'd:
By sev'ral Crowds of Wandring Thieves o're-run,
Often unpeopl'd, and as oft undone.
While ev'ry Nation that her Pow'rs reduc'd,
Their Languages and Manners Introduc'd.
From whose mixt Relicks our compounded Breed,
By Spurious Generation does succeed;
Making a Race uncertain and unev'n,
Deriv'd from all the Nations under Heav'n.
  The *Romans* first with *Julius Caesar* came,
Including all the Nations of that Name,
Gauls, Greeks, and *Lombards;* and by Computation,
Auxiliaries or Slaves of ev'ry Nation.
With *Hengist, Saxons; Danes* with *Sueno* came,
In search of Plunder, not in search of Fame.
Scots, Picts, and *Irish* from th' *Hibernian* Shore:
And Conqu'ring *William* brought the *Normans* o're.
  All these their Barb'rous Offspring left behind,
The Dregs of Armies, they of all Mankind;
Blended with *Britains* who before were here,
Of whom the *Welsh* ha' blest the Character.
  From this Amphibious Ill-born Mob began
That vain ill-natur'd thing, an Englishman.
The Customs, Sirnames, Languages, and Manners,
Of all these Nations are their own Explainers:
Whose Relicks are so lasting and so strong,
They ha' left a *Shiboleth* upon our Tongue;
By which with easy search you may distinguish
Your *Roman-Saxon-Danish-Norman* English.
  The great Invading *Norman* let us know
What Conquerors in After-Times might do.

To ev'ry *Musqueteer* he brought to Town,
He gave the Lands which never were his own.
When first the *English* Crown he did obtain,
He did not send his *Dutchmen* home again.
No Reassumptions in his Reign were known,
D'avenant might there ha' let his Book alone.
No Parliament his Army cou'd disband;
He rais'd no Money, for he paid in Land.
He gave his Legions their Eternal Station,
And made them all Freeholders of the Nation.
He canton'd out the Country to his Men,
And ev'ry Soldier was a Denizen.
The Rascals thus enrich'd, he call'd them *Lords,*
To please their Upstart Pride with new-made Words;
And *Doomsday-Book* his Tyranny records.
  And here begins the Ancient Pedigree
That so exalts our Poor Nobility:
'Tis that from some *French* Trooper they derive,
Who with the *Norman* Bastard did arrive:
The Trophies of the Families appear;
Some show the Sword, the Bow, and some the Spear,
Which their Great Ancestor, *forsooth,* did wear.
These in the Heralds Register remain,
Their Noble Mean Extraction to explain.
Yet who the Hero was, no man can tell,
Whether a Drummer or a Colonel:
The silent Record blushes to reveal
Their Undescended Dark Original.
  But grant the best, How came the Change to pass;
A *True-Born Englishman* of *Norman* Race?
A *Turkish* Horse can show more History,

200. *send his Dutchmen home:* See *An Encomium upon a Parliament,* headnote, pp. 45–46, above.

201. *Reassumptions:* See *On My Lord Somers,* headnote, pp. 195–96, above.

202. *Book:* Charles Davenant, *A Discourse upon Grants and Resumptions,* [November 1699 but dated] 1700.

203. *disband:* See *An Encomium upon a Parliament,* 7 *n.,* above.

212–24: "he's a Leveller, and though he flatters King *William,* is but for making one Estate of the Three the Nation is compos'd of, and reducing the People under the Government of the People, as in the Year 48" (*The True-Born Englishman: A Satyr, Answer'd,* p. 20).

To prove his Well-descended Family.
Conquest, as by the Moderns 'tis exprest,
May give a Title to the Lands possest:
But that the Longest Sword shou'd be so Civil,
To make a *Frenchman English,* that's the Devil.
These are the Heroes that despise the *Dutch,*
And rail at new-come Foreigners so much;
Forgetting that themselves are all deriv'd
From the most Scoundrel Race that ever liv'd.
A horrid Medly of Thieves and Drones,
Who ransack'd Kingdoms, and dispeopl'd Towns.
The *Pict* and Painted *Britain,* Treach'rous *Scot,*
By Hunger, Theft, and Rapine, hither brought.
Norwegian Pirates, Buccaneering *Danes,*
Whose Red-hair'd Offspring ev'ry where remains.
Who join'd with *Norman-French,* compound the Breed
From whence your *True-Born Englishmen* proceed.
And lest by Length of Time it be pretended,
The Climate may this Modern Breed ha' mended,
Wise Providence, to keep us where we are,
Mixes us daily with exceeding Care:
We have been *Europe*'s Sink, *the Jakes* where she
Voids all her Offal Out-cast Progeny.
From our Fifth *Henry*'s time, the Strolling Bands
Of banish'd Fugitives from Neighb'ring Lands,
Have here a certain Sanctuary found:
The Eternal Refuge of the Vagabond.
Where in but half a common Age of Time,
Borr'wing new Blood and Manners from the Clime,

229. *the Moderns: "Dr.* Sherl[ock] *De Facto" (E).* Sherlock was aware, as he said, that *"My taking the Oath of Allegiance to King* William *and Queen* Mary, *after so long a Refusal, has occasioned a great deal of talk, and a great many uncharitable guesses about it."* The truth, he insisted, was that he found justification for taking the oaths in Article 28 of the English convocation of 1603, which provided that even the de facto authority of a king who has no legal right to the throne, *"being always God's Authority . . . is ever . . . to be reverenced and obeyed"* (*The Case of the Allegiance Due to Soveraign Powers,* 1691, sig. A1r, p. 4). But when the deist Charles Blount elaborated the same doctrine in *King William and Queen Mary Conquerors* (1693), he was said "to destroy the very Fundamentals of the Constitution" and the House of Commons ordered his book to be burned by the common hangman (Oldmixon, p. 80).

256. *Borr'wing new Blood:* Cf. Shakespeare's *Henry V:* "For he to-day that sheds his blood with me,/Shall be my brother. Be he ne'er so vile,/This day shall gentle his condition" (IV.3.61–63).

Proudly they learn all Mankind to contemn,
And all their Race are *True-Born Englishmen.*
Dutch, Walloons, Flemings, Irishmen, and *Scots,*
Vaudois and *Valtolins,* and *Hugonots,*
In good Queen *Bess*'s Charitable Reign,
Suppli'd us with Three hundred thousand Men.
Religion, *God we thank thee,* sent them hither,
Priests, Protestants, the Devil and all together:
Of all Professions, and of ev'ry Trade,
All that were persecuted or afraid;
Whether for Debt or other Crimes they fled,
David at *Hackelah* was still their Head.
The Offspring of this Miscellaneous Crowd,
Had not their new Plantations long enjoy'd,
But they grew *Englishmen,* and rais'd their Votes
At Foreign Shoals of *Interloping Scots.*
The Royal Branch from *Pict-land* did succeed,
With Troops of *Scots* and Scabs from *North-by-Tweed.*
The Seven first Years of his Pacifick Reign,
Made him and half his Nation *Englishmen.*
Scots from the *Northern* Frozen Banks of *Tay,*
With Packs and Plods came *Whigging* all away:
Thick as the Locusts which in *Egypt* swarm'd,
With Pride and hungry Hopes compleatly arm'd:
With Native Truth, Diseases, and No Money,
Plunder'd our *Canaan* of the Milk and Honey.
Here they grew quickly Lords and Gentlemen,
And all their Race are *True-Born Englishmen.*
The Civil Wars, the common Purgative,
Which always use to make the Nation thrive,
Made way for all that strolling Congregation,
Which throng'd in Pious *Charles*'s Restoration.

260. *Valtolins:* natives of Valtellina, in the present canton of Grisons, Switzerland.

268. *David at Hackelah:* With about 600 of his followers, David sought refuge in the mountain of Hachilah from Saul's attempt against his life (1 Samuel 23:9–19).

272. *Interloping Scots:* The attempt of the Company of Scotland Trading to Africa and the Indies to establish a settlement at Darien, in the isthmus of Panama, in 1698–99, was greatly resented as a threat to English trade in the Caribbean.

278. *Whigging:* jogging along (*OED* quotes this line).

285–86. "It's but an odd sort of an Observation, that Countries *thrive by Civil Wars,* since it is evident that where the Seat of a War is, the Trade of that People is at a stand" (*The True-Born Englishman: A Satyr, Answer'd,* p. 25).

The *Royal Refugeé* our Breed restores,
With *Foreign Courtiers,* and with *Foreign Whores:*
And carefully repeopled us again,
Throughout his Lazy, Long, Lascivious Reign,
With such a blest and True-born *English* Fry,
As much Illustrates our Nobility.
A Gratitude which will so black appear,
As future Ages must abhor to hear:
When they look back on all that Crimson Flood,
Which stream'd in *Lindsey*'s, and *Caernarvon*'s Blood:
Bold *Strafford, Cambridge, Capel, Lucas, Lisle,*
Who crown'd in Death his Father's Fun'ral Pile.
The Loss of whom, in order to supply
With True-Born *English* Nobility,
Six Bastard Dukes survive his Luscious Reign,
The Labours of *Italian Castlemain,*
French Portsmouth, Tabby Scot, and *Cambrian.*

294. *Nobility:* "The extent to which the peerage in 1688 was of Stuart creation is very remarkable. . . . [Charles II] was responsible for no fewer than 64 [creations]" (A. S. Turberville, *The House of Lords in the Reign of William III,* Oxford, 1913, p. 2).

298. *Lindsey:* Robert Bertie, first earl of Lindsey, was killed at the battle of Edgehill, October 1642.

Caernarvon: Robert Dormer, earl of Carnarvon, was killed at the first battle of Newbury, September 1643.

299. *Strafford:* Thomas Wentworth, first earl of Strafford, was beheaded on 12 May 1641.

Cambridge: James Hamilton, second earl of Cambridge, was beheaded on 9 March 1649.

Capel: Arthur Capel, Lord Capel of Hadham, was beheaded 9 March 1649 "for his loyalty to King Charles the First," as the inscription reads on his monument at Hadham.

Lucas: Sir Charles Lucas was captured by the parliamentary army at the siege of Colchester, courtmartialed, and shot on 28 August 1648.

Lisle: Sir George Lisle suffered the same fate as Lucas. The two heroes are celebrated in Edward Howard, *Caroloiades, Or, The Rebellion of Forty One. In Ten Books. A Heroick Poem* (1689). pp. 324–26.

300. *Fun'ral Pile:* Cf. *CSPD 1660–1661,* p. 396: "Mary Lisle . . . Is the only survivor of her family; her two brothers were slain fighting for the late King, and her parents died of grief for their loss."

303–05. *Six Bastard Dukes:* James Scott, duke of Monmouth and Buccleuch (1649–85), the son of "Cambrian" Lucy Walter, "a private Welch woman of no good fame, but handsome" (Edward Hyde, Earl of Clarendon, *The Life of Edward Earl of Clarendon,* 2 vols., Oxford, 1857, 2, 18; Charles Fitzroy, duke of Southampton (1662–1730), Henry Fitzroy, duke of Grafton (1663–90), and George Fitzroy, duke of Northumberland

Besides the Num'rous Bright and Virgin Throng,
Whose Female Glories shade them from my Song.
This Offspring, if one Age they multiply,
May half the House with *English* Peers supply:
There with true *English* Pride they may contemn
Schomberg and *Portland,* new-made Noblemen.
French Cooks, *Scotch* Pedlars, and *Italian* Whores,
Were all made Lords, or Lords Progenitors.
Beggars and Bastards by his new Creation,
Much multipli'd the Peerage of the Nation;
Who will be all, e're one short Age runs o're,
As True-Born Lords as those we had before.
Then to recruit the Commons he prepares,
And heal the latent Breaches of the Wars:
The Pious Purpose better to advance,
H' invites the banish'd Protestants of *France:*
Hither for God's sake and their own they fled,
Some for Religion came, and some for Bread:
Two hundred thousand Pair of Wooden Shooes,
Who, God be thank'd, had nothing left to lose;
To Heav'n's great Praise did for Religion fly,
To make us starve our Poor in Charity.
In ev'ry Port they plant their fruitful Train,
To get a Race of *True-Born Englishmen:*

(1665–1716), the sons of "Italian Castlemain," Barbara Villiers, countess of Castlemaine and duchess of Cleveland; Charles Beauclerk, duke of St. Albans (1670–1726), the son of "Tabby Scot," Nell Gwyn; Charles Lennox, duke of Richmond (1672–1723), the son of "French Portsmouth," Louise de Kéroualle, duchess of Portsmouth.

311. *Schomberg:* See *The Foreigners,* 128 *n.,* above.

Portland: See *Advice to a Painter,* 31 *n.,* above.

312. *Scotch Pedlars:* One wonders on what basis Defoe attributes Scottish origins to Nell Gwyn's father, who is otherwise identified as "a poor royalist Welsh captain in the army" and keeper of a fruit-stall in Covent Garden (*N&Q, 12* [31 August 1867], 166; *1* [29 February 1868], 196).

Italian Whores: Presumably the reference includes the duchess of Cleveland (304, above) and Hortensia Mancini, the niece of Cardinal Mancini, and duchesse de Mazarin, who momentarily supplanted the duchess of Portsmouth as Charles' mistress but neither founded a family nor gained an English title.

321. *banish'd Protestants:* "They had begun to arrive a few years before the Revocation of the Edict of Nantes in October 1685" (Ogg, *3,* 41).

327. *Poor:* A law of 1662 entitled An Act for the better Relief of the Poor of this Kingdom (13 & 14 Charles II c. 12) provided in fact for the more rigorous application of the Elizabethan poor laws.

Whose Children will, when riper Years they see,
Be as Ill-natur'd and as Proud as we:
Call themselves *English,* Foreigners despise,
Be surly like us all, and just as wise.
  Thus from a Mixture of all Kinds began,
That Het'rogeneous Thing, *An Englishman:*
In eager Rapes, and furious Lust begot,
Betwixt a Painted *Britton* and a *Scot:*
Whose gend'ring Offspring quickly learnt to bow,
And yoke their Heifers to the *Roman* Plough:
From whence a Mongrel half-bred Race there came,
With neither Name nor Nation, Speech or Fame.
In whose hot Veins new Mixtures quickly ran,
Infus'd betwixt a *Saxon* and a *Dane.*
While their Rank Daughters, to their Parents just,
Receiv'd all Nations with Promiscuous Lust.
This Nauseous Brood directly did contain
The well-extracted Blood of *Englishmen.*
  Which Medly canton'd in a Heptarchy,
A Rhapsody of Nations to supply,
Among themselves maintain'd eternal Wars,
And still the Ladies lov'd the Conquerors.
  The *Western* Angles all the rest subdu'd;
A bloody Nation, barbarous and rude:
Who by the Tenure of the Sword possest
One part of *Britain,* and subdu'd the rest.
And as great things denominate the small,
The Conqu'ring Part gave Title to the Whole.
The *Scot, Pict, Britain, Roman, Dane* submit,
And with the *English-Saxon* all unite:
And these the Mixture have so close pursu'd,
The very Name and Memory's subdu'd:
No *Roman* now, no *Britain* does remain;
Wales strove to separate, but strove in vain:
The silent Nations undistinguish'd fall,
And *Englishman*'s the common Name for all.
Fate jumbl'd them together, *God knows how;*
Whate're they were, they're *True-Born English* now.

348. *Heptarchy:* the seven kingdoms of the Angles and Saxons in England.

The Wonder which remains is at our Pride,
To value that which all wise men deride.
For *Englishmen* to boast of Generation,
Cancels their Knowledge, and lampoons the Nation.
A *True-Born Englishman*'s a Contradiction,
In Speech an Irony, in Fact a Fiction.
A Banter made to be a Test of Fools,
Which those that use it justly ridicules.
A Metaphor invented to express
A man *a-kin* to all the Universe.
For as the *Scots,* as Learned Men ha' said,
Throughout the World their Wandring Seed ha' spread;
So open-handed *England,* 'tis believ'd,
Has all the Gleanings of the World receiv'd.
Some think of *England* 'twas our Saviour meant,
The Gospel should to all the World be sent:
Since when the blessed Sound did hither reach,
They to all Nations might be said to Preach.
'Tis well that Virtue gives Nobility,
Else God knows where we had our Gentry;
Since scarce one Family is left alive,
Which does not from some Foreigner derive.
Of Sixty thousand *English* Gentlemen,
Whose Names and Arms in Registers remain,

368. *Pride: "Pride* was wholly attributed to the *Spaniards* sometime before [82–95, above], but now 'tis the property of the *English" (The True-Born Englishman: A Satyr, Answer'd,* p. 30).

378. *as Learned Men ha' said:* John Cleveland, *The Rebel Scot:* "Had *Cain* been *Scot,* God would have chang'd his Doom,/Not forc'd him wander but confin'd him home" *(The Works of Mr. John Cleveland,* 1687, p. 41). "Our Author does very ill to make use of *Cleaveland's Word (Wandring)* unless he had been gifted with *Cleaveland's Wit" (The True-Born Englishman: A Satyr, Answer'd,* p. 31).

382. *Some think:* "I am apt to think, those are no ones Sentiments but his own" (ibid., p. 31).

386. *Virtue gives Nobility:* "Grosvenor motto" (ms. note in Yale copy of *G*). The motto of the Grosvenors of Eaton, Cheshire, is actually "Virtue, *not* ancestry" (*Virtus non stemma*) (GEC, *Baronetage, I,* 189).

390. *Sixty thousand:* Chamberlayne (1700, p. 297) puts the number of esquires and gentlemen at "above 6000"; Gregory King estimated 15,000 (George N. Clark, *The Later Stuarts,* Oxford, Clarendon Press, 1949, p. 25).

391. *Registers:* "The Gentry of *England* . . . are descended of ancient Families, that have always born a Coat of Arms." The records of coats of arms are kept in the College

We challenge all our Heralds to declare
Ten Families which *English-Saxons* are.
France justly boasts the Ancient Noble Line
Of *Bourbon, Mommorency,* and *Lorrain.*
The *Germans* too their House of *Austria* show,
And *Holland* their Invincible *Nassau.*
Lines which in Heraldry were Ancient grown,
Before the Name of *Englishman* was known.
Even *Scotland* too her Elder Glory shows,
Her *Gourdons, Hamiltons,* and her *Monroes;*
Dowglas, Mackays, and *Grahams,* Names well known,
Long before Ancient *England* knew her own.
But *England,* Modern to the last degree,
Borrows or makes her own Nobility,
And yet she boldly boasts of Pedigree:
Repines that Foreigners are put upon her,
And talks of her Antiquity and Honour:
Her *Sackvills, Savils, Cecils, Delamers,*
Mohuns and *Mountagues, Durases* and *Veres,*
Not one have *English* Names, yet all are *English* Peers.
Your *Houblons, Papillons,* and *Lethuilliers,*
Pass now for True-Born *English* Knights and Squires,
And make good Senate-Members, or Lord-Mayors.

---

of Heralds which in 1700 was located "upon St. *Bennet's* Hill, near *Doctors Commons, London*" (Chamberlayne, 1700, pp. 294, 401).

401. *Monroes:* "[The Family] of *Monroe,* which I never heard was Famous for any Member of it, but one Mr. *Monroe,* who is a celebrated Tobaconist" (*The True-Born Englishman: A Satyr, Answer'd,* p. 32). Members of one branch of the Munro family, of which the Black Baron (d. 1633) was the most celebrated representative, were hereditary chiefs of the clan Foulis. The representative of a collateral branch, Sir Robert Munro (d. 1746), was twenty-seventh baron and sixth baronet of Foulis.

409–10. The names are spelled out in the *Key.*

411. *Peers:* Charles Sackville, earl of Dorset; William Saville, marquis of Halifax; James Cecil, earl of Salisbury; John Cecil, earl of Exeter; Henry Booth, second Baron Delamere and first earl of Warrington; Charles Mohun, Lord Mohun; Charles Montagu, earl of Manchester; Edward Montagu, earl of Sandwich; Ralph Montagu, earl of Montagu: Louis de Duras, earl of Feversham; Aubrey de Vere, earl of Oxford.

414. *Members, or Lord Mayors:* Sir John Houblon (d. 1712), first governor of the Bank of England and master of the Grocers' Company, served as lord mayor of London in 1695. His younger brother, Sir James Houblon (d. 1700), deputy governor of the Bank of England, served the city both as alderman (1692–1700) and member of parlia-

Wealth, howsoever got, in *England* makes
Lords of Mechanicks, Gentlemen of Rakes.
Antiquity and Birth are needless here;
'Tis Impudence and Money makes a Peer.
  Innumerable City-Knights we know,
From *Blewcoat Hospitals* and *Bridewell* flow.
Draymen and Porters fill the City Chair,
And Footboys Magisterial Purple wear.
Fate has but very small Distinction set
Betwixt the *Counter* and the Coronet.
Tarpaulin Lords, Pages of high Renown,
Rise up by Poor Mens Valour, not their own.
Great Families of yesterday we show,
And Lords, whose Parents were *the Lord knows who.*

---

ment (1698–1700). Thomas Papillon (1623–1702) was candidate for mayor in the critical shrievalty election of 1682; he was subsequently elected alderman for Portsoken ward (1689). He was a Whig member of parliament for Dover (1673–81, 1689–95) and then for London (1695–1700). Sir John Lethuillier (c. 1629–1719), whose fat wife Pepys "admired so," served as sheriff (1674) and alderman for Cripplegate ward (1676) (Beaven, *2*, 191). He was succeeded in both of these offices by his younger brother, Sir Christopher Lethuillier (d. 1690), who served as alderman for Coleman Street ward (1687–90) and sheriff (1689).

420. *From Blewcoat Hospitals and Bridewell:* "*Christ-Church Hospital* . . . called by some the *Blue-coat Hospital;* all the Boys and Girls being cloathed in Blue Coats, very warm and decent, and provided with all suitable Necessaries. . . . Here's almost a Thousand poor Children, most of 'em Orphans, maintain'd . . . and some of those that have been put to Trades, have arrived to the highest Dignities in the City, even the *Praetorial Chair* hath been proud of being filled with one of these . . . . *Bridewell Hospital,* or Work-house, is a place where indigent, vagrant and idle People are set to work, and maintained with Clothing and Diet. . . . To this Hospital, divers hopeful and ingenious Lads are put Apprentices, and prove afterwards honest and substantial Citizens" (Chamberlayne, 1700, pp. 406–08).

424. *Counter:* The Counters were prisons and there were two of them in London, one on the north side of the Poultry and the other on Wood Street (Strype, *1*, 333, 350–51).

425. *Tarpaulin Lords:* persons of indifferent origins elevated to the peerage for distinguished naval service.

Pages of high Renown: "though *English* Pages for their Bravery at Sea are made Lords, it is not a thing to be wondered at" (*The True-Born Englishman: A Satyr, Answer'd,* p. 34).

428. *the Lord knows who:* "It is easie to observe in the late and present Parliament, that several Boroughs and some Counties have been represented by Persons, who little thought to have ever had such hopes before" (Swift, *Discourse,* pp. 126–27).

Part II

The Breed's describ'd: Now, *Satyr,* if you can,
Their Temper show, for *Manners make the Man.*
Fierce as the *Britain,* as the *Roman* Brave;
And less inclin'd to Conquer than to Save:
Eager to fight, and lavish of their Blood;
And equally of *Fear and Forecast* void.
The *Pict* has made 'em Sowre, the *Dane* Morose;
False from the *Scot,* and from the *Norman* worse.
What Honesty they have, the *Saxon* gave them,
And That, now they grow old, begins to leave them.
The Climate makes them Terrible and Bold;
And *English* Beef their Courage does uphold:
No Danger can their Daring Spirit pall,
Always provided that their Belly's full.
  In close Intriegues their Faculty's but weak,
For gen'rally whate're they know, they speak:
And often their own Councils undermine
By their Infirmity, and not design.
From whence the Learned say it does proceed,
That *English* Treasons never can succeed:
For they're so open-hearted, you may know
Their own most secret Thoughts, and others too.
  The Lab'ring Poor, in spight of Double Pay,
Are Sawcy, Mutinous, and Beggarly:
So lavish of their Money and their Time,
That want of Forecast is the Nation's Crime.
Good Drunken Company is their Delight;

430. *Manners make the Man:* proverbial; the full form is "Manners make a man, quoth William of Wickham" (Tilley M629).

434: *Forecast:* forethought, prudence.

437. *gave:* "A valuable sort of Gift, indeed, when according to his Challenge [390–93, above], out of 60000 Families, ten of them had not so much as a drop of [*Saxon*] Blood in them" (*The True-Born Englishman: A Satyr, Answer'd,* p. 35).

454. *Forecast:* See 434 *n.,* above.

455. *Good Drunken Company: "who can dispute our* Intemperance, *while an* Honest Drunken Fellow *is a Character in a Man's Praise?"* (*The True-Born Englishman,* Preface).

And what they get by Day, they spend by Night.
Dull Thinking seldom does their Heads engage,
But Drink their Youth away, and hurry on Old Age.
Empty of all good Husbandry and Sense;
And void of Manners most, when void of Pence.
Their strong Aversion to Behaviour's such,
They always talk too little, or too much.
So dull, they never take the pains to think;
And seldom are good-natur'd, *but in Drink.*
In *English* Ale their dear Enjoyment lies,
For which they'll starve themselves and Families.
An *Englishman* will fairly drink as much
As will maintain Two Families of *Dutch:*
Subjecting all their Labours to the Pots;
The greatest Artists are the greatest Sots.
The Country Poor do by Example live;
The Gentry Lead them, and the Clergy drive:
What may we not from such Examples hope?
The Landlord is their God, the Priest their Pope.
A Drunken Clergy, and a Swearing Bench,
Has giv'n the Reformation such a Drench,
As wise men think there is some cause to doubt,
Will purge Good Manners and Religion out.
Nor do the Poor alone their Liquor prize,
The Sages join in this great Sacrifice.
The Learned Men who study *Aristotle,*
Correct him with an Explanation-Bottle;
Praise *Epicurus* rather than *Lysander,*
And *Aristippus* more than *Alexander.*
The Doctors too their *Galen* here resign,
And gen'rally prescribe *Specifick Wine.*
The Graduates Study's grown an easier Task,
While for the *Urinal* they toss the *Flask.*
The Surgeons Art grows plainer ev'ry Hour,
And Wine's the Balm which into Wounds they pour.

476. *Reformation:* See *A Satyr against Wit,* headnote, pp. 129–31, above. Cf. "*All our Reformations are Banters, and will be so, till our Magistrates and Gentry Reform themselves by way of Example; then, and not till then, they may be expected to punish others without* blushing" (*The True-Born Englishman,* Preface).

484. *Aristippus:* "The Drunkard's Name for Canary" (*E*).

Poets long since *Parnassus* have forsaken,
And say the Ancient Bards were all mistaken.
Apollo's lately abdicate and fled,
And good King *Bacchus* reigneth in his stead:
He does the Chaos of the Head refine,
And Atom-Thoughts jump into Words by Wine:
The Inspiration's of a finer Nature;
As Wine must needs excel *Parnassus* Water.
Statesmen their weighty Politicks refine,
And Soldiers raise their Courages by Wine.
Caecilia gives her Choristers their Choice,
And lets them all drink Wine to clear the Voice.
Some think the Clergy first found out the way,
And Wine's the only Spirit by which they Pray.
But others less prophane than so, agree,
It clears the Lungs, and helps the Memory:
And therefore all of them Divinely think,
Instead of Study, 'tis as well to drink.
And here I wou'd be very glad to know,
Whether our *Asgilites* may drink or no.
Th' Enlight'ning Fumes of Wine would certainly
Assist them much *when they begin to fly:*
Or if a Fiery Chariot shou'd appear,
Inflam'd by Wine, they'd ha' the less to fear.
Even the gods themselves, as Mortals say,
Were they on Earth, wou'd be as drunk as they:

496. *Atom-Thoughts:* the smallest conceivable particles of idea.

510. *Asgilites:* John Asgill (1659–1738), by trade a lawyer and occasional Whig member of parliament for Bramber, Sussex (1699–1700, 1702–07), was, like Defoe, an enthusiastic and resourceful projector. He achieved his greatest notoriety in July 1700 when he published *An Argument Proving, that according to the Covenant of Eternal Life Revealed in the Scriptures, Man may be Translated from Hence into that Eternal Life, without Passing through Death.* Two months later Bishop Burnet ordered all unsold copies to be confiscated, "as containing things of dangerous consequence" (Luttrell, *4*, 691), and Defoe, also responding, as he said, to "the Danger . . . to Religion," wrote *An Enquiry into the Case of Mr. Asgil's Translation: Shewing that 'Tis not a Nearer Way to Heaven than the Grave.* This work, however, he suppressed while the sheets were still in the press, probably after he read *The Way to Heaven in a String; Or, Mr. Asgil's Argument Burlesqu'd* ("There are some things accounted real"), amusing doggerel which was widely circulated and reprinted (*POAS,* 1704, *3,* 443), and which called into question the seriousness of Asgill's argument. The word "Asgilites" first occurs in the latter work.

Nectar would be no more Celestial Drink,
They'd all take Wine, to teach them how to Think.
But *English* Drunkards, gods and men outdo,
Drink their Estates away, and Senses too.
Colon's in Debt, and if his Friends should fail
To help him out, must dye at last in Gaol:
His *Wealthy Uncle* sent a Hundred Nobles,
To pay his Trifles off, and rid him of his Troubles:
But *Colon, like a True-Born Englishman,*
Drank all the Money out in bright Champaign;
And *Colon* does in Custody remain.
Drunk'ness has been the Darling of the Realm,
E're since a Drunken Pilot had the Helm.
  In their Religion they are so unev'n,
That each man goes *his own By-way to Heav'n.*
Tenacious of Mistakes to that degree,
That ev'ry man pursues it sep'rately,
And fancies none can find the Way but he:
So shy of one another they are grown,
As if they strove to get to Heav'n alone.
Rigid and Zealous, Positive and Grave,
And ev'ry Grace, but Charity, they have:
This makes them so Ill-natur'd and Uncivil,
That all men think an *Englishman* the Devil.
  Surly to Strangers, Froward to their Friend;
Submit to Love with a reluctant Mind;
Resolv'd to be ungrateful and unkind.
If by Necessity reduc'd to ask,
The Giver has the difficultest Task:
For what's bestow'd they awkwardly receive,
And always Take less freely than they Give.

521. *Colon:* Cf. *The Dispensary, 2, 74 n.,* above.

529. *a Drunken Pilot:* Charles II, "a Prince whom [Defoe] had before [291–307, above] rendred infamous for a Vice which is not consistent with [drunkenness]" (*The True-Born Englishman: A Satyr, Answer'd,* p. 42).

530–40. "Any one may perceive he's for voting an Act of *Comprehension,* and that he would have all the straggling Sects whatsoever enjoy the same Privileges with those that are actually in common with the Establish'd Church" (ibid.).

547. *Take less freely than they Give:* "a Vertue we ought to be priz'd above our Neighbours for . . . , that makes us Superior to the rest of those Nations that People the World" (ibid., p. 43).

The Obligation is their highest Grief;
And never love, where they accept Relief.
So sullen in their Sorrows, that 'tis known,
They'll rather dye than their Afflictions own:
And if reliev'd, it is too often true,
That they'll abuse their Benefactors too:
For in Distress their Haughty Stomach's such,
They hate to see themselves oblig'd too much.
Seldom contented, often in the wrong;
Hard to be pleas'd at all, and never long.
  If your Mistakes their Ill Opinion gain,
No Merit can their Favour reobtain:
And if they're not Vindictive in their Fury,
'Tis their unconstant Temper does secure ye:
Their Brain's so cool, their Passion seldom burns;
For all's condens'd before the Flame returns:
The Fermentation's of so weak a Matter,
The Humid damps the Fume, and runs it all to Water.
So tho the Inclination may be strong,
They're pleas'd by Fits, and never angry long.
  Then if Good Nature shows some slender proof,
They never think they have Reward enough:
But like our *Modern Quakers* of the Town,
Expect your Manners, and return you none.
  Friendship, th' abstracted Union of the Mind,
Which all men seek, but very few can find:
Of all the Nations in the Universe,
None talk on't more, or understand it less:
For if it does their Property annoy,
Their Property their Friendship will destroy.
  As you discourse them, you shall hear them tell
All things in which they think they do excel:
No Panegyrick needs their Praise record;
An Englishman *ne're wants his own good word.*
His first Discourses gen'rally appear
Prologu'd with his own wondrous Character:
When, to illustrate his own good Name,

556–57. Cf. *Absalom and Achitophel,* 547–48.

He never fails his Neighbour to defame:
And yet he really designs no wrong;
His Malice goes no further than his Tongue.
But pleas'd to Tattle, he delights to Rail,
To satisfy the Lech'ry of a Tale.
His own dear Praises close the ample Speech,
Tells you how Wise he is; *that is, how Rich:*
For Wealth is Wisdom; he that's Rich is wise;
And all men Learned Poverty despise.
His Generosity comes next, and then
Concludes that he's a *True-Born Englishman;*
And they, 'tis known, are Generous and Free,
Forgetting, and Forgiving Injury:
Which may be true, thus rightly understood,
Forgiving Ill Turns, and Forgetting Good.
  Chearful in Labour when they've undertook it;
But out of Humour, when they're out of Pocket.
But if their Belly and their Pocket's full,
They may be Phlegmatick, but never Dull:
And if a Bottle does their Brains refine,
It makes their Wit as sparkling as their Wine.
  As for the general Vices which we find
They're guilty of in common with Mankind,
Satyr, forbear, and silently endure;
We must conceal the Crimes we cannot cure.
Nor shall my Verse the brighter Sex defame;
For *English* Beauty will preserve her Name.
Beyond dispute, Agreeable and Fair;
And Modester than other Nations are:
For where the Vice prevails, the great Temptation
Is want of Money, more than Inclination.
In general, this only is allow'd,
They're something Noisy, and a little Proud.
  An *Englishman* is gentlest in Command;
Obedience is a Stranger in the Land:
Hardly subjected to the Magistrate;
For Englishmen *do all Subjection hate.*
Humblest when Rich, but peevish when they're Poor;

And think whate're they have, they merit more.
  Shamwhig pretends t' ha' serv'd the Government,
But baulk't of due Reward, turns Malecontent.
For English *Christians always have regard*
To future Recompences of Reward.
His forfeit Liberty they did restore,
And gave him Bread, which he had not before.
But *True-Born English Shamwhig* lets them know,
His Merit must not lye neglected so.
As Proud as Poor, his Masters he'll defy;
And writes a *Piteous Satyr* upon *Honesty*.
  Some think the Poem had been pretty good,
If he the Subject had but understood.
He got Five hundred Pence by this, and more,
As sure as he had ne're a Groat before.
  In Bus'ness next some Friends of his employ'd him;
And there he prov'd that Fame had not bely'd him:
His Benefactors quickly he abus'd,
And falsly to the Government accus'd:
But they, defended by their Innocence,
Ruin'd the Traytor in their own Defence.
  Thus kick'd about from Pillars unto Posts,
He whets his Pen against the Lord of Hosts:
Burlesques his God and King in Paltry Rhimes:
Against the *Dutch* turns Champion for the Times;

624. *Shamwhig:* "To call *Tutchin* a *Shamwhig,* is directly to affirm, he has not half the ill Qualities of a *Whig.* . . . For my part, I must own, I think he has the particular Characteristic of that Rebellious and Whining Sect . . . Every Body knows *Tutchin* was deservedly order'd to be whip'd through the West Country Market-Towns, and that he was set at Liberty, and entertain'd by some People of no small note after the Revolution, and how that he like a *True Whig* and Villain, afterwards abus'd his Benefactors, by writing a *Satyr in Praise of Folly and Knavery*" (*The True-Born Englishman: A Satyr Answer'd,* p. 49).

633. *Satyr upon Honesty: A Search after Honesty. A Poem by Mr. Tutchin* ("In Silent Shades, upon the Banks of Thames"), dated 1697, but apparently published during Easter term, 1698 (Arber, *3,* 65).

641. *accus'd:* "This is also a Truth, which he has pick'd out of the *Reverse* [see *The Reverse,* 86–88, above] which . . . intimates [Tutchin] had a Place given him at the Victualling-Office; but accusing the Commissioners before the Lords of the Admiralty, and not able to make out what he charg'd 'em with, he himself was divested of his own Post" *(The True-Born Englishman: A Satyr, Answer'd,* pp. 49–50).

646. *Paltry Rhimes: The Foreigners.*

And Huffs the King, upon that very score,
On which he Panegyrick't him before.
Unhappy *England,* hast thou none but such,
To plead thy Scoundrel Cause against the Dutch?
This moves their Scorn, and not their Indignation;
He that Lampoons the Dutch, *Burlesques the Nation.*
The meanest *English* Plowman studies Law,
And keeps thereby the Magistrates in Awe:
Will boldly tell them what they ought to do,
And sometimes punish their Omissions too.
Their Liberty and Property's so dear,
They scorn their Laws or Governors to fear:
So bugbear'd with the Name of Slavery,
They can't submit to their own Liberty.
Restraint from Ill is Freedom to the Wise;
But Englishmen *do all Restraint despise.*
Slaves to the Liquor, Drudges to the Pots,
The Mob are Statesmen, and their Statesmen Sots.
Their Governors they count such dangerous things,
That 'tis their custom to affront their Kings:
So jealous of the Power their Kings possess'd,
They suffer neither Power nor Kings to rest.
The Bad with Force they eagerly subdue;
The Good with constant Clamours they pursue:
And did King Jesus reign, they'd murmur too.
A discontented Nation, and by far
Harder to rule in Times of Peace than War:
Easily set together by the Ears,
And full of causeless Jealousies and Fears:
Apt to revolt, and willing to rebel,
And never are contented when they're well.
No Government cou'd ever please them long,

649. *Panegyrick't him:* In *An Heroick Poem upon the Late Expedition of His Majesty to Rescue England from Popery, Tyranny, and Arbitrary Government* (1689) (Wing T3377), Tutchin hailed William as "a Godlike Hero," "our other Moses," the "mighty *Nassau*" who "Conquer'd by Goodness" rather than by might.

665. *The Mob are Statesmen:* Bishop Burnet observed in 1700 that "tho' we were falling insensibly into a Democracy, we had not learned the virtues, that are necessary for that sort of Government" (*2*, 247).

679. *No Government cou'd ever please:* See *Absalom and Achitophel,* 45, 48: "The *Jews,* a Headstrong, Moody, Murmuring race . . . No King could govern, nor no God could please."

Cou'd tye their Hands, or rectify their Tongue.
In this to Ancient Israel *well compar'd,*
Eternal Murmurs are among them heard.
It was but lately that they were opprest,
Their Rights invaded, and their Laws supprest:
When nicely tender of their Liberty,
Lord! what a Noise they made of Slavery.
In daily Tumults show'd their Discontent;
Lampoon'd their King, and mock'd his Government.
And if in Arms they did not first appear,
'Twas want of Force, and not for want of Fear.
In humbler Tone than *English* us'd to do,
At Foreign Hands for Foreign Aid they sue.
William *the Great Successor of* Nassau,
Their Prayers heard, and their Oppressions saw:
He saw and sav'd them: God and Him they prais'd;
To This their Thanks, to That their Trophies rais'd.
But glutted with their own Felicities,
They soon their New Deliverer despise;
Say all their Prayers back, their Joy disown,
Unsing their Thanks, and pull their Trophies down:
Their Harps of Praise are on the Willows hung;
For Englishmen *are ne're contented long.*
The Rev'rend Clergy too! and who'd ha' thought
That they who had such Non-Resistance taught,
Should e're to Arms against their Prince be brought?

681. *well compar'd:* See *Absalom and Achitophel,* 45.

692. *for Foreign Aid they sue:* Cf. *Letter of Invitation to William of Orange,* 30 June 1688: "We have great reason to believe we shall be every day in a worse condition than we are, and less able to defend ourselves, and therefore we do earnestly wish we might be so happy as to find a remedy before it is too late for us to contribute to our own deliverance. . . . If upon a due consideration of all these circumstances your Highness shall think fit to adventure upon the attempt, or at least to make such preparations for it as are necessary (which we wish you may), there must be no more time lost . . ." (*EHD,* pp. 120–21).

704. *Non-Resistance:* a doctrine elaborated by the Anglican clergy in the second half of the seventeenth century, that since the authority of the king derived solely from God, it could not be resisted even if it violated human law.

705. *to Arms:* Henry Compton, bishop of London, one of the seven signers of the letter of invitation to William, accepted a commission as colonel of cavalry in November 1688 and marched into Oxford "in a blew Cloak, and with a naked Sword" at the

Who up to Heav'n did Regal Pow'r advance;
Subjecting *English* Laws to Modes of *France.*
Twisting Religion so with Loyalty,
As one cou'd never live, and t'other dye.
And yet no sooner did their Prince design
Their Glebes and Perquisites to undermine,
But all their Passive Doctrines laid aside;
The Clergy their own Principles deny'd:
Unpreach'd their Non-Resisting Cant, and pray'd
To Heav'n for Help, and to the *Dutch* for Aid.
The Church chim'd all her Doctrines back again,
And Pulpit-Champions did the Cause maintain;
Flew in the face of all their former Zeal,
And Non-Resistance did at once repeal.
   The *Rabbies* say it would be too prolix,
To tye Religion up to Politicks:
The Church's Safety is Suprema Lex.
And so by a new Figure of their own,
Do all their former Doctrines disown.
As Laws *Post Facto* in the Parliament,
In urgent Cases have obtain'd Assent;
But are as dangerous Presidents laid by;
Made lawful only by Necessity.
   The Rev'rend Fathers then in Arms appear,
And Men of God became the Men of War.
The Nation, *fir'd by them,* to Arms apply;
Assault their Antichristian Monarchy;
To their due Channel all our Laws restore,
And made things what they shou'd ha' been before.
But when they came to Fill the Vacant Throne,
And the *Pale Priests* look'd back on what they had done;

---

head of his troop (Hearne, *1*, 304). Another militant cleric was George Walker (1618–90), vicar of Lissan, who served as military governor of Londonderry during the siege and was killed at the passage of the Boyne.

their Prince: James II.

736. *the Pale Priests:* "(meaning the Non-Jurants) . . . were Men of such Tender Consciences, as not to be led by any hopes of Gain to take Oaths to a Prince, who was established in the Throne during the Life of the King they had sworn to" (*The True-Born Englishman: A Satyr, Answer'd,* p. 57). Of the entire body of 9743 beneficed clergymen and 28 bishops, only about 400 clergymen and 8 bishops refused to take the

How *English* Liberty began to thrive,
And Church-of-*England* Loyalty out-live:
How all their Persecuting Days were done,
And their Deliv'rer plac'd upon the Throne:
The Priests, *as Priests are wont to do,* turn'd Tail;
They're *Englishmen,* and *Nature will prevail.*
Now they deplore the Ruins they ha' made,
And Murmur for the Master they Betray'd.
Excuse those Crimes they cou'd not make him mend;
And suffer for the Cause they can't defend.
Pretend they'd not ha' carry'd things so high;
And Proto-Martyrs make for Popery.
Had the Prince done as they design'd the thing,
Ha' set the Clergy up to rule the King;
Taken *a Donative* for coming hither,
And so ha' left their King and them together,
We had, say they, been now a happy Nation.
No doubt we had seen a Blessed Reformation:
For Wise Men say 't's as dangerous a thing,
A Ruling Priesthood, as a Priest-rid King.
And of all Plagues with which Mankind are curst,
Ecclesiastick Tyranny's the worst.
If all our former Grievances were feign'd,
King *James* has been abus'd, and we trepann'd;
Bugbear'd with Popery and Power Despotick,
Tyrannick Government, and Leagues Exotick:
The Revolution's a Phanatick Plot,
William a Tyrant, *Sunderland* a Sot:
A Factious Army and a Poyson'd Nation,
Unjustly forc'd King *James*'s Abdication.
But if he did the Subjects Rights invade,

---

oaths of allegiance to William and Mary; cf. *A Satyr on the French King,* headnote, p. 3 above.

757–58. Quoted in [Defoe], *Jure Divino. A Satyr,* 1706, p. xvii.

764. *Sunderland a Sot:* See *Advice to a Painter,* 57 *n.,* above. The insinuation that Sunderland was an important figure in bringing about the Revolution is accepted by William Pittis who finds "*S*[*underland*] . . . guilty of a greater Crime than Sottishness, for betraying so kind a Master" (*The True-Born Englishman: A Satyr, Answer'd,* p. 58). But for *A True Collection* in 1710, Defoe adopted the later reading, "*W*——— a Tyrant, and *K*—— *J*—— was not" and then glossed the line "William, King James" in the *Key.*

Then he was punish'd only, not betray'd:
And punishing of Kings is no such Crime,
But Englishmen *ha' done it many a time.*
  When Kings the Sword of Justice first lay down,
They are no Kings, though they possess the Crown.
Titles are Shadows, Crowns are empty things,
The Good of Subjects is the End of Kings;
To guide in War, and to protect in Peace:
Where Tyrants once commence, the Kings do cease:
For Arbitrary Power's so strange a thing,
It makes the *Tyrant,* and unmakes the *King.*
If Kings by Foreign Priests and Armies reign,
And Lawless Power against their Oaths maintain,
Then Subjects must ha' reason to complain.
If Oaths must bind us when our Kings do ill;
To call in Foreign Aid is to rebel.
By Force to circumscribe our Lawful Prince,
Is wilful Treason in the largest sense:
And they who once rebel, most certainly
Their God, and King, and former Oaths defy.
If we allow no Male-Administration
Could cancel the Allegiance of the Nation;
Let all our Learned *Sons of Levi* try,
This Eccles'astick Riddle to unty:
How they could make a Step to Call the Prince,
And yet pretend to Oaths and Innocence.
  By th' first Address they made beyond the Seas,
They're perjur'd in the most intense Degrees;
And without Scruple for the time to come,
May swear to all the Kings in *Christendom.*
And truly did our Kings consider all,
They'd never let the Clergy swear at all:
Their Politick Allegiance they'd refuse;
For Whores and Priests do never want excuse.

771–72. *Qui cessat regnare cessat judicare,* quoted in January 1689 by Sir Gilbert Dolben during the debate on James II's "withdrawal" (*Parl. Hist., 5,* 37).

773–78. An "Argument . . . heard every day over Coffee and Tea" (*The True-Born Englishman: A Satyr, Answer'd,* p. 60), of which the classical statement is John Locke, *Two Treatises of Government,* 1690, Chapter XVIII, "Of Tyranny."

774–75. Cf. *The Foreigners,* 178–79, above.

But if the *Mutual Contract* was dissolv'd,
The Doubt's explain'd, the Difficulty solv'd:
That Kings, when they descend to Tyranny,
Dissolve the Bond, and leave the Subject free.
The Government's ungirt when Justice dies,
And Constitutions are Non-Entities.
The Nation's all a Mob, there's no such thing
As Lords or Commons, Parliament or King.
A great promiscuous Crowd the Hydra lies,
Till Laws revive, and mutual Contract ties:
A Chaos free to chuse for their own share,
What Case of Government they please to wear:
If to a King they do the Reins commit,
All men are bound in Conscience to submit:
But then that King must by his Oath assent
To *Postulata's* of the Government;
Which if he breaks, he cuts off the Entail,

802. *Contract:* The question whether there was in fact a contract between king and people was debated in the House of Lords in January 1689 and upon a division, 53–46, it was decided that there was (Ralph, *2,* 37). Locke derived all political power "only from Compact and Agreement, and the mutual Consent of those who make up the Community" (*Two Treatises of Government,* 1690, p. 394).

806–07. These lines are quoted in *The Post Angel, 1,* (January 1701), 61.

808–19. "The design of this Paragraph, is to shew, that the Kingly Power is the Gift of the Subjects, and that whenever a Prince fails in the Duty of his Office, the People may recal their Gift, and bestow the Crown on whom they please. This Doctrine might do very well in *Poland* . . . an Elective Monarchy; but never will suit with a Nation, whose Kingdom has been Hereditary upwards of six hundred years" (*The True-Born Englishman: A Satyr, Answer'd,* p. 62). These lines in fact are a versification of Locke, *Two Treatises of Government,* 1690, pp. 439–40: "There is one way more, whereby such a Government may be dissolved, and that is, When he who has the supreme executive Power, neglects and abandons that charge, so that the Laws already made can no longer be put in execution. This is demonstratively to reduce all to Anarchy, and so effectually to dissolve the Government. For Laws not being made for themselves, but to be by their execution the Bonds of the Society, to keep every part of the Body Politick in its due place and function, when that totally ceases, the Government visibly ceases, and the People become a confused Multitude, without Order or Connexion. . . . In these and the like Cases, when the Government is dissolved, the People are at liberty to provide for themselves, by erecting a new Legislative, differing from the other, by the change of Persons, or Form." By the Corporation Act of May 1661 it was unlawful to take arms against the king "upon any pretence whatsoever" (13 Charles II Stat. II c. 1).

813. *Case:* outward covering, form.

817. *Postulata's:* demands, requirements (*OED* quotes this line); Defoe had used the word in *The Two Great Questions Consider'd,* [November] 1700, p. 7.

And Power retreats to its Original.
This Doctrine has the Sanction of Assent,
From Nature's Universal Parliament.
The Voice of Nations, and the Course of Things,
Allow that Laws superior are to Kings.
None but Delinquents would have Justice cease,
Knaves rail at Laws, as Soldiers rail at Peace:
For Justice is the End of Government,
As Reason is the Test of Argument.
No man was ever yet so void of Sense,
As to debate the Right of Self-Defence;
A Principle so grafted in the Mind,
With Nature born, and does like Nature bind:
Twisted with Reason, and with Nature too;
As neither one nor t'other can undo.
Nor can this Right be less when National;
Reason which governs one, should govern all.
Whate're the Dialect of Courts may tell,
He that his Right demands, can ne're rebel.
Which Right, if 'tis by Governors deny'd,
May be procur'd by Force, or Foreign Aid.
For *Tyranny*'s a Nation's Term for Grief;
As Folks cry *Fire,* to hasten in Relief.
And when the hated word is heard about,

819. *Original:* "all Power did . . . originally derive from the People" (John Toland, *Anglia Libera,* [June] 1701, p. 115).

823. *Laws superior are to Kings:* "For the King's Authority [is] given him only by the Law" (John Locke, *Two Treatises of Government,* 1690, pp. 426–27.

826. *Justice is the End of Government:* "The Legislative, or Supream Authority . . . is bound to dispense Justice" (ibid., p. 357).

829. *the Right of Self-Defence:* "this Fundamental, Sacred, and unalterable Law of Self-Preservation"; "it being out of a Man's power so to submit himself to another, as to give him a liberty to destroy him; God and Nature never allowing a Man so to abandon himself, as to neglect his own preservation" (ibid., pp. 370, 391).

834. *this Right:* the right of revolution; cf. "whenever the Legislators endeavour to take away, and destroy the Property of the People, or to reduce them to Slavery under Arbitrary Power . . . they forfeit the Power, the People had put into their hands, for quite contrary ends, and it devolves to the People, who have a Right to resume their original Liberty, and, by the Establishment of a new Legislative (such as they shall think fit) provide for their own Safety and Security, which is the end for which they are in Society" (ibid., pp. 441–42). Cf. "there remains still in the People a Supream Power to remove or alter the Legislative when they find the Legislative act contrary to the trust reposed in them" (ibid., pp. 369–70).

All men shou'd come to help the People out.
  Thus *England* groan'd, *Britannia*'s Voice was heard;
And Great *Nassau* to rescue her, appear'd:
Call'd by the Universal Voice of Fate;
God and the Peoples Legal Magistrate.
Ye Heav'ns regard! Almighty *Jove* look down,
And view thy Injur'd Monarch on the Throne.
On their Ungrateful Heads due Vengeance take,
Who sought his Aid, and then his part forsake.
Witness, ye Powers! it was Our Call alone,
Which now our Pride makes us asham'd to own.
Britannia's Troubles fetch'd him from afar,
To court the dreadful Casualties of War:
But where Requital never can be made,
Acknowledgment's a Tribute seldom paid.
  He dwelt in Bright *Maria*'s Circling Arms,
Defended by the Magick of her Charms,
From Foreign Fears, and from Domestick Harms.
Ambition found no Fuel for her Fire,
He had what God cou'd give, or Man desire.
Till *Pity* rowz'd him from his soft Repose,
His Life to unseen Hazards to expose:
Till *Pity* mov'd him in our Cause t' appear;
Pity! *that Word which now we hate to hear.*
But *English* Gratitude is always such,
To hate the Hand which does oblige too much.
  Britannia's Cries gave Birth to his Intent,
And hardly gain'd his unforeseen Assent:
His boding Thoughts foretold him he should find
The People, Fickle, Selfish, and Unkind.
Which Thought did to his Royal Heart appear
More dreadful than the Dangers of the War:
For nothing grates a Generous Mind so soon,
As base Returns for hearty Service done.

844. *England groan'd . . . And Great Nassau . . . appear'd:* "That is as much to say, after his own way of expressing himself, [that] *England cry'd Fire,* and a Neighbour came in an instant, and quench'd it, and receiv'd the House, and all the Furniture for his Pains" (*The True-Born Englishman: A Satyr, Answer'd*, p. 64).

876. *base Returns:* As early as March 1689, William complained to Halifax that "the

Satyr be silent, awfully prepare
Britannia's Song and *William*'s Praise to hear.
Stand by, and let her chearfully rehearse
Her Grateful Vows in her Immortal Verse.
Loud Fame's Eternal Trumpet let her sound;
Listen ye distant Poles, and endless Round.
May the strong Blast the welcome News convey
As far as Sound can reach, or Spirit fly.
To *Neighb'ring Worlds,* if such there be, relate
Our Hero's Fame, for theirs to imitate.
To distant Worlds of Spirits let her rehearse:
For Spirits without the helps of Voice converse.
May Angels hear the gladsome News on high,
Mixt with their everlasting Symphony.
And Hell it self stand in suspence to know
Whether it be the Fatal Blast, or no.

Britannia

The Fame of Virtue 'tis for which I sound,
And Heroes with Immortal Triumphs crown'd.
Fame built on solid Virtue swifter flies,
Than Morning Light can spread my Eastern *Skies.*
The gath'ring Air returns the doubling Sound,
And lowd repeating Thunders force it round:
Ecchoes return from Caverns of the Deep:
Old Chaos dreams on't in Eternal Sleep.
Time hands it forward to its latest Urn,
From whence it never, never shall return,
Nothing is heard so far, or lasts so long;
'Tis heard by ev'ry Ear, and spoke by ev'ry Tongue.
My Hero, with the Sails of Honour furl'd,

Commons used him like a dog" (*The Life and Letters of Sir George Savile, Bart., First Marquis of Halifax,* ed. Helen C. Foxcroft, 2 vols., 1898, 2, 207).

893. *sound:* "The Trumpeter's out of Tune at the first Note; that is, he has no manner of Musick in the first Line. . . . 'tis a comical sort of a sound indeed—the Devil-a-bit of any Eccho comes from it, which is the Beauty of Musick" (*The True-Born Englishman: A Satyr, Answer'd,* p. 67).

Rises like the Great Genius of the World.
By Fate and Fame wisely prepar'd to be
The Soul of War, and Life of Victory.
He spreads the Wings of Virtue on the Throne,
And ev'ry Wind of Glory *fans them on.*
Immortal Trophies dwell upon his Brow,
Fresh as the Garlands he has won but now.
By different Steps the high Ascent he gains,
And differently that high Ascent maintains.
Princes for Pride and Lust of Rule *make War,*
And struggle for the Name of Conqueror.
Some fight for Fame, and some for Victory.
He Fights to Save, and Conquers to set Free.
Then seek no Phrase his Titles to conceal,
And hide with Words what Actions must reveal.
No Parallel from Hebrew *Stories take,*
Of God-like Kings my Similies to make:
No borrow'd Names conceal my living Theam;
But Names and Things directly I proclaim.
'Tis honest Merit does his Glory raise;
Whom that exalts, let no man fear to praise.
Of such a Subject no man need be shy;
Virtue's above the Reach of Flattery.
He needs no Character but his own Fame,
Nor any flattering Titles, but his Name.
William'*s the Name that's spoke by ev'ry Tongue:*
William'*s the Darling Subject of my Song.*
Listen ye Virgins to the Charming Sound,
And in Eternal Dances hand it round:
Your early Offerings to this Altar bring;
Make him at once a Lover and a King.
May he submit to none but to your Arms;
Nor ever be subdu'd, but by your Charms.
May your soft Thoughts for him be all sublime;

921. *No Parallel:* While he resists the greatest poetical temptation of his day, the temptation to write in the manner of Dryden's *Absalom and Achitophel,* Defoe cannot eliminate all traces of this poem from his work; see lines 268, 556–57, 679, 681, 990–91.

933–936. *Virgins . . . Make him . . . a Lover:* "I am amaz'd to see him turn *Pimp,* while he is lab'ring at the painful Vocation of a *Panegyrist,* and seek out for *Maidenheads* for His Majesty" (*The True-Born Englishman: A Satyr, Answer'd,* p. 70).

And ev'ry tender Vow be made for him.
May he be first in ev'ry Morning Thought,
And Heav'n ne're hear a Pray'r where he's left out.
May ev'ry Omen, ev'ry boding Dream,
Be Fortunate *by mentioning his Name.*
May this one Charm Infernal Powers affright,
And guard you from the Terrors of the Night.
May ev'ry chearful Glass as it goes down
To William*'s Health,* be Cordials to your own.
Let ev'ry Song be Chorust with his Name.
And Musick pay her Tribute to his Fame.
Let ev'ry Poet tune his Artful Verse,
And in Immortal Strains his Deeds rehearse.
And may Apollo *never more inspire*
The Disobedient Bard with his Seraphick Fire.
May all my Sons their grateful Homage pay;
His Praises sing, and for his Safety pray.
Satyr return to our Unthankful Isle,
Secur'd by Heav'n's Regard, and *William*'s Toil.
To both Ungrateful, and to both Untrue;
Rebels to God, and to Good Nature too.
If e're this Nation be distress'd again,
To whomsoe're they cry, they'll cry in vain.
To Heav'n they cannot have the face to look;
Or if they should, it would but Heav'n provoke.
To hope for Help from Man would be too much;
Mankind would always tell 'em of the Dutch:
How they came here our Freedoms to maintain,
Were *Paid,* and *Curs'd,* and *Hurry'd home again.*
How by their Aid we first dissolv'd our Fears,
And then our Helpers damn'd for Foreigners.
'Tis not our *English* Temper to do better;
For *Englishmen* think ev'ry man their Debtor.
'Tis worth observing, that we ne're complain'd
Of Foreigners, nor of the Wealth they gain'd,
Till all their Services were at an End.

966–68. *Dutch . . . Hurry'd home:* See *An Encomium upon a Parliament,* headnote, pp. 45–46 and 7 *n.,* above.

970. *damn'd for Foreigners:* See *The Foreigners, passim,* above.

Wise men affirm it is the *English* way,
Never to Grumble till they come to Pay;
And then they always think their Temper's such,
The Work too little, and the Pay too much.
As frighted Patients, when they want a Cure,
Bid any Price, and any Pain endure:
But when the Doctor's Remedies appear,
The Cure's too Easy, and the Price too Dear.
Great *Portland* ne're was banter'd, when he strove
For Us his Master's kindest Thoughts to move.
We ne're lampoon'd his Conduct, when employ'd
King *James*'s Secret Councils to divide:
Then we caress'd him as the only Man,
Which could the Doubtful Oracle explain:
The only *Hushai* able to repell
The Dark Designs of *our Achitophel.*
Compar'd his Master's Courage to his Sense;
The Ablest Statesman, and the Bravest Prince.
On his Wise Conduct we depended much,
And lik'd him ne're the worse for being Dutch.
Nor was he valued more than he deserv'd;
Freely he ventur'd, faithfully he serv'd.
In all King *William*'s Dangers he has shar'd;
In *England*'s Quarrels always he appear'd:
The *Revolution* first, and then the *Boyne;*
In Both his Counsels and his Conduct shine.

987. *divide:* Bentinck served as intermediary first at The Hague, between the prince of Orange and the duke of Monmouth, and then (after William learned that Monmouth had declared himself king on 20 June 1685) in London, between the prince and James II. The king indiscreetly revealed to Bentinck his displeasure with the prince, his son-in-law (Echard, *3*, 755, 767).

989. *Oracle:* William of Orange [?].

990. *Hushai:* the friend of David who advises Absalom to "defeat the counsel of Ahithophel" (2 Samuel 15:32–34). In *Absalom and Achitophel* (888–97) he is Laurence Hyde, earl of Rochester.

991. *our Achitophel:* James II [?].

996–97. *deserv'd . . . serv'd:* Defoe is virtually quoting William's words. In reply to the Commons' protest against his grant to Portland of crown lands in Wales, the king said, "I have Kindness for my Lord *Portland,* which he has deserved of me, by long and faithful Services" *(CJ, 11,* 409).

1001. *Conduct:* Bentinck commanded a regiment of dragoons at the Boyne in July 1690 and during eight campaigns in Flanders. He was wounded during the confederates'

His Martial Valour *Flanders* will confess;
And *France* Regrets his Managing the Peace.
Faithful to *England*'s Interest and her King:
The greatest Reason of our Murmuring.
Ten Years in *English* Service he appear'd,
And gain'd his Master's and the World's Regard:
But 'tis not England'*s Custom to Reward.*
The Wars are over, *England* needs him not;
Now he's a *Dutchman,* and *the Lord knows what.*
  Schonbergh, the Ablest Soldier of his Age,
With *Great Nassau* did in our Cause engage:
Both join'd for *England*'s Rescue and Defence;
The Greatest Captain, and the Greatest Prince.
With what Applause his Stories did we tell?
Stories which *Europe*'s Volumes largely swell.
We counted him an Army in our Aid:
Where he commanded, no man was afraid.
His Actions with a constant Conquest shine,
From *Villa-Vitiosa* to the *Rhine.*
France, Flanders, Germany, his Fame confess;
And all the World was fond of him, but Us.
Our Turn first serv'd, we grudg'd him the Command.
Witness the Grateful Temper of the Land.
  We blame the King that he relies too much
On Strangers, *Germans, Hugonots,* and *Dutch;*
And seldom does his great Affairs of State,
To *English* Counsellors communicate.

---

defeat at Landen and distinguished himself on several other occasions (Luttrell, *2*, 61, 87; *3*, 146, 502, 521).

1003. *Managing the Peace:* See *A Satyr upon the French King,* 33 *n.,* above. It is true, of course, as *The Female Critick* was quick to point out (p. 112), "that my Lord was only the Trunk through which the King spake" in these transactions.

1011. *Schonbergh:* Friedrich Herman von Schönberg (1615–90) was a German nobleman whose mother was English and whose great-grandfather was Sir James Harrington, the political philosopher. He was not only one of the greatest field commanders but also one of the greatest military organizers of his day. His victory over the Spanish at Villa Viciosa (June 1665) completely established the independence of Portugal. He was the last Protestant to be made a marshal of France. He volunteered his services to William of Orange in 1688, was created duke of Schomberg in May 1689, and put in command of all English forces in Ireland. He died leading his troops across the Boyne on 1 July 1690.

1027–28. *seldom . . . communicate:* An anonymous memorandum on affairs in

The Fact might very well be answer'd thus;
He has so often been betray'd by us,
He must have been a Madman to rely
On *English* Gentlemens Fidelity.
For laying other Arguments aside,
This Thought might mortify our *English* Pride,
That Foreigners have faithfully obey'd him,
And none but *Englishmen* have e're betray'd him.
They have our Ships and Merchants bought and sold,
And barter'd *English* Blood for Foreign Gold.
First to the *French* they sold our *Turky*-Fleet,
And Injur'd *Talmarsh* next at *Camaret*.
The King himself is shelter'd from their Snares,
Not by his Merit, but the Crown he wears.
Experience tells us 'tis the *English* way,
Their Benefactors always to betray.
  And lest Examples should be too remote,

England in 1698 mentioned that William's "chief characteristic is great distrust, so that very few persons, even among those who are in office, are acquainted with his secrets . . . which are in the hands of his Dutch favourites" (Grimblot, *2*, 191).

1039. *sold our Turky-Fleet:* In May 1693 a merchant fleet of 300–400 vessels bound for the Levant sailed from Spithead. On the same day Nottingham, the Tory secretary of state, received intelligence that Tourville had sailed from Brest in command of the French grand fleet. Although Nottingham laid this information before the privy council, no action was thought necessary. On 17 June Tourville sighted the merchant fleet, under a convoy commanded by Vice-Admiral Sir George Rooke, in Lagos Bay. In the engagement which followed 100 merchant ships, worth about £1,500,000, were lost "And the disgrace of it," as Burnet observed, "was visible to the whole World" (*2*, 116). In November 1693, after hearing Rooke's testimony, the House of Commons resolved "That, upon Examination of the Miscarriage of the Fleet, and the Loss of the *Turkey* Company sustained this Summer, this House is of Opinion, That there hath been a notorious and treacherous Mismanagement of the Fleet this Year," whereupon the House divided on an amendment to leave out the word "treacherous" and voted 140–103 to let it stand (*CJ, 11*, 5).

1040. *Talmarsh:* Thomas Tollemache (1651?–94) was one of the two or three most successful English military leaders of his day. He commanded one of the regiments that landed with William at Tor Bay and subsequently distinguished himself at Aughrim and Landen. In January 1692, when Marlborough was dismissed, he was promoted lieutenant-general in his place. In 1694 he was placed in command of a descent upon Brest, in Camarets Bay, the plan for which was known to the French so far in advance that Louis was able to send Vauban to attend the fortifications (Luttrell, *3*, 328). It is not surprising, therefore, that the operation was a total failure and that Tollemache and almost the entire landing party were killed. Tollemache died believing that he had been betrayed by "the Government," that is, by the king's English ministers (Oldmixon, *4*, 92).

A Modern Magistrate of Famous Note,
Shall give you his own History by Rote.
I'll make it out, deny it he that can,
His Worship is a True-born *Englishman,*
In all the Latitude that Empty Word
By Modern Acceptation's understood.
The Parish-Books his Great Descent record,
And now he hopes e're long to be a Lord.
And truly as things go, it wou'd be pity
But such as he bore Office in the City:
While Robb'ry for Burnt-Offering he brings,
And gives to God what he has stole from Kings:
Great Monuments of Charity he raises,
And good St. Magnus *whistles out his Praises.*
To City-Gaols he grants a Jubilee,
And hires Huzza's from his own Mobile.

1046. *Modern Magistrate:* Sir Charles Duncombe (see *A Satyr against Wit,* 234 *n.)* was a Tory member of parliament for Hedon, Yorkshire (1685–87), Yarmouth, Isle of Wight (1690–95), Downton, Wiltshire, of which he was the proprietor (1695–98, 1702–11), and Ipswich, Suffolk (1701). In February 1698 he was expelled from the House for forgery (*A Conference,* 120 *n.,* above). He was knighted in October 1699 and elected alderman of Broad Street ward (1683–86), sheriff (1699), and alderman of Bridge ward (1700–11).

1052. *Great Descent:* "his father [was] a Haberdasher of Hatts in Southwark as some say; others that he was Steward to Sir Will. Tiringham of Tiringham in Bucks., Knt." (Le Neve, p. 468).

1055. *Office in the City:* The line probably refers to the mayoralty election of September 1700: in the poll of liverymen, Duncombe's name stood at the top of the list, but the aldermen voted 14–12 to elect a Whig, Sir Thomas Abney (Luttrell, *4,* 692). William Pittis, however, thought that the lines were looking forward to the next parliamentary election of January 1701 in London, which Duncombe contested unsuccessfully: "these Calumnies were written on purpose to lessen the Number of those who had espous'd [Duncombe's] Party, against the ensuing Election for Members of Parliament for the City" (*The True-Born Englishman: A Satyr, Answer'd,* p. 77). See textual note on this line.

1057. *gives to God:* The parish church of St. Magnus Martyr was burned down in the Great Fire and rebuilt. In 1700 Duncombe contributed a clock with "a curious dyal" which cost £485 5*s* 4*d* (Strype, *1,* 2174).

stole from Kings: In October 1688 Duncombe, while serving as a receiver of the customs, "stopt in his hands £60,000 of the kings money, upon account of his majestie oweing him as much" (Luttrell, *1,* 471).

1060. *Jubilee:* A jubilee was celebrated in 1700; during this time plenary indulgence could be obtained by a pilgrimage to Rome, the visiting of certain churches there, giving of alms, fasting three days, and the performance of other pious works (*OED*). During Duncombe's shrievalty, 1699–1700, he released from prison "above 170 persons that were in for Debt" (*The Post Boy,* No. 754, 6–8 February 1700).

Lately he wore the Golden Chain and Gown,
With which Equipt he thus harangu'd the Town.

Sir Charles Duncomb's Fine Speech, &c.

With Clouted Iron Shooes and Sheepskin Breeches,
More Rags than Manners, and more Dirt than Riches:
From driving Cows and Calves to *Layton*-Market,
While of my Greatness there appear'd no Spark yet,
Behold I come, to let you see the Pride
With which Exalted Beggars always ride.
Born to the Needful Labours of the Plow,
The Cart-Whip grac't me as the Chain does now.
Nature and Fate in doubt what course to take,
Whether I shou'd a Lord or Plough-Boy make;
Kindly at last resolv'd they wou'd promote me,
And first *a Knave,* and then *a Knight* they vote me.
What Fate appointed, Nature did prepare,
And furnish'd me with an exceeding Care.
To fit me for what they design'd to have me;
And ev'ry Gift *but Honesty* they gave me.
And thus Equipt, to this Proud Town I came,
In quest of Bread, and not in quest of Fame.
Blind to my future Fate, an humble Boy,
Free from the *Guilt and Glory* I enjoy.

1062. *wore the Golden Chain:* "[The Lord Mayor's] *State* and *Magnificence* is remarkable, when he appears abroad, which is usually on Horseback, with rich Caparison, himself always in long Robes, sometimes of Scarlet Cloth richly Furred, sometimes Purple, sometimes Puke; and over his Robes a Hood of Black Velvet, which some say, is a Badge of a Baron of the Realm, with a great Chain of Gold about his Neck" (Chamberlayne, 1700, p. 337). See 1055 *n.,* above.

1064. *Clouted Iron Shooes:* shoes having the sole protected with iron plates, or studded with large-headed nails (*OED*). Hertfordshire clubs and clouted shoon are proverbial symbols of rusticalness (Tilley C454).

1066. *driving Cows:* " 'Tis well known . . . that his Father had not wherewithal to educate him, as his sprightly Genius deserv'd; yet he was so far from making him a *Cow-Driver,* which sort of People are seldom thought to write and read, that he had all the Education necessary . . . to make his Fortune" (*The True-Born Englishman: A Satyr, Answer'd,* p. 78).

The Hopes which my Ambition entertain'd,
Were in the Name of *Foot-Boy* all contain'd.
The Greatest Heights from Small Beginnings rise;
The Gods were Great on Earth, before they reach'd the Skies.
Backwell, the Generous Temper of whose Mind,
Was always to be bountiful inclin'd:
Whether by his Ill Fate or Fancy led,
First took me up, and furnish'd me with Bread.
The little Services he put me to,
Seem'd Labours rather than were truly so.
But always my Advancement he design'd;
For 'twas his very Nature to be kind.
Large was his Soul, his Temper ever Free;
The best of Masters and of Men to me.
And I who was before decreed by Fate,
To be made Infamous as well as Great,
With an obsequious Diligence obey'd him,
Till trusted with his All, and then betray'd him.
All his past Kindnesses I trampled on,
Ruin'd his Fortune to erect my own.

1088. *Backwell (Key):* Edward Backwell (d. 1683), called Alderman Backwell (he was elected alderman for Bishopsgate ward in 1660, but paid a fine of £720 not to serve again), was a goldsmith who became the private banker of Cromwell and then of Charles II, and finally one of the first public bankers in London, doing business at the sign of the Unicorn in Lombard Street. He bought the estate of Sir William Tiringham, of Tiringham, Buckinghamshire, "and maried his son to Sir William's daughter and heir" (Le Neve, p. 24). Duncombe (see 1052 *n.,* above) began his career as an apprentice to Backwell.

1101. *betray'd him:* When Charles II ordered the exchequer to stop payments in 1672, Backwell lost nearly £300,000 and was forced out of business. Duncombe, however, who "was at that time banker to Lord Shaftesbury . . . received a timely warning of the projected closing of the exchequer . . . and by this means he was enabled to withdraw 'a very great sum of his own,' and £30,000 belonging to the Marquis of Winchester, afterwards the first Duke of Bolton" (*DNB, 6,* 176). Duncombe's methods are further elaborated in Thomas Brown, *A Continuation or Second Part of the Letters from the Dead to the Living,* 2nd ed., 1707, p. 150. Brown maintains that Duncombe represented Backwell's situation to be worse than it was, which enabled him to buy up Backwell's notes to the amount of £100,000 for an eighth of their value. He then presented these notes to Backwell for payment in full.

1103. *Ruin'd his Fortune:* "If he had ruin'd his Fortunes, the Son of that Honest and unhappy Bankrupt would have shewn his Resentments for it. But Mr. [*John*] *B*[*ackwe*]*ll* who is now living, is satisfy'd of other things, and none at this time has greater respect for Sir *Charles D*[*unco*]*mb,* and visits him oftner in the Country upon all Occasions" *(The True-Born Englishman: A Satyr, Answer'd,* p. 80).

So Vipers in the Bosom bred, begin
To hiss at that Hand first which took them in.
With eager Treach'ry I his Fall pursu'd,
And my first Trophies were *Ingratitude.*
Ingratitude's the worst of Human Guilt,
The basest Action Mankind can commit;
Which like the Sin against the Holy Ghost,
Has least of Honour, and of Guilt the most.
Distinguish'd from all other Crimes by this,
That 'tis a Crime which no man will confess.
That Sin alone, which shou'd not be forgiv'n
On Earth, altho perhaps it may in Heav'n.
Thus my first Benefactor I o'rethrew;
And how shou'd I be to a second true?
The Publick Trust came next into my Care,
And I to use them scurvily prepare:
My Needy Sov'reign Lord I play'd upon,
And Lent him many a Thousand of his own;
For which, great Int'rest I took care to charge,
And so my Ill-got Wealth became so large.
My Predecessor *Judas* was a Fool,
Fitter to ha' been whipt, and sent to School,
Then Sell a Saviour: Had I been at hand,
His Master had not been so cheap Trepann'd;
I wou'd ha' made the eager *Jews* ha' found,
For Thirty Pieces, Thirty thousand Pound.
My Cousin *Ziba,* of Immortal Fame,
(Ziba *and I shall never want a Name:*)

1118. *Publick Trust:* Duncombe was a receiver of the customs under Charles II and James II, and receiver-general of the excise under William III.

1120. *Sov'reign Lord:* Charles II.

1130. *Ziba:* "For Jonathan's sake" David restored to Mephibosheth, the crippled son of Jonathan and grandson of Saul, his grandfather's entire estate, including Ziba, Saul's slave who had gained his freedom (2 Samuel 9:1–13). Years later, during the revolt of Absalom, Mephibosheth intended to join David in his flight, but Ziba betrayed him and went off in pursuit of David with Mephibosheth's asses and provisions (2 Samuel 19:24–28). Catching up with David on the Mount of Olives, Ziba offered, as his own, Mephibosheth's asses and provisions, and accepted, as David's reward, Mephibosheth's entire estate (2 Samuel 16:1–4). "The Person whom he rails at under the Name of *Ziba,* has so signaliz'd himself in his Services to the *English* Government, that his envious Reflections on him, return upon himself" (*The True-Born Englishman: A Satyr, Answer'd,* p. 83).

First-born of Treason, nobly did advance
His Master's Fall, for his Inheritance.
By whose keen Arts old *David* first began
To break his Sacred Oath to *Jonathan:*
The Good Old King, 'tis thought, was very loth
To break his Word, and therefore broke his Oath.
Ziba's a Traytor of some Quality,
Yet *Ziba* might ha' been inform'd by me:
Had I been there, he ne're had been content
With half th' Estate, nor half the Government.
  In our late Revolution 'twas thought strange,
That I of all mankind shou'd like the Change:
But they who wonder'd at it, never knew,
That in it I did my Old Game pursue:
Nor had they heard of Twenty thousand Pound,
Which ne're was lost, yet never cou'd be found.
  Thus all things in their turn to Sale I bring,
God and my Master first, and then the King:
Till by successful Villanies made bold,
I thought to turn the Nation into Gold;
And so to Forgery my Hand I bent,
Not doubting I could gull the Government;
But there was ruffl'd by the Parliament.
And if I 'scap'd th' Unhappy Tree to climb,
'Twas want of Law, and not for want of Crime.

1135. *Sacred Oath:* David had sworn an oath to show the same kindness to Jonathan's descendants that he had shown to Jonathan himself (1 Samuel 20:14–19).

1137. *Word . . . Oath:* David's "Word" to Ziba (1130 *n.*, above) conflicted with his "Oath" to Jonathan (1135 *n.*, above), so he set a good precedent for Solomon by dividing Mephibosheth's estate between Ziba and Mephibosheth (2 Samuel 19:29).

1145. *Old Game:* In August 1696 it was reported that "the Dutch are to advance . . . £300,000 (on the security of these following persons) unto his majestie . . . viz. . . . Charles Duncomb." The following March it was reported that "Mr. Duncomb, the banker, has lent the king £10,000" (Luttrell, *4*, 92, 192).

1152. *Forgery:* In January 1698 Duncombe was charged with "having contrived and advised the making false Indorsements of Exchequer Bills" (see *Advice to a Painter,* 87 *n.,* above) and ordered to be held incommunicado in the Tower. Subsequently, "on Examination, and by the Confession of *Charles Duncomb* Esquire," he was expelled from the House of Commons and a bill for his punishment was ordered to be brought in (*CJ*, *12*, 63, 78).

1155. *Tree: "Gallows"* (*C*).

1156. *want of Law:* In February 1698 a bill to punish Duncombe for making false endorsements of exchequer bills passed the Commons upon a division, 138–103. Some

But my *Old Friend,* who printed in my Face
A needful Competence of *English* Brass,
Having more business yet for me to do,
And loth to lose his Trusty Servant so,
Manag'd the matter with such Art and Skill,
As sav'd his Hero, and threw out the Bill.
And now I'm grac'd with unexpected Honours,
For which I'll certainly abuse the Donors:
Knighted, and made a Tribune of the People,
Whose Laws and Properties I'm like to keep well:
The *Custos Rotulorum* of the City,
And Captain of the Guards of their *Banditti.*

---

members "were of opinion he had done nothing against the letter of the law, but only the intention of it" (*CJ, 12,* 133; Luttrell, *4,* 346). The lords however, "after a debate of near 3 hours," threw out the bill by a vote of 49–48 (Luttrell, *4,* 355; *LJ, 16,* 235). The Commons then addressed the king to prosecute Duncombe in the law courts. The case was tried in the court of king's bench in February 1699 but a mistake was found in the information and Duncombe "of course [was] found not guilty." Upon a retrial on 20 June 1699 "the jury, without going from the bar, [again] found him not guilty." That night Duncombe treated the jury to "a noble dinner at Locket's ordinary; 'tis said he gave them 5 guineas apeice, and declared the prosecution had cost him £10,000" (Luttrell, *4,* 480, 528).

1157. *Old Friend:* "The Devil" *(E).* Duncombe's "Old Friend" could not have failed also to suggest Charles Paulet, sixth marquis of Winchester and first duke of Bolton (1625?–99) (see 1011 *n.,* above), "a man of a profuse expence, and of a most ravenous avarice to support that" (Burnet, *2,* 225). In March 1698, before Duncombe's case came before the House of Lords, "The duke of Bolton brought into the lords house *Mr. Duncombs Case* printed, wherein he sets forth the severity of the bill, and gave every peer one to consider of." Two days later, when the bill was read for the first time, Bolton made a speech against it. Since the final vote closely followed party lines—the Tory leaders, Leeds, Rochester, Nottingham, and Peterborough all spoke against the bill—the vote of Bolton, who was a Whig, was decisive in the 49–48 division (Luttrell, *4,* 351–52, 355).

1165. *Knighted:* "Sir Charles Duncomb Sheriff of London Knighted at Kensington in bedchamber 20 of October 1699" (Le Neve, p. 468).

Tribune: Only a week after his acquittal by the court of king's bench, Duncombe was "without a poll" elected high sheriff of London. It was expected that he would pay the usual fine not to serve, so his decision to accept the post was "a great disappointment to the court of aldermen" (Luttrell, *4,* 530–31).

1167. *Custos Rotulorum:* The City did not boast such an official. The *custodes rotulorum* were the principal justices of the peace in the counties (and the liberty of Westminster); they had custody of the rolls and records of the sessions of the peace.

1168. *Captain:* This may refer to Duncombe's membership in the Artillery Company of London (Luttrell, *1,* 179), or more simply to a sheriff's "army" of deputies, catchpoles, and informers.

Surrounded by my Catchpoles, I declare
Against the Needy Debtor open War.
I hang poor Thieves for stealing of your Pelf,
And suffer none to rob you, but my self.
  The King commanded me to help Reform ye,
And how I'll do't, Miss *Morgan* shall inform ye.
I keep the best Seraglio in the Nation,
And hope in time to bring it into Fashion.
No *Brimstone-Whore* need fear the Lash from me,
That part I'll leave to Brother *Jeffery*.
Our Gallants need not go abroad to *Rome*,
I'll keep a Whoring Jubilee at home.
Whoring's the Darling of my Inclination;
A'n't I a Magistrate for Reformation?
For this my Praise is sung by ev'ry Bard,
For which *Bridewell* wou'd be a just Reward.
In Print my Panegyricks fill the Street,

1170. *Needy Debtor:* "he was so far from declaring War against *Needy Debtors*, that he made *even their Enemies to be at Peace with 'em*, and reconcil'd their Creditors to 'em, by assisting those that were Insolvent" (*The True-Born Englishman: A Satyr, Answer'd*, p. 85); cf. Luttrell, *4*, 570.

1173. *The King commanded:* William issued a proclamation in 1698 "ascribing the spread of vice to the magistrates' neglect to enforce the laws, and commanding them 'to be very vigilant and strict in the discovery and effectual prosecution and punishment' of all persons guilty of 'dissolute, immoral, or disorderly practices' " (A. C. Guthkelch, "Defoe's *True-Born Englishman*," *Essays and Studies by Members of the English Association*, *4* [1913], 150).

1174. *Miss Morgan:* Nothing is known about the lady but her name, which is supplied in *D;* see textual note.

1178. *Jeffery:* See *Reformation of Manners*, 103 *n.*, below.

1180. *Jubilee:* See 1060 *n.*, above.

1182. *Reformation:* See *A Satyr against Wit*, headnote, pp. 129–30 above.

1185. *Panegyricks:* The panegyrics began with William Hog's ode *Ad virum nobilissimum omnique laude dignissimum, Carolum Duncombum, equitem auratum, Londini serifum, cum ingentem pauperum numerum, qui in variis Londini carceribus detinebantur, magnifica sua munificentia libertati restitueret, aere illorum alieno liberaliter persoluto* (Wing H2351), which probably was published in October 1699 when Duncombe "discharged out of the prisons belonging to this citty all in for £5 and under" (Luttrell, *4*, 570). This was followed the next year by *The Dream to Sir Charles Duncomb. By Mr. R. Gold* ("On my hard Fate as late I pond'ring lay") (Wing G1418), published in May (and reprinted in *POAS*, 1703, *2*, 378) and *The Poet's Address to the Honourable Sir Charles Duncomb, Knight, and Alderman of the City of London* ("The Fair Augusta of all Lands the Pride") (Wing P2738A) published in October (*History of the Works of the Learned*, *2* [October 1700], 640).

And hir'd Gaol-birds their Huzza's repeat.
Some Charities contriv'd to make a show,
Have taught the Needy Rabble to do so:
Whose empty Noise is a Mechanick Fame,
Since for Sir *Belzebub* they'd do the same.

The Conclusion

Then let us boast of Ancestors no more,
Or Deeds of Heroes done in days of Yore,
In latent Records of the Ages past,
Behind the Rear of Time, in long Oblivion plac'd.
For if our Virtues must in Lines descend,
The Merit with the Families would end:
And Intermixtures would most fatal grow;
For Vice would be Hereditary too;
The Tainted Blood wou'd of necessity,
Involuntary Wickedness convey.
  Vice, like Ill Nature, for an Age or two,
May seem a Generation to pursue;
But Virtue seldom does regard the Breed;
Fools do the Wise, and Wise Men Fools succeed.
  What is't to us, what Ancestors we had?

1187. *Charities contriv'd to make a show:* In June 1700, after he had been elected alderman of Bridge ward and in expectation of being elected mayor in September, Duncombe offered to "build a house for all succeeding mayors to live in." In July it was rumored that "Mr. sherif Duncomb designs to build a stately armory for the artillery company." In September he provided a clock for the parish church in Bridge ward (see 1057 *n.*, above) and on election day it was rumored that "if sir Charles Duncomb be chose lord mayor, he will lay out £40,000 for the good of the citty, and will sett up the kings statue in brasse upon Cheapside conduit" (Luttrell, *4*, 660, 667, 692). For the sequel, see 1055 *n.*, above.

1188. *to do so:* to repeat their huzzas.

1198. *Vice . . . Hereditary:* Defoe denies that vice is hereditary despite Exodus 20:5: "for I the Lord thy God am a jealous God, visiting the iniquity of the fathers upon the children unto the third and fourth generation." Cf. 1216 *n.*, below.

1205. *What is't to us:* "That question is resolv'd without any Difficulty, for if our Ancestors were good, then the remembrance of their Brave Actions would excite us to tread in the same Paths of Honour; if Bad, the Reflections on their dishonourable Practices would create in us a Detestation of Vice, and make us endeavour to degenerate from 'em" (*The True-Born Englishman: A Satyr, Answer'd,* p. 88).

If Good, what Better? or what worse, if Bad?
Examples are for Imitation set,
Yet all men follow Virtue with Regret.
  Cou'd but our Ancestors retrieve their Fate,
And see their Offspring thus degenerate;
How we contend for Birth and Names unknown,
And build on their past Actions, not our own;
They'd cancel Records, and their Tombs deface,
And openly disown the vile degenerate Race:
For Fame of Families is all a Cheat,
'Tis Personal Virtue only makes us great.

FINIS.

1216. *Personal Virtue:* "[the author] may more properly be stil'd a *Bankrupt,* than a Dealer in that sort of Commodity" (ibid.). Defoe, of course, was a bankrupt, but Pittis thought that John Toland had written *The True-Born Englishman.* For the concept, see Jeremiah 31:29–30 and Ezekiel 18:20–21: "The son shall not bear the iniquity of the father. . . . But if the wicked will turn from all his sins . . . he shall surely live." It is also a theme of Juvenal's, summarized in the words, "nobilitas sola est atque unica virtus" (*Sat. 8,* 20), which Defoe's line translates.

William Walsh[?]

The Worcester Cabal, Or a very new Ballad to a very old Tune, call'd Packington's Pound. (*January 1701*)

William Walsh (1662–1708) was the eldest son of Joseph Walsh of Abberley, an ancient Worcestershire family. Upon the death of his father in 1682 he left Wadham College, Oxford, without taking a degree and proceeded to London where he set up as beau and wit. He sent one of his early poems to Dryden for criticism and by 1691 their friendship had progressed to the point where Dryden supplied a preface to Walsh's prose *Dialogue Concerning Women, Being a Defence of the Sex,* "a book of ladies cruelties," as it was called at the time. Walsh is certainly not "the best Critic of our Nation," as Dryden claimed in 1697 in the *Postscript* to his translation of Virgil, but no one would deny Pope's more modest claim that he was "the Muse's Judge and Friend." In August 1698, with the support of the lord chancellor, John Somers, he had been returned to parliament, without opposition, as a member for Worcestershire.

The biographical notices of Walsh all mention the fact that he was elected three times to the House of Commons "and once succeeded in a contest upon the Whig interest," and then hasten on to mention his appointment in 1702 as gentleman of the horse to Queen Anne. The reason, apparently, that nothing more is said about this contested election is that the details of the story have been hidden away in an unpublished poem. A major interest of this poem, therefore, is that it affords glimpses of the electioneering process in a provincial setting at the turn of the eighteenth century. The election was that of January 1701 when the tide was running against the Whigs all over the kingdom.

The Tory magnate in Worcestershire was Sir John Pakington (1671–1727) of Westwood, fourth baronet and great-great-grandson of Queen Elizabeth's favorite, Sir John Pakington "the lusty," for whom the tune of "Packington's Pound" is alleged to have been named (Chappell, *1*, 123). Pakington succeeded to the baronetcy in March 1688, nine months before James II fled London. "At the Revolution the doors of Westwood were open to some persons who scrupled to take the oaths to king William" in 1689 (Nash, *1*, 353). Among these was George Hickes, who there wrote most of his *Linguarum vett. septentrionalium Thesaurus grammatico-criticus* and dedicated it to Sir John. In March 1690, before his nineteenth birthday, Pakington was elected knight of the shire for Worcestershire and, except for the parliament of 1695–98, sat for that county until his death, "speaking his mind there," as his monumental inscription declares, "without reserve, neither fearing nor flattering those in power, but despising all their offers of title and preferment" (Nash, *1*, 539). Pakington's political orientation may be judged from the fact that in December 1699 he moved in the House of Commons that Bishop Burnet be removed as preceptor to Prince William, duke of Gloucester (HMC *Hope Johnstone MSS.*, p. 114). More precisely, Pakington was a High Church Tory and member of the October Club in the next reign.

In the subsequent election of January 1701, with which the poem is concerned, Pakington procured not only his own election for Worcestershire and Aylesbury, Buckinghamshire, of which he was lord of the manor, but that of Hugh Parker, his brother-in-law, for Evesham, Worcestershire, and of James Herbert, Danby's son-in-law, for Aylesbury, which Pakington declined (Walcott, pp. 211–12). On the evidence of the poem alone, Pakington's candidate for the other seat for Worcestershire was Sir Thomas Rouse, fourth baronet, of Rouse Lench, the scion of an ancient Worcestershire family said to be descended from William Rufus, the son of William the Conquerer (Nash, *2*, 85). Again on the evidence of the poem, the contest was carefully planned. Pakington convened, presumably at Westwood, a caucus of 15 influential Tories. No fewer than 10 members of the group—or 12 if the candidates themselves are included—were country squires, but it seems no longer possible to divide this group of 10 into "six Projectors" and "four Squires," according to the first line of the poem. Only three members of the cabal were city men: Thomas Twitty, Samuel Swift, and Thomas Chetle. The first product of this cabal was a manifesto, drafted by Thomas Twitty and stating the requirements for knights of the shire for Worcestershire. William Walsh, a Whig, the other sitting member for Worcestershire, obviously did not meet these requirements, as Pakington also made clear to him in a personal letter (line 73 *n.*).

Besides the manifesto and Sir John Pakington's letter to Walsh, the Tories also undertook an active campaign of personal vilification. "The story of Mr. Walsh's being a Socinian" was circulated among the clergy in full expectation that it would be repeated from the pulpit (*Diary of Francis Evans,* ed. David Robertson, Oxford, 1903, p. xxii). Alexander Pope, incidentally, described his friend in almost exactly the same terms to Jonathan Swift; Walsh, he said, "was not only a Socinian, but . . . a Whig" (Pope, *Corr., 1,* 200). On his side, Walsh campaigned aggressively, undertaking considerable "Charges and labour" (line 54). He also wrote a reply to the Tory manifesto, but neither the manifesto nor Walsh's reply seem to have survived. Twitty, in turn, wrote "a scandalous Libel" in reply to Walsh's paper and posted it on the door of St. Martin's Church in Worcester. The theme of Twitty's "Libel" seems to have been a favorite Tory complaint of the day against "placemen" (a pejorative term for anyone holding office in the government) sitting in the House of Commons. The present poem concludes with campaign speeches by Rouse and Pakington, both promising to refuse all offers of places if elected.

Pakington's speech, however, contains something more than this, "As by the *Sequel* shall be shown" (see *The Golden Age Restor'd,* headnote, p. 488 below). His high flying Tory principles are revealed in his use of such phrases as "the Priestriding Crew" for the broad churchmen whom William had consistently appointed to episcopal sees. We are also told, in the notes preserved in *B,* which must be considered an integral part of the poem, that Pakington was ready to introduce a bill "for taking the power of Nominating Bishops out of the Kings Hands" (line 76 *n.*).

Concerning the authorship of the poem, there are only two pieces of evidence. In *B* the author is stated to be "J[?]:P[?]. Esqr." but the initials are heavily scored through, perhaps because someone knew them to be wrong. The poem is attributed to Walsh in the succeeding poem in *B,* which is entitled *Quid Pro Quo, or The Worcester Ballad Burlesk'd,* by Henry Hall of Hereford ("Since in the last Sessions your Beau got the Better"). There is nothing inherently improbable in Hall's attribution and no one was in a better position than Walsh to know the contents of his own personal letters (lines 29 *n.*, 73 *n.*).

The Worcester Cabal,

Or a very new Ballad to a very old Tune, call'd Packington's Pound.

1.

Two Knights, six Projectors, four Squires, and Tom Twitty,
And Sam the profound, Representer o'th City;
With a New Cloath'd Lieutenant in the Colour of Claret,
Having all the perfections and Name of a Parrot,
With honest Tom Cheatle
As dull as a Beetle,
Who Warrants and Justice dispences by Retail:
In deep Consultation and Council did sit,
To find Knights for the Parliament proper and fit.

2.

Pert Tony was one of the first that was heard,
(For that He's a Statesman demonstrates his Beard)

1. *Tom Twitty:* Thomas Twitty (1660?–1728) studied law at Lincoln's Inn and became "An officious impertinent Attourny" (*B*) and churchwarden of the parish of Claines.

2. *Sam the profound:* Samuel Swift of Claines (d. 1718), called profound "from his great Insight into the Misteries of Hops, Sugar, Tobacco, &c." (*B*). He was mayor of Worcester in 1684, sheriff in 1693, and Tory member for the city of Worcester in every parliament from 1695 to 1714 (W. R. Williams, *The Parliamentary History of the County of Worcester,* Hereford, 1897, p. 100).

3. *a New Cloath'd Lieutenant:* Thomas Perrot of Belbroughton (1670–1737), "in a new-vampt Red Coat, the first he ever had in his Life" (*B*). In 1708 Perrot was appointed sheriff for Worcestershire (Nash, *1,* xxi).

5. *Tom Cheatle:* Thomas Chetle (1646?–1714), or Cheatle, as the name is now spelled, was an attorney and one of the proctors of the consistorial court at Worcester. He lived in the Wall-house, Hanbury (Nash, *1,* 553; H. Sydney Grazebrook, *The Heraldry of Worcestershire,* 2 vols., 1873, *1,* 111–12).

9. *proper and fit:* "Their words in the Manifesto" *(B).*

10. *Tony:* Anthony Lechmere (1675–1720), the elder son of Edmund Lechmere of Hanley Castle, was "a Beardless Prig, who drank Confusion to Mr. Walsh's Interest" (*B*). In 1710 he was returned for Bewdley, Worcestershire, but the Commons refused to seat him. In the next reign he served as a Whig member for Tewkesbury, Gloucestershire (1715–17).

And as if a Courant were to dance, turns out 's Toe,
And stood breaking Jests, and Confounding the Beau.
And then spoke plump Phinny
Of Clains, that great Ninny,
And utter'd such notable Things as wou'd Win Ye;
But the Joy and the Life, and the Soul of my Tale
Was Francis the blustring Commander o'th Vale.

3.

Another that mov'd in this Worshipfull Batch
Was Savage, who shou'd be ty'd up by Jack Ketch,
Then Oracle Lyggon, in dubious Report,
Talk'd Reserv'dly like Chairman in Synod of Dort.
But stout Captain Sands
Who lead the Train'd Bands,
And less rich in Brains than in Houses and Lands,
Spoke boldly for th' Barnets, as thinking no hurt,
No more than the Member that lives at Pool Court.

12. *Courant:* (accented on second syllable), the courante or coranto, a dance characterized by a running or gliding step.

13. *the Beau:* Samuel Johnson observed that William Walsh was not "merely a critick or a scholar, but a man of fashion, and, as Dennis remarks, ostentatiously splendid in his dress" (*Lives, 1,* 328).

14. *Phinny:* Phineas Jackson of Claines (1674–1725), "who never had a hand in any plot, but one like this" (*B*). In 1703 he was appointed sheriff for Worcestershire (Nash, *1,* xxi).

18. *Francis:* Francis Sheldon (1643–1700) of Abberton, near the vale of Evesham, "swore he'd bring in 1000 Men out of the Vale against Mr. Walsh, and came in alone" (*B*).

20. *Savage:* "Savage of Darmston [Dormston] who had been arraigned for a base murther" (*B*).

21. *Lyggon:* William Lygon (1642–1720) of Madresfield (Nash, *2,* 117–18). "He kept himself upon the Reserve, 'till he Sign'd the Manifesto, and made both parties believe they were sure of him" (*B*). The motto of the family was "Ex fortis fide."

23. *Sands:* Captain Samuel Sandys (1638–1701) of Ombersley, whose monumental inscription declares that he suffered "Pro monarchia, pro ecclesia, tot tantaque" (Nash, *2,* 218–23), represented Droitwich, Worcestershire, in three reigns: 1661–81, 1685–87, 1680–90. He was a consistent member of the court party under Charles but not under James (Browning, *3,* 156).

26. *th' Barnets:* the baronets, Sir John Pakington and Sir Thomas Rouse (66 *n.*).

27. *the Member:* Richard Dowdeswell (1653–1711) of Pull Court, Worcestershire, represented the borough of Tewkesbury, Gloucestershire, in every parliament from 1685 to 1710. In 1689 he was sheriff of Worcestershire and in 1698 one of the burgesses in Tewkesbury. Captain Sandys' poverty of intellect is illustrated here by his bumbling endorsement of Dowdeswell, who was a staunch Whig and friend of Somers (Walcott, p. 202).

4.

The next that made Speeches without Wit or Fear,
Was Samuel, the haughty Dictator of Kyre.
Then the Man who is Nam'd from the Tree we make Cyder,
Spoke in Tropes by a Muse that had Venus to guide her,
For honesty Noted
And to Valour devoted,
As Sherrington tells us, (if he may be quoted)
Declaring aloud for the Knights, said he wou'd
Bring 'em in fourscore Men, and himself if he cou'd.

5.

This Wight had a Brother by Marriage of a Sister,
That governs Delinquents about Kidderminster,
For Impudence famous, Assisted in Council,
And fits this Cabal, Sir, because he can bounce well.
Quoth this William the Bluff
In terms very rough
(Proceeding from Lipps thick and Oylie as Buff)

29. *Samuel:* Samuel Pitts (c. 1674–1729) of Kyre, "who in a Letter to Mr. Walsh told him he shou'd not be perpetual Dictator" (*B*). Pitts' first wife was the daughter of Samuel Sandys of Ombersley (23 *n.*). His seat at Kyre Park was said to be "a very pleasant habitation for the summer, but in the winter rather dirty" (W. R. Williams, *The Parliamentary History of Worcester,* p. 56; Nash, *2,* 70). In December 1699 Pitts had been chosen to represent Hereford "in room of Mr. Paul Foley, deceased," but in the present election of January 1701, he was "shamefully Outvoted" (*B*) by Thomas Foley, Paul Foley's elder son. In the next reign, as an October Club Tory, he sat for Worcestershire (1710–15).

30. *the Man:* John Appletree (d. 1711?) of Inkberrow, "who has a lewd Character" (*B*). In 1697 he served as sheriff for Worcestershire (Nash, *1,* xxi).

34. *Sherrington:* Richard Cherington (d. 1724) "the Organist of Worcester [cathedral] to whom [Appletree] is indebted for 2 years House Rent, and when Sherrington ask'd him for it, Appletree ran him (being a Naked Man) into the Belly" (*B*). Cf. John Noake, *The Monastery and Cathedral of Worcester,* 1866, p. 486.

35. *the Knights:* Pakington and Rouse (66 *n.*).

36. *if he cou'd:* "If the Bayliff would let him" (*B*).

37–38. *a Brother by Marriage . . . That governs Delinquents:* "William Vernon lately made Justice of Peace" (*B*). This must be the William Vernon (1654–1708) who "lived at Caldwell, in the parish of Kidderminster, in 1701" (Nash, *1,* facing p. 549). He served as sheriff of Worcestershire in 1698 (Nash, *1,* xxi). Ann Vernon, his sister, married John Appletree, of Inkberrow (30 *n.,* above) on 20 August 1681 (Marriage Licence Allegations, No. 1548, Worcester Record Office).

40. *bounce:* talk big, bluster, swagger, hector, bully.

43. *Buff:* leather made of buffalo-hide or ox-hide, dressed with oil.

Of Voters against Walsh, I will pour in whole Loads,
Or else I will swing for't like Jeremy Rhodes.

6.

Again Spoke the Squire, who for Hereford Town
Serv'd two months in one Session, and then return'd down
To be chosen again, but (a Plague take the Doters)
He lost the Election by many foul Voters:
Says he, Here's my word for't,
I care not a Turd for't,
These Knights shall Serve here: for the Baron of Burford
Shall send in his Tenants by me his next Neighbour,
And so Walsh shall lose all his Charges and labour.

7.

Encourag'd such Forces and Interest to find,
The Knights at request of these Governours, Join'd,
And that all the world might partake of the Jest too
They publish'd a delicate penn'd Manifesto
By Twitty the Prater,
That learn'd Commentator,
Who's equally Cunning at Bill, Bond, and Satyr,
More fam'd tho' for late Writ of Error he pasted
On the door of St. Martin's, for which he'll be basted.

45. *Jeremy Rhodes:* "whom [William Vernon] hang'd (when high Sheriff) because Rhodes had procur'd a Repreive with some Mony, of which he was to have no Share. Therefore [Vernon] hang'd him at five in the Evening because he knew the Repreive would come the next Morning, as it did" (*B*).

46. *the Squire:* Samuel Pitts, 29 *n.*

52. *Baron of Burford:* Thomas Cornwall of Burford (1652–1724), "told the Bishop he would bring in his Tenants against Mr. Walsh, but the Bishop brought 'em in himself single Voices for him" (*B*). "The family of Cornwall possessed from the time of Edward II, the manor of Burford, Salop, held of the King in chief by barony. They were never summoned to Parliament. But in Monumental Inscriptions, Church Registers, &c., of a late date, down to the close of the 17th century, they are frequently styled Barons of Burford. The reason for this appellation is unknown, unless it was to indicate their (illegitimate) descent from Richard, Earl of Cornwall, brother of Henry III" (GEC, 2, 421).

56. *Join'd:* agreed to stand together for the two Worcestershire seats.

62. *Writ of Error:* "After Mr. Walsh's answer to this Manifesto was dispers'd, Twitty posted a scandalous Libel against him on St. Martins Church Door, and in which he persuaded [sic] to make observations on Mr. Walsh's Answer" (*B*).

63. *St. Martin's:* a parish church in Worcester, adjacent to the Cornmarket.

8.

This Paper affords Us much matter of Sport,
Because it proclaims War 'gainst places at Court.
Sir Thomas the Subtle (in Politicks mask'd)
Denies like a Virgin before She is ask'd.
He'll not get th'Election
By such damn'd Projection,
But will shun all preferment as 'twere an Infection,
And Vows he'll refuse to be Keeper o'th Roll,
The Place which his Grandfather held under Noll.

9.

Then faithful Sir John made the same Protestation,
And Swore he'd mind nought but the Good of the Nation,
And promis'd Sincerely in Order thereto
He'd regulate the Bishops, and the Priestriding Crew.
And at this they're so mad,
That a Walsh must be had,
Their Rights to defend, against which plots are Laid;
Then Let town and Country with this news Abound
That Pakington's taken now in his own Pound.

64. *This Paper:* "Twitty's Paper" (*B*).

66. *Sir Thomas:* Sir Thomas Rouse (1664–1721) of Rouse Lench, fourth baronet, "whose Grandfather was Custos Rotulorum to Oliver Cromwell" (*B*). The Sir Thomas Rouse, first baronet, whom Cromwell appointed *custos rotulorum* of Worcester in 1656, was the fourth baronet's father, not grandfather (Henry Townshend, *Diary of the Civil War,* p. 39, Worcester Record Office).

67. *Denies:* refuses to accept.

73. *faithful Sir John:* Sir John Pakington, "alluding to the Stile of his own Letter to Mr. Walsh" (*B*).

75. *Sincerely in Order thereto:* "idem" (*B*).

76. *regulate the Bishops:* Sir John Pakington "has a Bill to be offer'd in parliament for taking the power of Nominating Bishops out of the Kings Hands" (*B*). The bill that Pakington introduced on 20 March 1701 (*CJ, 13,* 416) was to prevent the translation of bishops from one see to another, "by which they depend on the Crown, and are made votes for the Court" (*Original Letters,* p. 126).

76. *the Priestriding Crew:* "an Expression of his" (*B*). Sir John's expression alluded to the latitudinarian bishops who restrained the high flying tendencies of the lower house of convocation, which convened for the first time in more than 10 years in February 1700 (Thomas Lathbury, *A History of the Convocation,* 2nd. ed., 1853, pp. 346–62).

Daniel Defoe

A New Satyr on the Parliament
(June [?] 1701)

By April 1701, only six months after he had entrusted his government to Tories, William already regretted his choice. He particularly disliked Laurence Hyde, earl of Rochester, "of whose imperious and intractable temper, he complained much, and seemed resolved to disengage himself quickly from him." Rochester's party, he found, was "neither solid nor sincere, [but] actuated by passion and revenge, without any views with relation to our quiet at home, or to our affairs abroad" (Burnet, 2, 280).

Affairs abroad were indeed precarious. In February, while the House of Commons was preoccupied with hearings on contested elections, Louis XIV moved 60,000 French troops into the Lowlands. In March he reimposed the wartime capitation tax and in April he recalled his ambassador from London.

Affairs at home were hardly better. The Commons seemed reluctant to settle the crown on Sophia, the 71-year-old dowager electress of Hanover and granddaughter of James I. The committee to draft a succession bill was entrusted to Sir John Bolles, "who was then disordered in his Senses, and soon after quite lost them" (Burnet, 2, 271). Under Bolles' direction, hearings were postponed from one week to another. Every time the motion was called for, "the Members ran out of the House, with so much indecency, that the Contrivers seemed ashamed of this management" (ibid.). A similar fate had befallen the supply bill which was introduced on 25 February. Hearings had dragged on week after week, but by the end of April no money had yet been voted. In the meantime the Commons had amused itself by deciding all contested elections in favor of the Tory candidate and impeaching the Whig lords of the last administration for transacting the partition treaties of 1698 and 1700.

Worst of all, the new administration seemed compelled to attack the king. The attack on the partition treaties was a covert attack on the king, for the conduct of foreign affairs belonged to "The King only, and the King alone, by his Royal *Prerogative*" (Chamberlayne, 1700, p. 76). It soon became apparent that the ministry had so little control over the Commons that it was not able to "restrain them from doing unreasonable & Extravagant things only to lessen the King" (BM Add. MS. 7074, f. 15). André Bonet, the London resident of the new king of Prussia, observed that the recurrent theme of Tory propaganda in 1701 was to depreciate the king in the eyes of the people (BM Add. MS. 30000E, f. 151v).

"The King seemed to bear all this," as Burnet observed, "with his usual coldness" (2, 262), but finally, toward the end of April, he decided to act. His decision was to take his case to the people, whom he believed to be overwhelmingly in favor of containing the power of France and settling the crown on the house of Hanover.

How Defoe was received by the king and "how Employ'd," has been mentioned above (*The True-Born Englishman,* headnote, p. 264). It appears now that the Kentish petition, the Legion *Memorial,* and the present poem must all be included in this employment (Swift, *Discourse,* pp. 53–57). It was James Drake who observed that Defoe had "endeavoured to Bully the *House* as well in Rime as in *Prose*" (*The Source of our Present Fears Discover'd,* 1703, p. 32).

The evidence for Defoe's authorship of *A New Satyr on the Parliament* is completely circumstantial. *The Ballad, Or; Some Scurrilous Reflections in Verse, on the Proceedings of the Honourable House of Commons: Answered,* which includes the text both of *A New Satyr on the Parliament* and of the first answer to it ("Ye Slaves who make it your Pretence"), appears in *An Alphabetical Catalogue of an Extensive Collection of the Writings of Daniel De Foe* (1830), p. 5, and also, although prefixed with a question mark, in Lowndes (2, 616). More recently Defoe's authorship has been accepted by Moore (p. 15) on the basis of Defoe's quotation of it in later works (see lines 81–85 *n* and 174–175 *n.*, below). That *An Encomium upon a Parliament* and *A New Satyr on the Parliament* are companion pieces by the same author is reflected in the similarity of their first lines ("Ye worthy Patriots go on" and "Ye True-Born *Englishmen* proceed"), in the use of the same rhyme scheme, (a^4 b^3 a^4 a^4 b^3), and in the interdependence of their allusions. *A New Satyr* takes up exactly where *An Encomium* left off (see 3 *n.*, 17 *n.*, etc., below).

F. Elrington Ball's suggestion (*Swift's Verse,* 1929, pp. 49–50) that

Swift and Charles Davenant collaborated to write *The Ballad . . . Answered* cannot be accepted. Swift's political orientation in 1701 was identical with Defoe's, while Davenant was a leading Tory propagandist.

The first five lines of the poem appear in Cowper MS. Box 11 under the title, "Found in the Lobby of the House of Commons 29 April 1701," but this is too early a date for composition of the whole poem, which refers to two events of mid-May. The act of settlement was parliament's "Immediate care" (line 97) on 14 May when it passed the third reading in the House of Commons and was sent up to the Lords. Later in the same day the Commons undertook to draft the "wise Address" which is mentioned in lines 143–45 (*CJ, 13,* 540). *The Ballad . . . Answered* was advertised in *The Flying Post,* No. 958, 26–28 June 1701, so presumably *A New Satyr on the Parliament* was published a few weeks before. *The Miseries of England, from the Growing Power of Her Domestick Enemies* (1701) ("*Albion,* disclose thy drowsy Eyes, and see"), which was reprinted in *POAS,* 1707, *4,* 132, is partly a reply to *A New Satyr on the Parliament.*

A New Satyr on the Parliament

Ye True-Born *Englishmen* proceed,
Our trifling Crimes detect.
Let the Poor starve, Religion bleed,
The *Dutch* be damn'd, the *French* succeed,
And all by your Neglect.

Your actions all the World disgust,
The *French* are only glad;
Your friends your honesty distrust,
And while you think you're wise and Just,
The Nation thinks you mad.

1–5. These lines are included in BM MS. Stowe 305, p. 464 under the title *The Speaker found the following Lines put Into his Coate pockett;* see also headnote, p. 320.

2. *trifling Crimes:* The diplomatic representatives in London agreed that the impeachment charges brought by the House of Commons against the three leaders of the Whig junto were frivolous. "La verité," Bonet reported, "est qu'il n'y a aucune accusation importante à alleguer contre ces deux Lords [Somers and Orford]," and Poussin observed that the charges against Halifax "se reduisent à six articles assez faibles" (BM Add. MS. 30000E, f. 233; PRO Transcripts 31/3 188, f. 94).

3. *Poor starve:* Cf. *An Encomium upon a Parliament,* 72 *n.,* above; in his address at the opening of the session, the king reminded parliament for the fourth time that nothing had been done to relieve the poor (*Parl. Hist.,* *5,* 1191, 1199, 1200, 1233). A bill for the further relief and employing the poor of London was introduced but was defeated at the second reading (*CJ,* *13,* 485).

Religion bleed: Cf. *An Encomium upon a Parliament,* 76 *n.,* above; William did not again remind parliament that nothing had been done to suppress vice and immorality because it now seemed to him—with a grandson of His Most Christian Majesty on the throne of Catholic Spain—that "the preservation of the Protestant Religion in general" was at stake (*Parl. Hist.,* *5,* 1191, 1199, 1201, 1233). A bill for the better preservation of the Protestant religion received a second reading on 23 April (*CJ,* *13,* 501) but then was allowed to drop.

4. "As soon as our Parliament was opened," Burnet recalled (2, 257), "it appeared that the *French* had a great Party in it." Consequently, on 18 February 1701, when the king laid before the House of Commons a memorial from the Dutch appealing for help against French troops who had occupied all the barrier fortresses between Ostend and Luxemburg, the response was less than enthusiastic. "Some endeavoured," as Burnet said, "all that was possible to put this off for the present, pretending that [the Dutch] were not yet attacked." Troops were finally voted (*CJ,* *13,* 349, 523), but, as Burnet went on to explain, "This coldness and uncertainty in our Councils, gave the French great advantages in their Negotiations, both in *Germany* and in *Portugal*" (2, 263).

Are these the ways your wisdome takes,
To raise our Reputation,
To quarrel at a few mistakes,
Whilst *France* their own advantage makes,
And Laughs at all the Nation?

You are the people who of old
The Nations Troops disbanded,
And now you should your Friends uphold,
Your Friends and you are bought and sold,
As always was intended.

There's none but Fools in time to come,
Will Trust the *English* Nation;
For if they do, they know their doome,
That we'l be falling out at home,
And baulk their Expectation.

You are the Nations grand defence
Against Illegal power,
And yet, against both Law and Sence,
And sometimes too without pretence,
You send folk to the *Tower*.

Some Lords your anger have incurr'd,
For Treaty of Partition,

13. *mistakes:* See 2 *n.*, above.

17. *Troops disbanded:* See *An Encomium upon a Parliament,* headnote, pp. 45–46, above.

18. *Friends:* See *An Encomium upon a Parliament,* 7 *n.*, above.

21. *Fools:* See *An Encomium upon a Parliament,* 8, above.

30. *send folk to the Tower:* On 8 May 1701 five gentlemen from Kent (see illustration, p. 336) presented a petition to the House of Commons "setting forth the danger of that county in case of an invasion, prayeing them to lay aside their heats and animosities, and turn their addresses into bills of supplyes to enable his majestie (under whom we have happily lived so long) to defend us, and preserve the peace of Europe, before 'twas too late; upon which they were called in and examined, and their petition voted seditious, scandalous and insolent" (Luttrell, *5*, 47). The Kentish petitioners were remanded, not to the Tower, but to a spunging house "in *Fox-Court* in *Holborn*" and then to the Gate House (Defoe, *The History of the Kentish Petition*, 1701, p. 12).

31. *Lords:* Each of the impeached lords (see 2 *n.*, above), was accused of advising the king to conclude with France, the Empire, and the Netherlands a treaty of partition of the Spanish monarchy that was "highly injurious to the Protestant Religion, and manifestly tending to disturb the general peace of Europe" (*Parl. Hist.*, *5*, 1261, 1267, 1304).

32. *Treaty of Partition:* By two treaties with France, the Empire, and the Netherlands (see *The Foreigners*, 156 *n.*, above), signed September 1698 and February 1700, William

But if you'l take the Nations word,
Most People think it was absurd,
And empty of discretion.

For if that Treaty, as 'tis fam'd,
Gave part of *Spain* to *Gaul,*
Why should those Gentlemen be blam'd,
When you your selves are not asham'd,
To let them take it all.

Bribes and ill practices you found,
And some few felt your Power,
But soon you run your selves a-ground,
For had you push'd the matter round,
You all had gone to th'*Tower.*

Some Reformation hath from you,
In vain been long expected,

---

tried to settle, short of war, the issue of who was to succeed Carlos II on the throne of Spain. The junto lords had nothing to do with these transactions, which were entirely the prerogative of the crown. Somers and Orford, in fact, advised against the treaties.

34. *it:* impeaching the junto lords for advising the king to conclude the partition treaties.

37. *part of Spain:* According to the terms of the second partition treaty, the province of Guipuscoa, including the cities of Fuenterrabia and St. Sebastian, were ceded to France (HMC *Lords MSS.*, New Series, *4*, 254).

40. *take it all:* Carlos II, in his last will, named Philippe, duc d'Anjou, the 16-year-old second grandson of Louis XIV, as his successor on the throne of Spain. In order to accept the will, Louis simply tore up the second partition treaty, which he had signed only 10 months before. By "this pretence," as William III called it, Louis XIV made himself "the real Master of the whole Spanish Monarchy" (*Parl. Hist.*, *5*, 1330). Their eagerness to impeach the junto lords for advising the king to conclude the partition treaties forced the Tories to represent Louis' decision to accept "the whole Spanish Monarchy" as "the justest and most honourable part" (HMC *Portland MSS.*, *3*, 636).

41. *Bribes:* On 18 March 1701 the Commons resolved that Samuel Shepherd, senior, was guilty of "Bribery and corrupt Practices" in the elections for Wooton Bassett, Wiltshire, and four other boroughs, and committed him to the Tower. His son, Francis Shepherd, was found guilty of "corruptly exposing to Sale the Election of a Burgess" in Andover, Hampshire (*CJ*, *13*, 413).

42. *some few:* "In conclusion, the matter [of bribery] was so well proved, that several Elections were declared void: and some of the persons so chosen, were for some time kept in prison; after that they were expelled the House" (Burnet, *2*, 259). One director of the New East India Company who was expelled the House for "notorious Bribery," was Edward Allen (*CJ*, *13*, 408). Defoe's friend, Dalby Thomas, was summoned to testify in the case of Samuel Shepherd, another director of the New East India Company (ibid., pp. 400, 404).

46. *Reformation:* See 3 *n.*, above.

But when you shou'd the busines do,
Your privat quarrels you pursue,
  And th'Nation lyes neglected.

Long has the Kingdom born the weight
  Of your deficient Funds,
That Parliamentary publick Cheat;
Pray where's the difference of that
  And Plundring with Dragoons?

Are you the People that complain
  Of Arbitrary power?
Then shew the Nation if you can,
Where Kings have been since Kings began,
  Such Tyrants as you are.

When Kings with right and Law dispence
  And set up power despotick,
It has been counted Law and sence
To take up Arms against our Prince
  And call in aids Exotick.

But you, although your Powers depend
  On every Plowman's Vote,

49. *privat quarrels:* Even Edward Harley, the speaker's younger brother, admitted that the impeachments of the junto lords "tended only to expose the personal malice and folly of the impeachers" (HMC *Portland MSS., 5,* 646). Vernon (*3,* 88) records that Robert Harley remained "exasperated" with Somers even after Somers had been dismissed.

52. *deficient Funds:* See *An Encomium upon a Parliament,* 49 *n.,* above; on 27 February 1701, when the figures were laid before the House of Commons, the deficit amounted to £2,724,000 (*CJ, 13,* 359–61).

60. *Such Tyrants as you:* It was observed in April 1700 that the House of Commons had already begun to act "comme un souveraine, accordant des recompenses aux uns et excluant d'autres" (BM MS. Add. 17677UU, f. 203). During the next session this tendency revealed itself in the Commons' imprisonment of the Kentish petitioners and in its address to the king to exclude the junto lords from his presence and council forever, even before the impeachment charges against them had been drafted, much less tried. Accordingly, a Whig broadside in August 1701 argued that "Arbitrary Power [is] less terrible in the Hands of One, than of Many; since in the first Case Shame or Pity may sometimes prevail, but never in the other" (*Some Queries, which may deserve Consideration,* 1701).

61. Defoe expounds the right to revolt against a tyrant by "Force, or Foreign Aid" in *The True-Born Englishman,* 802–39, above.

Beyond the Law that Power extend,
To ruine those you should defend,
And sell the Power you bought.

The King Religion did Commend
To you, his *Law-Explainers;*
We know not what you may intend,
Nor how you should Religion mend,
Unless you will your Manners.

You are the Nations darling Sons,
The abstract of our Mobb;
For City Knights and Wealthy Clowns,
Stock Jobbers, Statesmen and Buffoons,
You may defye the Globe.

Toland insults the Holy Ghost,
Brib'd *Seymour* bribes accuses,
Good Manners and Religion's lost;

69. *ruine those:* Sunderland warned the king in September 1701 that "the Tories will not be satisfied without ruining my Lord Somers" (Hardwicke, 2, 446) and Vernon added that "nothing would satisfy them but the utter subduing of those whom they have sett themselves against" (BM MS. Add. 40775, Vol. 5, f. 116).

72. *Law-Explainers:* This may refer to 12 & 13 William III c. 3, An Act for preventing any Inconveniences that may happen by Privilege of Parliament, which was called "An Act explaining Privilege" (Burnet, 2, 271).

78. *City-Knights:* See *The True-Born Englishman,* 419, above.

79. *Stock Jobbers:* those engaged in "a sharp, cunning, cheating Trade of Buying and Selling Shares of Stock" (*New Dictionary,* sig. L6r).

Statesmen and Buffoons: See *Absalom and Achitophel,* 550.

81–85. Quoted on the title page of [Defoe], *A Farther Argument against Ennobling Foreigners,* 1717, as from a poem entitled *A Letter to a Member of Parliament.*

81. *Toland:* Toland insulted the Holy Ghost by denying that there were any mysteries in Christianity (*Christianity not Mysterious,* 1696, pp. 170–73). Although not a member of parliament, Toland is included here because he was working closely with Harley in the production of Tory propaganda. In March 1701 he published *Limitations for the Next Foreign Successor,* a trial balloon for the Act of Settlement.

82. *Brib'd Seymour:* See 41 *n.,* above; in May 1701, while Seymour was sitting as chairman of a committee to draw up a bill for preventing bribery and corruption in boroughs, one James Bulkley testified that Seymour had promised his constituents in Totnes a new organ for the parish church if he were re-elected. Bulkley was ordered to be taken into custody and imprisoned in the Gate House along with the Kentish petitioners (*CJ, 13,* 553; BM Add. MS. 30000E, f. 202v; PRO Transcripts 31/3 188, f. 68; *A List of One Unanimous Club of Members of the Late Parliament,* 1701, p. 2).

The King who was your Lord of Hosts,
The Raskal *How* abuses.

Your Statesman, *Granville,* with intent
To cultivate with care
The dignity of Parliament,
Plyes closely at the Dancing tent,
And manages *May*-Fair;

The True-Born Hero's diligence
For publick good appears;
There he refines his Wit and Sense,
That the next day in our defence,
May fill Committee Chairs.

84. *Lord of Hosts:* See *An Encomium upon a Parliament,* 26–27, above.

85. *How:* Five days after the opening of the session, John Howe, "that Scandal of Parliaments" (BM MS. Add. 30000E, f. 44v), attacked the king in such violent terms that Bonet declined to report them. Howe said that "the king's grants were squandered away upon buffoons and harlots, and even called the treaty of partition a felonious treaty of three thieves" (Alexander Cunningham, *History of Great Britain,* 2 vols., 1787, *1,* 208). Ten years later Defoe wrote a defense of the partition treaties ironically entitled *The Felonious Treaty* (Moore, p. 90).

86. *Granville:* John Granville or Grenville (1665–1707) was the second son of John Grenville, earl of Bath. In parliament, where he sat for Launceston, Cornwall (1685–87), Plymouth, Devonshire (1689–98), Newport, Cornwall (1698–1700), Fowey, Cornwall (January 1701–November 1701), and county Cornwall (1701–03), he was a country Tory "qui s'est toujours ouvertement declaré contre la Cour." He refused to subscribe to the Association for the defense of William III in 1696 and was reported to be a Jacobite in 1698 (BM MS. Add. 30000B, ff. 264v, 273v). During the session of 1701 he was one of the ringleaders, having, as *The Ballad . . . Answered* put it, "been lately bought/And Country left for Court" (p. 14).

90. *May-Fair:* May Fair was an annual rite held "in a Place called *Brook-Field,* in the Parish of St. *Martin in the Fields,*" between St. James's and Hyde Park, where young people "spent their Time and Money in Drunkenness, Fornication, Gaming, and Lewdness" (Strype, *2,* 84). Granville led the kind of life traditionally reserved for colonels of the guards, fighting duels with noblemen (Luttrell, *2,* 374) and intriguing with widows and "strowling Punks" (BM MS. Harleian 7315, f. 287v; Holkham MS. 686, pp. 130, 239).

95. *fill Committee Chairs:* John Granville was chairman of the standing committee of privileges and elections and, during 1701, served as chairman of the committee appointed to draft a reply to the Dutch memorial (BM Add. MS. 17677WW, f. 169; BM Add. MS. 30000E, f. 48; cf. 4 *n.,* above) and a member of at least four others, including the committee to draft impeachment charges against the "Lords Partitioners" (*CJ, 13,* 465; cf. 2 *n.,* above) and the committee to draft an address to the king on the occasion of the Legion *Memorial* (*CJ, 13,* 540; cf. 143 *n.,* below).

The Limitation of the Crown
Is your Immediate care;
If your *Wise Articles* go down,
Your Power will be so Lawless grown,
'Tis no matter who's the Heir.

Did we for this depose our Prince,
And Liberty assume,
That you should with our Laws dispense,
Commit Mankind without Offence,
And Govern in his Room?

You shou'd find out some other word
To give the Crowns *Accepter;*
To call him King wou'd be absurd,
For tho' he'l seem to wear the sword,
'Tis you have got the Scepter.

And now your wrath is smoaking hot
Against the *Kent* petition,
No man alive can tell for what,
But telling Truths which pleas'd you not
And taxing your Discretion.

96. *Limitation:* Settlement of the succession to the throne, made necessary by the death of the young duke of Gloucester, the last surviving child of Princess Anne, got under way on 3 March 1701 when Harley proposed to the Commons that since "Nothing pressed them at present . . . they would settle some Conditions of Government, as Preliminaries, before they should proceed to the Nomination of the Person." What these "Conditions" were to be was revealed a few days later in Toland's pamphlet, *Limitations for the Next Foreign Successor.* They were, again in Burnet's words, "such extravagant Limitations, as should quite change the Form of our Government, and render the Crown titular and precarious: The King was alarmed . . . for almost every particular, that was proposed, implied a reflection on him and his Administration" (Burnet, 2, 270).

99. *Power . . . so Lawless:* Bonet agreed with Defoe that "par ces limitations . . . le pouvoir sera presque dévolu au Peuple, ou plutot aux Chefs de la Chambre qui agissent par faction et par interet . . . En un mot que la balance de ce Gouvernement sera otée, que c'est le chemin a une Anarchie" (BM Add. MS. 30000E, f. 80). Defoe had already noted that "the People's Right to make Kings . . . is what these [Tory] Gentlemen are so fond of" (*The Two Great Questions Further Considered,* [December] 1700, p. 12).

107. *Crowns Accepter:* Defoe's prophecy is eminently fulfilled in the person of George I, "like whom," as Pope discovered, "None e'er has risen, and none e'er shall rise."

112. *the Kent petition:* See 30 *n.*, above.

If you those Gentlemen detain
By your unbounded power,
'Tis hop'd you'l never more complain
Of Bishops in King *James*'s Reign,
Sent blindly to the *Tower*.

A strange *Memorial* too there came,
Your Members to affront,
Which told you Truths you dare not name,
And so the paper scap'd the flame,
Or else it had been burnt.

Some said the Language was severe,
And into passion flew,
And some began to curse and swear,
And call'd the author *Mutineere,*
But all men said 'Twas True.

But oh! the Consternation now
In which you all appear!
'Tis plain from whence your terrours flow;
For had your guilt been less, you know,
So would have been your fear.

117. *unbounded power:* A similar complaint is made in a pamphlet attributed to Somers, *Jus Regium: Or, The King's Right to Grant Forfeitures,* [April] 1701, p. 35: " 'Tis hard to say what Parliaments cannot do: The Boundaries of their Power not being fix'd, 'tis difficult to determine when 'tis carried beyond the utmost extent of its Tether." The most violent Tories, however, were urging the Commons to wield "the whole Power" ([James Drake], *The History of the Last Parliament,* 1702, p. 141).

119. *Bishops:* See *POAS,* Yale, *4,* 215.

121. *Memorial . . . came:* On 14 May, as Charles Davenant recalled, "Out came *Legion,* of which there were dispers'd upwards of thirty thousand" (*Tom Double Return'd out of the Country,* 1702, p. 12). That morning the original *Memorial* was handed to the speaker by its author, Daniel Defoe, at the door of the House of Commons. It claimed to come from 200,000 Englishmen and it was signed "LEGION." The speaker himself was "commanded" to present it to the Commons. The *Memorial* that he read was an unequivocal assertion of the right of the people to resist arbitrary power "by Extra-Judicial Methods." It demanded that the Kentish petitioners be admitted to bail, that John Howe be ordered to ask pardon for "his vile Reflections" on the king, that all public debts be paid, and that *"Suitable Supplies"* be granted to the king. Finally it demanded that the French troops be obliged to leave Flanders, "or that His Majesty be address'd to declare War."

135. *fear:* Defoe claimed later that the *Memorial* was *"that Paper* which frighted Mr. *P*[*rior?*] and Mr. *H*[*arcour*]*t,* and several others into the Country; that Paper which Mr. *Howe* in a lamentable Tone told the House made him, *from the sense of his own*

In fifteen Articles you're told
You have our Rights betray'd,
Banter'd the Nation, bought and sold
The liberties you shou'd uphold;
No wonder you're afraid.

And now to make your selves appear
The more impertinent,
A wise Address you do prepare,
To have his Majesty take care
Rebellion to prevent.

No doubt his Majesty will please
To take your Cause in hand;
Besides the work is don with ease,
Full *Seven Thousand men* he has
The Nation to defend.

Guilt, afraid" (*Legion's New Paper,* 1702, p. 4). The diplomatic correspondents, however, reported that it was the Kentish petition that had caused the fears (PRO 31/3 188, f. 59v; BM Add. MS. 17677WW, f. 255v) and *The Ballad . . . Answered* (p. 18) insisted that "The House had other Fish to fry,/When *Legion*'s Libel came."

136. *fifteen Articles:* The 15 articles of the *Memorial* are followed very closely in the present poem: with Article I, "To raise Funds for Money . . . and then give subsequent Funds, without transferring the Deficiency of the Former, is a horrible Cheat on the Subject who lent the Money," cf. 51–53, above; with Article VII, "Deserting the *Dutch,* when the *French* are at their Doors, till it be almost too late to help them, is unjust to our Treaties . . . and shew you negligent of the Safety of *England,*" cf. 4–5 above, and with Article XIV, "Publicly neglecting the great Work of *Reformation of Manners,* tho' often pressed to it by the King . . . is a Neglect of your Duty," cf. 46–50.

138–39. *sold The liberties:* Article V of the *Memorial* complained that "Voting People guilty of Bribery and ill Practices, and committing them . . . without Bail, and then upon Submission, and kneeling to your House, discharging them; exacting exorbitant Fees by your Officers, is illegal, betraying the Justice of the Nation, selling the Liberty of the Subject." This seems to have been a common, and profitable, practice; see the case of John Perks, *CJ, 13,* 523, 524.

143. *Address:* The Commons responded to the *Memorial* by voting "to lay before his Majesty the Endeavours of several ill-disposed Persons [as Bonet pointed out, no one knew whether the *Memorial* was the work of one person or several] to raise Tumults and Sedition" and by urging him to "provide for the publick Peace and Safety" (*CJ, 13,* 540; BM Add. MS. 30000E, f. 193v). The first meeting of the committee appointed to draft the address was ordered to meet at five o'clock the same day, 14 May, in the speaker's chambers. "Having thought better of it," however, Harley never asked for a report from the committee "and the whole Affair was silently let fall" (Ralph, *2,* 953).

149. *Seven Thousand men:* See *An Encomium upon a Parliament,* headnote, p. 45 above.

One hundred Thousand Heroes more
Do our Train'd Bands compose;
If foraign Forces shou'd come o're,
Plant them and you upon the Shoar;
How bravely you'l oppose!

Then blush ye Senators to see
How all men stand dismay'd;
The Nation shou'd so patient be
To bear with all your Villany,
And see themselves betray'd.

It was our Freedom to defend,
That *We the People* chose you,
And *We the People* do pretend
Our power of Choosing may extend
To punish and depose you.

For since in vain are Hopes and Fears,
Petitions too are vain,
No Remedy but this appears,
To pull the House about your Ears,
And send you home again.

These are the Nations Discontents,
The Causes are too true;

152. *Train'd Bands:* the militia of England. Under the command of the lords lieutenant or deputy lieutenants of each county, troops were mustered twice a year for training and discipline. Every householder worth £500 a year was required to furnish a horse and horseman, and those worth £50 a year a foot soldier. "They are at present computed to be 200000 Horse and Foot" (Chamberlayne, 1700, p. 214).

162. *We the People:* See [Daniel Defoe?], *A Satyr upon King William, being the Secret History of His Life and Reign,* 1703, p. 21.

164. *power:* While Whig and Tory could agree that parliamentary power originated with the people, the Tories insisted that no power remained with the people after they had delegated it to their representatives in the House of Commons: "[the electors] have no Power to compel their Members to Vote or Act . . . tho' the whole Country . . . were of a contrary Opinion to that of their Representatives" (*England's Enemies Exposed,* [July] 1701, p. 30). Since "this Parliamentary Branch of Power," as Defoe said, "is no more Infallible than the Kingly," the Whigs maintained that the people had the same right to revolt against a tyrannical parliament as they did against a tyrannical king (*The Original Power of the Collective Body of the People,* 1702, pp. 9, 12).

The ploughman now his Choice repents,
For tho' he values Parliaments,
He's out of Love with *You.*

When to be chose, with Cap in hand,
You courted every Voice,
You were our Servants at command,
By which it seems you understand,
Untill we made our Choice.

If that be True, we let you know
Upon that very Score:
You'd best your present Hours bestow
In all the Mischiefs you can do,
For We'l ne're choose you more.

The Second Part

No Wonder *Powys, Finch* and *Shower,*
With others such as they,
For the French *King* so Loudly Roar,
And would do so for twenty more;
They always plead for pay.

How once was thought an honest Man;
But now the Tool of *Lory;*
He for his Country first began,

174–75. Years later, in one of his typical, self-deprecatory self-allusions, Defoe recalled that "in one of the worst of those numberless Pamphlets, which the Dr. [Davenant] takes notice of, among all the Gall against the Members of that House, it still appeared they had none against the Constitution, by this following Line. *For tho' we value Parliaments, we're out of love with you"* (*Some Remarks on the First Chapter in Dr. Davenants Essays,* 1704, p. 12).

186. *Powys, Finch and Shower:* These prominent Tory pleaders reappear below in *England's Late Jury,* lines 126, 66, and 86, respectively.

191. *How:* See *England's Late Jury,* 76 *n.,* 80 *n.,* below.

192. *Lory:* Laurence Hyde, Earl of Rochester; see *A Conference between King William and the Earl of Sunderland,* 127 *n.,* and headnote, p. 192 above.

But afterwards *turn'd Cat in pan,*
And stinks like any Tory.

Harcourt by *Musgrave*'s Compass sailes,
Whilst *Seymour* guides the Helm;
Their pole is *Gold* which never fails;
Their Aim's to Crown the Prince of *Wales*
And all our Rights o'rewhelm.

Blathwayt that Proud Imperious Beast,
Is to be bought and Sold.
'Tis all chimaera, 'tis a Jest
To think that he can stand the Test
Against the Power of Gold.

Those Mushrooms rais'd by *Dorset*'s hand
To save the King and State,
Would now his Majesty disband,
At Least with those go hand in hand
That do his Person hate.

Others I might have here set down,
Whose Venom is not weaker,
As they themselves have fully shewn
To Court, to Country and to Town;
I pray God Bless the Speaker.

194. *turn'd Cat in pan:* changed sides from motives of interest (*OED*); proverbial (Tilley C172).

196. *Harcourt . . . Musgrave:* See *Advice to a Painter. 1701,* 16 *n.,* 14 *n.,* below.

201. *Blathwayt:* William Blathwayt, secretary-at-war, member of the Board of Trade, and auditor-general of the royal revenues in Virginia and the West Indies, was a court Tory (Gertrude A. Jacobsen, *William Blathwayt,* New Haven, Yale University Press, 1932, pp. 480–81), who sat for Newtown, Hampshire (1685–87) and Bath, Somersetshire (1693–1710). Defoe puts him in the same company and again mentions his brassy willingness to be corrupted (Jeremiah 6:28) in *England's Late Jury,* 121–23, below.

206. *Dorset:* See *The Dispensary,* 2, 67 *n.,* above; cf. *England's Late Jury,* 118, below.

215. *the Speaker:* Robert Harley was elected speaker of the fifth parliament of William III on 11 February 1701.

William, while these Men govern thee,
  Our prospect is but sad;
For all Mens thoughts in this agree,
That thou art blind and canst not see,
  Or else thou art stark mad.

Advice to a Painter. 1701
(*July*[?] *1701*)

The Kentish petitioners (p. 322 above) became popular heroes almost as soon as they were arrested, particularly after one of them, Thomas Colepepper, made "his bold Escape to kiss his Wife" (*The Kentish Men. A Satyr* ["When Men, for want of Courage and of Sense"], 1701, p. 10). Even while in prison they received visits from all sorts of people and sat for their portraits by Robert White. As soon as they were released, when parliament was prorogued on 24 June, they were carried to the Guildhall and displayed to their admirers from a balcony (BM MS. Add. 17677WW, f. 309v). That evening the Fishmongers Company entertained them at a splendid banquet in Fishmongers Hall and made them free of their company. On Monday 30 June their portraits were published in a fine engraving, also by Robert White (see illustration, p. 336), with a bold motto, *Non Auro Patriam,* reflecting on the recipients of French gold (Luttrell, *5,* 66).

The next day, while their pictures were hawked about the streets, the Kentish petitioners were "nobly entertained" at Mercers Chapel in Cheapside. "The Entertainment was very splendid; there being present his Grace the Duke of Bolton, the Marquis of Hartington, and some other Noblemen," members of parliament, and more than 200 other persons of quality and citizens. On this occasion Daniel Defoe was seated next to the guests of honor; or as the Tory pamphleteer phrased it, "Next the Worthies was placed their Secretary of State, the Author of the *Legion Letter*" (*The Post Boy,* No. 956, 1–3 July 1701; *The Legionites Plot,* 1702, p. 18).

After the Kentish gentlemen had begun their triumphant homeward journey, the young earl of Huntingdon observed that the town was "very dusty and solitary."

Advice to a Painter. 1701 must have been written soon after 30 June, while the engraving was still being sold, for it would have had no relevance thereafter. *The Retrievement* ("Pamper'd in Kentish Meads with pickl'd feed"), dated 1703 but published on 27 November 1702 (Luttrell copy, Pickering & Chatto Catalogue 244, Item 11908), is partly an answer to the present poem.

Advice to a Painter. 1701

Painter, I've seen a Picture represent
The Five illustrious Gentlemen of Kent.

Painter, as I went t'other day to 'Change
The Poultry way, I saw a very strange
Piece of your Art upon a signe and stall:
Five heads with but three legs to walk withall;
The one the Bookeseller did represent,
The other the brave gentlemen of Kent.
Just such a Piece as that, for size, I'd have,
But for each Hero there pourtray a *Knave:*
Each Traytor's Guilt discover in his Face,
And let just Art detect their want of Grace.
  Draw *Robin Hood* a plotting in a Chair,
And *Little John* well pleas'd to see him there,
Brothers in Villany, as next in Shire.
Place *Harcourt* next, and then let *Finch* appear;

1. *'Change:* The speaker is to be imagined walking east, past T. Cockerill's print shop in the Poultry, toward the Royal Exchange.

4. *three legs:* T. Cockerill's shop was at the sign of the Bible and Three Legs, in the Poultry.

7. *size:* "The Effigies of the five Kentish Gentlemen" were "done from the Life; in one large sheet of Paper" (Arber, *3*, 258).

11. *Robin Hood a plotting:* Harley (*A Prophecy,* 24 *n.*, below) would have every reason to be plotting at the end of June 1701. He was in danger of being abandoned by both parties. On 27 June "and perhaps very often" during the next few days until the king went to Holland, he was at Hampton Court with Sunderland (*Advice to a Painter,* 57 *n.*, above). But he was not included in Sunderland's plan for a new ministry, which materialized during the summer, and by November he was, as his new friend, young Henry St. John said, "our *quondam* Speaker" (Hardwicke, *2*, 458; HMC *Downshire MSS.*, *1*, ii, 804, 811).

12. *Little John:* Although he represented New Radnor, Radnorshire, in parliament, Robert Harley had his seat at Brampton Castle, Hereford. His "Brother in Villany" is almost certainly John Howe of Stowell Park, who represented the neighboring county of Gloucester.

14. *Harcourt:* "Harcourt is in the secret with Robin," a correspondent wrote to Thomas Coke on 7 June 1701 (HMC *Cowper MSS.*, *2*, 428). Simon Harcourt (1661?–1727), of Stanton Harcourt and the Inner Temple, had been a schoolmate of Robert Harley and was now his close collaborator in the Commons, where he sat for Abingdon, Berkshire (1690–1705, 1710–13) and Cardigan, Cardiganshire (1710). During the

The Five Kentish Petitioners. Engraving by Robert White

Let *Tallard*'s Gold and *Sydney*'s Blood be there;
Then *Kit* the Trimmer, and when these you've drew,
The *Merry Andrew* of St. *Bartholomew*
Bring in with his Fool's Coat, and close the Shew.
  But hold—there are a Couple wanting yet,

---

session of 1701, he served on the committee that drafted the Act of Settlement (see *A New Satyr on the Parliament,* 96 *n.*, above) and managed the impeachment proceedings against Somers (*CJ, 13,* 401, 489).

Finch: Heneage Finch (see *The Dispensary, 1,* 50 *n.*, above), a member for Oxford University, was one of the reasons why Sunderland feared the eloquence of Tory orators in the Commons. He distinguished himself in the next session by offering an amendment "to the Clause, abjuring the Prince of *Wales,* so that it imported only an obligation not to assist him; [which] he pressed . . . with unusual vehemence, in a Debate that he resumed seventeen times in one Session, against all rules" (Burnet, *2,* 298).

15. *Tallard's Gold:* Camille d'Hostun, duc de Tallard, arrived in London as Louis XIV's ambassador in November 1700. In December it was observed that there were almost as many French *louis d'ors* in circulation in London as there were English gold guineas (BM Add. MS. 17677UU, ff. 353–53v). When Tallard was recalled in April 1701, 50,000 *louis d'ors* were dispatched to him to enable him to "pay his debts" (BM Add. 30000E, f. 25). If Simon Harcourt was a recipient of French gold, which was said to be his magnetic "pole" in *The Second Part* of *A New Satyr on the Parliament,* it may have been because the estates he inherited in 1688 were "in a very embarrassed condition" (*DNB, 8,* 1206).

Sydney's Blood: as Charles II's solicitor-general, Heneage Finch managed the state trial by which Algernon Sidney was wrongly convicted of high treason. The day after Sidney was beheaded on Tower Hill, it was prophesied that the perpetrators of this injustice would "tremble at the guilt" of Sidney's blood "untimely spilt" (*POAS,* Yale, *3,* 460).

16. *Kit the Trimmer: Sir Christopher Musgrave* (1632?–1704) owed his election as the second member for Oxford University "in a great measure" to Harley (HMC *Portland MSS., 4,* 14). Both his changing from side to side as interest dictated and his collaboration with Harley in 1701 were reported by L'Hermitage: "Musgrave se trouva un de ceux qui estoient le plus près de l'orateur . . . toujours distingué parmy ceux qui estoient oposéz à la cour, mais presentement il change de sentimens" (BM Add. MS. 17677WW, f. 295).

17. *Bartholomew:* Sir Bartholomew Shower (1658–1701), like Robert Harley a renegade dissenter, became a well-known lawyer and Tory politician, whose success could be measured in terms of "great gilt Coaches" (*The Grove: Or, the Rival Muses, POAS,* 1707, *4,* 359). He was knighted by James II in 1687, prosecuted the seven bishops in June 1688, defended Fenwick in November 1696 and Duncombe in June 1699. He was a political client of Sir Edward Seymour, with whom he shared the representation of Exeter, and of the old East India Company. In 1701 he was active in the impeachment proceedings against Lord Orford and made himself so obnoxious to the upper house that they struck his name from the list of commissioners to examine the public accounts, "for being a lawyer" (*CJ, 13,* 516; Vernon, *3,* 149–50). He died in December 1701, allegedly from "a debauch of ill wine" (HMC *Cowper MSS.,* 2, 441).

For whose Effigies thou art in *England*'s Debt,
Old *Ned;* and let me see—a Coronet,
A *Hide*-bound Carkass, that deserves no Name,
But what of old in *French* from *Dunkirk* came;
When his vile Sire that Fortress did betray,
To those his Son would *sell us all away.*
Now *Auro Patriam* for their Motto chuse,
And say, We have a Right to speak that lose.

21. *Old Ned:* Sir Edward Seymour; see *Advice to a Painter,* 108 *n.,* above; *A New Satyr on the Parliament,* 41 *n.,* 82 *n.,* above.

Coronet: Laurence Hyde, first earl of Rochester and brother-in-law to James II; see *A Conference between King William and the Earl of Sunderland,* 127 *n.,* above and *A New Satyr on the Parliament,* headnote, p. 318, above. In June 1701 Rochester delayed taking up his post as lord lieutenant of Ireland until he had reshuffled the deputy lieutenants and judges of the peace in England to prevent any further demonstrations like the Kentish petition (BM MS. Add. 17677WW, f. 322v).

22. *Name:* The word in French is presumably *traître.*

24. *Sire:* In October 1662 Rochester's father, Edward Hyde, first earl of Clarendon (1609–74), who was then lord chancellor of England, sold Dunkirk to France for 5,000,000 *livres* (*POAS,* Yale, *1,* 43, 91).

26. *Auro Patriam:* "The motto under the pictures of the 5 Kentish gentlemen is look't upon as a reflection, viz. Non auro patriam, or, They have not sold their countrey for gold" (Luttrell, *5,* 68).

A Paradox in Praise of War
(Before October 1701)

A Paradox in Praise of War and Addison's *The Play-House,* both of which appeared in the same number of *A Pacquet from Parnassus* in 1702, became poems on affairs of state by a kind of historical accident. Just as some people blamed the stage for the new immorality, so others, including the anonymous author of the present poem, were sure that peace was to blame.

The issue of peace or war had been the dominant one in England since November 1700 when Louis XIV tore up the second partition treaty and allowed his grandson, the duc d'Anjou, to be crowned Felipe V of Spain. The Whigs were the war party, convinced that the only alternative to war, as the earl of Shaftesbury said, was to "leave the Duke of Anjou on the Throne of Spain, and France in the consequence master of the world" (*Original Letters,* p. 160). The Tories were the party of peace, convinced that "all that Noise and Eagerness for a War with France" was designed to cover up the Whigs' peculations in the last war (*A Pacquet from Parnassus,* Vol. I, No. 1, 1702, 8). "What is't to us who's King of *Spain*" was the refrain of a popular Tory song (*Wit and Mirth,* 1714, *5,* 246).

In this context, the present poem, whatever its intent, could not help being read by Whigs with great satisfaction. As early as 9 May 1701, however, there were defections from the Tory position. "Jack Howe . . . came off from them, and declar'd a warr seem'd now necessary, the designs of France being so apparent" (*Original Letters,* p. 137) and a month later the Tory leaders, Rochester, Godolphin, Abingdon, Seymour, Musgrave, and Harcourt, meeting in secret caucus at Lord Nottingham's house, reluctantly agreed to the necessity for war (*CJ, 13,* 631; BM MS. Add. 30000E, ff. 283v–84). By October 1701 Charles Davenant, the leading Tory propagandist, was known to be writing a book "to shew the necessity and equity of a war against France" (Luttrell, *5,* 100). By this time, therefore, war and peace had virtually ceased to be a party issue and the present poem may be assumed to have been written before this. After England declared war on France, on 4 May 1702, it would have had no point at all.

A Paradox in Praise of War

Peace, thou Corrupter of Morality,
Mother of Shame and base Security:
Whose Beggar'd Womb so many Bastards brings,
Three parts must Starve; the rest, like Demy-Kings,
Reign o'er their Brothers; all maligne their Birth
To have One Father, yet are Slaves on Earth.
Aid me, ye Powers, whose influence got you Fame,
To rip the Womb of *Peace,* and shew her Shame:
Peace makes fair Show, but yet 'tis foul within,
Peace like to Rivers feeds a Sea of Sin.
Let War in Foreign Lands hunt drowzie *Peace,*
And in a just Cause Mans Renown Increase.
'Tis wholesome War dissolves the cause of Sin;
Men best Repent when Dangers near begin
To show their Faces; but while *Peace* does hold,
Our Strength is Weak, and our Devotion cold.
Safety from Worldly Danger makes Men think,
They that stand fast on Earth, shall never sink.
The Countrey Miser who his Bags preserves,
And feeds him Fat while many Thousands Starves,
Is this occasioned by this Sloathful *Peace,*
Which lessens Vertue, to make Vice increase.
'Tis fearless *Peace,* makes pleasure Mans chief God.
We want both Sight and Feeling of Wars Rod.
That Land more happy is that War doth nourish,
Causing the World in better State to flourish.
For danger makes us fear a sudden end,
War sads the Soul because it did offend.
The fear of Danger makes each Man prepar'd,
And of his ill-past life to have regard.
Danger calls Conscience to a strict Account,
Repentance makes a heavy Soul to mount.
'Tis soft Security lulls Men in Sin,
Where only Heav'n is Earths delight to win.

'Tis Idle Peace that breeds in us such Faction,
As kills at Home for want of Foreign Action.
The Valiant Man does hence his Fame increase;
Maintains himself by War, grows poor by Peace.
Hence flow the Fountains of detested Vice,
Sloath, Lust, Deceit, and filthy Avarice.
Extortion, Usury, and Gains excess,
Griping the Substance of the Fatherless:
So they by use or fraud their Bags may fill,
In Shew of Goodness they'll Commit all Ill;
Cheat their own Brother to get Worldly Dross,
And make them Poor by Law, who such dares cross.
For this Almighty Gold is of that force,
As Muffles Justice, and Exiles Remorse.
Gold in these Times can turn the Wheel of Fate,
And make them best Belov'd who merit Hate.
Gold can make Peace joyn Hands of deadly Foes,
Gold can make War again, Wound Peace with Blows.
'Tis Peace that makes this *Indian* God Ador'd,
This Golden Calf their Soveraign and Lord.
Gold in the Soul breeds such an Alteration,
That some desire it more than their Salvation.
Some cut Mens Throats for Gold, Committ all Evils,
Gold makes them Gods on Earth, and in Hell Devils.
Peace makes Religion Faint, and not regarded,
Vertue a Beggar, Learning unrewarded.

35–36. Cf. Defoe, *The Pacificator,* 27–32, and headnote, p. 157, above.

Daniel Defoe [?]

England's Late Jury
(November 1701)

The king came back to England for the last time on 4 November 1701 and the first decision he had to make, as Burnet says, was "whether the Parliament should be continued, or dissolved and a new one called" (Burnet, *2*, 295). The Tory leaders fought hard to prevent a dissolution, representing the dangers of another change of government in such perilous times. The people, on the other hand, wanted a new parliament; in one day "near 30 addresses were presented to the king, tending to dissolving the parliament" (Luttrell, *5*, 107). Vernon had warned the king in September that "great violence [was] intended next Sessions and that nothing would satisfy [the Tories] but the utter subduing of those whom they have sett themselves against" (BM MS. Add. 40775, Vol. 5, f. 116). When some of the Tory leaders actually told the king that "they would begin where they left off, and would insist upon [the] Impeachments" (*A New Satyr on the Parliament,* headnote, p. 318 and *2n.*, above) the king decided to dissolve his fifth parliament (Burnet, *2*, 295).

He had, besides, another motive. By recognizing the 13-year-old James Francis Edward, pretended prince of Wales, as king of England, Scotland, and Ireland, upon the death of James II at St. Germain in September, Louis XIV had done for William of Orange what the king had never been able to do for himself: he had made him popular. And now the king wanted to have this new popularity translated into a majority in the House of Commons that would vote the necessary supplies for the inevitable showdown with Louis XIV. So on 11 November 1701 he ordered writs for a new election.

The Whig propaganda machine was promptly cranked up for another contest with the New Country-Party. The present poem is an election pamphlet in verse. Probably the most effective, and certainly the most widely publicized of the Whig efforts was a black list of 167 members who were to be denied re-election. All of Defoe's "Jury" but Blathwayt are on this list.

The origins of the "Jury" can be traced back to 1695 when Thomas Bruce, earl of Ailesbury, who was himself negotiating with Louis XIV for "a competent number of troops" to restore James II, accidentally learned of the existence of a group of malcontents who "had entered into a sort of Association" for the same purpose. This group included "Sir Edward Seymour . . . , Mr. John How, Sir Chr. Musgrave, Mr. Heneage Finch . . . , Sir Simon Harcourt (the most zealous of all there) and others to the number of thirty Commoners" (Ailesbury, *1*, 359).

The effectiveness of the propaganda against the "Jury" may be measured by the fact that four of the 12 were not re-elected in December 1701: Charles Davenant, Anthony Hammond, John Howe, and Matthew Prior.

The evidence for Defoe's authorship of the present poem is very slight: lines 111–15 are reworked from lines 86–95 of *A New Satyr on the Parliament* and by a kind of literary Occam's razor it is easier to believe that Defoe did the reworking rather than some plagiarist; lines 43–45 and 89–90 supply typical examples of Defovian grammar, elliptical and telegraphic.

The date of the poem is less problematical. Since *England's Late Jury. A Satyr: With The Counter-Part, In Answer to it* was advertised in *The Post Boy,* No. 1022, 2–4 December 1701, the poem itself was presumably published in November.

England's Late Jury

Wisely an Observator said
(Who knew our State full well),
England need never be afraid,
Or seek out for a Foreign Aid,
Our Dangers to Repel.

But then he never did suppose
Our Army near so small;
Or Statesmen to oblige their Foes,
Should with seven Thousand wipe our Nose:
A Force like none at all.

This Vote made *Lewis* give a Smile
And Laugh within his Sleeve;
Scarce did he Credit it a while,
Brittain shou'd for his Glory toil,
Which now he does believe.

But when again such men were chose
As did our Force Disband;
He found our Ruine follow'd close,
And had no Reason to oppose
Such as went Hand in Hand.

Seymour forgets he was a Slave,
When in his Younger years,

7. *Army . . . so small:* By a bill introduced in December 1698 the army had been cut back to 7000 men; see Defoe, *An Encomium upon a Parliament,* headnote, pp. 45–46, above.

16. *again . . . chose:* All members of the "Jury" who sat in the fourth parliament of William III were re-elected (in January 1701) to the fifth Parliament. Three of them, however—Heneage Finch, Matthew Prior, and Sir Thomas Powys—did not sit in the fourth parliament.

21. *Slave:* Seymour "Was always suspected to be in the *French* Interest . . . and was openly visited by the *French* Ambassador" (Macky, pp. 111–12). It was during his term as speaker that a wooden shoe, the symbol of enslavement by the French, was left in

He was the Speaker and a Knave;
And not so much inclin'd to Save,
Or think upon our Fears.

But then there lay a Patent by
To Gratifie his Pride;
On which he often cast an Eye,
And on the Stop did wonder why
Totness was not supplyed.

---

the speaker's chair in the House of Commons, and as recently as June 1701 a mock resolution of the House of Commons had been circulated which "*Resolved,* That the Three Kingdoms be offered for Sale [and] *Ordered,* That Sir Edward Seymour inform the King of France" (HMC *Seventh Report,* 1879, p. 491; BM MS. Add. 17677WW, f. 282).

23. *Speaker and a Knave:* Although his election as speaker in February 1673 was unanimous, it was never seriously doubted that Seymour was totally dependent on the court, for he already held two lucrative offices in the navy and was appointed a privy councillor during the summer of 1673. Accordingly, in November 1673, with Black Rod at the door summoning the Commons to their prorogation, he avoided a motion "*That our Alliance with* France *was a Grievance*" simply by vacating the chair, and on another occasion he adjourned the House "by the Kings order," without even putting the question, and when some of the angry members offered to hold him in the chair, "he leaped from it very nimbly" (*Memoirs of Sir John Reresby,* ed. Andrew Browning, Glasgow, 1936, pp. 123–24). In the articles of impeachment that were exhibited against him in November 1680 he was accused of misappropriating funds which the Commons had voted "to enter into an actual War against the French" and other financial peculations (*CJ, 9,* 658–59; BM MS. Add. 9291, f. 1).

24. *not . . . inclin'd to Save:* Seymour was a noted gambler and it was objected to him as speaker that he compromised the honor of the House "in resorting to Gaming-houses . . . and ill places" (*Parl. Hist., 4,* 590). Despite his salary of £3000 a year as treasurer of the navy and another £3000 a year paid him out of the secret service funds, he was £16,000 in debt to the crown in 1688 and secured a special clause in the Act of Indemnity to release him from that debt ([Anthony Hammond], *Considerations upon the Choice of a Speaker,* 1698, rptd. *A Collection of State Tracts,* 3 vols., 1705–07, 2, 652).

26. *a Patent:* In October 1682 Rochester attempted to obtain the privy seal for Seymour (even though Charles had promised it to Halifax): "the Lord Rochester underhand did endeavour to obtean it for Mr. Seamure." So when Halifax got it, as well as the marquisate, which was supposed to compensate him for the loss, Seymour "retired from court into the country much disgusted" (*Memoirs of Sir John Reresby,* pp. 289–90; Luttrell, *1,* 232).

29–30. Perhaps these lines mean: when denied the privy seal, Seymour wondered why he was not made a marquis [e.g. of Totnes] as Halifax had been. In August 1682 there had been a rumor that he would be created baron Pomeroy. Such rumors, in fact, recurred frequently: in March 1692 it was reported that he would be created viscount Totnes; in December 1700 earl of Bristol (Luttrell, *1,* 213; *2,* 374; BM MS. Add. 17677UU, f. 360v).

Resenting an Affront like this,
He forthwith veers about,
Mad that he did Preferment miss,
(A Feather fit for Pride like his)
And Courts the fickle Rout.

But his Designs are understood,
The matter's very plain:
Pretending for his Countreys good,
He since has acted all he cou'd,
To keep his Prince in Pain.

For a long time he cou'd not Swear,
With a nice Conscience bred;
Nor take an Oath against an Heir,
That to a Monarch did Repair,
At least till he was Dead.

But when All-Conquering Gold was brought,
Which Glisten'd in his Eyes,
Quickly a Miracle was wrought,
(*Exeter* knows it was no Fault)
They that have Wealth are Wise.

Musgrave has Parts, and Eloquence,
And others say speaks well,
Tho' Young *Kit* met a Recompence,

40. *keep his Prince in Pain:* Seymour did this by supporting Monmouth in 1682–83, opposing standing armies in 1685, and refusing, in February 1689, to admit that the throne was vacant. Cf. *The Reverse,* 53–60 and notes, above.

43. *Oath:* William of Orange occupied Exeter on 9 November 1688. Seymour waited eight days before coming forward to offer his services. Then he proposed that all those about the prince should bind themselves by oath to support him. Two days later, when William marched on to London, he left all of Devonshire under Seymour's command (Burnet, *1,* 792–93). Seymour took the oaths of allegiance to William and Mary on 2 March 1689.

50. Cf. *The Dispensary, 2,* 94, above, and *The True-Born Englishman,* 592, above.

51. *Musgrave:* See *Advice to a Painter.* 1701, 16 *n.,* above. Burnet (*2,* 410–11) called him "the head of the opposition" to William III and "the wisest Man of the Party."

53. *Young Kit:* Christopher Musgrave, the second son of Sir Christopher by his first wife. His "Recompense" may have been the post in the ordnance to which he was appointed in July 1689. If this is the case, it did not "Bias" his father, for Sir

To bring his Father to his Sense,
Spight did the Guilt Repel.

Nothing can Bias stout Sir *Kit,*
Civility is Vain,
For he must Exercise his Wit,
And sometimes did at Random hit,
Which Credit did obtain.

Harcourt pretends unto the Law,
And makes a fearful din;
As little Sense as e'er I saw,
His Judgement brittle as a Straw,
And oftner out than in.

Finch, he has Sense and Rethorick,
And seems of *Seymour*'s Kidney.
His Lungs do to the Quarrel stick,
And once was very Politick,
And some think hard on *Sidney.*

Hammond, he runs among the Herd;
Is Violent and Strong;

Christopher's behavior in the Commons, as viscount Sydney observed in 1692, continued to be inexcusable (*CSPD 1689–1690,* p. 187; *CSPD 1691–1692,* p. 333).

60. *Credit:* Although "head of the opposition," Musgrave "gave up many points of great importance in the critical minute," for which, Burnet (2, 411) estimated, the king paid him "at different times" £12,000. Alexander Pope records an accident to a bag of gold guineas on one of these occasions (*Epistle III. To Allen Lord Bathurst,* 65–68).

61. *Harcourt:* See *Advice to a Painter. 1701,* 14 *n.,* above.

66. *Finch:* See *The Dispensary, 1,* 50 *n.,* above; *Advice to a Painter. 1701,* 14 *n.,* above.

67. *Seymour's Kidney:* Finch, Seymour, and Sir Christopher Musgrave were among the "very few" who voted against the motion that James II had abdicated the government (Luttrell, *1,* 499).

70. *Sidney:* See *Advice to a Painter. 1701,* 15 *n.,* above.

71. *Hammond:* Anthony Hammond (1668–1738), the Tory member for Huntingdonshire (1695–98), Cambridge University (1698–1701), Huntingdon, Huntingdonshire (1702–05), and New Shoreham, Sussex (1708), was, as Dr. Johnson said, "a man of note among the wits, poets, and parliamentary orators in the beginning of [the 18th] century" (*Lives, 2,* 313). He was particularly noted for "his noisy Tory eloquence" in the House of Commons, but he also wrote amatory verse and at least two political pamphlets, *Considerations upon the Choice of Speaker,* 1698, and *Considerations upon*

Wou'd fain seem Grave without a Beard:
But he needs never to be feard;
His Judgement is too Young.

Jack Howe sets up for one of Sense,
Does for a *Patriot* stand.
Most wonder at his Impudence,
That he thereto should lay Pretence,
Who was the Courts Disband!

He who was reckon'd the Buffoon,
In former Parliaments,
Fickle and Changing like the Moon,
Till *French* Gold came he was undone,
Now Vents his Discontents.

But most Men wonder that Sir *Batt*
So Eager is to rail:

Corrupt Elections, 1701 (Hearne, *9,* 264; *Philological Quarterly, 31* [January 1952], 45–53). He ran with the High Church "Herd," which was hot to enforce the penal laws against Catholics and to "make the Bishops less dependent upon the Crown" (Vernon, *2,* 428; Bodl. MS. Rawl. A.245, f. 83v).

75. *Judgement:* Lord Chesterfield, who enjoyed Hammond's company, observed that he had "all the senses but common sense" and another friend admitted that he "had but a small portion of solid understanding" (Johnson, *Lives, 2,* 313, n. 1; *DNB, 8,* 1124). In January 1698 Hammond was wounded in a duel with Lord William Paulet over an election dispute and two months later he was involved in a squabble over a cookmaid that required attention by the House of Commons (Luttrell, *4,* 337; *CJ, 12,* 140). In September 1701 he was seriously compromised by being discovered at supper with Jean Baptiste Poussin, the French *chargé d'affaires,* and some other dignitaries, when Poussin was served with orders to leave the country (HMC *Cowper MSS., 2,* 436).

76. *Jack Howe:* The member for Gloucestershire (see *Advice to a Painter,* 108 *n.,* above) was said to be "le plus hardi personnage de toute la Chambre de Communes" in his opposition to the court, "homme d'esprit, mais de peu de jugement" (BM MS. Add. 30000E, f. 43v).

80. *the Courts Disband:* Apparently this means the "discard" or "reject" of the court. Howe was in fact dismissed from his post as vice-chamberlain to Queen Mary in March 1692, allegedly for "singing bawdy Songs behind Her Closet at Chapel, in time of Divine Service, and for other lewd Tricks amongst the Ladies at Court" (*A New Dialogue between Monsieur Shaccoo and the Poussin Doctor,* 1701, rptd. *England's Late Jury. A Satyr: with The Counter-Part, In Answer to it,* 1702, p. 25).

84. *French Gold:* It was rumored that the favorite toast at Versailles and St. Germain during the summer of 1701 was "A la santé Monsieur Jaccou"; cf. *The History of the Kentish Petition,* 1701, sig. A3r; Oldmixon, p. 217.

86. *Sir Batt:* Sir Bartholomew Shower, or Batt Shoar, as he was familiarly designated, was the member for Exeter (see *Advice to a Painter. 1701,* 17 *n.,* above).

Yet why should we admire at that,
Since his Profession is to chat,
But seldom does prevail?

Some (he had heard) by Speeches rise,
And to Preferment leap;
But such had *Merit,* and were Wise,
And did not Foreigners despise,
Nor after Faction creep,

Never for Rebells did Harrangue,
Nor Tenter-Hook the Law;
But left the Criminal to Hang,
'Till one Foot did the other bang,
To keep Mankind in Awe.

The Fam'd *Civilian* who can write
Of Parliamental Power,
If he has Judgment he has Spite,
And goes beyond the matter quite,
A short of second *SHOWER.*

Upon Records he spends his Ink;
He Writes at such a Rate,

101. *Fam'd Civilian:* Charles Davenant, self-styled Doctor of Civil Laws. His books on "Parliamental Power" included *A Discourse upon Grants and Resumptions,* 1700, and *Essays upon I. The Ballance of Power. II. The Right of Making War, Peace, and Alliances,* 1701. He was the member for Great Bedwin, Wilts., and "faithfully voted with *How, Seymour, Shower, Harley,* &c." "That *Tallard* courted this *Davenant,* was apparent; that he corrupted him, was suppos'd" (Oldmixon, p. 217). Davenant was recruited by the French in August 1701 but his usefulness to them came to an abrupt end a month later when he, along with Anthony Hammond (71–75, above) and others, was discovered at supper with the French *chargé d'affaires* (Swift, *Discourse,* pp. 73–79). In December 1701 it was rumored that he was bringing action against Sir Richard Holford for "affronting him at Garaways coffee house, [and] calling him French pensioner, the Poussin doctor, count Tallards mercenary writer, &c." (Luttrell, *5,* 116).

106. *Records:* The 125 pages of *"Records Referr'd to in the Second Essay,"* which Davenant appended to his *Essays,* 1701, were the cause of much merriment: "he has taken a great deal of pains," it was pointed out, "in hunting for *Knowledge that lies under abundance of Rubbish"* (Davenant's own phrase, quoted in *Jus Regium: Or, The King's Right to Grant Forfeitures,* 1701, p. 14).

107. Davenant was described as "a certain *indefatigable Writer,* who as long as [Louis XIV's] Gold has lasted, has been very useful to [the Jacobite] Cause, and boldly

To prove what few did ever think,
Unless depriv'd of Sense in Drink,
Yet of a Plodding Pate.

Granville, he Stroles unto the Fairs,
To get himself Renown;
Yet for this Faction he declares,
And to their Club at Night Repairs,
To Regulate the Crown.

The times are likely sure to mend,
When *Prior* Rules the State;
Prior the Noble *DORSET*'s Friend
(For whom the Learned World Contend),
Justly deserves his Hate.

Blathwayt with Proud Imperious Face,
And Forehead made of Brass;
Forgets the Honour of his Place;
Does all true Policy Disgrace,
And for a Fool may pass.

---

defeated the dangerous Counsels of the *Whigs*" (*Letters from the Dead to the Living,* 2nd ed., 1702, p. 54).

111. *Granville:* John Granville was the member for Fowey, Cornwall; see *A New Satyr on the Parliament,* 86–95 and notes, above.

117. *Prior:* Matthew Prior began his career as a Whig: he "grew magnificently great;/ . . . with *M*[*ontag*]*ue* ally'd" (*An Epistle to Sr. Richard Blackmore,* 1700, p. 10) and enjoyed flattering notices from the Whig poets Garth (*The Dispensary, 4,* 227) and Blackmore (*A Satyr against Wit,* 252–55). But when the Tory Edward Villiers, earl of Jersey, was appointed secretary of state in May 1699, Prior accepted an appointment as undersecretary; in fact it was Prior, as Tallard explained to Louis XIV, "qui fait tout" (PRO 31/3 186, f. 15v). Then in the last months of 1700 the new Tory managers decided that Prior was to occupy one of the seats in the borough of East Grinstead, Sussex, controlled by the earl of Dorset. Consequently, when the Tory majority in the House of Commons undertook to impeach the ousted Whig leaders, Prior earned himself a place in the present poem by voting "against Those that had established him in the World": Somers, Portland, and Montagu, now Lord Halifax (Macky, p. 135).

118. *Dorset:* See *Reformation of Manners,* 584 *n.,* below.

121–25. *Blathwayt . . . a Fool:* See *A New Satyr on the Parliament,* 201 *n.,* above. Blathwayt's "foolish manner" was the subject of much merriment. Prior, who called him "the Elephant," said he was "jocular and ignorant, disguising his want of knowing what is going on by affecting to keep it secret" (Gertrude A. Jacobsen, *William Blathwayt,* New Haven, Yale University Press, 1932, pp. 258, 268).

Powys shall Marshal up the Rear,
With Rethorick Debate;
And tho' good Natur'd he appear,
Yet all his Services will steer
To undermine the State.

These are the Jury which were struck
To try *Britania*'s Claim:
And how cou'd we expect good Luck,
From such as did with *LEWIS* truck,
To their Eternal Shame?

Conclusion.

Others below the Dignity of Rhime,
Shall 'scape my Satyr till another time.
Twelve Men like these, a Nation might undo,
And let 'em, if again we trust 'em, too.
No, no, fair *Britain,* at her Wrongs awakes,
Finds what ye mean, and other methods takes.
Your Popularity at last Expires,
And Men of better Tempers she requires:
Dispis'd at home, mutter your Discontent,
And know the Nation spoke her mind by *KENT*.

126. *Powys:* Sir Thomas Powys (1649–1719) succeeded Heneage Finch as James II's solicitor-general in April 1685, upon which occasion he was "confidently said to be a papist" (Luttrell, *1,* 375–76). Knighted in April 1686, he was promoted to attorney-general in December 1687 and conducted the prosecution of the seven bishops in June 1688. In the next reign he held no public office until January 1701 when he was elected to represent the borough of Ludlow, Shropshire (1701–13). In 1696, however, he defended Sir John Fenwick (see *Advice to a Painter,* 14 *n.,* above) at the bar of both houses. Even in his maiden term in the Commons, he earned a great reputation for oratory, and it was said that "ev'ry Period falling from his Tongue/Reveals a Knowledge like his Reasons strong" ([William Pittis], *The Patriots,* 1702, p. 11). Cf. *The Golden Age Restor'd,* 21 *n.,* below.

136. *below the Dignity of Rhime:* Cf. *Absalom and Achitophel,* 570: "below the dignity of Verse." Defoe quotes Dryden's phrase exactly in *More Reformation,* 633, below.

The Fall of the House of Orange-Nassau

The death of two kings of England within six months stirred Grub Street to a veritable superfetation of elegy. James II died at St. Germain-en-Laye on 5 September 1701 "between Three and Four that Afternoon," and on the same day Louis XIV allowed James Francis Edward, the 13-year-old pretended prince of Wales to be proclaimed king of England, Scotland, and Ireland.

Within three days elegies to James II began to be hawked on the streets of London and since none of these works found their way into *Poems on Affairs of State,* a list of some of them, of which all but the last were folio half-sheets, may be included here:

On the Much Lamented Death of the Most Serene and Illustrious Prince, James VII and II, King of Great Britain, France and Ireland ("All-Conquering Death, and even Fortune too"), n.d.

An Elegie upon the Much Lamented Death of the Most Serene and Potent Prince, James VII ("Before Sin tainted the pure Universe"), n.d.

J. M., *An Ode: or Elegy on the Death of James the Second, Late King of England* ("See how the wrangling World in fumes arise"), 1701

An Ode on the Death of the Late King James. Written Originally in French at St. Germains ("My Muse, let sacred Truth be now thy guide"), 1701

An Elegy on the Death of James the Second, Late King of England ("'Tis true—when Death, Fate's Minister does call"), 1701

An Elegy on the Death of the Late King James ("What rumour's this, as does our Ears amuse?"), 1701 [Luttrell copy at Harvard dated 8 September 1701]

[William Pittis], *The Generous Muse. A Funeral Poem, in Memory of His Late Majesty King James the II* ("What? Shall the Croud his Injur'd Name blaspheme"), 1701

André Bonet, the London resident of the king of Prussia, was surprised that this Jacobite literature could circulate so freely and put it down to the "douceur" of the Tory ministry (BM MS. 30000E, f. 352v). John Tutchin reacted more violently. "Did you ever read the Poem, called, the *Generous Muse?*" he asked. "Is not there a fine piece of Stuff in commendation of K. *James*" (*The Mouse Grown a Rat,* [1702], p. 32). It was *The Generous Muse,* therefore, that precipitated Tutchin's *The British Muse: Or Tyranny Expos'd. A Satyr, Occasion'd by All the Fulsom and Lying Poems and Elegies, that have been Written on the Occasion of the Death of the Late King James* ("For Tyrants dead no Statues we erect"), 1702. *The British Muse* was reprinted in *POAS,* 1703, 2, 387–95, but since it is nowhere so effective as in its title, it has been omitted from the present collection.

One effect of Louis' recognition of James Francis Edward as king of England was to unleash a wave of popular sympathy for William III. Hundreds of addresses from all parts of England poured into London deploring the presumption of the French king and offering to stand by William with their authors' lives and purses. Upon the news of his majesty's landing at Margate, the citizens of Hereford gave vent to their feelings "by Ringing of Bells, Bonfires, and Illuminations, and all imaginable Demonstrations . . . of Loyalty, Duty, and Affection to His Majesty's Person and Government" (*The London Gazette,* No. 3758, 13–17 November 1701). Nothing like this had happened since November 1688.

But, unfortunately, William was dying. He lay ill at Loo almost the whole month of October. As soon as he was well enough, he returned to England, dissolved his fifth parliament, and issued writs to elect a new one. Godolphin resigned immediately and Rochester was expected to do so upon his arrival from Dublin. Sir Thomas Littleton, a Whig, was designated to succeed Harley as speaker and Somers translated into English the speech the king wrote to deliver at the opening of his sixth parliament on 31 December 1701. "It is fit I should tell you," he said, that

> the Eyes of all *Europe* are upon this Parliament; all Matters are at a stand till your Resolutions are known; and therefore no Time ought to be lost.
>
> You have yet an Opportunity, by God's Blessing, to secure to

The Death of William III. Anonymous engraving

> you, and your Posterity, the quiet Enjoyment of your Religion and Liberties, if you are not wanting to yourselves, but will exert the antient Vigour of the *English* Nation: But I tell you plainly, My Opinion is, If you do not lay hold on this Occasion, you have no Reason to hope for another.
>
> (*CJ, 13,* 647)

Whigs and Tories were so evenly divided in the sixth parliament that Harley was able to upset the king's calculations by winning the election for speaker by four votes (Ralph, *2,* 1005), but it made little difference since Whigs and Tories were now agreed on the necessity for reducing the exorbitant power of France.

Sometime this winter, in his garden at Hampton Court, the king told Portland "that he found himself so weak, that he did not expect to live another Summer" (*The Life of William III,* 2nd ed., 1703, p. 631). On 21 February his horse stumbled as he was putting him to the gallop and the king's collarbone was broken in the fall (see illustration, p. 364). "It [was] a strange thing," he said, "for it happened upon a smooth level ground" (*Parl. Hist., 5,* 1341). By 4 March the king felt well enough to take several turns in the picture gallery at Kensington, but on the same day he was seized with "an Ague Fit," as it was called, and two days later he knew that the end had come. He entrusted the key to his escritoire to Albemarle and reminded him that he knew what to do with the contents. About eight o'clock the next morning, "sitting upon his Bed in his Night-gown," the king died "in the Arms of Mr. *Sewell,* one of the Pages of the Back-Stairs" (see illustration, p. 355). Sir Richard Blackmore was one of the physicians in attendance.

Elegies to William appeared in the streets almost as soon after his death as those after the death of James II and in much greater number—in such numbers, in fact, that it would be not practical to list them all here. The first that is possible to date is an anonymous folio half-sheet entitled *An Ode on the Death of King William III* ("Great William, to the Shades of Death confin'd") of which the Luttrell copy, now in the Newberry Library, is dated 13 March 1702. But the elegies to William III did not need to remain anonymous. Nor were they confined to English: one in French was published in London, *Elegie sur la Mort du Trés-puissant Prince, Guillaume III. Roy d'Angleterre* ("Helas! il ne vit plus, Ah! perte irreparable"),

1702, and another published in London was translated from Dutch: *Batavia in Tears: or an Elegy from the Dutch, upon the Melancholy News of the Ever to be Lamented Death of that Glorious Monarch, William III* ("Ye Liquid Streams, which thro' our Sluces glide"), 1702.

Those elegies to William that were not printed anonymously are the following:

John Hughes, *The House of Nassau. A Pindarick Ode* ("Goddess of Numbers, and of Thoughts sublime"), 1702; reprinted *POAS,* 1703, 2, 325

Francis Manning, *The Shrine. A Poem Sacred to the Memory of King William III* ("Farewel thou Last and Greatest of thy Race"), [10 July] 1702

Joseph Harris, *A Poem Humbly Offer'd to the Pious Memory of His Late Sacred Majesty King William III* ("That Grecian Bard who sweetly Sung of old"), 1702

Richard Daniel, *A Dream; or, An Elegiack Poem Occasion'd by the Death of William III* ("The Shades of waning Night had now begun"), Dublin, 1702

John Dennis, *The Monument: A Poem Sacred to the Immortal Memory of the Best and Greatest of Kings, William the Third* ("What sudden Damp has seiz'd upon my Soul?"), [18 June] 1702

John Oldmixon, *A Funeral Idyll, Sacred to the Memory of K. William III* ("Oh thou, who lately by this silver Stream"), 1702

E. Lewis, *The Weeping Muse. A Poem Sacred to the Memory of His Late Majesty* ("Oh Muse! my only, and my last Relief!"), 1702

Gilbert Burnet, *An Elegy on the Death of that Illustrious Monarch William the Third, late King of England* ("Alas! 'tis so; no Virtue can withstand"), [March] 1702

J[oseph] S[tennett], *A Poem to the Memory of His Late Majesty William the Third* ("Where is the tuneful tribe that sang so well"), 1702

Even Sarah, countess of Marlborough, who had so long looked forward to the king's death, found that she felt "nothing of that satisfaction," which she once thought she "should have had upon this occasion" (*Account of the Conduct,* p. 120).

BRITTANIA's TEARS:
OR,
England's Lamentation.
IN AN
ELEGY.

Occaſion'd by the Death of Our ſo much Beloved Monarch, and Deliverer, His Late Moſt Gracious Majeſty, King *WILLIAM* III. Who Departed this Life, for the Obtaining a Crown of Glory, from the Hands of His Bleſſed Redeemer, *March* the 8*th*. 170$\frac{1}{2}$.

NO Longer, O thou God of Heav'n and Earth,
From whoſe Exiſtence all Things take their Birth:
No longer, O thou Sacred *Three* in *One*,
Who *knew all things*, before this World begun:
No longer, O thou God of *Nature*, ſave
This *Apoplectick Body* from the Grave;
Since the *firſt Spring*, which gave my Soul Delight,
Is vaniſh'd far above this Land of *Night*:
Oh, that my Head a Flood of Waters were,
And theſe Two blubb'ring Eyes both Fountains clear,
Then ſhou'd I, Day and Night, eſteem it beſt,
To *Sigh* ſome *Time* away, and *Weep* the Reſt.
Then ſhou'd my Widdow'd Soul exempt from Fears,
Moiſten its withring Limbs in Floods of Tears;
Then ſhou'd my Couch in Liquid Brine be made,
And I of Death, nor Nature be afraid:
Then wou'd I lie me down, and never Dream,
But Horror in my Sleep ſhould be ſupreme:
Nature ſhou'd know no Reſt, but loud Allarms
Of Fire and Plague; and all the illboding Harms
That ever in *Pandora*'s Box was known,
Should be amongſt thoſe, Murm'ring Mortals thrown.—

For why, *Brittania*, God has ta'en away
Thy Guardian Angel, whoſe Eternal Ray,
Shines more Reſplendant in a Glorious place,
Where Cherubs 'fore their Maker Vail their Face:

Ah, Heaven-born *WILLIAM*, Thou, whoſe Pious Soul
Darted its Virtues far above each Pole:
Thou, who was ſent by Heaven's ſtrict Decree,
To be our Man of War by Land and Sea:
Thou, who Eſpous'd the Mighty Cauſe of God,
And Puniſh'd Pop'ry with *JEHOVAH*'s *Rod*:
Why haſt Thou left us here, Depreſs'd with Grief,
And none behind like Thee, for our Relief?
Who ſhall Swim o'er the *Boyn*, to Fight our Cauſe,
Secure our Rights, Religion and our Laws?
Who ſhall indure Seven Toilſome Years Campaine,
And Run thoſe Riſques of Waſting o'er the Main?
Who ſhall Incourage Poor, and Suppreſs Vice,
And Study *England*'s Flouriſhing and Riſe?
Who ſhall Reduce a Faithleſs King to Reaſon,
And Puniſh Villians for their Helliſh Treaſon?
Who, who, I ſay, ſhall do ſuch mighty Things,
Now Thou art with thy God, the King of Kings:

None, poor *Brittania*, none, without *Jehove*,
Once more vouchſafes to Smile on us in Love.

Ah! bleſſed Monarch! Hear Thy Subjects Cryes,
Which do attend Thee to the Azure Skies;
Thou now art freed from all Conſpiracies,
All Machinations, Popiſh Treacheries:
God ſtill ſecur'd Thee from a ſudden Death,
And took Thy Soul as Calmly as Thy Breath:
He Crown'd Thy Reign, and ev'ry Glorious Action
With joynt Succeſs, to all our Satisfaction:
And now Thy Loſs is mourn'd by all, but thoſe
Who were to God and's People, ſecret Foes.

The Nation Weeps, now Prayers cann't avail,
And ev'ry Subject's Heart begins to fail,
For fear that *France* ſhould once Inſult again,
And Link us faſt unto his Slaviſh Chain:
The Soldier Weeps, becauſe his Monarch's Fled,
And fears he ne'er ſhall find another Head:
The Saylor Weeps, and makes the Ocean Swell,
And turns each Ship into a Weeping Well.
All who have any ſpark of Good, or Grace,
Appear abroad with a Dejected Face;
Our Foreign Neighbours Grieve he Dy'd ſo ſoon,
That *England*'s Sun ſhould Set before 'tis Noon;
The floating *Hollanders*, th' oppreſſed *Dutch*,
Bemoan his Loſs, and Heav'n the Jewel begrutch.

EPITAPH.

WILLIAM *the Third lyes here, th' Almighty's Friend,*
A Scourge to France, *a Check t' imperious* Rome,
Who did our Rights and Liberties defend,
And Reſcu'd England *from it's threaten'd Doom.*
Heav'n ſnatch'd Him from us whom our Hearts Carreſs'd,
And now He's King in Heav'n, among the Bleſt.
Grief ſtops my Pen:— Reader, pray Weep the Reſt.
Mœſtus Compoſuit, B. H.

London, Printed by *Benj. Harris*, at the Golden Boars-Head in *Grace-Church-Street*, 170$\frac{1}{2}$.

Britannia's Tears, a folio half-sheet, 1702

The first of the elegies listed above and two anonymous laments are included in *Poems on Affairs of State.* The anonymous elegies are *On King William the III* ("Great *Nassau,* from his Cradle to his Grave") (*POAS,* 1703, *2,* 468) and *Epitaph on King William, 1702* ("William the Third lies here, th' Almighty's Friend") (*POAS,* 1703, *2,* 267), which is only the epitaph of a folio half-sheet published under the title *Brittania's Tears: or, England's Lamentation. In an Elegy Occasion'd by the Death of Our So Much Beloved Monarch and Deliverer, His Late Most Gracious Majesty, King William III* ("No longer, O thou God of Heav'n and Earth"), dated 1701/2, and which included, in the style of the time (see illustration, p. 357), both elegy and epitaph. Despite its misleading subtitle (*A Satyr by Way of Elegy*), Defoe's *Mock Mourners* really belongs to the same category as the pure elegies.

From the critical point of view, however, by far the most interesting product of the king's death is the mock-elegies, a new genre in which Swift was to produce a minor masterpiece in 1722, *A Satirical Elegy on the Death of the Late Famous General.* These range in complexity from a very crude *Elegy on K.W.* ("Willie Nassau from the Hague,/The Isle of Britain's scourge and plague") (Chicago University MS. PR1195.M73, p. 71), which unfortunately suffers a collapse soon after this promising start, to the more sustained and sophisticated efforts that are included here.

1702

BEVIL HIGGONS[?]

The Mourners
(*March*[?] *1702*)

It had not been difficult to hate the king during his lifetime. His grotesque hooknose (see illustration, p. 513), his asthmatic cough and "ungraceful" laughter—even his bad habit of "folding down of the Leaves" of books of devotion that he read—provided ample reasons to dislike him. If the facts were disregarded it was even possible to believe him guilty of filial impiety: "s'il y a quelque justice sur la terre," Voltaire piously affirmed, "il n'appartenait pas . . . au gendre du roi jacques, de le chasser de sa maison" (Foxcroft, p. 193; *A Satyr upon King William,* 3rd ed., 1703, p. 32; [Voltaire], *Le Siècle de Louis XIV,* 2 vols., Berlin, 1751, *1,* 302).

Since it had been so easy to hate the king during his lifetime it is not surprising that the hatred survived his death. George Stepney attests to the variousness of the reaction:

> Let H[owe?] and S[ir?] I[ohn?] B[olles?] and thousands more
> Slander his Fame; let snarling S[edley?] roar,
> Sated with Spight . . . .
>
> (*Poems on Several Occasions,* 1703, p. 50)

The impression gained from the title given the following squib when it was reprinted in *POAS,* 1703, that copies were literally strewn in the streets of London is corroborated by *The Observator,* No. 25, 15–18 July 1702. The attribution to Bevil Higgons was made by Alexander Pope in his copy of *PRSA,* 1705, now in the British Museum (C.28.e.15). William J. Cameron, however, has demonstrated how unreliable these attributions may be (*N&Q, 203* [July 1958], 291–94).

The Mourners

In Sable Weeds the Beaux and Belles appear,
Dismal their out, what e'er their insides are.
Mourn on, you foolish fashionable things,
But mourn your own Condition, not the King's;
Mourn for the mighty Summs by him mis-spent,
Those prodigally given, those idly lent;
Mourn for the Statues, and the Tapestry too,
From *Windsor,* gutted to aggrandize *Loo.*
Mourn for the Miter long from *Scotland* gone,
And mourn as much the Union coming on.
Mourn for ten Years of War and dismal Weather,
For Taxes, strung like Necklaces together,

1. *Sable Weeds:* On 9 March 1702, the day after William died, the earl marshal ordered "the deepest mourning (long cloaks excepted)" for the dead king, "All Lords and Officers of the Household to cover their coaches with black cloth." For the citizenry, "Hatbands of black English Alamode covered with black crape" were *de rigueur* (Steele, No. 4312).

5. *mighty Summs:* See *Advice to a Painter,* 40 *n.,* above; *The Pacificator,* 17 *n.,* above. In December 1697 William was voted a civil list of £700,000 a year for life (see 14 *n.,* below).

7. *Statues, and . . . Tapestry: A mémoire* to the United Provinces, dated 24 July/3 August 1702, demanding repatriation of 17 tapestries and 32 paintings—including copies of the Raphael cartoons which had been at Windsor Castle—is preserved in BM MS. Add. 17677YY, ff. 26–27v.

9. *Miter . . . from Scotland gone:* William and Mary were crowned king and queen of Scotland on 11 May 1689. Since, as Burnet (2, 23) says, "the abolishing Episcopacy . . . was made a necessary Article of the new Settlement," an act of the Scottish parliament abolishing prelacy received the royal assent on 22 July 1689.

10. *Union:* In March 1689, only three months after his arrival in London, William recommended a union of the two kingdoms "living in the same island, having the same Language, and the same Common Interest of *Religion* and *Liberty.*" On 28 February, only a week before his death, he did "in the most earnest Manner" again recommended this matter to the consideration of the House of Commons (Oldmixon, pp. 25, 257). And the very evening before his death "he ask't a privy counsellor by him what the house of commons had done that day about an union with Scotland" (Luttrell, 5, 150).

11. *ten Years of War:* See *The Pacificator,* 13 *n.,* above.

12–13. Taxes on salt, malt, glass, and leather were all imposed for the first time during William's reign (*An Encomium upon a Parliament,* 66 *n.,* 67 *n.,* above). The

On Salt, Malt, Paper, Syder, Lights and Leather.
Much of the Civil List need not be said:
They truly mourn who're eighteen Months unpaid.
If matters then, my Friends, you see are so,
Tho now you mourn, 't had lessen'd much your Wo
Had *Sorrel* stumbled thirteen Years ago.

---

tax on cider, which had been 1*s*. 3*d*. per hogshead from the time of the Commonwealth, was increased to 2*s* 6*d* in 1690 (2 William & Mary Sess. 2 c. 10).

14. *Civil List:* the nonmilitary items of the national budget, including the civil service, judiciary, diplomatic and consular services, pension lists, royal household and privy purse. "William died with his Civil List heavily in debt, with more than a year's arrears unpaid on every branch of it." The debt amounted to £1,004,005 (*CTB 1695–1702*, p. xl; *CTB 1702*, p. 941).

18. *Sorrel:* See *Upon Sorrel,* 1 *n.*, below.

Thomas Smith [?]

Upon Sorrel
(*March*[?] *1702*)

On 16 April 1702, Dr. Thomas Smith, D.D. (1638–1710), in a long letter to his old friend Samuel Pepys, enclosed "a paper containing an epitaph upon the late high and mighty Dutch hero, as also some few heroic lines upon *Sorrell,*" which he warned Pepys to throw into the fire after a single reading (Pepys, *Corr., 2,* 262). Smith was an antiquarian—a fellow of the Royal Society and keeper of the Cottonian Library—who had been deprived of his fellowship in Magdalen College, Oxford, for refusing to take the oaths of allegiance to William and Mary. The epitaph is presumably the one preserved among Smith's papers in Bodl. MS. Smith 23, p. 121 ("Religion, loyalty and truth's perverter") and the "heroic lines upon *Sorrell*" are the Latin verses ("Illustris sonipes, certe dignissime coelo") of which the English translation is reproduced here. Much of what Smith wrote was in Latin—his prose style was said to be "somewhat intricate and too full of long periods"—and he is known to have written occasional verse—he contributed *To the Indefatigable Rhimer* ("O Somers, Talbot, Dorsett, Montague") to *Commendatory Verses* (1701). So he may have written both the Latin and English versions of *Upon Sorrel.* On the other hand, the verses must have been written somewhat earlier than mid-April, for the copy in BM MS. Add. 40060, f. 10v, is dated "Mar: 1701/2" and in his letter of 28 March to Pepys, Smith says nothing about verses, even while he is decrying James II's "unnaturall son in law and nephew" (Pepys, *Corr., 2,* 259). Alexander Pope, in his copy of *PRSA,* attributed *Upon Sorrel* to Bevil Higgons (but see *The Mourners,* headnote, p. 361, above).

Another translation of the same Latin epigram circulated with the first line, "Transcendent Sorrell worthy heav'n to grace" (BM MS. Add. 21094, f. 130), and this, in turn, generated an epigram, *Upon the Author of the Latin Epigram* ("Sorrell transform'd to Pegasus wee see") (Portland MS. Pw V 46, p. 309 and BM MS. Add. 21094, f.

The Fall of William III. Engraving by Reinier Vinkeles

130). The apotheosis of Sorrel is accomplished in *An Epitaph upon a Stumbling Horse* ("Here lyes a Horse beneath this Stone"), printed first in Tonson's *Sylvae: or, The Second Part of Poetical Miscellanies,* 3rd ed., 1702, pp. 182–83, then in *POAS,* 1703, 2, 195–96, and eventually in *The Remains of Mr. Tho. Brown,* 1720, pp. 61–63.

Upon Sorrel precipitated at least two replies. The first, in English, by John Tutchin ("Insulting Ass! who basely could'st revile") was reprinted in *POAS,* 1703, 2, 408, and the second, in Latin ("Pessime quadrupedum, Stygiis dignissime pratis"), was attributed to "the learned Mr. Edmund Chishull" (BM MS. Add. 6229, f. 30).

Upon Sorrel

Illustrious Steed, who should the Zodiac grace,
To whom the *Lion* and the *Bull* give place,
Blest be the Duggs that fed thee, blest the Earth
Which first receiv'd thee, and beheld thy Birth.
Did wrong'd *Iërne,* to revenge her slain,
Produce thee first, or murder'd *Fenwick*'s Strain?
Where e'er thou art, be now for ever blest,
And spend the Remnant of thy Days in rest;
No servile Use thy Sacred Limbs profane,
No Weight thy Back, no Curb thy Mouth restrain;
No more be thou, no more Mankind a Slave,
But both enjoy that Liberty you gave.

1. *Illustrious Steed:* Since Sir John Fenwick (*Advice to a Painter,* 14*n.,* above) had been attainted, his real and personal property fell to the crown upon his death. This fact may have provided the basis for the Jacobite belief that the horse which stumbled over a molehill and threw the king, breaking his collarbone, was a strawberry roan named Sorrel, formerly the property of Sir John Fenwick (NLS MS. 2910, f. 7v).

5. *Iërne:* Ireland. Nearly 16,000 officers and men in James II's army in Ireland are estimated to have been killed in the war of 1688–91 (George Story, *A Continuation of the Impartial History of the Wars of Ireland,* 1693, p. 317).

6. *Fenwick's Strain:* a literal translation of "stirps . . . Feniciana," i.e. the breed developed at Wallington Castle, Northumberland, the seat of the Fenwicks.

A Dialogue between the Illustrious Ladies,
the Countesses of Albemarle and Orkney,
Soon after the King's Death
(March[?] 1702)

Geertruid Johanna Quirina van der Duyn (after 1678–1741) had every reason to mourn the death of the king. Her father, Adam van der Duyn, heer van 's Gravenmoer, had been master of the buck-hounds to William III and one of the heroes of the late war. He served as quartermaster-general of the forces in Ireland, led a cavalry regiment across the Boyne in 1690, and commanded all the Dutch cavalry at Landen in 1693, when he was fatally wounded. In recognition of these services, the king had granted his widow, known in England as Lady Gravemore, 21,000 acres of forfeited estates in Ireland. When the Commons resumed these grants, the king awarded her an annual pension of £4000 in 1701 (*Nieuw Nederlandsch Biografisch Woordenboek,* ed. P. C. Molhuysen and P. J. Blok, 10 vols., Leiden, 1911–37, *4,* 541).

On 29 June of this same year, in the English church at The Hague, Geertruid married the king's favorite, Arnold Joost van Keppel, heer van der Voorst in Guelderland, baron von Keppel, and, since February 1696, earl of Albemarle in the English peerage. The king himself provided her dowry of 8000 guilders (Nesca A. Robb, *William of Orange,* 2 vols., Heinemann, 1962–66, *2,* 557) and in November 1701 the bride was installed in the earl's lodgings in Whitehall, where the king usually dined when he was in town. With a sure instinct she set about to redecorate the apartments, running up bills of £1694 15*s.* to plasterers, bricklayers, joiners, and glaziers, all of which remained unpaid at the time of the king's death (*CTB 1702,* p. 1065).

At court the new countess of Albemarle would be sure to see again the countess of Orkney, whom she had met in Holland. This was Elizabeth Villiers, late mistress to the king, whom Swift called the wisest woman he ever saw even if she did squint like a dragon (*Journal, 2,* 558, 570). She had been a maid of honor to Princess Mary at the court of the prince of Orange nearly 25 years before and was said to be the only Englishwoman to be a mistress of the king. As *maîtresse en titre,* she had also become a formidable *intrigante* and although William publicly put her aside in 1694 when Queen Mary died, she neither left the court nor abandoned her intrigues (Vernon, *3,* 8). She was an inveterate enemy of the Churchills and her jealousy of her sister Anne, who had married Willem Bentinck, earl of Portland, the king's first favorite, was said to be the reason why she had pushed forward Keppel as a rival (*DNB, 20,* 326).

So it is not surprising that the young wife of Keppel, now seven months pregnant and faced with the collapse of all her bright hopes, should be imagined in the following poem to appeal for sympathy to one of her few friends in England, that wise old dragon, the countess of Orkney. Nor is it surprising that she did not get any.

A Dialogue between the Illustrious Ladies, the Countesses of Albemarle and Orkney, Soon after the King's Death

A. Ah Madam, the King is—But words I may spare,
These Rivers of tears his Decease may declare.
Alas, we're undon! I am come to lament
His sad Death, which Hell could no longer prevent.
Let's joyn in our sorrows, let's mourn our sad fate,
Mourn the Downfall of vice, Mourn the good of the State.
O. And comst thou to me then, of all womankind?
From me dost thou hope any comfort to find?
A. Alas, and what other will Comfort afford?
You were Miss to my King and Bawd to my Lord,
Employments so honour'd, which brought so much Gain,
What Heart from lamenting the Loss can abstain?
Judge my Grief by your own: Oh! pitty my Case!
Oh pitty the Glories one Hour could Deface!
But yesterday saw Lords and Commons at strife
Which most they should honour, my Lord or his wife.
Our poor rotten King priz'd us more than his Crown:
We were Stars to the Court—
O. But a jest to the Town.
What? were you so pamper'd with fulsom damn'd Lyes
That a few honest Truths draw Tears from your Eyes?
Perhaps you were pleas'd with the nauseous dull Praise
Of two dirty poets in their Damnable plays,

11. *so much Gain:* On 30 May 1695 William settled upon Elizabeth Villiers nearly all of the Irish estates that had belonged to James II. These amounted to 95,649 acres and were reported to be worth £25,995 a year (HMC *Lords MSS.*, New Series, *4*, 54). This grant was revoked in 1700, but in 1700 and 1701 payments of £13,000 were made to the countess out of secret service funds (*CTB 1702*, pp. 872–925).

15. *Lords and Commons at strife:* This is presumably intended to reveal the countess' ignorance; Lords and Commons were indeed at strife in the session which began on 30 December 1701, but the issue was a bill for abjuring the pretended prince of Wales, James Francis Edward, the 13-year-old son of James II.

22. *plays:* George Farquhar's *Sir Harry Wildair* was published in May 1701 and dedicated to the earl of Albemarle. Richard Steele's *The Funeral: Or, Grief A-la-mode*

Where thy Spouse for his Vertue and Wisdom is fam'd,
And thy timorous Dad is a Hero proclaim'd,
Tho' to Valour tis known he'd as little Pretence
As thy Lord has to Breeding, good Nature, or Sense.

A. Ah Madam, these Truths are the least of my Care,
E'en the Death of the King with ease I could spare—
Not but I must own, to give due to the Devil,
Tho' crabbed to others, to us he was Civil;
Crown Jewels for me he would pilfer each morn,
And with spoils of his Crown would his Minion adorn.
Tho' to merit he would not one shilling disburse,
Yet so tender of me, he was Nick-nam'd my Nurse.
But should I behold—Hence, hence is my pain—
My Keppel reduc'd to his Livery again;
If the Queen bids I should those Jewels resign,
Or say she contemns them because they are mine,
I'm told there's a thing call'd the Mob, who have swore
They'll strip us of all our ill-gotten store.
For the Loss of my Grandeur and wealth is my Grief,
But from your wise Advice I hope some Relief.

O. Peace, peace! To thy native Dull Climate repair:
Hope nothing from hence but increase of thy Care.
What? think'st thou, however I flatter'd thy Pride,
That the thoughts of my wrongs I'll e'er lay aside?
The King I seduc'd from his Excellent Queen;
With contempt, by his Eyes, her Beauties were seen;
Dissension I sow'd, yet to me he prov'd just
Till thy damn'd Pathick Lord perverted his Lust;
And then, when to Him I grew useful, false He
My Int'rest forsook to be fetter'd to thee.

---

was published in December 1701 [dated 1702] and dedicated to the countess of Albemarle, "a Stranger in our Nation" (*The London Stage*, 2, 10, 17). Steele, of course, praised the countess' beauty and generosity.

23. *Vertue and Wisdom:* Farquhar "pays more Homage to [Albemarle's] Worth, than Adoration to [his] Greatness" (*Sir Harry Wildair*, 1701, sig. A2r).

24. *Dad:* In the dedication of *The Funeral*, Steele, who was at this time an ensign in the Coldstream Guards, mentions "the great Services" of the countess' father, Lieutenant-General Adam van der Duyn (see headnote, p. 367).

36. *Livery:* Keppel had worn the livery of the prince of Orange in 1688 when he accompanied William to England as a page of honor.

50. *Pathick Lord:* See *Advice to a Painter*, 51 *n.*, above.

When I posted to Holland to see you, Reflect
How I fawn'd, yet was us'd with the uttmost Neglect.
Am I in condition to lessen thy care
When vertue once more at the Court dares appear?
There's no word of Comfort that from me can fall,
But such as the Devil once utter'd to Saul:
From our wicked Crew Corrupt pow'r shall depart,
For the Crown rests on Her that is after God's Heart.

58. *Saul:* In the apparition conjured up by the witch of Endor, the false Samuel, a figment of the devil, affords Saul no comfort but death: "to morrow shalt thou and thy sons be with me" (1 Samuel 28:19).

Daniel Defoe

The Mock Mourners
(*12 May 1702*)

"A Satyr by Way of Elegy on King William," which the subtitle of *The Mock Mourners* announces, seems to portend a hopeless confusion of genres.

> Satyr and Flattery, both together joyn
> And thus he mixes up his false made Coyn,

is what the first critic of the poem proclaimed. "By way of" in the subtitle of the poem means "as a kind of," or "serving as," but a satire can be a kind of elegy only in mock-elegy, which *The Mock Mourners* certainly is not. What *The Mock Mourners* seems to be is not a satire at all, but an extended panegyric with satirical digressions (lines 184–277, 532–52).

Defoe seems to have known exactly what he was doing, however, when he called this mixture (L. *satura*) "A Satyr." He conceived of satire-written, in a characteristic commercial metaphor, as a kind of moral balance sheet—and of satire-writing as an act of running a trial balance, crediting the deserving here and debiting the undeserving there:

> Thou, Satyr, shalt the grateful Few rehearse,
> And solve the Nation's Credit in thy Verse.
>
> (520–21)

The nation's moral accounts failed to balance because a great debt of gratitude remained to be paid. A "thankless Devil," the devil of ingratitude, had seized the land (line 510), just as "Thankless *Israel,* when they were set free,/Reproach't the Author of their Liberty" (lines 274–75). So the emotional center of the poem, Britannia's song (lines 282–405), is "a grateful Trophy" (line 280), a monument of gratitude to the dead king, to redress the balance. The stiffnecked people whom William had led out of an Egyptian bondage of popery and wooden shoes into a promised land of Protestantism and prosperity, simply refused to be grateful. In the obscene pleasure that the "Sons of *Belial*" (line 141) took in the death of their king, Defoe knew that he had seen "Vertue fail" (line 36). And the contrast between two generations of German Schombergs dying on the battlefield for England while the scions of ancient English houses remained in London to murder actors and hackney coachmen was instructive enough to run the risk of an action for *scandalum magnatum*.

In order to strike a balance, therefore, Defoe found that William needed a great deal of praise and that the English nobility who failed to support him when he was alive and the Jacobites who rejoiced at his death required some blame. This is why four-fifths of the poem is panegyric and only one-fifth "satire." Defoe insisted that "Satyr be just" (line 406). By "just" he meant "true"; the subjects of satire must not be blamed for crimes they did not commit. Ten years later Defoe formulated this as a theory: "my Opinion of Satyr is, that *first of all* the Character should be *just*" (*Review, 8* [17 May 1712], 724). But the present context makes it clear that "justice" also includes the correct apportionment of praise and blame. Although he claimed that "To Write Panegyricks . . . is none of my business," panegyric turns out to be an important part of satire in Defoe's practice:

> Satyr be just, and when we lash their Crimes,
> Mingle some Tears for *William* with our Rhimes.
> (406–07)

Britannia is the chief mourner for William, but "Satyr" also sheds some tears.

These same facts account as well for the "official" tone of the poem. It sounds like a public utterance, like an announcement in the *Gazette,* because it is intended to speak for the nation. Like the *Gazette,* it tells the truth, but not the whole truth. This can be seen most clearly in what the poem says about the relationship beween William and Anne, the cousins who were also brother- and sister-in-law. The poem says that William governed so well that when he died there was nothing for Anne to do but "take up the Scepter he laid down" (line 57), and that "The Dying Hero . . . Gave her the Nations Blessing with the Crown" (line 112–13). The poem does not say that during William's lifetime Anne "was not made acquainted with publick Affairs; She was not encouraged to recommend any to Posts of trust and advantage: Nor had the Ministry Orders to inform her how matters went, nor to oblige those about her" (Burnet, 2, 312). Nor does the poem say that when the king was on his deathbed, "La Princesse Anne envoia aussi pour savoir si Elle ne pouvoit pas le voir; mais, on lui fit dire que non" (Lamberty, 2, 66). It might be argued that by suppressing facts of this kind, the poem is functioning in a *negative* way to redress the moral balance, for Jacobites and French agents were busily promoting the groundless lie that William had formed a plot to exclude Anne from the throne. But in no case can the suppression of these facts be used to argue that the poem is not "just." It tells the truth and nothing but the truth, but not of course the whole truth, which would be impossible.

One of the most delightful passages in the poem, outlining the "vast Machine" of the Revolution establishment, is simply an imaginative elaboration of the phrase "balance of power": God is the originator, the people are the owners, the king is the manager, the legislators are the engineers, the laws are the weights and springs, and the magistrates the wheels of a mechanism so delicate that it can be set in motion with a single hair (lines 82–95). More daring than this is Defoe's elaboration of William as an Old Testament patriarch: "*William*'s Modern Character" (line 346) is discovered to be morally superior to the Old Testament prototypes Moses, Joshua, David, and Solomon.

Finally, the poem includes a fine Defovian epigram (line 269; cf. *The True-Born Englishman,* 8, above, for another example) and a fine example of the Defovian variety of metaphysical paradox (lines 502–03; cf. *The Pacificator,* headnote, p. 158, above). Here Defoe argues that whereas ordinary merit may provide the basis for a man's posthumous fame, truly extraordinary merit simply arouses unbelief:

> So *William*'s Life, encreas'd by doubling Fame,
> Will drown his Actions to preserve his Name.

William's extraordinary "Actions," in short, must be forgotten so that his name can be remembered: a paradox worthy of Donne's Anniversaries.

Like *The True-Born Englishman, The Mock Mourners* results from a response to other literature, in this case the mock-elegies of William of which three examples are included above (pp. 361–71). Defoe may also have written a mock satire of William entitled *A Satyr upon King William; Being the Secret History of His Life and*

Reign (3rd ed., 1703). Nominally written in the person of a high flying Tory with a talent for "finding of Faults," this work hints broadly of a discrepancy between "the Face of the Book" and "the real Design" (sigs. A3r, B3r), and ends up being pure panegyric. *The Mock Mourners,* in its turn, evoked *An Answer to The Mock Mourners, by Way of Reflection on a Late Satyr, Pretended to be Written by the Author of The True-born English-man* (1702). The preface to this work is signed by "R. B.," who is confused by mock-elegies, *The Mock Mourners,* and mock satire, and too easily concludes that "None knows who mourns in earnest or in jest" (p. 8).

Since Defoe included *The Mock Mourners* in *A True Collection of the Writings of the Author of The True Born English-man* (1703), Narcissus Luttrell's attribution of it to "Dr. Barber," made on the title page of the copy in the British Museum (164.m.27), must be wrong. There is no reason, however, to doubt the date that Luttrell assigns to the poem: 12 May 1702.

The Mock Mourners

Such has been this Ill-Natur'd Nations Fate,
Always to see their Friends and Foes too late;
By Native Pride, and want of Temper led,
Never to value Merit till 'tis Dead:
And then Immortal Monuments they raise,
And Damn their Former Follies by their Praise,
With just Reproaches Rail at their own Vice,
And Mourn for those they did before despise:
So they who *Moses* Government defied,
Sincerely sorrow'd for him when he Died.
  And so when *Brittain*'s Genius fainting lay,
Summon'd by Death, which Monarchs must obey:
Trembling, and Soul-less half the Nation stood,
Upbraided by their own Ingratitude.
  They, who with true born Honesty before,
Grudg'd him the Trophies he so justly wore,
Were, with his Fate, more than himself dismay'd,
Not for their King, but for themselves afraid.
He had their Rights and Liberties restor'd,
In Battle purchas'd, and by Peace secur'd:
And they with *English* Gratitude began,
To feel the Favour and despise the Man.
But when they saw that his Protection ceas'd,
And Death had their Deliverer possest;

5. *Monuments:* Ten days after William's death, the privy council voted "that a monument be erected on him and his queen [in Westminster Abbey], and his statue on horseback set up in some publick place" (Luttrell, *5,* 154). Defoe(?) mentions *"the* New Mausoleum *Erecting to his Memory" (A Satyr upon King William,* 3rd ed., 1703, sig. A2v), but neither the monument nor the equestrian statue was ever raised.

10. *sorrow'd:* Although they rebelled against him and reverted to the worship of "gods of gold" (Exodus 32:31), when he died "the children of Israel wept for Moses in the plains of Moab thirty days" (Deuteronomy 34:8).

13. *Trembling:* Cf. John Evelyn's comment: "The King . . . died at Kensington . . . about 8 a clock, to the extraordinary disturbance of the whole Citty, & I feare, to the Interests of the whole nation, in this dangerous Conjuncture" (*5,* 491).

21. *English Gratitude:* See *The True-Born Englishman,* 867–68, above.

How Thunder struck they stood! What cries they rais'd!
They look't like Men Distracted and Amaz'd:
Their Terror did their Conscious Guilt explain,
And wish't their injur'd Prince Alive again.
They Dream't of Halters, Gibbets and Jails,
French Armies, Popery and Prince of *Wales*,
Descents, Invasions, Uproars in the State,
Mobs, Irish Massacres, and God knows what:
Imaginary Enemies appear'd,
And all they knew they Merited, they Fear'd.
'Tis strange that Pride and Envy should prevail,
To make Men's Sence as well as Vertue fail:
That where they must depend they should abuse,
And slight the Man they were afraid to lose.
But *William* had not Govern'd Fourteen Year,
To be an unconcern'd Spectator here:
His Works like Providence were all Compleat,
And made a Harmony we Wonder'd at.
The Legislative Power he set Free,
And led them step by step to Liberty,
'Twas not his Fault if they cou'd not Agree.
Impartial Justice He Protected so,
The Laws did in their Native Channels flow,
From whence our sure Establishment begun,
And *William* laid the first Foundation Stone:
On which the stately Fabrick soon appear'd,

30. *French Armies:* A French intelligence report of 14/25 March 1702 observed that it would be possible "de jeter quinze ou vingt mille hommes dans la rivière de Londres ou de Rochester avant qu'ils fussent en état de s'opposer à leur passage" (PRO 31/3 190, f. 31v).

31. *Uproars:* "Il a couru ces jours cy [23 March/3 April 1702] un faux bruit: que les Escossois s'estoient révoltés . . . et que le Duc d'Hamilton étoit le chef de la révolte" (ibid., f. 40).

32. *Irish Massacres:* The same source reported that "les Raperies [remnants of James II's army in Ireland who had turned to banditry] ont commis quelques brigandages" (ibid., f. 40). On 28 March 1702 the queen issued a proclamation restraining the spreading of false news or the publication of libels reflecting on the queen or her ministers (Luttrell, *5*, 157).

33. *Imaginary Enemies:* "[Les anglais] craignent la France, et quelque mal fondée que soit cette crainte, elle est si forte et si universelle que les meilleures raisons du monde ne feroient que blanchir contre leurs prétentions" (PRO 31/3 190, f. 28).

37. Cf. *The True-Born Englishman*, 544–45, above.

How cou'd they sink when such a Pilot steer'd?
He taught them due defences to prepare,
And make their future Peace their present care:
By him directed, Wisely they Decreed,
What Lines shou'd be expell'd, and what succeed;
That now he's Dead, there's nothing to be done,
But to take up the Scepter he laid down.
The Circle of this Order is so round,
So Regular as nothing can confound:
In Truth and Justice all the Lines commence,
And Reason is the vast circumference:
William's the moving Centre of the whole,
'T had else a Body been without a Soul.
Fenc't with just Laws, impregnable it stands,
And will for ever last in *Honest Hands*.
For Truth and Justice are the Immortal Springs,
Give Life to Constitutions and to Kings:
In either case, if one of these decay,
These can no more Command than those obey:
Right is the only Fountain of Command,
The Rock on which Authority must stand.
And if executive Power steps awry,
On either hand it splits on Tyranny:
Oppression is a plague on Mankind sent,
Infects the Vitals of a Government.
Convulsions follow, and such Vapours rise,
The Constitution Suffocates and Dies:
Law is the Grand Specific to restore,
And unobstructed, never fails to Cure,
All other Remedies compar'd to that,
Are Tampering and Quacking with the State.

56–57. The French intelligence report written upon the king's death concluded that "si le Roy Guillaume vient à mourir, les affaires iront toujours leur train . . . et la Princesse Anne reprendra les choses où le Roy Guillaume les aura laissées" (PRO 31/3 190, f. 29v).

59. *nothing can confound:* The same source observed that one might naturally expect divisions in the state upon the death of the king, but warned that such hopes would be "mal fondées" (ibid., f. 30v).

61. Cf. Blake, *The Marriage of Heaven and Hell* (K.149): "Energy is the only life, and is from the Body; and Reason is the bound or outward circumference of Energy."

66–67. See *The True-Born Englishman*, 806–07, above.

The Constitution's like a vast Machine,
That's full of curious Workmanship within:
Where tho' the parts unwieldly may appear,
It may be put in Motion with a Hair.
The Wheels are Officers and Magistrates,
By which the whole contrivance operates:
Laws are the Weights and Springs which make it move,
Wound up by Kings as Managers above;
And if they'r screw'd too high or down too low,
The movement goes too fast or else too slow.
The Legislators are the Engineers,
Who when 'tis out of Order make Repairs:
The People are the Owners, 'twas for them,
The first Inventor drew the Ancient Scheme.
'Tis for their Benefit it works, and they
The Charges of maintaining it defray:
And if their Governours unfaithful prove,
They, Engineers or Mannagers remove,
Unkind Contention sometimes there appears,
Between the Managers and Engineers,
Such strife is always to the Owners wrong,
And *once* it made the work stand still too long.
Till *William* came and loos'd the Fatal Chain,
And set the Engineers to work again:
And having made the wondrous thing compleat,
To *Anne*'s unerring hand he left the Helm of State.
Anne like *Elisha* when just *William* went,
Receiv'd the Mantle of his Government:
And by Divine Concession does inherit,
A Double Portion of his Ruling Spirit.
The Dying Hero loaded with Renown,

103. *once:* under James II.

108. *Elisha:* "And Elisha said, I pray thee, let a double portion of thy spirit be upon me . . . and Elijah went up by a whirlwind into heaven. And Elisha saw it, and he cried, My father, my father. . . . He took up also the mantle of Elijah that fell from him, and went back" (2 Kings 2:9–13).

111. *Double Portion:* Despite the biblical analogue (108 *n.*), Defoe can hardly have been unaware that he is describing Anne's succession in the same mock-epic terms that Dryden used to describe Shadwell's: "The Mantle fell to the young Prophet's part,/With double portion of his Father's Art" (*Mac Flecknoe,* 216–17).

Gave her the Nations Blessing with the Crown,
From God, the People, and the Laws her own.
Told her that he had Orders from on High,
To lay aside the Government and Dye:
What he had Fought for, gave her up in Peace,
And chear'd her Royal Heart with Prospect of Success.
While he, who Death in all its Shapes had seen,
With full Composure quiet and serene,
Passive and undisorder'd at his Fate,
Quitted the English Throne without Regret.
No Conscious Guilt disturb'd his Royal Breast,
Calm as the Regions of Eternal Rest:
Before his Life went out, his Heaven came in,
For all was bright without and clear within.
The blest Rewards did to his sight appear,
The Passage easie, and the prospect near:
His parting Eye the gladsom Regions spied,
Just so before, his Dear Maria *Dyed.*
His High concern for *England* he express't,
England, the Darling of his Royal Breast:
The Transports of his parting Soul he spent,
Her disunited Parties to Lament,

122. *without Regret:* The earl of Portland told Burnet that when he was encouraging the king, "from the good state his affairs were in, both at home and abroad, to take more heart; the King answered him, that he knew Death was that, which he had looked at on all occasions without any terror, sometimes he would have been glad to have been delivered out of all his troubles, but he confessed now he saw another Scene, and could wish to live a little longer" (Burnet, *2*, 303).

124. *Calm:* Burnet, who was an eyewitness, said that the king died "in a wonderful tranquillity" (*2*, 303–04).

125–26. Quoted in *A Satyr upon King William,* 3rd ed., 1703, p. 49.

130. *Dear Maria:* At his death, a bracelet of Queen Mary's hair, threaded through her gold wedding ring, was discovered on the king's left arm (Lamberty, *2*, 66–67; Kennett, *3*, 837).

131. *concern for England:* The king gave his assent on 22 December 1694, six days before Queen Mary died, to a bill requiring triennial elections, which he had vetoed the year before: "He came, on the second day of her illness," Burnet records, "and passed the Bill for frequent Parliaments; which if he had not done that day, it is very probable he would never have passed it" (*2*, 137).

134. *Parties to Lament:* In his speech opening his sixth parliament on 31 December 1701, the king had said: "I should think it as great a Blessing as could befal *England,* if I could observe you as much inclined to lay aside those unhappy fatal Animosities which divide and weaken you. . . . Let me conjure you to disappoint the only Hopes

His Wishes then supplied his want of Power,
And Pray'd for them, for whom he Fought before.
  Speak Envy, if thou canst, inform us what
Cou'd this unthankful Nation Murmur at?
But Discontent was always our Disease,
For *English-men* what Government can please?
We always had our Sons of *Belial* here,
Who knew no God nor Government to Fear:
No Wonder these dislik'd his Gentle sway,
Unwilling Homage to his Scepter Pay,
And only did for want of Power, Obey.
  Some soft excuse for them we might contrive,
Had he not been the Gentlest Prince Alive:
Had he not born with an exalted Mind,
All that was disobliging and unkind.
Peaceful and Tender Thoughts his Mind possess't,
And High Superior Love conceal'd the rest:
Our Discontents wou'd oft his Pity move,
But all his Anger was supprest by Love.
That Heaven-born Passion had subdu'd his Soul,
Possess't the greatest part, and Rul'd the whole:
This made him strive his People to possess,
Which he had done, had he oblig'd 'em less.
He knew that Titles are but empty things,
And Hearts of Subjects are the strength of Kings:
Justice and Kindness were his constant care,
He scorn'd to Govern Mankind by their Fear.

---

of our Enemies, by your Unanimity: I have shewn, and will always shew, how desirous I am to be the common Father of My People: Do you, in like manner, lay aside Parties and Divisions" (*CJ, 13,* 647).

140. *what Government can please: "And did King Jesus reign, they'd murmur too"* (*The True-Born Englishman,* 672).

141. *Sons of Belial:* "Certain men, the children of Belial . . . have withdrawn the inhabitants of their city, saying, Let us go and serve other Gods" (*Deuteronomy* 13:13; cf. *Paradise Lost, 1,* 502).

149. *disobliging and unkind:* See *An Encomium upon a Parliament,* 28 *n.,* above; *A New Satyr on the Parliament,* 96 *n.,* above.

152. *Pity:* Cf. *The True-Born Englishman,* 863–66, above.

161. *scorn'd to Govern . . . by . . . Fear:* When Louis XIV allowed his grandson to accept the crown of Spain in violation of the second partition treaty, William recognized that public opinion in England unaccountably favored Louis' action. "The blindness of the people here is incredible," he told Heinsius, but he set about

Their Universal Love he strove to Gain,
'Twas hard that we should make him strive in vain:
That he should here our English Humours find,
And we, that he had sav'd, shou'd be unkind.
By all endearing stratagems he strove,
To draw us by the secret springs of Love:
And when he could not Cure our Discontent,
It always was below him to Resent.
Nature was never seen in such excess,
All Fury when Abroad, at Home all Peace:
In War all Fire and Blood, in Peace enclin'd,
To all that's Sweet, and Gentle, Soft and Kind,
Ingratitude for this, must needs Commence,
In want of Honesty, or want of Sence.
When King's to Luxury and Ease Resign'd,
Their Native Countries just defence declin'd;
This High pretending Nation us'd to plead,
What they'd perform had they a King to lead.
What Wondrous Actions had by them been done,
When they had Martial Monarchs to lead on?
And if their Prince would but with *France* make War,
What Troops of English Heroes wou'd appear?
William the bottom of their Courage found,

---

doggedly to change this opinion: "I will engage people here, by a prudent conduct, by degrees . . . not being able to play any other game with these people than engaging them imperceptibly" (Grimblot *2*, 477–79).

171. Burnet observed a similar anomaly: "He spoke little and . . . with a disgusting dryness, which was his Character at all times, except in a day of Battle; for then he was all fire" (*2*, 304).

at Home all Peace: William told Heinsius in 1699 that it was "the interest of all Europe, and of us in particular, to prevent a war," and he acceded to the partition of the Spanish empire because he believed that this was "the only means of doing so." Portland even complained that the king "preferred calmness and mildness to what appeared to be the best for his own interest" (Grimblot, *2*, 236, 330).

172. *In War all Fire:* Although wounded the day before while reconnoitering the enemy, William led two cavalry charges during the passage of the Boyne in 1690, while James II watched the action from the safety of Dunmore Hill. In the disastrous defeat at Landen three years later, the king charged the French at the head of the earl of Galway's regiment and received musket shot through his sleeve, his sash, and his peruke. On the same occasion he shot a Dutch officer whom he saw running away from the battle (Oldmixon, pp. 43–45, 84–85; Luttrell, *3*, 154). He was a small man, but "He drew his Sword as if he meant to cut off six Heads at a Blow" (*A Satyr upon King William*, 3rd ed., 1703, p. 8).

False like themselves, meer emptiness and sound:
For call'd by Fate to Fight for *Christendom,*
They sent their King abroad, and stay'd at Home;
Wisely declin'd the hazards of the War,
To Nourish Faction and Disorders here.
Wrapt in Luxurious plenty they Debauch,
And load their Active Monarch with Reproach:
They stay at Home and teach him to command,
And Judge those Actions which they dare not mend.
Backward in Deeds, but of their Censures free,
And blame that Conduct they'r afraid to see:
Against the hand that saves them they exclaim,
And Curse the strangers, tho' they Fight for them.
Tho' some who wou'd excuse the matter say,
They did not grudge their Service, but their Pay:
Where are the Royal bands that now advance,
To spread his dreadful Banners into *France.*
Britannia's Noble Sons her Interest fly,
And Foreign Heroes must their place supply;
Much for the Fame of our Nobility.
Posterity will be asham'd to hear,
Great Britain's Monarch did in Arms appear,
And scarce an English Nobleman was there.
Our Ancestors had never Conquer'd *France,*
For Kingdoms seldom are subdu'd by Chance:
Had *Talbott, Vere* and *Montacute* with-held,

187. *stay'd at Home:* Of the 50 regiments raised in 1688–89 only 16 were commanded by Englishmen. German, Dutch, French Huguenot, Scottish, and Irish officers commanded the rest and even this proportion is misleading, for most of the company-grade officers of the regiment commanded by William Pierrepoint, fourth earl of Kingston, were Irish, and in the regiment commanded by Henry Herbert, fourth Lord Herbert of Cherbury, both officers and men were Welsh (Dalton, *3,* 2–8, 70, 113).

198. *some . . . say:* In his characteristic indirect fashion, Defoe introduces a quotation of himself (*The True-Born Englishman,* 976–77: "the *English* way,/*Never to Grumble till they come to Pay*").

210. *Talbott:* Gilbert Talbot, fifth Lord Talbot (1383–1418), accompanied Henry V to France in 1415 with 30 men-at-arms and 90 archers and was killed in the siege of Rouen (GEC, *12,* i, 617–19).

Vere: Richard de Vere, eleventh earl of Oxford (1385?–1417), also accompanied Henry V to France, with 39 men-at-arms and 60 archers; he was one of the English commanders at Agincourt (25 October 1415) (GEC, *10,* 235).

Montacute: John de Montagu, first baron Montagu (d. 1390), of the celebrated

The Glory, for the danger of the Field.
Had English Honesty been kept alive,
The Ancient English Glory would survive
But Gallantry and Courage will decline,
Where Pride and all Confederate Vices joyn.
Had we kept up the Fame of former Years,
Landen had been as Famous as *Poictiers;*
Ormond and *Essex* had not Fought alone,
The only English Lords our Verse can own:
The only Peers of whom the World can say,
That they for Honour Fought, and not for Pay.
A Regimented *Few* we had indeed,
Who serv'd for neither Pride nor Fame, but Bread:
Some Bully Lords, *Protection Peers,* and some
Went out, because they durst not stay at Home.
Loaded with Noxious Vices they appear,
A scandal to the Nation and the War:
Heroes in Midnight scuffles with the Watch,
And Lewd enough an Army to Debauch.

"coer . . . fier et agu," fought in the retinue of Edward, the Black Prince, both at Crécy (August 1346) and Poitiers (September 1356) (GEC, *9,* 86–87).

218. *Ormond:* James Butler, second duke of Ormonde (1665–1745), served in all of William's campaigns. While leading a cavalry charge at Landen, on 19 July 1693, he was wounded and his horse shot under him and in the resulting melee he was captured. He is the only "English" nobleman (he was born in Dublin of a Dutch mother) mentioned with distinction in an eyewitness account (D'Auvergne, 1693, p. 76).

Essex: Algernon Capell, second earl of Essex (1670–1710), also served in all of William's campaigns and commanded the fourth dragoons at Landen (GEC, *5,* 146).

224. *Bully Lords* (*Key*)*:* Charles Gerard, second earl of Macclesfield, whose career of violence began at 14 and included "breaking a boy's neck, when he was in his cups" (GEC, *8,* 330–32), commanded a regiment of horse. Edward Rich, sixth earl of Warwick, who later killed his friend (see *The Court,* 40 *n.,* above), put in for a regiment in December 1693 but had to settle for a captaincy in the queen's regiment of horse. In the same month (February 1694) Charles Mohun, fourth baron Mohun (1677–1712), who had already been twice tried for murder, was made captain of a troop in Macclesfield's regiment (GEC, *9,* 27–29; Dalton, *3,* 354). Richard Savage, fourth earl Rivers, "one of the greatest Rakes in *England,*" commanded the third troop of horse guards and "attended the King in all his Campaigns" (Macky, p. 60).

Protection Peers (*Key*): A protection is "a writing issued by the king granting immunity from arrest or lawsuit to one engaged in his service, or going abroad with his cognizance" (*OED*). Although Mohun had been acquitted, in February 1693, of the murder of William Mountfort (see 231 *n.,* below), there was always the danger that Mrs. Mountfort would appeal (Luttrell, *3,* 46, 48, 207) and Mohun must have been glad to go with his majesty to Flanders as a "volunteer" in March 1694 (ibid., *3,* 282).

Flesh't with cold Murthers and from Justice fled,
Pursu'd by Blood, in Drunken Quarrels shed:
In vain they strive with Bravery to appear,
For where there's Guilt, there always will be Fear.
These are the Pillars of the English Fame,
Such Peers as History must blush to Name.
When future Records to the World relate,
Marsaglia's Field and Gallant *Schombergs* Fate:
Warwick was Captive made, it was severe,
Fate took the *Honest Man,* and left the *Peer.*
The World owes Fame for Ages long before,
To the Great stile of *Warwick* which he bore:
But when we come the branches to compare,
'Tis a *Hero* Ancestor, a *Bully* Heir:
The Vertues the Posterity forsake,
And all their Gallant Blood is dwindl'd to a *Rake.*
More might be said, but *Satyr* stay thy Rhimes,
And mix not his misfortunes with his Crimes;
We need not Rake the Ashes of the Dead,

231. *Drunken Quarrels:* In one of the most notorious of these, in December 1692, Lord Mohun and Richard Hill, a captain in Thomas Erle's regiment, killed William Mountfort, a celebrated actor and playwright. It was established at Mohun's trial in the House of Lords that he and Hill had dressed in each other's clothes and lain in wait an hour before Mountfort's door. While Mohun "embraced" him, Hill stabbed Mountfort in the back and disappeared. The House of Lords acquitted Mohun by a vote of 69–14 (ibid., *3*, 27, 29).

237. *Schombergs Fate:* In 1691 Charles Schomberg, second duke of Schomberg (1645–93), raised an army of French Protestants to support Víctor Amadeo II (see *A Satyr upon the French King,* 105 *n.,* above) against the French. At Marsaglia, on 4 October 1693, Schomberg was mortally wounded and the confederate armies so disastrously defeated by Nicolas Catinat that suspicions were aroused that they had been betrayed (*Memoires of the Transactions in Savoy,* 1697, pp. 71–81).

238. *Warwick:* Edward Rich, sixth earl of Warwick (1673–1701), is known to have been present at the battle of Marsaglia (*CSPD 1693,* p. 412), but his capture does not seem to have been recorded elsewhere. He was back in London by December 1693 (Luttrell, *3,* 241).

243. *Hero Ancestor:* Among Warwick's hero ancestors was Henry Rich, first earl of Holland (1590–1649), who was beheaded in Palace Yard, Westminster, a few days after his master, Charles I (GEC, *6,* 538–40). Another was the puritan Robert Rich, second earl of Warwick (1587–1658), whose command of the fleet enabled parliament to dominate the seas during the civil wars (GEC, *12,* ii, 407–12).

247. *his misfortunes:* See *The Court,* 40 *n.,* above; Warwick died "very penitent" on 31 July 1701, aged 28 (GEC, *12,* ii, 417).

248. *the Dead:* Cf. [Defoe], *The Present State of Jacobitism Considered,* 1701, p. 22: "I have not ill nature enough to make Satyrs upon the Dead."

There's living Characters enough to Read.
How cou'd this Nation ever think of Peace?
Or how look up to Heaven for Success?
While lawless Vice in Fleets and Camps appear'd,
And Oaths were louder than their Cannon heard:
No wonder English *Israel* has been said,
Before the French *Philistines* Fleet t' ha' fled.
While *Torrington Embrac'd with Whores* appear'd,
And Vice it self the Royal Navy Steer'd.
William oppos'd their Crimes with steady hand,
By his Example First, and then Command,
Prompted the Laws their Vices to suppress,
For which no doubt the Guilty Lov'd him less.
Ye Sons of Envy, Railers at the Times,
Be bold like English-Men and own your Crimes:
For shame put on no Black, but let us see
Your Habits always, and your Tongues agree.
Envy ne'r Blushes: Let it not be said,
You Hate him Living and you Mourn him Dead:
No Sorrow show where you no Love profess,
There are no Hypocrites in Wickedness.
Great Bonfires make, and tell the World y' are glad
Y' have lost the greatest Blessing e're you had:
So Mad-Men sing in Nakedness and Chains,
For when the Sense is gone, the Song remains.
So Thankless *Israel,* when they were set free,
Reproach't the Author of their Liberty:
And wisht themselves in *Egypt* back again;
What pity 'twas they wisht, or wisht in vain.
Stop Satyr, let *Britannia* now relate

256. *Torrington* (*Key*): Arthur Herbert was created earl of Torrington in June 1689; see *The Pacificator,* 147 *n.,* above. Pepys describes his manner of life while in command of the Mediterranean fleet in 1680, "keeping a house on shore and his mistresses visited and attended one after another, as the King's are" (*The Tangier Papers of Samuel Pepys,* ed. Edwin Chappell [Navy Records Society], 1935, p. 138).

257. *Vice it self:* "'Ballocks' was the word that Herbert always called his chaplain by" (*ibid.,* p. 168).

260. *Laws:* See *An Encomium upon a Parliament,* 76 *n.,* above.

264–65. Cf. *The Mourners,* 1–2, above.

269. *Hypocrites in Wickedness:* who profess more vice than they practice.

275. *Reproach't the Author:* Exodus 16:1–2.

Her *William*'s Character, and her own Fate;
Let her to him a grateful Trophy raise,
She best can sigh his Loss that sung his Praise.

Britannia

Of all my Sons by Tyranny bereft,
A Widow desolate and Childless left,
By Violence and Injury opprest,
To Heaven I cast my Eyes, and sigh'd the rest.
I need but sigh, for I was always heard,
And *William* on my welcome Shores appear'd.
With Wings of speed to rescue me he came,
And all my Sorrows vanisht into Flame.
New Joys sprung up, new Triumphs now abound,
And all my Virgin Daughters hear the sound:
Eternal Dances move upon my Plains,
And youthful Blood springs in my ancient Veins.
With open Arms I yielded my Embrace,
And *William* saw the Beauties of my Face.
He had before the knowledge of my Charms,
For he had my Maria *in his Arms.*
While he remain'd, I gave eternal Spring,
Made him my Son, my Darling, and my King;
While all the wondring World my Choice approve,
Congratulate his Fate, and justifie my Love.
  Of *British* Blood in *Belgian* Plains he liv'd,
My only Foreign Off-spring that surviv'd.
Batavian Climates nourisht him a while,
Too great a Genius for so damp a Soil:
And freely then surrendred him to me,
For wise Men freely will the Fates obey.
Yet in my *William* they had equal Share,

281. *sung his Praise:* in *The True-Born Englishman,* 893–956, above.

302. *Of British Blood:* See *The Foreigners,* 29 *n.,* above.

308. *they: "Batavian* Climates"; when William was made captain-general of the United Provinces in February 1672 at the age of 21, the situation seemed utterly hopeless; Louis XIV was ready to invade the Lowlands at the head of a huge French

And he defended them with equal Care.
They were the early Trophies of his Sword,
His Infant Hand their Liberty restor'd.
His Nurse, the Belgick Lion, roar'd for Aid,
And planted early Lawrels on his Head.
His easie Victories amaz'd Mankind;
We wonder'd what the dreadful Youth design'd.
Fearless he Fought his Country to set Free,
And with his Sword Cut out their Liberty.
The Journals of his Actions always seem'd
So wonderful, as if the World had dream'd:
So swift, so full of Terror he went on,
He was a Conqueror before a Man.
The *Bourbon* Sword, tho' it was brighter far,
Yet drawn for Conquest, and oppressive War,
Had all the Triumphs of the World Engrost,
But quickly all those Triumphs to him lost.
Justice to *William* early Trophies brought;
William *for Truth and Justice always fought.*
He was the very Mystery of War,
He gain'd by't when he was not Conqueror.
And if his Enemies a Battle won,
He might be beaten, they wou'd be undone.
Antaeus-like from every fall he rose,
Strengthen'd with double Vigor to oppose;
Those Actions Mankind judg'd Unfortunate,
Serv'd but as secret Steps to make him Great.

army and the English fleet (which Louis XIV had paid to have fitted out) was ready to destroy the Dutch fleet in the Channel. By the end of the next summer, the situation was completely reversed: the English fleet had been virtually destroyed and the French army, by the prince's capture of Bonn, had been outflanked and forced to withdraw. "The *Dutch* were transported at this great and unexpected Turn of Affairs, and justly imputed it to the Wisdom and Conduct of the Prince of *Orange;* and therefore a greater Honour was done to him than to any of his illustrious Ancestors: For now the *States-General* not only confirm'd the Office of *Stadt-Holder* in the Person of his Highness during Life, but settled it likewise upon his Heirs Male" (Echard, *3,* 331).

316. *set Free:* See *The True-Born Englishman,* 918, above.

332. *Antaeus-like:* Antaeus was a Libyan giant, the son of Earth, who, in his famous fight with Hercules, received new strength from his mother every time he was thrown (Lucan, *Pharsalia, 4,* 598; Statius, *Thebaid, 6,* 893).

Then let them boast their Glory at *Landen,*
In vain th' Embattl'd Squadrons crowded in,
Their's was the Victory, the Conquest mine.
Of all the Heroes, Ages past adore,
Back to the first Great Man, and long before;
Tho' Virtue has sometimes with Valour join'd,
The Barren World no Parallel can find.
If back to *Israel*'s Tents I shou'd retire,
And of the *Hebrew* Heroes there enquire,
I find no Hand did *Judah*'s Scepter wear,
Comes up to *William*'s Modern Character.
Namure's Gygantick Towers he o'erthrew;
David did less when he *Goliah* slew.
Here's no *Uriah*'s for Adult'ry slain,
Nor Oaths forgot to faithful *Jonathan.*
And if to *Jesse*'s Grandson we ha' recourse,

336. *Landen:* The old duc de Luxembourg, *le tapissier de Notre Dame,* added 82 captured standards and colors to Louis XIV's collection in July 1693 when he defeated the confederate armies at Landen. After the battle he lined up the captured cannon and fired them three times in token of his victory and Louis ordered a *te deum* to be sung at Notre Dame. French losses, however, were so heavy that Luxembourg was unable to follow up his great victory (D'Auvergne, 1693, pp. 80–82). William, as Voltaire said, "always made excellent retreats" (*The Age of Louis XIV,* 2 vols., 1752, *1,* 265).

347. *Namure's Gygantick Towers:* The citadel of Namur, which Vauban was ordered to make "impregnable" after its capture by Louis XIV in 1692, is located on a rocky promontory at the junction of the Sambre and the Meuse, 479 feet above water-level. William recaptured it in August 1695. "And that which must elevate the Glory of His Majesty . . . above all that other Conquerors have done, is, That such Monarchs have made Conquests for themselves, Conquests to oppress their Neighbours, and to Raise a Mighty Empire upon their Ruine: But here His Majesty Expos'd Himself dayly to the greatest Dangers to Conquer for the good of *Europe,* to free it from Oppression, and to Establish its Peace and Liberties upon a Lasting foundation" (D'Auvergne, 1696, p. 172).

348. *Goliah:* 1 Samuel 17.

349. *Uriah:* When David fell in love with Bathsheba, the wife of one of his captains, a foreigner named Uriah, he ordered Uriah to be fatally exposed in battle (2 Samuel 11:2–21).

350. *Oaths . . . to . . . Jonathan:* See *The True-Born Englishman,* 1135 *n.,* above; David forgot about this oath until he had secured his position on the throne of Israel (2 Samuel 9:1).

351. *Jesse's Grandson:* Solomon, the son of David and Bathsheba. "But king Solomon loved many strange women" and stocked his harem with 700 wives and 300 concubines (1 Kings 11:1–3).

William his Wisdom had *without his Whores.*
Joshua might still ha' staid on *Jordan*'s Shore,
Must he, as *William* did the *Boyne,* pass o'er.
Almighty Power was forc'd to interpose,
And frighted both the Water and his Foes:
But had my *William* been to pass that Stream,
God needed not to part the Waves for him.
Not Forty Thousand *Canaanites* cou'd stand;
In spight of Waves or *Canaanites* he'd land:
Such Streams ne'er stemm'd his Tide of Victory;
No, not the Stream; no, nor the Enemy.
His Bombs and Cannon wou'd ha' made the Wall,
Without the Help of Jewish Rams-Horns, fall.
When his dear *Israel* from their Foes had fled,
Because of stoln Spoils by *Achan* hid:
He'd ne'er, like *Joshua,* on the Ground ha' laid,
He'd certainly ha' fought as well as pray'd.
The Sun would rather ha' been thought to stay,
Amaz'd to see how soon he had won the Day,
Than to give time the *Canaanites* to slay.
The greatest Captains of the Ages past,
Debauch'd their Fame with Cruelty at last:
William did only Tyrants subdue;
These conquer'd Kings, and then the People too:
The Subjects reap'd no Profit for their Pains,
And only chang'd their Masters, not their Chains;
Their Victories did for themselves appear,

353. *Joshua:* Considering the length and urgency of the exhortation that seems to have been necessary to embolden Joshua to cross the Jordan (Joshua 1:1–9), Defoe supposes that he might never have attempted it if he had been opposed, as William was at the Boyne, by "Forty Thousand *Canaanites.*"

358. *part the Waves:* Joshua 3:15–17.

363–64. *Wall . . . fall:* "the priests blew with the trumpets: and it came to pass, when . . . the people shouted with a great shout, that the wall fell down flat . . . and they took the city [Jericho]" (Joshua 6:20).

366. *Achan:* When they were defeated in a minor skirmish at Ai, Joshua fell to the ground and tore his clothes, regretting that he had led the Israelites across the Jordan. Yahweh then explained the reason for the defeat: one Achan, of the tribe of Judah, had appropriated to himself some of the spoils from Jericho that belonged to Yahweh (Joshua 7:1–26).

369. *Sun:* The sun stood still at Gibeon, "a great city," to give Joshua more time to kill Canaanites (Joshua 10:12–13).

And made their Peace as dreadful as the War:
But *William* sought Oppression to destroy,
That Mankind might in Peace the World enjoy.
The *Pompeys, Caesars, Scipios, Alexanders,*
Who croud the World with Fame, were great Commanders:
These too brought Blood and Ruin with their Arms,
But *William* always fought on other Terms:
Terror indeed might in his Front appear,
But Peace and Plenty follow'd in his Rear:
And if Oppression forc'd him to contend,
Calmness was all his Temper, Peace his End:
He was the only Man we e'er saw fit
To regulate the World, or conquer it.
Who can his Skill in Government Gainsay,
He that cou'd *England*'s brittle Scepter sway,
Where Parties too much rule, and King's obey?
He always reign'd by Gentleness and Love,
An Emblem of the Government above.
Vote me not Childless then in Christendom,
I yet have Sons in my suspended Womb;
And 'till just Fate such due Provision makes,
A Daughter my Protection undertakes.
Crowns know no Sexes, and my Government
To either Kind admits a just Descent.
Queens have to me been always fortunate,
E'er since my *English Phoenix* rul'd the State;
Who made my People rich, my Country great.

Satyr be just, and when we lash their Crimes,
Mingle some Tears for *William* with our Rhimes.

381. *Peace:* See 347 *n.,* above.

384. *Blood and Ruin:* The contribution of "your *Caesars,* or your *Alexanders*" to "Death's Eternal Empire" is related in *The True-Born Englishman,* 72–77, above.

387. *Peace and Plenty:* See illustration, p. 12.

392. *Skill in Government:* John Dunton called William "the Greatest Politician . . . of his Time" (*The Post Angel, 3* [May 1702], 289).

400. *A Daughter:* Queen Anne.

404. *Phoenix:* Queen Elizabeth.

406. *their:* The grammatical "antecedent" is supplied in line 408, the base and ungrateful.

Tho' Baseness and Ingratitude appear,
Thank Heaven that we ha' weeping Millions here:
Then speak our hearty Sorrows if you can,
Superior Grief in feeling Words explain:
Accents that wound, and all the Senses numb,
And while they speak may strike the Hearer dumb:
Such Grief as never was for King before,
And such as never, never shall be more.
  See how Authority comes weeping on,
And view the Queen lamenting on his Throne.
With just Regret she takes the Sword of State,
Not by her Choice directed, but his Fate;
Accepts the sad Necessity with Tears,
And mournfully for Government prepares.
The Peoples Acclamations she receives
With sadden'd Joy, and a Content that grieves.
  View next the sad Assemblies that appear,
To tell their Grief for Him, and Joy for Her.
The first confounds the last with such Excess,
They hardly can their noble Thoughts express.
The illustrious Troop address her to condole,
And speak such Grief as wounds her to the Soul:
They lodge their Sorrows in the Royal Breast;
The Harbour where the Nation looks for Rest.
  Next these, the Representatives arise,
With all the Nation's Sorrow in their Eyes.
The Epithets they righteously apply

414. *Grief as never was:* "And thus ended this Ceremony [William's funeral], at which were more weeping Eyes and aking Hearts, than had ever been known in the like Number of Assistants on the like Occasion" (Oldmixon, p. 261).

417. *the Queen lamenting:* Anne's first public pronouncement, made in a speech to the privy council the night of the king's death, began with these words: "My Lords, I am extremely sensible of the general Misfortune to these Kingdoms, in the unspeakable Loss of the King; and of the great Weight and Burden it brings in particular to my self" (Oldmixon, p. 273).

418. *the Sword of State:* curtana, the pointless sword borne before the monarch at the coronation, symbolic both of royal power and mercy.

424. *sad Assemblies:* The first to pay public homage to the new queen was Prince George of Denmark, the royal consort, and he was followed, in order of precedence, by the entire court.

434. *The Epithets:* The Commons' address of condolence to the queen began as follows: "Most gracious Sovereign, We, Your Majesty's most dutiful and loyal Subjects,

To the Restorer of their Liberty,
Are Tokens of their Sence and Honesty.
For as a Body we were always true,
But 'tis our Parties that our Peace undo.
Who can like them the Peoples Grief express?
They shew her all the Tokens of Excess:
O'erwhelm'd with Sorrow, and supprest with Care,
They place the Nation's Refuge now in her:
Nothing but her Succession cou'd abate
The Nation's Sorrow for their Monarch's Fate:
And nothing but his Fate cou'd their true Joy
For her Succession lessen or destroy.
The Civil Sword to her, as Heaven saw fit,
With general Satisfaction they commit:
How can it in a Hand like hers miscarry?
But who shall for us weild the Military?
Who shall the jarring Generals unite;
First teach them to agree, and then to fight?
Who shall renew'd Alliances contrive,
And keep the vast Confederacies alive?
Who shall the growing Gallick Force subdue?
'Twas more than all the World, but him, cou'd do.
Sighs for departed Friends are sensless things,
But 'tis not so when Nations mourn for Kings:
When wounded Kingdoms such a Loss complain,
As Nature never can repair again;
The Tyrant Grief, like Love, obeys no Laws,
But blindly views the Effect, and not the Cause.
Dark are the Works of Sovereign Providence,
And often clash with our contracted Sence:
But if we might with Heavens Decrees debate,

---

the Commons in Parliament assembled, having a deep and true Sense of the great Loss the Nation has sustained by the Death of our late Sovereign Lord King *William* the Third, of glorious Memory, who, under God, was our Deliverer from Popery and Slavery, humbly crave Leave to condole with Your Majesty, and express our Sorrow on this sad Occasion" (*CJ*, *13*, 784).

450. William settled this in June 1701 by appointing Marlborough commander-in-chief of the forces committed to the defense of the United Provinces (Luttrell, *5*, 58).

453. *Alliances:* William had also given Marlborough plenary powers to conclude a treaty of Grand Alliance with the Empire and the United Provinces, which was signed late in August 1701 (Trevelyan, *1*, 145).

And of our Maker's Works expostulate,
Why shou'd he form a Mind supreamly great,
And to his Charge commit the Reins of Fate,
And at one hasty Blow the World defeat?
A Blow so sudden, so severe and swift,
We had no time for Supplication left:
As if Almighty Power had been afraid,
Such Prayers wou'd by such Multitudes be made;
Such *Moses*'s wou'd to his Altars go,
To whom he never did, or wou'd say no;
He hardly cou'd know how to strike the Blow.
For Prayer so much the Soveraign Power commands,
Ev'n God himself sometimes as conquer'd stands,
And calls for Quarter at the Wrestler's Hands.
How Strenuous then had been the Sacred Strife,
While all the kneeling World had begg'd his Life,
With all that Earnestness of Zeal, and more
Than ever Nation begg'd for King before?
See how the neighbouring Lands his Fame improve,
And by their Sorrows testifie their Love;
Sprinkle his Memory with grateful Tears,
And hand his Glory to succeeding Years.
With what Contempt will *English* Men appear,
When future Ages read his Character?
They'll never bear to hear in time to come,
How he was lov'd abroad, and scorn'd at home.
The World will scarce believe it cou'd be true,
And Vengeance must such Insolence pursue.
Our Nation will by all Men be abhorr'd,
And *William*'s juster Fame be so restor'd.
Posterity, when Histories relate
His Glorious Deeds, will ask, *What Giant's that?*

474–75. *Moses:* Yahweh was about to abandon the Israelites after the golden calf episode (see 10 *n.*, above), but could not deny Moses' plea (Exodus 33:3–5, 12–14).

478–79. *God . . . calls for Quarter:* Hosea 12:2–4; cf. Genesis 32:24–30.

488–519. Quoted in *Review, 4* (27 March 1707), 79–80.

491. *lov'd abroad:* After they had been defeated at the Boyne, "the *Irish* themselves confest, *If the* English *chang'd Kings with them, they would fight the Battle over again.*" It was also said to be a common saying among the French troops, "*We want only such a King to make ourselves Masters of* Christendom" (Oldmixon, pp. 45, 85).

496–97. J. R. Moore cites *The Swedish Intelligencer* (Third Part, 1633), unpaged:

For common Vertues may Mens Fame advance,
But an immoderate Glory turns Romance.
Its real Merit does it self undo,
Men talk it up so high, it can't be true:
So *William*'s Life, encreas'd by doubling Fame,
Will drown his Actions to preserve his Name.
The Annals of his Conduct they'll revise,
As Legends of Impossibilities.
'Twill all a Life of Miracles appear,
Too great for Him to do, or Them to hear.
And if some faithful Writer shou'd set down
With what Uneasiness he wore the Crown;
What thankless Devil had the Land possest;
This will be more prodigious than the rest.
With Indignation 'twill their Minds inspire,
And raise the Glory of his Actions higher.
The Records of their Fathers they'll Deface,
And blush to think they sprung from such a Race.
They'll be asham'd their Ancestors to own,
And strive their Father's Follies to atone.
New Monuments of Gratitude they'll raise,
And Crown his Memory with Thanks and Praise.
  Thou, Satyr, shalt the grateful Few rehearse,
And solve the Nation's Credit in thy Verse;
Embalm his Name with Characters of Praise,
His Fame's beyond the Power of Time to rase.
  From him let future Monarchs learn to Rule,
And make his lasting Character their School.
For he who wou'd in time to come be Great,
Has nothing now to do but imitate.
Let dying Parents when they come to bless,
Wish to their Children only his Success.

"The Youth, hereafter, when Old Wives shall chat,/*Gustavus* high deeds, will aske *What Giant's that?*" (*The Library*, 5th series, *11* [September 1956], 165).

496–99, 502–07 Quoted in [Defoe?], *A Satyr upon King William*, 3rd ed., 1703, p. 51.

496–519: Quoted in *Review*, *4* (4 November 1707), 456.

509. *Uneasiness:* "as to his *Heroism*, the Prince of *Conti* who was an Eye-witness of it in Flanders said it was a Pity a Prince who deserv'd so well the Crown he wore, should have it disputed with him" (Oldmixon, p. 261).

521. *solve:* preserve.

Here their Instructions very well may end,
William's Example only recommend,
And leave the Youth his History t'attend.
  But we have here an Ignominious Croud,
That boast their Native Birth and English Blood,
Whose Breasts with Envy and Contention burn,
And now rejoice when all the Nations mourn:
Their awkward Triumphs openly they Sing;
Insult the Ashes of their injur'd King;
Rejoice at the Disasters of his Crown;
And Drink the Horse's Health that threw him down.
  Blush, Satyr, when such Crimes we must reveal,
And draw a silent Curtain to conceal.
Actions so vile shall ne'er debauch our Song;
Let Heaven alone, tho' Justice suffers long.
Her Leaden Wings, and Iron Hands, may show
That she is certain, tho' she may be slow.
His Foreign Birth was made the Fam'd Pretence,
Which gave our Home-Born Englishmen Offence.
But Discontent's the antient English Fashion,
The Universal Blemish of the Nation.
And 'tis a Question, whether God cou'd make
That King whom every Englishman wou'd *like?*
Nor is it any Paradox to say,
William *had more of English Blood than they;*
The *Royal Life* flow'd in his sprightly Veins,
The same that in the *Noble Stock* remains;
The same which now his Glorious Scepter wields,
To whom Three Nations just Obedience yields.
  ANNE, the remaining Glory of our Isle,
Well she becomes the Royal English Stile:

536. *rejoice:* "Les *Toris outrez* dans leurs libelles, dans leurs conversations, & dans leurs ballades, lachérent la bride à leur haine injuste, & à leur aveugle ressentiment. *Le chien est il mort?* dit un Ecclesiastique de distinction" (Emmanuel de Cize, *Histoire du Whigisme et du Torisme,* 1718, p. 221; quoted in Oldmixon, p. 262).

543. *Actions so vile:* "High Church *drank a Health to the little Gentleman dress'd in Velvet,* that is, *A Health to the Mole,* which made the Hole into which the King's Horse's Foot slipt when he fell" (Oldmixon, p. 262).

551–52. See 140 *n.*, above.

558. Cf. *The Rape of the Lock* (1714), III, 7: "Great *Anna!* whom three Realms obey."

In *William*'s Steps sedately she proceeds,
William*'s a Patern to immortal Deeds.*
Preserves his Memory with generous Care;
Forgetting him is Disobliging her;
Where shall the murmuring Party then appear!
Where wou'd the Nation, but for her, ha' found
So safe a Cure for such a sudden Wound?
And cou'd she but as well the Camp supply,
The World the sooner wou'd their grief lay by;
But there the Fatal Breach is made so wide,
That Loss can never, never be——supply'd.
Ye Men of Arms, and English Sons of War,
Now learn from him how you may Fight for her;
Your Grief for him express upon her Foes,
For William *lov'd such Funeral Tears as those.*
'Tis *William*'s Glorious Scepter which she bears,
Like *William* she for Liberty appears.
She Mounts to Honour by the Steps of Truth,
And his Example Imitates in Both.
'Tis you must make her blooming Fame Increase,
'Tis you must bring her Honour, Wealth and Peace;
And let it once more to the World be seen,
Nothing can make us Greater than a Queen.

563. *Preserves his Memory:* "Le prémier soin de la Reine *Anne* fut de défendre son Prédécesseur des insultes d'un parti qui avoit resolu de ternir la memoire de ce Prince aprés sa mort, comme il avoit troublé son repos pendant sa vie" (Emmanuel de Cize, *Histoire du Whigisme et du Torisme,* 1718, p. 221).

Daniel Defoe

Reformation of Manners
(*August*[?] *1702*)

The present poem may appear to be simply a blast of bird shot at such widely scattered targets as a country parson with delirium tremens, a homicidal barrister, an arsonous merchant, and a voyeuristic justice of the peace. But if it should develop that all of these gentlemen were members of the society for the reformation of manners, then the poem would be revealed in its proper perspective and connectedness. For it is, as Defoe said in the preface to *More Reformation* (1703), an attack on those who, "pretending to reform others, and Execute the Laws against Vice, have been the great Examples and Encouragers of it in their own Example and Practice."

The first society for the reformation of manners was founded by five or six private gentlemen, all "Members of the Church of *England,*" in the Tower Hamlets of London in 1690. It was "designed to controul Looseness, and to prevent the Youth of the City from being spoilt by Harlots and loose Women, and from spending their Time in Taverns or Ale-Houses, and distempering themselves by Excess of Drink and breaking the Sabbath" (Strype, *2,* [2]30). The wits, of course, eagerly responded to these earnest hopes and freely predicted that "Vice [would] be made to vanish throughout all *England,* like a Whiff of Tobacco" (*A Pacquet from Wills,* 1701, p. [50 misnumbered] 34). But vice proved more difficult to dispel—so difficult, in fact, that by the end of the century it seemed triumphant in London. One impressionable clergyman reported that Satan himself had been seen at a ball in masquerade (*The Note Book of the Rev. Thomas Jolly A.D. 1671–1693,* ed. Henry Fishwick, Manchester, 1894, p. 11) and another proclaimed that *"Hell* is broken loose among us" (Arthur Bedford, *The Evil and Danger of Stage-Plays,* 1706, p. 219).

In this situation Defoe adopted the *ingenu* pose that Swift was to attribute to Lemuel Gulliver seven months after the publication of *The Travels.* "Behold, I cannot learn," we can imagine Defoe saying, "that the societies for the reformation of manners have produced one single effect according to mine intentions . . . and it must be owned that ten years were a sufficient time to correct every vice and folly to which Man is subject." On this assumption there could be but one conclusion:

For shame your *Reformation-Clubs* give o'er,
And jest with Men, and jest with Heaven no more.
(1198–99)

Nor is the comparison between *Reformation of Manners* and *Gulliver's Travels* farfetched, for the two works precipitate an identical theme: you cannot reform the world; you can only reform yourself. This is a frequently recurring idea in Defoe: ". . . Examples, not Penalties, must sink this Crime" (*An Essay upon Projects,* 1697, p. 249); "If my own Watch goes false, it deceives me and none else; but if the Town-Clock goes false, it deceives the whole Parish" (*The Poor Man's Plea,* 1698, p. 17); "All our Reformations are Banters, and will be so, till our Magistrates and Gentry Reform themselves by way of Example" (*The True-Born Englishman,* 1700, sig. A4v); *". . . 'tis Example must reform the Times"* (*Reformation of Manners,* 1702, 1231); "If you will Reform the Nation, you that call your selves Reformers . . . , You must first Reform your selves" (*Review* [Edinburgh], *6* [7 April 1709], 15).

Thus the poem supplies evidence of how "Augustan" Defoe is, for *doubt* about the perfectibility of man in the mass is one of the distinguishing features of the succession from Dryden to Samuel Johnson, while *belief* in the possibility of mass reform is characteristic of all the great romantics from the third earl of Shaftesbury to Samuel Taylor Coleridge. Although the opposition to institutionalized reformation of manners came largely from Tories, all efforts to seize the reformation movement for the Whigs were unsuccessful. "If the Tories," as one nonconformist speculated, "will need have it that *a Satyr against Whoreing is a Satyr against them,* we cannot hinder them to apply it as they please" (John Dunton, *The Night-Walker,* October 1696, p. 2). But the Tories refused to be so obliging and the present poem remains markedly nonpartisan. "If a Vitious, Leud, Debauch'd Magistrate happen'd," as Defoe said, "to be a Whig, what then?" (*More Reformation,* 1703, sig. A3v).

The latter limit for the date of composition is determined by lines 578–79, urging the defeat of Sir John Bolles, which would be pointless after 5 August 1702 when Bolles lost the contest for Lincoln. On the other side, Defoe knew that Ormonde had "Embarkt for *Portugal* or *Spain*" (line 1033) on 20 June 1702 (Luttrell, *5*, 186). The internal evidence, therefore, indicates that most of the poem was written in July 1702. Internal evidence also makes it most unlikely that Defoe was a member of any of the societies for the reformation of manners in London at this time. He became a member of the Edinburgh Society for the Reformation of Manners in 1707, not because he sympathized with their methods but because it gave him, as he said, "occasion of influencing them" on behalf of the act of union (*Review of English Studies, 16* [July 1940], 307, 312).

One feature of the poem that seems never to have been observed is its remarkable prophetic strain. At line 400 Defoe observes simply that the writer of satire exposes himself to manifold hazards "From Laws, from Councils, and from Parliaments." At line 420 his friends fear that nothing but "Gaols and Gibbets" will crown his efforts and at line 1008 Defoe warns himself to be "well prepar'd for Martyrdom," which came in July 1703 when he was dragged out of Newgate "Gaol" and exposed, not on the "Gibbet," but on the pillory. By an even stranger coincidence three of the gentlemen of the long robe whom Defoe satirizes in the poem figure in his indictment and trial: Sir Robert Geffrey (line 103 *n.*) and Sir Salathiel Lovell (line 115 *n.*) were among the justices before whom the indictment was brought in February 1703, and Sir Simon Harcourt (line 573 *n.*) conducted the prosecution against Defoe on 7 July 1703 (Moore, *Daniel Defoe,* pp. 120, 129–31).

Reformation of Manners

How long may Heaven be banter'd by a Nation,
With broken Vows, and Shams of Reformation,
And yet forbear to show its Indignation?
 Tell me ye Sages, who the Conscience guide,
And Ecclesiastick Oracles divide,
Where do the Bounds of Sovereign Patience end,
How long may People undestroy'd offend?
What Limits has Almighty Power prepar'd,
When Mercy shall be deaf and Justice heard?
 If there's a Being Immortal and Immense,
Who does Rewards and Punishments dispense,
Why is he Passive when his Power's defy'd,
And his Eternal Government's deny'd?
Tell us why he that sits above the Sky,
Unreigns no Vengeance, lets no Thunders fly,
When Villains prosper, and successful Vice,
Shall human Power controul and Heavenly Power despise?
 If 'tis because the Sins of such a Nation,
Are yet too small to conquer his Compassion,
Then tell us to what height Mankind may sin,
Before Celestial Fury must begin.
How their extended Crimes may reach so high,
Vengeance must follow and of course destroy;
And by the common Chain of Providence,
Destruction come like Cause and Consequence.
 Then search the dark *Arcana* of the Skies,
And *if ye can,* unfold these Mysteries:
His clashing Providences reconcile
The partial Frown, and the unequal Smile.
Tell us why some have been destroy'd betimes,

2. *Shams of Reformation:* "Nay Reformation is grown a staple Commodity, and the dealers in it are suddenly to be made into a Corporation, and their privileges peculiar are to be *Perjury* without *Punishment,* and *Lying* with *Impunity*" (*Letters from the Dead to the Living,* 2nd ed., 1702, p. 72).

While *Albion*'s glittering Shores grow black with Crimes?
Why some for early Errors are undone,
Some *longer still, and longer still* sin on?
England with all her blackening Guilt is spar'd,
And *Sodom*'s lesser Crimes receiv'd a swift Reward:
And yet all this be reconcil'd to both
Impartial Justice, and unerring Truth?
Why *Ostia* stands, and no revenging hand
Has yet dismist her from the burthen'd Land;
No Plague, no sulphurous Shower her *exit* makes,
And turns her Silver *Thames* to *Stygian* Lakes,
Whose so uninhabitable Banks might flow
With Streams as black as her that made 'em so:
And as a Monument to future Times,
Should send forth Vapours nauseous as her Crimes?
  Tell us why *Carthage* fell a Prey to *Rome,*
And mourn the Fate of bright *Byzantium.*
Why ancient *Troy*'s embrac'd by Destiny,
And *Rome,* Immortal *Rome,* to Fate gives way,
Yet *Ostia* stands, more impious far than they?
  Where are the Golden Gates of *Palestine,*
Where High Superiour Glory us'd to shine?
The mighty City Millions dwelt within,
Where Heaven's Epitome was to be seen.
God's Habitation, sacred to his Name,
Magnificent beyond the Voice of Fame:
Those lofty Pinnacles which once were seen,
Bright like the Majesty that dwelt within.
In which Seraphick Glory cou'd reside,
Too great for human Vision to abide;
Whose glittering Fabrick, *God* the Architect,
The Sun's less Glorious Light, did once reject.
  These all ha' felt the Iron hands of Fate,
And Heaven's dear Darling City's desolate.
No more the sacred Place commands our Awe,

35. *Sodom's . . . Crimes:* Genesis 18:20–19:13.
38. *Ostia:* the port of Rome; here the antitype is London.
51–60. Revelation 21:9–22.
54. *Epitome:* tri-syllabic, accented on first syllable.
62. *Sun . . . reject:* Revelation 21:23.

But all's become a Curse, a *Golgotha.*
The Reverend Pile can scarce its Ruines show,
Forsook by him whose Glory made it so.
Yet *Ostia* stands, her impious Towers defie
The threatning Comets of the blazing Sky,
Foreboding Signs of Ruine she despises,
And all her teaching Saviour's Sacrifices;
The *Jews* are Fools, *Jerusalem*'s out-done,
We crucifie the Father, they the Son.
Within her Sacred Temples are allow'd
Worse Jews than those which crucified their God:
They kill'd a Man, for they suppos'd him so;
These boldly sacrifice the God they know,
His Incarnation, Miracles, deny,
And vilely Banter his Divinity;
Their old Impostor, *Socinus,* prefer,
And the long Voyage of Heaven without a Pilot steer.
Yet *Ostia* boasts of her Regeneration,
And tells us wondrous Tales of Reformation:
How against Vice she has been so severe,
That none *but Men of Quality* may swear:

67. *Ruines:* "Some houses neer the Temple of *Solomon,* and the Palace of *Herod* . . . but not many such: nor any thing but the ruins left of the antient buildings" (Peter Heylyn, *Cosmographie,* 1652, p. 396).

73–102. Defoe quotes these lines in *Review, 8* (24 July 1711), 211, but in the following order: 83–98, 73–74, 77–78, 99–102.

76. *Worse Jews:* deists, like Charles Blount and John Toland.

84. *wondrous Tales of Reformation:* "these *Endeavours* have had a very great Success, (particularly for the Suppressing of prophane *Swearing* and *Cursing, Drunkenness,* and *Prophanation* of the *Lord's-Day,* and the giving a great Check to the *open Lewdness* that was acted in many of our Streets)" ([Josiah Woodward], *An Account of the Progress of the Reformation of Manners,* 1701, p. 3) ". . . Thousands of Offenders . . . brought to Punishment for *Swearing, Drunkenness, and Prophanation* of the *Lord's-Day* . . . *Seventy* or *Eighty Warrants* a Week having been executed on these Offenders, in and about this City only . . . Nests for *Thieves, Clippers* and *Coiners,* &c. have been rooted out and suppressed; and . . . some *Thousands* of *Lewd Persons* have been *Imprisoned, Fined,* and *Whipt;* so that the *Tower-End* of the Town, and many of our Streets, have been much purg'd of that *pestilent Generation* of *Night-Walkers* . . . *Forty* or *Fifty* of them having been sent in a Week to *Bridewell,* where they have of late received such *Discipline,* that a considerable Number of them hath chose rather to be Transported to our *Plantations*" ([Josiah Woodward], *An Account of the Societies for Reformation of Manners,* 1699, pp. 11, 22).

86. *none but Men of Quality may swear: "The man with a Gold Ring and Gay Cloaths,* may Swear before the Justice, or at the Justice; may reel home through the

How Publick Lewdness is expell'd the Nation,
That *Private Whoring* may be more in fashion.
How Parish Magistrates, like pious Elves,
Let none be Drunk a Sundays, *but themselves.*
And Hackney Coach-men durst not Ply the Street
In Sermon-time, *till they had paid the State.*
These, *Ostia,* are the Shams of Reformation,
With which thou mock'st thy Maker, and the Nation;
While in thy Streets unpunish'd there remain
Crimes which have yet insulted Heaven in vain,
Crimes which our Satyr blushes to review,
And Sins thy Sister *Sodom* never knew:
Superiour Lewdness Crowns thy Magistrates,
And Vice grown grey usurps the Reverend Seats;
Eternal Blasphemies, and Oaths abound,
And Bribes among thy Senators are found.
Old Venerable *Jeph,* with trembling Air,
Ancient in Sin, and Father of the Chair,
Forsook by Vices he had lov'd so long,
Can now be vicious only with his Tongue;
Yet talks of ancient Lewdness with delight,
And loves to be the Justice of the Night:
On Baudy Tales with pleasure he reflects,
And leudly smiles at Vices he corrects.
The feeble tottering Magistrate appears
Willing to Wickedness, in spite of Years;
Struggles his Age and Weakness to resist,

---

open Streets, and no man take any notice of it; but if a Poor Man get drunk, or swears an Oath, he must to the Stocks without Remedy" (Defoe, *The Poor Man's Plea,* 1698, p. 10).

103. *Jeph:* Sir Robert Jeffries (*Key*), or Geffrey (1613–1704), was an important iron-monger who was knighted in 1673 upon his election as sheriff of London. He subsequently served as a Tory lord mayor (1685) and president of Bethlehem Hospital and Bridewell (1689–90, 1693–1704). Although he was, on account of his age and infirmities, excused from riding before the king in celebration of the peace of Ryswick in November 1697, he never failed in his duty of presiding over the flogging of prostitutes, who were stripped to the waist for this ceremony. He was also one of the judges before whom Defoe was arraigned on 24 February 1703 (*DNB,* 7, 988; Beaven, 2, 107; John R. Moore, *Defoe in the Pillory,* Bloomington, Indiana, 1939, pp. 26–27; *Daniel Defoe,* p. 120).

And fain wou'd sin, but Nature won't assist.
Lovel, the *Pandor* of thy Judgment-Seat,
Has neither Manners, Honesty, nor Wit;
Instead of which, he's plenteously supply'd
With Nonsence, Noise, Impertinence, and Pride;
Polite his Language, and his flowing Stile
Scorns to suppose Good Manners worth his while;
With Principles from Education stor'd,
Th' Drudgery of Decency abhor'd:
The *City-Mouth,* with Eloquence endu'd,
To Mountebank the listning Multitude,
Sometimes he tunes his Tongue to soft Harangues,
To banter Common Halls, and flatter Kings:
And all with but an odd indifferent Grace,
With Jingle on his Tongue, and Coxcomb in his Face;
Definitive in Law, without Appeal,
But always serves the Hand who pays him well:
He Trades in Justice, and the Souls of Men,
And prostitutes them equally to Gain:
He has his Publick Book of Rates to show,
Where every Rogue the Price of Life may know:
And this one Maxim always goes before,
He never hangs the Rich, nor saves the Poor.
God-like he nods upon the Bench of State,
His Smiles are Life, and if he Frown 'tis Fate:
Boldly invading Heaven's Prerogative;
For with his Breath he kills, or saves alive.
Fraternities of Villains he maintains,
Protects their Robberies, and shares the Gains,
Who thieve with Toleration as a Trade,
And then restore according as they'r paid,
With awkward scornful Phyz, and vile Grimace,
The genuine Talents of an ugly Face;
With haughty Tone, insults the Wretch that dies,

115. *Lovel* (*Key*): Sir Salathiel Lovell (1619–1713), serjeant at law, was elected recorder of London in April 1692 and knighted the following October. He was promoted to king's serjeant in May 1695 and to a judge of the Chester circuit the next year. In February 1703, in Justice Hall in the Old Bailey, he brought the indictment against Defoe for libel (*DNB, 12,* 175; Moore, *Daniel Defoe,* p. 120).

And sports with his approaching Miseries.
Furnese, for so sometimes unrighteous Fate
Erects a Mad-man for a Magistrate,
Equipt with Leudness, Oaths, and Impudence,
Supplies with Vices his defect of Sence;
Abandon'd to ill Manners, he retains
His want of Grace, as well as want of Brains.
Before the Boy wore off, the Rake began,
The Bully then commenc'd, and then the Man.
Yet Nature seems in this to do him wrong,
To give no Courage with a saucy Tongue;
From whence this constant Disadvantage flows,
He always gives the Words, and takes the Blows;
Tho' often Can'd, he's uninstructed by't;
But still he shews the Scoundrel with the Knight,
Still scurrilous, and still afraid to fight.
His Dialects a *Modern Billingsgate,*
Which suits the *Hosier,* not the Magistrate;
The same he from behind the Counter brought,
And yet he practis'd worse than he was taught;
Early debauch'd, in Satan's Steps he mov'd,

149. *Furnese* (*Key*): Sir Henry Furnese (1658–1712) began his career as "apprentice to a Stockin-seller in the exchange, . . . traded in poynt to Flanders by which it is said he gott an estate" (Le Neve, p. 436), and died a baronet and member of parliament. "Eminently known for wagering," he used his advance knowledge of allied successes in the Lowlands to win bets of £2500 in 1692. In 1694 he was elected one of the original directors of the Bank of England. He served as a receiver of the £2,000,000 loan which the New East India Company made to the government in 1696 and a trustee for circulating exchequer bills in the same year. During his term as sheriff of London in 1700 he entertained at dinner in Drapers Hall 600 guests, including three dukes, 20 other peers, and dozens of members of parliament. His efforts to secure his election to parliament ended in expulsion in February 1699 and disqualification in February 1701, but finally were successful in November 1701 when he secured the seat in Sandwich, which he held until his death. In June 1707 he was created the first baronet of Great Britain (Luttrell, *2,* 472, 473, 593, 595; *3,* 342; *4,* 483; *5,* 19–20; BM MS. Add. 17677UU, f. 358v; GEC, *Baronetage, 5,* 1).

165. *the Hosier:* Although Defoe insisted that he himself had "never been a Hosier" (*Review,* 2 [31 May 1705], 149), the truth is that, like Sir Henry Furnese, he had been "for many Years . . . a Hose Factor in Freemans Yard in *Cornhill,*" as he was officially designated in *The London Gazette,* No. 3879, 11–14 January 1703. Defoe's sensitivity on this point may have led him to cancel lines 164–67 when he revised the poem for inclusion in *A True Collection* (1703).

And all Mechanick Vices he improv'd:
At first he did his Sovereign's Rights invade,
And rais'd his Fortune by clandestine Trade;
Stealing the Customs, did his Profits bring,
And 'twas his Calling to defraud his King:
This is the Man that helps to Rule the State,
The City's New-reforming Magistrate.
To execute the Justice of the Law,
And keep less Villains than himself in awe;
Take Money of the Rich, and hang the Poor,
And lash the Strumpet he debauch'd before.
So for small Crimes poor Thieves Destruction find,
And leave the Rogues of Quality behind.
Search all the Christian Climes from Pole to Pole,
And match for Sheriffs *Sweetaple* and *Cole;*
Equal in Character and Dignity,
This fam'd for Justice, that for Modesty:
By Merit chosen for the Chair of State,
This fit for *Bridewell,* that for *Billingsgate;*
That richly clad to grace the Gaudy Day,
For which his Father's Creditors must pay:
This from the fluxing Bagnio just dismist,
Rides out to make himself the City Jest.
From some *lascivious Dish-Clout* to the Chair,
To punish Leudness and Disorders there;
The Brute he rides on wou'd his Crimes detest,
For that's the Animal, and this the Beast:
And yet some Reformation he began;
For Magistrates ne're bear the Sword in vain.
Expensive Sinning always he declin'd,

183. *Sweetaple* (*Key*): Sir John Sweetapple, a banker in Lombard Street, was sworn sheriff of London in September 1694 and knighted two months later. In March 1701 he went bankrupt "for a great sume, dyeing in the Mint" (Luttrell *3,* 376–77; *4,* 560; *5,* 28; Le Neve, p. 447).

183. *Cole* (*Key*): Sir William Cole, a dry salter, was indicted in February 1693 "for money levied on dissenters in the late reigns, and not paid into the exchequer" (Luttrell, *3,* 37). The next year, however, he was sworn sheriff "with Mr. Sweetapple" and knighted at Whitehall (ibid., *3,* 375–77; Le Neve, p. 447).

190. *fluxing Bagnio:* a bathhouse where mercury was administered to cure the pox and other ailments.

To *frugal Whoring* totally resign'd:
His Avarice his Appetite opprest,
Base like the Man, and brutish like the Lust:
Concise in Sinning, Nature's Call supply'd,
And in one Act two Vices gratified.
See what Good Husbandry in Vice can do,
Oblige the Lecher and the Nigard too;
Never was Oyster, Beggar, Cinder Whore,
So much caress'd by Magistrate before:
When Men are nice and squeamish in their Lust,
'Ts a sign the Vice is low, and wants a Gust;
But he that's perfect in th' Extreme of Vice,
Scorns to excite his Appetite by Price.
'Twas in his Reign we to Reform began,
And set the Devil up to mend the Man.
More might be said, but Satyr stay thy Rimes,
And mix not his Misfortunes with his Crimes.
Clayton superbly wise and grave of Life,
Cou'd every one reform, except his Wife:
Passive in Vice, he Pimps to his own Fate,
To shew himself a Loyal Magistrate.
'Tis doubtful who debauch'd the City more,
The Maker of the Masque, or of the Whore.
Nor's his Religion less a Masquerade;
He always drove a strange mysterious Trade:
With decent Zeal, to Church he'll gravely come,

216. *Clayton* (*Key*): Sir Robert Clayton (1629–1707), "a Scrivener by Trade," was another poor apprentice who amassed a fortune and left £40,000 to charity "to attone for his way of getting it, which was . . . per opus & usus" (Hearne, *2*, 27). He was sheriff of London in 1671 (knighted on 30 October 1671), lord mayor in 1679, and Whig member of parliament for London (1678–81, 1689–90, 1695–98, 1701–02, 1705–07 (and for Bletchingley, Surrey, which he controlled: 1690–95, 1698–1700, 1702–05). In *The Second Part of Absalom and Achitophel* (280–81) he is "Extorting *Ishban*," "Persu'd by a meagre Troop of Bankrupt Heirs." Although replaced as commissioner of customs in June 1697, he was still able to lend the king £30,000 in October to pay off the troops. His wife, Martha, daughter of Perient Trott, is described as "a free-hearted woman" (*DNB*, *4*, 474).

221. *Masque:* "the pageants performed at his cost on the day (29 October 1679) of [his] 'initiation and installation' [as lord mayor] were described by Thomas Jordan in a tract entitled 'London in Luster' " (*DNB*, *4*, 473).

To praise that God which he denies at home.
Socinian Toland's his dear Ghostly Priest,
And taught him all Religion to digest.
Took prudent Care he shou'd not much profess,
And he was ne're addicted to Excess.
And yet he *Covets* without Rule or End,
Will sell his Wife, his Master, or his Friend.
To boundless Avarice a constant Slave,
Unsatisfy'd as Death, and greedy as the Grave.
  Now, Satyr, let us view the numerous Fry,
That must succeeding Magistrates Supply,
And search if future Years are like to be
Much better taught, or better rul'd than we.
  The Senators of Hospital Descent,
The upper House of *Ostia's* Parliament,
Who from Destruction should their City save,
But are as wicked as they shou'd be grave:
With Citizens *in Petto,* who at need,
As these do those, so those must these succeed.
  Duncomb, the Modern *Judas* of the Age,
Has often try'd in vain to mount the Stage:
Profuse in Gifts and Bribes to God and Man,
To ride the City-Horse, and wear the Chain.
His Vices *Ostia,* thou hast made thy own,
In chusing him, thou writ'st thy own Lampoon:

226. *Toland* (*Key*): Toland's letter to Clayton in December 1694 on the occasion of the death of Clayton's nephew and heir is remarkably deficient in Christian consolation (John Toland, *The Miscellaneous Works,* 2 vols., 1747, *2,* 318–24).

238. *Hospital Descent:* "Several of our Aldermen have been Blew-Coat-Boys, or Charity Children" (*B*).

239. *upper House:* "The Court of *Common-Council,* consisting (as the Parliament of *England*) of Two Houses; one for the Lord Mayor and Aldermen, and the other for the Commoners; in which Court are made all By-Laws, which bind all the Citizens of *London*" (Chamberlayne, 1702, p. 344).

244. *Duncomb* (*Key*): See *The True-Born Englishman,* 1046 *n.,* above.

245. *try'd in vain:* With the support of Marlborough and Henry Guy, Duncombe placed first in the mayoral election of 1700, but the aldermen chose a Whig (*The True-Born Englishman,* 1055 *n.,* above; Kenyon, p. 319). In 1701 he was again nominated, but polled 500 votes less than Sir William Gore, whom the aldermen declared mayor (Luttrell, *5,* 95).

246. *Gifts and Bribes:* See *The True-Born Englishman,* 1187 *n.,* above.

Fancy the haughty Wretch in Chair of State,
At once the City's Shame and Magistrate;
At Table set, at his right Hand a Whore,
Ugly as those which he had kept before.
He to do Justice, and reform our Lives,
And *She* receive the Homage of our Wives.
Now Satyr, give another Wretch his Due,
Who's chosen to reform the City too;
Hate him, ye Friends to Honesty and Sence,
Hate him in injur'd Beauty's just Defence:
A Knighted Booby Insolent and Base,
"Whom Man no Manners gave, nor God no Grace.
The Scorn of Women, and the Shame of Men,
Matcht at Threescore to innocent Fifteen;
Hag-rid with jealous Whimsies, lets us know
He thinks he's Cuckold *'cause he should be so:*
His vertuous Wife exposes to the Town,
And fears her Crimes because he knows his own.
Here Satyr, let them just Reproach abide,
Who sell their Daughters to oblige their Pride.
The Chamberlain begins the doleful Jest,
As a *Memento Mori* to the rest;
Who fond to raise his Generation by't,
And see his Daughter buckl'd to a Knight:

252. *a Whore:* See *The True-Born Englishman,* 1174 *n.,* above.

253. *those . . . before:* "Two Wh[ores] by turns his vacant Hours employ;/Whom, as the Gout permits, he does enjoy" (*The Grove: Or, The Rival Muses, POAS,* 1707, *4,* 358).

256. *another Wretch:* "[Sir E]dward Wills [who marrie]d the Chamber[lain']s daughter" (University of Michigan copy of *A*). On 31 July 1699 Wills, who had served as sheriff and been knighted in 1695 (Luttrell, *3,* 537) and who was now a widower aged 50, received a license to marry "Ann Cuddon, of St. Lawrence, Old Jewry, Spinster, 18; [with] consent of her father Sir Thomas Cuddon, Kt." (*Allegations for Marriage Licenses Issued by the Bishop of London, 1611 to 1828,* ed. Joseph L. Chester and George J. Armytage, 2 vols., 1887, 2, 324).

270. *The Chamberlain:* Sir Thomas Cuddon (d. 1702), "descended from Suffolk," was knighted in November 1697. He was a Whig and held two lucrative posts in the city government: chamberlain of London (1696–1702), "to whom belongs the Receipts of the Rents and Revenues of the City," and receiver-general of the taxes (Le Neve, p. 459; Luttrell, *4,* 125, 127, 132; *5,* 251; Chamberlayne, 1708, p. 289). In addition to his daughter, who married Sir Edward Wills (256 *n.,* above), he left a son who succeeded him as receiver-general of taxes.

The Innocent unwarily betray'd,
And to the Rascal join'd the hapless Maid;
The Purchase is too much below the Cost,
For while the Lady's gain'd, the Woman's lost.
 What shall we say to common Vices now,
When Magistrates the worst of Crimes allow?
Ostia, if e'er thou wilt reform thy Gates,
'T must be another Set of Magistrates:
In Practice just, and in Profession sound;
But God knows where the Men are to be found.
In all thy numerous Streets 'tis hard to tell,
Where the few Men of Faith and Honour dwell:
Poor and despis'd so seldom they appear,
The *Cynick*'s Lanthorn wou'd be useful here.
 No City in the spacious Universe,
Boasts of Religion more, or minds it less;
Of Reformation talks and Government,
Backt with an Hundred Acts of Parliament:
Those useless Scare-Crows of neglected Laws,
That miss the Effect because they miss the Cause:
Thy Magistrates who should reform the Town,
Punish the poor Mens Faults, but hide their own.
Suppress the Players Booths in *Smithfield-Fair,*
But leave the *Cloysters,* for their Wives are there,
Where all the Scenes of Lewdness do appear.

291. *an Hundred Acts of Parliament:* "An Abstract of the Penal-Laws against Immorality and Prophaneness," included as an appendix to *An Account of the Societies for Reformation of Manners* (1699), lists 10 laws against "Prophanation of the Lord's Day," 7 against drunkenness, 5 against swearing, 1 against blasphemy, 12 against lewd and disorderly practices, and 3 against gambling.

296. *the Players Booths in Smithfield-Fair:* The cattle and trade fair in Smithfield during the first three days of Bartholomewtide was accompanied by the traditional sideshow activity. In booths named for the proprietors—Mrs. Mynn's booth, Holmse's booth—drolls, farces, freaks, feats, rope dancers, wild beasts, and other entertainments were presented. But the fair was also famous for "all sort of lewdnesse and disorder" (Luttrell, *2*, 270–71), and after a series of warning proclamations beginning in 1691, the sideshows were finally closed down and Tom Brown observed in September 1699 that "The Glory is departed from *Smithfield*" (Strype, *1*, ³285; Luttrell *4*, 268; *Familiar and Courtly Letters,* 1700, p. 194).

297. *the Cloysters:* "From *Kingstreet* is a passage into *Smithfield,* through a fair Cloister . . . On both sides of which are Rows of Shops most taken up by Semstresses and Milliners" (Strype, *1*, ³284–85).

Satyr, the Arts and Mysteries forbear,
Too black for thee to write, or us to hear;
No Man, but he that is as vile as they,
Can all the Tricks and Cheats of Trade survey.
Some in Clandestine Companies combine,
Erect new Stocks to trade beyond the Line:
With Air and empty Names beguile the Town,
And raise new Credits first, then cry 'em down:
Divide the *empty nothing* into Shares,
To set the Town together by the Ears.
The Sham Projectors and the Brokers join,
And both the Cully Merchant undermine;
First he must be drawn in and then betray'd,
And they demolish the Machine they made:
So conjuring Chymists, with their Charm and Spell,
Some wondrous Liquid wondrously exhale;
But when the gaping Mob their Money pay,
The Charm's dissolv'd, the Vapour flies away:
The wondring Bubbles stand amaz'd to see
Their Money Mountebank'd to *Mercury.*
Some fit out Ships, and double Fraights ensure,
And burn the Ships to make the Voyage secure:
Promiscuous Plunders thro' the World commit,
And *with the Money* buy their safe Retreat.
Others seek out to *Africk*'s Torrid Zone,
And search the burning Shores of *Serralone;*
There in unsufferable Heats *they fry,*
And run vast Risques to see the Gold, *and die:*

309. *Sham Projectors:* "A meer Projector then is a Contemptible thing, driven by his own desperate Fortune to such a Streight, that he must be deliver'd by a Miracle, or Starve . . . Thousands, and Hundreds of thousands are the least of his discourse, and sometimes Millions; till the Ambition of some honest Coxcomb is wheedl'd to part with his Money for it" (Defoe, *An Essay upon Projects,* 1697, pp. 33–34).

319–20. *ensure,/And burn the Ships:* Defoe may have felt that sharp practices like these contributed to his own bankruptcy in 1692, which was brought about by his losses as a merchant-insurer (Moore, *Daniel Defoe,* pp. 90–94).

323–32. These lines may reflect the exploits of John Hawkins (1532–95), an English interloper in the Spanish slave trade, as recounted by Richard Hakluyt, *The Principal Navigations, Voiages, and Discoveries of the English Nation,* 1589, pp. 528–29. Hakluyt records that Hawkins sought to buy slaves in Sierra Leone, where the "contageousnes of the place" claimed the lives of a number of his men, while "the hope they had to find golde" cost the lives of a number more. He finally bought a "great companie of Negroes" and sailed off to sell them to the Spanish in America.

The harmless Natives basely they trepan,
And barter Baubles for the *Souls of Men:*
The Wretches they to Christian Climes bring o'er,
To serve worse Heathens than they did before.
The Cruelties they suffer there are such,
Amboyna's nothing, they've out-done the *Dutch:*
Cortez, Pizarro, Guzman, Penaloe,
Who drank the Blood and Gold of *Mexico,*
Who thirteen Millions of Souls destroy'd,
And left one third of God's Creation void;
By Birth for Natures Butchery design'd,
Compar'd to these are merciful and kind;
Death cou'd *their* cruellest Designs fulfil,
Blood quench't *their* Thirst, and it suffic'd to kill:
But these the tender *Coup de Grace* deny,
And make Men beg in vain for leave to die;
To more than *Spanish* Cruelty inclin'd,
Torment the Body and debauch the Mind:
The lingring Life of Slavery preserve,
And vilely teach them both to sin and serve.
In vain they talk to them of Shades below,
They fear no Hell, *but where such Christians go;*

327. *trepan:* Cf. *Review, 5* (5 March 1709), 586: "the Interlopers . . . sometimes have trepann'd the innocent Natives on Board, on Pretence of Trade, and carry'd them away into Slavery."

330. *worse Heathens:* [Thomas Tryon], *Friendly Advice to the Gentlemen-Planters of the East and West Indies,* 1684, p. 85, makes the same point: "when we [slaves] come on Shore we find no better fare nor Treatment from our Christian Masters, most of them proving as sharp and Tyrranical as our own *Heathen.*"

332. *Amboyna:* See *The Pacificator,* 180 *n.,* above, from which this line is quoted.

333. Hernán Cortes (1485–1547), the conqueror of Mexico, Francisco Pizarro (1475?–1541), the conqueror of Peru, and Nuño de Guzman (d. 1550), Cortes' lieutenant and the conqueror of western Mexico, are variously estimated to have slaughtered "12, 15, or 20 millions of poore reasonable creatures, created (as our selves) after the image of the living God" and laid waste "thrice so much lande as christendome doth comprehende," which remains "unto this day . . . a wildernes and utter desolation" (Bartolomeo de las Casas, *The Spanish Colonies . . . Translated into English by M. M. S.,* 1583, sigs. 3v, 2r, A2r). Diego Dionisio de Peñalosa (1624–87), governor of New Mexico, explored the lower Missouri basin (John G. Shea, *The Expedition of Don Diego Dionisio de Peñalosa,* New York, 1882, pp. 8, 23).

338. *these:* slave traders. Defoe's argument here follows fairly closely that of [Tryon], *Friendly Advice to the Gentlemen-Planters of the East and West Indies,* p. 75 ff., in which Wylie Sypher found parallels to Friday in *Robinson Crusoe* (*Guinea's Captive Kings,* 1942, p. 68).

Of *Jesus Christ* they very often hear,
Often as his Blaspheming Servants swear,
They hear and wonder what strange Gods they be,
Can bear with Patience such Indignity.
They look for Famines, Plagues, Disease, and Death,
Blasts from above, and Earthquakes from beneath:
But when they see regardless Heaven looks on,
They curse our Gods, or think that we have none.
Thus Thousands to Religion are brought o'er,
And made worse Devils than they were before.
  Satyr, the Men of *Drugs* and *Simples* spare,
'Tis hard to search the latent Vices there;
Their *Theologicks* too they may defend,
They can't deceive, who never did pretend.
As to Religion, generally they show
As much as their Profession will allow:
But count them all Confederates of Hell,
'Till *Blackbourn* they with one Consent expel.
Blackbourn our Satyr startles at his Name,
The College Scandal, and the City's Shame:
Not satisfy'd his Maker to deny,
Provokes him with Lampoon and Blasphemy;

354. *Earthquakes:* ". . . unless God, to punish our Masters Inhumanity, should send an Earthquake" [Tryon], *Friendly Advice to the Gentlemen-Planters of the East and West Indies,* p. 103).

357. *to Religion . . . brought o'er:* meant, sarcastically, for "converted to devil worship," which, for Defoe, was the worst effect of slavery.

358. *made worse Devils:* "Nay, to the further shame of *Christians,* have you not by lewd Examples, *defiled* and *debauched* us . . . So that instead of learning us Virtue, and courting us to your Faith and Religion by *Sobriety* and *Godliness,* you set before us *destructive Presidents,* and make us more the Children of the Devil than we were before" [Tryon], *Friendly Advice to the Gentlemen-Planters of the East and West Indies,* pp. 198–99).

366. *Blackbourn* (*Key*): Richard Blackburne (1652–c. 1716) graduated A.B. from Trinity College, Cambridge, and M.D. from Leyden about 1677. In 1681 he published a Latin biography of Hobbes, from material supplied by John Aubrey, who characterized him as "A generall scholar, prodigious memorie, sound judgment," who "practises but little" (Aubrey, *1*, 107, 395). He was admitted honorary fellow in 1685 and fellow of the College of Physicians in April 1687 (along with Francis Bernard, Richard Blackmore, and other future dissidents). He served as censor in 1688 but was fined 4 *s.* for "unseemely Language" in 1691 and subsequently refused either to sign the bond to stand by the president (1695) or to subscribe to the dispensary (1696–97) (Munk, *1*, 451–52; *Annals, 6,* 9). "The Book of Mr. *Hobbs,* called *The Leviathan*" was particularly suspect of atheism, blasphemy, and profaneness (*CJ, 8,* 636).

And with Unpresidented Insolence,
Banters a God, and scoffs at Providence.
No Nation in the World, but ours, wou'd bear
To hear a Wretch blaspheme the Gods they fear:
His Flesh long since their Altars had adorn'd,
And with his Blood appeas'd the Powers he scorn'd.
But see the Badge of our Reforming Town,
Some cry Religion up, some cry it down:
Some worship God, and some a God defie,
With equal boldness, equal liberty;
The silent Laws decline the just Debate;
Made dumb by the *more silent Magistrate;*
And both together small distinction put
'Twixt him that owns a God, and him that owns him not:
The Modern Crime 'tis thought no being had,
They knew no Atheist when our Laws were made.
'Tis hard the Laws more freedom shou'd allow
With God above, than Magistrates below.
Blackbourn unpunish'd, may Heaven and Earth defie,
Dethrone Almighty Power, Almighty Truth deny;
Burlesque the Sacred, High, *Unuttr'd Name,*
And impious War with God himself proclaim:
While Justice unconcern'd looks calmly on,
And *Blackbourn* boasts the Conquests he has won;
Insults the Christian Name, and laughs to see
Religion Bully'd by Philosophy.
Blackbourn with far less hazard may blaspheme,
Than thou mayest, *Satyr,* trace thy Noble Theme:
The Search of Vice more Hazard represents
From Laws, from Councils, and from Parliaments.
Thou may'st be wicked, and less danger know,
Than by informing others they are so:
Thou canst no Peer, no Counsellor expose,
Or dress a vicious Member in his proper Cloaths;
But all the Bombs and Canon of the Law,
Are soon drawn out to keep thy Pen in awe:
By Laws *Post Facto* thou may'st soon be slain,
And *Inuendo*'s shall thy Guilt explain.

407. *Laws Post Facto:* Cf. *An Encomium upon a Parliament,* 36–37 *n.,* above.

Thou may'st Lampoon, and no Man will resent;
Lampoon but Heaven, and not the Parliament:
Our Trusties and our Welbelov'ds forbear;
Thou'rt free to banter Heaven, and all that's there;
The boldest Flights thou'rt welcome to bestow
O'th' Gods above, but not the God's below.
Blackbourn may banter Heaven, and *Asgill* Death,
And *Toland* poyson Souls with his infected Breath.
No Civil Government resents the Wrong;
But all are touch'd and angry at thy Song.
Thy Friends without the help of Prophesie,
Read Gaols and Gibbets in thy Destiny;
But *Courage springs from Truth,* let it appear,
Nothing but Guilt can be the Cause of Fear;
Satyr go on, thy keenest Shafts let fly,
Truth can be no Offence to Honesty;
The Guilty only are concern'd, and *they*
Lampoon themselves, when e're they censure thee.

Part II.

The City's view'd, now Satyr turn thine Eye,
The Country's Vices, and the Court's survey:
And from Impartial Scrutiny set down,
How much they're both more vicious than the Town.
How does our Ten Years War with Vice advance?
About as much as it hath done with France.
Ride with the Judge and view the wrangling Bar,
And see how lewd our *Justice-Merchants* are:
How *Clito* comes from instigating Whore,

411. *Trusties and . . . Welbelov'ds:* "Trusty and Well-Beloved, We Greet you well" is the formula by which the king addresses his subjects in a letter.

415. *Asgill:* See *The True-Born Englishman,* 510 *n.,* above.

416. *Toland:* See *A New Satyr on the Parliament,* 81 *n.,* above.

431. *Ten Years War:* The first society for the reformation of manners was organized in London in 1690 (Strype, 2, 230).

435. *Clito:* "Names without pointing to any particular Person" (*Key*). Defoe claimed in 1703 that "*the Lawyers have named me Twenty Men for my* Clitus" (*More Reformation,* 1703, sig. A4v). Despite Defoe's protestations, however, it is possible that Clito is Sir Robert Davers (1653–1722), second baronet, of Rougham, Suffolk, who married

Pleads for the Man he Cuckol'd just before;
See how he Cants, and acts the Ghostly Father,
And brings the Gospel and the Law together:
To make his pious Frauds be well receiv'd,
He quotes that Scripture which he ne're believ'd;
Fluent in Language, indigent in Sence,
Supplies his want of Law with Impudence.
See how he rides the Circuit with the Judge;
To Law and Leudness a devoted Drudge.
A Brace of Female-Clients meet him there,
To help debauch the *Sizes* and the *Fair:*
By Day he plies the Bar with all his might,
And Revels in St. *Edmund*'s Streets at Night:
The Scandal of the Law, his own Lampoon,
Is Lawyer, Merchant, Bully, and Buffoon,
In drunken Quarrels eager to engage,
Till Brother Justice lodg'd him in the Cage:
A thing the Learned thought could never be,
Had not the Justice been as drunk as he.
He pleads of late at *Hymen*'s Nuptial Bar,
And bright *Aurelia* is Defendant there.
He Courts the Nymph to Wed and make a Wife,
And swears *by God* he will reform his Life.
The solemn Part he might ha' well forbore;
For she alas! has been, *has been a Whore:*
The pious Dame, the sober Saint puts on,
And *Clito*'s in the way to be undone.
Casco's debauch'd, 'tis his Paternal Vice;

Mary, daughter of Thomas Jermyn, second baron Jermyn of St. Edmundsbury, in 1682, and served as Tory member of parliament for Bury St. Edmunds, Suffolk (1689–1701, November 1703–05) and for county Suffolk (1705–22). He was a big, red-faced man who could "neither write sence or true English" (S. H. A. Hervey, *Rushbrook Parish Registers,* Woodbridge, Suffolk, 1903, pp. 363–64; GEC, *Baronetage, 4,* 128). Defoe reported to Harley in September 1704 that Davers "rules" Bury and "carries matters very high" (HMC *Portland MSS., 4,* 136).

456. *Aurelia:* The lady remains unidentified. Her character however is not inconsistent with that of Aurelia in *The Grove: Or, The Rival Muses* (1701) who denies "The Joys of Wedlock" to "her trading Spouse," while *"Papirius* reaps the Harvest of her Charms" (*POAS,* 1707, *4,* 356).

463. *Casco:* "Cowper" (*Key*). William Cowper (1665?–1723), first earl Cowper and first lord chancellor of Great Britain, was the eldest son of Sir William Cowper, second baronet, of Ratling Court, Kent. He studied law at the Middle Temple (1682–88), married as his first wife Judith, daughter of Sir Robert Booth, a London merchant, in

For Wickedness descends to Families:
The tainted Blood the Seeds of Vice convey,
And plants new Crimes before the old decay.
Thro' all Degrees of Vice the Father run,
But sees himself out-sin'd by either Son;
Whoring and *Incest* he has understood,
And they subjoyn Adultery and Blood.
But some ha' Thought in Both he was Decoy'd,
The Mother that, the Negro this Enjoy'd.
This does the Orphan's Cause devoutly plead,

May 1688, and in November of the same year rode out in company with about 30 others to join the prince of Orange at Wallingford. He was appointed king's counsel in 1694. In the House of Commons, where he sat for Hertford (1695–1700) and Beeralston (1701–05), he made himself "very acceptable" to the Whigs and soon became known as "the Man who spoke the best of any" (Burnet, *2*, 426). In October 1705 he was made privy councillor and "the youngest Lord Keeper ever known . . . tho' of very bad Principles & Morals, being well known to have had two Wives at a time" (Hearne, *1*, 56). He was raised to the peerage as baron Cowper of Wingham in December 1706, made lord chancellor in May 1707, and created earl Cowper in May 1718.

467. *the Father:* Sir William Cowper (d. 1706), second baronet, of Ratling Court, Kent, and member of parliament for Hertford (1679–1700), was one of the first Whigs, joining Shaftesbury in the exclusion crisis of 1679–82. He was said to be "possess'd of a large Estate . . . an old *Debauchee,* given to irregular Pleasures, not such as the Laws of Nature seem to dictate . . . he dy'd suddenly in the midst of his Excesses" (Manley, *1*, 213).

468. *either Son:* William Cowper's younger brother, Spencer Cowper (1669?–1728), was educated at the Westminster School and studied law at Lincoln's Inn. He was appointed comptroller of the Bridge House estates, in June 1690, a post he held until 1705 when he succeeded his brother as member for Beeralston. He was one of the managers of the impeachment proceedings against Sacheverell in 1710 and ended his career as a judge of the common pleas, to which he was constituted in October 1727. He was the grandfather of William Cowper, the poet.

469. *Incest:* Spencer Cowper's "Lady [Pennington, daughter of John Goodeve] had been his Father's Mistress, and his Mother never forgave him his Marriage with her" (Manley, *1*, 229).

470. *Adultery:* The story of William Cowper's relationship with Elizabeth Culling, or Cullen, by whom he had two children (Hearne, *1*, 57; *The English Traveller,* 2 vols., 1746, *1*, 315; *Biographia Britannica,* 2nd ed., *4*, 388–89), is told in more detail by Delariviere Manley (473 *n.*, below).

Blood: The story of Spencer Cowper's involvement in the death of Sarah Stout is recounted below, 495 *n.*

473. *This:* Mary Manley recounts the story of William Cowper and Elizabeth Culling, or Cullen, in terms of Hernando and Louisa: "There was an *Orphan* left to his Care, her Fortune not large, but her Person very agreeable: *Hernando* was Amorous; he hated his Wife, tho' he liv'd civilly with her . . . *Louisa* was the Name of his beautiful Ward; she was brought up in the House with his Lady, who had a great kindness for her . . . [Louisa's] Mind had taken a natural bent to Orizons and Devotion . . .

Secures her Money and her Maidenhead:
And then perswades her to defend the Crime,
Evade the Guilt, and Banter off the Shame.
Taught by the subtile Counsellor, she shows
More nice Distinctions than *Ignatius* knows:
In Matrimony finds a learned flaw,
A Wife in Honour, and a Wife in Law.
"Choice is the Substance of the Contract made,
"And mutual Love the only Knot that's ty'd:
"To these the Laws of Nations must submit;
"And where they fail, the Contract's incomplete.
"So that if Love and Choice were not before,
"The last may be the Wife, the first the Whore.
Thus she securely sins with eager Gust,
And satisfies her Conscience, and her Lust:
Nor does her Zeal and Piety omit,
But to the Whore she joyns the Jesuit;
With constant Zeal frequents the House of Prayer,
To heal her prostituted Conscience there,
Without Remorse, adjourns with full Content,
From his lascivious Arms to th' Sacrament.

[Hernando] resolv'd to . . . undermine that seemingly invincible Chastity . . . introduced a learned Discourse of the lawfulness of Double Marriages . . . he urg'd Arguments innumerable . . . to perswade her to the lawfulness of Poligamy . . . till at length he almost convinc'd her, that the Law of Nature was prior, and ought to take place . . . *Louisa* had no very strong Head . . . Unknown to her self she lov'd him . . . she was become bold, as to Opinion, contented within her self, that she did nothing against the Laws of God and Nature . . . Having . . . fix'd this immoveable Principle in her Breast, she consented to marry him; she could admit of *Poligamy,* but would not hear a word of *Concubinage* . . . [Spencer Cowper, in clerical garb, "another colour'd Wig . . . and speaking *a la Francoise,"* married them in London] . . . *Louisa* prov'd with Child . . . [whereupon Lady Cowper] upbraided *Louisa* of breach of Hospitality; of violating the Laws of Friendship . . . 'twas more than Adultery, 'twas Incest . . . Throughly convinced of the Doctrine he had taught her, that Plurality of Wives were lawful . . . *Louisa* had two Children" (Manley, *1,* 214–44).

475. *defend the Crime:* Swift thought that Cowper himself had committed these arguments to writing, "with Intention to publish for the *general Good"* (*Prose, 3,* 57–58), but Delariviere Manley maintained that it was "Mr. Sambrook of *New Forest* [who] wrote the Defence of *Polygame"* (*The Key to Atalantis Part I*). Jeremy Sambrook, who succeeded as fifth baronet in 1740, was Elizabeth Culling's neighbor at Gobions, once the estate of Sir Thomas More.

486. *The last . . . the Wife:* "Mr. *Cowper* persuadeing his M[ist]r[es]s to think herself his *other wife"* was a feat that William Nicolson, bishop of Carlisle, recorded in his diary (8 February 1703) (Carlisle Public Library MS., no foliation).

The Brother less afraid of Sin than Shame,
Doubles his Guilt, to save his tottering Fame:
'Twas too much Risque for any Man to run,
To save that Credit which before was gone:
The Innocent lies unreveng'd in Death,
He stop'd the growing Scandal in her Breath:
Till Time shall lay the horrid Murther bare:

495. *The Brother:* Spencer Cowper, together with three other lawyers, was tried in July 1699 for the murder of a young woman named Sarah Stout, whose body had been found floating in the river at Hertford four months before. Cowper, who customarily stayed with the Stouts when he visited Hertford during assizes, and who handled the young woman's investments, was the last person to be seen with her before her death. The trial created a sensation and although Cowper was acquitted, a contemporary pamphleteer thought that "it certainly looks very darkly" (Howell, *13*, 1106–1250). Delariviere Manley, however, who tells the story in terms of Mosco and Zara, did not believe that Cowper was guilty of murder. Her version is as follows: "[Mosco] was sick at Heart of young *Zara* . . . a very pretty Girl, whose Mother liv'd in the same *Villa* with *Hernando,* but so great a Bigot, that *Zara* had seen nothing but their own forbidding Crew of Sectaries [Quakers] . . . Her Fortune was considerable for one of her rank; she had eight thousand Crowns in her own Hands . . . Her Father was dead . . . *Mosco* . . . was mightily taken with pretty *Zara* . . . The young Creature took a fatal Passion for him, which was not in her Power to conceal, not even from his Wife . . . she put all her little Matters in *Mosco*'s Hand; he it was that dispos'd of her Fortune . . . she . . . perpetually put her self in the Road where she might meet him . . . By the pretence of Business, he cou'd often see *Zara* at her Mother's House . . . [Zara discovers] he's cool'd! his fainting Ardors retain nothing of their first Sweetness! he ev'n avoids me . . . things are come to that height, I can't bear to live and not possess you all . . . Persons of our [Quaker] Persuasion, promise nothing but what they are sure to perform . . . [Zara threatens to expose Mosco to his wife] . . . he resolv'd to undeceive her, tho' it might possibly take her Affairs out of his Hands, and with it inconvenience his; yet her Persecutions were more intollerable, and he would be at rest from so troublesome an Amour . . . he took Horse, and arriv'd the same Night at the *Villa.* She was all Joy, and new Transport to see him . . . She told him he must lie there that Night . . . They supp'd with her Mother, who afterwards withdrew to order the Linen for his Bed. All the good Nature he was Master of could not force him to shew Tenderness where he had so strong an Aversion . . . Therefore having summon'd all his Resolution, he ask'd her if they should take a Walk by the River-side. The Servant was above ordering his Bed, but he was afraid what he had to say would make her so outragious, that the Family would hear her . . . Revenge and Despair work'd her up to the height of Lunacy . . . she flounc'd . . . into the River . . . Next Morning the Body was found down the River, where the Stream had carry'd it, and *Mosco* upon the Road . . . [Her friends] have advanc'd, That he had the Improvement of her Fortune in his Hands, which amounted to a considerable Sum, and [it] was not known to any but her self: That his Affairs would not then permit him to restore it; which if she had liv'd, and they had become Enemies, he must have done; and therefore to appropriate that, and rid himself of a troublesome Amour, in conjunction with two more of his Friends, they had first strangled, and then thrown her into the River" (Manley, *1*, 227–44).

No Bribes can crush the Writs of Error there.
Nor is the Bench less tainted than the Bar:
How hard's that Plague to cure that's spread so far!
'Twill all prescrib'd Authorities reject,
While they're most guilty who shou'd first correct.
Contagious Vice infects the Judgment Seats,
And Vertue from Authority retreats:
How shou'd she such Society endure?
Where she's contemn'd she cannot be secure.
Milo's Justice, they that made him so
Shou'd answer for th' oppressive Wrongs he'll do:
His Lands almost to *Ostia*'s Walls extend;
And of his heap'd up Thousands there's no end.
If Magistrates, as in the Text 'tis clear,
Ought to be such as Avarice abhor,
This may be known of the Almighty's Mind,
That *Milo*'s not the Man the Text design'd.
Satyr, be bold, and fear not to expose
The vilest Magistrate the Nation knows:
Let *Furius* read his naked Character,

502. *crush the Writs of Error:* In July 1700, Mary Stout, mother of the deceased, petitioned the new lord keeper, Sir Nathan Wright, for a writ of appeal. Sir Nathan, assisted by two lord chief justices, Sir George Treby and Sir Edward Ward, the master of the rolls, Sir John Trevor, and a puisne judge of common pleas, Sir John Powell, denied the petition (Howell, *13,* 1194–99). Burnet, who knew that "Money, as was said, did everything" with Wright, acknowledged that he had "never heard him charged with Bribery in his Court" (*2,* 379, 426).

511. *Milo:* "Tysson" (*Key*). Francis Tyson (d. 1710?), who lived near Hackney, was a merchant-adventurer and deputy governor of the old East India Company. Among the corporations he helped to found was the Royal Corporation "for the setting the poor at work," which received a charter in June 1691. In April 1695 during a parliamentary investigation of corrupt practices in the government, Sir Thomas Cooke, governor of the East India Company, testified that he gave Tyson £10,000 in November 1692 to use in securing passage of the Company's new charter in 1693. "Justice Tyson," as Luttrell refers to him, served as a deputy lieutenant in the Tower Hamlets (where the first society for the reformation of manners was founded in 1690). Luttrell reports that he died in November 1710, "leaving an estate of near 10,000*l.* per ann.," but according to another source he was still alive in April 1712 (HMC *Lords MSS.,* New Series, *1,* 552–53, 561, 569; *CSPD 1690–91,* 422, 459, 505; Luttrell, *6,* 659; HMC *Townshend MSS.,* p. 210).

515. *the Text:* The text is Exodus 18:21 and the judges whom the text designed were "able men, such as fear God, men of truth, hating covetousness."

521. *Furius:* "Old Justice Wroth" (*Key*). John Wroth (1647?–1708), of Loughton, Essex, refused to attend Cambridge but traveled abroad "for his better breeding." He

Blush not to write what he shou'd blush to hear;
But let them blush, who in a Christian State
Made such a Devil be a Magistrate.
In *Britain*'s Eastern Provinces he reigns,
And serves the Devil with excessive Pains:
The Nation's Shame, and honest Mens Surprize,
With Drunkard in his Face, and Mad-man in his Eyes.
The sacred Bench of Justice he prophanes,
With a polluted Tongue and bloody Hands:
His Intellects are always in a Storm,
He frights the People which he shou'd reform.
Antipathys may some Diseases cure,
But Vertue can no Contraries endure.
All Reformation stops when Vice commands,
Corrupted Heads can ne'er have upright Hands.
Shameless i' th' Class of Justices he'll swear,
And plants the Vices he should punish there.
His Mouth's a Sink of Oaths and Blasphemies,
And Cursings are his kind Civilities;
His fervent Prayers to Heaven he hourly sends,
But 'tis to damn himself and all his Friends;
He raves in Vice, and storms that he's confin'd,
And studies to be worse than all Mankind.

---

married the first of his three wives in 1666, the second in 1673, and the third in 1706. He served in the army (1667–78) but when Princess Anne made a brief halt at Loughton in her flight from London in November 1688, Lord Ailesbury described Wroth as "a blustering County Justice and a gentleman grazier." Wroth subsequently sat in the convention parliament (1688–89) for Essex and voted to proclaim the prince and princess of Orange king and queen. In 1703–04 he was deputy lieutenant for Essex (*CSPD 1703–1704*, p. 278). He engaged in several lawsuits with members of his own family: in fact he celebrated his attainment of majority by filing a bill of complaint against his guardian, who was also his uncle, and later he "declared his dislike of the settlement he had made [on his second wife], and threatened . . . that, if she would not consent to destroy it and accept one for her life only, he would not live with her." He also enjoyed bullying Joseph Brown, an ejected minister who kept a school at Nazeing. On one occasion Wroth ordered "Carts . . . brought to [Brown's] House, that carried away all his Goods, leaving nothing behind but a wooden Platter that was split in two" (A. G. Matthews, *Calamy Revised,* Oxford, 1934, p. 81). Roger Morice called him "debauched," but his vices may have been somewhat less "Exotick" than Defoe imagined. Two natural children, presumably by Mary Horne, who was buried at Loughton on 3 January 1703, were left "200*l.* apiece" in Wroth's will, but getting a wench with child does not, as Dr. Johnson ruled, qualify a man as a whoremonger (*Transactions of the Essex Archaeological Society, 8* [1903], 350–52; *CSPD 1703–1704,* p. 278).

Extremes of Wickedness are his Delight,
And's pleas'd to hear that he's distinguisht by't:
Exotick ways of sinning he improves,
We curse and hate, he curses where he loves;
So strangely retrograde to all Mankind,
If crost he damns himself, if pleas'd his Friend.
This is the Man that helps to bless the Nation,
And bully Mankind into Reformation,
The true Coercive Power of the Law,
Which drives the People which it cannot draw:
The Nation's Scandal, *England*'s true Lampoon,
A Drunken, Whoring, Justicing Buffoon.
With what stupendious Impudence can he
Punish a poor Man's Immorality?
How shou'd a Vicious Magistrate assent
To mend our Manners, or our Government?
How shall new Laws for Reformation pass,
If Vice the Legislation shou'd possess?
To see Old *Sidly* Blasphemy decry,
And *Seymore* vote to punish Bribery;
Lying exploded by a Perjur'd Knight,
And Whoring punish'd by a *Sodomite:*
That he the Peoples Freedom shou'd defend,
Who had the King and People too trepan'd.
Soldiers seek Peace, Drunkards prohibit Wine,
And Fops and Beaus our Politicks refine:
These are Absurdities too gross to hide,
Which wise Men wonder at, and Fools deride.
When from the Helm *Socinian Harcourt* flies,
And all the rest his Tenets stigmatize,

563. *Sidly* (*Key*): In February 1698 Sir Charles Sedley was appointed to a committee charged to bring in a bill against profaneness, immorality, and debauchery. What finally emerged was an Act for the more effectual suppressing of Blasphemy (9 & 10 William III c. 32). Cf. *Upon the Author of the Satyr against Wit,* headnote, pp. 130–31 above.

564. *Seymore* (*Key*): See Defoe, *A New Satyr on the Parliament,* 41 *n.,* 82 *n.,* above.

573. *Harcourt* (*Key*): Even one of Simon Harcourt's admirers agreed that "When young, he was wild," and Onslow called him "very able, but without shame" (Hearne, *9,* 334; John, Lord Campbell, *The Lives of the Lord Chancellors,* 2nd ed., 7 vols., 1846–47, *4,* 442). Despite his early heterodoxy, he prosecuted Daniel Defoe for blasphemous libel in July 1703 and by 1711 he had become baron Harcourt of Stanton Harcourt and "a great asserter of the Church of England" (GEC, *6,* 299).

And none remain that *Jesus Christ* denies.
Judas expell'd, Lewd, Lying *Cutts* sent home,
And Men of Honesty put in their room.
Blaspheming *Bolls* to his Fen-Ditches sent,
To bully Justice with a Parliament,
Then we shall have a Christian Government.
Then shall the wisht for Reformation rise,
And Vice to Vertue fall a Sacrifice:
  And with the Nautious Rabble that retire,
Turn out that Bawdy, Saucy Poet *Prior*.
A *Vintner*'s Boy, the Wretch was first preferr'd
To wait at Vice's Gates, and Pimp for Bread;
To hold the Candle, and sometimes the Door,
Let in the Drunkard, and let out the Whore:
But, as to Villains it has often chanc'd,
Was for his Wit and Wickedness advanc'd.

576. *Judas expell'd*: Judas is Sir Charles Duncombe (see *The True-Born Englishman*, 1124–29, above). Despite the fact that he had been expelled from the House in February 1698, he was returned for two boroughs in July 1702 and chose to represent Downton, Wiltshire.

Cutts (*Key*): See *Advice to a Painter*, 106 *n.*; *The Court*, 37–38 *n.*, above.

578. *Bolls* (*Key*): Sir John Bolles, of Scampton, Lincolnshire, fourth baronet (1669–1714), was educated at Christ Church, Oxford, and Gray's Inn. Before he was certified as a lunatic (HMC *Lords MSS.*, New Series, *8*, 273) he served 12 years as a Tory member for Lincoln (1690–1702). He refused to subscribe to the association for the king's safety in March 1696 (ibid., *2*, 209) and spoke of William "in the vilest terms," boasting that he had been elected in November 1701 "in spite of his teeth" (*CSPD 1700–1702*, pp. 499, 501, 505). In June 1702 a warrant was issued for his arrest "for having spoken scandalous and treasonable words of the Queen" (*CSPD 1702–1703*, p. 509) and he was not returned in July 1702.

584. *Prior* (*Key*): When his father died in the 1670s Matthew Prior was sent to live with his uncle, Arthur Prior, proprietor of the Rhenish (not the Rummer) tavern in Channel (now Cannon) Row. It was here, while keeping accounts at the bar, that Prior was "surprised" reading Horace and eventually sent back to Westminster School by the earl of Dorset (Charles K. Eves, *Matthew Prior*, New York, 1939, pp. 12–14). After his defection from the Whigs (see *England's Late Jury*, 117 *n.*, above) and his short-lived career in parliament (January–November 1701), Prior retained only his commission in the Board of Trade and Plantations. Since he was now "an intire Creature of my Lord *Jersey*'s," whom Anne reappointed lord chamberlain in April 1702, he "Hasten'd to Court, to beg a Place" (Macky, p. 135; Luttrell, *5*, 163; Prior, *Works*, *1*, 195). George Stepney mentions the violence of Defoe's attack on Prior in a letter from Vienna and congratulates himself that he is "out of the reach of such desperate Scandalls which is not to be wiped off during a whole life" (PRO, 105/68, f. 113v).

590. *Wit:* Defoe paid another grudging tribute to Prior's wit in *The Consolidator*, 1705, p. 27.

Let no Man think his new Behaviour strange,
No Metamorphosis can Nature change;
Effects are chain'd to Causes, generally
The Rascal born will like a Rascal die.
His Prince's Favours follow'd him in vain,
They chang'd the Circumstance, but not the Man.
While out of Pocket, and his Spirits low,
He'd beg, write Panegyricks, cringe and bow;
But when good Pensions had his Labours crown'd,
His Panegyricks into Satyrs turn'd,
And with a true Mechanick Spirit curst,
Abus'd his Royal Benefactor first.
O What assiduous Pains does *Prior* take,
To let great *Dorset* see he cou'd mistake!
Dissembling Nature false Description gave,
Shew'd him the Poet, and conceal'd the Knave.
Toland, if such a Wretch is worth our Scorn,
Shall Vice's blackest Catalogue adorn;
His hated Character, let this supply,
Too vile even for our University.
Now, Satyr, to one Character be just,
Mohun's the only Pattern and the first:

602. *Abus'd his Royal Benefactor:* After writing a series of flattering odes to the king between 1690 and 1700, Prior referred to him in 1701 as "our little disperited fr[igger]" in *Ballad* ("The Crown once again").

604. *Dorset:* Cf. 584 *n.*, above.

607. *Toland* (*Key*): In January 1694, after receiving an M.A. at Edinburgh and after further study at Leyden, Toland settled in Oxford. There his behavior was "so publick and notorious"—he was even thought to have "seduc'd" a number of students with "secret arts" (*Original Letters,* p. 227)—that the vice-chancellor, Dr. Henry Aldrich, ordered him to depart. When he returned to Oxford during Aldrich's absence, "Evidence was then offered upon Oath, of his Trampling on the Common prayer book, talking against the Scriptures, commending Commonwealths, justifying the murder of K. C[harles] 1st, railing against Priests in general, with a Thousand other Extravagancys" (*N&Q,* 3rd series, *1* [4 January 1862], 7).

612. *Mohun* (*Key*): Charles Mohun, fourth baron Mohun (1675?–1712), was "the greatest Debauchee and Bully of the Age" (Hearne, *3,* 486). His "Penitence" occurred when, after having been acquitted of two murders of which he probably was guilty, he was acquitted in March 1699 of a murder of which he probably was innocent: "On his being acquitted at the last Trial, he expressed his Confusion for the Scandal he brought upon his Degree as a Peer by his Behaviour, in very handsom Terms, and promised to behave himself so, for the future, as not to give farther Scandal" (Macky, p. 93). He was killed in a duel with James Douglas, fourth duke of Hamilton, in November 1712.

A Title which has more of Honour in't,
Than all his ancient Glories of Descent.
Most Men their Neighbours Vices will disown,
But he's the Man that first reforms his own.
Let those alone reproach his want of Sence,
Who with his Crimes have had his Penitence.
'Tis want of Sence makes Men when they do wrong,
Adjourn their promis'd Penitence too long:
Nor let them call him Coward, because he fears
To pull both God and Man about his Ears.
Amongst the worst of Cowards let him be nam'd,
Who having sin'd's *afraid to be asham'd:*
And to mistaken Courage he's betray'd,
Who having sin'd's *asham'd to be afraid.*
Thy Valour, *Mohun,* does our Praise prevent,
For thou hast had the Courage to repent:
Nor shall his first Mistakes our Censure find,
What Heaven forgets let no Man call to mind.
Satyr, Make search thro' all this sober Age,
To bring one season'd Drunkard on the Stage;
Sir *Stephen,* nor Sir *Thomas* won't suffize,
Nor six and Twenty *Kentish* Justices:
Your *Essex* Priesthood hardly can supply,
Tho' they'r enough to drink the Nation dry;
Tho' Parson *Bedford* has been steept in Wine,

633. *Sir Stephen:* "Sir *Stephen*" may be another name "without pointing to any particular Person" (435 *n.,* above). But since Defoe identified "Sir *Thomas*" in the 1710 *Key,* "Sir *Stephen*" may be equally particular. If so, one candidate is Sir Stephen Evance, a London goldsmith and business associate of Sir Thomas Cooke, who committed suicide under the mistaken apprehension that he was bankrupt (Luttrell, *2,* 395; Le Neve, p. 435).

Sir Thomas: "Sir Tho. Cook" (Key). The reading of the 1710 text, "Sir *T——s Cecil,*" is hypermetrical and presumably wrong. Sir Thomas Cooke (d. 1709), knighted in September 1690, was a London goldsmith, governor of the old East India Company, and a Tory member of parliament for Colchester, Essex (November 1694–October 1695, July 1698–April 1705). He was defeated in the election of October–November 1695 while a prisoner in the Tower on charges of bribing members of parliament to secure passage of a new charter for the East India Company in 1693. In 1699 he was fined £14,000 for a drawback in exported pepper (Le Neve, p. 434; Luttrell, *3,* 460–62, 519; *4,* 626; Beaven, *2,* 118).

637. *Bedford:* Hilkiah Bedford (1663–1724), "a learned conscientious Non-Juror," as Hearne calls him (*2,* 12 *n.*), graduated in 1684 from St. John's College, Cambridge, and was appointed a fellow the next year. In 1690, however, he was ejected as rector of

And sunk the Royal Tankard on the *Rhine,*
He's not the Man that's fit to raise a Breed,
Shou'd *P———k, Paul,* or *Robinson* succeed;
Or match the Size of matchless *Rochester,*
And make one long Debauch of Thirteen Year;
It must be something can Mankind out-do,
Some high Excess that's wonderful and new:
Nor will Mechanick Sots our Satyr suit,
'Tis Quality must grace the Attribute.
These like the lofty Cedars to the Shrub,
Drink *Maudlin-Colledge* down, and *Royston-Club.*
Such petty Drinking's a Mechanick Evil,
But he's a Drunkard that out-drinks the Devil:
If such can not in Court or Church appear,
Let's view the Camp, you'll quickly find 'em there.
Brave *Torrington,* who Revell'd Day and Night,

Wittering, Northamptonshire, for refusing to take the oaths to William and Mary. Hearne also mentions that he traveled abroad for several years as a traveling tutor (ibid., 2, 346). Later he kept a boardinghouse for students at Westminster School and acquired the "powerful Protection" of Robert Harley (*DNB, 2,* 110). In a lampoon of 1714 he and Defoe are incongruously associated as protégés of Harley: "The Priest and *De Foe,*/Pursue their wise Master's Direction" (*On Mr. Bedford's Sentence being remitted* ["When merry Sir *Lit*"], *Political Merriment,* Part I, 1714, pp. 38–40). In 1721 Bedford was consecrated a nonjuror bishop.

640. *P——k:* "Pembrook," the reading of *B,* makes no apparent sense, for the context requires a clergyman. Defoe may have intended Simon Patrick (1626–1707), bishop of Ely.

Paul: presumably William Paul (1678–1716), the Jacobite.

Robinson: presumably John Robinson (1650–1723), who succeeded Henry Compton as bishop of London in August 1713.

641. *Rochester:* John Wilmot, earl of Rochester. Rochester's chaplain could hardly conceal his wonder at the enormity of Rochester's sins; they "were like his Parts . . . all of them high and extraordinary. He seem'd to affect something singular and paradoxical in his Impieties, as well as in his Writings, above the reach and thought of other men" (Robert Parsons, *A Sermon Preached at the Funeral of the Rt. Honorable John Earl of Rochester,* 1680, pp. 8–9).

648. *Maudlin-Colledge:* a pun on maudlin drunk(?); cf. *New Dictionary,* sig. H3r: "*Mawdlin,* weepingly Drunk."

Royston-Club: The club met on the first Thursday of every month at the Red Lion inn in Royston, Hertfordshire, to "Settle all the affaires of the Country and carry all before them" (*Gentlemen's Magazine, 53* [October 1783], 814). The members, as Defoe told Harley, were "Entirely Church and all of the High Sort . . . They used to Drink Excessively, and do a Thousand Extravagant Things" (*The Letters of Daniel Defoe,* ed. George H. Healey, Oxford, 1955, p. 57).

653. *Torrington* (*Key*): See *The Mock Mourners,* 256 *n.,* above.

And always kept himself too drunk to fight;
And *Orford,* in a Sea of Sulphur strove
To let the *Spaniards* see the Vice we love.
Yet these are puny Sinners, if you'll look
The dreadful Roll in Fate's Authentick Book.
The Monument of *Bacchus* still remains,
Where *English* Bones lie heapt in *Irish* Plains:
Triumphant Death upon our Army trod,
And Revell'd at *Dundalk* in *English* Blood.
Let no Man wonder at the Dreadful Blow,
For Heaven has seldom been insulted so.
In vain brave *Schomberg* mourn'd the Troops that fell,
While he made Vows to Heaven and they to Hell.
Our Satyr trembles to review those Times,
And hardly finds out Words to name their Crimes;
In every Tent the horrid *Juncto's* sate,
To brave their Maker and despise their Fate;
The Work was done, Drunkenness was gone before,
Life was suspended, *Death could do no more.*
Five Regimented Heroes there appear,

655. *Orford:* See *A Conference,* 133 *n.,* above; a reference to Orford's drunkenness may be concealed in the following incident of February 1699: "it is reported that Lord Peterborough should brand Lord Orford with being a * * * and a coward" (Vernon, *2,* 264).

662. *Dundalk:* The English army encamped before Dundalk suffered frightful casualties during the winter of 1689–90. One Sunday in November it was reported that all the roads out of the city were crowded with wagons evacuating the dead and dying; "ever as the Waggons joulted, some of them died and were thrown off as fast." Although "a good quantity of Brandy [was] delivered out to every Regiment," it was "the unacquaintedness of the English to hardships, and indeed their lazy Carelessness" that was blamed for the deaths ([George Story], *A True and Impartial History of the Most Material Occurrences in the Kingdom of Ireland during the Two Last Years,* 1691, pp. 27–39).

665. *Schomberg:* See *The True-Born Englishman,* 1011 *n.,* above.

673. *Five Regimented Heroes:* five officers in the English army encamped before Dundalk in 1689. A manuscript note in the Michigan copy of *A* identifies four of them: "Sir Edw. Deeri[ng], Coll. [Wharton?], Sir Tho. Gowe[r], Coll. Hunger[ford], dead by excess [at?] Carlingford." Sir Edward Dering, of Surrenden Dering, Kent, third baronet (1650–89) and member of parliament for Kent (1678–81), was "known in his native county as the 'Black Devil of Kent'" (Dalton, *3,* 71). He commanded a regiment of foot and was buried in Dundalk church on 17 October 1689 (GEC, *Baronetage, 2,* 7; [George Story], *A True and Impartial History,* 1691, p. 29). Colonel Henry Wharton (1657–89), third son of Philip, fourth Baron Wharton, also commanded a regiment of foot. He was "a brisk, bold man" and there was said to be "much . . .

Captains of Thousands, mighty Men of War,
Glutted with Wine, and drunk with Hellish Rage,
For want of other Foes they Heaven engage.
Sulphur and ill extracted Fumes agree,
To make each drop push on their Destiny.
Th' Infernal Draughts *in Blasphemies rebound,*
And openly the Devil's Health went round:
Nor can our Verse their latent Crime conceal,
How they shook hands *to meet next day in Hell;*
Death pledg'd them, Fate the dreadful Compact Read,
Concurring Justice spoke, and Four of Five lay dead.
When Men their Maker's Vengeance once defy,
'Ts a certain Sign that their Destruction's nigh.
'Tis vain to single out Examples here,
Drunkenness will soon be th'Nation's Character:
The grand Contagion's spreading over all,
'Tis Epidemick now, and National.
Since then the Sages all Reproofs despise,
Let's quit the People and Lampoon the Vice.
Drunkenness is so the Error of the Time,
The Youth begin to ask if 'tis a Crime:
Wonder to see the grave Patricians come,
From City Courts of Conscience reeling home;
And think 'tis hard they shou'd no Licence make,
To give the Freedom which their Father's take.
The Seat of Judgment's so debauch'd with Wine,
Justice seems rather to be drunk than blind.
Lets fall the Sword, and her unequal Scale
Makes Right go down, and Injury prevail.
A Vice, 'tis thought, the Devil at first design'd

---

debauchery, and drinking" in his regiment (ibid., p. 32; Dalton, *3*, 109). He died on 29 October 1689. Sir Thomas Gower of Stittenham, York, third baronet (c. 1666–89), commanded a third regiment of foot and died "of a Feaver" on 28 October 1689 (GEC, *Baronetage, 1*, 147; [Story], *A True and Impartial History,* p. 32). Anthony Hungerford, son of Sir Edward Hungerford, knight, of Farley Castle, Wiltshire, was a captain in Gower's regiment. He died "A day or two after" Gower (Le Neve, p. 34; [Story], *A True and Impartial History,* p. 32).

689. *Contagion's spreading:* Defoe is certainly right, for the process culminating in Hogarth's Gin Lane was beginning its second decade. To stop the importation of French brandy, the distilling of domestic spirits was made taxfree in 1690. In 1694, 810,090 gallons of gin were distilled; in 1734 the figure had risen to 6,074,762 gallons.

Not to allure, but to affront Mankind;
A Pleasure Nature hardly can explain,
Suits none of God Almighty's Brutes but Man.
An Act so nautious, that had Heaven enjoyn'd
The Practice, as a Duty on Mankind,
They'd shun the Bliss which came so foul a way,
And rather forfeit Heaven, than once obey.
A double Crime, which by one Act we undoe
At once the Gentleman and Christian too:
For which no better Antidote is known,
Than t' have one Drunkard to another shown.
The Mother Conduit of expatiate Sin,
Where all the Seeds of Wickedness begin;
The Introduction to Eternal Strife,
And Prologue to the Tragedy of Life;
A foolish Vice, does needless Crimes reveal,
And only tells the Truth it shou'd conceal.
'Tis strange how Men of Sence shou'd be subdu'd
By Vices so unnatural and rude,
Which gorge the Stomach to divert the Head,
And to make Mankind merry, make them mad:
Destroys the Vitals, and distracts the Brain,
And rudely moves the Tongue to talk in vain,
Dismisses Reason, stupifies the Sence,
And wondring Nature's left in strange suspence;
The Soul's benumb'd, and ceases to inform,
And all the Sea of Nature's in a Storm;
The dead unactive Organ feels the Shock,
And willing Death attends the Fatal Stroke.
And is this all for which Mankind endure
Distempers past the Power of Art to cure?
For which our Youth Old Age anticipate,
And with Luxurious Drafts suppress their Vital Heat?
Tell us ye Learned Doctors of the Vice,
Wherein the high mysterious Pleasure lies?
The great sublime Enjoyment's laid so deep,
'Tis known in Dream, and understood in Sleep.
The Graduates of the *Science* first commence,
And gain Perfection when they lose their Sence:

Titles they give, which call their Vice to mind;
But Sot's the common Name for all the kind:
Nature's Fanaticks, who their Sence employ,
The Principles of Nature to destroy.
A Drunkard is a Creature God ne're made,
The Species Man, the Nature retrograde;
From all the Sons of Paradise they seem
To differ in the most acute Extreme;
Those covet Knowledge, labour to be Wise;
These stupifie the Sence, and put out Reason's Eyes;
For Health and Youth *those* all their Arts employ;
These strive their Youth and Vigour to destroy;
Those damn themselves to heap an ill-got Store;
These liquidate their Wealth, and covet to be poor.
  Satyr, examine now with needful Care,
What the rich Trophies of the Bottle are,
The mighty Conquests which her Champions boast,
The Prizes which they gain, and Price they cost.
  The Ensigns of her Order soon displace
Nature's most early Beauties from the Face,
Paleness at first succeeds, and languid Air,
And bloated Yellows supersede the Fair;
The flaming Eyes betray the Nitrous Flood,
Which quench the Spirits, and inflame the Blood,
Disperse the Rosie Beauties of the Face,
And Fiery Botches triumph in their place;
The tottering Head and trembling Hand appears,
And all the Marks of Age, *without the Years,*
Distorted Limbs, gross and unweildy move,
And hardly can pursue the Vice they love:
A *Bacchanalian* Scarlet dies the Skin,
A Sign what Sulphurous Steams arise within.
The Flesh emboss'd with Ulcers, and the Brain
Oppress'd with Fumes and Vapour, shews in vain
What once *before the Fire* it did contain.
  Strange Power of Wine, whose Vehicle the same
At once can both extinguish and inflame:
Keen as the Lightning does the Sword consume,
And leaves the untouch'd Scabbard in its room;

Nature burnt up with fiery Vapour dies,
And Wine a little while Mock-Life supplies:
Gouts and old Aches, Life's short Hours divide,
At once the Drunkard's Punishment and Pride:
Who having all his youthful Powers subdu'd,
Enjoys Old Age and Pain before he shou'd,
'Till Nature quite exhausted quits the Wretch,
And leaves more Will than Power to Debauch;
With Hellish Pleasure, past Excess he views,
And fain wou'd drink, but Nature must refuse:
Thus Drench'd, in artificial Flame he lies,
Drunk in Desire, forgets himself and dies.
In the next Regions he expects the same;
And Hell's no change, for here he liv'd in Flame.
  Satyr, *to Church,* Visit the House of Prayer,
And see the wretched Reformation there;
Unveil the Mask, and search the Sacred Sham:
For Rogues of all Religions are the same.
The several Tribes, their numerous Titles view,
And fear no Censure where the Fact is true;
They all shall have thee for their constant Friend,
Who more than common Sanctity pretend;
Provided they'll take care the World may see
Their Practices and their Pretence agree;
But count them with the *worst of Hypocrites,*
Whom Zeal divides, and Wickedness unites,
Who in Profession only are precise,
Dissent in Doctrine, and conform in Vice.
  They who from the Establish'd Church divide,
Must do it out of Piety or Pride:
And their Sincerity is quickly try'd.
For always they that stand before the first,
Will be the best of Christians, *or the worst.*
But shun their secret Councils, *O, my Soul!*
Whose Interest can their Consciences controul;

799. *Rogues:* adapted from Dryden's line, "For Priests of all Religions are the same" (*Absalom and Achitophel,* 99), which Defoe also quotes in *The Consolidator,* 1705, p. 42.

Those *Ambo-Dexters* in Religion, who
Can any thing dispute, yet any thing can do:
Those Christian-Mountebanks, that in disguise,
Can reconcile Impossibilities:
Alternately conform, and yet dissent,
And sin with both Hands, but with one repent.
The Man of Conscience all Mankind will love,
The Knaves themselves his Honesty approve:
He only to Religion can pretend,
The rest do for the Name alone contend;
The Verity of true Religion's known
By no Description better than its own:
Of Truth and Wisdom it informs the Mind,
And nobly strives to Civilize Mankind;
With potent Vice maintains Eternal Strife,
Corrects the Manners, and reforms the Life.
Tell us *ye Learned Magi* of the Schools,
Who pose Mankind with Ecclesiastick Rules,
What strange amphibious Things, are they that can
Religion without Honesty maintain,
Who own a God, pretended Homage pay,
But neither his, nor Human Laws obey.
Blush *England,* hide thy Hypocritick Face,
Who has no Honesty, can have no Grace.
In vain we argue from Absurdities,
Religion's bury'd just when Vertue dies:
Vertue's the Light by which Religion's known,
If this be wanting, Heaven will that disown.
We grant it merits no Divine Regard;
And Heaven is all from Bounty, not Reward:
But God must his own Nature contradict,
Reverse the World, its Government neglect,
Cease to be just, Eternal Law repeal,

817. *Ambo-dexters in Religion:* Occasional conformists took communion once a year in the Church of England to qualify themselves for public office, a practice to which Defoe was unalterably opposed: "I abhor both the Practices and the Persons" (*Peace without Union,* 1703, p. 11. Cf. [Defoe,] *An Inquiry into Occasional Conformity,* 1702, p. 28: "this scandalous *Ambo-dexter Conformity*").

845. *it:* virtue.

Be weak in Power, and mutable in Will,
If Vice and Vertue equal Fate should know,
And *that unbless'd*, or *this unpunish'd* go.
  In vain we strive Religion to disguise,
And smother it with Ambiguities:
Interest and Priestcraft, may, perhaps, invent
Strange Mysteries, by way of Supplement:
School-men may deep perplexing Doubts disclose,
And subtile Notions on the World impose;
Till by their Ignorance they are betray'd,
And lost in Deserts which themselves ha' made.
Zealots may Cant, and Dreamers may Divine,
And formal Fops to Pageantry incline,
And all with specious Gravity pretend
Their spurious Metaphysicks to defend.
  Religion's no divided Mystick Name;
For true Religion always is the same,
Naked and plain her Sacred Truths appear,
From pious Frauds, and dark Ænigma's clear:
The meanest Sence may all the Parts discern,
What Nature teaches all Mankind may learn:
And what's reveal'd, is no untrodden Path,
'Tis known by Rule, and understood by Faith,
The Negatives and Positives agree,
Illustrated by Truth and Honesty.
  And yet if all Religion was in vain,
Did no Rewards or Punishments contain,
Vertue's so suited to our Happiness,
That none but Fools cou'd be in love with Vice.
  Vertue's a Native Rectitude of Mind,
Vice the Degeneracy of Human-kind:
Vertue is Wisdom Solid and Divine,
Vice is all Fool without, and Knave within:
Vertue is Honour circumscrib'd by Grace,

870. Cf. Dryden, *Religio Laici* (1682), 151: "what is taught agrees with *Natures Laws.*"

879–910. *Vertue . . . Vice:* These lines repeat the Wit-Sense antitheses of *The Pacificator*, 355–96, above.

Vice is made up of every thing's that's base:
Vertue has secret Charms which all Men love,
And those that do not choose her, yet approve:
Vice like ill Pictures which offend the Eye,
Make those that made them their own Works deny:
Vertue's the Health and Vigour of the Soul,
Vice is the foul Disease infects the whole:
Vertue's the Friend of Life, the Soul of Health,
The Poor Man's Comfort, and the rich Man's Wealth:
Vice is a Thief, a Traytor in the Mind,
Assassinates the Vitals of Mankind;
The Poyson of his high Prosperity,
And only Misery of Poverty.
  To States and Governments they both extend,
Vertue's their Life and Being, *Vice* their End:
Vertue establishes, and *Vice* destroys,
And all the Ends of Government unties:
Vertue's an *English* King and Parliament,
Vice is a Czar of *Muscow* Government:
Vertue sets bounds to Kings, and limits Crowns,
Vice knows no Law, and all Restraint disowns:
Vertue prescribes all Government by Rules,
Vice makes Kings Tyrants, and their Subjects Fools:
Vertue seeks Peace, and Property maintains,
Vice binds the Captive World in hostile Chains:
Vertue's a beauteous Building form'd on high,
Vice is Confusion and Deformity.
  In vain we strive these two to reconcile,
Vain and impossible, the unequal Toil:
Antipathies in Nature may agree,
Darkness and Light, Discord and Harmony;
The distant Poles, in spight of space may kiss;
Water capitulate, and Fire make Peace:
But Good and Evil never can agree,
Eternal Discord's there, Eternal Contrariety.
  In vain the Name of Vertue they put on,
Who preach up Piety, and practice none.
Satyr resume the Search of secret Vice,

Conceal'd beneath Religion's fair Disguise.
Solid's a Parson Orthodox and Grave,
Learning and Language more than most Men have;
A fluent Tongue, a well-digested Stile,
His Angel Voice his Hearers Hours beguile,
Charm'd them with Godliness, and while he spake,
We lov'd the Doctrine for the Teacher's sake;
Strictly to all Prescription he conforms,
To Canons, Rubrick, Discipline, and Forms;
Preaches, disputes, with Diligence and Zeal,
Labours the Church's latent Wounds to heal:
'Twou'd be uncharitable to suggest,
Where this is found we should not find the rest:
Yet *Solid*'s frail and false, to say no more,
Dotes on a Bottle, and what's worse, a *Whore.*
Two Bastard Sons he educates abroad,
And breeds them to the Function of the Word.
In this the zealous Church-man he puts on,
And Dedicates his Labours to the Gown.
  Pelling, for so his Grace the Duke thought fit,

923. *Solid:* Solid suggests Lancelot Blackburne (1658–1743) who proceeded M.A. from Christ Church, Oxford, in 1683 and in the same year was appointed chaplain to Sir Jonathan Trelawny, bishop of Exeter, where he became a prebendary in 1691 and subdean in 1695. There was thought to be "something mysterious in the history and character of Dr. Blackbourne" (Noble, *3,* 68), however, and in 1702 he was forced to resign his subdeanery. In later years Thomas Blackburne, prebendary of Bilton, and Thomas Hayter, prebendary of Riccal, both in York Cathedral, were rumored to be his illegitimate sons, for Blackburne survived the early scandals to be consecrated archbishop of York in 1724 (*DNB, 2,* 585).

941. *Pelling: Key* reads "Pe—hum" and the 1710 text reads "Pel—n" but there is no doubt that the deluded parson is Edward Pelling (d. 1718), whom Defoe also invokes in *A New Test of the Church of England's Loyalty,* 1702, p. 16. He graduated B.A. from Trinity College, Cambridge in 1662, and D.D. in 1689. He was chaplain to Charles Seymour, sixth duke of Somerset, and chaplain-in-ordinary to the monarchs from Charles II to Queen Anne. In addition he was vicar of St. Helen's, London (1674–78), St. Martin's Ludgate (1678–91), prebendary of Westminster (1683–91), and finally rector of Petworth "in the Wild of Sussex" (1691–1718), where it was said that his parish was "perverted to Popery" (Bishop Nicolson's Diary, 10 February 1701, Carlisle Public Library, no foliation). "Having studied himself into the disorder of mind vulgarly called the hyp, (for he rarely quitted his study except during dinner-time), between the age of forty and fifty he imagined himself to be pregnant, and forebore all manner of exercise, lest motion should prove injurious to his ideal burden. Nor did the whim evaporate till his wife had assured him she was really in his supposed condition" (Samuel Johnson and George Steevens, *Supplement to the Edition of Shakespeare's*

Has in the Wild of *Sussex* made his Seat:
His want of Manners we cou'd here excuse,
For in his Day 'twas out of Pulpit-use;
Railing was then the Duty of the Day,
Their Sabbath-Work was but to Scold and Pray:
But when transplanted to a Country-Town,
'Twas hop'd he'd lay his fiery Talent down:
At least we thought he'd so much Caution use,
As not his Noble Patron to abuse.
But tis in vain to cultivate Mankind,
When Pride has once possession of his Mind.
Not all his Grace's Favours could prevail,
To calm that Tongue that was so us'd to rail.
Promiscuous Gall his Learned Mouth defil'd,
And Hypocondriack Spleen his Preaching spoil'd;
His undistinguish'd Censure he bestows,
Not by Desert, but as Ill-nature flows.
The Learned say the Causes are from hence,
An Ebb of Manners, and a Flux of Sence;
Dilated Pride, the Frenzy of the Brain,
Exhal'd the Spirits and disturb'd the Man;
And so the kindest thing which can be said,
Is not to say he's mutinous, but mad:
For less could *ne're* his Antick Whims explain,
He thought his Belly pregnant as his Brain;
Fancy'd himself with Child, and durst believe,
That he by Inspiration cou'd conceive,
And if the Hetrogoneous Birth goes on,
He hopes to bring his Mother Church a Son:
Tho' some Folks think the Doctor ought to doubt,
Not how't got in, *but how it will get out.*
Hark, Satyr, Now bring *Boanerges* down,

Plays, 2 vols., 1780, 2, 660). Pope adopted this fancy in *The Rape of the Lock* (1714), IV, 53.

973. *Boanerges:* Boanerges is the surname of two disciples of Jesus, the sons of Zebedee, who fail to learn the meaning of nonviolent action (Luke 9:54, Mark 9:38). Defoe may have intended David Jones (University of Michigan copy of *A*) (1663–1724?) who graduated from Westminster School and Christ Church, Oxford, and immediately achieved notoriety by the violence of his sermons. George Smalridge, who heard him preach at St. Mary's, Oxford, in 1697, observed "the impetuousness of his voice [and]

A Fighting Priest, a Bully of the Gown:
In double Office he can serve the Lord,
To fight his Battles and to preach his Word;
And double Praise is to his merit due,
He thumps the Pulpit and the People too.
  Then search my Lord of *London*'s Diocess,
And see what Rakes the Care of Souls possess;
Beseech his Lordship but to name the Priest,
Went sober from his Visitation Feast.
Tell him of sixteen Ecclesiastick Guides,
In whom no Spirit but that of Wine abides;
Who in contiguous Parishes remain,
And preach the Gospel once a Week in vain:
But in their Practices unpreach it all,
And sacrifice to *Bacchus* and to *Baal.*
  Tell him a Vicious Priesthood must imply
A careless or defective Prelacy.
But still be circumspect and spare the Gown,
The Mitre's full as Sacred as the Crown;
The Churches Sea is always in a Storm,
Leave them at *Latter Lamas* to reform.
If in their Gulph of Vice thou should'st appear,
Thou'lt certainly be lost and Shipwrack'd there:
Nor meddle with their Convocation Feuds,

---

the fantasticalness of his actions" (Nichols, *Illustrations, 3,* 268). Thomas Brown mentions his "celebrated Talent of censuring and railing" in *Novus Reformator Vapulans: Or, The Welch Levite Tossed in a Blanket,* 1691, sig. A2r.

979. *Lord of London* (*Key*): Henry Compton, bishop of London; see *The True-Born Englishman,* 705 *n.,* above. Burnet thought that he was "a generous and good-natured Man, but easy and weak, and much in the power of others" (*2,* 630).

980. *Rakes:* In *More Short Ways with the Dissenters,* 1704, pp. 3–4, Defoe mentions "the Reverend, but very Drunken Incumbent at *Wickam.*" This is probably Christopher Wragg, who in November 1689 was installed rector of Wickham Bishops, Essex, so-called "because the Bps. of *London* have been from time immemorial . . . Lords of the Mannor, and Patrons of the Rectory" (Richard Newcourt, *Reportorium Ecclesiasticum Parochiale Londinense,* 2 vols., 1708–10, 2, 657–58).

994. *at Latter Lamas:* never (*OED;* Tilley L90).

997. *Convocation Feuds:* Since the lower house of convocation, the deans, archdeacons, and representatives of the beneficed clergy, was overwhelmingly Tory and the upper house, the archbishops and bishops, was predominantly Whig, their relations were characterized by the bitterest acrimony. In the convocation summoned in February 1700, the lower house, under the prolocutorship of Henry Aldrich, dean of Christ's Church, challenged the right of the archbishop to prorogue the session and

The Church's Farce, the Clergy's Interludes;
Their Church Distinctions too let us lay by,
As who are *low Church Rakes* and who are *high*.
Enquire not who their Passive Doctrine broke,
Who swore at random, or who ly'd by Book:
But since their Frailties come so very fast,
'Tis plain they shou'd not be believ'd in hast.
  Satyr, for Reasons we ha' told before,
With gentle Strokes the *Men of Posts* pass o'er,
Nor within Gun-shot of St. *Stephen*'s come,
Unless thou'rt well prepar'd for Martyrdom;
Not that there's any want of Subject there,
But the more Crimes we have the less we'll hear.
And what hast thou to do with Sovereign Power?
Let them sin on and tempt the Fatal Hour.
'Tis vain to preach up dull Morality,
Where too much Crime and too much Power agree;
The hardn'd Guilt undocible appears,
They'll exercise their Hands but not their Ears.
Let their own Crimes be Punishment enough,
And let them want the Favour of Reproof.
  Let the Court-Ladies be as lewd as fair,
Let Wealth and Wickedness be *Musgrove*'s Care;
Let *Dorset* drench his Wit with his Estate,

---

forced the matter upon the reluctant attention of the privy council (White Kennett, *The History of the Convocation,* 1702, pp. 120–22, 182, 209–10).

1001. *Passive Doctrine:* See *The True-Born Englishman,* 704 *n.*, above.

1007. *St. Stephen's:* Since 1547 the House of Commons had met in the Chapel of St. Stephen, in Westminster Palace.

1020. *Musgrove* (*Key*): Despite the *Key* at least two readers assumed that *M*——— was Sarah Churchill, then countess of Marlborough (Rosenbach Library and University of Michigan copies of *A*). *"Musgrove"* may be a printer's error for *"Mulgrave,"* whom Defoe associated with Dorset and "Wealth" in *The Pacificator,* 136, 143 *n.*, above.

1021. *Dorset* (*Key*): Dorset, who was involved with Sir Charles Sedley in the notorious escapade at Oxford Kate's in 1663 (*Upon the Author of the Satyr against Wit,* 18 *n.*, above) and who was said to have bought his earldom by surrendering Nell Gwyn to the king in 1675, was 64 years old in 1702. One glimpse of him in 1700 is afforded in a lampoon entitled *Timon in Town, to Strephon in the Country* ("If to be born or not, Our Selves cou'd chuse,") and preserved in Osborn MS. Chest II, No. 2 (Phillipps 8302), f. 81. Dorset is discovered asleep at the Kit-Cat Club, but wakes up to propose "A Health to Jenny Roche" and promptly falls back asleep. Joan Roche was "a young married gentlewoman" whom Dorset finally married in October 1704. "After a thousand actions that plainly shew'd he had entirely lost his sences, [he] has compleated

And *Oxford* sin in spight of Age and Fate;
On the wrong side of Eighty let him Whore,
He always was, and will be, lewd and poor.
Let *Devonshire* be proud, and *Ormond* gay,
Lavish of vast Estates, and scorn to pay:
The Ancient Duke has sin'd *to's Heart's content,*
And but he scorns to stoop wou'd now repent;
Wou'd Heaven abate but that one darling Sin,
He'd be a Christian and a Peer again.
Let poor *Corinna* mourn her Maiden-head,

---

all by marrying Joany Roche . . . [who] had lain with Lord Nottingham's Black [Dick Squash], and being near the time of her delivery, grew very apprehensive she shou'd produce a little Negro, and has therfore run away to avoid the scandal" (John M. Kemble, *State Papers,* 1857, pp. 381–82).

1022. *Oxford* (*Key*): Aubrey de Vere, twentieth earl of Oxford (1626–1703), was actually four years on the right side of 80 in 1702. Macaulay called him "a man of loose morals" (*2,* 968), but the only one of his mistresses whose name is known is Elizabeth Davenport, an actress who created the part of Roxolana in Davenant's *Siege of Rhodes* and whom Oxford "snatched from the stage" in January 1662 (GEC, *10,* 260).

1025. *Devonshire* (*Key*): Devonshire, "the finest and handsomest Gentleman of his Time . . . of a princely Behaviour," the owner of a dozen estates, including Roehampton House, Putney, and Devonshire House, Piccadilly, and the builder of Chatsworth, "a Monument of Beauty and Magnificence that perhaps is not exceeded by any Palace in *Europe,*" was "Of nice Honour in every Thing, but the paying his Tradesmen" (Macky, p. 18).

Ormond (*Key*): James Butler, second duke of Ormonde (1665–1745), was known throughout Europe as "an example of the magnificence and splendour of the nobility of England." His house in St. James's Square quartered 41 servants, plus a gentleman of the horse and 10 stable hands, a chasseur, two chairmen, and 17 watermen (HMC *Ormonde MSS.,* New Series, *8,* vii, xxxiii *n.*).

1027. *sin'd to's Heart's content:* Devonshire, "this Great Man," also known on occasion as "the White Dog of Lady Fitzharding," was "famous for Debauchery, Lewdness, &c." (*A New Ballad to the Tune of Packington's pound 1691/92* ["Who w'd have thought that Romes Convert so neer"], Portland MS. Pw V 48, p. 114; Hearne, *2,* 39–40). He was said to have seduced "more Women than any Five Keepers of Quality besides." Three of these transactions are retailed by John Dunton, *The Hazard of a Death-Bed-Repentance, Fairly Argued from the Late Remorse of W——— late D— of D———,* 1708, pp. 26–27: "he took as much Pains to tempt and debauch *Mrs. H——ge* by whom he had Five Children) . . . as other Men do for the saving of their Souls . . . the Thousand Pound he gave to the L–dy *J——* to betray her own Daughter to his Adulterous Arms, how many *Bastard Children* he had by her, and how cold and indifferent he grew to her (*tho' a Woman of great Beauty*) for the Sake of an Actress . . . tempting an Actress out of the Play-House, (I mean Mrs. *Anne Campion*) and doating on her to that Degree, as to erect a *Tomb* to her Memory in *Latimer*'s *Chancel.*"

1031. *Corinna:* Although his grandfather lost Dublin for the king in August 1649 while toying with a mistress, the second duke of Ormonde seems to have lost a

And her lost Duke gone out to fight for Bread.
Be he Embarkt for *Portugal* or *Spain,*
She prays he never may return again;
For fear she always shou'd resist in vain.
Satyr, forbear the blushing Sex t' expose,
For all their Vice from Imitation flows;
And 'twou'd be but a very dull Pretence,
To miss the Cause, and blame the Consequence:
But let us make Mankind asham'd to sin,
Good Nature'l make the Women all come in.
This one Request shall thy Rebukes express,
Onely to *talk a little little less.*
  Now view the Beau's at *Will*'s, the Men of Wit,
By Nature nice, and for discerning fit:
The finish'd Fops, the Men of Wig and Snuff,
Knights of the Famous Oyster-Barrel Muff.
Here meets the *Dyet* of Imperial Wit,
And of their weighty Matters wisely treat;
Send Deputies to *Tunbridge* and the *Bath,*
To guide young Country Beau's in Wits unerring Path.
  Prigson from Nurse and Hanging-sleeves got free,
A little smatch of Modern Blasphemy;
A powder'd Wig, a Sword, a Page, a Chair,
Learns to take Snuff, drink Chocolate, and swear:
Nature seems thus far to ha' led him on,
And no Man thinks he was a Fop too soon;
But 'twas the Devil surely drew him in,
Against the Light of Nature thus to sin:
That he who was a Coxcomb so compleat,
Should now put in his wretched Claim for Wit.
Such sober Steps Men to their Ruine take,
A Fop, a Beau, a Wit, and then a Rake.
  Fate has the Scoundrel Party halv'd in two,
The Wits are shabby, and the Fops are Beau;
The Reason's plain, the Money went before,
And so the Wits are Rakish 'cause they'r poor;
Indulgent Heaven for Decency thought fit,

---

mistress while toying with Cadiz. Ormonde commanded the land forces in the unsuccessful descent upon Cadiz in August 1702; cf. *The Spanish Descent,* 3 *n.,* below.

1047. *Oyster-Barrel Muff:* a muff having the form of an oyster-barrel (*OED*).

That some shou'd have the Money, and some the Wit.
Fools are a Rent-Charge left on Providence,
And have Equivalents instead of Sence;
To whom he's bound a larger Lot to carve,
Or else they'd seem to ha' been born to starve.
Such with their double Dole shou'd be content,
And not pretend to Gifts that Heaven ne'er sent:
For 'twou'd reflect upon the Power Supream,
If all his Mercies ran in one contracted Stream:
If Men of Wit would by their Wealth be known,
Some wou'd have all the Good, and some ha' none.
The useless Fools wou'd in the World remain,
As Instances that Heaven cou'd work in vain.
  Dull *Flettumasy* has his Heart's Delight,
Gets up i'th' Morning to lie down at Night;
His Talk's a Mass of weighty Emptiness,
None more of Business prates, or knows it less;
A painted Lump of Idleness and Sloth,
And in the Arms of *Bacchus* spends his Youth:
The waiting Minutes tend on him in vain,
Mispent the past, unvallued those remain;
Time lies as useless, unregarded by,
Needless to him that's only born to die,
And yet this undiscerning thing has Pride,
And hugs the Fop that wiser Men deride.
  Pride's a most useful Vertue in a Fool,
The humble Coxcomb's always made a Tool;
Conceit's a Blockhead's only Happiness,
He'd hang himself if he cou'd use his Eyes.
If Fools cou'd their own Ignorance discern,
They'd be no longer Fools, because they'd learn.
From whence some wise Philosophers ha' said,
Fools may sometimes be sullen, but can't be mad.
'Tis too much thinking which distracts the Brain,
Crouds it with Vapours which dissolve in vain;
The fluttering Wind of undigested Thought
Keeps Mock Idea's in and true ones out:

1082. *Flettumasy: "the Lawyers have named me Twenty Men for my* Clitus, *and abundance more for* Fletumacy" (Defoe, *More Reformation,* 1703, sig. A4v).

These guide the undirected Wretch along,
With giddy Head and inconsistent Tongue;
But *Flettumasy*'s safe, he's none of them,
Bedlam can never lay her Claim to him,
Nature secur'd his unincumbred Scull,
For *Flettumacy* never thinks at all:
Supinely sleeps in *Diadora*'s Arms,
Doz'd with the Magick of her Craft and Charms;
The subtil Dame brought up in Vice's School,
Can love the Cully, tho' she hates the Fool:
Wisely her just Contempt of him conceals,
And hides the Follies he himself reveals.
'Tis plain the self-denying Jilt's i' th' Right,
She wants his Money, *and he wants her Wit.*
  Satyr, the Men of *Rhime* and *Jingle* shun,
Hast thou not Rhim'd thy self till thou'rt undone?
On Rakish Poets, let us not reflect,
They only are what all Mankind expect.
  Yet 'tis not Poets have debaucht the Times,
'Tis we that have so damn'd their sober Rhimes:
The Tribe's good-natur'd, and desire to please,
And when you snarl at those, present you these.
The World has lost its ancient Taste of Wit,
And Vice comes in to raise the Appetite;
For Wit has lately got the start of Sence,
And serves it self as well with Impudence.
  Let him whose Fate it is to write for Bread,
Keep this one Maxim always in his Head:
If in this Age he wou'd expect to please,
He must not cure, but nourish their Disease;
Dull Moral things will never pass for Wit,
Some Years ago they might, but now 'ts too late.
Vertue's the faint Green-sickness of the Times,
'Tis luscious Vice gives Spirit to all our Rhimes.
In vain the sober thing inspir'd with Wit,
Writes Hymns and Histories from sacred Writ;
But let him *Blasphemy* and *Bawdy* write,
The *Pious* and the *Modest* both will buy't.

1112. *Diadora:* not identified.

The blushing Virgin's pleas'd, and loves to look,
And plants the Poem next her Prayer-Book.
Wessly with Pen and Poverty beset,
And *Blackmore* Vers't in Physick as in Wit.
Tho' this of *Jesus,* that of *Job* may sing,
One Bawdy Play will twice their Profits bring:
And had not both carest the Flatter'd Crown,
This had no Knight-hood seen, nor that no Gown.
Had Vice no Power the Fancy to bewitch,
Dryden had hang'd himself as well as *Creech:*
Durfey had starv'd, and half the Poets fled
In foreign Parts, to pawn their Wit for Bread.
'Tis Wine or Lewdness all our Theams supplies,
Gives Poets Power to write, and Power to please:
Let this describe the Nation's Character,
One Man reads *Milton,* forty *Rochester.*
This lost his Taste, *they say,* when h' lost his Sight,
Milton had Thought, but *Rochester* had Wit.
The Case is plain, theTemper of the Time,
One wrote *the Lewd,* and t'other *the Sublime.*
And shou'd *Apollo* now descend and write,
In Vertue's Praise 'twou'd never pass for Wit.
The *Bookseller* perhaps wou'd say, *'Twas well:*
But *'Twou'd not hit the Times, 'Twou'd never Sell;*
Unless a Spice of Lewdness cou'd appear,
The sprightly part wou'd still be wanting there.
The Fashionable World wou'd never read,
Nor the Unfashionable Poet get his Bread.
'Tis *Love and Honour* must enrich our Verse,
The Modern Terms, *our Whoring to rehearse.*
The sprightly part attends the *God of Wine,*
The Drunken Stile *must blaze* in every Line.
These are the Modern Qualities must do,
To make the Poem and the Poet too.
Dear Satyr, If thou wilt reform the Town,

1146. *Wessly* (*Key*): Samuel Wesley; see *The Dispensary, 5,* 67 *n.,* above.

1147. *Blackmore* (*Key*): See *The Dispensary, 4,* 173 *n.,* above; *A Lent-Entertainment,* 89 *n.,* above.

1153. *Creech:* See *The Pacificator,* 419 *n.,* above.

1154. *Durfey:* See *A Satyr against Wit,* 180 *n.,* above.

Thou'lt certainly be beggar'd and undone:
'Tis at thy Peril, if thou wilt proceed
To cry down Vice, Mankind will never read.

Conclusion.

What strange Mechanick Thoughts of God and Man,
Must this unsteady Nation entertain,
To think *Almighty Science* can be blind,
Wisdom it self be banter'd by Mankind;
Eternal Providence be mockt with Lyes,
With Out-sides and Improbabilities,
With Laws, those *Rhodomonta's* of the State,
Long Proclamations, and the Lord knows what;
Societies ill Manners to suppress,
And new sham Wars with Immoralities,
While they themselves to common Crimes betray'd,
Can break the very Laws themselves ha' made:
With *Jehu*'s Zeal they furiously reform,
And raise false Clouds which end without a Storm;
But with a loose to Vice securely see
The Subject punish'd, and themselves go free.
For shame your *Reformation-Clubs* give o'er,
And jest with Men, and jest with Heaven no more:
But if you wou'd avenging Powers appease,
Avert the Indignation of the Skies;
Impending Ruin avoid, and calm the Fates,

1188. *Rhodomonta:* apparently intended to be a nonce-form of "Rhodomantado," which Defoe used, to mean "idle boast," in *Review, 1* (19 February 1704), 3.

1189. *Proclamations:* Royal proclamations against immorality had been issued in January 1692, February 1698, December 1699, and 26 March 1702. The last was reissued in February 1703 (Steele, Nos. 4076, 4246, 4269, 4314, 4354).

1192. *they:* members of parliament.

1194. *Jehu's Zeal:* Jehu's "zeal for the Lord" manifested itself in destroying worshippers of Baal, but not in reforming himself: "Jehu took no heed to walk in the law of the Lord" (2 Kings 10:16, 31).

1198. *Reformation-Clubs:* societies for the reformation of manners; see headnote, pp. 398–99 above. This line and 15 others are quoted in *Review, 6* (7 April 1709), 16, in the following order: 1208–09, 1230–31, 1236–37, 1242–43, 1260–61, 1198–1203.

Ye Hypocrites, reform your Magistrates.
Your Quest of Vice at *Church* and *Court* begin,
There lie the Seeds of high expatiate Sin;
'Tis they can check the Vices of the Town,
When e'er they please, but *to suppress their own,*
Our Modes of Vice from their Examples came,
And their Examples only must reclaim.
In vain you strive ill Manners to suppress,
By the Superlatives of Wickedness:
Ask but how well the drunken Plow-man looks,
Set by the swearing Justice in the Stocks;
And poor Street-Whores in *Bridewel* feel their Fate,
While *Harlot Morgan* rides in Coach of State.
The Mercenary Scouts in every Street,
Bring all *that have no Money* to your Feet,
And if you lash a Strumpet of the Town;
She only smarts *for want of Half a Crown:*
Your Annual Lists of Criminals appeare,
But no Sir *Harry* or Sir *Charles* is there.
Your Proclamations Rank and File appear,
To Bug-bear Vice, and put Mankind in fear:
These are the Squibs and Crackers of the Law,
Which hiss and make a Bounce, and then withdraw.

1215. *Morgan:* "Sir Cha. Duncomb's Miss[tress]" (*Key*). See *The True-Born Englishman,* 1174 *n.,* above.

1216. *Scouts:* Thomas Brown mentions that there were "At least five Hundred of those reforming . . . Ferrets" (*A Continuation or Second Part of the Letters from the Dead to the Living,* 2nd ed., 1707, pp. 184–85). One of the most famous of these was John Dent, "a great Hater of Sin and Wickedness," who busied himself "for 17 or 18 Years, in aiding and assisting at the apprehending and prosecuting of several Thousands of Lewd and Profligate Persons; and also of Sabbath-Breakers, profane Swearers, and Drunkards. In which Cause he was couragious, and feared no Encounter" (Strype, 2, 232).

1220. *Lists:* Beginning in 1695 the Society for the Reformation of Manners did "yearly set forth an Account of the Progress made in suppressing of Profaneness and Debauchery, by their means. The fourteenth Account came out *Decemb.* 1, 1708; wherein the Number of Persons prosecuted and proceeded against by the Magistrates for the Year before, was as follows: Lewd and Disorderly Men and Women, 1255; Keepers of Bawdy and Disorderly Houses, 51; Keepers of common Gaming-Houses, 30; Persons Exercising their Trades or ordinary callings on the Lord's Day, 1187; Profane Swearing and Cursing, 626; Drunkenness, 150" (Strype, 2, 231).

1221. *Sir Harry or Sir Charles:* presumably Sir Henry Furnese, 149 *n.,* above, and Sir Charles Duncombe, 244–55, above.

Law like the Thunder of Immortal *Jove,*
Rings Peals of Terror from the Powers above;
But when the pointed Lightnings disappear,
The Cloud dissolves, and all's serene and clear:
Law only aids Men to conceal their Crimes,
But 'tis Example must reform the Times,
Force and Authorities are all in vain,
Unless you can perswade, *you'll ne'er constrain;*
And all perswasive Power expires of Course,
'Till backt with good Examples to enforce.
The Magistrates must Blasphemy forbear,
Be faultless first themselves, and then severe;
Impartial Justice equally dispence,
And fear no Man, nor fear no Man's Offence:
Then may our Justices, and not before,
When they reprove the rich, correct the poor.
  The Men of Honour must from Vice dissent,
Before the *Rakes* and *Bullies* will repent;
Vertue must be the Fashion of the Town,
Before the Beau's and Ladies put it on;
Wit must no more be Bawdy and Profane,
Or Wit to Vertue's reconcil'd in vain.
The Clergy must be sober, grave and wise,
Or else in vain *they cant of Paradise:*
Our Reformation never can prevail,
While Precepts govern and *Examples fail.*
Were but the Ladies vertuous as they're fair,
The Beau's would blush as often as they swear;
Vice wou'd grow antiquated in the Town,
Wou'd all our Men of Mode but cry it down:
For Sin's a Slave to Custom, and will die,
Whenever Habits suffer a Decay;
And therefore all our Reformation here,
Must work upon our Shame and *not our Fear.*
If once the Mode of Vertue wou'd begin,
The poor will quickly be *asham'd to sin.*
Fashion is such a strange bewitching Charm,
For fear of being laught at they'll reform;
  And yet Posterity will blush to hear

Royal Examples ha' been useless here;
The onely *Just Exception* to our Rule,
Vertue's not learnt in this Imperial School.
In vain *Maria*'s Character we read,
So few will in her Path of Vertue tread.
In vain her Royal Sister recommends
Vertue to be the Test of all her Friends,
Backt with her own Example and Commands.
Our Church establisht, and our Trade restor'd,
Our Friends protected, and our Peace secur'd:
France humbl'd, and our Fleet's insulting *Spain,*
These are the Triumphs of *a Female Reign;*
At Home her milder Influence she imparts,
Queen of our Vows, and Monarch of our Hearts.
If Change of Sexes thus will change our Scenes,
Grant Heaven we always may be rul'd by Queens.

The Golden Age
(*November*[?] *1702*)

By the middle of the eighteenth century it had become a commonplace to represent the age of Queen Anne as a period of glory which established, in Oliver Goldsmith's phrase, "that excellence which now excites the admiration of Europe." But it is surprising to find the same attitude expressed in the present work (line 110) by an anonymous poet in the first year of Anne's reign.

Since this is a political satire, the poet anticipates this "Golden Reign" (line 62)—this second Restoration of the Stuarts—wholly in terms of party politics: Iron Age Whigs are to give way to aureate Tories. "The Queen had from her infancy," wrote the duchess of Marlborough, "imbibed the most unconquerable prejudices against the whigs. She had been taught to look upon them all, not only as republicans, who hated the very shadow of regal authority, but as implacable enemies to the church of England." It was no wonder, the duchess continued, "that as soon as she was seated in the throne, the tories . . . became the distinguished objects of the royal favour" (*Account of the Conduct,* pp. 123, 124). For the beneficiaries of this favor it was literally a golden age, and a note of heady self-congratulation is unmistakable in the tone of this poem.

Nor is it any wonder that the poet should have chosen the fourth eclogue of Virgil, with its riddling images of birth and peace and plenty, as the vehicle for his exultation. Dryden's translation, published in 1697, was available to be plundered for phrases (e.g. lines 96 *n.*, 97 *n.*) and is printed here on opposite pages to facilitate the comparison.

What the poet undertook, however, is not another translation, but an imitation. This genre, of which Pope's *Imitations of Horace* and Johnson's *London* are later examples, requires more than translation into the words of another language. It also seeks a modern equivalent for each detail of the ancient prototype; it attempts to restate the classical antitypes in modern terms. The excitement derives from the poet's ingenuity in finding "modern Instances": Partridge's almanac for the Sybilline books; Sir Samuel Dashwood, the new lord mayor of London, for C. Asinius Pollio, the new consul of Rome; Whig peculations for *priscae vestigia fraudis.*

But the fit is not perfect: 37-year-old Anne was hardly a type of "lovely Boy" (line 13). Since he was so ingenious, one wonders why the anonymous poet was not sufficiently imaginative and daring to find the antitype of the enigmatic, unborn child in an unborn child of Anne rather than in Anne herself. The answer must be that the anonymous poet was a Jacobite. He was looking forward not to the accession of a child of Anne but to the accession of Anne's half-brother, the son of James II, James Francis Edward, whom Louis XIV had already recognized as James III, king of England, Scotland, and Ireland. When Anne became pregnant again in 1703 the Jacobites were confounded; "it's beyond Description to tell you what an Alteration it made in some Peoples Countenances here at Court" (*Letters from the Living to the Living*, 1703, p. 22).

But neither is the fit imperfect: the messianic Boy, who was to rule, with his father's virtues—*patriis virtutibus*—a world at peace, is exactly what the Jacobites hoped would follow "the Mighty Months" of the reign of Anne.

Presumably the poem was written shortly before 3 December 1702, for after the earl of Ranelagh resigned his place on that day (Luttrell, *5*, 244), lines 45–46 would have no meaning. It was answered not only by *The Golden Age Restor'd* but also by *A Postscript to the Golden Age* ("Assist me, Muse, that in a glorious strain") preserved in Osborn MS. Chest II, No. 1 (Phillipps 8301).

The Fourth Pastoral of Virgil, Englished by Mr. Dryden

Sicilian Muse begin a loftier strain!
Though lowly Shrubs and Trees that shade the Plain,
Delight not all; *Sicilian* Muse prepare
To make the vocal Woods deserve a Consul's care.
The last great Age, foretold by sacred Rhymes,

The Golden Age

from the Fourth *Eclogue* of *Virgil,* &c.

Sicilian Muse, thy Voice and Subject raise,
All are not pleas'd with Shrubs and *Sylvan* Lays,
Or if we Shrubs and *Sylvan* Lays prepare,
Let 'em be such as suit a Consul's Ear.
Now *Merlin*'s Prophecies are made compleat,

5. *Merlin's Prophecies: Merlinus Liberatus* was the almanac published every year by John Partridge (1644–1715), whose death in 1708 was predicted by Jonathan Swift.

Renews its finish'd Course, *Saturnian* times
Rowl round again, and mighty years, begun
From their first Orb, in radiant Circles run.
The base degenerate Iron-off-spring ends;
A golden Progeny from Heav'n descends.

O chast *Lucina* speed the Mothers pains,
And haste the glorious Birth; thy own *Apollo* reigns!
The lovely Boy, with his auspicious Face,
Shall *Pollio's* Consulship and Triumph grace;
Majestick Months set out with him to their appointed Race.
The Father's banish'd Virtue shall restore,
And Crimes shall threat the guilty world no more.

And *Lilly*'s best Events with Credit meet;
Now Banish'd Justice takes its Rightful Place,
And *Saturn*'s Days return with *Stuart*'s Race.
With its own Lustre now the Church appears,
As one Year makes Amends for fourteen Years,
And Joys succeed our Sighs and Hopes succeed our Fears.
O Goddess, *Genius* of this Favourite Isle,
On thy own Work, this Revolution, smile,
Salute the Pleasures that come Rolling on,
And Greet the Wonders Heav'n and Thou hast done,
Worthy the Glorious Change inspire our Strains,
Now thy own *Anna* Rules, in Her own Kingdom Reigns.
And thou, *O Dashwood,* by peculiar Care
Reserv'd 'till now to fill *Augusta*'s Chair,
Behold the Mighty Months Progressive Shine!
See 'em begin their Golden Race in Thine!
Under thy Consulship, Lo! Vice gives way

6. *Lilly:* William Lilly (1602–81) came to London as a domestic servant, married his master's widow, and published his first almanac, *Merlinus Anglicus Junior,* and his first prophecy, *The English Merlin Reviv'd,* in 1644. Both of these continued to be published after Lilly's death by Henry Coley. Neither Partridge nor Coley predicted anything of interest for 1702, but a third astrologer, noting the conjunction of Saturn and Jupiter in this year, prophesied that "before these Two *Planets* will meet again (which will not be till the *Year 1722*), the Blessed *Millenium* (so much expected by some) will appear . . . [and] put an end to all *Controversies* and *Contentions* in the *World*" (William Andrews, *News from the Stars,* 1702, A1v).

10. *fourteen Years:* 1688–1702, the reign of William III.

18. *Dashwood:* Sir Samuel Dashwood, Knight (c. 1642–1705), was a London merchant, member of the Levant Company (1680–91), and deputy governor of the old East India Company (1700–02). A staunch Tory, he was elected sheriff in September 1683 and served two terms as member of parliament for the city (1685–87, 1690–95). From 1689 to 1696 he also served as a commissioner of the excise (Beaven, *2,* 109). He was defeated in his candidacies for lord mayor in 1698, 1700, and 1701, but upon the accession of Anne he was appointed to the commission for the lieutenancy of London in July 1702 and three months later was finally elected mayor (Luttrell, *4,* 432–33, 692; *5,* 95, 193, 220–21).

22. *Vice gives way:* Cf. *Reformation of Manners,* 84 *n.,* above.

The Son shall lead the life of Gods, and be
By Gods and Heroes seen, and Gods and Heroes see.
The jarring Nations he in peace shall bind,
And with paternal Virtues rule mankind.
Unbidden Earth shall wreathing Ivy bring,
And fragrant Herbs (the promises of Spring)
As her first Off'rings to her Infant King.
The Goats with strutting Duggs shall homeward speed,
And lowing Herds, secure from Lyons feed.
His Cradle shall with rising flow'rs be crown'd;
The Serpents Brood shall die: the sacred ground
Shall Weeds and pois'nous Plants refuse to bear,
Each common Bush shall *Syrian* Roses wear.
But when Heroick Verse his Youth shall raise,
And form it to Hereditary Praise;
Unlabour'd Harvests shall the Fields adorn,
And cluster'd Grapes shall blush on every Thorn.
The knotted Oaks shall show'rs of Honey weep,
And through the matted Grass the liquid Gold shall creep.

---

23. *Whigs . . . cease:* The Tory majority in the fifth parliament of William III had hoped to prevent the Whig junto (Somers, Halifax, and Orford) from ever coming into power again by impeaching them of high crimes and misdemeanors. The Whig majority in the House of Lords, however, dismissed the charges. After the election of July–August 1702 had reinforced their majority in the Commons, the Tories returned to the attack. One of the first acts of the first parliament of Anne was to vote 189–81, upon a motion of Sir Edward Seymour, "That Right hath not been done the Commons, upon the Impeachments, before the Lords, brought against divers Peers in the 13th Year of his late Majesty's Reign," and to threaten to reopen the impeachment proceedings (*CJ, 14,* 12).

33. *Halifax:* Charles Montagu, created baron Halifax of Halifax in December 1700, may have kissed the Queen's hand for his post of auditor of the exchequer (which he held for life), but he was struck off the list of privy councillors in March 1702 (GEC, *6,* 245).

34. *Somers:* Although dismissed as lord chancellor in April 1700, Somers remained "the life, the soul, and the spirit of his party" (*Miscellaneous State Papers, 2,* 446) and continued to direct its propaganda (*Swift's Discourse,* pp. 68–71). As a consequence, he was dismissed not only from the privy council, but even from the commission of the peace in March 1702 (GEC, *12,* i, 29).

And Whigs for ever cease to come again in Play.
The Life of Gods the Monarch shall partake,
Belov'd by Gods and Men for Virtues Sake,
As She from Heroes sprung, brave Acts prefers,
And Heroes Copy out their Fame from Hers,
As Kingdoms Rights She with her own maintains,
And where her Injur'd Father Govern'd, Reigns.
  Hail, Sacred Queen! Thy very Enemies own
Thy Lawful Claim, and Recognize thy Throne.
Dissembling Statesmen shall before thee stand,
And *Halifax* be first to Kiss thy Hand;
Somers shall change his Temper with his Fate,
And promise Duty where he vow'd his Hate,
Seeming for past Offences to Attone,
By Complementing Claims he would Postpone;
Had one but Liv'd, that rais'd him, to his Shame,
To let him Pack the Cards, and Win the Game.
Wharton shall to St. *James*'s House resort,
And leave his Master's Corps to make his Court;
Stamford quit the Practice of his Place,
Leave cutting Timber down in *Enfield* Chase,
To seek for Favour, and prevail for Grace.

38. *one:* William III.

40. *Wharton:* Although he had appointed Thomas, Lord Wharton to the lucrative post of warden of the royal forests south of Trent in April 1697, William balked at making him secretary of state. As recently as January 1702, Wharton had been made lord lieutenant of Buckinghamshire but in July 1702 he was removed from this and all other posts.

42. *Stamford:* Thomas Grey, second earl of Stamford (c. 1653–1720), was one of the first Whigs, suspected of complicity in the Rye House plot and Monmouth's rebellion. In William's reign he was appointed high steward of the honour of Leicester (1689), privy councillor (1694), commissioner of Greenwich Hospital (1695), first lord of trade and plantations (1699), lord lieutenant of Devonshire (1696), and chancellor of the duchy of Lancaster (1697). It was this last post that proved most troublesome. As Lord Ailesbury (2, 534) explained, this "poor headed Earl had a reasonable paternal estate, but entailed, so he cut down all the vast fine woods . . . and took money . . . and spent it." When he extended these depredations to crown lands in Lancaster, however, the House of Commons intervened and in May 1701, upon a division, voted 136–102 "That great Waste and Spoil hath been committed in *Enfield* Chace, belonging to his Majesty's Duchy of *Lancaster,* by destroying great Quantities of Wood and . . . That the Destruction of the Wood . . . happened through the Neglect of Duty, and Breach of Trust, of *Thomas,* Earl of *Stamford*" (*CJ, 13,* 572). In March 1702, therefore, Stamford was dismissed from all his offices.

Yet, of old Fraud some footsteps shall remain,
The Merchant still shall plough the deep for gain:
Great Cities shall with Walls be compass'd round;
And sharpen'd Shares shall vex the fruitful ground.
Another *Tiphys* shall new Seas explore,

---

45. *Ranelagh:* As paymaster-general of the army, Ranelagh handled vast sums of money "and God knows where it went; but after the King's death, it was found that twenty two millions stirling was not accounted for" (Ailesbury, *1*, 241). Although not removed from the privy council upon Anne's accession, he resigned his post as paymaster-general on 3 December 1702 to avoid a parliamentary inquiry. Subsequently convicted of misappropriation of funds, he was expelled from the House of Commons in February 1703. Ranelagh House in Chelsea, laid out on a scale "not to be seen in many Prince's Palaces" and painted by Canaletto, was "seiz'd for its Owner's Guilt" (J. Bowack, *The Antiquities of Middlesex*, 1705, p. 14; *Letters from the Living to the Living*, 1703, p. 222). Ranelagh's beautiful second wife, for whom he bought Cranbourne Chase, near Windsor, was Margaret, dowager baroness Stawell (Luttrell *4*, 647).

47. *Grid-iron:* "my Lord of *R*[*anelagh*], Poor Man, we are told his Lordship's Grid Iron has had no greater Sum fallen through it than *Two Millions* Sterling, and yet the P[arliament] takes him to Task" (*Letters from the Living to the Living*, p. 220).

51. *South with Sherlock:* See *The Dispensary, 5*, 31 *n.*, above.

Old *Ranelagh* shall thy Accession Sing,
Hoping to serve Thee as he serv'd the King;
To keep his Grid-iron while he keeps his Life,
And Build fresh Mansion-Houses for his Wife.
Lyons with Lambs United shall agree,
And Lambs like Lyons, Lyons Lambs shall be,
And *South* with *Sherlock* Hail and bow the Knee.
Kennett shall drop his Convocation Spleen,
And *Atterbury,* Quarrels with the Dean,
To join in our Allegiance with the Queen.
The Church-men and Dissenters shall combine
To pay the Tribute due to *Stuart's* Line,
As Presbyters with Bishops shall comply,
And Bishops shall fling out what Presbyters deny;
Like *Lambeth* Watermen, whose Tempers shew,
That look one way while they another Row.
  Yet shall some Footsteps of old Fraud remain,
And Ills be practic'd in thy Golden Reign;

52. *Kennett:* White Kennett (1660–1728) began his political career while an undergraduate at St. Edmund Hall by publishing a Tory pamphlet a few days before the parliament convened at Oxford in March 1681. In the next reign, however, he became *"Weather-cock Kennett"* when he opposed the measures of James II (Nichols, *Anecdotes, 1,* 393 *n.*). In 1700 he was created D.D. and presented to the rectory of St. Botolph, Aldgate. In the following year he became the archdeacon of Huntingdon, known as "the Anti-Convocationist" for maintaining, in his controversy with Atterbury, that "convocation had few inherent rights of independent action" (*Letters from the Living to the Living,* p. 213; *DNB, 11,* 3).

53. *Atterbury:* Francis Atterbury (1662–1732) began his career as a controversialist in 1687 while a tutor at Christ Church, Oxford, when he published an essay opposing James II's attempt to Romanize the university. He took orders the same year and in 1691 was appointed lecturer of St. Bride's, London, and chaplain to William and Mary in 1694. He was one of the Christ Church wits who opposed Richard Bentley in the Phalaris controversy of 1694–98 (see *The Dispensary, 5,* 74 *n.,* above). His *Letter to a Convocation Man* (1697), blaming the rampant immorality of the day partly on the refusal of the king to allow the convocation to assemble, precipitated an acrimonious controversy with White Kennett, William Wake, and Edmund Gibson. In February 1701, Sir Jonathan Trelawny, bishop of Exeter, presented Atterbury with the archdeaconry of Totnes in Devon, "worth 150*l.* per ann., for his great service in writing" *The Rights and Privileges of an English Convocation Stated and Vindicated* (Luttrell, *5,* 15).

Another *Argos* land the Chiefs, upon th' *Iberian* Shore.
Another *Helen* other Wars create,
And great *Achilles* urge the *Trojan* Fate:

---

63. *Munden:* Sir John Munden, Knight (d. 1719), failed to intercept a French squadron between Rochelle and Coruña in May 1702 and was tried at courtmartial on charges of negligence in July. Although he was acquitted, the queen yielded to popular clamor—*The London Gazette,* No. 3835, 10–13 August 1702, reported that he had failed in his duty—and ordered him to be dismissed from the service.

64. *Wade and . . . Kirkby:* Richard Kirkby was second in command of the squadron that sailed from Jamaica in May 1702 under Vice-Admiral John Benbow. Benbow's orders to engage the French fleet which was sighted near Santa Marta in August were not obeyed and in the half-hearted skirmish that resulted, Benbow himself was mortally wounded. Kirkby and Edward Wade, captain of the *Greenwich,* were tried at courtmartial in Jamaica in October and condemned to be shot for cowardice. The sentence was executed aboard the *Bristol* in Plymouth Sound on 16 April 1703 and brought to an end "the most disgraceful event" in British naval history (*DNB,* 2, 210).

65–66. *Hara . . . And Bellasis:* See *The Spanish Descent,* 199 *n.,* below.

67. *Ormond:* See *The Spanish Descent,* 3 *n.,* 299 *n.,* below.

69. *Marlborough:* William III had appointed Marlborough commander-in-chief of the English forces in the Lowlands in June 1701. A year later the allies responded by giving him sole command of the confederate army (Luttrell, *5,* 58, 188). "The Dutch [and] the Germans," as Dalrymple remarked, knew how to compliment the queen when they appointed her favorite, "an Englishman [who] had never commanded above 3000 men, to be general of the allied army" (*3,* 2244). As a result, Marlborough had "a more deciding influence than . . . even . . . K. William" (*Biographia Britannica, 5,* 3563 *n.*).

70. *Liege:* Marlborough's capture of Liége was reported in London on 23 October 1702 (Luttrell, *5,* 228).

71. *Sarum's huge Prelate:* Gilbert Burnet, bishop of Salisbury; see *The Brawny Bishop's Complaint,* headnote, p. 37 above.

73. *Worcester:* William Lloyd, the 75-year-old bishop of Worcester, was one of the seven bishops who had dared to oppose James II in 1688. Now, however, he had "Brow-beat his Clergy" to oppose Sir John Pakington for re-election in Worcestershire in July, and in November 1702 found himself in danger of being taken into custody for *scandalum magnatum* (Bishop Nicolson's Diary, 16 November 1702, Carlisle Public Library). He had spent "above twenty Years" trying to interpret the prophecies of *Revelation* "chronologically" and finally lost his mind amid the delusions of numerology (Burnet, 2, 204; Luttrell, 2, 213).

Munden at Sea shall in his Duty fail,
And *Wade* and Dastard *Kirkby* turn their Tail.
Hara at Land his Country shall abuse,
And *Bellasis* by Plund'ring, Conquest lose,
While *British* Troops with *Ormond* at their Head
Shall meet with Conquest, who from Conquest fled,
And *Marlborough* of *William*'s Post Possess'd,
Reducing *Liege,* shall *France* it self Invest.
Sarum's huge Prelate shall before thee Preach,
And his dead Lord to flatter thee, Impeach;
Old dreaming *Worcester,* once the Church's Pride,
Shall quit her Interest for another side,
Brow-beat his Clergy, and a Chief defame,
Spotless as is the Blood from whence he came;
And though a Prisoner made in dubious times,
Shall now deserve the *Tower* for real Crimes.
'Midst *Lords* and *Commons* shall Disputes arise,
And one diswade what t'other shall advise.

75. *a Chief:* Sir John Pakington; see *The Worcester Cabal,* headnote, pp. 310–11, above. Lloyd's unsuccessful efforts to secure the defeat of Pakington in the elections of November 1701 and July–August 1702 are also described in Henry Sacheverell, *The Character of a Low-Church-man,* 1702. Sacheverell assumes that Lloyd wrote *The True Character of a Churchman,* 1702, and sent copies of it by "his Officers the Apparitors, throughout the County of *Worcester* . . . to every Minister or Church-warden in the Diocese." Sacheverell also claimed that this "Lampoon" was "peculiarly levell'd, as a *Personal Brand* on that Worthy Gentleman, Sir *John Packington,*" whom he describes as "*High* for the *Divine Right of Episcopacy*" and "*High* for the *Uninterrupted Succession.*" On the other side, Sacheverell describes William Walsh as "a *Deist, Socinian,* or *Republican,* or anything . . . and in a Word, a *Thorough-Pac'd and Season'd Low-Church-Man*" (pp. 5, 26, 27). Although defeated in November 1701, Walsh was re-elected in August 1702.

76. *Spotless:* This line replies to Lloyd's aspersions of Pakington. "He aspersed me to his Clergy," Pakington told the House of Commons, "branding me, and my Ancestors, with several Vices" (*CJ, 14,* 37).

79. *Disputes:* Without even hearing the evidence on Lloyd's behalf, the Commons voted unanimously on 18 November 1702 that Lloyd's actions had been "Malicious, Unchristian and Arbitrary" and addressed the queen to remove him as her lord almoner. Alarmed at these proceedings, the Lords represented to her majesty next day that it was the right of every subject to be heard in his own defense, and humbly desired that Lloyd be retained until tried by due course of law. Sir Edward Seymour, however, who had attended the queen with the Commons' address, was pleased to inform the House on 20 November that her majesty had ordered Lloyd to be removed (Boyer, *Annals,* 1703, pp. 145–46).

But when to ripen'd Man-hood he shall grow,
The greedy Sailer shall the Seas forego;
No Keel shall cut the Waves for foreign Ware;
For every Soil shall every Product bear.
The labouring Hind his Oxen shall disjoyn,
No Plow shall hurt the Glebe, no Pruning-hook the Vine:
Nor wooll shall in dissembled colours shine.
But the luxurious Father of the Fold,
With native Purple, or unborrow'd Gold,
Beneath his pompous Fleece shall proudly sweat:
And under *Tyrian* Robes the Lamb shall bleat.

---

81. *Orford:* See *A Conference,* 133 *n.,* above. "Adriatick" may allude to Orford's success in 1694–95, when the fleet wintered at Cadiz, in bringing the doge of Venice to recognize William III (Burnet, 2, 129).

82–83. These lines allude to the first of the articles of impeachment drawn up against Orford in May 1701: "towards the Prosecution of [the] War, great Sums of Money have been given and levied by Authority of Parliament; and many Debts have been contracted, which remain a very heavy Burden upon the People of *England;* the said Earl being then of his Majesty's Most Honourable Privy Council, but always preferring his private Interest to the Good of the Publick, and taking Advantage of the ready Access he had to his Majesty's Person . . . hath procured from his Majesty . . . Grants of several Manors . . . and also of exorbitant Sums of Money, to be made to him . . . the Profits whereof he now enjoys" (*CJ, 13,* 520). Orford was removed from the privy council in March 1702.

Proud *Adriatick Orford* shall be known
To sink the Nation's Money for his own,
And fix the Courtier's *Thefts* upon the *Throne.*
Funds shall, as if no Funds there were, appear,
Millions be giv'n the Kingdom's Debts to Clear,
Yet shall we Owe the Millions that we gave,
And Pay for what we had not Wit to save,
Unless some Moths that Fret the threadbare State,
Prevent our Ruin by their timely Fate,
Unless a *Peer* more often *Accounts* keeps,
And gives the Queen the Crop which now he Reaps.
But when confirm'd in Arts of Empire grown,
Thou seest thy Reign Mature, and Fix'd thy *Throne,*
Both Land and Sea thy Soveraign Power shall own.
Fearless of loss, and confident of Gain,
The Merchant shall in Safety Plough the Main;
The lab'ring Hind shall cleave the Country Soil,
And Plenty rise and Court the Farmer's Toil.
As every Subject sees his Wrongs Redress'd,
Views Faction quell'd, and Anarchy Suppress'd,
And Prince and People Mutually Bless'd.

84. *Funds:* See *An Encomium upon a Parliament,* 49 *n.,* above. Despite her "unparalell'd goodnesse" in contributing £100,000 of her own revenue to reduce deficiencies in the funds, Anne had to observe with some concern, in her speech at the opening of parliament in October 1702, "That the Fonds given by the last Parliament have . . . faln short of the Sums propos'd to be Rais'd by them" and that consequently the deficiencies had increased (Luttrell, 5, 158; Boyer, *Annals,* 1703, p. 122).

90. *Peer:* See 45 *n.* above.

96. *Plough the Main:* Cf. "The Merchant still shall plough the deep for gain" (*The Fourth Pastoral of Virgil, Englished by Mr. Dryden,* 38).

97. *The lab'ring Hind:* Cf. "The labouring Hind his Oxen shall disjoyn" (*The Fourth Pastoral of Virgil, Englished by Mr. Dryden,* 49).

The Fates, when they this happy Web have spun,
Shall bless the sacred Clue, and bid it smoothly run.
Mature in years, to ready Honours move,
O of Coelestial Seed! O foster Son of *Jove!*
See, labouring Nature calls thee to sustain
The nodding frame of Heav'n, and Earth, and Main;
See to their Base restor'd, Earth, Seas, and Air,
And joyful Ages from behind, in crowding Ranks appear.
To sing thy Praise, wou'd Heav'n my breath prolong
Infusing Spirits worthy such a Song;
Not *Thracian Orpheus* should transcend my Layes,
Nor *Linus* crown'd with never-fading Bayes:
Though each his Heav'nly Parent shou'd inspire;
The Muse instruct the Voice, and *Phoebus* tune the Lyre.
Shou'd *Pan* contend in Verse, and thou my Theme,
Arcadian Judges should their God condemn.

---

118. *Tate:* Upon the accession of Queen Anne, Nahum Tate was reappointed poet laureate (but not also historiographer royal, as stated in *DNB, 19,* 380) (*CTB 1702,* pp. 426, 427; *CTP 1702–1707,* p. 355).

120. *Rowe:* Nicholas Rowe (1674–1718) was educated at Westminster School and the Middle Temple, but abandoned the law for a literary career when he inherited £300 a year upon the death of his father in 1692. He produced a blank verse tragedy, *The Ambitious Step-Mother,* in December 1700, with a dedication to Edward Villiers, earl of Jersey, the lord chamberlain, and fell in love with the leading lady, Anne Bracegirdle. A year later he produced a second tragedy, *Tamerlane,* for which Samuel Garth wrote a prologue ("To day a mighty Hero comes to warm,") (*POAS,* 1703, *2,* 312). This piece, in which history was warped to present a hero of "amiable moderation" who could be identified with William III, was dedicated to the duke of Devonshire and became virtually an article of Whiggish faith. It was "played annually at Drury Lane theatre on 5 November, the anniversary of William III's landing . . . until 1815" (*DNB, 17,* 341–42). Jersey, retained by Anne in the post of lord chamberlain, would have been most reluctant to "take [the] Part" of so violent a Whig as Rowe.

Such be thy Reign, the Fatal Sisters Cry,
And such Britannia's *Future Destiny.*
Arise, Auspicious Queen! the *Times* are come,
When *France* shall from thy Mouth expect her doom;
When Providence shall labour in thy Cause,
And trembling *Spain* acknowledge *English Laws;*
Arise, thou Bright Inspirer of my Song,
And Vindicate the Blood from whence thou'rt sprung.
See the consenting World adore thy Fame!
Heav'n, Earth, and Sea confess the Justice of thy Claim!
See us for *Thee* our Vows and Prayers Employ,
And Coming *Ages* Smile in Hopes of Coming Joy.
Oh! that this Life of mine so long would last,
As I might Sing thy future deeds and past,
As on thy Rising Glories I might swell,
And I in Verse, as thou in Fame, Excel!
Not thy own *Tate* though with thy Lawrels Crown'd,
Should touch a sweeter Pipe, or give a sweeter Sound;
Not Favourite *Rowe,* though *Jersey* took his Part,
Should boast more Judgment, or reveal more Art;
Not *Congreve,* stock'd with all his Patron's Praise,
Produce a Zeal like Mine, or equal Lays;
Though *Congreve Halifax*'s Friend should be,
Congreve, if *Halifax* were Judge, should yield to me.

122. *Patron:* Congreve's patron was Charles Montagu, later Lord Halifax, who appointed him in July 1695 to the minor post of commissioner for licensing hackney coaches. Although Congreve may have hurried to court in 1702, as William Pittis claimed (*The Patriots. A Poem,* 1702, p. 9), his patron was then in no position to help him.

Begin, auspicious Boy, to cast about,
Thy Infant Eyes, and with a smile, thy Mother single out;
Thy Mother well deserves that short delight,
The nauseous Qualms of ten long Months and Travail to
requite.
Then smile; the frowning Infants Doom is read,
No God shall crown the Board, nor Goddess bless the Bed.

Begin Great Queen, the *Stuart*'s Steps to tread,
And let thy *Living* Worth Exceed the *Dead;*
Happiest of Princes in this Climate Born,
Entirely *English,* above thy Enemies Scorn,
Thou ne'r wer'st dandled on an *Austrian*'s Knee,
Nor *Hanover* stood Godfather for thee,
But sprung directly from the *British* Strain,
Where thou first drew'st thy Breath, dost there commence thy Reign.

129. *Entirely English:* Anne's assurance, in her first address to parliament on 11 March 1702, three days after the death of the foreigner, William III, that she knew her "Heart to be entirely English," "raised a hum from all that heard her" (Trevelyan, *1,* 164). This single phrase, said to have been inserted in the queen's speech by her uncle, the earl of Rochester, raised the hopes of the Jacobites, thrilled the war party, stiffened the intolerance of the high churchmen, and encouraged a strain of xenophobia which was already flourishing in all strata of English society (William T. Morgan, *English Political Parties and Leaders in the Reign of Queen Anne,* 1920, p. 63).

131. *Godfather:* Anne's godfather was the high Tory archbishop of Canterbury, Gilbert Sheldon.

133. *first . . . Breath:* Anne was born in St. James's Palace on 6 February 1665 and proclaimed queen before the gate of the palace on 8 March 1702.

The Spanish Descent
(*December*[?] *1702*)

The Cadiz expedition of 1702 was the most considerable military adventure that the English had undertaken abroad for more than 100 years (*The Daily Courant,* No. 126, 12 September 1702) and it left behind an inevitable literary precipitate. "The *White-Friers* Ballad-Singers," we are told, "bawll nothing at *Shoe-Lane End,* and the *Porter's Block* in *Smithfield,* but *England's Happiness, or, A new Copy of Verses upon the Taking of the Plate-Fleet, Set to an Excellent New* Vigo *Tune*" (*Letters from the Living to the Living,* 1703, p. 210). It is by contrast with street ballads like this that Defoe's poem defines itself as literature.

The unexpected failure at Cadiz, followed by the even more unexpected success at Vigo, supplied a shape to events that Defoe was quick to detect and exploit. His poem begins on the streets, with the first news arriving from Cadiz; then it works its way through the failures and successes of the campaign—with a retrospective glance at the failures and successes of the war of 1689–97 (lines 70–114)—and ends in St. Paul's Cathedral with a magnificent tableau of queen, Lords, and Commons, drawn up in full regalia, singing hymns of thanksgiving.

Running unobtrusively through all this there is a theme. The events of August–October 1702 had not only arranged themselves in a convenient tragi-comic shape, they also supplied Defoe with evidence of God's providence. This is the theme that polarizes the scattered details of the poem: no mortal man could have foreseen that the failure at Cadiz was *necessary* to produce the success at Vigo, for "The vast Designs of Fate remain unknown" (line 65). Just as the treaty of Ryswick was "Imperfect" because it ignored the designs of providence (lines 96–102), so the French at Vigo were helpless because they opposed "Almighty Fate" (line 297). Thus it is right—both formally and psychologically—that the poem should end in St. Paul's Cathedral with the functionaries of church and state drawn up in ordered ranks and singing praises to the power that brought about the victory. Defoe probably believed literally that "the Sword of *God*" (line 104) had been unsheathed at Vigo.

Since the duke of Ormonde would have had no concern for his journal of the Cadiz expedition until 10 December 1702 when the House of Lords ordered him to lay it before the House (line 193 *n.*), the poem may have been written and published in December 1702, rather than in November as William Lee surmised (*1,* xxix).

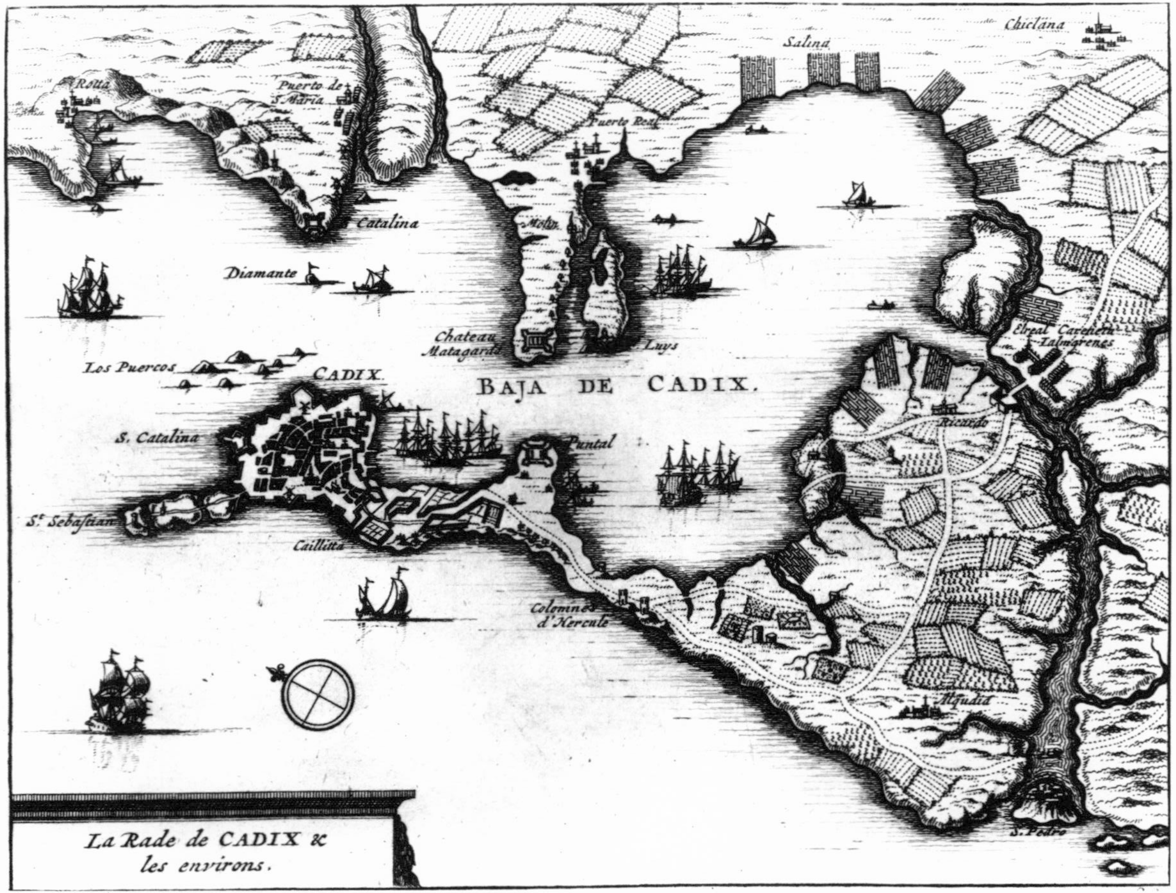

La Rade de CADIX &
les environs.

The Bay of Cadiz

The Spanish Descent

Long had this Nation been amus'd in vain
With Post from *Portugal,* and News from *Spain,*
With *Ormond*'s Conquests, and the Fleets Success,
And Favours from the *Moors* at *Maccaness.*
The Learned *Mob* bought Compasses and Scales,
And every Barber knew the Bay of *Cales,*
Show'd us the Army here, and there the Fleet,
Here the Troops Land, and there the Foes Retreat,
There at St. *Maries* how the *Spaniard* runs,
And listen close as if they heard the Guns,
And some pretend they see them Swive the Nuns.

2. *News:* "the whole Town is at present so deeply engag'd about the success of your Expedition at *Cadiz,* that scarce any body will afford themselves leisure to mind any thing but the News Papers. The coming in of every fresh *Mail* puts the whole Town in an uproar, and People assemble themselves in . . . Crouds at the *Old Exchange, Pauls* Church, *Covent Garden* Piazza, and *Westminster* Abby, upon the arrival of a Packet-Boat, and the noise of a new Express" (*Letters from the Living to the Living,* 1703, p. 182).

3. *Ormond's Conquests:* Ormonde captured the undefended villages of Rota and El Puerto de Santa María and the small fortress of Santa Catalina, but failed to capture the larger fortress of Matagorda, which dominated the approaches to Cadiz (see illustration, p. 469).

the Fleet: The combined English and Dutch fleet under the command of Sir George Rooke boasted "196 Vessels great and small" (*The Daily Courant,* No 127, 14 September 1702), with 14,000 troops aboard under the command of James Butler, second duke of Ormonde.

4. *Favours from the Moors:* Muley Ismail the Bloodthirsty, emperor of Morocco, who had declared war against Spain in June 1702, sent an envoy to Rooke with assurance of his "friendship for the English nation [and] made some offers about the redemption of thirty slaves" (*The Journal of Sir George Rooke,* ed. O. Browning, 1897, pp. 197–98).

8. *the Troops Land:* The landing was effected on 15 August about a mile from the fort of Santa Catalina. More lives were lost from drowning in the heavy surf than from the very light resistance of the Spanish (*The London Gazette,* No. 3845, 14–17 September 1702).

9. *St. Maries:* From the beachhead the troops first secured Rota, where Ormonde set up his headquarters, and then turned back to take El Puerto de Santa María on 21 August against 600 Spanish troops who "retreated, and at last march'd off into the Country" (*An Impartial Account of all the Material Transactions of the Grand Fleet and Land Forces,* 1703, p. 13).

11. *Swive:* Both *A* and *B* read "——" but the desideratum is supplied in the Yale

Others describe the Castle and *Puntalls,*
And tell how easie 'tis to Conquer *Cales;*
Wisely propose to let the Silver come,
And help to Pay the Nation's Debts at Home.
But still they count the Spoils without the Cost,
And still the News comes faster that the Post.
The graver Heads, like Mountebanks of State,
Of Abdication and Revolts Debate,
Expect a Revolution should appear
As Cheap and Easie as it had done here;
Bring the revolting *Grandees* to the Coast,
And give the Duke *De Anjou* up for Lost;
Doom him to *France* to seek Relief in vain,
And send the Duke of *Austria* to Spain;
Canvas the Council at *Madrid,* and find
How all the *Spanish* Courtiers stand enclin'd;
Describe the strange Convulsions of the State,
And Old *Carreroe* Sacrific'd to Fate.

---

copy of *A*. In view of line 214, "Kiss," the reading of the *Key,* is apparently intended as a jest. Cf. *Letters from the Living to the Living,* pp. 167–68: "I suppose by this time you have heard strange stories of some part of the *Soldiery* and the *Nuns:* I know not how much the snow-ball may have gather'd in the rowling, but I assure you the devout *Seraglio* had no other usage from us than what I am Confident they were well pleas'd with . . . and therefore, what ever was done to the dishonour of *Popery,* and the Glory of the Reform'd Churches, I hope can be thought no evil by a *True-Blue-Protestant.*"

12. *the Castle and Puntalls:* The Castle (Castillo de Matagorda) and Puntals (Castillo de San Lorenzo del Puntal), on either side of the bay, controlled the harbor of Cadiz.

14. *Silver:* Cadiz was the usual destination of the Plate fleet, which transported the year's production of American silver to Spain, and before the English forces left there it was reported (erroneously) in London that the Plate fleet was making the best of its was to Cadiz (*The Daily Courant,* No. 124, 10 September 1702).

17. Proverbial: "The lame Post brings the truest news" (Tilley P489).

19. *Revolts:* John Tutchin had boldly prophesied that great numbers of Spaniards would take advantage of Ormonde's protection to desert the French, "for those People seem only to want an opportunity to declare for the Emperour" (*The Observator,* No. 39, 2–5 September 1702). But when Ormonde set up the imperial standard with the arms of the archduke Charles and issued a declaration exhorting nobility and clergy alike to join him in defending the rights of the Habsburgs to the throne of Spain, no one took the opportunity to do so (Lamberty, 2, 250; *The Daily Courant,* No. 127, 14 September 1702).

25. *Duke of Austria:* The archduke Charles (1685–1740), second son of the emperor Leopold I, was proclaimed king of Spain on 1/12 September 1702 in Vienna.

29. *Carreroe:* It was principally Luis Manuel Fernandez de Portocarrero (1635–1709), archbishop of Toledo and "an old Covetous Cardinal," who had secured the throne

Then all the Stage of Action they Survey,
And wish our Generals knew as much as they.
  Some have their Fancies so exceeding Bold,
They saw the Queens fall out, and heard 'em Scold:
Nor is the thing so strange, for if they did,
It was but from *Toledo* to *Madrid.*
  And now the Farce is acting o'er again,
The meaning of our Mischiefs to Explain.
The Learned *Mob o'er-read* in Arms and Law,
The Cause of their Miscarriages foresaw;
Tell us the Loitering Minutes were mis-spent,
Too long a going, and too few that went;
Exalt the *Catalonian* Garrison,
The New made Works, the Platform, and the *Town;*
Tell us it was Impossible to Land,
And all their Batteries sunk into the Sand.
  Some are all Banter, and the Voyage Despise—
For fruitless Actions seldom pass for Wise—
Tell us 'twas like our *English* Politicks,
To think to wheedle *Spain* with *Hereticks.*

---

of Spain for Philippe d'Anjou, but soon after the coronation he "lost much of the Esteem which he had formerly in this Court" (*The Present State of Europe, 13* [June 1702], 239; *The Daily Courant,* No. 116, 1 September 1702).

33. *Queens:* The dowager queen was Maria Ana of Neuburg, the second wife of Carlos II, whom Philippe had caused to be removed to Toledo before his arrival in Madrid. The queen was the young Maria Luisa of Savoy (1688–1714), who married Philippe in October 1701 (William Coxe, *Memoirs of the Kings of Spain,* 2nd ed., 5 vols., 1815, *1,* 98, 146).

40. *Minutes . . . mis-spent:* On 12 October 1702 it was reported in the press "That the English and Dutch [had] made no attempt at Cadiz, since they rose from before the Matagorda Fort on the 16th [September]" (*The Daily Courant,* No. 152, 12 October 1702) and Trevelyan cites the expert opinion of Marlborough: "What can be said for staying 26 days at Port St. Mary? For if Cadiz was to be attacked, they should not have staid there. And if the taking of Cadiz was not thought feasible, then they should not have lost time, but have reimbarked to have attempted what was in their instructions" (*1,* 265).

43. *New made Works:* The construction of new defenses at Cadiz was reported in June 1702 and reinforcements for the garrison began to arrive the same month (*The London Gazette,* No. 3829, 20–23 July 1702).

45. *Batteries sunk:* A battery of four artillery pieces opened fire on the fortress of Matagorda on 2 September, but "the Ground was so low, and on a Morass, that our Battery sunk by our firing" (*An Impartial Account,* 1703, p. 15).

49. *Hereticks:* The commander of the garrison at El Puerto de Santa María replied to Ormonde's declaration (19 *n.*), "We *Spaniards* neither change our Religion or King" (*An Impartial Account,* 1703, p. 13).

The disproportion'd Force they Banter too;
The Ships too many, and the Men too few.
Then they find fault with Conduct, and condemn
Sometimes the Officers, sometimes the Men:
Nor scapes his Grace the *Satyr* of the *Town;*
Whoever fails Success, shall fail Renown.
Sir *George* comes in among the Indiscreet;
Sometimes the Army's censur'd, then the Fleet;
How the abandon'd *Country* they destroy'd,
And made their early Declarations void;
Too hasty Proofs of their Protection gave,
Plundering the People they came there to Save;
As if the *Spaniards* were so plagu'd with *France,*
To fly to Thieves for their Deliverance.
But amongst all the Wisdom of the *Town,*
The vast Designs of Fate remain unknown,
Unguest at, unexpected, hid from Thoughts,
For no Man look'd for Blessings in our Faults.
Mischances sometimes are a Nation's Good,
Rightly Improv'd, and Nicely Understood.
Ten Years we felt the Dying Pangs of War,
And fetch'd our Grief and Miseries from far.

54. *Satyr:* Ormonde seems to have been the subject of some feeble panegyric (e.g. *POAS,* 1703, *2,* 409, 415), but of no real satire.

58. *abandon'd Country . . . destroy'd:* When the refugees from Cadiz and the neighboring villages returned after the confederate fleet had sailed away, they "view'd with Horrour the Churches profan'd and the Images defac'd or beaten down by the Hereticks," which made nonsense, of course, of Ormonde's declaration that he had come to defend the Spanish against "the Insupportable Slavery whereto they are brought and sold to *France"* (*The Daily Courant,* No. 178, 11 November 1702; *The London Gazette,* No. 3843, 7–10 September 1702).

61. *Plundering:* El Puerto de Santa María was found to be almost empty of inhabitants when it was captured on 21 August. The next day, however, the houses were found to be "full of riches" and "for a week following there was nothing but Drunkenness and Confusion." Ormonde's order of 26 August to stop the plundering was ignored either because Ormonde "was not able, or, thro' a gentleness of temper, was not willing to proceed to extremities." Vast quantities of goods and plate were loaded aboard the men-of-war and when the fleet sailed it left behind "such a filthy stench among the Spaniards that a whole age will hardly blot it out," as an English eyewitness reported (*An Impartial Account,* 1703, pp. 13–14; Burnet, *2,* 331; Bishop Nicolson's Diary, 30 December 1702, Carlisle Public Library; Steele, No. 4339; *CSPD 1702–1703,* p. 303).

70. *Ten Years:* Defoe's usual approximation of the length of King William's war, 1688–97; cf. *The Pacificator,* 13, above.

Our *English* Millions Foreign War maintains,
And *English* Blood has Drencht the Neighbouring Plains.
Nor shall we Blush to Boast what all Men own,
Uncommon *English* Valour has been shown;
The forward Courage of our *Ill Paid Men,*
Deserves more Praise than Nature spares my Pen.
What cou'd they not Perform, or what Endure,
Witness the Mighty Bastions of *Namure!*
We fasted much, and we attempted more,
But ne'er cou'd come to giving Thanks before,
Unless 'twas when the Fatal Strife was o're.
Some secret *Achan* Curst our Enterprize,
And *Israel* fled before her Enemies.
Whether the Poisonous Particles were hid
In Us that Follow'd, *or in Them that Led:*
What Fatal Charm benumb'd the Nations Sense,
To struggle with Eternal Providence:
Whether some Curse, or else some *Perjur'd Vow,*
Or some strange Guilt that's expiated now:
Was it the *Pilots* who ill steer'd the State;
Or was it the Decisive Will of Fate;
'Tis hard to tell; but this too well we know,
All things went backward, or went on too slow;
Small was the Glory of our High Success,
A Tedious War, and an Imperfect Peace;

72–73. *English Millions . . . English Blood:* Estimates of the cost of William's war in money and lives are given in *The Pacificator,* 17 *n.,* above.

79. *Namure:* The capture of Namur by the armies of Louis XIV in 1692 is celebrated in Boileau's famous *Ode sur la prise de Namur.* When William recaptured the town in August 1695, Prior wrote *An English Ballad,* parodying Boileau's ode, which he reprinted on the facing pages.

83. *Achan:* Joshua 7:1–26; see *The Mock Mourners,* 366 *n.,* above.

85. *Poisonous Particles:* The 250 shekels of gold and silver that Achan withheld are called "an accursed thing" in Joshua 7:13. Defoe seems to be making the common Tory charge that the enormous fortunes amassed by war profiteers had made it impossible to gain a clear-cut victory in the last war.

96. *Imperfect Peace:* The treaty of Ryswick signed by the English in September 1697 was "Imperfect" because it ignored the problem of who was to succeed the childless Carlos II on the throne of Spain. As Tutchin said, "That Peace of *Ryswick* was more prejudicial to the *English* Nation, than was the whole War . . . by that opportunity given the *French* King of Recruiting his Forces, and thereby putting *Anjou* into possession of the Kingdom of *Spain*" (*The Observator,* No. 38, 29 August–2 September 1702).

Peace Dearly purchas'd, and which Cost us more
Great Kingdoms than we Conquer'd Towns before.
  Actions may miss of their deserv'd Applause,
When Heaven approves the Men, and not the Cause;
And well contriv'd Designs miscarry when
Heaven may approve the Cause, but not the Men;
Here then's the Ground of our Expence of Blood,
The Sword of *Gideon*'s, not the Sword of *God.*
The Mighty and the Wise are laid aside,
And Victory *the Sex* has Dignified;
We have bin us'd to *Female Conquests* here,
And Queens have bin the Glory of the War,
The Scene Revives with Smiles of Providence,
All things Declin'd before, and Prosper since;
And as if ill Success had been Entail'd,
The Posthume Projects are the last that fail'd;
As Heaven, whose Works are hid from Humane View,
Would blast our Old Designs, and bless our New.
  And now the Baffl'd Enterprize grows stale,
Their Hopes decrease, and juster Doubts prevail:
The Unattempted *Town* Sings Victory,
And scar'd with Walls, and not with Men, we Fly;
Great Conduct in our safe Retreat we shew,
And bravely Re-imbark when none Pursue;
The Guns, the Ammunition, put on Board,
And what we could not Plunder, we Restor'd.
And thus we Quit the *Andalusian* Shores,
Drencht with the *Spanish* Wine, and *Spanish* Whores.

97–98. *Cost us . . . Kingdoms:* The reference is to the partition treaties of 1698–1700 by which England divided the vast Spanish empire between France and Austria without taking anything for herself.

104. *The Sword of Gideon's:* Three hundred Israelites routed a numberless host of Midianites by blowing trumpets and shouting "The sword of the Lord and of Gideon" (Judges 7:15–23). At Cadiz, Defoe implies, the sword of Yahweh remained sheathed.

112. *Posthume Projects:* The failure at Cadiz was blamed on its having been proposed by the late king; the success at Vigo was the first under the new queen. Tutchin expresses the idea of lines 105–14 much less cryptically: "King *William*'s Design upon *Cadiz* was the Occasion of Queen *Ann*'s Destroying the Ships at *Vigo*" (*The Observator,* No. 58, 7–11 November 1702).

118. *we Fly:* News of the duke of Ormonde's defeat and the fleet's withdrawal from Cadiz on 19 September reached London on 6 October 1702 (Luttrell, *5,* 222).

124. *Whores* (*Key*).

With Songs of Scorn the *Arragonians* Sing,
And loud *Te Deums* make the Valleys Ring.
Uncommon Joys now raise the Hopes of *Spain,*
And *Vigo* does their Plate-Fleet Entertain;
The vast Galeons Deep-Balasted with Ore,
Safely reach Home to the *Galitian* Shore.
The Double Joy spreads from *Madrid* to *Rome,*
The *English* Fled, the Silver Fleet come Home:
From thence it reaches to the Banks of *Po,*
And the loud Cannons let the *Germans* know.
The ratling Volleys tell their Short-liv'd Joys,
And roar *Te Deum* out in Smoak and Noise.
To *Milan* next it flies on Wings of Fame,
There the Young Monarch and his Heroes came,
From sad *Luzara,* and the *Mantuan* Walls,

128. *Plate-Fleet:* Seventeen Spanish galleons with a cargo estimated to be worth 60,000,000 pesos and under a French convoy commanded by François Louis de Rousselet, marquis de Chateaurenault, vice-admiral of France, reached Vigo, a port in Galicia, on 22 September 1702 (*The Daily Courant,* No. 153, 13 October 1702; Luttrell, *5,* 222).

133. *the Banks of Po: "From the Imperial Camp near* Luzzara, *Octob.* 22. The 16th Instant . . . The Enemy . . . made a treble Discharge of their great and small Arms, upon the occasion . . . of the *English* and *Dutch* Fleets being sailed from before *Cadiz,* and of the Arrival of the *Spanish* Plate Fleet at *Vigo"* (*The London Gazette,* No. 3860, 5–9 November 1702).

137. *Milan next:* "on the 17th *Ult. Te Deum* was sung in the Cathedral of that City, with firing of Cannon, &c. for the Retreat of the Confederates from before Cadiz" (*The Daily Courant,* No. 174, 6 November 1702).

138. *the Young Monarch:* Philippe d'Anjou (1683–1746), the second grandson of Louis XIV, was crowned Felipe V of Spain on 21 April 1701, before his eighteenth birthday. A year later he put himself at the head of the Spanish troops in the French army commanded by Louis Joseph, duc de Vendôme, who was opposing the incursions of Prince Eugene into Italy.

139. *Luzara:* Luzzara, on the banks of the Po, was the scene of the climactic battle in the campaign of 1702 between the forces of France and those of the Empire. To encourage his troops by his presence, the young king of Spain eluded those whom his grandfather had appointed to take care of him and exposed himself "several times" to cannon and musket fire (*The Daily Courant,* No. 118, 3 September 1702). Despite Philippe's efforts, the Germans inflicted 12,000 casualties on the French and Spanish forces and remained master of the field at nightfall (Luttrell, *5,* 208; *The London Gazette,* No. 3838, 20–24 August 1702). On 12 October (see 137 *n.,* above) Philippe entered Milan, which was then a Spanish possession, and was received with much ceremony (*The Daily Courant,* No. 168, 30 October 1702).

Mantuan Walls: Philippe did not join the French army until July 1702, a month after Vendôme's appearance in the field with 40,000 troops had forced Prince Eugene to abandon the siege of Mantua (Luttrell, *5,* 179).

To seek New Dangers, and to rescue *Cales.*
His Joy for Welcome Treasure he exprest,
But grieves at his good Fortune in the rest:
The Flying *English* he had wisht to stay,
To Crown with Conquest One Victorious Day.
The Priests, in high Procession, shew their Joy,
And all the Arts of Eloquence Employ,
To feed his Pride of fancy'd Victories,
And raise his untry'd Valour to the Skies.
The flattering *Courtiers* his vain Mind possess
With Airy Hopes of Conquest and Success,
Prompt his young Thoughts to run on new Extreams,
And Sycophantick Pride his Heart Enflames.
His *Native Crime* springs up, his Pulse beats high,
With Thoughts of Universal Monarchy;
Fancies his Foreign Enemies supprest,
And Boasts too soon how he'll subdue the rest.
Princes, like other Men, are blind to Fate;
He only sees the Event who does the Cause create.
From hence through *France* the Welcome Tydings fly,
To mock his Ancient Sire with Mushroom Joy.
Raptures possess the Ambitious Heads of *France,*
And Golden Hopes their new Designs advance.
Now they Consult to Crush the World agen,
And talk of rifling *Christendom* for Men.
New Fleets, new Armies, and new Leagues contrive,
And swallow Men and Nations up alive;
Prescribe no Bounds to their Ambitious Pride,
But first the Wealth, and then the World, Divide.
Excess of Pride to Airy Madness grows,
And makes Men strange Romantick things propose:

149. *flattering Courtiers:* Although Philippe seems to have been both timid and indolent, and already suffered from attacks of depression during which he did not speak, his courtiers flattered him with the title *El Animoso* (Coxe, *Memoirs of the Kings of Spain, 1,* 207–10).

165. *new Armies:* "The New Levys for the Armys of France both by Sea and Land are to be compleated by the end of February next, and will amount to 68000 Foot and 10000 Horse" (*The Daily Courant,* No. 137, 25 September 1702).

170. *strange Romantick things: "Paris, June 26, N.S.* The Court is daily contriving new Methods of raising Money to supply the King's urgent occasions . . . and the many Edicts lately issued for that purpose being not sufficient, one was published this

The Head turns round, and all the Fancy's vain,
And makes the World as Giddy as the Brain.
Men that Consult such Weighty Things as those,
All Possible Disasters should suppose:
In vain great *Princes* mighty things Invent,
While Heaven retains the Power to prevent:
He that to General Mischief makes Pretence,
Should first know how to conquer Providence.
Such strive in vain, and only shew Mankind,
How Tyrants cloath'd with Power are all enclin'd.
  Mean while our melancholy Fleet steers Home,
Some griev'd for past, for future Mischiefs some:
Disaster swells the Blood, and Spleen the Face,
And ripens them for glorious Things apace.
With deep Regret they turn their Eyes to *Spain,*
And wish they once might Visit her again.
Little they dreamt that Good which Heaven prepar'd;
No Merit from below, no Signs from Heaven appear'd;
No Hints, unless from their high-ripen'd Spleen,
And strange ungrounded Sympathy within.
  The silent Duke, from all Misconduct Free,
Alone enjoys the Calm of Honesty:
Fears not his Journal should be fairly shown,
And sighs for *England*'s Errors, not his own.
His Constant Temper's all serene and Clear;
First free from Guilt, and therefore free from Fear.
  Not so the rest, for conscious Thoughts become
More restless now the nearer they come Home.
The Party-making Feuds on Board begin:

---

week, by which the King offers to give the Title of Gentleman to 200 Persons, paying 6000 Livres each" (*The London Gazette,* No. 3822, 25–29 June 1702).

193. *Journal:* Once back in England, Ormonde demanded a parliamentary inquiry into the miscarriage at Cadiz—or the "*Cales farce,*" as Tutchin called it (*The Observator,* No. 95, 17–20 March 1703). Consequently, on 10 December 1702 the House of Lords moved that "the Duke of *Ormond*'s Journal of his Expedition to *Cadiz* and *Vigo*" be taken into consideration on 15 December and at the same time ordered that "the original Journals of all the Flag Officers . . . who were in the late Expedition" be laid before the House on 14 December (*LJ, 17,* 188).

199. *Feuds on Board:* When Ormonde discovered that his two immediate subordinates, Lieutenant-General Sir Henry Bellasis, Knight (d. 1714), and Major-General Sir Charles O'Hara, Knight (1640?–1724), were involved in the looting of El Puerto de

For People always Quarrel when they Sin.
Reflect with Shame upon the things mis-done,
And shift their Faults about from One to One,
Prepare Excuses, and compute their Friends,
And dread the Fate which their Desert attends.
Some wish for Storms, and curse the Wind and Sails,
And Dream, no doubt, of Gibbets, and of Jayls;
Imaginary Punishments appear,
And suited to their secret Guilts, their Fear,
Their hast'ning Fate in their own Fancies Read,
And few, 'tis fear'd, their Innocence can plead.
Then their sweet Spoils to trusty Hands convey,
And throw the *rifl'd Gods of Spain* away;
Disgorge that Wealth they dare not entertain,
And wish the Nuns *their Maiden-Heads again;*
Dismiss their Wealth for fear of Witnesses,
And purge their Coffers and their Consciences,
Cursing their *Ill-got Trifles,* but in vain,
For still the Guilt, and still the Fears, remain.
Tell us, ye Rabbies of abstruser Sense,
Who jumble Fate and Fools with Providence;
Is this the chosen Army, this the Fleet,
For which Heaven's Praises sound in every Street?
Cou'd Heaven provide them one Occasion more,
Who had so Ill discharg'd themselves before?
That Fleet so many former Millions Lost,

Santa María, he immediately drew up charges against them. Then, acting on instructions he received the day before the descent on Vigo, he ordered the two officers to be placed under arrest. Upon return of the fleet to England both of the officers were removed from their commands for coming ashore at Deal without orders. Bellasis, who had just been re-elected member of parliament for Durham city, pleaded privilege of parliament. In courtmartial proceedings Bellasis was dishonorably discharged from the service but O'Hara was acquitted and was subsequently created baron Tyrawley in the Irish peerage (Dalton, *2,* 228 *n.,* GEC, *12,* ii, 106–07; Luttrell, *5,* 237; Boyer, *Annals, 1,* 129).

212. *rifl'd Gods:* See 58 *n.,* above; cf. Boyer, *Annals, 1,* 88: "Churches . . . [were] despoiled of their most precious Ornaments."

225. *That Fleet:* The English fleet entered the Mediterranean twice during the war of 1688–97. In June 1693, under the command of Sir George Rooke, it suffered the disastrous loss of the Turkey fleet (*The True-Born Englishman,* 1039 *n.,* above). The next year, under the command of Admiral Russell (later Lord Orford), the fleet

So little had Perform'd, so much had Cost:
That Fleet, so often Mann'd with Knaves before,
That serv'd us all the War to make us Poor;
That Twice had made their fruitless Voyage to *Spain,*
And saw the *Streights,* and *so came Home again:*
Our *Wooden Walls* that should Defend our Trade,
And many a Witless *Wooden* Voyage ha' made;
How oft have they been fitted out in Vain,
Wasted our Money, and destroy'd our Men,
Betray'd our Merchants, and expos'd their Fleets,
And caus'd Eternal Murmurs in our Streets?
The Nation's Genius sure prevails above,
And Heaven conceals his Anger, shows his Love:
The Nation's Guardian Angel has prevail'd,
And on her Guardian Queen new Favours has entail'd.
  Now let glad *Europe* in her Turn Rejoice,
And Sing new Triumphs with exalted Voice.
See the glad Post of Tidings wing'd with News,
With suited Speed the wondring Fleet pursues:
His Haste discern'd, increases their Surprize,
The more they wonder, and the more he flies.
Nor Wind, nor Seas, proportion'd Speed can bear;
For Joy and Hope have swifter Wings than Fear.
With what Surprize of Joy they meet the News!
Joys, that to every Vein new Spirits infuse.
The wild Excess in Shouts and Cries appear;
For Joys and Griefs are all irregular.

---

maneuvered but failed to prevent the French from returning to Toulon and after wintering in Cadiz it was equally unsuccessful in August 1695 in an attempt to recover Palamos, in Cataluña, from the French (John Ehrman, *The Navy in the War of William III,* Cambridge, Cambridge University Press, 1953, pp. 499–502, 517–19, 544–53). "What had You don, had you attacq'd the place?" asked a contemporary ballad, "But your sage judgement took a wiser hint/And did conclude there might be danger in't" (*On Admiral Russells return from the Streights* ["Wellcome great Russell from the Coast of Spain"], BM MS. Add. 29497, f. 105).

242. *Sing new Triumphs: "Vienna,* December 2. Two days ago the Imperial Court went to the Cathedral of St. Stephen, where *Te Deum* was sung for the Success of the Allies at Vigo" (*The Daily Courant,* No. 206, 14 December 1702).

243. *glad . . . Tidings:* Captain Thomas Hardy, in command of the *Pembroke,* accidentally learned when he put into Lagos for water that the Plate fleet had just reached Vigo. He reported this news to Rooke on 6 October 1702 (Rooke, *The Journal of Sir George Rooke,* 1897, p. 247; *The Daily Courant,* No. 171, 3 November 1702).

Councils of War for sake of Forms they call,
But Shame admits of no Disputes at all:
How should they differ where no Doubt can be
But if they shou'd accept of Victory?
Whether they shou'd the great Occasion take,
Or baffle Heaven, and double their Mistake?
Whether the naked and defenceless Prize
They should accept, or Heaven and that Despise?
Whether they shou'd Revive their Reputation,
Or sink it Twice, and Twice Betray the Nation?
Who dare the horrid Negative design?
Who dare the Last suggest, the First decline?
Envy her self; for *Satan's always there,*
And keeps his Councils with the God of War.
Tho' with her swelling Spleen she seem'd to burst,
Will'd the Design while the Event she Curs'd.
The Word's gone out, and now they spread the Main
With swelling Sails, and swelling Hopes, for *Spain:*
To double Vengeance prest where-e'er they come,
Resolv'd to pay the Haughty *Spaniard* home:
Resolv'd by future Conduct to atone
For all our past Mistakes, and all their own.
New Life springs up in every *English* Face,
And fits them all for Glorious Things apace:
The Booty some Excites, and some the Cause;
But more the Hope to gain their lost Applause.
Eager their sully'd Honour to restore,
Some Anger whets, some Pride and Vengeance more.
The lazy Minutes now pass on too slow,
Fancy flies faster than the Winds can blow:
Impatient Wishes lengthen out the Day;

253. *Councils of War:* The next day, 7 October, Rooke convened a council of flag officers wherein it was decided that in order "to reduce the Exorbitant Power of *France,* the Fleet should make the best of their Way to the Port of *Vigo,* and fall on immediately with the whole Line" (*Present State of Europe, 13* [November 1702], 435).

265, 268. *Envy . . . Design . . . Event:*

Tell the bleak Fury [Envy] . . .
. . . what th'Event, unless her Care enclines
To blast their Hopes, and baffle their Designs.
(*The Dispensary, 1,* 177–80)

They chide the loitering Winds for their delay.
But Time is Nature's faithful Messenger,
And brings up all we Wish, as well as all we Fear.
The Mists clear up, and now the Scout discries
The Subject of their Hopes and Victories:
The wish'd for Fleets embay'd, in Harbour lye,
Unfit to fight, and more unfit to fly.
Triumphant Joy throughout the Navy flies,
Eccho'd from Shore with Terror and Surprize.
Strange Power of Noise! which at one simple sound
At once shall some Encourage, some Confound.
In vain the Lion tangl'd in the Snare
With Anguish roars, and rends the trembling Air:
'Tis vain to struggle with Almighty Fate;
Vain and Impossible the weak Debate.
The Mighty Boom, the Forts, resist in vain,
The Guns with fruitless Force *in Noise* complain.
See how the Troops intrepidly fall on!
Wish for more Foes, and think they fly too soon.
With eager Fury to their Forts pursue,
And think the odds of Four to One too few.
The Land's first Conquer'd, and the Prize attends;
Fate beckens in the Fleet to back their Friends:
Despair succeeds, they struggle now too late,
And soon submit to their prevailing Fate:
Courage is Madness when Occasion's past,
Death's the securest Refuge, and the last.
And now the rolling Flames come threatning on,

299. *The Mighty Boom, the Forts:* The descent upon Vigo was not totally unexpected by "the United Crowns of *France* and *Spain*," as they were now described. In August, "Monsieur Renaud, a French Ingenier" had been sent there to fortify the port "against any Attempt that the English and Dutch" might make and as soon as the Plate fleet made harbor, Chateaurenault ordered a nine-foot-thick boom "made up of Masts, Yards, Cables, Top-Chains and Casks" to be placed across the mouth of the harbor so the ends could be covered by shore batteries in the forts. After a task force under Ormonde had taken the Castillo de Randa on 11 October and silenced the batteries on the left bank, Thomas Hopsonn, vice-admiral of the white and second in command under Rooke, broke through the boom in his flagship, the *Torbay,* and cleared a passage for the rest of his squadron (*The Daily Courant,* No. 111, 26 August 1702; No. 123, 9 September 1702; *Present State of Europe, 13* [November 1702], 436; *An Impartial Account,* 1703, pp. 21–22).

311. *Flames:* "When the Confederate Vessels had pass'd the Boom, the Enemy, fol-

And mighty Streams of melted Gold run down.
The flaming Oar down to its Center makes,
To Form new Mines beneath the Oazy Lakes.
Here a Galleon with Spicy Drugs enflam'd,
In Odoriferous folds of Sulphur stream'd.
The Gods of Old no such Oblations knew,
Their Spices weak, and their Perfumes but few.
The frighted *Spaniards* from their Treasure fly,
Loth to forsake their Wealth, *but loath to Die.*
Here a vast Carrack flies while none pursue,
Bulg'd on the Shore by her Distracted Crew:
There like a mighty Mountain she appears,
And groans beneath the Golden Weight she bears.
Conquest perverts the Property of Friend,
And makes Men Ruin what they can't Defend:
Some blow their Treasure up into the Air,
With all the wild Excesses of Despair.
Strange Fate! that War such odd Events shou'd have;
Friends would destroy, and Enemies would save:
Others their Safety to their Wealth Prefer,
And mix *some small Discretion* with their Fear.
Life's the best Gift that Nature can bestow;
The first that we receive, the last which we forego:
And he that's *vainly Prodigal of Blood,*
Forfeits his Sense to do his Cause no good.
All Desparation's the Effect of Fear;
Courage is Temper, Valour can't Despair.
And now the Victory's compleatly gain'd;
No Ships to Conquer now, no Foes remain'd.
The mighty Spoils exceed what e'er was known

lowing the Example of M. *Chasteaurenaud,* fir'd and blew up several of their ships, and ran others ashoar" (*Present State of Europe, 13* [November 1702], 437). "For some time," it was reported, "there was nothing to be heard or seen but cannonading, burning, [and] men and guns flying in the air." To a witness aboard an English ship in the harbor it was "altogether the most lively scene of horror and confusion that can be imagined," but to an English soldier safely ashore, " 'twas . . . unexpressible fine" (*Life of Captain Stephen Martin,* ed. Clements R. Markham, 1895, p. 58; *An Impartial Account,* 1703, p. 25).

315. *Spicy Drugs:* The fireship by which the French set on fire Hopsonn's flagship, the *Torbay,* happened to have on board a large quantity of snuff, "the blast of which as she blew up extinguished the flames" aboard the *Torbay* (*DNB, 9,* 1239).

341. *Spoils:* Without the loss of a single ship the confederates captured an entire

That Vanquish'd ever lost, or Victor won:
So great, if Fame shall Future Times remind,
They'll think she Lies, and Libels all Mankind.
Well may the Pious Queen New Anthems raise,
Sing her own Fortunes, and Her Maker's Praise;
Invite the Nation willing Thanks to pay;
And well may all the Mighty Ones Obey.
So may they sing, be always so preserv'd,
By Grace unwish'd, and Conquest undeserv'd.
Now let us Welcome Home the Conquering Fleet,
And all their well aton'd Mistakes forget:
Such high Success shou'd all Resentments drown'd,
No thing but Joy and Welcome should be found.
No more their past Miscariages Reprove,
But bury all in Gratitude and Love;
Let their high Conduct have a just Regard,
And meaner Merit meet a kind Reward.
But now what Fruits of Victory remain?
To Heaven what Praise? What Gratitude to Man?
Let *France* sing Praise for Shams of Victories,
And Mock their Maker with Religious Lies:
But *England* blest with thankful Hearts shall raise,
For mighty Conquests, mighty Songs of Praise.
She needs no false Pretences to Deceive:

---

fleet: 12 Spanish galleons and 15 French men-of-war. The loss of prestige to the united crowns was incalculable, but the loss of plate was not nearly so great as had been feared. A French officer told Rooke that all the king's silver, worth about £3,000,000, had been unloaded and removed to Lugos before the English arrived (*The Journal of Sir George Rooke*, p. 234). What was left was silver belonging to private persons, including even some Dutch and English merchants. Enough gold and silver went to the bottom to support successful salvage operations in Vigo Bay even in recent years. And such quantities of merchandise were privately looted by English officers and men that the government published a proclamation on 13 December 1702 ordering the plunder to be surrendered and offering one-fifth of the value of the recovered goods as a reward to informers. "O, what a rich Cordial is Plunder and Plate!" as the words of a current popular song expressed it (*The Sailor's Account of the Action at Vigo* ["Muse will have her song; hark! she merrily sings"], Exon., 1702; *The Daily Courant,* No. 193, 28 November 1702).

345. *Anthems raise:* On 3 November Anne appointed a "Day of Thanksgiving for the Good Success of Her Majesty's Arms this Campaign" with the bishop of Exeter to preach in St. Paul's Cathedral "on Thursday next" (12 November) (Steele, No. 4337; *The Daily Courant,* No. 180, 13 November 1702).

351. *Welcome Home:* Rooke sailed into the Downs on 7 November and Ormonde reached London the following day (*The London Gazette,* No. 3860, 5–9 November 1702).

What all Men see, all Men must needs believe.
Our Joy can hardly run into Excess,
The well known Subject all our Foes confess:
We can't desire more, they can't pretend to less.
ANNE, like her Great Progenitor, sings Praise:
Like her she Conquers, and like her she Prays;
Like her she Graces and Protects the Throne,
And counts the Lands Prosperity her own:
Like her, *and long like her,* be Bless'd her Reign,
Crown'd with new Conquests, and more Fleets from *Spain.*
See now the Royal Chariot comes amain,
With all the willing Nation in her Train,
With humble Glory, and with solemn Grace,
Queen in her Eyes, and Christian in her Face.
With Her, Her represented Subjects join;
And when She Prays, th'whole Nation says, *Amen.*
With Her, in Stalls the Illustrious Nobles sat,
The Cherubims and Seraphims of State:
ANNE like a Comet in the Center shone,
And they like Stars that circumfere the Sun.
She Great in them, and they as Great in Her;
Sure Heaven will such Illustrious Praises hear.
The crouding Millions Hearty Blessings pour:
Saint Paul *ne'er saw but one such Day before.*

376. *the Royal Chariot:* On 12 November "Her Majesty, Habited in Purple, wearing her Collar and George, [rode from St. James's Palace to St. Paul's] in her Body Coach drawn by Eight Horses, in which were also the Countesses of *Marlborough* and *Sunderland*" (*The London Gazette,* No. 3862, 12–16 November 1702).

382. *With Her . . . Nobles sat:* "Her Majesty being entred into the Choir, seated Her Self on Her Throne of State, which was placed near the West end of the Choir, opposite the Altar; The Peers had Seats in the Area . . . the Commons in the Stalls and upper Galleries" (ibid.).

388. *crouding Millions:* "The Publick Demonstrations given by the Inhabitants of this great and populous City . . . were suitable to so great and solemn an Occasion; and the Night ended with ringing of Bells, Bonfires, Illuminations, and other Rejoycings" (ibid.).

389. *one such Day before:* "Queen *Elizabeth* also, after her great Success in Ruining King *Philip* the Second's *Invincible Armada,* order'd a Day of Publick Thanksgiving for her Glorious Victory to be solemniz'd all over the Kingdom, and upon the Day prefix'd, pass'd her self, attended by a numerous Train of Nobility and Gentry, through the Streets of *London,* hung with Blue Cloth, to the Cathedral of S. *Paul,* where several of the Banners taken in the Engagement were placed in View, and there perform'd the Duties of the Day" (*Present State of Europe, 13* [November 1702], 442).

1703

William Walsh

The Golden Age Restor'd
(January 1703)

According to John Oldmixon, "A little after King *William*'s Death, Mr. *Walsh* wrote a State Poem, called the *Golden Age restor'd,* a kind of Imitation of the Fourth Eclogue of *Virgil*" (*The Life and Posthumous Works of Arthur Maynwaring,* 1715, p. 21). It is possible that Walsh *intended* to write an "Imitation" (see *The Golden Age,* headnote, p. 449 above) of Virgil's fourth eclogue, but if he did, he was forestalled by the anonymous author of *The Golden Age* and had to content himself with a reply to an imitation of Virgil's fourth eclogue. *The Golden Age Restor'd* owes more to *The Golden Age* than it does to Virgil; it is in fact "a kind of Imitation" (in the generic sense) of *The Golden Age.* The wit of the poem arises partly from Walsh's ingenuity in finding ironical analogues for corresponding details of the earlier poem: "old *Ranelagh expires*" (line 14) for "Vice gives way" (line 22); "Pacifick" Rooke for *"Adriatick Orford,"* and Tory poetasters Henry St. John, Henry Davenant, and John Tredenham for Whig poets Nahum Tate, Nicholas Rowe, and William Congreve. There are occasions when the descent into bathos can be traced through the three poems and represented graphically:

Dryden (line 12)	thy own *Apollo* reigns
The Golden Age (line 17)	Now thy own *Anna* Rules
Walsh (line 10)	now thy own *Bromley* reigns

Pollio's consulship (line 14) reduces to Dashwood's mayoralty (lines 18–19) and terminates in Scobell's membership in the commission to take the public accounts (lines 11–12), with the implication that it would be difficult to sink lower.

"This Poem," Oldmixon goes on to say, "Mr. *Walsh* brought to Mr. *Maynwaring,* who corrected and improv'd it, and it was reported, that he was the Author of it: 'Twas mightily talk'd of, the Wit and the Turn of it were equally applauded, and as the Satyr struck a certain prevailing Faction very home, the Heads of it were extreamly offended with the Poem and the Poet." Mainwaring had to assure Godolphin that he was *not* "the Author of it" ([John Oldmixon], *The Life and Posthumous Works of Arthur Maynwaring,* 1715, pp. 21–22).

For Walsh, however, *The Golden Age Restor'd* was more than a literary exercise; it was the payment of a political debt to William Lloyd, the 75-year-old lord bishop of Worcester, which Walsh had incurred during the elections of November 1701 and July–August 1702. Lloyd had "stood as in the front of the battel all King *James*'s reign" (Burnet, *1,* 190), and when he was released from the Tower on bail in June 1688 he was unable to get through Palace Yard by reason of the crowds kissing his hands and garments (Henry Hyde, Earl of Clarendon, *Correspondence,* 2 vols., 1828, *2,* 177). In April 1695 William had appointed him to a commission "to recommend fit persons to all ecclesiastical preferments" (Luttrell, *3,* 466; Foxcroft, p. 406).

As he had threatened to do during the election campaign of January 1701 (*The Worcester Cabal,* headnote, p. 312 above), Sir John Pakington introduced in the next session of parliament a bill for the better preservation of the protestant religion and for preventing the translation of bishops from one see to another (*CJ, 13,* 416). This was not only a blow against Lloyd, whom William had translated from St. Asaph to Lichfield and Coventry in October 1692 and from Lichfield and Coventry to Worcester in January 1700, but also an invasion of the royal prerogative. Upon the failure of his bill to pass during the session of February–June 1701, Pakington published two pamphlets in support of the bill—"Two Libels, full of horrible Lies," according to Lloyd—and had them sent "in a blank Case" to the freeholders of Worcestershire (*The Evidence Given at the Bar of the House of Commons upon the Complaint of Sir John Pakington against Wiliam Lord Bishop of Worcester,* 1702, pp. 8, 11).

When William decided to call a new parliament in November 1701, Lloyd, who was then in London, responded to Pakington's attack by commanding his bailiffs to urge every freeholder in their manor to "vote for Mr. Bromley and Mr. Walsh" and not for Sir John Pakington (*Diary of Francis Evans,* ed. David Robertson, Oxford, James Parker & Co., 1903, p. 57). This effort was a failure, however, for Pakington and William Bromley (not the Tory William Bromley of Bagington, Warwickshire, but a Whig William Bromley who died in 1707) were returned.

When Anne determined to call a new parliament in July 1702, Lloyd undertook a more intensive campaign. He sent into the country "a great number" of copies of a folio half-sheet entitled *The True Character of a Church-Man, Shewing the False Pretences to that Name,* allegedly "written against Sir J. P. for hindering his Election." When he came down to the country himself, he was confronted with "a Third Libel," as he said, "written against me in particular" (*The Evidence Given at the Bar of the House of Commons upon the Complaint of Sir John Pakington against Wiliam Lord Bishop of Worcester,* pp. 11, 13). This was a pamphlet by Henry Sacheverell, entitled *The Character of a Low-Church-Man* (1702), claiming that Lloyd had *"Run* Mad . . . *with Prophecy and Enthusiasm,"* that he had no fixed principles but republicanism and presbytery, and that he only "Personates the Character of a True Church-Man, *more Dextrously to betray it"* (*The Character of a Low-Church-Man,* 1702, pp. 5, 23, 24).

Shocked at the violence of this anonymous attack, Lloyd responded by increasing his efforts against Pakington. He enlisted the help of his son, William Lloyd, and his secretary, Francis Evans, to write letters urging the freeholders to vote for Bromley and Walsh. He himself did not scruple to browbeat his tenants by threatening to put a mark against their names in his rent book so their leases would not be renewed, or to call Sir John "a Whoremonger, Drunkard, and Swearer," "so full of Jacobitism, that it could not be rooted out." Nor did his secretary hesitate to inform one honest freeholder that "he had as good Vote for the Prince of *Wales* as for Sir *John Pakington."* The voters responded this time by returning Pakington—and William Walsh (*The Evidence Given at the Bar of the House of Commons upon the Complaint of Sir John Pakington against Wiliam Lord Bishop of Worcester,* pp. 17–20, 22).

The parliament convened on 20 October 1702. On 2 November Sir John Pakington complained at the bar of the House that the lord bishop of Worcester had violated his rights and privileges. Sir John presented no fewer than 15 witnesses, one of whom was the churchwarden, Thomas Twitty (see *The Worcester Cabal,* 1 *n.,* above). Without even hearing the evidence on the bishop's side, the House voted *nemine contradicente* that the proceedings of the lord bishop were "in high Violation of the Liberties and Privileges of the Commons of *England*" (*CJ, 14,* 37) and upon an address from the House, Queen Anne removed the lord bishop from his place as her lord almoner (Luttrell, *5,* 238).

When Lloyd was attacked in *The Golden Age* (lines 73–78), Walsh had additional reasons to write a reply. In composing his poem he seems to have worked with both versions of *The Golden Age* (p. 778 below). The evidence for this is that in line 34 he parodies *The Golden Age,* line 68, which is not in *B,* and in line 47 he parodies a line in *B* (textual note 27, pp. 778–79 below) which is not in *A*.

The date of one manuscript of the poem, BM MS. Add. 40060, ff. 17–20, subscribed "Jan. 1702/3," is confirmed by another, Bodl. MS. Rawl. D.361, ff. 343–45v, which is inscribed: "A Satyr on the present tymes given mee by a freind, Feb. 7, 1702 [i.e. 1703]."

Although the poem is said in one manuscript to be the work of Charles Montagu, Lord Halifax (Bodl. MS. Add. B.105, f. 83), there can be no doubt that Walsh wrote it. It was attributed to him by his young friend Alexander Pope (*PRSA,* 1705, p. 496, BM copy: C.28.e.15), by John Oldmixon (p. 487 above), and by Giles Jacob (*Historical Account,* p. 224).

The Golden Age Restor'd

The 4th Eclogue of *Virgil*,
Supposed to have been taken from a *Sybilline* Prophecy,
Imitated.

—Paulo majora canamus.

Sicilian *Muse, begin a loftier Flight,*
Not all in Trees and lowly Shrubs delight:
Or if your Rural Shades you still pursue,
Make those Shades worthy of a Statesman's view.
The time is come, by antient Bards foretold,
Restoring the *Saturnian* Age of Gold:
The Vile, Degenerate Whiggish Offspring ends,
A High-Church Progeny from Heaven descends.
O Learned *Oxford* spare no Sacred Pains
To nurse the Glorious Breed, now thy own *Bromley* reigns,
And thou, Great *Scobell,* Darling of the Land,
Do'st foremost in that fam'd Commission stand;
Whose deep Remarks the listening World admires,

4. *Statesman:* a member of the government, as opposed to a patriot, or member of the opposition; see *An Encomium upon a Parliament,* 1 *n.,* above.

10. *Bromley:* William Bromley (1664–1732) graduated B.A. from Christ Church, Oxford, in 1681. During the grand tour he visited James II at St. Germain and later became known as "a violent Tory, and . . . great Favourer of Jacobites" (Nichols, *Illustrations, 3,* 242; Burnet, *2,* 428). After serving as knight of the shire for his native Warwickshire from February 1690, he was returned for Oxford University in March 1701 and awarded an honorary D.C.L. in August 1702. Thereafter he continued to represent Oxford University until his death in February 1732. His name appears on 10 division lists between 1696 and 1705, invariably as a Tory.

11. *Scobell:* Francis Scobell (1664–1740) was educated at the Middle Temple and married a daughter of Sir Joseph Tredenham (113 *n.,* below). He served as a Tory member for five Cornish boroughs: Michael (1690–95), Grampound (1699–1708), St. Germans (1708–10), Launceston (1710–13), and St. Mawes (1713–15), and was numbered among the True Churchmen in 1705 (J. L. Vivian, *The Visitations of Cornwall,* Exeter, 1887, p. 492; *Numerical Calculation*). In 1701 he picked up the Tory cry of "millions unaccounted for" and was elected a member of the commission for taking the public accounts in the first parliament of Anne. In November 1702, along with William Bromley and Henry St. John, he signed the commission's report which led to the resignation of the earl of Ranelagh (Luttrell, *3,* 381; *4,* 490; HMC *Cowper MSS., 2,* 428; *CJ, 14,* 30).

By whose auspicious Care old *Ranelagh* expires;
Whose mighty Power no common Rules can bind:
Who punish Men for Crimes that they want time to find.
Senates shall now like Holy Synods be,
And Holy Synods Senate-like agree.
Mackworth and *Mostyn* here instruct the Youth,
There *Bincks* and *Kimberly* maintain the Sacred Truth.

14. *Ranelagh:* See *The Golden Age,* 45 *n.,* above.

19. *Mackworth:* Sir Humphrey Mackworth, Knight (1657–1727), Tory politician, propagandist, and projector, was educated at Magdalen College, Oxford, and the Middle Temple. Since he was "a younger Brother, without any Fortune, or Name in his Profession . . . [and] had been Knighted . . . for Revelling, not Law," he soon turned projector. On 3 October 1698, the first day the books were open, £26,490 was subscribed to his mine adventure in Wales, but on 1 April 1710 the House of Commons *nem. con.* found Mackworth "guilty of many notorious and scandalous frauds and indirect practices, in violation of the charter granted to the said company, in breach of his trust, and to the manifest wrong and oppression of the proprietors and creditors of the said company" (*The True Patriots Vindicated,* 1711, p. 5; Luttrell, *4,* 434; *6,* 564). Another project, referred to in the text, was more successful. In March 1699 Mackworth was one of four laymen who met with Dr. Thomas Bray and drew up by-laws for a society "to raise Charity Schools, for teaching poor Children, for cloathing them and binding them out to Trades; Many Books were printed," as Burnet (*2,* 318) goes on to explain, "and sent over the Nation by them, to be freely distributed: These were called Societies for propagating Christian Knowledge." Mackworth's motives seem not to have been wholly philanthropic, however, for his project also included work-houses where the poor were to be employed—at a profit—and he was indefatigable in his efforts to secure passage of a bill to provide "the most effectual Ways, for setting the Poor on Work" (*CJ, 14,* 12, 20, 21, 231, 256, 351, 383). In parliament Mackworth was a Tory member for Cardiganshire, Wales (February 1701–December 1701, 1702–05, 1710–13), and for Totnes, Devon (1705–08). He published two works in defense of his party in the Commons: one of these, *A Vindication of the Rights of the Commons of England* (1701), was noticed by Swift in *A Discourse of the Contests and Dissentions* (1701), and the other, *Peace at Home: or A Vindication of the Proceedings of the Honourable the House of Commons* (1703), was answered by Defoe in *Peace without Union* (1703).

Mostyn: Sir Roger Mostyn, of Mostyn, Flintshire, third baronet (c. 1675–1739), matriculated at Jesus College, Oxford, but may have been overcome by a "kind of lethargy, caused . . . by the air of this place," as his friend George Smalridge described it, for he does not seem to have graduated (Nichols, *Illustrations, 3,* 248). He served as Tory member for Flintshire, Wales (December 1701–July 1702, 1708–13, 1715–34), Cheshire (1702–05), and Flint borough (1705–08, 1713–15). In July 1703 when he married a daughter of the earl of Nottingham, it was rumored that he would be raised to the peerage. A list dated December 1703 of the members of a secret committee of the Commons includes not only the names of Mackworth and Mostyn but also many of the other members mentioned below: Sir Christopher Musgrave, Henry St. John, Sir Thomas Powys, John Howe, and James Graham (HMC *Downshire MSS., 1,* ii, 817).

20. *Bincks:* William Binckes (c. 1653–1712), whom Thomas Hearne called "a Man of Learning" (*3,* 381), graduated B.A. from St. John's College, Cambridge, in 1674, was

Powis and *Hoblin* here with equal Claim,
Thro wide *West-Saxon* Realms extend their Fame;
There *Birch* and *Hooper* Right Divine convey,

---

instituted to prebendaries in Lincoln and in Lichfield, and in 1699 took the degree of D.D. On 30 January 1702, while proctor of the diocese of Lichfield in the lower house of convocation, Binckes preached a sermon before the house "in which he drew a Parallel between King *Charles*'s Sufferings and those of our Saviour: and, in some very indecent Expressions," as Burnet said (2, 316), "gave the preference to the former." The House of Lords resolved that these "Expressions . . . give just Scandal and Offence to all Christian People" (*LJ, 17,* 132) and ordered Binckes to be reprimanded by his bishop, John Hough. The court responded by appointing him dean of Lichfield in May 1703 and in 1705 he was elected prolocutor of the convocation (Luttrell, *5,* 298, 609).

Kimberly: Jonathan Kimberley (1651–1720), whom Thomas Hearne called "honest" (7, 104), which usually, in Hearne's Aesopian language, means "Jacobite," graduated B.A. from Pembroke College, Oxford, in 1671. Soon after he became "a famed preacher in the university, which carried him to the vicaridge of Trinity church in . . . Coventry" (Wood, *4,* 2327, 335). He supported Atterbury in the convocation controversy and in November 1710 was chosen chaplain to the Tory speaker of the House of Commons, William Bromley (Luttrell, *6,* 659). In 1713, he succeeded William Binckes as dean of Lichfield (Hearne, *4,* 158).

21. *Powis:* See *England's Late Jury,* 126 *n.,* above. Upon the accession of Anne, Sir Thomas Powys was appointed serjeant at law and her majesty's serjeant. He continued to represent Ludlow, Shropshire (January 1701–August 1713), and was one of the managers for the bill against occasional conformity. He was finally promoted to a seat on the queen's bench in 1713 but was removed the next year for his Jacobite sympathies (Luttrell, *5,* 185, 259; *Numerical Calculation;* Edward Foss, *The Judges of England,* 9 vols., 1848–64, *8,* 56).

Hoblin: John Hoblyn (1665–1706) was born at Nanswhyden, Cornwall, educated at the Middle Temple, and called to the bar in May 1682 at the same time as Humphrey Mackworth (19 *n.,* above). He served as a Tory member for Bodmin, Cornwall (1696–1705) and was numbered among the True Churchmen in 1705. His "Fame" in "*West-Saxon* Realms" may refer to his real estate transactions, some of which are calendared in the treasury papers: in 1690 he was £900 in arrears on the rent of one estate; in 1693 he leased another holding in Boynton; in 1704 he was accused of "malicious opposition" to the renewal of a lease (*Register of Admissions to . . . the Middle Temple,* ed. H. A. C. Sturgess, 1949, p. 204; *Middle Temple Records,* ed. Charles H. Hopwood, 4 vols., 1904–05, *3,* 1346; *Numerical Calculation; CTP 1557–1696,* p. 125; *CTB 1693–1696,* p. 44; *CTB 1704–1705,* p. 190).

23. *Birch:* See *On Dr. Birch,* headnote, p. 541 below.

Hooper: George Hooper (1640–1727), whom Thomas Madox called "incomparably learned" (Hearne, *3,* 177), graduated B.A. from Christ Church, Oxford, in 1660 and was collated to the rectory of Lambeth in 1675. Upon the marriage of Princess Mary in 1677, Hooper was appointed her almoner in The Hague, and it was here that the prince of Orange assured him that he would never be a bishop. Mary appointed him to the deanery of Canterbury during the king's absence in 1691 but, as Burnet observed, Hooper "thought he deserved to be raised higher" (2, 282). In February 1701 he was elected prolocutor to the lower house of convocation and became one of those "Angry men" whose attacks on episcopal authority seemed so absurd to Burnet (2, 338).

And treat their Bishops in no human Way.
  Now all our Factions, all our Fears shall cease,
And Tories rule the promis'd Land in Peace.
Malice shall die, and noxious Poisons fail,
Harley shall cease to trick, and *Seymour* cease to rail:
The Lambs shall with the Lions walk unhurt,
And *Halifax* with *Howe* meet civilly at Court.
Viceroys, like Providence, with distant Care,
Shall govern Kingdoms where they ne'er appear:
Pacifick Admirals, to save the Fleet,

"It seemed strange," he said, "to see men, who had so long asserted the Divine Right of Episcopacy . . . now assume to themselves the most important Act of Church Government, the judging in Points of Doctrine" (*2*, 283). Hooper finally was preferred to the bishopric of St. Asaph in June 1703 and translated to Bath and Wells in December 1703 (Luttrell, *5*, 304, 368).

28. *Harley:* On 30 December 1701 Robert Harley was elected speaker over Sir Thomas Littleton by the narrow margin of four votes (216–212), but in October 1702 he was the unanimous choice (Luttrell, *5*, 125, 227). The opinion of historians that Harley was "universally allowed to have been one of the most reserved and mysterious of all politicians" (*The Works of Jonathan Swift,* ed. John Hawkesworth, 12 vols. 4°, 1755, *1*, 11) is amply corroborated by contemporary evidence. The duchess of Marlborough describes "that wonderful talent Mr. HARLEY possessed . . . of confounding the common sense of mankind," and also that "ambiguous and obscure way of speaking, [so] that he could hardly ever be understood" (*Account of the Conduct,* pp. 218, 262). Even his admirers noted Harley's deviousness. In September 1701 Henry St. John referred jokingly to "that laudable custom" Harley had "of never meaning what he says" (HMC *Downshire MSS., 1*, ii, 808).

Seymour: To "Huff like *N[ed] S[eymou]r*" (*Aesop in Select Fables,* 1698, sig. D8r) had become a commonplace in the reign of William. And after Seymour had been promoted to two lucrative posts in April–May 1702—comptroller of the royal household and ranger of Windsor Forest—Burnet was still able to report that "the indecent scorn with which *Seimour* . . . treated the *Scots*" in the House of Commons was a clear indication that the posts he had been brought into had not changed his temper (Burnet, *2*, 315). "There never yet," as Henry St. John told Harley, "was more gravity and less thought, more noise and less mirth" (HMC *Portland MSS., 4*, 73).

30. *Halifax:* cf. *The Golden Age,* 33 *n.,* above.

Howe: Dismissed from court in March 1692 (*England's Late Jury,* 80 *n.,* below) John Howe returned almost exactly 10 years later. He was one of the four Tories chosen to the privy council to replace Halifax and Somers in April 1702.

31–32. *Viceroys . . . ne'er appear:* The earl of Rochester was appointed lord lieutenant of Ireland in December 1700 but delayed his departure "very long" (*Advice to a Painter. 1701,* 21 *n.,* above). He finally left London late in August 1701, only to return in December. William dismissed him from the post in January 1702, but Anne reappointed him in March. Finally, on 1 February 1703 the queen had to order him to Ireland but three days later he resigned "in great wrath" (Burnet, *2*, 290–91; Luttrell, *5*, 83, 122, 135, 154; *Account of the Conduct,* p. 141).

33–34. *Admirals . . . fly:* See *The Golden Age,* 63–68, above; cf. *The Spanish Descent,* 3 *n.,* 118 *n.,* above.

Shall fly from Conquest, and shall Conquest meet:
Commanders shall be prais'd at *William*'s Cost,
And Honour be retriev'd before 'tis lost.
 But as they stronger grow, and mend their strain
By choice Examples of King *Charles*'s Reign,
Bold *Bellasis* and Patriot *Davenant* then,
One shall employ the Sword, and one the Pen:
Troops shall be led to plunder, not to fight,
The Tool of Faction shall to Peace invite,
And Foes to Union be imploy'd the Kingdoms to unite.
Brereton and *Burnaby* the Court shall grace,

36. *retriev'd:* Anne sought to reward the earl of Marlborough for his success in the campaign of 1702 by creating him a duke and granting him an annual pension of £5000 during her lifetime. This occasioned a violent debate in the Commons. The pension was refused on the grounds that "the Revenue of the Crown . . . has been so much reduced by exorbitant Grants in the last Reign" (see *Advice to a Painter,* 40 *n.,* above). A Whig motion to add "and by the extraordinary Pensions, charged on the Revenue by King *Charles* the 2d, and King *James* the 2d," was defeated 195–74. The House acknowledged, however, that Marlborough had, "by his Conduct of the Army, retrieved the ancient Honour and Glory of the *English* Nation," "the word *Retrieved,*" as Burnet explained, "implying that it was formerly lost" (*CJ, 14,* 85, 87; Burnet, *2,* 334). A Whig motion to remove the word "retrieved" was defeated by "a great Majority; All that had favour at Court, or hoped for any, going into it" (Burnet, *2,* 334). Lines 25–36 are quoted in Tindal's account (*4,* 1574 *n.*) of this incident.

37. *mend their strain:* improve the breed; the figure, as in lines 10, 48–49, is horticultural. The reading of *ABC,* "Right(s) maintain," represents an attempt to make "sense" of the couplet in nonmetaphorical terms.

39. *Bellasis:* See *The Spanish Descent,* 199 *n.,* above.

Davenant: "Patriot" Davenant (see *England's Late Jury,* 101 *n.,* above) had become a "Statesman" in October 1702 when he was appointed secretary to the commissioners for the union with Scotland at £1000 a year (Luttrell, *5,* 227–28).

43. *Foes to Union:* Of the 23 members whom the queen named in 1702 to the commission for a union with Scotland (Boyer, *Annals,* 1703, pp. 155–56), eight are mentioned in the present poem: the duke of Somerset, the earls of Pembroke, Rochester, Marlborough, Nottingham, Sir Charles Hedges, Sir Christopher Musgrave, and Robert Harley.

44. *Brereton:* Edward Brereton (1640–1705?) was educated at Oriel College, Oxford, and Lincoln's Inn. As the Tory member for Denbigh, Wales (1688–1705), he was another West Saxon who was "very warm in the Interest of High-Church" and very cool in other things. He refused to subscribe to the association in defense of the king in 1696 and, as comptroller of the Inner Temple, refused to allow William Sherlock, master of the Temple, to preach there in December 1697. In July 1699 he was charged with inciting a riot during a local election in Denbigh. He received his reward in June 1703 when he was appointed one of the commissioners for prizes and deputy lieutenant for the northern counties of Wales (Luttrell, *4,* 325, 533; *CTB 1703,* p. 315; *CSPD 1703–1704,* p. 278).

Burnaby: Anthony Burnaby entered the Middle Temple in 1695 and two years later petitioned for a place in the commission of the excise "setting forth his claims

And *Howe* shall not disdain to share a Place.
Forgotten *Molineux* and *Mason* now
Revive and shine again in *Fox* and *Howe*.
Yet still some Whigs among the Peers are found,
Like Brambles flourishing in barren Ground.
Somers maliciously imploys his Care
To make the Lords the Legislature share.
Burnet declares how French Dragoons arose;

---

to that employment as the projector of the new duty on malt" (*An Encomium upon a Parliament,* 66 *n.,* above). He was elected to parliament for Stockbridge, Hampshire, in November 1701 and sat until May 1705. In his first session he voted for the impeachment of the Whig lords and was rewarded in June 1702 with the secretaryship of the commission of prizes (of which Edward Brereton was a commissioner), worth £100 a year. Unfortunately the commissioners had to report in 1704 that "Mr. Burnaby had not application equal to the employment" (*Register of Admissions to . . . the Middle Temple,* ed. Sturgess, p. 237; *CTP 1697–1702,* p. 30; *CTB 1702,* p. 250; *CTP 1702–1707* p. 266).

45. *Howe:* The place that Howe shared was paymaster-general of the army, which the earl of Ranelagh resigned on 3 December 1702 (*The Golden Age,* 45 *n.,* above). He shared it with Charles Fox; Howe was made paymaster of guards and garrisons, and Fox paymaster of the army abroad (Luttrell, *5,* 247).

46. *Molineux and Mason:* Sir Francis Molyneux, of Teversall, Nottinghamshire, fourth baronet (c. 1656–1742), and Charles Mason (1661–1732?) were appointed comptrollers of the Mint in December 1696 and displaced after some scandal in May 1701 (Luttrell, *4,* 160; *5,* 48). Molyneux was the Whig member for Newark, Nottinghamshire (January 1693–July 1698), and for Nottinghamshire (December 1701–April 1705). Mason was the Whig member for Bishop's Castle, Shropshire (October 1695–December 1700, November 1701–September 1710, 1715–1727). He was also returned in January 1701 but the committee of elections in April 1701 found him guilty of bribery and not elected (Luttrell, *5,* 44).

47. *Fox:* Charles Fox (1659–1713), the eldest son of Sir Stephen Fox, Knight, was born in Brussels and named after his godfather, Charles Stuart. He succeeded his father as paymaster-general in 1680, was dismissed by James II, restored by William III, but finally displaced by Lord Coningsby in 1698. As a member for Salisbury, Wiltshire (1698–1713), his place required him to vote for a standing army in January 1700; otherwise his record is solidly Tory. In December 1702 he was made paymaster-general of the army abroad and in April 1705 he became engaged to marry Lady Catherine Hyde, daughter of the earl of Rochester (Luttrell, *5,* 536).

50. *Somers:* By encouraging the Lords to adhere to their amendments, Somers and the other leaders of the opposition were able to defeat the bill to prevent occasional conformity (Luttrell, *5,* 258–59; *The Mitred Club,* headnote, pp. 507–08 below).

52. *Burnet:* Burnet visited France in 1685, after Louis XIV had revoked the Edict of Nantes, and witnessed the "terrible effect" of the dragoons who were quartered upon "those of the [Protestant] Religion, committing all possible insolencies, till they should force them to abjure their religion" (Foxcroft, p. 203). In *Some Letters Containing an Account of what Seemed Most Remarkable in Switzerland, Italy, &c.,* Amsterdam, 1686, p. 255, he explains that it is the clergy who "animate" these enforced conversions.

And Bishops Persecuting Bills oppose,
Till *Rochester*'s cool Temper shall be fir'd,
And *North*'s and *Nottingham*'s strong Reas'ning be admir'd.
But when due Time their Counsels shall mature,
And fresh Removes have made the Game secure;
When *Somerset* and *Devonshire* give place
To *Windham*'s *Bedford,* and to *Richmond*'s Grace,

53. *Persecuting Bills:* the bill to prevent occasional conformity, which, as Burnet says, was opposed by "the greater number of the Bishops," including Burnet himself. Burnet agreed that it was the principle of toleration that was "aimed at" in the bill (*2,* 337, 338; Luttrell, *5,* 258–59).

54. *Rochester:* The temper of the earl of Rochester did not grow any less "imperious and intractable" (Burnet, *2,* 280) after the accession to the throne of his niece, Anne; cf. 31–32 *n.,* above.

55. *North:* William North, sixth lord North (1678–1734) left Magdalene College, Cambridge, without taking a degree and after the grand tour and other dissipations took his seat in the House of Lords in January 1699. He was promoted to a captaincy in the foot guards in March 1702 and became known as "a great courtier." He argued strongly (but vainly) for the bill against occasional conformity and in January 1703 succeeded to the command of Sir Bevil Grenville's regiment. He was eventually created earl North by the titular James III and imprisoned in the Tower on suspicion of treason in October 1722 (GEC, *9,* 658–59).

Nottingham: Daniel Finch, second earl of Nottingham (1647–1730), the scourge of poets (he confined Defoe to the pillory and Swift to the deanery of Dublin), served William III as secretary of state from 1689 until 1693, when he was forced to resign over the disaster of the Turkey fleet (*The True-Born Englishman,* 1039 *n.,* above). Within weeks of William's death he was reappointed secretary of state. Nottingham's real obsession, however, for which he finally abandoned even the Tory party, was religious conformity. He first conceived of a bill against occasional conformity in 1689 during debate on the Toleration Act and he was probably responsible for clauses prohibiting occasional conformity in Sir John Pakington's bill of March 1701 (headnote, p. 312 above) and Heneage Finch's amendment to the abjuration bill of 1702 (*CJ, 13,* 750; Feiling, p. 358), both of which were defeated. In November 1702 Nottingham persuaded William Bromley to introduce a bill against occasional conformity in the House of Commons, for he "thought great use might be made of it" (Burnet, 1823, *5,* 49 *n.*). On 2 December the bill was sent to the Lords where Nottingham himself undertook (vainly) to secure its passage.

58. *Somerset:* In July 1702 "the proud Duke" of Somerset was removed as lord president of the council and sworn master of the horse to her majesty (Luttrell, *5,* 192).

Devonshire: The duke of Devonshire was retained in all his posts, but his successful management of the opposition to the bill against occasional conformity, which "The Court put their whole strength to carry," did not win any favor at court (Burnet, *2,* 338).

59. *Windham:* Catherine Leveson Gower (c. 1670–1704), daughter of Sir William Leveson Gower, fourth baronet, by Jane, eldest daughter of John Grenville, first earl of Bath. In May or June 1687 she married Sir Edward Wyndham, of Orchard Windham, Somersetshire by whom she had two children. Wyndham died in June 1695 (*GEC,*

Both Converts great, when Justice is refin'd,
And Corporations garbled to their Mind;
Then Passive Doctrines shall with Glory rise;
Before them hated Moderation flies,
And Antichristian Toleration dies.

Baronetage, 3, 238). His "Fantastick Widdow," with her duck-like walk and Billingsgate language, was said to have grown so ugly by 1699 that she would no longer be "a Toast/But that her Uncle Jack is still her freind" (BM MS. Harleian 7315, f. 287v). "Uncle Jack" is John Granville (*A New Satyr on the Parliament,* 86 *n.,* 90 *n.,* above). But her uncle's cousin, George Granville, represents her as "a Tyrant . . . Proud of the ravage that her Beauties make" (*A New Collection of Poems on Several Occasions,* 1701, p. 157). Arthur Maynwaring and James Vernon, Jr., were among her other conquests.

Bedford: Wriothesley Russell (1680–1711) was the eldest son of William, Lord Russell, the Whig martyr. In May 1695, aged 14, he married Elizabeth Howland, also aged 14 and said to be worth £100,000. In September 1700 when he succeeded his grandfather as second duke of Bedford, he was the richest peer in England, said to be worth £30,000 a year and with expectations of an eventual £45,000 a year. He was one of the lords of the bedchamber to William III and in January 1702 took his seat in the House of Lords, where he voted with the Whigs. On 14 March 1702, together with the earl of Marlborough, he was elected knight of the garter, not for any merit on his part, but because William had promised the first duke that his grandson would have a garter (Luttrell, *3,* 472, 476; *4,* 685; *5,* 152, 162; HMC *Portland MSS., 3,* 487).

Richmond: Charles Lennox, duke of Richmond (1672–1723), was the youngest of the "Six Bastard Dukes" (*The True-Born Englishman,* 303 *n.,* above). He professed the Catholic faith in October 1685 in the presence of Louis XIV at Fontainebleau but returned to the Anglican communion in May 1692. After his marriage a year later it was said that "[il] s'y perdit de vin et de débauches" (GEC, *10,* 836–38). Although professedly "a staunche Whig" (HMC *Lonsdale MSS.,* p. 121), he was suspected of Jacobitism in 1696. At the coronation of Anne he bore the scepter with dove.

61. *garbled:* Whig voters weeded out. According to Burnet (*2,* 337), "All believed, that the chief design of this Bill [against occasional conformity] was, to [new-]model Corporations, and to cast out of them all those, who would not vote in Elections for Tories."

62. *Passive Doctrines:* The doctrines of *jure divino* (*A Satyr upon the French King,* 22 *n.,* above) and nonresistance (*The True-Born Englishman,* 704 *n.,* above). Defoe uses the phrase "Passive Doctrine" in *Reformation of Manners,* 1001, above.

63. *Moderation:* "all moderate men" were said to be against the bill to prevent occasional conformity (Burnet, *2,* 338). In the Tories' lexicon of abuse the word "Moderation" deteriorated between 1701 and 1711 from "a mark of Sincerity" to "nothing but Anarchy" (*The Claims of the People of England, Essayed,* 1701, p. 89; *A Collection of Poems, &c. For and Against Dr. Sacheverell. The Fourth Part,* 1711, p. 30).

64. *Toleration:* By the Toleration Act of 1689 (*More Reformation,* 318 *n.,* below) Protestant dissenters (except Unitarians) had been granted the right of public worship. Burnet (*2,* 336) believed that the bill against occasional conformity was really intended to revoke even this limited toleration; he was afraid that "such a breaking in upon the Toleration . . . would undermine it."

Granvile shall seize the long expected Chair,
Godolphin to some Country-Seat repair;
Pembroke from all Employments be debar'd,
And *Marlborough* for antient Crimes receive his just Reward.
France, that this happy Change so wisely has begun,
Shall bless the great Design, and bid it smoothly run.
Come on, Young *James's* Friends, now is the Time, come on;
Receive just Honours, and surround the Throne.
Boldly your Loyal Principles maintain;
Hedges now rules the State, and *Rooke* the Main.

65. *Granvile:* John Granville was one of the three unsuccessful Tory candidates for speaker in December 1698, when it was hoped that "les grands profits qui sont annexés à la Charge d'Orateur, et l'esperance d'en obtenir de plus grands, l'addouciroient, et l'apprivoiseroient avec la Cour" (BM MS Add. 30000B, f. 264v). He was reconciled to the court by other means in 1701 (*A New Satyr on the Parliament,* 86 *n.*, above) and showered with posts in the new regime: in April 1702 he succeeded Godolphin as lord lieutenant of Cornwall, in May he was made lieutenant-general of the ordnance, in June appointed to the privy council, and in March 1703 raised to the peerage as baron Granville of Potheridge (GEC, *6,* 88).

66. *Godolphin:* After agreeing in November 1700 to serve with the earl of Rochester as first lord of the treasury in a Tory ministry (*A Conference,* headnote [p. 212], 127 *n.*), Godolphin resigned a year later when the king decided to dissolve the fifth parliament and call a new one. On 6 May 1702 he reluctantly agreed to serve with the earl of Marlborough in another Tory ministry: "The Lord *Godolphin* was made Lord Treasurer: This was very uneasy to himself, for he resisted the motion long; but the Earl of *Marlborough* pressed it in so positive a manner, that he said he could not go beyond Sea to command our Armies, unless the Treasury was put in his hands; for then he was sure that remittances would be punctually made to him" (Burnet, *2,* 313).

67. *Pembroke:* The earl of Pembroke had reluctantly accepted the office of lord high admiral in January 1702. He had taken "great pains" to put the fleet in order to sail and assumed that he would undertake its active command. Upon the accession of Anne, however, Sir George Rooke was given command of the fleet and on 20 May 1702 Pembroke was replaced as lord high admiral by Prince George of Denmark, Anne's consort. "Yet the respect paid the Queen," Burnet adds, "made that no publick question was made of this." Pembroke was offered "a great Pension," which he generously refused, and retired to Wilton. In July 1702 he succeeded Somerset as lord president of the council (Burnet, *2,* 313–14; Luttrell, *5,* 175, 192).

68. *Marlborough:* From the Tory point of view (which Walsh assumes throughout the poem), Marlborough's "antient Crimes" were (a) his betrayal of James II in November 1688 (James Macpherson, *Original Papers,* 2 vols., 1776, *1,* 280–84), and (b) his alarming influence over Princess Anne: the earl of Dartmouth was warned in 1701 that if Anne succeeded to the throne, "it would be making lord Marlborough king" (Burnet, 1823, *4,* 540 *n.*).

71. *James:* James Francis Edward (1688–1766), the product of the warming pan in Whig mythology and the Jacobites' prince of Wales, whom Louis XIV had recognized as James III of England in September 1701.

74. *Hedges:* Sir Charles Hedges, Knight (c. 1650–1714), graduated B.A. from

Grahme is at hand the Members to reward,
And Troops are trusted to your own *Granard*.
The faithful Club assembles at the *Vine*,
And *French* Intrigues are broach'd o'er *English* Wine.
Freely the Senate the Design proclaims,
Affronting *William* and applauding *James*.

Magdalen Hall, Oxford, in 1670 and D.C.L. in June 1675. In June 1689 he was appointed judge of the admiralty court and knighted. In the Commons, where he sat for Dover (January 1701–November 1701), Malmesbury, Wiltshire (1701–02), Calne, Wiltshire (1702–05), West Looe, Cornwall (1705–13), and East Looe (1713–14), he was said to be "a better Companion than a Statesman . . . [but] very zealous and industrious for his Party" (Macky, pp. 127–28). The duchess of Marlborough's claim that in William's reign he voted with the Whig party is partly true: he voted with the court Whigs in January 1700 for a standing army, but then voted to impeach the leaders of the court Whigs in April 1701. The reason for this switch may be that in November 1700, through the influence of the earl of Rochester, he was appointed secretary of state. Again according to the duchess of Marlborough, Hedges had "no capacity, no quality" and not even any interest; he was therefore asked to resign in December 1701. "The first Remarkable Occurrence . . . after the Queen's Coronation, was, the Choice"—this time at the insistence of the earl of Nottingham—of Hedges to be secretary of state. He now became a great favorite at court, accompanying the queen to Bath in August 1702 (*Account of the Conduct*, pp. 168, 170; Boyer, *Annals*, 1703, p. 28; Luttrell, *5*, 124, 207).

Rooke: See 67 *n.*, above.

75. *Grahme:* James Graham (1649–1730), or Grahme, as he preferred to write his name, was the younger brother of Sir Richard Graham, second baronet and viscount Preston in the Scottish peerage, who was secretary of state to James II in exile. In 1671 he was commissioned by Louis XIV as captain in an English infantry regiment in the French service. He became a great favorite at the court of Charles II and a confidant of James II, by whom he was appointed keeper of the privy purse, master of the buckhounds, and deputy lieutenant of Windsor Castle. He also sat for Carlisle in James' only parliament (1685–87). Graham remained active in Jacobite plots until James' death in September 1701 when he finally took the oaths of allegiance to William III. Thereafter he sat for Appleby, Westmoreland (1702–05) and county Westmoreland (1708–27).

76. *Granard:* Arthur Forbes, second earl of Granard in the Irish peerage (c. 1656–1734), was colonel of the eighteenth regiment in the army of James II. He refused to serve under William and was sent to the Tower on suspicion of treason. In the next reign, however, his fortunes improved: his £500 annual pension was confirmed by royal patent in July 1703 "in consideration of his . . . services to the crown" and in September it was rumored that he would be made governor of Jamaica (John Lodge and M. Archdall, *The Peerage of Ireland*, 9 vols., 1789, *2*, 147; Luttrell, *5*, 338). He finally took the oaths in August 1707.

77. *the Vine:* The Vine tavern in Longacre, "Where Friends to *France* do often dine," had long been known to be a Jacobite center (*Political Merriment*, 1714, p. 3; *The States-Men of Abingdon*, 1702, p. 3).

80. *Affronting William:* After the election of July 1702 the parliament "met full of fury against the Memory of the late King" (Burnet, *2*, 334); see 36 *n.*, above.

James: See 71 *n.*, above.

Good antient Members with a solemn Face,
Propose that Safety give to Order place;
And what they dare not openly dissuade,
Is by their Methods ineffectual made;
Nor be surpriz'd if those you most advance
Now roar aloud to stop the Post with *France;*
'Tis with no cruel but a kind Design,
As jealous Lovers Mistresses confine.
E'en *Finch* and *Musgrave,* whom the Court caress,
Exalt its Praises, but its Power depress;
And that Impartial Justice may be seen,
Confirm to Friends what they deny the Queen.
Bishops who most advanc'd Good *James*'s Cause

82. *that Safety give to Order place:* that the strict "Order" of succession, set aside for "the Safety, Peace, and Quiet of this Realm" by the Act of Settlement (12 & 13 William III c. 2), be reinstated (so that James III might succeed to the throne).

85. *you:* James III.

86. *stop the Post with France:* According to Abel Boyer, the Tories insisted that all correspondence with France be stopped because Nottingham had discovered "an unlawful Intercourse of Bills of Exchange, between some *French* Bankers at *Paris,* and some Citizens of *London*" presumably Whigs (*Annals,* 1703, p. 172; Luttrell, *5,* 287).

89. *Finch:* By June 1702 it was already rumored that "the Eloquent Mr. *Finch,*" the member for Oxford University, would be raised to the peerage. In August, upon the occasion of the queen's visit to Oxford, Finch presented a complimentary address and in March 1703 he was created Lord Guernsey and sworn of the privy council (Boyer, *Annals,* 1703, p. 219).

Musgrave: Less than a week after the death of William III it was rumored that Sir Christopher Musgrave would be reappointed to the post of lieutenant-general of the ordnance, a post he had held under James II. In June 1702 he was appointed one of the tellers of the exchequer (Luttrell, *5,* 152, 187).

93. *Bishops:* Of the seven bishops who "made the Tow'r their Choice" in June 1688 by opposing James II, three were still alive at the accession of Queen Anne. One of the three, Thomas Ken, then bishop of Bath and Wells, refused to take the oaths to William and Mary and so belongs in the next category. Of the two remaining bishops, Sir Jonathan Trelawny, third baronet, now the bishop of Exeter, who had sided with Marlborough against William III (*The Reverse,* 115 *n.,* above), was asked by Anne to preach at St. Paul's in the thanksgiving service for the military successes of 1702 (*The Spanish Descent,* 345 *n.,* above), while William Lloyd, now the bishop of Worcester, who had served William III on a commission for recommending ecclesiastical preferments, was condemned without a hearing in the House of Commons as "Malicious, Unchristian, and Arbitrary," and removed from his post as the queen's lord almoner (*The Golden Age,* 79 *n.,* above). On the other side, there were 18 bishops who did *not* go to the Tower in June 1688. Of these, seven were still alive. And of these seven, four received unusual marks of the queen's favor: Robert Frampton, the deprived bishop of Gloucester, was offered the see of Hereford; Henry Compton, bishop of London, replaced Lloyd as the Queen's lord almoner and was installed in lodgings at St. James's Palace from which Burnet had been evicted (Luttrell, *5,* 238, 257);

In Church and State, now reap deserv'd Applause:
While those who rather made the Tow'r their Choice,
Are stil'd Unchristian by the Nation's Voice.
Avow'dly now St. *David*'s Cause they own,
And *Jones*'s Votes for Simony atone.
Archbishop *Ken* shall from *Longleat* be drawn,

Thomas Sprat, bishop of Rochester, read the service for the day at the coronation and is said to have been offered the primacy of Ireland (ibid., 166, 251); and even Thomas Watson, who had been deprived of the bishopric of St. David's for simony in August 1699, continued to sit in the House of Lords until 22 January 1705 (97 *n.*, below). The case of the deprived bishop of Bath and Wells, Thomas Ken (1637–1711), is the most remarkable of all. Almost immediately upon the death of William, it was made known that Anne would herself dispose of all ecclesiastical preferments belonging to the crown "and not leave it to the archbishop of Canterbury and 5 other bishops, as the late king did" (Luttrell, *5,* 157). "The first bishoprick that fell vacant, after the accession of Anne, was that of Carlisle. Lord Weymouth, who was of the Queen's Privy Council, at once made interest for restoring his friend Ken to Bath and Wells, by the translation of Kidder to Carlisle. Kidder consented to this through the Archbishop of York: but when it was proposed to Ken, he declined" ([J. L. Anderdon], *The Life of Thomas Ken,* 2nd ed., 2 vols., 1854, *2,* 700). The offer is also said to have included the prospect of succeeding to the primacy in case of a vacancy at Lambeth (Tenison was then 66). (E. H. Plumtre, *The Life of Thomas Ken,* 2 vols., 1889, *2,* 119).

97. *St. David's:* Thomas Watson (1637–1717), whom Clarendon called a "very bad" man (HMC *Buccleuch and Queensberry MSS., 2,* i, 32), was promoted to the bishopric of St. David's by James II in June 1687. In 1694–95 it was "proved, that the Bishop had collated a Nephew of his to a great many of the best Preferments in his Gift, and that . . . he had taken the whole profits of these to himself, keeping his Nephew very poor . . . But, as he was advanced by King *James,* so he stuck firm to that Interest; and the [Tory] Party, tho' ashamed of him, yet were resolved to support him, and with great zeal" (Burnet *2,* 226–27). Although deprived of his bishopric in August 1699 and excommunicated in May 1701, he was so skillfully defended by the Tory lawyers Sir Thomas Powys and Sir Bartholomew Shower that it was not until January 1705 that the House of Lords finally confirmed the decree of deprivation (Luttrell, *4,* 516, 545; *5,* 49, 511).

98. *Jones:* Edward Jones (1641–1703), bishop of St. Asaph, was charged with simony and other "crimes and excesses" in March 1697 (Luttrell, *5,* 63). Proceedings dragged on until June 1701 when he was finally found guilty. Burnet explained that "the thing was new, and the House [of Lords] was not yet well apprized of it" (Burnet, *2,* 250–51), but the earl of Dartmouth assumed that "The bishop knew a better reason for delay in Jones's case; which was that he always voted with the court" (Burnet, 1823, *4,* 450 *n.*).

99. *Ken:* Thomas Ken (1637–1711), who was raised in the household of Isaac Walton, graduated B.A. from New College, Oxford, in 1661, and D.D. in 1679. He then served as chaplain to Princess Mary at The Hague and in November 1684 was appointed bishop of Bath and Wells. Although he resisted James II, he refused to take the oaths to William and was deprived of his bishopric in April 1691. Thereafter he lived largely at Longleat, the seat of viscount Weymouth, and "continued," as Burnet said, "in a very warm opposition to the Government" (*2,* 7); see 93 *n.*, above.

While firm *Nonjurors* from behind stand crowding
the Lawn.
And thou, Great *Weymouth,* to reward thy Charge,
Shall sail to *Lambeth* in his Grace's Barge.
See by base Rebels *James* the Just betray'd,
See his Three Realms by vile Usurpers sway'd;
Then see with Joy his lawful Heir restor'd,
And erring Nations own their injur'd Lord.
O would kind Heaven so long my Life maintain,
Inspiring Raptures worthy such a Reign!
Not *Thracian St. John* should with me contend,
Nor my sweet Lays harmonious *Hammond* mend:
Not tho young *Davenant St. John* should protect,

101. *Weymouth:* Thomas Thynne (1640–1714) graduated from Christ Church, Oxford, and then represented Oxford University (1674–79) and Tamworth, Staffordshire (1679–81) in parliament. In December 1682 he was created viscount Weymouth. Upon the flight of James II in November 1688 he and the earl of Pembroke carried to the prince of Orange the invitation of the peers and privy council. According to Lord Dartmouth, he was not "so well received by the prince as the earl of Pembroke, which he expected, [and] immediately espoused king James's interest, with great zeal" (Burnet, 1823, *3,* 331 *n.*). Dartmouth called him "a weak, proud man, with a vast estate . . . [and] very liberal to nonjurors . . . which occasioned his house being constantly full of people of that sort" (ibid.). One of them was Thomas Ken, on whom he settled a pension of £80 a year.

105. *lawful Heir:* See 82 *n.,* above.

109. *St. John:* Henry St. John (1678–1751), created viscount Bolingbroke in July 1712, was just emerging into fame in 1701–02. He was first elected to parliament in February 1701 as a member for Wootton-Basset, Wiltshire, a borough that his family controlled. He attached himself to Robert Harley and was immediately successful as a speaker. He was re-elected in July 1702 and awarded an honorary doctor of laws degree at Oxford upon the occasion of the queen's visit in August. In the next session he served in two important roles: together with William Bromley and Arthur Annesley, he managed the bill against occasional conformity in the House of Commons and in conference with the Lords, and he was also one of the commissioners appointed to examine the accounts of the earl of Ranelagh. His literary career had been somewhat less distinguished; he contributed a copy of commendatory verses to to Dryden's Virgil in 1697, a prologue to George Granville's tragedy, *Heroic Love* (1698), a pindaric ode, *Almahide* ("I long have wander'd from the Muses Seat") which was published in *A New Miscellany of Original Poems,* 1701, pp. 98–114, and some other trifles (*The Book Collector, 14* [1965], 531–32). His name appears on the title page of volumes 2 and *3* of *POAS* (1703–04), but no poem in either volume is attributed to him. He is (ironically) called "Thracian" as a type of Orpheus (cf. *The Fourth Pastoral of Virgil, Englished,* 66, above).

110. *Hammond:* See *England's Late Jury,* 71 *n.,* above.

111. *young Davenant:* Henry Davenant, the son of Charles Davenant, and "a very giddy-headed young Fellow" (Macky, p. 154), was appointed her majesty's secretary at

Or the shrewd Doctor *Hammond*'s Lines correct.
Nay, should *Tredenham* in St. *Maws* compare his Songs with mine;
Tredenham, tho St. *Maws* were Judg, his Laurel should resign.
  Prepare, Auspicious Youth, thy Friends to meet;
Sir *George* already has prepar'd the Fleet.
Should Rival *Neptune* (who with envious Mind
In times of Danger still this Chief confin'd)

Frankfurt in December 1702 (Luttrell, *5,* 244; *British Diplomatic Representatives,* pp. 68–69; BM MS. Add. 4291, f. 3).

112. *the shrewd Doctor:* Charles Davenant was more commonly called "the Poussin doctor" (*England's Late Jury,* 101 *n.,* above). Like William Binckes (20 *n.,* above) he found himself in serious difficulties for making Tory propaganda. On 12 May 1702 the House of Lords voted 39–34 that a pamphlet entitled *Tom Double Return'd out of the Country, or The True Picture of a Modern Whig Set Forth in a Second Dialogue between Mr. Whiglove and Mr. Double at the Rummer Tavern, in Queen Street,* "of which 'tis said Dr. Davenant is the author" (Luttrell, *5,* 171, 172), was scandalous and seditious, and ordered that the author be discovered and prosecuted. The offending passage insinuated that there had been a Whig plot to exclude Anne from the throne (*LJ, 17,* 125). Davenant was then summoned to appear before the Lords in a totally different cause nine days later and only escaped conviction on a bribery charge by a vote of 21–28 (Luttrell, *5,* 175).

113. *Tredenham:* John Tredenham (1668–1710) was the son of Sir Joseph Tredenham, Knight, who controlled the Cornish borough of St. Mawes, and the grandson of Sir Edward Seymour (Le Neve, p. 99). He matriculated at Christ Church, Oxford, in May 1684 and a year later contributed verses to the university's collection celebrating the accession of James II. As a member for St. Mawes (April 1690–1705, November 1707–10), he refused to subscribe to the association in defense of William III and in eight recorded divisions between 1696 and 1703 invariably voted Tory. He was the third of the Poussineers, the unfortunate Tories who were discovered at supper with the French chargé d'affaires in September 1701. Davenant and Hammond, in fact, made "lame excuses about being trepanned into it by Tredenham," which as Robert Jennens pointed out, was "of little service to them" (HMC *Cowper MSS., 2,* 436). His literary interest is also mentioned by the author of *The Character of a Sneaker,* 1705, p. 2, who calls him *"Poet-Laureat* to *Monsieur Poussin"* and points out an example of his *"St. Maws Muse"* in *The Diverting Post,* No. 13, 13–20 January 1705. This is a modest ode *To the Duke of Marlborough* ("While with a steady and a skilful Hand").

115. *Auspicious Youth:* James, the pretended prince of Wales, 71 *n.,* above.

116. *Sir George:* Sir George Rooke; see 67 *n.,* above. On the morning of 12 October 1702, when the English and Dutch detachment under the command of Sir Thomas Hopsonn and Philip van der Goes broke into Vigo Bay, Rooke was far from the scene of action, incapacitated by the gout. Back in London, while Ormonde was being followed through the streets by cheering mobs, Rooke remained aboard the *Royal Sovereign,* ill with the gout (Trevelyan, *1,* 270, 272). Ormonde was so enraged by his caution that he demanded a full parliamentary inquiry. Rooke was found to have behaved like a brave commander and Ormonde was sent off to Ireland as lord lieutenant. But before either of these events occurred, it was announced that George Churchill would command the fleet in 1703 (Luttrell, *5,* 256, 266, 269).

Now send the Gout, your Hero to disgrace,
Honest *George Churchill* may supply his Place.

120. *George Churchill:* George Churchill (1654–1710), the younger brother of the then earl of Marlborough, was "a coarse fat Man, much marked with the small Pox" (Macky, p. 167). He "seems to have been ignorant, incapable, and overbearing, and to have rendered himself hated by almost all who came in contact with him" (*DNB, 4,* 314). In parliament, where he sat for the borough of St. Albans, Hertfordshire (1685–1708), he was known as a Tory, but he subscribed to the association for the defense of William in 1696, was put down as a Whig in a manuscript list of 1698, and voted against William Bromley for speaker in October 1705. He is correctly described as a "High Church Courtier" (*Numerical Calculation*), but rather more courtier than high church. In May 1702 when he was appointed a commissioner of the admiralty, almost his first act was to promote himself one rank higher than Matthew Aylmer, Lord Aylmer, who had been advanced over Churchill's head in 1693. Through his influence over Prince George, the nominal lord high admiral, Churchill was able to control the navy until October 1708, when he retired to enjoy the great fortune he had amassed.

Henry Hall [?]

The Mitred Club
(January [?] 1703)

Ever since Sunday 7 November 1697 when the new lord mayor of London, Sir Humphrey Edwin, who had not scrupled the week before to take the sacrament according to the rites of the Church of England, went to an Independent meeting at Pinners Hall in the full regalia of his office and attended by his sword bearer (Luttrell, *4*, 299, 303), the Tories had been determined to put a stop to the practice of occasional conformity. John Howe immediately moved "to bring in a bill to prevent hypocrisy in religion; without further design," as he told the earl of Dartmouth, "than to expose the dissenters and shew what rogues they were" (Burnet, 1823, *5*, 49 *n.*). And Daniel Defoe, who deplored occasional conformity as much as Howe but for different reasons, published *An Enquiry into the Occasional Conformity of Dissenters, In Cases of Preferment. With A Preface to the Lord Mayor, Occasioned by his carrying the Sword to a Conventicle.*

When the first election in the new reign returned an overwhelming Tory majority, William Bromley, Arthur Annesley, and Henry St. John were given leave to bring in a separate bill against "that abominable hypocrisy, that inexcusable immorality," as Bromley called it (Bodl. MS. Ballard 38, f. 137, cited in W. A. Speck, *The House of Commons 1702–1714,* unpub. D. Phil. thesis, Oxford University, 1965, p. 31; *CJ, 14,* 14).

The bill easily passed the House and on 28 November 1702 Bromley was ordered to carry it to the House of Lords. It provided that all those, like Sir Humphrey Edwin, who took the sacrament required by the Test Act to qualify themselves for public office and then resorted to "any Conventicle, or Meeting under Colour of any Exercise of Religion, in other Manner than according to the Liturgy and Practice of the Church of *England*" should be removed from office and fined £100 plus £5 for every day they remained in office thereafter (Calamy, *Abridgement, 1*, 624–25).

In the House of Lords, where it received a first reading on 2 December 1702, the bill occasioned a long and perplexing debate. The queen was most zealous for the bill and threw the whole weight of the court behind it, even sending her consort, Prince George, himself an occasional conformist, to vote against occasional conformity. Under these circumstances the leaders of the opposition to the bill in the House of Lords, Thomas, Lord Wharton, and Gilbert Burnet, bishop of Salisbury, did not dare to oppose the bill in principle. Instead, they adopted the familiar tactic of overloading it with amendments. On 9 December the Lords informed the Commons that they had agreed to the bill—with nine amendments and five additional clauses. One of the amendments, the eighth, reduced the fine to be levied on violators, thus raising the constitutional question of whether the Lords could amend a money bill. And one of the additional clauses, the fifth, excluded all municipal and local officials from the bill, confining its provisions to officers of the state only (*CJ, 14,* 76–77), a change "so drastic," as Trevelyan has said, that it undermined the very purpose of the bill (Trevelyan, *1,* 280).

The Commons found it could agree with only three of the nine amendments and one of the additional clauses, and called for a conference with the Lords on 17 December. Just as Wharton expected, the Commons refused to allow the Lords to meddle with the fines and a long wrangle ensued during which the managers for the Commons raised the possibility of tacking the bill to a money bill. After the conference and on the following day the Lords, upon a division, voted 52–47 to adhere to their amendments and 61 peers signed an agreement "not to receive any money bills from the commons which have clauses tack't to them foreign to the bill" (*LJ, 17,* 192–95; Luttrell, *5,* 248).

A second free conference failed to make any progress and when a third conference was convened on 16 January 1703, there was such a crowd in the Painted Chamber that the managers for the Commons, William Bromley, Henry St. John, Heneage Finch, Sir Simon Harcourt, and Sir Thomas Powys, were unable to get in (*LJ, 17,* 243). When they were finally admitted, they argued that the intent of the bill was to enact nothing new but simply to put a stop to "a very scandalous Practice; which is a Reproach to Religion, gives Offence to all good Christians, and to the best among the Dissenters" (*CJ, 14,* 180) (including, of course, Daniel Defoe). They argued further that the only effective way of preserving a national church was "by keeping the civil Power in the hands of those, whose Practices and Principles are conformable to it," and that the Act of Toleration (1689) was intended only "for the Ease of tender and scrupulous Consciences, and not to give a Licence for occasional Conformity," a practice which they were particularly "surprised to hear a Prelate [Burnet] speak in Defence of" (*CJ, 14,* 181–83).

That night the Lords sat until 11 o'clock (*LJ, 17,* 244) and Burnet observed that there were "above an hundred and thirty Lords in the House, the greatest number that had ever been together." When "it came to the final Vote *of Adhering,*" he said, "the Lords were so equally divided, that in three Questions, put on different heads, the *Adhering* was carried but by one voice in every one of them; and it was a different person that gave it in all the three Divisions" (Burnet, *2,* 338). Luttrell gives the figures in one division as 65–63, confirming Burnet's estimate of the size of the House (*5,* 258), and Evelyn recorded in his diary that the bill against occasional conformity "lost by one Vote" (*5,* 527).

A fourth free conference on 1 February failed to resolve anything (*LJ, 17,* 264). The managers for the Commons complained that the managers for the Lords, the duke of Devonshire, the earl of Peterborough, the bishop of Salisbury, Lord Somers, and Lord Halifax, "were against the Bill, which they had seem'd to Agree to." Finally, on 5 February when the Commons voted to "adhere to their disagreeing," "the Bill came to nothing" (Calamy, *Abridgement, 1,* 633, 634; *CJ, 14,* 183).

In one manuscript (*F*), the poem is attributed to "H. Hall Organist of Hereford." This is Henry Hall, the younger (d. 1713), who wrote a reply to *The Worcester Cabal* (p. 312 above). Other verse by Hall—including *A Catch upon the Vigo Expedition* ("Whilst this Bumper stands by me, Brimful of *Cydero*")—appears in *The Grove* (1721) and in Pope's *Miscellany Poems,* 5th ed., 2 vols., 1727, *2,* 265. Two more—including a "banter upon the Whiggs" entitled *A Farther Explanation of the Oxford Almanack* (1706) ("As Man in Westminster to each that comes")—are preserved in Hearne (*1,* 205; *5,* 50). But the bulk of Hall's verse remains unpublished in two manuscript volumes in the Brotherton Collection at the University of Leeds.

There is no external evidence for the date of composition. The action imagined in the poem might have taken place on the nights of 8 December 1702, 17 December 1702, or 15 January 1703, but the poet's assumption that the bill to prevent occasional conformity had already been lost could be made more easily after 16 January 1703, when the Lords voted a second time to adhere to their amendments. One of the manuscripts (*E*) is dated 1703.

The Mitred Club

To give the last Amendments to the Bill,
Which to the Saints portended so much Ill,
To Curb the Commons, and their Ends defeat,
Right Reverend Twelve last Night at *Lambeth* met.
Tho' much of Lawn did round the Room appear,
Yet none but *Moderate-Men* of God were there,
Nor had been Mitr'd more than Thirteen Year.
The Tea remov'd, the grave Assembly sate,
The Business of the Day fell in Debate;
This way and that their various Censures tend,
And some wou'd pass the Bill, but more amend:
At length with usual Vehemence aloud,
A Brawny Bishop thus Harangu'd the Crowd:
  "Far off from us let Persecution Reign,
Slav'ry in *France,* and Bigottry in *Spain.*
The best of Kings, the best of Gifts bestow'd,

4. *Twelve:* The identity of the 12 can be inferred from the 11 lords spiritual who voted against the *second* bill to prevent occasional conformity on 14 December 1703 (*Parl. Hist., 6,* 171): Thomas Tenison (January 1692 Lincoln; 1695 Canterbury), William Lloyd (October 1680 St. Asaph; 1692 Lichfield; 1699 Worcester), Gilbert Burnet (March 1689 Salisbury), Simon Patrick (October 1689 Chichester; 1691 Ely), John Hough (May 1690 Oxford; 1699 Lichfield), John Moore (July 1691 Norwich), Richard Cumberland (July 1691 Peterborough), James Gardiner (March 1695 Lincoln), John Williams (December 1696 Chichester), William Talbot (September 1699 Oxford), John Evans (January 1702 Bangor), plus two more who are mentioned in the poem (and who voted against the second bill to prevent occasional conformity by proxy): Edward Fowler (July 1691 Gloucester), and John Hall (August 1691 Bristol). The date of elevation to the episcopal bench (and translation to other sees) is given in parenthesis.

Lambeth: Lambeth House, across the Thames from the Horse Ferry in Westminster, is the "most noble ancient Palace belonging to the Archbishops of *Canterbury*" (Strype, 2, 483).

6. *Moderate-Men:* See *The Golden Age Restor'd,* 63 *n.,* above.

7. *Thirteen Year:* With the exception of William Lloyd, all of the bishops mentioned in 4 *n.,* above, had been raised to the episcopal bench by William III between March 1689 and January 1702, a space of 13 years.

13. *Brawny Bishop:* See *The Brawny Bishop's Complaint,* headnote, p. 37 above.

16. *The best of Kings:* William III, to whom, as Burnet said in a speech in the House of Lords in December 1703, "we owe our present happiness, and that we are now sitting here" (*Parl. Hist., 6,* 161).

And Toleration by a Law allow'd,
And bid us go to God which way we wou'd.
Shall Moderate-Men from Top Preferments fall,
Because they can't agree with us in all?
We may Esteem the Ore, yet drive the Dross,
May be good Christians, yet Condemn the Cross;
May hate Cathedral Hymns, yet *Hopkins* sing,
And propagate without a Pagan Ring:
No doubt the Bill by some well-meaning Men,
Was but sent up to be sent down again:
The Sacramental Test caus'd no Debates;
That but their Souls, this touches their Estates;
It needs must give weak Consciences Offence,
Rogues can't be so without a vast Expence.
Should this unchristian bitter Bill succeed,
'Twoud be a Woe to Hypocrites indeed.
Away with it, 'tis one of *Bonner*'s Bills;

17. *Toleration:* See *The Golden Age Restor'd,* 64 *n.,* above.

21. *drive the Dross:* reject the worthless impurities. At a free conference with the Commons on 16 January 1703, one of the managers for the Lords (which included Burnet) argued "that the Dissenters are Protestants, and differ from the Church of *England* only in some little Forms" (*CJ, 14,* 182).

22. *Condemn the Cross:* See *More Reformation,* 408 *n.,* below.

23. *Hopkins:* See Prologue to *The Pilgrim,* 35 *n.,* above.

27. *Sacramental Test:* a bill for suppressing the growth of popery, or the Test Act as it came to be known, was passed by the Cavalier parliament in March 1673 with only one division (on a minor amendment proposed by the Lords) recorded in the journals (*CJ, 9,* 259–68). It prevented all persons who refused to take the oaths of allegiance and supremacy and the sacrament according to the rites of the Church of England from public employment, military or civil.

29. *weak Consciences:* The Commons' managers argued "That the Toleration was intended only for the Ease of tender and scrupulous Consciences, and not to give a Licence for occasional Conformity" (*CJ, 14,* 182).

32. *Woe to Hypocrites: "Vae vobis hypocritę"* (Matthew 23:13) appears on the title page of the quarto editions of *Reformation of Manners* (1702).

33. *Bonner:* Edmund Bonner (1500?–69) served as Henry VIII's envoy to the papal court in 1532, and was consecrated bishop of London in 1540. In Mary's reign he became "the chiefest instrument of this persecution" of protestants and a major villain in Foxe's *Actes and Monuments* ([1563], p. 1703). Burnet describes him extorting a confession from one Thomas Tompkins by holding his hand "in the Flame of the Candle, so long, till the Sinews and Veins shrunk and burst" (*The History of the Reformation of the Church of England,* 2 vols., 1679–81, *2,* 307) and Fox illustrates this act with a woodcut in *Actes and Monuments* (p. 1101). Bonner was "so hated, that every illfavoured fat fellow that went in the street, they would say, that was *Bonner*" (Sir John Harington, *A Briefe View of the State of the Church of England,* 1653, p. 16).

I'm not for Saving Saints against their Wills."
He said; from all a Kind contented Nod,
The Reformation Writer's Thoughts applaud.
When streight a most melodious Sound was heard,
And lo! in White, a Rev'rend Form appear'd,
His Hand a Crosier, a Mitre grac'd his Head,
And whilst sweet Odours round the Room were spread,
Thus to them all the Sacred Shadow said:
"Since Time at length turns up the happy Hour,
And Providence hath put it in your Power
To Cote the Flock, to Fence from out the Fold
The Proling Wolf; will you your Hands with-hold?
Shall that pure Church for which the Martyrs bled,
And for which too, I Sacrific'd my Head,
Be by her Bishops into Bondage led?
Think, think, such Times may never come again,
Seldom such Senates, never such a Queen.
Your Church's Fate you falsely fear from *Rome,*
Out of the *North* more likely 'tis to come:
One Faith's Defender having hurt Her more
Than all the Kings that ever Reign'd before,
Make then your legal Dams 'gainst Schism so high,
No Spring-Tide of Succession may destroy."

36. *Reformation Writer:* Gilbert Burnet, *The History of the Reformation of the Church of England* was published in two folio volumes in 1679–81 (Wing B5797).

38. *a Rev'rend Form:* William Laud (1573–1645), "Admirable in his Naturalls, Unblameable in his Morals" (Thomas Fuller, *The History of the Worthies of England,* 1662, p. 93), was consecrated archbishop of Canterbury in 1633. In 1640 he was "accused . . . of a design to bring in Popery," impeached by the Long Parliament, treated "with all the rudeness, reproach, and barbarity imaginable" and finally beheaded on 10 January 1645 in the 72nd year of his age (Edward Hyde, earl of Clarendon, *The History of the Rebellion,* 3 vols., 1702–04, 2, 440).

45. *Proling:* ME prollen, to move about in search of prey. The change to "prowl," originally only orthographic, finally came to affect the pronunciation (*OED*).

50. *such Senates:* "the Tories in the House of Commons were at least double the number of the Whigs" (Burnet, 2, 334).

such a Queen: See *The Golden Age,* 129 *n.,* above. To the Lords' argument that in time of war it was dangerous to antagonize the dissenters, the Commons replied "That no Time could be more seasonable for this Bill than the Present, because good Laws may be obtain'd most easily in the best Reigns" (Calamy, *Abridgement, 1,* 631, 633).

53. *One Faith's Defender:* William III.

55. *Schism:* The Commons argued "That, to separate from a Church, which has

William and Mary. Medal by George Bower

He ceas'd, and lo! a Cloud refulgent Bright,
Bore up the Saint to Realms of lasting Light.
Fear and a just Confusion fell on all;
Old *Samuel*'s Truths with trembling shook each *Saul;*
Shame and Confusion sat on every Face,
And even *Sarum* felt some shocks of Grace:
The Heav'nly Vision quite had chang'd their Will,
And all, without Amendments, now would pass the Bill.
—When Strange!
After an Earthquake, and a Flash of Flame,
Into the Room a Meagre Phantom came;
His bending Bulk a Purple Robe hung o're,
And in his Hands the Regal Ensigns bore.
Struck with Surprize, each Reverence arose,
And Homage paid, and Recogniz'd his Nose.
When casting on them all a dreadful Look,
With Indignation, thus the Spectre spoke:
"False to your Faith, and t'your Creator too,
To be to what's against your Interest, true.
Have I been lab'ring Thirteen Years and more,
That to destroy, which you would now restore?
Did I not Cull you out amongst the Crowd,
And make you all Right Reverend Things in God?
Did I not thro' the Surplice see the Saint,
Churchmen in shew, but *Calvinists* in Cant;
Forc'd you the Chair Episcopal to fill,
And Mitred you almost against your Will.
And will you now at last Apostatize?

---

nothing in it against a Man's Conscience to conform to," as the occasional conformists did, "is Schism" (*CJ, 14,* 181; cf. *More Reformation,* 413 *n.,* below). To this the Lords replied "That there can be no Schism, where the Differences are not in Essentials of Religion" (*CJ, 14,* 182).

60. *Samuel's Truths:* "old and gray-headed," Samuel imparted his "Truths" to the Israelites at Gilgal where Saul "foolishly" ordered burnt offerings and "all the people followed him trembling" (1 Samuel 12:2, 13:1–14).

67. *a Meagre Phantom:* William III.

71. *Nose:* See illustration, p. 513.

74. *Creator:* See 7 *n.,* above.

81. Cf. Charles Leslie, *The Rehearsal,* No. 82 (19 January 1706): "whom do they mean by *Low-Church?* . . . The *Non-Conformists* of the *Church.*"

Think better on't, my former Friends, be Wise.
Is this a Reign in which you e'er can rise?
Can *Worcester* tell with his Prophetick Vein,
When e'er he'll be Lord Almoner again?
Does *Gloucester, Bristol,* or does *Oxford* know
The happy Time when they shall not be so.
Throw off the Mask, and boldly now appear
The very Men the World once thought you were."
In Shapeless Air the Royal Bubble broke,

87. *Worcester:* See *The Golden Age,* 73 *n.,* above.

88. *Lord Almoner:* See *The Golden Age,* 79 *n.,* above.

89. *Gloucester:* Edward Fowler (1632–1714), the son of a nonconformist minister, graduated B.A. from Corpus Christi College, Oxford, in 1653 and M.A. from Trinity College, Cambridge, c. 1655. In 1662 he chose conformity, took the oaths, and in 1681 was instituted to the vicarage of St. Giles, Cripplegate, in London. To justify his decision he published *The Principles and Practices of certain Moderate Divines . . . called Latitudinarians* (1670) and *The Design of Christianity* (1671). The latter work aroused a ferocious reply from John Bunyan, who was still languishing in Bedford jail for refusing to take the oaths. Addressing himself directly to Fowler, Bunyan began on page 1 with "the rottenness of your heart" and by page 90 was still occupied with "the rottenness of your Doctrine" (*A Defence of the Doctrine of Justification, by Faith in Jesus Christ: Shewing, True Gospel-Holiness flows from Thence. Or, Mr. Fowler's Pretended Design of Christianity, Proved to be nothing more then to trample under Foot the Blood of the Son of God; and the Idolizing of Man's own Righteousness,* 1672). Fowler replied in kind with *Dirt wipt off: Or A Manifest Discovery of the Gross Ignorance, Erroneousness, and Most Unchristian and Wicked Spirit of one John Bunyan, Lay-Preacher in Bedford,* 1672. In the next reign, however, Fowler was found "guilty of whigism" and suspended from his vicarage. In April 1687 he led the opposition to James II's declaration of indulgence and four years later was rewarded with the see of Gloucester.

Bristol: John Hall (1633–1710), "one of the Rebel Bishops," as Hearne called him (*2,* 343), came from a puritan family, matriculated at Pembroke College, Oxford, and was "educated there among presbyterians and independents" (Wood, *4,* 900). He was elected a fellow of the college in 1653. After taking the oaths of allegiance and supremacy in 1662, he was elected master of Pembroke College (1664–1710) and rector of St. Aldate's. He became "a great Admirer & Favourer" of "the Whiggish Party" and was consecrated bishop of Bristol in August 1691 (Hearne, *3,* 50).

Oxford: William Talbot (1659?–1730), a relation of Charles Talbot, duke of Shrewsbury, graduated B.A. from Oriel College, Oxford, in 1677 and in April 1691 succeeded the nonjuror, George Hickes, as dean of Worcester. He was consecrated bishop of Oxford in September 1699. In 1710 he was one of four bishops who supported the impeachment of Sacheverell. Hearne called *The Bishop of Oxford His Speech in the House of Lords on the First Article of the Impeachment of Dr. Henry Sacheverell* (1710), "a malicious and Republican, Whiggish, Libell" (*2,* 72; *3,* 11). Talbot lived to spoil Henry Hall's prophecy, for he was translated to Salisbury (worth £3500 a year) in April 1715 and finally to Durham (worth £8700 a year) in October 1721.

And that thin Form their wond'ring Eyes forsook.
—When see,
What great Success the Infernal Mission finds,
How soon the Mitred Courtiers chang'd their Minds.
What feign'd Obedience the Apostates paid,
To Venerable *Laud*'s Angelick Shade;
At first occasionally Good for Fear,
But the Surprize once vanish'd; as they were.
Thus 'midst his Pains a Debauchee Diseas'd
Grew Penitent, and Piety profess'd;
But once Reliev'd, again the Gods he brav'd,
Disown'd his Short-liv'd Grace, and swore he Rav'd:
Thus *Burnet* first asham'd of Meaning well,
Began, and whilst his Poys'nous Accents fell,
The rest, with Ears prickt up, attend their Oracle:
"My Lords, shall *Sarum* Live and not Maintain
The Ancient League, 'twixt Godliness and Gain;
Far be the Starving Thought; full well you know
What to our Unconforming Friends we owe;
By them intrusted with the Power we bear,
The Orphan-Church was given to our Care;
So to the Kite's Protection Chicken are.
Laud, had he been less obstinately Good,
Might here as once, with us to Night have stood,
Not Cloath'd in Fluid Air, but Flesh and Blood.
But he, weak Man, ne'er Learnt at *Amsterdam*
That Conscience, and Preferment, were the same;
Believ'd it Justice, when he knew the Will,
Deprav'd to tye Men up from doing Ill;
And thought that Persecution only True,
Which Blood, for Causes of Religion, drew.

112. *Unconforming Friends:* Collaboration between the low churchmen and the nonconformists was what Charles Leslie called *The New Association of those Called, Moderate-Church-Men, with the Modern Whigs and Fanaticks, to Under-mine and Blow-up the Present Church and Government* (1702).

119. *Amsterdam:* Upon the accession of James II, Burnet received permission to travel abroad. After visiting Italy and France, he remained at The Hague, where he had "free access" to the prince of Orange, until January 1688 when James II demanded his banishment. "I went no more to court," Burnet said (Foxcroft, pp. 250, 251), and he withdrew to Amsterdam where he lived "in great splendor" until his return to England in November 1688 as William's chaplain (Luttrell, *1*, 427, 434).

To Seal this Truth he dy'd, But should I be
Retrench'd, but from One Gallon of *Bohee,*
To all the list'ning World I'd make appear
What Persecuting Folks, the Church of *England* are.
But after all, did *Laud* indeed appear?
No, no, 'twas but the Creature of our Fear,
Whilst we the Bus'ness of this Bill discuss,
What have Celestial Forms to do with us?
But Oh! the watchful Genius of our Cause,
His, without doubt a true Appearance was.
Not all the Antick Vizor Masks in Hell
Could Represent our *Sovereign Lord* so well;
Such Lines of Terror in that Visage dwell:
And then what Truths th'Illustrious Vision said,
How fiercely our Apostacy Upbraid;
False to your Faith—No mighty Matter that;
But false to Interest, was a heinous Fault."
  At Interest's powerful Name, the Factious Crowd
Impatient grew and clamorously Loud.
Then rose th'Assembly, *Una Voce* cry'd,
"Great is *Diana!* Let's throw the Bill aside."
  Which did their Breasts with Resolution fill,
So fixt to act the Dictates of his Will,
They'd Damn themselves, but they'd Throw out the Bill.

126. *Bohee:* the finest kinds of black tea (*OED*); cf. 8, above.

128. Dissenters "call every thing *Persecution* that excludes them from *Power!*" ([Charles Leslie], *The New Association, Part II,* 1703, p. 10).

145. *Great is Diana:* Demetrius of Ephesus, who manufactured silver images of the great goddess Diana, warned his workmen that Paul's preaching against idols not only profaned their deity but endangered their profits, "And when they heard these sayings, they were full of wrath, and cried out, saying, Great is Diana of the Ephesians" (Acts 19:21–28).

The Golden Age Revers'd (*February 1703*)

The Golden Age Revers'd is an anonymous reply to *The Golden Age Restor'd,* or in other words a reply to a reply to an imitation of the fourth eclogue of Virgil. It is not surprising, therefore, that the Virgilian element has almost disappeared and remains only in the opening couplet and in the envoy beginning "O that my languid Numbers I could raise,/High as their Merits, sounding as their Praise," which imitates Virgil's "o mihi tum longae maneat pars ultima vitae,/spiritus et quantum sat erit tua dicere facta."

The effectiveness of the poem does not depend upon finding ironic equivalents for details of *The Golden Age Restor'd.* There are a few examples of these (e.g. 3 *n.,* 83 *n.,* 102 *n.*)—a sufficient number to remind the reader that it *is* Walsh's poem which is being "Revers'd"—but the poem does not proceed on these analogues. Instead it depends, first, on the anonymous author's clear insight into the shakiness of the Tories' dominance in 1702–1703, undermined as it was by Sarah Churchill's control of the queen and by Godolphin's "Advances" to the Whigs—and the pointed omission of any reference to Marlborough should be included here—and, second, on the unusual recklessness of the attack on the Whigs. As George Stepney wrote from Vienna on 11/22 April 1703, "I find a great deal of humour in the answer calld the golden age rever[s]ed, thô a man of Coll. Stanhopes fire ought hardly to put up [with] such infamous Terms . . . If that be their Play, I think a man is happy to be out of the reach of such desperate Scandalls which is not to be wiped off during a whole life" (PRO 105/68, f. 113v). The author could risk "such desperate Scandalls" only by remaining anonymous and he was so successful that no evidence of his identity seems to have survived. From internal evidence, however, it might be supposed that he is either the author or the plagiarist of *Advice to a Painter* (1698), for the use made of that poem is indeed remarkable.

William Pittis claimed that he was "one of the first that vindicated [Queen Anne] and her Ministry . . . from the Aspersions cast upon them in a Libel call'd The Golden Age [Restor'd]" (*A Hymn to Confinement,* 1705, sig. a2v), but there is nothing to connect this claim with the present poem.

The only external evidence for the date of the poem is in BM MS. Add. 40060, f. 26r, where it is subscribed "feb: 1702/3."

The Golden Age Revers'd

Sicilian Goddess, whose Prophetick Tongue
Reveals Fate's dark Decrees in Sacred Song;
The present vile degenerate Age disdain,
And sound the Glories of a Future Reign:
When Whigs again shall rouse the drooping Land,
Unnerv'd and weaken'd by a Female Hand.
Stamford for his great Wealth and Wisdom known,
Already has ador'd the Rising Sun,
Secur'd the Faction's Cause, and made the Game their own.
Then *Somerset,* in whose capacious Mind
Learning and solid Sense with Wit are join'd,
Judiciously in Council shall preside;
And ev'ry deep Design, and ev'ry Project guide.
Then *Halifax,* by Nature form'd to please,
Humble in Greatness, easy of Access,
With unaffected Air the Court shall grace,
And safe from Angry Votes enjoy his Place.
Tonson and he in frequent close Debate

3. *vile degenerate:* Cf. *The Golden Age Restor'd,* 7.

7. *Stamford:* See *The Golden Age,* 42 *n.* After being dismissed from all his places, Stamford left England in July 1702 for an extended visit to the elector of Hanover and the dowager electress at Hanover and Zell (GEC, *12,* i, 222). Cf. Shakespeare, *Richard II,* III. 2. 47–50.

10. *Somerset:* See *The Golden Age Restor'd,* 58 *n.* The quality of Somerset's "Mind" may be judged from a note to Burnet's *History.* Dartmouth explained to Godolphin that since the Venetians did not allow their subjects to converse with foreign ministers, all that was needed in an ambassador was a man of quality who could make a good figure at an audience. Godolphin asked if he meant the duke of Somerset (Burnet, 1823, *5,* 140 *n.*).

14. *Halifax:* See *Advice to a Painter,* 81 *n.,* above. Macky (p. 53) observes that "His quick Rise made him haughty" and that he "prudently got himself made a Lord; and as a Screen from all Objections against his Administration, quitted his Management of Commissioner [of the Treasury], to serve as Auditor." On 26 January 1703 the House resolved "That *Charles* Lord *Halifax,* Auditor of the Receipt of the Exchequer, hath neglected his Duty, and is guilty of a Breach of Trust" (*CJ, 14,* 140).

18. *Tonson:* Halifax (and Somers) supplied many of the themes for Whig propaganda and occasionally revised the authors' copy, which was then consigned to "their Trusty Secretary," Jacob Tonson, "to Babble it Abroad by the Hawkers." Tonson was also

Shall joyn their Heads and weigh the Business of the State.
Then *Devonshire,* whose elevated Chin
Proclaims the happy Vacancy within,
Shall shuffle with his Creditors no more,
But pay his Debts and quitt his Dice and Whore.
Wharton, for Vertue and for Truth renown'd,
Whose ev'ry Action is with Justice crown'd,
Whose innocent and undesigning Life
Was always free from Faction, free from Strife,
Shall be invested with his old Command,
And wrest the Staff from haughty *Seymour*'s hand.
Somers, tho weak in Body, strong in Mind,
No Pox can taint a Substance so refin'd!
With just Applauses shall resume the Mace;
For now, neglecting Health, and private Ease,
He heals Divisions, and promotes the Publick Peace.
Orford shall lord it o'er the subject Main,
Eager of Battel, negligent of Gain.
Mohun shall put on a Politician's Face,

---

a member (and founder, according to Edward Ward) of the Kit-Cat Club, where many Whig propaganda lines originated (*A Vindication of the Whigs,* 1702, pp. 8–10; *The Secret History of Clubs,* 1709, pp. 360–63).

20. *Devonshire:* See *Reformation of Manners,* 1025 *n.,* 1027 *n.,* above; *The Golden Age Restor'd,* 58 *n.,* above.

24. *Wharton:* See *The Golden Age,* 40 *n.,* According to Lord Dartmouth, "Wharton had the most provoking insolent manner of speaking . . . ever observed in any man, without any regard to civility or truth; and . . . went amongst his own party by the name of honest Tom Wharton" (Burnet, 1823, *5,* 228 *n.*). In politics he affirmed that "a lie well believed is as good as if it were true" and in religion he affirmed nothing: "an atheist grafted on a presbyterian," was what he was called. Rebelling against a strict Presbyterian upbringing, this " 'emancipated precisian' . . . early acquired and retained to the last the reputation of being the greatest rake in England" (*DNB, 20,* 1329, 1330). He was appointed comptroller of the royal household in February 1689 and held this post until he was replaced by Sir Edward Seymour in April 1702 (Luttrell, *5,* 164).

30. *Somers:* For Somers' pox, see *Advice to a Painter,* 26–30, above. As the head of his party (*The Golden Age,* 34 *n.,* above) and the central figure in the impeachment proceedings of 1701, Somers was at the center of "la double division" which Poussin observed between Whig and Tory and between the House of Commons and the House of Lords (PRO 31/3 189, f. 5v). Henry St. John, for example, felt that the acquittal of "this little fellow" in "a sham trial" (*The Golden Age,* 23 *n.,* above) was a defeat for "all the gentlemen of England" (HMC *Downshire MSS., 1,* ii, 803).

35. *Orford:* See *The Spanish Descent,* 225 *n.,* above.

37. *Mohun:* See *Reformation of Manners,* 612 *n.,* above. Lord Mohun, who inherited

For Sense with Riches always does increase;
By Railing now, he'll then deserve a Place.
What if sometimes when Strumpet lewd appears,
The Rake confessing, he the Sage cashiers?
So Puss transform'd, the Mouse could not refrain,
But re-assum'd her Shape, and mew'd again,
For Nature will in spite of Art remain.
Hastings, tho now he struts with Comick Mien,
And sneers and jokes with Countenance serene,
Shall gravely quit his Jests, and lisping praise
The glorious Prospect of these golden Days.
Young *Sunderland,* of honest Parents born,
Mature in Council, shall the Board adorn,
Shall emulate his Father's spotless Fame,
And with a Faith like his secure a lasting Name.
Burnet, the Glory of the Lawn he wears,

---

the entire real estate of Charles Rivers, second earl of Macclesfield, in December 1702, apparently decided to "purge, and leave sack/And live cleanly as a nobleman should do" (GEC, *8,* 331–32).

42. *Puss transform'd:* The phrase may be borrowed from John Sheffield, earl of Mulgrave, and John Dryden, *An Essay upon Satire,* (1679): "So cat transform'd sat gravely and demure/Till mouse appear'd and thought himself secure" (*POAS,* Yale, *1,* 406 *n.*), but the motif is proverbial (Tilley C135).

45. *Hastings:* George Hastings, eighth earl of Huntingdon (1677–1705), styled Lord Hastings until 30 May 1701. William gave him a commission in the first regiment of foot guards, which he threw over in 1702 to serve as a volunteer under Marlborough and distinguish himself at the capture of Venlo in September. He was said to have "a great deal of Wit," "a slow lisping Speech," and to be "something of a Libertine" (Macky, p. 79).

49. *Young Sunderland:* See *Advice to a Painter,* 114 *n.,* above. Charles Spencer succeeded as third earl of Sunderland upon the death of his father on 28 September 1702. Although 15 to 25 years younger than they were, he soon joined Somers, Halifax, Wharton, and Orford in the junto that controlled the Whig party during the reign of Anne. This was a role for which his father had prepared him by arranging a marriage with Anne, "the little Whig," the second daughter of Marlborough, in January 1700. William Petty, first marquis of Lansdowne, called him "the most passionate man of his time." Macaulay deplored his "violent temper and crooked politics" (GEC, *12,* i, 488) and Trevelyan agreed that he was "intemperate and unwise" (*1,* 200).

53. *Burnet:* Although Burnet "had declared much against Clergymen's meddling in secular affairs," he himself "had run . . . so deep in them" that there was no backing out. Most recently, while admitting that the bill to prevent occasional conformity "seemed to favour the Interests of the Church," Burnet had borne a large part in the debates that defeated it in the House of Lords and still seemed surprised that "Angry men took occasion from hence, to charge the Bishops as enemies to the Church" (*1,* 380; *2,* 338).

Firm in the Church's Interest appears,
Asserts and vindicates her injur'd Cause,
Whene'er invaded by Conforming Laws:
This holy Man shall *Tennison* succeed,
Tall *Tennison,* the Church's awful Head,
Whose venerable Fabrick fills the Eye
With solemn Apostolick Majesty.
Lambeth rejoice, when one great Prelate dies,
Another, great as he, shall soon arise,
Of equal Gravity, of equal Size.
Then *Hartington,* the Commons mighty Chief,
Who with undaunted Zeal oppos'd the word *Retrieve,*
Shall baffle *Harcourt*'s Reasoning, *Harley*'s Reach,
Musgrave's Experience, *Seymour*'s lofty Speech.
Jekyl, who was by his own Merits rais'd

58. *Tennison:* The size of Thomas Tenison, archbishop of Canterbury, is mentioned in *Advice to a Painter,* 22, and *A Conference,* 147, above.

63. *Size:* The size of Burnet is mentioned in *The Golden Age,* 71, above.

64. *Hartington:* William Cavendish, marquis of Hartington (c. 1673–1729), the eldest son of the duke of Devonshire, served with the army in Flanders in 1692 and then became "a considerable Figure in the House of Commons," where he sat for Derby (November 1695–November 1701), Castle Rising, Norfolk (1701–02), and Yorkshire (1702–07). He was a country Whig and "a constant Opposer of Mr. *Howe*" (Macky, p. 47). During the impeachment proceedings in April 1701 he scandalized even his own party by his "puerilitées" and narrowly missed being sent to the Tower when he challenged that "venerable vieillard," Sir Christopher Musgrave, to settle their differences outside the House. This, as Poussin drily remarks, "excita la risée de toute l'assemblée" (PRO 31/3 188, f. 24v).

65. *Retrieve:* See *The Golden Age Restor'd,* 36 *n.,* above.

66. *Harcourt:* See *Advice to a Painter. 1701,* 14 *n.,* above. Harcourt continued to work very closely with Harley. They "were two of the chief that contriv'd and drew up the Abjuration Oath [March 1702] and the Act about the Succession [June 1701]" (Hearne, *6,* 226–27; *7,* 93). Upon the accession of Anne, Harcourt was sworn solicitor-general on 30 May 1702 and knighted the following day. In the next session he was one of the managers of the bill to prevent occasional conformity.

Harley: See *A Prophecy,* 24 *n.,* below. Jonathan Swift observed that Harley "knew how to prevail on the House with few words and strong reasons" (*Prose, 5,* 260).

67. *Musgrave:* See *England's Late Jury,* 51 *n.,* above.

Seymour: See *Advice to a Painter,* 108 *n.,* above.

68. *Jekyl:* Sir Joseph Jekyll (1663–1738) owed at least part of his success to his marriage with a sister of Lord Somers, then lord high chancellor of England. He studied at the Middle Temple, was called to the bar in 1687, and in June 1697 was made lord chief justice of Chester and knighted in December (W. R. Williams, *The History of the Great Session in Wales,* Brecknock, 1899, p. 44). In parliament where he sat for Eye, Suffolk (November 1695–1700, 1702–13), New Lymington, Hampshire (1713–22), and Reigate, Surrey (1722–38), he was called a low church courtier, but he

Shall justly be by all admir'd and prais'd.
Jessop and he with *Finch*'s Tongue shall vie,
And ev'ry Period, ev'ry Trope supply:
Bromley's clear Notions, *Granvile*'s Vehemence
Shall yield to *Jervois* Wit and *Pawlet*'s Sense.
Then *Boyle, like Sampson,* for his Hair renown'd,

---

was "more of a Whig than of a courtier" (*Numerical Calculation; DNB, 10,* 725). His characterization, in the latter source, as "somewhat puzzled-headed" seems borne out by his subsequent history. Upon her accession in 1702 the queen renewed the commissions of all the judges except two. Jekyll was one of these and "though much threatened with a prosecution, stood it out . . . and continued in the office by virtue of his old appointment" until July 1717 when he was made master of the rolls (Burnet, 1823, *5,* 12 *n.*).

70. *Jessop:* William Jessop (1665–1734) fought his first battle for nonconformity in a "brabble" with Sir John Reresby in 1682. He was admitted to Gray's Inn the next year and was called to the bar in 1690. In parliament he sat for Aldborough, Yorkshire (1702–13, 1715–34) and fought a duel with a Tory member, William Levinz, in January 1709 (*The Rev. Oliver Heywood, B.A., 1630–1702; His Autobiography,* ed. Joseph H. Turner, 4 vols., Brighouse, Yorkshire, 1881–85, *2,* 293; Williams, *The History of the Great Session in Wales,* p. 65).

Finch: See *Advice to a Painter. 1701,* 14 *n.,* above.

72. *Bromley:* See *The Golden Age Restor'd,* 10 *n.,* above. William Bromley, "the Champion of our Cause," as William Pittis described him, was elected chairman of the committee of elections and a member of the commission for taking the public accounts in October 1702, presented the case against Lord Ranelagh in November, and was one of the managers of the bill to prevent occasional conformity in November–December (*The Patriots,* 1702, p. 8; Luttrell, *5,* 229, 234–35, 259).

Granvile: John Granville (*A New Satyr on the Parliament,* 86 n.); "sa rage" was noticed by Bonet in 1698 (BM MS. Add. 30000B, f. 264v).

73. *Jervois:* Thomas Jervoice (c. 1668–1743) of Herriard, Hampshire, was the son of Sir Thomas Jervoice, Knight. He was a lawyer and a deputy lieutenant for Hampshire in 1700–01. In parliament, where he sat for Stockbridge, Hampshire (May 1691–95), Hampshire (July 1698–1702, 1705–10), and Hindon, Wiltshire (November 1704–05), he was a Whig, serving with Robert Walpole as teller on several divisions of the House. But he was also included in the list of those members "said to have been influenc'd by M. *Poussin,* the French Agent" in 1701 (*A Collection of White and Black Lists,* 4th ed., 1715, pp. 15–18). In July 1702 he was returned for Plympton, Devonshire, but he was charged with bribery in the election and on 28 January 1703 the House voted 138–104 that he had not been duly elected (*CSPD 1700–1702,* p. 252; Luttrell, *5,* 259, 262; *CJ, 14,* 149–51).

Pawlet: See *Advice to a Painter,* 125 *n.,* above.

74. *Boyle:* See *Advice to a Painter,* 127 *n.,* above. Henry Boyle, whose nickname was Sugar Plum, seems to have been completely bald (*Advice to a Painter,* textual note 127–30, p. 716 below; *A Prophecy,* textual note 33, p. 787 below). His voting record reveals a remarkable number of turnabouts, including three in 1696 when he voted with the Tories in the division on the council of trade in January, subscribed to the association for the defense of William III in April, and rejoined the Tories in November to vote against the attainder of Fenwick. Then he voted with the Court Whigs in

One was with Strength and one with Beauty crown'd.
Shall make no scruple to wheel round again,
For he, sweet Soul! complies with ev'ry Reign.
King in a mixt Capacity shall shine,
The Lawyer here, and there the Tub Divine.
Cowper shall leave his Whoring, and grow chast;
For such excessive Lewdness ne'er can last.
Now *Littleton* disdains to buy a Place,
But then the long forbidden Chair shall grace;
All his Debates shall be from trifling free,
Nor Tale be heard, nor idle Repartee.
Strickland shall coolly talk, and cease to rant;
And *Fagg* forget his formal tedious Cant.
Stringer no longer shall a Bully seem;

---

opposing the disbanding of the army in January 1699 but was included with the Tories in the Black List of 1701. Finally he voted with the Whigs again in 1705 against William Bromley for speaker. Upon the accession of Anne he was reappointed chancellor of the exchequer and a privy councillor.

78. *King:* Peter King (1669–1734), whose father was a grocer and whose mother was a first cousin of John Locke, was knighted in 1708 and raised to the peerage as Lord King, baron of Ockham, in May 1725. "He was put an apprentice to a grocer in Exeter & from thence came to London to study the lawe . . . he hath Published a book of divinity & is an ingenious worthy gentleman" (Le Neve, p. 500). Actually he studied law at Leyden but was admitted to the bar from the Middle Temple in June 1698. The book of divinity is *An Enquiry into the Constitution, Discipline, Unity and Worship, of the Primitive Church,* 2 vols., 1691. He was elected to parliament for Beeralston, Devonshire (January 1701–15).

80. *Cowper:* See *Reformation of Manners,* 463 *n.,* 473 *n.,* above.

82. *Littleton:* The "Place" that Sir Thomas Littleton disdained to buy must have been in the commission of the treasury, which he held from 1696 to 1699, for he was reappointed treasurer of the navy in June 1702 (Luttrell, *5,* 184). Although he had been speaker of the Commons in 1698–1700, he was not a candidate in February 1701 or in October 1702. In December 1701, however, he lost to Harley by four votes (Luttrell, *5,* 15, 125, 227).

83. This line replies to *The Golden Age Restor'd,* 65, above.

86. *Strickland:* See *Advice to a Painter,* 110 *n.,* above. Sir William Strickland, one of the Whig leaders in parliament, had to be enjoined in May 1701 not to prosecute his quarrel with John Howe outside the House. He is also reported to have been involved in "a drunken bout" with Lord William Paulet in 1709 and some "foul play" in the election of 1713 (*CJ, 13,* 540; *CSPD 1699–1700,* p. 310; HMC *Portland MSS., 4,* 520, 614).

87. *Fagg:* Thomas Fagg (d. 1705) was a Whig member for Rye (November 1701–April 1705) whose election in 1702 was challenged because five of the 40 voters for him "were Dissenters . . . and had not received the Sacrament within a Year" (*CJ, 14,* 89–90).

88. *Stringer:* Thomas Stringer (1661–1706), the second son of Sir Thomas Stringer, Knight, was commissioned captain in the earl of Danby's regiment of volunteer

The Tories Terror, and the Whigs Esteem.
Stanhope, that Offspring of unlawful Lust,
Begot with more than Matrimonial Gust,
Who thinks no Pleasure like *Italian* Joy,
And to a *Venus* Arms prefers a Pathick Boy,
Shall thunder in the Senate and the Field,
And reap what Fame, or Arts or Arms can yield.
Godolphin, who this mighty Change foresees,
Advances to their Cause by just degrees;
And happy they who can secure his Heart,
Unvarnish'd with the false disguise of Art:
His Thoughts are free, sincere and unconfin'd,
His Words the dictates of an open Mind.

---

dragoons in July 1690, fought in all of William's campaigns in the Lowlands, and was promoted to colonel in February 1702 (*CSPD 1700–1702,* p. 512). In January 1693 he was wounded in a duel with Peregrine Osborne and in February 1695 fought another duel with Osborne in which both were wounded (Luttrell, *3,* 3, 445). As a Whig member for Clitheroe, Lancashire (1698–1706), he was accused of bribery and other corrupt practices in the election of July 1702, but his return was upheld by the committee on elections nonetheless (*CJ, 14,* 258–59).

90. *Stanhope:* James Stanhope (1673–1721), the grandson of Philip Stanhope, first earl of Chesterfield, was born in Paris, where his father was secretary of the embassy. This fact, together with his swarthy complexion—Macky called him "a handsom black Man"—may account for the insinuation in the text regarding his conception. He began his military career in 1691 as an aide-de-camp to Charles, duke of Schomberg, fighting the French in the Savoy. Thereafter he served with distinction in four campaigns in the Lowlands (1694–97), and was promoted to colonel in February 1702. In October 1702 he was mentioned in Ormonde's dispatches for gallantry in the Vigo landing. His diplomatic career, in which he was to become "one of the brightest ornaments of Europe," began in 1698 when he was appointed second secretary in the embassy at Paris. Heavy gambling, debauchery, and dueling—he killed his opponent in a duel in Brussels in 1694—occupied his leisure time until March 1702 when he was elected to parliament for Newport, Isle of Wight, in place of his friend John, Lord Cutts, who elected to serve for Cambridgeshire instead. Thereafter he sat for Cockermouth, Cumberland (1702–13, 1715–April 1717), Wendover, Buckinghamshire (March 1714–15), and Newport again (April–July 1717). He was of course a Whig, eventually the only serious rival to Robert Walpole within the party, but in 1705 he was called a high church courtier and included in Harley's list of Tories who might be influenced to tack the occasional conformity bill to the land tax. He voted against the tack, however (*Parl. Hist., 6,* 363) and in April 1718 was created earl Stanhope.

90–93. Cf. *Advice to a Painter,* 115–17, above.

96–97. *Godolphin:* These lines provide an interesting example of prescience. In May 1702 with great reluctance Godolphin assumed the leadership of a Tory ministry which "by just degrees" became a Whig ministry, the leadership of which Godolphin gave up with even greater reluctance in August 1710.

But *Sarah* sure, who now surrounds the Throne
With her Innumerable Pigmy-spawn,
Can never hope a more Auspicious Reign,
A kinder Mistress or a greater Queen.
Leeds, Weymouth, Abingdon and *Normanby,*

102. *Sarah:* Sarah Churchill (1660–1744), countess of Marlborough, as she then was, admitted that she had been "distinguished . . . by so high a place in [Anne's] favour, as perhaps no person ever arrived at a higher with queen or princess." Upon the accession of the queen, the countess "began to be look'd upon as a person of consequence, without whose approbation, at least, neither places, nor pensions, nor honours were bestowed by the crown" (*Account of the Conduct,* pp. 11, 122). The countess herself was showered with places: keeper of the privy purse, groom of the stole, and first lady of the bedchamber (Luttrell, *5,* 160). This line replies to *The Golden Age Restor'd,* 72, above.

103. *Pigmy-spawn:* Since Sarah Churchill and her daughter Anne, now Lady Spencer, were both ladies of the bedchamber (Luttrell *5,* 163) and since the queen liked to have both of them with her on state occasions (*The Spanish Descent,* 376 *n.,* above), it must have seemed to many that "the Throne" was beset with Churchills.

106. *Leeds:* Sir Thomas Osborne (1631–1712), successively first earl of Danby, marquis of Carmarthen, and duke of Leeds, had no real political power after 1694. But "that old English hero," as John Dunton called him, remained at the council board and in the House of Lords as a reminder of Tory greatness. "Despite his great age and increasing bodily infirmities, the duke never relaxed his efforts to recover some of the ground he had lost. In December 1702 he made a fierce personal attack in the House of Lords on Charles Montagu, baron (afterwards earl of) Halifax, asserting that his family was 'raised by rebellion.' A duel was anticipated, and Halifax and the duke's son, the Marquis of Carmarthen, were both bound over by the council not to accept a challenge" (HMC *Beaufort MSS.,* p. 96, cited in *DNB, 14,* 1196).

Weymouth: Viscount Weymouth, who held no public office under William III and even refused to subscribe to the association in defense of the king, was, upon the accession of Anne, made first lord of trade and foreign plantations in May and sworn of the privy council in June 1702 (HMC *Lords MSS.,* New Series, *2,* 206, 212–13; Luttrell, *5,* 180, 185).

Abingdon: Montagu Bertie, second earl of Abingdon (d. 1743), was a nephew of the duke of Leeds and "very high for the Monarchy and Church" (Macky, p. 96). In parliament, where he sat for Berkshire (1689–90) and Oxfordshire (1690–99), he voted solidly Tory and refused to sign the association for the defense of William III. Accordingly, upon the accession of Anne, he was sworn of the privy council (April 1702), appointed constable of the Tower of London (May 1702), and in June 1702 made lord lieutenant of Oxfordshire and chief justice in eyre, south of Trent, two places from which Lord Wharton had just been dismissed.

Normanby: Like Abingdon, John Sheffield, third earl of Mulgrave, was "violent for the *High Church,*" but in his case Macky (p. 20) was forced to add: "yet seldom goes to it." After a distinguished military career, Mulgrave was banished from the court of Charles II for presuming to make love to Princess Anne (then 17). Upon the accession of James II, however, Mulgrave was restored to all his places and sworn to the privy council. In November 1686 he succeeded Rochester in the court of high commission. During the next reign he distinguished himself for his opposition to the court except during the period 1694–96 when he was granted an annual pension of

Rooke, Nottingham and *Rochester* shall fly
To some Recess, and there obscurely die.
For their unequal Sense can ne'er support
The vast Ambitious Aims of such a Court.
Manchester, Bolton, Haversham, Carlisle,

£3000, sworn to the privy council, and created marquis of Normanby. But in March 1696, when he refused to subscribe to the association for the defense of William III, he was dismissed from the privy council, and returned to the opposition. Upon the accession of Anne, "to the admiration of all men," as Burnet said (2, 314) he was made lord privy seal and again sworn to the privy council in April 1702. Finally, on 23 March 1703, he was created duke of Buckingham and of Normanby (Luttrell, *5*, 165, 182, 209; *CSPD 1702–1703*, p. 502).

107. *Rooke:* Sir George Rooke (1650–1709) was vice-admiral of the blue in the battle of La Hougue in May 1692, in which the French fleet was virtually destroyed, and William III came aboard his ship the next February at Portsmouth and knighted him (Luttrell, *3*, 39). In parliament, where he sat for Portsmouth, Hampshire (1698–1708), Rooke "signalized" himself in the impeachment proceedings against the Whig lords in 1701 and came to be numbered among the high church courtiers. In May 1702 he was restored to the commission of the admiralty and put in command of the fleet (Luttrell, *5*, 172, 177). In July "Queen Anne and the prince were godfather & godmother" of his only son (Le Neve, p. 444) and in November Rooke returned to London as the hero of Vigo, to receive the "Favour of her Majesty, and . . . the loud Acclamations of the People." On the 21st, when he resumed his seat in the Commons, Harley read a unanimous resolution of the House thanking him for the great and signal services that he had performed for the nation (*CJ, 14*, 39). On the same day he was sworn of the privy council (Luttrell, *5*, 239) and two years later Daniel Defoe reported to Harley from Bury St. Edmunds that Rooke's health "is now drunk by those here, who won't drink the Queen's, nor yours" (HMC *Portland MSS., 4*, 137).

Nottingham: See *The Golden Age Restor'd,* 55 *n.,* above.

Rochester: Anne restored her uncle to the lord lieutenancy of Ireland, named his daughter one of her ladies of the bedchamber (Luttrell, *5*, 163), and seemed determined to forget his "ill behaviour . . . to her" during the late reigns (*Account of the Conduct,* p. 133). Rochester responded by encouraging the zeal of the lower house of convocation—even arguing that the convocation was part of the parliament (and so could not be dissolved but by the queen)—and supporting the bill against occasional conformity in the House of Lords (Burnet, *2*, 317).

111. *Manchester:* Charles Montagu, fourth earl of Manchester (c. 1662–1722), "a Gentleman of greater Application than Capacity" (Macky, p. 57), was one of the first noblemen to take arms for the prince of Orange in November 1688. His embassies to Venice (1697–98) and to France (1699–1701), and his term of office as seceretary of state—from January to May 1702, when he was replaced by Sir Charles Hedges—were equally unremarkable.

Bolton: Charles Paulet, Pawlet, or Powlett (1661–1722), second duke of Bolton, sat in parliament as a Whig member for Hampshire from 1681 to 1698. He went to Holland in 1688 and returned to England with the prince of Orange. He is alleged to have been involved in a plot to exclude Princess Anne from the throne in favor of the electress Sophia (Burnet, 1823, *4*, 540), but at the same time the earl of Shaftesbury thought that he was "entangled in the [Tory] netts" (*Original Letters,* p. 139). In any

The Pride and Glory of our British Isle,
Shall undertake and execute the noble Toil.
O that my languid Numbers I could raise,
High as their Merits, sounding as their Praise!
Not *Maynwaring,* tho all his Club should join,
And *Somerset* himself correct each Line,

---

case, although Bolton soon accommodated himself to the new regime, he failed to "make any Figure at Court" (Macky, p. 38). Swift, who knew him well, called him "A great Booby" and Lady Cowper added that he was generally to be seen with his tongue lolling out of his mouth. Hearne characterized him as "A most lewd, vicious man, a great dissembler and a very hard drinker" (GEC, 2, 212).

Haversham: John Thompson (c. 1648–1710), "a short red Faced Man," was "a Dissenter by Principle, and always turbulent" (Macky, p. 104). Although created a baronet in 1673, he became a solidly Whig member of parliament for Gatton, Surrey (1685–96) and a commissioner for the public accounts in 1695. In May 1696 he was created baron Haversham of Haversham, Buckinghamshire, and appointed to the commission of the admiralty (June 1699–December 1701). During the impeachment proceedings in 1701 he lost his temper and accused the Commons of using the proceedings for an ulterior "Design." As an occasional conformist himself, he was violent in his opposition to the bill to prevent occasional conformity.

Carlisle: Charles Howard (1669–1738), sat in parliament for Morpeth, Northumberland (1689–92) until he succeeded his father as third earl of Carlisle in April 1692. It was he who precipitated the addresses demanding dissolution of William's fifth parliament (*England's Late Jury,* headnote, p. 343 above), and in December 1701 he replaced Godolphin in the commission of the treasury. On Anne's accession to the throne, "he was dismissed from his Employments at Court" (Macky, p. 59).

116. *Maynwaring:* Arthur Mainwaring (1668–1712) was born in Ightfield, Shropshire, where his family had been distinguished since the fifteenth century. In November 1683 he matriculated at Christ Church, Oxford, but left without taking a degree. About 1690 he came to London to study law and write poetry. In poetry "he gave himself mostly to Satyr" ([John Oldmixon], *The Life and Posthumous Works of Arthur Maynwaring,* 1715, p. 9), and since his tutor at Oxford had been the Jacobite George Smalridge, and his uncle, Francis Cholmley, had been sent to the Tower for refusing to take the oaths to William III, it is not surprising that these early satires were violently Jacobite. Two of them, *Tarquin and Tullia* (1689) and *The King of Hearts* (1689), were good enough to be attributed to Dryden and to be included in *POAS,* Yale, 5. But within a few years Mainwaring had been taken up by Charles Montagu (later Lord Halifax) and Lord Somers, made a member of the Kit-Cat Club, and came "to be as much in Love with the Establishment, as he had before been averse to it" (ibid., p. 15). This change from Jacobite to Whig, of which *The Brawny Bishop's Complaint* (1699) may represent a transitional point, must have been completed by November 1701 when Mainwaring was appointed to Sir Walter Yonge's place in the commission of the customs, worth £1200 a year (Luttrell, 5, 110). Thereafter, Mainwaring became one of the most effective of the Whig propagandists.

117. *Somerset:* It was "the proud Duke," to whom Mainwaring was related through his Cholmondeley connections, who introduced him "to the Company of Men of Sound Principles" in London (i.e. the Whig junto) ([Oldmixon], *The Life and Posthumous Works of Arthur Maynwaring,* p. 15).

Could e'er produce Diviner Lays than mine.
Nay, tow'ring *Halifax,* that Giant Wit,
Tho he transcrib'd and own'd what *Prior* writ,
Could e'er pretend to reach the matchless Strain,
The Poet's Envy, and the Critick's Pain.

119. *Halifax:* See *The Dispensary, 4,* 236 *n.,* above. "Some people," possibly including the author of *The Golden Age Revers'd,* believed that Halifax wrote *The Golden Age Restor'd.* But George Stepney, in Vienna, doubted that "my noble friend was so imprudent to have an hand in the Ecclogue, thô some people who envy him in his employment were glad of that or any other occasion that might put him in the danger of losing it" (PRO 105/68, f. 113).

120. *what Prior writ:* Cf. *The Dispensary, 4,* 236 *n.,* above.

A Prophecy
(*June*[?] *1703*)

Prophecy as a subgenre of satire was domesticated in England in January 1672 when *Nostradamus' Prophecy* (*POAS,* Yale, *1,* 185–89) began to circulate in manuscript. This work, which also establishes the "When . . . When . . . When . . . Then" structure of the present poem, was derived from the famous prophecies of Michel de Notredame (Latinized to Nostradamus) published in Lyons in 1555. Nostradamus' work, called *Les Prophéties,* is divided into *Centuries* and written in decasyllabic quatrains rhyming *abab,* which the anonymous writer of the present work imitates as decasyllabic triplets.

Besides the structure and metrical pattern, the style of the present work also derives from Nostradamus, or from the English translations of his work which began to appear in 1672 (Wing N1397-1401). These prophecies are deliberately cast in a riddling, anagrammatic (e.g. *Nicole* for *Lincoln*), ambiguous style so that they can be interpreted in a dozen different ways. Quatrain 89 of Century IV, for example, has been applied to the Revolution of 1688. It reads:

> Trente de Londres secret conjureront
> Contre leur Roy, sur le pont l'entreprise:
> Leuy, satalites là mort de gousteront,
> Un Roy esleut blonde, natif de Frize.

Subjects in London did conspire secretly with the prince of Orange against their king, James II, and William was in a sense "elected" king, but he was *not* blonde and was only a native of Friesland by a wild synecdoche. So the quatrain has also been interpreted to apply to earlier conspiracies against Charles I.

This riddling style makes annotation extremely problematical but it offered obvious advantages to the Whig writer of the present poem who was willing to risk the pillory to make his satirical sallies.

As the subgenre developed after 1672 it acquired two more differentia, only one of which is present in *A Prophecy*. The first is the fiction that the poem is reprinted from an ancient manuscript or inscription, long lost but recently recovered. This is illustrated by the title of a poem of 1696: *A Prophecy found on the 29th of January 1696 by Some Workmen digging up the Ruins in the Privy Garden, And by them Carry'd to the Usher of the Black Rod as it was written in a Scroll of Parchment.* Jonathan Swift adopts this fiction in *The Windsor Prophecy* (1711) and develops it with typical panache: "About three Months ago at *W–nd—r,* a poor Knight's Widow was buried in the Cloysters. In digging the Grave, the Sexton struck against a small Leaden Coffer, about half a Foot in length, and four Inches wide. The poor Man expecting he had discovered a Treasure, opened it with some difficulty; but found only a small Parchment, rolled up very fast, put into a Leather Case; which Case was tied at the top, and sealed with a St. *George,* the Impression on black Wax, very rude and *Gothick*" (*Poems, 1,* 146).

The second feature that prophecy (in the generic sense) acquired after 1672 was marginal annotation. In the first line of the 1696 poem, "Knight of the North" is glossed "Sir John Fenwick." In one manuscript of *A Prophecy,* however, the marginalia are elaborated to a degree where they may be considered part of the work. These marginalia, which appear in the TCD MS. I.5, 2, 20–23, are cited in the footnotes below as (*A*).

The only evidence of authorship of the poem is a note in one manuscript (BM MS. Harleian 6914, f. 103) that reads "by H: Mor". This may refer to Henry Mordaunt (c. 1663–1720), the second son of John Mordaunt, first Viscount Mordaunt of Avalon, who graduated B.A. from Christ Church, Oxford, in 1684, was commissioned colonel of a foot regiment in 1694, and sat as a Whig member for Brackley, Northamptonshire (January 1692–98, January 1701–02, November 1705–08) and Richmond, Yorkshire (1708–20) (G. F.) Russell Barker and Alan H. Stenning, *The Record of Old Westminsters,* 2 vols., 1928, *2,* 661–62). The title page of *POAS,* 1704, *3,* lists "Col. *Mordaunt*" among "*the greatest Wits of the Age*" whose works are included in that volume, but no work therein is attributed to Mordaunt. (And in *POAS,* 1707, *4,* in which *A Prophecy* was first printed, Mordaunt's name does not appear on the title page).

In four witnesses (*CEHJ*) the poem is dated 1703 and in one (*G*) it is dated June 1703, which agrees well enough with line 77.

A Prophecy

When Great *Nassau* is dead and gone,
That Hero of the First Renown,
Whose Equal never will be known.

When Rogues bare-fac'd appear in Packs,
When State Physicians are all Quacks,
And Privy Councillors are *Jacks*.

When Contradictions do meet,
And Knaves are at the Helm of State,
Tho faithless and unfortunate.

When *Marlborough, Godolphin, Lory,*
Have acted over the old Story,
And *Ireland* has been rul'd by Tory.

When *Seymour, Harley,* and *Jack How*
Agree the Nation to undo,
Tho each would hang the other two.

1. *Nassau:* William III.

2. *Hero:* The address to the queen in October 1702 in which the Commons said that Marlborough had "retrieved" the honor of the English nation (*The Golden Age Restor'd,* 36 *n.,* above) was resented by the Whigs, who thought that it alluded to "the success of [William's] wars being tarnished with the frequency of his defeats" (Dal-*rymple, 3,* [2]244).

6. *Jacks:* Jacobites (*OED*).

10. *Marlborough, Godolphin, Lory:* Marlborough has replaced Sunderland in the traditional formulation of the three chits, the first (Tory) ministry of Charles II (1679): "Sunderland, Godolphin, Lory [Laurence, earl of Rochester]/Turn politics to jests" (*POAS,* Yale, *2,* 340). The implication is that Marlborough, Godolphin, and Rochester will re-enact for Anne the arbitrary measures which Sunderland, Godolphin, and Rochester executed for her uncle.

12. *Ireland:* On 4 February 1703 Anne appointed the duke of Ormonde to replace Rochester as lord lieutenant of Ireland (Luttrell, *5,* 266). Both of course were Tories.

13. *Seymour:* See *Advice to a Painter,* 108 *n.; England's Late Jury,* 21 *n.,* above.
Harley: See 24 *n.,* below.
How: See *Advice to a Painter,* 108 *n.,* above.

When nauseous *Jack* can quiet sit,
That is, when all his Venom's spit,
Of Constitution and of Wit.

When *Gloucester* has smelt out the Knave,
And Patriot *Jack* Recourse must have
To Foreign Borough to inslave.

When *England*'s Interest is seen clearly,
When Parties carry matters fairly,
And Trimming is left off by *Harley*.

16. *Jack:* In December 1701, after he had been blacklisted by the Whigs (*A List of One Unanimous Club of Members of the Late Parliament,* 1701, p. 3), the name of John Grubham Howe stood at the bottom of the poll in Gloucestershire. In July 1702, therefore, he made an extraordinary effort to be re-elected. He drew "a Party in that County to join with him in an Address to the Queen," Burnet (2, 334–35) said, "in which, reflections were made on the danger and ill usage she had gone thro' in the former Reign; this Address was received by the Queen, in so particular [*i.e.* markedly favorable] a manner, that it looked like the owning that the Contents of it were true; but she made such an excuse for this, when the offence it gave was laid before her, that probably, she was not acquainted with the matter of the Address, when she so received it."

19. *Gloucester:* As part of his extraordinary campaign for re-election, Howe stood for three constituencies besides Gloucestershire: Gloucester borough and the "Foreign" boroughs of Newton, Lancashire, and Bodmin, Cornwall. The result was equally extraordinary: Howe was returned for all four constituencies and chose to sit for Gloucestershire. His rehabilitation was completed at the assizes in August when he was awarded £400 against one Prinn "for speaking scandalous words of him" (Luttrell, *5*, 203). At the opening of the session in October, however, the defeated candidate, Sir John Guise, of Elmore, Gloucestershire, second baronet, who was Howe's brother-in-law, claimed that the high sheriff "was prevailed upon, by undue and illegal Practices, to return the said Mr. *How* . . . [and] shewed himself very partial against the Petitioner, illegally adding to, and changing, the Votes, and adjourning the Poll at his Pleasure" (*CJ, 14,* 5–6). The Commons heard the evidence on 19 November 1702 and upon the motion of Sir Simon Harcourt voted, "By a great and shameful majority" (221–90), that Howe had been duly elected (Burnet, 1823, *5*, 47 *n.*).

24. *Harley:* Robert Harley (1661–1724) entered parliament in a by-election of 6 April 1689 for the Cornish borough of Tregony and thereafter sat for New Radnor, Radnorshire (1690–May 1711). By 1703 he had already changed sides twice. He began as a Whig, voting with Thomas Wharton and Edward Russell for the Sacheverell clause in 1690 (Oldmixon, p. 36) and ordering bonfires and free cider when William was proclaimed joint monarch. In 1696, although he voted against the Whigs' recoinage bill and the attainder of Fenwick, he held back from the most violent Tories by signing the association for the defense of the king. But by January 1699 his successful management of the disbanding bill gained him the leadership of the New Country Party of Sir Edward Seymour and Sir Christopher Musgrave. In February 1701 he was duly elected speaker and so successfully pushed through the impeachments of the

When *Seymour* scorns Salt-Petre Pence,
When *Bolles* to *Bedlam* 'as no pretence,
Or any *Bertie* can talk Sense.

When *Hedges,* richly worth the Gallows,
For what the *Magdalen* Records tell us,
Shall represent those very Fellows.

When Worth's prefer'd without the Ready,
When wav'ring *Boyle* is once fixt steddy,
When *Hedges* is less Knave than *Ady*.

Whig lords that he was included among the Poussineers and blacklisted by the Whigs at the next election. Already, however, Harley must have decided to move back toward the Whigs, for in June 1701 the most violent Tories boasted that "Robin's nose was brought to the grindstone" (HMC *Cowper MSS., 2,* 428). This phase was completed in March 1705 when Harley brought into the ministry as lord privy seal John Holles, duke of Cavendish, one of the most powerful Whigs in England. In 1708 Harley made a final turnabout and rejoined the Tories.

25. *Seymour:* "a Bribe from the Old East India Company" (*A*); see *A New Satyr on the Parliament,* 41 *n.,* above. Saltpeter, for the manufacture of gunpowder, was one of the major imports of the East India Company. Peter's pence was an annual tax on land paid to the papal see, discontinued in England in 1534 (*OED*).

26. *Bolles:* See *Reformation of Manners,* 578 *n.,* above. On one occasion during the assizes at Lincoln, Bolles became "somewhat disorder'd on the bench . . . [and] told Mr. justice [Henry Gould] that he came down with the kings commission to enslave the people . . . and that he and his brother judge (meaning the lord cheif justice Holt) should come down on their knees in parliament: he gave the judge the lye, and kickt the sherif" (Luttrell, *4,* 545).

27. *Bertie:* See *The Brawny Bishop's Complaint,* 27 *n.,* above, and *The Golden Age Revers'd,* 106 *n.,* above.

28. *Hedges:* "Secretary to the Ecclesiastical Commission in K: James's time" (*A*). In his attack on Magdalen College, Oxford, in 1687 James II (1) tried to appoint Anthony Farmer, "notable for debauchery even in that age," as president of the college, (2) expelled 26 fellows and declared them incapable of holding any church preferment, and then (3) filled up the presidency and fellowships with Roman Catholics (Ogg, *3,* 183–85). In all of these proceedings, which were tried before the court of ecclesiastical commission, Charles Hedges, himself a graduate of Magdalen Hall, Oxford, was the king's counsel. He supplied farfetched precedents, read the king's mandate to the fellows, and on one occasion ordered the door of the fellows' common room to be forced open (J. R. Bloxam, *Magdalen College and King James II,* Oxford, 1886, pp. 112, 191, 195). In July 1702 Hedges "talk'd of being Member of Parliament for the University of Oxford" (*A*).

32. *Boyle:* See *The Golden Age Revers'd,* 74 *n.,* above.

33. *Ady:* Malmesbury, Wiltshire, was a corporation borough "chiefly notable for its extreme corruption . . . it had only thirteen voters and the high steward and his deputy had the chief influence" (VCH, *Wiltshire, 5,* 218). From 1698 to 1705 Sir Charles

When *Musgrave,* who long seem'd proof-Place,
The first that's vacant does embrace,
To Goose and Gander's the same Sauce.

When honest Men dare shew their Faces,
And Wit and Sense are no Disgraces,
And *Coningsby* has no minc'd Places.

When *Ranelagh* has left his Puns,
And *Cutts* has nothing but Coach Duns,
And *Jack*'s Lieutenant of the Guns.

Hedges was high steward and William Adey was his deputy. Of these 13 voters Adey was said to control "8 or 9" (*Wiltshire Archaeological and Natural History Magazine, 46* [December 1932], 76). On one occasion he boasted that "that Gentleman that would give him most Money should be Parliament-Man for *Malmesbury*" for "he had so many Voices at his Command" that he could return whom he pleased (*CJ, 12,* 622). These practices had been complained of in parliament twice before the election of November 1701 (*CJ, 12,* 351; *13,* 408), when Hedges himself was returned for Malmesbury. On 14 January 1702 Daniel Park, the defeated candidate, claimed that Adey "did corruptly treat and contract with several Persons" to vote for Hedges (*CJ, 13,* 679). Three days later Hedges was appointed to a committee to bring in a bill for the better preventing of bribery and corruption in elections (*CJ, 13,* 683). On 29 January 1702 Adey created a sensation when he appeared at the bar of the House with "a Bag of Gold, and a Bank Bill for Two Hundred Pounds, which, he said, he had received from *Daniel Park.*" Without even a division the House resolved that Hedges had been duly elected (*CJ, 13,* 711).

34. *Musgrave:* See *England's Late Jury,* 56–60, 60 *n.,* above. Less than 10 days after the king's death it was rumored that Musgrave would replace the old Williamite, Sir Henry Goodricke, second baronet, as lieutenant-general of the ordnance, a place Musgrave had held from 1681 to 1687. Actually the post went to John Granville, but in June 1702 Musgrave was appointed one of the tellers of the exchequer, worth £1000 a year (Luttrell, *5,* 152, 187).

39. *Coningsby:* Although one of William's favorites (*Advice to a Painter,* 102 *n.,* above), Lord Coningsby was reappointed to all his old posts, including that of the vice-treasurer of Ireland, said to be worth £7000 a year, and even appointed to a new one, treasurer of war in Ireland "with a fee of 6*d.* out of every £1 he pays out" (*CSPD 1702–1703,* pp. 143, 391, 400; *CSPD 1703–1704,* p. 170). The latter must be the place which "Lady Marlborough [was] said to share" (*A*).

40. *Ranelagh:* See *A Conference,* 131 *n.,* above; Ranelagh was said to be "very happy in Jests and Repartees" (Macky, p. 82).

41. *Cutts:* See *Advice to a Painter,* 106 *n.,* above. Cutts confessed to the king in 1699 that his debts were £17,500 and when he died in Dublin in January 1707 his aides de camp had to contribute "10*l.* a piece to bury him" (HMC *Seventh Report,* Appendix, p. 246).

42. *Jack:* John Granville (*A*) was appointed lieutenant-general of the ordnance in May 1702 (Luttrell, *5,* 174).

When he has Places in Possession,
For having open made Profession,
Against the Protestant Succession,

That chief of the informing kind,
To whom old *Escrick*'s Soul we find
By wondrous Transmigration join'd.

When *England*'s Bulwark, our great Fleet,
That never should fear odds they meet,
Shall barely on the Square, retreat.

When comes to nought our great Descent,
And most Men think 'twas never meant,
When *Rooks* are on such Errands sent.

When *Somers,* whom all Knaves do dread,
The truest *Britan* e'er was bred,
Shall therefore lose that able Head.

When *Wright* one prudent thing has done,
T'exchange the lopt one for his own;
Better have that that's off than none.

When Church to Charity is given,
That is, when Numbers odd are even,
Or *Rowe*'s in Chappel of St. *Stephen.*

46. *chief of the informing kind:* presumably Daniel Finch, earl of Nottingham, who as principal secretary of state (May 1702–May 1704) controlled the secret service funds by which intelligence operations were financed and informants paid.

47. *Escrick:* William Howard, third baron Howard of Escrick (1626?–94), "this vile Whig traitor and informer" (GEC, *6,* 587 *n.*), by giving credence to the false accusations of Titus Oates, contributed to the death of his own kinsman, William Howard, Lord Stafford, in 1680. When arrested himself in the Rye House plot (1683) he provided evidence that sent Lord William Russell and Algernon Sidney to the scaffold.

51. *barely on the Square:* face to face with the enemy (*OED,* s.v. square, a., III, 11a); see *The Golden Age,* 64 *n.,* above.

52. *Descent:* See *The Spanish Descent,* 3 *n.,* 118 *n.,* above.

55. *Somers:* See *The Dispensary, 1,* 51 *n.,* above.

58. *Wright:* Sir Nathan Wright succeeded Somers as lord keeper in May 1700 (*A Conference,* headnote, p. 212 above). According to the duchess of Marlborough, he was "a man despised by all parties [and] of no use to the crown . . . whose weak and wretched conduct in the court of *chancery,* had almost brought his very office into contempt" (*Account of the Conduct,* p. 147).

63. *Rowe:* Anthony Rowe was returned to the Convention parliament as a member

When the dull *Dutch* turn merry Grigs,
When true-born *Englishmen* turn Prigs,
And Bishops are condemn'd for Whigs.

When *Sarum* shall leave off to wive,
And under *Compton* Trade shall thrive,
The dullest Clergy-man alive.

When *Western* Prelates swear and rant,
And 't does appear that there's no want
Of Sense in Honest *Tom* of *Cant.*

---

for Penryn, Cornwall (1689–90), but thereafter failed to be re-elected. In a by-election of 20 November 1693 he was returned for Stockbridge, Hampshire, by bribes so flagrant that not only was the election declared "corrupt and . . . void" but a bill was introduced to disenfranchise the borough. In October 1695 and January 1701 he was returned for Michael, Cornwall, but again the elections were declared void (*CJ, 11,* 36–37, 361–62; *13,* 416–17). It was said to be his misfortune "Not to *Bribe* the Right Electors, or the Majority, and so was always put to *Petitioning:* Or if he got in, for his *Reputation* and *Integrity* of downright *Bribery* was always turn'd out: So that even the *disfranchised Borough* of *Stockbridge* was his last Refuge, and both he and his Borough made Martyrs together" (*The Old and Modern Whig Truly Represented,* 1702, p. 28).

66. *Bishops:* See *The Golden Age Revers'd,* 53 *n.,* above. "King William's bishops," as they were called, voted solidly against the bill to prevent occasional conformity. On one critical occasion, when the House divided 50–47, it was Archbishop Tenison and seven bishops who provided a majority for the Whigs (*Letters of Eminent Men Addressed to Ralph Thoresby,* 2 vols., 1832, *1,* 436; Klopp, *10,* 222).

67. *Sarum:* Burnet's first wife, whom he married in 1671, was Lady Margaret Kennedy (1630?–85?), daughter of John Kennedy, sixth earl of Cassilis. In May 1687 he married Mary Scott (c. 1660–98), by whom he had seven children. In May 1700 he was reported to have married "one Mr. Barclay's widdow of Worcestershire" (Luttrell, *4,* 649). Actually he married Elizabeth Blake (1661–1709), a spinster, by whom he had two children who died in infancy (Foxcroft, pp. 492–93, 508–09).

68. *Compton:* Henry Compton, bishop of London, the only bishop to sign the invitation to William of Orange in 1688, was overlooked for the primacy in 1691 and 1695 and became the only bishop to vote against the deprivation of the Tory bishop of St. David's for simony in 1699. In 1702 he was appointed a commissioner of trade and plantations *pro tempore* and in January 1705 succeeded Lord Weymouth as a permanent member at £1000 a year (Chamberlayne, 1702, p. 619; Luttrell, *5,* 504). His "defects of . . . intellect" are noted in DNB, *4,* 903.

70. *Western Prelates:* See *The Golden Age Restor'd,* headnote, pp. 488–90 above.

72. *Honest Tom of Cant.:* See 66 *n.,* above. In debate, Thomas Tenison, archbishop of Canterbury, was said to have "all the good qualities of a tailor's goose, which were, being very hot and heavy" (Burnet, 1823, *4,* 238 *n.*), but his sincerity was sometimes questioned. Thomas Hearne agreed that Tenison was "a man of some Learning, but of no Principles of Honesty and Conscience" (*5,* 153).

When *Ned,* omniscient Proto-Martyr,
To calver'd Salmon shall give Quarter,
Or leave his Trade of following after.

When *Essex* shall forswear the *Rummer,*
And spend with his own Wife a Summer,
And for *St. Albans* leave dear *Plummer.*

When *Wyndham*'s crooked fulsom Relict,
Of Scent and Shape intirely *Belgick,*
Shall be by *Bedford* deem'd *Angellick.*

When Men can fancy such a Whale,
And such old stuff is made a Stale,
To catch our silly Dukes withal.

73. *Ned:* "L[or]d Edward Russell" (*A*) (c. 1663–1714) was the third son of William Russell, first duke of Bedford, and the younger brother of Lord William Russell, the Whig martyr. He was a Whig member of parliament for Bedfordshire (1695–1705, 1708–13). Upon the accession of Anne he was replaced as treasurer of the chamber (1694–1702) by another Whig member, John Berkeley, viscount Fitzhardinge (Chamberlayne, 1694, p. 237; Luttrell, *4,* 708; *5,* 163).

74. *calver'd:* an epithet of various meanings applied to salmon; "A good deal of evidence points to the condition of a fish, the dressing or cooking of which has begun while it is still alive" (*OED*).

76. *Essex:* Algernon Capel, second earl of Essex (1670–1710), whose father was another Whig martyr, was known as "the lewdest young man of the town" (GEC, *5,* 146 *n.*). He was gentleman of the bedchamber to William III (1691–1702), with whom he served with distinction in Flanders as colonel of the 4th Dragoons (1693–1710). In February 1692 he married Lady Mary, eldest daughter of the earl of Portland, who was said to be "no Man's pleasure," but who bore a son and two daughters (Collins, 1741, *2,* 311–12; Holkham MS. 686, p. 264). Essex was said to have "no Genius for Business, nor will ever apply himself that Way." Although otherwise "well shaped," his "Gaping Mouth" was frequently noticed (Macky, p. 70; Holkham MS. 686, p. 125).
the Rummer: a tavern in Queen Street famous for its cooking (Thomas Brown, *Letters from the Dead to the Living,* 2nd ed., 1702, p. 15; Portland MS. Pw V 47, p. 199).

78. *St. Albans:* Essex's seat, Cassiobury Park, Hertsfordshire, is six miles southwest of St. Albans; its "fine Gardens and pleasant Groves" are noticed by Collins (1741, *2,* 311).
Plummer: The lady remains unidentified.

79. *Wyndham's . . . Relict:* See *The Golden Age Restor'd,* 59 *n.,* above.

81. *Bedford:* See *The Golden Age Restor'd,* 59 *n.,* above.

When Tear-shirt *Wharton,* fam'd for wenching,
His Whores and Gardens is retrenching,
Or shall consent to let the *French* in.

When *France* shall faithfully keep Leagues,
When *Maintenon* leaves State Intrigues,
And Men are born with two left Legs.

When these Strange things shall come to pass,
England will be, or I'm an Ass,
The strangest Queendom ever was.

85. *Wharton:* See *The Golden Age Revers'd,* 24 *n.,* above.

86. *Gardens:* Wharton's gardens were in Buckinghamshire, where he had two estates, one at Upper Winchendon, which he preferred, and another at Wooburn, "standing under the shadow of the richly-wooded hills, and adorned by a stately row of poplars," on which his father is said to have spent "nearly £40000" on improvements (Bryan Dale, *The Good Lord Wharton,* Congregational Union of England and Wales, 1901, pp. 42, 47).

88. *Leagues:* Louis XIV broke the second partition treaty with England and the Netherlands in November 1700 when he recognized his second grandson, Philippe d'Anjou, as Felipe V of Spain. Then he broke the treaty of Ryswick in September 1701 when he recognized James Francis Edward, the pretended prince of Wales, as James III, king of England, Scotland, and Ireland.

89. *Maintenon:* See *A Satyr upon the French King,* 91 *n.,* above. It was widely believed that "this Female Upstart," as she was called, "governs all absolutely" (Thomas Brown, *Letters from the Dead to the Living,* sig. A3r; Coxe, p. 540).

90. *two left Legs:* "Jacob Tonson" (*A*); cf. *Faction Display'd,* 377–79 *n.,* below.

On Dr. Birch
(June 1703[?])

"The King died," as the duchess of Marlborough remarked, "and the Princess of Denmark took his place" (*Account of the Conduct*, p. 121). But for the lower clergy of the Church of England there was no such nerveless transfer of power; there were fervent hopes for changes in the way this power was to be administered. Only three weeks after William's death Dr. Thomas Smith told Samuel Pepys (Pepys, *Corr.*, 2, 259) that "a numerous party" of the clergy who had "been kept under by Tenison and Burnett"

> greatly rejoyce that now, having got a Church of England Lady in the Throne, they shall have their share in the best and highest ecclesiastical dignityes and preferments as they shall become vacant.

The lower clergy hoped that the commission which William had established in April 1695 "to recommend fit persons to all ecclesiastical preferments" and which included, besides Tenison and Burnet, John Sharp, archbishop of York, Simon Patrick, bishop of Ely, and William Lloyd, bishop of Worcester, would be dissolved and that her majesty herself would dispose of all ecclesiastical preferments (Foxcroft, p. 406; Luttrell, 5, 157).

Even before there were vacancies, there were candidates: early in May 1702 it was said that Thomas Sprat, bishop of Rochester and dean of Westminster, was to be the queen's lord almoner, instead of the Whiggish bishop of Worcester; when Michael Boyle finally died on 10 December 1702, aged 92, it was rumored that Sprat would succeed him as lord primate of Ireland and that Dr. Peter Birch would be installed dean of Westminster (Luttrell, 5, 171, 251). On 23 December 1702 *The London Post* published the rumor that may have precipitated the present poem:

> We hear that Dr. Sprat, Bishop of Rochester and Dean of Westminster, will be made Archbishop of Armagh in Ireland,

And Lord Primate of all that Kingdom, and that Dr. Birch, Rector of St. Bride's, will succeed him in the See of Rochester.

Peter Birch (1652?–1710) was the fourth son of one of Cromwell's colonels. He compounded with his Presbyterian faith, however, to graduate B.A., M.A., and finally D.D. (1688) from Christ Church, Oxford. He was appointed chaplain to the duke of Ormonde, then to the House of Commons, and was installed a prebendary of Westminster in October 1689. He succeeded Tenison as rector of St. James, Piccadilly, in July 1692, but the House of Lords in January 1695 upheld the queen's presentation of this living to Dr. William Wake (HMC *Lords MSS.*, New Series, *1*, 399–400). Birch was consoled with St. Bride's, Fleet Street, to which he was instituted rector in March 1695 (James P. Malcolm, *Londinium Redivivum*, 2 vols., 1803, *1*, 358). By this time he had come to be "a great Stickler for the High-Church Party" and even Francis Atterbury was shocked at the boldness of his sermon on 30 January 1703 reflecting on the last reign (Boyer, *History*, p. 254; Atterbury, *Works*, *1*, 155).

There can be no doubt that Birch expected a miter. The bishopric of Rochester and the deanery of Westminster together were worth £2400 a year (Beatson, *1*, 215). Comparable figures for a prebendal stall in Westminster and the rectory of St. Bride's are difficult to estimate, but in 1680 these were put down at £60 and £16, respectively (*A Book of the Valuations of all the Ecclesiasticall Preferments in England and Wales*, 1680, pp. 190–91). In 1702 they may have been worth £300, so by "putting in for the Bishoprick" Birch was putting in to increase his stipend about eight times, and "money, as Peter Birch said, is a serious thing" (HMC *Portland MSS.*, *7*, 454).

There is no evidence to indicate who wrote this poem and there is conflicting, or at least equivocal, evidence about its date of composition. In one manuscript, *G* (probably a late one), the poem is dated 1702, and the particular rumor embodied in the subtitle of *FG* would cease to have any currency after 10 February 1703 when Narcissus Marsh was translated to Armagh. But the "action" of the poem—Birch's solicitation of the patronage of the duchess of Marlborough and the earl of Nottingham—occurs after the death of the young marquis of Blandford on 20 February 1703 (8 *n.* below). Furthermore, the titles of the earlier manuscripts are not at all specific and rumors involving Birch continued to circulate. In May 1703 it was said that "Dr. Birch stands fair for the bishoprick of St. Asaph, vacant by the death of Dr. Jones" (Atterbury, *Works, 1,* 211 *n.*). But most important of all may be the possibility that lines 51–55 refer to the death of Birch's third wife on 28 May 1703 (Luttrell, *5,* 298). So June 1703 may be the best guess for the date of composition.

On Dr. Birch

Among the little Pages that were sent
With Morning How-d'yes and a Compliment,
Was seen a lofty Member of the Church,
Whose Name I think they said was Dr. *Birch*.
With Primitive Humility he sate,
Fawning and cringing at the Lady's Gate,
Trying t'ingage the Porter in Discourse,
Whether her Grace were better now or worse:
In hopes by just Degrees he might ascend,
And to the waiting Maid his Business recommend.
The honest Porter, easy of Access,
Began his Brother Gown-man to caress:
And soon familiar grown, in close Debate
Told him some secret Mysteries of State.
The would-be Prelate vainly now began
To think he should the Dignity obtain;
And pleas'd with the new Friendship he had gain'd,
Hasted forthwith to kiss black *Dicky*'s hand;
Dicky the black, whose great and favorite Name

2. *Morning How-d'yes:* "Among Persons of any Fashion, it is the sole Employment of one Man to *register* the *Visits paid,* the *How-d'ye's sent,* the *Messages left;* that the Lady may repay the *same Visits,* return the *same How-d'ye's,* and send a Servant to leave the *same Messages*" (*The Man of Manners,* 3rd ed., n.d., p. 46).

5. *Primitive Humility:* meekness worthy of a Christian in the earliest and purest times.

6. *Fawning and cringing:* "it is in vain to imagine there is any so *good natured,* as that their *visits* . . . are without *particular ends.* . . . The first caution therefore that they are to observe, is, that their *language* be *full of submission, humility,* and *such deference* as also tendeth to the *debasing* of our selves: for we are born in an Age that is *extravagantly complemental*" (Henry Stubbe, *The Arts of Grandeur and Submission: Or, A Discourse concerning the Behaviour of Great Men toward their Inferiours; and of Inferiour Personages towards Men of Greater Quality,* 2nd ed., 1670, pp. 4, 25).

the Lady: Sarah Churchill, duchess of Marlborough.

8. *better now or worse:* "after the Death of her Son" (*FG*). Lady Marlborough's only son, John, born 13 January 1690, died of smallpox at Trinity College, Cambridge, on 20 February 1703.

18. *black Dicky:* "Dick Squash, the Ld. Nottinghams Black [page]" (*D*).

Is known as far as that of *Nottingham;*
Dicky, who to the Church was ever kind,
Thrice shook his Hand, thrice swore he'd be his Friend.
Slighted, contemn'd, and scorn'd by Men of Sense,
Noted for Ignorance and Impudence,
Thus meanly is he forc'd t'implore the Aid
Of Porter, Valet, Page, and Chambermaid.
  Now let us trace him to the Western Quire,
And see with what Applause he fills the Chair.
With such a Graceful Boldness does he teach,
You'd swear all was his own that he did preach.
So gay in borrow'd Feathers does he shine;
But *Sprat* and *South* are known in every Line.
For *South*'s deep Learning always will appear,
And *Sprat* will be distinguish'd by the Ear.

20. *Nottingham:* "Lord Nottingham," as the disappointed candidate for the bishopric of Carlisle, wrote in June 1703, "lays his hand on all church preferment. His brother, his chaplains, and his favourites are all taken care of" (HMC *Bagot MSS.,* p. 337). Nottingham had already succeeded in getting his brother, Henry Finch, promoted to the deanery of York, and his "favourites," Humphrey Prideaux to the deanery of Norwich, and William Nicolson to the bishopric of Carlisle (Luttrell, *5,* 164, 171).

24. *Ignorance and Impudence:* Hearne (*1,* 231) records that Birch was "a forward, illiterate Man." In 1693 or 1694, in St. James's, Piccadilly, of which he was then the rector, Birch preached a sermon for the king's birthday on the text, *Sufficient to each Day is the Evil thereof,* which gave "great Offence to the Court" (Boyer, *Annals,* 1711, p. 421); cf. 37 *n.,* below.

27. *the Western Quire:* Stowe records that a monastery built in 605, "partly from the Situation to the West, and partly from the Monastery or Miste . . . began to take the Name of *Westminster*" (Strype, *2,* [3]8). Birch had occupied a prebendal stall in Westminster since October 1689.

28. *Applause:* John Evelyn recorded several occasions on which Birch had given "an excellent discourse," or even "a very excellent discourse" (*Diary, 4,* 488, 529; *5,* 136–37).

31. *borrow'd Feathers:* "Dr. Pet. Birch of Xt Church has publish'd several Sermons, & preach'd some that are none of his own, particularly some of the Bp. of Rochester's and one of Dr. South's whilst the Dr. was present at the Hearing of it in the Abbey Church of Westminster: which occasion'd this Raillery of the Poet [quoting lines 35–38, below]" (Hearne, *1,* 231). South and Birch were both graduates of Christ Church, Oxford, and both prebendaries of Westminster.

33. *South's deep Learning:* Burnet (*2,* 213) agreed that South was "a learned but an ill-natur'd Divine."

34. *Sprat:* Thomas Sprat (1635–1713), bishop of Rochester and dean of Westminster, whose "Name deserves principally to be recorded in History, for his Mastery in the Art of *Oratory,* and his raising the *English* Language to that Purity and Beauty, which former Writers were wholly Strangers to, and those who come after him can but imitate" (Boyer, *History,* 260).

My Brother *Birch,* crys *Sprat* in Courtly Tone,
Hath to my Sermons too much Honour done.
Whilst rugged *South,* made of a coarser Mould,
Swears he's a Thief, and scandalously bold.
Some do indeed admire his wondrous Height,
As if he could support the Church's Weight;
That he alone could bear the Ballance down,
'Gainst Whiggish Primate and the *Scotish* Loon:
With Care he will the Right Divine maintain,
And many Female Proselytes he'll gain.
With the fair Sex Knaves still will most prevail,
Hypocrisy with them can never fail.
The crafty Priest well knows this subtle Art,
And will continue still to act his Part:
Whether in Midnight Healths the Bowl goes round,
Whether at Dice he is with Fortune crown'd;
Whether he forms some dark and deep Design,
(For killing Wives he never thought a Crime);

37. *South:* "Dr. *South* has another Volume of Sermons ready for the Press. . . . There is a Preface to one of these Sermons that concludes with a very severe Reflection upon Dr. *Birch* . . . who had the Impudence to preach one of his printed Sermons in the Collegiate Church of *Westminster* when the Author himself was present" (Hearne, *1,* 106).

42. *Whiggish Primate:* Thomas Tenison, archbishop of Canterbury; see *A Conference,* 147 *n.,* above.

Scotish Loon: Gilbert Burnet, bishop of Salisbury, was born in Edinburgh, educated at Marischal College, Aberdeen, became a probationer in the Church of Scotland while it was still under presbyterian government (1661), and was presented with his first living at Saltoun, in East Lothian (*DNB, 3,* 394–95).

52. *killing:* If this insinuation alludes to the death of Birch's third wife, the following incident related by Francis Atterbury may be relevant: "Dr. Birch buried his wife on Friday night last; your Lordship may judge with how little concern, when I tell you that on the evening before, while his wife lay dead, he went to my Lord Fitzharding's, and there married Mr. Chetwynd to my Lord's daughter; after Dr. Smalridge had been applied to, and had refused to do it, it being an uncanonical hour and place, and there being no extraordinary dispensation to warrant him. Dr. Birch overleaped all these formalities, for the sake of five or ten guineas, which helped to bear the charges the next day of his wife's interment" (*Works, 1,* 210–11).

Wives: Birch "had good Luck by rich Wives," as Thomas Hearne observed (*1,* 231). The first was Mary Waller, favorite daughter of the poet Edmund Waller (Aubrey, *2,* 280; *Poems, &c. . . . By Edmond Waller, Esq; The Tenth Edition, with Additions. To which is Prefix'd The Author's Life,* 1722, pp. xxxvi, xl); the second was Sybil Wyrley, youngest daughter and co-heir of Humphrey Wyrley, Esq., of Hampstead (John Booker, *A History of the Ancient Chapel of Birch,* Manchester, 1859, pp. 102–03); and the third was Martha, daughter of Samuel Viner, Esq., and relict of Francis

Whether his false deluding Tongue does move
To Matrimonial or Incestuous Love,
The——————————.
  But here my Muse, be silent as the Night
In which he acts those Scenes of leud Delight,
Lest thou transgress the bounds of Satyr's Laws,
Or Mother-Church espouse her Bully's Cause.

Millington, Esq., "a widdow worth £20,000" (Luttrell, *4*, 284), whom Birch married in September 1697 and who died on 28 May 1703, aged 50, "and left a considerable sum of money to the Doctor" (*The London Post*, 2 June 1703, cited in Atterbury, *Works, 1,* 211 *n*.).

Daniel Defoe

More Reformation. A Satyr upon Himself (*16 July 1703*)

The *hypocrites lecteurs* whose vices had been exposed in *Reformation of Manners* reacted predictably. They threatened violence, which made Defoe "Be cautious" how he went "abroad by Night" (line 772, below), and they charged Defoe with the same vices himself. "The vicious Party," as Defoe called them in the preface to *A True Collection of the Writings of the Author of the True Born English-man* (1703), "who are touch'd too warmly, in some of the Satyrs, are most industriously ransacking my Character, to make it, if possible, look like themselves" (sig. A5v).

More Reformation, in short, originated as a gesture of self-defense. By 2 January 1703, when he was arrested for publishing *The Shortest Way with the Dissenters,* Defoe had already begun a poem that would include "a State of the Case between my Errors and theirs; not at all to lessen my own, but [to] settle Matters between Vice and Repentance a little" (ibid. sig. A6r). At the height of his prosperity he was willing to "act the Pharisee a little" (*More Reformation,* 1703, sig. A4r) to provide a vehicle for further satire on the real "Scribes and Pharisees, hypocrites . . . full of extortion and excess." And for this presumption he was struck down immediately in what must have seemed to him an act of divine providence.

Most of the poem was written during the five months when Defoe was a fugitive from justice and it was finished in Newgate where he had been committed to prison during the queen's pleasure when he had literally nothing left to defend.

Although taken into custody on 2 January 1703 by the queen's messengers, Defoe managed somehow to escape—"to Jump out of the Window," according to one account (*The Shortest Way with the Dissenters: Or, Proposals for the Establishment of the Church. With its Author's Brief Explication Consider'd,* 1703, p. 22). He left his house in Tilbury and moved about London incognito. On 11 January 1703 a £50 reward was offered for information leading to his arrest and on 14 January the offer was repeated in *The London Gazette,* this time accompanied by the famous physical description of the fugitive (line 669 *n.,* below). On 24 February in the Old Bailey he was indicted in absentia for high crimes and misdemeanors in publishing *The Shortest Way with the Dissenters.* The next afternoon the House of Commons might be said to have prejudiced his case when it found this work "full of false and scandalous Reflections upon this Parliament, and tending to promote Sedition" and ordered it to be burned by the common hangman (*CJ, 14,* 207). If Defoe was still in London on 26 February he could have witnessed *The Shortest Way with the Dissenters* going up in flames in New Palace Yard, Westminster. The next day, when the queen came to the House of Lords to prorogue parliament, her speech from the throne convinced Defoe that *The Shortest Way with the Dissenters* had even offended her majesty, for what she said clearly cut off all hope of a pardon: "I think it might have been for the Publick Service," she said, "to have had some further Laws for restraining the great Licence, which is Assumed, of Publishing and Spreading Scandalous Pamphlets and Libels; but as far as the present Laws will extend, I hope you will all do your Duty in your respective Stations, to Prevent and Punish such Pernicious Practices" (*The Observator,* No. 73, 30 December 1702–2 January 1703; [Charles Gildon], *The Life and Strange Surprizing Adventures of Mr. D—— DeF—, of London, Hosier,* 1719, p. xi; *The London Gazette,* Nos. 3878–79, 7–14 January 1703; Moore, *Daniel Defoe,* pp. 120–21; Boyer, *Annals,* 1703, p. 225).

What had set this all in motion was Defoe's publication on 1 December 1702 of his most celebrated pamphlet, *The Shortest Way with the Dissenters* (line 690 *n.,* below) and Harley's insistence a few weeks later that it was "absolutely necessary for the service of the Government that [Nottingham] should endeavor to discover who was the author of it" (BM MS. Add. 29589, f. 400, cited in Moore, *Daniel Defoe,* p. 113). It would be futile now to speculate about the motives of Harley's action, but there can be no doubt about its result: "imprisonment," as John Robert Moore has said, "delivered Defoe . . . into Harley's hands" (*Defoe in the Pillory and Other Studies,* Bloomington, Indiana, 1939, p. 4).

Perhaps it was when he despaired of a royal pardon that Defoe "left his Lodging where he had been hid for some time, and removed to *Barnet* on the Edge of *Hertfordshire;* intending, as soon as he had settled some Family Affairs, to go away North into *Scotland;* But before he went away he was obliged to come once more to *London,* to sign some Writings for the securing some Estate, which it was fear'd might be seized by Out-law, if the Prosecution had gone on so far." While at Barnet Defoe dreamed that "he saw two Men come to the Door, who said they were *Messengers,* and produced a Warrant from [Nottingham] the Secretary of State to apprehend him, and that accordingly they seiz'd upon and took him." Eventually he did go to London and on 21 May 1703 "was taken by the Messengers, just in the very Manner as he had been told in his Dream" (*An Essay on the History and Reality of Apparitions,* 1727, pp. 220–22). At the time, however, he claimed that he had "surrendred at Discretion" and voluntarily submitted himself to "the Publick [not the royal] Clemency" (*More Reformation,* sig. A4v). But since someone collected the £50 reward for betraying him to the queen's messengers (Moore, *Daniel Defoe,* pp. 124, 126), Defoe's recollection 25 years after the fact is likely to be more accurate than his claim at the time. He was released on bail on 5 June and tried on 7 July in the Old Bailey for the crime of publishing a scandalous and seditious libel.

Defoe was ill advised by his counsel to plead guilty (Moore, *Daniel Defoe,* p. 129) and Sir Simon Harcourt, the new solicitor-general who had been knighted by the queen only a month before, by "bullying the Author then *at the Bar*" (*Review, 6* [27 December 1709], 454), emboldened the judges (lines 234–47, 795–815, below) to impose an unusually heavy sentence on the prisoner (line 854 *n.,* below).

The Shortest Way with the Dissenters was published three days after the House of Commons had passed a bill for preventing occasional conformity. On 28 February 1703 Defoe rushed into print another pamphlet explaining that *The Shortest Way with the Dissenters* had no intention of influencing pending legislation, but was merely employing "an *Irony not unusual*" to answer some pamphlets like Charles Leslie's *New Association* (1702) ([Defoe], *A Brief Explanation of a Late Pamphlet, Entituled, The Shortest Way with the Dissenters,* 1703, p. 2; Moore, p. 21). But even this explanation came too late, for the bill to prevent occasional conformity had been lost on 5 February when the Commons voted to "adhere to their disagreeing with the Lords in the Amendments made by their Lordships" (*CJ, 14*, 51, 183; [William Pittis], *The Proceedings of Both Houses of Parliament, In the Years 1702, 1703, 1704, upon the Bill to Prevent Occasional Conformity,* 1710, p. 35).

Defoe was unalterably opposed to the practice of occasional conformity (line 282 *n.*, below). He called it "*playing Bo-peep* with God Almighty" and considered it "sinful against God, scandalous to the Dissenters, and . . . fatal to their Interest" ([Defoe], *An Enquiry into the Occasional Conformity of Dissenters,* 1697, p. 17; *A True Collection,* sigs. A5v-A6r). So he was one of the few dissenters to support the bill against occasional conformity (line 339 *n.* below). This delighted the high flyers, of course, and worried low churchmen like young Benjamin Hoadly, but Edmund Calamy must have been right when he said, "I don't think Mr. *Foe* had so many followers or Abettors among the Dissenters, as our Author [Hoadly] seems to apprehend" (Edmund Calamy, *A Defence of Moderate Non-Conformity,* Part I, 1703, p. 226).

While he opposed occasional conformity as "a Religious Error," Defoe saw clearly that the Tories opposed it "as a Politick One" because "it lets the *Whigs* into Places, and State Employments" ([Defoe], *The Sincerity of the Dissenters Vindicated,* 1703, pp. 1–2) He saw as clearly as Gilbert Burnet that the purpose of the bill to prevent occasional conformity was "to [new-]model Corporations, and to cast out of them all those, who would not vote . . . for Tories" (*2*, 337). "Why is this Great Out-cry rais'd against the Dissenters for their *Occasional Communion,*" he asked. "These Gentlemen are Exasperated at it, as it lets the Dissenters into the Publick Exercise of the Government, and joins them to the Low Churchmen; and what a late Reverend Clergyman and no less a Statesman, said of this Case: 'The Sacramental Test was not Contriv'd in order to Rejoin the Whigs to the Church, but to keep them out of the State' " ([Defoe], *A New Test of the Church of England's Honesty,* 1704, p. 19).

Even more than the autobiographical interest, and even more than the attempts to define and limit the "Business" of satire, it is this unresolved political conflict that bristles in the verse of *More Reformation.* Defoe wanted dissenters in "the Publick Exercise of Government," but he did not want dissenters in government at the cost of their conscience. Even the title, *More Reformation,* implies this, for more reformation was not only the *basis* of dissent—"You think separation your duty in order to a *farther reformation,*" Hoadly sneered at them—but also the *condition* for dissenters to return to *"Constant Communion"* in the Church of England (Benjamin Hoadly, *The Reasonableness of Conformity to the Church of England,* Part II, 2nd ed., 1703, p. 114).

The date of publication of the poem, 16 July 1703, is given in the Luttrell copy in the British Museum (164.m.30).

More Reformation. A Satyr upon Himself

He that in Satyr dips his angry Pen,
To lash the Manners, and the Crimes of Men;
Pretends to bring their Vices on the Stage,
And draw the proper Picture of the Age:
If he be Mortal, if he be a Man,
They'l make a Devil of him if they can.
The meanest slip shall in a Glass be shown,
That by his Faults they may excuse their own:
So guided by their Passions, Pride, or Fate,
That they who should reform, recriminate:
And he that first reforms a vicious Town,
Prevents their ruin, but completes his own;
For if he was an Angel from on high,
He cannot 'scape the general Infamy:
They who resolve, they never will amend,
Assault him first, their Vices to defend;
And when his Lines may happen to convince,
They miss the Passions, tho' they touch the Sense.
By secret Pride, of which we all partake,
We'll hate the Doctrine for the Teacher's sake:
Scorn the Instruction, or, with high Disdain,
Tho' we receive the hint, abuse the Man;
As School Boys, when Corrected for a Fault,
Like what they learn, but hate the Man that taught.
Ill Nature is conspicuous enough
In Mankind's strong aversion to Reproof,
In which their Passions contradict their Sence,

2–3. *lash the . . . Vices:* Defoe clearly understood the risks he was running and as early as July or August 1702 anticipated that legal action might be taken against him. In the preface to *Reformation of Manners* he foresaw that "the Party" of vice would "suppress the Poet rather than the Crime" (*Reformation of Manners,* 1702, sig. A2v). Defending *The Shortest Way with the Dissenters,* publication of which was the pretext for the legal proceedings against him, was "no part of the Design" of the present poem (*More Reformation,* 1703, sig. A4v).

20. *hate the Doctrine:* Cf. *Reformation of Manners,* 928, above.

While Shame and Pride shut out their Penitence.
For Pride's the Native regent of the Mind,
And where it rules, it ruins all Mankind;
He that pretends to storm it, may as well
Assault the very Counterscarp of Hell:
Ten Thousand lesser Devils stand within,
To garrison their Frontier Town of Sin:
Whom e're this swelling Vapour does possess,
It never fails their Reason to suppress;
To struggle with it, is a vain pretence,
It masters all the Manners and the Sence;
But above all things, 'tis distinctly shown,
In that our least Mistakes we scorn to own:
Go on in Vice, because we hate to mend,
And won't acknowledge what we can't defend:
And if the sawcy Priests, or Poets, dare
To Lash the fashionable Vice we wear;
Nay, tho' their Language should convince the Age,
We'll hiss the grave Instructor off the Stage.
Shame, Pride's young Sister, and her self a Vice,
Prompts Nature next, Repentance to despise;
She talks of Honour, Scandal of the Times,
Blushes at Reformation, not at Crimes.
Men must be vicious, when they have begun,
The scandal of Acknowledgment to shun;
They must go on in Vice, because they're in,
Asham'd t'repent, but not asham'd to sin:
These Mens destruction no Man can prevent,
For Modesty has made them impudent.
The Difficulty in this Riddle lies;
The Virtue shou'd reform them is their Vice.
No proper Language can describe the case,
Too little Honesty, and too much Grace:
Cowards, whom Nature too much Courage lent,
Who dare to sin, but dare not to repent:
Fools, who unhappily are curst with Wit,

29–30. *Pride . . . ruins all Mankind:* Cf. Pope, "Nor Virtue, male or female, can we name,/But what will grow on Pride, or grow on Shame" (*An Essay on Man, II,* 193–94).

And know not how to Own what they commit.
These Arguments the latent Cause contain,
Why Mankind are so oft reprov'd in vain:
Their Modesty's the new uncommon Evil,
'Tis bad to sin, but to repent's the Devil.
He that offends, may ha' been Vice's Tool,
But to acknowledge, makes a Man a Fool;
Puts him quite out of Fashion in the Town,
And he that *Once* reforms, is *Twice undone.*
Satyr, while Men upon such Maxims move,
Expect no quarter, if thou wilt reprove;
If e're unhappily thou step'st awry,
Thy general Virtue's all condemn'd to die:
With a full Cry they'l join to hunt thee down,
By th' Universal Clamour of the Town.
Then first examin with a careful Hand,
And search the Ancient Statutes of the Land,
And if you miss the matter on Record,
See what assistance Reason will afford;
Enquire among the Sages, often try
The Rules of Wisdom and Philosophy,
And learn, if possible, from wiser Men,
Who us'd to be allow'd our Vices to condemn.
If Innocence alone must Guilt remove,
Where lives the Man that's fitted to reprove?
Whose Life will Scandal and Reproach prevent,
And never had occasion to repent?
If in our Circle such a Star should shine,
Thy Whips and Scorpions, *Satyr,* must resign:
He only cou'd a right of Scandal claim,
And he alone might honestly defame.
But since Mankind are all alike so frail,
That Crimes with life, come like Estates in tail;
All have an equal Title to reproach,
Except some few, who sin a Knot too much:

72. *Twice undone:* i.e. he admits he was undone (wrong doing) before and now undoes (repudiates) himself again; for a similar argument, see 347, below.

87–88. Cf. "If none but faultless Men must reprove others, the Lord ha' Mercy upon all our Magistrates; and all our Clergy are undignified and suspended at a Blow" (*Reformation of Manners,* sig. A2r).

He that has all his own Mistakes confest,
Stands next to him who never has transgrest,
And will be Censur'd for a Fool by none,
But they who see no Errors of their own:
For Innocence in Men, can not be meant
Of such as ne're offend, but as repent;
Therefore of them that Vices reprehend,
'Tis not requir'd, that they should ne'er offend:
But this they always owe to Gods and Men,
Not to commit the Vices they Condemn;
Nor to be quite subdu'd by general Crimes,
Not first Debauch, and then Reform the Times.
 Satyr is Nonsense, when it comes from those
Who practise all the Errors they expose;
This is reforming of the World by halves,
And all the Satyr points upon themselves;
Directly tells us, their own Names are meant,
As if they sin'd on purpose to repent.
 Yet is it not thy Business to decry
The vulgar Errors of Society?
Humane Infirmities are not the Crimes,
For which thou art to scandalize the Times;
Nor is it fit for thee to call to mind,
Or banter the Misfortunes of Mankind;
For if their Sins and Sorrows must come in,
Thy Satyr must upon thy self begin.
Since none that ever wrote a Line before
Of *these,* has had, so many of *those,* has more:
 Malice shall write thy Character in vain,

99–102. Quoted on the title page of John Dunton, *The Life and Errors,* 1705.

99. *Mistakes confest:* "I began this Satyr, with Owning, in my self, those Sins and Misfortunes which I am no more exempted from than other Men, and as I am far from pretending to be free from Humane frailties, but forwarder to confess any of the Errors of my Life, than any Man can be to Accuse me" (*More Reformation,* sig. A3r).

108. "That no Man is qualified to reprove other Mens Crimes, who allows himself in the Practice of the same, is very readily granted, and is the very Substance and Foundation of the following Satyr" (*Reformation of Manners,* sig. A2r).

119. *Infirmities:* "Nor does the *Satyr* assault private Infirmity, or pursue Personal Vices" (*Reformation of Manners,* sig. A2v). "I have always carefully avoided lashing any Man's private Infirmities, as being too sensible of my own" (*More Reformation,* sig. A3r).

127. *thy Character:* "Satyr's" (i.e. Defoe's) character.

Thou know'st more Faults than thy Describers can;
But let the Man that pens thy History
Correct his own, and first repent like thee:
He's welcome then his Satyr to advance,
And gorge his rising Spleen with thy Mischance:
'Tis vain, against thy Crimes to raise a Storm,
Let those recriminate who first reform:
Let them expose thy Errors to the Town,
As freely as if they themselves had none:
Thou shalt go unreprov'd, 'till they repent,
But first let them reform, and thou'rt content.
   If ever yet thou did'st pretend to be
From Passions, Pride, or from Misfortunes free,
In this thou hast been guilty of a Crime,
Blacker than all the Vices of the Time.
   Nay, if it should be thy severer Fate,
That those thou hast reprov'd, recriminate;
And as, in Malice, it is often found,
Should forge on thee the Crimes with which themselves abound;
Thy Pen shall never plead thine Innocence,
Nor write one angry Line in thy Defence;
Because thy guilty Thoughts can call to Mind
More secret Crimes, than ever they could find.
   Yet tell them who their darling Vices love,
Thou still retain'st a Title to reprove;
For this thy Satyr's Credit shall Restore,
Thy faults are less, and thy Repentance More.
   Nor will Recrimination ever do't,
For common Vices are not in Dispute;
But let the Men who think thou dost 'em wrong,
And are so touch'd and angry at thy Song,
Rummage the bottom of thy Character,
To find the Crimes which thou hast banter'd there;

128. *Faults:* "they that search for Faults may find them plenty" (Defoe, *A True Collection,* sig. A6r).

138. *reform:* "the only way to make him do them Justice is to reform" (*Reformation of Manners,* sig. A2v).

148. *Defence:* "I scorn to make a Satyr the Method of showing my private Resentment" (*More Reformation,* sig. A3r).

160. *Crimes:* "I am not a Drunkard, or a Swearer, or a Whore-master, or a busy

And if with Truth of Conduct they can find
Those Crimes in thee, for which thou blam'st Mankind,
Then let them blast thy Satyr and condemn
The Partial Malice of thy ill-bred Pen,
Then let thy Rhymes be Curst, *but not till then.*
Gildon Writes Satyrs, rails at Blasphemy,
And his next Page Lampoons the Deity;
Exposes his *Darinda*'s Vitious Life,
But keeps six Whores, and starves his modest Wife;
Sets up for a Reformer of the Town,
Himself a First Rate *Rake* below Lampoon.
To Sin's a Vice in Nature, and we find
All men to Error and Mistakes enclin'd,
And Reprehension's not at all uncivil,
But to have *Rakes reprove us,* that's the Devil.
Seaton, if such a thing this Age can show,
Sets up for an instructing sober *Beau,*
An Air of Gravity upon his Brow,
And wou'd be Pious too, if he knew how;
His Language Decent, very seldom Swears,
And never fails the Play-House, nor his Prayers;
Vice seems to ha' been banish'd from his Doors,
And very, very, very seldom Whores.
His Brother Fops he drags to Church to Pray,

Body, or Idle, or Revengeful, &c. . . . and I challenge all the World to prove the contrary" (*More Reformation,* sig. A4r).

166. *Gildon* (*Key*): These lines may refer to "Satires and Fables," pp. 22–44 of *Examen Miscellaneum* (1702), of which Gildon is usually supposed to have been only the editor (*CBEL, 2,* 576). The anonymous satirist does indeed adopt a moral tone that would be appropriate to Charles Leslie's most celebrated convert (*The Pacificator,* 272 *n.,* above), but there seems to be nothing that "Lampoons the Deity." Part of Defoe's antipathy to Gildon proceeds from Gildon's revival of John Wilmot, earl of Rochester (190–91, below). Gildon edited the second volume of Rochester's *Familiar Letters* (1697) and included Rochester's verse in *Examen Miscellaneum.*

168. *Darinda:* These lines identify Gildon as the author of *Cleon to Dorinda* in *A New Miscellany of Original Poems on Several Occasions,* 1701, pp. 134–41. Since Dorinda is faithless, Cleon leaves his "tedious home,/To seek some Desart where no Women come," an affectation that Defoe exposes in the next line: "But keeps six Whores, and starves his modest Wife." Theophilus Cibber records that "to crown his other imprudences, [Gildon] married, without improving his reduced circumstances thereby" (Cibber, *Lives, 3,* 326).

176. *Seaton* (*Key*): unidentified.

And checks the Ladies if they talk too Gay:
But *Seaton* most unhappily has fix'd
On two Extreams which never can be mix'd;
For it will all the Power of Art out-do,
To join the new Reformer and the Beau.
Some that look out for Wit, and love to Read,
Are raising Bully *Strephon* from the Dead;
His vitious Lines they say will Vice Lampoon,
And *Rochester* shall now Convert the Town:
What tho' the Baudy runs thro' all he Writ,
The more the Wickedness, the more the Wit.
The vilest Scene which in his Verse appears,
Will ruin Leudness by the Dress she wears;
And thus with lame pretences they revive
Those Lines when Dead, he blush'd at whilst alive:
As if Mankind could not discern their Evil,
Without a naked Vision of the Devil.
Like some Gay Ladies who, as Authors say,
First for the vitious part approve the Play;
But threaten they would all the work refuse,
Did not the Wit the Leuder part excuse.
These worse than *Rochester* prepare to sin,
And act the Follies he left off, again:
Like him they boldly venture on the Crime,
But think not of Repenting too like him.
Pleas'd with the Lines he wish'd he had not Writ,
They Court his Folly, and pass by his Wit.
Some, *Satyr,* make thy sharp Rebukes in vain,
Whose Reformation no Man can Explain:
The fault which they're reprov'd for, they forsake,
And change of Vices not of Manners make,
Transpose their Crimes, which they by turns commit,
And manage their Repentance by their Wit.
These from thy Satyr always were secure,
Fenc'd by the Mask of Penitence they wore;

191. *Strephon:* "[John Wilmot, earl of] Rochester" (*Key*); see *Reformation of Manners,* 641 *n.*, above. New editions of Rochester's *Poems, &c. On Several Occasions* were published in 1691, 1696, and 1701, and a second volume of his *Familiar Letters,* edited by Charles Gildon, appeared in 1697.

197. *by the Dress:* i.e. by dressing "Leudness" unattractively.

Busie to Cure the Error of the Times,
But shams of Reformation hide their Crimes.
The course of Nature does their faults renew,
And when they lay one down, they take up two.
These are the *Royal Companies* of Vice,
Whose Reformation in their out-side lies;
Who Shift their Crimes about from hand to hand,
And *Stock-job* Sin, as men transfer their Land;
The *Devil's Brokers* for Exchanges, who
Old *Whiston, Haynes,* or Leuder *Crisp* out-do.
These are *Dissenters* from the Modes of Vice,
But hold *Occasional Conformities;*
A general Virtue openly profess,
But *as occasion offers,* can Transgress.
D——d's a Penitent, his Former Days
Were spent in all the high Extremes of Vice;
At *Rome,* at *Paris,* and where'ere he came,
The Bravoes knew his Face, the Whores his Fame.
His Bully Sword he now forbears to draw,
Repents of Blood, and Murthers now by Law;
Reforms his open Leudness, and begins
To mingle some Discretion when he Sins;

221. *shams of Reformation:* Cf. *Reformation of Manners,* 2 *n.,* above.

229. *Whiston:* There was a James Whiston, a projector (Luttrell, *3,* 258, 264; cf. *Reformation of Manners,* 319 *n.,* above), but nothing more is known of him.

Haynes: probably Joseph Haines or Haynes (c. 1648–1701), actor, playwright, and "Secretary of State to the Nine" (Wood, *4,* 527; Portland MS. Pw V 48, p. 214). His specialty was speaking prologues while mounted on an ass and several anecdotes "of indescribable nastiness" are told about him (*DNB, 8,* 888). One of his poems, *The City Regiment* (1689), is included in *POAS,* Yale, *5.*

Crisp: presumably not Henry Crisp, the common serjeant ([Defoe], *A New Discovery of an Old Intreague,* 1691, p. 34), who died in October 1700 (Luttrell, *4,* 699), but "Crisp the Broker," who went bankrupt in 1703 (BM MS. Add. 4291, f. 29).

231. *Occasional Conformities:* See headnote, pp. 549–50 above.

234. *D——d:* "D——d, K— . . . [are] no particular Persons, but put in to introduce the Characters" (*Key*). Despite this disclaimer, Robert Dashwood (c. 1687–1728), eldest son of Sir Robert Dashwood, of Northbrooke, Oxfordshire, first baronet, is a good candidate. In August 1703 he was issued a passport to travel to Holland, but later in the same month he fought a duel with Lord Wharton and they had to be parted by the guards. He died in Paris (*CSPD 1703–1704,* p. 321; Luttrell, *5,* 334; James Townsend, *The Oxfordshire Dashwoods,* Oxford, 1922, p. 13). He was a first cousin of Sir Samuel Dashwood, the Tory lord mayor of London (*The Golden Age,* 18 *n.,* above), who was one of the judges before whom Defoe was indicted in February and tried in July 1703.

Has learnt to blush, and pleads in Scripture Phrase,
And shakes his Head at his own leuder Days.
The outside of Repentance may proceed,
But still the Devil and the Man's agreed:
He changes publick Crimes for private Vice,
And where's the Reformation pray of this?
  K—'s a Dissenter and severe of Life,
Instructs his Household, and *Corrects his Wife;*
Reproves a Stranger, if he hears him Swear,
For Vice and he ha' been some Years at War;
But Sins of Inclination will remain,
Eclipse the Christian, and Expose the Man:
For Wine's the darling Devil of his Life;
This reconciles the Anti-Christian strife
Betwixt the Convert and his former Friends,
And for his Reformation makes amends.
Religion seems to have possest his Soul,
But Vice Corrupts the Parts, and Taints the whole,
Infects his painted Piety and Zeal,
And shows the Hypocrite he'd fain conceal.
The Bottle Conquers all his Reformation,
And makes Religion stoop to Inclination.
Lectures and Sermons he frequents by Day,
But yet comes home at Night too Drunk to Pray;
Yet too much Piety is his Disease,
Thank Heaven! there's few such Hypocrites as these;
That wipes his Mouth, and acts without remorse,
Sins and Repents, Repents and sins in course.
  All this to true Religion's no Disgrace.
For Hypocrites encrease in every place.
The Church may the Dissenters then despise,
When they themselves are free from men of Vice;
And Whigs may Church Integrity decry,

248. *K*—. This may be William King (1663–1712), "miscellaneous writer" *(DNB, 11,* 161). He was an advocate in Doctors' Commons, a Tory and high churchman, who published *Dialogues of the Dead* (1699) attacking Richard Bentley, and *Some Remarks on the Tale of a Tub* (1704) attacking Swift.

268. *wipes his Mouth:* Cf. [Defoe], *An Enquiry into the Occasional Conformity of Dissenters,* 1697, pp. 24–25: "[Occasional conformists make] the Sacred Institutions of Christ Jesus . . . Pimps to their Secular Interest, and then wipe their Mouths, and sit down in the Church, and say, *They have done no Evil.*"

When none are so but men of honesty;
For Party Vice can no Religion blame,
But Knaves of all Religions are the same;
The Villain in his Heart will still be so,
Tho' he to Church or *Conventicles* go.
The Sacred Mask put on, the Man may come
And joyn with all the sorts in Christendom.
Satyr forbear to touch the *honest few,*
Who are to Honour and to Conscience true;
Whom no Occasional Pretence can bribe,
No byass turn, or human force prescribe.
These are the Favourites of God and Man,
Whom Kings need never fear, nor Laws restrain;
They never study to embroil the State,
Nor Mortgage their Religion to be Great.
Tho' Oaths or Sacraments they may decline,
'Tis not from subtle Reasons, but Divine;
The private scruples in the Conscience fix'd,
From int'rest free, and with design unmix'd:
And therefore when by Fear or Honour mov'd,
Their Native Honesty is quickly prov'd.
This with a just contempt they can defie,
And *that* with equal constancy deny.
With steady Faith they serve the Government,
In Judgment, not in Charity dissent:
To the Establish'd Church they yield the hand,
For Conscience only they dispute Command;
And those few Doubts which force them to divide,
Are from Necessity and not from Pride:

277. *Knaves:* See *Reformation of Manners,* 759 *n.*, above.

282. *the honest few:* dissenters who refused to conform occasionally to the Church of England to qualify for a place in the government. "Occasional Communion," Defoe said, "is contrary to the very Nature and Being of a Dissenter; who, if he can Conform, ought to Conform; and if he can for a Place of Preferment, ought to do it without that Preferment" (*An Enquiry into Occasional Conformity,* 1702, p. 26).

284. *Pretence:* e.g. "to make themselves room in the Publick Advancements, and Glittering Gawdy Honours of the Age" ([Defoe], *An Enquiry into the Occasional Conformity of Dissenters,* 1697, p. 14).

302. *few Doubts:* according to Defoe, the dissenters agreed with the Church of England "in all the Fundamentals of Doctrine, and Sign to 36 of your 39 Articles" (*More Short-Ways with the Dissenters,* [April] 1704, p. 12).

Events or Causes are not their pretence,
These they resign with Peace to Providence:
They seek no Place for Profit or Applause,
Are Friends to *Caesar* and to *Caesar*'s Laws:
In Quietness and Peace is their delight,
And always where they can't obey, submit:
For the Establish'd Government they Pray,
To the Establish'd Government they Pay,
With hearty Zeal, Sincerity and Love,
Which both the Christian and the Subject prove:
The *English* Crown they chearfully maintain,
And wish that where it is, it may remain.
The Church they can't Conform to they defend,
Its Civil Power uphold, its Sacred Power befriend;
With Tolleration they are well content,
And these are they the Tolleration meant:
No Government would such as these oppress,
Or wish to make their little numbers less.
What tho' we think their Consciences mis-led,
Conscience is positive, and must b' obey'd;
And he that's faithful to its Dictates, goes
Direct and steady to the Truth he knows;
And they that find a nearer way than he,
May blame his Knowledge, not his Honesty.
But he's the Hypocrite who both ways bends,
Whose doubling Conscience serves his private Ends;

308. *Quietness:* "For points obscure are of small use to learn;/But *Common quiet* is *Mankind's concern*" (Dryden, *Religio Laici,* 449–50).

318. *Tolleration:* The Act of Toleration (May 1689)—"the Great Charter of religious liberty," as Macaulay called it—exempted Protestant dissenters from the penal laws requiring attendance in the Church of England, if they would take oaths of allegiance to William and Mary and subscribe to a declaration against transubstantiation. The dissenting clergy were exempted from the penal laws if they would, in addition, subscribe to 34 of the 39 articles. It is remarkable that Defoe should be "content" with this arrangement, for (in Macaulay's words again) "the Toleration Act recognized persecution as the rule, and granted liberty of conscience only as the exception" (Macaulay, *3,* 1386–92; Ogg, *3,* 231–33).

329. *doubling Conscience:* Cf. "First, Sir, I am to tell you, that I am, and acknowledge my self to be, possess'd with a strong Aversion to Doubling and Shifting in Points of Religion" ([Defoe], *A Letter to Mr. How, by Way of Reply to His Considerations,* 1701, pp. 4–5).

To day can from the Establish'd Church divide,
To morrow can his Conscience sell to avarice and Pride;
Alternate Oaths and Sacraments can take,
Alternate Sacraments and Oaths can break;
On one hand can the Establish'd Church defie,
And when *occasion offers* can comply:
No *Tollerating Laws* can these defend,
To these no *Royal Promises* extend;
The Nation should determine this dispute,
By Timely Laws, lest Heaven it self shou'd do't.
  In vain to Honesty they may pretend,
Vain are the shifts the Practice to defend;
He never can be steady to the Truth,
Who builds with one hand, and pulls down with both.
  They that for Conscience sake at first Dissent,
Can ne're Conform again till they repent:
The actions of themselves so distant lye,
They stab the first Dissent when they comply:
The scruple's banish'd by instructing light,
As Day succeeds the darkness of the Night.
  But some to distant Ages will retire,

337. *Royal Promises:* In her speech proroguing parliament on 25 May 1702 Anne had promised to "be very careful to preserve and maintain the Act of Toleration, and to set the Minds of all my People at Quiet" (Boyer, *Annals,* 1703, p. 42). Then, after allowing Archbishop Sharp to convince her that the bill against occasional conformity would not undermine the Act of Toleration (*Letters of Eminent Men Addressed to Ralph Thoresby,* 2 vols., 1832, *1,* 436), she mobilized all the resources of the court to secure passage of the bill, which disturbed the minds of all her people. In her speech at the conclusion of the next session, therefore, she found it necessary to repeat her assurances—in slightly different but very significant terms: "I hope that such of [my Subjects] as have the Misfortune to Dissent from the Church of *England,* will rest Secure and Satisfied in the Act of Toleration, which I am firmly resolved to Maintain" (Boyer, *Annals,* 1703, p. 224).

339. *Laws:* i.e. against occasional conformity. As a dissenter who supported the bill to prevent occasional conformity, Defoe was attacked on all sides, "like a Dog with a Broom at his Tail" (*More Reformation,* sig. A2v).

343. *builds . . . pulls down:* "None but Protestants halt between *God* and *Baal;* Christians of an Amphibious Nature, that have such Preposterous Consciences, that can believe one Way of Worship to be right, and yet serve God another way themselves . . . 'Tis like a workman, that Builds with one Hand, and pulls down with t'other" [(Defoe] *An Enquiry into the Occasional Conformity of Dissenters,* p. 10).

347. Cf. ibid., p. 13: "by Conforming I deny my Dissent being lawful."

And of the Church's Infant Years enquire;
And there from Apostolick Practice try
To back the grand Mistake with Scriptural Authority:
St. *Paul,* they tell us, sometimes did refuse,
And sometimes joyn'd in Worship with the *Jews:*
To Day would Christian Proselytes Baptise,
To Morrow Hebrew Converts Circumcise.
Crowds of Dissenting Christians from them draw,
Exalt the Gospel, and Preach down the Law;
Yet as occasion offer'd, too, thought fit
To Synagogues and Sanhedrims submit.
And this they very Learnedly apply,
To their Occasional Conformity.
No Man can certainly be thus mistaken,
But he that's of his Senses first forsaken;
Since he that has but half an Eye may see
The Reasons differ, tho' the Facts agree;
The distant Circumstances soon will tell,
The Lame and Incoherent parallel.
For *Law* and *Gospel* were the very same,
From one Divine Original they came:
Law was but *Gospel* under Types conceal'd,
And *Gospel* was those Types and *Laws* reveal'd;
The Sacred Institution only dy'd,
Because the thing was come it signifi'd;
The Types and Figures could no more remain,
Because the Substance made the Shadows plain,
The meaning of the Law was not destroy'd,
Only the Gospel made th' Occasion void;
The Sacred Substance still remain'd alive,
In its Eternal Representative.
The equal Object equally will last,
That of a Christ to come, *this* of a Jesus past.

351. *Infant Years:* "And if *John*'s Ministry was *the beginning of the Gospel,* as St. *Mark* calls it, Christianity had its first beginning in *Occasional Conformity*" ([James Owen], *Moderation a Virtue,* 1703, p. 7).

354. *St. Paul:* "St. *Paul,* the Apostle of the *Gentiles,* was eminent for *Occasional Conformity* . . . He judges the *Occasional Use* of the *Levitical* Ceremonies *lawful* . . . but the *Constant Use* of 'em to be *sinful* . . . And therefore he Circumcises *Timothy,* but would not Circumcise *Titus*" (ibid., p. 8).

Thus both in equal strength remain alive,
That Antecedent, *this* the Relative;
The Circumstances to one Center came,
And were not two Religions, but the same.
Their high successive Order was Divine,
Where *that* determin'd, *this* was to begin;
So that the Man who did with *this* comply,
Did not by Consequences *that* deny.
The Knife with which the Rabby Circumcis'd,
The Font in which the Christian was Baptis'd,
Were all the same, the same they signifi'd,
And only one another they supply'd;
Both had their Sanction from the high Command,
And the same thing by both we understand:
No scruple therefore justly cou'd arise,
Whether to cut the *Foreskin* or Baptise.
The same in Ceremonies holds as true,
The Jewish Rites the Christian Doctrines view;
Their *Altars, Sacrifices, Incense, Smoke,*
Attonements, Sprinklings, Blood, and *Priests* t'invoke;
The *Temple, Holy-place,* and *Mercy Seat,*
Feasts, Passovers, New-Moons, forbidden Meat,
All these the great *Messias* represent,
For him they all were made, and him they meant.
Human Inventions were not here impos'd;
Where Heaven Commands the Conscience is foreclos'd.
And all the Scruples that cou'd here remain,
Was but where *this* shou'd end, or *that* begin:
Here was no Civil Power or Military,
To make indifferent *things* be necessary:
Nothing was insignificant or vain,

408. *Human Inventions:* This was one of the things which dissenters were said to dissent against, "Human Mixtures in the Ministration, as the Cross, Surplice, &c." ([Defoe], *The Sincerity of the Dissenters Vindicated, from the Scandal of Occasional Conformity,* 1703, p. 15).

413. *indifferent things:* This was a technical phrase in the language of dissent. The apologists for nonconformity justified their separation from the Church of England on the grounds that the Church imposed "things own'd to be indifferent, as Terms of Communion," or things "otherwise indifferent, [but] made necessary by . . . the Civil Magistrate." This point worried Defoe, for, as he said, if "the Difference between Us and the Establish'd Church be only in dubious and small Matters . . . I know not

Nothing was doubtful, nothing was humane;
'Twas all from Heaven, and tho 'twas near its end,
Its great beginning did their awe Command.
If this be all we find to justifie
This Modern Hetrodox Conformity,
The lame Precedent no Example draws,
But leaves the Practice Modern as the Cause.
Besides, if 'twill not thus be understood,
Jewish Conformity may still be good:
Christians may when they think it fit Baptise,
Or as *Occasion* offers Circumcise;
The Talmud use instead of Common Prayer,
Altars and Sacrifices now prepare:
We may their Feasts, New-Moons, and Fasts divide,
And *Pentecost* observe for *Whitsontide;*
If we the Apostle's Practice will avow,
Because 'twas Lawful then, *'tis Lawful now;*
Christians their Ancient Rites may first refuse,
And then *Occasionally* turn to Jews.
But if to Scripture Periods we refer,
We find no Mystery, nor Wonder there;
The Matter's plain, the Difficulty's solv'd,
The Type was in the Typifi'd dissolv'd:
But 'till the Perfect Union, 'tis as plain,
'Till one was fixt, the other might remain.
How readily a sinking Cause applies
To weak and unassisting Vanities!
And how industriously will men defend
The Faults on which their Interest does depend!
Satyr, thou may'st the farther search refrain,

---

how we shall Ward off the Blow of being guilty of Schism" (*A Letter to Mr. How, By Way of Reply to his Considerations,* 1701, pp. 16, 17).

419. *Hetrodox Conformity:* Cf. *Reformation of Manners,* 817 *n.,* above.

421. *Practice Modern:* Defoe argued that "the Practice of this Scandalous Conformity was new" and that the Anabaptist Sir John Shorter, whom James II had made lord mayor of London in 1687, was the first instance of it (*An Enquiry into the Occasional Conformity of Dissenters,* 2nd ed., sig. A2r; Evelyn, *4,* 562 *n.*). James Owen replied that "*Occasional Conformity* is no new Thing, but is warranted in some Cases by the most sacred and uncontestable Precedents" (*Moderation a Virtue,* p. 7).

423. *Jewish Conformity:* Defoe depends upon his readers' anti-Semitism to reduce Owen's arguments to an absurdity.

And let the latent Arguments remain;
He that his baffl'd Conscience can defie,
Will Arguments and Principles deny:
To talk where Pride and Profits are to come,
Is preaching Gospel to a Kettle-Drum.
  Interest, like one of *Jeroboam*'s Calves,
In all Religions will at least go halves;
But where it gets a little oversway,
It hurries all our Honesty away.
If Conscience happens to maintain its ground,
And is too long on the Defensive found,
The vigorous Siege is carry'd on so fast,
'Tis ten to one but it's subdu'd at last.
But if the Scruple happens to remain,
Religion's twisted up, that Scruple to Explain.
To this great Idol, Conscience learns to bow,
And what was *Error* once, is *Order* now.
  Satyr, forbear, industriously refrain,
The Sacred Name of *Conscience to prophane;*
Cunning and Craft may take up the Disguise,
But *Conscience* must be under some Surprise:
And, when he's well recover'd, will raise a storm,
'Tis ten to one 'twill make them all reform:
He can the strongest Resolution break,
And *will be heard,* when he thinks fit to speak:
The stoutest Courage never could sustain
The shocks of Conscience, the Attempt's in vain.
  The Atheist feels *this trifle* in his breast,
And, while he Banters, trembles at the Jest;
The secret Trepidation racks his Soul,

449. *preaching Gospel to a Kettle-Drum:* Cf. [Defoe], *An Argument, Shewing, That the Prince of Wales, Tho' a Protestant, Has no Just Pretensions to the Crown of England,* 1701, p. 24: "What's the Gospel to a Kettle-Drum" (*Huntington Library Quarterly, 28* [November 1964], 55).

450. *Jeroboam's Calves:* Jeroboam, first king of Israel, established rival religious centers to Jerusalem at Dan and Bethel and set up in each a golden figure of Mnevis, the sacred calf of Heliopolis, with the legend: "Behold thy God which brought thee up out of the land of Egypt" (1 Kings 12:28–33; Nehemiah 9:18).

471. *shocks of Conscience:* Cf. *The Mitred Club,* 62, above; *An Elegy on the Author of the True-Born-English-Man. With an Essay on the Late Storm,* 1704, p. 48: "Even *Vile Blackbourn* felt some shocks of Grace."

And when he says, *No God;* replies, *Thou Fool.*
Of *Sleep* it robs their Nights, of *Joy* the Day,
Makes Monarchs stoop to Fear, *and Kings obey;*
Distracting thoughts in all their Mirth 'twill raise,
And strange regret to pleasant acts conveys.
Kingdoms and Governments it keeps in awe,
For Conscience is superior to the Law.
No Acts of Parliament can here constrain,
But Force or Fraud are equally in vain.
Dispensing Power has here a legal force,
For Laws to conquer Conscience *cease of course;*
And where a Law commands a Man to sin,
The Law goes out, and lets the Libel In.
Men never could commit Mistakes, would they
This *Constant wakeing Centinel obey;*
Would they within this Cabinet retire,
And of this *Faithful Councellor* enquire,
Of every action, they might quickly know
Whether it was an honest one or no.
Conscience must be the only thing that's meant,
When we express our Reasons for Dissent;
They who another Argument can make,
Let them stand up, and bid their Reasons speak:
For he that can Dissent, and yet comply,
I own has learnt a Doctrine more than I.
Satyr, with them thy future Portion seek,
Who use no Arts their Conscience to bespeak;
But listening to his honest dictates, they
With care enquire, and then with care obey.
If e're thou turn thy Pen *to banter these,*
May all thy power of Satyr from thee cease;

480. *it:* conscience.

486. *Law commands a Man to sin:* Defoe probably refers to occasional conformity: while the Test Act (1673) did not actually command a man to sin (conform occasionally), it provided both an incentive and a sanction for this practice, which the bill to prevent occasional conformity would have removed.

495. *Reasons:* In *The Sincerity of the Dissenters Vindicated, from the Scandal of Occasional Conformity,* 1703, p. 15, Defoe lists five of the reasons commonly given for dissenters to dissent, including the one mentioned above, 408 *n.,* and comments: "This is a Satyr upon the Church of *England* and the True and Real Grounds of a Dissenter's Separation."

May Heaven deny thee Wit as well as Bread,
Thou cease to Write, and wise Men cease to Read.
For against these it is in vain to Write;
Sharp will not here find out his Hypocrite,
And were we all like these, *there's none wou'd try't.*
Hoadly would answer *Callamy* in vain,
Only to help him baffle him again:

509. *Sharp:* John Sharp (1645–1714) graduated B.A. from Christ's College, Cambridge, in 1663 and soon became one of the best preachers of the day. He survived the persecutions of James II's court of ecclesiastical commission to enjoy "no small favour" at the court of William and Mary and was installed archbishop of York in October 1691. He was said to be *"not absolutely attached to a party"* until the accession of Anne, but then the influence of his lifelong patron, the earl of Nottingham, "brought him over to be head of the high church party." He preached the sermon at the coronation, succeeded Lloyd as the queen's lord almoner, and managed the bill against occasional conformity in the House of Lords. He was *"a plain-dealing man* . . . who neither disguised his sentiments on any occasion, nor feared at any time to take the liberty of following his own judgment" and he had expressed his opinion of occasional conformists in 1684, when he called them "false Pretenders to Conscience" (*DNB, 17,* 1346–47; Thomas Sharp, *The Life of John Sharp,* 2 vols., 1825, *1,* 253, 254; *Letters of Eminent Men Addressed to Ralph Thoresby,* 2 vols., 1832, 1, 436–37; [John Sharp], *A Discourse concerning Conscience,* 1684, p. 40).

511. *Hoadly:* Benjamin Hoadly (1676–1761), the Anglican apologist and bishop, in succession, of Bangor (1715–21), Hereford (1721–23), Salisbury (1723–34), and Winchester (1734–61), graduated from Catherine Hall, Cambridge, in January 1696 and was elected fellow the next year. In 1701 he was appointed lecturer at St. Mildred's, in the Poultry. His "answer" to Calamy, published in two parts in 1703, undertook "to induce *You* who can *Communicate occasionally,* to *Communicate constantly,* with the *Church of England"* (*The Reasonableness of Conformity to the Church of England,* Part II, 2nd ed., 1703, p. 183).

Callamy: Edmund Calamy (1671–1732) was the son of an ejected minister and the grandson of Edmund Calamy, one of the five nonconformists who called themselves Smectymnuus and for whom John Milton wrote an apology. After studying at Utrecht he settled down in Oxford in 1691 to ponder "the whole range of questions at issue between conformists and nonconformists" (*DNB, 3,* 683). He was ordained a Presbyterian minister by Samuel Annesley in London in June 1694 and chosen lecturer at Salter's Hall in October 1702. In 1702 he published a work of historical scholarship, *An Abridgement of Mr. Baxter's History of His Life and Times. With an Account of the Ministers, &c. who were Ejected after the Restauration of King Charles II,* in two volumes. Chapter X of this work, "The Grounds of the Nonconformity of the Ministers who were Ejected," concludes in a defense of occasional conformity as the only way in which the nonconformists can "show their Love and Charity unto those from whom they ordinarily separated" until "a farther Reformation" of the Church of England had made possible "an Happy Settlement" (2nd ed., 2 vols., 1713, *1,* 285).

511–12. a characteristic Defovian ellipsis, which may be construed as follows: Hoadly's "answer" to Calamy's exposition of "The Grounds of . . . Nonconformity" would have been "vain" if Calamy had limited his "Grounds" to one—the operation of conscience—and had not tried to justify occasional conformity. In this case Hoadly's

Sachevrell's Standard never had been spread,
And *High Church Spleen* would hide her angry head.
The Church her self would so much candour feel,
To own their Honesty, and *spare their Zeal:*
The general Charity would quickly flow,
And Christian wou'd be all the Names they'd know:
Here wou'd be then no Parties nor no strife,
The Nation wou'd be easie as they're safe;
The Church might Govern, and have no pretence
To crush the Party in their own defence,
For what have men to fear from innocence?
  Then they could find no colour to oppress,
And if the hate remain'd, *the Cause would cease.*
No Prince, no Church could such a Race destroy,

arguments would have served only to reveal the weakness of the Anglican position and thus to "help" Calamy "baffle" Hoadly in his reply.

513. *Sachevrell:* According to the duchess of Marlborough, Henry Sacheverell (1674?–1724) was "an ignorant, impudent incendiary . . . who was the scorn even of those, who made use of him as a tool" (*Account of the Conduct,* p. 247). Although he found "*nothing worth seeing*" in the Bodleian (Hearne *3,* 376), he graduated B.A. from Magdalen College, Oxford, in June 1695 and was elected a fellow in 1701. His ambition overheated by the queen's assurance that she would "Countenance [i.e. promote to higher dignities in the Church] those who have the truest Zeal to support it" (Boyer, *Annals,* 1703, p. 42), Sacheverell began waving "the *Bloody Flag* . . . of Defiance" at the dissenters in a sermon preached at Oxford on 2 June 1702. This was immediately published under the conciliatory title, *The Political Union. A Discourse Shewing the Dependence of Government on Religion in General: and of the English Monarchy on the Church of England in Particular,* but as Defoe was soon to point out, "*Sacheverell's* Bloody Flag of Defiance is not the Way to Peace and Union; *the shortest Way to Destroy, is not the shortest Way to Unite;* Persecution . . . is not the Way to this Union" (*A Challenge of Peace,* [November] 1703, p. 3).

516. *Zeal:* After February 1703 when Anne repeated her assurance that "upon all Occasions of Promotions to any Ecclesiastical Dignity, I shall have a very just regard to such as are Eminent and Remarkable for their . . . Zeal" (Boyer, *Annals,* 1703, pp. 224–25), there was a marked increase of this commodity in England; "it first proceeded from a *Notion* into a *Word,* and from thence in a hot Summer, ripned into a *tangible Substance*" (Swift, *Prose, 1,* 86).

519. *Parties:* Demands to abolish "the damn'd Names and Distinctions of Parties" (*Division our Destruction: Or, A Short History of the French Faction in England,* 1702, p. 16) were heard on all sides. "At the bottom," Defoe said, "the whole Quarrel is guided by the Interests of Parties, Places, Preferments, to get Some in, and Some out, this seems the main Thing in hand. Parties Contend to get into the Executive Power, that they may put all their Friends into the great Places, and Offices of the Crown" (*A Challenge of Peace,* p. 5; cf. *The True-Born Englishman,* 14 *n.,* above).

525. *the Cause:* Defoe reduces the causes of hatred of nonconformists to the practice of occasional conformity.

Without the blackest brand of Tyranny.
Religion, *if there's any in the Land,*
Would own the Party, and the Cause defend:
And all the Clamour, at their long Dissent,
Must bow to *Conscience* which they can't prevent.
  Now, *Satyr,* all thy Grievances rehearse,
And so *retrieve* the Honour of thy Verse.
No more shalt thou old *Marvell*'s Ghost lament,
Who always rally'd Kings and Government:
Thy Lines their awful Distance always knew,
And thought that Debt to Dignities was Due.
Crowns should be counted with the things Divine,
On which Burlesque is rudeness and profane;
The *Royal Banter* cannot stand the Test,
But where we find the Wit, we lose the Jest.
Poets sometimes with Royal Praise appear,
And sometimes too much Flattery prepare,
Which wiser Princes hardly will Dispence,
Tho' 'tis a Crime of no great Consequence.
But Satyr has no business with the Crown,
No Wit can with good Manners there be shown.
He that the Royal Errors will Expose,
His Courage more than his Discretion shows.
Besides his Duty shou'd his Pen restrain,
And blame the Crime, but not describe the Man:
His proper Parallel of Vice may bring,
Expose the Error, not Expose the King.
  Be faithful, *Satyr,* and thy Lines address;
Before Mankind accuses thee, Confess;
And where thy Pen has thy own Maxims broke,
Recal thy Senses, and the Crime revoke:

528. *Religion, if there's any:* Cf. "Incredulity is strangely increas'd and almost become fashionable" ([William Stephens], *A Letter to His Most Excellent Majesty King William III,* 3rd ed., 1699, p. 10).

533. *retrieve the Honour:* See *The Golden Age Restor'd,* 36 *n.,* above.

534. *Marvell's Ghost:* Marvell rallied kings in a dozen poems and is lamented in John Ayloffe, *Marvell's Ghost* (1678) (*POAS,* Yale, *1,* 284).

536. *Thy: "Satyr's,"* i.e. Defoe's satire.

540. *Royal Banter:* Defoe's "Banter" of Charles II (*The True-Born Englishman,* 289–307, above) does not fail "the Test" of comparison with Marvell.

544. *Dispence:* permit, allow, give dispensation (obsolete in this sense) (*OED*).

Thy Swift persuit of Vice a while adjourn,
To Panegyricks all thy Satyrs turn;
Let Guilt take Breath, and all *the Sons of Sin*
Have time with thee to mend their Manners in:
Cease now to lash the Errors of the Town,
And turn thy pointed Satyr at *thy Own.*
Thy needless care from Vices to abstain,
Thy Virtue and thy Temperance all's in Vain;
Since the First slip of thy unhappy Pen
Levels thy Fame beneath the worst of Men:
Unhappy Poets! when they strive t' excel,
Perish in the Extremes of doing well.
Promiscuous Gall, unwarily let flye,
May hit the Honest, pass the Guilty by:
But when at Soveraign Power 'tis loosly thrown,
'Tis Treason in the Verse, and all the Crime's our Own.
When thy *Luxuriant Fancy* soar'd too high,
And scorch'd its Wings with Beams of Majesty,
Like hasty *Icarus,* depriv'd of Flight,
It sunk Beneath the Ignorance of Night.
Herein much more than others thou hast sin'd,
Because thy Lines against thy Light offend;
Hast broke thy own firm constituted Laws,
Hast been thy self th' Effect, thy self the Cause;
And it must be the Devil drew thee in,
Against thy Sense and Custom thus to sin,
Since thou hast always own'd that Heaven thought fit,
Want of Manners should pass for Want of Wit.
Well grounded Satyr's Physick for the Times,
But operates on nothing but our Crimes;
And turns to rankest Poyson, if let flye
At Virtue, Innocence, or Majesty.
Satyr on Kings and Queens is all Lampoon,

559. *Panegyricks:* Cf. [Defoe], *Reasons against a War with France,* 1701, p. 1: "to Write Panegyricks . . . is none of my business."

575. *scorch'd . . . with Beams of Majesty:* In April 1703, while he was still in hiding, Defoe told Nottingham that there was nothing "that I would not submit to, to obtain her Majesty's favour . . . [and] I omitted nothing to express the unfeigned sense I had upon my mind of having offended her Majesty" by publishing *The Shortest Way with the Dissenters* (HMC *Portland MSS., 4,* 61).

And he that writes it ought to be undone.
'Tis Wits High-Treason, and, for punishment,
The Poet ought to lodge *i' th' City's Tenement.*
  Bedlam's the County Jayl, the Wits should know,
Where all *Apollo*'s Mad-Men ought to go;
The Muses *Bridewell* to Correct such Fellows
As Merit not the Favour of the Gallows;
A worser Dungeon *than the Last below,*
Where, if men are not mad, it makes them so:
For he that wou'd not rather chuse to Dye,
And from St. *Bedlam* to St. *Tyburn* flye,
Must have no Senses left to be his Guide,
Must certainly be Lunatick and Mad.
  Satyr go on, and search the rankl'd wound,
For *more Mistakes of thine* are to be found;
And if thou should'st not all thy Faults confess,
Mankind will mind reforming theirs the less:
The Country Justice may disturb the Peace,
The Clergy Drink and Whore, the Gospel cease,
The Doctors Cavil, and the Priests contend,
And Convocation-Quarrels see no end;
The *High* and *Low Church* strife embroil the State,
And subdivide us all for God knows what;
Physicians fetch their Poisons from afar,
And Soldiers studdy to protract the War;
Give thanks for Victories when they retreat,
And find out Conquests in their own Defeat;
Occasional Conformity prevail,
And looseness on our Principles entail.
Thou art not qualifi'd to lash the Crimes,
Or heal by searching Verse the vitious Times;
Lest in persuance of thy stated Law,
Thy own Mistakes should keep thy Pen in awe.
  Then first confess that, with unwary touch,

608–14. In these lines Defoe refers to some objects of satire in *Reformation of Manners,* above: "The Country Justice" (427 ff.); "Clergy" (921 ff.); "Convocation-Quarrels" (997); "*High and Low Church* strife" (1000); "Physicians" (359 ff.).

616–17. *Victories . . . Defeat:* Cf. *The Golden Age Restor'd,* 34: "fly from Conquest, and shall Conquest meet."

618. *Occasional Conformity:* See headnote, pp. 549–50 above.

Thou lashest some too little, some too much;
And humbly ask the Pardon of Sir *John,*
For thinking him too much below Lampoon:
Not that he less than others loves a Whore,
Not that he's less than those debauch'd, *but more.*
For when to Beasts and Devils men descend,
Reforming's past, and Satyr's at an end.
No decent Language can their crimes rehearse,
They lye below *the Dignity of Verse.*
But if among thy Lines he would have place,
Petition him to *Counterfeit some Grace,*
Let him like something of a Christian sin,
Then thou't ha' some pretence to bring him in.
  Then thou art blam'd for Winking at a Lord
Whose Rapes and Vices stand upon Record,
And call'd a partial Coward, for passing by
Such open Crimes, because of Quality;
But here thy Courage has too much been Proof,
And to thy loss, hast anger'd Lords enough;
But if 'tis Criminal, my Lord may see
Thy Veneration for Nobility;
Since their Sublimer Quality might lead,
To guess they're meant, when other Names are read.
  Satyr's Imperfect, and the Title's Lame,
Till Men may read their Crimes without the Name,
And Characters the Persons best explain,
When by the Picture all men know the Man;
For if the Picture does the Person shew,

626. *Sir John:* Pakington?; cf. *The Golden Age Restor'd,* headnote, pp. 488–89 above.

627. *below Lampoon:* "I am assaulted by two or three Gentlemen of another sort, and of no mean Quality, who are angry that they are left out in some Characters in the Satyr called, *Reformation of Manners;* the Gentlemen are displeased, thinking I did not suppose them bad enough to be Lampoon'd" (Defoe, *A True Collection,* sig. A5r). Cf. Colley Cibber, *The Careless Husband,* 1697, Prologue: "such abject Trash/ Deserve not Satyrs but the Hangman's Lash").

633. *below the Dignity of Verse:* Cf. *England's Late Jury,* 136 *n.,* above.

638. *a Lord:* "Ld Mo," according to the Yale copy of the 4° edition of 1703, presumably Lord Mohun, whom Defoe cited in *Reformation of Manners,* 627–30, above, for his "Valour."

They're certain signs that the Description's true.
The Poet is not taken upon Trust,
For all Men know the Characters are just;
But if the Names are needful to Impart,
There must be a Deficiency of Art,
Like the *Dutch* Painter with his *Man* and *Bear,*
Who writes beneath to tell us what they are,
As if the Picture would not let us know,
Which was the properest Booby of the Two.
  And wou'dst thou now describe a *Modern Tool,*
To wit, to Parties, and himself a Fool,
Embroil'd with State to do his Friend no good,
And by his Friends themselves misunderstood;
Misconstru'd first in every word he said,
By these unpitied, and by those unpaid,
All men would say the Picture was thy own,
No Gazet Marks were half so quickly known.
  Thou that for *Party-Interest* didst Indite,
And thoughtst to be Excus'd for *meaning right.*
This Comfort will thy want of Wit afford,
That now thou'rt left a *Coxcomb* on Record;
England had always this one Happiness,
Never to look at Service, but Success;
And he's a Fool that Differing Judgment makes
And thinks to be rewarded for Mistakes.
  If thou canst name the long forgotten Days,
When Men for *Good Intentions* met with Praise;

658. *the Dutch Painter:* Cf. *More Reformation,* sig. A2v: "All the Fault I can find in my self as to these People is, that when I had drawn the Picture I did not like the *Dutch*-man, with his Man and Bear, write under them, *This is the Man,* and *This is the Bear,* lest the People should mistake me." The phrase may be proverbial; Maximillian E. Novak points out a variant in Elkanah Settle, *Notes and Observations on the Empress of Morocco Revised,* 1674, p. 39: "like the piece of painting with the superscription of *this is the Dog, and this is the Hare.*"

669. *Gazet Marks:* The advertisement in *The London Gazette,* No. 3879, 11–14 January 1703, offering a £50 reward for information leading to his arrest, described Defoe as "a middle sized spare Man, about 40 years old, of a brown Complection, and dark-brown coloured Hair, but wears a Wig, a hooked Nose, a sharp Chin, grey Eyes, and a large Mold near his Mouth."

675. *Success:* Cf. [Defoe], *Royal Religion Being some Enquiry after the Piety of Princes,* 1704, p. 7: "Success sanctifies all the Frauds of Life."

If in our antient Records you can find
True English Men to Gratitude enclin'd.
If it has been the Talent of the Land,
Merit without Success to Understand,
Then you might have expected a Reward,
And then ha' thought the Disappointment hard.
Endeavour bears a Value more or less,
Just as 'tis recommended by Success;
The lucky Coxcomb every man will prize,
And Prosperous Actions always pass for Wise.
Poet take heed of *Ironies* again,
You'll meet with more than *Labour for your Pain;*
If thinking to oblige them you offend,
'Tis as they Think, and not as you Intend;
For if you miss what Honestly you meant,
The Error's not excus'd by the Intent;
The Custom of the Age will fix th' Offence,
Not in your Meaning, but your Ignorance.
The Reason's plain, the Subject is with-held,
The Fact's express'd, but the Intent's conceal'd.

681. *Gratitude:* See *The True-Born Englishman,* headnote, pp. 262–63 above.

690. *Ironies:* In *The Shortest Way with the Dissenters* (1702) Defoe adopted the method of total irony, "*personating* some of these *Violent Church-men*" ([Charles Leslie], *The New Association. Part II,* 1703, p. 6) like Henry Sacheverell and Charles Leslie, and a title mimicking two of Leslie's earlier pamphlets, *A Short and Easie Method with the Deists* (1698) and *A Short and Easie Method with the Jews* (1699). In this guise Defoe could propose a final solution to the problem of dissent, repeating in jest what he knew the high flying Tories were saying in earnest: "Hang, and Quarter all the *Roundheads* and extirpate the Race of 'em from the Face of the Earth" (*The Exorbitant Grants of William the III Examin'd and Question'd . . . With Reflections on Each Paragraph,* 1703, pp. 27–28). And the Tories rose eagerly to the bait. Years later Defoe could recall "Innumerable Testimonies of the Pleasure with which the Party Embrac'd the Proposal of sending all the Dissenters Ministers to the Gallows, and the Galleys—Of having all their Meeting-Houses Demolish'd, and being let loose upon their People, to Plunder and Destroy them" (*Review,* 2 [11 August 1705], 277–78). But at the time he found himself more involved with the perils than with the triumphs of irony. "I fell a Sacrifice," he said, "for writing against the Rage and Madness of that High Party, and in the Service of the Dissenters," or, as Charles Gildon made him say, "by a plaguy Irony, I got myself into the damnable *Nutcrackers*" ([Defoe], *An Appeal to Honour and Justice,* 1715, p. 11; [Charles Gildon], *The Life and Strange Surprizing Adventures of Mr. D—— DeF—, of London, Hosier,* 1719, p. xii).

693. *as they Think, and not as you Intend*: Defoe exposes the intentional fallacy some 250 years before it was formulated.

Nor will this Reason form a just Pretence
To plead there is no need of Penitence:
If thou hast err'd, tho' with a Good Intent,
One merits Pity, t'other Punishment.
Deal with the Times as they ha' dealt with thee;
If they mistake, what's that Mistake to me,
Be unconcern'd at that, and let them kno',
Thou'lt own the Error *'cause they think 'tis so;*
For 'tis a Debt to Sovereign Power due,
Always to let them think *that they say true;*
And he that strives to make the Matter known,
In opening first their Eyes, *puts out his Own.*
Dear *Satyr,* thou wer't of thy Wits forsaken,
To leave them any room to be mistaken;
For if a Poet's Meaning is not plain,
The World allows no Leisure to explain;
He dies for the first Crime he can commit,
For want of Cunning, not *for want of Wit;*
If double Meaning hangs upon his Tongue,
He's always certain to be taken wrong,
And Misconstructions are his constant Fate,
Which he in vain corrects, when 'tis too late.
Then *Satyr,* justify thy self no more,
Thou wilt be only where thou was't before;
For till the World thy Meaning understood,
They ought to think thy Meaning was not good.
To b' Unintelligible is a Crime
Almost as bad *in Prose* as 'tis in *Rhyme.*
An Author who we can not understand,
Is like a Resty Horse at no Command;
And 'tis Convenient in a Land of Peace,
With Care to cause Disturbances to cease;

708. *Sovereign Power:* See *The True-Born Englishman,* 808–19, above. Cf. [Defoe], *Some Remarks on the First Chapter in Dr. Davenant's Essays,* 1704, p. 21: "if *Vox Populi* be *Vox Dei,* here is a plain Divine Right." Defoe's aesthetic proceeds directly from his belief in the sovereignty of the people.

713. *room to be mistaken:* Cf. *More Reformation,* sig. A2r: "he that writes any thing which may be misunderstood *Ought to expect to be Misunderstood . . .* and the Reason is, because he that knew the Defect of Custom, ought to have fenc'd against it."

Besides, *a State Enigma* put in print,
Has something really Seditious in't.
Unless the Exposition suit the Times,
For Negatives in Authors pass for Crimes;
Then let thy Penitence for this be known,
And when thou writ'st again, thy Meaning own,
Or honestly Declare that thou hast none.
He that Dares write and leave the World to guess,
Will *Fall like Thee,* and he deserves no less;
Yet be not sullen, Satyr, and *give o're,*
But never Trust 'em with thy Meaning more.
For if thou but a Hypocrite Describe,
The Clergy search for him *among their Tribe,*
If one *Sir Harry* in thy Lines appear,
All the Sir Harry's think themselves are there.
If to Describe a Blockhead we Intend,
The *Beaus* take Arms, and think they're all design'd;
Each Man takes up the Part that suits him best,
And strives to knock thy Brains out for the rest.
There's not a Drunken Justice in these Lands,
But for himself thy *Furius* understands,
Because so much Similitude appears
Betwixt the Practice and the Characters.
How many has thy *Fletumacy* Own'd,
Of his Supine Accomplishments, how fond,
How Satisfy'd to be from *Bedlam* free,
Pleas'd to be thought as rich and blind as he;
The Ladies who in Fops and Fools delight,

733. *something really Seditious:* In January 1704 Defoe published *An Essay on the Regulation of the Press,* advocating not another licensing act but a law "to settle what an Author may or may not do" (p. 18).

742. *never Trust 'em:* Despite this warning, it may have been Defoe who employed the method of total irony, which by 1710 had come to be called "the Method of *Daniel de Foe,*" in *A Satyr on K. William III,* 1703 (*The Tale of the Cock-Match* ["The World I don't question has heard of the trial"] n.d. 2° half-sheet). Both this work and *King William's Affection to the Church of England Examin'd* (1703) are written in the person of a high churchman.

745. *Sir Harry:* See *Reformation of Manners,* 149, above.

752. *Furius:* See *Reformation of Manners,* 521, above.

755. *Fletumacy:* See *Reformation of Manners,* 1082, above.

Wou'd all be *Diadora*'s for her Wit:
What tho' she stands a Whore upon Record,
They'll never baulk the Practice of the Word,
They'd gladly be as much a Jilt as she,
To get a Cully half so blind as he.
'Tis strange that Men so forward should appear,
Fond to be thought more Wicked than they are.
He that to such a Pitch in Vice is brought,
Is quite as Wicked as he wou'd be thought.
B———'s an Atheist, and so Angry's grown,
That *Blackbourn*'s Character is not his own.
Dear *Satyr,* if thou dost not do him right,
Be cautious how thou goest abroad by Night.
In Impudence he can not be out-done,
Thinks if there's any Gods, himself is one;
He raves to see our Verse should be so blind,
To search for Atheists and leave him behind.
In Wickedness he is so Nice and odd,
He will not Swear, lest he should own a God:
Corrects his Vice for Fear the Crimes should tend,
To prove the Deity which they offend.
Beau *Powell* shows himself in *Tunbridge* Walks,
Of strange Amours and Numerous Actions talks;
His Levee's crowded up with Billet Deux,
He Haunts the Court, the Playhouse, and the Stews;
Eternal Tattle dwells upon his Tongue,

760. *Diadora:* See *Reformation of Manners,* 1112, above.

770. *Blackbourn:* "Dr. Blackburn" (*Key*): see *Reformation of Manners,* 367–96, 415, above.

781. *Powell* (*Key*): George Powell (1658?–1714) "grew up in the theatres, as his father, Martin Powell, was a member of the King's Company." His first recorded role was that of Don Cinthio in Aphra Behn's farce, *The Emperour of the Moon* (c. March 1687). Although "formed by nature for a first rate actor," Powell is said "to have ruined himself in a great measure by his negligence and drunkenness." Vanbrugh describes him "drinking his Mistresses Health in *Nants* Brandy, from six in the Morning, to the time he wadled on upon the Stage" to play Worthy, the fine gentleman in *The Relapse* (John Vanbrugh, *The Relapse,* 1697, sig. A3r). Defoe may have assumed that Powell was playing in Thomas Baker's comedy, *Tunbridge Walks,* which opened at Drury Lane in January 1703 (while Defoe was a fugitive from justice) and was repeated five times that year. Actually, however, Powell left Drury Lane after the season of 1699–1700 to join Thomas Betterton's company at Lincoln's Inn Fields and did not return until June 1704 (*London Stage, 1,* xcix, 356, 531; *2,* 12, 31, 69; Genest, *2,* 146).

Eternal Bawdy fills up every Song;
Whores are his Daily Consorts and Delight.
Is Lewd all Day, but very Chaste at Night.
Fate may a Stone upon his Grave bestow,
Tho' Niggard Nature has deny'd him two;
'Tis strange that Vice on Nature shou'd prevail
To fill the Head, and yet forget the Tail.
Supply his Want of Lewdness with his Wit,
And make him Boast of Sins he can't Commit.
But *Satyr,* that which most Concerns thee now,
Is what if Heav'n prevent not feelingly thou'lt know.
That when a *Learned Mouth*'s describ'd by thee,
Lovel of all Mankind should think 'twas He!
Without Dispute the Characters were true,
But that 'twas *Lovel*'s none but *Lovel* knew.
What tho' to Likeness he might make Pretence,
Similitude can not be Evidence.
But, *Satyr,* of his Anger, have a Care,
Or speedily for Martyrdom Prepare;
For if within his Reach you Chance to Come,
You've Sung your Last, a Fool may read your Doom,
Tho' no more Poets liv'd in *Christendom.*
Grave *Inuendo* in his Forehead sits,
Able to Banter Fools, and Punish Wits.
From his Resentment, *Satyr* flee amain,
Like Death, there's none returns from him, again;
'T will be in vain to make a long Defence,
In vain 'twill be to Plead thy Innocence.

786. *Song:* George Powell wrote or adapted for the stage seven plays. *Alphonso King of Naples. A Tragedy* (1691) included three songs, one of which, "When *Silvia* is kind, and Love plays in her Eyes," was set to music by John Eccles and published in *Joyful Cuckoldom* (c. 1695). *Bonduca; or, The British Heroine, A Tragedy* (1696) included songs set by Henry Purcell. *The Single Songs* from *A New Opera; Called Brutus of Alba: or, Augusta's Triumph* (1697), set by Daniel Purcell, were entered in the Stationers Register in November 1696, and four songs from *Imposture Defeated: or, A Trick to Cheat the Devil. A Comedy* (1698) were first printed in *A Collection of New Songs* (1697). Powell also wrote at least one number of William Pittis's *Heraclitus Ridens* (*London Stage, 1,* 392, 452–53, 468, 485–86; *Modern Philology, 33* [November 1935], 182). All of these are unexceptionably chaste.

798. *Lovel* (*Key*): See *Reformation of Manners,* 115–48, above.

808. *Inuendo in his Forehead sits:* Lovell was one of the justices before whom Defoe was tried and sentenced in 7 July 1703 (Moore, *Daniel Defoe,* p. 131).

His Breath Concludes the Sentence of the Day,
He kills at once, For 'tis his *Shortest Way.*
Satyr go on, do Pennance for thy Crimes,
And own thy Rhyming Errors in thy Rhymes;
Blush not thy Native Folly to make known,
The Pen that has offended must attone,
But if *thou Poet* shouldst be Obstinate,
And load thy Satyr with thy Verses Fate,
His Blood will certainly be on thy Head,
And *Haunt the Poet* when the *Poem*'s Dead.
With *Whitney's Horses* 'twill in Judgment rise,
And all thy later Penitence Despise.
Kneel then upon the *Penitential Stool,*
And Freely tell the World that thou'rt a *Fool,*
Which from thy Mouth, if they will not believe,
Thy Verse shall *lasting Testimonies* give.
A Fool indeed to Advocate for such,
As load thee Daily with unjust Reproach;
A Fool as by the Consequence appears,
To put thy own Eyes out, *to Open theirs.*
A Fool to tell the Nation of their Crimes,
And knock thy Brains out to Instruct the Times.
From hence old *Rauleigh*'s Cautious Rule Obey,

824. *Whitney's Horses:* In one of Thomas Brown's *Letters from the Dead to the Living* (2nd ed., 1702, p. 49) Charon complains to Jack Ketch of a session at the Old Bailey of 16–17 July 1701 in which "none received sentence of death" (Luttrell, 5, 72). "Was it then possible," Charon exclaims, "the most worshipful Sir senceless *L[ovel]l* . . . upon the Bench and no Man hang'd! Well, as assuredly as the Blood of the Horses will rise up in Judgment against our Friend *Whitney,* this Maiden Session shall rise up in Judgment against him." This, in turn, refers to an absurd speech that Lovell is supposed to have made in 1693 upon sentencing to death Captain James Whitney, the celebrated highwayman, warning him "that the blood of the horses he had slain on the highway would rise up in judgment against him" (John R. Moore, *Defoe in the Pillory,* Bloomington, Indiana, Indiana University Publications Humanities Series No. 1, 1939, p. 33).

830. *such:* the nonconformists.

836. *Rauleigh's Cautious Rule:* "And as Dogs bark at those they know not, and accompany one another in their Clamours, so it is with the unthinking Multitude; which led by uncertain Reports, condemn without hearing, and wound without Offence given; contrary to the Counsel of *Syracides.* Against this vanity of Vulgar Opinion, *Seneca,* giveth a good Rule; Let us satisfie our own Consciences, and not trouble our selves about the Censures of others, be it never so ill, as long as we deserve well" (*An Abridgment of Sir Walter Raleigh's History of the World,* 1698, sig. A4r, A1v).

And nere Reform the World the *Shortest Way;*
Reproof the Grave Reprover will Undo,
They'll always Hate thee if the Matter's true.
Simpson the Grave thy Labours has Condemn'd,
And wisely says he knows what we Intend.
Two Fam'd Harangues the Orator has made,
Tho' Talking's *not his Talent, but his Trade:*
Yet has his Wit betray'd him to thy Fate,
For no man understands what he'd be at;
And as his first Discourses seem'd to Fail,
For being all Head, but born without a Tail,
So these were Damn'd again, as has been said,
For being all Tail, indeed, without a Head.
Unhappy Satyr, now Review thy Fate,
And see the *Threatning Anger* of the State!
But learn thy sinking Fortunes to despise,
And all thy *Coward Friends* turn'd Enemies.
Before thee stands the Power of Punishment,
In an Exasperated Government.
Behind the Vacant Carpet fairly Spread,
From whence thy *too well serv'd Allies* are fled.
At a remoter Distance, there they stand,
And Mock thy *Folly;* but thy *Fault* Commend;
Freely thy former Services Disown,
And slily Laugh to see thee *first Undone;*

840. *Simpson* (*Key*): possibly Sidrach Simpson (d. 1704), the rector of Stoke Newington, Middlesex (1665–1704) when Defoe was a student at Newington Academy. He was said to be "somewhat severe with dissenters" (*DNB,* 18, 278), but his "Two Fam'd Harangues" have not been identified.

854–926. The poem ends in contempt for "the Tribe" of dissenters, who, as Defoe told William Paterson, "lift up the first dagger at me; I confess it . . . gives me the more regret that I suffer for such a people" (HMC *Portland MSS., 4,* 61).

854. *Punishment:* On 7 July 1703 Defoe was sentenced to pay "a fine of 200 marks [£133 6*s*] . . . and to stand upon a pillory, one day in Cornhill by the Exchange, London, and another day in Cheapside near the Conduit there, the third day in Fleet Street by Temple Bar, for one hour between the hours of eleven before noon and two after noon, whichever one he likes, with a paper on his head on which his offences are written, and that the said Daniel de Foe should find good sureties to be of good behaviour for the space of seven years," which, in Moore's words, was "severe beyond all expectation" (Moore, *Daniel Defoe,* p. 131).

857. *Allies:* Charles Leslie referred to "Mr. *De Foe,* the Common Advocate of the *Dissenters*" (*The Rehearsal,* 2, No. 30 [21 January 1707/8]).

Of thy plain *Action* wou'd invert the *Sense,*
And rail, and counterfeit an *Ignorance,*
As if 'twas possible thou should'st intend,
In one Point Blank two Opposites Offend.
These seem'd provok'd because they will not know
Thy Easy Sense, and Those because they do.
  Satyr, 'twould certainly appear a Crime,
Not to *Applaud* their Policy in Rhyme,
Who when Poor *Authors* in their Quarrel write,
Can to *their Safety* Sacrifice the Wit.
Wait for the *Safe Event,* and wisely try,
Whether with *Truth* or *Int'rest* to Comply,
As Prospects govern, and Success directs,
Their Cunning this *Approves,* or that *Rejects.*
  Blush for them, *Satyr,* who thy Name abuse,
And by Reproach wou'd *Gratitude Excuse,*
And tell them as thou mayst be Understood,
Their Temper's Wicked, tho their Cause is Good.
Yet never thy just Principles forsake,
For that wou'd be to sin, because thy Friends Mistake.
But bid 'em tell thee, if they can tell how,
What are the Crimes for which they treat thee so.
What horrid Fact, what Capital offence
Could bar thee from the Priests Benevolence,
That they their Benediction should deny,
And let thee live unbless'd, *unpray'd for Die.*
Thieves, Highway-men, and Murtherers are sent
To *Newgate* for their future Punishment,
But all Men pity them when they Repent.
Religious Charity extorts a Prayer,
And *How* shall freely visit *Whitney* there;

865. *two Opposites:* Firing at point blank elevation (i.e. horizontally) would make it impossible to hit two opposite targets, "These" nonconformists (866) and "Those" high churchmen (867), at the same time.

885. *the Priests Benevolence:* In July 1703 after he had been sentenced and committed to Newgate, Defoe invited three nonconformist ministers. John Howe, John Spademan, and Robert Fleming, to pray with him. They all refused, although Howe had "visited Whitney the Highway man when he declined praying for the Author when in his Trouble" (*Key*).

890. *Repent:* Whitney "seemed to dye very penitent" (Luttrell, *3*, 27).

Yet three Petition'd Priests have said thee nay,
And vilely scorn'd so much as but to Pray;
Refus'd the weighty Talent of the Tribe,
And let their Heat their Piety prescribe;
Strange Power of Fear upon the Minds of Men,
Which neither Sence, nor Honour can restrain.
Ask them why they're Exasperated so,
To baulk the cheapest Gift they can bestow.
Satyr, it must ha' been some Mortal Sin,
Some strange Apostacy of thy unhappy Pen,
That has the Reverend Fathers so perplex'd,
And disoblig'd the Masters of the Text.
What, tho' the Scurvy Humours of thy Head,
In House of Tribulation made thy Bed,
And Fate, which long thine Enemy was known,
Had Cloath'd thy Tenement in Walls of Stone?
I know the Learned Orthodoxly say,
That after Death there is no room to Pray;
But yet no Article I ever Read,
Has counted Men in *Newgate* with the Dead.
Satyr, look back, and former Days review,
How stood it once betwixt the Tribe and you,
In Prosperous Days their Conscious Pride must know
You fed those Priests that Scorn to own you now.
With Constant Charity reliev'd their Poor,
For which they'll stone thee Now 'tis in their Power.
With just Contempt look back upon their pride,
And now despise the Gift which they deny'd;
But let thy Charity their Crime outlive,
And what they seldom practise, now forgive.
For Heaven, without their Help, upholds thee here,
He only claims thy thanks who hears thy Prayer,
He can the Royal Clemency incline,
For Humane Grace is center'd in Divine.

A Hymn to the Pillory
(29 July 1703)

This is the poem that Defoe "made in Derision of [the high churchmen], and publish'd the very Day they expos'd him" in the pillory ([Defoe], *The Present State of the Parties in Great Britain,* 1712, p. 21). "The Indignity of the Pillory" was what Defoe had feared most, and what he remembered longest; it was, he told Nottingham, "worse to me than Death" (Review, [9] [7 May 1713], 183; *Athenaeum, 67* [22 December 1894], 862). It was to avoid the pillory that he had offered, on 9 January 1703, to serve in her majesty's armies in the Lowlands—a privilege frequently extended even to convicted felons—and it was to avoid the pillory that he had agreed to plead guilty at his trial on 7 July. "This Poem," he said in 1705, "was the Author's Declaration, even when in the cruel Hands of a merciless as well as unjust Ministry; that the Treatment he had from them was unjust, exorbitant, and consequently illegal" (*A Second Volume of the Writings,* sig. A5r). The most striking feature of the poem is the recklessness of its tone, and Defoe is reckless, as James Sutherland has said, "because he is right" (*Defoe,* Philadelphia and New York, J. B. Lippincott Co., 1938, p. 97).

"This Satyr or Poem, call it which you please," was published on 29 July 1703, the first of the three days in which Defoe stood in the pillory (*A Second Volume of the Writings,* sig. A5v). On this day the pillory was set in front of the Royal Exchange, in Cornhill, just around the corner from Freemans Yard where Defoe had lived from 1684 to 1700. He had been warned that the dissenters would not stand by him and that he could be expected to be pelted with rotten eggs. But what was intended to be a degrading ordeal turned out to be a triumph (Moore, *Daniel Defoe,* p. 104; *The Shortest Way with Whores and Rogues,* 1703, sig. a1v).

The transaction is a matter of history, as G. E. Cokayne would say. Defoe's account of what happened is fully corroborated by the accounts of his worst enemies: he was "expos'd . . . for the Mob to laugh at him for a Fool . . . and the People, that it was expected would have treated this Man very ill, on the contrary *Pitied him*" ([Defoe], *The Consolidator: Or, Memoirs of Sundry Transactions from the World in the Moon,* 1705, pp. 68, 69). "*The Party,*" as Charles Leslie complained, "caus[ed] his *Books* to be *Hauk'd* and Publickly *Sold* about the *Pillory,* while he stood upon it (in *Triumph!*) for Writing them" (*The Wolf Stript of His Shepherd's Cloathing,* 1704, p. 74). *A Hymn to the Pillory* and *A True Collection of the Writings of the Author of The True Born English-man,* which had been published only the week before, on 22 July, with a portrait of Defoe engraved by Michael Van der Gucht, were not only sold but publicly read at the pillory and the author toasted, as William Pittis reported ([Pittis], *The True-Born-Hugonot,* [1703], p. 4):

> . . . the Mob . . .
> That *Dirt* themselves protected him from *Filth,*
> And for the *Faction*'s Money drank its *Health.*
> The Brainless Fools that Prais'd his Hymn when read,
> Rail'd against *Monarchy* at a *Monarch*'s Head.

And finally, at the end of the long hour, the mob "exprest their Affections, by *loud Shouts* and Acclamations, when he was taken down," or, in Pittis' words again, they "Hallow'd him down from his Wooden Punishment, as if he had been a *Cicero* that had made an Excellent Oration on it" ([*Pittis*], *Heraclitus Ridens,* No. 2, 3–7 August 1703). On the two succeeding days the process was repeated in Cheapside and at Temple Bar and with exactly the same results.

For this popular poem Defoe adapted to the purposes of satire the popular "Pindarick Way," as Abraham Cowley, its inventor, had called it (*Ode. Upon Liberty* [1668], p. 115). "All the boys and girls caught the pleasing fashion," as Samuel Johnson said, "and they that could do nothing else could write like Pindar" (*Lives, 1,* 48). The standard definition of the Pindaric stanza is supplied by Edward Bysshe: "The Stanzas of Pindarick Odes are neither confin'd to a certain number of Verses, nor the Verses to a certain number of Syllables, nor the Rhyme to a certain Distance. Some Stanzas contain 50 Verses or more, others not above 10, and sometimes not so many. Some Verses 14, nay 16 Syllables, others not above 4: Sometimes the Rhymes follow one another for several Couplets together, sometimes they are remov'd 6 Verses from each other; and all this in the same

Stanza" (*The Art of English Poetry,* 2nd ed., 1705, p. 34). Generically the poem is not a hymn, but a direct address—to the pillory. And Defoe imposes on a subject matter that ranges from puritan martyrs to short sellers in the Royal Exchange, in a free and unpredictable stanza form, a recurrence of epithets—*"Hi'roglyphick* State *Machin . . . Speaking Trumpet of Mens Fame . . . Herald of Reproach"*—which holds the poem together. Perhaps the best description of the poem is that by George Chalmers. "In this ode," he said, "the reader will find satire, pointed by [Defoe's] sufferings, generous sentiments, arising from his situation, and an unexpected flow of easy verse" (*The History of the Union between England and Scotland, with A Collection of Original Papers relating thereto. By Daniel De Foe . . . To which is Prefixed, A Life of Daniel De Foe by George Chalmers,* 1786, p. viii).

Besides a satiric imitation, Thomas Brown, *A Dialogue between the Pillory and Daniel de Foe* ("Awake, thou busy Dreamer, and arise"), which was published in a folio half-sheet in 1703, the poem generated a reply, *Remarks on the Author of the Hymn to the Pillory. With an Answer to the Hymn to the Funeral Sermon* ("Forbear thou great Destroyer of Mens Fame"), of which the Luttrell copy in the British Museum (164.m.34) is dated 9 October 1703, and a sequel, *A Hymn to Tyburn. Being a Sequel of the Hymn to the Pillory.* The latter, of which two editions were published in 1703, repeats many of the motifs of *A Hymn to the Pillory.*

A Hymn to the Pillory

Hail! *Hi'roglyphick* State *Machin,*
Contriv'd to Punish Fancy in:
Men that are Men, in thee can feel no Pain,
And all thy *Insignificants* Disdain.
Contempt, that false New Word for shame,
Is without Crime, an empty Name,
A Shadow to Amuse Mankind,
But never frights the Wise or Well-fix'd Mind:
Virtue despises Humane Scorn,
And Scandals Innocence adorn.
Exalted on thy *Stool of State,*
What Prospect do I see of Sov'reign Fate;
How the *Inscrutables* of Providence,
Differ from our contracted Sence;
Here by the Errors of the Town,
The Fools look out, the Knaves look on.
Persons or Crimes find here the same respect,
And Vice does Vertue oft Correct,
The undistinguish'd Fury of the Street,
With Mob and Malice Mankind Greet:
No Byass can the Rabble draw,
But *Dirt* throws *Dirt* without respect to Merit, or to Law.

Sometimes the *Air of Scandal* to maintain,
Villains look from thy *Lofty Loops* in Vain:
But who can judge of Crimes by Punishment,
Where Parties Rule, and Law's Subservient.
Justice with Change of Int'rest Learns to bow,
And what was Merit once, is Murther now:

1. *Hi'roglyphick:* having a hidden meaning, symbolic, emblematic (*OED*).

4. *Insignificants:* lack of (1) meaning, (2) importance.

22. *Dirt throws Dirt:* When that "sorry Rascal" William Fuller stood in the pillory in June 1702 he was "severely pelted by the mob with rotten eggs, dirt, &c." (Luttrell, 5, 189).

26. *Parties:* See *More Reformation,* 519 *n.,* above.

Actions receive their Tincture from the Times,
And as they change are Vertues made or Crimes.
Thou art the *State-Trap of the Law,*
But neither can keep Knaves, nor Honest Men in Awe;
These are too hard'nd in Offence,
And those upheld by Innocence.

How have thy *opening Vacancys* receiv'd,
In every Age the Criminals of State?
And how has Mankind been deceiv'd,
When they distinguish Crimes by Fate?
Tell us, *Great Engine,* how to understand,
Or reconcile the Justice of the Land;
How *Bastwick, Pryn, Hunt, Hollingsby* and *Pye,*
Men of unspotted Honesty;
Men that had Learning, Wit and Sence,
And more than most Men have had since,

41–46. Quoted in *Heraclitus Ridens,* No. 2, 3–7 August 1703.

41. *Bastwick, Pryn:* The Puritan propagandists Dr. John Bastwick (1593–1654), William Prynne (1600–69), and Henry Burton (1578–1648) "had their Ears cut off for several Seditious Libels" on 30 June 1637 (Samuel Butler, *Hudibras,* ed. Zachary Grey, 2 vols., Cambridge, 1744, *1,* 205 *n.;* William Knowler, ed., *The Earl of Straforde's Letters,* 2 vols., 1739, *2,* 85).

Hunt: Thomas Hunt (c. 1627–88), "a bold republican," as Dryden called him (*Prose, 2,* 115), was born in London and educated at Queen's College, Cambridge, and Gray's Inn, whence he was called to the bar in February 1659 (Reginald J. Fletcher, *The Pension Book of Gray's Inn,* 2 vols., 1901–10, *1,* 427). He soon became famous "among certain schismatical persons for several things that he has written" (Wood, *4,* 181–84). The most celebrated of these was a bold attack on the quo warranto proceedings against the ancient liberties of the city of London, entitled *A Defense of the Character and Municipal Rights of the City of London* (1683), to which Dryden replied in *The Vindication: . . .* [*of*] *The Duke of Guise* (1683). In this work, which Saintsbury called one of Dryden's "happiest controversial passages" (Dryden, *Works, 7,* 145), Hunt is called *"magni nominis umbra*—the most malicious, and withal, the most incoherent ignorant scribbler of the whole party" (Dryden, *Prose, 2,* 125). But even while Dryden was writing, Hunt's pamphlet was cited as a criminal libel and "he fled into Holland in June, or thereabouts" (Luttrell, *1,* 247).

Hollingsby: unidentified.

Pye: Robert Pye was born in London and educated at Peterhouse, Cambridge, and the Inner Temple, whence he was called to the bar in 1595, but "The career of this Robert was not happy." He involved himself in some discreditable action against another lawyer, "was brought before the Star Chamber, was found guilty of perjury . . . and was sentenced to a fine of 1000 marks, to pillory and the loss of his ears and to perpetual imprisonment" (Thomas A. Walker, *A Biographical Register of Peterhouse Men,* 2 vols., Cambridge, Cambridge University Press, 1930, *2,* 104).

Could equal Title to thee claim,
With *Oats* and *Fuller,* Men of later Fame:
Even the Learned *Selden* saw,
A Prospect of thee, thro' the Law:
He had thy *Lofty Pinnacles* in view,
But so much Honour never was thy due:
Had the Great *Selden* Triumph'd on thy Stage,
Selden the Honour of his Age;
No Man wou'd ever shun thee more,
Or grudge to stand where *Selden* stood before.

Thou art no shame to Truth and Honesty,
Nor is the Character of such defac'd by thee,
Who suffer by Oppressive Injury.
Shame, like the Exhalations of the Sun,
Falls back where first the motion was begun:
And he who for no Crime shall on thy *Brows* appear,
Bears less Reproach than they who plac'd him there.

But if Contempt is on thy *Face* entail'd,
Disgrace it self shall be asham'd;

46. *Oats:* Titus Oates (1649–1705), whose perjuries condemned to death hundreds of innocent men during the Popish Plot (1678–81), was himself convicted of perjury in May 1685 and condemned to be stripped of his clerical habit, to pay a fine of 2000 marks, to be whipped from Aldgate to Newgate and from Newgate to Tyburn three days later, to stand in the pillory five times a year, and to remain in prison for life. After his first whipping he could not stand, so he was dragged in a sledge from Newgate to Tyburn while the common hangman applied the whip (Luttrell, *1,* 343). Set at liberty in 1689, he promptly resumed his clerical garb and petitioned the crown for a pension, which was increased to £300 a year in 1698. For a time in 1691 he encouraged William Fuller in the fabrication of a Jacobite plot (*DNB, 14,* 746–47).

Fuller: William Fuller (1670–1733), called "the Evidence," flourished as a Jacobite courier and double agent but overreached himself when he turned informer and in November 1692 was fined 200 marks and sentenced to stand in the pillory. His most celebrated project was *A Brief Discovery of the True Mother of the Prince of Wales* (1696) and a series of later works that revived and elaborated the warming-pan legend (*The Golden Age Restor'd,* 71 *n.,* above). Again he failed to produce any evidence for his allegations and in May 1702 was fined 1000 marks and sentenced to appear in all the courts in Westminster with a paper in his hat describing his crimes, to stand in the pillory three times, to be whipped in Bridewell, and to remain there a year at hard labor (see 22 *n.,* above).

47. *Selden:* John Selden (1585–1654), the parliamentarian and jurist, stood in danger of the pillory in March 1629 when he was committed to the Tower for his opposition to enforced loans and arbitrary imprisonment in the previous session of parliament.

Scandal shall blush that it has not prevail'd,
    To blast the Man it has defam'd.
Let all that merit equal Punishment,
Stand there with him, and we are all Content.

    There would the Fam'd *Sachevrel* stand,
With Trumpet of Sedition in his Hand,
Sounding the first *Crusado* in the Land.
He from a Church of *England* Pulpit first
    All his Dissenting Brethren Curst;
    Doom'd them to Satan for a Prey,
    And first found out *the shortest way;*
With him the Wise Vice-Chancellor o'th'Press,
Who, tho' our Printers Licences defy,
    Willing to show his forwardness,
    Bless'd it with his Authority;
He gave the Churche's Sanction to the Work,
As *Popes* bless Colours for Troops which fight the *Turk.*
    Doctors in scandall these are grown,
For *Red-hot Zeal* and Furious Learning known:
Professors in Reproach and highly fit,
For *Juno*'s Academy, *Billingsgate.*

68–74. Defoe quotes these lines in *Review, 6* (27 December 1709), 454.

68. *Sachevrel (Key)*: See *More Reformation,* 513 *n.,* above.

69. *Trumpet:* Cf. [Defoe], *More Short-Ways with the Dissenters,* [April] 1704, p. 8: "Mr. *Sachevrell* of *Oxford* has blown his second Trumpet [Henry Sacheverell, *The Nature and Mischief of Prejudice and Partiality Stated,* Oxford, 1704], to let us know he has not yet taken down his Bloody Flag, and that he was the Real Author of the *Shortest Way,* tho' another was Punish'd for it."

74. *the shortest way:* See *More Reformation,* 690 *n.,* above. *Cf.* [Charles Leslie], *The Wolf Stript of his Shepherd's Cloathing,* 1704, p. 74: "And in his *Verses* since Publish'd, [Defoe] often brings in for *Rime,* and the Burden of his *Song—The Shortest way* —So far is he . . . from thinking the *Pillory a Shame,* in such a *Cause!*"

75. *Vice-Chancellor:* Henry Sacheverell, *The Political Union* (1702) (see *More Reformation,* 513 *n.,* above), was published under the imprimatur of Roger Mander (1649–1704), the master of Balliol College, Oxford (1687–1704), and vice-chancellor of the university (1700–04).

84. *Juno's Academy, Billingsgate:* Cf. *Review,* 7 (16 December 1710), 455: "my Father forgetting *Juno*'s Royal Academy, left *Language of Billingsgate* quite out of my Education." Defoe was scornful of the *"Oxford* Rhetorick" of Sacheverell and Leslie, which reduced dissenters to *"Spawn of Rebels, and Vermin not fit to Live"* ([Defoe], *A Serious Enquiry into this Grand Question,* 1704, pp. 17, 19; cf. [Defoe], Peace without Union, 4th ed., 1704, sig. A2r).

Thou like a True-born *English* Tool,
Hast from their Composition stole,
And now art like to smart for being a Fool:
And as of *English* Men, 'twas always meant,
They'r better to Improve than to Invent;
Upon their Model thou hast made,
A Monster makes the World afraid.

With them let all the States-men stand,
Who Guide us with unsteady hand:
Who Armies, Fleets, and Men betray;
And Ruine all *the shortest way.*
Let all those Souldiers stand in sight,
Who're Willing to be paid and not to fight.
Agents, and Collonels, who false Musters bring,
To Cheat their Country first, and then their King:
Bring all your *Coward Captains* of the Fleet;
Lord! What a Crow'd will there be when they meet?
They who let *Pointi* 'scape to *Brest,*
Whom all the Gods of *Carthagena* Blest.
Those who betray'd our *Turkey* Fleet;
Or Injur'd *Talmash* Sold at *Camaret.*

85–86. *Thou . . . Hast . . . stole:* Defoe wrote *The Shortest Way with the Dissenters* in the person of Henry Sacheverell and Charles Leslie (see *More Reformation,* 690 *n.,* above).

87. *Fool:* Cf. *More Reformation,* 830–35, above.

91. *Monster:* There is much evidence that readers were puzzled by *The Shortest Way with the Dissenters.* Edmund Calamy insisted upon interpreting literally what was intended ironically: "It was very Sharp and Poignant," he said, "and some on both Sides were at first amus'd with it, as questioning what its Design was; but it was not long before that was sufficiently discover'd . . . [i.e.] to pull up this Heretical Weed" of nonconformity (Calamy, *Abridgement, 1,* 634). Thomas Salmon had a different wrong idea: "This Book," he said, "very broadly hinted that the Parliament were about to enact sanguinary Laws, to compel the Dissenters to Conformity" (*A Review of the History of England,* 2 vols., 1724, *2,* 141).

102. *Pointi:* In December 1696 when it was learned that Jean Bernard Louis Desjean, baron de Pointis (1645–1707), had sailed from Brest to prey upon Spanish commerce in the Caribbean, Vice-Admiral John Neville was ordered to "traverse" his designs. Neville not only failed to prevent de Pointis from plundering Cartagena to the bare walls, but allowed him, although outnumbered two to one, to convoy this loot, said to be worth £11,000,000 safely back to Brest without losing a ship (Luttrell, *4,* 150, 171, 237, 262, 498).

104. *Turkey Fleet:* See *The True-Born Englishman,* 1039 *n.,* above.

105. *Talmash:* See *The True-Born Englishman,* 1040 *n.,* above.

Who miss'd the Squadron from *Thoulon,*
And always came too late or else too soon;
All these are Heroes whose great Actions Claim,
Immortal Honours to their Dying Fame;
And ought not to have been Denyed,
On thy *great Counterscarp,* to have their Valour try'd.

Why have not these upon thy *spreading Stage,*
Tasted the keener Justice of the Age;
If 'tis because their Crimes are too remote,
Whom leaden-footed Justice has forgot?
Let's view the modern Scenes of Fame,
If Men and Management are not the same;
When Fleets go out with Money, and with Men,
Just time enough to venture home again?
Navyes prepar'd to guard th' insulted Coast,
And Convoys settl'd when Our Ships are lost.
Some Heroes lately come from Sea,
If they were paid their Due, should stand with thee;
Papers too should their Deeds relate,
To prove the Justice of their Fate:
Their Deeds of War at *Port Saint Mary*'s done,
And set the Trophy's by them, which they won:
Let *Ormond*'s Declaration there appear,
He'd certainly be pleas'd to see 'em there.
Let some good Limner represent,
The ravish'd Nuns, the plunder'd Town,
The *English* Honour how mispent;
The shameful coming back, and little done.

The *Vigo* Men should next appear,
To Triumph on thy *Theater;*

106. *Thoulon:* See *The Spanish Descent,* 225 *n.,* above.

122. *Some Heroes:* See *The Spanish Descent,* 199 *n.,* above.

124. *Papers:* Part of Defoe's sentence was to stand in the pillory "with a paper on his head on which his offences are written" (Moore, *Daniel Defoe,* p. 131; see *More Reformation,* 854 *n.,* above.)

126. *Port Saint Mary:* See *The Spanish Descent,* 61 *n.,* above.

128. *Ormond (Key):* See *The Spanish Descent,* 19 *n.,* 58 *n.,* above.

131. *Nuns:* See *The Spanish Descent,* 11 *n.,* above.

They, who on board the Great Galoons had been,
Who rob'd the *Spaniards* first, and then the Queen:
Set up the praises to their Valour due,
How Eighty Sail, had beaten Twenty two.
Two Troopers so, and one Dragoon,
Conquer'd a *Spanish* Boy in Pantalone.
Yet let them *Ormond*'s Conduct own,
Who beat them first on Shore, or little had been done:
What unknown spoils from thence are come,
How much was brought away, *How little home.*
If all the Thieves should on thy *Scaffold* stand
Who rob'd their Masters in Command:
The Multitude would soon outdo,
The City Crouds of *Lord Mayor*'s *show.*

Upon thy *Penitential stools,*
Some People should be plac'd for Fools:
As some for Instance who while they look on;
See others plunder all, and they got none.
Next the Lieutenant General,
To get the Devill, lost the De'll and all;
And he some little badge should bear,
Who ought, in Justice, to have hang'd 'em there:
This had his Honour more maintain'd,
Than all the Spoils at *Vigo* gain'd.

Then Clap thy *Wooden Wings* for Joy,
And greet the Men of Great Employ;
The Authors of the Nations discontent,
And Scandal of a Christian Government.

137. *rob'd . . . the Queen:* Not only did the queen find it necessary to say in her speech at the opening of parliament on 21 October 1702 that she had ordered an investigation of "Disorders and Abuses Committed at *Port S. Maries*" (Boyer, *Annals*, 1703, p. 122), but on 13 December 1702 she issued a proclamation ordering the Vigo plunder to be surrendered to the commissioners of prizes and offering one-fifth of the value of the recovered goods as a reward to informers (Steele, No. 4339).

141. *Pantalone:* a one-piece garment including stockings and breeches of the same material (*OED*).

142. *Ormond* (*Key*): See *The Spanish Descent*, 299 *n.*, above.

154. *the Lieutenant General:* Sir Henry Bellasis; see *The Spanish Descent*, 199 *n.*, above.

Jobbers, and *Brokers* of the City Stocks,
With forty Thousand Tallies at their backs;
Who make our Banks and Companies obey,
Or sink 'em all *the shortest way.*
Th' Intrinsick Value of our Stocks,
Is stated in their Calculating Books;
Th' Imaginary Prices rise and fall,
As they Command who toss the Ball;
Let 'em upon thy lofty Turrets stand,
With *Bear-skins* on the back, *Debentures* in the hand,
And write in Capitals upon the Post,
That here they should remain,
Till this *Ænigma* they explain,
How Stocks should Fall, when Sales surmount the Cost,
And rise again when Ships are lost.

Great *Monster of the Law,* Exalt thy Head;
Appear no more in Masquerade,
In Homely Phrase Express thy Discontent,
And move it in th' Approaching Parliament:
Tell 'em how Paper went instead of Coin,
With Int'rest eight *per Cent.* and Discount Nine.
Of *Irish* Transport Debts unpaid,

173. *Bear-skins:* a bear skin jobber (*OED* cites Defoe, *The Political History of the Devil*) was a short seller (a trader who sold stock which he did not own in the expectation of buying it back at a lower price); a short sale was called "selling the bearskin," which *OED* (s.v. Bear sb.1 8) suggests may have originated in the proverb "To sell the bear's skin before one has caught the bear" (Tilley B132).

Debentures: a government voucher "certifying to the recipient the sum due to him for goods supplied, services rendered, salary, etc., and serving as his authority in claiming payment" (*OED*). Unpaid debentures like the Irish Transport debentures of 1695 (185 *n.,* below) were traded in the market.

176–78. Quoted twice in *Review 3* (1 August 1706), 366, and [*9*] (14 March 1713), 139.

177–78. *Stocks . . . rise . . . when Ships are lost:* this part of the "*Ænigma*" is explained by *Reformation of Manners,* 319–20. The practice was so common that in February 1703 a law was passed "for punishing of Accessaries to Felonies . . . and to prevent the wilful burning and destroying of Ships" (*LJ, 17,* 320).

183. *Paper:* Exchequer bills (*Advice to a Painter,* 87 *n.*) circulated as currency but were traded at a discount.

185. *Irish Transport Debts:* The interest on this debt, which the government incurred in 1689–91 and which was still outstanding, amounted to nearly £20,000 a year (*CTB 1693–1696,* p. 321). Defoe's concern for this particular detail of the national debt may indicate that he had bought some of the debentures himself.

Bills false Endors'd, and long Accounts unmade.
And tell them all the Nation hopes to see,
They'll send the Guilty down to thee;
Rather than those who write their History.

Then bring those Justices upon thy Bench,
Who vilely break the Laws they should defend;
And upon Equity Intrench,
By Punishing the Crimes they will not Mend.
Set every vitious Magistrate,
Upon thy *sumptuous Chariot of the State;*
There let 'em all in Triumph ride,
Their Purple and their Scarlet laid aside.
Let none such *Bride-well* Justices Protect,
As first debauch the Whores which they Correct:
Such who with Oaths and Drunk'ness sit,
And Punish far less Crimes than they Commit:
These certainly deserve to stand,
With Trophies of Authority in Either Hand.

Upon thy *Pulpit,* set the Drunken Priest,
Who turns the Gospel to a baudy Jest;
Let the Fraternity Degrade him there,
Least they like him appear:
There let him, his *Memento Mori* Preach,
And by Example, not by Doctrine, Teach.
Next bring the Lewder Clergy there,
Who Preach those Sins down, which *they can't forbear;*
Those *Sons of God* who every day *Go in,*
Both to *the Daughters* and *the Wives* of Men;
There Let 'em stand to be the Nations Jest,
And save the Reputation of the rest.

Asgill who for the Gospel left the Law,
And deep within the Clefts of Darkness saw;

186. *Bills false Endors'd:* See *The True-Born Englishman,* 1152 *n.,* above. *Accounts unmade:* See *The Golden Age,* 45 *n.,* above.

189. *History:* Defoe wrote Sir Charles Duncombe's "History" in *The True-Born Englishman,* 1045–1190.

212. *Sons of God:* "when the sons of God came in unto the daughters of men . . . they bare children to them" (Genesis 6:4).

216. *Asgill (Key):* See *The True-Born Englishman,* 510 *n.,* above.

Let him be an Example made,
Who durst the Parsons Province so Invade;
To his new Ecclesiastick Rules,
We owe the Knowledge that we all are Fools:
Old *Charon* shall no more dark Souls convey,
Asgill has found the shortest way:
Vain is your funeral Pomp and Bells,
Your Grave-stones, Monuments and Knells;
Vain are the Trophyes of the Grave,
Asgill shall all that Foppery save;
And to the Clergy's great Reproach,
Shall change the *Hearse* into a *Fiery Coach:*
What Man the Learned Riddle can receive,
Which none can Answer, and yet none Believe;
Let him Recorded, on thy *Lists* remain,
Till he shall Heav'n by his own Rules obtain.

If a Poor Author has Embrac'd thy *Wood,*
Only because he was not understood,
They Punish Mankind but by halves,
Till they stand there,
Who false to their own Principles appear:
And cannot understand themselves.
Those *Nimshites,* who with furious Zeal drive on,
And build up *Rome* to pull down *Babylon;*
The real Authors of *the Shortest Way,*
Who for Destruction, not Conversion pray:
There let those Sons of Strife remain,
Till this Church Riddle they Explain;
How at Dissenters they can raise a Storm,
But would not have them all Conform;
For *there* their certain Ruine would come in,
And Moderation, *which they hate,* begin.
Some Church-men Next should Grace thy *Pews,*

235. *not understood:* Cf. *More Reformation,* 713 *n.,* above.

238. *false to their own Principles:* See *More Reformation,* 578–85, above.

240. *Nimshites:* Jehu, the son of Nimshi, who "driveth furiously" (2 Kings 9:20), is Defoe's "Type" of high flying clergy.

241. *build up . . . pull down:* Cf. *More Reformation,* 343 *n.,* above.

242. *real Authors:* See 69 *n.,* above.

Who Talk of Loyalty they never use;
Passive Obedience well becomes thy *Stage,*
For both have been the banter of the Age.
  Get them but Once within thy reach,
Thoul't make them practice what they us'd to Teach.

  Next bring some Lawyers to thy *Bar,*
By *Inuendo* they might all stand there;
  There let them Expiate that Guilt,
And Pay for all that Blood their Tongues ha' spilt;
  These are the Mountebanks of State,
Who *by the slight of Tongue* can Crimes create,
And dress up Trifles in the *Robes of Fate.*
  The *Mastives* of a Government,
To *worry* and run down the Innocent;
  The Engines of Infernall Wit,
  Cover'd with Cunning and Deceit:
Satan's Sublimest Attribute they use,
  For first they Tempt, and then Accuse;
No Vows or Promises can bind their hands,
  Submissive Law Obedient stands:
When Power concurrs, and Lawless Force stands by,
He's Lunatick that Looks for Honesty.

  There Sat a Man of Mighty Fame,
Whose Actions speak him plainer than his Name;
In vain he struggl'd, he harangu'd in vain,
To bring in *Whipping Sentences* again:
And to debauch a Milder Government,
With *Abdicated kinds of Punishment.*
  No wonder he should Law despise,
  Who *Jesus Christ* himself denies;

252. *Passive Obedience:* Defoe ridiculed the high church doctrine that obedience to a king must be absolute. "The Laws are the Test . . . of . . . Obedience," he said, "and to pretend to more Obedience than the Law requires, is abusing your Prince, and abusing your Selves" (*A New Test of the Church of England's Loyalty,* 1702, p. 32).

273. *a Man of Mighty Fame:* Sir Simon Harcourt, the solicitor-general, as these lines imply, may have demanded that whipping be included in Defoe's sentence, as it had been in William Fuller's (46 *n.*, above).

280. *Jesus Christ . . . denies:* Defoe called him *"Socinian Harcourt"* in *Reformation of Manners,* 573.

His Actions only now direct,
What we when he is made a Judge, expect:
Set *Lovell* next to his Disgrace,
With *Whitney's Horses* staring in his Face;
There let his Cup of Pennance be kept full,
Till he's less Noisy, Insolent and Dull.

When all these Heroes have past o'er thy *Stage*,
And thou hast been the Satyr of the Age;
Wait then a while for all those Sons of Fame,
Whom present Pow'r has made too great to name:
Fenc'd from thy hands, they keep our Verse in Awe,
Too great for Satyr, and too great for Law.
As they their Commands lay down,
They all shall pay their Homage to thy *Cloudy Throne:*
And till within thy reach they be,
Exalt them in Effigie.

The Martyrs of the by-past Reign,
For whom new Oaths have been prepar'd in vain;
Sherlock's Disciple first by him trepan'd,
He for a Knave and they for Fools should stand.
Tho' some affirm he ought to be Excus'd,
Since to this Day he had refus'd;

283. *Lovell (Key)*: See *Reformation of Manners,* 115–48, 115 *n.,* above.

284. *Whitney's Horses:* See *More Reformation,* 824 *n.,* above.

297. *Martyrs:* nonjurors (*The True-Born Englishman,* 736 *n.,* above).

299. *Sherlock (Key)*: "the famous Dr. *S———k,*" as Defoe called him, "Who having stood out long in his old antiquated Doctrine of Passive Obedience, and confirm'd the Faith of his Suff'ring Brethren, by strong and wonderful Arguments, at last, at the powerful Instigation of a Wife, and a good Salary, *has Sold all his Loyalty for a Mess of Pottage*" (*A New Test of the Church of England's Loyalty,* pp. 16–17).

Disciple: There is some evidence that the nonjuror Thomas Wagstaffe (1645–1712), who was secretly consecrated bishop of Ipswich in February 1694 and who openly maintained a brisk trade in Jacobite pamphlets, had been Sherlock's "Disciple" before Sherlock took the oaths to William and Mary. In 1690 Sherlock supplied him with notes and engaged him to write "a Vindication of the Principle of Passive-Obedience" (Bodl. MS. Tanner 27, f. 188, cited in [J. L. Anderton], *The Life of Thomas Ken,* 2nd ed., 2 vols., 1854, *2,* 547 *n.*). It is difficult to imagine how Defoe could have known of this transaction.

300. *He . . . they:* Wagstaffe(?) . . . the other nonjurors.

301. *he:* Sherlock.

302. *this Day:* 25 September 1690, when Sherlock "at last resolved to take the oaths . . . [and] kist his majesties hand" (Luttrell, *2,* 108).

And this was all the Frailty of his Life,
He Damn'd his Conscience, to oblige his Wife.
But spare that Priest, whose tottering Conscience knew
That if he took but one, he'd Perjure two:
Bluntly resolv'd he wou'd not break 'em both,
And Swore by God he'd never take the Oath;
  Hang him, he can't be fit for thee,
  For his *unusual Honesty.*

  Thou *Speaking Trumpet of Mens Fame,*
  Enter in every Court thy Claim;
Demand 'em all, for they are all thy own,
Who Swear to Three Kings, but are true to none.
  Turn-Coats of all sides are thy due,
And he who once is false, is never true:
To Day can Swear, to Morrow can Abjure,
For Treachery's a Crime no Man can Cure:
Such without scruple, for the time to come,
May Swear to all the Kings in Christendom;
  But he's a Mad Man will rely
  Upon their lost Fidelity.

They that in vast Employments rob the State,
Let them in thy *Embraces* meet their Fate;
Let not the Millions they by Fraud obtain,
Protect 'em from the Scandal, or the Pain:
  They who from Mean Beginnings grow
  To vast Estates, but *God knows how;*
  Who carry untold Summs away,
From little Places, with but little Pay:
  Who Costly Palaces Erect,
  The Thieves that built them to Protect;
The *Gardens, Grotto's, Fountains, Walks,* and *Groves*
Where Vice Triumphs in Pride, and Lawless Loves:

305. *that Priest:* Wagstaffe(?).

314. *Three Kings:* Not all Anglican parsons were as agile as the vicar of Bray, but 95 per cent of them took the oaths to Charles II, James II, and William III (*The True-Born Englishman,* 736 *n.,* above).

327. *Mean Beginnings:* Cf. *The True-Born Englishman,* 428 *n.,* above.

331. *Palaces:* Cf. *The Golden Age,* 45 *n.,* above.

Where mighty Luxury and Drunk'ness Reign'd,
Profusely Spend what they Prophanely Gain'd:
Tell 'em their *Mene Tekel's* on the Wall,
Tell 'em the *Nations Money* paid for all:

  Advance thy *double Front* and show,
And let us both the Crimes and Persons know:
  Place them aloft upon thy *Throne,*
Who slight the Nation's Business for their own;
Neglect their Posts, in spight of Double Pay,
And run us all in Debt *the Shortest Way.*

  Great Pageant, Change thy Dirty Scene,
For on thy Steps some Ladies may be seen;
When Beauty stoops upon thy Stage to show,
She laughs at all the Humble Fools below.
Set *Sapho* there, whose Husband paid for Clothes
Two Hundred Pounds a Week in *Furbulo's:*
There in her Silks and Scarlets let her shine,
She's Beauteous all without, all Whore within.

  Next let Gay URANIA Ride,
Her Coach and Six attending by her side:
  Long has she waited, but in vain,
  The City Homage to obtain:
The Sumptuous Harlot long'd t' Insult the *Chair,*
And Triumph o'er our City Beauties there.
Here let her Haughty Thoughts be Gratifi'd,
    In Triumph let her Ride;

  Let DIADORA next appear,
And all that want to know her, see her there.

337. *Mene Tekel:* "Mene Mene, Tekel Upharsin" was the handwriting on the wall which prophesied the end of Belshazzar's empire (Daniel 5:25).

345–68. These lines with their generalized "Characters of Women" based on particular cases may have supplied the pattern for Pope's *Epistle to a Lady.*

349. *Sapho:* glossed "Ranelah" in the Victoria and Albert Museum copy of *A,* presumably Margaret, countess of Ranelagh (*The Court,* 49 *n.,* above; *The Golden Age,* 45 *n.,* above).

353. *Urania:* See *Reformation of Manners,* 1215 *n.,* above.

361. *Diadora:* See *More Reformation,* 759–64, above.

What tho' she's not *a True-Born English Whore?*
  French Harlots have been here before;
Let not the Pomp nor Grandeur of her State
  Prevent the Justice of her Fate,
But let her an Example now be made
To Foreign *Whores* who spoil the English Trade.

Let *Flettumacy* with his Pompous Train,
  Attempt to rescue her in vain;
  Content at last to see her shown,
Let him despise her Wit, and find his own:
Tho' his Inheritance of Brains was small,
Dear-bought Experience will Instruct us all.

  Claim 'em, thou *Herald of Reproach,*
Who with uncommon Lewdness will Debauch;
Let *Crisp* upon thy Borders spend his Life,
'Till he Recants the Bargain with his Wife:
  And till this Riddle both Explain,
  How neither can themselves Contain;
How Nature can on both sides run so high,
As neither side can neither side supply:
  And so in Charity agree,
He keeps two Brace of Whores, two Stallions she.

What need of *Satyr* to Reform the Town?
  Or Laws to keep our Vices down?
  Let 'em *to Thee* due Homage pay,
This will Reform us all *the Shortest Way.*
Let 'em *to thee* bring all the Knaves and Fools,
  Vertue will guide the rest by Rules;
They'll need no Treacherous Friends, no breach of Faith,
No Hir'd Evidence with their Infecting Breath;
  No Servants Masters to Betray,
  Or Knights o'th' Post, who Swear for Pay;

369. *Flettumacy:* See *More Reformation,* 755–58, above.
377. *Crisp* (*Key*): See *More Reformation,* 229–33, 229 *n.*, above.
394. *Knights o'th' Post:* professional perjurers; proverbial (Tilley K164).

No injur'd Author'll on thy Steps appear,
Not such as *won't be Rogues,* but such *as are.*

The first Intent of Laws
Was to Correct th' Effect, and check the Cause;
And all the Ends of Punishment,
Were only Future Mischiefs to prevent.
But Justice is Inverted when
Those Engines of the Law,
Instead of pinching Vicious Men,
Keep Honest Ones in awe;
Thy Business is, as all Men know,
To Punish Villains, not to make Men so.

When ever then thou art prepar'd,
To prompt that Vice thou should'st Reward,
And by the Terrors of thy *Grisly Face,*
Make Men turn Rogues to shun Disgrace;
The End of thy Creation is destroy'd,
Justice expires of Course, and Law's made void.
What are thy Terrors? that for fear of thee,
Mankind should dare to sink their Honesty?
He's Bold to Impudence, that dare turn Knave,
The Scandal of thy Company to save:
He that will Crimes he never knew confess,
Does more than if he knew those Crimes transgress:
And he that fears thee more than to be base,
May want a *Heart,* but does not want a *Face.*
Thou like the Devil dost appear
Blacker than really thou art by far:
A wild Chimerick Notion of Reproach,
Too little for a Crime, for none too much:
Let none th' Indignity resent,
For Crime is all the shame of Punishment.

Thou *Bug-bear of the Law* stand up and speak,
Thy long Misconstru'd Silence break,
Tell us who 'tis upon thy *Ridge* stands there,

So full of Fault, and yet so void of Fear;
And from the Paper in his Hat,
Let all Mankind be told for what:

Tell them it was because he was too bold,
And told those Truths, which shou'd not ha' been told.
Extol the Justice of the Land,
Who Punish what they will not understand.
Tell them he stands Exalted there,
For speaking what we wou'd not hear;
And yet he might ha' been secure,
Had he said less, or wou'd he ha' said more.
Tell them that this is his Reward,
And worse is yet for him prepar'd,
Because his Foolish Vertue was so nice
As not to sell his Friends, according to his Friends Advice;
And thus he's an Example made,
To make Men of their Honesty afraid,

That for the time to come they may,
More willingly their Friends betray,
Tell 'em the Magistrates that plac'd him here,

431. *Paper:* See 124 *n.,* above.

440. *said more:* Even after he had been sentenced on 7 July, but before he stood in the pillory, Defoe was visited in prison by two distinguished personages: the new duke of Buckingham and Normanby, lord privy seal, and the earl of Nottingham, the principal secretary of state (Moore, *Daniel Defoe,* pp. 137–39). "What he said in *Newgate* to two Peers" ([William Pittis], *The True-Born-Hugonot,* 1703, p. 4), is not recorded, but it was clearly not enough to reduce his sentence.

444. *sell his Friends:* Defoe said later that "the Author of the *Review* was set in the Pillory . . . *for speaking the Truth . . . since 'tis well known, he could have deliver'd himself from that Ignominy, if he would have sold his Friends for his own Liberty, and betray'd the Memory of his Master King* William." On another occasion he recalled that his friends who had raised £1000 bail for him on 5 June 1703 "were so apprehensive for me, and for my Family, that they earnestly pressed me to go away; and offered to give it me under their Hands, that they had given me their Free Consent" (*Review, 5* [25 December 1708], 466; [9] [7 May 1713], 184).

445. *Example:* Even the Presbyterian minister Edmund Calamy, who knew "what its Design was," agreed that Defoe "must be made an Example, for the Terror of others," for publishing *The Shortest Way with the Dissenters* (*An Abridgement of Mr. Baxter's History,* 2nd ed., 2 vols., 1713, *1,* 634, 635).

449–52. Defoe quotes these lines in *Review,* 2 (11 August 1705), 278.

449. *Magistrates:* The six justices who presided at Defoe's trial were Sir Edward

Are Scandals to the Times,
Are at a loss to find his Guilt,
And can't Commit his Crimes.

Ward, lord chief baron of the exchequer, Sir Samuel Dashwood, the lord mayor (cf. *More Reformation,* 234 *n.,* above), three aldermen: Sir John Fleet, Sir Edward Clarke, and Sir Thomas Abney, and the recorder, Sir Salathiel Lovell, who pronounced the sentence (*Reformation of Manners,* 115–48; *More Reformation,* 797–815).

451. *at a loss:* cf. [Defoe], *More Short-Ways with the Dissenters,* 1704, p. 1: "that noble Lord [Nottingham(?)], who told the Author of his Extraordinary Guilt, wou'd be puzzl'd to find a Crime in it."

1704

On the King of Spain's Voyage to Portugall
(January[?] 1704)

The two short poems following are a selection of those that record the Tories' increasing disenchantment with Queen Anne. The first of these converts the case of the archduke Charles of Austria into a cautionary tale.

Charles of Habsburg (1685–1740), second son of the emperor Leopold I, was a cousin and nephew (by marriage) of the dead king of Spain, Carlos II. He had been named heir to the entire Spanish empire except the grand duchy of Milan, Naples, and Sicily, in the second partition treaty, which France, England, and the Netherlands signed in February 1700. But the emperor denounced the partition treaty and claimed the entire inheritance for himself. When Carlos died in October 1700 and left the entire inheritance to Philippe, duc d'Anjou, the second grandson of Louis XIV (*The Spanish Descent,* 138 *n.,* above), Leopold began to reconsider. In September 1702 he declared war on Louis XIV and his grandson, who, he said, had been "intruded" as king of Spain. Then he prepared a manifesto "to be sent to Spain to declare the archduke Charles king thereof." To Charles he granted a patent "and a great number of declarations" investing him with the crown of Spain. Finally, in June 1703 he concluded a treaty with Portugal, England, and the Netherlands whereby Charles was to marry Doña Teresa, the infanta of Portugal (then seven years old), and be established on the throne of Spain by the armed forces of the confederates (Luttrell, *5,* 220, 221; Lamberty, *2,* 213; [John Colbatch], *An Account of the Court of Portugal,* 1700, p. 260).

This ambitious plan was set in motion in Vienna on 1/12 September 1703 when Charles was proclaimed king of Spain and sent off a week later to claim his throne and his bride. To avoid the French armies in Bavaria and the Lowlands, he proceeded to The Hague (where he was to take shipping for Portsmouth and Lisbon) by way of Prague, Leipzig, Halle, Halberstadt, Düsseldorf, and Rotterdam.

He traveled in great state—his equipage alone was said to have cost £15,000—and everywhere was received with all possible marks of respect, including the discharge of cannon, and "a very fine *Italian* Opera" at Düsseldorf, where he also granted a private audience to the duke of Marlborough. In the meantime the queen's upholsterer had been sent down to Portsmouth to hang with crimson velvet the cabin of the *Royal Catherine,* which was to carry the king to Lisbon, and a new standard was made for him in London "curiously wrought with the arms of Spain and the house of Austria." Finally, on 9 November at Oranjepolder, he boarded the royal yacht *Peregrine* to cross the Channel (*The London Gazette,* No. 3950, 16–20 September 1703; No. 3957, 11–14 October 1703; No. 3969, 22–25 November 1703; Luttrell, *5,* 318, 332, 340).

On the same day, at the opening of the second session of her first parliament, Anne declared that "recovering the Monarchy of *Spain* from the House of *Bourbon* and restoring it to the House of *Austria*" was government policy of "the highest Importance imaginable" (*CJ, 14,* 211). The expenses of "the king of Spain's voyage to Portugal" were already said to be £105,000 "at her majesties charge" (Luttrell, *5,* 352).

The *Peregrine,* however, was driven back to port by violent winds, which reached a climax in the great storm of 27 November and prevented Charles from setting foot in England until 28 December 1703. Then, after a week's entertainment at Petworth and Windsor Castle, he set sail from Portsmouth with a vast fleet of English and Dutch men-of-war under the command of Sir George Rooke and transports sufficient for an army of 24,000 men. Two weeks later, within sight of the Spanish coast, this entire flotilla was forced by contrary winds all the way back to England and Charles again found himself the guest of the duke of Somerset at Petworth. He sailed from Portsmouth a second time on 13 February and on 25 March/5 April 1704 finally reached Lisbon, where he was entertained "with great Magnificence." But "the infanta of Portugal, whom the king of Spain was to have married," had died the month before of smallpox (*The London Gazette,* No. 3979, 27–30 December 1703; No. 3981, 3–6 January 1704; Luttrell, *5,* 382–83 391 400).

In three witnesses (*ABC*) the poem is dated 1703/4 and in two more (*KL*) it is dated 1704. No evidence of authorship has been discovered.

On the King of Spain's Voyage to Portugall

Backt with Confederate Force the Austrian goes,
To find in Spain strong Friends and Feeble Foes.
But oh! Unthinking Anna, have a care
How with Your Troops you Wage a Distant War,
Whilst an Apparent Danger Dwells so near.
And Whilst You would a Settled Prince Dethrone,
And durst Dispute a Title to a Crown,
The World enquires by what You hold Your own.
How long has our Vile Gazeteer mistook:

2. *strong Friends and Feeble Foes: The London Gazette* claimed not only that Portugal had already raised a force of 27,000 men, but that "the Spanish Forces lessen daily, as well by Sickness, as by the Desertion of their Soldiers" to the Portuguese "in whole Companies" (No. 3961, 25–28 October 1703; No. 3975, 13–16 December 1703; No. 3984, 13–17 January 1704).

4. *Your Troops:* According to the terms of the Methuen treaty (May 1703) (*EHD*, pp. 876–78) Pedro II was required to provide 28,000 troops of which the cost of 13,000 was to be borne by the confederates. The confederates in turn were required to provide 12,000 "foreign veteran soldiers" each, but since "the imperial treasury [was] much exhausted," England had to assume this share as well (Luttrell, *5*, 295, 329). Thus England (and the Netherlands, which the poet ignores) ended up providing or paying for the entire force.

5. *an Apparent Danger:* News of the Scotch plot (*An Address to Our Sovereign Lady*, headnote, p. 615 below) began leaking out in December 1703. Luttrell first mentions "a design of inviting the prince of Wales into England" on 11 December 1703, but it was not until 29 January 1704 that Nottingham laid before the House of Lords "several depositions relating to the plot for introducing the prince of Wales" (Luttrell, *5*, 368, 385).

8. *by what You hold:* Anne was queen of England not by divine right but by act of parliament and the failure of William and Mary to leave issue. The Bill of Rights (December 1689), which "declared" William and Mary king and queen of England, also provided that "for default of [their] issue" the crown devolve upon Princess Anne of Denmark (*EHD*, p. 124).

9. *Gazeteer: Robert Yard* (d. 1705) was a protégé of Sir Joseph Williamson, who sent him to The Hague in October 1666 to learn languages. Yard's position as Williamson's clerk gradually evolved into the important post of permanent under-secretary of state and in this capacity he served the duke of Shrewsbury, the earl of Jersey, and James Vernon in William's reign, and the earl of Nottingham in Anne's. He was also appointed a clerk of the signet (March 1678), secretary to the lords justices (July 1698), and commissioner of prizes (June 1702). He began to compile *The London Gazette* from foreign newsletters and diplomatic correspondence in 1671 while a clerk in the State Paper office, and this post evolved into that of Gazetteer to which Yard was

First Made him Monarch, then Redubb'd him Duke?
Phillip was King of Spain two Months ago,
And now (the Lord be Prais'd) Duke Charles is so;
Why i'n't th'Equivocating Rogue Arraign'd for't,
For making Spain so near Resemble Brentford?
Two Kings of Spain at once is all a Jest;
Phillip is King, while Phillip is Possess'd.
Mere Title, Charles, will ne'er thy Cause Advance;
You're King of Spain as Anne is Queen of France.

---

reappointed in the new reign (*CSPD 1666–1667*, pp. 17, 52, 104, 419; *CSPD Addenda 1660–1685*, p. 403; *CSPD 1678*, p. 71; *CSPD 1695*, p. 243; Luttrell, *4*, 404, 517, 661, 705; *5*, 169, 182, 336; *CTB 1702*, p. 196).

10. *Monarch . . . Redubb'd . . . Duke:* Philippe, duc d'Anjou, was called king of Spain in *The London Gazette* from November 1700 when he was proclaimed in Paris to May 1703. From May to October 1703 Yard solved the problem of what to call Philippe by not printing any news from Spain. Finally, at the end of October after Charles had been proclaimed in Vienna, Yard demoted Philippe to duke of Anjou (*The London Gazette,* No. 3653, 11–14 November 1700; No. 3916, 20–24 May 1703; No. 3961, 25–28 October 1703).

12. *Charles:* The archduke Charles was proclaimed king of Spain in Vienna on 1/12 September 1703 (*The London Gazette,* No. 3950, 16–20 September 1703).

14. *Brentford:* The reference is to George Villiers, second duke of Buckingham, *The Rehearsal* (1672). "The chief hindge of this Play," Bayes explains, "is, that I suppose two Kings to be of the same place" (I, i).

18. *Queen of France:* Anne's title was "*Dei Gratia* of England, Scotland, France, *and* Ireland, Queen, *Defender of the Faith.*"

On the 8th of March 1703/4
(March 1704)

The occasion for the next of the Jacobite satires on Queen Anne was a resolution of the House of Commons to celebrate the second anniversary of "her Majesty's Inauguration Day at the Church of *St. Margaret's, Westminster*" on 8 March 1704. Francis Atterbury, the high flying archdeacon of Totnes, was invited to preach, and the Lords, not to be outdone, invited the Whiggish bishop of Chichester, John Williams, to preach to them in Westminster Abbey on the same occasion. Since Ash Wednesday also fell on 8 March this year, the irony of a feast day to be celebrated on a fast day was not lost on the anonymous author of the present poem (*CJ*, *14*, 366; Luttrell, *5*, 398).

On the 8th of March 1703/4

Hail Queen of Hearts! to whose true English praise
The faithfull Commons vote new holy-days,
Turn fasts to feasts, and bless with gratefull Cant
A day, the Subject of a double Lent;
How happy thou in such a Loyall House
Of Atheists, Rakes, Enthusiasts and Beaux.
How happy Church and State in those and Thee,
Choice Subjects of an English Jubilee;
'Twas thus thy grateful Father Sanctify'd
The joyfull day on which his brother dy'd
And since We must Your Brother's death pursue
With the like Cant, and Gratitude for You,
For Yours, what shall we not have cause to do?

4. *day:* Ash Wednesday, "pulvis es et in pulverem reverteris," the first day of Lent.

8. *Jubilee:* See *The True-Born Englishman,* 1060 *n.,* above.

9. *grateful:* Charles II died on 6 February 1685 and according to Lord Ailesbury (*1,* 98) James succeeded him "with an inward as well as outward joy."

Sanctify'd: According to Burnet (*1,* 610), Charles II's funeral was "very mean. He did not lie in state: No mournings were given: . . . Many . . . said, that he deserved better from his brother."

11. *Your Brother:* William III.

13. *Yours:* Anne's death.

Arthur Mainwaring[?]

An Address to Our Sovereign Lady
(5 April 1704)

Narcissus Luttrell called this poem "A scandalous libel on the Commons in Parliament." While it might more accurately be called a libel on the Tory majority in the Commons in parliament, there can be no doubt that it is scandalous, for it accuses them collectively of treason. Again, it would be more accurate to say that it is the Tory majority in the Commons who condemn themselves, for it is their speaker who must be imagined to deliver the words of the poem. Generically, therefore, the poem is a mock address to the throne. The scene is the throne room in the palace of St. James, with Robert Harley and 31 members of the Committee for the Address of Thanks drawn up in the presence of the queen. After the usual ceremonies of obeisance, the speaker begins to read, pausing at one point to make an embarrassing reference to Sir John Pakington. So the poem is also a dramatic chorus, providing wry, riddling comment on the action of the Tory majority during the parliamentary session that began in November 1703. The author, in short, makes ironic use of the attitudes of frustration and disenchantment that were expressed literally in the two preceding poems.

The occasion for this choric comment was the discovery in December 1703 of the Scotch plot, or the Queensberry plot as it is known in Scotland. This affair, which has been called "another of the many mysteries of Scottish history" (P. Hume Brown, *History of Scotland,* 3 vols., Cambridge, Cambridge University Press, 1900–09, *3,* 91) turns around the enigmatic figure of Simon Fraser, who, as Lord Lovat, was beheaded in the Tower in April 1747 for high treason. In pursuit of his own tangled ambitions or his personal vendetta with John Murray, first duke of Atholl, Fraser, who was himself traveling in Scotland in May 1703 under orders signed by James III, convinced James Douglas, second duke of Queensberry, the royal high commissioner to the parliament of Scotland, that Atholl was plotting an insurrection on behalf of the pretender.

Queensberry had his own reasons for hating Atholl—whom Fraser later admitted to be "notoriously the incorrigible enemy of king James"—and reported this alarming news to Nottingham (*Memoirs of the Life of Simon Lord Lovat,* 1797, p. 175; James Macpherson, *Original Papers,* 2nd ed., 2 vols., 1776, *1,* 630–31).

Nottingham, too, had ample reason to believe in the reality of a plot. All summer long he had been busy intercepting treasonable correspondence and arresting spies from France. His agents reported again and again that "There is something pernicious to the Queen and Government working in England, Scotland, and Ireland . . . some notorious contrivances against the Queen and Government." He was warned that "the French come ashore frequently and boldly" at Cuckmere, in East Sussex, and from there scatter through the country "to kindle an unnatural war" (*CSPD 1703–1704,* pp. 54, 134, 183, 250).

In July Nottingham began to catch bigger game. He intercepted letters in cipher to David Lindsay in Edinburgh, who had been "much trusted at *St. Germains*" as undersecretary to John Drummond, earl of Melfort, and Charles Middleton, second earl of Middleton, James II's secretaries of state. In November Nottingham arrested Sir John Maclean, fourth baronet, Catholic chief of the Highland clan which he had led against William's army at Killiecrankie in 1689. Maclean and his wife, who had been delivered of a child only 11 days before, had crossed the Channel in a small boat and landed secretly at Folkestone in Kent. Finally, on 12 December Nottingham intercepted another boatload of Jacobites at Eastbourne, only a few miles from Cuckmere. These included Major James Boucher, an aide-de-camp to James Fitzjames, duke of Berwick, James II's illegitimate son, a marshal of France, and a most successful military leader (*CSPD 1703–1704,* pp. 60–61, 478; Burnet, *2,* 371–73).

These ominous events were made public on 14 December 1703 when Richard Lumley, earl of Scarbrough, read to the House of Lords a provocative letter to his brother, Lieutenant-General Henry Lumley, from James Boucher, "lately come out of *France.*" Nottingham assured the Lords that the matter was already before the queen and that details would be forthcoming in a few days. Then the Lords turned to consider the second bill to prevent occasional conformity, which the Commons had passed a week before. There can be no doubt that Scarbrough's revelations influenced the Lords in their debate: Wharton "took notice of the distracted State of *Scotland*" and argued that nothing ought to be done to increase divisions in England; Lord Mohun "did not stick to say, that *if they pass'd this Bill, they had as good Tack the pretended Prince of Wales to it.*" After long debate the bill was defeated 71–59, even before a second reading (*LJ, 17,* 348; Boyer, *Annals,* 1704, p. 189; Luttrell, *5,* 369; cf. [William Pittis], *The Proceedings of Both Houses of Parliament in the Years 1702, 1703, 1704,* 1710, pp. 53–55).

The next day, the Lords, observing "that there was a general Remissness . . . in the taking, searching, and looking into such Prisoners" (*LJ, 17,* 372) (cf. 11 *n.,* below), ordered Maclean and Boucher to be brought to the House for examination. While the Lords went ahead, on 18 December, to appoint a select committee to examine the prisoners, the Commons framed an address to the queen expressing absolute confidence in the "Directions" that the queen had already given. On 20 December, when they learned of the Lords' actions, the Commons appointed John Howe, Sir Simon Harcourt, Sir Humphrey Mackworth, Sir Roger Mostyn, Sir Christopher Musgrave, William Bromley, Sir Edward Seymour, and 25 more members, to a committee, of which Henry St. John was chairman, to draft a second address to the queen. It is this address, presented to the Queen on 23 December and immediately ordered to be published, that provided the occasion for the present poem (*CJ, 14,* 254–55, 257). "It was an amazing thing," Burnet said, "to see a House of Commons affirm, in so publick a manner and so positively, that the Lords taking Criminals into their own Custody, in order to an Examination, was without Warrant or Precedent; when there were so many Instances, fresh in every Man's Memory, especially since the Time of the Popish Plot, of Precedents . . . that went much further" (Burnet, *2,* 374).

According to the Luttrell copy (now in the Newberry Library), the poem was published on 5 April 1704, two days after Anne finally put an end to this second session of her first parliament. Presumably it was written shortly after 23 December 1703, the date of the occasion it celebrates. In one of the manuscripts (*C*) the poem is subscribed "Robert Wisdome," which may be a pseudonym. *The History and Fall of the Conformity Bill* ("God bless our gracious Sovereign Anne"), a similar Whiggish satire dated January 1704, is also subscribed "Thus sung Robert (or Robin) Wisdom" in five manuscripts (Trumbull MS. Add. 17, BM MS. Add. 40060, Osborn MS. Chest II, No. 58, Portland MS. Pw V 42, and Cowper MS. Box 46) and in two printed books (*POAS,* 1704, *3,* 425, and *PRSA,* 1705, p. 557). But Alexander Pope wrote in his copy of *PRSA,* 1705 (BM C.28.e.15): "Certainly written by Mr. Congreve." Oldmixon, however, in *The Life and Posthumous Work of Arthur Maynwaring,* 1715, p. 40, records that this "merry Ballad" was variously said to be written by Henry Mordaunt or "Lord *H*[*alifax*], but Mr. *Maynwaring* was the Author of it." So the best guess may be that "Robert Wisdom" is a pseudonym for Arthur Mainwaring.

An Address to Our Sovereign Lady

We Address you to Day in a very new Fashion,
And tell you of nothing but Force and Invasion,
Tho some folks will Laugh when they hear the Occasion;
Violation's the Word, not a Tittle o'th' Church,
For as *Johnny* says Plainly, You've left that in the Lurch:
That Sham's at an End which made such a pother,
And we're plaguily put to our Trumps for another:
For since the Curst Lords have thrown out the Bill
And have chose a Committee which Piss in a Quill,
Who (if we be silent) will find out the Plot,
(Then *Nottingham*'s Merit will soon be forgot

4. *Violation's the Word:* On 21 December 1703 when the first paragraph of the address to the queen drafted by Henry St. John was read in the Commons—"We, your Majesty's most dutiful and loyal Subjects, the Commons of *England,* in Parliament assembled, beg Leave humbly to lay before your Majesty the great and just Concern we are under to see any Violation of your royal Prerogative"—a motion was made to leave out "are under, to see any Violation" and to insert "have of the Preservation," but upon a division the House voted 180–142 to retain "Violation" with its "amazing" reflection upon the House of Lords (*CJ, 14,* 259).

5. *Johnny:* Glossed "Packington" in a copy of *A* at Balcarres, the reference is apparently to Sir John Pakington (*The Golden Age Restor'd,* headnote, pp. 488–89 above). Although not a member of the committee that drafted the address of 23 December 1703, Pakington published *A Speech for the Bill against Occasional Conformity* [January 1704?], which reminded the queen of her "Title of *Defender of the Faith*" (*The Observator,* No. 89, 9–12 February 1704). "The Church . . . Which has of late been left i'th' lurch/By her own Sons and Heirs" appears in *The History and Fall of the Conformity Bill,* another poem subscribed "Sic Cecinit Rob. Wisdom" (headnote, p. 617 above).

6. *That Sham:* the second bill to prevent occasional conformity.

8. *thrown out the Bill:* The Lords rejected the second bill against occasional conformity on 14 December 1703 (Luttrell, *5,* 369).

9. *a Committee:* The select committee of the House of Lords to examine witnesses in the Scotch plot included seven Whigs: the dukes of Devonshire and Somerset, the earls of Sunderland and Scarbrough, and Lords Townshend, Wharton, and Somers (*LJ, 17,* 353–54).

11. *Nottingham's Merit:* On 20 December 1703 the Commons began to consider the case of Captain Robert Middleton, a retired officer in James II's Scotch Guards, who had come over from Calais to Dover without a passport early in July, been arrested at Hull, but released on Nottingham's orders on 14 August (*CSPD 1703–1704,* pp. 66–67, 88). The debate was resumed the next day and lasted late into the night, "not without some

And some of us, probably, may go to Pot),
We are forc'd to Invent, in this Dangerous Crisis,
Some pretty New Whim to Confound their Devices:
Why Madam, You're Ravisht, Your Queenshipp's Invaded,
And we must Squeal out till of this You are perswaded.
But who are the Villains, perhaps You will ask,
And if we did not tell You, 'twou'd be a hard Task
To Guess or Perceive You had any Abuse,
So that we come on purpose to tell you the News.
'Tis the Whole House of Lords, those Damnable Lords,
Who have done this sad thing upon most of our Words:
O Madam, take care of Prerogative Royal.
We were never till Now so Confoundedly Loyal
For Extending your Power to be humbly Addressing,
But You see we Conform, on Occasion so pressing,

---

severe Reflections upon his Lordship," but at last it was resolved, "That the Earl of *Nottingham,* one of her Majesty's principal Secretaries of State, for his great Abilities and Diligence in the Execution of his Office, for his unquestionable Fidelity to the Queen, and her Government, and for his steady adhering to the Church of *England,* as by Law established, hath highly merited the Trust her Majesty hath reposed in him" (Boyer, *Annals,* 1704, p. 194; *CJ, 14,* 260).

22. *this sad thing:* In the third paragraph of the address the Commons said, "We are therefore surprised to find, that, when several Persons, suspected of treasonable Practices against your Majesty, were taken into Custody by your Messengers, in order to be examined, *the Lords, in violation of the known Laws of the Land, have wrested them out of your Majesty's Hands, and, without your Majesty's Leave, or Knowledge, in a most extraordinary Manner taken the Examination of them solely to themselves;* whereby a due Enquiry into the evil Practices, and Designs, against your Majesty's Person and Government, may, in great measure be obstructed" (*CJ, 14,* 259, italics added).

our Words: The second paragraph of the address reads: "Your faithful Commons believe the Administration of the Government best secured, when it is left to your Majesty, with whom the Law has entrusted it; and have so firm a Dependence upon your Majesty's Affection to your People, and your great Wisdom, that they can never apprehend so little Danger from any Conspiracy, as *when the Examination thereof is under your Majesty's Direction*" (*CJ, 14,* 259, italics added).

23. *Prerogative:* The fourth paragraph of the address reads: "Your loyal Commons do therefore most earnestly desire your Majesty, to suffer no Diminution of that Prerogative, which, during your Majesty's Reign, they are confident will always be exerted for the Good of your People" (*CJ, 14,* 259).

24. *Loyal:* The last paragraph reads: "And we humbly beg Leave to assure your Majesty, that, as we are resolved, by timely and effectual Supplies, to enable your Majesty to carry on the War, which we have so gloriously begun; so we will, to the utmost of our Power, support your Majesty in the Exercise of your just Prerogative at home, and in the Assertion of it against all Invasions whatsoever" (*CJ, 14,* 259).

To Glut our Revenge, Moderation to foil,
The Peers to Affront, the State to Embroil:
This Glorious Quarrel we come to Advance,
Much Dearer to Us, than that against *FRANCE*.

27. *Revenge:* Cf. Burnet (2, 373): "The Commons were in an ill humour against the Lords, and so they were glad to find Occasions to vent it."

The Seven Wise Men
(January–March[?] 1704)

"The Lords Committee appointed to consider of the *Scottish* Conspiracy" was balloted on 18 December 1703, held almost daily meetings in Northumberland house, and presented its final report to the Lords on 28 March 1704. The members of the committee (*An Address to Our Sovereign Lady,* 9 *n.,* above) were such noted Whigs that the purpose of the present poem was to associate them with those secret committees of the Commons in 1641 who appropriated the power of king, lords, and commons into their own hands.

This in fact is exactly the association that the Commons was trying to make. On 18 February 1704 they complained that by excluding the other two estates, the Lords did "appropriate to their own House only . . . the Name of a Parliament; an Instance, not to be parallelled, unless by that very Assembly, that subverted the Monarchy." Again on 29 February they resolved "that the establishing of a Committee of Seven Lords, for the sole Examination of the said Conspiracy, is of dangerous Consequence, and may tend to the Subversion of the Government." Structurally the present poem consists of "characters" of these "Seven Lords" set in a slight framework of prologue and epilogue. It is the "characters" of course that provide the interest of the poem (*CJ, 14,* 344, 362).

It will be noted that this is satire written on a very different plan from that of Defoe. Defoe refused to attack "any Man's private Infirmities," but the present poem does not spare Somerset's speech impediment or Somers' uncured clap. Defoe also refused to make "any Man's Disasters and Misfortunes the Subject of . . . Satyr." "I never Lampoon'd a Man," he said, "for his being a Cuckold." The present poem attributes this misfortune to Somerset as well as to Wharton. Defoe also refused "to make Satyrs upon the Dead," but the present poem discovers that the first Lady Wharton, dead for nearly 20 years, had been guilty of adultery (*More Reformation,* [1703], sig. A3r, A3v; *The Present State of Jacobitism Considered,* 1701, p. 22).

Defoe did not deny that details in his satires were drawn from individuals, but he insisted that the finished "characters" were those of "a whoreing drunken Clergy-man, [or] a leud debauch'd Justice of the Peace," *not* of individuals. "I have singl'd out but one of a Sort," he said (*More Reformation,* [1703], sig. A4r, A4v). The "characters" in Defoe's satires, in other words, are not individuals but sorts. In the present satire they are individuals.

The Seven Wise Men

Seven Sages in our happy Isle are seen,
The Glory and Support of *Albion*'s Queen,
Whose mighty Names and Worth *Recorded,* stand,
Vested with *Pow'r,* and with *Supreme Command;*
Champions of *Truth,* and *Saviours* of the *Land.*
No *Plots* escape their All-discerning Eye,
Tho' wrap'd in Languages unknown they lie.
Unstable *Britain* may like *Delos* float,
Yet still *she*'s safe while *Patriots* guide the *Boat.*
First stands recorded in the *List* of Fame,
The Gen'rous, Brave, the Humble *Somerset's* Name,

7. *Languages unknown:* Some of the intercepted letters to David Lindsay (*An Address to Our Sovereign Lady,* headnote, p. 616 above) were written in cipher and had to be sent to John Wallis, the great mathematician at Oxford, while others "were writ in gibberish, so the Lords moved, that a reward should be offered, to anyone who should decypher these" (*CSPD 1703–1704,* p. 60; *LJ, 17,* 449–50, 502).

8. *Delos:* The island of Delos in the Aegean floated free until Zeus fastened it down to provide a birthplace for Apollo (Callimachus, *Hymn to Delos,* 34–54).

11. *Somerset:* Charles Seymour, sixth duke of Somerset (1662–1748), "the proud Duke," was descended from Anne Seymour, third wife of Henry VIII and mother of Edward VI, and his Whig friends did not ridicule his pretensions to the throne in default of the Hanover line. As the first Protestant peer of the realm, he officiated with great pomp in the coronations of James II, William and Mary, Anne, George I, and George II. He was gentleman of the bedchamber to Charles II and James II and commanded the Somerset militia *ex parte regis* in Monmouth's rebellion (1685). In 1689 he was elected chancellor of Cambridge University but he held aloof from William's government until June 1701 when he was sworn of the privy council. Bonet called him a "nouveau Whig" in November 1701 and reported that he had revealed to his new party the entire strategy of the Tories for the next session of parliament (BM MS. Add. 30000E, f. 405. William responded by making him president of the privy council (January–June 1702), but "by reasons of a great hesitation in his speech," he could not have been very effective in this post. Swift added that his judgment was so poor that he seemed "hardly [to have] common sense." Although he was said to be "a pretender to the greatest Courage and steddiness," Lord Dartmouth found that he "always acted more by humour than reason." Anne very appropriately made him her master of the horse. He was said to be "a Lover of Musick and Poetry," but the poets did not always respond to his enthusiasm. One of them, in *The Assembly at Kensington* (1699), suggested that he was both pathologically vain and impotent: "His Quality makes him vain to a disease,/He Ogles all but none can please" (BM MS. Harleian 7315, f. 288). His red headed wife, whom Swift called Carrots, was Elizabeth Percy (1667–1722), daughter of Joceline

Learnings great Ornament, the Muses Pride,
By Nature form'd in Councils to preside.
The *Poets* who in Crowds his *Table* throng,
Applaud the *Gibberish Language* of his *Tongue,*
And by *Appollo's* Sons the Duke display'd,
Is Vouch'd a *Statesman,* and his Bride a *Maid.*
  A gentle Duke comes next in close Debate,
To search into the deep Intrigues of State,
But scarce had he in Council taken place,
When *Campiana* call'd away his Grace;
In Liberties of Love, she told her Lord
His Talent was not for the Council-board.
Her tender *Limberham* she did implore
To quit those *Factious* Follies at *Threescore,*
And pleaded that his Name was only given,
To have one Man of *Honour* in the *Seven.*
  Vainly does next young *Sunderland* aspire
To tread the Steps of his accomplish'd Sire;
Unequal to the matchless Statesman's Part,
He wants the Head, tho' he has all the Heart.
With Praise, 'tis true th'Informers Part he play'd;
The Sire *Converted,* and the Son *Betray'd;*
While poor *Clancarty* leads a wretched Life,

Percy, the last earl of Northumberland of that family. When she married Somerset in May 1682 at the age of 15, she was not "a *Maid*" (17), but the widow both of Henry Cavendish, earl of Ogle, and of Thomas Thynne, who had been murdered only three months before (GEC, *12,* i, 77).

18. *A gentle Duke:* "Gentle" of course is ironical, for Devonshire was a violent man. The stories of his duel with half a dozen insulted French officers at the opera house in Paris in 1669 and his caning of Colonel Culpepper in the presence of the king and queen at Whitehall in 1687 were well known (William Montagu, seventh duke of Manchester, *Court and Society from Elizabeth to Anne,* 2 vols., 1864, *2,* 237–38). "He was not," as Dr. Johnson regretted to say, "a man of superiour abilities" (James Boswell, *The Life of Samuel Johnson,* 2 vols., 1791, *2,* 165).

21. *Campiana:* "Mrs. Campion" (*C*); see *Reformation of Manners,* 1027 *n.,* above.

24. *Limberham:* Besides Wycherley and Dryden, *OED* cites Thomas Brown, *A Declamation in Praise of Poverty* (c. 1704): "he's a true *limberham,* a prodigal cully to the jilt he keeps for the use of the publick" (*Works,* 7th ed., 1730, *1,* 99).

28. *Sunderland:* See *The Golden Age Revers'd,* 49 *n.,* above.

32. *th'Informers Part:* Cf. *A Conference,* 45, above.

34. *Clancarty:* Donogh Maccarty, fourth earl of Clancarty (1668–1734), raised a Protestant, was decoyed from Oxford when barely 16 and forced to marry Elizabeth, the earl of Sunderland's younger daughter, aged 13. He was soon converted to Catholi-

Banish'd his *Country,* Shackled to his *Wife.*
Let him in Libraries consume his Days,
And labour to deserve *James Forbes*'s Praise.
To Learning, 'tis allow'd, he has some Pretence,
For he abounds in *Books,* tho' not in *Sense.*
O valiant *Scarbrough,* with unan'mous Voice,

---

cism (by Sunderland himself, according to line 33) and commanded a troop of horse for James II in Ireland (J. P. Kenyon, *Robert Spencer Earl of Sunderland,* Longmans, Green, 1958, pp. 102–03). Captured at the capitulation of Cork in September 1690, he was imprisoned in the Tower and his vast estates in Ireland were confiscated. In October 1694 he boldly escaped from the Tower and made his way to St. Germain. There he assumed command of a troop of James II's horse guards and fought in all the remaining campaigns against William III. In December 1697 he returned to London secretly and joined his wife, who was living in Sunderland's house in St. James's Square. That same night the news of Clancarty's arrival was brought to Lord Spencer, who did not hesitate to betray his brother-in-law. "He went straight to Whitehall, where he was lucky enough to find James Vernon working late. The Secretary wrote out a warrant on the spot, collected a few soldiers and a messenger, and went back with him to St. James's Square. They hauled Clancarty out of bed and consigned him to Newgate" (ibid., p. 302). William, however, was prevailed upon to pardon Clancarty and grant him a pension of £1000 a year on condition he live abroad. In May 1698, therefore, the man who might have enjoyed 149,000 acres in Cork and Kerry set out with his wife to spend the rest of his life on an island in the Elbe, salvaging debris that floated down the river (GEC, *3,* 216).

36. *Libraries:* "The great library of Charles Spencer, third Earl of Sunderland contained . . . some 20,000 printed books: it was particularly strong in incunabula (many being printed on vellum), in Bibles, in first editions of the classics and in Continental literature of the fifteenth and sixteenth centuries . . . Sunderland was a lavish and even extravagant buyer" (Seymour de Ricci, *English Collectors of Books & Manuscripts,* Cambridge, Cambridge University Press, 1930, p. 38).

37. *James Forbes:* James Forbes (d. 1711), who was said "to be often with the Duke of Monmouth," apparently was turned around to spy on his former associates after he had been interrogated by the king and privy council in July 1683 for his involvement in the Rye House plot (*CSPD July–September 1683,* pp. 90, 106). A year later Henry Guy paid one "Mr. Forbes" £250 for secret services (*CTB 1681–1685,* p. 1183). But this did not prevent a warrant being issued in May 1685 for his arrest, along with such noted conspirators as Major John Wildman, John Trenchard, John Freke, and Sir Walter Yonge (*CSPD February–December 1685,* p. 157). He survived the counter-terror to be knighted in August 1689 and appointed a clerk of the greencloth in the royal household, a post to which he was not reappointed under Anne (Luttrell, *1,* 572; *5,* 164). J. P. Kenyon calls him the second earl of Sunderland's "toady" (Kenyon, *Robert Spencer Earl of Sunderland,* p. 314). He is Phaleg in *The Second Part of Absalom and Achitophel* (1682), 330–50.

40. *Scarbrough:* Richard Lumley (c. 1650–1721), grandson and heir to viscount Lumley of Waterford, commanded the cavalry troop that captured Monmouth in July 1685 and was one of the seven peers who signed the invitation to the prince of Orange in June 1688. Accordingly, in February 1689 he was made a gentleman of the bedchamber, privy councillor, colonel of the first troop of life guards, lord lieutenant of

The Nation do's applaud, the Senates Choice.
Grown old in Wars, thou may'st in Council sit;
For Councils now, as once for actions fit.
Thy penetrating Sense can soon unfold,
Mysterious truths in thy own Ciphers told;
Justly with Hero's we enroll thy Name,
Thy *Hosier*'s Letter's the foundation of their fame.
Next a raw Youth of the *Patrician* Race
In that *August Assembly* claims a Place,
Only with aweful Silence to attend,
And by their Precepts form his tender Mind.
Our modern *Sages* prudently admit
Young *Townshend* shou'd in the Committee sit,
Provided still the Saint-like Stamp he bear,

Northumberland, and in April 1690 created earl of Scarbrough in the English peerage. As one of the few English friends of William III, with whom he served at the Boyne and in all the campaigns in the Lowlands, he was anathema to the Jacobites. According to one source he sold most of his appointments before Queen Mary died and began to assume a more active political role, voting against the impeachments of Somers, Orford, and Montagu in June 1701. In the new reign he was made a privy councillor and lieutenant-general of all the forces, while his wife was appointed a lady of the bedchamber (GEC, *11*, 508–10).

46. *Hero's:* the seven members of the select committee (headnote).

47. *Hosier:* It was Scarbrough who made public the Scotch plot (*An Address to Our Sovereign Lady,* headnote, p. 616 above). The implication seems to be that he passed off bills from his hosier as documents purporting to establish the existence of a plot.

48. *Youth:* Charles Townshend, second viscount Townshend (1675–1738), was descended from "LODOVIC, a noble Norman, who coming into England in Henry the First's reign [1100–35], assumed the surname of TOWNSHEND, and took to wife Elizabeth, the daughter and heir of Sir Thomas de Havile, in whose right he became possessed of the manor of Havile, in Rainham [Norfolk], where his posterity have ever since continued to have their principal residence" (Collins, *2*, 454). He was educated at Eton and King's College, Cambridge, and took his seat in the House of Lords in December 1697. Like Somerset and Devonshire, he was a recent convert to Whiggism, for as recently as June 1701 he had signed a protest against the acquittal of Somers, Orford, and Montagu. In April 1709, however, when he was appointed plenipotentiary to negotiate a treaty of peace with France, Burnet described him as "by much the most shining Person of all our young Nobility" (Burnet, *2*, 528) and in July 1713 he was admitted to the inner circle when he married the sister of Robert Walpole, whom "Lord Wharton [had] keept" (GEC, *12*, i, 805).

54. *the Saint-like Stamp:* Townshend's father, Horatio Townshend, first viscount Townshend (1630–87), was an enthusiastic parliamentarian. He served the Commonwealth as commissioner of militia for Norfolk (1648–49, 1659), member of parliament for Norfolk (1656–60), and councillor of state (May–December 1659). It was not until 1682 that he was reported "entirely come over to the court party" (Luttrell, *1*, 161).

And like the Infant *Carthaginian* swear,
Immortal hatred to his Father's Foes,
And ever to support *The good Old Cause.*
Unheard, came creeping out sly *Cataline,*
Father of *Faction;* who with Force unseen,
Rowls on with steddy Pace, the *Great Machine.*
Of antient Stock, in covert *Saw-pits* bold,
In Plots consummate, and in Tricks grown old,
Since among Knaves he holds the foremost place,
Old *Ferguson*'s footsteps, who so well can trace;
Tho' twice his Marriage-bed has been betray'd,

55. *the Infant Carthaginian:* Hannibal (274–183? B.C.) was only nine years old when his father made him swear on the altar of Zeus "immortal" enmity to the Roman people (Polybius *3,* 11; Livy, *21,* 1); cf. Dryden, *Mac Flecknoe* (1676?), 112–13: "As *Hannibal* did to the Altars come,/Sworn by his *Syre* a mortal Foe to *Rome.*"

57. *The good Old Cause:* "Rebelling against Kings" (Butler, *Hudibras* [1662–78], *3,* i, 1275; cf. Dryden, *Absalom and Achitophel* [1681], 82).

58. *Cataline:* Wharton, whom William III thought "too much a Republican to be intrusted with the Administration of State Affairs" (Macky, p. 91), became "The most active manager in the Whig Junto" in the reign of Anne. "In the Lords he led the party with equal energy and craft" (Trevelyan, *1,* 194–95). His classical prototype is Lucius Sergius Catilina (c. 108–62 B.C.), whose clumsy republican conspiracies, usually involving remission of debts, were exposed and defeated by Cicero (Plutarch, *Life of Cicero*).

61. *Of antient Stock:* Although the Whartons appear to have been lords of the manor of Wharton, Westmorland, in the reign of Edward I (1272–1307), the family pedigree begins with Thomas Wharton, member of parliament for Appleby, Westmorland (1436–37) (GEC, *12,* ii, 594 *n.*).

Saw-pits: Wharton's father, Philip, fourth Lord Wharton, is alleged to have concealed himself in a sawpit during the battle of Edgehill (1642) (*POAS,* Yale, *4,* 199). The slander was revived in 1677 when Wharton was sent to the Tower with Shaftesbury: "What Couper designes Sawpit darres not oppose" (HMC *Le Fleming MSS.,* p. 143).

64. *Ferguson:* Robert Ferguson responded quite characteristically to the Scotch plot, about which he learned in London from Simon Fraser. He immediately betrayed Fraser to the duke of Atholl (*An Address to Our Sovereign Lady,* headnote, p. 615 above) and then published a declaration that "there is not a Nonjuror, or one reckoned a Jacobite, engaged in a plot." On 25 March 1704 the Lords voted Ferguson's declaration "false, scandalous, and seditious" and committed him to Newgate (James Ferguson, *Robert Ferguson, The Plotter,* Edinburgh, 1887, pp. 341–42, 345; *LJ, 17,* 525).

65. *Marriage-bed:* Wharton's first wife, whom he married in September 1673, was Anne Lee (c. 1659–85), second daughter of Sir Henry Lee, of Quarrendon, Buckinghamshire, and Ditchley, Oxfordshire, third baronet. It is surprising that she is said here to have been unfaithful to Wharton for her character was supposed to be "the very Reverse of Gaiety and Gallantry." Whatever her morals, she brought him £10,000 down and £2500 a year. Wharton's second wife was Lucy Loftus (c. 1670–1717), daughter and heiress of Adam, viscount Lisburne in the Irish peerage. Swift recorded that Wharton bore the gallantries of this Lady Wharton "with the Indifference of a Stoick" and Lady

Good Reasons still his Vengeance have allay'd.
The Injury his former Spouse has done,
The large Estate she left did well attone.
He is content his present Spouse shou'd strole,
To gain young Cully's to the *Kit-kat* Bowl.
Sommers, thou mighty Genius, next arise,
Nor let young *James* thy vigilance surprise,
Let neither Guilt of Crimes, nor sence of pain
Distract the Projects of thy teeming Brain;
Thy labours may be crown'd another reign.
With thy accustom'd Art expound the Laws,
Weighing the Party's Merit, not the Cause.
The Plot of *Lancashire,* Begot and Nurs'd
By thee, was with a Fate untimely Curs'd:
Yet this adopted One, Success attends,
Tho' Ridicul'd by all, it serves thy Ends.
Destin'd to greater Honours shalt thou live,
Loaded with *Guilt,* and with *Impeachments* Thrive,
And to Crown all, *Hobs*'s ill Cures survive.
Hail *Great Cabal,* in whose wise Conduct's shewn
The Artful Steps pursued of *Forty One;*
Thus *Pym* and *Hambden* did support the Throne.

Mary Wortley Montagu added that she was "as abandoned and unscrupulous" as Wharton himself (GEC, *12,* ii, 607).

70. *Kit-kat Bowl:* A toast to the second Lady Wharton, presumably engraved on a "*Kit-kat* Bowl," was published in *POAS,* 1704, *3,* 398:

> When *Jove* to *Ida* did the Gods invite,
> And in immortal Toastings pass'd the Night,
> With more than Bowls of Nectar they were bless'd,
> For *Venus* was the *Wharton* of the Feast.

74. Cf. *Advice to a Painter,* 87, above.

78. *Plot of Lancashire:* The Lancashire plot of 1694 was mainly a fabrication of John Lunt, a Jacobite courier who had defected, and an apostate Catholic priest who called himself John Taaffe. Seven Lancashiremen were indicted for high treason, but the plot was "Curs'd" in October 1694 when the government witnesses completely discredited themselves at the trial and the king's counsel, Sir William Williams, abandoned the prosecution (HMC *Kenyon MSS.,* pp. 292–301, 309–94; *Lords MSS.,* New Series, *1,* 435–55; Luttrell, *3,* 388; Ralph, *2,* 523–31).

80. *this adopted One:* the Scotch plot.

84. *Hobs's ill Cures:* See *The Golden Age Revers'd,* 30 *n.,* above.

87. *Pym:* It was John Pym (1584–1643), the leader of the opposition to Charles I, who moved the impeachment of Laud (*The Mitred Club,* 38 *n.,* above) and of Strafford.

Illustrious *Off-spring* of that *Factious Race,*
Each Feature in Great *Clarendon* we trace.
Thus did the *Few,* the *Many* then *Seduce,*
Secret *Committees* did the World *Amuse,*
And with like *specious Shews* Mankind *Abuse.*
O *Albion,* on these Shoulders ne'er Repose,
These are thy *Dangerous, Intestine Foes,*
These are the Tyrants who would thee Enthral,
Resolv'd to *Govern,* or o'erthrow the *Ball,*
Tho' they, like *Sampson,* in the Ruin *fall.*

He voted for the root and branch bill in May 1641, served on the secret committee for defense, and drafted the Grand Remonstrance.

Hambden: John Hampden (c. 1595–1643), who refused to pay the ship-money, became Pym's most important lieutenant. He too voted for the root and branch bill, supported the Grand Remonstrance, and served on the committee of public safety in 1642.

89. *Clarendon:* The earl of Rochester had published the first volume of *The History of the Rebellion and Civil Wars in England,* by his uncle Edward Hyde, earl of Clarendon, in 1702. It was this volume (p. 147) that included the characters of Pym and Hampden.

Daniel Defoe [?]

The Address
(*April*[?] *1704*)

It must have seemed an act of providence to Defoe that he had never attacked Robert Harley as he had attacked every other prominent member of the New Country-Party of which Harley had assumed the leadership in 1700. In April 1703, while he was still a fugitive from justice, he told William Paterson, with an irony that may not have been wholly unconscious, that if he had offended Harley, it was "only because he did not know him." On 4 November 1703 Godolphin told Harley that he had "taken care in the matter of De Foe"; the fine of "200 marks of the lawful money of England" was somehow paid; sureties for his "good Behaviour for the Space of Seven Years" were somehow found, and Defoe walked out of Newgate a free, if heavily mortgaged, man. (HMC *Portland MSS.*, *4*, 62, 75; Moore, *Daniel Defoe*, p. 131).

Immediately he set about to pay off the mortgage. It was as "a mortified stranger" eager "to dedicate [his] life and all possible powers to the interest of so generous . . . benefactors" that he appears in his first, undated letter to Harley. Harley of course knew exactly how to exploit these proffered "powers." Soon he began meeting Defoe in coffeehouses "carefully concealed from all the world" and on Saturday 19 February 1704 *A Weekly Review of the Affairs of France: Purg'd from the Errors and Partiality of News-writers and Petty-Statesmen, of all Sides,* began publication. Defoe kept it up week after week for nine years, until 11 June 1713 when the treaty of Utrecht had been signed and nothing further could be done to prevent Harley's great fall (HMC *Portland MSS.*, *4*, 75, 76, 83).

The Address is the first poem that Defoe published in the interest of his new benefactors, but it takes up exactly where *An Encomium upon a Parliament* (1699), *A New Satyr on the Parliament* (1701), and *England's Late Jury* (1701) left off. One looks in vain for unequivocal evidence of Harley's influence on the poem. Instead one finds a remarkable independence: Defoe defends William's Irish grants (71 *n.*) and treaties of partition (87 *n.*, 93 *n.*), which Harley had bitterly opposed; he even taunts Harley for failing to order the printing of the Commons' debates on the second bill to prevent occasional conformity (66–67 *n.*). Harley's influence may account for Defoe's support of the licensing bill (211 *n.*) and his demand for a new election (251–52), but these suppositions cannot yet be documented.

One remarkable shift of opinion reflected in *The Address* was clearly *not* influenced by Harley. In *More Reformation* (July 1703) Defoe had, quite consistently, opposed the practice of occasional conformity and supported the bill to prevent it (lines 328–39). In *The Address,* however, he flatly opposes the second bill (lines 41–65). But this change had been effected even before Defoe encountered Harley. The last attack that Defoe wrote on the practice of occasional conformity to qualify for public office was in *The Sincerity of the Dissenters Vindicated, from the Scandal of Occasional Conformity,* published in September 1703. Here Defoe limits himself to the casuistical issue and does not even mention the political problem (p. 26). But in his next pamphlet, also written in Newgate and entitled *The Case of the Dissenters as affected by the Late Bill Proposed in Parliament for Preventing Occasional Conformity,* published on 18 September 1703, Defoe comes out flatly against the bill. Leaving aside "the Matter of Conscience," he considered only the "Prudential and Political" problem, and concluded that the bill was unconstitutional because it would take away from the dissenters "what they enjoyed before by Law." "This Bill," he said, "draws over all their Heads a dismal Cloud of Incapacity" (pp. 7, 19, 24). What he had learned was that civil rights are more important than flawless casuistry. And what he had lost in consistency he had more than made up in political mobility. By supporting the first bill to prevent occasional conformity Defoe had found himself in the same camp with extremists like Charles Leslie, Sir John Pakington, and the earl of Nottingham. By deciding to oppose the second bill he found himself in agreement with moderates like Harley.

After what he had written about ingratitude in *The True-Born Englishman,* it is not surprising that Defoe should have been, as he said, "the gratefullest wretch alive" (headnote, pp. 262–63). The truth seems to be that he wanted and expected "orders" from Harley, but since he did not always get them, he continued to write what he pleased. And what he pleased in the present case was another satire, in the same five-line stanza ($a^4b^3a^4a^4b^3$), on the aberrations of the Tory majority in the Commons during a single session of parliament. This was the session in which the Lords observed that "the Steps the Commons have made . . . will hardly be believed" (*LJ, 17,* 540). In *The Address* Defoe explains more bluntly that these were "Steps" toward usurpation of the whole power of government:

> And now you stand in Peer's Records,
> *Usurpers* of the Nation,
> (226–27)

and in *Legion's Humble Address to the Lords,* probably published in the same month, he adds that "it cannot be Just . . . that the People may endure the Tyranny of 500 Usurpers more than of One" (HMC Portland MSS., *4,* 83, 89, 106; *Legion's Humble Address to the Lords,* 1703, recto).

The Address was attributed to "our *Legionite*" in the verse reply to the poem entitled *The Whig's Scandalous Address Answered Paragraph by Paragraph,* 1703, sig. A4v, apparently in allusion to *Legion's Humble Address to the Lords,* widely known to be Defoe's (HMC *Portland MSS., 4,* 93, 138). The attribution to Defoe (Moore, p. 31) is supported by the similarity of the poem to other works known to be Defoe's. Many lines, for example, simply versify, in the same order, the same points that are made in prose in *Legion's Humble Address to the Lords* (28 *n.,* 32 *n.,* 71 *n.,* 152 *n.*).

The latest event to which *The Address* seems to allude is the Lords' address of 28 March 1704 (152 *n.,* 170 *n.,* 227 *n.*). On the other side, Defoe's demand that the Commons address the queen to dissolve the parliament (251–52) would not have been actionable after 3 April 1704 when parliament was prorogued. It may be assumed therefore that the poem was written late in March 1704 and published shortly after.

The Address

Ye Men of Might, and Muckle Power,
Our Representing Knaves;
Who *High-Church* Zealots to restore,
And Tolleration Acts devour,
Would make us all your Slaves.

You lately told her Majesty,
You would retrieve her Honour;
'Tis plain you meant it to deceive,
And you'l the Nation's Faults retrieve,
By bringing new ones on her.

If you would have us think you're true,
Let actions make it known;
The Nation's Happiness persue,
Her old Miscarriages review,
But don't forget your own.

1. Quoted verbatim in [Defoe], *An Elegy on the Author of the True-Born-Englishman,* 1704, p. 28.

3. *High-Church Zealots:* The two nonjuring bishops whom Anne offered to restore were Robert Frampton and Thomas Ken (*The Golden Age Restor'd,* 93 *n.,* above).

4. *Tolleration Acts devour:* Cf. *The Golden Age Restor'd,* 53 *n.,* above. Defoe argued that since the Act of Toleration had exempted the dissenters "from all Penalties . . . for Dissenting," the bill to prevent occasional conformity would impose an unconstitutional "Penalty on their Dissenting again" (*A Serious Inquiry into This Grand Question; Whether a Law to Prevent the Occasional Conformity of Dissenters, would not be Inconsistent with the Act of Toleration, and a Breach of the Queen's Promise,* 1704, p. 12).

7. *retrieve:* See *The Golden Age Restor'd,* 36 *n.,* above.

11. *true:* Defoe may refer to the formula: "your Majesty's most dutiful and loyal Commons . . . Your loyal Commons . . . Your faithful Commons" (*CJ, 14,* 343–44), which recurs so frequently in addresses to the throne.

14. *old Miscarriages:* On 2 March 1704 the Commons resumed its inquiries into the accounts of the earl of Ranelagh "to the Year 1692" (cf. *The Golden Age,* 45 *n.,* above) and on 11 March it voted 60–57 that the earl of Orford's delays in making up his accounts when he was treasurer of the navy (April 1689–May 1699) (cf. *A Conference,* 133 *n.,* above) had "rendered the examining and passing the said Accounts very difficult, and may be of great Loss to the Publick" (*CJ, 14,* 366, 369, 375).

Tell us, ye Sons of Emptiness,
  Explain this Contradiction;
How can Contention bring forth Peace,
Or how a Nation have Success,
  Without the Law's protection?

You that in Lawyers so abound,
  And Men of Elocution;
Your *Mackworth, Wright,* and *Northey* send,
See if they can your Works defend,
  As well as Constitution.

You meet in Clubs, and strong Cabals,
  To Controvert Elections;
But Party Interest there prevails,

18. *Peace:* In the speech—drafted by Godolphin and Harley—which she delivered at the opening of parliament on 9 November 1703, Anne made a plea for "perfect Peace and Union" among her subjects and urged them to avoid "any Heats or Divisions" that might "give Encouragement to the common Enemies of our Church and State" (Feiling, p. 371; *CJ, 14,* 211). The Tories, however, chose to ignore this warning and introduced the second bill to prevent occasional conformity on 27 November. At the end of the session, therefore, Anne recalled to the House that "At the Opening of this Session, I did earnestly express My Desires of seeing you in perfect Unity among yourselves, as the most effectual Means imaginable to disappoint the Ambition of our Enemies, and reduce them to an honourable and lasting Peace" (*LJ, 17,* 562).

23. *Mackworth:* Cf. *The Golden Age Restor'd,* 19 *n.,* above. "This Gentleman," Defoe said, "descends to Defend the Letter of the late [bill to prevent occasional conformity], and advances to the World that it is no breach of the Toleration Act . . . [whereas it is] directly contrary both to the Act of Toleration, and of it self Destructive of the Liberty of Conscience" (*Peace without Union. By Way of Reply to Sir H. M.'s Peace at Home,* 1703, p. 7).

Wright: Sir Nathan Wright, who succeeded Somers as lord keeper in May 1700 (*A Conference,* headnote, p. 212 above), presided over the court of chancery.

Northey: Sir Edward Northey (1652–1723) was educated at St. Paul's school, Queen's College, Oxford, and the Middle Temple, whence he was called to the bar in 1674. He succeeded Sir Thomas Trevor as attorney-general in July 1701 (Luttrell, *5,* 68) and was knighted by Queen Anne a year later. In April 1703 he prosecuted John Tutchin for libel. Tutchin had been bold enough to defend *The Shortest Way with the Dissenters* in *A Dialogue between a Dissenter and the Observator* (1703), but the obstensible charge was "reflecting on the earl of Albemarl" (ibid., *5,* 257). Tutchin, however, claimed that the indictment was for writing against papists and the grand jury ignored the bill. But as Godolphin wrote to Harley, "Mr. Attorney [Northey] has no great success in his prosecutions of any kind" (HMC *Bath MSS., 1,* 59).

28. *Party Interest . . . prevails:* The committee on elections and privileges normally resolved controverted elections on the basis of party. "No one pretended," as Trevelyan

Merit and Sense of Honour fails,
And meets with no protection.

With House of Peers you're wondrous Nice,
And of Reputation tender;
But they see thro' the thin disguise,
And where you're foolish, they're as wise,
And they're our true Defenders.

In Reason, Management, and Law,
They turn you round and round;
No Age such Bubbles ever saw,
The lines of Justice thwart you draw,
And all your Plots confound.

---

has said, "that justice was done on the evidence" (2, 20). The first such case in the present session was that of Sudbury, in Suffolk, where the incumbent, George Haskin Styles, a London merchant independent of party, was opposed in the election of July 1702 by George Dashwood (c. 1680–1762), eldest son of Sir Samuel Dashwood, the Tory lord mayor of London (*More Reformation,* 234 *n.,* above). Styles was returned, but in December 1702 the election was declared void. In February 1703 the freemen of Sudbury again returned Styles, 365–344. As soon as the next session was convened in November 1703 and William Bromley had been elected chairman, the committee on elections entertained Dashwood's petition that Styles had been wrongly returned. On 6 December, without even a division, the House agreed to the committee's resolution that Dashwood be returned (Luttrell, *5,* 248; *CJ, 14,* 244–45). Cf. *Legion's Humble Address to the Lords,* 1704, p. 2: "To Throw-out and Put-in Members of Parliament at Committees of Elections, by Interest of Parties . . . , not prescribing that Vote by the True Merit of the Case, and Plain Majority of the Electors; is Destroying the Peoples Right of Elections."

32. *of Reputation tender:* In the celebrated case of Ashby *vs.* White (Trevelyan, 2, 20–25), the committee on elections ruled on 26 January 1704 that the Lords' action in reversing the decision of the queen's bench in disenfranchising one Matthew Ashby of Aylesbury, was "a high Breach of the Privilege of this House" (*CJ, 14,* 308). Cf. *Legion's Humble Address to the Lords,* p. 2: "To Deprive any Freeholder of his Right in Election of Members to Serve in Parliament . . . as was Practised in the Case of the Election at *Aylesbury;* is a Manifest Invasion of those very Liberties which it is the House of Commons Business to Protect and Defend."

35. *our true Defenders:* John Tutchin, under prosecution by the Commons in this session, called the Lords "a Barrier to the People, against the Oppressions of Great Men in Offices . . . above the reach of *Bribery*" (*The Observator,* No. 97, 8–11 March 1704). Cf. *A Postscript to the Golden Age* (1704) ("Assist mee Muse, that in a Gloriouse straine"): "Oh Rightfull Queen confirme thy mighty power,/Stand by the peers & then wee'r all Secure" (Osborn MS. Chest II, No. 1 [Phillipps 8301]).

39. *thwart:* across the course of, so as to obstruct (*OED*).

With mighty Votes, and furious Bill,
You keep a wretched pother;
But *Mackworth* manag'd it so ill,
The Cheat came out against your Will,
And Sav'd Dissenting Brother.

The Blund'ring Orator Betray'd
The *Snake of Persecution;*
The *Trojan Ass* so loudly Bray'd,
It made the Nation all afraid,
In spight of Elocution.

He told you Places were ingross'd,
In all the wiser Nations,

41. *Votes:* The second bill to prevent occasional conformity passed the Commons with increasing majorities. The House voted 173–130 to bring in the bill on 25 November, 210–132 to commit it upon the second reading on 30 November, and 223–140 to pass it after the third reading on 7 December (*CJ, 14,* 238, 241, 246).

43. *Mackworth:* See 23 *n.,* above. Cf. Boyer, *History,* p. 103: "Sir *Humphrey Mackworth,* another Gentleman of the same [high church] Principles, put out a small Treatise on [*Peace at Home, or a Vindication of the Proceedings of the House of Commons on the Bill for Preventing Danger from Occasional Conformity* (1703)]; which Pamphlet, however, contain'd little else, besides the Arguments used a Year before on the same Subject."

46. *Orator:* In the preface to *Peace at Home* (1703) Mackworth insisted that "Art and Oratory" were unnecessary and that "this plain Discourse [was] recommended with no Oratory, no Address" (sigs. A2r, B2r). In *Peace without Union* (1703) Defoe had already glanced at these deficiencies: "so much an Orator, and so much a Statesman" (p. 1).

47. *Persecution:* "Is the meer Preservation of the Establish'd Government in Church and State," Mackworth asked, "to be esteemed no less then Persecution of Dissenters" (*Peace at Home,* p. 3). And Defoe replied, " 'Tis plain the Design . . . of this Author seems to be . . . to keep Men out of the Government . . . for being Dissenters" (*Peace without Union,* p. 13). Later in the *Review* he added: "[by] this True High-Church Principle; Destruction of Dissenters is proved to be no more Persecution, than Hanging of High-way-men" (2 [11 August 1705], 278). Tutchin also noticed "that Flaw in our Constitution; to mend which, Sir *Humphry,* is now Erecting his Scaffolds" (*The Observator,* No. 69, 1–4 December 1703).

48. *The Trojan Ass:* Henry Sacheverell(?); cf. *A Hymn to the Pillory,* 69–70, above; cf. [John Phillips], *Typhon: or The Gyants War with the Gods,* 1665, p. 91: "*Silenus*'s ass . . . with his noise did fright/Philistins fierce from heat of fight."

51. *Places . . . ingross'd: "Henry* the Third of *France* . . . exclud[ed] *Hugonots* from Publick Offices and Employments" (Mackworth, *Peace at Home,* sig. B1r). Cf. [Defoe], *The Dissenters Answer to the High-Church Challenge,* 1704, pp. 16, 42.

By those that worship God the most;
But we have found it to our cost,
'T has here been out of fashion.

For Rogues get into Church and State,
And wise men Circumvent;
Leudness directs the Magistrate,
Knaves Rule *the Cash,* and Fools *the Fleet,*
And *both* the Parliament.

With Royal Faith her Majesty
Had back'd the Tolleration;
And you, with *English* honesty,
Wou'd have her Faith and Vows deny,
And ruine all the Nation.

No wonder you're asham'd to Print
The Votes of your Proceeding;
The Nation soon knew what you meant,
And that there would be something in't,
That would not bear the reading.

Of *William*'s Grants you now complain,
Without regard to Merit;

61. *Royal Faith:* Cf. [Defoe], *A Serious Inquiry into This Grand Question; Whether a Law to Prevent the Occasional Conformity of Dissenters, would not be Inconsistent with the Act of Toleration,* p. 14: "she has given us her Royal Promise, that she will continue her Protection of the Dissenters in . . . the Toleration Establish'd." Cf. *More Reformation,* 337 *n.* above.

66–67. *Print/The Votes:* On 3 January 1704 "Mr. Speaker [Harley] acquainted the House, That there were come into his Hands several written Papers, which had been dispersed at Coffee-houses; wherein the Proceedings of the House are misrepresented, and several false Things inserted, as if they had been the Votes of the House," whereupon it was *"Ordered,* That no News-writers do, in their Letters, or other Papers . . . presume to intermeddle with the Debates, or any other Proceedings, of this House" *(CJ, 14,* 270).

69. *something in't:* "There was now such a division upon this matter," Tindal explains, "that it was fairly debated in the House of Commons; whereas before it went [through] with such a torrent, that no opposition to it could be hearkned to. Those who opposed the bill, went chiefly upon the ground . . . that it was a breach upon the Toleration . . . That things of this kind could have no effect, but to imbroil the Nation with new distractions . . . [and] That it was necessary to continue the happy quiet, that the Nation now enjoyed, especially in this time of war, in which even the severest of persecutions made their stops" (Tindal, *4,* 1628).

71. *Grants:* The Tory majority in the Commons had resumed William's grants of forfeited estates in Ireland in 1699 (*Advice to a Painter,* 40 *n.,* above) and had re-

For the lewd Gifts of former Reigns
To *Whores* and *Papists,* you maintain,
  And *Bastards* may inherit.

You Recognize wise *Nottingham,*
  As one that did his Duty,
And there are other Rogues of Fame,
To whom you ought to do the same,
  Because they are so true to ye.

But here the Mischief of it lyes,
  Your Character's a Scandal;
For *any Knaves* in Church-disguise,
And *any Fool* you like's as wise,
  When we're to be Trapan'd all.

You are the Men that once Cry'd down
  The Treaty of Partition;
After the mighty things y'have done,
Pray have you not reduc'd the Crown
  Into a worse Condition?

We wou'd be glad you'd make it plain,
  And fain we would believe it,

---

peatedly tried to resume the rest of his grants, most recently by introducing a bill for this purpose on 14 January 1704. This bill quickly passed a second reading but then, after being committed from week to week in February and March, was finally lost when the session was prorogued on 3 April (*CJ, 14,* 282, 285). Cf. *Legion's Humble Address to the Lords,* p. 3: "Resolving to Reassume the Grants of King *William* on whatsoever Merit or Valuable Consideration they were made, and at the same time Continue the Extravagant Dispositions of former Reigns, in which the stated Revenues of the Crown are alienated to Whores, Bastards, and Papists, and the Publick Enemies of the Nation, is a Partial and Malicious Proceeding, Contriv'd to Reflect upon His Late Majesty, and lessen the Value all True *English-men* have for his Memory; and shews the Degeneracy in the Principle of the Present House of Commons, from Those that Join'd with that Glorious Monarch in the Redemption of this Nation from Slavery and Arbitrary Government."

76. *Nottingham:* See *An Address to Our Sovereign Lady,* 11 *n.,* above.

87. *Treaty of Partition:* See *A New Satyr on the Parliament,* 31–40, 32 *n.,* above. *Cf.* [Defoe], *Royal Religion Being Some Enquiry after the Piety of Princes,* 1704, p. 13: "Tis to King *William*'s Memory, they lay the Blame of a Partition Treaty, whose Conditions, 'twill be well for us, if we can ever come up to."

When better Terms you'l for us gain,
And how those better Terms maintain,
That we might all perceive it.

The very day you first began
Dissenters to reform,
Heaven told you 'twou'd be all in vain,
And did its just dislike explain,
In a prodigious Storm.

But Heaven those Men corrects in vain,
Who are for Judgments worse;
Who still their Vices will retain,
Who first the Blessing dare disdain,
And then despise the Curse.

In all the Grand Faux-Pa's you make,
Cou'd you be curs'd alone,
Wou'd Heaven such proper vengeance take,
We might not suffer for your sake,
You were welcome to go on.

93. *better Terms:* Defoe means "better" than the grandiose terms that Godolphin and Harley laid down in Anne's speech at the opening of the session on 9 November 1703, namely, "recovering the Monarchy of *Spain* from the House of *Bourbon,* and restoring it to the House of *Austria*" (*CJ, 14,* 211). After Ramillies (May 1706), as Trevelyan has said, "No Peace without Spain" became a Whig shibboleth, "and it took the whole strength of the reunited Tory party to overcome it and give peace to Europe at Utrecht" (*1,* 303). The remarkable stability of Defoe's principles amid the sway and creak of party platforms may be judged by comparing what he says here with what he said nine years later, the very month the treaty of Utrecht was signed: he explains that the purpose of the partition treaties was to "have given the Ballance of Power into [England's and Holland's] Hands; so that they should never have been again in fear of Popish Exorbitance, whether *French* or *Austrian* . . . . This was the Glorious design of King *William,* in the *Treaty of Partition;* a Treaty which I had the Honour to hear his Majesty say, too Prophetically, *That* England *would be glad to make Peace, upon worse Terms, after seven Years War;* and which we have now found fatally true" (*Review,* [9] [14 March 1713], 140).

100. *Storm:* About one o'clock in the morning of 27 November 1703 the worst storm "in the Memory of Man," as *The London Gazette* reported, struck England from the southwest. It lasted only six hours but in its fury it laid thousands of acres under water in the Severn Valley, leveled 2000 of John Evelyn's beloved oaks, and almost destroyed Ostend. On the same day, as if in defiance of this augury, William Bromley reintroduced the bill to prevent occasional conformity and guided it successfully through its first reading (Luttrell, *5,* 363, 366, 370; *The London Gazette,* No. 3972, 2–6 December 1703; Evelyn, *5,* 550–51).

Then you might all your selves undo,
  And for the time to come,
Make out this riddle to be true,
How you can foreign Wars persue,
  By raising Feuds at home.

When you look back on *William*'s Reign,
  And his Mistakes disclose,
Of his bad Conduct you complain,
But if you'd view it o're again,
  'Twou'd all your own expose.

Your want of temper to the last,
  Did his Designs Defeat,
Always too slow, or else too fast,
Too Backward, or in too much haste,
  Too cold or else too hot.

We wish you would look back upon
  The modern things you boast,
The great Exploits your Fleets have done,
The Glory gain'd, the Conquest won,
  And how much all has cost.

With wonted Courage and Success
  Sir *Rook* invaded *Spain,*

114–15. Cf. *An Address to Our Sovereign Lady,* 29–30.

128. *Exploits:* "The great Exploits" of Admiral Sir John Munden and Captains Kirkby and Wade are recounted above (*The Golden Age,* 63 *n.,* 64 *n.*). More recently Vice-Admiral John Graydon had been dismissed from the service for failing to engage a fouled and undermanned French squadron in the Caribbean in April 1703, Commodore Bennett Allen and Captain Josias Crow were courtmartialed for failing to attack an outnumbered French force in the Channel in August 1703, and Captain Abraham Tudor, in command of the 26-gun man-of-war *Queenborough,* was courtmartialed and dismissed from the service for allowing himself to be chased into Dover harbor by two small French privateers (Luttrell, *5,* 290, 325, 327, 400, 403, 405; *The Observator,* No. 97, 8–11 March 1704.

132. *Rook:* Defoe may refer either to the failure of Rooke to take Cadiz in September 1702 or to the even more inconsequential campaign of 1703. In April of that year Rooke was placed in command of a fleet of 25 men-of-war and transports for six marine regiments, four regiments of foot, and 5000 Dutch troops, for a descent on the French coast. He set sail in May, suffered an attack of gout, was back in Bath

His wonted Conduct we confess,
And all men own the Happiness,
That he's come home again.

The Lords have now thrown out your Bill,
Which moves your indignation;
But you betray your want of Skill,
And manage your Revenge so ill,
You're the jest of all the Nation.

Your Ancestors, with one consent,
Complain'd of Lawless Power;
Made Laws our Bondage to prevent,
And you of those good Deeds repent,
And all those Laws devour.

You are the first that e're apply'd,
T'exalt the Encroaching Crown,
As if you did not kno' that *Pride*
When mounted up, and ask't to ride,
Wou'd pull Religion down.

"for recovery of his health" in June, and rejoined the queen and the prince at Windsor Castle in August (Luttrell, *5*, 287, 291, 312, 326). As Feiling has said, "Outside England the year was one of disaster" (p. 371). It is most likely, however, that Defoe refers to the unexpected return to Spithead in January 1704 of the even more formidable fleet under Rooke's command (*On the King of Spain's Voyage to Portugall,* headnote, p. 610 above) which was under orders to convoy the archduke Charles to Lisbon and then to continue into the Mediterranean to bombard and destroy all the maritime towns in Andalusia that refused to recognize Charles III as king of Spain (Luttrell, *5*, 382, 452).

136. *Now:* The Lords rejected the second bill to prevent occasional conformity on 14 December 1703 (*LJ, 17,* 348); cf. *An Address to Our Sovereign Lady,* headnote, pp. 616–17 above.

139. *Revenge: See* 14 *n.,* 66–67 *n.,* 71 *n.,* above.

141. *Ancestors:* See *The Seven Wise Men,* 87 *n.,* above.

146–90. These lines refer to the Commons' addresses to the throne of 21 December 1703, 18 February, and 29 February 1704 and the Lords' replies of 13 January, 17 January, and 28 March 1704 (*CJ, 14,* 259, 343–45, 362–63; *LJ, 17,* 367, 371–74, 538–41), which, according to Burnet, "were drawn by the Lord *Somers,* and were read over and considered and corrected very critically, by a few Lords, among whom I had the honour to be called for one" (Burnet, *2,* 378).

147. *exalt the . . . Crown:* The Lords observed that "Your Majesty's great Judgement cannot but readily discern, whither it does naturally tend, for One House of Parliament to be exciting and earnestly desiring the Sovereign to exert a real or supposed Prerogative against the other House" (*LJ, 17,* 374).

Your Strange Unparallell'd Address
No less affronts the Queen,
Prompts her the lawful Power t'abuse,
Tells her she holds the Reins too loose,
And knows not how to Reign.

Did ever *House of Knaves* but you,
Like this betray the Nation?
Is this our Freedom to pursue;
Pray what's Prerogative to you,
In *representing Station?*

Your business is, as all men kno',
Our *Grievance to redress,*
Supply the Crown, Support it too,
But not to Prompt, *the Lord kno's who,*
The People to Oppress.

151. *Unparallell'd:* On 13 January the Lords resolved that the Commons' first address was "unparliamentary, groundless, and without Precedent." Four days later they complained that "the House of Commons have made an Appeal directly to the Throne against the House of Lords, and charged them, though most unjustly, with Attempts of the highest Nature. Nothing like this was ever done before" (*LJ, 17,* 367, 374).

152. *affronts the Queen:* "the House of Commons . . . depart from their Pretences of Respect to Your Majesty; and censure Your Conduct, in assisting our Examination, as if you had thereby done an Injury to Your Prerogative" (*LJ, 17,* 538). Cf. [Defoe], *Legion's Humble Address to the Lords,* pp. 3–4: "to Address Her Majesty to Extend her Prerogative, and thereby to Embroil Her Majesty with the Privilege of the Peers; is the most Aggravated piece of Treachery that ever House of Commons was, or ever can be Guilty of. 1. As 'tis an Affront to Her Majesty, and Reproaching her with not knowing how to Manage her Government. . . . 5. As 'tis the most Unparallel'd, Unpresidented Attempt upon the Liberties of the People."

153. *Power . . . abuse:* The Lords concluded their third address by "expressing the just Sense we have of that virtuous and truly Royal Moderation which Your Majesty has shewn upon this Occasion, in not suffering Yourself to be prevailed upon to do any Thing to the Prejudice of the Constitution, from whatsoever Hands the Invitation comes" (*LJ, 17,* 541).

159. *Prerogative:* Cf. *An Address to Our Sovereign Lady,* 22 *n.* "And we hope," the Lords said in their second address, that "the House of Commons will, in all Times to come, speak and act with that Regard to the Prerogative, which they seem to have taken up lately" (*LJ, 17,* 374).

164. *the Lord kno's who:* This may glance at the Tory ministers, Nottingham, Ormonde, Jersey, et al. The Lords maintained that denying them the right to examine witnesses in criminal matters "cannot but be of dangerous Consequence . . . especially . . . where ill Ministers abuse their Favour towards the oppressing or enslaving of the People" (*LJ, 17,* 372).

In former Times, when Tyrants Reign'd,
Your Treatments were too rough,
But if you'd have your Sense Explain'd,
You give the Queen to understand,
She's not Severe Enough.

Is this the blessed way you take
Our Freedoms to defend,
To force the Queen her Vowes to Break,
And all her soft Resolves forsake,
And abs'lute Power extend?

This Nation has had Kings enough,
That rul'd with Power Despotick,
Who of Tyrannick Arts made proof,
And us'd the Nation much too rough,
By Means and Ways Exotic.

At these you always snarl'd, and show'd
Your discontented Spirit,
And now you wou'd be understood,
Because you have a Queen too good,
You know not how to bear it.

With humble Cant, and lowly Speech,
How you besiege her Throne,
Tell her she is too mild, *by Mich,*
That she must whip the Nation's Britch,
And make her Power be known.

167. *Treatments . . . too rough:* "There is no Passage in our History more notorious than that the pretended House of Commons, in the Year 1648, when they could not prevail with the House of Lords then sitting to join with them in the intended Murder of their King, took upon them first to abolish the House of Lords by a Vote, and then to proceed to do that execrable Fact by themselves" (*LJ, 17,* 539).

170. *not Severe Enough:* On 29 February the Commons voted 149–93 to address the queen, "That she will be pleased to re-assume the just Exercise of her Prerogative, and take to herself the Examination of the Matters, relating to the Conspiracy" (*CJ, 14,* 362). A month later the Lords confessed that they were "still at a Loss to know what [the Commons] truly mean, by Your Majesty's re-assuming Your just Prerogative" (*LJ, 17,* 541).

173. *Vowes:* See *More Reformation,* 337 *n.,* above.

Have Patience, till by Management
  You bring your King from *France;*
'Tis plain, the scope of your intent
Is there, *or else the Devil's in't,*
  And you're all mad by chance.

When your young Hero mounts the Throne,
  You'll quickly have a proof;
He'll quickly make the difference known,
And take just care to have it shown,
  He'll Tyrannize enough.

What pity 'tis you shou'd be Fool'd,
  And bauk'd in your Petition;
They who with Scorpions will be rul'd,
And they who will be ruin'd, *should,*
  And mock'd in their submission.

If e're Tyrannick Powers possess
  And Re-reduce the Nation,
They'l bear their date from this Address,
And you'll too late your Crimes confess,
  But merit no Compassion.

Now you fall foul upon the Press,
  And talk of Regulation;
When you our Libelling suppress,
Pray Drop your Votes among the rest,
  For they Lampoon the Nation.

192. *your King:* See *The Golden Age Restor'd,* 71 *n.,* above.

211. *the Press:* On 15 December 1703 three Tories (Sir Simon Harcourt, Francis Gwyn, and John Howe) and two Whigs (John Smith and the marquis of Hartington) were given leave to bring in a bill to restrain the licentiousness of the press. In what must have seemed to him an act of penance, Defoe set to work to write in support of the bill and on 7 January 1704 he published *An Essay on the Regulation of the Press,* in such haste that the four signatures of the book were printed on four different presses. Despite this effort, the bill encountered opposition in the House and only passed the second reading upon a division, 127–90, on 18 January. A month later, in a committee of the whole house, it was so encumbered with amendments that it was finally allowed to die in committee (*CJ, 14,* 249, 287, 347; Moore, p. 28).

You are the *Monkeys* of the State,
And *Ape* our true Defenders;
Heaven Guard us from the hasty Fate,
Which wise men look for from the Cheat,
Of all such vile Pretenders.

You are the Nation's True Lampoon,
In Banter be it spoken,
If you wou'd save us, *'Tis too Soon;*
And 'tis *too late* to be undone,
Because our Eyes are open.

And now you stand in Peer's Records,
Usurpers of the Nation;
No Men regard your forfeit words,
The Nation's Eyes are on *the Lords,*
And There's our Expectation.

Your *G——s, W——s, R——s* shall there
Their due Deserts Encounter,

227. *Usurpers:* While the Lords did not actually call the Commons *"Usurpers,"* they hinted at the possibility, in their third address, by referring to the Danish revolution of 1660: "we are surprized that the House of Commons should single out the Instance of a Revolution in a neighboring Country, where the Clergy and the Commons were prevailed upon, by the Management of the Court, to carry their Resentments against the Lords so far, that they delivered up the Authority of the Lords, the Freedom of the People, and made a total Alteration of the Government [from a limited to an absolute monarchy]. We cannot imagine what is meant by calling this Treachery of the Commons and Clergy, in betraying the Liberties of their Country, their uniting in the Publick Defence. . . . We hope there is no Danger of such a Union amongst us, for such Purposes" (*LJ, 17,* 540).

231. *G——s:* probably James Graham (*The Golden Age Restor'd,* 75 *n.,* above). *W——s:* There are several Tory members whom Defoe may have intended here: John Williams, a member for Herefordshire (February 1701–05) who became one of the directors of the South Sea Company and was knighted in 1713, or John Wilkins, a member for Leicestershire (1698–November 1701, 1702–08) who was blacklisted by the Whigs for "Constant Voting" with the Poussineers in 1701 and who supported Bromley for speaker in 1705. The most likely candidate may be Sir William Whitlock (d. 1717), of Henley, who was called to the bar from the Middle Temple in 1671, knighted by William III in 1689, and returned to parliament for Great Marlow, Buckinghamshire (1689–95) and Oxford University (1702–17). Although the second son of Bulstrode Whitelocke, Cromwell's lord keeper, Sir William came to be a sound Tory and True Churchman. In 1705 he voted for the tack and supported Bromley for speaker (Le Neve, pp. 420, 509; Charles H. Hopwood, *Middle Temple Records,* 4 vols., 1904–05, *3,* 1261; *Numerical Calculation*).

R——s: presumably Sir George Rooke, Vice-Admiral of England (132 *n.,* above) and Tory member for Portsmouth (*The Golden Age Revers'd,* 107 *n.,* above).

And in due time *Vile Rochester*
And *Nottingham* may both appear
  To give a Black account there.

Assure yourselves, the Nation will
  The House of Lords defend,
You've lost your interest and your Skill,
And never will regain it, 'till
  Your Manners come to mend.

That you betray the People's Trust,
  The Nation knows 'tis true,
Are Arbitrary and Unjust,
And if we will be sav'd, we must
  Find *other men than You.*

And now you Cavil with the Lords,
  Because they first reprov'd you;
Your Manners just Remarks affords,
But most of all your Decent words
  Have Rogues and Scoundrels prov'd you.

Go home, for shame; *But first the Queen*
  Address *for Dissolution,*
No more in that high House be seen,
Where such a Scandal you have been,
  To the *English* Constitution.

243. *Arbitrary and Unjust:* Cf. *A New Satyr on the Parliament,* 60 *n.,* above; [Defoe], *The History of the Kentish Petition,* 1701, p. 25: "To see one Tyrant banish'd from his Home,/*To set Five Hundred Traytors in his Room";* headnote, p. 633 above.

249. *Decent words:* The Lords observed that "The Expressions in the Address of the House of Commons [of 21 December] are so very harsh and indecent, that, we may truly affirm, the like were never used of the House of Peers in any Age; not even by that Assembly, which, under the Name of the House of Commons, took upon them not only to abolish the House of Lords, but to destroy the Monarchy" (*LJ, 17,* 372).

WILLIAM SHIPPEN

Faction Display'd
(April[?] 1704)

"The Influence of Dryden," which the textbooks postulate for the eighteenth century, is nowhere more apparent than in *Faction Display'd.* Three of its 533 lines (377–79), many of its scattered details (e.g. 129, 301, 473), and even something of its tone (533 *n.*), come straight from Dryden. Defoe struggled against this influence (*The True-Born Englishman,* 921 *n.,* above), but Shippen surrendered to it. His friend C. D., who wrote a prefatory sonnet *To the Concealed Author of this Excellent Poem,* recognized that *Faction Display'd* aspired to "the same Majesty of Verse;/The same just Stile, [and] the same deep Sense" that Dryden achieved in *Absalom and Achitophel.*

The structure and the theme of the poem, however, derive not from *Absalom and Achitophel* but from Sallust's *Bellum Catilinae.* The operative fiction in *Faction Display'd* is the Mafia-style *conversazione* that Lucius Catilina convened in a back room of his house in Rome in 64 B.C. Upon this occasion Catilina was the only speaker and the other conspirators simply sealed their guilt in a libation of human blood. This model is obviously much less susceptible of dramatic development than Dryden's model for *Absalom and Achitophel,* Book IX of *Paradise Lost,* but Shippen does the best he can with it. Not one but eight of the conspirators are made to speak and further dramatic complication is introduced when Sigillo praises Clodio's speech and even finds it worthy of Cethego (lines 247–52). But in spite of this effort, *Faction Display'd,* like its model, remains static and oratorical. It is essentially a gallery of *caricaturas* of the Whig leaders in the early years of the reign, very much in the style of Dryden's portraits of the first Whigs in *Absalom and Achitophel,* lines 543–681.

Shippen insists that he is writing history, not fiction: "I have not form'd an Imaginary Poetical Design," he says in the preface to the poem, "but described a real one." But whether this is true or not, the theme of Shippen's poem clearly derives from Sallust. The weakness that Sallust attributes to Lucius Catilina is the same that Shippen imputes collectively to the Whig conspirators on the night of 8 March 1702: it is the limitlessness of their desires. "His shattered mind," Sallust said (V, 5), "always craved the monstrous, the incredible, the immeasurable heights." Shippen reverts to this theme again and again: "no Ties can bind [the Whig conspirators]" (line 179); they soar above "The little Tyes of Gratitude and Love" (line 264); their "Course" is "boundless" (line 406); they acknowledge "no fixt Rule" (line 464). And if restored to power, their government would be equally "boundless" (line 476).

Even the angry Whigs who wrote replies to *Faction Display'd* did not deny that it was a poem "of the very first form" or that it had obtained "great Vogue and Credit" (Bodl. MS. Rawl. poet. 152, f. 42v; *Some Critical and Politick Remarks on a Late Virulent Lampoon, Call'd Faction Display'd* 1704, p. 3). The most impressive of the replies in verse is *Faction Display'd. The Second Part* ("Distant a little from the *Gallick* Shore"), 1704. This work, sprinkled throughout with Scotticisms, creates a Tory counterpart to the Whig cabal in Northumberland House, which is interrupted by the ghost of Sir John Fenwick. Less impressive is *Faction Display'd Burlesqued* ("Say Muse, for thou'rt a quick-ey'd Goddess"), which seems to have circulated only in manuscript. Here the joke is simply to turn *Faction Display'd* into octosyllabic couplets to make the author's "malice . . . barefac'd, & obvious [to] every reader." A third reply in verse is mentioned below. Of the two replies in prose, the first, *Faction Display'd. A Poem. Answer'd Paragraph by Paragraph,* 1704, attributes the poem to Matthew Prior, while the second, *Some Critical and Politick Remarks on a Late Virulent Lampoon, Call'd Faction Display'd,* 1704, pointedly refuses even "to guess at the Author, whether it is Mr. *D*[*urfey?*], Dr. *A*[*tterbury?*] or Mr. *P*[*ittis?*]" (p. 22).

Since the poem was published anonymously and never acknowledged, it has been attributed to a number of Tory writers, of whom Matthew Prior was the most distinguished and the most embarrassed. In the beginning of the new reign, Prior had done "very well at Court," but in January 1704 he discovered that the duke and duchess of Marlborough believed him to be "the author of some Libel" against the duke. Prior hurried to Godolphin to deny the rumor and Godolphin "seemed fully satisfied and said he would endeavour to let my Lady Marl: know." In April 1704, therefore, when *Faction Display'd,* with its scurrilous couplet about the duchess's ancestry (lines 431–32), was publicly attributed to "good Mr. *Pr—r,*" Prior wrote to Godolphin in a panic: "I . . . Repeat to your Lordship, that before God, Angels, and Men I neither did write that Book, or any Line in it, nor do I directly or indirectly know who wrote the whole or any part of it" (L. G. Wickham Legg, *Matthew Prior,* Cambridge, Cambridge University Press, 1921, pp. 128, 129–30; Prior, *Works, 2,* 797) (cf. 377–79 *n.,* below). The next year, in August 1705, Thomas Hearne was told that "Mr. *Priaulx*" was the author of "those two ingenious Poems," *Faction Display'd* and *Moderation Display'd* (Hearne, *1,* 31). If Priaulx is not simply a homonym for Prior, it may refer to Peter Priaulx (c. 1662–1740) who graduated B.A. from University College, Oxford, in 1685 and became the vicar of Elsfield, Oxfordshire, and rector of Elmley, Kent, and Buckland, Surrey (*Alumni Oxonienses, 3,* 1201). Finally, as late as 1710, William Pittis disclosed that Bertram Stote, a Tory member of parliament for Northumberland, was the author of the same "two excellent Poems" (Nichols, *Illustrations, 4,* 336; [Pittis], *The Proceedings of Both Houses of Parliament in the Years 1702, 1703, 1704 upon the Bill to Prevent Occasional Conformity,* 1710, p. 56 [the last reference was very kindly called to my attention by Professor Henry L. Snyder of the University of Kansas]). But Alexander Pope identified the poem in his copy of *PRSA,* 1705 (BM: C.28.e.15), as "By W. Shippen, Esq;" and Giles Jacob confirmed the attribution in *An Historical Account,* 1720, p. 306.

Shippen presumably began the poem after the death of William III (8 March 1702) (5 *n.* below) and before the death of Robert Spencer, earl of Sunderland (28 September 1702) (251 *n.* below). It is said to have been "handed . . . about at first in Manuscript" (*Some Critical and Politick Remarks on a Late Virulent Lampoon, Call'd, Faction Display'd,* 1704, p. 3). A *terminus ad quem* for publication of the poem is provided by some doggerel verses entitled *Faction Display'd, in Answer to Faction Display'd, a Poem* ("Good People give ear, I'll declare to you all"), 1704. The Luttrell copy of this folio half-sheet, at Harvard, is dated 22 April 1704.

Charing Cross and Northumberland House. Drawing by Antonio Canale (Canaletto)

VIEW here the *POURTRAIT* of a Factious Priest,
Who (spight of Proverbs) dares defile his Nest:
And where he shou'd defend the Church's Cause,
Basely deserts her, and arraigns her Laws.
Such, and no better is the Man that dares
With his Superiors wage litigious Wars:
And to *malignant Answers* set his Hand,
To Sermons publish'd by *supreme Command*.
If this be meritorious, let him find
Preferment suited to so vile a Mind:
A Mitre ne'er can fit that impious Head,
Who has his Conscience, and his Trust betray'd.
Such the *Satyrick Muse* did well describe,
When thus (provok'd) she sung the factious Tribe:

Unhappy Church! by such Usurpers sway'd,
How is thy Native Purity decay'd?
How are thy Prelates chang'd from what they were
When Laud *and* Sancroft *fill'd the sacred Chair?*
When for establish'd Faith they shou'd contend,
Meekness and Christian Charity pretend;
But with a blind enthusiastick Rage,
For Schism and Toleration they engage;
With strange Delight and Vehemence espouse
Occasional Conformists shameful Cause;
Oppress thy Friends, and vindicate thy Foes.
Faction, a restless and repining Fiend,
Curdles their Blood, and gnaws upon their Mind,
Offspring of Chaos, Enemy to Form,
Who, raging, swells the World into a Storm.
She taught the Giants to attempt the Sky,
And Jove's *avenging Thunder to defy:*
She rais'd the AXE *that struck the fatal Blow,*
Which murder'd Gods Vicegerent here below;
And still pursues him with relentless Hate,
Arraigns his Mem'ry, and insults his Fate.

[Faction display'd.]

Engrav'd, and Printed at *AMSTERDAM:* 1710.

Benjamin Hoadly. A folio half-sheet, reprinting lines 145–48, 155–61, 9–18 of *Faction Display'd*

Faction Display'd

Say, Goddess Muse, for thy All-searching Eyes
Can Traytors trace thro' ev'ry dark Disguise,
Can penetrate Intriguing Statesmen's Hearts,
Their deepest Plots, and all their wily Arts.
Say, how a Fierce *Caball* Combin'd of late,
Imploy their anxious Thoughts t'embroil the State;
What angry Pow'r inspires 'em to Complain
In *Anna*'s Gentle and Propitious Reign.
  Faction, a restless and repining Fiend,
Curdles their Blood, and gnaws upon their Mind;
Off-spring of *Chaos,* Enemy to *Form,*
By whose destructive Arts the World is torn.
She taught the Giants to attempt the Sky,
And *Jove*'s avenging Thunder to defy.
She rais'd the Hand, that struck the Fatal Blow,
And Martyr'd *Jove*'s Vicegerent here below;
She still pursues him with relentless Hate,
Arraigns his Mem'ry, and Insults his Fate.
'Tis She, that wou'd, for ev'ry slight Offence,
Depose a True Hereditary Prince;

5. *Caball:* The classical analogue of the Whig "Caball" convened at Northumberland House on the night of William's death is the meeting that Lucius Catilina convened at his own house in 64 B.C. Sallust supplies the names of the conspirators, but the only one that Shippen appropriates is that of Gaius Cethegus (251 below) (Sallust, *Bellum Catilinae,* XVII, 2–4).

of late: "8 Mar. 1702 when K. Wm died" (Bodl. copy of *POAS,* 1707, *4,* 83 [Thorn Drury d. 27]).

9. *Faction:* Cf. *The Dispensary, 1,* 64, above, and illustration, p. 651.

16. *Jove's Vicegerent:* Charles I.

18. *Insults:* Besides "the *Calves-Head-Feast*" (86 below), the worst offender was John Toland, who wound up his exposé of John Gauden's authorship of *Eikon Basilike; The Pourtraicture of His Sacred Majestie in His Solitudes and Sufferings* (1648) with the gratuitous assumption that Charles I "was really of neither [the Anglican nor the Roman] Church, but believed the Pretences of both to be Credulity or Craft" and a year later published a list of Charles I's "immoral Practices" (*A Complete Collection of the Historical, Political, and Miscellaneous Works of John Milton,* 3 vols., Amsterdam, 1698, *1,* 130; *Amyntor: Or, A Defence of Milton's Life,* 1699, pp. 166–69).

20. *Prince:* James II.

That would *Usurpers* for their Treason Crown,
Till Time and Vengeance drag them headlong down,
And *Exil'd Monarchs* Reassert their rightful Throne.
No Constitution in the World can boast
A Scheme of Laws more Rational, more Just,
Than *England*'s are; where Sov'reign, Kingly sway,
Is *mixt* and qualify'd with such Allay,
That Free-born Subjects willingly Obey.
Nor yet so basely *mixt,* as that our Kings
Are only Tools of State, and Pow'rless Things.
For tho', indeed, they can have no Pretence
With *Fundamental Contracts* to *Dispence,*
(For that were Conquest) yet, those Rights maintain'd,
Prerogative is High, and unrestrain'd.
In equal Distance from Extremes we move,
Nor Tyranny, nor Commonwealth approve.
Nor Tyranny, that Savage Brutal Pow'r,
Which not protects Mankind, but does devour.
Nor Commonwealth, a Monster, Hydra State,
Whose many Heads threaten each others Fate,
And load their Body with unweildy Weight.
But a Successive Monarchy we own,
With all the Lawful Sanctions of a Crown.
Such was our old Establish'd *English* Frame,
Which might have flourish'd Ages yet the same,
But for this Envious Fiend; who still prepares
To sow the Seeds of long Intestine Wars.
Near the Imperial Palace's Remains,

21. *Usurpers:* William and Mary.

23. *Exil'd Monarchs:* James Francis Edward, recognized as James III by Louis XIV.

27. *mixt:* The Tories agreed that in a "Mixt Government," like England's, the three estates "(or *Tres Ordinis Regni*) are so *mixt,* as the Soveraignity is joyntly in them all . . . as in [a] *Corporation*" (J. H[owe?], *Letters to Parliament-Men in Reference to Some Proceedings in the House of Commons,* 1701, p. 21); cf. Pope, *An Essay on Man,* III, 294: "jarring int'rests of themselves create/Th'according music of a well-mix'd State."

32. *Dispence:* Shippen rejects the power that James II assumed to dispense with the laws in the interests of all his subjects.

48. *Palace's Remains:* Whitehall, the palace that Henry VIII had seized from Cardinal Wolsey in 1529, still lay in ruins, having burned to the ground in January 1698 (Evelyn, 5, 283).

Where nothing now but Desolation reigns;
(Fatal Presage of Monarchy's decline,
And Extirpation of the Regal Line!)
There stands an Antique Venerable Pile,
Whose Lords were once the Glories of our Isle:
But now it Mourns that Race of Heroe's dead,
And droops, and hangs its Melancholy Head.
This Pile (howe'er for better Ends design'd,
An Emblem of the Noble Founder's Mind)
Is *Faction*'s Refuge; where she keeps her Court,
Where all her darling Votaries Resort.
Here, when their glorious *Nassau* fell, they met
On new Resolves and Measures to Debate.
  Say then, my Muse, their secret Thoughts display,
Expose their dark Designs to open Day.
  This Grand *Caball* was held at dead of Night,
(For Ghosts and Furies always shun the Light)
Despair, and Rage, and Sorrow kept 'em dumb,
Till *Moro* rose (the Master of the Dome)
A Stamm'ring Hot, Conceited, Laughing Lord,
Who yet presided o're the Council Board,
By *Nassau*'s choice, by Nature's wise decree,
For empty Levity will upwards fly.
With much adoe his Fetter'd Tongue broke loose;
  I take it as an Honour that you've Chose
For this Debate, your humble Servant's House.
The House henceforward shall Recorded stand,
As the *Palladium* of the sinking Land;

52. *Venerable Pile:* Northumberland House, in the Strand at Charing Cross (see illustration, p. 653), was "a noble and spacious Building; having a large square Court at the Entrance, with Buildings round it; at the upper End of which Court, is a Piazzo, with Buildings over it, sustained by Stone Pillars, and behind the Buildings there is a curious Garden, which runneth down to the *Thames*" (Strype, 2, 376).

57. *the Noble Founder:* Algernon Percy, tenth earl of Northumberland (1602–68), the favorite of Charles I, acquired Northumberland House by his marriage to Lady Elizabeth Howard in October 1642. It was originally built (c. 1612) by Henry Howard, earl of Northampton, and called Northampton House.

60. *when . . . Nassau fell:* See 5 *n.* above.

67. *Moro:* "[Charles Seymour, duke of] Somerset" (*BB*3); see *The Seven Wise Men,* 11 *n.,* above.

76. *Palladium:* the image of the goddess Pallas, in the citadel of Troy, on which the safety of the city was believed to depend (*OED*).

And I to future Ages be renown'd,
The *Party*'s Bullwark, and the Nation's Mound.
Now *Nassau,* the immortal *Nassau*'s gone,
We justly his untimely Herse Bemoan.
O that I could restore his Life again!
For who can bear a Woman's Servile Chain?
  Full of such Stuff, he would have giv'n it vent,
But that black *Ario*'s fierceness did prevent,
A *Scotch,* Seditious, Unbelieving Priest,
The Brawny Chaplain of the *Calves-Head-Feast;*
Who first his Patron, then his Prince Betray'd,
And does that Church, he's Sworn to guard, Invade.
Warm with Rebellious Rage, he thus began;
  To talk of calling Life agen is vain.
Peace to the *Glorious* dead. We justly mourn
His Ashes, ever Sacred be his Urn:
But here, my Lords, we are together met,
To vow to *Anna*'s Sceptre endless Hate.
For since my hope of *Winton* is expir'd,
With just Revenge and Indignation fir'd,
I'll write, and talk, and preach her Title down,
My thund'ring Voice shall shake her in the Throne;
Do you the Sword, and I'll engage the Gown.
  A Pause ensu'd, till *Patriarcho*'s Grace,
Was pleas'd to rear his Huge unweildy Mass;

84. *Ario:* "[Gilbert Burnet, bishop of Salisb]ury" (*B*).

86. *Calves-Head-Feast:* See *The Reverse,* headnote, p. 228 above.

87. *Patron:* Burnet's "Patron" was John Maitland, second earl and first duke of Lauderdale (1616–82), Charles II's secretary of state in Scotland. In 1671 he offered Burnet his choice of four Scottish bishoprics and the following year he offered him a bishopric again, with the added promise of the first archbishopric that should fall vacant. Burnet refused both and soon suffered Lauderdale's displeasure. Consequently, in April 1675, when Burnet revealed to a committee of the Commons what he knew of Lauderdale's unconstitutional designs (*Parl. Hist., 4,* 683), he was, as he said, "much blamed for what [he] had done" (Burnet, *1,* 380). "Treacherous villain," was Swift's comment (*Prose, 5,* 276).

Prince: James II; cf. *The Mitred Club,* 119 *n.,* above.

88. *Church . . . Invade:* Cf. *The Golden Age Revers'd,* 53–56, above.

95. *Winton:* The possibility of Burnet's translation to the rich bishopric of Winchester was lost when Peter Mews (1619–1706) failed to predecease William III.

98. *thund'ring Voice:* Cf. *The Mitred Club,* 12, above.

100. *Patriarcho:* "[Thomas] Tenison, archbishop of Canterbury" (*BB2B3*); see *The Golden Age Revers'd,* 58 *n.,* above.

A Mass unanimated with a Soul,
Or else he'd ne're be made so vile a Tool;
He'd ne're his Apostolick Charge Prophane,
And *Atheists,* and *Socinians* Cause maintain.
At length, as from the Hollow of an Oak,
The Bulky Primate Yawn'd, and Silence broke;
  I much approve my Brother's Zealous Heat,
Such is the Noble Ardour of the Great,
On which Success and Praise will ever wait.
But I'm untaught in Politician's Schools,
Unpractic'd in their Arts and studied Rules;
By which they make the Wisest of us Fools.
The Task be therefore yours, to Forge some Plot,
And I'll be Ready with my trusty Vote,
Nor e're give your Commands a Second Thought.
Tho' I were Mute, you must confess I've Stood,
Fixt as a Rock, amidst the beating Flood.
Witness St. *Asaph*'s, and St. *David*'s Cause,

105. *Socinians Cause maintain: "The* Maidstone *Lecture"* (*ABC*). While the exact reference has not been found, the general outlines are apparent from *Faction Display'd. A Poem. Answer'd Paragraph by Paragraph,* 1704, p. 7: "where there is a Tolleration by Act of Parliament . . . it belongs not to the Episcopal Function to disturb any Persons in the Exercise of their several Religions, and the *Maidstone* Lecture is no other than what should result from Royal Indulgence, since the Grant of it has been confirm'd from the Throne, both from this and the precedent Reign, and such Lectures by the Dissenting Clergy have been allow'd of, and Weekly held in all the principal places of *England*."

107. *Bulky:* Cf. *Advice to a Painter,* 22, above; *A Conference,* 147 *n.,* above.

115. *trusty Vote:* On 25 November 1703, during the debate on the second bill to prevent occasional conformity, Sir John Pakington bantered the archbishop for opposing the bill: "I did wonder," he said, "to hear so many B[ishop]s against this Bill, but that wonder ceas'd, when I consider'd whom they ow'd their Preferment to. The A[rch]b[isho]p of *C*[*anterbur*]*y,* I think, was promoted to that See by my Lord *S*[*underlan*]*d*'s interest; and being ask'd what Reasons he had against this Bill, Replyed, he had not well consider'd the Bill, but that my Lord *S*[*ome*]*rs* told him it ought not to pass. This was a very weighty Reason for the Head of our C[hurc]h to give; and yet, I dare say, none of the rest of them could give a better One" ([Sir John Pakington], *A Speech for the Bill against Occasional Conformity* [1704], pp. 2–3).

119. *St. Asaph's . . . Cause:* See *The Golden Age Restor'd,* 98 *n.,* above. Although Tenison received complaints of Edward Jones' "corruption, negligence and oppression" (*DNB, 10,* 985) in March 1697, legal proceedings were not instituted until June 1700 (Luttrell, *4,* 652–53). Unlike Thomas Watson, who stubbornly maintained his innocence, "Drunken *A*[*sap*]*h* . . . with his Red Fiery Face" (*The Town Display'd* ["My Dear *Amintor,* on a Summer's Day"], 1701, p. 14), confessed that he was guilty of most of the 36 charges against him. In June 1701 Tenison sentenced him to be suspended for less

Where obstinately I transgress'd the Laws,
And did in either Case Injustice show,
Here sav'd a Friend, there Triumph'd o're a Foe.
  Then old *Mysterio* shook his Silver Hairs,
Loaded with Learning, Prophecy, and Years,
Whom Factious Zeal to fierce *Unchristian* Strife,
Had hurry'd in the last Extream of Life;
Who, Jumbling Numbers in his heated Brain,
Rome's sudden Fall had long foretold in vain.
Strange Dotage! thus to Sacrifice his Ease,
When Nature whispers Men to Crown their days
With sweet Retirement and Religious Peace!
Fore-knowledge struggled in his heaving Breast,
E're he in these dark Terms his Fears exprest:
  The Stars rowl adverse, and malignant shine,
Some dire Portent! Some Comet I divine!
I plainly in the *Revelations* find,
That *Anna* to the Beast will be inclin'd.
Howe're, tho' She and all the Senate frown,
I'll wage eternal War with *Packington*,

than a year. "The chief difference between their cases," according to Lord Dartmouth, "was, that Watson took the money himself, (being a bachelor,) and Jones's wife received it for him" (Burnet, 1823, *4*, 407 *n*.). But Burnet explained that whereas Watson, the Tory, was guilty of "direct simony," Jones, the Whig, was guilty only of "simoniacal practices" (ibid.).

St. David's Cause: See *The Golden Age Restor'd*, 97 *n*., above. In October 1695, five months after he was installed as archbishop, Tenison, by a very rarely exercised right, deprived Thomas Watson of the bishopric of St. David's on charges of simony and extortion. The court of arches, over which Tenison presided, sustained the decree of deprivation in April 1699. In his appeal before the court of delegates of Serjeant's Inn, Watson's lawyers argued "that there was no president for the archbishop of Canterbury alone, without a convocation, to deprive a bishop; and if allowed, in an ill reign the archbishop might deprive most of the bishops in the kingdom" (Luttrell, *3*, 541; *4*, 506, 589).

123. *Mysterio:* "[William] Lloyd, bishop of Worcester" (*BB*3); cf. *The Golden Age*, 73 *n*., above.

129. *Strange Dotage:* Cf. *Absalom and Achitophel*, 165–66: "why should he [Zimri], with Wealth and Honour blest,/Refuse his Age the needful hours of Rest?"

137. *the Beast:* The beast in Revelation 13, with seven heads and ten horns, "and his number is Six hundred threescore and six," was identified first with the Anti-Christ and then, by Puritan divines, with the Roman church.

139. *Packington:* See *The Golden Age Restor'd*, headnote, pp. 488–89 above.

And venture Life and Fame to pull him down.
As he went on, his Tongue a trembling seis'd,
And all his Pow'r of Utterance suppress'd.
So when the Sibyll felt th'inspiring God,
She raving lost her Voice, and Speechless stood.
Unhappy Church, by such Usurpers sway'd!
How is thy Prim'tive Purity decay'd!
How are thy Prelates chang'd from what they were,
When *Laud* or *Sancroft* fill'd the Sacred Chair!
Laud, tho' by some traduc'd, with Zeal adorn'd,
Whilst *Patriarcho* is despis'd and Scorn'd,
Shall be by me for ever Prais'd, for ever Mourn'd.
Sancroft's unblemish'd Life, divinely Pure,
In its own heav'nly Innocence Secure,
The teeth of Time, the blasts of Envy shall endure.
When for th'Establish'd Faith they should contend,
Meekness and Christian Charity pretend;
But with a blind and unbecoming Rage,
For *Schism* and *Toleration* they engage;
With strange Delight and Eagerness espouse
Occasional Conformists shameful Cause;
Oppress thy Friends, and Vindicate thy Foes.
Thy guardian Laws to weaken they Combine,
And tamely thy Essential Rights resign.

148. *Laud:* See *The Mitred Club,* 38 *n.,* above.

Sancroft: William Sancroft (1617–93) succeeded as archbishop of Canterbury in November 1677. Although it was said at the time that he had been "set up by the Duke of York against [Henry Compton, bishop of] London" (*DNB, 17,* 735), Sancroft refused to serve on James' court of high commission and vigorously opposed the Declaration of Indulgence in 1688. He seems nonetheless to have retained James' confidence and declared that the offer of the crown to William of Orange was unconstitutional: "if it be done at all," he said, "it must be done by force of conquest" (ibid., *17,* 737). He was deprived in February 1690 and a year later initiated the nonjuror succession by delegating the archepiscopal authority to William Lloyd, the deprived bishop of Norwich. In August 1691 he retired to Fressingfield, Suffolk, his birthplace. He is "Zadock the Priest . . . shunning Power and Place" in *Absalom and Achitophel* (864) and "divine SANCROFT" in young Jonathan Swift's unfinished pindaric ode (Swift, *Poems, 1,* 40).

158. *Schism:* Cf. *The Mitred Club,* 55 *n.,* above; *More Reformation,* 413 *n.,* above. *Toleration:* Cf. *The Golden Age Restor'd,* 64 *n.,* above.

159–60. *espouse/Occasional Conformists . . . Cause:* Cf. *The Golden Age Restor'd,* 53 *n.,* above; *A Prophecy,* 66 *n.,* above.

Thy antient Truths with Modern Glosses blend,
Destroying the Religion they would mend.
So have they broke thy Pale and Fences down,
Such Arts have Christianity o'rethrown:
For *Scepticism,* that now triumphant reigns,
Condemns her Captive to inglorious Chains,
Where She Forlorn, Contemn'd, Despairing lies,
Nor hopes a Refuge, but her Native Skies.
But Muse proceed, nor dwell on Thoughts too long,
That would Inflame thy Satyrizing Song.
Clodio with kindling Emulation heard,
What this Triumvirate of Priests declar'd.
Clodio, the Chief of all the Rebel-Race,
Uncheck'd by Fear, unhumbled by Disgrace;
Whose Working, Turbulent, Fanatick Mind
No Tenderness can move, no Ties can bind.
To gain a Rake he'll Drink, and Whore, and Rant,
T'engage a Puritan will Pray and Cant.
So Satan can in diff'ring Forms appear,
Or Radiant Light, or gloomy Darkness wear.
Thrice he Blasphem'd, and thrice he frantick Swore
By ev'ry Terrible, Infernal Pow'r;
Then wav'd his Staff, and said:
Tho' *Nassau*'s Death has all our Measures broke
Yet never will we bend to *Anna*'s Yoke.
The glorious *Revolution* was in vain,
If Monarchy once more its Rights regain.
Let all be Chaos, and Confusion all,
E're that damn'd Form of Government prevail.

164. *Modern Glosses: "B[urne]t's* Exposition of the Articles" (*AC*). *An Exposition of the Thirty-Nine Articles of the Church of England,* which Burnet published in 1699, was censured by the Lower House of Convocation in May 1701 in the following terms: "1. that the said Book tends to introduce such a Latitude and Diversity of Opinions, as the Articles were fram'd to avoid. 2. . . . many Passages in the *Exposition* of several Articles . . . appear . . . to be contrary to the true meaning of them. 3. . . . some Things in the said Book . . . seem . . . to be of dangerous Consequence to the Church" ([White Kennett], *The History of the Convocation,* 1702, p. 179).

174. *Clodio:* "[Thomas Wharton, Lord] Wharton" (*BB2B3*); cf. *The Golden Age Revers'd,* 24 *n.,* above. Wharton's classical antitype is P. Claudius Pulcher, "the boldest and vilest" Roman demagogue in the first century B.C. (Plutarch, *Pompey,* XLVI, 4).

John Toland(?) presenting the Act of Settlement to the Dowager Electress Sophia of Hanover. Anonymous engraving

O had he liv'd to Perfect his Design,
We ne're had been Subjected to her Reign,
But rooted out the *Stuarts* hated Line!
Howe're, since Fate has otherwise decreed,
We may on his unfinish'd Scheme proceed.
We may 'gainst Pow'r repos'd in One inveigh,
And call all Monarchy Tyrannick Sway.
We may the Praises of the *Dutch* advance,
Rail at the Arbitrary Rule of *France,*
Extol the Commonwealth in *Adria*'s Flood,
Which for ten rowling Centuries has stood;
Argue how th'*Roman,* and *Athenian* State
Were only when Republicks truly Great;
'Tis easy the Unreas'ning Mob to guide,
For they are always on the Factious side.
This labour'd here, 'twill be our second Thought,
To Manage and Cajole *Sophia*'s Court.
Toland alone for such a work is fit,
In all the Arts of Villany Compleat.
For this from Publick Justice have we screen'd,
For this his Impious Heresies maintain'd.
The *Scotch,* a Rough, Revolting, Stubborn Kind,

193. *to Perfect his Design:* "King *William* was hardly cold in his Death-Bed" before the rumor began to circulate "That there were some Papers found in his strong Box, whereby it appear'd, that he had form'd the Design of Advancing the Elector of *Hanover* to the Crown, to the Exclusion of Queen ANNE." A commission appointed to examine the dead king's private papers duly reported that the rumor was "Groundless, False, Villanous and Scandalous" (Boyer, *Annals,* 1703, pp. 33–34).

202. *Commonwealth:* Venice had existed as an independent state since 697.

210. *Toland:* In July 1701 William III appointed two noted rakes (Charles Gerard, earl of Macclesfield, and Charles Mohun, Lord Mohun) and one supposed atheist (John Toland) to present to the electress Sophia a copy of *Anglia Libera, or the Limitation and Succession of the Crown of England Explained and Asserted,* which Toland had written to interpret the Act of Settlement (June 1701) by which Sophia "and the Heirs of her Body, being Protestants," were made heirs presumptive to the throne of England (Luttrell, *5,* 67); see illustration, p. 659.

212. *screen'd:* Cf. *Reformation of Manners,* 607 *n.,* above. In September 1697 the Irish parliament ordered *Christianity not Mysterious* (1696) to be burned by the common hangman; Toland avoided further punishment by escaping to England (HMC *Portland MSS., 3,* 586).

214–17. *The Scotch . . . Rebellion:* See *Address to Our Sovereign Lady,* headnote, p. 615 above.

Have long at *England*'s growing Pow'r repin'd.
Nor need we, with unnecessary Care,
Endeavour to foment Rebellion there.
For scarce our *Nassau*'s Empire they endur'd,
Tho' he their antient Liberties restor'd,
And murm'ring now they ask a foreign Lord.
But (Health suppos'd) to *Ireland* I'll repair,
And right or wrong Usurp the Common's Chair;
That Point once gain'd, we'll soon secure our Cause,
Soon undermine our hot-brain'd towring Foes.
At least I'll substitute some Wealthy Friend,
Who shall with Heat and Arrogance contend
To thwart the Court in ev'ry just Command.
  So *Catiline* the Fate of *Rome* design'd,
And when h'had form'd the Scheme within his mind,
In such a warm Harangue his Friends addrest,
And open'd all the Secret of his Breast.
This hit *Sigillo*'s Thoughts, and made him cool,
Tho' just before he scarcely could Controul
The stormy Passion swelling in his Soul;
His restless Soul, that rends his sickly Frame,
Worn with a poys'nous and corroding Flame.
  An unjust Judge, and blemish of the Mace,
Witness the *Bankers* long depending Case.

219. *antient Liberties:* See *The Mourners,* 9 *n.,* above.

220. *a foreign Lord:* A rebellious Scottish parliament in September 1703 passed the Act of Security, providing that upon the death of Queen Anne, her successor in Scotland was to be a Protestant and a Stuart but not the same person as the king of England. The queen withheld her assent to the bill until 5 August 1704 (Trevelyan, 2, 235–36, 242).

222. *Usurp the . . . Chair:* "This Project was once talk'd of" (*ABB2B3*). Wharton's intervention in Irish politics is reflected in Swift's statement that he sold William Conolly a place in the commission of the revenue for £3000 in September 1710 (*Journal to Stella,* ed. Harold Williams, 2 vols., Oxford, Clarendon Press, 1948, *1,* 31–32).

228–31. *Catiline:* Cf. *The Seven Wise Men,* 58 *n.,* above. Catiline "form'd the Scheme" (*consilium cepit*) of overthrowing the government, called the conspirators together in a private room (*in abditam partem*) of his house, and delivered "a warm Harangue" (*orationem*) (Sallust, *Bellum Catilinae,* XVI, 4; XX, 1).

232. *Sigillo:* "[John Somers, Lord] Somers" (*BB3*).

236. *corroding Flame:* See *Advice to a Painter,* 28–30, above.

238. *the Bankers . . . Case:* Williamson *vs.* Regem was the most important case that came before Somers in the court of chancery. It originated in Charles II's stop of the exchequer in 1672. By that act the king appropriated about £1,300,000 which should

A shallow Statesman, tho' of mighty Fame,
For who can e're that curst *Partition* name,
But to his foul Disgrace, and to his Shame?
Besides, in spight of all his loud Defence,
He shew'd a want of Honesty or Sense,
In passing ev'ry Plund'ring Courtier's *Grants.*
He is (for Satyr dares the Truth declare)
Deist, Republican, Adulterer.
Thus his lov'd *Clodio,* for his Speech he prais'd,
And Joy and Wonder in the Hearers rais'd:
    There spoke the Guardian Genius of our Cause,

---

have been applied to the repayment of loans granted by the bankers. Instead of repaying the money, Charles paid the bankers interest at the rate of six per cent out of the hereditary excise. These payments were continued until 1683, but James II and William III both refused to recognize the obligation. In 1689 the bankers brought suit to recover the arrears and were upheld by the barons of the exchequer. The attorney-general, Sir Thomas Trevor, then appealed the case to the court of exchequer chamber. "No judgment so elaborate had ever been delivered in Westminster Hall as that by which, in November 1696, [Somers] reversed the decision of the court of exchequer" (Howell, *14,* 1–3, 39 *n.*, 107; *DNB, 18,* 632). Lord Dartmouth observed that the decision was based "upon political reasons, without any regard to law and equity," and in January 1700, "after a very warm debate," the House of Lords set aside Somers' reversal and "gave judgment that the bankers ought to be paid" (Burnet, 1823, *4,* 432; Luttrell, *4,* 606).

240. *Partition:* In August 1698 when he was negotiating the secret treaty by which the Spanish empire was to have been partitioned between France, Austria, and the Netherlands, William III wrote to Somers, asking him, if he approved, to send full powers, under the great seal of England, to ratify the treaty. Although he did not approve, Somers ordered James Vernon, the secretary of state, to draw up a blank commission. Then he affixed the great seal and sent it off to William at Loo, where it was signed by the English plenipotentiaries. When Somers was impeached by the Commons in April 1701, the first article exhibited against him charged that he "did not, according to the Trust and Duty of his said several Offices, dissuade, or endeavour to obstruct" the ratification of the treaty (*CJ, 13,* 546).

244. *passing . . . Grants:* See *Advice to a Painter,* 40 *n.*, above. Grants from the crown are initiated by a petition to the throne and completed in the office of the lord keeper of the great seal or the lord chancellor (offices that Somers held from March 1693 to April 1700). "If the Grant be exorbitant, if it be made to an undeserving Person . . . , if it occasions Obloquy to the Government or Discontent among the People," as Charles Davenant explained, this officer is "bound in Duty and by his Oath not to fix the Great Seal to the said Grant" (*A Discourse upon Grants and Resumptions,* 1700, pp. 296–97).

246. *Deist:* In April 1700 during the bitter debate on the bill to resume the king's grants of estates in Ireland, Sir Edward Seymour "reflected on [Somers] for his judgment in the bankers' case, and for his religion, that he was a Hobbist" (Vernon, *3,* 13).

Adulterer: See *Advice to a Painter,* 26 *n.*, above.

Whose ev'ry word deserves divine Applause.
Not ev'n *Cethego*'s self could form a Plot,
More nicely Spun, more exquisitely wrought,
Tho' he, to his immortal envied Fame,
The Glory of the Revolution claim.
'Twas his profound unfathomable Wit,
Did *James* and all his *Jesuit-train* defeat.
He knew Reveal'd Religion was a Jest,
Impos'd upon the World by some designing Priest,
Nor therefore fear'd, but to their Idols Bow'd,
Prevaricating with his King, his God.
A *Proteus,* ever acting in Disguise,
A finish'd Statesman, Intricately Wise,
A second *Machiavel,* who soar'd above
The little Tyes of Gratitude and Love;
Whose harden'd Conscience never felt Remorse,
Reflection is the Puny Sinner's Curse.
But why should I *Cethego*'s Praise pursue,
When all his Vertues, *Clodio,* shine in you.
You can another Revolution frame,
The same your Principle, your Skill the same.
Whilst then the wav'ring *Irish* are your Care,
Believe we'll use our utmost Efforts here,
Nor Time, nor Pains, nor Health, nor Money spare.
Cethego in your Absence shall preside
O're our Debates, and ev'ry Consult guide;
Like the Supream directing Hand of *Jove,*
Shall act unseen, and all around him move.
I, as the Moderator of the Laws,
Will find a way to sanctify our Cause,
Will prove, in *Passive Jacobites* despight,
Rebellion is a Freeborn Peoples Right.
Then as we take our Circuits thro' the Land,

251. *Cethego:* "[Robert Spencer,] Ld. Sunderland. The person here represented was living at the time of this Cabball" (*ABB2B3*). Sunderland died on 28 September 1702; see 5 *n.,* above.

256. *James . . . defeat:* See *Advice to a Painter,* 57 *n.,* above.

261. *Proteus:* Cf. *Advice to a Painter,* 57, above.

278. *Moderator of the Laws:* Cf. *Advice to a Painter,* 26, above.

281. *Right:* Cf. *The True-Born Englishman,* 834 *n.,* above.

We'll sound how all the Counties Interests stand,
And mould the Stern Freeholders to our Hand.
When with our faithful City Friends we Dine,
We'll mingle Treason with the flowing Wine.
We'll plant in ev'ry Coffeehouse a Spy,
That boldly shall the Ministry decry;
Shall Praise the past, the present Reign Condemn,
And all their Measures, all their Councils Blame;
Shall spread a thousand idle, groundless Tales,
Of foreign Gold, the Pope, and Prince of *Wales;*
Shall never fail Objections still to raise,
(Whatever is transacted with Success)
And turn their greatest Honour to Disgrace,
This Chimick Art, perverting Nature's Law,
From sweetest Things will rankest Poysons draw.
Narcisso next, Magnificently Gay,
Smil'd his Assent, but not a word would say.
He fear'd to strain his Voice by Talking loud,
Nor was his Quail-pipe made for such a Crowd.
A batter'd Beau, yet youthful in Decay,
Who Dresses, Whores, and Games his Time away;
Fond of Sedition, but indulging Ease
With ev'ry vain and riotous Excess,
With all that Wealth, profusely spent, supplies.
And yet this Debauchee pretends to claim
An injur'd Patriot's Meritorious Name.
Then squeal'd *Orlando,* but his furious Heat,

292. *foreign Gold:* Cf. *Advice to a Painter. 1701,* 15 *n.,* above.

297. *sweetest Things will rankest Poysons draw:* proverbial: *corruptio optimi est pessima* (Tilley W470).

298. *Narcisso:* "[William Cavendish, duke of] Devonshire" (*B2B3*); cf. *Reformation of Manners,* 1027 *n.,* above.

301. *Quail-pipe:* throat. Dryden used the phrase twice in his translation of Juvenal (VI, 107, 500).

309. *Orlando:* "[Charles Mordaunt, third earl of] Peterborough" (*BB2B3*). This identification is confirmed by annotations in two manuscripts (BM MS. Lansdowne 852 and Add. 21094) and in several printed copies, including three in the NLS (3.1543[36], L.C. 690, NG.1168. c. 24[14]) and another copy of *B3* in the editor's possession. Charles Mordaunt, third earl of Peterborough and first earl of Monmouth (c. 1658–1735), was educated at Westminster School and Christ Church, Oxford. About 1678 he married Carey Fraser, a maid of honor who was "discovered to be with child" (GEC, *10,* 501). He began his political career as a violent Whig, being one of the 16 peers who signed

Shew'd him for cool mature Debates unfit,
Nor will we here the Blust'ring Speech repeat.
A Bully Lord, whose wild mad Looks proclaim
His Bosom warm'd with more than Heroe's Flame.
Fighting and Railing are his Chief Delight,
Promiscuously opposing wrong and right.
What e're he does is always in Extreams,
Sometimes the Whig, sometimes the Tory damns.
His various Temper and impetuous Mind,
To ev'ry Party is by Starts inclin'd.
He never was, nor e're will be Content
With any Prince, with any Government.
  Last rose *Bathillo,* deck'd with borrow'd Bays,
Renown'd for others Projects, others Lays.

---

a petition against the parliament meeting at Oxford in 1682. As early as 1686 he urged the prince of Orange "to undertake the business of *England*" (Burnet, *1,* 762). Created earl of Monmouth in April 1689, he served William as colonel of a regiment of foot (1688–94), gentleman of the bedchamber (1689–97), privy councillor (1689–97), and 1st lord of the treasury (1689–90). In December 1692 he quarreled violently with the king over the conduct of the war and went into opposition. He even promised Sir John Fenwick to save his life if he would accuse the junto lords, Shrewsbury and Orford, of plotting to restore James II. But since "his secrets were soon known," he was imprisoned in the Tower himself from January to March 1697. Then, "by the Assistance of Dr. D'Avenant," he wrote a book making the same charges and published it in the name of Matthew Smith, a notorious intelligence "Novelist." He was "brave and generous," but "always in Debt and very poor," and "his natural Giddiness, in running from Party to Party" cost him the favor of "all honest Men." "He affects Popularity," Macky said, "and loves to preach in *Coffee-Houses,* and publick Places; [and] is an open Enemy to *Revealed Religion*" (Macky, pp. 64–66). Jonathan Swift, who "love[d] the hangdog dearly," agreed that Macky's character was "for the most part true" (*Journal to Stella,* ed. Williams, *2,* 600; *Prose, 5,* 259). In January 1702 the House of Commons voted 141–56 that Peterborough's pursuit of "Popularity" had involved him in flagrant bribery in procuring the election of Daniel Park for the borough of Malmesbury, Wiltshire (*CJ, 13,* 711–12). Upon the accession of Queen Anne, he was reappointed lord lieutenant of Northamptonshire (1702–15). In March 1705 he was restored to the privy council and the next month he was appointed general of the allied forces in Spain. His inclusion in the poem indicates that he had rejoined the Whigs, probably because he opposed the occasional conformity bill (*Parl. Hist. 6,* 168, 171).

321 Textual Note. *Penurio:* the duke of Marlborough. Since Marborough voted for the bill to prevent occasional conformity in December 1703 "while taking steps to get it killed behind the scenes," Shippen may have suspected that he was already half Whig (Winston S. Churchill, *Marlborough,* 4 vols., George G. Harrap, 1933–38, *2,* 180).

322. *Bathillo:* "[Charles Montagu, Lord] Halifax" (*BB2B3*); cf. *The Golden Age Revers'd,* 14 *n.,* above.

A gay, pragmatical, pretending Tool,
Opinionately wise, and pertly dull.
A Demy-Statesman, Talkative and Loud,
Hot without Courage, without Merit proud;
A Leader fit for the unthinking Crowd.
With dapper Gesture, but with haughty Look,
His lewd Associates vainly he bespoke:
  Do you perform the Politician's Part,
I'll bring th'Assistance of the Muses Art.
The Poet-Tribe are all at my Devoir,
And write as I Command, as I inspire.
Congreve for me *Pastora*'s Death did Mourn,
And her white Name with Sable Verse adorn.
Rowe too is mine, and of the Whiggish Train,
'Twas he that Sung immortal *Tamerlane,*
Tho' now he dwindles to an humbler Strain.
I help'd to Polish *Garth*'s rough, awkward Lays,
Taught him in Tuneful Lines to Sound our Party's praise.
Walsh Votes with us, who, tho' he never writ,
Yet passes for a Critick and a Wit.
Van's Bawdy, Plotless Plays were once our Boast,

325. *Opinionately:* in one's own opinion (*OED,* citing this line, in the reading of *B*3).

335. *Pastora:* Pastora is Queen Mary in Congreve's elegy, *The Mourning Muse of Alexis. A Pastoral. Lamenting the Death of our late Gracious Queen Mary* (1695), the refrain of which, "*I mourn* Pastora *dead, let* Albion *mourn,/And Sable Clouds her Chalkie Cliffs adorn,*" is paraphrased in the next line.

337. *Rowe:* Cf. *The Golden Age,* 120 *n.,* above. In a poem published in 1702 Shippen had called Rowe "A faithful Friend, a guardian Deity" ("*An* Epistle to N. Rowe, Esq; *By* William Shippen, Esq; Translated from the Latin by H. Lloyd, Esq;", *A New Miscellany of Original Poems,* 1701, pp. 42–46).

338. *Tamerlane:* Rowe's second tragedy, *Tamerlane,* for which Garth wrote a prologue that was suppressed (*POAS,* 1703, 2, 312), probably opened at Lincoln's Inn Fields in December 1701 and was published in January 1702.

339. *humbler Strain: The Fair Penitent* (*ABB*2*B*3), Rowe's next tragedy, opened at Lincoln's Inn Fields in May 1703 and was published the same year. It recreates a kind of Romeo and Juliet situation.

342. *Walsh . . . never writ:* Shippen may not have been aware that since *A Funeral Elegy upon the Death of the Queen* (1695), Walsh had written (but had not published) *The Worcester Cabal* (1701) and *The Golden Age Restor'd* (1703), which was published anonymously in *POAS,* 1703.

344. *Van:* Since *The Provok'd Wife* (1697), which had fallen afoul of Jeremy Collier (*A Satyr against Wit,* headnote, p. 131 above), John Vanbrugh had produced only two

But now the Poet's in the Builder lost.
Addison had a Pension to be ours,
And still we justly claim his hireling Verse.
Thro' *Alpine* hills he shall my Name resound,
And make his Patron known in *Classick Ground.*
These pay the Tribute to my Merit due,
Call me their *Horace,* and *Maecenas* too.
Princes but sit unsettled on their Thrones,
Unless supported by *Apollo*'s Sons.
Augustus had the *Mantuan,* and *Venusian* Muse,
And happier *Nassau* had his *Montagues.*
But *Anna,* that Ill-fated Tory Queen,
Shall feel the Vengeance of the Poet's Pen.
  Triton, who like the vast *Leviathan,*
Long wallow'd in the Treasures of the Main,
Was all Attention, and suspended hung,
For ev'ry Rebel Heart has not a Tongue.

---

feeble adaptations: *The Pilgrim* (March 1700), to which Dryden had contributed a prologue (p. 199 above), and *The False Friend* (January 1702). Most of his energies since 1701 had gone into the building of Castle Howard, in Yorkshire, for Charles Howard, third earl of Carlisle. In 1703 he also began a house at Whitton Hall, near Hounslow, for Sir Godfrey Kneller, and the Queen's Theatre in the Haymarket (*DNB, 20,* 88–89).

346. *Pension:* Halifax arranged a Treasury grant of £200 and in July 1699 Addison set off on his grand tour. In 1704 Addison published *A Letter from Italy, to the Right Honourable Charles Lord Halifax,* in which he compared his patron's verse with Virgil's (*Poetical Miscellanies: The Fifth Part,* 1704, pp. 4–5, 12).

349. *Classick Ground:* Cf. Addison: "Poetick Fields encompass me around,/And still I seem to tread on Classic Ground" (ibid., p. 2); cf. *The Dunciad* (B), IV, 321.

350. *the Tribute:* John Dennis said that Halifax "receiv'd more Addresses of this Nature, than any Man of his Time" (*Critical Works, 2,* 251). Congreve dedicated *The Double Dealer* (1693) and *The Birth of the Muse* (1698) to him and Garth flattered him in *The Dispensary, 2,* 67.

354. *Mantuan, and Venusian Muse:* Mantua, in Etruria, and Venusia, in Apulia, were the birthplaces of Virgil and Horace.

355. *Montagues:* See *The Dispensary, 4,* 236 *n.*, above. After 1690 Halifax wrote only a few lines of occasional verse and his true opinion of literature may have been revealed when he said, "I wou'd not be a Poet if I cou'd" (*Journal of English and Germanic Philology, 32* [1933], 68). Another Montague was William, who published *The Delights of Holland* in 1696. Shippen seems to imply that, for *his* Virgil and Horace, William III had an antipoet and an obscure hack; cf. "The Pindars, and the Miltons of a Curl" (*The Dunciad* (B), III, 164).

358. *Triton:* "[Edward Russell, Lord] Orford" (*B2B3*); see *A Conference,* 133 *n.*, above.

359. *Treasures of the Main:* See *The Golden Age Revers'd,* 35–36, above.

Besides, there stood a Num'rous Train of Peers,
Below the Notice of Recording Verse.
Beaus, Biters, Pathicks, Buggerers and Cits,
Toasters, Kit-Kats, Divines, Buffoons and Wits
Compos'd the Medly Crew; but I forbear
To give 'em any Place, or Mention here.
For since the Muse would Blush to paint their Crimes,
Let Decency restrain th'Invective Rhimes.
  When thus their Chiefs had spoke, thro' all the *Throng*
Repeated Peals of Acclamations rung.
Not antient *Demagogues,* with more Applause,
Asserted, and Espous'd the Rabble's Cause.
  Now the Assembly to adjourn prepar'd,
When *Bibliopolo* from behind appear'd,
As well describ'd by th'old Satyrick Bard,
With leering Looks, Bullfac'd, and Freckled fair,
With two left Legs, and Judas-colour'd Hair,
And Frowsy Pores, that taint the ambient Air.
Sweating and Puffing for a-while he stood,
And then broke forth in this Insulting Mood:
  I am the Touchstone of all Modern Wit,
Without my Stamp in vain your Poets write.
Those only purchase everliving Fame,
That in my Miscellany plant their Name.
Nor therefore think that I can bring no Aid,
Because I follow a Mechanick Trade,

363. See *England's Late Jury,* 136 *n.,* above.

365. *Toasters:* See *The Brawny Bishop's Complaint,* 9 *n.,* above.

375. *Bibliopolo:* "[Jacob] Tonson" (*BB*3); see *A Satyr against Wit,* 239 *n.,* above.

376. *th'old Satyrick Bard:* John Dryden.

377–79. The origin of these lines is recounted in a letter of 14 July 1698 from Richard Powys to Matthew Prior: "Sir Godfrey Kneller hath drawn at length the picture of your friend Jacob Tonson, which he shewed Mr. Dryden, who desired to give a touch of his pencil, and underneath it writ these three verses: With leering look, bull-faced, and freckled fair,/With frowsy pores, poisoning the ambient air,/With two left legs, and Judas-coloured hair" (HMC *Bath MSS., 3,* 238–39; cf. Nichols, *Anecdotes, 1,* 293; Dryden, *Prose, 1,* i, 525).

385. *Miscellany: Miscellany Poems,* published by Tonson, appeared under various titles from 1684 to 1716 (Macdonald, pp. 67–78). The 1704 volume included the first edition of Addison's *Letter from Italy, to the Right Honourable Charles Lord Halifax* (346 *n.,* above). Cf. [Sir Richard Blackmore], *The Kit-Cats, A Poem,* 1708, p. 4: "[Tonson] still caress'd the unregarded Tribe,/And did to all their various Tasks prescribe."

I'll print your Pamphlets, and your Rumours spread.
I am the Founder of your lov'd *Kit-Kat,*
A Club that gave Direction to the State.
'Twas there we first instructed all our Youth,
To talk Prophane and Laugh at Sacred Truth.
We taught them how to Toast, and Rhime, and Bite,
To Sleep away the Day, and drink away the Night.
  Some this Fantastick Speech approv'd, some Sneer'd;
The Wight grew Cholerick, and disappear'd.
  Mean time the Fury smil'd, who all this while
Sat hov'ring on the Summet of the Pile.
A secret and exulting Joy she finds,
To see her Influence brooding in their Minds;
And the bare prospect of such Noble Ills
Her thoughts with rapt'rous Speculations fills.
Then She:
  With what delight do I my Sons behold,
So resolutely Brave, so fiercely Bold.
Sure nothing can resist their boundless Course,
Nothing subdue their well united Force.
Volpone, who will solely now Command
The Publick Purse, and Treasure of the Land,
Wants Constancy and Courage to oppose
A Band of such exasperated Foes.
For how should he, that moves by Craft and Fear,
Or ever greatly think, or ever greatly dare?
What did he e're in all his Life perform,
But shrunk at the approach of ev'ry Storm;
But when the tott'ring Church his aid requir'd,
With *Moderation-Principles* Inspir'd,
Forsook his Friends, and decently Retir'd.

389. *Kit-Kat:* See *The Golden Age Revers'd,* 18 *n.,* above. n 1703 the Kit-Cat Club moved from the Fountain tavern in the Strand to Tonson's new house at Barn Elms, Surrey, about six miles from London, where Sir Godfrey Kneller's Kit-Cat portraits were hung (Nichols, *Anecdotes, 1,* 295).

397. *the Fury:* Faction (9, above).

408. *Volpone:* "[Sidney Godolphin, Lord] Godolphin" (*BB2B3*); see *The Golden Age Revers'd,* 96–101, above.

417. *Moderation-Principles:* Cf. *The Golden Age Restor'd,* 63 *n.,* above. Like Marlborough, Godolphin voted for the second bill to prevent occasional conformity while working behind the scenes to defeat it.

Nor has he any real just Pretence
To that vast Depth of Politicks and Sense.
For where's the Depth, when Publick Credit's high,
To manage an o'reflowing Treasury?
Or where the Sense to know the Tricks of Gain,
Since *Sims,* Sir *James,* and *Holloway* may claim
A Knowledge as profound as his, as loud a Fame?
I fear the Man, who dares the Truth assert,
Who never plays the Double-dealing Part;
The Patriot's Soul disdains the Trimmer's Art.
Such *Celsus* is, but I foresee his Fate
To be supplanted by *Sempronia*'s Hate,

421–22. This couplet asks the question that Dryden answered in *Absalom & Achitophel,* 894–95, alluding to Godolphin's predecessor, the earl of Rochester, who served Charles II as first lord of the treasury in 1679–85: " 'Tis easy conduct when Exchequers flow,/But hard the task to manage well the low."

424. *Sims, Sir James, and Holloway:* "common Sharpers" (*Faction Display'd. A Poem. Answer'd Paragraph by Paragraph,* 1704, p. 18). Godolphin, as Burnet said, "loved gaming the most of any man of business I ever knew" (*1,* 478), but a friendly critic questioned "the Wit of comparing a Gentleman, because he plays sometimes, to three scandalous Sharpers" (*Some Critical and Politick Remarks on a Late Virulent Lampoon, Call'd, Faction Display'd,* 1704, p. 14). Holloway may be Charles Holloway, who matriculated at Oriel College, Oxford, in December 1670, and became "a Goldsmith in the Strand" (*Alumni Oxonienses, 2,* 733; Le Neve, p. 378). In October 1704 it was reported that Godolphin had returned from Newmarket, "where the duke of Somerset's horse won the queens plate; and it's said Mr. Holloway got £2000" (Luttrell, *5,* 473–74). Sims may be "Richard Sims Esq; commonly called Beau Sims," who died in May 1728 (Abel Boyer, *The Political State of Great Britain, 35* [January–June 1728], 518). According to the heavily cropped gloss in the TCD copy of *B*2 Sir James is "[Sir James] of the peake," whom Henry L. Snyder has identified as James Ashburne (d. 1712), a one-eyed gambler, member of the Board of Commissioners of Appeal (of the excise), and the original of Steele's Monoculus in *The Tatler,* No. 36, 30 June–2 July 1709 (*Books and Libraries at the University of Kansas, 4* [November 1966], 3–5).

429. *Celsus:* "[Laurence Hyde, earl of] Rochester" (*B*2*B*3). After his dismissal in February 1703 (*The Golden Age Restor'd,* 31–32 *n.,* above) and the loss in December 1703 of the second bill to prevent occasional conformity, on which he had staked all his political capital, Rochester surrendered the leadership of the high church party to Nottingham. Lines 433–51 make a deliberate contrast with 408–18.

430. *Sempronia:* duchess of Marlborough (*BB*3). Sarah Jennings (1660–1744) married John Churchill early in 1678. According to Samuel Johnson, she was "a bold frontless woman, who knew how to make the most of her opportunities in life" (James Boswell, *The Journal of a Tour to the Hebrides,* 1785, p. 202). And these opportunities were so considerable that, as she said herself, the princess Anne "distinguished me by so high a place in her favour, as perhaps no person ever arrived at a higher with queen or princess" (*Account of the Conduct,* p. 11). The historical Sempronia was a former prostitute whom Catiline recruited to his party. By birth, beauty, husband, and children,

(*Sempronia* of a Lewd *procuring* Race,
The Senate's Grievance, and the Court's Disgrace.)
'Tis well he cannot long his Ground maintain,
For Hell wou'd then employ her Fiend in vain.
He never knew to Prostitute the State,
Never by being Guilty to be Great.
Nor yet when publick Storms came rowling on,
Did he or Danger or his Duty shun.
Rome's subtle Priests with Sophistry essay'd,
With Wealth and Honour in the Ballance lay'd,
To shock his Faith; but nothing could controul
The firm Resolves of his unbyass'd Soul,
True to his Conscience, as the Needle to the Pole.
Ally'd in Blood and Friendship to the Throne,
He nobly makes his Country's Cause his own;
Whilst others keep their int'rest still in view,
And meaner Spirits meaner ends pursue.
So the fixt Stars harmoniously comply
With the *first Publick Motion* of the Sky,
Whilst wand'ring Planets oppositely move,
Within the narrow Orbs of *private* Love.
She stopp'd—for now her Anger 'gan to rise,
Flush'd in her Cheeks, and sparkl'd in her Eyes.
And well it might a Fury's Passion raise,
That she was forc'd the Worth she hates, to Praise.
The Dawn dispers'd the Crowd, she took her flight
To the low Regions of Eternal Night.
O *England* how revolving is thy State!
How few thy Blessings! how severe thy Fate!

---

she was singularly favored, but lust and wild extravagance made her desperate (Sallust, *Bellum Catilinae,* XXV).

431. *a Lewd procuring Race:* "if he had called her Mother a *Bawd* in one word, it had been altogether as Witty and Poetical" (*Some Critical and Politick Remarks on a Late Virulent Lampoon, Call'd Faction Display'd,* p. 15).

445. *his Country's Cause:* "Many people think [Rochester] a Jacobite," Leibniz said in June 1702, "but I believe they do him wrong, at least I cannot see that they found their suspicions on anything real. The English . . . exaggerate everything" (John Kemble, ed., *State Papers,* 1857, p. 306).

448. *fixt Stars:* "the Advocates for this Lampoon, will have that [similitude] of the *Fixt Stars* and *Planets* to be entirely new, and unparalelled in any other Poem. I will freely acknowledge, that it is a noble Compliment" (*Some Critical and Politick Remarks on a Late Virulent Lampoon, Call'd, Faction Display'd,* p. 15).

O destin'd Nation, to be thus betray'd
By those, whose Duty is to serve and aid!
A griping vile degen'rate viper Brood,
That tear thy Vitals, and exhaust thy Blood.
A varying Kind, that no fixt Rule pursue.
But often form their Principles anew;
Unknowing where to lodge supreme Command,
Or in the King, or Peers, or People's hand.
One while the People's Sov'raignty they own,
To vex and goad a Peaceful Monarch's Crown;
Who to his Subjects when at length *Restor'd,*
Without distinction was their common Lord.
What Party else to *David*'s happy Throne,
Would have preferr'd a giddy *Absalon?*
But when a King is moulded to their Mind,
Then they to him would have all sway confin'd;
Nor in their own despotick boundless Reign,
Of Injur'd Rights, and *Property* complain:
Nay with a *Standing Force* thy Sons wou'd awe,
The Subject's Slavery, the Tyrant's Law.
But if nor King nor Commons will comply
With their detested Acts of Villany,
They strive the Peers declining Pow'r to raise,
And get *Impeachments* voted into Praise.
Blest Patriots these, who Liberty employ,
T'elude thy Laws, and Liberty destroy!
  Where is the Noble *Roman* Spirit fled,
Which once inspir'd thy antient Patriots dead?
Who were above all private Ends, and joy'd,
When bravely for the publick Weal they dy'd:
Who spread, like Branching Oaks, their Arms around,
To shelter and Protect the Parent Ground;
Tho' Storms of Thunder rattl'd o're their Head,

469. *a Peaceful Monarch:* Charles II.

473. *a giddy Absalon:* James Scott, duke of Monmouth. In Dryden it is the "Rabble" who are "giddy" (*The Second Part of Absalom and Achitophel,* 118).

474. *a King:* William III.

478. *a Standing Force:* See *An Encomium upon a Parliament,* headnote, pp. 45–46 above.

483. *Impeachments:* See *The Golden Age,* 23 *n.,* above.

Yet all was safe beneath their Guardian Shade.
Or sure Historians on our Faith impose,
And never such a Race of Men arose;
Or Nodding Nature to a Period draws;
Or Providence, incens'd by Guilty Times,
With-holds his Grace, and dooms us to our Crimes.
  Pardon (for Harmony will bring Relief,
Will sooth thy anxious Cares, and charm thy Grief)
If my Condoling Mournful Muse Presume
To Visit thy *Marcellus* Sacred Tomb.
For his Hereditary Gifts alone
Could have *Retriev'd* thy Fame, and carried down
The Glorious Scene of Triumphs *Anna* has begun.
O may thy Angel Guard her Royal Mind,
That *Trimmers* not Seduce, nor *Fav'rites* Blind.
For 'tis on Her thy Church and State depend,
With Her will Flourish, and with Her will End.
But my shok'd Thoughts the sad Idea shun,
(The sad Idea gives Eternal Moan)
When she shall late, but ah! too soon comply
With Nature, to Adorn her Kindred Sky.
For who can then pretend to wear her Crown?
Who represent the Mother, but the Son?
O! had the Pow'r, that governs humane Fate,
His years extended to a longer Date,
To what transcendence had his Genius sprung,
Which was so Ripe, so Perfect, yet so Young;
But when fresh blooming Youth seem'd to proclaim
The lasting Structure of his Beauteous Frame,
When Health and Vigour with a kind presage,

497. *Providence:* "I wonder so high a *Flyer,* so errant a *Jackdaw,* should have any Tang of the *Geneva*-Principles. This is the very Spirit of *Calvin*" (*Some Critical and Politick Remarks on a Late Virulent Lampoon, Call'd, Faction Display'd,* p. 17).

502. *Marcellus:* "[William, duke of] G[louceste]r" (B^3), the only one of Anne's 17 children to survive infancy, died of smallpox in July 1700, at age 11.

504. *Retriev'd:* See *The Golden Age Restor'd,* 35–36 *n.,* above. Lines 503–04 may allude to *The Address,* 6–7, above.

507. *Trimmer:* one who inclines to each of two opposite parties as interest dictates (*OED,* citing this line).

510. *shok'd:* The term, but not the sixteenth century spelling (*OED*), may derive from Dryden. Henri IV is "Shock'd" in *Astraea Redux,* 101.

Promis'd the hoary happiness of Age;
Then with a Momentary swift decay,
Thy Pride, thy darling Hope was snatch'd away.
So, by the Course of the revolving Sphears,
Whene'er a new discover'd Star appears,
Astronomers with Pleasure and Amaze
Upon the Infant Luminary gaze.
They find their Heav'n enlarg'd, and wait from thence
Some Blest, some more than common Influence,
But suddenly alas! the fleeting Light
Retiring leaves their Hopes involv'd in endless Night.

533. The alexandrine recaptures the tone of the concluding alexandrine in Dryden's *To the Memory of Mr. Oldham* (1684), but the phrases "involv'd in gloomy Night" and "in endless Night" occur in Dryden's translation of the *Aeneid* (IV, 173, 992). The couplet alludes specifically to the evanishing ghost of Marcellus in the *Aeneid,* VI, 866: *sed nox atra caput tristi circumvolat umbra,* which Dryden translates, "But hov'ring Mists around his Brows are spread,/And Night, with sable Shades, involves his Head" (VI, 1198–99).

Thomas Brown

Upon the Anonymous Author of, Legion's Humble Address to the Lords

To that Most Senseless Scondrel, the Author of Legion's Humble Address to the Lords, Who Wou'd Perswade the People of England to Leave the Commons, and Depend upon the Lords
(May[?] 1704)

The most celebrated case in constitutional law to be tried in the reign of Queen Anne was that of Matthew Ashby, a burgess in the town of Aylesbury, Buckinghamshire, who brought an action at common law against the constables of Aylesbury "for having by Contrivance fraudulently and maliciously hindered him to give his Vote at an Election." The original verdict for him was set aside by the court of queen's bench and upon a writ of error brought in the House of Lords Ashby "obtained Judgement, to recover his Damages for the Injury; and afterwards had Execution upon that Judgement" (Howell, *14*, 695). When five more burgesses in the town of Aylesbury brought actions to recover their damages, they were committed to Newgate by the House of Commons on 5 December 1703 "as having acted . . . in Contempt of the Jurisdiction, and in Breach of the Privilege, of that House." Subsequently the Commons declared that the Lords' action in reversing the decision of the queen's bench was also "a high Breach of the Privilege of this House" (*CJ*, *14*, 308). Finally, after a series of conferences with the Commons, the Lords, on 13 March 1704, drew up a statement of the case on which an address to her majesty could be drafted.

The theme of this brief is that the action of the Commons in imprisoning the five Aylesbury burgesses is such that "The most arbitrary Governments cannot shew more direct Instances of Partiality and Oppression" (*LJ*, *17*, 699). In *Legion's Humble Address to the Lords* (p. 2) Defoe calls it "Exercising the same Arbitrary Power they are sent thither to Suppress."

Defoe, however, expanded the pamphlet he published about April 1704 to take in eight points at issue between the two Houses and in every case he decides against "our Degenerated Representatives," as he calls them. Exactly as in January 1703, the machinery of suppression was promptly set in motion: on 29 May 1704 a warrant was issued for the author's arrest, a reward was offered, and Defoe may even have found it necessary to leave London again. On 14 June 1704 an informant told Harley that if Defoe was wanted for writing *Legion's Humble Address to the Lords,* he might be found "at Captain Roger's at the city of Canterbury." The pamphlet must have enjoyed a good sale, for as late as September 1704 "one Sammen a weaver, a tool of De Foe's," was arrested for dispersing it, but the author was never discovered. This time he enjoyed the protection, not the hostility, of the secretary of state (Luttrell, *5,* 429; HMC *Portland MSS., 4,* 93, 138).

Thomas Brown's two poems are witty attempts to discredit both the author and that "mock authoritative Manner," as Swift called it, in which without a snicker Defoe represents the Lords as "the Sanctuary and Safety of this Nation" (*Legion's Humble Address to the Lords,* 1704, p. 4).

Upon the Anonymous Author of, Legion's Humble Address to the Lords

Thou Tool of Faction, Mercenary Scribe,
Who Preachest Treason to the *Calveshead* Tribe,
Whose fruitful Head, in Garret mounted high,
Sees Legions, and strange Monsters, in the Sky;
Who wou'dst with War and Blood thy Country fill,
Were but thy Power as rampant as thy Will:
Well may'st thou boast thy self a *Million* strong,
But 'tis in Vermine that about thee throng.

2. *Preachest:* Cf. *The Reformer Reform'd: Or, The Shortest Way with Daniel D'Fooe,* 1703, pp. 4, 6: "the *Calves Head Club,* of which Mr. *D'Fooe* is a worthy Member . . . Mr. *D'Fooe* [is] known to be a Preacher at a Conventicle."

4. *Legion:* Defoe's 1701 *Memorial* (Moore, *Daniel Defoe,* pp. 105–06) was subscribed, "Our Name is LEGION, and we are many."

7. *Million: Legion's Humble Address to the Lords* (1704) was subscribed, *"Our Name is* Million, *and We are more."*

To that Most Senseless Scondrel, the Author of Legion's Humble Address to the Lords, Who Wou'd Perswade the People of England to Leave the Commons, and Depend upon the Lords

What *Demons* mov'd thee, what malicious Fiends,
To tempt the People from their surest Friends?
Sooner thou might'st embracing Floods disjoyn,
And make the Needle from its North decline:
Or teach the graceful *Heliotrope* to run,
A diff'rent Motion from th'enlivening Sun.
Our Peers have often for themselves rebell'd;
When did they for the People take the Field?
Led not by Love, but Interest and Pride,
They wou'd not let the Prince their Vassals ride.
That pow'r they to themselves reserv'd alone,
And so through thick and thin they spurr'd *Old Roan*.
To Fact and long Experience I appeal,
How fairly to themselves they justice deal:
For if my Lord, o'erpower'd by Wine and Whore,
The next he meets, does through the Entrails scow'r,
'Tis pity, his relenting Brethren cry,
That for his first Offence the Youth shou'd dye:
Come, he'll grow grave; Virtue and he'll be Friends,
And by his Voting, make the Crown amends.
'Tis true, a most magnificent Parade
Of Law, to please the gaping Mobb, is made.
Scaffolds are rais'd in the Litigious Hall,
The Maces glitter, and the Serjeants bawl.
So long they wrangle, and so oft they stop,
The wearied Ladies do their moisture drop.

8. *take the Field:* Defoe said that the Lords had "frequently Taken Arms, and Pull'd down Bloody Tyrants; Deposing their Power, and Rescuing [the] Country from Slavery and Oppression" (*Legion's Humble Address to the Lords,* 1704, p. 1).

15. *my Lord:* probably Charles Mohun, fourth Lord Mohun (*Reformation of Manners,* 612 *n.,* above).

20. *Voting:* Lord Mohun voted against the second bill to prevent occasional conformity in December 1703 (*An Address to Our Sovereign Lady,* headnote, pp. 616–17 above).

This is the Court (say they) keeps all in awe,
Gives Life to Justice, vigour to the Law.
True, they quote *Law,* and much they prattle on her,
What's the result? *Not Guilty, upon Honour.*
  Should I who have no Coronet to show,
Fluster'd in Drink, serve the next Comer so,
My Twelve blunt Godfathers wou'd soon agree,
To doom me, sober, to the fatal Tree.
  Besides how punctually their Debts they pay,
There's scarce a Cit in London but can say.
By peep of morn the trusting Wretch does rise,
And to his Grace's Gate, like Lightning flies:
There in the Hall this poor believing Ass,
With gaping on bare walls Seven Hours does pass,
And so does Forty more in the same Class.
At last my Lord, with Looks erect and hardy:
"Troth, Friends, my Tenants have been somewhat tardy:
"But for the future, this shall be redrest,
"Delays and Losses may befall the best.
This said, he presses with regardless Pride,
Between the opening Squadrons on each side:
Calls for his Page, then slips into his Chair,
And so, *good Gentlemen,* you're as you were.
  Cease Scribler then, our Grandees to defame,
With feign'd Encomiums, which they scorn to claim:
What they can challenge by the Laws o' th' Land,
We freely give, while they no more demand:
But let not in their praise the *Plot* be brought,
Thou know'st the Proverb: *Nothing due for naught.*

35. *Debts:* probably William Cavendish, first duke of Devonshire (*Reformation of Manners,* 1025 *n.,* above). Devonshire "spoke loud" against the second bill to prevent occasional conformity in December 1703 (Boyer, *Annals,* 1704, p. 189).

38. *Gate:* At this time the duke of Devonshire lived in Arlington House (on the present site of Buckingham Palace) (Strype, 2, 377). The duns also assemble "at his Lordships Gate" in Swift, *A Description of the Morning* (1709), 13.

54. *the Plot:* Defoe praised the Lords' "Zeal, Courage, and Fidelity . . . in Searching after the Deeply laid Contrivances of Her [Majesty's] Enemies in the late [Scotch] Plot" (*Legion's Humble Address to the Lords,* p. 4); cf. *An Address to Our Sovereign Lady,* headnote p. 617 above.

55. *Nothing due for naught:* perhaps a variant of Thank you for nothing (Tilley N277).

The Tryal of Skill:
or,
A New Session of the Poets.
Calculated for the Meridian of Parnassus,
In the Year, MDCCIV.
(8 August 1704)

The session-of-the-poets, as Dr. Johnson said, is "a mode of satire by which, since it was first introduced by Suckling, perhaps every generation of poets has been teazed" (*Lives, 1,* 15). Sir John Suckling (1609–42), therefore, figures twice in the present poem: once when he invented the genre (or domesticated an Italian *gèner* in England), and again, in lines 153–56, when he explodes in rage over Thomas Cheek's adaptation of his play *The Goblins,* which was first produced in 1638.

In Suckling's poem *A Session of the Poets,* written early in 1637 before Ben Jonson's death but not published until 1646, Jonson, Thomas Carew, and William Davenant are passed over and the laurel is bestowed on an anonymous alderman (Sir John Suckling, *Fragmenta Aurea,* 1646, p. 7). Thirty years later, in 1676, another poem of the same title ("Since the *Sons* of the *Muses* grow num'rous, and loud") began to circulate in manuscript, attributed variously to George Villiers, second duke of Buckingham, and to Elkanah Settle. In 1680, however, it was included in the *Poems on Several Occasions* of *"the Incomparable* Earl of Rochester," as he is designated in the preface to the present poem (*POAS,* Yale, *1,* 352). It is Suckling's poem and this work of 1676, in which George Etherege, William Wycherley, and Thomas Shadwell are passed over in favor of Thomas Betterton, the actor, that provide the chief models for *The Tryal of Skill.* Two more recent works, however, are also in the background. These are Daniel Kenrick, *A New Session of the Poets, Occasion'd by the Death of Mr. Dryden* (September 1700) ("As in our late Elective Monarchies") and *An Epistle to Sr. Richard Blackmore, Occasion'd by The New Session of the Poets* (November

1700) ("Not that you need Assistance in your Wars"), which a manuscript note in the Yale copy attributes to "Tho. Phillips." Both of these poems set down many of the failed candidates of *The Tryal of Skill* and both of them pay particular attention to the candidacy of Samuel Garth (573 *n.*, below) (*The Grove; Or, A Collection of Original Poems, Translations, &c.*, 1721, p. 129; *History of the Works of the Learned*, 2 [September 1700], 575; Macdonald, pp. 298, 299).

The interest of *The Tryal of Skill* lies partly in its spirited verse, in anapestic stanzas rhyming $a^4b^3a^4b^3$, and partly in its encyclopedic scope: it provides unique information on most of its 24 candidates for the laurel. And since half of the poets included in the present volume are among these candidates, *The Tryal of Skill* is a most appropriate poem with which to conclude this volume.

The author of the poem remains unidentified. On internal evidence alone, a case might be made for Thomas Brown (cf. 80 *n.*, 419 *n.*). But Brown died on 16 June 1704 and it seems unlikely that his name would be withheld from such an important posthumous publication. Another candidate is William Pittis, Brown's close friend and occasional imitator (cf. 56 *n.*, 307 *n.*).

The date of publication indicated in the Luttrell copy, 8 August 1704 (Macdonald, p. 222, *n.* 3), is confirmed by advertisements for the poem in *The Daily Courant* of 8 August and 18 August 1704.

The Tryal of Skill:
or,
A New Session of the Poets. Calculated for the Meridian of Parnassus, In the Year, MDCCIV.

Apollo perplext with Poetical Duns
  For Preferment and Places of Trust,
Was pleas'd to Convene all his whimsical Sons
  In Order to do what was just.

And scarce had he signified what was his Will,
  By making it publickly known,
But to Court run the Scribes that belong'd to the Quill,
  And surrounded the God on his Throne.

Amongst all the rest that stood up for the Bays,
  Monsieur would first enter his Claim,
And left dealing in *China* to Traffick for Praise,
  And Company's Sales to get Fame.

Your Majesty knows, said the Bard, my deserts,
  Which have me a free Citizen made,
How I'm got into Business by dint of my Parts,
  And have bragg'd my self into a Trade.

10. *Monsieur:* Peter Motteux; see *The Pacificator,* 169 *n.,* above.

11. *dealing in China:* Motteux "kept a large East India warehouse in Leadenhall Street," "filled and adorned with Tea, China, and Indian Ware" (Baker, *1,* 528). "China" included more than tableware and a "warehouse" included retail salesrooms. In Motteux's warehouse in 1712 Steele saw "Silks of various Shades and Colours, rich Brocades . . . the most delicate Cambricks, Muslins, and Linnens" (*Spectator,* No. 552, 3 December 1712).

12. *Company's Sales:* In September 1705 one "Matteux" bought goods at "A General Court of Sales" held by the old East India Company (Robert N. Cunningham, *Peter Anthony Motteux,* Oxford, Basil Blackwell, 1933, p. 182).

14. *Citizen:* In his will, dated 23 February 1709, Motteux described himself as "Citizen and Grocer of London" (ibid., p. 197).

My *Gentleman's Journal,* my Farces and Plays,
My Madrigals, Catches and Puns,
Are enough to determine whom first you should rise
'Fore the rest of your Indigent Sons.

Says He so, said the God, Go, *Mercury,* strait,
And whisper the Fool in the Ear,
That the best way for him to get an Estate,
Is at *Leaden-Hall* Sales to appear;

Not but even there he will want good Advice,
To Manage the Trading Concern,
For he that bids more than th' Accustomèd price,
By the rest of the Dealers should Learn.

Besides, its his Business that gave him the Post,
Of which he does now stand possess'd,
For the Cringes and Scrapes, he receiv'd to his Cost,
With another such Place to Invest.

As for my part, if for this Pretender to Wit,
I was any Office to Chuse,
Not one in my Service could ere be so fit,
As a *Penny Post Man*'s to the *Muse.*

Since none could go over more ground in a Day,
Than that Author of *Beauty Distress'd,*

24. *Leaden-Hall:* Leadenhall, in Limestreet ward, provided marketing, display, and warehouse facilities for East India merchants (Strype, *1,* 289).

29. *the Post:* Motteux "had a very genteel place in the General Post-Office, relating to the foreign letters, being master of several languages" (Baker, *1,* 528).

36. *Penny Post:* The penny post, a project of William Dockwra, which began operation in 1680, made it possible to send letters and parcels anywhere within London or seven miles around "almost as soon as they can be sent by a Messenger," as Daniel Defoe discovered (Howard Robinson, *The British Post Office,* Princeton, Princeton University Press, 1948, pp. 70, 85).

38. *Beauty Distress'd:* Motteux's only tragedy, *Beauty in Distress,* was produced at Lincoln's Inn Fields in 1698 and published the same year. The action, which requires "no more Time than the Representation takes up," is characterized by a "great number of Turns," and, as Motteux confessed, "they came on somewhat too fast." Dryden noted this defect in his prefatory verses: "Thy Incidents," he said, "perhaps too thick are sown" (*Beauty in Distress,* 1698, pp. vii, xxviii).

And none run about for a Swinging Third Day,
To a Comedy without a Jest.

However this did not discourage at all
Another *Jack Frenchman* to come,
Resolv'd where true Merit should stand or should fall,
To wait and attend for his Doom.

With his *Annals* and other such Riff Raff of Prose,
And some Scantlings of Sorrowful Verse,
He Petition'd the God-head that he might be chose
For Endowments Uncommon and Scarce;

But was told the Court wonder'd, He blush'd not to send
A Petition so fruitless and Vain,
Amongst Men of Parts and Good Sence to attend,
For Preferment He never could gain.

That his Wit was *Uncommon* and *Scarce* was allow'd,
Since none e'er yet Scribbl'd so Dull,
And not a Phantastical Soul in the Croud
Had such a Jejune Hungry Skull.

And Orders were given that he should be dismiss'd
To wait at his Last Patron's Gate:

39. *Third Day:* The proceeds of every third performance of a play were traditionally reserved for the author.

40. *Comedy:* presumably Motteux's first play, *Love's a Jest,* which was produced at Lincoln's Inn Fields in July 1696 and published the same year.

42. *Another Jack Frenchman:* Abel Boyer (1667–1729) was another French Protestant who fled France upon revocation of the Edict of Nantes in October 1685. He suffered "great poverty" until 1691 when he secured appointment as tutor to Allen Bathurst, later Lord Bathurst and Pope's great friend. His prose works include two miscellanies, *Letters of Wit, Politicks and Morality* (1701) and *The English Theophrastus* (1702), a *Dictionnaire Royal Français et Anglais* (1702) to which his friend Richard Savage contributed 1000 words and phrases, *The History of King William the Third* (1702–03), and *The History of the Reign of Queen Anne, Digested into Annals* (1703–13) (Baker, *1*, 52–54).

46. *Verse:* Boyer published no separate volume of verse but poems are occasionally mingled in his prose works. One that can be attributed to him is *Cupid's Revenge,* which occurs in a letter from "*Mr.* B—r *to* Diana" (*Letters of Wit, Politicks and Morality,* 1701, p. 385).

56. *Jejune Hungry:* cf. "hungry Jejune Lines" ([William Pittis?], *Letters from the Living to the Living,* 1703, p. 217.).

58. *Last Patron:* Boyer tried at first to avoid political commitment by dedicating *Letters of Wit, Politicks and Morality* to Halifax and the first volume of *The History*

Or Incur, if he durst in his Claim to persist,
His own *Iphigenia*'s Fate,

Since *Northumberland* House was the fittest Resort
For a Conceited Ignorant Sot,
Who to Favour and Pop'lar Esteem made his Court,
With the Devil a bit of a Plot.

Tom D'Urfey next stutter'd for some Annual Pence,
For his Footman and Dear *Musidora;*
But had Intimation that a Man of no Sense
Ought to keep neither Footman nor Whore-a.

Nor Footman nor Whore! said the Mortal aghast,
Odzooks such a Mortification!
Please your Majesty, Damn me for ever to fast,
So I look but in Quality Station.

No Sence? that's the chiefest of Titles I plead,
To Preferment to make my approach,
And since I scarce know how to write or to read,
Like others I should keep my *Coach.*

---

of the Reign of Queen Anne, Digested into Annals to Ormonde, but in the second volume of *Annals* (1704) he came down squarely on the Whig side with a dedication to Charles Seymour, duke of Somerset, of Northumberland House in the Strand, particularly for his zeal in uncovering the Scotch plot (cf. *The Seven Wise Men,* headnote, p. 622 above).

60. *Iphigenia's Fate:* Boyer's adaptation of Racine's *Iphigénie* was produced at Drury Lane late in 1699 as *Achilles: or, Iphigenia in Aulis* and published the next year. "The First run of this Play was but short," Boyer explained in the preface. "The Reason of it is obvious: This Tragedy came out upon the Neck of another of the same Name [John Dennis, *Iphigenia*], which being the product of a *Giant-Wit,* and a *Giant-Critick* . . . had miserably balk'd the World's Expectation; and most People having been tir'd at *Lincolns-Inn-Fields,* did not care to venture their Patience at *Drury-Lane.*" "To which he might have added," in the words of the advertisement to the second edition of 1714, "That the Dutchess of Marlborough, who at that Time bore an irresistable Sway, bespoke the Comedy then in Vogue [George Farquhar, *The Constant Couple: or, A Trip to the Jubilee*], during the Run of *Iphigenia in Aulis.*"

64. *the Devil a:* no.

65. *D'Urfey:* See *A Satyr against Wit,* 180 *n.,* above.

66. *Footman:* Steele mentions D'Urfey's footboy in *The Lover,* No. 40, 27 May 1714, and Pope complains in *The Dunciad,* IV, 128 *n.,* that "no Poet [has] had a *Page* since the death of Mr. Thomas Durfey."

Musidora: The lady has not been identified.

His Claim was allow'd for being reasonably Good,
And He'd not made Addresses in Vain,
Had the Chatterpye learn'd but to be understood
And spoke as he Swore and Sung, *Plain.*

But what was enjoyn'd him, to no purpose he try'd,
Not a Souse for poor Footman and Whore,
When he would have spoke *plain,* he seem'd as *Tongue-ty'd,*
Though he was *understood* when he *Swore.*

The next that advanc'd 'mong th' illiterate Class,
Was the Finnikin Yeoman of *Kent,*
And equip'd with a Suit, and some Gold that would pass,
His Works to the Court would present.

What's here, cry'd Don *Phoebus,* an Attorney turn'd Fool,
Whose Profession it is to turn Knave?
Let the Clerk of the Crown give the Blockhead a Rule,
Still in Metre to drudge on and Slave.

For he ne'er can arrive at the Fame he pretends,
To acquire from Abilities Raw,
And has as small a Claim, in spight of his Friends,
To Advancement by Wit, as by Law.

77. *reasonably Good:* Some of D'Urfey's farces, John Dunton said, "wou'd make a Body laugh" (*The Life and Errors,* 1705, p. [245 misnumbered] 239).

80. *Swore . . . Plain: "Durfey . . .* speaks plain when he Swears" (Thomas Brown, *Amusements Serious and Comical,* 1700, p. 51).

85. *The next:* Thomas Baker (c. 1680–1731?), "Son of an eminent Attorney . . . in the City of *London*" (Mottley, pp. 166–67), matriculated at Brasenose College, Oxford, in March 1697 and graduated B.A. from Christ Church in 1700 (*Alumni Oxonienses, 1,* 59). Besides five comedies produced between 1701 and 1708, he is also said to have written *The Female Tatler* (1709–10). Like Abel Boyer, he dedicated his first play, *The Humour of the Age* (1701), to a Whig, Lord Halifax, and the next, *Tunbridge Walks: or, The Yeoman of Kent* (1703), to a Tory, John Howe. He may be the same Thomas Baker who was rector of Bolnhurst, Bedfordshire, in 1711 and vicar of Ravensden, Bedfordshire, in 1716–31 (Venn, *1,* 72).

86. *Finnikin:* The character of Francis Maiden, a transvestite, in *Tunbridge Walks: or, The Yeoman of Kent,* "in which effeminacy is carried to an height beyond what any one could conceive to exist in any man in real life," is said to have been "absolutely, and without exaggeration, a portrait of the author's own former character" (Baker, *3,* 358).

95. *Friends:* Three of Baker's friends supplied prefatory verses to *Tunbridge Walks: or, The Yeoman of Kent* and one of them, Charles Vaughan, imagined Apollo ordering Baker to be crowned with bays as "My Youngest, my Renown'd, my Fav'rite Son."

Besides he's recorded a Convict in Court,
For daring my Sons to abuse,
And presuming to make both a Jest and a Sport,
Of *Oxford,* the Seat of the Muse.

However, that he mayn't Incessantly grieve,
And lay this Reception to Heart,
I consent that the Scribe of a Mortal have leave
To *think* himself full of Desert;

To imagine, because with his Trifles some bear,
And the Town has Vouchsaf'd them their Sight,
Because he can look and can dress with an *Air,*
That he with an *Air* must needs write.

This Enrag'd him so far, that resolv'd to resent
What he judg'd was unjust and was hard,
He his Malice and Nonsence would Instantly Vent,
Without any Thought or Regard.

And strait a dull Prologue and Epilogue wrote,
Good Sence to Abuse and Lampoon,
In Praise of the Battle that *Marlborough* Fought,
And gave the Town Captain *Shabroon.*

99–100. *make . . . a Jest . . . Of Oxford:* Baker's third play, which was denied a license for the stage, was entitled *An Act at Oxford.* Baker resented "the Imputation so industriously spread on my want of Sense as well as Manners, to have rudely treated that LEARNED BODY for which I have the highest Deference and Esteem." He protested quite rightly that he had done little more than to lay the scene in Oxford, for the play is much less abusive of fat dons and fornicating students than it is of drunken country squires and reforming City justices (*An Act at Oxford. A Comedy,* 1704, sig. A4r).

113. *Prologue and Epilogue:* The advertisement of Aphra Behn's *The Emperor of the Moon* in *The Daily Courant* for 11 August 1704 mentions only "a new Prologue occasion'd by the good News that arriv'd yesterday, of the Great Victory gain'd over the French and Bavarians, by his Grace the Duke of Marlborough," but a marginal note in the first edition of the present poem (p. 5) mentions both *"A Prologue and Epilogue Spoke by* Will. Pinkethman, *representing a* Bavarian *Officer on that Occasion."* These are presumably the verses that Baker wrote, but no copy is known to have survived.

116. *Shabroon:* a disreputable person. *OED* cites Edward Ward, *The London Spy, 15* (1706), 366: "loose Shabroons in Bawdy-Houses Bred."

Make way, said the Cryer, and in came a Bard,
Three Yards round about in the Wast,
And desired without more adoe to be heard,
For He was in very great hast;

And his Bottle Companions would sit *a la Mort,*
Without any Distic or Song,
Should a Man of his Worth be detain'd by the Court,
Or kept from the Tavern too long.

When the Judges reply'd, He might go when he pleas'd,
For the Bench would ne're offer the Bays
To a Man with a sort of *Enthusiasm* seiz'd,
That had nothing but *Quakers* in Plays.

Besides, any Man in his Senses must know
Where *Wilkinson*'s Talent lay most,
If he'd sit up to Drink for a Rump, So and So,
'Twas the Devil to think of this Post.

When *Cheek* notwithstanding His Case was his own,
As a Candidate press'd through the Throng,

117. *a Bard:* Richard Wilkinson is a very shadowy figure about whom there may be more biographical information in this poem than in all other sources. He wrote one play, *Vice Reclaim'd; or, The Passionate Mistress. A Comedy,* of which there were five performances at Drury Lane in July 1703. Despite the lateness of the season, the play "met with very good success" (Baker, *3,* 379), was revived at Lincoln's Inn Fields in the season of 1719–20 as *The Quaker's Wedding,* played twice as a benefit in 1721, and apparently was revived again in 1723 when a new edition was published under the new title (ibid., p. 188; *London Stage, 2,* 39, 552, 553, 558, 565, 629, 632).

121. *a la Mort:* as if dead.

127. *Enthusiasm:* the pretense of special divine revelation, characteristic of nonconformists (*OED*).

128. *nothing but Quakers:* There is only one Quaker in *Vice Reclaim'd* and that is the rich Widow Purelight, whom an aged debauchee traps into marriage by pretending to be a Quaker. The central figure in the play is the demimondaine, Mrs. Haughty, who traps her keeper into marriage.

131. *Drink for a Rump, So and So: OED* cites Hearne, 2, 329: the "word *Rump* . . . was given to those scandalous headstrong, rebellious members [of the Long Parliament] that strenuously oppos'd the King." "To Drink for a Rump, So and So," therefore, may mean, "to drink toasts to this or that republican leader." In any case, the tavern scenes in Act V of *Vice Reclaim'd* are drawn with an authenticity that indicates long habituation.

133. *Cheek:* presumably Thomas Cheek (d. 1713?) of Hertfordshire, who was admitted a fellow commoner at Queens' College, Cambridge, in June 1676 (Venn, *1,* 328), the

And protested by Day-break he'd surrender to none,
  What of right to his *Muse* did belong.

As for his part, he sat up five Nights in a Week,
  To get the Repute of a Wit,
And had Drank 'till his Guts were e'en ready to break,
  For a Place for which other Folks Writ.

Besides, though he had not Voluminous been,
  Or a very Great Friend to *Duck-Lane,*
There were those that in Print his Composures had seen,
  And his Merry Poetical Strain.

How *Garth* had accepted his Distics of Praise,
  That Sung his Dispensary's Fame,
And had Scratch'd him again thro' good Nature to raise
  His Friend a Poetical Name.

---

same year that Samuel Garth matriculated at Peterhouse. In London he joined the circle of Whig poets and by 1700 Abel Boyer could describe him as "a Gentleman, who both by his Education, and his converse with the best Authors, and most ingenious Men of the Age, has acquir'd a true Taste of Poetry, and Prosaick Writings. He is also famous for writing a great many Songs, full of Wit and inimitable Graces." Although he was said to have "a new Play upon the Stocks" in August 1700, nothing but his occasional pieces have survived (*Letters of Wit, Politicks and Morality,* pp. 219, 251).

139. *Drank:* "That C[*heek*] Drinks hard, and late in Taverns sits," was observed in *Discommendatory Verses,* 1700, p. 16 and confirmed in *Letters of Wit, Politicks and Morality,* p. 251: "Our Friend, Mr. C[*hee*]*k* has neither forsaken his *Jest,* nor his *Bottle.*"

142. *Duck-Lane:* Duck Lane, leading into Smithfield, is "taken up by Booksellers for old Books" (Strype, *1,* ³122); cf. Pope, *An Essay on Criticism* (1711), 444–45).

143. *Composures:* Cheek's "Composures" include a song for Thomas Southerne's *The Wives Excuse* (1692), "Corinna I excuse thy Face," which was set by Henry Purcell; another song, "Bright Cynthia's pow'r divinely great," for Southerne's *Oroonoko* (1696); a third song, "When, Cloe, I your Charms survey," for John Dennis' *A Plot and No Plot* (1697); some prefatory verses, "To my Friend Dr. G—*th,* the Author of the *Dispensary,*" which were prefixed to the second edition of *The Dispensary* (May 1699); a prologue to Abel Boyer's *Achilles; or, Iphigenia in Aulis* (1700); and a squib, "To the Canting Author of the *Satyr against Wit,*" in *Commendatory Verses* (1700) (*London Stage, 1,* 403, 454, 519; John Dennis, *The Select Works,* 2 vols., 1718, *2,* 330).

145. *Garth:* see 573 *n.,* below.

147. *Scratch'd:* By what means Garth "Scratch'd" (flattered?) Cheek has not been discovered.

Apollo was mute when the Doctor was nam'd,
  And has like t' have declar'd of his Side,
Since a Man *Garth* spoke well of could not be disclaim'd,
  Or in any Request be deny'd.

But *Suckling* let fly a whole Volly of Curses,
  And accosted the God in a Rage,
With, Mine *Arse* for the Scribes *Panegyrical* Verses,
  He has murder'd my *Goblins* each Page;

Has damn'd in one Day, what had held more than Three,
  And had well been receiv'd by the Town,
Had not such a Cursed Corrector as He,
  Flung out my best Lines for his own.

Nay then, said the God to the Cryer, Go tell
  The Pretender his Suit to give o're;
For though I respect my Son *Garth* very well,
  I must own I love *Suckling* much more.

Stiff *Manning* stalk'd in, the next Claimant to Wit,
  With a Bundle of Words without Thought,
And snuff'd up his Nostrils as if 'twas beshit,
  And he smell'd to the Nonsence he brought.

156. *Goblins:* Cheek may have revised Sir John Suckling's *The Goblins* (1646) for a revival. If it was played, it must have been a private performance, for no public performances are known after 1667; cf. *The Goblins. A Comedy. Presented at the Private House in Black-Fryars, by His Majesties Servants,* Printed in the Year, 1694, in *The Works of Sir John Suckling,* 1696, p. 243.

165. *Manning:* Francis Manning (c. 1674–c. 1752), the son of Thomas Manning of London, matriculated at Trinity College, Oxford, in March 1689 at the age of 15. Subsequently he is said to have studied at the Middle Temple and the Inner Temple. His first published work seems to have been a translation of Valentin Esprit Fléchier, *The Life of the Emperour Theodosius the Great* (1693). He published "something in the *Gentleman's Journal* [1692–94]," as Anthony à Wood said (*4,* 1691), and "On Sir *R——— Bl——re's* Noble Project to Erect a Bank of Wit" in *Commendatory Verses.* His first play, *The Generous Choice,* was produced at Lincoln's Inn Fields, and published in March 1700. Another comedy, *All for the Better; or, The Infallible Cure,* with a prologue by George Farquhar, was produced at Drury Lane, and published in November 1702. The latter part of his life was spent in the diplomatic service and in 1716 he was appointed minister to the Swiss Confederation. *Poems Written at Different Times on Several Occasions, By a Gentleman who Resided Many Years Abroad in the Last Two Reigns with a Publick Character* (1752) (BM: 11607.h.5) probably represents his posthumous work (*Alumni Oxonienses, 3,* 966; *CBEL, 2,* 780; *British Diplomatic Representatives,* pp. 146–47; *London Stage, 1,* 524; *2,* 28; Baker, *1,* 489–90).

There were Verses on *Namur,* and on *Greenwich hill,*
  And Plays that deceas'd at their Birth,
With a Thousand Abortives that had drop'd from his Quill,
  And Elegies, that had made Mirth.

At which the Court smil'd, and strait pass'd a Decree
  In favour of Learning and Sence,
That such shallow pated Pretenders as he,
  Should be instantly banish'd from thence;

Yet since with his Nature he could not well part,
  And Passions with which he was born,
He was left to make use of the Crutches of Art,
  That another guess'd Genius had worn,

And permitted to Father the Works were produc'd
  From other Men's Labour and Toil,
And since what h' had written himself was refus'd,
  To adopt things was written by *Boyle.*

Is it so then? said *Farquhar,* My Matters are safe,
  By St. *Patrick* my Business is done,
For it's known I have made Pit and Gallery laugh
  Without any ones help but my own.

My Jubilee *Dicky,* and Airy Sir *Harry,*
  Will Vindicate what I have said,

169. *Namur:* Manning published *A Congratulatory Poem: Humbly Offered to the King upon His Return Home after Taking Namur* in 1695.

Greenwich hill: Manning published *Greenwich-Hill. A Poem* in 1697.

172. *Elegies:* In 1695 Manning published *A Pastoral Essay, Lamenting the Death of our Most Gracious Queen Mary, of Blessed Memory* and in 1702 he published *The Shrine. A Poem Sacred to the Memory of King William III.*

180. *another guess'd:* of another sort or kind (*OED*); cf. 339, below.

184. *Boyle:* See *The Dispensary, 5,* 74 *n.,* above.

189. *Jubilee Dicky:* Farquhar's second comedy, *The Constant Couple; or, A Trip to the Jubilee,* opened at Drury Lane in November 1699 and played to "some fifty Audiences in five months." Even Abel Boyer, whose *Achilles* was forced off the stage by it, acknowledged that Farquhar's play deserved its "great success." Clincher, Jr., the gay Jubilee beau, was played by William Bullock, and his manservant, Dicky, by Henry Norris, Jr., thereafter "commonly call'd Jubilee Dicky" (*London Stage, 1,* 517–18, *2,* 39; [Abel Boyer], *The English Theophrastus,* 2nd ed., 1706, p. 13).

Sir Harry: The sequel to *The Constant Couple, Sir Harry Wildair,* opened at Drury Lane in April(?) 1701, was published in May, but not revived thereafter (*London Stage, 2,* 10–11).

And none but myself has a Title to carry
 The Laurels away on my Head.

By your leave, Brother *Teague,* reply'd *Mac Fleckno*'s Ghost,
 Our Country Men are better known,
The Beauties are borrow'd of which you thus boast,
 But the Faults, I dare swear, are your own.

Tho' the Town allows, what you wou'd have 'em all take
 For granted, with no one you joyn,
Since none but a Man of your Judgment could make
 Such Language to such a Design.

And I can't but applaud the Resolve you have ta'en,
 In the present employ which you chuse,
For it's nobler in Red to make a Campaign,
 Than to Butcher an innocent Muse.

The Funeral next was held up as a Piece
 More Accomplish'd than any yet brought,
And was said to out do those of *Rome* and of *Greece*
 In Choice both of Stile and of Thought.

Abundance of Red-Coats and Men of the Sword
 In defence of this Comedy stood,
And not one among 'em but swore by the Lord,
 What the Captain had written was good.

193. *Mac Fleckno's Ghost:* presumably the patriotic ghost of Thomas Shadwell, aroused by an Irishman's claim to pre-eminence.

196. *Faults:* Pope also dismissed Farquhar as a "farce writer" (Spence, *1*, 208).

202. *present employ:* In March 1704 Farquhar was commissioned lieutenant in a regiment of foot that Charles Boyle, fourth earl of Orrery, had been asked to raise (*The Complete Works of George Farquhar,* ed. Charles Stonehill, 2 vols., Nonesuch Press, 1930, *1*, xxv).

205. *The Funeral:* Richard Steele's first play, *The Funeral; or, Grief à la Mode,* produced in December 1701, was an immediate success (*London Stage, 2,* 17). " 'Tis a dangerous Matter to talk of this Play," Charles Gildon said, "the Town has given it such applause, 'twill be an ungrateful undertaking to call their Judgments in question" (*A Comparison between the Two Stages, With an Examen of The Generous Conqueror; And Some Critical Remarks on The Funeral, or Grief Alamode,* 1702, p. 145).

210. *defence:* In the prologue to *The Funeral* Steele appealed to his fellow soldiers in the audience to "save the Poet" and in the preface to the printed play (1702) he thanked them "for their Warmth and Zeal in my behalf."

Apollo look'd pale at the Noise which they made,
And thought it the best to Speak fair,
Well knowing there's not such a Mischievous Blade,
As a Candidate train'd to the War,

And besought him, to hold himself easy that he
Was Advanc'd to a Troop of Dragoons,
For undoubtedly he nere a Collonel would be,
If he Studyed no Schemes but Lampoons.

While a Poet, He did well enough to declaim
Against *Russel,* and Laugh at his Trade,
Since he only Embalms Men of Wealth and of Fame,
And undertakes not the poor Dead.

But now he might one Day make use of his Art,
And pass out of the World in State;
'Twere but fitting he play'd a Political part,
And repented of Folly, though late.

If he'd merit the Common Respecte of the Court,
That avoids all Occasions of Heat,
Or behind him hereafter would leave a Report,
Like the Bodies that *Russel* kept sweet.

218. *Advanc'd:* Steele probably enlisted in the second troop of Life Guards in March 1692 while still an undergraduate at Merton College, Oxford. He fought in the disastrous battle of Steinkirk during his first campaign. In 1695 he transferred to the Coldstream Regiment, under the command of the "Salamander," Lord Cutts. In April 1697 he was commissioned ensign in the headquarters company of the second battalion, which was assigned to guard duty in London. At the same time he was appointed Cutts' private secretary and brevetted to the rank of captain (Calhoun Winton, *Captain Steele,* Baltimore, Johns Hopkins Press, 1964, pp. 39, 42, 45–46).

222. *Russel . . . his Trade:* See *The Dispensary, 3,* 166 *n.,* above. Charles Gildon agreed that Steele had "touch'd . . . the Knavery of those Undertakers very luckily" and that this was what was "new" in *The Funeral* (*A Comparison between the Two Stages,* p. 156).

228. *Folly:* Steele's reputation as "a rakish, wild, drunken Spark" was well earned. His "Occasions of Heat" (230) to date had produced one duel (in which he almost killed his adversary) and two illegitimate children (Hearne, *4,* 325; Winton, *Captain Steele,* pp. 49, 54).

229. *Court:* Calhoun Winton supposes that Steele was first seen at court in the company of Lord Cutts (ibid., p. 46).

For Popery and Slavery were now out of Doors,
And English Elections were Free,
Not the least to be Rul'd by the Threats or the Powers
Of such Termagant Lobsters as he.

Harry Hall was attentive to what was declar'd,
And deliver'd as Matter of Fact,
And Requested he might have a Poet's Regard,
Since he like a Poet could Act.

For Thanks to *Dan Kendrick* who wrote what he sent
To his Friends as his own up to Town,
For a Poet among certain Judges he went,
And deserv'd the Poetical Crown.

What! to Game it away? said *Apollo,* 'Tis plain
My Lord *Shandois* will never admit,

234. *Elections:* Steele began his political career managing elections for Lord Cutts. "In 1700 Cutts was engaged in a dispute with the burgesses of Newport, Isle of Wight, in respect of their having returned a certain mayor after another person had been appointed to the office by Cutts." Earlier in the same year Cutts had been accused of bribery in the election of Henry Greenhill to represent Newport in parliament. How well Steele learned these early lessons is shown by the "merry trick" he used himself to win election to parliament for Wendover, Buckinghamshire, in March 1722 (ibid., pp. 47, 67; *DNB, 5,* 369; *CJ, 13,* 111–13; HMC *Seventh Report,* Appendix, pp. 247–48).

237. *Hall:* See *The Mitred Club,* headnote, p. 508 above.

241. *Kendrick:* Daniel Kenrick or Kendrick (c. 1650–c. 1721), the son of Samuel Kenrick of Leigh, Gloucestershire, matriculated at Christ Church, Oxford, on 30 May 1666, aged 16. He graduated B.A. in 1670 and M.A. in 1674 (*Alumni Oxonienses, 2,* 844). He practiced medicine at Worcester, but since he was not wearing doctor's robes when he had his portrait painted in 1685 (when he was said to be 32 years old), he was relegated to the empirics by James Granger (*4,* 545). In the preface to *The Grove,* however, he is said to have taken "Degrees both in Divinity and Physick, and being a Person of Vivacity and Wit, entertain'd his Leisure Hours in Poetical Compositions." Henry Purcell and Aphra Behn seem to have been among his friends and in 1700 he published *A New Sessions of the Poets, Occasion'd by the Death of Mr. Dryden,* which was attributed to John Sheffield, marquis of Normanby. Twenty-two of his "Posthumous Pieces" are included in *The Grove* (*The Grove; or, A Collection of Original Poems, Translations, &c.,* 1721, pp. iii–iv; *CSPD 1700–1702,* p. 119). Although evidence for Hall's plagiarism from Kenrick is lacking, there are indications of their close relationship: In *To Your Lordship after Being Ruin'd at Play* Hall leaves "Rhimeing well" to Kenrick; in the same manuscript some lines of Kenrick's, "though of so different a nature," are "clapp'd" onto the end of a poem by Hall through "The ignorance of the Transcriber," as a marginal note explains (University of Leeds MS. Lt.q.5, pp. 34, 90).

246. *Shandois:* This line apparently identifies the noble lord to whom Hall addressed his verse letter *To Your Lordship after Being Ruin'd by Play* ("Dun'd by the Bills, I

Though he flung at his Clothes, that he set him a Main
 So Small as the Trophies of Wit.

What if just now we put by a Man of the Sword,
 Must we needs chuse a Man of the Gown?
You a Candidate fit for a Place? You a Turd;
 We must have a more Worthy or None.

Not but if any *Muse,* that was Fleshly Inclin'd,
 Would have what makes a Virgin be Spoil'd,
She need not go very much farther to find
 A Parson would get her with Child.

But as for this Office to which you lay claim,
 Sweet Sir, you are hugely mistaken,
It belongs to a Person of Learning and Fame,
 And not to a Scandalous Deacon.

Tate heard what was said, and not doubting the least,
 But he was the Person was meant,

---

roase from Bed"). "Shandois" is James Brydges, eighth Lord Chandos of Sudeley (1642–1714). He served Charles II as ambassador to Constantinople, and refused to sign the association to defend William III in 1696. In the next reign it was rumored that he was to be Anne's first ambassador to Hanover, but he was not appointed (Luttrell, *4,* 22; *5,* 194). Hall's "Awkard Doggrell Letter" was written "By way of Bond, to own the Debt" that left him, as he said, at his lordship's "mercy,/By force of *Noverint universi*" (University of Leeds MS. Lt.q.5, pp. 34–35).

247. *Main:* In eighteenth-century dice play, or hazard, the main is the number (5–9 inclusive) called by the thrower before the first roll of the dice. If the main comes up on the first throw, the roller wins the stake set by the banker. Otherwise he loses the stake the next time he throws the main. In *To Your Lordship after Being Ruin'd by Play* Hall complained: "Was Eight the Maine, I threw Eleven." Although the exigencies of rhyme enforce a slight anomaly (it is the stake that is "set," not the main), the meaning of 246–48 is clear: even though Hall might be willing to wager his very clothing to win the laurel crown, Lord Chandos, as banker, would never set a stake so low.

256. *Parson:* Hall refers to himself as a clerk (but not a priest) in *The Humble Petition of that Priest and Henry Hall to Edmund Addys Gent* (University of Leeds MS. Lt.q.5, p. 95).

with Child: In *To Your Lordship after Being Ruin'd at Play* Hall confessed that his skill was greater at love: "The Bargain here is quickly driven,/And Miss turns sooner up than seven . . ./Thô some nine Months, or there abouts/What you threw in, too oft comes out" (ibid., p. 34) .

Stepp'd into the Court to be laugh'd at and hiss'd,
For Misconstruing the Royal Intent.

He manag'd himself with abundance of Form,
Appearing Devout and Precise,
And endeavour'd to seem not too cold nor too warm,
And to put upon *Phoebus* his Eyes.

But he saw him throughout and bid him take care
That his Principles might be conceal'd,
For should his Respect for *John Calvin* take Air,
He might be from St. *James*'s expell'd.

As for her part, the *Queen* might e'en do what she wou'd,
And admit Men to Service like him,
But nothing like low Church Dissembler e'er shou'd
Creep into his Royal esteem.

Besides, Poor King *David* had made his Complaint
And had enter'd his Mournful protest,
That by his means his numbers seem'd languid and faint
And his Energy cramp'd and oppress'd;

That his Praises and Prayers had both lost their Force
Through the Damps of Expressions he chose,
And pretending to mend, had abus'd him much worse,
Than the former Assassines, his Foes.

Wherefore he was bid to make the best of his Way,

264. *Misconstruing:* trisyllabic, with the accent on the second syllable: mis-con-string.

266. *Precise:* puritanical (*OED*); cf. 127 *n.*, above. Tate was said to be "remarkable for a downcast look" (Baker, *1*, 703).

268. *to put upon:* to impose upon, deceive (*OED*), s.v. put, v.[1] 23f).

269. *he:* Apollo.

273. *Queen:* See *The Golden Age,* 118 *n.*, above.

277. *David:* See *The Pacificator,* 271 *n.*, above. Resentment of *A New Version of the Psalms* (1696), by Nahum Tate and Nicholas Brady, flared up again in 1703 when the volume was licensed for use in the churches by the queen (*DNB, 19,* 380).

284. *former Assassines:* The earlier version, *The Whole Booke of Psalmes Collected into Englysh* (1562), by Thomas Sternhold and John Hopkins, had long been the standard for bad verse (Prologue to *The Pilgrim,* 35 *n.*, above.)

Lest the Court fall asleep, and should Nod,
They'd be sufferers themselves, perhaps, should he stay;
He that us'd a King ill, would a God.

When Silence commanded above and below,
And the Marshal's Men clearing the Way,
The Cryer call'd out for *Daniel de Foe*
To tell the Bench what he 'ad to say.

Why truly, my Liege, said the Prophet, not much.
For the Place, I'm not earnest about it,
My *Reviews* bring me in, what with Scandal keeps touch,
And I can do Mischief without it.

However, since Merit alone should receive,
What only to Merit is due,
I'll accept of the Post, by your Sovereign leave,
And give you in Bail to be True.

To govern just like a Dissenter in Power,
And hold in the Rein and the Bit,
And be as Malignant and Peevish and Sour,
As e'er Man in Office was yet.

Not a Syllable farther for fear of a Gaol,
Be content with Crimes pardon'd before,
'Tis enough, said the God, you're got off with *Sham Bail,*
If you're Wise, never talk of *Bail* more.

288. *us'd a King ill:* The allusion is probably to Tate's version of Shakespeare's *Richard II,* which was suppressed on 14 December 1680 after two performances at Drury Lane. It was revived "in Disguise" the next month but again banned and the theatre ordered to be closed. It was supposed to offer "too close a parallel with the political situation of the time" (*London Stage, 1,* 293, 294; *DNB, 19,* 379).

295. *Reviews:* See *The Address,* headnote, p. 631 above.

300. The line may be paraphrased: "And offer security that I will faithfully perform the office of laureate."

307. *Sham Bail:* Cf. [William Pittis?], *Heraclitus Ridens,* No. 2, 3–7 August 1703: "Mr. *De Foe* is . . . acquainted with some Knights that look as big as Aldermen. . . . They must get other than Sham Bail for him." None of Defoe's bailsmen on 5 June 1703 were "Aldermen" but since they urged him to abscond, they may be said to have offered "Sham Bail" (*A Hymn to the Pillory,* 444 *n.,* above; Moore, *Daniel Defoe,* p. 128).

He was hush'd and sneak'd off to correct his *Reviews,*
With abundance of Shame and Regret,
And faulty Himself to find fault with the News,
That has worsted his Censure as yet.

Next *Pittis* came in, with two Quarts in his Guts,
And his Eyes dropping out of his Head,
And declared to the Bench, that they could not be Sots,
Who were drunk with Omnipotent Red.

Here's a Health to King *Phoebus,* the Candidate cry'd,
As he guzl'd down Two in a Hand;
Can His Majesty be of another Man's side,
Or refuse me the Bays when I stand?

None has ventur'd his Neck more than I for the Cause,
Or deeper in Scandal has sunk,
And fish'd in the Mud for the Party's Applause,
Whether found to be Sober or Drunk.

The Deity smil'd at the Merry Conceit,
And Commanded the Fool to withdraw,
Since Fellows like him that reproach Church and State,
And Offend, should be punish'd by Law.

Besides the two Glasses fill'd up to the Brim,
And the Zeal he now shew'd to Extreams,
Made it plain that the Health he drunk was not to him,
But his Favourite Idol, Young *James.*

Therefore, if he pleas'd, he might e'en buy a Brush
And away to his Club, and talk Treason;
To be plain with him, his Majesty car'd not a Rush
For a Flash without Substance or Reason.

313. *Pittis:* See *The Pacificator,* 270 *n.,* above. Since 1700 Pittis had written replies to *The True-Born Englishman* and to *The History of the Kentish Petition,* an elegy to James II entitled *The Generous Muse* (1701), a panegyric to the leaders of the New Country-Party in *The Patriots. A Poem* (1702), and had undertaken a new periodical in the guise of *Heraclitus Ridens* (August 1703–March 1704). Defoe characterized him as "that Mighty, Judicious, Papistical Author" (*Moderation Maintain'd,* 1704, p. 26).

333. *a Brush:* to brush off "the Mud" (323)?

334. *his Club:* Pittis frequented the Rose tavern in Russell Street (*Modern Philology, 33* [February 1936], 283–87).

Charles Gildon took Heart, and assur'd of the Place,
Was all Joy at the Sentence last past,
And told the Court his was another guess Case
Than the *Jacobite*'s they flung out last.

As for his part, 'twas known that his Principles were
Of a downright Fanatical Strain.
And he'd be Tooth and Nail for a *Hanover* Heir,
Or for any other for Gain.

Though the Doctrines he follow'd not long since were
Romish,
Which he blush'd not before 'em to own,
Now, thanks to *Spinosa,* though formerly Squeamish,
Such a Thing as Religion he'd none.

A *Matchiavel* this without doubt, said the God,
And a wonderful Sort of a Plea:
To pretend Divine Beings of Gods to explode,
Is to make no such Being of me.

Take care of him, Gaoler, to the Gibbets and Forks
Such an Author as this should be Sped;
Not an Infidel amongst the *Jews* or the *Turks,*
But for half this would forfeit his Head.

He was loath to be Hang'd, and before he'd depart,
In Arrest of the Sentence, he pray'd,
That the Court would consider his Judgment and Art,
And first suffer his Plays to be read.

337. *Gildon:* See *The Pacificator,* 272 *n.,* above.

339. *another guess Case:* See 180 *n.,* above. Cf. John Dunton, *The Life and Errors,* 1705, p. [247 misnumbered] 241: "Mr. Gildon . . . writes with a peculiar Briskness, which the common Hacks can't boast of, in Regard, they want the Life and Spirit, and the same *Liberty,* and Extent of *Genius.*"

347. *Spinosa:* The English reputation of Benedict de Spinoza (1632–77), "this famous atheist," as Hume called him, began to take shape in the seventeenth century. In 1683 when Charles Blount published a translation of chapter six of *Tractatus Theologico-Politicus* (1670) under the title *Miracles, no Violation of the Laws of Nature,* it was said that Blount's whole design was "To instill the Principles of *Deisme* or *Atheisme* into the minds of his Readers" ([Thomas Browne], *Miracles Work's Above and Contrary to Nature,* 1683, p. 2). Although Gildon did not include this translation in *The Miscellaneous Works of Charles Blount, Esq.* (1695), it is not likely that he was ignorant of it.

'Twas agreed, and he toss'd them *The Patriot* first,
  In hopes 'twould Reverse the Decree,
But never was Mortal so Storm'd at and Curs'd,
  As he was by Murder'd *Nat Lee.*

Ye Gods meet with Gods and make hast to my Aid,
  Cry'd the Bard, take the Profligate hence,
What a Fool of a Hero my *Brutus* is made!
  How perverted my meaning and Sense!

Against this Assassin for Justice I call,
  O Grant me so Lawful a Claim;
By more than one Death such a Traytor should fall,
  That had made bold with more than Ones *Fame.*

Then *Oldmixon* brought some Epistolary Verse,
  To rescue his Friend in Distress;
But *Drayton* gave him such a Kick of the Arse,
  As defeated the Intended Success.

For he too, must needs be a Dabling in Print.
  And amending good things for the worse,
As he, what bore just weight, had new Stampt in his Mint,
  And Allay'd both its Beauty and Force.

361. *The Patriot: The Patriot; or, The Italian Conspiracy* was the last of five plays that Gildon adapted for the stage. This one, produced at Drury Lane, published in December 1702 (but dated 1703) and never revived, was an "Alteration" of Nathaniel Lee's tragedy, *Lucius Junius Brutus* (1680), which was banned by the lord chamberlain after it played three performances during the time of the popish plot. The "Alteration," as Gildon explains in the preface, was similarly refused a license until he had moved the scene from Rome to Florence, translated Brutus into Cosmo de' Medici, "taken away all Reflections on Monarchy," and changed the title.

372. *made bold:* Giles Jacob observed that Gildon's "Style . . . [was] too near an Imitation of Mr. *Lee's*" (*Poetical Register,* pp. 116–17).

373. *Oldmixon:* John Oldmixon published *Amores Britannici. Epistles Heroical and Gallant, In English Heroic Verse* in 1703. In the dedicatory epistle he acknowledged that he had taken "the hint of the following Letters from Mr. *Drayton,* whose Language is now obsolete, his Verses rude and unharmonious." What he took was more than a "hint," however; he rewrote all 24 of Drayton's *England's Heroical Epistles* (1597) much in the way that Pope "Versify'd" Donne's satires, and then added six more of his own.

Stern *Dennis* concern'd at his Comrades mischance
  Would have held a Dispute on his side,
But the Critick was ask'd what he had to advance
  Why he should not himself be deny'd.

Sure you Jest, said the Bard, what occasion's to speak?
  My performance it self may suffice,
And my skill in Italian, French, Latin, and Greek,
  Must of Consequence get me the Prize.

Not a Kitcat but owns what you seem to suspect,
  And submits to my determination,
Wherefore, since my Merit is matter of Fact,
  You must think I bid fair for this Station.

I have stood the Lord *Dorset*'s distinguishing Test,
  And have made half the Kingdom to know it,
And if *Halifax* once would have made me a *Priest,*
  Sure I shan't be refus'd for a *Poet.*

The Names of those Peers made the Judges demur,
  And Consult how to shew their Behaviour,
For their good Opinions were known to go far,
  And 'twas half done to be in their Favour.

When Madam *Thalia* rose up from her Seat,
  And her Judgment was pleas'd to declare,

381. *Stern Dennis:* John Dennis was said to be "A very severe Critic on other Mens Writings" (Mottley, p. 209).

his Comrade: John Oldmixon had been known to Dennis for at least 10 years (Dennis, *Critical Works, 2,* xl, xlviii).

389–90. *Not a Kitcat but . . . submits:* Although Dennis was not a member of the Kit-Cat Club (Oldmixon, p. 479), several of his friends and connections were among its most prominent members: Charles Seymour, duke of Somerset, Charles Montagu, Lord Halifax, Arthur Mainwaring, William Congreve.

391. *Merit:* Giles Jacob called Dennis "the greatest Critick of this Age" (*Historical Account,* p. 257).

393. *Dorset's . . . Test:* See *A Satyr against Wit,* 353 *n.,* above.

395. *Priest:* There is no evidence that a living in the church was among the "repeated Encouragements" which Dennis acknowledged from Halifax in 1696 (*Critical Works, 1,* 52; *2,* xxi).

That to have the Good Word and Report of the Great,
  Was not always to Merit the Chair.

Since some are spoke well of for sinister Ends,
  As Factions each others oppose,
And *Liberty Asserted* had those for its Friends,
  That were reckon'd the Monarchy's Foes.

This Caution of hers made the Court put him by,
  And Command him forthwith to be gone,
They advis'd him in others *less Faults* to espie,
  Or offend 'em with *Less* of his own.

Sir *Richard* rejoic'd at his Critick's Rebuke,
  Stood up with the Volumes he writ,
And desir'd of the Bench, they would please next to look
  On his *Arthurs,* and *Satyr against Wit.*

But a Goddess that sat there to give him a Rub,
  Told him, he his Addresses might spare,
And a Man that had tir'd out the *Patience of Job*
  Would Infallibly be tiresome to theirs.

Yet nothing abash'd, he went on with his Tale,
  And harangu'd in Defence of his Lays,
Declaring that what went off best in the Sale,
  Best deserv'd their Opinion and Praise,

405. *sinister Ends:* Despite the implication, Dennis never condescended to write for a party. He identified himself as a solid Whig, however, when he published an attack on Sacheverell, *The Danger of Priestcraft to Religion and Government* (1702).

407. *Liberty Asserted: Liberty Asserted. A Tragedy* was Dennis' most successful work for the stage. It opened at Lincoln's Inn Fields in February 1704 and was acted "with very great Applause" for 11 performances (*London Stage, 2,* 59–62; Jacob, *Poetical Register,* p. 68). In the preface Dennis denied that the play favored either party, but he acknowledged that it was widely held to be "a Whiggish Play" or even "a Republican Play" (*Critical Works, 1,* 321, 322). Many of its "Friends" were Whig propagandists: Thomas Southerne, Anthony Henley, Arthur Mainwaring, and, surprisingly enough, Daniel Defoe (ibid., *2,* lvi; Defoe, *Review, 3* [10 August 1706], 381). This is the play that is said to have so annoyed Louis XIV "that he never would make Peace with England, unless the delivering Mr. *Dennis* was one of the Articles of it" (*The Life of Mr. John Dennis,* 1734, p. 23).

413. *Sir Richard:* Richard Blackmore; see *A Satyr against Wit,* 180 *n.,* above.

419. *Job:* See *A Lent-Entertainment,* 89 *n.,* 94 *n.,* above.

And his Chapmen the *Churchills* could Witness from thence
That his Verses were Teirce, and were good,
For if good Luck's a Token and Sign of good Sence,
To reject his Pretensions was Rude.

With his Bombast enrag'd, the God took him up short,
And had made him be laid by the Heels,
For attempting with Nonsence to Murder the Court,
As he did his poor *Patients* with *Pills.*

But consider'd 'twas Lawful both for *Gibbeline* and *Guelph,*
For Saint and for Sinner to Write,
And his Satyr on *Wit,* had been one on himself,
While he try'd other Authors to Bite.

As for Satyr, said *Burnaby,* let me alone,
That's a Province to which I lay Claim,

425. *Churchills:* Awnsham and John Churchill, Locke's publishers, also published Blackmore's verse, which Locke so recklessly admired. It was John Dunton's opinion that Locke and Blackmore "receiv'd no small Advantage by coming abroad thro their Hands . . . [for] they never starve an Undertaking to save Charges" (*The Life and Errors,* 1705, p. 280).

426. *Teirce:* terse; in the obsolete sense of polished, smooth (*OED*).

437. *Burnaby:* William Burnaby (c. 1673–1706) was born in London, the son of a wealthy brewer, and educated at Merton College, Oxford, where he matriculated the same year as Richard Steele. When his father died he took up residence in the Middle Temple and his first published works, both of which appeared in May 1694, were *The Satyr of Titus Petronius Arbiter . . . Made English by Mr. Burnaby of the Middle Temple, and Another Hand* and "Upon a Lady singing" in *The Gentleman's Journal.* After an absence of nearly two years, Burnaby returned to London in 1698, was received into the Will's coffeehouse circle (*Letters of Wit, Politicks and Morality,* p. 216), and may have contributed "To the Cheapside Knight on his Satyr against Wit" to *Commendatory Verses.* "On a *Wednesday* in *Lent,*" 1700, his first play, *The Reform'd Wife,* was produced at Drury Lane and "met with the general Approbation" (ibid., p. 220). At the same time he was sued for assault by John Hawks during an altercation over "the said Hauks's sister's Chastity" and ordered to pay £32 damages (*The Dramatic Works of William Burnaby,* ed. Frederick E. Budd, Scholartis Press, 1931, p. 42). Thereafter he wrote three more plays: *The Ladies Visiting Day* (1701), *The Modish Husband* (1702), and *Love Betray'd; or, The Agreeable Disappointment* (1703), and contributed half a dozen epilogues to the plays of his friends, Susannah Centlivre, John Dennis, and Charles Gildon. About 1704, through the efforts of his brother, a Tory member of parliament, he was appointed a subcommissioner for prizes at Hull, worth £300 a year, but when he died in November 1706 he left "very little Assetts or effects behind him," as his friend, Mary Holmes, deposed (ibid., pp. 66, 71). He was buried in the Poet's Corner of Westminster Abbey (*The Gentleman's*

Witness the Characters I have fly-blown,
And the Virtues I'm known to defame.

Male and Female Confess with what Force I can strike,
As I point at their Faults in my Play,
And Uncivilly use both the Sexes alike,
Sparing no one that comes in my way.

But *Apollo* gave Orders to tell him that *Smut*
Was a thing not at all to the Matter,
And He might as well call his a *Play* 'thout a *Plot,*
As a Scandalous Invective a Satyr.

With respect 'twas a Gentleman's business to treat
The Methods and Ways of the Fair,
And he that expos'd their Proceedings should meet
What was due to those gave Secrets Air.

Journal, 3 [May 1694], 113; *London Stage, 1,* 525; *2,* 4, 6–7, 8, 10, 18, 19, 31, 33; Thomas Brown, *Works,* 4 vols., 1707–11, *4,* 79).

439. *Characters:* The only contemporary figures who have been identified in Burnaby's comedies are Elizabeth, duchess of Albemarle, and Ralph Montagu, first earl of Montagu. In *The Ladies Visiting Day* (1701) Thomas Courtine woos the eccentric Lady Lovetoy in the guise of Prince Alexander the Muscovite, which may conceal an allusion to Montagu's courtship, 10 years before, of "the mad Duchess," widow of Christopher Monck, second duke of Albemarle, and daughter and co-heir of Henry Cavendish, the vastly wealthy second duke of Newcastle. "Montagu wooed and won her in the character of the Emperor of China, and he kept her in a sort of confinement at Montagu House, where she was always served upon the knee as the Empress of China" (GEC, *9,* 108).

fly-blown: contaminated, spoiled (*OED*).

445. *Smut:* When Mr. Triffle, in Burnaby's second play, *The Ladies Visiting Day,* mentions a new play "call'd, *The Ladies Visiting-Day,*" Lady Lovetoy cries out, "O—out a'pon't, 'tis the smuttiest thing!" The laugh, however, is on Lady Lovetoy, for Burnaby's "care to avoid any thing that might shock the Ladies" made his comedies remarkably innocent. There may be a Shakespearean quibble on "lay" in *The Reform'd Wife,* but the worst that the anonymous author of *A Representation of the Impiety and Immorality of the English Stage* (1704) could discover in *The Modish Husband* was "The Devil fetch him" (*The Dramatic Works of William Burnaby,* ed. Budd, pp. 152, 195, 254).

447. *'thout a Plot:* Three of Burnaby's comedies turn about a wife's (unsuccessful) attempt to cuckold her husband. Burnaby himself admitted that his third play, *The Modish Husband* (1702), was "a Thing without . . . Design" (ibid., p. 275).

451. *expos'd their Proceedings:* Burnaby reveals something of "the Fashionable Mysteries of Lying, Hypocrisy, and Intriegue" and "Gaming, Drinking, and Cuckolding . . . Husbands," but the ladies emerge from these proceedings as innocent as grace itself (ibid., pp. 154, 220).

Though few could expect other Treatment from one
  Of his Temper, than *Visiting Days,*
And he that in English *Petronius* had done,
  Was expected to write *Bawdy Plays.*

Clarenceux King at Arms, then made his Approach,
  And enter'd his Prayer to be heard,
With a *Muse* that was Cloy'd with Dramatick Debauch,
  Yet in the Debauch persever'd.

A Projector, a Poet, a Herald, what's here?
  Cry'd the Deity, set him a Fine;
He'll advise me to Build till I'm *Bankrupt,* I fear,
  Should I grant him this Office of Mine.

E'en give him a *Trowel,* a *Rule* and a *Spade,*
  What a Pox should he do with a Pen?
Does he think by improving the *Bricklayer*'s Trade,
  To attain to the Knowledge of *Ben.*

'Tis impossible; no one to *Johnson* can rise,
  That without *Johnson*'s Genius was born,

457. *Clarenceux:* In March 1704 Charles Howard, third earl of Carlisle, for whom Vanbrugh had designed and was building Castle Howard in Yorkshire, secured for Vanbrugh the lucrative post of Clarenceux king-of-arms (Luttrell, *5,* 408), which required him to marshal and arrange the funerals of all baronets, knights, and esquires south of the river Trent. Since Vanbrugh "was known to take a humorously sceptical view of the importance of heraldic functions (which he had publicly ridiculed in his comedy of *Aesop*), his appointment was not popular" (*DNB, 20,* 89).

459. *Debauch:* Four players were indicted in the court of king's bench "for using indecent expressions" in *The Provok'd Wife* (1697) and Jeremy Collier devoted a whole chapter in *A Short View of the Profaneness, and Immorality of the English Stage* (1698) to *The Relapse* (1696). Vanbrugh boldly "persever'd" by writing *A Short Vindication of the Relapse and the Provok'd Wife* (1698). "The Business of Comedy," he said, "is to shew People what they shou'd do, by representing them upon the Stage, doing what they shou'd not" (Luttrell, *5,* 111; *The Complete Works of Sir John Vanbrugh,* ed. Bonamy Dobrée and Geoffrey Webb, 4 vols., Nonesuch Press, 1927, *1,* 206).

468. *Ben:* "Johnson *the Poet is said to have been a* Brick layer" [marginal note]. Ben Jonson told William Drummond of Hawthornden that he was taken from school and "put to ane other craft (I think was to be a . . . Bricklayer), which he could not endure" (*Ben Jonson's Conversations with William Drummond of Hawthornden,* ed. R. F. Patterson, Blackie & Son, 1923, p. 23).

Translations may Glisten and *Put* on Mens Eyes,
And the Trinkets of *France* may be worn,

But Originals only, discover and Sound
The Depth and the Strength of the Mind;
And English Invention would suffer a Wound,
Were his Patent ordain'd to be Sign'd.

For his part in *Treloby* was what stood accus'd,
Of tending good Manners to spoil,
And in *Aesop,* his Country he had so much abus'd,
He should go again to the *Bastile.*

When *Congreve* brim full of his Mistresses Charms,
Who had likewise made bold with *Molier,*
Came in piping hot from his *Bracegirdle*'s Arms,
And would have it his Title was clear.

471. *Translations:* Of the eight plays that Vanbrugh had produced by 1704, four were translations: *Aesop* (1697) and *Aesop. Part II* (1697) were translated from Edmé Boursault, *Les Fables d'Ésope* (1690); *The False Friend* (1702) was adapted from Alain René Le Sage, *Le Traître puni* (1700), and *Squire Treloby* (477 *n.*, below) was derived from Molière, *Monsieur de Pourceaugnac* (1670) (*DNB, 20,* 87–88).

Put on: impose upon, deceive; see 268 *n.* above.

477. *Treloby:* Although the following lines do not solve "the *Squire Treloby* puzzle," as it has been called, they provide some interesting evidence. *Squire Treloby* was a French farce which, when it was revived on 23 May 1704, was said to have been "perform'd before Her Majesty on Her Birth-day [6 February 1704]." The first public performance, however, was advertised for 30 March 1704. Congreve, Vanbrugh, and Walsh translated the play from Molière, *Monsieur de Pourceaugnac* (1670). "Each did an act," as Congreve wrote to his friend Joseph Keally, and on the evidence of the following lines it appears that Congreve "did" Act I (487), Vanbrugh Act II, and Walsh Act III (512, 519–20). Samuel Garth contributed a prologue, but the play was apparently not published and no manuscript or prompt copy is known to exist (*Review of English Studies, 4* [1928], 404–13).

478. *Manners:* John Ozell claimed that *Squire Treloby* was "a Party-Play made on purpose to ridicule the whole Body of *West-Country* Gentlemen [i.e. Tory squires]" (*The Complete Works of William Congreve,* ed. Montague Summers, 4 vols., Nonesuch Press, 1923, *3,* 115).

480. *Bastile:* In 1690 Vanbrugh was arrested in Calais on suspicion of espionage for entering France without a passport. He was "clapt up in the Bastile" in February 1692 and released nine months later (*DNB, 20,* 86–87; Luttrell, *2,* 355, 621).

482. *Molier:* See 477 *n.* above.

483. *Bracegirdle:* Anne Bracegirdle (c. 1663–1748), the most celebrated actress of the age, was said to have been Congreve's "Wife" (499 below), but seems actually to have been his mistress from 1693 to 1707. Their relationship is celebrated in terms of

What he rendred in English, was nothing like *Smut;*
For he wisely had taken his Choice;
And though the first Act in this Version might not,
Yet his Prudence should give him their Voice.

Said *Apollo,* You did most discreetly to take
A Part that was easiest and best;
Though the Rules of Behaviour Distinction should make,
And you'd not done amiss to chuse last.

But never pretend to be Modest or Chast,
Th' Old Batchelor speaks you Obscene,
And *Love for Love* shews, notwithstanding your hast,
That your Thoughts are Impure and Unclean.

That meaning's Lascivious your Dialogues bear,
Fit to grace the foul Language of *Stews,*
And though you are said to make a Wife of a Play'r,
You in those make a Whore of your Muse.

Then *Walsh,* who the Learned Triumvirate clos'd,
That English'd the Subscription Farce,
Expecting by none to be baulk'd or oppos'd,
Brought in his Oblation of Verse.

His Equipage made such a flourishing Shew,
And his Courtly Behaviour so pleas'd,
That for his Soul, the God could not say no,
And with Silence, as if Dumb, was seiz'd.

But recover'd, at last, with a seeming Concern,
He was told he might carry the Day,
If he'd only submit to be Taught and to Learn
How to chuse the best *Act* of a Play.

Valentine and Angelica, the lovers of *Love for Love* (1695), in *The Benefits of a Theatre* ("Prithee *Jerry* be quiet, cease railing in vain") (*POAS,* 1707, *4,* 49).

502. *Subscription Farce: Squire Treloobу* was acted at a "Subscription Musick" in Lincoln's Inn Fields on 30 March 1704.

505. *Shew:* John Dennis called Walsh "a Man of a very good Understanding, in spight of his being a Beau" (*Critical Works, 1,* 416).

512. *the best Act:* If Walsh translated the third act of *Squire Treloobу* (477 *n.,*

Since he that for Judgment was formerly fam'd,
  In Judging had very much err'd;
And deserv'd by the Court to be mightily blam'd,
  'Stead of being advanc'd and preferr'd.

For if through a Temper too Courteous and Free,
  He surrender'd the Choice was his Right,
Or He knew not which Act was the best of the Three,
  For want of an Accurate Sight.

Either this or that made him be put by a Course,
  And would render his Projects in Vain;
Though those that are Rich ha'nt defects in the *Purse,*
  They may chance to have Faults in the *Brain.*

Tom Southerne Petition'd the next, and besought
  The Court, that he must be preferr'd,
For he two Fat Places already had got,
  And most grievously wanted a Third.

When the Judges amaz'd at his Temper and Suit,
  Remanded him back to *White-hall,*
And declar'd, who had lost his Esteem and Repute,
  Was not fit for their Business at all.

---

above), this line is strangely prophetic, for when the play was revived in January 1706, the third act had to be "entirely" rewritten (*London Stage, 2,* 115).

513. *Judgment:* In 1697 Dryden had called Walsh "the best Critick of our Nation" (*Prose, 3,* 563).

518. *Choice was:* probably an ellipsis for "Choice which was."

521. *put by a Course:* If the text is not corrupt, this may mean "diverted from this plan" (*OED* s.v. Put v.1 40d).

527. *Places:* That Southerne deserted his Tory principles to acquire a lucrative post is also alleged in *The Last Will and Testament of Mr. Tho. Brown, Archi-Poetae Celeberrimi: "Item.* To *S*[*outhe*]*rn,* who for Gain/And Place of Trust, turn'd Cat in Pan" (*A Letter from the Dead Thomas Brown, to the Living Heraclitus,* 1704, p. 30, quoted in *Modern Language Review, 28* [October 1933], 430). In 1692 Southerne was a commissioner for assessments in Leicestershire county and 20 years later he served as secretary to Charles Boyle, fourth earl of Orrery, the Tory envoy to the Netherlands (January 1711–June 1713) (*CTB 1689–1692,* p. 1471; John W. Dodds, *Thomas Southerne Dramatist,* New Haven, Yale University Press, 1933, p. 6 *n.*).

Not but *Oroonoko* some Merit might plead,
  And take off from the weight of's Offence,
Were but every Character Just which we read,
  And Consistent with Reason and Sence.

Were his Heroine but like his Heroe, not Fair,
  Since their Breath in one Country they drew,
And She that was Born in an *Indian* Air,
  Set forth in an *Indian* Hue.

Yet for all that Mistake, it would be worth his while,
  And his Interest might not be lost,
For if this Contradiction he could reconcile,
  He might stand assur'd of the Post.

How Treason and Loyalty could e'er agree,
  And he could the World's Censure evade,
That meanly accepted an Agent to be,
  Where Pendergrass Collonel was made?

537. *Heroine . . . Fair:* Oroonoko is a negro, "Son and Heir to the great King of *Angola,*" married to Imoinda, the white daughter of an European adventurer (*Oroonoko: A Tragedy,* 1696, pp. 13, 23–24).

543. *this Contradiction:* described in lines 545–48.

547–48. These lines are partly explained by three letters from Southerne calendared in *CSPD 1703–1704* and transcribed in full by Clifford Leech (*Modern Language Review, 28* [October 1933], 422–25). Two of these are impassioned pleas to Nottingham to intercede for Major James Boucher (*An Address to Our Sovereign Lady,* headnote, p. 616 above), who had been sentenced to death in the Scotch plot. Southerne had known Boucher in 1685–88 when they both served in the duke of Berwick's regiment. The third letter is addressed to Harley, asking him to appeal to the House of Commons. In return for Boucher's pardon, Southerne offered to provide evidence of treasonable activities on the part of half a dozen Irish Catholic officers. For whatever reason, Boucher was pardoned in April 1704 and ordered to depart the kingdom in December 1706 (Luttrell, *5,* 415; *6,* 112).

548. *Pendergrass:* Sir Thomas Prendergast or Pendergrass (c. 1660–1709) was a Jacobite and Catholic who turned king's evidence in the plot to assassinate William III in February 1696. It was largely on his testimony that five of his fellow conspirators were executed. In May 1696 he received £3000 from the treasury and a grant worth £500 a year from a forfeited estate in Ireland and in June 1699 he was created a baronet. He entered the army and in June 1707 was created a lieutenant-colonel of the fifth regiment of foot. He was a frequent satirical target of Swift, who described him as "Footman, Traytor, vile Seducer,/Perjur'd Rebel, brib'd Accuser" (*Poems, 3,* 831).

Such a Question as this drew the Blood into's Face,
And away from the Querists he ran,
Well knowing how near it came up to his Case,
That so lately had turn'd *Cat in Pan.*

Rowe said 'twas his turn to *throw* for the Post,
He could *Nick* it, for the *Box* was his;
And though his Estate and Money was lost,
What was *Set* him he could not well miss.

No *Levants,* I beseech you, cry'd *Phoebus,* a *Cover,*
You may win it and wear't, I'm Content;
And down he flung *Tamerlain* and *The Step Mother,*
With his Idol *The Fair Penitent.*

But the *Cast,* since the *Stake* was not *Cover'd,* was *barr'd,*
Till with something Momentous was back'd,
Since Words were but Wind, and should have no regard,
Without what was Matter of Fact.

The first was all *Flattery,* and falsly *apply'd,*
The Second was half of it *Stole,*

552. *turn'd Cat in Pan:* changed sides; cf. 527 *n.* above. The phrase is proverbial (Tilley C172).

554. *Nick it:* make a winning throw of the dice in hazard; cf. 247 *n.,* above.

555. *Estate:* Upon his father's death in 1692 Rowe inherited an estate worth £300 a year (Spence, *1,* 349).

556. *Set:* Rowe feels lucky enough to win any wager that is set; cf. 247 *n.,* above.

557. *Levants:* bets made with the intention of absconding if they are lost (*OED*).

Cover: Rowe wants to roll dice for the laurel crown. Apollo is willing to gamble, but insists that Rowe cover the bet, that is, put up an equal sum in case he loses. Rowe then flings down his three plays.

565. *Flattery . . . falsly apply'd:* See *The Golden Age,* 120 *n.,* above. Edmund Gibbon, recalling Tamburlaine's "abominable trophies . . . or pyramids of human heads," was equally amused by the "amiable moderation" of Rowe's hero (*The History of the Decline and Fall of the Roman Empire,* 6 vols., 1776–88, cap. LXV, *n.* 71).

566. *half . . . Stole:* It has been pointed out that "the design" of *The Ambitious Step-Mother* (1700) "seems to have been taken from the establishing of Solomon on the throne of David, by Bathsheba, Zadock the Priest, and Nathan the Prophet" (2 Samuel 11; 1 Chronicles 1:5–49), but no evidence of plagiarism has been uncovered (Baker, *2,* 23; Ludwig Stahl, *Nicholas Rowes Drama The Ambitious Step-Mother,* Rostock, Carl Hinstorff, 1909, pp. 24–39).

And the Third could have none that were *good* on its side,
  Since his *Fair One* was wicked and *Foul.*

Yet to shew by the Court, some distinction was made,
  Betwixt Men of Merit and None,
He was told the God lik'd him the best of the Trade,
  And advis'd to persist and write on.

Till *Clio* call'd out, for her *Garth* to appear,
  Rising up with his Works in her Hand,
And said to the God, Sh' had a Candidate there,
  Would their Votes and their Wishes Command.

A Bard, that for Judgment, Expression and Thought,
  For sweetness of Style and Address,
Had never yet known such a thing as a Fault,
  And that only was fit for the Place.

Parnassus confess'd his approach, and each Muse
  At his Entrance transported arose,
Nor was it in *Phoebus* to put by or refuse,
  What the General Suffrage had chose;

568. *Fair One was . . . . Foul:* Cf. Cibber, *Lives, 3,* 276: "Mr. Rowe is guilty of a mis-nomer; for his Calista has not the least claim to be called the Fair Penitent, which would be better changed to the Fair Wanton, for she discovers not one pang of remorse till the last act."

571. *the best of the Trade:* This was a common opinion: "I think he may stand the first Man in the List of our present Dramatists" (*A Comparison between the Two Stages,* 1702, p. 183); "In his Writings there is a beauty of Expression, a masterly Wit, a nervous Strength, and a Diction more exactly Dramatick than appears in the Works of any other Modern Author" (Jacob, *Poetical Register,* p. 212).

573. *Garth:* Garth's reputation rested squarely on "his admirable Poem, *The Dispensary*" (Jacob, *Historical Account,* p. 58), and since he had written almost nothing else since 1699 but was personally "one of the best-natured men in the world" (Spence, *1,* 44), his reputation continued to grow. In the first of two session-of-the-poets poems published in 1700 Garth is a strong contender to succeed Dryden but loses out (to the de facto laureate, Nahum Tate) because of "some fulsome Couplets" in *The Dispensary* flattering Whig politicians ([Daniel Kenrick], *A New Session of the Poets, Occasion'd by the Death of Mr. Dryden,* 1700, p. 9). In the second, however, Dryden's "Mantle falls to G[*arth*] by Destiny" (*An Epistle to Sr. Richard Blackmore, Occasion'd by the Death of Mr. Dryden,* 1700, p. 8). By 1709 both Dryden and Shadwell *"resign the Crown when* Garth *appears"* ([Edward Ward], *The Secret History of Clubs,* 1709, p. 15).

With all Rapture, Enjoyment, Surprize and Desire,
He had heard *The Dispensary* read;
As he seem'd to out Rival the Nine with their Lyres,
And himself fix'd the Bays on his Head.

While the Laureat Elect begg'd leave to decline,
What was due to his Learning and Wit,
Though at last over-rul'd by th' Applause of the Nine,
He was forc'd to give way and submit.

When even his Rivals, confess'd it was just,
That he was install'd in Witt's Throne,
And rejoyc'd, that the Place that they stood for was *lost,*
Since a Bard of his Merit had *Won.*

Nor was one to be seen that Repin'd or that Mourn'd,
That the Present on *Garth* was bestow'd,
But said, when the Court during his Life adjourn'd,
That the God paid no more than he ow'd.

593. *just:* Because the choice of laureate in the earlier session-of-the-poets is frequently ironical (headnote, p. 679 above), the question of tone arises here. The possibility of irony seems to be ruled out in the preface, where the author says, "but if after all, I am mistaken in the Account of some of the *Candidates,* I have the Satisfaction to be assur'd, I am not in the Choice of the *Laureat,* I have given the *Bays* to; for if this *Election* were Real, which is Poetical and Fictitious, and *Apollo* was to determine it, the same Judge would make Choice of the same Man."

TEXTUAL NOTES

In the notes below, sigma, Σ, stands for the sum of the unspecified witnesses (W. W. Greg, *The Calculus of Variants,* Oxford, Clarendon Press, 1927, p. 14). A line number (or numbers) followed immediately by the bracket, indicates that the variants to the right of the bracket replace the whole line (or lines). Letters in parentheses, e.g. *F—(ch),* stand for letters that are found in some unspecified witnesses but not all.

A Satyr upon the French King

Copy text: A Satyr upon the French King, Written by a Non-Swearing Parson, and drop'd out of his Pocket at Samm's Coffee-House, London, Printed for Will. Jac-about, in the Year of Peace (folio half-sheet; Bodl. copy: Firth b. 21 [40]).

Collation: The text survives in two traditions. There are three witnesses to the better of these: the first folio half-sheet edition (*A*), which is derived from the same source as Osborn MS. Chest II, No. 4, pp. 34–35 (*B*), and the first collected edition of *The Works of Mr. Thomas Brown,* 1707, *1,* 189 (*C*), which derives from a source different from that of *A* and *B*. A second folio half-sheet edition, *Tom. Brown's Letter from the Shades, to the French King in Purgatory,* London: Printed for Will. Jack-about (Wing T1782), is a fragmentary version fitted out with a new title and new first line, "And wilt thou leave Young *Jemmy* in the lurch?" to make it conform to events of 1715 when the death of Louis XIV in September virtually insured the failure of James Francis Edward's last attempt to seize the throne of England. Subsequent editions of the poem in *The Works of Mr. Thomas Brown,* 1708, 1715, 1720, and 1730, derive from *C*.

There are four witnesses to the inferior tradition: Bodl. MS. Rawl. poet. 173, pp. 129–32, (*D*), University of Chicago MS. PR1195.C72, pp. 111–13 (*E*), and two printed sources, *POAS,* 1703, 2, 258–61 (*F*), and *A New Collection . . . of Miscellaneous Poems,* Dublin, 1721, pp. 50–54 (*G*). The poem also appears in *PRSA,* 1705, p. 479, which derives from *F*. *EFG* derive from a common source different from the source of *D*.

4 Would] That *ACDEFG.* 20 no bigger than] not worth *B.* 22 the Plague will become] a plague become's *D* the Plague will come *G.* 25 a] one *B.* 26 things] words *G.* 27 Thou] Tho' *EG.* 28 distress'd] oppress'd *D.* 29 that] who *BD.* 42 buy] get *D.* 50 bilk] baulk *B.* 53 spent of] bestow'd of *B* spent on *EFG* such] good *B.* 58 grown] turn'd *D.* 60 for] to *D.* 62 primitive] modern *D.* 66 for] to *D.* 68 in] on *D.* 70 E're] But *B* monstrous] wondrous *B.*

72 on] of *B*. 76 from the] from his *B* down from *D*. 78 And] As *B*. 84 Since thou] Since then thou'st *ABDEFG*. 86 ly] goe *B*. 90 of the Polish] of Polish *BDEFG*. 95 The] May *C*. 96 Dozens] th'Dozens *D*. 104 own Hugonots] own poor Hugonots *DEFG*.

Advice to a Painter

Copy text: POAS, 1703, 2, 428–32 (Princeton copy).

Collation: The text survives in three traditions, two of which are represented wholly by manuscripts and the third by manuscripts and printed books. The best tradition, which also includes some of the worst corruptions, is represented by the following witnesses:

BM MS. Sloane 3516, f. 160	*A*
BM MS. Sloane 1731A, ff. 148r–49v	*B*
BM MS. Add. 40060, ff. 12v–15r	*C*
Osborn MS. Box 214, No. 8	*D*
TCD MS. I.5, 2, 107–12	*E*
BM MS. Lansdowne 852, pp. 21–24	*F*
Osborn MS. Chest II, No. 1 (Phillipps 8301)	G

A and *B* preserve half a dozen unique readings of manifest superiority, but *B* renders "diverted to their private use" (line 77) as "converted to the publick use," which is nonsense, and *A* renders "abhors the Name" (line 120) as "Ahores the Same." *A,* in fact, may have been taken down from dictation: it reproduces "Sloan baits Seymour" (line 108) as "Sloan Bates Seamer" and "rote" (line 135) as "Wrote."

The printed texts derive from (γ), not one of the best manuscripts of the *ABCDEFG* tradition, and are collateral with BM MS. Stowe 305, ff. 265r–67r (*H*). These relationships may be represented as follows:

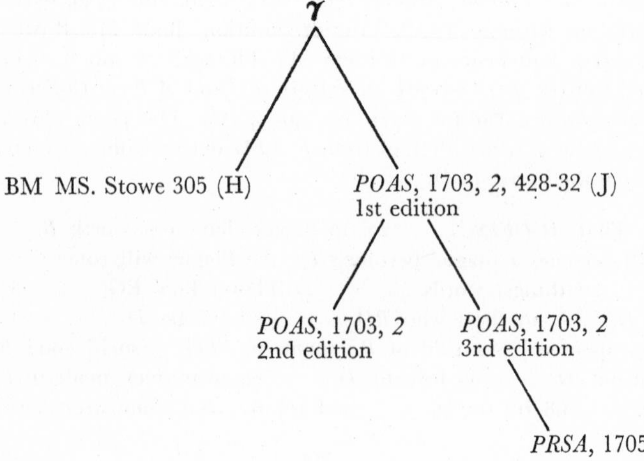

An inferior tradition is preserved in the following manuscripts, which derive collaterally from a source different from the source of *ABCDEFG* or the source of *HJ:*

Portland MS. Pw V 44, pp. 221–29	*K*
BM MS. Harleian 7315, ff. 270v–74r	*L*
Portland MS. Pw V 48, pp. 225–31	*M*
Holkham MS. 686, pp. 210–16	*N*
Huntington MS. EL 8734, ff. 52r–56v	*O*

Variants from two more manuscripts are recorded in the margins of George Thorn-Drury's copy of *POAS,* 1703, *2,* preserved in the Bodleian. These are described as a "(17th Cent.) transcript on 5½ p. small fo. lent to me by Percy Dobell" (*P*), and the "Fraser Ms." The "transcript" seems to have been made from *O,* or a very similar manuscript. The Fraser MS. is now known as Portland MS. Pw V 48 (*M*).

The manuscript said by Mary T. Osborne (*Advice-to-a-Painter Poems 1633–1856,* Austin, University of Texas, 1949, p. 58) to include an eight-line "character" of Walter Moyle not found in other manuscripts is probably the TCD MS. I.5 (*E*), which has a unique eight-line variant of the "character," not of Walter Moyle, but of Henry Boyle (see textual notes, lines 127–30).

Title: Advice to a Painter *ABDFGHLO* The Tory's Advice to a Painter *E* Advice to a Painter, 1697 *CJ* 1698. Advice to a Painter *KN* Advice to a Painter. 1698/9 *M.*

1 Skill] art *CGL.* 2 To] And *CDEK.* 3 w'indite] *AB* we write Σ. 6 With Master-] With th(e) Master *MNO.* 8 vast] *AB* large Σ. 10 but] paint *HJ.* 11 Youth] Youths *KLMNO.* 12 and at] *A* Spilt and *B* spilt or Σ. 13–14 *omitted CD.* 13 invoke] provoke *B.* 14 cruel] Barbarous *E* fatal *HJKLMNO.* 16 Laws] law *HJ.* 19 set] Sit(t) *AB.* 21 There] Then *D* This *GKMNO* Thus *L.* 25 in] *BC* with Σ. 28 Flame] brains *AB* brain *CKL.* 29–30] *AB omitted* Σ. 31 place] stands *CD.* 33 undescended] undiscovered *B* undeserved *C* undistinguish'd *E.* 34 not discover'd] not distinguish'd *E* undiscover'd *KLMNO.* 37 his] this *ADEKLMN.* 39 Lust] Ca(ba)lls[?] *B* Lusts *EFGHJ.* 43–44 *omitted CD.* 44 Name] man *HJ* Land *L.* 45 retire] withdraw *BCD* Insolence] Impudence *KLMNO.* 46 T'expose] T'Express *BE.* 47 Moments] minutes *BHJK.* 48 Hellish] *AB* guilty Σ Ears] *ABC* eyes Σ. 49 you] they *E* we *KLMNO* the] their *AB* a *G.* 51 *Keppell*] W— *AB.* 52 Omen] Omens *EFG.* 54 let me] may I *KLMNO.* 56 even] every *D* now thy *HJ.* 57 the] *ABC* shifting *E* that Σ. 59 Principles] Principle *KNO.* 60 Disguises] disquiet *AB.* 62 supple] *ADEFHJ* subtle Σ. 63 Trusted, yet always] *AB* Still Trusted, and still *E* Confided in, still *F* Confident Still, Still *G* Confided still, still Σ forfeiting] *ACDEF* failing in *HJ* forfeited Σ. 65 *omitted CD* prostituted Faith alone] *AB* Witchery and prosti-

tuted Faith *HJ* Treachery and Prostituted Faith Σ. 66 And this] *AB* This *KLM* That *NO* Yet this Σ. 67 sinking] *CDOP* falling Σ. 71 set] Sit(t) *AB.* 73 Darling] darlings *DELMNO.* 78 Bounty] *AB* Bounties *FGHJ* pensions Σ. 79 Liberty] *ABCKN* Liberties Σ. 83 monstrous] *AB* matchless Σ. 84 successful Villanies] *AB* successful Villany *HJ* consummate Villanyes *K* consummate Villany Σ. 86–87 *omitted CD.* 87 Product] *AB* Project Σ. 88–89 *omitted CDE.* 88 Profit] *AB* prospect Σ conduces] *AB* conductive *F* conducting *H* conducing *J* conducive Σ. 90–91 *omitted CD.* 90 Things] *ABE* Terms Σ. 92–96 *MS. torn A.* 92–101 *omitted CDG.* 93 Principles] Liberties *EKLMNO.* 95 Thus] So *EFKLMNO.* 96 Couch] Croutch *F* Creep *EKMNO* Keep *L.* 97 some lucky] *AB* some fatall *EFHJ* a Fatal Σ. 98 Fraud opprest] Frowne opprest *B* Usage prest *EKLMNOP.* 99 Resentment] Resentments *AEKMNO.* 106 the florid warlike] the warlike *ABO.* 108 *Sloan*] Hartington *LM* H—n *O.* 110 *Yorkshire*] Northern *CD.* 113 Rancour] temper *ABEFGHJ.* 115 roiling wither'd] *A —withered B* wither'd sowered *FG* weak sour *J* wither'd sour Σ. 117 Joys] *AEK* Joy Σ. 118 the] this *CDE* that *FHJ.* 121 for Liberty] of Liberty *ABC.* 122 In th' House for Millions, out for] Votes Millions talks of *C* He votes for Millions, talkes for *D.* 124 The] *ABD* That Σ. 125–26 *omitted F.* 125 Near] Next *ABCD.* 126 his] Chit's *HJ.* 127–30 *omitted CD.* 127–30]

One hasty Sketch, Painter on B—l bestow
For Sugar Plumms grown an Apostate too:
Whose bubl'd Youth not true to Any Side,
Shifts with each Wind, and Turns to ev'ry Tide
Deprav'd by Nature, and the Lust of Change,
To some young hoyden Wench inclin'd to Range
By her Imprudence does her Flame destroy
Is mark'd for Whore, and never Tastes the Joy. *E*

127 our] Crop Ear'd *KLMNOP.* 130 Buggery] beggary *A* Begging *B.* 132 *Hobart*] Scrib Lownds *A.* 133 *Hawles*] *FHJ* Boyl *CD* the rest *E — GO* P— *P* Ra(ne)la(u)gh Σ. 135 poll] *C* baule Σ. 136 And] To *HJ.* 138 Reason] Vertue *KLMNO* lies] dyes *CDE.* 139–46 *MS. torn A.* 139 still] yet *BHJ.* 140 *omitted C.* 142 Ruin] ruines *BG.* 143 the] a *EKLMNO* some *G.* 145 undiscover'd, yet will us] *C* sly and undiscover'd yet *B* undiscovered yet with ease *DEFGHJ* Undiscover'd yet, will us with Ease Σ.

The Play-House

Copy text: A Pacquet from Parnassus, Vol. I, No. 2, 1702, 18–21 (Yale copy: Z17.217).

Collation: Assumed to represent the archetype most closely are the copy text (*A*) and University of Chicago MS. PR1195.C72, pp. 130–33, identical witnesses except that the latter reads "who" for "that" in line 31. The text of the poem in *POAS,* 1703, 2, 374–77, is derived from *A,* and that in *A New Collection of Poems,* Dublin, 1721, pp. 59–63, in turn, is derived from *POAS,* 1703. The text of *PRSA,* 1705, pp. 486–89 (*B*), however, may represent an independent derivation from the archetype.

In 1706 the poem was revised upon the occasion of the reopening of the playhouse at Dorset Garden, which was also under the management of Christopher Rich (*London Stage,* 2, xxiii–xxiv). The revised poem, entitled *A Description of the Play-House in Dorset-Garden,* was published in a folio half-sheet of which the Luttrell copy (in the Newberry Library) is dated 23 July 1706. The witnesses that seem to represent the archetype of the revised poem most closely, however, are those in *The Poetical Works of the Honourable Sir Charles Sedley,* 1707, pp. 202–07 (*C*) and in Osborn MS. Box 22, No. 20, ff. [33v–36] (*D*). Another witness, BM MS. Harleian 7315, ff. 288–90v (*E*), derives from a source different from the source of *CD.* It was, however, from the source of *E,* and not from the source of *CD,* that the 1706 broadside was set up.

Title: The Play-House: A Satyr. By T. G. *Gent. A The Play-House: A Satyr, By Mr.* A. D——n *B The Play-House.* By *J. Addison,* Esq; *C* Mr. Adison of Magd:s Poem on Ye Playhouse 1699 *D* The Play House/1699 *E.*

1] Where gentle *Thames* through stately Channels Glides *CD* Where gently Thames in stately Channells glides *E.* 2] To pick up Cullies to increase the Stock *B* And *Englands* proud Metropolis divides *CD* All Englands proud Metropolis devides *E.* 4 round the Place] o'er the Waves *CDE.* 7 *Rich*] *R— AB* Heroes] Monarchs *AB.* 10 draines the Town] Rakes the Stews *CDE.* 24 Trees] Streets *D.* 27 rising] Neig(h)b(ou)ring *AB.* 30–31 *omitted D.* 33 fits] acts *D* fills *E.* 34 Swagging Belly] swaggering Belly *AB* swagging Bellys *E.* 35 Pale] But *C.* 38 Tone] voice *D* *Farquhar*] *F——r AB Congreve CDE.* 40 Mincing] Whineing *C.* 41 Character] Character's *ABD.* 42 haughty] mighty *AB.* 44 Royal] regall *D* awful] Haughty *AB.* 46 Vassals] Rascalls *AB.* 51 a] her *D.* 52 Sallow] Ghastly *ABCE.* 59 last] length *ABD.* 62 and . . . Nature] in . . . Nature's *E.* 67 There] Then *D.* 75 Where] There *CD* Here *E.* 76 cares that wait] care that waits *AB.* 77 painted] pointed *AB.* 80 Patches] Washes *CDE.* 83 Beauties run in] Beauty run in *ABC* Beauty run as *E.* 86 So the same] So the fam'd CE Thus the famd D. 87 that] and D. 94 mealy] meager *AB.* 96 Swords and Shields] Shields and Swords *CE* Helms and Sheildes *D.* 105 Lawrells] honours *D.* 110 in his own vile Tatters stinks] is in *Statu quo,* himself *AB.*

The Brawny Bishop's Complaint

Copy text: POAS, 1704, *3,* 372–73 (Yale copy).

Collation: The text survives in two traditions, of which the superior is represented by 10 factory manuscripts, and the inferior by five independent manuscripts and six printed editions. The large number of manuscripts may reflect the fact that no broadside edition was published, presumably because the poem was intentionally libelous. The factory manuscripts are the following:

BM MS. Add. 21094, ff. 65v–66	*A*
Holkham MS. 686, pp. 333–35	*B*
Bodl. MS. Rawl. poet. 172, f. 121	*C*
Folger MS. M.b.12, ff. 199v–200v	*D*
Portland MS. Pw V 44, pp. 240–42	*E*
Portland MS. Pw V 48, pp. 245–47	*F*
BM MS. Add. 27408, f. 26	*G*
Osborn MS. Chest II, No. 1 (Phillipps 8301)	*H*
BM MS. Harleian 7315, ff. 281–82	*J*

The text of BM MS. Lansdowne 852, ff. 118v–119, is derived from *J* and has no independent value.

The inferior tradition is represented by the following witnesses:

BM MS. Add. 40060, ff. 3–4	*K*
Bodl. MS. Firth b.21 (57)	*L*
Portland MS. Pw V 41, f. 131	*M*
TCD MS. I.5, *1,* 65–67	*N*
BM MS. Stowe 305, ff. 234v–35	*O*
POAS, 1704, *3,* 372–73	*P*

It is likely that the derivation of *K* and *L* is successive rather than collateral, but lack of evidence makes it impossible to determine the direction. *M* is a fragmentary manuscript lacking lines 23–45.

There is evidence of conflation between the two groups. In *H,* for example, lines 10–11 are omitted, but have been supplied, in a different hand, from a manuscript of the inferior group. Conversely, at line 34 the unique reading of *H* has been altered to conform to the reading of the superior group. At line 39 the scribe of *L* originally wrote "a Protestant Reign," which is the reading of *KP,* and then overwrote "the Protestant Reign," which is the reading of *ABCDEFGH.* At line 41 the scribe of *O* first wrote "are all," the reading of *ABCDEFJN,* and then overwrote "all are," the reading of *GHKLOP.*

All the printed versions derive from *POAS,* 1704, *3*. The most probable relation among them is represented in the following diagram:

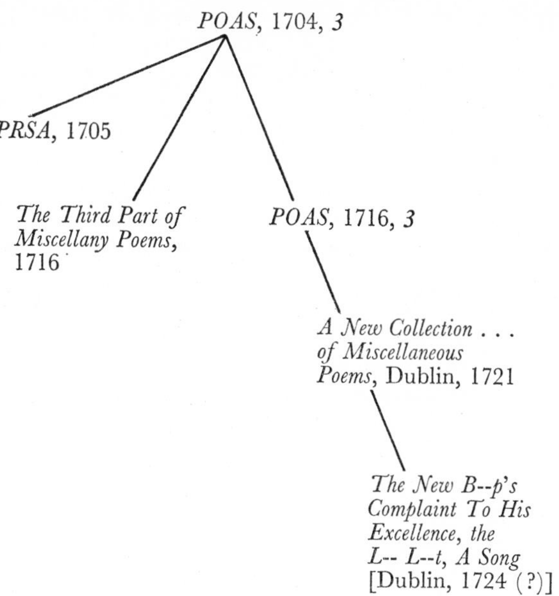

The Dublin folio half-sheet edition is a reworking of the poem to fit a new situation, just as was done in the case of *A Satyr upon the French King* (p. 713, above).

Title: An Excellent New Ballad to the Tune of Packington's Pound *ABCDFJ* A Ballad on the Bishop of Salisbury To the Tune of Packington's Pound *E* A New Ballad to the Tune of Packington's Pound *GN* An Excellent Ballad to the Tune of Packington's Pound *H* A Ballad to the Tune of Packington's Pound *K* A Ballad on Building up the Seats in St. James's Chappel to the Tune of Packington's Pound *L* On Building up the Pews at St. Jameses Chappell *O* A New Ballad, call'd The Brawny Bishop's Complaint. To the Tune of Packington's Pound *P.*

1 perceiv'd that the] perceived the *P.* 2 Who] That *O* flock] flock'd *JKLP* holy] hilly *P.* 3 their Lovers above their] their Lovers their *ABN* the Lovers above their *K* their Lovers about their *O* their Lovers the kindest *P.* 4 not at him] not him *H* not on him *KLMNOP* when he] that *O* while he *P.* 5 the Princess] Princes *M.* 6 With a pious] With pious *NOP.* 7 This . . . ill] These . . . ills *L.* 8 said] quoth *P* our Religion's quite] our Religion is *ABCFGHJKMNP* all Religion is *L* Religion is *O.* 9 thus] they *G.* 10 observes] observe *G* observed *HJ* perceives *KL* sees *M* labour'd] *A* labour Σ. 11 raise] whet[?] *K.*

12 And sure] Sure *O* preach] speake *O* will] must *L*. 13 That their] Their *K* pointed at] fix'd upon *E* pointed on *P*. 14 can] can't *P*. 15 No] One *P*. 16 My Parts] My prayers *K* As my Parts *P* or] nor *ABCDEFKN* Person] Presence *P*. 17 a] the *JMO* one feminine] a feminine *NO* any one *P*. 18 those] that *K* and] or *L*. 19 These] Those *BJ* The *K* Truth] Ruth *O*. 25 'Tis a Mercy] 'Tis mercy *J*. 26 Shape] Shapes *KOP* Fancies] Fancy *GH*. 27 me] not *E* the] their *DFG* his *O*. 30 may] will *K* men *O* so] as *L* for *P*. 31 Who] To *OP* in the] in a *B* at the *H* on the *O*. 32 Therefore pray] Therefore *K* Then pray *P*. 33 end] mend *ELN*. 34 Vineyard those] Vineyard these *GO* Vines those lewd *H* Vineyard the *KL* Vineyards such *P*. 35 Beauties] Ladys *O*. 37 Importunity] opportunity *J* Importunities *P*. 38 his Reasons, allow'd his Request] the Person respected the Priest *KL*. 39 *Britain*'s] Brittish *O* in this Protestant] in Protestant *J* in a Protestant *KP*. 41 they] we *L* all are] are all *ABCDEFJN*. 42 For as] As *P*. 44 from her Bondage] from the Bondage *LNO* from Bondage *P*. 45 Lady] Lass *P* the] a *K*.

An Encomium upon a Parliament

Copy text: POAS, 1703, 2, 241–45 (Princeton copy).

Collation: Eighteen witnesses to the text have survived in manuscript. Seven of these are derived collaterally from a common source:

Bodl. MS. Firth b.21, pp. 45–46	*A*
BM MS. Sloane 2717, pp. 70–71	*B*
BM MS. Stowe 305, f. 235	*C*
BM Harleian 7315, ff. 282–84v	*D*
Portland MS. Pw V 48, pp. 248–53	*E*
Folger MS. M.b.12, pp. 200–05	*F*
Portland MS. Pw V 44, pp. 263–70	*G*

Since BM MS. Lansdowne 852, ff. 119–20v is derived from *D,* its variants have not been recorded.

The remaining manuscripts derive from a common source different from the source of *ABCDEFG*. These are:

Harvard MS. 606, pp. 31–35	*H*
Osborn MS. Chest II, No. 58, no fol.	*J*
Osborn MS. Chest II, No. 2 (Phillipps 8302), f. 91	*K*
BM MS. Add. 29497, ff. 107–08	*L*
Portland MS. Pw V 41, ff. 123–26	*M*
TCD MS. I.5, 2, 35–36	*N*

BM MS. Stowe 747, f. 138 *O*
Osborn MS. Chest II, No. 18, pp. 13–19 *P*
Bodl. MS. Rawl. poet 169 (1) *Q*

N is a fragmentary manuscript of lines 1–45 only. Two more fragmentary manuscripts, *O* and *P,* omit lines 41–45 and 16–20, respectively. The readings of a fourth fragmentary manuscript, Bodl. MS. Rawl. poet 169 (17), which may be a memorial reconstruction, are not included in the apparatus. Of the two branches of the manuscript tradition, the first, *ABCDEFG,* is slightly superior.

The printed texts, which derive from the source of *HJKLMNOPQ,* are the following:

POAS, 1703, 2, 241–45 *R*
PRSA, 1705, pp. 381–84 S

The second and third editions of *R* are successive line-by-line resettings of *R,* but *S* was set up from the third edition of *R* corrected by a manuscript similar to *HJ.*

Four stanzas of the poem, lines 21–25, 41–45, 86–95, are quoted (from a manuscript of the *HJKLMNOPQ* type) in *Cursory Remarks upon Some Late Disloyal Proceedings in Several Cabals,* 1699 (Wing C7687), together with seven additional stanzas that appear in no other witness. The added stanzas, however, were immediately recognized to be the work of "the *Remarker,*" not of the "late bold Encomiaster," Defoe (*A Just Rebuke of a Late Unmannerly Libel, in Defence of the Court: Entituled, Cursory Remarks upon Some Late Disloyal Proceedings, &c.,* 1699, p. 11).

Title: An Encomium upon a Parliament *ABCEFGKL* An Encomium upon the Parliament *DO* A Satyr on the Parliament *H* Upon the Parliament of Paris *N* The Parliament *P* The Patriots *RS.*

1 Ye] Goe *A* You *LMO* Ye worthy Patriots] Ye Patriots *R* Patriots] Patrons *A.* 3 but your] but not your *A.* 4 *omitted BC* but] and *JKL.* 6 Freedom] *AJLNQRS* Friends *B* forces *C* Freedoms Σ secure] Restore *J.* 7 And all our Friends] And all our Troops *N* Our ffriends for to *Q.* 8 Fools] Men *HRS* ffolks *M* Tooles *Q.* 9 knew no better than to] know us noe better than to *AB* knew us no better than to *C* know no better than *D* knew's no better than *EF* knows no better than *G* were such fools as to *HRS* knew no better than *JK* knows no better than to *O* were such fools for too *Q.* 10 help] save *L.* 11 And] Then *JM* hear] hears *GJKLOS.* 12 relieve] relieves *GJKL.* 13 like those without their] without your thanks or *ADEFG.* 14 with] in *J.* 16–20 *omitted P.* 16 e're] once *MN.* 17 This] Thy *L.* 18 list] 'list *O.* 19 your] the *NORS.* 20 To be like us] And so be all *N* like us to be *O.* 21 bestow'd] disposs'd *A.* 24 Would] will *MN.* 26 ye have] You did *N* once you *S.* 28 You have] You in *ACJKPRS*

You *H* have him *LO* was on *M* You him *NQ* Request] Suit have *AHR*. 31 that] who *MO*. 33 fear] hate *A*. 34 And have] have *HNOQRS* that have *M*. 35 mortify] Rob us of *N* our] *HMNO* there *A* your *RS* the Σ. 37 Laws] Law *AJ* Laws made *ex*] Laws ex *BEFG*. 38 Who] And *P*. 39 married Women] *CHQRS* make a Whore to *D* can make marryed women *M* Married Strumpetts *N* make marryed women Σ. 41–45 *omitted O*. 41 purify the] purge the men of *H*. 42 the] all *N*. 43 send] bring *H*. 44 get] you *H*. 46 to reestablish] for to establish *RD*. 47 our] your *HL*. 49 And borrow on] And on borrowed *H* Borrow on *OQ* Funds that will ne'er] *MPQ* friends ne'er to *O* Funds will ne'er Σ. 51 our] your *LM* Gold] good *Q*. 53 what] that *S*. 55 Or let them all] if not lett them *L*. 56 Missives] messages *P* you] now *BCEQ* round about] all about *HJLO* about *P*. 59 Which] *RS* Whom Σ believe] *RS* obey Σ. 60 no] the *E*. 61 You] With *RS*. 64 want] meet *M*. 65 that] this *CM*. 66 our] the *B* your *G*. 67 On . . . and Glass and] On . . . Glasse and *A* On . . . on Glasse and *CDKQR* On . . . on Glass on *GJPS* Our . . . and glasse and *H* and . . . and glass and *LM* on . . . glass ware and *O*. 68 in] on *M*. 69 Then] *JL* And Σ drop] dropt *DHMPRS*. 70 sink] sunk *DHPQRS* cheat *L*. 71 piously] Jealously *M*. 73 your] *AHMRS* that Σ. 74 pay the neglected] pay neglected *AHRS*. 75 make] *BCDEFHQ* makes Σ. 78 And] but *LPQ* your] the *RS*. 79 that e'er were] that e'er we *BCFG* were ever *P*. 80 And the] But the *C* And *RS*. 81 'Twas] You *L* once] first *H*. 82 Whoring] whoredom *L*. 84 grow so] be too *H* grow too *LMOPQ*. 86 your] their *AJ*. 89 would soon have] had quickly *M*. 92 work] make *BCDEFG*. 94 things that have] that which hath *H*. 96 choicely] merrily *A* employ'd] improv'd *KL*. 100 Debts which are] Deponent *A* Debts *HMO* Deponents *RS*. 101 leave this] leave off this *BEFP*.

The Dispensary

*Sigla:**

1699¹ The Dispensary: A Poem . . . 1699.
1699² The Dispensary: A Poem . . . The Second Edition . . . 1699.
1699³ The Dispensary: A Poem . . . The Third Edition . . . 1699.
1700 The Dispensary. A Poem . . . The Fourth Edition . . . 1700.
1703 The Dispensary. A Poem . . . The Fifth Edition . . . 1703.
1703A The Dispensary. A Poem . . . The Fifth Edition . . . 1703, Yale Medical Library copy with MS. emendations.
1706 The Dispensary. A Poem . . . The Sixth Edition . . . 1706.
1714 The Dispensary. A Poem . . . The Seventh Edition . . . 1714.
1718 The Dispensary. A Poem . . . The Eighth Edition . . . 1718.

Copy text: 1699[2] was chosen as copy text because the intention of this edition is to present *The Dispensary* in its historical context as an event of 1699. Although *1718,* published less than a year before his death, obviously represents Garth's final revision of the text, it does not, with its allusions to Marlborough's victories and dismissal in 1712, represent the poem which originated in a controversy of 1687–99 and which elicited replies in 1699–1700. Furthermore, the poem is readily available in its final form since all subsequent editions derive from *1718.* The decision to base the text on the second edition was also made in the belief that *1699*[2] is a better poem than *1718.* This was the opinion of Thomas Killigrew, who imagined the ceremony by which Garth was "made free of *Parnassus*" in these terms:

> Before him was carried the *Dispensary* . . . but I was surpriz'd to find, that the Book that was carry'd before him was in *Quarto;* which made me suppose it was the first Edition.
>
> (*Miscellanea Aurea,* 1720, p. 32)

It was the opposite opinion, however, that became a commonplace of eighteenth-century criticism. Pope's dictum that "there was hardly an alteration of the innumerable ones through every edition, that was not for the better" (Jonathan Richardson, *Richardsoniana,* 2 vols., 1776, *1,* 195–96 *n.*) was canonized in 1779 when it was quoted by Samuel Johnson in his *Life of Garth,* but this opinion would not be shared by many readers today. Many of the additions are repetitions of situations or turns of phrase already in the poem. Others are clearly adventitious or anachronistic. Still others are merely hackneyed. The fact that *1718* deletes 16 of the lines that were added in *1714* indicates that Garth himself did not believe that "Every Thing he added hath been an Embellishment to his *Poem,*" as Richardson Pack claimed in 1719 (*Miscellanies in Verse and Prose,* 2nd ed., 1719, pp. 96–97).

Wilhelm Leicht, who edited *The Dispensary* in 1905, chose as his copy text the first collected edition of Garth's works, published by F. Cogan in 1749, which he called *W*. Leicht explained that "Mit ein Grund, *W* für diese kritische Ausgabe zu benutzen, war der Umstand, dasz, wie aus den Varianten zu ersehen ist, in *W* verschiedene Änderungen an Versen vorgenommen sind, die sich in keiner der Einzelauflagen finden. Wer diese Änderungen vornahm, ist mir unbekannt. *W* ist auszerdem die erste Ausgabe, die die Schreibung insofern normalisierte, als sie sämtliche Wörter mit Ausnahme des Zeilenanfangs und der Eigennamen klein schrieb" (p. 20). Actually, however, there is no mystery about these "variants." They are deleted passages from earlier editions, printed in *1749* as footnotes. Otherwise *1749* is a line-by-line resetting of *1718.* Furthermore, it is by no means the first attempt to normalize the accidentals of the text. Similar attempts were made in *1703* and *1706.* All that *1749* does is to normalize the text according to printing-house practice of the mid-eighteenth century: it reduces capitals to lower case (even where capitals are now required, as in "Christian," the "Rose" tavern, and the goddess "Earth"), and omits italics and the final "k" from words like "critick."

1699^2 was chosen rather than *1699*^{1} for quite different reasons. Despite some careless presswork *1699*^{2} is more carefully edited and more accurately printed than *1699*^{1}. It is, in fact, an "authorized version" of *1699*^{1}. Besides the 72 lines that Garth revised, *1699*^{2} corrects nearly all of the 40-odd misprints in *1699*^{1} and introduces only about a dozen new ones. These new ones have been silently corrected in the present edition. The following changes have also been made without being recorded in the *apparatus criticus:*

1. letters omitted from proper names have been supplied;
2. direct discourse is introduced by a colon and the first word is capitalized;
3. wherever necessary in order to avoid misunderstanding (in about two dozen cases), punctuation is supplied or brought into conformity with modern usage;
4. the spelling of "yew" and "haste" has been normalized to prevent confusion with "ewe" and "hast," as the words sometimes appear in *1699*^{2}.

Otherwise the text of the present edition, both in substance and accident, is that of *1699*^{2}. The fact that it reads "bloted" at *2,* 17 and "Bloated" at *6,* 123 is a condition of the language, not merely of typographical practice of the period, and to normalize these inconsistencies would be to conceal linguistic facts.

Collation: 1699^1 is the "bad quarto" of *The Dispensary*. Garth himself was not surprised to find it "uncorrect," for he knew that the poem, in some still undetermined manner, "stole into the World." Evidence of "the Publisher's Precipitation," of which Garth complained in the preface to *1699*^{2}*,* is to be found on nearly every page. Besides some 40-odd misprints in the text, there are "Errours of the Printer" in the running titles ("Canto I" for "Canto II" on D4r and "Canto III" for "Canto IV" on K3r and K4r), catchwords ("These" for "Some" on K4r, and none on E3v), and signatures (M2 is missigned L2). The volume includes the text of 1418 lines and a few marginal notes, with no frontispiece, no prefatory material, and of course no Key. As an earlier editor has remarked, "Die erste Auflage ist in ziemlich schmucklosen Gewand hergestellt" (Leicht, p. 20). Its publication was advertised in *The Post Boy* for 6–8 May 1699.

1699^2*,* the first octavo edition, was advertised in *The Post Boy* for 25–27 May 1699. It is a line-by-line resetting of *1699*^{1} and bears the marks of careful editing but careless presswork; 72 lines are revised by the author and nearly all the 40-odd misprints of *1699*^{1} are corrected. But more than a dozen new ones are introduced and early copies of the run, represented by the Yale Medical Library copy, are full of errors in pagination, catchwords, and running titles. In later copies, represented by the Newberry Library copy, the errors in pagination are corrected, but not the misprints or other mechanical errors. This is the first edition that includes as a frontispiece Michael Van der Gucht's engraving of the Cutlerian Theatre, the part of the Royal College of Physicians facing Warwick Lane. *1699*^{2} also includes, for the first time, the prefatory material that appears in all subsequent editions: the Dedication to Anthony

Henley, The Preface, The Copy of an Instrument . . . in relation to the Sick Poor subscribed by 53 members of the Royal College of Physicians, and commendatory verses signed C. Boyle, Chr. Codrington, Tho. Cheek, and H. Blount. Garth also added 2 lines (*2*, 60–61) to the text.

1699³ was advertised in *The Post Boy* for 13–15 June 1699. It retains most of the misprints of *1699²*, of which it is a line-by-line resetting, adds about 20 new textual errors and a number of misprinted headlines ("Canto I" for "Canto II" on C1r, "Canto II" for "Canto III" on C8r, "Canto III" for "Canto IV" on D7r and D8r, and "Canto V" for "Canto VI" on F8r). The Northwestern University copy, however, includes a later state of the outer forme of sheet G which corrects the misprints in that forme, and there may be other copies with further corrections. The copy in the library of the Royal College of Physicians, which bears on its title page the signature of "S. Codrington" (presumably Samuel, the first cousin of Christopher Codrington), adds, in marginal annotation, most but not all of the readings of *1706*. For *1699³* Garth made only the slightest changes: he revised five lines, deleted six, and added nothing new.

For *1700*, which was advertised in *The Post Boy* for 9–11 April 1700, Garth revised 43 lines and added 34 new ones to bring the total to 1448. The printer responded by cutting down the number of misprints to about a dozen and almost eliminating mechanical errors (only a few catchwords, on [A]3v, a7r, a7v, a8v, and F1v, are omitted). The Chicago University copy is one of several in which two of the lines omitted from *1699³* (*4*, 97–98) are restored in a manuscript note.

1703 is a line-by-line resetting of *1700* with changes in accidentals only. It seems to be the first edition in which some consistency in styling is attempted. The compositor almost invariably changes " 'l" to " 'll", "Battel" to "Battle", "faulter'd" to "falter'd", "ne're", "e're" and "o're" to forms in " 'er", and terminal "y" or "ye" to "ie". The punctuation is also normalized. Some of the misprints of *1700* are corrected, but an equal number of new ones are introduced. *1703* also omits the same catchwords as *1700* and misnumbers page 73 as 37. The copy that Garth presented to Alexander Pope is now in the library of the Victoria & Albert Museum. Five of Pope's observations (incorporated into the footnotes of the present edition at *2*, 1, 37; *5*, 172; *6*, 44–47, 96) are recorded, in his own hand, on the flyleaf, but the annotation in the rest of the volume is in another hand.

1703A is an interleaved copy of *1703* in which extensive manuscript revisions have been made, in a hand not Garth's, both on the blank leaves and in the text itself. These changes amount to 414 lines added, 82 revised, and 104 deleted, making a poem of 1753 lines, a fourth longer than the earlier version. The additions include an attack on Francis Atterbury, whom readers identified with Urim (textual note *1*, 132), a "vision" of Queen Anne (textual note *2*, 47–69), the much-quoted lines on death, "To Die, is landing on some silent Shoar,/ Where Billows never break, nor Tempests roar" (textual note *3*, 174), and a "pre-romantic" evening song," The Ev'ning now with blushes warms the Air,/ The Steer resigns the Yoke, the Hind his Care" (textual note *4*, 237).

There is no evidence that *1706* was not set up directly from *1703A* with further corrections—46 lines revised and five deleted—being made in proof. If, on the other hand, the likelihood of the printer's copy text surviving seems slight, it may be assumed that *1703A* is a fair copy of the text that actually went to the printer. In any case, *1706* contains a few more misprints than *1703* and two misprinted catchwords ("And" for "How" on B1v and "Her" for "Here" on H4r). Otherwise it represents a second attempt to normalize the text. The compositor consistently capitalizes all nouns (and some pronouns, adjectives, and verbs as well), introduces apostrophes liberally in words like "list'ning," "am'rous," and even in "lou'd," and consistently prints forms like "Gyants," "Skyes" and "noysom" with an "i." The Yale Medical Library copy 1 is a large-paper copy that Garth presented to Charles Boyle, who had succeeded as fourth earl of Orrery in 1703. Alexander Pope's copy, with autograph annotations, is in the Huntington Library. The annotations, however, are disappointing. Some 40 of them are scattered through the first four cantos and there are none thereafter. Pope locates the gravel pits (*3*, 174 *n.*) in Kensington and surmises that Spadillio (see textual note *4*, 237) is the famous gambler, Boucher, but otherwise he offers nothing worth recording.

In 1709 there appeared two pirated editions, the first by Henry Hills. This edition prints the 1448 lines of *1700* and *1703* but with readings from *1699¹* and *1699²*, e.g. at *4*, 217 "gentle" (the reading of *1699¹–1699²*) instead of "courtly" (the reading of *1699³–1703*). The text, therefore, is a conflation of earlier editions with no independent value. All copies examined include the Van der Gucht plate of the Cutlerian Theatre, the prefatory material, and the booklist of Henry Hills. Some copies, such as the Newberry Library copy, also include *A Compleat Key to The Dispensary*, which, since it mentions "the late Lord Somers," who died in 1716, is probably a piracy of the *1718* Key published by James Roberts, which was bound into unsold copies of Hill's edition.

The second pirated edition in 1709 was published by John Bradford, who was referred to in 1709 as "a printer of other men's copies" (Plomer, p. 46). The pseudo-occasion for this edition is explained on the title page:

> Having seen an Edition of this Poem, printed by *H. Hills* in *Black-Fryers*, I had the Curiosity to Compare it with one I had in my Study, and upon Examination, found near *200* Lines omitted, which had been added by the Author to a later and better Impression; with several Errors Corrected through the whole: Which to oblige the Publick, I lent to the Printer of this Volume, being entirely satisfied it is a much more Correct and Authentick Copy than any hitherto printed; besides having the Advantage of the *Key* to Explain the *Persons* hinted at, and a Solution of every Thing that seems difficult to understand.

Very little of this is true, but it does demonstrate that *The Dispensary* was becoming a "difficult" poem only ten years after its first publication. There is no key in Bradford's edition, but it is the first edition to print some of the proper names in full, and others are identified in marginal notes. Copy text for Bradford's edition was apparently taken from *1699¹*, with additions (but none of the deletions) from later editions. This ran the text up to 1741 lines, nearly 300 lines more than Hill's edition, but still a dozen lines less than *1706*. Canto 2, for example, includes 212 lines: the 210 lines of *1699*[1] (five lines as revised in *1699*[2], but without the two lines that were added in *1699*[2]) plus two lines added in *1700*. The resultant hodge-podge has no value and is miserably printed.

In *1714 The Dispensary* became one of Jacob Tonson's duodecimo classics. When Tonson acquired the copyright he commissioned the Huguenot engraver Louis Du Guernier, who had done the plates for John Nutt's edition of *A Tale of a Tub,* to execute a new frontispiece and one plate illustrative of each of the six cantos of *The Dispensary*. The volume is also adorned with printer's ornaments in every available space. For this edition Garth made his last extensive revision of the text, adding 118 lines, revising 142, and deleting seven. It is unfortunate, therefore, that this is probably the worst printed of all authorized editions of *The Dispensary*. Obviously working from a revised copy of *1706,* the compositor managed to introduce some 50-odd misprints and more than a dozen mechanical errors; his punctuation introduces a whole new dimension of unintended humor into the poem. Compared with those of *1703A,* there is also a noticeable difference in the length and quality of the additions in *1714*. In *1703A* most of the 414 lines added are contained in more than a dozen long passages, but in *1714* most of the additions are short, only two (textual notes *3,* 40 and *5,* 83–88) being longer than six lines. In *1714* there are very few additions of which the reader will regret the omission from the present edition. After refusing for 15 years to vulgarize his text, Garth faltered and introduced urinal-throwing into the mock-epic battle in Canto *5:* "On *Stentor*'s Crest the useful Chrystal breaks,/And Tears of *Amber* gutter'd down his Cheeks" (textual note *5,* 206).

1718 is a line-by-line resetting of a revised, but uncorrected, copy of *1714*. In this last edition before his death in January 1719, Garth made no additions to the text, but revised four lines and deleted 16. Most of the misprints and some of the mechanical errors in *1714* are retained, but since the compositor corrected more than a dozen misprints, *1718* is a slightly improved text. It reprints all the prefatory material of the earlier editions and the seven Du Guernier plates added in *1714*. Some copies (e.g. the Yale Medical Library copy) are bound with *A Compleat Key to the Eighth Edition of The Dispensary,* printed for J. Roberts in 1718 and separately-paginated, but other copies (e.g. the Newberry Library copy) are not.

Canto 1

3 Whence 'twas] And why *1706–1718* frugal] cautious *1703A–1718*. they still] their Search *1706–1718*. 21–22]

Wrapt in the Shades of night the Goddess lies
Yet to the learn'd unveils her dark Disguise,
But shuns the gross access of vulgar Eyes. *1703A–1718*.

After 30 *1700–1718 add:*

How lambent Flames from life's bright Lamp arise,
And dart in emanations through the eyes;

31 How] While *1700–1703* briny] gentle *1703A–1718.* 32 T'extinguish] To slake a *1703A–1718* Heats] heat *1703A–1718.* 40 T'extend] To work *1703A–1706* T'exert *1714* recent Form, and stretch] brittle being up *1703A–1706* primogenial Heat and stretch *1714.* 48 *Scarsdale*] *S——* *1699*[1]*–1718.* 49 at th'*Olympick's*] at *Olympick's* 1706–1718. 50 *Finch*] *F—(ch)* *1699*[1]*–1718* *Sloan*] *S—(n)* *1699*[1]*–1718.* 51–52]

How Matter, by the vary'd shape of Pores,
Or Idiots frames, or solemn Senators. *1714–1718.*

52 *Methuen*] *M(e)——(n)* *1699*[1]*–1706* *Montague*] *M——gue* *1699*[1]*–1706.* 60 Substances, and Things] Figure, and a Form *1714–1718.* *After* 60 *1714–1718 add:*

How quick their Faculties the Limbs fulfil,
And act at ev'ry Summons of the Will.

63 those great . . . no more] no grand . . . descry'd *1714–1718.* 64 And . . . skulks] Mean . . . reigns *1714–1718* Learning shone before] Knowledge shou'd preside *1714–1718.* *After* 64 *1714–1718 add:*

Feuds are encreas'd, and Learning laid aside.
Thus *Synods* oft, Concern for Faith conceal;
And for important *Nothings* show a Zeal:

70 empty] sullen *1714–1718.* 74 The careless Deity supinely] Supine with folded Arms he thoughtless *1703A–1718.* 75–76]

Indulging Dreams his Godhead lull to Ease,
With murmurs of soft Rills, and whisp'ring Trees.
The Poppy and each numming Plant dispense
Their drowsy Virtue, and dull Indolence. *1703A–1718*

79 dull] dark *1703A–1718.* 80 bedew his thoughtless] bedew his gracious *1700–1703* hang ling'ring o'er his *1703A–1718.* 98 their swol'n] swelling *1714–1718.* 100 curling] with curl'd *1699*[1]. 103 Then, half erect, he rubb'd his op'ning] Listless he stretch'd, and gaping rubb'd his *1703A–1718.* 104 And] Then *1703A–1718.* 106 born] bless'd *1699*[3]. 107 Mortals hourly] 'tis, that Mortals *1699*[1]. 117 inactivity] Joys the night, in Vows

1703A–1718. 119 Some Rev'rend Worthies of the Gown can] My bright and blooming Clergy hourly *1699*[1]. *After* 132 *1703A–1718 add:*

Urim was civil, and not void of sense,
Had humour, and a courteous Confidence.
So spruce he moves, so gracefully he cocks;
The hallow'd Rose declares him Orthodox.
He pass'd his easie Hours, instead of Pray'r,
In Madrigals, and Phillising the Fair.
Constant at Feasts, and each Decorum knew,
As soon as the Dessert appear'd, withdrew.
Always obliging and without offence,
And fancy'd for his gay Impertinence.
But see how ill mistaken Parts succeed;
He threw off my Dominion, and would read;
Engag'd in Controversie, wrangl'd well,
In Convocation-Language could excell.
In Volumns prov'd the Church without Defence,
And guarded but by helpless Providence:
How Grace and Moderation disagree;
And Violence advances Charity.
Thus writ till none would read, becoming soon
A wretched Scribler, of a rare Buffoon.

135 in return, I ask but some Recess] all I ask are Shades and silent Bow'rs *1714–1718.* 136] To rellish the lov'd Extasies of Peace *1703A–1706* To pass in soft Forgetfullness my Hours *1714–1718.* *After* 136 *1714–1718 add:*

Oft have my Fears some distant *Villa* chose,
O'er their *Quietus* where fat *Judges* dose,
And lull their Cough and Conscience to repose:
Or if some *Cloyster*'s Refuge I implore,
Where holy *Drones* o'er dying Tapers snore:

137–38]

The Peals of *Nassau*'s Arms these Eyes unclose,
Mine he molests, to give the World Repose. *1714–1718.*

139 Still my Indulgence] That Ease I offer *1714–1718.* 141 Nor Skies nor] No threatning *1700–1703* Nor Climes, nor *1703A–1718.* 143–44]

With Arms resistless o're the Globe he flies,
And leaves to *Jove* the Empire o' the Skies. *1700–1718.*

147–48 *omitted 1703A–1718.* 149–50 *omitted 1703A–1706 restored 1714–1718* (see textual note *1*, 136). 151–58 *omitted 1703A–1718.* 153] Now since he has vouchsaf'd the World a Peace *1699¹* Since on the World his blessings he bestows *1700–1703*. 154 bid *Bellona* cease] settl'd a Repose *1700–1703*. 159 here, alas! I thought I might] in this rev'rend dome I sought *1703A–1718*. 161–64]

Here have I rul'd long and undisturb'd with Broils,
And laugh'd att Heroes, and their glorious Toils.
My Annals are in mouldy Mildews wrought, *1703A–1718*
With strong unlabour'd Impotence of Thought. *1703A–1706*
[With easie Insignificance of Thought. *1714–1718*].

165 I find some enterprizing] some busie Wretch's feavourish *1699¹* some busye enterprising *1703A–1718*. 173–75]

Or where dull Criticks Author's Fate foretel;
Or where stale Maids, or meager Eunuchs dwell. *1703A–1718*.

179 her Care enclines] she streight enclines *1700–1718*.

Canto 2

1 with gentle Sighs the ev'ning Breeze] the Ev'ning veil'd the Mountains Heads *1714–1718*. 2–3 *omitted* 1714–1718. 3 to wrap] had wrap'd *1699¹*. 4 While] And *1714–1718*. *After* 4 *1714–1718 add:*

Whilst sick'ning Flow'rs drink up the Silver Dew,
And *Beaus,* for some *Assembly,* dress anew;
The City Saints to Pray'rs and Play-house haste;
The Rich to Dinner, and the Poor to Rest:

5 did with speed prepare] then prepar'd with Care *1714–1718*. 7 He often sought] Oft he attempts *1700–1718*. 10 The hissing of her Snakes proclaim'd] He found, by th' hissing of her Snakes *1699¹*. 15–16]

In a dark Grott the balefull Haggard lay,
Breathing black vengeance, and infecting Day.
But how deform'd and worn with Spightfull Woes, *1703A–1718*
Rapacious Verres, late a Statesman, knows. *1703A–1706*
[When *Accius* has Applause *Dorsennus* shows. *1714–1718*]
The chearfull blood her meager Cheeks forsook,
And Basilisks sate brooding in her Look. *1703A–1718*.

18 The] And *1699¹*. 19–22]

From her chapp'd Nostrils scalding Torrents fall,
And her sunk Eyes boil o'er in Floods of Gall.

Volcano's labour thus with inward Pains
Whilst Seas of melted Oar lye [lay *1714–1718*] waste the Plains.
Around the Fiend in hideous Order sate
Foul bawling Infamy, and bold Debate;
Gruff Discontent, thro' Ignorance miss-led,
And clam'rous Faction at her Party's Head,
Restless Sedition, still dissembling Fear,
And sly Hypocrisie with Pious Leer.
Glouting with sullen spight the Fury shook
Her clotter'd Locks, and blasted with each Look. *1703A–1718.*

23 Then] And *1699*[1] rends] tore *1703A–1718.* 28 That, the fam'd] And That, the *1699*[1]. 30 all pale, th'expiring] like setting Stars, the *1700–1718.* 36 the Glorious] th'immortal *1699*[1] *1714–1718* the wondrous *1700–1706* of] on *1699*[1]. 37 th'airy] the light *1703A–1718.* 41 essay'd] convey'd *1703A–1718.* 42 T'inform the Fiend, then] His Errand, then he *1703A–1718.* 45 She] Then *1703A–1718.* 47–69]

Thus she—Mankind are bless'd, they riot still
Unbounded in exorbitance of Ill.
By Devastation the rough Warrior gains,
And Farmers fatten most when Famine reigns;
For sickly seasons the Physitians wait,
And Politicians thrive in Broils of State.
The Lover's easie when the Fair one sighs,
And Gods subsist not but by Sacrifice.
Each other Being some Indulgence knows,
Few are my Joys, but infinite my Woes.
My present pain Britannia's Genius wills,
And thus the Fates record my future Ills.
A Heroine shall Albion's Scepter bear,
With Arms shall vanquish Earth, and Heav'n with Pray'r.
She on the World her Clemency shall Show'r,
And only to preserve, exert her Pow'r.
Tyrants shall then their impious Aims forbear,
And Blenheim's Thunder, more than Ætna's, fear. *1703A–1718.*

51 *Tenison's*] *Te——ns* *1699*[1]*–1703.* 52 At last has rais'd him] Has rais'd his Virtues *1699*[1]. 53 *Somers*] *S(o)—rs* *1699*[1]*–1703.* 54 are oppress'd] now need weep *1699*[1]. 55 *Pembroke*] *Pem—ke* *1699*[1]*–1703.* 57 *Ormond*] *O—nd* *1699*[2]*–1703.* 57–58]

Unshaken is the Throne and safe its Lord,
Whilst *Macclesfield* or *Ormond* wears a Sword. *1699*[1].

59–60]

When *Devonshire* appears, all Eyes confess
An easie Grandeur graces his Address. *1700–1703.*

60 *Devonshire*] *De——re 1699*[1]*–1699*[3]. 61–62 *omitted 1699*[1]. 61 *Macclesfield*] *M——ld 1699*[2]*–1703*. 63 radiant] shining *1699*[1]. 64 *Portland*] *P—land 1699*[1]*–1703* *Jersey*] *I—sey 1699*[1]*–1703*. 66 *Montague*] *M—gue 1699*[1]*–1703*. 68 *Vernon's*] *V—ns 1699*[1]*–1703*. 70 by no Arts I therefore] *therefore* by no Arts I *1699*[1]. 78 he'd] did *1714–1718*. 81 starch'd Urbanity his] vain Formality his *1699*[1] trifling Show his Tinsel *1714–1718*. 82 Form the want of Intellects] th'empty Head's defects, the Band *1699*[1]. *After* 82 *1714–1718 add:*

In Aspect grand and goodly He appears,
Rever'd as Patriarchs in primaeval Years.

85–86]

The Patient's Ears remorsless he assails,
Murthers with Jargon where his Med'cine fails. *1703A–1718*.

92 T'increase their Ills, and throng] For ruine throng, and pay *1703A–1718*. 93 *Wight* all Mercenary] *Visionarie* various *1714–1718*. 100 *Brownlow*] *B(r)—(w) 1699*[1]*–1718* *Grace*] *G—(ce) 1699*[1] *1706–1718 F—— 1699*[2]*–1699*[3] *—— 1700–1703*. 104 bright] lov'd *1714–1718*. 105 that a Thousand Pound supplies] such bright Heraldry can prove *1714–1718*. 106] The vile *Plebeian* but the third from *Jove*. *1714–1718*. 130 Enquire when courteous] Wou'd know how soon kind *1699*[1]. 139 must] wou'd *1700–1718*. 149 Bleak Envy these . . . with Pleasure sees] With pleasure those . . . bleak Envy sees *1699*[1]. 164 but the great] to't, but the *1699*[1]. 170 Mortars utter their Attempts] their attempts their Mortars speak *1699*[1]. 181 of *Physicians*] insolently *1714–1718*. 183 *Crabs* Eyes as well] Then let *Crabs* Eyes *1706–1718* Use may] Virtue *1706–1718*. 188 spightfully th'intrinsick Value] their true Value treacherously *1714–1718*. 189–190]

Nay more: Inhumanly They'l force us soon
T'exert our Charity, and be undone;
Whilst We, at our expence, must persevere,
And, for another World, be ruin'd here. *1700–1706*
Nay, They discover too, (their spight is such,)
That Health, than Crowns more valu'd, costs not much.
Whilst we must steer our Conduct by these Rules,
To cheat as Tradesmen, or to starve as Fools. *1714–1718*.

203 But] Yet *1700–1718*. 206 Bethought th'Assistant of] By *Squirt*'s nice Hand apply'd *1700–1718*. 207 Whose Steam the Wight no sooner did] The Wight no sooner did the Steam *1700–1718*. 211 The Great *Pelides, Thetis* found] *Pelides* did blue *Thetis* see *1699*[1]. 212 Fishy Smell] oozy scent *1703A–1706* Sea-weed Scent *1714–1718* th'Azure Goddess own'd] own'd her Deity *1699*[1].

Canto 3

4 spoke] said *1714–1718.* 6 *Salmon's*] *S—(nd's) 1699¹–1718.* 7 all those] those bless'd *1706–1718.* 11–12]

> The Earth has rowl'd twelve annual turns, and more,
> Since first high Heav'ns bright Orbs I've number'd ore. *1699¹*

14 I once thought] Some granted *1714–1718.* 22] You'l hardly e're convince a Fool, He's so: *1700–1703* You'll ne'er convince a Fool, himself is so: *1703A–1718.* 24 Pleasure lies in] only Pleasure's *1700–1718.* 27 Prospects at distance please, but when we're near, *1699¹.* 34 despise] they leave *1706–1718.* 36 grows a] becomes *1700–1718.* *After* 40 *1714–1718 add:*

> So proud of Praise, for That their Ease they slight;
> Yet never think the Rabble in the right.
> Thus Priests their Pagan Gods profanely mock;
> And know that Sacrifice is only Smoke.
> They find, if some great Enterprise they view,
> Oft more to Folly, than to Prudence due.
> Or if some matchless Conduct shou'd appear,
> They call the Valour, Heat; the Caution, Fear. *1714*
> So false their Censure, fickle their Esteem,
> This Hour they Worship; and the next Blaspheme. *1714–1718*
> Tho' honour'd as some God a *Heroe* shines,
> And Valour executes what Skill designs;
> Tho' rescu'd Nations their Deliv'rance own,
> And Monarchs sit unshaken on a Throne,
> Whilst proud Oppressors their vain Hopes give o'er,
> And tremble at the Chains They forg'd before;
> Yet if th'amazing Issue we survey,
> We find that *Fame* has Wings, and flies away. *1714.*

45–46]

> Be aw'd, if puny Emmets wou'd oppress;
> Or fear their Fury, or their Name caress? *1714–1718.*

After 54 *1714–1718 add:*

> Drums, Trumpets, Haut-boys wake the slumbring Pair;
> Whilst Bridegroom sighs, and thinks the Bride less fair.

63 you assume] thou assum'st *1699¹.* 68 hies] flies *1703–1718.* 69 flies] rise *1706–1718.* *After* 82 *1714–1718 add:*

The Griper *Senna,* and the Puker *Rue,*
The Sweetner *Sassafras* are added too;

84] Of *Sulphur, Turpentine* and *Mastick* Wood: *1714–1718.* *After* 84 *1714–1718 add:*

Gums, Fossiles too the Pyramid increas'd,
A *Mummy* next, once Monarch of the East.

88 smoth'ring] smouldring *1699¹.* 92 soft Indulgence we perceive] kind indulgencies we taste *1703A–1706* kind Indulgence we discern *1714–1718.* 93–94]

Thou well canst boast thy num'rous Pedigree
Begot by sloth, maintain'd by Luxury.
In gilded Palaces thy Prowess reigns,
But flyes the humble Sheds of Cottage swains.
To you such might and Energy belong,
You nip the blooming, and unnerve the strong.
The purple Conqueror in Chains you bind,
And are to us your Vassals onely kind. *1703A–1718.*

96 T'extend] To fix *1703A–1718.* 108 the Off'ring] and th'Off'ring *1699¹.* *After* 118 *1703A–1718 add:*

In healing Tears how Myrrha mourn'd her Fall,
And what befel the beauteous Criminal. *1703A–1706*
[How mournful, *Myrrha* for her Crimes appears,
And heals hysterick Matrons still with Tears. *1714–1718*]
How Mentha and Althea, Nymphs no more,
Revive in sacred Plants, and Health restore. *1703A–1718.*

127 We here had met on some] We'd met upon a more *1699¹* serene] more safe *1714–1718.* 130 Interest had taught us to obey] int'rest had directed us t'obey *1699¹* Int'rest then had taught us to obey *1706* Int'rest then had bid us but obey *1714–1718.* 131 Then we'd this only Emulation] This only Emulation we had *1706–1718.* 134 Which threatens] And threatens *1699¹* Which ruins *1714–1718.* 136 Whilst] And *1699¹.* *After* 140 *1700–1718 add:*

Who-e're throws Dust against the Wind, descries
He throws it, in effect, but in his Eyes.

146 live to] breathe, and *1714–1718.* 148 go to *Aix* or *Bourbon*] yield to Fine for Sheriff *1699¹.* *After* 148 *1700–1718 add:*

Then Priesthood thriv'd, and Piety decay'd;
And Senates gave their Votes as They were paid.
Right was adjudg'd as Favour did prevail,
And Burgesses were made by nappy Ale. *1700–1703*
[Then Priests increas'd, and Piety decay'd,
Churchmen the Church's Purity betray'd;
Their Lives and Doctrine Slaves and Atheists made.
The Laws were but the hireling Judge's Sense;
Juries were sway'd by venal Evidence.
Fools were promoted to the Council-Board,
Tools to the Bench, and Bullies to the Sword.
Pensions in private were the Senate's Aim;
And Patriots for a place abandon'd Fame. *1703A–1718*]
But now no influencing Art remains,
For *S—rs* has the Seal, and *Nassau* reigns.
And we, in spight of our Resolves, must bow,
And suffer by a Reformation too. *1700–1718.*

149 But] For *1700–1718.* 150 For] And *1700–1718* th'Effect] Effect *1706–1718.* 154 advance] proceed *1714–1718.* *After* 156 *1703A–1718 add:*

Send swarms of Patients, and our Quarrels end.
So awful *Beadles,* if the *Vagrant* treat,
Strait turn familiar, and their *Fasces* quit. *1714–1718*
In vain we but contend, that radiant [that Planet's *1714–1718*] Pow'r
Those vapours can disperse it rais'd before. *1703A–1718*

157–158]

As He prepar'd the Mischief to recite,
Keen *Colocynthis* paus'd and foam'd with Spight, *1714–1718.*

After 158 *1714–1718 add:*

Sow'r Ferments on his shining Surface swim,
Work up to Froth and bubble o'er the Brim:
Not *Beauties* fret so much if Freckles come,
Or Nose shou'd redden in the Drawing-Room;
Or *Lovers* that mistake th'appointed Hour,
Or in the lucky Minute want the Pow'r.

159 Thou Scandal of the mighty] Thus He—Thou Scandal of great *1714–1718.* 162 th'Itch] Itch *1706–1718.* 167 imperious] despotick *1714–1718.* 169 The tow'ring] Th'aspiring *1699*[1]. *After* 172 *1714–1718 add:*

Allys at *Wapping* furnish us new Modes,
And *Monmouth* street, *Versailles* with Riding-hoods;

173 sooner shall] in pale Throngs *1714–1718*. 174 *Essex*] *Kentish 1706–1718*. *After* 174 *1703A–1718 add:*

Our Properties must on our Arms depend;
'Tis next to conquer, bravely to defend.
'Tis to the Vulgar, Death too harsh appears;
The Ill we feel is onely in our Fears.
  To Die, is Landing on some silent Shoar,
Where Billows never break, nor Tempests roar:
E'er well we feel the friendly Stroke, 'tis o're.
The Wise thro' Thought th'Insults of Death defy;
The Fools, thro' bless'd insensibility.
'Tis what the Guilty fear, the Pious crave;
Sought by the Wretch, and vanquish'd by the Brave.
It eases Lovers, sets the Captives free;
And, tho' a Tyrant, offers Liberty.

175 No, no, the Faculty] Sound but to Arms, the Foe *1703A–1718*. 180 as immense a Pow'r as] no less wondrous Pow'r than *1700–1718*. 183 Whole Troops] Legions *1714–1718*. 189 the times] the time *1699*[3] *1706–1718* time *1700–1703A*. 191–192]

On Dangers past, serenely think no more;
And curse the Hand that heal'd the Wound before. *1714–1718*.

202 But th'Elder] The Elder *1706–1718*. 203 Then] Thus *1706–1718*. *After* 204 *1700–1718 add:*

But e're we once engage in Honour's Cause,
First know what Honour is, and whence it was. *1700–1718*
  'Tis Pride's Original, but Nature's Grave; *1700–1703*
  [Scorn'd by the Base, 'tis courted by the Brave, *1703A–1718*]
The Heroe's Tyrant, and the Coward's Slave.
Born in the noisy Camp, it lives on Air;
And both exists by Hope and by Despair.
Angry when e're a Moment's Ease we gain,
And reconcil'd at our Returns of Pain.
It lives, when in Death's Arms the Heroe lies,
But when his Safety he consults, it dies. *1700–1718*
Bigotted to this Idol, we disclaim
Rest, Health, and Ease, for nothing but a Name. *1703A–1718*.

205 But let us, to the] But to the fatal *1699*[1] Then let us, to the *1700–1718* move] fly *1699*[1]. 206] We'll first reflect, and then consider why. *1699*[1]. 217–20]

If Reason could direct, e'er now each Gate
Had born some Trophy of Triumphal State.
Temples had told how Greece and Belgia owe
Troy and Namur to Jove and to Nassau. *1703A–1718.*

227 a servile Air they] feign'd Airs they poorly *1714–1718.* 228 their Clandestine Arts] boast their Politicks *1714–1718.* 235 when] thus *1699*[1] all the *Gyants*] when the *Gyants 1699*[1] Earth's big Offspring *1714–1718.* 236 T'invade] To scale *1714–1718.*

Canto 4

1 most famous] frequented *1700–1718.* 8 scarce a Mortal, but himself] none, but such as rust in health *1703A–1718.* 9 luckily than He] Fitly to impart *1706–1718.* 10] His known Experience, and his healing Art. *1706–1718.* 11 *Burgess*] *Bu(r)—ss 1699*[1]*–1718.* 13 *Freeman*] *F——(n) 1699*[1]*–1718.* 17 happy] darling *1714–1718.* *After* 20 *1700–1718 add:*

The Criticks each advent'rous Author scan,
And praise or censure as They like the Man. *1700–1718*
The Weeds of Writings for the Flowers They cull;
So nicely Tasteless, so correctly Dull! *1714–1718.*

34 Th'*Apothecaries*] Apothecaries *1706* The trading Tribe oft *1714–1718.* 35 Elbow-room's supply'd] Elbow-room supply *1714–1718.* 48 Yet that's a Trifle] Such Arts are Trifles *1706–1718.* 71 other Arms than] Arms but such as *1714–1718.* 75 Younger] th'Younger *1699*[1]. 82 trifle] puzzle *1714–1718.* 86 Flood had curs'd young *Peleus*'s Arm] horned River then had curs'd *1714–1718.* 87 For troubling his choak'd Streams with heaps of] Young *Peleus*' Arm, that choak'd his Stream with *1714–1718.* 96 sly] shrill *1703A–1718.* 97 worthless] stubborn *1699*[3]*–1706* zealous *1714–1718.* 98–99 *omitted 1699*[3]*–1718.* 103 th'envenom'd] the righteous *1714–1718.* 106 Dull] Grave *1699*[3]*–1703A* Good *1706* Slow *1714–1718.* 107 much ado explaining] painful Pauses mutt'ring *1714–1718.* 108–09]

His Sparks of Life in spight of Drugs retreat,
So cold, that only *Calentures* can heat. *1714–1718.*

112–13] *omitted 1699*[3]*–1718*

Legions of Lunaticks about him press, *1700–1718*
'Tis He that can lost Intellects redress. *1700–1703*
[His Province is lost Reason to redress. *1703A–1718*].

114–15 *omitted 1699*[3]. 118 Fry] Throng *1714–1718.* 119 Consulting less their Reason than] And deaf to Reason still consult *1714–1718.* 120

And] Well *1706–1718* it stands in greater stead] the World will often find *1714–1718*. 121 well] out *1706* 121] To catch the Eye is to convince the Mind *1714–1718*. 130 shelves] Walls *1714–1718*. 131 *Danish*] Runick *1703A–1718*. 132 And hither, rescu'd from the *Grocers*] Hither, retriev'd from *Cooks* and *Grocers* *1706–1718*. 133 *More*'s] *M—* *1699*[1]*–1718* *Bloom*] *B(l)—m* *1699*[1]*–1718*. 134 *Collins*] *C——(s)* *1699*[1]*–1718*. 148 Wren's] Wren *1706–1718*. 149 *Colt*] *C—(t)* *1699*[1]*–1718* *Rowe*] *R—e* *1699*[1]*–1718*. 152 For future glory, while the Scheme is] And whilst the Scheme for future Glory's *1699*[1]. 155 We'll] Let's *1699*[1]. 158 Which way He pleases, he can mould a] At pleasure he can mould the passive *1703A–1706* For Fees, to any Form he moulds a *1714–1718*. 165 *Orford*] *Or—(r)d* *1699*[1]*–1718* *Duncombe*] *D—(comb)* *1699*[1]*–1718*. 166 Let's then to Law] To Law then Friends *1714–1718*. 169 T'assist, and be propitious to our] To prove propitious to future *1706–1718*. 194 noysom] rufull *1714–1718* pensive Temples] meager Forehead *1714–1718*. 195 parch'd] furr'd *1714–1718*. 205 Th'offensive Discord] The Dissonance *1699*[3]*–1718* hideous] unequal *1699*[3]*–1706* untuneful *1714–1718*. 211 *Wycherley*] *W——(y)* *1699*[1]*–1718* *Dryden*] *D—(den)* *1699*[1]*–1718*. 214 *Dorset's*] *D—(set)s* *1699*[1]*–1718*. 217 gentle] courtly *1699*[3]*–1703*. 217–18 *omitted* *1703A–1718*. 218 *Normanbys*] *N(o)—bys* *1699*[1]*–1703*. 219 And] The *1703A–1718*. 220 *Addison*] *A—(so)n* *1699*[1]*–1718*. 221 *Congreve*] *C—(gre)ve* *1699*[1]*–1718*. 226 *Stepny*] *St—(ny)* *1699*[1]*–1718*. 227 *Prior*] *P—(r)* *1699*[1]*–1718* what *Apollo* dictates, *Prior*] *P—r* some Facetious Fancy *1699*[1]. 236 *Montague*'s] *M—(g)ue*'s *1699*[1]*–1718*. *After* 237 *1703A–1718 add:*

The Fury paus'd, till with a frightfull sound
A rising Whirlwind burst th'unhallow'd ground.
Then She—The Deity we Fortune call,
Tho' distant, rules and influences all.
Strait for her favour to her court repair,
Important Embassies claim [ask *1714–1718*] wings of Air.
Each wondrous [wond'ring *1706–1718*] stood, but Horoscope's great Soul
That Dangers ne'er alarm, nor doubts control;
Rais'd on the Pinions of the bounding wind,
Outflew the Rack, and left the Hours behind.
The Ev'ning now with blushes warms the Air,
The Steer resigns the Yoke, the Hind his Care.
The Clouds aloft [above *1714–1718*] with golden Edgings glow,
And falling Dews refresh the Flow'rs [Earth *1714–1718*] below.
The Bat with sooty wings flits thro' the Grove,
The Reeds scarce rustle, nor the Aspine move,
And all the feather'd Folks forbear their Lays of Love.
Thro' the transparent Region of the Skyes,
Swift as a wish the missionary flies.
With wonder he surveys the upper air,

And the gay gilded Meteors sporting there.
How lambent Jellies kindling in the Night,
Shoot thro' the Æther in a trail of Light,
How rising Streams [Steams *1706–1718*] in th'Azure fluid blend,
Or fleet in Clouds, or in soft Show'rs descend;
Or if the stubborn Rage of Cold prevail,
In flakes they fly, or fall in moulded hail.
How Hony Dews embalm the fragrant Morn,
And the fair Oake with luscious Sweats adorn.
How Heat and Moisture mingle in a Mass,
Or belch in Thunder, or in Lightning blaze.
Why nimble coruscations strike the Eye,
And bold Tornado's bluster in the Sky.
Why a prolifick Aura upwards tends,
Ferments, and in a living Show'r descends.
How Vapours hanging on the tow'ring Hills
In Breezes sigh, or weep in warbling Rills;
Whence Infant Winds their tender Pinions try,
And River Gods their thirsty Urns supply.
The wond'ring Sage pursues his airy Flight,
And braves the chill unwholsome Damps of Night;
He views the tracts where Luminaries rove,
To settle Seasons here, and Fates above,
The bleak Arcturus still forbid the Seas,
The stormy Kidds, the weeping Hyades;
The shining Lyre with Strains attracting more
Heaven's glitt'ring Mansions now, than Hell's before.
Glad Cassiopeia circling in the Sky,
And each bright [brave *1718*] Churchill of the Galaxy.
Aurora on Etesian Breezes born,
With blushing Lips breaths out the Sprightly Morn;
Each Flow'r in Dew their short-liv'd Empire weeps,
And Cynthia with her lov'd Endymion sleeps.
As thro' the Gloom the Magus cuts his way,
Imperfect Objects tell the doubtfull Day.
Dim he discerns Majestick Atlas rise,
And bend beneath the Burthen of the Skies.
His tow'ring brows aloft no Tempest know,
Whilst Lightning flies, and Thunder rolls below.
Distant from hence, beyond a Waste of Plains,
Proud Teneriff his Giant Brother reigns;
With breathing Fire his pitchy Nostrils glow,
As from his Sides he shakes the fleecy Snow.
Around their [this *1714–1718*] hoary Prince from wat'ry Beds,
His Subject Islands raise their verdant Heads;
The waves so gently wash each rising Hill,

The Land seems floating, and the Ocean still.
Eternal Spring with smiling Verdure here
Warms the mild Air, and crowns the youthfull Year.
From Crystal Rocks transparent Riv'lets flow,
The Rose still blushes, and the [The Tub'rose ever breathes, and *1714–1718*]
Vi'lets blow.
The Vine undress'd her swelling clusters bears,
The lab'ring Hind the mellow Olive cheers;
Blossoms and Fruit at once the Citron shows,
And as she pays, discovers still she owes. *1703A–1718*
And the glad Orange courts the am'rous Maid *1703A–1706*
With golden Apples, and a silken Shade. *1703A–1706*
[The Orange to the Sun her Pride displays,
And gilds her fragrant Apples with his Rays. *1714–1718*]
No blasts e'er discompose the peacefull Sky,
The Springs but murmur, and the winds but sigh.
The tunefull Swans on gliding Rivers float,
And warbling Dirges, die on ev'ry note.
Where Flora treads her Zephyr Garlands flings,
Shaking rich [And scatters *1714–1718*] Odours from his purple wings;
And [Whilst *1714–1718*] Birds from Woodbine Bow'rs and Jasmin Groves
Chaunt their glad Nuptials, and unenvy'd Loves.
Mild Seasons, rising Hills, and silent Dales,
Cool Grotto's, Silver Brooks, and flow'ry Vales, *1703A–1718*
In this bless'd Climate all the circling Year prevails. *1703A–1706*
[Groves fill'd with balmy Shrubs in pomp appear,
And scent with Gales of Sweets the circling Year. *1714–1718*]
These happy Isles, where endless Pleasures wait,
Are stil'd, by tunefull Bards—The Fortunate.
On high, where no hoarse Winds nor Clouds resort
The hoodwink'd Goddess keeps her partial Court.
Upon a Wheel of Amethyst she sits,
Gives and resumes, and smiles and frowns by fits.
In this still Labyrinth around her lye
Spells, Philters, Globes, and Schemes of Palmistry:
A Sigil in this Hand the Gypsie bears,
In th'other a prophetick Sive and Sheers.
The Dame by divination knew that soon
The Magus would appear—and then begun
Hail, sacred Seer! thy Embassie I know,
Wars must ensue, the Fates will have it so.
Dread Feats shall follow, and Disasters great,
Pills charge on Pills, and Bolus Bolus meet:
Both sides shall conquer, and yet both shall fall;
The Mortar now, and then the Urinal.
To thee alone my Influence I owe;

Where Nature has deny'd, my Favours flow,
'Tis I that give (so mighty is my pow'r)
Faith to the Jew, complexion to the Moor.
I am the Wretch's Wish, the Rook's Pretence,
The Sluggard's Ease, the Coxcomb's Providence.
Sir Scrape Quill, once a supply smiling Slave,
Looks lofty now, and insolently grave,
Builds, settles, purchases, and has each hour
Caps from the Rich, and Curses from the poor.
Spadillio, that at Table serv'd o' late,
Drinks rich Tockay himself, and eats in Plate;
Has Levees, Villas, Mistresses in Store,
And owns the Racers, which he rubb'd before.
  Souls heav'nly born my faithless Boons defy,
The Brave is to himself a Deity.
Tho' bless'd Astrea's gone, some Soil remains,
Where Fortune is the Slave, and merit reigns.
  The Tyber boasts his Julian Progeny,
Thames his Nassau, the Nile his Ptolemy,
Iberia, yet for future Sway design'd,
Shall, for a Hess, a greater Mordaunt find.
Thus Ariadne in proud Triumph rode,
She lost a Heroe, and she found a God. *1703A–1718.*

238–41 *omitted 1703A–1718.* 238 The Fury said; and vanishing from] She said; and as She vanisht from their *1699¹.* 239 Cry'd out] She cry'd *1699¹.*

Canto 5

9 He finds no respite from his] No Respite he can find from *1706.* 12 Glutted with Fees, and mighty in] And great as my Ambition's my *1699¹* Cumber'd with Fees, and glutted with *1706* Oppress'd with Fees and deafen'd with 1714–1718. 13 There's none can] None e'er cou'd *1706–1718.* 14 be] were *1706* was *1714–1718.* 21 Then] And *1699¹.* 21–22]

Shall one of such Importance now [then *1714–1718*] engage
In noisie Riot, and in civil Rage? *1703A–1718.*

24 Preserve] I save *1699¹* Honour] Character *1703A–1718* my Person] Person *1706–1718.* 27 *Mirmillo* reas'ning in his Bed] Mirmillo's Anguish, then begun *1703A–1718.* 28] In sullen [peevish *1714–1718*] Accents to express her own; *1703A–1718.* 31 *South*] *S—(th) 1699¹–1718* *Sherlock*] *S(h)—(lock) 1699¹–1718.* 33 *Ferguson*] *F(er)—(son) 1699¹–1718.* 36 more] most *1718.* 39 T'embroyl] To curse *1706–1718.* 47 I come,

altho' at Midnight] At dead [Noon *1714–1718*] of Night I hasten *1703A–1718*. 49 my Friend, that you were by] I heard your heaving Sighs *1703A–1718*. 50] Nay saw the Tears debating in your Eyes. *1703A–1718*. 51 sure] Threats *1714–1718*. 52 Grief] Storms *1703A–1706* Low'r *1714–1718* Tempests] Terror *1703A–1706* rankle *1714–1718*. 55 Erroneous] Mistakes in *1703A–1718*. 58 but too impertinent] a fruitless Industry *1703A–1718*. 59–62]

My Safety first I must consult, and then
I'll serve our suff'ring Party with my Pen.
All shou'd, reply'd the Hag, their Talent learn,
The most attempting oft the least discern.
Let P—h speak, and V—k write,
Soft *Acon* court, and rough *Caecinna* fight:
Such must succeed, but when th'enervate aim
Beyond their Force, they still contend for shame. *1700–1718*

63 *Colbatch*] *C——(h) 1699[1]–1718*. *Saffold*] *S—fold 1699[1]–1718*. 65 themselves] their Kind *1714–1718*. 67 *Wesley*] *W(e)—(y) 1699[1]–1718*. 74 *Bentley*] *B—(l)y 1699[1]–1718* *Boyle*] *B—(l)e 1699[1]–1718*. 80 Penury] Magazine *1714–1718*. 81 awkardly you've] aukward have you *1706–1718*. 83 soon, what They've exalted They'l] they [Those *1706*] that can exalt, can soon 1703A–1706. 83–88]

Then haste and join your true intrepid Friends,
Success on Vigour and Dispatch depends.
Lab'ring in Doubts *Mirmillo* stood, then said,
'Tis hard to undertake, if Gain disswade;
What Fool for noysie Feuds large Fees wou'd leave?
Ten Harvests more, wou'd all I wish for give.
True Man, reply'd the Elf; by Choice diseas'd,
Ever contriving Pain, and never pleas'd.
A present Good they slight, an absent chuse,
And what they have, for what they have not, lose.
False Prospects all their true Delights destroy,
Resolv'd to want, yet lab'ring to enjoy.
In restless Hurries thoughtlessly they live,
At Substance oft unmov'd, for Shadows grieve.
Children at Toys, as Men at Titles aim;
And in effect both covet but the same.
This *Philip*'s Son prov'd in revolving Years;
And first for Rattles, then for Worlds shed Tears.
The Fury spoke, then in a moment fir'd
The Heroe's Breast with Tempests, and retir'd. *1714–1718*.

88 satisfy'd, in Smiles] smil'd, and sullenly *1699[1]* nodded, and in Smiles *1706*. 89 boding] ominous *1699[1]*. *After* 90 *1714–1718 add:*

Till the pale *Pleiads* clos'd their Eyes of Light.

91 smiles] glows *1714–1718* Sky] Skies *1714–1718*. 92] The Larks in Raptures thro' the *Æther* rise, *1714–1718*. 93 rising] Azure *1714–1718*. 95 *Vi'lets* ope their Buds, *Cowslips* their] *Amaranth* opes its Leaves, the *Lys* its *1714–1718*. 100 *Querpo* in his Armour shone] mighty Querpo charm'd [fill'd *1714–1718*] the Eys *1703A–1718*. 101 Shield was wrought] Arms were made *1703A–1718*. *After* 102 *1703A–1718 add:*

Of temper'd Stibium the bright Shield was cast,
And yet the work the Metal far surpass'd.

103 dissembl'd *Senna*] the Vulnerary *1714–1718*. 104 its] the *1706–1718*. *After* 104 *1714–1718 add:*

Around the Center Fate's bright Trophies lay,
Probes, Saws, Incision Knives, and Tools to slay.

105 its] the *1706–1718*. 110 But] And *1703–1703A*. 111 And whilst one] Whilst one *1703A–1706* Whilst each *1714–1718* another plys] his learn'd Collegue tires *1703A–1718*. 112 starch'd] quaint *1703A–1706* learn'd *1714–1718* Civilities] Impertinence *1703A–1718* Patient dyes] Sick expires *1703A–1718*. 122 But] And *1706–1718* he'd] wou'd *1706–1718*. *After* 124 *1703A–1718 add:*

As Querpo tow'ring stood in Martial might,
Pacifick Carus sparkl'd on the Right.
An Oran Outang o'er his shoulders hung,
His Plume confess'd the Capon whence it sprung.
His motly Mail scarce could the Heroe bear,
Haranguing thus the Tribunes of the War.
    Fam'd Chiefs,
For present Triumphs born, design'd for more,
Your Virtue I admire, your Valour more.
If Battel be resolv'd, you'll find this Hand
Can deal out Destiny, and Fate command.
Our Foes in throngs shall hide the Crimson Plain,
And their Apollo interpose in vain.
Tho' Gods themselves engage, a Diomed
With ease could shew a Deity can bleed.
    But War's rough Trade should be by Fools profest,
The grossest [truest *1714–1718*] rubbish fills a Trench the best.
Let Quinsies throttle, and the Quartan shake,
Or Dropsies drown, and Gout and Colicks rack;
Let Sword and Pestilence lay waste, whilst we
Wage bloodless Wars, and fight in Theory.
Who wants not Merit needs not arm for Fame;

The Dead I raise my Chivalry proclaim.
Diseases baffl'd, and lost Health restor'd,
In Fame's bright List my Victories record.
More Lives from me their Preservation own,
Than Lovers lose if fair Cornelia frown.
Your cures, shrill Querpo cry'd, aloud you tell,
But wisely your miscarriages conceal.
Zeno, a Priest, in Samothrace of old,
Thus reason'd with Philopidas the bold;
Immortal Gods you own, but think 'em blind
To what concerns the State of human kind.
Either they hear not, or regard not Pray'r,
That argues want of Pow'r, and this of Care.
Allow that Wisdom infinite must know,
Pow'r infinite must act. *I grant it so.*
Haste strait to Neptune's Fane, survey with Zeal
The Walls. *What then?* reply'd the Infidel.
Observe those num'rous Throngs in Effigy,
The Gods have sav'd from the devouring Sea.
'Tis true their Pictures that escap'd you keep,
But where are theirs that perish'd in the deep.
Vaunt now no more the triumphs of your skill,
But, tho' unfee'd, exert your arm and kill.
Our scouts have learn'd the posture of the foe;
In War, surprizes surest conduct shew.

125–26]

But Fame, that neither good nor bad conceals,
That Pembroke's Worth, and Ormond's Valour tells,
How Truth in Benting, how in Candish reigns
Varro's magnificence with Maro's Strains. *1703A–1718.*

127 And] But *1703A–1718.* 128 *Winnington*] *W(i)—(ton) 1699¹–1718* *Onely*] *O—(l)y 1699¹–1718.* 128 but plead, or *Onely*] plead, or *S——* or *O——y 1703A–1718.* 131–40]

Confusion in each Countenance appear'd,
A Council's call'd, and Stentor first was heard;
His lab'ring lungs the throng'd Praetorium rent,
Addressing thus the Passive President. *1703A–1718.*

136 aim'd at] courted bus'ness *1699¹* and none succeeded] or knew it *1699¹.* 150 scatter] humble *1714–1718.* 151–64]

Our Spight, they'll find, to their Advantage leans,
The End is good, no matter for the Means.

So modern *Casuists* their Talents try,
Uprightly for the sake of Truth to lye. *1714–1718*
He had not finish'd, till th'Out-guards descry'd
Bright Columns move in formidable Pride.
The passing Pomp so dazzl'd from afar,
It seem'd a Triumph rather than a War.
Tho' wide the Front, tho' gross the Phalanx grew,
It look'd less dreadfull as it nearer drew.
The adverse Host for Action strait prepare;
All eager to unveil the Face of War.
Their Chiefs lace on their Helms, and take the Field.
And to their trusty Squires resign their Shield:
To paint each Knight, their Ardour and Alarms,
Wou'd ask the Muse that sung the frogs in Arms.
And now the Signal summons to the Fray;
Mock Falchions flash, and paltry Ensigns play.
Their Patron God his Silver Bow-string twangs;
Tough Harness rustles, and bold Armour clangs.
The piercing Causticks ply their spightfull pow'r;
Ementicks ranch, and keen Catharticks scour.
The deadly Drugs in double Doses fly,
And Pestles peal a martial Symphony. *1703A–1718*.

165 Then] Now *1703A–1718*. 179 an ample] a spacious *1703A–1718*. 183 And th'empty Vessels the] Whilst empty Jarrs the dire *1703A–1718*. 191 sinewy Arm an] Arm a massy *1703A–1718*. 193–94 *omitted 1703A–1718*. 195 *Japix*] *Sertorius 1703A–1718* *Rhubarb*] *Buckthorn 1714–1718*. 197 And] But *1700–1718* a dauntless and disdainfull] an angry and revengefull *1699*[1]. 199–200]

Chiron attacked Talthibius with such might,
One pass had paunch'd the huge Hydropick Knight,
Who strait retreated to evade the Wound,
But in a Flood of Apozem was drown'd.
This Psylas saw, and to the Victor said,
Thou shalt not long survive th'unwieldy dead,
Thy Fate shall follow; then to [follow; to *1714–1718*] confirm it, swore
By th'Image of Priapus, which he bore;
And rais'd an Eagle-Stone, invoking loud
On Cynthia, leaning o're a silver Cloud.
Great Queen of Night, and Empress of the Seas,
If faithfull to thy midnight Mysteries,
If still observant of my early Vows,
These hands have eas'd the mourning Matron's throws;
Direct this rais'd avenging Arm aright,

So may loud Cymbals aid thy lab'ring Light.
He said, and let the pond'rous Fragment fly
At Chiron, but learn'd Hermes put it by.
 Tho' the haranguing God survey'd the War,
That day the Muse's Sons were not his Care.
Two Friends, Adepts, the Trismegists by Name,
Alike their Features, and alike their Flame.
As simpling near fair Tweed each sung by Turn,
The list'ning River wou'd neglect his Urn.
Those Lives they fail'd to rescue by their Skill,
Their Muse cou'd make Immortal with her Quill.
But learn'd Enquiries after Nature's state
Dissolv'd the League, and kindl'd a Debate.
The One, for lofty Labours fruitfull known,
Fill'd Magazines with Volumes of his Own.
At his once favour'd Friend a Tome he threw
That from its birth had slept unseen till now.
Stunn'd with the Blow the batter'd Bard retir'd,
Sunk down, and in a Simile expir'd.
 And now the Cohorts shake, the Legions ply,
The yielding Flanks confess the Victory. *1703A–1718.*

201 And *Querpo,* warm'd with more than mortal] Stentor, undaunted still with noble *1703A–1718.* 202 *Stentor*] *Querpo* *1703A–1718.* *After* 206 *1714–1718 add:*

On *Stentor*'s Crest the useful Chrystal breaks,
And Tears of *Amber* gutter'd down his Cheeks.

207 as] whilst *1700–1718* bold *Stentor*] the Champion *1714–1718* eager of Renown] (as late rumors tell,) *1700–1718.* 208 fatal Stroak] sure decisive Stroke *1714–1718* he tumbl'd down] the Hero fell *1700–1706* he fell *1714–1718.* 209 whilst] as *1700–1718.* 214 Reflect] Think *1699*[1] young *Querpoïdes* thy] *Querpoides* thy darling *1699*[1]. 215 Then pity mine; for] Mine's small as He, just *1699*[1]. 216 Sports] Smiles *1714–1718.* 217 by] near *1703A–1718.* *After* 220 *1714–1718 add:*

At this the *Victors* own such Extasies,
As *Memphian* Priests if their *Osiris* sneeze;
Or Champions with Olympick Clangour fir'd;
Or simpring Prudes with sprightly *Nantz* inspir'd;
Or Sultans rais'd from Dungeons to a Crown;
Or fasting Zealots when the Sermon's done.

221 The Chief at this] A while the Chief *1714–1718.* 226 mortal Indignation] more than mortal Fury *1703A–1718.* 229 *La Chase* shall with the

Jansenists] The Jesuits and Jansenists *1703A* The Jesuit and Jansenists *1706* *Jansenius* and the *Jesuits 1714–1718.* 230 The Inquisition] And th'Inquisition *1699*^{1}. 231 unmov'd] unshook *1703A–1706* *Stillingfleet*'s] *S(t)—(fleet)s 1699*^{1}*–1706.* 231–32]

Warm Convocations own the Church secure,
And more consult her Doctrine than her Pow'r. *1714–1718.*

232 *Lock*] *L—k 1699*^{1}*–1706.* 233 unsheathing an Incision Knife] he drew a Lancet in full [his *1714–1718*] Rage *1703A–1718.* 234] To puncture the still supplicating Sage *1703A–1718.* 235 Act] Stroke *1714–1718.* 239 I've] We've *1699*^{1} *1700–1718.* 245 so] thus *1699*^{1}.

Canto 6

6 *Cecil*'s] *C—(l)l(e)*'s *1699*^{1}*–1718.* *Grafton*'s] *G—ton*'s *1699*^{1}*–1718.* 7 *Ranelagh*'s] *R—agh*'s *1699*^{1}*–1718.* 8 *Churchill*'s] *Ch—ill*'s *1699*^{1}*–1718* *Berkley*'s] *B—kley*'s *1699*^{1}*–1718.* *After* 8 *1714–1718 add:*

On *Iris* thus the differing Beams bestow
The Die, that paints the Wonders of her Bow,

9 her bright Lips] the fair Nymph *1714–1718.* 10 As] Whilst *1699*^{1}. 15 He'll soon] soon He'll *1706–1718.* 16 terminate] mollify *1714–1718.* 27 soon as e'er th'imperial] when the bold imperial *1706–1718.* 36 Th'obedient] The willing *1706–1718.* *After* 39 *1714–1718 add:*

Thus *Numa* when to hallow'd Caves retir'd,
Was by *Ægeria* guarded and inspir'd.

After 47 *1703A–1718 add:*

Hence the chaste lillie rises to the Light,
Unveils her snowy breasts, and charms the Sight.

50 verdant Temples] laurel'd forehead *1703A–1718.* 57 Where hateful] And there the *1699*^{1}. 58 Where] There *1699*^{1}. *After* 59 *1714–1718 add:*

Here their new Form the numb'd *Erucae* hide,
Their num'rous Feet in slender Bandage ty'd:
Soon as the kindling Year begins to rise,
This upstart Race their native Clod despise,
And proud of painted Wings attempt the Skies.

70 th'Arms] th'op'ning Arms *1699¹* those more yeilding] these lov'd *1699¹*. 75 living Floods of Merc'ry] Floods of living Silver *1703A–1718.* 76 Beams] Looks *1703A–1718.* 77 While] And *1706–1718* Silver] Golden *1703A–1718* Golden] Amber *1703A–1718.* *After* 77 *1703A–1718 add:*

Where Light's gay God descends to ripen Gems,
And lend a lustre brighter than his Beams.

89 Which] And *1699¹ 1706–1718.* *After* 93 *1703A–1718 add:*

The warring winds unmov'd Hygeia heard,
Brav'd their loud Jars, but much for Celsus fear'd.
Andromeda, so whilst her Heroe fought,
Shook for his danger, but her own forgot.

102–03]

To these dark Realms much learned Lumber creeps,
There copious M—— safe in Silence sleeps; *1703A–1718.*

103 *Philipps'*] *P——p's 1699¹–1703.* 104 silently retire] in Oblivion lye *1703A–1718.* 105 with Decency expire] like other Monsters dye *1703A–1718.* 112 In the close Covert of a] I'th'middle of a dusky *1699¹.* 114 most formidably] with awful Horror *1714–1718.* *After* 115 *1703A–1718 add:*

Confus'd, and wildly huddl'd to the Eye,
The Beggar's Pouch, and Prince's Purple lye.
Dim Lamps with sickly Rays scarce seem to glow;
Sighs heave in mournfull Moans, and Tears o'reflow. *1703A–1718*
Restless Anxiety, forlorn Despair,
And all the faded Family of Care, *1714–1718*
Old mouldring Urns, pale Fear, and dark [Urns, Racks, Daggers and *1714–1718*] Distress
Make up the frightfull Horror o' the Place. *1703A–1718.*

128 She's] Still *1706–1718.* 147 *Charon* ne'er refuses] *Charon*'s present still at *1700–1718.* 156 careful] mournful *1700–1718.* 163 valu'd] firmest *1714–1718.* 171 To] And *1706–1718.* 173 rigid is] moving's *1699¹.* *After* 175 *1703A–1718 add:*

Insipid as your late Ptisans you lye,
That once were sprightlier far than Mercury.
At the sad Tale you tell, the Poppies weep,
And mourn their vegetable Souls asleep.
The unctuous Larix, and the healing Pine
Lament your Fate in tears of Turpentine.

But still the offspring of your Brain shall prove
The Grocer's care, and brave the Rage of Jove.
When Bonfires blaze, your vagrant Works shall rise
In Rockets, till they reach the wondring Skyes.

191]

Soft Infant Blossoms their chast Odours pay;
And Roses blush their fragrant Lives away. *1714–1718.*

192 Cold] Cool *1699*[1] *1706–1718.* 195 there] here *1700–1718.* *After* 195 *1703A–1718 add:*

The Morn awakes the Tulip from her bed;
E'er Noon in painted Pride she decks her Head:
Roab'd in rich dye she triumphs on the Green,
And ev'ry Flow'r does Homage to their Queen.
So when bright Venus rises from the Flood,
Around in throngs the wondring Nereids crowd;
The Tritons gaze, and tune each vocal Shell,
And ev'ry Grace unsung, the Waves conceal.

After 199 *1703A–1718 add:*

Here Jealousie with Jaundice Looks appears,
And broken slumbers, and Fantastick Fears.
The Widow'd Turtle hangs her moulting Wings,
And to the Woods in mournfull Murmurs sings.

204 His Mistress] Olivia *1703A–1718.* 207 mournful] dying *1714–1718.* 212 Cold and] All o're *1703A–1718.* 215 Then softly in these gentle words] As to the cold-complexion'd Nymph *1703A–1718.* 219 unfriendly] relentless *1714–1718.* 220 pale Complexion your late] languid looks, your late ill *1700–1718.* *After* 221 *1703A–1718 add:*

Stabb'd with th'unkind Reproach, the conscious Maid
Thus to her late insulting Lover said;
When Ladies listen not to loose desire,
You stile our Modesty, our want of Fire.
Smile or Forbid, Encourage or Reprove,
You still find Reasons to believe we love:
Vainly you think a liking we betray,
And never mean the peevish things we say. *1703A–1718*
Few are the Fair Ones of Rufilla's make,
Unask'd she grants, uninjur'd she'll forsake:
But sev'ral Caelias, sev'ral Ages boast
That like, where Reason recommends the most.

Where heav'nly Truth and Tenderness conspire,
Chast Passion may perswade us to desire. *1714–1718*
Custom, reply'd the Lover, is your Guide,
Discretion is but Fear, and Honour, Pride. *1703A–1706*
[Your Sex, he cry'd, as Custom bids, behaves;
In Forms the Tyrant tyes such haughty Slaves. *1714–1718*]
To do nice Conduct right, you Nature wrong;
Impulses are but weak, where Reason's strong.
Some want th'assurance oft, but [want the Courage, but how *1714–1718*] Few the Flame;
They like the Thing, That startle at the Name.
The lonely Phoenix, tho' profess'd a Nun,
Warms into Love, and kindles at the Sun.
Those Tales of spicy Urns and fragrant Fires,
Are but the Emblems of her scorch'd desires. *1703A–1718.*

234 next to] more than *1714–1718.* 235] With so much Lustre your bright Looks endear, *1703A–1718.* 236 when you are there] where those appear *1703A–1718.* 240 mean] foul *1714–1718.* 241] How your sad sick'ning Art now hangs her Head *1703A–1718.* 242 what was once a Science, now's] once a Science, is become *1703A–1718.* *After* 244 *1714–1718 add:*

Not so when *Rome* to th'*Epidaurian* rais'd
A Temple, where devoted Incence blaz'd.
Oft Father Tyber views the holy [lofty *1718*] Fire,
As the learn'd *Son* is worship't like the Sire:
The Sage with Romulus like Honours claim;
The Gift of Life and Laws were then the same.

251 *Ent*] *Bates 1699¹ 1703A–1718.* 256 Physick her lost Lustre] her lost Health your Science *1703A–1718.* 262 cuts] grinds *1714–1718.* 267 th'Emblems] Emblems *1703A–1718.* 276 He] His Life *1699¹ 1700–1718* as Immortal] immortal *1699¹* as lasting *1700–1718* Name] Fame *1700–1718.* 283 but *Apollo* some great Bard] Phoebus, or his Granvil, but *1703A–1718.* 284 With] Their *1703A–1718.* *After* 293 *1714–1718 add:*

When late, *Jove*'s Eagle from the Pyle shall rise
To bear the Victor to the boundless Skies,
Awhile the God puts off Paternal Care,
Neglects the Earth, to give the Heav'ns a Star.
Near Thee, *Alcides,* shall the Heroe shine;
His Rays resembling, as his Labours, Thine.

294 Hero] Patriot *1714–1718.* 296 *Latian* Liberties] sinking *Latian* Power *1699¹.* 297] *Rome* had erected Columns ev'ry hour; *1699¹.* 298] Loud *Io*'s her [the *1703A–1718*] proud Capitol had shook *1699¹ 1703A–1718.* 299 The Statues of the Guardian] And all the Statues of the *1699¹ 1703A–1718.*

A Satyr against Wit

Copy text: A Satyr against Wit, 1700 (Wing B3084).

Collation: The first edition of the poem, printed for Samuel Crouch in 1700, is a folio volume of which the Yale copy has been collated (*A*). The copy in the Boston Public Library, apparently the Luttrell copy, is dated "23 Nov. 1699." *A Satyr against Wit. The Second Edition,* so-called (Wing B3085), is really a second issue of the first edition. The need for more copies apparently became evident while the type for Sheet A was being distributed. So Sheet A was reset, *"The Second Edition"* substituted for a printer's device on the original title page, and new marginals supplied throughout.

The second edition, called *"The Third Edition"* on the title page (Wing B3086), is a word-for-word resetting of *A*. Emendations at lines 212, 328, and 377, and the omission of two couplets, lines 236–37 and 358–59, make it likely that Blackmore himself corrected the copy. Collation of the Harvard copy (*B*) is recorded below.

A Dublin piracy, also dated 1700 (Wing B3087), is mainly interesting on account of its title, which makes an important point about the poem: *A Satyr against Wit: Design'd an Answer to a Poem Stil'd the Dispensary.* It is a word-for-word resetting of the first edition (probably of the second issue).

Blackmore subsequently revised the poem for inclusion in his *Collection of Poems on Various Subjects,* published in 1718. Working from a copy of *B*, he struck out 42 lines, revised 88, and restored lines 236–37, which he had omitted from *B*. The result is a thorough-going revision, of which the readings of the Yale copy (*C*) are recorded below.

A fragmentary manuscript of the poem survives in Folger V.a.308. It is entitled *Some Lines taken out of the Satyr against Wit. 1700* and seems to have been copied from the second issue of *A*. Its existence, together with Samuel Crouch's repeated underestimation of the demand for copies, testifies to the popularity of the work.

7 Have surely] Must sure have *C*. 8 Fierce] Whence *C*. 17 Detesting both alike] And did alike detest *C*. 18 They justly Wits and Fools believ'd] For Wits and Fools they justly thought *C*. 20 would never quit] did long retain *C*. 21 dissolve in Wit] soft Arts disdain *C*. 24 Then she] Which then *C*. 27 all turn'd] sunk to *C*. 28 Our Learning daily sinks, and Wit] Learning and Sense decay, while Jest *C*. 29 senseless Conversation of the] Conversation of the laughing *C*. 30–31]

Where manly Virtues, which we once could boast,
Unnerv'd by Mirth and Levity, are lost *C*.

32 The Plague of] So far this Plague *C* 'tis] in *C*. 33 Now to attempt its Fury] We now attempt its Progress *C*. 37 loose] vile *C*. 38 some

only Wits] and some *C*. 43 first this] this sore *C*. 50 th'Infection] the Poison *C*. 56 *Dryden*] *D——n ABC*. 63 Pity that so much Labour should be] Yet happily his Care and Pains are *C*. 64 such a healthful] his *Athletick C*. 68 Wit] Jests *C*. 69 Vice] Sin *C*. 70 To Wickedness pretend, that's] Boastful pretend to Vices *C*. 71 A Bantring Spirit] Since this vain Humour *C*. our Men] the Realm *C*. 72 Wisdom is become] sober Heads are grown *C*. 73–74 *omitted C*. 75 Wise Magistrates leud Wit do therefore] Men arm'd with Pow'r should this light Spirit *C*. 76 The Bane of Virtue's Treason to] That saps the Church, and undermines *C*. 77 Honour] Wisdom *C* Honesty] Probity *C*. 79 well-form'd Government or State] Throne is safe, what Government *C*. 80 Wit has laid the Peoples] impious Wits have laid all *C*. 81 *Mob* of Wits] laughing Mob *C* to storm] and range *C*. 82 To pull all Virtue and right] With Jests and Noise they bear all *C*. 83 Quite to subvert] Subvert Divine *C* sacred] envy'd *C*. 84 To set up] Set up loose *C*. 88 *Smalwood*] *S———d ABC*. 93 will no *Alldridge, Mill,* or *Charlett*] will no *All———e, M—ll,* or *Ch———t AB* 'll of the Schools not One Supporter *C*. 94 But the leud] But chief the *C*. 95 unless they've] till they have *C* *Bently*'s] *B——ly*'s *ABC*. 97 rarest] finest *C* e'er was] has been *C*. 105 just] did *C* appear'd] appear *C*. 106 *Bentley*] *Newton C*. 110 famous] the fam'd *C*. 112 *Tyson*'s] *Ty—n*'s *ABC*. 114–15 *omitted C*. 114 *Tyson*] *Ty—n AB*. 116 For next to Virtue, Learning they] Learning they next to Vertue most *C*. 118 A Wit's an idle, wretched] For a loose Wit's an Idle *C*. 120 Wit] Mirth *C*. 121 Business] Action *C*. 122 useless is a sauntring empty] mean a Trifler is a saunt'ring *C*. 125 Wit have learned] this light Vein have *C*. 128 Wit] that *C* *Treby*'s] *T—by*'s *ABC*. 129 *Somers*'] *S——r*'s *ABC*. 130–34 *omitted C*. 130 *Holt*] *H—lt AB*. 131 *Finch*] *F—ch AB*. 132 *Powys*] *P——s AB*. 135 the bant'ring] this jesting *C*. 136 A *Sloan* may sometimes there] There Blockheads may *C* *Sloan*] *Sl—— AB*. 137–42 *omitted C*. 137 *Radcliffe*] *R—t——ffe AB*. 141 *Colbatch*] *C———h AB*. 143 *Gibbons*] *G——ns ABC* *How*] *H—w ABC*. 145–46 *omitted C*. 150–53 *omitted C*. 154 Despise their Spite] Let Malice rage *C*. 157–60]

> Had not this merry Sickness of the Head,
> This Plague in Fashion o'er the Nation spread,
> Proud of her Sons, *Britannia* might have seen
> Vast Numbers more of great and generous Men. *C*.

159 *Garth*] *G—— AB*. 160 *Smalwood*] *S———d AB* *Addison*] *Ad—son AB*. 161 An able Senator is lost] She had not lost a Senator *C* *Moyle*] *M—l ABC*. 162 And] Nor *C* sunk by Wit in] in the hopeful *C* *Boyle*] *B—l ABC*. 163 After] Now, since *C*. 173 Nothing can be expected] All Hope will be extinguish'd *C*. 179–83 *omitted C*. 182–83] O *S—er, T—bot, D—set, M——gue,/Gr—y, Sh———ld, C——d—sh,*

P———ke, V——n, you *AB.* 184 Who in *Parnassus* have Imperial] Ye noble Patrons, who *Parnassus C.* 185 Subjects here] tuneful Sons *C.* 194 Sense] Wit *AB.* 197 *St. Evremont* and *Rymer* both are] *St. E——m—t* and *R——r* both are *AB R——r* and *E—r——t* are Judges *C.* 198 Coining] Stamping *C.* 199 Essay] Assay *B.* 200 They'll every Piece of Metal touch and] For they will every Piece of Metal *C.* 201 light, which has] light, or has *C.* 204 *Congreve, Southern . . . Wycherly*] *C———e, S———n . . . W———ly ABC.* 206 *Dryden*] *D——n ABC.* 210–11 *omitted C.* 212 Those who will] The Men who *BC Dennis*] *D—n—s AB D——s C.* 214 Do, as th'] Copy the *C.* 216–19 *omitted C.* 218 *Somers' . . . Talbot's*] *S——r's . . . T—bot's AB.* 225 for Wit and] of Sterling *C.* 228 *Somers, Dorset, Sheffield, Montague*] *S—(e)r, D—set, Sh———ld, M———gue ABC.* 229 but their] their great *C.* 231 They] Who *C.* 236–37 *omitted B.* 242 *Vanbrugh . . . Congreve*] *V——e . . . C———e ABC.* 252 *Prior*] *P——r ABC.* 253 nobler] Lyrick *C* happy] finer *C.* 256 *Tate*] *T—e ABC.* 258–61 *omitted C.* 261 *Freek*] *Fr—k AB.* 262 *Lock, Fleetwood*] *L—k, Fl———d AB.* 265 *Garth . . . Urwin's*] *G—(th) . . . Ur——'s ABC.* 269 *Tonson*] *T——n ABC.* 280 Sword] Foe *C.* 284 It does] The Beds *C.* 287 Ev'n these] Who since *C Dryden*] *D——n ABC.* 289 just] fit *C.* 290 Licentiousness] licentious Course *C.* 303 Poetic] The strictest *C.* 304 soon the Muses State] Schools of Learning soon *C.* 305 an honest Man can't peep] a vertuous Pen scarce peeps *C.* 315 *Garth*] *G—— ABC.* 316 others] Merchants *C.* 326 he's allow'd] he acquires *C* Sense] Fame *C.* 328 his] the *A.* 329 *Dryden*] *D——n ABC.* 333 a Wit] his Parts *C.* 334 him forbear] *Darfel* cease *C.* 340 Sense] Brains *C.* 343 what generous *Oran*] *Pausanias* had not *C.* 344 Had ne'er been Standard, sheer] With *Spartan* Judgment, and *C.* 350 *Elliot's*] *Ell——t's ABC.* 351 *Smalwood*] *S———d ABC.* 353 *Dorset's*] *D—set's ABC.* 354 *Dorset's*] *D—set's ABC.* 358–59 *omitted BC.* 361 good Sense] true Worth *C* Merit] Vertue *C.* 362 *Dorset*] *D—set ABC.* 373 It takes their Heads before] Their Heads grow giddy e'er *C.* 376–77 *omitted C.* 377 'tis known was likely to have] unhappy Youth, had almost *B.* 389 Med'cines make, and] make up Medicines *C.* 390 Let 'em pound Drugs, they have no Brains to] And out of pounded Drugs their Dinner *C.*

The Pacificator

Copy text: The Pacificator. A Poem, 1700.

Collation: The text of the poem exists only in two printed versions: a separate folio (*A*) published by John Nutt in February 1700 (Moore, p. 10) and an octavo collection (*B*), *A Second Volume of the Writings of the Author of the True-Born Englishman,* which appeared early in 1705 (Moore, p. 36). The versions in the second volume of the so-called "Third Edition" of *A True Collection of the Writings of the Author of the True-Born English-Man,* which Defoe advertised in the *Review,* 7 (28 December 1710), 476 (Moore, p. 197), and in the second volume of the so-called "3rd Edition, corrected" of *A True Collection* which was advertised on 25 June 1713 in *The Daily Courant* and which William Lee called the fourth edition (Lee, *1,* xxx), are in fact the same edition as *B.*

The Yale copy of the first volume of *A True Collection* (1710)(Ik.D362.C703c) has two title pages, of which the first is *The Genuine Works of Mr. Daniel D'Foe, Author of the True-born English-Man, A Satyr. Containing Thirty Nine Scarce and Valuable Tracts, upon many Curious and uncommon Subjects. To which is added a Complete Key to the Whole, Never before Printed.* Between signatures A and B of this volume are inserted the separately paginated "Key to the first Vol." and "Key to the second Vol." (sig. *4). Both of these are cited in the annotation as *Key.*

The copies of *A* and *B* that have been collated are in the Yale University Library.

33] O *Gr——ll, Harcourt, Saymour,* and *Ja. How B.* 34–35 *omitted B.* 38 your] our *B.* 89 *Collier*] *C——r AB.* 99 *Collier's*] *C——r's AB.* 113 *Milburn*] *M——n AB.* 136 *Dorset, Montague,* and *Normanby*] *D——, M——,* and *N—— AB.* 147 *Russel . . . Herbert*] *R—— . . . H—— AB.* 148 *Orford . . . Torrington*] *O—— . . . T—— AB.* 155 *Dennis*] *D——s AB.* 169 *Congreve . . . Dryden, Hopkins* and *Motteaux*] *C——e . . . D——n, H——s* and *M——x AB.* 170 *Durfey*] *D——y AB.* 173 Flesh'd] Flush'd *B* *Collier's*] *C——'s AB.* 184 *Tonson . . . Tonson*] *T—— . . . T—— AB.* 207 *Garth*] *G——h AB.* 217 *Garth*] *G——h AB.* 228 *Garth*] *G——h AB.* 236 *Dryden, Congreve, Addison* and *Sanders*] *D——n, C——e, A——n* and *S——s AB.* 239 *Durfey*] *D——y AB.* 244 *Dryden*] *D——n AB.* 247 *Dryden*] *D——n AB.* 268 *Congreve, Hughs*] *C——e, H——s AB.* 269 *Dennis, Durfey, Tuchin . . . Motteaux*] *D——s, D——y, T——n . . . M——x AB.* 270 *Brewer, Wessly, Pettys*] *B——r, W——y, P——s AB.* 271 *Tate . . . Brady . . . Traherne*] *T——e . . . B——y . . . T——e AB.* 272 *Gildon . . . Brown*] *G——n . . . B——n AB.* 277 *Davenant*] *D——t AB.* 284 *Dryden*] *D——n AB.* 295 *Dorset, Dorset, Mountague*] *D——, D——, M—— AB.* 372 *Devil*] *D—— AB.* 374 *Parliament*] *P——t AB.* 378 *Arse*] *A— AB.* 419 *Dryden . . . Creech*] *D——n . . . C——h AB.* 420 *Durfey . . . Tate*] *D——y . . . T——e AB.* 421 *Prior*] *P——r AB.* 422 *Ratcliff . . . Wicherly*] *R——ff . . . W——y AB.* 423 *Congreve . . . Foe*] *C——e . . . F——e AB.* 424 *Wessly . . . Milburn*] *W——ly . . . M——n AB.* 437 *Dennis*] *D——s AB.* 438 *Motteaux*] *M——x AB.* 441 *Milburn*] *M——n AB.*

Upon the Author of the Satyr against Wit

Copy text: *The Miscellaneous Works of the Honourable Sir Charles Sedley, Bart.*, 1702, p. [1]114 (Yale copy).

Collation: No manuscript copy of the poem has been discovered and the only printed versions of any authority are those in *Commendatory Verses* (1700) (Case 217), p. 2, and *The Miscellaneous Works of the Honourable Sir Charles Sedley, Bart. Containing Satyrs, Epigrams, Court-Characters, Translations, Essays and Speeches in Parliament. Collected into one Volume. To which is added, The Death of Marc Antony: A Tragedy never before Printed. Published from the Original Manuscripts, by Capt. Ayloffe* (1702). The latter restores to the poem the final couplet, which is anticipated in line 2 and without which the poem is incomplete. It introduces no other substantive variants but is a more carefully edited version than that in *Commendatory Verses* and completely bears out Vivian de Sola Pinto's supposition "that whatever manuscript works the poet had by him at the time of his death passed into Ayloffe's hands" (*The Poetical and Dramatic Works of Sir Charles Sedley*, ed. Vivian de Sola Pinto, 2 vols., London, Constable, 1928, *1*, viii). In the preface to his edition, William Ayloffe mentions his "Affinity" to Sedley—he was a nephew by Sedley's bigamous marriage to Ann Ayscough—and claims that he had printed Sedley's poems from copies "corrected by his own Hands." The present edition reproduces this text *literatim.*

A Lent-Entertainment

Copy text: Commendatory Verses: Or, A Step towards a Poetical War, betwixt Covent-Garden and Cheap-side, 1702, pp. 29–30 (Case 217b) (Harvard copy).

Collation: Both Case and Boys (*Sir Richard Blackmore and the Wits*, p. 37 *n.*) mention a 30-page issue of *Commendatory Verses* (1700), but since no copy can now be found, it was necessary to take the 1702 issue as copy text. In 1708 the poem was reprinted, with no substantive variants, in *The Third Volume of the Works of Mr. Thomas Brown*, 1708, pp. [3]110–13.

On My Lord Somers

Copy text: *The Diverting Post*, 2 (12–19 May 1705) (BM copy).

Collation: The text of the poem is preserved in four collateral manuscripts and the printed version (*D*), which supplies the copy text. Three of the manuscripts, BM MS. Lansdowne 852, f. 20v (*A*), Harleian 6914, f. 93v (*B*), and TCD MS. I.5, 2, 366 (*C*) are almost identical, while BM MS. Add. 21094, f. 153v (*E*) is a later version (omitting lines 3–4) in which "Sarrah" has been substituted for "Somers" in line 2 and the result entitled *On the Dutches of Marlborough.*

1 Spurr'd] push't *E.* 2 read] see *E.* 3–4 *omitted E.* 3 Attempts] *A* Efforts *BCD.* 5 Efforts] attempts *BCD* atempt *E.* 6 close] Joyn *E.* 8 that] the *CDE* strove] thought *B.*

Prologue to "The Pilgrim"

Copy text: The Pilgrim; a Comedy: As it is Acted at the Theatre-Royal in Drury-lane. Written Originally by Mr. Fletcher, and Now Very Much Alter'd, with Several Additions. Likewise a Prologue, Epilogue, Dialogue, and Masque, Written by the Late Mr. Dryden Just before His Death, being the Last of His Works (1700) (Macdonald, p. 135; Yale copy IK.V275.700P).

Collation: If the poem was first published separately in a folio half-sheet, as seems likely, no copy is known today. The first extant edition is that in *The Pilgrim; a Comedy* (1700) (*A*), of which the British Museum copy is dated "the 5 of May Monday." But 5 May 1700 fell on a Sunday and *The Pilgrim; a Comedy* was not published until 18 June (*The London Gazette,* No. 3610; *The Post Man,* No. 765). The text of the prologue includes four errors, which, in the Yale copy, have been corrected in an old hand.

The work advertised in *The Post Boy,* No. 806, 6–8 June 1700, as *Songs in the Revis'd Comedy, call'd, The Pilgrim* (J. Walsh), is *A Collection of New Songs with a Through Bass to Each Song for the Harpsichord. Compos'd by Mr. Daniel Purcel. Perform'd in the Revis'd Comedy Call'd The Pilgrim, Being the Last Writeings of Mr. Dryden,* but it does not include the Prologue (which is not, of course, a song).

The Prologue next was printed in *The Comedies, Tragedies, and Operas Written by John Dryden, Esq; with a Secular Masque* (*B*) (Macdonald, p. 149) which was advertised in *The London Gazette,* No. 3698, 17–21 April 1701. Here the poem is erroneously entitled *Prologue to the Masque,* but the four errors in *A* are corrected.

The Prologue was also included in *A Collection of Poems* printed for Daniel Brown and Benjamin Tooke in 1701, of which a second edition was advertised in *The London Gazette,* No. 3815, 1–4 June 1702. The text of the Prologue is a line-by-line resetting of *B.*

16 *Maurus*] *Marus A.* 26 lower] longer *A.* 29 flounders] founders *A.* 40 in for gain] in again *A.*

Epitaph upon Mr. John Dryden

Copy text: *Deliciae Poeticae; Or, Parnassus Display'd,* 1706 (Harvard copy).

Collation: More than a dozen witnesses to the text have survived in two closely related traditions both of which include manuscripts as well as printed versions. The better of these is the following:

Luttrell, *4,* 655	*A*
Hearne, *2,* 69	*B*
Flyleaf of Yale copy of *Luctus Britannici: Or The Tears of the British Muses; for the Death of John Dryden, Esq.,* 1700	*C*
BM MS. Burney 523, f. 111	*D*
Deliciae Poeticae; Or, Parnassus Display'd, 1706, p. 150	*E*
BM MS. Stowe 305, f. 242	*F*
Bodl. MS. Add. B.105, f. 6v	*G*
BM MS. Sloane 3065, f. 73	*H*
BM MS. Harleian 6914, f. 93	*J*

The inferior tradition is represented by the following:

University of Chicago MS. PR1195.C72, p. 106	*K*
TCD MS. I.5, *2,* 313	*L*
POAS, 1704, *3,* 379	*M*
PRSA, 1705, p. 536	*N*

Title: [none] *ACDFHJ* *Epitaph upon Mr. John Dryden B* *On Mr. John Dryden E* *Upon Mr. Dryden G* *On the Death of Mr. Dryden KLMN.*

1 *John Dryden*] Here lyes John Dryden, who *B* Here lyes old John who *C* (John) Drydens *JK.* 3 The fustian knight] Sir Dick he quick- *C* Sir Dick to Jack *DE* Against the Knight *F* The doughty Knight *GKLMN* The Knight he beat *H* The Knight was quick- *J* was forc'd] -ly made *C* he held *F* out of *H* -ly forc'd *J* to yield] the field *FH.* 4 The other two] But Nick and Jer *CH* maintain'd] ry kept *C* did make *F* ry made *H* still keep *J* have kept *KLMN* the Field] him yield *FH.* 5 the Poet's Life been] our poet's life been *B* his Life been somewhat *GH* the Poet had been *J* his Life been something *KLMN.* 6 beat] o'recome *A* knick't *B* foil'd *GKLMN.*

A Conference
Between King William and the Earl of Sunderland.
In a Letter to a Friend.
June 1700.

Copy text: BM MS. Lansdowne 852, f. 283.

Collation: The text survives only in manuscripts, none of sufficient authority to provide any confidence that the archetype can be totally recovered. These eight witnesses divide themselves equally into two groups. The independent manuscripts are immediately recognizable from the speech ascriptions, "C:" and "K:", in the left-hand margin. As in the case of *Advice to a Painter,* the independent manuscripts represent the best tradition but also include some of the worst corruptions (e.g. line 34, below). Two of them, BM MS. Sloane 1731A, f. 140 (*A*) and Egerton 1717, f. 49 (*B*), are fragmentary versions of only 50 lines, plus a 10-line "Postscript" probably by another, and inferior, hand. The copy text, BM MS. Lansdowne 852, f. 283 (*C*), by contrast, contains 155 lines. Of these, 34 (11–12, 53–56, 61–62, 69–74, 79–82, 85–88, 91–98, 161–62, 165–66) are not found in any other manuscript and 16 more (51–52, 57–60, 75–78, 83–84, 89–90, 163–64) are found only in *AB*. BM MS. Lansdowne 852, f. 41 (*D*), with 104 lines, shows evidence of contamination from the second group.

The factory manuscripts, all of which derive collaterally from a common source, are the following:

BM MS. Harleian 7315, f. 295v	*E*	115 lines
Portland MS. Pw V 48, p. 284	*F*	117 lines
Folger MS. M.b.12, f. 226v	*G*	100 lines
Portland MS. Pw V 44, p. 336	*H*	101 lines

E and *F* contain 10 lines (135–44) not found in any other manuscript. *G*, in addition to 100 lines of the text, also includes a 20-line version of the postscript mentioned above. The copy of the poem in Bodl. MS. Eng. poet. e.50 is George Thorn Drury's transcript of *F*. Three more witnesses, Cowper MS., Box 11, TCD MS. I.5, 2, 92, and Huntington MS. EL 8915, are not included in the apparatus.

Since the copy text includes no punctuation, a minimum has been supplied.

Title: [none] *AB* Letter June 1700 *CD* A Conference between K: W: and the E(arl) of Sund(er)l(an)d In a Letter to a Friend June 1700 *EFG* 1700. A Conference Between King William and the Earle of Sunderland In a Letter to a Friend *H*.

6 Not more in the Dumps] *AB* More pensive then Σ. 8 perceive] *AB* am told Σ. 9 Sacrament, swore] 'Tis thou said *AB* thou hast] *BC* that

has *A* you have made *D* you have *E* you've made *FHG.* 11–12 *omitted ABDEFGH.* 13–14 *omitted AB.* 17–30 *omitted AB.* 20 my] *CD* the *EFGH.* 22 three sworn] *CD* absolute *E* all sworn *FGH.* 25 *omitted G.* 27–28 *omitted ABDGH.* 28 Man] *EF* Keeper *C. After* 28 *EF add:* And now you may guess, if or no I have hit it. 31 I confesse] much *AB.* 32 be what will] *B* what will be *A* what ere be Σ. 33 like poor hen] *AB* like hen Σ. 34 but first] *A* and then *B* and Σ. 35 I designed to have given it to the man you were] You know the man I design'd you know *A* You know I design'd it, the man you were *B* I intended to have given it the Man you were *CD* I intended to have given it to the Man you was *EFG* I intended to have given it to the Man you are *H.* 37 bred up] *A* bred Σ. 38 Twere monstrous for him to] *AB* I must not let Methuen Σ. 39 lookeing] *ABC* growing Σ cry'd] *AB* said Σ. 41 I have sent] I'le send *E.* 43–50 *omitted AB.* 48 *omitted GH.* 48 you know] *CDF* you doe know *E.* 51–52 *omitted DEFGH.* 53–56 *omitted ABDEFGH.* 57–60 *omitted DEFGH.* 57 displacing] *AB* disgraceing *C.* 58 More Credit I've lost than can ere] *AB* The Credit I have lost can nere *C.* 59 With] *AB* With such *C* sure never before] *AB* never was heretofore *C.* 61–62 *omitted ABDEFGH.* 63 I must tell you] *AB* you know *C* said the King Σ I plainly] *AB* too late Σ. 64 taking] *AB* following Σ. 65–74 *omitted AB.* 67 that is] *C* that sure's *D* that's *E* 'tis *FG* it is *H.* 69–74 *omitted ABDEFGH.* 75–78 *omitted DEFGH.* 76 Kings to Change theires do think it no Shame] *C* Princes, you know, commanded the same *A* Princes (you know) have committed the same *B.* 79–82 *omitted ABDEFGH.* 83–84 *omitted DEFGH.* 84]*C* Religion's a Tool both to you and to mee *AB.* 85–88 *omitted ABDEFGH.* 89–90 *omitted DEFGH.* 89 He gets] I get *AB* To get good *C.* 90 By private agreement the Profit to] *A* by previous agreement the profitts to *B* But then of the Profitts hath always a *C.* 91–98 *omitted ABDEFGH.* 99 But ministers should] *AB* King's Ministers ought *C* A minster ought Σ. 100 their Councells receiv'd] *AB* their faithful Councells *C* his cunning Schemes Σ. 101 Honest] *ABC* able Σ. 105–06 *omitted AB.* 108 Seal] *ABC* Great Seal Σ be given to none but to] *AB* have been bestow'd upon Σ. 109–62 *omitted AB.* 109 these] *EFGH* the *CD.* 115–16 *omitted ABE.* 119 *omitted ABGH.* 120 *omitted ABCGH.* 120 National] *EF* Nation's *D.* 122 on another]*CD* and another *EFGH.* 131 Skip] *EF* Ship *CDGH.* 134 Though his Cowardly] *CDEF* To this Cowards *GH.* 135–44 *omitted ABCDGH.* 138 poisonous] *E* Poys'ning *F.* 146 Us Kings] *EF* all things *CGH* all Kings *D.* 150 tales] *DEFGH* things *C.* 151 all] *C* both *D* just *EFGH.* 152 be] *DEFGH* *are C.* 156 Arts] *CFGH* Art *DE.* 159 And after] *C.* After *DEFGH.* 161–62 *omitted ABDEFGH.* 163–64 *omitted DEFGH.* 164] *AB* You are so perfectly like one another *C.* 165–66 *omitted ABDEFGH.* *G* adds 167–86, of which 171–72 and 177–84 also occur in *AB:*

With the King in his Closset, the Count did contest,
That Religion and Government make but a Jest.
He, that two Kings hath betray'd and undone,
With his Councel alone can be faithful to none;
When the Chancellor turn'd out, his Enemy's thought
They all shou'd have been into the Government bro't.
But now like to rise no higher than they are,
They all of Preferment begin to despair.
Of advancement there is but a two fold Sort
The one to the Gallows, the other to th' Court.
Seym—r Harl—, and Harc——t with their Jacobite Crew,
All hanging deserve if they had but their due.
Their Tryal, Condemnation, and Tyburn Confession
I hope to send you the next Parliament Session.
But Methwyn's sad fate to his Surgeon's great Shame
Is to dy of a Mallady with an ill Name;
Besides being clap't, the Knave is but poor,
All Wages being Shar'd by his Patron and Whore.
Of all my Lord Somer's Foes, may the Hope
Of their Court Expectations end in Pox or a Rope.

The Foreigners

Copy text: The Foreigners. A Poem. Part I (1700) (Wing T3375) (Yale copy: Ij.T88.+700).

Collation: There are two witnesses to the text of *The Foreigners:* the copy text, a folio published by Ann Baldwin on 6 August 1700 (*A*), and a collateral manuscript, Osborn Chest II, No. 4, ff. 1–2 (*B*). The manuscript is corrupt and may have been taken down from dictation; it reads "a Mighty Jove" for "Almighty *Jove*" (90) and "An other Kingdom" for "And other Kingdoms" (156), but it retains at least one reading that corrects the folio.

The poem was also printed as the first item in the second volume of *POAS*, 1703, but the text is a word-for-word resetting of *A*. The second and third editions of *POAS*, 1703, are set up from the first. The text of the poem in *A New Collection of Poems Relating to State Affairs* (1705), in turn, is a word-for-word resetting of the third edition of *POAS*, 1703. (The relationship between these reprints is the same as that diagrammed above for *Advice to a Painter*).

76 noisy] riseing *B*. 147 untun'd] untoward *B*. 204 Bays that] Badges *A*.

The Reverse

Copy text: The Reverse: Or, The Tables Turn'd. A Poem . . . The Second Edition, Corrected (John Nutt) 1700 (TCD copy).

Collation: Despite the claims of the publisher, there is only one edition of *The Reverse* (Wing D1041), that published by John Nutt on 24 August 1700 (*A*). Corrections were made, probably by the author while the type was still standing, and with a new title page announcing *"The Second Edition, Corrected,"* this reissue (*B*) was advertised a week later (*The Post Boy,* No. 842, 29–31 August 1700).

4 These] Those *AB* Those] These *AB*. 11 Fiends] Friends *B*. 50 Reward] Rewards *A*. 79 they'd] they'll *A*. 116 groundless] thoughtless *A*. 166 still] hush *A*. 207 Jockey] Jockney *AB*.

The Court

Copy text: BM MS. Add. 21094, ff. 167v–168.

Collation: The text of the poem, which seems never to have been printed, is preserved in two closely related manuscripts, BM MS. Add. 21094 (*A*) and Huntington MS. EL 8904 (*B*). These in turn are derived collaterally from the same source as that of Portland MS. Pw V 48, pp. 277–80 (*C*). Bodl. MS. Eng. poet. c.50, ff. 34–38 is George Thorn Drury's transcript of *C*, formerly the property of Sir William Augustus Fraser. BM MS. Harleian 7315, ff. 291v–93v (*D*) seems even more remote from the archetype, and Bodl. MS. Rawl. poet. D.361, ff. 201v–04 (*E*) is an answer to *The Court,* in the form of an expanded paraphrase, cast into two separate poems. But since even this *pasticcio* seems to include some original readings, it is included in the apparatus.

Title: The Court *AB* To Damon 1700 *CD* Damon, Damon Parraphras'd *E*.

2 Coxcombs] *E* Coxcomb Σ. 10 *omitted E*. vicious] *BCD* various *A*. 13 *omitted E* 't'as] *D* has *ABC*. 19 Theams] *E* Things Σ. 21 *Architectus*] *Artichetus A* Artitchlechas *B* *Artichectas CD* Juvenal, or Perseus *E*. 22 Drunk] *ABE* Punk *CD*. 28 preach] plead *E*. 30 others] Darnell *E*. 34 Boucher] Bourcher *A*. 35 this one turn] *ABC* this Wom'n turn *D* Offley be *E*. 40 *omitted E* Morton] *A* Moreton *BCD*. 41 *omitted E*. England's] *BCD* England *A*. 46 Whores that] *AB*

Whores who *C* very Whores who *D* verry Whores they *E*. 54 but] and *D*. 55 Garrat] *ACD* Jarrat *B* Garret *E*. 59 Thô] *E* The Σ may] *E* may not *ABC* mayn't *D*. 60 They] The *A*. 61 or] and *A*. 68 purleing] *E* parting Σ. 71 too] *DE* to *ABC*. 75 make-ing] *E* Wryting Σ. 78 in peace] in a peace *C*.

The True-Born Englishman

Copy text: The True-Born Englishman. A Satyr, 1700 (Wing D850, Foxon D62) (Yale copy: Ik.D362.700T).

Collation: Lines 1064–1190, "Sir Charles Duncomb's Fine Speech, &c.," comprise the earliest part of the poem, having been written upon the occasion of Duncombe's election as sheriff of Middlesex county on 24 June 1699. Entitled *The New Tribune,* or *The Devil upon Dunne* (the proverbial horse in the mire), these lines circulated as an independent work and were even anthologized before *The True-Born Englishman* was written. They are preserved in the following manuscripts:

BM MS. Harleian 7319, pp. 755–61	*A*
Folger MS. M.b.12, ff. 220–222v	*B*
BM MS. Stowe 305, ff. 242v–243	*C*
Osborn MS. Chest II No. 1 (Phillipps 8301)	*D*

If it did not read "keep" at line 1180, *B* could be assumed to be a copy of *A;* both *A* and *B* are parts of a manuscript anthology and probably represent Defoe's original draft more closely than the other witnesses. *C* appears to be an extract from a private commonplace book, and *D* is a fragmentary manuscript lacking 20 lines, probably a factory product made to be sold separately.

Other parts of the poem which, on the basis of internal evidence, seem to be "detachable" and may have existed in draft before *The True-Born Englishman* was begun, are lines 893–956, Britannia's song in praise of William III, and lines 624–53, the "character" of "Shamwhig" Tutchin. The publication of Tutchin's *The Foreigners* on 6 August 1700 provided the catalyst that jostled these disparate elements into a single poem.

The main line of the argument is laid down in lines 1–623, 654–956, ending with Britannia's song in praise of the foreigner-king. Lines 957–1063 make the transition to the "character" of Duncombe, now introduced as an example of English ingratitude, and lines 1191–1215 provide a conclusion. The "character" of Tutchin (624–53), inserted in the midst of the argument against xenophobia, provides another example of English ingratitude. Defoe must have recognized almost immediately the irrelevance of his personal attack on Tutchin, for it is omitted from all authorized editions after the first.

Some 50 editions of *The True-Born Englishman* were published before 1750 but only four of these, *EFGH,* have any importance for establishing the text. As soon as the poem was published, the demand for copies was so great *"that besides Nine Editions of the Author,"* as Defoe recalled, the poem was *"Twelve Times printed by other Hands; some of which have been sold for* 1d. *others* 2d. *and others* 6d., *the Author's Edition being fairly printed, and on good Paper, and could not be sold under a Shilling.* 80000 *of the Small Ones have been sold in the Streets for* 2d. *or at a Penny"* (*A True Collection,* 1705, sig. A3r). Of these 21 editions only 10, five authorized and five pirated, have been identified (David F. Foxon, "A specimen of a catalogue," *The Library, 20* [December 1965], 277–97). A search of the major libraries in the United States, Great Britain, and Ireland has failed to find any more.

The first "true" edition (*E*), a quarto (D62), of which the Yale copy (Ik.D362.700T) has been collated, is easily distinguishable from the first pirated edition, an octavo volume also dated 1700 (Foxon D67). The publisher was "Captain [John?] *Darby* in St. *Martins-Lane,"* who, it is said, would have made a great deal of money "had not the Pirates invaded his Property," and Defoe estimated his own loss to be "above £1000" (*The True-Born Englishman: A Satyr, Answer'd,* 1701, p. 88; *The Post Angel, 1* [April 1701], 312–13; *A True Collection,* 1705, sig. A3r).

The second edition (*F*), of which the Yale copy (Ik.D362.C701 v. 1) has been collated, is another quarto, dated 1701 (Foxon D63). Like two of the three succeeding editions (Foxon D64 and D66), D63 collates A–H4. All four of these editions, in fact, must be very closely related in time, for sheets G and H of D64, D65, and D66 are not reset at all, but are successive reimpressions of D63. Sheets A–F of D64, however, appear to have been revised by Defoe. The Yale copy (Ik.D362.700Tb) has been collated (*G*).

D65, called "The Ninth Edition" on the title page, is not a new edition at all. Unsold copies of D64 were bound up with a new sheet A, bearing a new title page and "An Explanatory Preface," which was inserted before the old sheet A. The Yale copy of the resulting volume (Ik.D362.700tj) collates A4A3B–H4.

Sheets A–F of D66, called "The Tenth Edition" on the title page, are reset, not from D65, but from D63. The Clark Library copy (*PR3404.T861.1701h) has been collated.

The pirated editions have not been collated. The one described in *The Post Boy,* No. 907 for 28–30 January 1701, which "the White-Friars Sham-Printer has lately put out . . . and has so mangled the Sense and maim'd the Connections of one Paragraph with another, having left out more than half of the Original," is probably D68. This edition, which collates A–C4, omits lines (e.g. 861–66, 879–90) without any rhyme or reason. Yet even of this miserable edition two impressions were required. In what is presumably the first (Harvard copy: *EC7.D3823.701te), among the innumerable printer's errors there was one, a marginal note on page 5 which read "**Dr.* Archer" (a mistake for **Or* Archer), and another on page 21, which read "A enedful Comptence." In some copies (Yale: Ik.D362.706je) these errors have been "corrected" to "*Dr. Atcher" and "A ueedful Comptence."

As advertised in *The Post Boy,* No. 907, the text of the poem, which appeared in [William Pittis], *The True-Born Englishman: A Satyr, Answer'd Paragraph by Paragraph,* published on 31 January 1701 (*The London Post,* No. 48, 29–31 January 1701; Luttrell copy preserved at Harvard), was reset "from the true [i.e. first] Edition."

Next the poem was anthologized in:

A Collection of the Writings of the Author of the True-Born English-Man, [17 April] 1703, pp. [6]–41

A True Collection of the Writings of the Author of the True Born English-man, [22 July] 1703, sig. B1–p. 40.

POAS, 1703, 2, 7–46.

PRSA, 1705, pp. 277–315.

The relation of these editions to the authorized editions is shown in the diagram below.

Most surprising of all is the fact that two complete manuscript copies of the

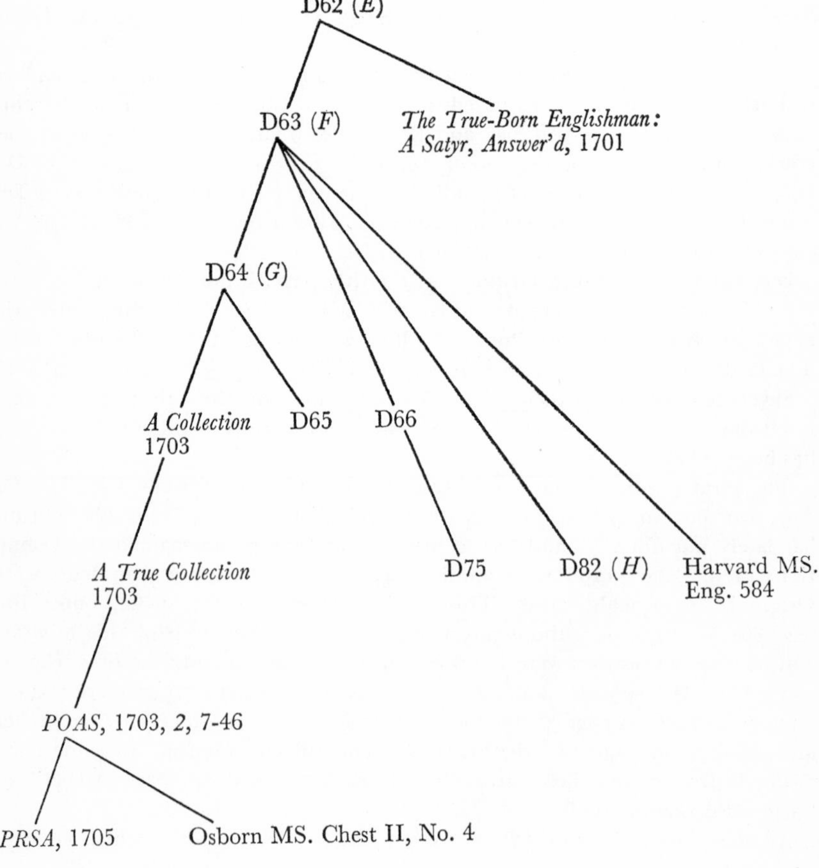

poem have been preserved. One of these, Osborn MS. Chest II, No. 4, pp. 3–18, was copied into a commonplace book from *POAS*, 1703, 2. The other, Harvard MS. Eng. 584, pp. 71–116, despite the fact that its title page attributes the poem to "An unknown Hand. 1703," is copied from the second authorized edition, *F*.

The fourth substantive edition (*H*) was published in 1716, a political generation after 1700. For this edition Defoe took the second edition (*F*) as his copy text, "mended some Faults" here and there, and added 59 lines. Retaining "An Explanatory Preface" added in "The Ninth Edition" (D65), he deleted the original Preface, probably because he felt it focused too narrowly on events of 1700—after the treaty of Utrecht there was an entire *new* set of reasons for English guilt to be warped into hatred of the Dutch—and wrote a new and very interesting "Preface by the Author," which concluded in diverting the praise of William III to a new foreigner-king, George I. Of this edition the Boston Public Library (**Defoe 21.T76. 1716) has been collated.

Title [lines 1064–1190]: The New Tribune *A* The New Tribune 1699 *B* The devil upon Dunne: 1700 *C* [none] *D* Sir Charles Duncomb's Fine Speech, &c. *EFGH.*

77 Empire's maintain'd] Empire's well maintain'd *H.* 79 Lords Justices] L—— J——— *EFG.* 87 *would in wise hands*] *in wise Hands wou'd H.* 88 Genius was] native Genius *H.* 98 livid] living *E.* 237 Medly of] Crowd of Rambling *FGH.* 288 *Charles*'s] *Ch——s*'s *EFGH.* 302 Nobility] N——ty *FG.* 304 *Castlemain*] *C———n EFG Castl——n H.* 305 *Portsmouth, Tabby Scot*] *P———h, Tabby S——t EFG Ports——th, Tabby Scot H.* 311 *Schomberg* and *Portland*] *S———g* and *P———d EFG Scom—g* and *Post—d H.* 387] How shall we else the want of Birth and Blood supply? *G* Other Pretence our Gentry must defy; *H.* 409] Her *S———lls, S——ls, C——ls, De——M—rs, EFG* Her *Sack—lls, Sav—ls, Ce—ls, Delam—rs, H.* 410] *M——ns* and *M——ues, D——s* and *V——rs, EFG Moh—ns* and *Mont—ues, Dura—s* and *Ve—rs, H.* 412] Your *H———ns, P——llons,* and *L——liers, EFG.* Your *Houb—ns, Pap—llons,* and *Leth—liers, H.* After 464 *H adds:*

The gen'ral Business of the meaner Sort,
Is drudging, drinking, quarrelling, and Sport:
Tho' these divide their Time, 'tis hard to say
Which of the four is Labour, which is Play.
So hard they ply the Bottle and their Trade,
Their Pleasure's equal to their Labour made.
The rugged Temper runs thro' ev'ry Part;
Their Sport's like Fighting, and their Fighting Sport.

494 reigneth] governs *FGH.* 500 And] As *FH.* *After* 540 *H adds:*

From all the World they differ in their Spleen,
So soon made mad, so soon restor'd again.

Pleasant in Broils, they smile when they engage;
There's something strangely calm in all their Rage;
Yet to their Disadvantage 't must be said,
'Tis all mere Nature, 'tis not in their Head;
'Tis neither Manners nor Philosophy;
'Tis all they know not how, and know not why.
  Their personal Quarrels they as ill persue,
As any Creatures bless'd with Souls can do;
A little while they're manag'd with the Tongue,
Then fight, before they judge of Right or Wrong;
Then cease, take Breath, argue about their Right,
And so alternately they scold and fight.
  For Strife's the natural Physick to their Phlegm,
Poyson to other People, Food to them.
And yet it must be own'd they seldom hate,
Harbour no ranc'rous Thoughts of ancient Date,
Or Father-Feuds entail'd with the Estate.
Their Sense of Injury's so very quick,
The least Delay in Payment makes them sick.
They keep no smother'd Malice in their Mind;
The Reason's plain, they always pay in Kind.
Swift in Return, impatient of the Wrong,
They hate to be in Debt for Mischief long;
And if they can't decide the warm Dispute,
They ne'er adjourn the Cause, but fight it out.
Then the next Age concerns themselves no more,
Than if they had been always Friends before.
  Their strange litigious Temper runs so high,
And they so oft fall out, they know not why;
That 'twas their Father's study to invent,
For uncouth foolish Crimes, a suited Punishment.
Such are their *Ridings,* Ducking Stools, and Juries,
For Husband-Drivers, Scolds, and Household-Furies;
The awkward Execution plainly shews
'Twas less contriv'd to punish, than expose.
And 'twas but just indeed to have Compassion
On Crimes entail'd by Blood upon the Nation.
  Some think their brangling Temper's kept in Awe
By Justice and the Iron Hands of Law:
But wiser Heads have thought it does them Harm,
And prompts the Humour which it should disarm;
For under Skreen of Justice, they engage
In all the most unhappy Parts of Rage;
The Life-Blood of their Fortunes freely draw,
And Beggars spend the Parish-Alms at Law:
The strange litigious Gust appears so keen,
They'll starve their Children, to supply their Spleen.

576 their] the *FH.* 582 first] Long *FGH.* 584 When,] But First *FGH.* 624–53 *omitted FGH.* 724 Do all their former Doctrines] Their former Doctrines all at once *FGH.* 772 They are no] They're no more *H.* 794 Seas] Sea *H.* 795 Degrees] Degree *H.* 801 do] will *FGH.* 884 Spirit] Spirit can *G* Spirits can *H.* 912 won] worn *E.* 978 Temper's] Temper *F.* 1055 bore Office in] should represent *FGH.* 1067 Greatness there appear'd no] future Greatness, not a *ABCD.* 1068 Behold I] Appear'd; I'm *ABCD.* 1079 Gift] Thing *ABCD* they] She *ABC.* 1083 I enjoy] I now Injoy *ABC.* 1086–87 *omitted D.* 1093 Labours rather than] Labours then, & since *A* Labours, than *B* rather Labour, then *D.* 1096 ever] alwaies *ABC.* 1103 Fortune] Fortunes *CEFGH.* 1104–05 *omitted D.* 1105 which] who *AB.* that *C.* 1106 eager] equall *AB.* 1108–09 *omitted D.* 1108 *Ingratitude*'s] Ingratitude *ABCG.* 1112 other Crimes by] other Sins, but *AB* Sins by *C* other sins by *D.* 1115 perhaps it may] it may perhaps *AB.* 1116 my first Benefactor I] My Benefactor I *B* I, my first Creator *D.* 1117 a second] another *ABCD.* 1122–23 *omitted D.* 1122 great Int'rest] good Interest *ABC* great Int'rests *EFGH.* 1123 so] thus *ABC.* 1132 Treason] Treachery *ABCD.* 1136–37 *omitted D.* 1136 'tis] 'twas *C.* 1141 nor half the Government] *omitted AB* till all from him we shd vent *C.* 1142–47 *omitted D.* 1147 yet never cou'd be] nor never yet was *FG* and never yet was *H.* 1152 And so to Forgery my Hand I] And so to Forgery my Hand was *AB* My hand to Forgery I therefore *D.* 1153 gull] cheat *ABCD.* 1156 'Twas . . . and not for] 'Twas . . . not *C* It was for . . . not *D.* 1157 printed in] first endow'd *ABC* had endow'd *D.* 1158 A needful Competence of *English*] With a necessary Competence of *ABC* As all men know, with its full share of *D.* 1159–60 *omitted D.* 1160 Servant] Broker *ABC.* 1161 the matter . . . Art] their honours . . . Gold *D.* 1166 Properties] Liberties *ABCD.* 1168 Guards of their] Guard of their *B* Squadron of *D.* 1169 by my] with my *ABC* with the *D.* 1170 Debtor] Merchants *AB.* 1171 Thieves] Rogues *AB.* 1174 Miss *Morgan* shall] Miss D—— can *AB* Davis & Morgan can *C* Miss Morgan can *D* Miss —— shall *E* Miss *M——n* shall *FH* Miss shall *G.* 1177 fear] feel *AB.* 1179 go] Run *ABD.* 1180 keep] make *ACD.* 1183–84 *omitted D.* 1184 just] fit *ABC.* 1188 Needy] blinded *ABD* blindest *C.* 1204 do the Wise] for wise Men *H.* *After* 1216 *H adds:*

Vice is down-hill; and when we do offend,
'Tis Nature all, we act what we intend.

The Worcester Cabal

Copy text: Osborn MS. Chest II, No. 1 (Phillipps 8301), ff. [68r–69r].

Collation: The text survives only in three manuscripts: Lechmere MS. B.A. 1531/40(i), pp. 8–9 (*A*), Osborn MS. Chest II, No. 1 (Phillipps 8301) (*B*), and

Portland MS. Pw V 41 (*C*). *B* and *C* seem to derive from a common source, different from the source of A.

Title: The Worcester Caball or a very New Ballad to a Mighty Old Tune, call'd Packingtons Pound *A* The Worcester Cabal, Or a very new Ballad to a very old Tune, call'd Packingtons Pound. The Second Edition with Annotations & Ammendments. By J[?]:P[?]. Esqr. *B* The Worcester Cabal: A new Ballad, to an Old-Tune. P: P: *C.*

1 six] 9 *AC* four Squires] 3 Esquires *A* 3 Squires *C.* 2 Representer] Representitive *C.* 3 in the Colour] in Colour *BC* of Claret] of Carrot *B* of a Carrot *C.* 9 for the Parliament] for Parliament *B.* 12 as if a Courant were] as if Courant Was *B* if a Courant was *C.* 13 Jests, and] of Jests *C.* 16 And] Who *B* notable Things as] words that it *A* noble things that *C.* 18–27 *omitted AC.* 30 Then the] the *C.* 34 tells us, (if] tells, if *C.* 36 fourscore Men, and] fourscore, and *B.* 37 of a Sister] of Sister *B.* 40 And fits] And fit for *B* fits *C* Cabal, Sir, because] Cabal, because *BC.* 41 Quoth this William] Quoth William *BC.* 45 swing] hang *C.* 46 Spoke the Squire] the Esquire Spake *A* Spake the Squire *C.* 53 his] their *BC.* 56 request of these] request these *A.* 57 And that all] And all *C* might] may *C.* 61 Who's] is *C.* 62 for late Writ of Error he] for's new Witt, that he had *A* for new writt of erour he *C.* 63 On the door] On door *B.* 67 like a] 'em, like *B.* 70 But will] He'll *BC.* 74 Swore he'd] vow'd he wou'd *A* said hee'd *C.* 76 regulate the Bishops] regulate Bishops *BC.* 77 at this] if *C.* 79 Their] Those *B* against which plots are Laid] this Cabal wou'd invade *B.* 80] Whilst all their wise Councils, themselves do Confound *A.* 81 That] And *B* taken now] now taken *B.*

A New Satyr on the Parliament

Copy text: A Poem [n.d.] (Harvard copy: 25242.72PF* [92]).

Collation: Although seven editions, three manuscripts, and half a dozen reprints of this poem have been preserved, it is not now possible to determine which of these most accurately embodies the author's intentions. None of the manuscripts antedates the earliest printed texts and it may be that no copy of the first edition has survived.

The earliest extant edition seems to be an anonymous folio half-sheet (Foxon X42) bearing no imprint and entitled simply *A Poem* (*A*). Such precaution is not surprising, however, for it was extremely dangerous to publish, while parliament was still in session, an attack on a House of Commons which had already imprisoned the Kentish petitioners for "taxing [its] Discretion" (115) so much more politely.

What little evidence that there is indicates that four almost identical quarto editions derive from the folio in the following line of descent:

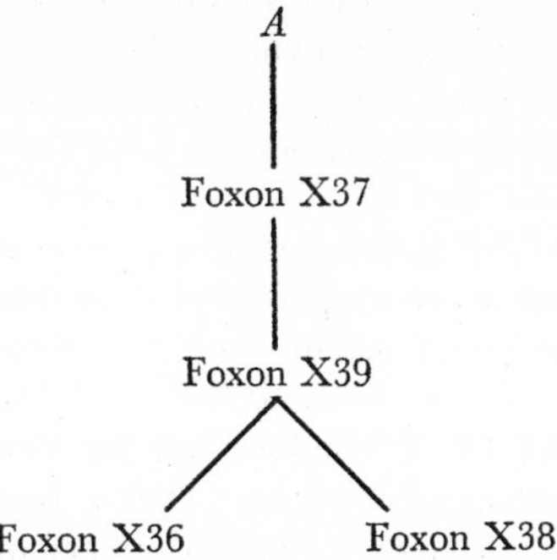

Since there are no substantive variants, the evidence for these relationships is of the following kind:

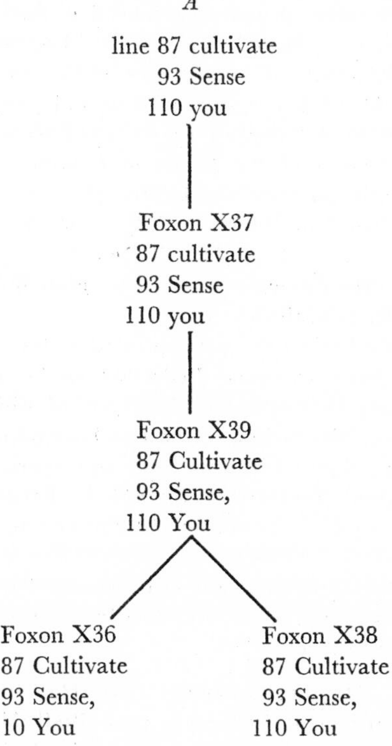

X37, X39, and X38 are the products of hurried and careless presswork, perhaps in John Darby's garret, where, if William Pittis is correct, his "Servants . . . work Tooth and Nail to get ready Seditious Pamphlets soon enough to be cry'd about the Streets next Morning" (*Letters from the Living to the Living,* 1703,

p. 153). All of them, for example, print "neglelcted" at line 50 and "or're" at line 153. X36, however, seems to be a corrected edition—corrected by a proof-reader and not by the author, who presumably would have emended such obvious errors as "you knew" for "you know" (134).

One manuscript of the poem, Harvard MS. 606, pp. 36–43, probably derives from X38. Another, Bodl. MS. Rawl. 361, ff. 205v–10, derives either from X37, X39, or X36.

A slightly different textual tradition is preserved in three remaining witnesses. The first of these, another undated quarto with no title and no imprint (Foxon X40) (*B*), but apparently published in Dublin, is fitted out with "The Second Part" ("No Wonder *P——s, F—ch,* and *Sh——r*") and "A Dialogue between the Old Horse at Charing Cross, London, and the Young One over against the Trustee's Court on Colledge-green Dublin" ("Dear Brother or Sire, for I'm sure we're a Kin"). The press corrector, failing to understand how "deficient Funds" could be a "publique Cheat," altered line 53 to make parliament itself the cheat. And the compositor, discovering that he had omitted lines 151–55, simply tacked them on to the end of the poem where they make no sense at all. Yet despite all this, *B* preserves three or four readings that are superior to any of the London editions and it is the only witness for "The Second Part."

Collaterally derived from the same source as that of the Dublin quarto is a manuscript, Osborn MS. Chest II, No. 3, of no independent value, and another folio half-sheet, entitled *A Coppy of Verses, Expressing the Peoples Dissatisfaction with the Proceedings of the House of Commons* (Foxon X41), with no imprint but apparently published in Edinburgh. The compositor, at any rate, substitutes "ye" for "you," introduces an elegant Scoticism, "inhauns'd," into the text at line 110, and turns "King *James*'s Reign" (119) into the more familiar "King Jamie's time." He also omits lines 91–96, probably because, like the editor of *B,* he did not understand them.

A New Satyr on the Parliament was reprinted at least half a dozen times, first in *The Ballad, Or; Some Scurrilous Reflections in Verse, on the Proceedings of the Honourable House of Commons: Answered,* of which the text is probably taken from Foxon X37, the earliest of the London quartos. Besides four London editions (Foxon X43–X46), this work was also reprinted in Dublin as *The Memorial, alias Legion, Answered, Paragraph by Paragraph: With a Reply to the Scurrilous Reflections in Verse, on the Proceedings of the House of Commons.*

A New Satyr on the Parliament was next reprinted in *A Collection of Poems on State Affairs* (1712), pp. 3–11, and finally in *A Collection of Scarce and Valuable Tracts,* 1748, *3,* 5–11.

Title: A Poem *A* On the Parliament 1701 (Harvard MS. 606, p. 36) A new Satyr On the Parliament June 28th. 1701 (Bodl. MS. Rawl. D.361, f. 205v) [no title] *B* A Coppy of Verses, Expressing the Peoples Dissatisfaction with the Proceedings of the House of Commons (Foxon X41) cf. 81–85 *n.,* above.

1 Ye] You *B.* 2 Our] Some *B.* 5 by] thro' *B.* 8 distrust] Mistrust *B.* 10 you] you're *B.* 11 wisdome takes] Wisdoms take *B.*

14 France . . . makes] the *French* . . . make *B.* 15 Laughs . . . the] Laugh . . . our *B.* 19 Your Friends and you are] Instead, you have them *B.* 20 was] you *B.* 25 And baulk] Baulk all *B.* 48 the] our *B.* 53 That Parliamentary] Of *Parliaments,* that *B.* 79 Statesmen] Tradesmen *B.* 93 he refines his] to Refine our *B* Sense,] Sense *A.* 109 seem to wear the] serve to wear a *B.* 128 And some] Some too *A.* 133 flow] flew *A.* 134 know] knew *A.* 143 Address] address *A.* 154 the] our *B.* 155 you'l] you'd *B.* 156 ye] you *B.* 166 are] our *A.* 176 Cap] Caps *A.* 186–220 *omitted A.*

Advice to a Painter. 1701

Copy text: POAS, 1707, *4,* 126–37.

Collation: There are only two witnesses to the text of *Advice to a Painter. 1701,* with no substantive variants between them: BM MS. Stowe 305, ff. 258–258v, and a fragmentary version in *POAS,* 1707, *4,* 126–27. The manuscript begins with the two lines that are printed here as an epigraph and continues with lines 1–6. The printed version omits lines 1–6. Both witnesses include lines 7–27. The epigraph has been separated from the text of the poem because it seems to supply a generalizing proem, rather than a true beginning to lines 1–6.

A Paradox in Praise of War

Copy text: A Pacquet from Parnassus, Vol. I, No. 2, 1702, pp. 15–16 (Yale copy).

Collation: Only two witnesses to the text have been recovered:

A Pacquet from Parnassus, Vol. I, No. 2, 1702, pp. 15–16 *A*
A Collection of Poems on State-Affairs, 1712, pp. 23–24 (Bodl. copy) *B*

B appears to represent the author's revision of *A.*

1 Morality] Mortality *AB.* 35 such] much *B.* 36 As] And *B.* 45–48 *omitted B.* 51–54 *omitted B.* 55 in the Soul breeds] breeds in the Soul *B.* 56 That some] As Men *A.*

England's Late Jury

Copy text: England's Late Jury: A Satyr, 1701 (Lambeth Palace copy).

Collation: There are two states of the folio half-sheet edition, of which the first is represented by copies at Harvard and the University of Texas and the second by the Lambeth Palace and BM (G.559[4]) copies. The uncorrected state omits the word "Foreign" in line 4, but otherwise there are no substantive variants.

The text of the poem, set up from the corrected state of the first edition, was also included in *England's Late Jury. A Satyr: With The Counter-Part, In Answer to it,* 1702, of which the BM copy (11631.bb.23) has been collated. Other reprints of the poem derive from the first edition according to the following scheme:

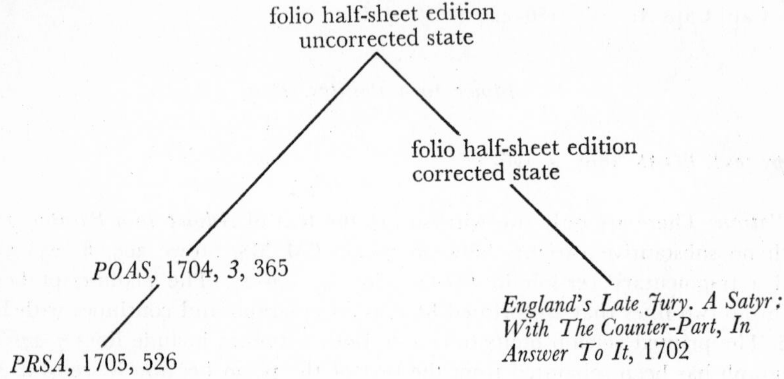

The Mourners

Copy text: POAS, 1703, 2, 320 (Princeton copy).

Collation: The text of *The Mourners* survives in two traditions, the better of which is represented by:

Bodl. MS. Mus. Sch. c.81, f. 24	*A*
Bodl. MS. Smith 23, f. 107	*B*
BM MS. Add. 27989, p. 28	*C*

The inferior tradition is represented by:

BM MS. Add. 40060, f. 11	*D*
Bodl. MS. Rawl. poet. D.361, f. 55	*E*
Osborn MS. Box 37, No. 16	*F*
POAS, 1703, 2, 320	*G*

Bodl. MS. Rawl. poet. 173, f. 129 and *PRSA,* 1705, pp. 483–84 are independently derived from *G.* Bodl. MS. Rawl. poet. 169, f. 9v, in turn, is derived from *PRSA,* 1705.

Two more witnesses have not been included in the apparatus: one of these is Kent Archives Office U442.Z26/3, a manuscript similar to *ABC*, and the other is a printed text, *The Observator*, No. 18, 20–24 June 1702, from which *G* seems to derive.

Title: An Answer to the Mock Mourner *A* The Mourners *BDF* A Satyr on K. Wm. *C* The Mourners. A Satyr Writ on the Death of King William Anno 1702 *E* The Mourners: Found in the Streets, 1702 *G*.

1 the] your *G*. 2] Dismall their outsides, what e're their insides are *BC* And cloud the coming Beauties of the Year *DEFG*. 4 Condition] Misfortunes *DEFG*. 5 Summs by him] Masse of Coyn *DFG* Summs of Coyne *E*. 6 those idly] and those idly *BC* or idly *DF* and idly *G* lent] spent *EG*. 7 for the Statues, and the Tapestry] for the Tapestry and Statues *DE* for your Tapestry and Statues *F* your Tapestry and Statutes *G*. 8 From *Windsor*, gutted to aggrandize] From gutted Windsor, to agrandize *A* And gutted Windsor to aggrandize *BC* And Windsor gutted to Adorn the *DE* Windsor gutted to adorne the *F* And *Windsor* gutted to adorn your *G*. 9–10 *follow line* 6 *in A*. 9 from *Scotland*] since *BC*. 10 mourn as much the] mourne much more for the *B* mourn much more the *CDEF* much more mourn your *G*. 11 ten Years of] a ten Years *AEG* a wicked ten years *B* a Ten years' wicked *C* dismal] *omitted BC*. 12 For] And *BCFG*. 14 of] to *BC* for *DEFG* need] shall *ABC*. 15 eighteen] fifteen *DEFG*. 16–18 *omitted C*. 16 If matters then, my Friends] If matters, then, yee Sots *B* well then (my Friends) Since things *DEFG*. 17 Tho now you mourn, 't had lessen'd] Let's e'en Mourn on: 'twould lessen *D* E'ne Lett's Mourn on! It had *E* lett's e'ne Mourne on 'twould lessen *FG*. *After* 18 *BC add:*

Wisely ourselves from Popery to secure,
Wee first attaint the Prince, and then abjure.
No doubt the Senate takes a proper course,
If oaths with us have still their proper force:
The very men, who caus'd the Martyr's fate,
First swore by God, they'd make him wondrous great:
And they that 'gainst the Son Swore once againe
To keep him out, were those that brought him in.

Upon Sorrel

Copy text: The Observator, No. 4, 22 April 1702.

Collation: The six witnesses to the text of *Upon Sorrel* include four manuscripts and two printed versions:

BM MS. Add. 40060, f. 10v *A*
Chicago University MS. PR1195.M73, p. 130 *B*
The Observator, No. 4, 22 April 1702 *C*
Bodl. MS Smith 23, p. 121 *D*
Downshire MS. Trumbull Add. 18 *E*
POAS, 1703, 2, 323 (Princeton copy) *F*

The versions in BM MS. Add. 6229, f. 30 and Essex R.O. MS. D/DW.z4 are copies of *C*. Osborn MS. Box 37, No. 16, with a similar first line ("Illustrious Sorrell shall the Zodiacke grace"), is a different work, a variation on the original theme by an inferior hand. The version in *PRSA,* 1705, p. 485, is derived from *F,* and Bodl. MS. Rawl. C.986, f. 15v, in turn, is derived from *PRSA,* 1705.

Title: [none] *ABCE* Upon Sorrell *D* *On* S——l *F.*

2 whom] thee *F* and the Bull] Bull and Bear *E.* 3 Duggs] Dam *DF* the Earth] that Earth *CD.* 4 beheld thy] first gave thee *F.* 5 wrong'd *Iërne*] Glenco breed thee *A* wrong'd *Hibernia F.* 6 Produce thee first, or] Or didst thou rise from *A.* *After* 6 *F adds:* Or barbarously massacred *Glencoes Claim.* 7 Where] Who *BCD* Which *E* Whence *F* now] thou *F.* 9 Sacred] Noble *DEF.* 12 you] thou *B.*

A Dialogue between the Illustrious Ladies,
The Countesses of Albemarle and Orkney,
Soon after the King's Death

Copy text: Downshire MS. Trumbull Add. 18.

Collation: The text of *A Dialogue between the Illustrious Ladies* has been preserved only in the Downshire MS. It is reproduced here with punctuation and spelling normalized.

The Mock Mourners

Copy text: The Mock Mourners. A Satyr, By way of Elegy on King William. The Second Edition Corrected. 1702 (Foxon D41) (Yale copy: Ik.D362. C701. v.1).

Collation: Of the 13 entries under *The Mock Mourners* in Foxon (D40–D52), only five are separate editions and only one of these is a substantive edition. This is the first (D40), of which the Yale copy (Ik.D362.702m) has been collated

(*A*). The second impression of the first edition (D41), called "The Second Edition Corrected," was chosen as copy text because it embodies corrections that are undoubtedly authorial (*B*). The second edition of the poem (D42, D43) is a Dublin piracy, also entitled "The Second Edition Corrected," which is a line-by-line reprint of *B*. The Boston Public Library copy of this volume (**Defoe 21.M61.1702A) has been collated.

All of these volumes are quartos, but the third edition of the poem is an octavo volume (D47) entitled "The Fifth Edition Corrected." This volume, of which the Yale copy (Ik.D362.702me) has been collated, is another line-by-line reprint of *B*. The quarto editions called third, fourth, and fifth on the title pages (D44, D45, D46) are successive reimpressions of *B*. A sixth edition (D48) is described in W. T. Morgan, *A Bibliography of British History (1700–1715)*, 2 vols., Bloomington, Indiana, 1934–37, *1*, 209: "36 pp. 4°, 1702," but a search of the major libraries in the United States, Great Britain, and Ireland has failed to find a copy. The quarto called "The Seventh Edition Corrected" (D49), of which the Boston Public Library copy (**Defoe 21.M61.1702E) has been collated, is the fourth edition of the poem. The two octavo editions, D50 and D51, entitled respectively "The Seventh Edition Corrected" and "The Ninth Edition Corrected," are the same edition as D47 but with new title pages. Of these, the Yale copy (Ik.D362.702mg) and the Bodl. copy (Vet. A3.e.237) have been collated. The fifth edition of the poem, set up from D49, is an Edinburgh piracy (D52) entitled "The Eighth Edition Correected" (NLS copy: 3/2861 [1]).

The text of *The Mock Mourners* in *A Collection of the Writings of the Author of the True-Born English-Man*, 1703, was also set up from "The Seventh Edition Corrected" (D49). The versions that appeared in *POAS*, 1703, *2*, 291, and in *A True Collection of the Writings of the Author of the True Born English-man*, 1703, pp. 41–63 (*C*) are both derived collaterally from *A*. In the latter, however, the reading "Infects" at line 75 must have been supplied by Defoe. Of this volume, the Brown University copy was collated.

These complicated relationships are represented in the diagram on p. 776.

38 lose] loose *AB*. 42 And] Which *AC*. 75 Infects] To infect *A*. 85 may] will *B*. 90 And] Which *B*. 137 thou canst] you can *AC*. 192–95]

> Backward in Deeds, but of their Censures free,
> And slight the Actions which they dare not see.
> At Home they bravely teach him to Command,
> And Judge of what they are afraid to mend: *AC*.

224 Lords . . . *Peers*] L——s . . . *P——s* *ABC*. 225 durst] dare *AC*. 231 Drunken Quarrels] Drink and Darkness *B*. 238 *Warwick*] W——— *ABC*. 241 *Warwick*] *W*——— *ABC*. 247 misfortunes] misfortune *AC*. 312 the] that *AC*. 393 cou'd] can *AC*.

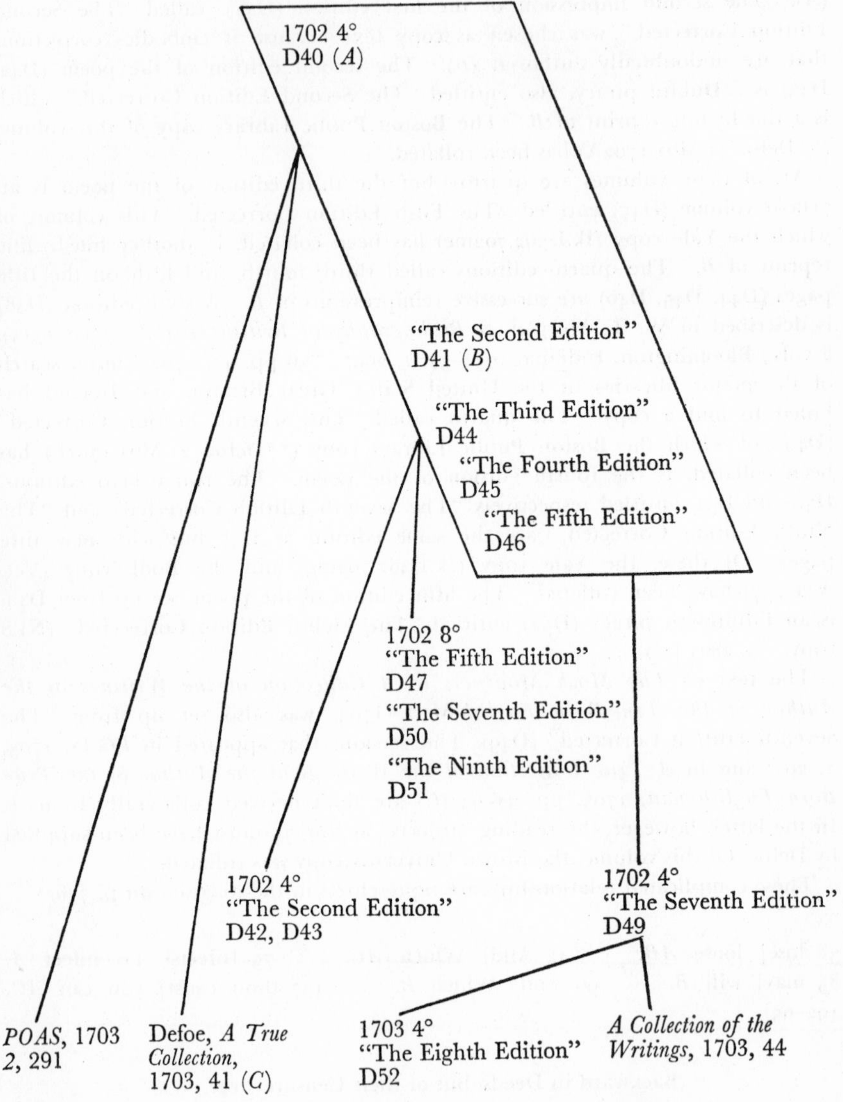

Reformation of Manners

Copy text: *Reformation of Manners, A Satyr*, 1702 (Foxon D54) (Boston Public Library copy).

Collation: The text is preserved in six printed editions and a fragmentary manuscript. The first edition seems to be Foxon D54, of which the copy in the Boston Public Library has been collated (*A*). Of the two remaining quarto editions, D55 is derived from D54 and D56 from D55. The version in the pirated *Collection of the Writings of the Author of the True-Born English-Man* (1703) was set up from D55, while the authoritative version in *A True Collection of the Writings of the Author of the True Born English-man* (1703) was set up from D56. For the latter, Defoe took the opportunity to add and subtract a few lines and to revise a few dozen more. The Yale copy of this revised text has been collated (*B*).

The text of the poem in *POAS*, 1703, 2, 340–74, was set up from *A*.

Lines 463–502 have also been preserved in a manuscript, BM MS. Lansdowne 852, f. 48, and in a folio half-sheet (omitting lines 471–72) entitled *Casco, and His Brothers; As Describ'd in the Satyr, call'd, The Reformation of Manners, By Daniel De Foe. In the first Vol. (Page 81.) of His Works,* n.p., n.d. (Essex R.O., D/DBy. 25). Both of these derive collaterally from *B*.

The readings of *B* have been incorporated into the text where they correct seeming errors in the meaning (e.g. 222, 537) or in the meter (e.g. 75, 313) of *A*, but not where they represent stylistic preferences (e.g. 212, 293).

66 all's] all *A*. 75 Sacred Temples] Reprobate Gates there *A*. 81 Imposter] Imposture *B*. 115 *Lovel*] *L——l AB*. 144 they're] their *A*. 149 *Furnese*] *F———e A Fur——e B*. 152 defect] defects *B*. 155 wore] were *B*. 164–67 *omitted B*. 171 Fortune] Fortunes *B*. 172 the] of *B*. 183 *Sweetaple*] *S———ple AB* *Cole*] *C–le AB*. 197 Magistrates] Magistrate *AB*. 204–5 *omitted A*. 208 When Men] They that *A*. 212 'Twas in his Reign we to Reform] Our Reformation in his Reign *B*. 216 *Clayton*] *C———n AB*. 222 Nor's] Nor *A*. 226 *Toland's*] *T——d's A Tol—d's B*. 244 *Duncomb*] *D———b AB*. 264 Whimsies, lets] Whimsies let *AB*. 293 the Effect because they miss] th' Effect by missing first *B*. 313 with their] who with a *A*. 316 Charm's] Cheat's *B*. 361 too they may] they may well *B*. 362 *did*] *do A*. 366, 367, 389, 394, 397, 415 *Blackbourn*] *B——— A B——bourn B*. 392 God] *Jove A*. 394 Conquests] Conquest *A*. 400 Parliaments] *P——— A P———ts B*. 403 Peer] *P—r A*. 404 Member] *M——r A M—ber B*. 410 Parliament] P——— *AB*. 415 *Asgill*] *A——l A*. 416 *Toland*] *T——d A*. 420 Gaols] Goals *AB*. 424 Offence] affront *B*. 448 *Edmund's*] *Ed——'s A*. 471–72 *omitted A*. 485 were] went *B*. 537 i' th'] its *A*. 542 to] *omitted A*. 563 *Sidly*] *S——y A S—ly B*. 564 *Seymore*] *S——e AB*. 573 *Harcourt*] *H———t AB*. 574 Tenets] Tenents *A*. 576 *Cutts*] *C—— A C–tts B*. 578 *Bolls*] *B——— A B–lls B*. 584, 603 *Prior*] *P—— A P—or B*. 603 O What] What strange *B*. 604 *Dorset*] *D——— A D—set B*. 607 *Toland*] *To——d A To–and B*. 608 adorn;] *B* adorn *A*. 612 *Mohun's*] *M——n's A Moh–n's B*. 627 *Mohun*] *M—— AB*. 631 this] the *B*. 633 *Thomas*] *T——s Cecil B*. 635 *Essex*] *E——x A*. 637 *Bedford*] *B———d A*. 640 *P———k, Paul,* or *Robinson*] *P———k, P—l,* or *R———n A*. 653 *Torrington*] *T———n A Toring—n B*. 655 *Orford*] *O——d A Orf—d B*. 655 *brave*] *old B*. 710 rather

forfeit Heaven] forfeit Heaven, rather *A.* 711 which by] by which *AB.* 714 t'have one Drunkard] when one Drunkard's *B.* 719 does] will *B.* 721 how] that *B.* 757 needful] heedful *A.* 768 their] the *AB.* 799 *Religions*] *Religion B.* 855 Priestcraft] Priest—— *A.* 871 And] Even *A.* 929 conforms] adheres *B.* 930 Forms] Prayers *B.* 936 *Whore*] *W—— A.* 941 *Pelling*] *P—— A Pel——n B.* 944 Day] *Time B.* 979 Lord of *London's*] *L—* of *L—— A* Lord of *L—— B.* 980 Rakes] R—— *A.* 981 Lordship] *L—— A L——p B.* 984 In] On *A.* 998 Farce] F—— *A.* 1000 *Rakes*] *R—— A.* 1011 Sovereign Power] *S—— P—— A.* 1020 *Musgrove's*] *M—— A Musgr—s B.* 1021 *Dorset*] *D—— A Dar—'t B.* 1022 *Oxford*] *O—— A Oxf—d B.* 1025 *Devonshire*] *D—— A D——shire B* Ormond] *O—— A Orm—d B.* 1027 Duke] D— *A.* 1030 Peer] P— *AB.* 1032 Duke] D— *AB.* 1033 *Portugal* or *Spain*] *P——* or *S—— A.* 1078 If] The *AB.* 1099 because they'd learn] *omitted A.* 1118 Jilt's] Jilt *A.* 1146 *Wessly*] *W—ly A Wess–ly B.* 1147 *Blackmore*] *Bl——re A Black—re B.* 1160 when h' lost his] as well as *B.* 1215 *Morgan*] *M——n AB.* 1256 will] will'd to *A.*

The Golden Age

Copy text: The Golden Age from the Fourth Eclogue of Virgil, &c., 1703 (BM copy 11385.e.16).

Collation: The only witness to the text of the poem (*A*) is the first edition, a 4° volume which collates A-B [2] (Yale copy: Poems 17; BM copy: 11385.e.16). Another 4° volume with the same title and date—but which collates [A] [4] and bears a different printer's device and no place of publication on the title page —is not a second edition of *A* but a new, and inferior, poem (BM copy: 11375.ee.37) worked up from fragments of the old. It is inferior because the plain Jacobitism of the original has been sophisticated by the omission of lines 10, 28–29, and 130–31 and because the addition of 97 lines (after 27) representing the Elizabethan age as a "*Golden Age* of Peace" to be "reviv'd in *Ann*" has no counterpart in Virgil's fourth eclogue, which the poem pretends to "imitate." But since it may represent the work of the same author, most of the textual variants are included below (*B*).

The version of the poem that was reprinted in *POAS,* 1703, 2, 441–45, is reset from *A*. The text in *PRSA,* 1705, in turn, derives from *POAS,* 1703.

4 Ear] Year *AB.* 10 *omitted B.* 14 Pleasures] Pleasure *A* Rolling] reeling *B.* *After 27 B adds 97 lines, of which the last nine are:*

> Forgotten *Willoughby* in *Cuts* is seen,
> And Great *Eliza*'s Fame revives agen,
> In just so Bright a *Court,* so Good a *Queen,*
> Deserving *Walsingham* and *Hunsdon* now

Revive again in *Nottingham* and *How,*
Mildmay, by *Mostin*'s Virtues is pursu'd
Norris, by *Seymour* in his Countreys good;
Howard and *Hawkins,* are by *Rook* supply'd,
While *Bacon*'s Learning, *Holt* and *Wright* divide.

28–29 *omitted B.* 30 Queen! Thy . . . Enemies] PRINCESS! whose . . . Foes do *B.* 33 *Halifax*] *H——— AB.* to] will *A.* 34 *Somers*] *S—— AB.* 36–48 *omitted B.* 40 *Wharton*] *W——— A.* 42 *Stamford*] *S——— A.* 43 *Enfield*] *E——d A.* 45 *Ranelagh*] *R——— A.* 51–54 *omitted B.* 51 *South . . . Sherlock*] *S—— . . . S——— A.* 52 *Kennett*] *K——— A.* 53 *Atterbury*] *Att——y A.* 57–60 *omitted B.* 59 *Lambeth*] *L———*'s *A.* *After* 62 *B adds:*

Faction (like Rebels) seldom wants pretence
To taint the Glorious Actions of a Prince,
Nor will till Murm'ring Envy cease her Spite,
Or Bards for Spleen and Int'rest cease to write.

63 *Munden*] *M—en AB.* 65–66 *omitted B.* 65 *Hara*] *H——— A.* 66 *Bellasis*] *B——— A.* *After* 66 *B adds:*

But where Great Marlborough does his Arms employ,
The Union *Rook,* or *Cuts*'s Ensigns fly,
Conquest and Terrour shall their Foes subdue,
While they to Fame, and to their Int'rest true,
Shall bring their Laurels home Great Queen to you;
Till Crown'd with *Glory* and Eternal *Peace,*
You sit and smile, and see the Lands encrease.

68 who from Conquest Fled] by his Valour led *B.* 71–91 *omitted B.* 71 *Sarum*'s . . . Prelate] *S——*'s . . . P——te *A.* 73 *Worcester*] *W——— A.* 78 *Tower*] *T—r A.* 81 *Orford*] *O—— A.* 90 *Peer . . . Accounts*] *P— . . . A——ts A.* 118 Tate] Fate *AB.* 120 Favourite *Rowe . . . Jersey*] Favourite *R— . . . I——y A B——y . . . D——s B.* 122 *Congreve*] *C——ve AB.* 124 *Congreve Halifax*'s] *C——— H———* his *AB.* 125 *Congreve . . . Halifax*] *C——ve . . . H——— AB.* 130–31 *omitted B.* 132 But sprung directly] Directly springing *B.*

The Spanish Descent

Copy text: The Spanish Descent. A Poem. By the Author of The True-Born Englishman, 1703, 8° (Harvard copy).

Collation: All of the printed texts of the poem derive from *The Spanish Descent. A Poem. By the Author of the True-Born Englishman,* 1702, 4° (*A*), of which the Yale copy has been collated. Several copies of this edition (Yale, BM, Clark Library) have been corrected, in the same hand, at line 3, where "*Ormond's*" is changed to "*Or—d's*" and line 82, where "were" is corrected to "was." The large number of printer's errors (e.g. "ptepare" for "Prepare" in the catchword on p. 15) indicate that *A* was very hurriedly and carelessly put together. For this reason, the second edition, an octavo of 1703, which corrects many of the errors of *A,* has been chosen as copy text.

The text of the poem in the pirated *Collection of the Writings of the Author of the True-Born English-Man* (1703), of which the Yale copy has been collated, is a line-by-line resetting of *A.* In preparing the poem for inclusion in *A True Collection of the Writings of the Author of the True Born English-man* (1703), however, Defoe took the pirated edition for his copy text but then made changes that produced a substantive edition (*B*), of which the Yale copy has been collated. The second edition of *A True Collection* (1705) is a line-by-line resetting of *B,* but the text of the poem in the so-called third and fourth editions of *A True Collection* (Moore *197* and *258*) is identical with *B.*

11 Swive] —— *AB.* 12 Castle] Castles *B.* 17 comes] came *A.* 19 Abdication] Abdications *A.* 35 It was but] 'Twas Talking *A.* 82 was] were *A.* 113 are] were *B.* 121 Ammunition] Ammunitions *A* Ammunition's *B.* 124 Whores] W——s *AB.* 132 Fleet] Fleets *A* Fleet's *B.* 186 her] them *A.* 369 to] no *B.*

The Golden Age Restor'd

Copy text: POAS, 1703, *2,* 422–25 (Princeton copy).

Collation: More than 20 witnesses to the text of the poem have survived in manuscript and print. Those in manuscript, all of which are derived collaterally from a common source, are the following:

BM MS. Lansdowne 852, ff. 7v–9	*A*
BM MS. Add. 40060, ff. 17–20	*B*
BM MS. Stowe 222, ff. 274–76	*C*
Bodl. MS. Thorn Drury d.25 (C)	*D*
Trumbull MS. Add. 17	*E*
BM MS. Egerton 924, ff. 26–27	*F*
BM MS. 4457, ff. 22–24	*G*
BM MS. Stowe 305, ff. 268v–70	*J*
BM MS. Add. 28253, ff. 66–67v	*K*
TCD MS. I.5, *1,* 228–32	*L*
Bodl. MS. Add. B.105, ff. 164v–65	*M*
Osborn MS. Box 89, No. 3	*N*
Lilly MS., Indiana University	*O*
Osborn MS. Chest II, No. 28	*P*
Bodl. MS. Montagu e. 13, pp. 70–75	*Q*

Bodl. MS. Rawl. poet. 81, ff. 36v–38v	*R*
Portland MS. Pw V 41, pp. 11–16	*S*
BM MS. Add. 27989, ff. 70–72v	*T*
Bodl. MS. Rawl. D.361, ff. 343–45v	*U*
Portland MS. Pw V 44, pp. 388–96	*V*
Folger MS. M.b.12, pp. 274–78	*W*

ABCD (which probably represent the archetype most nearly), *J, U,* and *V* preserve four lines (85–88) which are omitted in the other witnesses. In G the missing lines are added at the end in another hand. Four more manuscripts (all omitting lines 85–88) have not been included in the apparatus. These are Hertfordshire R.O. Cowper MS. Box 46 (2 exemplars), Cowper MS. Box 11, and Essex R.O. MS. D/DW.Z3.

Some variant readings from three more manuscripts which are now otherwise unavailable are recorded in George Thorn Drury's copy of *POAS,* 1703, 2, preserved in the Bodleian. Two of these, *(A),* a manuscript similiar to *ABC,* and (*B*), a manuscript similar to *E,* include nothing worth recording. But the third, (*C*), "On 4¼ pages sm. 4°," which is also similar to *ABC,* includes interesting marginalia and variants which are indicated as *D* in the textual apparatus.

K has been folded in a legal fold but the endorsement is cropped so that only "4 Egl. of Virgile/The Golden Age" remains. *M* is a fragmentary manuscript of lines 1–20 only.

The printed texts include: *POAS,* 1703, 2, 422–25 (*H*) and *The Works of William Walsh Esq., in Prose and Verse* (E. Curll), 1736, pp. 71–76 (*X*). *H,* which is collateral with *J,* is the source of the printed texts in *PRSA,* 1705, pp. 496–99, *A New Collection . . . of Miscellaneous Poems,* Dublin, 1721, pp. 67–71, *The Works of the Most Celebrated Minor Poets,* 2 vols., 1749, 2, 127–30, and *The Second Part of Miscellany Poems,* 4th ed. (J. Tonson), 1716, 2, 209–12. X, in turn, is the source of the texts of the poem in *Mr. Pope's Literary Correspondence. Volume the Fifth,* 1737, pp. 71–76, *The Works of Celebrated Authors,* 2 vols., 1750, 2, 146–49, *The Minor Poets, or the Works of the Most Celebrated Authors,* 2 vols., Dublin, 1751, 2, 85–89, and *The Poetical Works of William Walsh,* 1802, pp. 39–42. The relationship of the various printed texts is shown in the following diagrams:

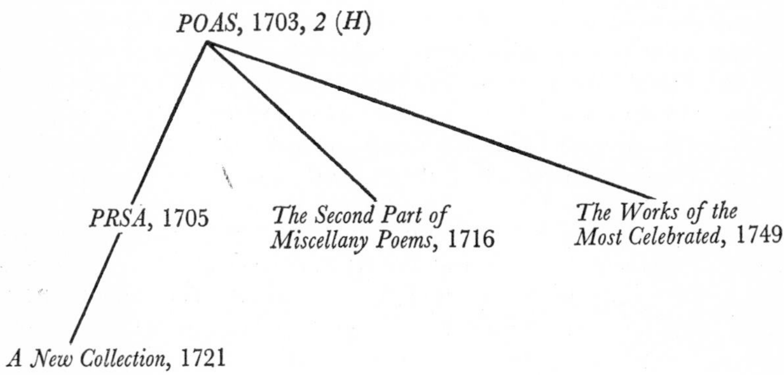

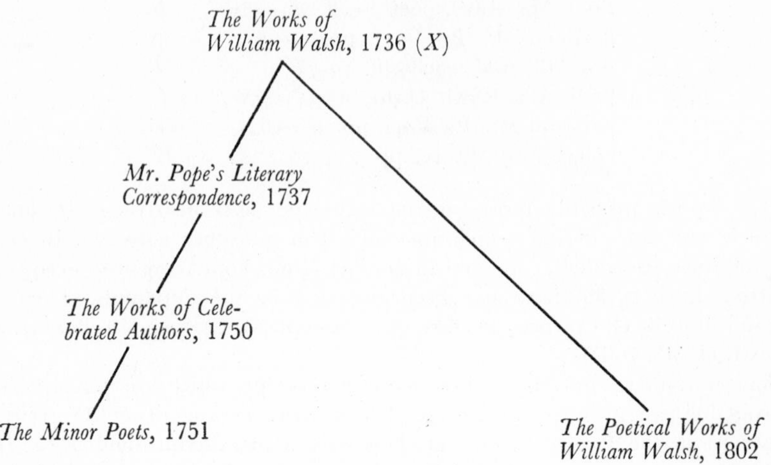

Title: The Golden Age restor'd Or the 4th Eclogue of Virgil, supposed to be taken from a Sybilline Prophecy *A* The Golden Age Restor'd. A Poem in imitation of the fourth Pastoral of Virgil; suppos'd to have been taken from a Sibylline Prophecy *H* The Golden Age reviv'd. A poem in Imitation of the gt pastorall of Virgill, Supposed to have bin taken from a Sybilline prophesy *J* The Golden Age restor'd. The fourth Eclogue of Virgil imitated, suppos'd to have been taken from a Sybilline prophecy *M* The Golden Age Restor'd. The 4th Eclogue of Virgil translated. Suppos'd to have been taken from a Sybelline Prophecy *Q* The Golden Age restored, or the 4th Eclogue of Virgil translated, supposed to be taken from a Sibylline Prophecy *R* The Golden Age Restor'd, 1703. An Imitation of the Fourth Eclogue of Virgil. Supposed to have been taken from a Sybilline-Prophecy *X* The Golden Age retreivd Or the fourth Ecclogue of Virgil translated suppos'd to be (have been) taken from a Sybilline prophesy *BCEFGKLTUVW* The Golden Age retreiv'd or the fourth Eclogue of Virgil supposed to be taken from a sublime Prophesy *D* The Golden Age retrieved. Or the Fourth Eclogue of Virgill, Supposed to have been taken from a Sibilline Prophecy, translated *S* The Golden Age retrived in Imitation of the 4th Eclogue of Virgill *N* The Golden age retreivd *OP*.

3 *still*] will *ALN*. 4 *those*] *MNO* your Σ worthy of a] *EFN* worthy of the *ABC* fitt for the *J* fit for able Σ. 11 *Scobell*] *S——l H* *Scarsdale X* the] *ANPQ* this Σ. 12 that] the *ANOPQ*. 15 Whose . . . Power no common] *ABC* Your . . . Genius no Strict Σ. 16 Who] *ABCEF* You Σ Crimes] Faults *A* they] *ABC* you Σ. 19 *Mackworth*] *M———th H* *Monmouth X*. 21 *Hoblin*] *H—lin H* *Hamlin X*. 24 And] *EF* But *GL* Nor Σ no] *EFG* their *L* a Σ human] *AGHQWX* Fathers *L* humane Σ. 26 And Tories] Torys shall *EF*. 30 with] and *BKPQSX*. 37–43 *follow* 47 *HJX*. 37 mend their strain] Right(s) maintain *ABC*. 41 *omitted C*. 44–47 *follow* 36 *HJX*. 48–120

follow 43 *HJX*. 51 Legislature] Legislative *BRTU*. 52 Dragoons arose] *A* Dragooners rose *BC* Dragooning rose Σ. 55 Reas'ning] *AEFJKOPQST* Reasons *LR* Reas'nings Σ. 59 *Bedford*] *B——d H Bradford X*. 71 now] *AB* this Σ. 75 *Grahme*] *Graham(e) DEF Grimes* Σ. 76 *Granard*] *Gremard D Gr—rd H Gerhard X*. 77–78 *omitted V*. 77 Club assembles] Club(s) assemble *HJKNTU*. 84 their Methods] *ABCD* Expedient(s) Σ. 85–88 *omitted EFHKLNOPQRSTWX*. 86 Post] *AGJ* Posts *BCDUV*. 88 Mistresses] *BCDGJUV* their Mistress *A*. 89 *Musgrave*] *Mu——ve H Mulgrave X*. 92 deny] *ABDEF* refuse(d) Σ. 97–98 *omitted BCD*. 98 *Jones's*] *J—es's H* Tories *O James's X*. 109 *St. John*] *AFGKLNORTUX St. J(oh)ns* Σ. 111 *St. John*] *AFGKLNORSTX St. J(oh)ns* Σ. 113 Songs] *Song BCP* lines *KLSU* with] *ABEFRU* to Σ. 118 this] his *CLR* that *PQ*. 119 your] the *CHPX* this *JR* that *Q*. 120 his] *ACEFHKNQUX* the Σ.

The Mitred Club

Copy text: The M——'d C—b; Or, The L——th Consultation. Et tu Brute? Acheronta Movebo: From a Correct Copy. London, MDCCIV (Yale copy).

Collation: The text is preserved in two closely related traditions, each of which is represented by manuscripts as well as by printed texts. The better tradition is represented by the following witnesses, all of which are derived from the same source:

Huntington MS. HM 183, ff. 31r–32v	*A*
The M——'d C—b; Or, The L——th Consultation (1704)	*B*
BM MS. Add. 27407, ff. 41–41v	*C*
Portland MS. Pw V 41, ff. 137–40	*D*
BM MS. Lansdowne 852, pp. 28–31	*E*
BM MS. Add. 25490, ff. 13–14	*F*
BM MS. Stowe 305, pp. 533–34	*G*
Portland MS. Pw V 41, ff. 111–13	*H*

A is a fragmentary manuscript of lines 1–36 only. *B* adds 53 lines that are preserved in no other witness. *H* shows some evidence of memorial reconstruction, as in lines 89 and 92.

The inferior tradition is represented by the following witnesses, derived from a common source different from the source of *ABCDEFGH:*

Bodl. MS. Rawl. poet. 173, pp. 136–38	*J*
Osborn MS. Chest II, No. 18, pp. 26–29	*K*
BM MS. Add. 27408, ff. 138–39v	*L*
POAS, 1704, *3*, 392–95	*M*

L has been heavily written over, perhaps from memory of the *ABCDEFGH* tradition; thus lines 59–60 are written in the margin:

> Fear & a like amazement fell on all
> As when the Prophet spoke his truths to Saul.

The remaining revisions of *L* do not seem to be authorial and have not been recorded. Another witness similar to *LM,* Osborn MS. Box 22, No. 8, pp. 150–56, has not been included in the apparatus.

The texts in *PRSA,* 1705, pp. 542–44, and in *POAS,* 1716, *3,* 352–55, are independently derived from *M.* That in *A New Collection . . . of Miscellaneous Poems,* Dublin, 1721, pp. 107–10, derives from *PRSA,* 1705.

Title: The M——'d C—b; Or, The L——th Consultation 1704 *AB* Et tu Brute *CDK* The Mitred Cabal *E* A Poem upon the Bill of Conformity *F* Koej ou Téknon *G* To give (the last) Amendment(s) to the Bill *HJ* A Consultation of the Bishops *LM.*

1 Amendments] amendment *CDFJKLM.* 2 Which] That *EGHK.* 4 last Night at *Lambeth*] in close Cabal were *EF.* 6 *Moderate-Men*] *ABC* modern men Σ. 9 fell] came *E* was *JKLM.* 10 tend] bend *GH.* 11 amend] *AB* will mend *H* would mend Σ. 13 A Brawny] The Brawny *CD.* 17 And] Kind *CDEFGJK.* 18 God] Heaven *EGH.* 19 Shall] *AB* Must Σ. 21 yet] tho' *CD* drive] drein *AB* mixt *CD* sl(e)ight *JKLM.* 22 Christians] Churchmen *GH.* 24 a] *AB* the Σ. 25–26 *omitted FGH.* 25 the] *ABC* this Σ. 27–28 *follow* 29–30 *CDEFGHJKLM* Debates . . . Estates] Debate . . . Estate *CDEJ.* 30 Rogues can't be so] Which can't be Rogues *CD.* 31–32 *omitted F.* 31 Bill] Pill *GH.* 32 Woe] Rod *GH.* 34 Saints] folks *CD* Souls *FJ* men *GH.* 35 He] *ABH* This Σ from all a Kind] All with a *F* and all by kind *GH* they all with a *JLM* contented] *AB* consenting Σ. 39 His Hand a Crosier] *B* A Cross his hand(s) Σ. grac'd] *BGHJ* deck'd Σ. 40 And whilst sweet Odours round the Room were] While round the roome Ambrosian odours *GH.* 42 at length] it self *B.* 44 Cote] Save *B* cacth[?] *D* call *E* to Fence from out] which sever from *CD* and fence from out *EGH* and sever from *FJKLM.* 45 will you] will then *BE* would yet *C* let not *D.* 46 Martyrs] *BC* Martyr Σ. 48 by her] *BEF* By *HJ* by its Σ. 49 think, such Times may never] *B* such a Time may rarely *E* such a time will hardly *GH* such a Time may never Σ. 50 Senates] Commons *HJ.* 52 more] most *GH.* 53 Her] it *JKLM.* 55 then] now *CD.* 56 Tide] Tides *EFGKLM.* 57 lo!] *omitted CD* then *GH.* 59 Confusion] conviction *CDEFGH* fell on all] shook each soul *JKLM.* 60 Old] Thus *GH* And *JLM* Truths] *BEFG* Truth Σ shook each *Saul*] struck each Saul *GH* fell on All *JKLM.* 68 Bulk] back *H.* 69 *omitted E* Hands] Hand *CDGH.* 71 And Homage] Then Homage *E* Their Homage *FH.* 72 dreadful] *BHJ* direfull Σ. 74 Creator] *BFGH*

Creation Σ. 78 Did I not Cull you out amongst] Did I not call you out among(st) *CDEKL* Was itt for this I call'd you from *GH.* 79 And make] And made *BGH* To make *JKLM.* 81 but *Calvinists*] in Calvinists *C* but Calvins *DEFKLM* and Calvins *GH* in Cant] *BCJ* in their Cant *E* in your Cant Σ. 86 Reign] Trick *B.* 87 Vein] Strain *H.* 88 e'er he'll] he shall *CDFJLM* he shall ever *H.* 89 or does *Oxford*] Zealous O——rd *B* or Pet——h *H* or St. Asaph Σ. 90 they shall not be so] they'l be more than so *CD.* 91 and] *BCDF* then Σ. 92 thought you were] Took you for *H.*

The Golden Age Revers'd

Copy text: POAS, 1703, 2, 438–41 (Princeton copy).

Collation: The text of *The Golden Age Revers'd* is preserved in 16 manuscripts and two printed books. The manuscripts, all collaterally derived from the same source, are the following:

BM MS. Add. 40060, ff. 23v–26	*A*
BM MS. Add. 27407, ff. 32–33	*B*
Portland MS. Pw V 48, pp. 326–39, 396	*C*
Portland MS. Pw V 44, pp. 396–405	*D*
Folger MS. M.b.12, ff. 240–42v	*E*
BM MS. Egerton 924, ff. 27v–28v	*F*
Bodl. MS. Montagu e.13, ff. 121–23	*G*
Huntington MS. EL 8902	*H*
Lilly MS., Indiana University	*J*
Bodl. MS. Rawl. poet. 81, ff. 39–41v	*K*
BM MS. Lansdowne 852, pp. 18–21	*L*
BM MS. Add. 27989, ff. 76v–79	*M*
Osborn MS. Chest II, No. 18	*N*
Bodl. MS. Rawl. C.986	*O*
BM MS. Stowe 305, ff. 270–72v	*P*
BM MS. Add. 28263, ff. 68–69v	*Q*

A, which seems to represent the archetype most closely, is an independent manuscript (not the product of a scriptorium, like *BCDE*), written in a loose and sprawling hand. *B* might be mistaken for two fragmentary manuscripts, for lines 1–93 are copied in one hand, and 94–122 in another. But both parts of the manuscript represent the same tradition and the two hands may represent two scribes copying from the same exemplar. *C* exhibits the same characteristic: lines 1–70, 71–113, and 114–22 have been copied by three different hands, but again there is no evidence that the three parts are not derived from the same exemplar. *G* is a fragmentary manuscript omitting lines 20–23, 40–44, 59–60, 69–73, 80–95.

The two printed texts are: *POAS,* 1703, 2, 438–41 (*R*) and *PRSA,* 1705, 505–08. *PRSA,* 1705, is derived from *R.* Essex R.O. MS. D/DW.z4, another witness with the same lineation as *B* (textual note 68–71), has not been included in the apparatus.

Title and date: [none] [subscribed] feb: 1702/3 *A* The Golden Age Revers'd *BCFHJKMNOPQR* 1702. The Golden Age Revers'd *DE* A Copy of Verses *G* 1702/3. The Golden Age Revers'd *L.*

5 rouse] Rule *DEFG.* 6 Unnerv'd] Ennerv'd *BCDEFGJKLNOPQ* Injur'd *H.* 8 Already has] *ABC* Has in the Faction's Name Σ. 9 Faction's Cause] *ABC* Point Σ. 12 Judiciously] Industriously *DH.* 13 and ev'ry Project] and Project *HJKLM.* 18 *Tonson*] *Thompson AF Tennison Q.* 19 joyn their Heads and] *ABC* pond'ring Σ. 23 and quitt] *ABNOP* and leave *HJK* forsake Σ. 24 Vertue] *HJK* Valour Σ. 31 taint] wast *OP.* 46 sneers] swears *HM.* 48 golden] *ABC* happy Σ. 51 emulate] imitate *ACJKP.* 54 in] *LM* to Σ. 56 Laws] *FGL* Foes Σ. 63 Gravity, of] Gravity and *CHJ.* 68–71 *follow* 77 *B.* 69 justly] Jointly *CDE.* 82–85 *follow* 77 *CDEFGHJKLMNOPQR.* 84 trifling] *CDE* Trifles Σ. 86 coolly] wisely *R.* 92 like *Italian*] like the Italian *HJKL.* 93 And] But *AB.* 112 our] the *HJKLM.* 113 the noble Toil] the Glorious Toil *DE* the Toil *KMN.* 119 Giant] *R* mighty Σ. 121 e'er] *ABCJL.* not *DEFHKMOPQR* never *G* once *N.*

A Prophecy

Copy text: POAS, 1707, *4,* 58–62 (Yale copy).

Collation: Nine witnesses to the text have been found, all derived collaterally from a common source:

TCD MS. I.5, 2, 20–23	*A*
Cowper MS. Box 46	*B*
POAS, 1707, *4,* 58–62	*C*
BM MS. Lansdowne 852, f. 289	*D*
BM MS. Harleian 6914, ff. 103–05v	*E*
Portland MS. Pw V 46, pp. 321–25	*F*
BM MS. Add. 40060, ff. 27v–29v	*G*
Folger MS. M.b.12, ff. 249–52	*H*
Portland MS. Pw V 44, pp. 420–27	*J*

A and *B* appear to represent the archetype most nearly. *C* includes nine lines, of doubtful authority, not found in any other witness. *D* is a fragmentary manuscript, in three different hands, of 38 lines only. *F* bears the unmistakable marks of oral transmission. *H* and *J*, products of the same scriptorium, include another three lines, again of doubtful authority, not found in the other witnesses.

Title: A Prophecy *ABDEF* The Prophecy *CGHJ*.

2 First Renown] *British* Throne *C*. 6 are *Jacks*] are all Jacks *DEG*. 9 faithless] *B* faithful Σ and] But *HJ*. 10] When *M———h, G———n, L—y BCEF*. 13–15 *omitted D*. 13] When *S———, H——,* and *Jack H— BC*. 19 smelt] found *G*. 20 Patriot] petticoat *F* patient *G*. 22–24 *omitted D*. 24 Trimming] tricking *F* *Harley*] *H——y C*. 25 *Seymour*] *S——r BC*. 27 Or] And *CG* To *F* *Bertie*] Bromley *B* party *F*. 28 *Hedges*] *H—ges BC*. 29 Records tell] *College* tells *C*. 32 *Boyle*] *B—le C* Balls *F* fixt] held[?] *D* grown *FG*. 33 *Hedges*] *He—s BC* *After* 33 *C adds:*

When *Harry B—le* shall keep less Pother
With his no Hair, and be no Lover,
Or be as honest as his Brother.

When *B——gton* is in Disgrace,
'Cause he won't vote to get a Place,
Tho promis'd, is not call'd his Grace.

When Tories fall into a Trance,
And give up dear Non-Resistance,
And cease to wish Success to *France*.

34 *Musgrave*] *M——ve BC* long seem'd] was once *F*. 36 Goose] Geese *BC* Gander's] Ganders *CE* Gander *DFGHJ*. 38 And Wit] When Wit *C*. 39 And] When *C* *Coningsby*] *Con——by BC* minc'd] mind to *F* more minct *G*. 40 *Ranelagh*] *Ran—h BC*. 41 And] When *BCDEF* *Cutts*] *C—ts C* nothing but] only his *C*. 43–48 *omitted D*. 43 he] Tate *F*. 44 *omitted G*. 46–48 *omitted E*. 46 chief] Chitt *F*. 49 great] brave *DE*. 51–93 *omitted D*. 51 barely] basely *BCEFG* Safely *HJ*. 54 *Rooks*] *R—ks C*. 55 *Somers*] *S——s C*. 57 that] his *C*. 58 *Wright*] *W——t C*. 59 lopt] Lost *HJ*. 60 that that's off than none] thats of then his own *F*. 61 When Church] *BC* When the Church Σ. 62 are] or *C*. 64–72 *omitted HJ*. 66 And] When *C*. 67 *Sarum*] *S—m C* wive] swive *C*. 68 *Compton*] Com—ns *BC* common *EF* Complotts *G*. 72 *Tom*] *T— C*. 76–78 *omitted EF*. 76 *Essex*] *E—x C* forswear] leave of *A* Forbear *HJ*. 78 *St. Albans . . . Plummer*] *St. A——s . . . P———r C* *After* 78 *HJ add:*

Which Plummer if You will be Nice
Is little better than the Vice
. . . .

79 *Wyndham's* crooked] Crooked Wyndham's *A* *W———m's* crooked *C* Wyndhams fulsom *F*. 80 Scent] Sense *CF* extent *G*. 81 *Bedford*] *B———d C*. 85 *Wharton*] *W———n C* fam'd for] shall leave *HJ*. 92 will] shall *CF*.

On Dr. Birch

Copy text: POAS, 1707, *4*, 66–68 (Yale copy).

Collation: The text of *On Dr. Birch* is preserved in two closely related traditions, one of which is represented by:

POAS, 1707, *4*, 66–68	*A*
BM MS. Stowe 305, ff. 281v–282	*B*
Portland MS. Pw V 46, pp. 316–18	*C*

The other, slightly inferior tradition is represented by four manuscripts, all collaterally derived from a source different from the source of *ABC:*

Osborn MS. Chest II, No. 18, pp. 76–78	*D*
BM MS. Lansdowne 852, ff. 36–36v	*E*
Portland MS. Pw V 44, pp. 413–17	*F*
Folger MS. M.b.12, ff. 246–47v	*G*

Another witness of the second type, Essex R.O. MS. D/DW.Z3, is not included in the apparatus.

Title: Upon Dr. B's Suit to the E. of N for a Bishoprick *A* On Dr. Birch *BE* [none] *C* Satyr on Dr. B—— *D* On Doctor Birch He/Birch's putting in for the Bishoprick of Rochester, in case that Bishop had been made Primate of Ireland *FG*.

1 that] who *DEFG*. 8 were] was *CDEFG*. 16 the] a *ABC*. 18 forthwith] away *DEFG*. 19 *Dicky* the black, whose] Dicky whose *CDEFG* great and] great Desert and *FG*. 22 Hand] head *CDE*. 30 all] it *CDEFG*. 33–34 *omitted C*. 35 crys *Sprat* in] Sprat cries with *CDEFG*. 44 he'll] will *FG*. 47 this] his *ABC*. 48 will continue] well continues *BDEFG*. 49 Bowl goes] Bowls go *AB*. 52 Crime] Sin *EFG*. 55 *omitted ABC*. 59 Or] And *CF*.

More Reformation. A Satyr upon Himself

Copy text: More Reformation. A Satyr upon Himself. By the Author of The True Born English-Man, 1703 (Foxon D53).

Collation: There appear to be only two witnesses to the text of the poem: the quarto edition of 1703 and *A Second Volume of the Writings of the Author of The True-Born Englishman,* 1705, pp. 27–64. The substantive variants between these texts, of which the Yale copies of both have been collated—"descry" for "decry" at line 117 and "Sense" for "Scene" at line 196—seem more likely to be compositor's errors than author's emendations. Having taken more care than usual in seeing the quarto edition through the press, Defoe apparently decided that no further corrections were necessary for the collected edition in 1705.

The copy text has been emended as follows:

46 We'll] They'll. 188 it] they. 189 To] Can. 690 *Ironies*] *Irony's* 737 writ'st] writes 759 Ladies] Lady's

A Hymn to the Pillory

Copy text: A Hymn to the Pillory. The Second Edition Corrected, with Additions, 1703 (Foxon D25) (TCD copy).

Collation: Confirming what might be inferred from the external evidence, the first edition of *A Hymn to the Pillory,* 1703 (*A*), of which Yale copy 2 has been collated, presents every symptom of hurried presswork. Besides the usual mechanical errors—reversed letters and hapless pointing—the compositor encountered unusual difficulty in reading Defoe's hand. Twice he read "see" for "set"; once he read "See" for "Let" and twice he read "Let" for "Set". The first edition of the poem, therefore (Foxon D24), does not recommend itself as a copy text. Different locations of signature B in some copies do not indicate different impressions of the first edition, because otherwise the sheets are identical.

For "The Second Edition Corrected, with Additions" (Foxon D25), also published in 1703, sheet B was not reset, but corrected and reimposed. Sheets C and D, however, which add 20 lines to the poem, are corrected and reset. Since it appears that Defoe made the corrections (as well as the additions), the second edition, of which the TCD copy has been collated, was chosen as copy text (*B*).

The so-called "Third Edition Corrected, with more Additions" (Foxon D26) is not a new edition, but simply a new issue of *B* with 14 lines of Latin verse, inscribed A. D. D. F. on the verso of the half-title. A manuscript copy of this edition is preserved in the National Library of Scotland (MS. 3/1543[24]). It reveals its national origin in such variants as "ane" for "an" and "meitt" for "meet" and one wonders whether its existence indicates that the demand for printed copies could not be met, or that the copyist preferred not to demand one.

The true third edition of the poem is a quarto pamphlet wretchedly printed in two columns (Foxon D27). Probably a piracy, with no date or place of publication, it is a line-by-line resetting of *A*. A fragmentary copy of this edition, BM MS. Harleian 7332, ff. 250–51v, breaks off in the middle of line 83. A variant of this edition, in which the two columns are divided by a rule, is described by Foxon (D28).

In 1705 Defoe included the poem in *A Second Volume of the Writings of the Author of The True-Born Englishman.* For this edition (*C*), of which the Yale copy has been collated, he took *B* as his copy text and made a number of unimportant corrections. H. Hills' piracy, an octavo volume published in 1708 (Foxon D29), is a line-by-line resetting of *A*. Another octavo edition (Foxon D30), probably published in 1721, was set up from the corrupt third edition.

16 the] and *A*. 26 Law's] L....s *ABC*. 32 can] canst *BC*. 60 he] they *A*. 61 him] 'em *A*. 68 *Sacheverell*] *S———ll ABC*. 103 Whom] With *AB* Who *C*. 112 *spreading*] swelling *A*. 128, 142 *Ormond's*] *Or—d's ABC*. 138 the] their *A*. 141 in Pantalone] a Pampalone *A* at Pampalone *BC*. 198 none] no *A*. 203 Either] Each *A*. 205 baudy] daily *A*. 216, 223, 227 *Asgill*] *A—ll ABC*. 232 thy *Lists*] the List *A*. 235 was] has *A*. 238 false to] 'gainst *A*. 242 Authors] Author *A*. 250–55 *omitted A*. 265–72 *omitted A*. 282 Judge] J—e *BC*. 283 *Lovell*] *L—ll ABC*. 299 *Sherlock's*] *She——k's ABC*. 300 Knave . . . Fools] K—— . . . F—s *ABC*. 368 *Whores*] Wh—s *ABC*. 369–74 *omitted A*. 377 *Crisp*] *C—— ABC*. 396 Not . . . *won't*] Nor . . . *wou'd A*. 449 Magistrates] Men *A* M— BC. 450 Scandals] Friends unto *A* Sc——ls *BC*.

On the King of Spain's Voyage to Portugall

Copy text: Folger MS. M.b.12, f. 252.

Collation: A slightly superior textual tradition is preserved in four manuscripts:

Folger MS. M.b.12, f. 252	*A*
Portland MS. Pw V 44, pp. 428–29	*B*
BM MS. Harleian 6914, f. 101v	*C*
Osborn MS. Chest II, No. 58	*D*

The remaining witnesses are collaterally derived from a source different from that of *ABCD:*

Bodl. MS. Rawl. poet. 81, f. 42	*E*
BM MS. Add. 27989, ff. 90v–91	*F*
Osborn MS. Chest II, No. 18, p. 79	*G*
BM MS. Stowe 305, ff. 292–292v	*H*
Bodl. MS. Firth b. 21, f. 29	*J*
BM MS. Lansdowne 852, pp. 41–42	*K*
POAS, 1707, *4,* 128	*L*

L is a fragmentary version of only six lines (1–2, 9–12).

Title: On the King of Spain's Voyage to Portugall 1703/4 *ABC* On the two Kings of Spain *DEK* Satyr on Charles the 3. of Spain *F* On the King of Spain *G* On the Portugall expedition *H* [none] *J* On K. Charles's Voyage to Spain 1704 *L.*

2 Feeble] feebler *KL.* 5 Dwells] is *DE* lyes *HJ.* 7 durst] dare *DEFG* darst *H* a Title] his Title *EFGHJK.* 10 First Made him] To make a *FK* First dub'd a *H* To create a *J* then] and then *FJ* him] a *HL.* 11 two] some *EFJK.* 13–14 *omitted* *H.* 13 Why i'n't] Why's not *CFK* Why an't *D.* 14 Resemble] Resembling *DF* akin to *J.* 17 Mere] More *FK.*

On the 8th of March 1703/4

Copy text: Osborn MS. Chest II, No. 18, pp. 73–74.

Collation: The text of the poem is preserved in seven manuscripts, with no substantive variants:

Osborn MS. Chest II, No. 18, pp. 73–74	*A*
Folger MS. M.b.12, ff. 246–47	*B*
Portland MS. Pw V 44, pp. 419–20	*C*
TCD MS. I.5, 2, 17	*D*
Cowper MS. Box 46	*E*
Cowper MS. Box 46	*F*
Cowper MS. Box 9, *6*, 75	*G*

Title: The 8th of March 1703/4 *A* 1703/4 On the 8th of March *BC* A Poem on the 8th of March 1703/4 *D* On the Eight of March *E* The Eight of March *F* To the Queen G.

An Address to Our Sovereign Lady

Copy text: An Address to Our Sovereign Lady [n.d.] (2° half-sheet, Newberry Library copy).

Collation: The five witnesses to the text seem to be derived collaterally from the archetype. They are:

An Address to Our Sovereign Lady [n.d.]	*A*
POAS, 1704, *3*, 409–10	*B*
Cowper MS. Box 11 [no foliation]	*C*

Portland MS. Pw V 42, pp. 455–57	*D*
BM MS. Add. 27407, f. 42	*E*

The text in *PRSA*, 1705, pp. 455–56, was set up from *B*.

Title: An Address to Our Sovereign Lady *A* An Address *B* Upon the Commons Address to the Queen Concerning the Occasional Bill *C* The House of Commons most Humble Address to her Majestie Die Jovis 23 Decembris 1703 *D* [none] *E*.

2 And tell] To tell *DE*. 5 *Johnny*] Sir John *C* that] us *BCDE*. 6 That] The *B*. 7 plaguily put] plainly put *C* sadly put *D* put *E*. 8 For] That *BCDE* the Curst Lords] their Curs'd Lordships *DE*. 11 *Nottingham's*] *Nott——s A N———m's B*. 12 probably, may] surely must then *B* shall as sure *CDE*. 14 Whim] Whims *BC* Thing *DE*. 15 Queenshipp's] Q——shipp's *A*. 16 Squeal] Squal *C* Squeek *DE*. 18 'twou'd be] 'twill prove *E*. 22 this sad] this said *AE* the sad *B*. 23 of Prerogative] of Your Prerogative *AB*. 24 were never till Now] ne'er were before *BE* were never before *CD*. 30 Much Dearer] Which is as dear *B* And tis Farr more Dear *C* And 'tis as Dear *DE*.

The Seven Wise Men

Copy text: The Seven Wise Men, 4°, 1704 (University of Cincinnati copy).

Collation: Four witnesses to the text derive collaterally from a common source. These are:

The Seven Wise men, 4°, 1704	*A*
Osborn MS. Chest II, No. 18, pp. 68–72	*B*
TCD MS. I.5, 2, 39–42	*C*
The Seven Wise Men, 2°, 1704 (Rylands Library copy)	*D*

A is assumed to represent the archetype most nearly, while *B* and *CD* represent successive stages of a kind of generalizing revision. Since it reveals a remarkable economy of means, this revision is assumed to have been undertaken by the author. The phrase, "inflame the Ball," for example, was transferred from the conclusion of *B* (textual note, 96) to the Phaeton image introduced in *CD* (textual note, 28–35), where it is vastly more appropriate.

The original poem was apparently intended to say that rumors of plots—and similar abuses of language—were being used to unsettle, and hopefully to overthrow, the monarchy. In the revision, most (5–7, 58, 78–81, 92), but not all (45,

62) references to plots were deleted. At the same time the poem was further generalized by the omission of such details as those at 16–17, 34–35, 46–47, and 84. The most obvious principle on which the revision was undertaken, however, is an aesthetic one. Of the seven triplets in *AB* (3–5, 58–60, 73–75, 82–84, 85–87, 90–92, 96–98), all but two (73–75, 96–98) were eliminated.

Both editions of the poem (*AD*) were printed on the same press, but even these temporizing revisions could not embolden the printer to put his name on the title page. Both editions claim equally to have been set "From a Correct Copy."

The text of the fifth witness, *POAS*, 1707, *4*, 28–30, was set from *D*.

Title: The Se(a)ven Wise Men *ABCD*.

1 our happy Isle] these latter Times *CD*. 3 mighty Names and Worth *Recorded,* stand] wisdom will the *Gordian Knot* undo *CD*. 4] And be our Isle's *Palladium* 'gainst the Foe *CD*. 5–7 *omitted CD*. 9 *she*'s] we're *BC* guide] Steer *B*. 11 *Somerset*'s] *S*——'s *ABD*. 12 great] good *D*. 15 Applaud the *Gibberish Language*] Are ravish'd with the *Accents BCD*. *After* 15 *BCD add:*

The Rhiming Guests are fed with sumpt'ous Fare,
Rewards can make his *Gibbrish Language* clear.

16–17 *omitted CD*. 21 *Campiana*] fond *Lucinda CD*. 22 Liberties] Liberty *C*. 28 *Sunderland*] *S*——*d AB*. 28–35]

Next giddy *Phaethon* begins his Flight,
And boldly dares ascend the Orb of Light.
But the rash Youth will soon inflame the Ball,
And with Confusion from his Chariot fall.
Those *Jackdaws* eyes can never bear the *Test,*
Tho' they were nourish'd in an *Eagles* Nest.
Those artless Hands, and that untimely Zeal
May harm, but ne'er preserve the *Commonweal. CD*

34 *Clancarty*] *C*——*y A*. *After* 35 *CD add:*

Then to his Library, let him confine
The undigested Notions of his Brain,

36 Let him in Libraries consume] In curious Speculations spend *CD*. 37 deserve] preserve *D* *James Forbes*'s] *J—s F–rb–s*'s *AD*. 38 allow'd] confess'd *D*. 40 O] Thee *B* *Scarbrough*] *Sc*—— *ABD* unan'mous] com-

mon *B.* 41 do's applaud] greets, approves *B.* 44 can] will *B.* 45 truths] truth *AD.* 46–47 *omitted ACD.* 48 Next] As *CD.* 51 their] the Sire's wise *CD.* 53 *Townshend*] *T—s—d ABD.* 54 Saint-like] first like *D.* 58 out] next *BCD* sly *Cataline*] a crafty Bard *CD.* 59 Who *Faction*'s business never did retard *CD.* 60 *omitted CD.* 63–64 *omitted A.* 64 *Ferguson*'s] Fergus's *B* *Fer——n*'s *D.* 68 The large Estate she left did well] A large Estate most amply did *ACD.* 69 He is content his present Spouse] His present Bride he is content *B* He is content his present Bride *C.* 70 Cully's] Bully's *D.* 71 *Sommers*] *S——* *AD* S——rs *B* next arise] last arise *B* arise *C.* 72] An Exhalation glaring in the Skyes *B* *James*] *J—es AD.* 73–75 *follow* 77 *B.* 73 sence of] nightly *B.* 75 Thy] Those *ACD.* 78 *Lancashire*] *L——re A.* 78–83]

Above the *Common Honour* of a Peer,
Thy restless Soul disdains that *Humble Sphere.*
A Blazing Comet to amaze the Sight,
And with a *Fiery Tail* the People fright.
Thus, for *a while,* thou may'st with Lustre shine,
But *soon* to *Primitive Dregs* thou must return again. *CD*

84–92 *omitted CD.* 89 *Clarendon*] *C——n A.* 96 o'erthrow] inflame *B.*

The Address

Copy text: The Address, 1704 (Foxon X1).

Collation: The text survives in a 1704 quarto, of which the Bodl. copy (Firth b.21 [55]), has been collated, and in *POAS,* 1707, *4,* 68–76. Variants in the latter, of which the Yale copy has been collated, seem to exceed what might be expected from a press corrector. At lines 204–05, for example, "ruin'd, *should,*/And mock'd" is amended (incorrectly) to "ruin'd, should/Be mock'd," which may indicate the existence of another quarto, or folio half-sheet, edition.

23 *Mackworth, Wright,* and *Northey*] *M——h, W——t,* and *N——y 1704.* 43 *Mackworth*] *M—— 1704.* 76 *Nottingham*] *N——m 1704.* 132 *Rook*] *R—k 1704.* 231 *G——s, W——s, R——s*] *G——s, W——'s, R——s 1704* 233 *Rochester*] *R——r 1704.* 234 *Nottingham*] *N——m 1704*

Faction Display'd

Copy text: Faction Display'd. A Poem, 1704 (Bodl. copy: G Pamph. 1747[8]).

Collation: Despite an apparent profusion of witnesses, only the following are of any significance:

BM MS. Harleian 6947, ff. 171–80v (533 lines)	*A*
Faction Display'd. A Poem, 1704. 4° (526 lines)	*B*
Faction Display'd. A Poem, 1705. 8° (502 lines)	*C*

Collateral with *A* is BM MS. Lansdowne 852, ff. 1–7v, of 510 lines, which preserves no variant worth recording but the heavily ironic subtitle: "Dedicated to The Duke of Somerset/—Sed non Authore furoris/Sublate cecidit rabies./—To be Printed for Jacob Tonson—." It may be surmised, however, that there were some lines in the archetype that are preserved in neither of these manuscripts. The long speech of Clodio (lines 187–227) seems incomplete as it now stands; it should not end anticlimactically with Wharton's "Wealthy Friend" who is to be introduced as speaker of the Irish House of Commons. It needs a generalizing summary of the kind Shippen tried to supply in *C* when he revised lines 276–77 to read, "Like the Supreme directing Hand of *Jove,*/We'll Act unseen, and all around us Move," and inserted them immediately before line 228. Otherwise, *A* preserves a sufficient number of unique lines of undoubted authority (e.g. 212–13, 346–47) to establish its priority to *B. C,* however, of which the Bodl. copy: G. Pamph. 1602(8) has been collated, presents a more difficult problem. It is possible that it includes material earlier than A, but the assumption that is made here is that all of its variants are later.

The title page of *C* claims that the poem is "Now first Correctly Published, with large Amendments, and the Addition of several Characters omitted in former Editions," but the additions are only two: the new "Character" of Penurio (textual note, line 321) and the lines on Clarendon's *History of the Rebellion* (textual note, line 442). The "Amendments" are numerous, but whoever was making them must have soon tired, for there are almost none in the last third of the poem. Most of them are deletions, although some (e.g. line 118) seem to point up the satire and a larger number (e.g. line 40) seem to regularize the sound effects of the poem: the "Amendments" at lines 194, 294, 387 and 443 eliminate triplets, and that at line 402 eliminates an unpleasing cacophony. The result is a thorough-going revision of the poem, presumably by the author. The economy of Shippen's procedure may be illustrated by the fact that from the longest passage that he cut out (269–97), he salvaged four of the best lines (280–81, 291–92) and added them to Clodio's speech, and another (284), which he transferred to the new "Character" of Penurio (textual note, line 321). All of this, therefore, seems to be more accurately described in the words of Thomas Hearne (*I,* 31), who called *C* "a new Edition printed from a correct copy [*B*], with Improvements," than it is by the words of the title page, which imply that *C* derives from a source anterior to *B*.

The remaining witnesses are all derived from *B*, in the following order:

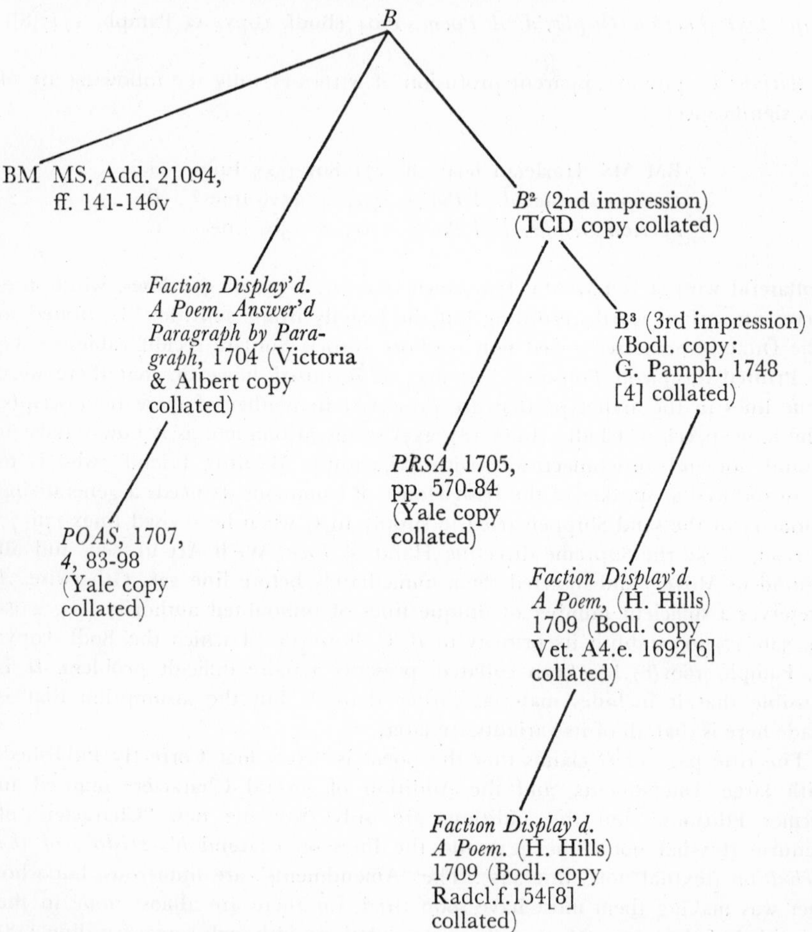

The three impressions of *B* may be distinguished by the following variants:

	B	B^2	B^3
p. 6	by some	with some	with some
p. 9	foment Rebellion	foment Rebellion	foment Religion

The two impressions of Henry Hills' edition may be distinguished in the same way:

	1st	2nd
p. 10	Coutier's	Courtier's

Another pirated edition of which there are copies in the BM (11626.c.44[7]) and the NLS (1.265[17]), is described in a printed notice on the title page of an uncropped copy of B^3 in the NLS (1.193[6]):

> A Counterfeited Edition is lately Published, it may be discovered by being Printed in Old Letter, hardly legible, and full of Errors, no Lines over *To the Reader,* and particularly in Page 18, after Line 9, the Verse so run into another as makes it Nonsense.

Otherwise these witnesses hold few surprises. The fact that the *POAS* text derives from a reprint of the poem in an answer rather than from *B* indicates the haphazard methods of the editor of *POAS,* 1707.

12] Who raging swells the World into a Storm *C.* 14 Thunder] Thunders *A.* 16 And] Which *BC.* 19 for ev'ry slight Offence] on ev'ry vain pretence *C.* 24–34]

> Here is maintain'd a *mixt* Monarchic sway,
> Which Freeborn Nations willingly obey.
> For in the due Proportion of the State
> The Subject's happy as the Monarch Great *C.*

36 Nor Tyranny] No Tyranny *B.* 40 threaten] attempt *C.* 42–43 *omitted C.* 44 Such was our old Establish'd] Just is the Model of our *C.* 45 Which might have flourish'd Ages yet] That might for ever Flourish still *C.* 46 still] thus *C.* 47 Seeds] Seed *B.* 69] Who prov'd his want of Sense in ev'ry word *BC.* 70–71 *omitted BC.* 72 With much adoe] When hissing thus *B* When thus at length *C.* 82 for who can bear a Woman's Servile] My Manly Spirit spurns a Woman's *C.* 83 Stuff, he would have giv'n it vent] Nonsence lisping on he went *C.* 84] Till *Ario* interposed his Spleen to Vent *C.* 95 *Winton*] *W—ton BC.* 97 write, and talk] boldly Write *C.* 102 unanimated with a] unacted with a *Reas'ning C.* 103 Or else he'd] Else would he *C.* 104 He'd] Would *C.* 105 *Socinians*] *Fanaticks BC.* 118 *C adds* Witness a Conscience drench'd in *Fenwick*'s Blood. 127–28 *omitted BC.* 138 the] her *BC.* 146 Prim-'tive] Native *C.* 157 and unbecoming] Enthusiastick *C.* 159 Eagerness] Vehemence *C.* 166–71 *omitted C.* 194 *omitted C.* 195 But rooted out the *Stuarts*] We soon had rooted out the *C.* 196 otherwise] that great Change *C.* 208 second Thought] next Resort *BC.* 212–13 *omitted BC.* 214–27 *omitted C.* 242 Besides, in spight . . . loud] Nay, spight . . . loud and vain *C.* 269–75 *omitted C.* 276–77 *follow* 295 *C.* 277] We'll Act unseen, and all around us Move. *C.* 278–79 *omitted C.* 280–81 *follow* 205 *C.* 282 *omitted C.* 283 *omitted BC.* 284] *B adds:*

> Awe their Elections, and their Votes command.

C transfers the resulting couplet to follow 321. 285–86 *omitted C.* 287–90, 293, 295 *follow* 211 *C.* 291–92 *follow* 281 *C.* 294 *omitted C.* 296–97 *omitted C.* 304 Ease] Vice *BC.* 305 *omitted BC.* *After* 321 *C adds:*

Penurio lov'd the Cause, but silent sat,
Nor listen'd to their close intense Debate.
For on his Wealth ran all his Thoughts and Care,
Unblest with *thirty thousand Pound a Year.*
Scriv'ners Attorneys Bankers are his Train,
The Miser's Equipage, the Orphans Bane.
A narrow Soul amidst the boundless Store,
Who shuns the Wretch, that dares be Just and Poor;
Who Charity and Virtue but esteems
As the Priests Cant, and empty moral Names.
But Factious Zeal sometimes Dilates his Breast,
To Mould the Stern Freeholders to his Hand,
Awe their Elections, and their Votes Command.
But where's the end of this immod'rate Toil?
To make a Puny Girl a Golden Spoil.

325 Opinionately] Opinionatively *AB* Opiniatively *C.* 346–47]

On *A—son* we safely may depend,
A Pension never fails to gain a Friend. *BC.*

379 *And*] *With ABC.* 387 *omitted C.* 400 in] on *BC.* 401 Noble] Glorious *C.* 402 Speculations] Speculation *C.* 423 Gain] Game *BC.* 424 *Sims,* Sir *James,* and *Holloway*] *S–ms, Sir James,* and *H–ll–way B.* *After* 442 *C adds:*

Descended of a Sire, whose *Loyal* Pen
So well describes *Rebellion*'s bloody Scene,
Nor *Livy* nor *Thucydides* can Vie
With his Superior Sense, and Majesty.
(A History might teach succeeding Kings,
Whence the long Train of all their Sorrow Springs,
What draws their Subjects Love, what moves their Hate,
Who would support their Crowns, who work their Fate.
Reception in *Misguided Princes* Minds.)

443 *omitted C.* 446 int'rest] Interests *A.* 507 *Trimmers . . . Fav'rites*] *Fav'rites . . . Trimmers BC.* 510 shok'd] shockt *A* shock'd *C.*

Upon the Anonymous Author of Legion's Humble Address to the Lords

Copy text: [Thomas Brown], *The Second Volume of Miscellaneous Works, Written by George, Late Duke of Buckingham,* 1705, p. ^{2}93 (Harvard copy).

Collation: Only the witnesses in the copy text and in *The Works of Mr. Thomas Brown,* 2 vols., 1707, *1,* ^{2}21, have been found. There are no substantive variants between the Amherst College Library copy of the latter and the copy text.

To that Most Senseless Scondrel, the Author of Legion's Humble Address to the Lords

Copy text: [Thomas Brown], *The Second Volume of Miscellaneous Works, Written by George, Late Duke of Buckingham,* 1705, pp. ^{2}94–97 (Harvard copy).

Collation: Only the witnesses in the copy text and in *The Works of Mr. Thomas Brown,* 2 vols., 1707, *1,* ^{2}21–23, have survived. Between the Amherst College Library copy of the latter and the copy text there are the following variants:

23 in the Litigious] in Litigious *1705.* 29 much they] they do *1707.* 51 which] that *1707.*

The Tryal of Skill

Copy text: The Tryal of Skill: or, A New Session of the Poets. Calculated for the Meridian of Parnassus, In the Year, MCCCIV, 1704.

Collation: The text seems to have survived only in the copy text, a folio volume of 22 pages (of which p. 22 is misnumbered "20"). The Yale copy has been reproduced above, with a few corrections and the following emendations:

51 Amongst] And amongst. 231 Report] Repo s. 241 *Dan*] *Don.* 275 like] but. 487 this] its. 585 With] But. 586 He had heard] He heard. 598 That] At.

INDEX OF FIRST LINES

A Grave Physician, us'd to write for Fees, 187
Ah Madam, the King is—But words I may spare, 369
Among the little Pages that were sent, 543
And hast thou left Old *Jemmy* in the Lurch? 6
Apollo perplext with Poetical Duns, 681
Backt with Confederate Force the Austrian goes, 611
Blown up by Faction, and by Guilt Spurr'd on, 198
Damon forbear, and don't disturb your Muse, 251
Hail! *Hi'roglyphick* State *Machin,* 588
Hail Queen of Hearts! to whose true English praise, 614
Haveing thankt me so much for the Newes in my last, 214
He that in Satyr dips his angry Pen, 552
How long may Heaven be banter'd by a Nation, 401
How wretched is the Fate of those who write! 202
Illustrious Steed, who should the Zodiac grace, 366
In Sable Weeds the Beaux and Belles appear, 362
Israel had still, if *Israel* had been true, 231
John Dryden had Enemies three, 209
Long had this Nation been amus'd in vain, 469
Long time had *Israel* been disus'd from Rest, 230
Near to the *Rose* where Punks in numbers flock, 31
Painter, as I went t'other day to 'Change, 336
Peace, thou Corrupter of Morality, 341
Phoebus the witty, gay and bright, 190
Say, Goddess Muse, for thy All-searching Eyes, 651
Seven Sages in our happy Isle are seen, 624
Sicilian Goddess, whose Prophetick Tongue, 519
Sicilian Muse begin a loftier strain! 450
Sicilian *Muse, begin a loftier Flight,* 491
Sicilian Muse, thy Voice and Subject raise, 451
Speak, Goddess! since 'tis Thou that best canst tell, 63
Speak, *Satyr;* for there's none can tell like thee, 265
Such has been this Ill-Natur'd Nations Fate, 376
Thou Tool of Faction, Mercenary Scribe, 676
To give the last Amendments to the Bill, 510
Two Knights, six Projectors, four Squires, and Tom Twitty, 313
We Address you to Day in a very new Fashion, 619
What *Demons* mov'd thee, what malicious Fiends, 677
What *English* Man, without Concern, can see, 160
What Hand, what Skill can form the Artful Piece, 15
When *Burnet* perceiv'd that the beautiful Dames, 40
When Great *Nassau* is dead and gone, 532
Who can forbear, and tamely silent sit, 135
Wisely an Observator said, 345
Ye Men of Might, and Muckle Power, 634
Ye True-Born *Englishmen* proceed, 321
Ye worthy Patriots go on, 49

INDEX OF PROPER NAMES

Italicized entries refer to the text of the poems

Abbot, Robert, 147

Abingdon, second earl of. *See* Bertie, Montagu

Abney, Sir Thomas, 301; at Defoe trial, 604

Act explaining Privilege, 325

Act for the better Relief of the Poor of this Kingdom, 275

Act of Security (Scottish), 660

Act of Settlement, 325, *327,* 659

Act of Toleration, 497, 498, 563, 634, 635, 655; described, 562

Adams, T., 178

Addison, Joseph, *142,*. 143, *171,* 251, *666, 798;* quoted, xxxv; biographical note, *103; The Play-House,* 339, headnote, 29–30, text, 31–34; *A Letter from Italy . . . ,* 666, 667

Adey, William, *534,* 535

Advice to a Painter: headnote, 12–14; text, 15–25

Advice to a Painter. 1701: headnote, 334–35; text, 336–38

Aglionby, William, 167

Ailesbury, earl of. *See* Bruce, Thomas

Albemarle, countess of. *See* Villiers, Elizabeth

Albemarle, duchess of. *See* Elizabeth, duchess of Albemarle

Albemarle, duke of. *See* Monck, George

Albemarle, second duke of. *See* Monck, Christopher

Albemarle, first earl of. *See* Keppel, Arnold Joost van

Aldrich, Henry, *138,* 425, 438

Alexander the Great, 64, 71, *391*

Allen, Commodore Bennett, 641

Allen, Edward, 323

All Souls College, Oxford, 111, 178, 179

Amphion, 32

Anglesey, countess of. *See* Darnley, Lady Catherine

Anglesey, fifth earl of. *See* Annesley, James

Anjou, duke of. *See* Felipe V

Annandale, earl of. *See* Johnstone, William

Anne, countess of Macclesfield, 254

Anne, dowager countess of Kingston, *41*

Anne, Queen, xxvii, *396,* 397, 453, *463,* 494, 495, 527, *643, 644, 658, 659, 666, 672,* and reformation of manners, xxviii; as Princess Anne, 18, 37, 40, 89, 239, 327, 373–74, 526; succession, 378, *379;* attitude toward Whigs, 449; children, 450, 672; on deficiencies in funds, 461; "entirely *English,*" *465;* birth, coronation, *465;* and Cadiz expedition, 474; and victory at Vigo, *483, 484;* and conformity bill, 507; on "scandalous pamphlets," 548; and Act of Toleration, 563; on ecclesiastical promotions, 570; quoted, 594; Tories' disenchantment with, 609; and Charles of Habsburg, 610; and Charles' Portugal visit, satirized, *611–12* (*On the King of Spain's Voyage . . .*); full title, 612; inauguration day to be celebrated, 613; satirized, *614* (*On the 8th of March 1703/4*); speech to parliament (9 November 1703), 635

Annesley, Arthur, 503; and conformity bill, 506

Annesley, James, fifth earl of Anglesey, 41

Annesley, Samuel, 569

Apostates, The, 208

Apothecaries, Company of. *See* Society of the Art and Mystery of Apothecaries

Appletree, John, biographical note, *315*

Ardglass, earl of. *See* Cromwell, Thomas

Argument Shewing that a Standing Army is Inconsistent with a Free Government, An, 161

Ariosto, *Orlando Furioso,* 70

Aristotle, *Poetics,* quoted, 260

Arlington, first earl of. *See* Bennet, Henry

Arthur, Henry and John, 181–82
Asgill, John, *416*, 596, 597; *An Argument Proving, that . . . Man may be Translated . . . into . . . Eternal Life . . .*, 282; biographical note, *282*
Ashburne, James, *669*
Ashby, Matthew, 636, 674
Ashby *vs.* White, 636
Ashton, Edmund, *On the Same Author upon His British Princes*, quoted, 170
Ashurst, Sir Harry, 131
Assembly at Kensington, The, quoted, 624
Atholl, first duke of. *See* Murray, John
Atterbury, Francis, archdeacon of Totnes, 68, 541, 545, 613, 649, 725, *729*; et al., *Dr. Bentley's Dissertations . . . Examin'd*, 108; biographical note, *457*; *Letter to a Convocation Man*, 457; convocation controversy, 493
Atticus, T. Pomponius, *65*
Aubigné, Françoise d', Marquise de Maintenon, *539*; biographical note, *10*
Aubrey, John, 173, 414
Augsburg, League of, 11
Augustus II, 10
Aurelia, *417*
Aylmer, Matthew, Lord Aylmer, 505
Ayloffe, John, *Marvell's Ghost*, 571
Ayloffe, William, 755
Ayscough, Ann, 755

B., R., *An Answer to The Mock Mourners . . .*, 375
Backwell, Edward, 146; biographical note, *303*
Badger, John, 76, 89
Baker, Thomas: *Tunbridge-Walks: Or, The Yeoman of Kent*, 161, 579, 685; biographical note, *685*; *The Female Tatler*, 685; *The Humour of the Age*, 685; *An Act at Oxford*, 686
Baldwin, Ann, 235, 760
Baldwin, Richard, 235
Ball, F. Elrington, 319
Balliol College, Oxford, 173
Bank of England, 25, 146, 147, 278, 406
"Barber, Dr." 375
Bart, Jean, 4
Bastwick, John, *589*
Batavia in Tears . . ., 356
Bateman, John, 60, 119, 124; biographical note, 118
Bath, earl of. *See* Granville, John
Bathurst, Allen, 683
Bayes, John, quoted, 612
Bayle, Pierre, 65
Baynard, Edward, *151*; *Melancholy Reflections on the Deficiency of Useful Learning*, 153, 175; and Blackmore, *153*; *Epitaph upon Mr. John Dryden*, headnote, 208, text, 209
Beauclerk, Charles, duke of St. Albans, 275
Beaumont, Francis, 131; (and Fletcher,) *A King and No King*, quoted, 94
Bedford, first duke of. *See* Russell, William
Bedford, Hilkiah, biographical note, *426–27*
Behn, Aphra, 178, 693; biographical note, *166*; *The Emperour of the Moon*, 579, 686
Bellamont, earl of. *See* Coote, Richard
Bellasis, Sir Henry, 458, *459*, *495*, 594; courtmartialed, 477–78
Benbow, John, 458
Bennet, Frances, biographical note, 117
Bennet, Henry, first earl of Arlington, 117
Bennet, Isabella, biographical note, 117
Bennet, Simon, 117
Bentinck, Ann, Lady Portland, 368
Bentinck, Hans Willem, first earl of Portland, 7, *16–17*, 118, 195, *221*, 225, *236*, *240*, *241*, *244*, *275*, 355, 368; biographical note, 16–17; as ambassador to France, *74*; military career, *238*, *298–99*; in privy council, 240; signs partition treaty, *242*; quoted, 380
Bentley, Richard, bookseller, *91*
Bentley, Richard, classics scholar, *108*, 138, *139*, 252, 459, 560
Berkeley, Charles, second earl of Berkeley, 253
Berkeley, Elizabeth, 253
Berkeley, John, third baron Berkeley, 117
Berkeley, John, viscount Fitzhardinge, 538
Berkshire, first earl of. *See* Howard, Thomas
Bernard, Francis, 79, 92, 95, *99*, 100, 112, 127, 414; biographical notes, 75–76, 139; library, 77
Bertie, Montagu, second earl of Abingdon, 339; biographical note, *526*
Bertie, Peregrine, *42*
Bertie, Robert, first earl of Lindsey, *274*
Bertie, Robert, third earl of Lindsey, 42
Berwick, duke of. *See* Fitzjames, James
Bethlehem Hospital, 136, 140

Betterton, Thomas, 579, 679
Bill of Rights, 51
Binckes, William, biographical note, *492–93*, 504
Birch, Peter, *493;* biographical note, 541; satirized, 543–46 (*On Dr. Birch*)
Birch, Samuel, *75, 114*
Black Baron, 278
Black Box controversy, 105
Blackburne, Lancelot, biographical note, *436*
Blackburne, Richard, *415, 416, 579;* biographical note, 414
Blackburne, Thomas, 436
Blackmore, Sir Richard, xxx, 61, 73, 76, 92, 94, *108,* 112, 127, 151, 154, 158, 165, 171, *174, 175,* 189, 201, *202, 209,* 252, 355, 414, *444, 701; A Satyr against Wit,* xxviii, 62, 149, 150, 157, 169, 175, 181, 199, *701, 702,* headnote, 129–34, text, 135–54; biographical note, *100*–01; *King Arthur. An Heroick Poem. In Twelve Books,* 101, 149, 157, *163,* 181, 191, 203, 204, quoted, 133; *Prince Arthur. An Heroick Poem. In ten Books,* 101, 113, 130, 143, 149, 157, *162, 163,* 181, 191, 202, 203, quoted 119–20, 199; *Essay upon Wit,* quoted, 131–32; ridiculed, 147; *A Short History of the Last Parliament,* 149, 185; and Sydenham, 132; and Baynard, 153; knighted, 163, *205;* lampooned, 181–86, 187–88 (*Upon the Author of the Satyr against Wit*), 187, 190–94 (*A Lent Entertainment*); *A Paraphrase on the Book of Job . . . ,* 192, 200, 203, *701;* and Dryden, 199; attacked in Prologue to "The Pilgrim"; 199–201, 202–05; his religion, 204–05; *The Kit-Cats, A Poem,* quoted, 667; publishers of, *702*
Blake, Elizabeth, 537
Blake, William, quoted, 378
Blandford, marquis of, 541
Blathwayt, William, *221,* 343, *351;* biographical note, *332*
Blome, Richard, *97*
"Blount, Madam," 16
Blount, Charles, 403; *King William and Queen Mary Conquerors,* 272; *Miracles, no Violation of the Laws of Nature,* 698
Blount, H., 725
Board of Commissioners of Appeal, 669
Board of Trade, 332
Boileau, Nicholas: *Le Lutrin,* quoted, 67, 68, 69, 71, 75, 80, 83, 99, 105–06; *Ode sur la prise de Namur,* 10, 473
Bolingbroke, viscount. *See* St. John, Henry
Bolles, Sir John, 318, 400, *534;* biographical note, *424*
Bolton, first duke of. *See* Paulet, Charles
Bolton, second duke of. *See* Paulet, Charles
Bonet, André, 326, 329, 354, 523; quoted, 215, 217, 321; on Tory propaganda, 319; on Somerset, 624
Bonner, Edmund, biographical note, *511*
Booth, Henry, second baron Delamere, first earl of Warrington, *278*
Booth, Judith, 417
Booth, Sir Robert, 417
Boscawen, Hugh, 22
Boucher, Maj. James, 616, 617, 708
Boufflers, Louis François, duc de, 7
Bourbon, François-Louis de, prince de Conti, biographical note, *9*–10, 395
Bourbon-Condé, duc de. *See* Louis III
Bourchier, Richard, *252;* biographical note, 253
Bourgogne, duc de. *See* Louis, duc de Bourgogne
Boursault, Edmé, *Les Fables d'Ésope,* 705
Bowman (unidentified), 22
Box, a druggist, 254
Boyer, Abel: quoted, 61, 133, 136, 226, 501, 688; biographical note, *683; Cupid's Revenge,* 683; *Dictionnaire Royal Français et Anglais,* 683; *The English Theophrastus,* 683; *The History of King William the Third,* 683; *The History of the Reign of Queen Anne . . . ,* 683, 684; *Letters of Wit, Politicks and Morality,* 683; *Achilles . . . ,* 684, 688, 690
Boyle, Arethusa, *41*
Boyle, Charles (*1676–1731*), 136, 138, *142, 221, 690,* 691, 707, 725, 726; biographical note, *108;* et al., *Commendatory Verses, on the Author of the Two Arthurs and the Satyr against Wit,* 134; *Dr. Bentley's Dissertations . . . Examin'd,* 139
Boyle, Charles, baron Clifford of Lanesborough, 24, 41
Boyle, Charles, second earl of Burlington and Cork, 41
Boyle, Henry, *523–24, 534, 716, 787;* biographical note, 24
Boyle, Honora, *41*
Boyle, Juliana, Lady Burlington, *41*
Boyle, Michael, 41, 540
Boyle, Richard, first earl of Burlington and second earl of Cork, 24, 787

Boyle, Robert, 111
Boyne, battle of, 21, 72
Bracegirdle, Anne, 65, 462; and Congreve, *705;* biographical note, 705–06
Brady, Nicholas, 695; biographical note, *173; Epigram, Occasion'd by the Passage in the Satyr against Wit . . . ,* 173; (and Tate), *A New Version of the Psalms of David,* 173
Brasenose College, Oxford, 173, 685
Bray, Thomas, 492
Brereton, Edward, 496; biographical note, *495*
Brett, Henry, 254
Brewer, *172*
Brewster, John, 84
Bridgeman, Sir Orlando, 173
Briscoe, Samuel, 185; biographical note, *91*
Bristol (ship), 458
Brittania's Tears . . . , 357
Brome, Richard, *The City Wit,* quoted, 252
Bromley, William (Tory), 493, *523,* 524, 617, 636, 646; biographical note, 491; and conformity bill, 497, 503, 506, 507, *523,* 640
Bromley, William (Whig), 488–89
Brown, Joseph, 422
Brown, Thomas, 165, 172, *173,* 175, 208, *256,* 303, 680; quoted, xxviii, 23, 108, 134, 182, 214, 411, 437; *A Satyr upon the French King,* headnote, 3–5, text, 6–11; *Mr.* Brown's *Character of the Jacobite Clergy . . . ,* 4; career and works, 4–5; *Tho. Brown's Recantation of his Satyr on the French King,* quoted, 5; poetry described, 5; contributor to *Commendatory Verses, on the Author of the Two Arthurs and the Satyr against Wit,* 134; *The Life of Erasmus,* 138; *A Lent-Entertainment,* headnote, 189, text, 190–94; on Richard Baldwin, 235; on reformers, 446; *Letters from the Dead to the Living,* quoted, 235, 401, 581; *A Dialogue between the Pillory and Daniel de Foe,* 587; *A Declamation in Praise of Poverty,* quoted, 625; *Upon the Anonymous Author of Legion's Humble Address to the Lords,* headnote, 674–75, text, 676; *To That Most Senseless Scondrel, the Author of Legion's Humble Address to the Lords,* headnote, 674–75, text, 677–78
Brownlow, Sir William, biographical note, 77
Bruce, Thomas, earl of Ailesbury, 344; quoted, 422, 456, 614
Brutus, *65*
Brydges, James, eighth Lord Chandos, *693;* biographical note, 694
Buccleuch, duke of. *See* Scott, James
Buckingham, duke of. *See* Sheffield, John
Buckingham, second duke of. *See* Villiers, George
Bulkeley, Robert, second viscount Bulkeley of Cashel, 255
Bulkley, James, 325
Bullock, William, 690
Bunyan, John, 165, 514
Burdett, Thomas, 41
Burgess, Daniel, biographical note, 92
Burlington, earl of. *See* Boyle, Richard
Burlington, Lady. *See* Boyle, Juliana
Burnaby, Anthony, biographical note, *495*–96
Burnaby, William, 136; biographical note, *702; The Ladies Visiting Day,* 702, 703; *Love Betray'd . . . ,* 702; *The Modish Husband,* 702, 703; *The Reform'd Wife,* 702, 703; *The Satyr of Titus Petronius Arbiter . . . ,* 702; "Upon a Lady Singing," 702
Burnet, Gilbert, bishop of Salisbury, 247, 252, 282, 311, 380, *459, 510,* 540; quoted, 12, 17, 19, 21, 22, 65, 196, 211, 214, 220, 300, 319, 321, 327, 343, 438, 493, 494, 497, 498, 499, 501, 502, *513,* 527, 614, 642, 656, 669; biographical note, 37–38; favor with Princess Anne, 40; satirized, 40–42 (*The Brawny Bishop's Complaint*); *History of His Own Time,* 152; on Somers, 195, 216; *The History of the Reformation of the Church of England, 239,* 512; on democracy, 287; *An Elegy on the Death . . . William the Third . . . ,* 356; on Wright, 421; and conformity bill, *496,* 507, 508, *521,* 550; on William III, 510; on Bonner, 511; in Amsterdam, *515;* physical stature, 458, 522; wives, *537;* on Birch, 544; early career, *545;* on Scotch plot, 617; on Townshend 627; his "patron," *654; An Exposition of the Thirty-Nine Articles of the Church of England,* 658
Burton, Henry, 589
Busby, Richard, 92, 256
Butler, James, second duke of Ormonde, 244, 255, 400, 458, *459, 469, 477,* 504, 541, *593, 594,* 643, 684; biographical notes, *73, 384;* loses mistress, *440–41;* and Cadiz expedition, 468–74 passim; and

Butler, James (*cont.*)
Vigo victory, 481, 483; replaces Rochester, 532
Bysshe, Edward, quoted, 586–87

Cadiz expedition, 467–68; as poem subject, 469–84 (*The Spanish Descent*)
Caius College, Cambridge, 167
Calamy, Edmund, nonconformist, *569*
Calamy, Edmund, grandson of nonconformist: quoted, 550, 592; biographical note, *569; An Abridgement of Mr. Baxter's History . . .*, 569; Presbyterian, 604
Calves' Head Club, described, 227–28; *237, 654, 676*
Cambridge, second earl of. *See* Hamilton, James
Cambridge University, *175*, 348, 624; Sidney Sussex College, 144; King's College, 148, 627; Pembroke College, 164; Trinity College, 103, 104, 166, 251, 414, 436, 514; Trinity Hall, 167; Caius College, 167; Queens' College, 168, 589, 687; St. John's College, 222, 426, 492; Magdalene College, 497; Catherine Hall, 569; Christ's College, 569; Peterhouse, 60, 589
Cameron, William J., 40, 361; *New Light on Aphra Behn*, 166
Camillus, M. Furius, 72
Campbell, Thomas, 82
Campion, Anne, 440, *625*
Capel, Arthur, Lord Capel of Hadham, *274*
Capell, Algernon, second earl of Essex, 384; described, 538
Carew, Thomas, 679
Carlisle, third earl of. *See* Howard, Charles
Carlos II, 242, 323, 471, 609; described, *243;* successor, 473
Carnarvon, earl of. *See* Dormer, Robert
Case, John, biographical note, *89*
Cassilis, sixth earl of. *See* Kennedy, John
Catherine Hall, Cambridge, 569
Catilina, L. Sergius, *100, 628*, 648–49, 651, *660*, 669
Cato Uticensis, 100
Cavendish, duke of. *See* Holles, John
Cavendish, Henry, earl of Ogle, 625
Cavendish, Henry, second duke of Newcastle, 703
Cavendish, William, fourth earl and first duke of Devonshire, *73, 143*, 144, 462, *520*, 522, *528*, 619, *663;* quoted, 196; described, *440*, 625; and conformity bill, *497*, 508, 678
Cavendish, William, marquis of Hartington, biographical note, *522*
Caesar, Julius, 100
Cecil, James, third earl of Salisbury, 117
Cecil, James, fourth earl of Salisbury, 117, *278*
Cecil, John, earl of Exeter, *278*
Cecil, Margaret, 255; biographical note, *117*
Centlivre, Susannah, 74, 702
Certain Verses Written by Several of the Authors Friends . . ., 181
Cervantes, Miguel de, *Don Quixote*, 129, 132, 168
Chalmers, George, quoted, 587
Chamberlayne, Edward, 277
Chamberlen, Hugh, 61, 154; biographical note, *114*
Chandos, eighth Lord. *See* Brydges, James
Character of a Sneaker, The, quoted, 504
Charles of Habsburg (Charles III), 242, *470*, 642; biographical note, 609–10; satirized, *611*–12 (*On the King of Spain's Voyage . .*)
Charles I, 230, *231;* beheaded, 227, 385; religion, 651
Charles II, 18, *57*, 89, 98, 104, 127, 130, 143, 144, 230, *495*, 500, 571, 660, *671;* children, 117; quoted, 185; Catholicism, *218;* landing at Dover, 232; peers created, 274; mistresses, 274–75; as drinker, *283;* orders stop on exchequer, 303; funeral, 614; and Williamson *vs.* Regem, 660–61
Charlett, Arthur, 75, 76, *138;* biographical note, 139
Chateaurenault, marquis de. *See* Rousselet, François de
Cheek, Thomas, 136, 137, 679, 725; *The Antient and Modern Stage Survey'd*, 137; biographical note, 687–88; and Suckling's *Goblins*, 689
Cherington, Richard, biographical note, *315*
Chesterfield, first earl of. *See* Stanhope, Philip
Chetle (or Cheatle), Thomas, *313;* in Tory cabal, 311
Chishull, Edmund, 365
Chivers, Henry, 54
Cholmley, Francis, 528
Christ Church College, Oxford, 74, 110,

126, 138, 147, 173, 256, 424, 436, 457, 491, 493, 503, 504, 528, 531, 541, 663, 685, 693
Christ-Church Hospital, 279
Christ's College, Cambridge, 569
Chudleigh, Lady Mary, xxxiv
Church of England, 3, 511; and occasional conformity, 506; and honest dissenters, 561; and Act of Toleration, 562
Churchill, Awnsham and John, 149, *702*
Churchill, Anne, 484, 521, 526; biographical note, *117*
Churchill, George, 504; biographical note, *505*
Churchill, John (*1690–1703*), 543
Churchill, John, duke of Marlborough, 117, 210, 239, 300, 368, 393, 409, *459*, 498, 505, *532*, 669, *686*, 779, 798; military influence, 458; on Cadiz expedition, 471; rewarded for military success, 495; "antient crimes," *499;* and Charles of Habsburg, 610; and *Faction Display'd,* 649–50; and conformity bill, 664, 668
Churchill, Sarah, duchess of Marlborough, 239, 261, 356, 368, 439, 484, 517, 535, 536, 541, *543*, *670*, 684; quoted, 449, 540; on Harley, 494; on Hedges, 500; in Anne's favor, *526;* on Sacheverell, 570; and *Faction Display'd,* 649–50; biographical note, *669–70*
Cibber, Colley, 31, 200, 254; *Love's Last Shift,* 130; *The Careless Husband,* 574
Cibber, Theophilus, 557, 710
Cicero, 99
Clancarty, fourth earl of. *See* Maccarty, Donogh
Clarendon, first earl of. *See* Hyde, Edward
Clarke, Edward, *24*, biographical note, 25
Clarke, Sir Edward, 604
Claudius Pulcher, P., 658; biographical note, *99–100*
Clayton, Martha, 408
Clayton, Sir Robert, *146*, 147, 409; biographical note, *408*
Cleveland, John, 260; *A Character of a Diurnall-Maker,* quoted, 251; *The Rebel Scot,* quoted, 277
Clifford, Baron. *See* Boyle, Charles
Clubmen of the House of Commons, The, 166
Cockerill, T., 336
Cocles, P. Horatius, 72
Codrington, Sir Christopher, 138, 179, 185, 204, *252*, 725; et al., *Commendatory Verses on the Author of the Two Arthurs and the Satyr against Wit,* 134; biographical note, *147–*48; *A Short and True History of the Author of the Satyr against Wit,* 148
Codrus, *108*
Cokayne, G. E., xix, 585
Coke, Sir Edward, *140*
Coke, Thomas, 336
Colbatch, Sir John, *141;* biographical note, *107*
Coldstream Regiment, 692
Cole, Sir William, *407*
Colepepper, Thomas, 334
Coleridge, S. T., xxxi, xxxiii, 399
Coley, Henry, 453
Collection of New Songs, A (1697), 580
College, Stephen, xxvii
College of Heralds, 277-78
College of Physicians. *See* Royal College of Physicians
Collier, Jeremy, 29, 30, 137, 143, *163*, *164*, *168*, *209*, 250, 665; *A Short View of the Immorality, and Profaneness of the English Stage,* 29, 129–30, 147, 150, 157, 163, 167, 704; *A Defence of the Short View . . . ,* 164
Collins, Samuel, *97*, 111, *114; A Systeme of Anatomy . . . ,* 97
Colt, Henry Dutton, biographical note, *98*
Colyear, Sir David, Lord Portmore and Blackness, *254*
Commendatory Verses on the Author of the Two Arthurs and the Satyr against Wit, 152, 153, 158, 175, 181, 189, 688, 702; quoted, 204
Committee for the Address of Thanks, 615
Company of Apothecaries. *See* Society of the Art and Mystery of Apothecaries
Company of Parish Clerks, 85
Company of Scotland Trading to Africa and the Indies, 273
Compton, Henry, bishop of London, 427, 501, 657; as soldier, 288–89; characterized, *438*, *537*
Conference between King William and the Earl of Sunderland, A, 13; headnote, 210–13; text, 214–23
Congress of Ryswick, 103
Congreve, William, 91, *103*, 136, 142, *147*, 164, 167, *168*, *171*, *172*, *179*, 248, *251*, 487, 618, *665*, *706; The Birth of the Muse. A Poem,* 103; *The Mourning*

Congreve, William (*cont.*)
Muse of Alexis. A Pastoral, 103; wit, *145; The Double Dealer,* 149; *The Way of the World,* 202; and Montagu, *463;* Kit-Cat member, 700; and Anne Bracegirdle, *705*–06; et al., *Squire Trelooby* (trans. from Molière), 705, 706
Coningsby, Thomas, baron Coningsby of Clanbrassil, *221,* 496, *535;* biographical note, *20*
Conolly, William, 660
Conti, prince de. *See* Bourbon, François-Louis de
Cooke, Sir Thomas, 421, *426*
Cooper, Anthony Ashley, third earl of Shaftesbury, 399; quoted 339, 527
Coote, Richard, 254
Coote, Richard, earl of Bellamont, 20
Cork, second earl of. *See* Boyle, Richard
Cornwall, earl of. *See* Richard, earl of Cornwall
Cornwall, Thomas, 316
Corpus Christi College, Oxford, 514
Cortes, Hernán, *413*
Court, The: headnote, 248–50; text, 251–56
"Covent-Garden Wits," 181, 188
Cowley, Abraham, 144, *165,* 260, 586
Cowper, Lady, 528
Cowper, Spencer, 419; biographical note, *418;* and death of Sarah Stout, *420,* 421
Cowper, William (*1665?–1723*), first Earl Cowper, *524;* biographical note, *417*–18, and Elizabeth Culling, 418–19
Cowper, William (poet), 261, 418
Cowper, Sir William (*d. 1706*), 417; biographical note, *418*
Coxe, Daniel, quoted, 132
Creech, Thomas, *444;* biographical note, *178*–79
"Crisp the Broker," *559, 602*
Cromwell, Oliver, 317
Cromwell, Thomas, earl of Ardglass, baron Cromwell, 41
Crow, Capt. Josias, 641
Cuddon, Ann, *410*
Cuddon, Sir Thomas, biographical note, *410*
Cuffe, Francis, 41
Culling (or Cullen), Elizabeth, affair with Cowper, 418–19
Culpeper, Nicholas, quoted, 86
Cumberland, Richard, 510
Curll, Edmund, 103
Curtius, Marcus, 72
Cutler, Sir John, 63, 112
Cutts, John, baron Cutts of Gowran, 187, *253, 424,* 525, 692, 693, *778, 779;* biographical note, *21;* debts, *535*
Cyrus, 72

D., C., *To the Concealed Author of this Excellent Poem,* 648
Dalrymple, Sir John, quoted, 458
Danby, first earl of. *See* Osborne, Sir Thomas
Daniel, Richard, *A Dream . . . ,* 356
Dante, Alighieri, quoted, 96
Daphnis: Or, A Pastoral Elegy . . . , 179
Darby, John, 763, 769
Darius, 71
Darnell, Sergeant, 99
Darnley, Lady Catherine, 41
Dartmouth, Lord, 502, 506, 661; on Weymouth, 503; on Wharton, 520; on Somerset, 624; quoted, 656
Dashwood, George, 636
Dashwood, Robert, biographical note, *559*
Dashwood, Sir Robert, 559
Dashwood, Sir Samuel, 449, 487, 559, 636; biographical note, *453;* in Defoe trial, 604
Davenant, Charles, 160, 320, 331, *495; 664;* biographical notes, *173*–74, *350; Essays,* 174, 350; *A Discourse upon Grants and Resumptions,* 174, *271,* 350; *Circe. A Tragedy,* 174; *Tom Double Return'd out of the Country . . . ,* 504; quoted, 266, 328, 661; on war with France, 339; election defeat, 344; as Tory propagandist, *504*
Davenant, Henry, 487; diplomatic post, *503*
Davenant, Sir William, 173, 181, 679
Davenport, Elizabeth, 440
Davers, Sir Robert, biographical note, *416*–17
Dawks, Ichabod, 181
Decius Mus, Publius, 71
Defoe, Daniel, xxx, xxxii–iii, 21, 95, 105, 107, 161, 226, 682, *696,* 701; *Reformation of Manners,* xxviii, headnote, 398–400, text, 401–48, 547, 573, 574; *A New Satyr on the Parliament,* xxix, 48, headnote, 318–20, text, 321–33, 631; oracular tone, xxix; *The Address,* xxx, headnote, 631–33, text, 634–47; *Legion's Humble Address to the Lords,* xxx, 633, 674–75, quoted, 643, lampooned, 676 (*Upon the Anonymous Author . . .*), 677–78 (*To that Most*

Senseless Scondrel . . .); as poet, xxxi–xxxii; *The True-Born Englishman,* xxxi, 158, 227, 324, 596, 632, headnote, 259–64, text, 265–309; satiric purposes, xxxii–xxxiii; *More Reformation. A Satyr upon Himself,* xxviii, 398, 632, headnote, 547–51, text, 552–84; quoted, 45, 331; and glass-tax legislation, 55; *An Enconium upon a Parliament,* 105, 158, 210, 319, headnote, 43–48, text, 49–57; *The Genuine Works,* 158; *A Second Volume of the Writings of the Author of the True-Born Englishman,* 158–59; forms of his name, *179;* on Sedley, 185; *The Pacificator,* 248, headnote, 157–59, text, 160–80; on satire, 262; *An Enquiry into the Case of Mr. Asgil's Translation . . . ,* 282; *The Two Great Questions Consider'd,* 292; denies hereditary vice, 308; *An Alphabetical Catalogue of an Extensive Collection of the Writings of Daniel De Foe,* 319; *Memorial,* 226, 319, *328,* 329; *A Farther Argument against Ennobling Foreigners,* 325; *The Felonious Treaty,* 326; *England's Late Jury,* 332, headnote, 343–44, text, 345–52, 631; at entertainment for petitioners, 334; *The Mock Mourners,* 357, headnote, 372–75, text, 376–97; *A Satyr upon King William . . . ,* 374; *A True Collection of the Writings of the Author of The True Born English-man,* 375, quoted, 290, 547; *Reformation of Manners,* headnote, 398–400, text, 401–48, quoted, 552, 554, 555, 556; bankruptcy, 412; *Robinson Crusoe,* 413; *A New Test of the Church of England's Loyalty,* 436; *The Spanish Descent,* headnote, 467–68, text, 469–84; *Peace without Union,* 492; quoted, 637; in pillory, 497, 582, 585–86; *An Enquiry into the Occasional Conformity of Dissenters . . . ,* 506, quoted, 560; and occasional conformity, 433, 506, 507, 549–51, 632, 634, 635; on Rooke, 527; as fugitive from justice, 547–49, 675; *The Shortest Way with the Dissenters,* 547, 548, 549, 572, 576, 592; *An Argument, Shewing, That the Prince of Wales . . . Has no Just Pretensions to the Crown . . . ,* 567; *The Sincerity of the Dissenters Vindicated . . . ,* 568, 632; *Reasons against a War with France,* quoted, 572; *Royal Religion, Being some Enquiry after the Piety of Princes,* 575, quoted, 639; use of total irony, 576, 578; *Some Remarks on the First Chapter in Dr. Davenant's Essays,* quoted, 577; *An Essay on the Regulation of the Press,* 578, 645; *King William's Affection to the Church of England Examin'd,* 578; *A Hymn to the Pillory,* headnote, 585–87, text, 588–605; on absolute obedience to the king, 598; scruples on lampooning, 622–23; and Harley, 631–33; *A Weekly Review of the Affairs of France . . . ,* 631; *An Elegy on the Author of the True-Born-Englishman,* 634; *A Serious Inquiry into this Grand Question,* 265, 591, 638, on partition treaties, 640; *The History of the Kentish Petition,* quoted, 647; bailsmen for, 696; on Pittis, 697

Deists, 403

Delamere, second baron. *See* Booth, Henry

Delaune, Gideon, 86

Denbigh, third earl of. *See* Feilding, William

Denham, John, *15*

Dennis, John, 74, *146, 172,* 183, 193, *252, 700, 701,* 702; literary output, *143; A Plot and No Plot,* 143, 688; *Remarks on a Book Entituled, Prince Arthur, An Heroick Poem,* 143, 157, 163, 167; biographical note, *167*–68; *The Usefulness of the Stage . . . ,* 167, quoted, 239; quoted, 204, 224; *The Reverse,* headnote, 227–29, text, 231–47; on Swan, 255; on Walsh, 314, 706; *The Monument . . . ,* 356; on Halifax, 666; *Iphigenia,* 684; Kit-Cat friends, 700; *Liberty Asserted. A Tragedy,* 701; as Whig, 701

Dent, John, 446

Dering, Sir Edward, biographical note, 428

Desjean, Jean Bernard Louis, baron de Pointis, 592

Devil and the Collier, The, 209

Devonshire, fourth earl and first duke of. *See* Cavendish, William

Diadora, *443, 579, 601*

Dialogue between Captain Tom and Sir H—n D—n C—t, A, 98

Dialogue between the Illustrious Ladies, the Countesses of Albemarle and Orkney, A, headnote, 367–68, text, 369–71

Digby, Kenelm, 66

Dillon, Wentworth, fourth earl of Roscommon, *166,* quoted, 146, 198

Dionysius II, *9*

Discommendatory Verses, 185
Dockwra, William, 682
Dolben, Sir Gilbert, 291
Doña Teresa, 609, 610
Donne, John, 94; satires, 699
Dorchester, first marquis of. *See* Pierrepoint, Henry
Dormer, Robert, earl of Carnavon, 274
Dorset, sixth earl of. *See* Sackville, Charles
Douglas, James, fourth duke of Hamilton, 377, 425
Douglas, James, eleventh earl of Morton, biographical note, *254*
Douglas, James, second duke of Queensberry, and Scotch plot, 615–16
Douglas, William, duke of Hamilton, 254
Dove, Tom, *202*
Dowdeswell, Richard, biographical note, *314*
Drake, James, 137; quoted, 5; *To Dr. Garth, on the Fourth Edition of His Incomparable Poem, The Dispensary,* 175; on Defoe, 319
Drayton, Michael, *England's Heroical Epistles,* 699
Drummond, John, earl of Melfort, 616
Drummond, William, 704
Dryden, John, 37, 71, 74, 88, 91, 94, *102,* 129, 136, *137, 145, 149,* 164, 167, *168, 171, 174, 178,* 248, *256,* 260 352, 399, *444,* 528, 625, 663, 672, 682, 710; death, xxviii, 201; *Absolom and Achitophel,* xxxi, 262, 296, 298, 648, quoted, *174,* 230, 232, 287, 288, 352, 432, 657, 669; quoted, 38, 120, 158, 170, 199, 261, 379, 432, 434; *Mac Flecknoe,* 58, 107, 121, 171, 189, 379; *The Works of Virgil . . . Translated,* 103, 149, 310, 503, 673; on Southerne, 145; on Shakespeare, 146; (and Tate,) *The Second Part of Absolom and Achitophel,* 148, 203, 671; on Milbourne, 165; (and Mulgrave,) *An Essay on Satire,* 167, 521; on Hopkins, 168; *The Indian Emperour,* quoted, 171; and Pittis, 172; *Essay of Dramatic Poesy,* 185; and Blackmore, 199, 204; *Fables Ancient and Modern,* quoted, 199; *To My Honour'd Kinsman, John Driden, of Chesterton,* 199, 202; Prologue to *"The Pilgrim,"* headnote, 199–201, text, 202–05; *The Wife of Bath Her Tale,* quoted, 203; funeral described, 206–08; epitaph, 209 (*Epitaph upon Mr. John Dryden*); on Walsh, 310, 707; *Religio Laici,* quoted, 434, 562; *The Fourth Pastoral of Virgil, Englished by Mr. Dryden,* text, 450–64; *The Vindication . . .* [of] *The Duke of Guise,* quoted, 589; his influence, 648; on Tonson, *667; To the Memory of Mr. Oldham,* 673
Du Guernier, Louis, 727
Duke, Richard, 178
Duncombe, Sir Charles, *253,* 261, 262, 263, *302–08,* 337, *409, 424, 446,* 596, 762; biographical notes, *100, 146–47, 301;* expelled from Commons, *220,* 305; imprisoned, 220; and Backwell, *303;* government positions, *304;* elected high sheriff, 306; offers gifts to London, *308;* mistress, 446
Dunton, John, 91; quoted, 259, 391, 399, 702; *The Hazard of a Death-Bed-Repentance . . . ,* 440; on Danby, 526; on D'Urfey, 685; on Gildon, 698
Duras, Louis de, earl of Feversham, *278*
D'Urfey, Thomas, 164, *168, 171, 172,* 173, *179,* 248, *251, 444,* 649, *684,* 685; biographical note, *143; The Comical History of Don Quixote,* 143, 149
Dutch guards, disbanded, 46, *49;* William attempts to retain, 51–52
Dutch wars, 169
Duyn, Adam van der, 367, *370*
Duyn, Geertruid Johanna Quirina van der; becomes countess of Albemarle, 367–68; satirized, 369–71 (*A Dialogue*)

East India Company, *219,* 221, 337, 421, 426, 453, 534, 681; new Company created, *53,* 55 (*see* New East India Company)
Eccles, John, 580
Edict of Nantes, 683; revoked, 496
Edinburgh Society for the Reformation of Manners, 400
Edward III, *17*
Edwin, Sir Humphrey, 506
Elegie sur la Mort du Très-puissant Prince, Guillaume III . . . , 355
Elegie upon the Much Lamented Death of the Most Serene and Potent Prince, James VII, An, 353
Elegy on the Death of the Author of the Characters &c. Of the Ladies Invention . . . , 172
Elegy on the Death of James the Second, Late King of England, An, 353
Elegy on the Death of the Late King James, An, 353

Elegy on K. W., 357
Elizabeth, duchess of Albemarle, 703
Elizabeth I, *231*, 310, *391*, 484
Elliot, John, *The Grace of God Asserted*, 152
Elliot, Robert, biographical note, *152*
Ellis, John, 50
England's Happiness . . ., 467
English Gentleman Justified, The, 264
English Men no Bastards . . ., 264
Ent, Sir George, *126*
Epistle to Sr. Richard Blackmore . . ., 679
Epitaph on King William, 1702, 357
Erle, Maj. Gen. Thomas, 187
Essex, second earl of. *See* Capell, Algernon
Etherege, George, 679
Eton College, 627
Eugene, Prince, 475
Evance, Sir Stephen, *426*
Evans, Francis, 489
Evans, John, 510
Evelyn, John, quoted; 24, 37–38, 40, 45, 148, 178, 376, 508, 544
Examen Miscellaneum, 557
Exeter, earl of. *See* Cecil, John
Exeter College, Oxford, 142
Extempore verses on the Author of the Satyr against Wit, 133

Fabian, M., 208
Fable of the Cuckoo, The, 264
Faction Display'd. A Poem. Answer'd Paragraph by Paragraph, 649; quoted, 655. *See also* Shippen, William, *Faction Display'd*
Faction Display'd. The Second Part, 649. *See also* Shippen, William, *Faction Display'd*
Faction Display'd Burlesqued, 649
Fagg, Thomas, *524*
Farmer, Anthony, 534
Farquhar, George, *32*, 370, 689, *690*, 691; *Love and a Bottle*, 30; *Sir Harry Wildair*, 369, 690; *The Constant Couple . . .*, 684, 690; as lieutenant, 691
Fathers nown Child, quoted, 16
Feilding, William, third earl of Denbigh, 41
Feiling, Keith, quoted, 52, 642
Felipe V: as Philippe, duc d'Anjou, 323, *470*, 471, 473, 476, 539, 609, *612;* crowned, 339, *475*
Female Critick . . . , The, 264, 267
Fénelon, François de Salignac de la Mothe, archbishop of Cambrai, 116
Fenwick, Sir John, 19, 21, 25, 337, 352, 366, 523, 531, 533, 649, 664; as martyr, *15*–16; prosecution, 21, 22
Ferguson, Robert: biographical note, *105;* and Scotch plot, *628*
Feversham, earl of. *See* Duras, Louis de
Finch, Daniel, second earl of Nottingham, 217, 300, 306, 339, 492, 495, 500, 501, *527*, *536*, 541, 569, 585, 604, 605, 611, 632, *639*, 643, 669, *779;* biographical note, *497;* and church preferment, *544;* and Defoe arrest, 548, 549, 572; and Scotch plot, 611, 616, 708; Commons commends, *619*–*20*
Finch, Heneage, Lord Guernsey, *65*, *140*, *331*, *336*, 344, 345, 352, 497, *501*, *523;* amendment on Prince of Wales, 337; supports James II, *348;* and conformity bill, 507
Finch, Henry, 544
Fishmongers Company, 334
Fitzgerald, Col. John, 165
Fitzhardinge, viscount. *See* Berkeley, John
Fitzjames, James, duke of Berwick, 616
Fitzroy, Charles, duke of Southampton, 274
Fitzroy, George, duke of Northumberland, 274
Fitzroy, Henry, duke of Grafton, 117, 274
Flatman, Thomas, 178
Fleet, Sir John, 604
Fleetwood, William, biographical note, *148*
Fléchier, Valentin Esprit, *The Life of Emperour Theodosius the Great*, 689
Fleming, Robert, 583
Fletcher, Andrew, 239, 242
Fletcher, John, 131, 137; *The Island Princess*, 29, 38; (and Beaumont), *A King and No King*, quoted, 94; *The Pilgrim*, Dryden's prologue to, headnote 199–201, text, 202–05
Flettumasy, *442*–*43*, *578*, *602*
Flying Post, The, 5, 226, 320
Foley, Paul, 44, 109, 315; biographical note, *19*
Foley, Thomas, baron Foley of Kidderminster, 315; biographical note, 109
Foley, Thomas, of Stourbridge, 19, 109
Forbes, Arthur, second earl of Granard, biographical note, *500*
Forbes, James, biographical note, *626*

Fowler, Edward, 510; biographical note, *514; The Design of Christianity,* 514; *Dirt wipt off . . . ,* 514; *The Principles and Practices of certain Moderate Divines . . .* 514
Fox, Charles, biographical note, *496*
Fox, Sir Stephen, 496
Foxe, John, *Actes and Monuments,* 511
Frampton, Robert, 501, 634
France, xxviii, 231, 627; and second partition treaty, 242; troops raised against, 321; agitation for war against, 339–40; and battle at Luzzara, 475; and battle at Vigo, 481–83; and Scotch plot, 616
François, Louis, duc de Boufflers, 7
Fraser, Carey, 663
Fraser, Simon, Lord Lovat: and Scotch plot, 615–16; betrayed, 628
Freke, John, 626; biographical note, *148; The History of Insipids,* 148
Fuller, William, 588, 598; quoted, 226; biographical note, *590; A Brief Discovery of the True Mother of the Prince of Wales,* 590
Fuller's plot, 105
Furnese, Sir Henry, *446; biographical* note, *406*
Freeman, Samuel, *92*

Gaffney, *20,* 221
Gallus, C. Cornelius, biographical note, *102*
Gauden, John, *Eikon Basilike . . . ,* 651
Gardiner, James, 510
Gardiner, Thomas, 75; as apothecary officer, *87–88*
Garrard, Sir Samuel, biographical note, 255
Garth, Samuel, 72, 75, 86, 118, 129, 132, 136, *142, 143, 149,* 152, *170,* 204, 206, 207, *252, 665,* 680, *688, 689; The Dispensary,* xxxiv, 16, 150, 152, *710, 711,* headnote, 58–62, text, 63–128; literary importance, xxxiv; quoted, 12, 64, 480; *The Dunciad,* 58; *MacFlecknoe,* 58; biographical notes, 60–61; on Bernard, 76; as delegate, 119; *vs.* Blackmore on medical study, 132; *To the Merry Poetmaster at Sadlers-hall, in Cheapside,* 175–76; prologue to *Tamerlane,* 462
Gay, John, *The Beggar's Opera,* 39
Geffrey, Sir Robert, *307,* 400; biographical note, *404*
Gelsthorp, Peter, 75; biographical note, 86
Gentleman's Journal, The, 172, 689, 702
Gentleman's Magazine, The, 22
George, Prince, 505; and conformity bill, 507
George I, 327
Gerard, Anne, countess of Macclesfield, 52, 254
Gerard, Charles, second earl of Macclesfield, 50, 659; biographical note, 73–74; divorce, 52, 254; violent career, 384
Germain, Lady Elizabeth. See Berkeley, Elizabeth, 253
Germain, Sir John: biographical note, *252–53;* marriage, 254
Germany, 243; and battle at Luzzara, 475
Gibbon, Edmund, 709
Gibbons, William, 76, *93, 104, 106, 109,* 127, *141,* 200; biographical note, *92*
Gibson, Edmund, 457
Gildon, Charles, 136, *557,* 576, *698,* 702; biographical note, *173; The History of the Athenian Society,* 173; *Miscellaneous Letters and Essays . . . ,* 173; (ed.,) *The Miscellaneous Works of Charles Blount, Esq.,* 173; *The Roman Brides Revenge . . . ,* 173; *Cleon to Dorinda,* 557; quoted, 691, 692; *The Patriot,* 699
Gill, Thomas, 81; *The State of Physick in London . . . ,* 113
Gin, 429
Glisson, Francis, biographical note, *126*
Gloucester, duke of. *See* William, Prince, duke of Gloucester
Godolphin, Sidney, Lord Godolphin, 53, 210, 212, 218, 265, 488, *525, 532,* 631, 635, 640, 649; biographical note, *220;* at secret Tory caucus, 339; resigns, 354, 499; "advances" to Whigs, 517; and conformity bill, *668;* as gambler, 669
Goes, Philip van der, 504
Gold, R., *The Dream to Sir Charles Duncomb,* 307
Gold (or Gould), William, biographical note, *98*
Golden Age, The, 487, 490; headnote, 449–50; text, 451–66
Golden Age Restor'd, The, 518, headnote, 487–90; text, 491–505
Golden Age Revers'd, The, 13; headnote, 517–18; text, 519–29
Goldsmith, Oliver, xxvii; quoted, 449
Goodall, Charles (*1642–1712*), biographical note, *111;* 115
Goodall, Charles (*1671–89*), *Poems and Translations . . . ,* 115
Goodeve, John, 418
Goodricke, Sir Henry, 535

Gore, Sir William, 409
Gosse, Edmund, 166
Gould, Henry, 534
Gould, Robert, *The Play-House,* quoted, 29
Gould (or Gold), William, biographical note, 98
Gower, Sir Thomas, 428; biographical note, 429
Gower, Sir William Leveson, 497
Grafton, duke of. *See* Fitzroy, Henry
Graham (or Grahme), James, 492, *646;* biographical note, *500*
Graham, Sir Richard, 500
Granard, second earl of. *See* Forbes, Arthur
Granger, James, xix, 693
Granville, George, 498; on Wycherley, 145; *Heroic Love,* 503
Granville (or Grenville), John, earl of Bath, 244, 326, 497
Granville (or Grenville), John, son of earl of Bath, 351, 498, *523;* biographical note, 326; speaker candidate, *499;* ordnance post, *535*
Gravemore, Lady, 367
Graydon, Vice-Adm. John, 641
Gray's Inn, 144, 165, 424, 523, 589
Greenhill, Henry, 693
Grenville, Sir Bevil, 497
Grey, Forde, earl of Tankerville, 196, 267
Grey, Thomas, second earl of Stamford, 519; biographical notes, *143*–44, *455*
Grocers' Company, 83, 278
Groenevelt, John, 87
Gucht, Michael Van der, 586
Guernsey, Lord. *See* Finch, Heneage
Guidot, Thomas, *On Don Quicksilver,* 98
Guise, Sir John, 533
Guy, Henry, 212, 409, 626
Guzman, Nuño de, *413*
Gwyn, Francis, 645
Gwyn, Nell, 275, 439

Haines (or Haynes), Joseph, *559*
Hakluyt, Richard, *The Principal Navigations, Voiages, and Discoveries of the English Nation,* 412
Halifax, baron. *See* Montagu, Charles
Halifax, marquis of. *See* Saville, Sir George
Hall, John, 510; biographical note, *514*
Hall, Henry, 145; *The Mitred Club,* 189, headnote, 506–09, text, 510–16; *Quid Pro Quo, or The Worcester Ballad Burlesk'd,* 312; *To Your Lordship after Being Ruin'd at Play, 693,* 694; *The Humble Petition of that Priest and Henry Hall . . . ,* 694
Hamilton, duke of. *See* Douglas, William
Hamilton, fourth duke of. *See* Douglas, James
Hamilton, George, earl of Orkney, 254
Hamilton, James, second earl of Cambridge, *274*
Hammond, Anthony, 350, *503, 504;* election defeat, 344; biographical note, *348*–49; *Considerations upon the Choice of Speaker,* 348; *Considerations upon Corrupt Elections,* 348–49; judgment questioned, 349
Hampden, John, 24, *629,* 630
Hanmer, Sir Thomas, 117
Hannibal, *628*
Hanover, house of, 319, 624
Harcourt, Sir Simon, 328, *332,* 337, 344, *348,* 400, *533,* 617, 645, *760;* biographical note, *336*–37; at secret caucus, 339; wild youth, *423;* and Defoe prosecution, 549, *598;* and conformity bill, 507; and Harley, *522*
Hardy, Capt. Thomas, 479
Harley, Edward, 56; quoted, 217, 324
Harley, Robert, 16, 19, 20, 23, 25, 44, 109, 174, 184, 210, 215, 218, 265, 324, 325, 329, 350, 354, 417, 427, 495, 503, *522,* 527, *532,* 615, 635, 640, 675, 708, *760;* and Defoe, xxxii, 548, 631–33; leads fight to disband army, 45–46; quoted, 49, 51, 212, 327, 638; proposes militia bill, 50; elected speaker, *332,* 355; excluded by Sunderland, *336;* aids Musgrave, 337; political prowess, *494;* Whig-Tory record, *533*–34; "great fall," 631
Harrington, Sir James, 299
Harris, Joseph, *A Poem Humbly Offer'd to the Pious Memory of His Late Sacred Majesty King William III,* 356
Harrow, 167
Hartington, marquis of, 334, 645
Harvey, William, *118,* 126, 127
Hastings, George, eighth earl of Huntingdon: quoted, 334; biographical note, *521*
Haughton, James, 75
Haversham, baron. *See* Thompson, John
Havile, Elizabeth de, 627
Havile, Sir Thomas de, 627
Hawkins, John, biographical note, 412
Hawkes, John, 702
Hawles, John, biographical note, *25*
Hayter, Thomas, 436

Hearne, Thomas: quoted, 118, 178, 179, 492, 493; on Hall, 514; on Bolton, 528; on Tenison, 537

Hebron, *230*, 234, *238*, *246*, *247*

Hedges, Sir Charles, 495; biographical note, *499*–500; as high steward, *534*–35

Heinsius, Antonie, 46, 51, 381, 382; quoted, xxvii

Helmsley Castle, 147

Henley, Anthony, 152, 701, 724

Henry III, king of England, 316

Henry III, king of France, 637

Henry V, *272*, 383

Henry VIII, 624, 652

Herbert, Arthur, earl of Torrington, *167*, *386*, *427*

Herbert, Henry, fourth lord Herbert of Cherbury, 383

Herbert, James, 311

Herbert, Philip, seventh earl of Pembroke, 255

Herbert, Thomas, eighth earl of Pembroke, *143*, 144, 220, *252*, 495, 503; as admiral, 499; biographical note, *73*

Heveningham, Henry, biographical note, *41*–42

Hickes, George, 311, 514

Higgons, Bevil, *The Mourners*, headnote, 361; text, 362–63

Hill, Richard, 385

History and Fall of the Conformity Bill, The, 617–18, 619

Hoadly, Benjamin, 550, 570; quoted, 551; biographical note, *569;* illustrated, 651

Hobart, Henry, *24;* biographical note, 25

Hobbes, Thomas, surgeon, *16*, *123*, 200

Hobbes, Thomas, 144, *The Leviathan*, 414

Hoblyn, John, biographical note, *493*

Hog, William, *Ad virum nobilissimum . . .*, 307

Holford, Sir Richard, 350

Holland, first earl of. *See* Rich, Henry

Holles, John, duke of Cavendish, 534

Hollingsby (unidentified), *589*

Holloway, Charles, biographical note, *669*

Holmes, Mary, 702

Holt, Anne, 78

Holt, Sir John, 78, *140*, 215, 217, *252*, 254, 779; biographical note, *65*

Hooper, George, biographical note, *493*–94

Hopkins, Charles, biographical note, *168; The Art of Love*, 252; *The History of Love: a Poem*, 252

Hopkins, John, 173, *511;* biographical note, *203;* (and Sternhold,) *The Whole Booke of Psalmes*, 203, 695

Hopsonn, Sir Thomas, 481, 482, 504

Horace, 74, 189, 192, 207, 249, 261, *666*

Hostun, Camille, d', duc de Tallard, 350; quoted, 53, 216, 217, 351; arrival in London, *337*

Houblon, Sir James, *278*

Houblon, Sir John, *278*

Hough, John, 510

House of Commons, 13, 17, 19, *20*, 21, 23, 44, 53, 98, 195–96, 210, 211, 215, 220, 233, 237, 255, 272, 300, *369*, 418, 439, 615, 643, 647, 661; in fourth parliament, 43–48 passim; acts to disband army, 45–47; reply to king on Dutch guards, 51–52; and economic deficiencies, 54; placemen in, 13, 184, 312; impeaches Ranelagh, 221; William complains about, 294–295; and Duncombe case, 305–06; satirized, 49–57 (*Encomium upon a Parliament*); 313–17 (*Worcester Cabal*), 321–33 (*A New Satyr on the Parliament*); hears *Memorial*, *328*, 329; impeachment charges against Whig junto, 321; and Kentish petitioners, 324, 325; Whig election pamphlet in verse, 343–44, 345–52 (*England's Late Jury*); censures Stamford, 455; censures Lloyd, 459, 501; prosecutes Mackworth, 492; conformity bills, 497, 503, 510–16, 549–50 (*first*), 616, 632, 634, 635, 637, 638 (*second*); proportion of Tories, 512; certifies Howe's election, 533; prejudices Defoe's trial, 548; and Scotch plot, 617, 619, 620, 622; ill humor against Lords, 621, 644; Tory majority lampooned, 634–47 (*The Address*); Committee on elections, 635; and Irish grants, 638–39; and Aylesbury burgesses, 674–75

House of Lords, 60, 220, 254, *369*, 613; and East India Company, 53; and original contract, 292; acquits Mohun, 385; dismisses impeachments, 454; on Lloyd, 459; and Ormonde, 468; and Cadiz expedition, 477; deprives Watson, 502; and conformity bills, 506–13, 550, 569 (*first*), 642 (*second*); and Scotch plot, 611, 616, 619, 678, lampooned, 624–30 (*The Seven Wise Men*); on Ferguson, 628; and Williamson *vs.* Regem, 661; and Aylesbury burgesses, 674

Howard, Charles, third earl of Carlisle, 527, 666; biographical note, 528; aids Vanbrugh, 704

Howard, Lady Elizabeth, 653
Howard, Henry, earl of Northampton, 653
Howard, Robert: biographical note, *166; The Committee,* 166; *Five New Plays,* 166
Howard, Thomas, first earl of Berkshire, 166
Howard, Thomas, duke of Norfolk, sues for divorce, 252–53, 254
Howard, William, third baron Howard of Escrick, *536*
Howard, William, Lord Stafford, 536
Howe, George, 76, 92, 100, *106, 110,* 127, *141;* biographical note, *95*–96
Howe, John, 95, *583*
Howe, John Grubham, *21,* 51, 331, 336, 339, 350, *532, 533,* 617, 645, 685, *779;* biographical note, 22; amendment to disbanding bill, 45–46, 49; attack on king, *326,* 328; election defeat, 344; dismissed as vice-chamberlain, *349;* on secret committee, 492; returned to court, *494;* as paymaster, *496;* and conformity bill, 506; quarrel with Strickland, 524; re-election efforts (*1701*), *533*
Howe, Philip, 110
Howe, Scrope, 22
Howland, Elizabeth, 498
Hughes, John: biographical note, *172; The Court of Neptune . . . ,* 172; *The Triumph of Peace . . . ,* 172; *The House of Nassau . . . ,* 356
Huguenots, *11*
Humble, Sir George, biographical note, *255*–56
Hume, David, quoted, 698
Hungerford, Anthony, 429
Hungerford, Sir Edward, 429
Hunt, Thomas: biographical note, *589; A Defense of the Character and Municipal Rights of the City of London,* 589
Huntingdon, eighth earl of. *See* Hastings, George
Hyde, Lady Catherine, 496
Hyde, Edward, first earl of Clarendon, 220, *338,* 630
Hyde, Laurence first earl of Rochester, 53, 212, 218, 265, 298, 306, 318, *331, 338,* 346, 354, 465, 495, 496, 526, *527, 532,* 630, *647, 669;* biographical note, *220;* at Tory caucus, 339; Irish post, *494,* 527; temper, *497;* surrenders leadership, 669; alleged Jacobite, 670
Hymenaeus Cantabrigiensis, 103, 104
Hymn to Tyburn . . . , A, 587

Infallible Astrologer, The, 204
Inner Temple, 172, 495, 589, 689
Innocent XII, 10, *116*
Ireland, 17, 18, 20, 50, 53; war of *1688–91,* 366; massacres, 377; parliament, 659
Irish transport debts, 595
Italy, and second partition treaty, 242

Jackson, Phineas, *314*
Jacob, Giles, xx, 490, 650; on Gildon, 699; on Dennis, 700
Jacobites, xxxiii, 157, 174, 184, 326, 374, 450, 465, 491, 493, 499, 500, 528, *532,* 590, 613, 616, 627, 670
James I, 86, 230, *231,* 318; and male beauty, 16
James II, 6, 7, 16, 18, 22, 51, 99, 143, 184, *198,* 201, 214, *216, 230, 231, 233,* 239, *266, 290, 298,* 337, 344, 369, 379, 382, 495, *500, 501, 503,* 616, *651,* 652, *654, 662;* on control of the press, xxvii; and Louis XIV's concession to confederates, 3–4; against lewdness, drunkeness, 130; abjures Protestantism, *218;* mistress of, 254; death, 353; bishops oppose, 458; attack on Magdalen College, Oxford, 534; and Williamson *vs.* Regem, 661
James Francis Edward (pretended prince of Wales; James III), *6,* 369, 497, *501, 503, 504,* 539, 615, 629, 645, *663, 697,* 713; and Louis XIV, 343, 353, 354, 450, *499,* 652
Jansen, Cornelius, *Augustinus,* 116
Jansenism, 116
Jebb, R. C., quoted, 108
Jeffreys, Lady Charlotte, 248, *254*
Jeffreys, George, 172
Jeffreys, John, second baron Jeffreys, 206, marriage, 255
Jekyll, Sir Joseph, biographical note, 522–23
Jennings, Sarah, 669. *See* Churchill, Sarah
Jermyn, Mary, 417
Jermyn, Thomas, second baron Jermyn of St. Edmundsbury, 417
Jersey, earl of. *See* Villiers, Edward
Jervoice, Thomas, biographical note, *523*
Jervoice, Sir Thomas, Knight, 523
Jessop, William, biographical note, *523*
Jesus College, Oxford, 492
Jews, 287, 576
Johnson, Ayfara, 166
Johnson, Francis, 118
Johnson, Samuel (*1709–1784*), quoted, xxvii, 190, 260, 399, 422, 679; on Blackmore, 132, 133, 146, 147, 187, 204, 205;

Johnson, Samuel (*cont.*)
on Roscommon, 166; on Hughes, 171; on Walsh, 314; on Hammond, 348; *London,* 449; on Pindaric ode, 586; on Devonshire, 625; on duchess of Marlborough, 669; on *The Dispensary,* 723

Johnson, Samuel (*1649–1703*), 235, biographical note, *161; Julian the Apostate,* 161

Johnstone, William, earl of Annandale, 228

Jones, David, *437*

Jones, Edward, guilty of simony, *502;* death, 542; suspended, *655–56*

Jones, Margaret, countess of Ranelagh, *117,* 248, *255,* 456, *457, 601*

Jones, Richard, first earl of Ranelagh, 45, 51, 117, *457, 461,* 487, 503, 523; biographical note, *221;* marriage, 255; resigns as paymaster, 450, *456,* 491, *492,* 496; fondness for puns, 535

Jonson, Ben, 679; as bricklayer, *704*

Jordan, Thomas, "London in Luster," 408

Joyce, James, on Defoe, xxxiii

Joyful Cuckoldom, 580

Juvenal, *108,* 309

Keally, Joseph, 705

Ken, Thomas, 501, *634;* biographical note, *502;* pension, 503

Kennedy, John, sixth earl of Cassilis, 537

Kennedy, Lady Margaret, 537

Kennett, White, xxi, 49; biographical note, *457*

Kenrick, Daniel: biographical note, *693; A New Sessions of the Poets . . . ,* 693, 679

Kenrick, Samuel, 693

Kentish petitioners, 319, *327,* 328, 329, 647; imprisoned, 322, 324, 325; become popular heroes, 334; portrayed in engraving and poem, 336-38 (*Advice to a Painter. 1701*)

Kenyon, J. P., quoted, 214, 626

Keppel, Arnold Joost van, first earl of Albemarle, 17, *221,* 244, 255, 355, 370, 635; biographical note, *18;* marriage, 367

Kéroualle, Louise de, duchess of Portsmouth, *274,* 275

Kidder, Richard, 502

Killigrew, Thomas, *Miscellanea Aurea,* quoted, xxxiv, 723

Kimberley, Jonathan, *492;* biographical note, 493

King, Edmund, biographical note, *78*

King, Gregory, 277

King, Peter: biographical note, *524; An Enquiry into the Constitution, Discipline, Unity and Worship, of the Primitive Church,* 524

King, William: biographical note, 560; *Dialogues of the Dead,* 560; *Some Remarks on the Tale of a Tub,* 560

Kings College, Cambridge, 148, 627

Kings Playhouse. *See* Theatre Royal

Kingston, countess of. *See* Pierrepoint, Mary

Kingston, dowager countess of. *See* Anne, dowager countess of Kingston

Kingston, second earl of. *See* Pierrepoint, Henry

Kingston, fourth earl of. *See* Pierrepoint, William

Kingston, fifth earl of. *See* Pierrepoint, Evelyn

Kinsley, James, xviii, quoted, 200, 203

Kirkby, Capt. Richard, 458, *459,* 641

Kirke, Diana, *41*

Kirleus, Thomas, biographical note, *89*

Kit-Cat Club, xxxiv, 117, 165, 207, 439, 520, 528, 629, *667, 700;* moves to Tonson's house, *668;* prominent members, 700

Kneller, Sir Godfrey, 117, 666, 667; Kit-Cat portraits, 668

Knight, Sir John, quoted, 224

"Knight of the North," 531

Knights of the Bath, 244, 246

Knights of the Toast, *40,* 41, 42, *667*

Knipe, Thomas, biographical note, *256*

La Chaise, François de, biographical note, *116*

Lambeth House, *510*

Lancashire plot, *629*

Lansdowne, first marquis of. *See* Petty, William

Laud, William, *515;* biographical note, *512;* impeached, 629, *657*

Lauderdale, second earl and first duke. *See* Maitland, John

Lechmere, Anthony, biographical note, *313*

Lechmere, Edmund, 313

LeClerc, Jean, 65

Lee, Anne, Lady Wharton, 622, 628

Lee, Sir Henry, 628

Lee, Nathaniel, *Lucius Junius Brutus,* 699

Lee, William, xxi, 468; quoted, 158, 263

Leech, Clifford, 708
Leeds, duke of. *See* Osborne, Thomas
Leicht, Wilhelm, 723
Leibniz, Gottfried Wilhelm, baron von, quoted, 670
Leke, Robert, third earl of Scarsdale, *64,* 65
Le Neve, Oliver, 25
Lennox, Charles, duke of Richmond, 275; biographical note, *497,* 498
Leopold I, 242, 243, 470, 609
Le Sage, Alain René, *Le Traître puni,* 705
Leslie, Charles, 152, 515, 557, 576, 592; *The Rehearsal,* 513; *New Association,* 549; *A Short and Easie Method with the Deists,* 576; *A Short and Easie Method with the Jews,* 576; on Defoe, 582; quoted, 586; and conformity bill, 632
L'Estrange, Sir Roger, 22; *Twenty Select Colloquies out of Erasmus,* 138
Lethuillier, Sir Christopher, *278,* 279
Lethuillier, Sir John, *278,* 279
Letter from the Grecian Coffee-house . . . , 16
Letter to a Member of Parliament, A, 325
Levant Company, 453
Levellers, 271
Leveson Gower, Catherine. *See* Wyndham, Lady
Levinz, William, 523
Lewis, E., 356
Licensing Act, xxvii, 248
Life Guards, 692
Lilly, William, biographical note, *453; The English Merlin Reviv'd,* 453; *Merlinus Anglicus Junior,* 453
Linacre, Thomas, *63*
Lincoln College, Oxford, 141
Lincoln's Inn, 418
Lincoln's Inn Fields theatre, 579, 665, 682, 683, 684, 689, 701, 706
Lindsay, David, 616, 624
Lindsey, first earl of. *See* Bertie, Robert
Lindsey, third earl of. *See* Bertie, Robert
Lisburne, viscount. *See* Loftus, Adam
Lisle, Mary, 274
Lister, Martin, biographical note, *114*
Littleton, Sir Thomas, 44, *54,* 354, 494, *524;* biographical note, *21–22*
Lloyd, William, bishop of Worcester, 239, 501, 510, *514,* 540; *656;* opposes Pakington, 458, *459,* 488–90; biographical note, 458; dismissed by queen, 459; *The True Character of a Churchman . . . ,* 489
Lloyd, William (non-juror), 657
Lloyd, William (son of Bishop Lloyd), 489
Locke, John, 25, 54, 65, *116,* 133, *139, 148,* 291, 524, 702; *Two Treatises of Government,* xxxi; quoted, 132, 292, 293
Lodovic, 627
Loftus, Adam, viscount Lisburne, 628
Loftus, Lucy, 628
London Gazette, The, 163, 192, 458, 548, 611, 640
London Post, The, 540
Lorraine, duchy of, 242
Louis, duc de Bourgogne, marriage, 11
Louis le Dauphin, 243
Louis III, duc de Bourbon-Condé, 9
Louis XIV, 69, 160, 216, 318, *345,* 351, 381, 387, 388, 475, 498, 500, 609, *713;* and Treaty of Ryswick, 3–4; exposes Turks to defeats, 6; flexible code of honor, 7; and Conti's loss of Polish throne, 9–10; offers bribe to Orford, 100; quoted, 240; as gambler, 253; and second partition treaty, 323, 339; and James Francis Edward, 343, 353, 354, 450, 499, 652; treaty-breaker, 539; and Dennis, 701
Louis Joseph, duc de Vendôme, 475
Lovat, Lord. *See* Fraser, Simon
Lovell, Sir Salathiel, 400, *580,* 581, *599,* 604; biographical note, *405*
Lower House of Convocation, 658
Lowther, Sir John, first viscount Lonsdale, 220
Lucas, Sir Charles, *274*
Lucas, Richard, quoted, 51
Lumley, Lt. Gen. Henry, 616
Lumley, Richard, earl of Scarbrough, and Scotch plot, 616–17, 619; biographical note, *626*–27
Lunt, John, 629
Luttrell, Narcissus, quoted, 159, 421, 508, 615
Luxembourg, duc de, 389
Lycurgus, *98*
Lygon, William, *314*

M., J., *An Ode: or Elegy on the Death of James the Second, Late King of England,* 353
Macaulay, Thomas, xxii, quoted, 13, 440, 521

Maccarty, Donogh, fourth earl of Clancarty, 17; biographical note, *625–26*

Maclean, Sir John, 616, 617

Macclesfield, countess of. *See* Gerard, Anne, countess of Macclesfield

Macclesfield, earl of. *See* Gerard, Charles; Rivers, Charles

Mackworth, Sir Humphrey, 493, 617, *635, 637;* biographical note, *492; Peace at Home . . . ,* 492; *A Vindication of the Rights of the Commons of England,* 492

Macky, John, xxii, quoted, 18, 22, 24, 38, 664

Madox, Thomas, quoted, 493

Maecenas, Cilnius, *74*

Magdalen College, Oxford, 364, 492, *534,* 570

Magdalen Hall, Oxford, 500

Magdalene College, Cambridge, 497

Maintenon, marquise de. *See* Aubigné, Françoise d'

Mainwaring, Arthur, 487, 488, 498, 618, 701; *The Brawny Bishop's Complaint,* headnote, 37–39, text, 40–42; biographical note, *528; The King of Hearts,* 528; *Tarquin and Tullia,* 528; *An Address to Our Sovereign Lady,* headnote, 615–18, text, 619–21; Kit-Cat member, 700

Maitland, John, second earl and first duke of Lauderdale, *654*

Malone, Edmund, xviii, 39, 40, 185; quoted, 41, 165

Manchester, fourth earl of. *See* Montagu, Charles

Mancini, Hortensia, duchesse de Mazarin, *275*

Mander, Roger, 591

Manley, Delariviere, 418; quoted, 418–19, 420

Manlius Capitolinus, M., 72

Manning, Francis, biographical note, *689,* 690; *The Shrine . . . ,* 356, 690; *All for the Better . . . ,* 689; *The Generous Choice,* 689; *Poems Written at Different Times . . . ,* 689; *A Congratulatory Poem . . . ,* 690; *Greenwich-Hill,* 690; *A Pastoral Essay . . . ,* 690

Manning, Thomas, 689

Maria Ana of Neuburg, 471

Maria Luisa of Savoy, 471

Mark Antony, 102

Marlborough, duchess of. *See* Churchill, Sarah

Marlborough, duke of. *See* Churchill, John

Marsh, Narcissus, 541

Marvell, Andrew, xxxi, xxxiv, 95, *571*

Martial, 249

Mary of Modena, quoted, 4; biographical note, *6*

Mary II, formerly Princess Mary of York, xxviii, 16, 38, *294, 380, 448,* 493, 513, *665. See also* William and Mary

Mason, Charles, *496*

Masson, David, 228

Massue, Henri de, marquis de Ruvigny, 50, 234, 238, 240

Matthews, John, xxvii

Maximilian Emmanuel II, 253

May Fair, described, *326*

Mazarin, duchesse de. *See* Mancini, Hortensia

Melfort, earl of. *See* Drummond, John

Merrett, Christopher, 76, 82; quoted, 58–59

Merton College, Oxford, 118, 692, 702

Methuen, John, 212, *215, 216,* 760; biographical note, *66;* and Sunderland, *216*

Methuen, Paul, 216

Methuen treaty, 611

Mews, Peter, 654

Middle Temple, 142, 148, 417, 491, 492, 493, 495, 522, 524, 635, 646, 689, 702

Middleton, Charles, second earl of Middleton, 616

Middleton, Capt. Robert, 619

Milan, duchy of, 242

Milbourne, Luke, *165, 179, 180;* biographical note, *164; Notes on Dryden's Virgil . . . ,* 164

Militia, *50, 330*

Mill, John, *138;* biographical note, 139

Millington, Martha, 545–46

Millington, Thomas, 100, *118,* 154; biographical note, *111–12*

Milo of Croton, *65, 198*

Milo Papianus, T. Annius, *99*

Milton, John, *165,* 228, *444,* 569; *Paradise Lost,* quoted, 67, 86, 110, 121, 122, 166, 381

Miscellanies over Claret, 172

Miscellany Poems, 667

Miseries of England, from the Growing Power of Her Domestick Enemies, The, 320

Moestissimae ac Laetissimae Academiae Cantabrigiensis affectus, 104

Mohun, Charles, fourth baron Mohun, 73, *278, 520–21,* 617, 659; as murderer, *384,* 385; as debauchee, *425–26;* valor, *574;* and conformity bill, 677

Molière, Jean, 705
Molinos, Miguel de, 116
Molyneux, Sir Francis, *496*
Monck, Christopher, second duke of Albemarle, 703
Monck, George, duke of Albemarle, 244
Monmouth, duke of. *See* Scott, James
Monmouth, earl of. *See* Mordaunt, Charles
Monmouth's rebellion, 105, 172, 455, 624
Monroe, *278*
Montagu, Charles, baron Halifax of Halifax, 13, 20, 21, 22, 45, 53, 54, *66*, *74*, 98, 103, *104*, *143*, 146, *166–67*, *175*, 207, 212, 215, 218, *219*, *220*, 267, 351, 490, *494*, *519*, 526, 528, *529*, 618, *664*, 683, 685; biographical note, *19*; *An Epistle to the Right Honourable Charles Earl of Dorset and Middlesex . . .*, 104; (and Prior,) *The Hind and the Panther transver'd*, 104, 166–67; literary career, *104*; on Defoe, 261; impeached, 321, *454*, 627; and Congreve, *463*; and conformity bill, 508; and Whig propaganda, 519; in Whig junto, 521; quoted, 666; Kit-Cat member, *700*
Montagu, Charles, fourth earl of Manchester, 278, *527*
Montagu, Edward, earl of Sandwich, 278
Montagu, Edward Wortley, biographical note, *251*
Montagu, John de, first baron Montagu, *383*–84
Montagu, Lady Mary Wortley, 251; quoted, 628–29
Montagu, Ralph, first earl of Montagu, 278, 703
Montgomery plot, 105
Moore, John, 510
Moore, John Robert, 394; quoted, 548, 582
Mordaunt, Charles, third earl of Peterborough and first earl of Monmouth, 38, 306, 508; biographical note, *663*–64
Mordaunt, Henry, second earl of Peterborough, 252
Mordaunt, Colonel Henry, 618; biographical note, 531
Mordaunt, John, first viscount Mordaunt of Avalon, 531
Mordaunt, Lady Mary, duchess of Norfolk, 252, 254
More, Henry, *97*
Morgan, Miss, *307*, *446*
Morice, Roger, 422
Morley, Christopher Love, 176
Morocco, 469
Morton, Charles, 107
Morton, eleventh earl of. *See* Douglas, James
Morton, Richard, 81
Mostyn, Sir Roger, 617, *779*; biographical note, *492*
Motteux, Peter, *172*, *681*; *The Island Princess* (opera), 29, 38; *The Confederates . . .* (opera), 38; translation of *Don Quixote*, 129; translation of Rabelais, 172; biographical note, *168*; death, *179*; East India merchant, 681; *Beauty in Distress*, 682; *Love's a Jest*, 683
Mountfort, William, murdered, 384, 385
Mountfort, Mrs. William, 384
Moyle, Walter, 167; biographical note, 142; (and Trenchard,) *A Second Part of the Argument Shewing that a Standing Army is Inconsistent with a Free Government*, 161
Muley Ismail the Bloodthirsty, 469
Mulgrave, third earl of. *See* Sheffield, John
Munden, Sir John, 458, *459*, 641
Munro, Robert, 278
Munro family, 278
Murray, John, first duke of Atholl, 628; and Scotch plot, 615–16
Musgrave, Christopher, son of Sir Christopher, *347*
Musgrave, Sir Christopher, 43, 49, *332*, 344, 495, *522*, 533, *535*, 617; debt to Harley, *337*; at secret caucus, 339; behavior in Commons, *347*–48; accepts bribes, *348*; on Commons committee, 492; exchequer post, *501*
Musidora, *684*

Nassau van Zuylesteyn, Willem Hendrik, 234, 238
Natives: An Answer to The Foreigners, The, 227
Neale, Thomas, 52, 117
Neustria, kingdom of, *162*
Netherlands, the, 47, *234*, 267; and second partition treaty, 242; British troops voted to aid, *321*
Neville, John, 592
Newcastle, second duke of. *See* Cavendish, Henry
New College, Oxford, 172
New Country-Party, 157, 210, 213, 343, 533, 631; founded, 43; takes initiative in Commons, 45–47; gains majority, 195
New East India Company, *219*, 323, 406

Newton, Isaac, 65
Nicolson, William, 419, 436, 459, 544
Noel, Henry, 41
Norfolk, duchess of. See Mordaunt, Lady Mary
Norfolk, duke of. *See* Howard, Thomas
Normanby, marquis of. *See* Sheffield, John
Norris, Henry, Jr., 690
Norris, Thomas, 21
Norris, William, biographical note, *20–21*
North, William, sixth Lord North, biographical note, *497*
Northampton, earl of. *See* Howard, Henry
Northey, Sir Edward, biographical note, 635
Northumberland, duke of. *See* Fitzroy, George
Northumberland, tenth earl of. *See* Percy, Algernon
Northumberland House, *653*
Norton, Richard: *Pausanias the Betrayer of His Country,* 103, *151; A Merry Ballad on the City Bard,* 152
Nostradamus, *Les Prophéties,* 530
Nottingham, second earl of. *See* Finch, Daniel
Novak, Maximillian E., 575

Oates, Titus, 7; biographical note, *590*
October Club, 311, 315
Ode, on the Death of the Late King James. . . . , An, 353
Ode on the Death of King William III, 355
O'Faolain, Sean, 260
Ogg, David, xxiii, quoted, 46, 54
Ogilby, John, 165; biographical note, *107*
Ogle, earl of. *See* Cavendish, Henry
O'Hara, Sir Charles, baron Tyrawley, acquittal of, *459,* 477–78
Oldmixon, John, xxiii, 49, 490, *699, 700;* quoted, 5, 487–88; *Poems on Several Occasions,* 163; *A Funeral Idyll, Sacred to the Memory of K. William III,* 356; *The Life and Posthumous Work of Arthur Maynwaring,* quoted, 618; *Amores Britannici . . . ,* 699
On Dr. Birch, headnote, 540–42; text, 543–46
Onely, Nicholas, biographical note, *110–11*
On the King of Spain's Voyage to Portugall, headnote, 609–10; text, 611–12
On King William the III, 357
On the 8th of March 1703/4, headnote, 613, text, 614
On the Much Lamented Death of the Most Serene and Illustrious Prince, James VII and II . . . , 353
On My Lord Somers, headnote, 195–97; text, 198
On Sir William Williams Sollicitor Generall, 99
Onslow, Arthur, quoted, 218
On Some Votes against the Lord S., 197
Orford, earl of. *See* Russell, Edward
Oriel College, Oxford, 495, 514, 669
Orkney, countess of. *See* Villiers, Elizabeth
Orkney, earl of. *See* Hamilton, George
Ormonde, second duke of. *See* Butler, James
Orrery, fourth earl of. *See* Boyle, Charles
Osborne, Peregrine, 525
Osborne, Sir Thomas, first earl of Danby, duke of Leeds, 65, 215, 218, 306, 311; biographical notes, *220–21, 526*
Osler, William, 76
Otway, Thomas, 164, 178
Overkerke, count. *See* Nassau, Willem Hendrik
Owen, James, 566
Oxford, eleventh earl of. *See* Vere, Richard de
Oxford, twentieth earl of. *See* Vere, Aubrey de
Oxford University, 49, *175,* 337, 425, *491,* 569, 646, *686;* Christ Church College, 74, 110, 126, 138, 147, 173, 256, 424, 436, 457, 491, 493, 503, 504, 528, 531, 541, 663, 685, 693; University College, 139, 141, 650; Lincoln College, 141; Exeter College, 142; New College, 172, 502; Balliol College, 173; Brasenose College, 173, 685; All Souls College, 111, 178, 179; Wadham College, 98, 178, 310; St. Edmund Hall, 202–03, 457; Trinity College, 253, 689; Magdalen College, 364, 492, 534, 570; Jesus College, 492; Pembroke College, 493, 514; Oriel College, 495, 514, 669; Magdalen Hall, 92, 500; Corpus Christi College, 514; Queen's College, 635; Merton College, 118, 692, 702
Ozell, John, quoted, 705

Pack, Richardson, *Miscellanies,* quoted, 723
"Packington's Pound" (tune), 39
Pacquet from Parnassus, A, 339
Packington, Sir John (*1671–1727*), *314, 317,* 458, *459, 574,* 615, *619, 656;* convenes Tory cabal, 310–12; dispute with Lloyd, 488–90; and conformity bill,

497, 632, 655; *A Speech for the Bill against Occasional Conformity,* 619
Pakington, Sir John, "the lusty," 310
Palmes, William, biographical note, 22
Papillon, Thomas, *278,* 279
Paradox in Praise of War, A: headnote, 339–40; text, 341–42
Park, Daniel, 664; quoted, 535
Parker, Hugh, 311
Parliament: passes anti-vice act, 130–31; revokes Irish estate grants, *238;* explains laws, 325; Oxford, 664; Long, 687; third of William III, 44; fourth of William III, 43–48, 49–57, 195, 345; fifth of William III, 48, 332, 343, 345, 455; sixth of William III, 354–55, 380–81. *See also* House of Commons; House of Lords
Parsons, Robert, 427
Partition treaties (*1698, 1700*), 195, *242,* 243, 318, *322–23,* 381, 382, *539,* 609, *639,* 640
Partridge, John, *7; Merlinus Liberatus,* 449, *451,* 453
Patch, 98
Paterson, William, 582, 631
Patrick, Simon, bishop of Ely, *427,* 510, 540
"Patriot," *49*
Paul, William, *427*
Paulet, Charles, sixth marquis of Winchester, first duke of Bolton, 23, 303, *306,* 334
Paulet, Charles, second duke of Bolton: quoted, 211; biographical note, *527–28*
Paulet, Lord William, 21, 152, *523;* biographical note, *23–24;* duel with Hammond, 349; "drunken bout" with Strickland, 524
Pedro II, 611
Pelling, Edward, biographical note, *436–37*
Pembroke (ship), 479
Pembroke, seventh earl of. *See* Herbert, Philip
Pembroke, eighth earl of. *See* Herbert, Thomas
Pembroke College, Cambridge, 164
Pembroke College, Oxford, 493, 514
Penãlosa, Diego Dionisio de, *413*
Pepys, Samuel, 279, 364, 540; quoted, 150; on Torrington, 386
Percy, Algernon, tenth earl of Northumberland, *653*
Percy, Elizabeth, biographical note, 624–25
Peregrine (royal yacht), 610
Perks, John, 329
Perrot, Thomas, biographical note, *313*
Perrott (apothecary), 81
Peterborough, second earl of. *See* Mordaunt, Henry
Peterborough, third earl of. *See* Mordaunt, Charles
Peterhouse, Cambridge, 60, 589
Petition of Tom Brown . . . , 5
Petty, William, first marquis of Lansdowne, quoted, 521
Phalaris, 108, 138, 457
Philippe, duc d'Anjou. *See* Felipe V
Philipps, Sir John, introduces morality bill, 56, 121–22
Phillips, John, 91
Phillips, Thomas, 680
Phocion, *98*
Physicians, dispute with apothecaries, satirized in *The Dispensary,* 58–62, 63–128. *See also* Royal College of Physicians
Pierrepoint, Evelyn, fifth earl of Kingston, 41
Pierrepoint, Lady Grace, 77
Pierrepoint, Henry, first marquis of Dorchester, second earl of Kingston, 77
Pierrepoint, Lady Mary (Mrs. Wortley Montagu), 251; quoted, 628–29
Pierrepoint, Mary, countess of Kingston, 41
Pierrepoint, William, fourth earl of Kingston, 383
Pierce, Michael, 89
Pindaric stanza, defined, 586–87
Pitcairne, Archibald, biographical note, *174*
Pittis, Thomas, 172
Pittis, William, 208, 309, 463, 649, 650, 680, *697; The Patriots. . . . ,* 48, 352, *697;* biographical note, *172; An Epistolary Poem to John Dryden, Esq.,* 172; *An Epistolary Poem to N. Tate, Esquire,* 172; *Tom Brown Arrested by the Devil,* 172; quoted, 259, 260, 261, 301, 518; *The True-Born Englishman: A Satyr, Answer'd,* 264; *The True Born Hugonot . . . ,* 264, quoted, 586; on Sunderland, 290; *The Generous Muse . . . ,* 353, 354, 697; on Bromley, *523; Heraclitus Ridens,* 580, 696, 697
Pitts, Samuel, *316;* biographical note, *315*
Pizarro, Francisco, *413*
Pix, Mary, 168
Plummer (unidentified woman), *538, 787*
Poems on Affairs of State (original series), 353, 357, 361, 365

Poet's Address to the Honourable Sir Charles Duncomb . . . , The, 307
Pointi, Jean Bernard Louis Desjean, baron de, *592*
Polignac, Abbé Melchior de, 9
Poland, Conti's loss of throne of, 9–10
Pope, Alexander, xxxiv, 31, 72, 76, 78, 88, 136, 261, 348, 361, 364, 490, 650, 725, 726; quoted, xxx, 63, 70, 95, 99, 103, 113, 119, 121, 553, 618; *An Essay on Criticism,* 70, 688; *The Dunciad,* 149, 158, 189, 666, 684; on Milbourne, 164; *An Epistle . . . to Dr. Arbuthnot,* 262; *The Rape of the Lock,* 252, 437; and Walsh, 124, 310, 312; on George I, 327; *Imitation of Horace,* 449; *Epistle to a Lady,* 601; *An Essay on Man,* 652; on Farquhar, 691; and Donne's satires, 699; on *The Dispensary,* 723
Popish Plot, 590
Portland, first earl of. *See* Bentinck, Hans Willem
Portland, Lady. *See* Bentinck, Anne
Portocarrero, Cardinal Luis Manuel Fernandez de, court influence, *470–71*
Portsmouth, duchess of. *See* Kéroualle, Louise de
Portugal, 611
Post Boy, The, 61, 70, 133, 228–29, 344
Post Man, The, 133
Postscript to the Golden Age, A, 450
Poussin, Jean Baptiste, 349; quoted, 321, 520, 522
Poussineers, 504, 534
Powell, George: biographical note, *579,* 580; *Alphonso King of Naples,* 580; *Bonduca . . . ,* 580; *Brutus of Alba . . . ,* 580; *Imposture Defeated . . . ,* 580
Powell, Sir John, 217, 421
Powys, Sir Littleton, biographical note, *141*
Powys, Richard, quoted, 667
Powys, Sir Thomas, *331,* 345; biographical note, *352;* on secret committee, 492; court posts, *493;* defends Watson, 502; and conformity bill, 507
Prendergast, Sir Thomas, biographical note, *708*
Priaulx, Peter, biographical note, 650
Prideaux, Humphrey, 544
Prior, Arthur, 424
Prior, Matthew, xxiv, 3, 74, *148,* 167, *179,* 197, 214, 328, 345, *529,* 667; biographical notes, *103, 424;* (and Montagu), *The Hind and the Panther transvers'd,* 103, 166–67; election defeat, 344; political career, *351;* quoted 425; *An English Ballad,* 473; and *Faction Display'd,* 649–50
Propertius, 74
Prophecy, A, headnote, 530–31; text, 532–39
Prophecy found on the 29th of January 1696 . . . , A, 531
Protogenes, 94
Prussia, 319, 354
Prynne, William, *589*
Purcell, Daniel, 580
Purcell, Henry, 6, 152, 580, 688, 693
Pye, Robert, biographical note, *589*
Pym, John, biographical note, *629–30*

Queenborough (man-of-war), 641
Queensberry, second duke of. *See* Douglas, James
Queensberry plot, 615. *See* Scotch plot
Queens' College, Cambridge, 168, 589, 687
Queen's College, Oxford, 635
Queen's Theater, 666
Quietism, *116*

Rabelais, François, 168, 172
Radcliffe, Alexander, *179;* biographical note, *165; Captaine Ratcliffs Debauch,* 165; *A Satyre upon Love and Women,* 165
Radcliffe, Dr. John, 61, 110, 154, *252;* biographical note, *141*
Radziejowski, Cardinal Michal, 9–10
Raleigh, Sir Walter, 581
Ranelagh, countess of. *See* Jones, Margaret
Ranelagh, first earl of. *See* Jones, Richard
Rapin, René, *Reflections sur la poëtique,* 144
Reede de Ginkel, Godard van, 234, 241
Remarks on the Author of the Hymn to the Pillory . . . , 587
Renaud, Bernard, 481
Reresby, Sir John, 523
Retrievement, The, 335
Rhodes, Jeremy, *316*
Rich, Christopher, biographical note, 29, *31*
Rich, Edward, sixth earl of Warwick, *254,* 384, *385*
Rich, Henry, first earl of Holland, 385
Rich, Robert, second earl of Warwick, 385
Rich, Sir Robert, 25; biographical note, *24*

Richard, earl of Cornwall, 316
Richard III, *169*
Richmond, duke of. *See* Lennox, Charles
Ridley, Humphrey, biographical note, *113*–14
Rivers, fourth earl. *See* Savage, Richard
Rivers, Charles, earl of Macclesfield, 521
Robinson, John, *427*
Roche, Joan, 439–40
Rochester, earl of. *See* Hyde, Laurence; Wilmot, John
Rogers, Capt., 675
Roman Catholics, *241*, 498, 534; and Quietism, 116; penal laws against, 349
Romney, earl of. *See* Sidney, Henry
Rooke, Sir George, 300, 469, *472*, 478, 479, 487, *494*, *499*, 500, *536*, 610, *646*, *779*, and Vigo victory, 480, 481, 483; cautious nature, *504;* biographical note, *527;* return to Spithead, *641*–42
Roper, Abel, 4
Roscommon, fourth earl of. *See* Dillon, Wentworth
Rose Tavern, *31*, 172, 173, 697
Rouse, Sir Thomas, of Rouse Lench, first baronet, 317
Rouse, Sir Thomas, of Rouse Lench, fourth baronet, 311, *314*, *315*, *317*
Rousselet, François de, marquis de Chateaurenault, 475, 481, 482
Rowe, Anthony: biographical note, *98*–99; bribes electors, *536*–37
Rowe, Nicholas, 136, *463*, 487, *709*, *710; The Ambitious Step-Mother,* 462, 709–10; biographical note, 462; *Tamerlane,* 462, *665*, 709; *The Fair Penitent, 665*
Royal Catherine (ship), 610
Royal College of Physicians, 58, 59, 60, 61, *63*, 66, 76, *80*, 86, 90, 107, 111–12, 115, 118, 126, 153, 175, 207, 414; legal title, 83; delegates, 119; new charter (*1663*), *127*
Royal Exchange, 587
Royal Sovereign (ship), 504
Royston Club, *427*
Ruvigny, marquis de. *See* Massue, Henri de
Russell, Edward, earl of Orford, *100*, *167*, *221*, 351, 460, *520*, 634, 664, *666;* biographical note, *221;* against partition treaties, 323; impeached, 321, 337, 454, 460, *461*, 627; drunkenness, 428; failures, 478–79; in Whig junto, 218, 521
Russell, Lord Edward, 533, *538*
Russell, Lord William, 65, 161, 221, 239, 498, 538; hanged, 536
Russell, William, the undertaker, *88*, 206, 207
Russell, William, first duke of Bedford, 538
Russell, Wriothesley, *497*, *538*, biographical note, 498
Rye House plot, 105, 455, 626
Rymer, Thomas, 143; *Edgar, or the English Monarch,* 144; *A General Draught and Prospect of Government in Europe,* 144; *The Tragedies of the Last Age,* 144; *A Short View of Tragedy,* 144–45; biographical note, *145*–46; *Foedera,* 145
Ryswick, treaty of, xxviii, 3, 4, 6, *8*, 12, *69*, 73, 160, 467, *473*, 539

Sacheverell, Henry, 418, 576, *591*, 592, *637; The Character of a Low-Churchman,* 459, 489; biographical note, *570; The Political Union . . . ,* 570, 591
Sackville, Charles, sixth earl of Dorset, 19, *74*, *102*, *143*, 146, 152, *153*, *166*, *175*, *278*, *332*, *351*, 424, *425*, *700; Petition of Tom Brown . . . ,* 5; *On Mr. Edward Howard . . . ,* 152; sells office, 166; marriage, *439*–40
Saffold, Thomas, *107*
St. Albans, duke of. *See* Beauclerk, Charles
St. Augustine's, 148
St. Botolph's Bishopsgate, 172
St. Edmund Hall, Oxford, 100, 202–03, 457
St. Évremond, Charles Marguetel de St. Denis de, biographical note, *144*
St. George of Cappodocia, *17*
St. James, Piccadilly, congregation described, 37–38
St. James's Palace, 139
St. John, Henry, viscount Bolingbroke, 487, 491, 492, *503*, 520; on Garth, xxxiv; on Harley, 336, 494; *Almahide,* 503; biographical note, 503; and conformity bill, 506, 507; chairman of Commons committee, 617, 619
St. John's College, Cambridge, 103, 222, 426, 492
St. Leonard's, Shoreditch, 164
St. Martin's, Worcester, 316
St. Paul's school, 635
Saintsbury, George, quoted, 589
St. Simon, quoted, 74
Salisbury, third earl of. *See* Cecil, James
Salisbury, fourth earl of. *See* Cecil, James
Sallust, *Bellum Catilinae,* 648, 649

Salmon, Thomas, quoted, 592

Salmon, William, 83, quoted, 80; biographical note, *81–82*; *Rebuke to the Authors of A Blew Book . . .*, 80, 82

Salter's Hall, 569

Sambrook, Jeremy, 419

Sammen, 675

Sam's coffeehouse, 3, *6*

Sancroft, William, biographical note, *657*

Sandwich, earl of. *See* Montagu, Edward

Sandys, Capt. Samuel, *314*, 315

Satyr, On a True Born Dutch-Skipper, A, 264

Satyr upon a Late Pamphlet, Entituled, A Satyr against Wit, 133

Satyr against Satyrs, A, 248

Saunders, Charles, *170*; *Tamerlane the Great*, 170

Savage, Richard, 52, 683

Savage, Richard, fourth earl Rivers, 254, 384

Savage of Dormston, *314*

Saville, Sir George, first marquis of Halifax, 294

Saville, William, second marquis of Halifax, 278

Savoy, duke of. *See* Victor Amadeo II

Scarbrough, earl of. *See* Lumley, Richard

Scarron, Paul, *Typhon*, quoted, 91

Scarsdale, third earl of. *See* Leke, Robert

Schomberg, first duke of. *See* Schönberg, Friedrich Herman von

Schomberg, second duke of. *See* Schomberg, Charles

Schomberg, third duke of. *See* Schomberg, Meinhardt

Schomberg, Charles, second duke of Schomberg, *385*

Schomberg, Meinhardt, third duke of Schomberg, 240

Schönberg, Friedrich Herman von, first duke of Schomberg, 234, 238, 275, 299, *428*

Scobell, Francis, 487; biographical note, *491*

Scotch Guards, 619

Scotch plot, 611, *659*, *678*, 684; action against, 615–17; Lords' committee on, 619, lampooned, *624*–30 (*The Seven Wise Men*)

Scott, James, duke of Monmouth and Buccleuch, 274, 298, 347, 626, *671*

Scott, Mary, 537

Scott, Sir Walter, quoted, 164

Seaton, *557*, *558*

Second Advice to a Painter, quoted, 15

Second Tunbridge Lampoon, The, quoted, 96

Sedley, Catherine, countess of Dorchester, 41, 254

Sedley, Sir Charles, 78, 130, 183, 254, *423*, 439; *Upon the Author of the Satyr against Wit*, xxix, headnote, 181–86, text, 187–88; excrementizes, 188

Selden, John, *590*

Settle, Elkanah, 183; biographical note, *253–54*; *The Character of a Popish Successour . . .*, 253; *The Grove . . .*, described in, 253; *An Heroick Poem on the Coronation of the High and Mighty Monarch, James II . . .*, 253; *The Triumphs of London*, 253; *Notes and Observations on the Empress of Morocco Revised*, quoted, 575; poem attributed to, 679

Seven Wise Men, 13, headnote, 622–23; text, 624–30

Sewell, 355

Seymour, Anne, 624

Seymour, Charles, sixth duke of Somerset, *436*, 495, *497*, 499, *519*, 610, 619, *653*; as cuckold, 622; speech impediment, 622, 624; biographical note, *624–25*; and Scotch plot, 684; Kit-Cat member, 700

Seymour, Sir Edward, 22, 43, 224, *233*, *241*, *247*, *332*, 337, *338*, 344, 350, *423*, 459, 504, 520, *522*, *532*, 533, *534*, 617, *760*, *779*; biographical note, *21*; alleged bribe by, *325*; career summarized, *235*; at secret caucus, 339; accused of French sympathies, *345–46*; supports Monmouth, *347*; supports James II, *348*; moves to reopen impeachments, 454; described, *494*; on Somers, 661

Seymour, William, second duke of Somerset, 24

Shadwell, Thomas, 74, 148, 254, 262, 679, 691, 710

Shaftesbury, earl of. *See* Anthony Ashley Cooper, third earl of Shaftesbury

Shakespeare, William, 146; *Romeo and Juliet*, quoted, 77; *King Lear* (Tate's version), 148; *Henry V*, quoted, 272; *Richard II*, 265, (Tate's version) 695

Sharp, John, archbishop of York, 540, 563; biographical note, *569*

Sheffield, John, third earl of Mulgrave, marquis of Normanby, later duke of Buckingham, 65, *143*, 144, *146*, *166*, 167, 183, 439, 604, 693; biographical note, *102–03*; (and Dryden), *An Essay*

on Satire, 167, 521; *The Character of a Tory . . . ,* 167; *An Essay on Poetry,* 167; as gambler, 253; court posts, *526–27*
Sheldon, Francis, *314*
Sheldon, Gilbert, 465
Shepherd, Francis, 323
Shepherd, Samuel, 53; committed to Tower, 323
Sherlock, William, *105, 457,* 495, *599;* quoted, 272
Shippen, William: *Faction Display'd,* xxx, xxxi, 13, 40, 213, headnote, 648–50, text, 651–73; importance, xxxiii–xxxiv; *Moderation Display'd,* xxxiii, possible early works, 13; *A Conference,* 213; *An Epistle to N. Rowe,* 665
Shooter's Hill, *150*
Shorter, Sir John, 566
Shower, Sir Bartholomew, *331, 349, 350;* biographical note, *337;* and Watson, 502
Shrewsbury, twelfth earl and first duke of. *See* Talbot, Charles
Sidney, Algernon, 239, *348;* beheaded, xxvii, *337,* 536
Sidney, Henry, earl of Romney, 65, 138; biographical note, *220*
Sidney Sussex College, Cambridge, 144
Signetur statute, 90, *115,* 150
Simpson, Sidrach, *582*
Sims, Richard, *669*
Sloan, James, 13, *65, 141, 252;* biographical note, *21*
Smalridge, George, 528; et al., *Dr. Bentley's Dissertations . . . Examin'd,* 108; quoted, 437, 492
Smalwood, James, *142;* biographical note, *138; Mr. Smalwoods Verses to the Ladies When he was Praevaricator,* 138; *To Sir R— Bl— upon his Unhappy Talent at Praising and Railing,* 138
Smectymnuus, 569
Smith, John, 645; biographical note, *22–23*
Smith, Matthew, 664
Smith, Thomas, *To the Indefatigable Rhimer,* 364; *Upon Sorrel,* headnote, 364–65, text, 366; on Queen Anne and clergy, 540
Snyder, Henry L., 261, 650, 669
Sobieski, Jan, 9
Society of the Art and Mystery of Apothecaries, 58, 59, 60, 76, 79, 83, 86, 93, 107, 125; dispute with physicians, satirized in *The Dispensary,* 58–62, 63–128
Society for the Reformation of Manners, 130, 446
Soldier and a Sailor, A (tune), 105
Solms, Count, 15
Some Critical and Politick Remarks on a Late Virulent Lampoon, Call'd Faction Display'd, 649
Somers, John, baron Somers of Evesham, *16, 73, 127, 140, 143, 146, 151,* 168, 184, 195, 222, 267, 310, 325, 351, 354, 494, 528, *536,* 619, *629,* 642, *660, 662;* quoted, 43, 45; biographical note, *65;* dismissal from office, 195–97, 265, account of, 210–23 (*A Conference . . .*); attacked in epigram, 198 (*On My Lord Somers*); origins, 198; alleged adulterer and embezzler, 222, 661; impeached, 321, 454, *455,* 520, 627; and partition treaties, 323, 661; *Jus Regium . . . ,* quoted, 329; and conformity bill, *496,* 508; and Whig propaganda, 519; in Whig junto, 454, 520, 521; pox, *16, 520,* 622, *629,* 660
Somerset, second duke of. *See* Seymour, William
Somerset, sixth duke of. *See* Seymour, Charles
Sophia, dowager electress of Hanover, 318, *659*
Sorrel, 355, 363, 364–66, *396*
South, Dr., prebendary of Westminster, *105, 457, 544, 545*
Southampton, duke of. *See* Fitzroy, Charles
Southerne, Thomas, 701; biographical note, *145; Oroonoko,* 145, 688, 708; *The Wives Excuse,* 688; as officeholder, 707
South Sea Company, 646
Spademan, John, 583
Spain, *42,* 46, *68, 268,* 339, *463, 510;* and second partition treaty, 242; claimants to throne, *243,* 323; and Cadiz expedition, 467–68, 469–84 (*The Spanish Descent*); and battle at Vigo, 481–84
Speck, W. A., 506
Spectator, The, 169
Spence, Joseph, xxv, 42, 145
Spencer, Charles, third earl of Sunderland, 13, 117, 216, 619, *625,* biographical note, *23;* in Whig junto, *521;* betrays Clancarty, 625–26; library, 626
Spencer, Robert, second earl of Sunderland, 13, *23,* 45, 210, 216, 325, 337, 532,

Spencer, Robert **(cont.)** 625, *662;* biographical note, *18;* quoted, 44, 65, 73; resigns as lord chamberlain, 44–45; buys Dorset's office, 166; and Somer's dismissal, 211, 212, 214–223 (*A Conference*); role in Revolution, *290;* plan for new ministry, 336; and Tenison, 655
Spingarn, J. E., xxv, quoted, 130, 150
Spinoza, Benedict de, 144, *698*
Sprat, Thomas, bishop of Rochester, 207, 502, 540, *545;* oratory, *544*
Squash, Dick, 440, *543, 544*
"Stacy, Mr.," *An Answer to the Satyr upon the French King,* 4
Stafford, Lord. *See* Howard, William
Stamford, second earl of. *See* Grey, Thomas
Stanhope, James, 136, 517; biographical note, *525*
Stanhope, Philip, first earl of Chesterfield, 525
Stanhope, Philip Dormer, fourth earl of Chesterfield, 349
Stanley, Col. James, 187
State of Physick in London . . . , The, 88
Stawell, John, Lord, 117
Stawell, baroness. *See* Jones, Margaret
Steele, Richard, 183, 669, *691–92,* 702; *The Christian Hero,* 21; quoted, 169, 681; *The Funeral,* 369–70, *691,* 692; *The Lover,* 684; amatory career, 692; military career, 692; manager for Lord Cutts, 693
Steenkerke, battle of, *15*
Stennett, Joseph, *A Poem to the Memory of His Late Majesty William the Third,* 356
Stephens, Edward, biographical note, *237*
Stepney, George: biographical note, *103;* quoted, 214, 361, 424, 517; on Halifax, 529
Step to Oxford . . . , 179
Sternhold, Thomas, 173; et al., *The Whole Booke of Psalmes,* 203, 695
Steward, Elizabeth, 38, 200
Stillingfleet, Edward, *140;* biographical note, *116*
Stote, Bertram, 650
Stout, Mary, 421
Stout, Sarah, death of, 418, *420,* 421
Stowe, John, quoted, 544
Strafford, first earl of. *See* Wentworth, Thomas
Strickland, Sir William, *22, 524*
Stringer, Thomas, biographical note, *524–25*
Stringer, Sir Thomas, Knight, 524
Stuarts, second Restoration of, 449
Stubbes, Henry, 76
Styles, George Haskin, 636
Suckling, Sir John: *A Session of the Poets,* 679; *The Goblins,* 689
Sunderland, second earl of. *See* Spencer, Robert
Sunderland, third earl of. *See* Spencer, Charles
Sutherland, James, 47; quoted, 585
Swan, Owen, 182
Swan, R., *255*
Sweetapple, Sir John, *407*
Swift, Jonathan, 108, 135, 220, 226, 253, 255, 312, 320, 451, 497, 560, 657, 660; *A Tale of a Tub,* xxviii n.; on Defoe, xxix, 675; *Advice to a Painter* wrongly attributed to, 13–14; quoted, 18, 23, 157, 173, 419; on D'Urfey, 143; on Hughes, 171; on Tenison, 222; *A Satirical Elegy on the Death of the Late Famous General,* 357; *Gulliver's Travels,* 398, 399; *A Discourse of the Contests and Dissentions,* 226, 492; on Harley, 522; on Bolton, 528; *The Windsor Prophecy,* quoted, 531; on Somerset, 624; on Wharton, 628; on Lauderdale, 654; on Peterborough, 664; *A Description of the Morning,* 678; on Prendergast, 708
Swift, Samuel, 311; biographical note, *313*
Sydenham, Thomas, 129, 132
Sydney, viscount, 348
Sypher, Wylie, 413

Taafe, John, 629
Talbot, Charles, twelfth earl and first duke of Shrewsbury, 44, 74, *146,* 184, 185, 198, *220,* 514, 611, 664; biographical note, *143;* and Somers' dismissal, 211, 212; resigns as chamberlain, 265–66
Talbot, Gilbert, fifth Lord Talbot, *383*
Talbot, William, 510; biographical note, *514*
Tallard, duc de. *See* Hostun, Camille d'
Tankerville, earl of. *See* Grey, Forde
Tanner, Thomas, 76
Tate, Nahum, *173,* 178, *179, 463,* 487, *694–95,* 710; biographical note, *148;* version of *King Lear,* 148; (and Dryden), *The Second Part of Absalom and*

Achitophel, 148; (and Brady), *A New Version of the Psalms of David,* 173, *695;* reappointed laureate, 462; version of *Richard II,* 695
Taverner, William, 168
Telephos, 33
Tempest, Mrs., 124
Temple, Jane Martha, biographical note, *117*–18
Temple, Sir William: *Essay on Ancient and Modern Learning,* 108
Tenison, Thomas, archbishop of Canterbury, *73,* 510, *537,* 540, 541, *545, 654, 657;* Tory view of, *16;* size, *222,* 522, *655;* suspends Jones, 655–56
Test Act, 506, *511,* 568
Theatre Royal (Drury Lane), 29, 30, 31, *91,* 200, 579, 684, 689, 690, 699, 702
Thersites, 77
Thomas, Dalby, 52, 323
Thomas, Elizabeth, account of Dryden's funeral, 206, 207
Thompson, John, baron Haversham of Haversham, *527;* biographical note, 528
Thynne, Thomas, 625
Thynne, Thomas, viscount Weymouth, 502; biographical note, *503;* court post, *526*
Timon in Town, to Strephon in the Country, 439
Tiringham, Sir William, 301, 303
Toland, John, 293, 309, *325,* 403, *416,* 651, *659; The Danger of Mercenary Parliaments,* 43; on standing army, 45, 267; *Limitations for the Next Foreign Successor,* 325, 327; letter to Clayton, *409;* behavior, *425; Anglia Libera . . . ,* 659
Tollemache, Thomas, biographical note, *300, 592*
Tompkins, Thomas, 511
Tonson, Jacob, *149, 169,* 185, *539, 667;* and Whig propaganda, *519*–20
To the Poetical Knight, who would have no Body spoil Paper but Himself, 186
To the Quibling, Dribling, Scribling Poetaster . . . , 9
Torbay (ship), 481, 482
Torcy, marquis de, quoted, 23
Tories, xxxv, 12, 19, 22, 24, 49, 53, 54, 109, 121, 139, 143, 174, 184, 188, 195, 210, 211, *217, 218,* 255, 266, 323, 348, 351, 355, 424, 426, 438, 457, 492, *494,* 496, 497, 499, 505, 533, 559, 624; shift to ministry of, xxviii; and Fenwick assassination, 15–16; and grants of Irish estates, 17, 638–39; and New Country-Party, 43, 185; xenophobia, 224; electioneering, 310–12; October Club, 311, 315; satirized, 313–17 (*Worcester Cabal*); control of Commons, 318–20, 321–33 (*A New Satyr on the Parliament*); *vs.* Whigs on delegation of power, 330; as party of peace, 339; against dissolution of fifth parliament, 343; and reformation of manners, 399; beneficiaries of Queen Anne, 449; impeach Whig junto, 454; poetasters, 487; proportion in Commons, 512; and occasional conformity, 550; against dissenters, 576; majority in Commons satirized, 615, 619–21 (*An Address to Our Sovereign Lady*), 634–47 (*The Address*)
Torrington, earl of. *See* Herbert, Arthur
To the Tune of Lilly Bolero (song), 66, 216
Tourville, 300
Townshend, Charles, second viscount Townshend, 619; biographical note, *62*
Townshend, Horatio, first viscount Townshend, biographical note, *627*
Traherne, Thomas, biographical note, *173; A Serious and Pathetical Contemplation of the Mercies of God,* 173
Treby, Sir George, 215, 217, 421; biographical note, *140*
Tredenham, John, 487; biographical note, *504*
Tredenham, Sir Joseph, 491, 504
Trelawny, Maj. Gen. Charles, 187
Trelawny, Sir Jonathan, 436, 457, 501; biographical note, *239*
Trenchard, John, 160, 626; (and Moyle,) *A Second Part of the Argument Shewing that a Standing Army is Inconsistent with a Free Government,* 161
Trevelyan, George Macaulay, xxv, 471; quoted, 507, 521, 635–36
Trevor, Sir John, 215, 421
Trevor, Sir Thomas, 212, 217, 226, 635; and Williamson *vs.* Regem, 661
Trinity College, Cambridge, 103, 104, 111, 166, 251, 414, 436, 514
Trinity College, Dublin, 145, 148, 168
Trinity College, Oxford, 253, 689
Trinity Hall, Cambridge, 167
Trott, Perient, 408
"True-Born Englishman, The" (anonymous author), 264. *See also* Defoe, Daniel, *The True-Born Englishman*
True-Born Welshman, The, 264

True Character of a Churchman, The, 463
Trumbull, William, 74
Tryal of Skill . . . . ., The, xxviii; headnote, 679–80; text, 681–711
Tryon, Thomas, *Friendly Advice to the Gentlemen-Planters of the East and West Indies,* quoted, 413
Tudor, Capt. Abraham, 641
Turenne, Marshall, 238
Tunbridge Lampoon, 98
Turner, Francis, 184
Tutchin, John, 228, 235, *237, 241, 245,* 249, 259, *286–87,* 365, 762; *An Heroick Poem upon the Late Expedition of His Majesty . . . ,* 172, 287; *A New Martyrology . . . ,* 172; *Poems on Several Occasions,* 172; biographical note, *172; A Description of Mr. Dryden's Funeral . . . ,* 208; *The Foreigners,* 208, 250, 259, headnote, 224–27, text, 230; *The Mouse Grown a Rat,* 225; career summarized, 225–26; on Whig junto, 232; *The Apostates . . . ,* 264; as Whig, *286; Search after Honesty, 286; The British Muse . . . ,* 354; on Cadiz expedition, 470, 474, 477; on Ryswick treaty, 473; prosecuted, for libel, 635; on House of Lords, 636
Twitty, Thomas: in Tory cabal, 311; "libel" reply to Walsh, 312, 316, 317; biographical note, *313;* witness for Pakington, 489
Tyrawley, baron. *See* O'Hara, Sir Charles
Tyson, Edward, 61, *108, 140,* 154, 172; biographical note, *96*
Tyson, Francis, biographical note, *421*

Unitarians, 498
University College, Oxford, 139, 141, 650
University of Edinburgh, 152
Upon the Author of the Latin Epigram, 364
Urwin, Will, *149*
Utrecht, treaty of, xxxii, 631

Vanbrugh, John, 136, *147,* 164, 183, 200, *665, 704; The Provok'd Wife,* 131, 147, 665, 704; *The Relapse . . . ,* 147, 579, 704; success of plays, *147;* on Powell, 579; *The False Friend,* 666; *The Pilgrim,* 666; *Aesop,* 704; *A Short Vindication of the Relapse and the Provok'd Wife,* 704; translations, 705; et al, *Squire Trelooby* (trans. from Molière), 705, 706; arrested, 705
Van der Gucht, Michael, 724
Vauban, Sébastien le Prestre de, 300, 389
Vaughan, Charles, quoted, 685
Vere, Aubrey de, twentieth earl of Oxford, 41, *278;* mistresses, *440*
Vere, Richard de, eleventh earl of Oxford, *383*
Vernon, James, xxvi, *143,* 144, *222,* 325, 611, 626, 661; quoted, 22, 43, 47, 57, 98, 195–96, 214, 216, 218, 343; biographical note, *74–75*
Vernon, Thomas, 217
Vernon, William, 316; biographical note, *315*
Víctor Amadeo II, duke of Savoy, biographical note, 11
Vigo, naval attack on, 467, 468, *475,* 479–83, 504, 525
Villiers, Barbara, 117, 254
Villiers, Edward, earl of Jersey, 196, 211, 266, 462, *463,* 611, 643; biographical notes, *74, 222;* signs second partition treaty, 242; as secretary of state, 351
Villiers, Sir Edward, 254
Villiers, Elizabeth, countess of Orkney, 74, 222, 254, 367; and countess of Albemarle, satirized, 369–71 (*A Dialogue*)
Villiers, George, second duke of Buckingham, 147, 262; *The Rehearsal,* quoted, 612; poem attributed to, 679
Vindication of the Memory, of the Late Excellent . . . Mr. Thomas Firmin . . . , A, 165
Viner, Martha, 545
Viner, Samuel, 545
Vine Tavern, *500*
Virgil, fourth eclogue (Dryden translation), 449, 450–64; tenth eclogue, 102; 115, 123, 125, 165, 171, 189, 249, *256,* 487, 517, 666
Voltaire, 61; quoted, 361, 389
Vox Populi, Vox Dei, xxviii

Wade, Edward, 458, *459,* 641
Wadham College, Oxford, 98, 178, 310
Wagstaffe, Thomas, *599, 600*
Wake, William, 457, 541
Wales, prince of, 17
Wales, prince of, pretended. *See* James Francis Edward
Walker, George, 289
Wall, James, *252*
Waller, Edmund, 144, *166,* 178, 545
Wallis, John, 111, 624
Walpole, Robert, 525, 627

Walsh, Joseph, 310
Walsh, William, 38, 124, 136, 183, 261, *459, 665, 707;* biographical note, 310; *The Worcester Cabal . . . ,* 39, 488, 665, headnote, 310–12, text, 313–17; *Dialogue Concerning Women . . . ,* 310; *The Golden Age Restor'd,* 450, 517, 665, headnote, 487–90, text, 491–505; et al., *Squire Treloohy* (trans. from Molière), 705, 706
Walter, Lucy, 274
Walton, Isaac, 502
Ward, Sir Edward, 215, 421; at Defoe's trial, 604
Ward, Edward, 73, 248; on Garth, xxxiv; *An Answer to An Encomium on a Parliament,* 47; *A Journey to Hell,* 107; at Dryden's funeral, 207–08; *The London Spy,* 686
Warrington, first earl of. *See* Booth, Henry
Warton, Joseph, quoted, xxvii
Warwick, second earl of. *See* Rich, Robert
Warwick, sixth earl of. *See* Rich, Edward
Watson, Thomas, *655;* biographical note, *502;* deprived of bishopric, 656
Watts, Isaac: *To David Polhill, Esq.,* 14; *Stanzas to My Lady Sunderland . . . ,* 117
Way to Heaven in a String . . . , The, 282
Webb, Col. John, 187, 188
Weekly Comedy, 47–48
Weekly Review of the Affairs of France . . . , A, 631
Wentworth, Thomas, first earl of Strafford: beheaded, *274;* impeached, 629
Wesley, John, 107
Wesley, Samuel, 103, *172, 179, 444;* biographical note, *107*
Westminster School, 138, 173, 256, 418, 424, 427, 663
Weymouth, viscount. *See* Thynne, Thomas
Wharton, Goodwin, 25; biographical note, *24*
Wharton, Col. Henry, biographical note, 428–29
Wharton, Philip, fourth baron Wharton, 24, 428, 628
Wharton, Thomas, 628
Wharton, Dr. Thomas, *126*
Wharton, Thomas, Lord Wharton, 21, 22, 24, 45, *520,* 533, 619, *658;* officeholder, *455;* and conformity bill, 507, 617; in Whig junto, 521, *628;* estates, *539;* duel with Dashwood, 559; as cuckold, 622, *628–29;* intervention in Irish politics, *660*
Wheatley, H. B., quoted, 41
Whigs, xxxv, 7, 13, 19, 20, 22, 23, 24, 25, 53, 54, 65, 74, 98, 139, 143, 144, 147, 148, 157, 161, 184, 185, 187, 210, *217, 218,* 251, 279, 286, 301, 306, 310, 324, 351, 354, 355, 409, 410, 418, 424, 438, 449, 495, 496, 498, 505, 533, 627; shift from ministry of, xxviii; junto, xxxii, xxxiv, *232,* 266, 521, 528, 628, impeached, 321, 454, *455;* and Fenwick assassination, 15–16; and New Country-Party, 43; justices of the peace, 56, 195; resignations, 195; laureate, 253; and Tory cabal, 311, 312; and partition treaties, 318; *vs.* Tories on delegation of power, 330; as war party, 339; and reformation of manners, 399; and *Tamerlane,* 462; poets, 487; court Whigs, 500, 523; alleged plot to exclude Anne, 504; minority in Commons (*1702*), 512; propaganda, 519–20, 701; and prophecy, 530; bishops support, 537; and conformity bill, 550, 664; and Scotch plot, 619, 622; leaders caricatured, 651–73 (*Faction Display'd*)
Whig's Scandalous Address Answered Paragraph by Paragraph, The, 633
White, Robert, 334
Whitehall, 367; burned to ground, *652*
Whitelocke, Bulstrode, 646
Whitlock, Sir William, biographical note, *646*
Whitney, Capt. James, *581, 583, 599*
Whiston, James, *559*
Wildman, Maj. John, 626
Wilkes, John, 253
Wilkins, John, biographical note, *646*
Wilkins, W. Walter, ed., *Political Ballads of the 17th and 18th Centuries,* xxix
Wilkinson, Richard, *Vice Reclaim'd . . . , 687*
William, Prince, duke of Gloucester, 37, 40, 311; death, 327, *672–73*
William III, 4, 11, 12, 37, *51, 57, 64, 69, 74,* 101, 103, *128, 160,* 173, 184, 198, 201, 204, 210, 212, 214–23, 230, *233, 237,* 238, *252, 256,* 264, *266, 288, 294, 295–97, 326, 329, 333,* 355, 364, 370, *455,* 465, 494, *495, 500,* 501, *512, 513, 516, 532,* 540, *614, 653, 654, 658, 660,* 661, 666, 671; use of the press, xxvii;

William III (*cont.*)
and reformation of manners, xxviii; death, xxviii, 355–57, poems on, 362–63 (*The Mourners*), 369–71 (*A Dialogue*), 376–97 (*The Mock Mourners*); plans for celebration after Ryswick treaty, 12; vetoes placemen-exclusion bill, 13; plot to assassinate, 15, 708; favorites, 16, 18; as William of Orange, 18, 21, 50–51, 99, 118, 232, *233*, *239*, 347, 388, 503; concern for public morality, 44, 56, 130–31, *307*; on his third parliament, 44; on his fourth parliament, 46–47; urges employment of poor, 44, 55-56; plans to abdicate, 46; quoted, 47, 50, 51, 57, 100; urges trade legislation, 53; mistress of, 74, 254, 367–71; appoints physician-in-ordinary, 101; and Talbot, 143; and Somers, 195; ancestry, 232; and partition treaties, 243, 323, 382; as gambler, 253; visits to Netherlands, 267; on House of Commons, 294–95; on Portland, 298; distrustfulness, 300; and Rochester, 318; asks for troops to aid Dutch, 321; dissolves fifth parliament, 343; wave of popularity prior to death, 343, 354; speech to sixth parliament, 354–55, 380–81; disagreeable traits, 361; urges union with Scotland, 362; military prowess, 382, 387–88, 389; and Cadiz expedition, 474; Irish grants, *17*, 195–96, 632, *638*–39, 661; alleged plan to exclude Anne, *659;* and Wharton, 628; and Williamson *vs.* Regem, 660–61; and Peterborough, 664.
William the Conquerer, 311
William and Mary, 362, *652;* oaths to, 3, 7, 152, 184, 239, 272, 290, 311, 347, 364, 426–27, 513, 562, 599, 611. *See also* Mary II; William III
William Rufus, 311
Williams, Lady Ellen, *255*
Williams, John, 646
Williams, John, bishop of Chichester, 510, 613
Williams, Sir William, *100*, 629; quoted, 60; biographical note, *99*
Williams, Sir William, of Vaynol, 255
Williamson, Sir Joseph, 611
Williamson *vs.* Regem, 660–61
Willis, Thomas, 111; biographical note, *126*
Wills, Sir Edward, *410*
Will's coffeehouse, *136*, 138, 142, 149, 167, 173, *175*, 182, 188, 254, 255, *441*, 702
Wilmot, John, earl of Rochester, *165*, 174, *444*, *558*, 679; sins of, *427; Familiar Letters*, 557, 558; *Poems, &c. On Several Occasions*, 558
Winchester, sixth marquis of. *See* Paulet, Charles
Windsor, Arthur L., xxxii
Windsor, John, first viscount Windsor of Blackcastle, 248, *255*
Winnington, Sir Francis, biographical note, *110*
Winton, Calhoun, 692
Wisdome, Robert, 617, 619
Wise, Thomas J., 48
Witwoud, quoted, 202
Wolsey, Thomas Cardinal, 63, 652
Wood, Anthony à, 118, 173, 174, 689; quoted, 25, 126
Wotton, William, *Reflections upon Ancient and Modern Learning*, 108
Wragg, Christopher, 438
Wragg, William, 96
Wray, Sir Bourchier, 255
Wren, Christopher, quoted, 38
Wright, Sir Nathan, 212, 267, 421, *635*, *779;* as lord keeper, *536*
Wroth, John, biographical note, *421–22*, *578*
Wycherley, William, 74, 91, *102*, 136, 142, *145*, 167, *179*, 625, 679
Wyndham, Catherine Leveson Gower, Lady, *497*–98, *538*
Wyndham, Sir Edward, *497*
Wyrley, Humphrey, 545
Wyrley, Sybil, 545

Yard, Robert, biographical note, *611–12*
Yonge, Sir Walter, 528, 626; biographical note, *24*–25
York, James, duke of, 657